Addictive Behaviors

NEW READINGS ON ETIOLOGY, PREVENTION, AND TREATMENT

EDITED BY

G. Alan Marlatt and Katie Witkiewitz

AMERICAN PSYCHOLOGICAL ASSOCIATION
WASHINGTON, DC

Chapters 1 and 21 were authored or coauthored by an employee of the United States government as part of official duty and are considered to be in the public domain.

Published by
American Psychological Association
750 First Street, NE
Washington, DC 20002
www.apa.org

To order
APA Order Department
P.O. Box 92984
Washington, DC 20090-2984
Tel: (800) 374-2721; Direct: (202) 336-5510
Fax: (202) 336-5502; TDD/TTY: (202) 336-6123
Online: www.apa.org/books/
E-mail: order@apa.org

In the U.K., Europe, Africa, and the Middle East, copies may be ordered from
American Psychological Association
3 Henrietta Street
Covent Garden, London
WC2E 8LU England

Typeset in Goudy by Circle Graphics, Columbia, MD

Printer: Edwards Brothers, Inc., Ann Arbor, MI
Cover Designer: Berg Design, Albany, NY
Technical/Production Editor: Harriet Kaplan

The opinions and statements published are the responsibility of the authors, and such opinions and statements do not necessarily represent the policies of the American Psychological Association.

Library of Congress Cataloging-in-Publication Data

Addictive behaviors : new readings on etiology, prevention, and treatment / edited by G. Alan Marlatt and Katie Witkiewitz. — 1st ed.
        p. ; cm.
    "Reprinted from American Psychological Association journals."
    Includes bibliographical references and index.
    ISBN-13: 978-1-4338-0402-1
    ISBN-10: 1-4338-0402-6
  1. Substance abuse. 2. Compulsive behavior. I. Marlatt, G. Alan. II. Witkiewitz, Katie. III. American Psychological Association.
    [DNLM: 1. Substance-Related Disorders—etiology—Collected Works. 2. Behavior, Addictive—Collected Works. 3. Substance-Related Disorders—prevention & control—Collected Works. 4. Substance-Related Disorders—therapy—Collected Works. WM 270 A22473 2009]

    RC564.A314 2009
    362.29—dc22
                                    2008014394

British Library Cataloguing-in-Publication Data
A CIP record is available from the British Library.

Printed in the United States of America
First Edition

Addictive Behaviors

CONTENTS

Contributors xi

Introduction 3
G. Alan Marlatt and Katie Witkiewitz

I. Role of Psychology and Behavioral Science
   in Addiction Research and Treatment 17

Chapter 1.   Contributions of Behavioral Science
               to Alcohol Research: Understanding
               Who Is at Risk and Why 19
               Enoch Gordis

Chapter 2.   Why Psychologists Should Treat Alcohol
               and Drug Problems 33
               William R. Miller and Sandra A. Brown

II. Epidemiological Overview and Etiology 57

Chapter 3.   Etiologic Connections Among Substance
Dependence, Antisocial Behavior, and Personality:
Modeling the Externalizing Spectrum 59
Robert F. Krueger, Brian M. Hicks,
Christopher J. Patrick, Scott R. Carlson,
William G. Iacono, and Matt McGue

Chapter 4.   Etiological Contributions to Heavy Drinking
From Late Adolescence to Young Adulthood 89
Serena M. King, S. Alexandra Burt,
Stephen M. Malone, Matt McGue,
and William G. Iacono

Chapter 5.   Trends in Ecstasy Use in the United States
From 1995 to 2001: Comparison With Marijuana
Users and Association With Other Drug Use 117
Silvia S. Martins, Guido Mazzotti,
and Howard D. Chilcoat

III. Prevention and Harm Reduction 135

Chapter 6.   Toward a Psychology of Harm Reduction 137
Robert J. MacCoun

Chapter 7.   Adolescent Substance Use Outcomes in the Raising
Healthy Children Project: A Two-Part Latent
Growth Curve Analysis 159
Eric C. Brown, Richard F. Catalano,
Charles B. Fleming, Kevin P. Haggerty,
and Robert D. Abbott

Chapter 8.   Project DARE: No Effects at 10-Year Follow-Up 187
Donald R. Lynam, Richard Milich, Rick Zimmerman,
Scott P. Novak, TK Logan, Catherine Martin,
Carl Leukefeld, and Richard Clayton

IV. Initiation and Progression in Adolescence 197

Chapter 9.   A Longitudinal Analysis of Friendships
and Substance Use: Bidirectional Influence
From Adolescence to Adulthood 199
Thomas J. Dishion and Lee D. Owen

Chapter 10. Conjoint Developmental Trajectories
of Young Adult Alcohol and Tobacco Use 225
Kristina M. Jackson, Kenneth J. Sher,
and John E. Schulenberg

V. Family Dynamics and Family Impact 257

Chapter 11. The Roles of Familial Alcoholism
and Adolescent Family Harmony in Young
Adults' Substance Dependence Disorders:
Mediated and Moderated Relations 259
Qing Zhou, Kevin M. King, and Laurie Chassin

Chapter 12. Family Risk Factors and Adolescent Substance Use:
Moderation Effects for Temperament Dimensions 287
Thomas Ashby Wills, James M. Sandy, Alison Yaeger,
and Ori Shinar

VI. Screening and Assessment 321

Chapter 13. Test–Retest Reliability of Alcohol Measures:
Is There a Difference Between Internet-Based
Assessment and Traditional Methods? 323
Elizabeth T. Miller, Dan J. Neal, Lisa J. Roberts,
John S. Baer, Sally O. Cressler, Jane Metrik,
and G. Alan Marlatt

Chapter 14. The Neuropsychological Test Performance
of Drug-Abusing Patients: An Examination
of Latent Cognitive Abilities and Associated
Risk Factors 343
William Fals-Stewart and Marsha E. Bates

Chapter 15. Immediate Antecedents of Cigarette Smoking:
An Analysis From Ecological Momentary
Assessment 367
Saul Shiffman, Chad J. Gwaltney, Mark H. Balabanis,
Kenneth S. Liu, Jean A. Paty, Jon D. Kassel,
Mary Hickcox, and Maryann Gnys

VII. Treatment Approaches and Models **401**

Chapter 16.   Relapse Prevention for Alcohol and Drug Problems:
That Was Zen, This Is Tao 403
Katie Witkiewitz and G. Alan Marlatt

Chapter 17.   Brief Treatments for Cannabis Dependence:
Findings From a Randomized Multisite Trial 429
The Marijuana Treatment Project Research Group

Chapter 18.   Smoking Cessation: Progress, Priorities,
and Prospectus 459
Raymond Niaura and David B. Abrams

Chapter 19.   Risk Factors and Neuropsychological Recovery
in Clients With Alcohol Use Disorders Who
Were Exposed to Different Treatments 497
*Marsha E. Bates, Danielle Barry, Erich W. Labouvie,
William Fals-Stewart, Gerald Voelbel,
and Jennifer F. Buckman*

Chapter 20.   Alcohol and Tobacco Cessation
in Alcohol-Dependent Smokers:
Analysis of Real-Time Reports 515
*Ned L. Cooney, Mark D. Litt, Judith L. Cooney,
David T. Pilkey, Howard R. Steinberg,
and Cheryl A. Oncken*

Chapter 21.   Addictive Disorders in Context: Principles
and Puzzles of Effective Treatment and Recovery 537
Rudolf H. Moos

Chapter 22.   Abstinence-Based Incentives in Methadone
Maintenance: Interaction With Intake Stimulant
Test Results 559
*Maxine L. Stitzer, Jessica Peirce, Nancy M. Petry,
Kimberly Kirby, John Roll, Joseph Krasnansky,
Allan Cohen, Jack Blaine, Ryan Vandrey,
Ken Kolodner, and Rui Li*

VIII. Issues in Specific Populations 573

Chapter 23.   Preventing Substance Abuse in American Indian
               and Alaska Native Youth: Promising Strategies
               for Healthier Communities 575
               Elizabeth H. Hawkins, Lillian H. Cummins,
               and G. Alan Marlatt

Chapter 24.   Examination of Ethnicity in Controlled Treatment
               Outcome Studies Involving Adolescent Substance
               Abusers: A Comprehensive Literature Review 623
               Marilyn J. Strada, Brad Donohue,
               and Noelle L. Lefforge

Chapter 25.   Measuring Adolescent Drug Abuse
               and Psychosocial Factors in Four Ethnic Groups
               of Drug-Abusing Boys 657
               Ken C. Winters, William W. Latimer,
               Randy D. Stinchfield, and Elizabeth Egan

Chapter 26.   Meta-Analyses of *ALDH2* and *ADH1B*
               With Alcohol Dependence in Asians 677
               Susan E. Luczak, Stephen J. Glatt,
               and Tamara L. Wall

Author Index 713

Subject Index 751

About the Editors 777

CONTRIBUTORS

Robert D. Abbott

David B. Abrams

John S. Baer

Mark H. Balabanis

Danielle Barry

Marsha E. Bates

Jack Blaine

Eric C. Brown

Sandra A. Brown

Jennifer F. Buckman

S. Alexandra Burt

Scott R. Carlson

Richard F. Catalano

Laurie Chassin

Howard D. Chilcoat

Richard Clayton

Allan Cohen

Judith L. Cooney

Ned L. Cooney

Sally O. Cressler

Lillian H. Cummins

Thomas J. Dishion

Brad Donohue

Elizabeth Egan

William Fals-Stewart

Charles B. Fleming

Stephen J. Glatt

Maryann Gnys

Enoch Gordis

Chad J. Gwaltney

Kevin P. Haggerty

Elizabeth H. Hawkins

Mary Hickcox

Brian M. Hicks

William G. Iacono

Kristina M. Jackson

Jon D. Kassel

Kevin M. King

Serena M. King
Kimberly Kirby
Ken Kolodner
Joseph Krasnansky
Robert F. Krueger
Erich W. Labouvie
William W. Latimer
Noelle L. Lefforge
Carl Leukefeld
Rui Li
Mark D. Litt
Kenneth S. Liu
TK Logan
Susan E. Luczak
Donald R. Lynam
Robert J. MacCoun
Stephen M. Malone
The Marijuana Treatment Project
    Research Group
G. Alan Marlatt
Catherine Martin
Silvia S. Martins
Guido Mazzotti
Matt McGue
Jane Metrik
Richard Milich
Elizabeth T. Miller
William R. Miller
Rudolf H. Moos
Dan J. Neal

Raymond Niaura
Scott P. Novak
Cheryl A. Oncken
Lee D. Owen
Christopher J. Patrick
Jean A. Paty
Jessica Peirce
Nancy M. Petry
David T. Pilkey
Lisa J. Roberts
John Roll
James M. Sandy
John E. Schulenberg
Kenneth J. Sher
Saul Shiffman
Ori Shinar
Howard R. Steinberg
Randy D. Stinchfield
Maxine L. Stitzer
Marilyn J. Strada
Ryan Vandrey
Gerald Voelbel
Tamara L. Wall
Thomas Ashby Wills
Ken C. Winters
Katie Witkiewitz
Alison Yaeger
Qing Zhou
Rick Zimmerman

Addictive Behaviors

INTRODUCTION

G. ALAN MARLATT AND KATIE WITKIEWITZ

Since the publication of the *Addictive Behaviors Reader* in 1997, there have been major advances in the research, prevention, and treatment of addictive behaviors, many of which are documented by chapters in the current volume of readings. Gary VandenBos, coeditor of the earlier volume, contacted us in 2007 to see if we would be interested in putting together a new collection of readings from over the past decade. We thank Gary for his devotion to this topic and support of this edited collection.

One major development over the past decade has been the current definition of addiction as a "brain disease" as promoted by the National Institute on Drug Abuse and other authorities. Given that the neuroscience of addiction has made great strides in recent years, including analyses of how drug taking impacts various pleasure centers in the brain (many mediated by dopamine release that often enhances the rewarding consequences of drug use), it is no surprise that considerable research activity has been devoted to the development of new pharmacotherapies that are designed to reduce drug craving or block the rewarding effects of various substances on brain functioning. Research findings show that although pharmacotherapy (e.g., naltrexone, acamprosate, buprenorphine, methadone, etc.) can have beneficial therapeutic effects (e.g., reducing craving and urges to use), the effects are often enhanced if the treatment program combines pharmacotherapy with a behavioral intervention (e.g., relapse prevention, cognitive–behavior therapy, motivational interviewing).

Behavioral research on addictive behaviors has also grown exponentially over the past 10 years. Many of the findings and controversies identified in the 1990s have now been replicated, expanded, and extended to different populations or different types of addictive behavior. As will be evident in this collection of readings, the field has greatly benefited from advances in computer technology and increases in the National Institutes of Health budget from 1995 to 2002. Clinical trials are larger, more powerful, and have produced better data. Methodology, particularly statistical and assessment techniques, has changed the face of conducting research on addictive behaviors. Statistical methods and software that were previously unused by many psychological researchers are recently being introduced into the mainstream. This fact becomes blatantly evident when one browses through the more recent issues of the journal *Psychology of Addictive Behaviors*, where nearly every article has at least one figure of a complicated structural equation model or latent growth curve model. Assessment techniques have largely benefited from advances in computing technology. The growth of the Internet has made way for many Web-based psychological assessment tools and interventions delivered online. In this volume, E. T. Miller et al. (chap. 13) provide an introduction to Web-based assessment and test its reliability compared with traditional methods. In vivo methods for data collection, such as ecological momentary assessment (EMA) via handheld computers and interactive voice response systems, have provided real-time assessment of addictive behavior as it is happening in a person's daily life. Shiffman et al. (chap. 15) and Cooney et al. (chap. 20) provide examples of applications using EMA.

The intensity of treatment for addictive behaviors has also shifted over the past decade. In the traditional approach, anyone diagnosed with an addiction problem was referred to an intensive residential treatment program. Most such programs lasted for a month (28 days or longer) and combined medical detoxification and intensive treatment based on the disease model of addiction. More recently, there has been a shift in emphasis to embrace the "stepped-care" model. In this approach, initial intervention is usually brief and may consist of a single session or professional advice, often in settings such as primary care, medical emergency rooms, and trauma centers. The aim of the brief intervention is to engage the client or patient to participate in a self-help group or structured outpatient treatment—to get him or her started in taking action. If the brief intervention is successful, no more treatment is necessary. If it is not successful, the client could be encouraged to "step up" to a more intensive treatment (e.g., attending a 12-step group or signing up for inpatient treatment). Intensive rehab is more often reserved as a last resort if less intensive therapy is unsuccessful.

The expansion of available treatment goals is also a noteworthy development of the past decade. Traditional abstinence-only or "high-threshold" intervention programs are typically based on the disease model of addiction and a 12-step program for recovery. More recently, clients who are unwilling or unable to make a commitment to abstinence have been offered alternative treatment goals (an approach known as *harm reduction*). Originally associated with interventions for IV drug users such as needle exchange (to reduce the potential harm of HIV infection) or methadone maintenance (to reduce the risk of overdose or other problems associated with illegal drug use), harm reduction strategies have been applied to other high-risk addictive behaviors such as problem drinking (e.g., moderation management, brief alcohol screening and intervention for college students). Harm reduction therapy is a low-threshold approach that is willing to "meet people where they are at" instead of a confrontational top-down approach that mandates treatment goals that require total abstinence for successful recovery.

The addictive behaviors treatment field is also working to develop an integrated treatment approach for working with clients who are experiencing co-occurring substance abuse and mental health problems. Many clients that we see in our clinical programs are using alcohol and/or other drugs to self-medicate other personal problems such as anxiety, depression, or personality disorders. Typically, such clients are referred back and forth between mental health professionals ("You are drinking excessively because you are trying to reduce the intensity of your depression symptoms") and substance abuse treatment professionals ("Your depression is caused by your alcoholism"). Such clients often fall between the cracks of these frequently opposing professional perspectives and may give up and drop out of treatment altogether. As a result, there is a strong need to provide an integrated treatment approach, one that ties together both sides of the presenting problem, and offers a flexible approach to choosing treatment goals (including both harm reduction and abstinence).

AN OVERVIEW OF THE CHAPTERS

The articles reprinted in this collection of readings were all selected from American Psychological Association (APA) journals published since 1997. The selection of representative articles was determined by impact on the field, quality of research methodology, and topic coverage. Key articles in eight topic areas were selected (each represented in a different section of the book): (a) the role of behavioral science in addiction research and the treatment of addiction (Part I); (b) epidemiology and etiology of addictive behaviors (Part II); (c) prevention and reducing the harm associated with addictive behaviors (Part III); (d) the initiation and progression of addictive behaviors in adolescence (Part IV); (e) the role of familial factors, including family history of addiction (Part V); (f) the screening and assessment of addictive behaviors (Part VI); (g) treatment approaches and models of addiction (Part VII); and (h) addictive behaviors in specific populations (Part VIII).

We started with abstracts from every article published in APA journals since 1997 that were related to the topic of addictive behaviors. This voluminous list was then reduced to 86 articles that were deemed "exceptional" by the editors, three advanced graduate students (Sharon Hsu, Diane Logan, and Joel Grow), and one postdoctoral fellow (Susan Collins) at the University of Washington, Seattle. A final selection of 26 articles was chosen for this collection. Because of space limitations and to avoid overlap of topic areas, many excellent and ground-breaking articles were left out of the final selection.

Role of Psychology and Behavioral Science in Addiction Research and Treatment

Part I of the book contains two chapters written by top researchers in the field of addictive behaviors. Enoch Gordis (chap. 1), former director of the National Institute of Alcohol Abuse and Alcoholism, provides a thorough overview of the role of behavioral science in the prevention and treatment of alcohol use disorders. He highlights genetics research, gaining knowledge of neural systems, and medications development as important for elucidating the relationship between biology and behavior as well as how advances in these areas will improve the efficacy and effectiveness of alcohol prevention and intervention methods. Gordis also describes future challenges for behavioral scientists, all of which are still relevant today: diagnostic issues, adolescent drinking, the role of stress hormones, and increasing biobehavioral (including neural systems) and etiology research.

The chapter by W. R. Miller and Brown (chap. 2) makes a compelling case for how and why psychologists, who may or may not have formal addictions training, can and should provide assessment and treatment of addictive behaviors. The chapter focuses on the qualities and special expertise of psychologists that make them suited for working with individuals who have alcohol and/or drug problems. Substance use disorders are the most prevalent form of mental health problem and frequently co-occur with other mental health disorders. Thus, psychologists who treat other psychological problems will likely have several clients who are also struggling with an addictive behavior. Fortunately, many studies have shown that basic clinical skills (e.g., empathy, reflection) are predictors of favorable treatment outcomes. W. R. Miller and Brown also address some of the barriers for psychologists in the routine treatment of substance use disorders and provide several recommendations for future training and research.

Epidemiological Overview and Etiology

Part II of the book includes three chapters that address etiology and epidemiology. The first two chapters tackle some of the main challenges to behavioral scientists described by Gordis in Part I: genetics, biobehavioral research, and substance use in adolescence. Krueger et al. (chap. 3) propose a biometric model of the "externalizing spectrum" that encompasses comorbid substance use, antisocial behavior, and personality style. The chapter provides a thorough review of genetic research to date and examines the genetic and environmental influences on the externalizing spectrum in 626 twin pairs. The results support a hierarchical model in which the co-occurrence among alcohol dependence, drug dependence, conduct disorder, adolescent antisocial behavior, and disinhibitory personal style could all be partially explained by a heritable externalizing factor. Because all of the variance was not explained by heritability the authors concluded that both general environmental and specific etiologic factors play a role in predicting externalizing behaviors and substance dependence diagnoses.

Using the same data from the Minnesota Twin Family Study as Krueger et al., King, Burt, Malone, McGue, and Iacono (chap. 4) examine genetic and environmental predictors of heavy drinking from late adolescence to adulthood. The chapter explores whether heavy drinking and onset of heavy drinking among 1,252 twin pairs from ages 17 to 20 can be partially explained by genetic, environmental, or neurological predictors. The results show that biological predictors of heavy drinking are more influential among male twins compared with female twin pairs and that changes in heavy drinking are largely attributable to nonshared environmental factors for both males and females. The authors recommend future research to examine specific genetic and environmental factors.

The final chapter in this section addresses trends in ecstasy and other drug use from 1995 to 2001, a time when the increase in ecstasy use in the United States was considered an "epidemic." Martins, Mazzotti, and Chilcoat (chap. 5) look at data from the National Household Survey on Drug Abuse, which provides a nationally representative sample across the United States. The results show that lifetime ecstasy use prevalence more than doubled from 1995 (1.6%) to 2001 (3.6%) and that this increase was particularly notable for younger age groups (18- to 25-year-olds). In addition, users of ecstasy were likely to report using many other drugs, including alcohol, marijuana, cocaine, crack, heroin, LSD, and stimulants. The authors suggest prevention and harm reduction strategies for educating adolescents and young adults about ecstasy.

Prevention and Harm Reduction

The issue of harm reduction was a hotly debated topic throughout the 1990s and into the new millennium. In the first chapter of Part III,

MacCoun (chap. 6) addresses the American drug policy and a framework for integrating strategies to reduce harmful consequences of substance use and other behaviors. The strategies described in the article—prevalence reduction, quantity reduction, and harm reduction—have been evaluated quite differently in the domain of drug control, where the primary strategy has traditionally been "use reduction" via strict prohibition and enforcement. As of 2006, the Department of Justice had reported that 53% of federal prison inmates were drug offenders, and the trend of increased prison populations due to drug-related convictions continues. MacCoun takes a "frank look" at opposition to harm reduction and provides hypotheses for making harm reduction more successful and palatable.

The most effective and cost-saving way to reduce harm from substance use is through prevention. In the 1990s there was a flurry of large-scale preventive interventions targeting youth development and substance use. One such intervention, the Raising Healthy Children project, was designed to target developmentally appropriate risk and protective factors by implementing, school-, student-, and family-level intervention strategies that were targeted to the developmental stage of the child. Brown, Catalano, Fleming, Haggerty, and Abbott (chap. 7) examined the developmental trajectories of substance use from Grades 6 through 10 in 959 participants in this project. Using an innovative growth modeling strategy, the authors report that the intervention was effective in reducing the frequency of both alcohol and marijuana use during these years but not eliminating use entirely. Returning to the idea of harm reduction, Brown et al. conclude that although the intervention did not prevent use, it did potentially reduce the harm that has been associated with frequent substance use in adolescence.

In the final chapter of this section, Lynam et al. (chap. 8) examine 10-year outcomes of the most widely disseminated and ineffective drug-prevention program in the United States, Project Drug Abuse Resistance Education (DARE). DARE is a federally funded, school-based education program, which is delivered by uniformed police officers over 17 weekly sessions. Despite the widespread popularity of the program and the federal cost of implementing it, several outcomes studies have concluded that DARE has no short-term effects on actual drug use. Lynam et al. examine the affects of DARE (compared with a standard drug-education curriculum) on drug use in 1,002 individuals 10 years after they received the DARE curriculum. As in nearly all studies to date, the chapter concludes that DARE is not effective at reducing drug use or changing attitudes toward drug use. The authors provide some potential reasons why DARE advocates persist in promoting the program despite the overwhelming evidence that the program is not efficacious.

Initiation and Progression in Adolescence

As described by Gordis in chapter 1, the challenge of preventing and treating substance use in adolescence is a major target for addictive behaviors researchers. The two chapters in Part IV provide a longitudinal analysis of the development of substance use from adolescence into young adulthood. Dishion and Owen (chap. 9) examine the bidirectional relationship between deviant friendships and substance use from age 13 to age 23 in a sample of 206 boys. The results are consistent with previous research in showing that the strongest predictor of adolescent substance use is belonging to a peer group that also uses substances. One unexpected finding described in the article is the identification of a subgroup of adolescents who used substances during adolescence and escalated to dangerous drug use in young adulthood but did not have a deviant peer group. The authors conclude that aside from this small subgroup, most adolescents might benefit from preventive interventions that target peer group behavior and school- or community-wide prevention interventions.

In the next chapter, Jackson, Sher, and Schulenberg (chap. 10) examine trajectories of alcohol and tobacco use during young adulthood using data from the Monitoring the Future study. Using growth mixture modeling, the authors extracted seven classes of drinking/smoking, with individuals expected to be in the largest class (56%) reporting no drinking or smoking. In addition, the authors examine predictors of alcohol and tobacco trajectories and conclude that parent education, gender, race, and religiosity predicted specific developmental courses for both alcohol and tobacco use across time. The methodology used in the chapter has the potential to greatly increase our understanding of addictive behavior over time.

Family Dynamics and Family Impact

Family history of alcohol problems has been consistently shown to predict increased risk for drinking problem. In addition, family-level variables (e.g., family harmony, family conflict) have been shown to be strong predictors of substance use. The two chapters in Part V provide an investigation into the role of family in the development of substance use and abuse during adolescence and young adulthood. In the first chapter, Zhou, King, and Chassin (chap. 11) examine the interaction between family history of alcoholism and family harmony during adolescence in the prediction of alcohol and drug dependence during young adulthood. In their study, the authors assessed 732 participants from 393 families over five time points spanning the course of roughly 13 years (from average ages 13 to 26). The results are consistent with previous findings regarding the direct effects of family history of alcohol on offspring substance use dependence and family harmony as a protective factor related to decreased drug dependence during young adulthood. In addition, the authors show that family harmony during adolescence partially mediated the direct effect of family history on young adult development of substance use dependence.

In the second chapter, Wills, Sandy, Yaeger, and Shinar (chap. 12) provide a slightly different slant by examining potential moderators of adolescent substance use, including family risk factors and a variety of temperament characteristics. The application of latent growth modeling to test moderation effects, a large sample size ($N = 1,810$), and obtaining information from multiple reporters (adolescents and teachers) are particular strengths of the study. The chapter reports that family relationships and family stress are significant and unique predictors of adolescent and peer substance use. In addition, several temperament factors were found to moderate this association. For adolescents with positive emotionality and task attention, the relationship was weakened, whereas for those adolescents with high negative emotionality and high activity level the impact of family risk factors was heightened. The chapter concludes by examining these opposing resiliency and vulnerability effects within a broad theoretical context.

Screening and Assessment

As described above, one of the most notable changes since the publication of the *Addictive Behaviors Reader* in 1997 is the advances in computing technology and an exponential increase in the number of Internet users. Since the early 1990s, researchers have been incorporating Web-based computer technology and handheld computers as useful research tools, and the applications of computing to research questions have greatly expanded our ability to gather large amounts of data from a wide variety of people. The first and third chapters in Part VI describe two such applications. E. T. Miller et al. (chap. 13) conducted the first test–retest reliability study comparing Internet-based assessment and traditional paper-based methods of assessment. The authors conducted two assessments within 1 week in which 255 participants were randomized to complete either Internet or paper-based assessments. The results strongly support the test–retest reliability of Internet-based assessment and show no differences between assessment techniques, suggesting that Internet-based methods are a suitable and cost-efficient alternative to traditional paper-based measures.

Advances in statistical software are evident in the second study in Part VI. Fals-Stewart and Bates (chap. 14) examine the neuropsychological functioning of 587 participants recruited from substance use treatment programs using a multimethod approach and latent variable modeling. The authors describe four cognitive factors (executive, verbal, speed, and memory) that sufficiently represent 15 different neuropsychological test scores. In addition, the authors identify several risk factors that have predicted neuropsychological functioning, including premorbid functioning, years of education, alcohol career length and recent drinking quantity, polydrug dependence, family history of alcoholism, and several biological measures.

The final chapter in Part VI revisits the issue of expanding research questions by incorporating computing technology. In 1994, Stone and Shiffman published their seminal work on EMA, which is an assessment approach that attempts to take the laboratory to the person by providing an assessment instrument that is delivered in real-time in real-world contexts. Using handheld computers, participants complete electronic diaries of their daily life based on scheduled, random and self-initiated assessments. EMA greatly reduces problems of recall and enhances ecological validity. Shiffman and his colleagues have conducted several studies to date (Shiffman et al., 1997, 2000; Shiffman, Paty, Gnys, Kassel, & Hickcox, 1996), and their research has provided volumes of knowledge about the immediate antecedents and consequences of engaging in a variety of addictive behaviors. The work that we selected for this volume (Shiffman et al., chap. 15) examines the situational cues that precede smoking in real time. The authors recruited 304 smokers who recorded smoking and nonsmoking situations over the course of 1 week. In total, the authors collected 10,084 and 11,155 reports from smoking and nonsmoking situations, respectively. Using generalized estimating equations the authors show that smoking urges, consumption of coffee and food, and the presence of other smokers were the strongest predictors of ad lib smoking. Negative or positive affect and arousal were not related to smoking, which is contrary to prior studies that have consistently shown a strong relationship between self-reported affect and smoking behavior. It is important to note that these prior studies relied heavily on self-report via retrospective recall and were therefore not sensitive to the momentary experiences of the smoker. EMA and other in vivo methods of assessment (e.g., interactive voice response, text messaging) have the potential to greatly expand our understanding of addictive behavior.

Treatment Approaches and Models

Seven articles were selected for Part VII, each describing a different treatment approach for a variety of addictive behaviors. It is important to note that no single approach appears to be more effective than others in the treatment of addictive behavior problems and a wide variety of treatment alternatives are currently available. The chapters in this section describe several different treatment models, as well as some outcome data from studies that have implemented various treatments. Relapse, or the return to problematic substance use after a period of abstention or moderate drinking, remains one of the most common outcomes following treatment and is possibly one of the most frustrating aspects of the treatment of addictive behavior. In the first article (Witkiewitz & Marlatt, chap. 16), we provide a review and synthesis of relapse prevention for alcohol and drug problems. We included this chapter because it offers a comprehensive review of the multitude of risk factors for relapse as well as methods for assessment and treatment. The chapter also provides an extensive description of future research strategies that may help elucidate the relapse process and enhance relapse prevention interventions.

The second chapter, authored by The Marijuana Treatment Project Research Group (chap. 17), examines the efficacy of two brief interventions for cannabis dependence. The multisite randomized control trial recruited 450 participants and randomly assigned them to either two sessions of motivation enhancement treatment (MET), nine sessions of a multicomponent treatment including MET and cognitive–behavioral techniques, or a delayed-treatment control condition. Both active treatment conditions were significantly more effective in reducing marijuana use relative to the control condition, and individuals in the nine-session treatment experienced significantly greater reductions in cannabis use and related consequences compared with the two-session treatment.

Niaura and Abrams (chap. 18) review the state of the art for smoking cessation treatment in the third chapter in this section. Tobacco use is the leading cause of preventable death in the United States, and nicotine has been described as one of the most addicting substances. Several treatments have been developed for smoking cessation, from behavioral intervention to nicotine patches to hypnotherapy. Interventions have been implemented across a variety of contexts including individual treatment, community-based interventions, health-care-delivered intervention, and public health approaches. Niaura and Abrams provide a thorough overview of the field of smoking cessation interventions as well as offer recommendations for smoking cessation guidelines and future research for behavioral research related to smoking cessation.

Using similar methods as described by Fals-Stewart and Bates (chap. 14) in the previous section, Bates et al. (chap. 19) examine neuropsychological functioning among 1,726 participants who received alcohol treatment in the Project MATCH study. Project MATCH was a multisite study that was conducted to examine potential patient-treatment matching effects following three active treatments: cognitive–behavioral treatment, MET, and 12-step facilitation. The results suggest that initial neuropsychological abilities as well as a variety of risk factors predicted neuropsychological recovery at 15 months following treatment initiation.

Cooney et al. (chap. 20) also used electronic diaries for EMA in a study examining relapse precipitants in the first 2 weeks following discharge from treatment in a sample of 102 alcohol-dependent smokers. Overall, 90.2% of participants did not lapse to alcohol use during the monitoring period, but the abstinence rates for smoking were 5.8% and 24.0% for brief and intensive treatments, respectively. Momentary predictors of the first drink and first cigarette included urges to smoke and drink, self-efficacy, and mood. The data also provided evidence that alcohol urges increased following smoking episodes, supporting a cross-substance cue reactivity model. These are exciting data and future research needs to be conducted to extend the EMA follow-up period further.

In the next chapter in this section, Moos (chap. 21) ponders the seven principles and unresolved puzzles of effective addictive behavior treatment and recovery processes. He provides a detailed review of research studies that have either provided support or refuted the prevailing wisdom in addiction treatment. In conclusion, Moos provides a brief discussion of the concerns commonly voiced by clinical providers who are often least familiar and most suspicious of "evidence-based" treatments. In many ways, this chapter is essential reading for all psychologists who are practitioners treating or researchers researching addictive behavior.

In the final treatment approach chapter, Stitzer et al. (chap. 22) describe an innovative and evidence-based treatment for stimulant abuse and dependence. The introduction of incentives as part of addiction treatment was based on a basic behavioral principle: If a behavior is reinforced, it is more likely to occur in the future. Starting in the early 1990s, researchers began to systematically evaluate whether providing incentives, a treatment called *contingency management*, would result in lasting changes beyond the period when incentives for behavior were stopped. According to behavioral theory, there will be decay of the behavior after reinforcement ceases, and this has commonly been found to be the case in addiction treatment. Stitzer et al. look at a specific aspect of contingency management within a sample of 386 methadone maintenance patients. The question they address is whether intake stimulant test results (i.e., providing stimulant negative or positive urine tests at the initiation of treatment) would mediate the relationship between incentives and treatment outcomes. Analyses reveal that both groups of individuals (stimulant positive and stimulant negative at intake) reported reduced during-treatment drug use relative to a non-incentive-based control condition. The results from this particular study run contrary to a commonly held belief that incentives should only be offered for individuals with less severe drug abuse.

Issues in Specific Populations

In Part VIII, the final section of the book, four chapters examine issues for specific populations with substance abuse problems. As identified by Gordis in the first chapter of this collection, understanding and preventing adolescent substance use is an enormous challenge for addictive behaviors researchers and clinicians. Thus, for the first three chapters in this section, we included articles that focused on adolescent populations. In the first chapter of Part VIII, Hawkins, Cummins, and Marlatt (chap. 23) provide a thorough literature review on preventing substance use in American Indian and Alaskan Native adolescents. In the first section of the chapter, the authors provide an introduction to substance use prevalence rates as well as risk and protective factors for abusing specific substances among Native populations. In the last two sections Hawkins et al. provide a review of prevention efforts and offer recommendations for future research and preventive strategies that are most promising for substance abuse prevention among Native adolescents. The chapter concludes with a description of a program that was codeveloped by researchers at the University of Washington and Native elders from the Seattle Indian Health Board. The "Canoe Journey" is a culturally congruent prevention program that is unique to the cultural experiences of tribes in the Pacific Northwest. Drawing on the Northwest Native tradition of the canoe journey, a metaphor was constructed in which the canoe journey, as well as other Native symbols, served as a metaphor to teach skills such as communication, decision making, and goal setting as well as providing information about alcohol and drug use and its consequences.

The Hawkins et al. chapter provides a convincing example of how ethnicity and cultural values should be incorporated into treatment of substance use as well as how an existing prevention program can be successfully modified to accommodate culturally relevant variables. In counterpoint to the Hawkins chapter, Strada, Donohue, and Lefforge (chap. 24) provide a comprehensive review of how poorly the field has responded to this need. The authors reviewed 18 adolescent drug treatment outcome studies to examine whether ethnicity was systematically incorporated into the analysis or interpretation of findings across all studies. In total, 94% of the studies mentioned ethnicity to some extent and 28% incorporated ethnicity into their design, but only 6% of studies included specific analyses to examine ethnicity as a potential moderator of treatment responding. The authors conclude that the addictive behaviors research community needs to invest energy in the examination of ethnicity in existing controlled outcome studies and the development or adaptation of treatments to accommodate culture-relevant variables.

Winters, Latimer, Stinchfield, and Egan (chap. 25) focus specifically on the validation of a multiscale assessment tool for adolescent drug abusers called the Personal Experience Inventory, which was primarily developed in White samples. The authors sampled 3,191 adolescent boys (13 to 18 years old) from 30 different adolescent drug abuse programs, representing four groups: White, African American, Native American, and Hispanic. Although the results do provide strong support for the validity and commonality of the Personal Experience Inventory across ethnic groups, there were discrepancies across all ethnic groups on test–retest reliability in which some scales had inadequate reliability and some had discrepancies on response probabilities and distortions.

In the final chapter of this collection, Luczak et al. (chap. 26) provide an update and meta-analysis of two genes, *ALDH2* (aldehyde dehydrogenase) and *ADH1B* (alcohol dehydrogenase), which have been shown to offer protection from alcohol dependence, particularly among Northeast Asian populations. The chapter reviews the genetic influence and the potential mediators and moderators for the effects of these genes on alcohol dependence. In general, the authors conclude that an additive model of genetic influence (in which one gene allele is good and possession of two gene alleles is even better) provides an appropriate means for modeling the relationship between *ALDH2* and alcohol dependence, whereas a partial dominant or dominant model explains the influence of *ADH1B*. The article also describes several moderators of these effects, including being Japanese, recruiting samples from treatment settings, and gender (with men showing greater protection from *ADH1B*). It is interesting that this finding is consistent with the results from King et al. (chap. 4) presented in Part II of this volume.

CONCLUDING REMARKS AND ACKNOWLEDGMENTS

This collection of readings from articles published by the APA provides a small sampling of psychological research on addictive behaviors. As mentioned earlier, because of space constraints, the collection excludes several articles of equal importance to the ones that were chosen. In addition, because the focus of the book is on APA-published works, several ground-breaking articles from *Journal of Studies on Alcohol and Drugs*, *Addictive Behaviors*, *Addiction*, and other non-APA publications were not included. Also, several large-scale studies, most notably the COMBINE study, have recently been published in medical journals, including the *Journal of the American Medical Association* and the *New England Journal of Medicine*. The interested reader is referred to the references at the end of each chapter in this collection, which provide a further wealth of studies.

In closing, we thank Gary VandenBos for initiating the process for this new volume. We are also indebted to the great work conducted by Susan Collins, Joel Grow, Sharon Hsu, and Diane Logan in the identification of articles to be included in this collection.

REFERENCES

Shiffman, S., Balabanis, M. H., Paty, J. A., Engberg, J., Gwaltney, C. J., Liu, K. S., et al. (2000). Dynamic effects of self-efficacy on smoking lapse and relapse. *Health Psychology, 19,* 315–323.

Shiffman, S., Engberg, J., Paty, J. A., Perz, W., Gnys, M., Kassel, J. D., & Hickcox, M. (1997). A day at a time: Predicting smoking lapse from daily urge. *Journal of Abnormal Psychology, 106*, 104–116.

Shiffman, S., Paty, J. A., Gnys, M., Kassel, J. D., & Hickcox, M. (1996). First lapses to smoking: Within-subjects analyses of real-time reports. *Journal of Consulting and Clinical Psychology, 64*, 366–379.

Stone, A. A., & Shiffman, S. (1994). Ecological momentary assessment in behavioral medicine. *Annals of Behavioral Medicine, 16*, 199–202.

I

ROLE OF PSYCHOLOGY AND BEHAVIORAL SCIENCE IN ADDICTION RESEARCH AND TREATMENT

1

CONTRIBUTIONS OF BEHAVIORAL SCIENCE TO ALCOHOL RESEARCH: UNDERSTANDING WHO IS AT RISK AND WHY

ENOCH GORDIS

Alcoholism, like many other serious diseases, results from the interaction between complex biological and behavioral systems. Understanding the systems involved in the development of alcoholism and its consequences, how individual components of biological and behavioral systems separately and together act to protect against or increase risk for disease, and how to interrupt this process to prevent disease and reduce harm are the major goals of alcohol research.

Over the past 30 years, alcohol research has made major progress toward understanding alcohol use, abuse, and dependence. Behavioral science has been an active partner in this progress by helping to elucidate many of the key questions in alcohol research, including why some people who drink develop problems while others do not, the influence of the environment on genetic risk for alcoholism, and how alcohol's effects in the brain relate to alcohol-seeking behavior. In recent years, behavioral science and biological science have combined to help link biological findings to specific alcohol use behaviors.

I acknowledge the contributions of Brenda G. Hewitt and Richard K. Fuller to the preparation of this chapter.

Reprinted from *Experimental and Clinical Psychopharmacology*, 8, 264–270 (2000). In the public domain.

This chapter explores some of the actual and potential contributions of behavioral science in two increasingly rich fields of study: the genetics of alcoholism and alcohol's effects in the brain. It is from these two fields that the merging of biological and behavioral sciences can be seen most dramatically and from which will come both the pharmacological and behavioral methods to improve the prevention and treatment of alcohol-related problems.

ALCOHOLISM, GENES, AND BEHAVIOR

One of the key questions in alcohol research is why some individuals are vulnerable to developing alcoholism and others are not. Human population genetic studies with twins and adoptees have demonstrated clearly that about 50% of the vulnerability to becoming alcoholic has a genetic basis. Because alcoholism is a complex disease, there are likely to be many genes involved in increasing an individual's risk for alcoholism. Scientists are looking for these genes and have found likely locations on chromosomes. We now must determine what these genes are and whether they are specific for alcohol or define something more general, such as differences in temperament or personality, that increase an individual's vulnerability to alcoholism.

Collaborative Study on the Genetics of Alcoholism

One important contributor to the study of the genetics of alcoholism is the Collaborative Study on the Genetics of Alcoholism (COGA), a multisite study at six centers. COGA investigators have interviewed hundreds of probands and families, developed a complex computerized pedigree database, and have applied statistical genetics and molecular biology techniques to "informative" families, that is, families with many alcoholic members. Phenotypic markers shown previously to be relevant to alcohol are incorporated in the study, including biochemical markers, evoked potential responses, and tests of initial sensitivity to alcohol.

COGA scientists have found highly suggestive evidence for chromosomal *"hot spots"* (areas of potential linkage to alcohol dependence) on Chromosomes 1 and 2, and more modest evidence on Chromosomes 4 and 7 (Reich et al., 1998). In addition, locations for the genes involved in the expression of evoked potential responses, a high-risk marker for alcoholism, have been tentatively identified (Begleiter et al., 1998). These findings bring us a step closer to finding the genes underlying the genetic vulnerability to this chronic disease.

Behavioral science has contributed immensely to this work. The first 2 years of the COGA project were devoted to creating the diagnostic interview instruments. A special interview instrument that was created with major contributions from behavioral scientists was designed to deliver diagnoses from the *Diagnostic and Statistical Manual of Mental Disorders,* third edition, revised (*DSM–III–R*; American Psychiatric Association, 1987) and the *International Classification of Diseases,* tenth edition (*ICD–10*; World Health Organization, 1992). This instrument has been translated into several languages and used all over the world for similar purposes, providing the potential for comparing research findings across studies.

Finding the genes for alcoholism is an important goal in alcohol research. The discovery of a specific genetic effect on the development of alcoholism would be beneficial for at least three reasons: (a) It would lead to the identification of some people at risk who could act to avoid developing alcohol-related problems; (b) it may help clarify the role of environmental factors that are critical in the development of alcoholism; and (c) it may lead to better treatments based on new understandings of the physiological mechanisms of alcoholism.

Although it is important to find the genes for alcoholism, this is just the first step. Knowledge of which neural systems are affected by alcohol and how these systems are, in turn, affected by the genes for alcoholism will be necessary before this information can be used to develop highly effective prevention, early identification, and treatment programs. Behavioral scientists already have contributed to our understanding about several neural systems. These include the study of stress; reward and aversion; appetite and satiety; and memory, craving, and tolerance, which all may be related. The genes involved in the development of alcoholism may be involved in many different functions. Behavioral science will help us to determine which of these functions relate to alcoholism and which do not. For example, in one recent study, low initial sensitivity to alcohol was shown to be a strong predictor of later alcoholism (Schuckit & Smith, 1996), suggesting the possibility of a biological marker for identifying individuals, as well as groups, who are at greatest risk of developing alcoholism. However, we do not yet know if there are genes that code for this sensitivity or if the initial sensitivity is related to some entirely different mechanism.

Finally, behavioral science can help us to better understand cognition and its relationship to the vulnerability to developing alcoholism. It is possible, for example, that an individual's ability (or inability) to relate the memories of drinking to its consequences is the result of genetic deficiencies or genetic loading. If this is true, how such cognitive impairments may increase the vulnerability to alcoholism must be determined before this knowledge can be used in efforts to prevent alcohol dependence.

Animal Genetics

The alcohol field has been a leader in the field of animal genetics, and behavioral scientists have had a major role in developing animal lines selective to responses to alcohol. There are many effects for which animal lines have been developed. One of the most important effects concentrates on preference for drinking. There are several rat strains, for example, where, after breeding for many generations, animals exhibit the extremes of preference for drinking alcohol or rejecting it, and very reliably so. Further, when animals drink heavily, they model many of the aspects of human alcoholism. In some of these models the animals develop tolerance or dependence.

"Knockout" technology has become a very valuable tool in alcohol research. A knockout is a transgenic animal developed from molecular biological techniques that eliminate, or knock out, a specific gene from an animal. Behavioral scientists have had a prominent role in the development of several alcohol-relevant knockouts, including the PKCγ, Serotonin 1β, and NPY knockouts. Alterations in the animal's behavior or health before and after the elimination of the gene allow scientists to deduce that the missing gene is important in the mechanism that is being studied.

Using this technology, scientists have demonstrated that PKCγ alters the ability of alcohol to affect the γ-aminobutyric acid (GABA) receptor, the major inhibitory neurotransmitter in the brain. In this knockout model, animals showed reduced sensitivity to the effects of alcohol on the loss of righting reflex and hypothermia (Harris et al., 1995). PKCγ also was shown to play an important role in the initial sensitivity and tolerance to ethanol; however, its impact is modulated by the background genotype (Bowers et al., 1999). In the Serotonin 1β knockout, the animals were found to drink much more heavily than their normal wildlife litter mates and to develop tolerance but not physical dependence (Crabbe et al., 1996). This is an interesting finding because it distinguishes the mechanisms of tolerance and physical dependence, which had been thought to be related.

Scientists also are using animals to identify the location of genes responsible for the genetically influenced traits that are thought to underlie responses to alcohol. These traits are known as "quantitative traits." More than one gene influences the magnitude of a trait. A section of DNA on a chromosome that is thought to influence a quantitative trait is known as a quantitative trait locus (QTL). Using powerful new genetic analysis techniques, including knockout technology, researchers have begun to map these loci. Through QTL mapping and analysis, researchers can locate and measure the effects of a single QTL on a trait, or phenotype, and ultimately gain knowledge of the complex physiologic underpinnings of alcohol-related behavior. For example, scientists have identified two loci—Alcp1 and Alcp2—that appear to have significant gender-specific effects on alcohol consumption in mice (Melo, Shendure, Pociask, & Silver, 1995). This finding suggests that preference for alcohol, a quantitative trait, may be controlled by different genetic mechanisms in men and women.

Alcohol, Genes, and the Environment

Although a significant portion of the vulnerability to the development of alcoholism is inherited, not everyone with a family history that is positive for alcoholism develops the disease. Consequently, it is important to identify the environmental factors that are involved in the risk for developing alcoholism and the manner and extent to which these factors interact with genetic factors. For example, it has been known for some time that many individuals of Asian descent inherit an ALDH2 (aldehyde dehydrogenase) mutation that causes a "flushing" reaction when these individuals consume alcohol. Although we can predict that an Asian individual inheriting this mutation will be much less likely to develop alcoholism than an individual not inheriting this mutation, more precise prediction of outcome requires additional knowledge of that individual's cultural context and alcohol-specific expectancies. Greater knowledge of how an individual's environmental circumstances contribute to the development of alcohol problems will enable the design of prevention and early intervention strategies that focus on changing environmental risk factors for alcohol abuse and alcoholism.

In recent years, alcohol behavioral researchers have begun to test and apply models that emphasize the process by which environmental factors can transform heritable characteristics to either promote or impede the expression of alcohol problems and the reciprocal influence that biological and nonbiological factors can impose over time. An example of this type of research is the now-classic adoption studies (Cloninger, Bohman, & Sigvardsson, 1981; Cloninger, Sigvardsson, & Bohman, 1996) that have identified two alcoholism subtypes that differ in inheritance patterns as well as other characteristics. Type 1 alcoholism, which affects both men and women, requires the presence of a specific genetic background, as well as certain environmental factors (low socioeconomic status of the father). Mild or severe alcohol abuse, adult onset of the disease, a loss of control over drinking, and guilt and fear about alcohol dependence characterize this alcoholism subtype. Individuals with this type of alcoholism generally exhibit high harm avoidance and low novelty-seeking personality traits and drink primarily to relieve anxiety. In contrast, Type II alcoholism, which occurs more commonly in men than in women, primarily requires a genetic predisposition; environmental factors only play a minor role in its development. Type II alcoholism is associated with early onset (before age 25) of both alcohol abuse and antisocial behavior and an inability to abstain from alcohol. Type II alcoholics exhibit high novelty-seeking personality characteristics and unconcern for the consequences of drinking.

Finally, we need to understand much more about the longitudinal changes in gene expression, that is, genes that are expressed at different points of life. In molecular biology, every cell in the body has the same genes but *not all of them are expressed at the same time*. What makes the brain different from the liver, even though they have the same genes, is that different genes are being expressed in these organs continually. We know little about this area now, but finding out which genes are expressed, when, and which environmental triggers turn them on is fundamental to our understanding of the role of genetics in the development of alcoholism. Behavioral science will have a major role in answering what changes risk to disease and when during the life span the expression of specific genes is likely to interact with the environment to produce alcoholism.

ALCOHOLISM, BRAIN, AND BEHAVIOR

The last quarter of the 20th century has produced a growing body of evidence that biological processes involved in the development of alcoholism reside largely in the brain. Research over the past 2 decades has dramatically increased our understanding of the neural processes that underlie alcohol-seeking behavior. Several lines of investigation using animal models have helped scientists to discover two factors, reinforcement and cellular adaptation, that may explain alcohol-dependent behavior.

Alcohol Reinforcement

Alcohol is considered to be reinforcing because the ingestion of alcohol, or withdrawal from chronic long-term alcohol use, increases the probability that an individual will drink. One explanation for reinforcement is that alcohol appears to interact with the brain's reward system, thus stimulating continued use. This is termed "positive reinforcement." Relief of abstinence, or negative reinforcement, is another possible mechanism of reinforcement. For example, alcohol-dependent rats undergoing withdrawal have been shown to perform lever press responses for alcohol in an apparent attempt to alleviate withdrawal symptoms (Schulteis, Hyytia, Heinrichs, & Koob, 1996).

Cellular Adaptation

When alcohol is chronically present in the brain, some neurons seem to adapt to this physiological change by enhancing or reducing their response to normal stimuli. This adaptation is hypothesized to lead to the development of tolerance and dependence. A primary question under investigation is the mechanism of cellular adaptation to the long-term presence of alcohol. One successful approach to exploring cellular adaptation is through molecular genetic studies. Alcohol scientists have uncovered evidence that alcohol can cause changes in cellular communication and functioning by directly influencing the function of specific genes. Sophisticated genetic mapping techniques and related technology may pinpoint exactly which genes are involved. Researchers can selectively investigate the effects of alcohol on specific receptor constituents by directly manipulating genetic material. Data obtained from studies such as these will provide major advances in understanding the process of cellular adaptation to alcohol and thus provide clues about the mechanisms of alcohol dependence, tolerance, and withdrawal.

Alcohol investigators also have evidence that the cellular adaptive changes that occur with alcohol exposure can alter the degree of reinforcement experienced. Thus, adaptation and reinforcement, acting in concert, determine a person's short-term or acute response to alcohol, as well as the long-term or chronic craving for alcohol that characterizes dependence. Some adaptive changes may be permanent and are hypothesized to produce the persistent sense of discomfort during abstinence that again leads to relapse. Because relapse is very common among recovering alcoholics, understanding the mechanisms that cause or enable relapse is critical to designing effective behavioral and pharmacologic treatments for alcohol dependence tailored to individual physiology and psychology.

Because alcohol affects every cell in the body, the challenge is to sort out the critical effects that cause uncontrolled drinking in the face of negative consequences and the manner in which alcohol causes brain damage. Following the discovery of complex cell membranes, neuroscientists began probing the way in which the brain controls thinking, behavior, movement, and other key bodily functions. Current research strongly suggests that alcohol, unlike illicit drugs, affects multiple neurotransmitter systems in the brain. The specific neurotransmitters involved in the behavioral aspects of alcoholism, the mode of release, and the corresponding receptors involved in these effects are now under investigation.

MEDICATIONS DEVELOPMENT

One of the principal payoffs of both genetics and neurosciences research is their potential to improve alcohol prevention and treatment. The identification of genetic markers for alcoholism, as previously noted, would allow the early identification of individuals at risk for developing alcohol problems. Once the genes are identified that code for alcoholism and other alcohol-related behaviors, medications may be developed that prevent or interrupt the expression of these genes and, thus, the development of severe alcohol problems. This, of course, is a long-range objective.

Neuroscience research already has provided the groundwork for new medications for treating alcoholism. Researchers now are looking for new medications that target the mechanisms of the addiction itself, such as drugs that interfere with the reward properties of alcohol. It is likely that no one medication will be effective for everyone or that there will be the proverbial silver bullet of pharmacotherapies for alcoholism. Just as there are different types of medications with different mechanisms of action to treat complex diseases like diabetes, it is likely that there will be a range of medications coupled with verbal therapies available to clinicians as adjuncts to traditional alcoholism therapy.

Two such medications, the products of neuroscience research, already are in use, and more are certain to follow. In 1995, the opiate antagonist naltrexone, under the brand name ReVia 7, was approved for use in the United States to help prevent relapse in recovering alcoholics. An opiate antagonist, naltrexone is the first medication approved to help maintain sobriety after detoxification from alcohol since disulfiram's approval in 1949. In Europe, acamprosate has been tested and used successfully for several years for the same purpose and currently is awaiting approval for use in the United States. These two medications appear to work through different mechanisms in the brain to achieve the same effect; naltrexone may be blocking positive reinforcement, whereas acamprosate may block the effect of negative reinforcement.

Evaluating Alcohol Treatment

Many of the behavioral treatments that have been used in treating alcoholism evolved informally on the basis of clinical judgment and anecdotal information about what works best. Only during the past decade have modern standards of evaluating treatment outcomes, including the use of controls, blinding, and random assignment of subjects, been used to evaluate existing alcoholism treatments. For example, although disulfiram has been used to treat alcoholism since 1949, it was not until 1986 that the efficacy of this medication was subjected to research methods.

A significant advance in understanding what works in alcoholism treatment resulted from a large multisite clinical trial (Project MATCH) initiated by the National Institute on Alcohol Abuse and Alcoholism (NIAAA). The hypothesis that patients who are appropriately matched to treatments will show better outcomes than those who are unmatched or mismatched is well founded in medicine and behavioral science. In the alcohol field, evidence from a number of smaller studies led investigators to believe that alcoholism treatment outcomes would be improved for patients who were matched to treatments based on patient characteristics. In the 8-year, multisite trial, patients were matched to the three specific treatment approaches: twelve-step facilitation, cognitive–behavioral coping skills therapy, and motivational enhancement therapy. Contrary to investigators' expectations, on the basis of prior research evidence, Project MATCH found that patient-treatment matching does not substantially alter treatment outcome. Treatment in all three approaches resulted in substantial reductions in drinking, with reductions sustained over a 12-month period. Alcoholism treatment also was found to result in decreased alcohol-related problems, other drug use problems, and depression, and improvements in liver functioning (Project MATCH Research Group, 1997).

What are the implications of these findings? One is that, given the skill and the scientific basis with which behavioral research was applied to this study, both alcohol treatment providers and patients can have confidence that any one of the treatments tested, if well delivered, represents the state of the art in behavioral treatments. The second implication is that science must now look for ways to improve treatment effectiveness beyond those that are based solely on behavioral therapy.

Combined Therapies

Combining behavioral therapies with pharmacotherapies is likely to be the next important advance in alcoholism treatment. Several studies (O'Malley et al., 1992, 1996; Volpicelli, Alterman, Hayashida, & O'Brien, 1992) have found that naltrexone used in combination with verbal therapy prevented relapse more than standard verbal therapy alone. Project COMBINE, a new large-scale randomized study supported by the NIAAA, will take advantage of the knowledge learned from Project MATCH to further explore the coupling of verbal and pharmacological therapies. In Project COMBINE, mixed pharmacological and behavioral approaches will be evaluated in an effort to determine what combinations work best in the treatment of alcohol dependence.

There are several ways in which behavioral and pharmacological therapies could work together. One way is that one therapy may continue to function if the other failed. This resembles treatments using two antibiotics, where one medication can serve as backup if resistance to another develops. A second way is that each therapy may increase the efficacy of the other. For example, verbal therapy may enhance compliance with pharmacological therapy, which in turn reduces craving, allowing the patient's more complete attention to the verbal therapy. A third way illustrates the possibility that verbal and pharmacological therapy are not as radically different as they seem: they may act on the same neural circuits. For example, in a study of obsessive-compulsive disorder Baxter et al. (1992) compared positron emission tomography (PET) scans of patients before and after behavioral treatment with PET scans of patients before and after pharmacological treatment. In Baxter et al.'s study, changes in glucose utilization in the head of the caudate nucleus in patients who had responded to the behavioral treatment resembled changes seen in patients who had responded to the pharmacological treatment. Even though this study has limitations, these observations are striking because they indicate that successful verbal therapies and pharmacological therapies may work on the same system.

FUTURE CHALLENGES

In recent years, there have been two very important signals as to which way the future is going in alcohol research. One is the recognition of the importance of behavioral work in itself. Although the work in genetics is of vital importance to future improvements in health, the fact is that in alcoholism as in many other behavioral diseases, *genes are not destiny*. This recognition has led to increasing emphasis by investigators on the importance of understanding the cognitive as well as the biological processes involved in alcoholism. As a result, we have begun to learn how cognitive processes such as expectancies (where some of the actions of alcohol are produced because they are expected, not because of the pharmacology of the drug itself) and craving (e.g., whether craving exists intrinsically or whether it is dependent on cues from the environment) affect the etiology and course of alcohol dependence. The study of craving is of particular value because it is thought to play a major role in the chronic relapse that is typical in this disease.

In addition to continued clarification of the role of expectancies and craving in alcoholism, behavioral science can make significant contributions by improving the *DSM*, *ICD*, and other diagnostic instruments; in understanding the behavioral factors influencing adolescent drinking; and in longitudinal research.

Diagnostic Criteria

The *DSM* is the principal source of diagnostic criteria for alcohol use problems in the United States. Although these criteria were carefully developed on the basis of both scientific evidence and clinical experience, they tell us very little about how human drinking behavior affects the etiology and course of alcohol abuse and alcohol dependence. The kind of detail that has been done so well by behavioral scientists especially in the animal research arena is missing in people.

Adolescent Drinking

Another important area for behavioral science attention is adolescence. An analysis of data from the NIAAA National Longitudinal Alcohol Epidemiology Survey found that individuals who begin drinking before age 15 are four times more likely to develop alcohol dependence during their lifetime than those who begin drinking at age 21 (Grant & Dawson, 1998). This risk for developing alcoholism due to age of drinking onset applies both to individuals with and without a family history of alcoholism. The question then is why age of use is linked to future alcoholism regardless of one's family history. One possible reason that we have learned from

behavioral science is that many individuals experience lifestyle changes, such as beginning careers and marriage, in their 20s. These lifestyle changes tend to protect against alcohol abuse. Therefore, if there is less drinking before these protective lifestyle changes, there is less time for dysfunctional drinking patterns to be established. There may be other factors that are equally important to understanding the risk for alcoholism as a function of the age at which an individual begins to use alcohol. One question is the role of plasticity; that is, does early drinking cause changes in the brain that make an individual less responsive to environmental influences as time goes on through adolescence? Another important question is whether the age of drinking initiation is simply a surrogate for something entirely different.

Alcoholism and Subjective States

Finally, there is an area where behavioral science has something to tell us that other fields cannot: the effect of subjective states such as stress on drinking and on alcoholism. Here, I am referring mainly to stress as it is commonly, rather than scientifically, described. Scientifically, stress involves variations in neuronal systems; for example, high corticotropin releasing factor (CRF) in the brain, the measure of plasma adrenocorticotropin hormone (ACTH). However, most people understand stress in a very personal way. Being stuck in traffic and late for a job interview is stress! An individual's CRF and ACTH may be high, but the stress he or she describes as a result of this situation is a subjective state that neuroscience does not know how to measure. I believe that behavioral science can help them to do so. The same is true of other human subjective states, such as fear.

Biobehavioral Research

The second major trend for the future is the growing reciprocal work between the biological and behavioral sciences. Of the two trends, I believe this is the more important one. Examples of this type of work can be found in the study of the effects of alcohol on the fetus. On the one hand, we have excellent behavioral studies of children with fetal alcohol syndrome and other alcohol-related birth defects. On the other hand, we are learning from improved scanning technology available in the past few years about the tremendous structural changes in the brains of these children as a result of their exposure to alcohol. We also are learning about the proper connectivity among neurons. In this work, it appears that alcohol actually prevents the appropriate expression of certain genes. This is an area where the tools of behavioral science and behavior, imaging, neuroscience, and genetics are working in concert to produce findings that one day may help reduce the harm caused by alcohol abuse and dependence.

Behavioral Science in Disease Etiology

Even in the face of a growing melding of disciplines, the importance of behavior in disease etiology cannot be overemphasized. It is in this area that behavioral scientists can play a major role. There are many important areas of alcohol-related behavior to be investigated.

1. The microanalysis of drinking itself, with taste and reactions to taste, for example, studying tongue and face positions as a measure of animal reaction to what is being presented.
2. The analysis of drinking intervals, both drinking bouts and interbout intervals, and how various neural systems relate to these occurrences.
3. Reward, aversion, and associated behaviors.
4. Cues and conditioning also are important as we discuss the operational meaning of craving and relapse. The understanding of these phenomena has been significantly advanced through behavioral science studies.
5. Memory and learning, which come up in several ways in alcoholism. The neural circuits of memory, for example, the ability to remember the consequences of one's decision to drink, are probably related to the important issue of tolerance.
6. Affect, that is, the mood that alcohol may be sought after to relieve or the mood that it perhaps creates. The study of these moods, which are sometimes dysphoric and sometimes pleasant, is also very much in the province of the behavioral sciences.
7. Development of research-based prevention approaches for high-risk young people identified early by their genes or deviant behavior.

CONCLUSION

The rapid advance of medical science holds great promise for improvements in the human condition. Alcohol research almost certainly will contribute to this new era of improved health as findings from research on the genetics of alcoholism and on alcohol's effects in the brain are applied to improve preventive, diagnostic, and treatment tools for these problems. Such improvements will lead to reduced personal, social, and economic consequences of alcohol-related problems and give rise to hope in those affected by alcohol abuse and alcoholism that their lives can be better.

REFERENCES

American Psychiatric Association. (1987). *Diagnostic and statistical manual of mental disorders* (3rd ed., rev.). Washington, DC: Author.

Baxter, L. R., Schwartz, J. M., Bergman, K. S., Szuba, M. P., Guze, B. H., Mazziotta, J. C, et al. (1992). Caudate glucose metabolic rate changes with both drug and behavior therapy for obsessive–compulsive disorder. *Archives of General Psychiatry, 49*, 681–689.

Begleiter, H., Porjesz, B., Reich, T., Edenberg, H. J., Goate, A., Blangero, J., et al. (1998). Quantitative trait loci analysis of human event-related brain potentials: P3 voltage. *Electroencephalography and Clinical Neurophysiology, 108*, 244–250.

Bowers, B. J., Owen, E. H., Collins, A. C., Abeliovich, A., Tonegawa, S., & Wehner, J. M. (1999). Decreased ethanol sensitivity and tolerance development in gamma-protein kinase C null mutant mice is dependent on genetic background. *Alcoholism: Clinical and Experimental Research, 23*, 387–397.

Cloninger, C. R., Bohman, M., Sigvardsson, S. (1981). Inheritance of alcohol abuse: Cross-fostering analysis of adopted men. *Archives of General Psychiatry, 38*, 861–868.

Cloninger, C. R., Sigvardsson, S., & Bohman, M. (1996). Type I and Type II alcoholism: An update. *Alcohol Health and Research World, 20*, 18–23.

Crabbe, J. C., Phillips, T. J., Feller, D. J., Hen, R., Wenger, C. D., Lessov, C. N., & Schafer, G. L. (1996). Elevated alcohol consumption in null mutant mice lacking 5-HT sub 1B serotonin receptors. *Nature Genetics, 14*, 98–101.

Grant, B. F., & Dawson, D. A. (1998). Age at onset of alcohol use and its association with *DSM–IV* alcohol abuse and dependence: Results from the National Longitudinal Alcohol Epidemiologic Survey. *Journal of Substance Abuse, 10*, 163–173.

Harris, R. A., McQuilkin, S. J., Paylor, R., Abeliovich, A., Tonegawa, S., & Wehner, J. M. (1995). Mutant mice lacking the gamma isoform of protein kinase C show decreased behavioral actions of ethanol and altered function of gamma-aminobutyrate type A receptors. *Proceedings of the National Academy of Sciences of the U.S.A., 92*, 3658–3662.

Melo, J. A., Shendure, J., Pociask, K., & Silver, L. M. (1995). Identification of sex-specific quantitative trait loci controlling alcohol preference in C57BL/6 mice. *Nature Genetics, 13*, 147– 153.

O'Malley, S. S., Jaffe, A. J., Chang, G., Rode, S., Schottenfeld, R., Meyer, R. E., & Rounsaville, B. (1996). Six-month follow-up of naltrexone and psychotherapy for alcohol dependence. *Archives of General Psychiatry, 53*, 217–224.

O'Malley, S. S., Jaffe, A. J., Chang, G., Schottenfeld, R. S., Meyer, R. E., & Rounsaville, B. (1992). Naltrexone and coping skills therapy for alcohol dependence: A controlled study. *Archives of General Psychiatry, 49*, 881–887.

Project MATCH Research Group. (1997). Matching alcoholism treatments to client heterogeneity: Project MATCH posttreatment drinking outcomes. *Journal of Studies on Alcohol, 58*, 7–29.

Reich, T., Edenberg, H. J., Goate, A., Williams, J. T., Rice, J. P., Van Eerdewegh, P., et al. (1998). Genome-wide search for genes affecting the risk for alcohol dependence. *American Journal of Medical Genetics (Neuropsychiatric Genetics)*, *81*, 207–215.

Schuckit, M. A., & Smith, T. L. (1996). An 8-year follow-up of 450 sons of alcoholic and control subjects. *Archives of General Psychiatry*, *53*, 202–210.

Schulteis, G., Hyytia, P., Heinrichs, S. C., & Koob, G. F. (1996). Effects of chronic ethanol exposure on oral self administration of ethanol or saccharin by Wistar rat. *Alcoholism: Clinical and Experimental Research*, *20*, 164–171.

Sinha, R., & O'Malley, S. S. (1999). Craving for alcohol: Findings from the clinic and laboratory. *Alcohol and Alcoholism*, *34*, 223–230.

Volpicelli, J. R., Alterman, A. I., Hayashida, M., & O'Brien, C. P. (1992). Naltrexone in the treatment of alcohol dependence. *Archives of General Psychiatry*, *49*, 876–880.

World Health Organization. (1992). *The ICD–10 classification of mental and behavioral disorders: Clinical descriptions and diagnostic guidelines* (10th ed.). Geneva, Switzerland: Author.

2

WHY PSYCHOLOGISTS SHOULD TREAT ALCOHOL AND DRUG PROBLEMS

WILLIAM R. MILLER AND SANDRA A. BROWN

It is no coincidence that the American Psychological Association's (APA's) College of Professional Psychology selected treatment of substance use disorders as the first proficiency area for specialist certification (S. A. Brown, 1996). There are persuasive reasons why all practicing psychologists should be proficient in assessing and treating alcohol/drug problems and why psychologists should be contributing to treatment systems, policy, and research in this area.

PREVALENCE AND IMPACT OF ALCOHOL AND DRUG PROBLEMS

Surveys since the 1960s have consistently found that about 1 in 10 American adults in the general population has significant problems related

Preparation of this chapter was supported by Grants K05-AA00133 and R01-AA07033 from the National Institute on Alcohol Abuse and Alcoholism.
    Reprinted from *American Psychologist, 52*, 1269–1279 (1997). Copyright 1997 by the American Psychological Association.

to his or her own use of alcohol (Cahalan, 1970; National Institute on Alcohol Abuse and Alcoholism [NIAAA], 1993). Approximately one quarter of U.S. adults are regular users of tobacco, and about 7% currently use illicit drugs (U.S. Department of Health and Human Services, 1996). Together, substance use disorders represent the most frequently occurring mental health problem (Regier et al., 1990). Furthermore, the prevalence of problematic alcohol/drug use is reliably higher in health care delivery settings than in the general population (Helzer & Pryzbeck, 1988). Depending on specialization and setting, between one quarter and one half of clients being treated by health care professionals for other medical and psychological problems evidence problems related to alcohol or other drug involvement (Kiesler, Simpkins, & Morton, 1991). Substance use disorders, in fact, are the most frequently occurring comorbid disorders among those with mental health problems (e.g., Brady, Castro, Lydiard, Malcomb, & Arana, 1991; Regier et al., 1990) and adversely affect the clinical course and prognosis for other mental health problems (e.g., Hesselbrock, Meyer, & Keener, 1985; Rounsaville, Dolinsky, Babor, & Meyer, 1987). Add to this the fact that problem drinking and drug use also adversely affect the lives of others (e.g., Billings & Moos, 1983; Newcomb & Bentler, 1988; Sher, 1991), and it is likely that substance abuse affects a significant proportion of the caseload of any mental health professional. At the very least, alcohol and other drug problems represent one of the most serious threats to clients' lives and health (Anderson, Cremona, Paton, Turner, & Wallace, 1993). Alcohol and tobacco constitute two of the three leading contributors to preventable death in the United States (McGinnis & Foege, 1993). Tobacco use alone is the largest preventable cause of illness, disability, and premature death in our society. Alcohol is involved in nearly half of traffic fatalities and a substantial proportion of violent deaths, suicides, drownings, falls, and other fatal accidents, constituting (after AIDS) the leading contributor to death among young people (Stinson, Dufour, Steffens, & DeBakey, 1993). Furthermore, alcohol and other drug involvement is associated with increased occurrence of high-risk sexual behaviors, HIV exposure, and AIDS. Approximately one third of all documented adolescent and adult AIDS cases in the United States are directly or indirectly attributable to injection drug use (Centers for Disease Control and Prevention [CDC], 1994). Alcohol/drug problems represent a primary contributor to health problems and medical hospitalization (Atkinson & Schuckit, 1981; Chen, Scheier, & Kandel, 1996). Alcohol abuse alone is involved in at least 100,000 premature deaths per year (McGinnis & Foege, 1993) and contributes a significant share to health care costs. Failure to deliver effective treatment for alcohol problems results in later escalating medical problems and health care costs (Kranzler, Babor, & Lauerman, 1990). The failure to recognize, assess, and effectively treat substance use disorders is a most serious omission in any clinical setting.

Given the prevalence and intertwining of substance use disorders with mental health problems, health care organizations are increasingly requiring that clinical providers demonstrate competency in the treatment of substance use disorders prior to approval to deliver more general mental health services. This reflects a trend toward the reasonable requirement that all mental health service providers be knowledgeable about substance abuse and competent to recognize and address these problems. Professionals without such expertise may eventually find themselves excluded from managed care systems (Horvath, 1993). Despite the prevalence of substance use disorders and the broad array of clinical contexts in which people with alcohol or other drug problems present for treatment, psychologists have often presumed that these disorders can only or best be treated in specialized programs. In the United States, the predominant treatments for alcohol/drug problems developed independent of scientific study, and education in this area has seldom been incorporated into the routine clinical training of psychologists. Thus, although the prevalence of substance-related problems is very high, psychologists have often been uncomfortable in assessing and treating these disorders as a routine part of their clinical activities.

WHAT PSYCHOLOGISTS HAVE TO OFFER

On the more positive side, there is reason to assert that psychologists are particularly qualified by their training to treat alcohol/drug problems. This assertion runs contrary to the common notion that treating substance abuse and dependence requires an entirely separate knowledge and expertise and a unique set of therapeutic procedures that are best delivered by those with personal experience (e.g., who are themselves recovering from such problems). In fact, as we discuss below, the most effective treatments are not idiosyncratic to substance use problems, and there are many reasons to expect that the accustomed skills and training of psychologists are of central importance in treating these behavioral problems. Furthermore, a large body of evidence consistently has shown that recovering professionals are neither more nor less effective than others in treating addictions (McLellan, Woody, Luborsky, & Goehl, 1988).

The Nature of Alcohol and Other Drug Problems

Popular stereotypes of substance use disorders construe them as primarily biological problems with predominantly genetic bases, which require medical treatment such as hospitalization and medication. Research, however, shows no persuasive advantage for inpatient over outpatient treatment of alcohol/ drug problems (Institute of Medicine, 1990a; McLellan et al., 1994; U.S. Congress, Office of Technology Assessment, 1983). Even acute detoxification, the period of greatest medical concern, can be handled safely and effectively on an outpatient basis in the vast majority of cases (Schuckit, 1995; Sparadeo et al., 1982; Whitfield et al., 1978). Although psychoactive substances by definition provoke significant physiological and neurochemical changes and behavioral–genetic research clearly points to hereditary risk factors for alcohol and drug dependence, most of the clinical activity that occurs even in medically oriented treatment programs is psychosocial in nature and focuses on rehabilitation. There is every reason to view substance abuse primarily as *behavior* that responds to the same psychological principles that govern behavioral problems more generally. For example, outcome after specialist treatment for substance use problems is strongly driven by posttreatment adjustment factors such as social resources, employment, and family environment (Billings & Moos, 1983; S. A. Brown, Myers, Mott, & Vik, 1994; Moos, 1994; Moos, Finney, & Cronkite, 1990). Relapse is predictable from cognitive factors such as drug expectancies (S. A. Brown, 1993a; Connors, Tarbox, & Faillace, 1993) and social and environmental resources (S. A. Brown, Vik, Patterson, Grant, & Schuckit, 1995; Tucker, Vuchinich, & Gladsjo, 1991), and the presence of behavioral coping skills is a protective factor against relapse for both adolescents and adults (S. A. Brown, 1993a; Marlatt & Gordon, 1985; Miller, Westerberg, Harris, & Tonigan, 1996; Myers, Brown, & Mott, 1993). Furthermore, psychoactive substance use responds to classical (Siegel, 1978, 1989; Vogel-Sprott, 1992) and operant learning (S. A. Brown, Mott, & Stewart, 1992; Tracey & Nathan, 1976) as well as modeling influences (e.g., Caudill & Lipscomb, 1980). In both alcohol/drug-dependent and nondependent individuals, substance use increases and decreases in response to ordinary principles of learning and conditioning. A person's status on various psychosocial dimensions (e.g., depression, conduct disorders, and social support) is clearly related to the likelihood of relapse (Hesselbrock et al., 1985; Myers & Brown, 1996; Rounsaville et al., 1987). In sum, evidence strongly supports a view of problematic alcohol/drug use as behavior that is modifiable by ordinary psychological principles and not as a mysterious, anomalous entity requiring only medical intervention and somehow impervious to psychosocial influence.

Comorbidity

As pointed out earlier, clients who present with mental health concerns have a substantially higher incidence of substance abuse as compared with the general population. The reverse is also true. People with an alcohol or other drug abuse dependence diagnosis have markedly higher lifetime risk for other diagnosable mental disorders (Regier et al., 1990; Robins, Helzer, Pryzbeck, & Regier, 1988), and clients who present for treatment of alcohol/drug problems show significantly elevated rates of many other mental disorders (S. A. Brown, Irwin, & Schuckit, 1991; S. A. Brown, Inaba, et al., 1994; Helzer & Pryzbeck, 1988). Although emotional and psychosocial problems often remit when alcohol/drug use is stopped or reduced (e.g., S. A. Brown & Schuckit, 1988; Miller, Hedrick, & Taylor, 1983), professionals who treat substance abuse must be prepared to recognize, assess, and address affective and anxiety disorders, marital problems, personality disorders, psychoses, sleep disorders, sexual dysfunctions, and posttraumatic stress disorders, all of which are overrepresented among people with alcohol and other drug problems (Hesselbrock et al., 1985) and may often persist or even worsen with abstinence. For this reason, it is advantageous for substance use disorders to be treated by professionals with both specialized and more general mental health expertise.

Obviously, the interactions between substance abuse and other mental disorders are complex. Clinical research demonstrates that alcohol and drug use may, in some cases, provoke depressive episodes or panic attacks, whereas for others, substances may be used to self-medicate persistent emotional problems such as social phobia or generalized anxiety disorder (e.g., Kushner, Sher, Wood, & Wood, 1994). In the latter case, referral to traditional treatment programs that focus exclusively on substance abuse may be less efficient and effective than treating both disorders in the context of individually tailored psychological interventions, particularly if specialist programs are not specifically designed to make those important comorbidity distinctions and offer effective interventions for the coexisting mental health disorder.

Thus, although it was once thought sufficient for a recovering counselor to handle all alcohol/drug problems, it is now abundantly clear that other significant mental health problems are most often one part of a constellation of sociopsychological difficulties in both adolescents (S. A. Brown, Gleghorn, Schuckit, Myers, & Mott, 1996; Jessor & Jessor, 1977; Kaminer, Tarter, Buksten, & Kabene, 1992) and adults with substance use disorders (Miller & Brown, 1991). Those who have only addiction expertise and who expect all other problems to remit with addiction treatment are ill-prepared to recognize other mental health problems or to provide individually tailored, comprehensive, and integrated assessment and therapeutic services.

In addition to the heterogeneity of problems accompanying addictive disorders, the heterogeneity of clients requires sensitivity and adaptation to individual differences. Age, gender, ethnicity, legal status, and a variety of other personal characteristics, including involvement with multiple substances (Miller & Bennett, 1996), can invoke special assessment and intervention needs among those with addictive disorders. Whereas "alcoholics" and "addicts" were once assumed to have homogeneous pathology and common personality traits, the data instead point to broad diversity among substance-dependent individuals. Such heterogeneity cannot be accommodated by a one-size-fits-all approach to assessment and intervention. For example, adolescents use a wide variety of strategies to make and maintain successful changes in their problematic alcohol/drug involvement, with only about half of teens following common behavioral prescriptions offered by treatment programs (S. A. Brown, 1993b). Given the complexity and comorbidity of substance use disorders, professionals who are trained in psychological assessment and who can offer an array of effective change strategies are well prepared to make important psychodiagnostic distinctions and to individualize treatment plans for those with substance use disorders.

Effective Treatment

A third persuasive reason why psychologists should treat alcohol/drug problems is that the treatment methods with documented efficacy for substance use disorders are primarily psychological in nature. Such documented efficacy will likely assume increasing importance as health care services undergo transition to managed care models. A series of reviews of the outcome literature on alcohol treatment, for example, has pointed to cognitive–behavioral strategies as those with most evidence of efficacy (Finney & Monahan, 1996; Institute of Medicine, 1990a; Miller, Brown, et al., 1995; Miller & Hester, 1980, 1986). Many of the effective treatments for alcohol/drug problems do not focus exclusively or even primarily on substance use but address the complex array of adjustment problems that are related to risk for relapse (Institute of Medicine, 1990a). These include social skills training (Monti, Abrams, Kadden, & Cooney, 1989; Monti, Rohsenow, Colby, & Abrams, 1995), behavioral marital therapy (O'Farrell, 1993, 1995), relapse prevention (Zackon, McAuliffe, & Ch'ien, 1993), stress management (Monti, Gulliver, & Myers, 1994; Stockwell, 1995), and the community-reinforcement approach (Higgins et al., 1993, 1995; Meyers & Smith, 1995). Behavioral and harm-reduction strategies compare favorably with other approaches when cost-effectiveness is the criterion (Finney & Monahan, 1996; Holder, Longabaugh, Miller, & Rubonis, 1991; Marlatt, Larimer, Baer, & Quigley, 1993). Psychoanalytically oriented and biologically focused treatments, by contrast, have at best a modest track record of success with alcohol problems. Although certain medications (e.g., acamprosate, disulfiram, naltrexone) have been found to decrease the frequency or severity of relapse to drinking and pharmacotherapy has played an important role in the management of other drug problems (e.g., methadone, nicotine patch), most experts agree that such medications are best regarded not as stand-alone treatments but rather as one part of effective therapeutic programs (Fuller, 1995; Hughes, 1995; Mason & Kocsis, 1994; O'Malley, Jaffe, Chang, & Schottenfeld, 1992).

For no particularly good reason, psychologists who detect a substance abuse problem often refer the client to a specialist program, even in cases where a solid therapeutic relationship has already been established. Presumably, the motivation behind this practice is to provide the client with a targeted treatment that is not within the professional's area of competence. Oddly enough, however, the treatment methods that have been traditionally practiced by many specialized alcohol/drug programs in the United States are among those least supported by scientific evidence (Miller, Brown, et al., 1995; Miller & Hester, 1986). There is little reason to expect that clients who are referred to such programs will be better served than by treatment from a competent professional with expertise in substance use disorders as well as other mental health problems. American substance abuse treatment services, like those for mental health problems more generally, have evolved on the basis of factors other than empirical evidence for their efficacy (Miller, 1992; Narrow, Regier, Rae, Manderscheid, & Locke, 1993).

This is not to say that general case management or undifferentiated supportive care will suffice to address substance use disorders. In fact, relatively undefined forms of counseling and psychotherapy have a poor track record (Miller, Brown, et al., 1995). A variety of treatment manuals have emerged from clinical research and can be useful in guiding therapeutic interventions for substance use disorders (e.g., Kadden et al., 1992; Meyers & Smith, 1995; Nowinski, Baker, & Carroll, 1992; Zackon et al., 1993). Knowledge of specific problems and risks attached to particular kinds of drug use (e.g., withdrawal risk and need for detoxification) is vital. Assuming that psychologists have the requisite knowledge and therapeutic skills (e.g., empathy, training in cognitive–behavioral approaches), clients with substance abuse may have at least as good a chance for recovery when receiving integrated psychological treatment as when referred to specialist programs.

The dramatic shift away from inpatient and residential treatment programs toward community-based care is also noteworthy. Although this is a relatively recent development in the United States and is partially driven by broader changes in health care, most other nations have long deemphasized residential treatment of substance use disorders, if they ever emphasized it at all. To be sure, there are reasons why hospitalization may be an important precaution in certain cases (e.g., acute suicidal risk, medical complications). As noted above, however, even detoxification can be handled on an ambulatory basis in the majority of cases, and controlled trials indicate that inpatient programs may yield no more favorable outcomes than those associated with outpatient treatment. Alcohol and other drug use are embedded in the fabric of clients' everyday lives, and prolonged remission often involves lifestyle change (Marlatt & Gordon, 1985). It is sensible, therefore, that in many cases, effective outcomes can be achieved by treatment within the client's community context, rather than by removal of the person from his or her natural environment. In any event, there clearly are a number of avenues to success for those attempting to recover from substance abuse (S. A. Brown, 1993b; Hester & Miller, 1995; Project MATCH Research Group, 1997;

Schuckit, 1995), and therapists trained to deal with diverse problems and approaches are likely to be well prepared to facilitate change among those with alcohol or other drug problems.

The findings of the Project MATCH Research Group (1993, 1997) are instructive in this regard. In the largest randomized trial of psychotherapies conducted to date, this multisite study compared three well-specified individual outpatient treatment approaches designed to differ substantially in both rationale and practice: cognitive–behavioral skill training (Kadden et al., 1992), 12-step facilitation therapy (Nowinski et al., 1992), and a briefer (4 vs. 12 sessions), motivational enhancement therapy (Miller, Zweben, DiClemente, & Rychtarik, 1992). The study enrolled 1,726 clients with alcohol abuse or (primarily) dependence, who were treated by more than 80 therapists. Statistically significant differences in outcomes did emerge among treatments at various points during 15 months of follow-up, but they were small in absolute magnitude, and the more striking pattern was the high degree of improvement on multiple dimensions in all three treatment conditions. This further illustrates that psychologically based treatments are associated with substantial improvement in alcohol use and problems and argues empirically for mutual respect among those pursuing different, specific approaches to the treatment of substance abuse.

It is also worth noting that effective intervention can be provided long before severe problems develop. For example, a variety of low-threshold, low-intensity interventions are available for at-risk drinkers (e.g., Bien, Miller, & Tonigan, 1993; World Health Organization Brief Intervention Study Group, 1996) and can be offered independently or readily integrated into ongoing psychotherapeutic activities. Given the high comorbidity of substance use disorders and the mental health problems that ordinarily bring people to the attention of psychologists, it is sensible to screen routinely for alcohol/drug problems and to offer at least brief intervention in the context of psychological practice (e.g., NIAAA, 1995). Behavioral intervention approaches, developed by psychologists and cost-effective from a health services perspective, are available to deter the progression of alcohol/drug involvement and reduce future risk and harm (e.g., Brettle, 1991; Institute of Medicine, 1990a; Marlatt et al., 1993). Thus, in contrast to the common perception that substance abuse must be treated in specialized programs outside the context of psychotherapy, a diversity of rather easily administered behavioral programs are available to psychologists for use in standard clinical practice.

Motivation for Change

Recent evidence also suggests that motivation is a key issue in treating substance use disorders. In the past, motivation was sometimes regarded as if it were a client attribute, without which therapeutic efforts were likely to be futile (Miller, 1985). Traditional confrontational programs have required high motivation to enter and persist in treatment (Marlatt et al., 1993). More recent studies suggest that motivation fluctuates over time even without formal treatment and that environmental factors and personal experiences can dramatically alter one's motivation and readiness to reduce substance involvement or to seek treatment (e.g., Beattie et al., 1993; Cunningham, Sobell, Sobell, Agrawal, & Toneatto, 1993; Hasin, 1994). Psychological models of motivation have substantial applicability to alcohol/drug problems (e.g. Janis & Mann, 1977; Miller & Brown, 1991; Prochaska, DiClemente, & Norcross, 1992). The transtheoretical model of change (Prochaska et al., 1992), originally developed through studies of smokers who were attempting to quit smoking, points to strategies for helping those who are unaware of problems, are ambivalent about change, or are otherwise not yet ready for change.

The contexts in which alcohol or other drug problems are first identified and discussed provide a unique opportunity to enhance motivation for change and to intervene at earlier points in problem development (Bucholz, Homan, & Helzer, 1992). Given fluctuations in motivation to change substance use patterns, intervention efforts that can be quickly implemented by trusted professionals in the context of broader health care offer some persuasive advantages. Clinical trials have demonstrated, with surprising consistency, that even relatively brief interventions (one to three sessions) can have a significant beneficial impact on problem drinking (Bien, Miller, & Tonigan, 1993). More specifically, brief motivational interventions have been found to exert a substantial impact on the drinking outcomes of both self-referred problem drinkers (e.g., Miller, Benefield, & Tonigan, 1993) and clinical samples of alcoholics (Bien, Miller, & Boroughs, 1993; J. M. Brown & Miller, 1993). Beneficial effects of motivational therapies have also been demonstrated with marijuana (Stephens & Roffman, 1993), heroin (Saunders, Wilkinson, & Phillips, 1995), and polysubstance abuse (Henggeler, 1993). In fact, such brief interventions may exert a long-term benefit similar in magnitude to that of more extensive specialized treatment (e.g., Chapman & Huygens, 1988; Edwards et al., 1977; Miller, Taylor, & West, 1980). Taken together, these findings do not fit the classic notion that characterologic denial is inherent in substance use disorders. Rather, they suggest even brief psychological intervention can induce motivational shifts and long-term change in substance use problems. Motivationally focused treatments should be well within the comfortable repertoire of most clinically trained psychologists (Miller & Rollnick, 1991). Such treatments also appear to be associated with relatively rapid progress in treatment, an increasingly important factor with growing health care cost-containment concerns (Goodman, Holder, Nishiura, & Hankin, 1992).

Therapist Characteristics

Another strikingly consistent finding in the addiction literature is the impact of therapist characteristics (Najavits & Weiss, 1994). Clients assigned at random to therapists within the same program, who use ostensibly the same treatment approach, may experience substantially different outcomes (e.g., Luborsky, McLellan, Woody, O'Brien, & Auerbach, 1985; Miller et al., 1980). Research points to the Rogerian quality of therapist empathy as a predictor of favorable outcomes (Miller et al., 1980, 1993; Valle, 1981). Although accurate empathy is a common nonspecific element in the general training of mental health professionals, it stands in stark contrast to American notions of an effective counseling style for alcohol/drug abuse, which have emphasized aggressively confronting denial and dishonesty and breaking down defenses (Fox, 1967; Miller, 1985). Such aggressive therapist responses, actively discouraged by most psychology training programs in the treatment of other disorders, unfortunately have been portrayed in recent decades as normative and necessary in substance abuse treatment (Miller & Rollnick, 1991).

In fact, therapist responses do appear to play a key and enduring role in client motivation and change in the area of alcohol/drug problems. For example, problem drinkers assigned to therapists who were low in empathy were found to fare worse than if they had been left to self-help efforts (Miller et al., 1980). More aggressive confrontational tactics have a less than stellar record in alcohol treatment outcome research (Miller, Brown, et al., 1995) and may be particularly disadvantageous for clients with low self-esteem (Annis & Chan, 1983). Furthermore, professionally trained psychologists are less likely to be steeped in a dispositional disease model, belief in which has been linked to inflexibility in therapists (Moyers & Miller, 1993) and relapse in alcoholic clients (Miller, Westerberg, et al., 1996).

CHANGING THE ZEITGEIST

To summarize discussion thus far, substance use disorders are the most prevalent form of mental health problems and are frequent concomitants of many other diagnoses. Alcohol/drug abuse significantly threatens the lives, health, and welfare of clients and those around them. Substance use is a behavior that responds to ordinary principles of learning. A variety of effective treatment methods are already available, most of which are substantially psychological in focus. Motivation, a common issue in psychological intervention, appears to play a crucial role in the maintenance and treatment of alcohol/drug problems. Therapeutic skills that are commonly acquired by psychologists have been linked to successful client recovery. Alcohol/drug problems are commonly accompanied by a matrix of psychosocial problems and psychological disorders.

Why, then, have so few psychologists identified themselves as having expertise in this area, and why have so few reported treating alcohol/drug problems in their practices? There appear to be several barriers for psychologists in routinely treating substance use disorders. Perhaps chief of these has been the fact that, like other health professionals, many practicing psychologists received limited addiction-focused training during their graduate and postgraduate careers. It is true that substance use disorders seem to respond to the same general therapeutic processes that are effective with other forms of psychopathology and that treatment often involves addressing a broader range of psychosocial problems. Yet, as with other disorders such as depression and schizophrenia, there is a certain amount of specific knowledge needed for professional competence in assessment and treatment of addictive disorders (e.g., Donovan & Marlatt, 1988; Hanson & Venturelli, 1995; Hester & Miller, 1995; Miller & C'de Baca, 1995). The training of psychologists has usually failed to provide this piece of the puzzle (S. A. Brown, 1994). Thus, although psychologists are in general well prepared to deal with alcohol/drug problems for the reasons stated above, they have too often lacked the specific training, encouragement, and confidence to treat these common disorders. We are not advocating extensive specialist training, although that can also be of value. The emergence of specialist training and certification programs represents an opportunity for some psychologists to develop deeper expertise in addiction research and treatment. It is neither realistic nor necessary, however, for all psychologists to receive intensive specialized training in this area, but all psychologists do need a certain level of proficiency to deal with these highly prevalent problems. Precisely because of the more general nature of substance use disorders, training in this area is best integrated with, rather than segregated from, the routine graduate education of psychologists. Indeed, addictive behaviors provide excellent examples of and a superb field for studying ordinary principles of learning, self-control, cognition, behavior change, and clinical therapeutics (Baumeister, Heatherton, & Tice, 1994; S. A. Brown, 1994; Logan, 1993; Orford, 1985).

A second barrier for psychologists in routinely treating alcohol/drug problems in their practice is our failure to disseminate modern, clinical research findings to practitioners and to psychologists in training. Substance abuse clinical research historically lagged behind treatment research for disorders such as depression and schizophrenia, but the past 3 decades have produced a surge of new knowledge about the nature of addictive behaviors and of efficacious treatment and prevention. Although a unitary disease model continues to dominate popular opinion and media coverage of alcohol/drug problems in the United States, psychological (e.g., Marlatt & Gordon, 1985; Orford, 1985; Peele, 1985) and medical experts (e.g.,

Institute of Medicine, 1990a) have been moving dramatically toward a rather different understanding. Diagnosis has moved away from older conceptions (such as "alcoholism") toward dimensional concepts such as abuse (problems) and dependence (American Psychiatric Association, 1994; Miller, Westerberg, & Waldron, 1995). These are understood as lying along a behavioral continuum, varying quantitatively (in severity) but not qualitatively from normality (Institute of Medicine, 1990a). Thus, emphasis has shifted away from whether an individual does or does not "have" a disease, toward thinking of alcohol/drug abuse as a multidimensional public health problem. In this way, the evaluation and treatment of alcohol/drug problems are being integrated into our larger systems of health care, including preventive medicine, primary care, and health psychology. Therefore, psychologists need to be trained to be familiar with and prepared to assess and treat substance use disorders.

As this conceptual transition occurs, we may also move away from what has been another insidious barrier for psychologists in treating alcohol/drug problems: our sociopolitical history. Historically, these problems have been stigmatized, carrying negative moral connotations. Ironically, the disease model that was supposed to diffuse moralistic judgment has instead become intertwined with it (Moyers & Miller, 1993; Peele, 1989; Szasz, 1974). One result of this stigma, and of the idea that one either "is" or "isn't" an alcoholic/ addict, is that people are dissuaded from recognizing a concern and seeking help until their problems have become severe and recalcitrant. Scientific evidence supports nothing like a black-or-white diagnostic picture but rather a continuum of severity, as occurs with most psychological problems. Psychologists have a responsibility to assess routinely for alcohol/drug problems (including dependence) and to address such problems when they are part of the clinical picture. Such routine screening and assessment afford the opportunity for secondary prevention, to intervene earlier in the development of problems when behavior is likely to be more malleable and severe harm can be averted.

In sum, psychologists should not and realistically cannot avoid treating substance use disorders. They affect a substantial proportion of the general population and are particularly common among people seen for health and psychological care. Effective treatment of alcohol/drug problems is not a mysterious art. In fact, scientific evidence is abundant and points to the efficacy of therapeutic styles and common treatment approaches that are well within the repertoire of many psychologists. The specialist mystique that has surrounded substance abuse treatment in the United States has needlessly dissuaded psychologists from offering assessment and effective treatment and is perhaps partly responsible for the limited routine coverage of this area in the training of psychologists. Psychological models, assessment, and treatments have much to offer in the care of people with these common problems that are the source of so much suffering and mortality. Psychologists need at least basic competence to recognize, evaluate, and address addictive behaviors (S. A. Brown, 1994). This is likely to happen only if such preparation becomes a routine part of the training of clinical psychologists.

IMPLICATIONS FOR TRAINING OF PSYCHOLOGISTS

It is unlikely that new courses in alcohol and other drug problems will be added to the already extensive requirements in the training of clinical psychologists. To be sure, it is highly desirable that graduate programs offer specialized elective courses and practicums in substance abuse, but even when this is done, only a minority of clinical students may avail themselves of such training (Miller & C'de Baca, 1995).

A more achievable means is needed if we are to provide psychologists with competence and confidence in substance abuse intervention during their training. What is needed is not a radical expansion of clinical training curricula but rather an intentional and substantial inclusion of alcohol/drug problems in the core course work and training of psychologists in psychopathology, assessment, and treatment. First and foremost, psychologists in training need to be encouraged and expected from the beginning to think of substance abuse as a necessary and vital problem area to be included within their range of their professional competence, just as is the case for depression, anxiety disorders, and psychoses. The very skills that are often learned during the course of clinical training (e.g., accurate empathy, structured assessment, motivational enhancement, coping-skills training) are directly applicable and effective in treating substance abuse and dependence. Rather than leaving psychologists to refer to specialty programs when substance abuse happens to be discovered, clinical programs should be educating trainees routinely to screen for, assess, and treat these behaviors. An important element here is instilling a positive attitude toward the study and treatment of alcohol/drug problems, for such optimism is indeed warranted on the basis of outcome research.

Second, there is a core of knowledge about substance use disorders that should be part of the information base of all psychologists, not only those specializing in this field. Such core knowledge should consistently be included in graduate courses that are commonly required for clinical students (e.g., psychopathology, assessment, and developmental and social psychology). For example, all psychologists should be taught reliable and valid procedures to screen for and assess these common problems. This process would be greatly facilitated by the preparation of clear guidelines for the teaching of core knowledge within the context and time frames of clinical psychology training. Such guidelines for psychology training with regard to alcohol were commissioned over a decade ago by NIAAA, but unfortunately the volume completed by Sobell and Sobell (n.d.) was never released. APA Division 50

(Division on Addictions) developed knowledge-based objectives for substance abuse that could serve as a catalyst for incorporating substance abuse information into graduate training, and McCrady and Epstein's (1999) edited volume provides a comprehensive resource.

Third, substance abuse should be explicitly incorporated into the practicum training of clinical, counseling, and educational psychologists. One means to accomplish this is by having specialist substance abuse programs among the possible placement options. However, unless a specialist treatment program is advanced in its approaches, students placed in such a setting may not be exposed to the most current and effective methods for conceptualizing and treating substance use disorders (Pritchard, Wolfe, Waldron, & Miller, 1997). Optimally, screening for and assessing alcohol/drug use should be incorporated as a component of standard training practicums, When this is done, it is likely that a significant proportion of clients being treated for other presenting complaints will be found also to show substance use problems. The treatment of such problems should be considered a normal part of the training of psychologists in both professional schools and scientist-practitioner programs.

The general tenor here is to draw substance abuse into the mainstream of psychological expertise. Given the striking prevalence of these disorders, their potential for devastation, and their interweaving with so many other psychological and health problems, it is unethical not to train psychologists to recognize, assess, and treat these disorders. Furthermore, given the emerging demand within health care for the use of demonstrably cost-effective approaches, psychologists are well suited to incorporate substance abuse treatment as part of standard care. The core knowledge is conveniently assembled and is accessible free of charge (e.g., Allen & Columbus, 1995; NIAAA, 1993; National Institute on Drug Abuse, 1991). Highly effective psychological treatments are available (e.g., CDC, 1996; Hester & Miller, 1995; Institute of Medicine, 1990a, 1990b). Many psychometrically sound assessment methods have been developed (Allen & Columbus, 1995; McLellan et al., 1992; Miller, Tonigan, & Longabaugh, 1995). Clients with substance use disorders abound, whether or not identified, in nearly all clinical settings. What remains is for psychology training programs to see that the psychologists of the future will be consistently encouraged and prepared to use their expertise in the alleviation of this common, major source of human suffering.

CONCLUSION

Alcohol and other drug problems are so prevalent in American society and so commonly accompany other psychological and medical disorders that clinical and counseling psychologists should be trained routinely in their recognition, screening, diagnosis, assessment, prevention, and treatment. The incidence, morbidity, and mortality of substance use disorders warrant a priority at least equal to that for affective and anxiety disorders. As a behavioral science, psychology has much to contribute in this area. A variety of effective prevention and treatment methods are already available, most of which fall easily within the repertoire of cognitive-behaviorally trained psychologists. Although there is a body of specialized knowledge to be acquired for competence, psychologists are well prepared by their training to treat alcohol/drug disorders, particularly because of their comorbidity with many other psychosocial problems. A personal history of addiction and recovery is unrelated to therapists' effectiveness in treating substance use disorders. Psychologists have a vital role to play in addressing these common, devastating, and highly treatable problems.

REFERENCES

References marked with a dagger indicate material that is available free of charge from the National Clearinghouse for Alcohol and Drug Information, P.O. Box 2345, Rockville, MD 20847-2345.

†Allen, J. A., & Columbus, M. (Eds.). (1995). *Assessing alcohol problems* (NIAAA Treatment Handbook Series No. 4). Rockville, MD: National Institute on Alcohol Abuse and Alcoholism.

American Psychiatric Association. (1994). *Diagnostic and statistical manual of mental disorders* (4th ed.). Washington, DC: Author.

Anderson, P., Cremona, A., Paton, A., Turner, C., & Wallace, P. (1993). The risk of alcohol. *Addiction, 88,* 1493–1508.

Annis, H. M., & Chan, D. (1983). The differential treatment model: Empirical evidence from a personality typology of adult offenders. *Criminal Justice & Behavior, 10,* 159–173.

Atkinson, J. H., Jr., & Schuckit, M. A. (1981). Alcoholism and over-the-counter and prescription drug misuse in the elderly. In C. Einsdorfer (Ed.), *Annual review of gerontology and geriatrics* (Vol. 2, pp. 225–284). New York: Springer.

Baumeister, R. F., Heatherton, T. F., & Tice, D. M. (1994). *Losing control: How and why people fail at self-regulation.* New York: Academic Press.

Beattie, M. C., Longabaugh, R., Elliott, G., Stout, R. L., Fava, J., & Noel, N. E. (1993). Effect of the social environment on alcohol involvement and subjective well-being prior to alcoholism treatment. *Journal of Studies on Alcohol, 54,* 283–296.

Bien, T H., Miller, W. R., & Boroughs, J. M. (1993). Motivational interviewing with alcohol outpatients. *Behavioural and Cognitive Psychotherapy, 21,* 347–356.

Bien, T. H., Miller, W. R., & Tonigan, J. S. (1993). Brief interventions for alcohol problems: A review. *Addiction, 88,* 315–336.

Billings, A. G., & Moos, R. H. (1983). Psychosocial processes of recovery among alcoholics and their families: Implications for clinicians and program evaluators. *Addictive Behaviors, 8,* 205–218.

Brady, K., Castro, S., Lydiard, R. B., Malcomb, R., & Arana, G. (1991). Substance abuse in an inpatient psychiatric sample. *American Journal of Drug and Alcohol Abuse, 17*, 389–397.

Brettle, R. P. (1991). HIV and harm reduction for injection drug users. *A.I.D.S., 5*, 125–136.

Brown, J. M., & Miller, W. R. (1993). Impact of motivational interviewing on participation and outcome in residential alcoholism treatment. *Psychology of Addictive Behaviors, 7*, 211–218.

Brown, S. A. (1993a). Drug effect expectancies and addictive behavior change. *Experimental and Clinical Psychopharmacology, 1*, 55–67.

Brown, S. A. (1993b). Recovery patterns in adolescent substance abuse. In J. S. Baer, G. A. Marlatt, & R. J. McMahon (Eds.), *Addictive behaviors across the life span* (pp. 161–183). Beverly Hills, CA: Sage.

Brown, S. A. (1994). Addiction training needs for psychologists. In W. M. Cox (Chair), *Education and training in addictive behavior.* Symposium conducted at the 102nd Annual Convention of the American Psychological Association, Los Angeles.

Brown, S. A. (1996). Division 50 and the College of Professional Psychology. *The Addictions Newsletter, 3*(2), 4–7.

Brown, S. A., Gleghorn, A., Schuckit, M. A., Myers, M. G., & Mott, M. A. (1996). Conduct disorder among adolescent alcohol and drug abusers. *Journal of Studies on Alcohol, 57*, 314–324.

Brown, S. A., Inaba, R. K., Gillin, J. C., Stewart, M. A., Schuckit, M. A., & Irwin, M. R. (1994). Alcoholism and affective disorder: Clinical course of depressive symptoms. *American Journal of Psychiatry, 152*, 45–52.

Brown, S. A., Irwin, M., & Schuckit, M. A. (1991). Changes in anxiety among abstinent male alcoholics. *Journal of Studies on Alcohol. 52*, 55–61.

Brown, S. A., Mott, M. A., & Stewart, M. A. (1992). Adolescent alcohol and drug abuse. In C. E. Walker & M. C. Roberts (Eds.), *Handbook of clinical child psychology* (2nd ed., pp. 677–693). New York: Wiley.

Brown, S. A., Myers, M. G., Mott, M. A., & Vik, P. W. (1994). Correlates of success following treatment for adolescent substance abuse. *Applied and Preventive Psychology, 3*, 61–73.

Brown, S. A., & Schuckit, M. A. (1988). Changes in depression among abstinent alcoholics. *Journal of Studies on Alcohol, 49*, 412–417.

Brown, S. A., Vik, P. W., Patterson, T. L., Grant, I., & Schuckit, M. A. (1995). Stress, vulnerability and adult alcohol relapse. *Journal of Studies on Alcohol, 56*, 538–545.

Bucholz, K. K., Homan, S. M., & Helzer, J. E. (1992). When do alcoholics first discuss drinking problems? *Journal of Studies on Alcohol, 53*, 582–589.

Cahalan, D. (1970). *Problem drinkers: A national survey.* San Francisco: Jossey-Bass.

Caudill, B. D., & Lipscomb, T. R. (1980). Modeling influences on alcoholics' rates of alcohol consumption. *Journal of Applied Behavior Analysis, 13*, 355–365.

Centers for Disease Control and Prevention. (1994). *HIV/AIDS surveillance report*. Atlanta, GA: Author.

Centers for Disease Control and Prevention. (1996). *Smoking cessation* (Clinical Practice Guideline No. 18). Washington, DC: U.S. Government Printing Office.

Chapman, P. L. H., & Huygens, I. (1988). An evaluation of three treatment programmes for alcoholism: An experimental study with 6- and 18-month follow-ups. *British Journal of Addiction, 83,* 67–81.

Chen, K., Scheier, L. M., & Kandel, D. B. (1996). Effects of chronic cocaine use on physical health: A prospective study in a general population sample. *Drug and Alcohol Dependence, 43,* 23–37.

Connors, G. J., Tarbox, A. R., & Faillace, L. A. (1993). Changes in alcohol expectancies and drinking behavior among treated problem drinkers. *Journal of Studies on Alcohol, 54,* 676–683.

Cunningham, J. A., Sobell, L. C., Sobell, M. B., Agrawal, S., & Toneatto, T. (1993). Barriers to treatment: Why alcohol and drug abusers delay or never seek treatment. *Addictive Behaviors, 18,* 347–353.

Donovan, D. M., & Marlatt, G. A. (Eds.). (1988). *Assessment of addictive behaviors*. New York: Guilford Press.

Edwards, G., Orford, J., Egert, S., Guthrie, S., Hawker, A., Hensman, C., et al. (1977). Alcoholism: A controlled trial of "treatment" and "advice." *Journal of Studies on Alcohol, 38,* 1004–1031.

Finney, J. W., & Monahan, S. C. (1996). The cost effectiveness of treatment for alcoholism: A second approximation. *Journal of Studies on Alcohol, 57,* 229–243.

Fox, R. (1967). A multidisciplinary approach to the treatment of alcoholism. *American Journal of Psychotherapy, 123,* 769–778.

Fuller, R. K. (1995). Antidipsotropic medications. In R. K. Hester & W. R. Miller (Eds.), *Handbook of alcoholism treatment approaches: Effective alternatives* (2nd ed., pp. 123–133). Boston: Allyn & Bacon.

Goodman, A. C., Holder, H. D., Nishiura, E., & Hankin, J. R. (1992). An analysis of short-term alcoholism treatment cost functions. *Medical Care, 30,* 795–810.

Hanson, G., & Venturelli, P. J. (1995). *Drugs and society* (4th ed.). Boston: Jones & Bartlett.

Hasin, D. S. (1994). Treatment/self-help for alcohol-related problems: Relationship to social pressure and alcohol dependence. *Journal of Studies on Alcohol, 55,* 660–666.

Helzer, J. E., & Pryzbeck, T. R. (1988). The co-occurrence of alcoholism with other psychiatric disorder in the general population and its impact on treatment. *Journal of Studies on Alcohol, 49,* 219–224.

†Henggeler, S. W. (1993). Multisystemic treatment of serious juvenile offenders: Implications for the treatment of substance abusing youth. In L. S. Onken, J. D. Blaine, & J. J. Boren (Eds.), *Behavioral treatments for drug abuse and dependence* (Research Monograph 137, pp. 181–199). Rockville, MD: National Institute on Drug Abuse.

Hesselbrock, M. N., Meyer, R. E., & Keener, J. J. (1985). Psychopathology in hospitalized alcoholics. *Archives of General Psychiatry, 42,* 1050–1055.

Hester, R. K., & Miller, W. R. (Eds.). (1995). *Handbook of alcoholism treatment approaches: Effective alternatives* (2nd ed.). Boston: Allyn & Bacon.

Higgins, S. T., Budney, A. J., Bickel, W. K., Badger, G. J., Foerg, F. E., & Ogden, D. (1995). Outpatient behavioral treatment for cocaine dependence: One-year outcome. *Experimental and Clinical Psychopharmacology, 3,* 205–212.

Higgins, S. T., Budney, A. J., Bickel, W. K., Hughes, J. R., Foerg, F. E., & Badger, G. J. (1993). Achieving cocaine abstinence with a behavioral approach. *American Journal of Psychiatry, 150,* 763–769.

Holder, H., Longabaugh, R., Miller, W. R., & Rubonis, A. V. (1991). The cost effectiveness of treatment for alcoholism: A first approximation. *Journal of Studies on Alcohol, 52,* 517–540.

Horvath, A. T. (1993). Enhancing motivation for treatment of addictive behavior: Guidelines for the psychotherapist. *Psychotherapy, 30,* 473–480.

†Hughes, J. R. (1995). Clinical implications of the association between smoking and alcoholism. In J. B. Fertig & J. P. Allen (Eds.), *Alcohol and tobacco: From basics to clinical practice* (pp. 171–186). Washington, DC: U.S. Department of Health and Human Services, Public Health Service, National Institutes of Health, National Institute on Alcohol Abuse and Alcoholism.

Institute of Medicine, National Academy of Sciences. (1990a). *Broadening the base of treatment for alcohol problems.* Washington, DC: National Academy Press.

Institute of Medicine, National Academy of Sciences. (1990b). *Treating drug problems.* Washington, DC: National Academy Press.

Janis, I. L., & Mann, L. (1977). *Decision-making: A psychological analysis of conflict, choice, and commitment.* New York: Free Press.

Jessor, R., & Jessor, S. (1977). *Problem behavior and psychosocial development: A longitudinal study of youth.* New York: Academic Press.

†Kadden, R., Carroll, K., Donovan, D., Cooney, N., Monti, P., Abrams, D., et al. (1992). *Cognitive–behavioral coping skills therapy manual: A clinical research guide for therapists treating individuals with alcohol abuse and dependence* (Vol. 3, Project MATCH Monograph Series). Rockville, MD: National Institute on Alcohol Abuse and Alcoholism.

Kaminer, Y., Tarter, R. E., Buksten, O. G., & Kabene, M. (1992). Comparison between treatment completers and noncompleters among dually diagnosed substance-abusing adolescents. *Journal of the American Academy of Child and Adolescent Psychiatry, 31,* 1046–1049.

Kiesler, C. A., Simpkins, C. G., & Morton, T. L. (1991). Prevalence of dual diagnosis of mental and substance abuse disorders in general hospitals. *Hospital and Community Psychiatry, 42,* 400–403.

Kranzler, H. R., Babor, T. F., & Lauerman, R. J. (1990). Problems associated with average alcohol consumption and frequency of intoxication in a medical population. *Alcoholism, Clinical and Experimental Research, 14,* 119–126.

Kushner, M. G., Sher, K. J., Wood, M. D., & Wood, P. K. (1994). Anxiety and drinking behavior: Moderating effects of tension-reduction alcohol outcome expectancies. *Alcoholism: Clinical & Experimental, 18,* 852–860.

Logan, E A. (1993). Animal learning and motivation and addictive drugs. *Psychological Reports, 73,* 291–306.

Luborsky, L., McLellan, A. T., Woody, G. E., O'Brien, C. P., & Auerbach, A. (1985). Therapist success and its determinants. *Archives of General Psychiatry, 42,* 602–611.

Marlatt, G. A., & Gordon, J. R. (1985). *Relapse prevention.* New York: Guilford Press.

Marlatt, G. A., Larimer, M. E., Baer, J. S., & Quigley, L.A. (1993). Harm reduction for alcohol problems: Moving beyond the controlled drinking controversy. *Behavior Therapy, 24,* 461–503.

Mason, B. J., & Kocsis, J. H. (1994). Desipramine in the treatment of depressed alcoholics. *American Journal of Psychiatry, 151,* 1248.

McCrady, B. S., & Epstein, E. E. (Eds.). (1999). *Addictions: A comprehensive guidebook.* New York: Oxford University Press.

McGinnis, J. M., & Foege, W. H. (1993). Actual causes of death in the United States. *Journal of the American Medical Association, 270,* 2207–2212.

McLellan, A. T., Alterman, A. I., Metzger, D. S., Grissom, G. R., Woody, G. E., Luborsky, L., & O'Brien, C. P. (1994). Similarity of outcome predictors across opiate, cocaine, and alcohol treatments: Role of treatment services [Special section]. *Journal of Consulting and Clinical Psychology, 62,* 1141 – 1158.

McLellan, A. T., Kushner, H., Metzger, D., Peters, R., Smith, I., Grissom, G., et al. (1992). The fifth edition of the Addiction Severity Index. *Journal of Substance Abuse Treatment, 9,* 199–213.

McLellan, A. T., Woody, G. E., Luborsky, L., & Goehl, L. (1988). Is the counselor an "active ingredient" in substance abuse rehabilitation? An examination of treatment success among four counselors. *Journal of Nervous and Mental Disease, 176,* 423–430.

Meyers, R. J., & Smith, J. E. (1995). *Clinical guide to alcohol treatment: The community reinforcement approach.* New York: Guilford Press.

Miller, W. R. (1985). Motivation for treatment: A review with special emphasis on alcoholism. *Psychological Bulletin, 98,* 84–107.

Miller, W. R. (1992). The evolution of treatment for alcohol problems since 1945. In P. G. Erickson & H. Kalant (Eds.), *Windows on science: 40th anniversary scientific lecture series* (pp. 107–124). Toronto, Ontario, Canada: Addiction Research Foundation.

Miller, W. R., Benefield, R. G., & Tonigan, J. S. (1993). Enhancing motivation for change in problem drinking: A controlled comparison of two therapist styles. *Journal of Consulting and Clinical Psychology, 61,* 455–461.

Miller, W. R., & Bennett, M. E. (1996). Treating alcohol problems in the context of other drug abuse. *Alcohol Health & Research World, 20,* 118–123.

Miller, W. R., & Brown, J. M. (1991). Self-regulation as a conceptual basis for the prevention and treatment of addictive behaviours. In N. Heather, W. R. Miller, & J. Greeley (Eds.), *Self-control and the addictive behaviours* (pp. 3–79). Sydney: Maxwell Macmillan Publishing Australia.

Miller, W. R., Brown, J. M., Simpson, T. L., Handmaker, N. S., Bien, T. H., Luckie, L. E., et al. (1995). What works? A methodological analysis of the alcohol treatment outcome literature. In R. K. Hester & W. R. Miller (Eds.), *Handbook of alcoholism treatment approaches: Effective alternatives* (2nd ed., pp. 12–44). Boston: Allyn & Bacon.

Miller, W. R., & C'de Baca, J. (1995). What every mental health professional should know about alcohol. *Journal of Substance Abuse Treatment, 12,* 355–365.

Miller, W. R., Hedrick, K. E., & Taylor, C. A. (1983). Addictive behaviors and life problems before and after behavioral treatment of problem drinkers. *Addictive Behaviors, 8,* 403–412.

Miller, W. R., & Hester, R. K. (1980). Treating the problem drinkers: Modern approaches. In W. R. Miller (Ed.), *The addictive behaviors: Treatment of alcoholism, drug abuse, smoking and obesity* (pp. 11–141). Oxford, England: Pergamon Press.

Miller, W. R., & Hester, R. K. (1986). The effectiveness of alcoholism treatment methods: What research reveals. In W.R. Miller & N. Heather (Eds.), *Treating addictive behaviors: Processes of change* (pp. 121–174). New York: Plenum Press.

Miller, W. R., & Rollnick, S. (1991). *Motivational interviewing: Preparing people to change addictive behavior.* New York: Guilford Press.

Miller, W. R., Taylor, C. A., & West, J. C. (1980). Focused versus broad spectrum behavior therapy for problem drinkers. *Journal of Consulting and Clinical Psychology, 48,* 590–601.

†Miller, W. R., Tonigan, J. S., & Longabaugh, R. (1995). *The Drinker Inventory of Consequences (DrInC): An instrument for assessing adverse consequences of alcohol abuse. Test manual* (Vol. 4, Project MATCH Monograph Series). Rockville, MD: National Institute on Alcohol Abuse and Alcoholism.

Miller, W. R., Westerberg, V. S., Harris, R. J., & Tonigan, J. S. (1996). What predicts relapse? Prospective testing of antecedent models. *Addiction, 91*(Suppl.), S155–S171.

Miller, W. R., Westerberg, V. S., & Waldron, H. B. (1995). Evaluating alcohol problems. In R. K. Hester & W. R. Miller (Eds.), *Handbook of alcoholism treatment approaches: Effective alternatives* (2nd ed., pp. 61–88). Boston: Allyn & Bacon.

†Miller, W. R., Zweben, A., DiClemente, C. C., & Rychtarik, R. G. (1992). *Motivational enhancement therapy manual: A clinical research guide for therapists treating individuals with alcohol abuse and dependence* (Vol. 2, Project MATCH Monograph Series). Rockville, MD: National Institute on Alcohol Abuse and Alcoholism.

Monti, P. M., Abrams, D. B., Kadden, R. M., & Cooney, N. L. (1989). *Treating alcohol dependence: A coping skills training guide.* New York: Guilford Press.

Monti, P. M., Gulliver, S. B., & Myers, M. G. (1994). Social skills training for alcoholics: Assessment and treatment. *Alcohol and Alcoholism, 29,* 627–637.

Monti, P. M., Rohsenow, D. J., Colby, S. M., & Abrams, D. B. (1995). Coping and social skills training. In R. K. Hester & W. R. Miller (Eds.), *Handbook of alcoholism treatment approaches: Effective alternatives* (2nd ed., pp. 221–241). Boston: Allyn & Bacon.

Moos, R. H. (1994). Why do some people recover from alcohol dependence, whereas others continue to drink and become worse over time? *Addiction, 89,* 31–34.

Moos, R. H., Finney, J. W., & Cronkite, R. C. (1990). *Alcoholism treatment: Context, process, and outcome.* New York: Oxford University Press.

Moyers, T. B., & Miller, W. R. (1993). Therapists' conceptualizations of alcoholism: Measurement and implications for treatment. *Psychology of Addictive Behaviors, 7,* 238–245.

Myers, M. G., & Brown, S. A. (1996). The adolescent relapse coping questionnaire: Psychometric validation. *Journal of Studies on Alcohol, 57*(1), 40–46.

Myers, M. G., Brown, S. A., & Mott, M. A. (1993). Coping as a predictor of adolescent substance abuse treatment outcome. *Journal of Substance Abuse, 5,* 15–29.

Najavits, L. M., & Weiss, R. D. (1994). Variations in therapist effectiveness in the treatment of patients with substance use disorders: An empirical review. *Addiction, 89,* 679–688.

Narrow, W. E., Regier, D. A., Rae, D. S., Manderscheid, R. W., & Locke, B. Z. (1993). Use of services by persons with mental and addictive disorders: Findings from the National Institute of Mental Health Epidemiologic Catchment Area Program. *Archives of General Psychiatry, 50,* 95–107.

†National Institute on Alcohol Abuse and Alcoholism. (1993). *Alcohol and health: Eighth special report to the U.S. Congress.* Rockville, MD: Author.

†National Institute on Alcohol Abuse and Alcoholism. (1995). *The physicians' guide to helping patients with alcohol problems.* Rockville, MD: Author.

†National Institute on Drug Abuse. (1991). *Drug abuse and drug abuse research: The third triennial report to Congress from the secretary, Department of Health and Human Services.* Rockville, MD: Author.

Newcomb, M. D., & Bentler, P. M. (1988). *Consequences of adolescent drug use.* Newbury Park, CA: Sage.

†Nowinski, J., Baker, S., & Carroll, K. (1992). *Twelve step facilitation therapy manual: A clinical research guide for therapists treating individuals with alcohol abuse and dependence.* (Vol. 1, Project MATCH Monograph Series). Rockville, MD: National Institute on Alcohol Abuse and Alcoholism.

O'Farrell, T. J. (Ed.). (1993). *Treating alcohol problems: Marital and family interventions.* New York: Guilford Press.

O'Farrell, T. J. (1995). Marital and family therapy. In R. K. Hester & W. R. Miller (Eds.), *Handbook of alcoholism treatment approaches: Effective alternatives* (2nd ed., pp. 195–220). Boston: Allyn & Bacon.

O'Malley, S. S., Jaffe, A. J., Chang, G., & Schottenfeld, R. S. (1992). Naltrexone and coping skills therapy for alcohol dependence: A controlled study. *Archives of General Psychiatry, 49,* 881–887.

Orford, J. (1985). *Excessive appetites: A psychological view of addictions.* New York: Wiley.

Peele, S. (1985). *The meaning of addiction: Compulsive experience and its interpretation.* Lexington, MA: Lexington Books.

Peele, S. (1989). *Diseasing of America: Addiction treatment out of control.* Boston: Houghton Mifflin.

Pritchard, H. E., Wolfe, B. L., Waldron, D. J., & Miller, W. R. (1997). What services are being offered by whom? A survey of substance abuse programs in New Mexico. *Alcoholism Treatment Quarterly, 15,* 47–61.

Prochaska, J. O., DiClemente, C. C., & Norcross, J. C. (1992). In search of how people change: Applications to addictive behaviors. *American Psychologist, 47,* 1102–1114.

Project MATCH Research Group. (1993). Project MATCH: Rationale and methods for a multisite clinical trial matching patients to alcoholism treatment. *Alcoholism: Clinical and Experimental Research, 17,* 1130–1145.

†Project MATCH Research Group. (1997). Matching alcoholism treatments to client heterogeneity: Project MATCH posttreatment drinking outcomes. *Journal of Studies on Alcohol, 58,* 7–29.

Regier, D. A., Farmer, M. E., Rae, D. S., Locke, B. Z., Keith, S. J., Judd, L.L., & Goodwin, F. K. (1990). Comorbidity of mental disorders with alcohol and other drug abuse. *Journal of the American Medical Association, 264,* 2511–2518.

Robins, L. N., Helzer, J. E., Pryzbeck, T. R., & Regier, D. A. (1988). Alcohol disorders in the community: A report from the Epidemiologic Catchment Area survey. In R. M. Rose (Ed.), *Alcoholism: Origins and outcome* (pp. 15–29). New York: Raven Press.

Rounsaville, B. J., Dolinsky, Z. S., Babor, T. F., & Meyer, R. E. (1987). Psychopathology as a predictor of treatment outcome in alcoholics. *Archives of General Psychiatry, 44,* 505–513.

Saunders, B., Wilkinson, C., & Phillips, M. (1995). The impact of a brief motivational intervention with opiate users attending a methadone programme. *Addiction, 90,* 415–424.

Schuckit, M. A. (1995). *Educating yourself about alcohol and drugs: A people's primer.* New York: Plenum Press.

Sher, K. H. (1991). *Children of alcoholics: A critical appraisal of theory and research.* Chicago: University of Chicago Press.

Siegel, S. (1978). A Pavlovian analysis of morphine tolerance. In N. A. Krasnegor (Ed.), *Behavioral tolerance: Research treatment implications* (pp. 9–19). Rockville, MD: National Institute on Drug Abuse.

Siegel, S. (1989). Pharmacological conditioning and drug effects. In A. J. Goudie & M. W. Emmett-Oglesby (Eds.), *Psychoactive drugs* (pp. 115–169). Clifton, NJ: Humana Press.

Sobell, M. B., & Sobell, L. C. (n.d.). *Alcohol abuse curriculum guide for psychology faculty* (Health Professions Education Curriculum Resources Series, No. PH-188). Unpublished document, National Institute on Alcohol Abuse and Alcoholism.

Sparadeo, F. R., Zwick, W. R., Ruggiero, S. D., Meek, D. A., Carloni, J. A., & Simone, S. S. (1982). Evaluation of a social-setting detoxification program. *Journal of Studies on Alcohol, 43,* 1124–1136.

Stephens, R. S., & Roffman, R.A. (1993, January). Extended versus minimal intervention with marijuana dependent adults: Preliminary results. In J. M. Brown (Chair), *New applications of motivational interviewing and brief intervention.* Symposium conducted at the Sixth International Conference on Treatment of Addictive Behaviors, Santa Fe, NM.

Stinson, F. S., Dufour, M. C., Steffens, R. A., & DeBakey, S. (1993). Alcohol-related mortality in the United States, 1979–1989. *Alcohol Health & Research World, 17,* 251–260.

Stockwell, T. (1995). Anxiety and stress management. In R. K. Hester & W. R. Miller (Eds.), *Handbook of alcoholism treatment approaches: Effective alternatives* (2nd ed., pp. 195–220). Boston: Allyn & Bacon.

Szasz, T. S. (1974). *Ceremonial chemistry: The ritual persecution of drugs, addicts, and pushers.* Garden City, NY: Anchor Press/Doubleday.

Tracey, D. A., & Nathan, P. E. (1976). Behavioral analysis of chronic alcoholism in four women. *Journal of Consulting and Clinical Psychology, 44,* 832–842.

Tucker, J. A., Vuchinich, R. E., & Gladsjo, J. A. (1991). Environmental influences on relapse in substance use disorders. *International Journal of the Addictions, 25,* 1017–1050.

U.S. Congress, Office of Technology Assessment. (1983). *The effectiveness and costs of alcoholism treatment.* Washington, DC: Author.

†U.S. Department of Health and Human Services. (1996). *Smoking cessation.* Washington, DC: Centers for Disease Control and Prevention, Public Health Service, Agency for Health Care Policy and Research.

Valle, S. K. (1981). Interpersonal functioning of alcoholism counselors and treatment outcome. *Journal of Studies on Alcohol, 42,* 783–790.

Vogel-Sprott, M. (1992). *Alcohol tolerance and social drinking: Learning the consequences.* New York: Guilford Press.

Whitfield, C. L., Thompson, G., Lamb, A., Spencer, V., Pfeifer, M., & Browning-Ferrando, M. (1978). Detoxification of 1,024 alcoholic patients without psychoactive drugs. *Journal of the American Medical Association, 239,* 1409–1410.

World Health Organization Brief Intervention Study Group. (1996). A randomized cross-national clinical trial of brief interventions with heavy drinkers. *American Journal of Public Health, 86,* 948–955.

†Zackon, F., McAuliffe, W. E., & Ch'ien, J. M. N. (1993). *Recovery training and self-help: Relapse prevention and aftercare for drug addicts.* Rockville, MD: National Institute on Drug Abuse.

II

EPIDEMIOLOGICAL
OVERVIEW AND ETIOLOGY

3

ETIOLOGIC CONNECTIONS AMONG SUBSTANCE DEPENDENCE, ANTISOCIAL BEHAVIOR, AND PERSONALITY: MODELING THE EXTERNALIZING SPECTRUM

ROBERT F. KRUEGER, BRIAN M. HICKS, CHRISTOPHER J. PATRICK,
SCOTT R. CARLSON, WILLIAM G. IACONO, AND MATT McGUE

Common mental disorders are often correlated with each other, co-occurring at greater than chance rates in both clinical and epidemiological samples (Clark, Watson, & Reynolds, 1995; Lilienfeld, Waldman, & Israel, 1994; Sher & Trull, 1996; Widiger & Sankis, 2000). What is the meaning of this "comorbidity" phenomenon? Krueger and colleagues (Krueger, 1999b, 2002; Krueger, Caspi, Moffitt, & Silva, 1998; Krueger, McGue, & Iacono, 2001) have proposed that this phenomenon may result from common mental disorders acting as reliable indicators of latent factors, or hypothetical core psychopathological processes, that underlie putatively separate disorders. To date, this hypothesis has been supported by data gathered from unrelated persons. Such data have allowed for multivariate analyses of observed, phenotypic correlations among mental disorders. These analyses have revealed a broad, latent factor linking substance dependence and antisocial behavior disorders in late adolescence and adulthood. Following the lead provided by multivariate analyses of emotional and behavioral problems in children

The Minnesota Twin Family Study is supported in part by U.S. Public Health Service Grants AA00175, AA09367, DA05147, and MH65137.

Reprinted from *Journal of Abnormal Psychology*, *111*, 411–424 (2002). Copyright 2002 by the American Psychological Association.

(Achenbach & Edelbrock, 1978, 1984), this factor has been labeled *externalizing* (cf. Kendler, Davis, & Kessler, 1997).

In the analyses presented herein, we extended this line of research by addressing three specific questions in a genetically informative sample. First, what is the etiologic basis for the phenotypic externalizing factor? Second, are there etiologic factors that distinguish among specific externalizing disorders? Third, are disinhibitory personality traits part of the externalizing spectrum?

THE ETIOLOGIC BASIS OF THE EXTERNALIZING FACTOR

Recent research suggests the hypothesis that genetic factors play an important role in the etiology of the externalizing factor in adolescence and adulthood. First, many large-scale, well-conducted studies now point to genetic factors in the etiology of specific antisocial behavior disorders (Bock & Goode, 1996; Carey & Goldman, 1997; DiLalla & Gottesman, 1989; Gottesman & Goldsmith, 1994; Krueger, Hicks, & McGue, 2001; Lyons et al., 1995; Rutter, 1997; van den Bree, Svikis, & Pickens, 1998) and substance use disorders (Heath et al., 1997; McGue, Pickens, & Svikis, 1992; Pickens et al., 1991; Prescott & Kendler, 1999; Tsuang et al., 1996). Second, in contrast to earlier adoption studies that suggested genetic differentiation of antisocial and substance use disorders (Bohman, Sigvardsson, & Cloninger, 1981; Cadoret, O'Gorman, Troughton, & Heywood, 1985; Cadoret, Troughton, & O'Gorman, 1987; Cloninger, Bohman, & Sigvardsson, 1981; Crowe, 1974; Goodwin, Schulsinger, Hermansen, Guze, & Winokur, 1973), a number of recent twin studies have begun to point to common genetic factors linking antisocial behavior and substance use disorders. Grove et al. (1990) presented evidence for substantial genetic overlap between antisocial and alcohol problem symptom counts in a small sample of identical, or monozygotic (MZ), twins reared apart. Pickens, Svikis, McGue, and LaBuda (1995) compared cross-twin correlations between alcohol dependence and antisocial personality in small samples of both MZ and fraternal, or dizygotic (DZ), twins. For male pairs, the MZ cross-twin, cross-trait correlation was similar to the within-person correlation between alcohol dependence and antisocial personality but higher than the DZ cross-twin, cross-trait correlation, suggesting that the phenotypic correlation was partially due to genetic factors shared between alcohol dependence and antisocial personality.

The most extensive and thorough study documenting significant genetic links between antisocial behavior and substance use disorders was reported by Slutske et al. (1998). A sample of 2,682 adult Australian twin pairs retrospectively reported symptoms of childhood conduct disorder and alcohol dependence. Both disorders were substantially heritable; in addition, genetic influences accounted for 76% and 71% of the phenotypic, observed association between conduct disorder and alcohol dependence in men and women, respectively.

These twin studies have made fundamental contributions to our understanding of the meaning of comorbidity by suggesting that a significant portion of the covariance between substance dependence and antisocial behavior disorders can be traced to common genetic factors. This finding is compatible with the idea of a heritable factor that connects multiple substance use and antisocial behavior disorders (cf. Iacono, Carlson, Taylor, Elkins, & McGue, 1999; Krueger, 1999b; Tarter, 1988). Nevertheless, we are aware of only one study to directly examine genetic and environmental contributions to such a factor (Young, Stallings, Corley, Krauter, & Hewitt, 2000). Young et al. (2000) modeled genetic and environmental contributions to a latent factor linking child-reported symptoms of conduct disorder, attention-deficit hyperactivity disorder, substance experimentation (number of substances used on more than five occasions), and the personality trait of novelty seeking in 334 twin pairs ages 12 to 18 years. The majority of the variance in the latent factor (84%) was attributed to genetic factors.

The current study therefore endeavored to extend the existing literature by assessing both conduct disorder and adolescent antisocial behavior symptoms, along with alcohol and illicit substance dependence, simultaneously in a sample of 524 male and female 17-year-old twin pairs who were assessed with both maternal and self-report. Thus, our study extends the existing literature by fitting multivariate models to a range of severe externalizing problems that are observed in older adolescents and young adults. In addition, as evidence suggests that parents and children both contribute unique information regarding children's maladjustment (Achenbach, McConaughy, & Howell, 1987), we were able to extend existing work by using information provided by both mothers and children in determining the presence of externalizing symptoms in our participants.

DISTINCT ETIOLOGIC FACTORS LINKED TO DISTINCT EXTERNALIZING SYNDROMES

The externalizing factor accounts for the variance shared among substance dependence and antisocial behavior disorders. Yet when this shared variance is taken into account, significant variance remains uniquely associated with each disorder (Krueger, 1999b; Krueger et al., 1998; Krueger, McGue, & Iacono, 2001). In addition, as noted earlier, adoption studies suggest greater genetic specificity for antisocial behavior and substance use disorders in comparison with twin studies. How might we account for evidence of a broad externalizing factor, unique variance in specific substance use and antisocial disorders, and distinctive findings from adoption and twin studies? These observations might be reconciled if at least a portion of the unique variance in each externalizing syndrome reflects unique etiologic factors, distinct from the etiology of the broad externalizing factor. That is, it may be the case that there are broader factors that impact on the risk for externalizing disorder in general, along with specific factors that differentiate among specific disorders in the externalizing realm.

This hypothesis has considerable appeal because it can accommodate evidence from both adoption and twin studies, that is, evidence for both genetic generality and specificity. Along these lines, the hypothesis also has the potential to provide an ecumenical resolution to ongoing debates between nosologists who posit that a few broad syndromes can account for most psychopathologic variation ("lumpers"), and those who believe that there are many mental disorders, each with unique etiologies and pathophys-iologies ("splitters"). If the unique variance in each externalizing syndrome can be shown to have an etiologic basis not in common with the etiologic basis for the broad externalizing factor, then lumping and splitting positions might be reconciled. Rather than arguing principally for a lumping versus a splitting position, or for genetic generality versus specificity, such data would instead support a hierarchical model of the externalizing disorders.

A hierarchical model organizes individual difference variables from those that are narrow, more specific, and at lower levels of a hierarchy to those that are broader, more general, and at higher levels of a hierarchy (Krueger & Finger, 2001). In this way, comorbidity among mental disorders can be explicitly modeled through the influence of variables at higher hierarchical levels on variables at lower levels. For example, Mineka, Watson, and Clark (1998) proposed a hierarchical model to account for patterns of comorbidity among unipolar mood and anxiety disorders. This model posits a broad, higher order dimension of temperament, namely, negative affect, that influences all disorders within this realm. However, in this model, each separate disorder also has its own unique component of variance. Thus, anxiety and unipolar mood disorders are significantly influenced by negative affect, thereby accounting for their comorbidity. Yet each disorder also contains unique variance, thereby explaining why negative affect can be manifested in diverse ways, that is, as distinguishable, but often comorbid, unipolar mood and anxiety disorders.

Recently, Widiger and Clark (2000) reviewed research on the classifi-cation of psychopathology in anticipation of the fifth edition of the *Diagnos-tic and Statistical Manual of Mental Disorders* (*DSM–V*). Referring to the potential of the Mineka et al. (1998) model to inform the classification of mood and anxiety (internalizing) disorders, Widiger and Clark (2000) also noted that "on the basis of Krueger et al.'s (1998) results . . . researchers will need a parallel model to account for the externalizing disorders" (p. 954). The work reported herein represents an attempt to develop this type of model. In addition to examining genetic and environmental contributions to the externalizing factor (i.e., to the variance shared among conduct disorder, adolescent antisocial behavior, alcohol dependence, and illicit substance dependence), we were able to examine the genetic and environmental etiology of the residual variance in each of these syndromes. Thus, we were able to evaluate the level of empirical support for a hierarchical model of the externalizing disorders—a model including etiologic factors influencing both the broad, higher order externalizing factor and the residual aspects of specific syndromes within the externalizing realm.

We have discussed how antisocial behavior and substance dependence might define an etiologically coherent spectrum of externalizing disorders. Yet Widiger and Clark (2000) also noted that, like negative affect in the realm of internalizing disorders, the bipolar personality trait of disinhibition–constraint is pervasively linked with disorders in the externalizing spectrum. Thus, in the research presented here, we also examined how this trait fits into the externalizing spectrum.

LINKING EXTERNALIZING DISORDERS AND DISINHIBITORY PERSONALITY TRAITS

The idea that disorders involving substance dependence and antisocial behavior represent syndromes of disinhibition is not new (Gorenstein & Newman, 1980; Zuckerman, 1979). Extensive research documents correlations between externalizing disorders and personality traits such as novelty seeking, impulsivity, and disinhibition (Howard, Kivlahan, & Walker, 1997; Krueger, Caspi, Moffitt, Silva, & McGee, 1996; McGue, Slutske, & Iacono, 1999; McGue, Slutske, Taylor, & Iacono, 1997; Patrick & Zempolich, 1998; Sher & Trull, 1994; Verona & Patrick, 2000; Watson & Clark, 1993). However, most research in this area has examined cross-sectional, phenotypic correlations between mental disorders and personality traits. The problem with this design is that it is ambiguous regarding the causal direction of the personality–psychopathology correlation. That is, a cross-sectional correlation between a disinhibited personality style and psychopathology might be observed because an antisocial, substance-abusing lifestyle leads to impulsivity and disregard for the future consequences of one's actions (cf. Nathan, 1988) or because impulsivity leads to involvement with criminal behavior and substance use (cf. Tarter, 1988). Determining which of these two models is the more plausible requires either longitudinal or genetically informative data.

Longitudinal studies support the latter model. Higher novelty seeking in children is associated with subsequent substance use and abuse (Cloninger,

Sigvardsson, & Bohman, 1988; Masse & Tremblay, 1997) as well as subsequent delinquency (Tremblay, Pihl, Vitaro, & Dobkin, 1994). Indeed, impulsivity observed as early as age 3 foretells alcohol dependence and criminal behavior in early adulthood (Caspi, Moffitt, Newman, & Silva, 1996). Moreover, a lack of constraint in late adolescence predicts substance dependence and antisocial behavior in early adulthood, even after controlling for contemporaneous levels of substance dependence and antisocial behavior in late adolescence (Krueger, 1999a).

Genetically informative studies (e.g., twin studies) can also evaluate the possibility that disinhibitory personality traits are causally linked to externalizing disorders because they can discern the extent to which etiologic (genetic and environmental) contributions to personality and psychopathology are shared versus distinctive. For example, twin studies have indicated that a significant portion of the phenotypic relationship between the personality trait of neuroticism and the diagnosis of major depression can be traced to genetic factors shared between these variables (Kendler, Neale, Kessler, Heath, & Eaves, 1993; Roberts & Kendler, 1999). Nevertheless, the twin study approach has rarely been used to examine the etiologic basis for phenotypic connections between personality traits and externalizing disorders. Jang, Vernon, and Livesley (2000) recently reported an investigation documenting substantial genetic correlations between a four-item measure of self-reported alcohol misuse (excessive consumption and alcohol-related problems) and dissocial behavior (a self-reported, continuous personality factor resembling the antisocial personality diagnosis from the *DSM*). However, this study was somewhat limited by its reliance on a sample of volunteer twin pairs and assessment conducted solely by mailed self-report questionnaire. The study by Young et al. (2000) also supports genetic connections between the personality trait of novelty seeking, involvement in illicit substance use, and childhood symptoms of attention-deficit and conduct disorder, but this study is limited by its sole reliance on self-report data and limitation to milder symptoms characteristic of younger children.

The current research therefore endeavored to extend the existing literature by modeling the personality trait of disinhibition–constraint (Tellegen, 1985; Watson & Clark, 1993) as a potential indicator of the externalizing factor in genetically informative data. Our sample consisted of 17-year-old twins from the Minnesota Twin Family Study (MTFS), a birth record-based epidemiological study of twins born in the state of Minnesota. Twins and their mothers were interviewed in person to assess the twins' childhood antisocial behavior and alcohol and illicit substance dependence, and twins were also interviewed regarding their adolescent antisocial behavior. Twins also completed a self-report index of disinhibition. The fit of a model postulating that these measures were valid indicators of a hypothesized externalizing factor was evaluated. In addition, the genetically informative nature of the data allowed us to extend the existing literature by modeling genetic and environmental influences on both the externalizing factor and the unique, residual variance in each of the measured indicators of the externalizing factor.

METHOD

Research Participants

Participants were twin pairs from the MTFS. A comprehensive description of the goals and design of the MTFS has been provided elsewhere (Iacono et al., 1999). Briefly, the MTFS is an ongoing epidemiological–longitudinal study designed to identify the genetic and environmental factors that contribute to substance abuse and related psychopathology. The study used a population-based ascertainment method in which all twins born in Minnesota were identified by public birth records. Initial assessment was conducted during the year the twins turned either 11 or 17 years old. The present investigation involved the 17-year-old cohort, identified from birth records for the years 1972 to 1978 in the case of male twins and 1975 to 1979 in the case of female twins. The study was able to locate at least 90% of all twin pairs born during these years in which both members were still living. Families were excluded from participation if they lived further than a day's drive from our Minneapolis laboratories, or if either twin had a physical or intellectual disability that would preclude his or her completing the day-long, in-person assessment. Of the eligible families, 17% declined to participate. A brief self-report survey or telephone interview was obtained from 83% of the nonassessed families. Socioeconomic status levels were slightly, albeit significantly, lower for nonparticipating families, in that parents who participated had 0.25 more years of education, on average, than parents from families that did not participate. However, participating and nonparticipating families did not differ significantly on a brief screening measure of psychopathology, indicating that the MTFS sample is likely representative of twins born in Minnesota during the target years. Consistent with the demographics of Minnesota, 98% of the twins were Caucasian.

Zygosity was determined by agreement of questionnaires completed by (a) parents and (b) MTFS staff regarding the physical similarity of the twins as well as (c) an algorithm that compared twins on ponderal and cephalic indices and fingerprint ridge count. If the three estimates did not agree, a serological analysis was conducted. After intake, the sample size of the 17-year-old cohort consisted of 626 (223 female MZ, 188 male MZ, 114 female DZ, 101 male DZ) twin pairs. The preponderance of MZ twins reflects both an excess of MZ over same-sex DZ twins in the population from which the sample was drawn (Hur, McGue, & Iacono, 1995), as well as a slightly increased likelihood of MZ relative to DZ agreement to participate.

Measures

Clinical Assessment

All twins were interviewed separately and concurrently by different interviewers to assess lifetime mental disorders according to criteria from the *Diagnostic and Statistical Manual of Mental Disorders* (3rd ed., revised; *DSM–III–R*; American Psychiatric Association, 1987). (The *DSM–III–R* was the current diagnostic system at the time of intake.) Mothers were also interviewed about their children's psychopathology. Interviewers had either a bachelor's or master's degree in psychology and underwent extensive training. Maternal reports of child antisocial behavior and substance disorder symptoms were obtained with the use of the parent version of the Diagnostic Interview for Children and Adolescents—Revised (DICA–R; Welner, Reich, Herjanic, Jung, & Amado, 1987). Twins were assessed for child (before age 15) and adolescent (after age 15) antisocial behavior with a structured interview developed by MTFS staff (Holdcraft, Iacono, & McGue, 1998). Twins were assessed for substance abuse and dependence with the Substance Abuse Module (SAM) of the Composite International Diagnostic Interview (Robins, Babor, & Cottler, 1987).

Interview data were then reviewed in a clinical case conference by at least two graduate students with advanced training in descriptive psychopathology and differential diagnosis. All items that scored positive, or about which there were any questions regarding scoring, were reviewed. Symptoms were confirmed on the basis of consensus between the two diagnosticians and were tracked by informant (child or mother). A symptom was considered present if reported by either the twin or the mother, with the exception of adolescent antisocial behavior symptoms, for which only the twin reported.

The current investigation made use of four symptom count variables: adolescent antisocial behavior, conduct disorder, alcohol dependence, and drug dependence. Adolescent antisocial behavior consists of 9 of the 10 Criterion C symptoms of antisocial personality disorder. Symptom 9 ("has never sustained a totally monogamous relationship for more than 1 year") was not assessed due to the young age of the participants. Adolescent antisocial behavior was used instead of antisocial personality disorder because of the DSM requirement that an individual must be at least 18 years old to receive the latter diagnosis. In addition, this investigation sought to distinguish between child and adolescent symptoms of antisocial behavior, a distinction confounded by the antisocial personality disorder diagnostic requirement that at least three symptoms of conduct disorder be present before the age of 15 (Elkins, Iacono, Doyle, & McGue, 1997; Iacono et al., 1999). Conduct disorder, alcohol dependence, and drug dependence consist of the Criterion A symptoms of their respective disorders. In the case of conduct disorder, Symptom 9 ("has forced someone into sexual activity with him or her") was not assessed to avoid potential mandated reporting. Drug assessment covered amphetamines, cannabis, cocaine, hallucinogens, inhalants, opioids, phencyclidine, and sedatives. The substance for which the participant had the greatest number of symptoms was used as their drug dependence variable.

Reliability of the assessment process was estimated by an independent review of over 600 cases representative of the entire MTFS sample and yielded the following kappa statistics: .95 for adolescent antisocial behavior, .81 for conduct disorder, and greater than .91 for substance dependence disorders.

Personality

Personality was assessed with a shortened (198-item) version of the Multidimensional Personality Questionnaire (MPQ; Tellegen, 1992). The current investigation focused on behavioral disinhibition as indexed by the higher order MPQ factor of Constraint. Persons high on Constraint tend to inhibit behavioral impulses, to prefer boring but safe activities to exciting but dangerous activities, and to endorse conventional values. The primary MPQ scales Control, Harm Avoidance, and Traditionalism load principally on Constraint (Krueger, 2000; Tellegen, 1985). In this investigation, Constraint was reverse scored so that high scorers tended to exhibit greater behavioral disinhibition. This was done to ease interpretation of results, as all predicted relationships among variables would then be positive.

MPQs were mailed to families prior to their on-site, intake assessment. Participants were asked to bring their completed MPQ with them to their in-person visit. If a completed MPQ was not obtained by the end of the day-long intake assessment, participants were asked to complete it at home and return it by mail. One telephone prompt was made if a completed MPQ was still not received. Complete MPQs were available for 524 (188 female MZ, 156 male MZ, 103 female DZ, 77 male DZ) twin pairs. Female twins were more likely than male twins to complete the MPQ (91% vs. 86%).

To determine whether the final sample was representative, we compared returners and nonreturners on the four *DSM–III–R* symptom count scales in separate analyses for male and female adolescents. Because of the nonnormal distributions of the symptom count variables, we used the Mann–Whitney (a nonparametric test) rather than t tests to compare groups. Female nonreturners ($n = 64$) did not differ from female returners ($n = 610$) on any of the symptom count scales. Male nonreturners ($n = 82$), however, exhibited more symptoms than male returners ($n = 496$) for adolescent antisocial behavior, conduct disorder, alcohol dependence, and drug dependence (Mann-Whitney $Zs = -2.98, -2.90, -2.44$, and -2.57, respectively, all $ps < .02$, two-tailed). To provide an estimate of the impact of the higher levels of psychopathology in the male nonreturners, we fit the final best-fitting model without the Constraint variable on the total sample of persons observed on the symptom count variables. These analyses yielded nearly identical parameter estimates to those that included Constraint (i.e., the median absolute standardized parameter estimate discrepancy was .02).

Data Analysis

We used structural equation modeling to determine the genetic and environmental structure of the externalizing disorders and Constraint. The phenotypic variance of any trait can be decomposed into three causal latent factors—additive genetic effects, shared or common environmental effects, and nonshared or unique environmental effects. Twin methodology allows the estimation of these effects by comparing the similarity of MZ and DZ twins. Because MZ twins share all their genetic material, and DZ twins share on average 50% of their segregating genes, additive genetic effects have a correlation of 1.0 for MZ twins and 0.5 for DZ twins. Twin similarity may also be due to shared environmental effects. Because all twin pairs participating in the MTFS were reared together, shared environmental effects have a correlation of 1.0 for both MZ and DZ twins. Nonshared environmental effects are factors whose influences are unique to an individual and therefore are uncorrelated for both MZ and DZ twins. Nonshared environmental effects also include random and unsystematic variance (e.g., measurement error).

Structural equation modeling can be used to model the MZ and DZ correlations in order to estimate genetic and environmental effects and test relationships among multiple variables. We examined the fit of three multivariate biometric models: the Cholesky or triangular decomposition model, the independent pathway model, and the common pathway model (Neale & Cardon, 1992; Waldman & Slutske, 2000). In the Cholesky model, the phenotypic, observed variances and covariances among the five phenotypes (each of the four disorders evaluated plus Constraint) are decomposed into genetic, shared environmental, and nonshared environmental variances and covariances. The Cholesky model is the least parsimonious of the three models because it allows for all possible genetic and environmental variances and covariances to be freely estimated. That is, the Cholesky model does not impose a particular structure on the genetic and environmental variances and covariances.

The independent pathway model, in contrast, is more parsimonious than the Cholesky model because it imposes a structure on the genetic and environmental variances and covariances. In this model, genetic and environmental effects are of two types: general and specific. This model specifies general latent genetic, shared environmental, and nonshared environmental factors that load on each of the five phenotypes as well as specific genetic and environmental factors that are specific to each of the five phenotypes.

The common pathway model is the most parsimonious of the three models. This model augments the independent pathway model by hypothesizing that the general genetic, shared environmental, and nonshared environmental effects of the independent pathway model are mediated by a latent phenotype. In this model, rather than loading directly on each measured phenotype, the general effects are mediated through a latent phenotype that represents the variance shared among the measured phenotypes. As in the independent pathway model, the common pathway model also allows for additional effects that are specific to each observed phenotype.

Symptom counts were used rather than diagnoses for the following reasons. First, symptom counts retain information that is lost when collapsing into a dichotomous variable (cf. Krueger & Finger, 2001). For example, the Developmental Trends Study reported that over a 4-year period, the number of conduct disorder symptoms fluctuated above and below the number necessary for a definite diagnosis, suggesting that some persons who would be included in a negative diagnostic category are actually more similar to individuals who meet full criteria for the disorder (Lahey et al., 1995). Second, symptom counts provide greater statistical power, especially in a community-based sample such as the MTFS where diagnostic prevalence rates are lower than in a clinically referred sample. Third, there is empirical evidence to support measuring at least some forms of externalizing psychopathology as a quantitative trait (Doyle, 1998). For example, there is a linear relationship between the number of symptoms of conduct disorder and impairment criteria (Robins & Price, 1991). Finally, other investigations have shown that the patterns of genetic and environmental influence are similar for categorical and dimensional models of adolescent antisocial behavior and conduct disorder as well as other forms of psychopathology (Doyle, 1998; Livesley, Jang, Jackson, & Vernon, 1993).

As is typical in a population-based sample, the symptom count variables were positively skewed. In order to better approximate normality, variables were Blom transformed and rank normalized prior to model fitting. A Blom transformation replaces each raw score with its rank value. Ties were resolved by assigning the mean of the ranks being contested. The ranks were then referenced to the normal distribution and expressed in z-score units. A simulation study by van den Oord et al. (2000) has shown that of the available procedures for behavioral genetic analysis of psychiatric symptom count data, this procedure resulted more often in the selection of the true model from a set of alternative models. Though not markedly skewed, reversed Constraint scores were also transformed to maintain consistency across variables. Transformations were conducted by sex but without regard to zygosity. In addition, the data were double entered, a procedure that constrains the variance of Twin A and Twin B to be equal in order to remove any variance associated with this arbitrary designation. However, equating the variances reduces the degrees of freedom because some statistics in the variance–covariance matrix are no longer free to vary.

Model fitting to the variance–covariance matrices for the transformed symptom count scales and Constraint (reversed) was carried out by maximum likelihood estimation with the statistical modeling program (Neale, 1997). One standard index of model fit is the root-mean-square error of approximation (RMSEA), which is used to evaluate the absolute fit of a model. That is, RMSEA is used to determine whether a specific, isolated model fits the data, but it is not used to select the most optimal model from among a series of competing models. RMSEA values less than .05 indicate a close fit of the model (Browne & Cudeck, 1993). To evaluate the comparative fit of competing models within the present study, we report the Bayesian information criterion (BIC = $\chi^2 - df \ln N$; Raftery, 1995). BIC provides a quantitative index of the extent to which each model maximizes correspondence between the observed and model predicted variances and covariances while minimizing the number of parameters. Better fitting models have more negative values, and the difference in BIC values relates to the *posterior odds*—the odds ratio formed by taking the probability that the second model is correct, given the data, over the probability that the first model is correct given the data. When comparing models, a difference in BIC of 10 corresponds to the odds being 150:1 that the model with the more negative value is the better fitting model and is considered "very strong" evidence in favor of the model with the more negative BIC value (Raftery, 1995).

RESULTS

Descriptive Statistics

Prevalence rates for the *DSM–III–R* defined disorders were calculated separately for men ($n = 466$) and women ($n = 582$) in order to provide an estimate of the level of psychopathology in the final sample. *DSM–III–R* requires the presence of three or more Criterion A symptoms for a diagnosis of conduct disorder, alcohol dependence, or drug dependence. A clinically significant level of adolescent antisocial behavior was operationalized as the presence of four or more Criterion C symptoms of antisocial personality disorder, as is required by *DSM–III–R* for the latter diagnosis. Conduct disorder symptoms are not included in the adolescent antisocial behavior symptom count.

Table 3.1 provides lifetime prevalence rates at the definite level (all criteria satisfied) and the probable level (all but one symptom present). Table 3.1 also contains the means, standard deviations, and range of the

TABLE 3.1
Prevalence Rates for Lifetime Diagnoses and Descriptive Statistics
for Symptom Count Scales

| Disorder | Prevalence rate (%) | | Symptom count scale | | | |
| | | | *M* | *SD* | Range | |
	Definite	Probable			Min	Max
Male adolescents (*n* = 466)						
Adolescent antisocial behavior	4.7	9.2	0.73	1.16	0	6
Conduct disorder	19.7	33.3	1.37	1.77	0	10
Alcohol dependence	8.8	12.9	0.53	1.26	0	8
Drug dependence	3.2	4.9	0.22	1.03	0	8
Constraint (reversed)			52.6	9.40	23.0	97.0
Female adolescents (*n* = 582)						
Adolescent antisocial behavior	1.5	3.4	0.39	0.93	0	7
Conduct disorder	3.6	11.9	0.47	0.97	0	9
Alcohol dependence	5.8	8.9	0.41	1.26	0	9
Drug dependence	3.4	5.0	0.22	0.97	0	9
Constraint (reversed)			47.9	9.97	18.8	84.4

Note. A diagnosis at the *definite* level meets full criteria from the *Diagnostic and Statistical Manual of Mental Disorders* (3rd edition, rev.; American Psychiatric Association, 1987). A diagnosis at the *probable* level requires all but one symptom to be present. Hence, the probable group contains the definite group. Conduct disorder symptoms are not included in the adolescent antisocial behavior symptom count. Constraint (reversed) is scaled so that the total sample has a mean of 50 and a standard deviation of 10. Min = minimum; Max = maximum.

symptom count scales for male and female participants. Male participants exhibited significantly more symptoms for adolescent antisocial behavior, conduct disorder, and alcohol dependence (Mann–Whitney $z = -6.10$, -10.83, and -2.71, respectively, all $ps < .01$) but not for drug dependence ($z = .73$, ns). The mean value of reversed Constraint was also significantly higher for male participants. That is, male participants exhibited greater behavioral disinhibition than female participants, $t(1046) = -7.86, p < .001$, two-tailed. The range of the symptom count scales was broad and similar for both genders. These results show that the MTFS sample covers a wide spectrum of behavioral adjustment and maladjustment including a number of persons with clinical levels of psychopathology.

Correlations

Correlations among the Blom-transformed variables were computed to provide initial indications of the magnitude of phenotypic covariation and the relative genetic and environmental contributions to their expression and covariation. Table 3.2 contains the intraclass correlation matrices for the transformed symptom count scales and reversed Constraint, considered

TABLE 3.2
Correlation Matrices for Adolescent Antisocial Behavior, Conduct Disorder, Alcohol Dependence, Drug Dependence, and Constraint (Reversed)

Disorder	Twin A					Twin B				
	AAB	CD	ALD	DD	CON	AAB	CD	ALD	DD	CON
	Male adolescents									
Twin A										
AAB	—	.49	.49	.39	.33	.51	.33	.46	.24	.28
CD	.57	—	.27	.25	.32	.33	.56	.23	.22	.22
ALD	.51	.49	—	.36	.22	.46	.23	.53	.36	.14
DD	.32	.39	.50	—	.17	.24	.22	.36	.48	.15
CON	.43	.37	.23	.22	—	.28	.22	.14	.15	.54
Twin B										
AAB	.24	.16	.28	.23	.17	—	.49	.49	.39	.33
CD	.16	.31	.30	.12	.09	.57	—	.27	.25	.32
ALD	.28	.30	.45	.21	.08	.51	.49	—	.36	.22
DD	.23	.12	.21	.28	.15	.32	.39	.50	—	.17
CON	.17	.09	.08	.15	.14	.43	.37	.23	.22	—
	Female adolescents									
Twin A										
AAB	—	.36	.56	.54	.40	.35	.30	.43	.43	.27
CD	.50	—	.35	.36	.27	.30	.57	.29	.25	.20
ALD	.63	.41	—	.55	.30	.43	.29	.61	.44	.28
DD	.50	.31	.54	—	.33	.43	.25	.44	.48	.22
CON	.43	.25	.27	.31	—	.27	.20	.28	.22	.54
Twin B										
AAB	.18	.11	.13	.19	.01	—	.36	.56	.54	.40
CD	.11	.40	.12	.02	-.01	.50	—	.35	.36	.27
ALD	.13	.12	.25	.24	.08	.63	.41	—	.55	.30
DD	.19	.02	.24	.41	.07	.50	.31	.54	—	.33
CON	.01	-.01	.08	.07	.24	.43	.25	.27	.31	—

Note. Monozygotic twin correlations are above the diagonal; dizygotic twin correlations are below the diagonal. All variables in the table have been Blom transformed. Because of the double-entry procedure, corresponding elements in the upper left and lower right portions of the matrices (within-twin, cross-trait correlations), as well as corresponding elements above and below the diagonal of the lower left and upper right portions of the matrices (cross-twin, cross-trait correlations), are equal within zygosity. Correlations significant at $p < .01$ (two-tailed) are in boldface. AAB = adolescent antisocial behavior; CD = conduct disorder; ALD = alcohol dependence; DD = drug dependence; CON = Constraint (reversed).

separately for male and female adolescents, with MZ correlations above the diagonal and DZ correlations below the diagonal. Elements in the upper left-hand and lower right-hand portions of the matrices contain the within-twin, cross-trait correlations. These correlations describe the phenotypic relationships among the disorders and Constraint, and therefore should be similar across zygosity. The magnitude of these correlations is evidence of the moderate phenotypic covariation among these variables.

The elements in the lower left-hand and upper right-hand portions of the matrices contain the cross-twin, within-trait (along the diagonal) and cross-twin, cross-trait correlations (off-diagonal elements). Cross-twin, within-trait correlations provide information about the status of Twin B if the status of Twin A on that trait is known. For example, the level of adolescent antisocial behavior in Twin B can be predicted if the level of the same disorder in Twin A is known. Cross-twin, cross-trait correlations allow for the prediction of Twin B's status on a trait if the status of Twin A on a *different* trait is known. For example, Twin B's level of adolescent antisocial behavior can be predicted if Twin A's level of alcohol dependence is known.

Cross-twin, within-trait correlations can be used to decompose the variance of a trait into its genetic, shared environmental, and nonshared environmental components, whereas the cross-twin, cross-trait correlations can be used to decompose the covariance between traits into those components. The magnitude of the difference between the MZ and DZ twin correlations describes the relative contribution of the genetic and environmental effects to the expression and covariation of the phenotypes. MZ correlations twice that of DZ correlations suggest that genetic factors are the primary cause of twin similarity and trait covariation. MZ correlations that are nearly equal to DZ correlations suggest that shared environmental factors are the primary cause of twin similarity and trait covariation.

The generally higher MZ, as compared with DZ, correlations in Table 3.2 suggest that genetic effects contribute substantially to the expression and covariation of the disorders and Constraint. The similar pattern of correlations for males and female adolescents suggests that although the prevalence of the disorders is higher in men, the covariation and genetic–environmental structure of the disorders and Constraint are unlikely to differ across gender.

Model Fitting

Fitting an explicit statistical model to the data can better summarize the patterns visible in Table 3.2. We fit sex-variant and sex-invariant versions of Cholesky, independent pathway, and common pathway models to the data. Sex-variant models allowed parameters to differ for men and women, whereas sex-invariant models constrained the parameters to be equal for men and women. RMSEA was less than .05 for each of the models. Comparative fit indices for these models are presented in Table 3.3.

As is evident in Table 3.3, when the models are evaluated with a comparative index of fit (BIC), the sex-invariant models fit better than the sex-variant models. Whereas the prevalence for the disorders is higher in males (with the exception of drug dependence), the covariation and genetic–environmental structure of the disorders does not appear to differ by gender. In addition, the largest, negative BIC value was obtained for the sex-invariant common pathway model. That is, compared with the other models listed in Table 3.3, the sex-invariant common pathway model achieved the best balance of fit and parsimony. Moreover, the BIC value for the sex-invariant common pathway model

TABLE 3.3
Comparative Fit Indices for Sex-Variant and Sex-Invariant Confirmatory Biometric Models

Model	χ^2	df	BIC
Cholesky			
Sex variant	92.57	30	−95.23
Sex invariant	158.65	75	−310.85
Independent pathway			
Sex variant	142.06	60	−233.54
Sex invariant	180.79	90	−382.61
Common pathway			
Sex variant	184.14	76	−291.60
Sex invariant	216.61	98	−396.87

Note. For all chi-squares, $N = 524$. BIC = Bayesian information criterion; Sex variant = parameters were free to differ between sexes; Sex invariant = parameters were not allowed to differ between sexes.

was more than 10 points lower than the BIC value for its closest competitor (the sex-invariant independent pathway model), providing "very strong" (cf. Raftery, 1995) evidence in favor of the sex-invariant common pathway model. Specifically, the odds are greater than 150:1 that the common pathway model provides a better balance of fit and parsimony than any of the other models listed in Table 3.1.[1] Figure 3.1 displays the standardized parameter estimates and 95% confidence intervals (bounded at 0) for the sex-invariant common pathway model. Path coefficients in the figure must be squared to determine the percentage of variance contributed by a given path. Because the parameter estimates are standardized, the sum of the squares of the paths pointing at a variable sum to 100% (with tolerance for rounding error). Thus, additive genetic factors accounted for 81% (.90 × .90) of the variance of the latent phenotype, Externalizing, with the remaining variance (.43 × .43, or 19%) attributable to nonshared environmen-

---

[1]Akaike's information criterion (AIC = $\chi^2 - 2$ df; Akaike, 1987), a statistic often used in behavior genetic modeling, ranks the models in Table 3.3 somewhat differently than does the BIC, preferring the sex-invariant independent pathway model to the sex-invariant common pathway model. In addition, a chi-square difference test comparing these two models indicates that the gain of 8 degrees of freedom in the sex-invariant common pathway model is associated with a significant increase ($p < .05$) in chi-square over the sex-invariant independent pathway model. We did not rely on chi-square difference tests to select the most optimal model from the models given in Table 3.3 because such tests are highly dependent on sample size. In larger samples, chi-square tests tend to prefer complex, "overparameterized" models to more straightforward models because there is more statistical power to detect even minor and substantively trivial differences between model-predicted and observed variances and covariances (Tabachnick & Fidell, 1996). Indeed, this is the reason statistical modelers have turned to indices such as AIC and BIC that attempt to overcome this problem. Both AIC and BIC attempt to identify the "most optimal" model from a competing set of models, where "most optimal" means the model that reproduces the observed variances and covariances with the greatest degree of parsimony (i.e., while invoking as few unknown, estimated parameters as possible). However, BIC differs from AIC in that it is interpreted in Bayesian terms, that is, in terms of the odds of one model being more optimal than another. Hence, BIC provides a very meaningful basis for comparing the degree of support for various models that is not provided by AIC, which is why we have chosen to use BIC to guide model selection in the research presented in this chapter.

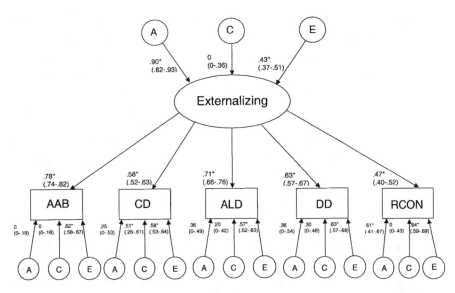

Figure 3.1. Common pathway model for externalizing phenotypes. Coefficients on the diagram are standardized, and 95% confidence intervals are presented in parentheses beneath each coefficient. Effects whose confidence intervals do not include zero are marked with an asterisk. The percentage of variance accounted for by a given variable in another variable can be determined by squaring the path coefficient on the path connecting the first with the second variable. A = additive genetic effects; C = shared environmental effects; E = nonshared environmental effects; AAB = adolescent antisocial behavior; CD = conduct disorder; ALD = alcohol dependence; DD = drug dependence; RCON = constraint (reversed).

tal factors. In addition, all the disorders and reversed Constraint have significant loadings on Externalizing. Nevertheless, a model constraining the loadings to be equal across the five variables resulted in a less optimal fit, $\chi^2(102, N = 524) = 279.18$, BIC $= -359.34$ (difference in BIC compared with the Figure 3.1 model $= 37.53$). Thus, the loadings are all significant but differ in magnitude across the five variables.

Latent variables at the bottom of Figure 3.1 are specific or residual genetic, shared environmental, and nonshared environmental effects: factors that contribute to the expression of a particular observed phenotype but not to the expression of any other observed phenotype in the model. As such, specific genetic and environmental effects are etiologic factors that contribute to differences among the observed phenotypes. The common pathway model describes how these specific effects lead to the different phenotypic expressions of the underlying Externalizing factor. As with the loadings, the specific effects differed across the five variables, $\chi^2(110, N = 524) = 343.14$, BIC $= -345.46$ (difference in BIC compared with the Figure 3.1 model $= 51.41$).

Constraint (reversed) was the only variable for which the specific genetic loading (.61) was significant, indicating that there are genetic effects that contribute to the expression of Constraint but not to any of the disorders. Whereas the specific genetic loadings were not significant for any of the disorders, the confidence intervals were relatively large (with the exception of adolescent antisocial behavior). Conduct disorder was the only variable for which the specific shared environmental loading (.51) was significant, suggesting that there were shared environmental effects that were unique to the expression of conduct disorder. Specific nonshared environmental effects were significant for all of the observed variables. This result suggests that there were nonshared environmental effects specific to the expression of a given variable and to the differentiation of that variable from the other variables included in the model.

DISCUSSION

Substance dependence, antisocial behavior, and disinhibitory personality traits commonly co-occur, yet the reasons for these patterns of co-occurrence have not been fully elucidated. In the research presented here, we have proposed and evaluated a biometric model designed to provide a better understanding of patterns of comorbidity among these "externalizing" syndromes. Our model is hierarchical, involving a general factor linking externalizing syndromes, as well as distinct etiologic factors that differentiate among distinct externalizing syndromes.

This hierarchical model achieved a good fit to our data. Our analyses indicated that co-occurrence among alcohol dependence, drug dependence, conduct disorder, adolescent antisocial behavior, and a disinhibitory personality style assessed in late adolescence can be traced to a highly heritable externalizing factor. Yet this factor did not account for all of the variance in each of its indicators; significant causal variance in each specific syndrome remained after accounting for the general externalizing factor. Thus, our model accommodates evidence for both general and specific etiologic factors in the externalizing realm.

Nevertheless, some important limitations must be borne in mind when considering these results. First, our study is limited by the size of the confidence intervals around some of our parameter estimates (see Figure 3.1). Although our sample is large by most standards (1,048 individual members of complete twin pairs provided complete data for our study), and although the confidence intervals around most parameter estimates were reasonable, there were wider confidence intervals around our estimates of specific genetic and environmental effects on specific externalizing syndromes. In pursuing large-scale, population-based twin research, there are inevitable trade-offs among sample size, representativeness, and comprehensiveness of assessment. Along these lines, we note that strengths of our sample include its representativeness of the population from which it was drawn, and in-person assessments of mental disorder in which both mothers and their children provided data. Although information from multiple reporters is more difficult to obtain, the use of information from multiple reporters appears to enhance the validity of assessments of mental disorder. For example, combined mother and child reports are better predictors of teacher reports than either mother or child reports taken alone (e.g., Burt, Krueger, McGue, & Iacono, 2001). Nevertheless, future research could complement the work presented here by applying our model to data obtained from a larger sample assessed with the use of alternative data-collection strategies (e.g., mailed surveys completed by twins recruited from a wider range of birth cohorts or from a wider geographical area). In addition, we note that we have converged on our model through a Bayesian approach to model comparison that seeks the model that best reproduces the observed data while invoking the fewest number of unknown, estimated parameters. Although we feel that this is a compelling approach, in that it allowed us to compare models in terms of their odds of providing the most optimal fit to the data, other approaches to model comparison are also possible. Ultimately, adoption of a model within a specific area of research depends on the model's heuristic value, that is, the ability of a model to organize research and to lead to novel ideas and findings. We look forward to extensions of the work reported here that evaluate the heuristic value of our model in other contexts (e.g., in terms of specific biological and psychosocial factors that impact on risk of disorders within the externalizing spectrum).

Finally, our study is limited in its ability to delineate specific genetic and environmental causes of variance within the externalizing spectrum. In our study, genetic and environmental effects were inferred; such effects were not linked to specific genetic polymorphisms, nor to specific measured environmental variables. Future studies could endeavor to link the effects documented here to specific genes and environments by including more direct measures of genes and environments in models of the externalizing spectrum.

In spite of these limitations, our findings advance the existing literature. We have provided evidence supporting a specific model of co-occurrence among alcohol dependence, drug dependence, conduct disorder, adolescent antisocial behavior, and a disinhibitory personality style, assessed in late adolescence, with data from both genders and from multiple reporters, in a genetically informative sample. As such, our findings provide answers to the three questions we posed earlier regarding (a) the etiologic basis for the phenotypic externalizing factor, (b) etiologic factors that distinguish among specific externalizing syndromes, and (c) etiologic bases for phenotypic links between disinhibitory personality traits and externalizing disorders.

Heritability of the Externalizing Factor in Late Adolescence

Our results support the hypothesis of significant heritability of the externalizing factor in late adolescence. Previous research documented a phenotypic Externalizing factor linking substance use and antisocial behavior disorders in late adolescence and adulthood (Kendler et al., 1997; Krueger, 1999b; Krueger et al., 1998; Krueger, McGue, & Iacono, 2001). Only one prior study (Young et al., 2000) delineated genetic and environmental contributions to a similar latent factor, identified with a somewhat different set of variables (i.e., symptoms of conduct disorder, attention-deficit hyperactivity disorder, substance experimentation, and novelty seeking). Yet our findings and those reported by Young et al. (2000) are reassuringly similar. Indeed, we estimated the heritability of externalizing at 81%, and Young et al. (2000) estimated the heritability of their latent factor at 84%.

This finding of very high heritability of the latent externalizing factor, now demonstrated independently by two distinct research groups, has key implications for research on externalizing syndromes. The general tendency in this area (and in psychopathology research more generally) has been to study single syndromes in isolation from other syndromes, under the assumption that "pure," single-disorder groups are more etiologically homogeneous than "impure," multidisorder groups. The comorbidity phenomenon presents a challenge to this research strategy because pure cases tend to be rare and unrepresentative of individuals who meet criteria for the target disorder (Clark et al., 1995). An alternative strategy is to study "all comers," that is, persons who meet criteria for a disorder of interest, regardless of other disorders for which they meet criteria. However, this strategy is also problematic because, in studies of this kind, it is difficult to determine whether the findings are due to the target disorder or to the specific mix of comorbid disorders found in the study (Sher & Trull, 1996).

Our model offers a new perspective on how to design research on externalizing syndromes. Specifically, the high heritability of the externalizing factor makes it an attractive and novel target for research. Rather than focusing on individual disorders such as alcohol dependence or conduct disorder, research could instead focus on the variance shared among these syndromes, that is, the continuous externalizing factor that links the syndromes. From this perspective, comorbid cases are highly informative because they represent the high pole of the externalizing factor. This strategy circumvents problems inherent in comparing disorder-free controls with persons who meet criteria for specific disorders by conceiving of individual syndromes as facets of externalization. A *facet* is a variable that defines one aspect of a broader construct; for example, spatial and verbal talent are facets of intelligence (Jensen, 1980). Thus, alcohol dependence, drug dependence, conduct disorder, adolescent antisocial behavior, and a disinhibitory personality style can be viewed as facets of an externalizing factor, rather than as entirely separate and distinct phenomena. In this way, comorbidity among these disorders is accommodated, rather than ignored or controlled for, as in many contemporary research designs.

In addition to accommodating the comorbidity phenomenon, our model offers the externalizing factor as a highly heritable vulnerability dimension that can be directly measured in samples of unrelated persons. It therefore represents a logical target for future research on the psychobiology of the externalizing disorders. That is, by focusing on the externalizing factor per se, researchers working with samples of unrelated persons can study an individual difference variable closely linked to genetic differences among persons. Nevertheless, our results also indicate that specific facets of the externalizing factor contain unique etiologic variance, a topic to which we now turn.

Distinct Etiologic Bases for Distinct Externalizing Syndromes: Evidence Supporting a Hierarchical Model

Although the broad externalizing factor represents a promising target for continued research, our analyses also support etiologic distinctions among specific externalizing syndromes. The hierarchical nature of our model accommodates evidence for both etiologic generality and specificity by allowing for causal influences on the broad externalizing factor, as well as etiologic influences on each specific syndrome within the externalizing spectrum. As noted earlier, however, confidence intervals around estimates of specific genetic and environmental contributions to specific syndromes were wider than confidence intervals around other estimates. Hence, we focus our discussion on specific point estimates whose confidence intervals did not include zero. These estimates document (a) a unique, shared environmental effect on conduct disorder, (b) unique nonshared environmental effects on each facet of externalizing, and (c) unique genetic effects on a disinhibitory personality style.

Shared Environmental Factors Contributing Uniquely to Conduct Disorder

Shared environmental effects on each of the five phenotypes we studied, as well as on the higher order externalizing factor, were generally small and not significantly different from zero. The sole exception was conduct disorder, for which the impact of unique, shared environmental factors (which might include influences such as neighborhoods or family dysfunction; Caspi, Taylor, Moffitt, & Plomin, 2000; Patterson, DeGarmo, & Knutson, 2000) was significant, accounting for 26% of the variance (i.e., $.51 \times .51$; see Figure 3.1). This finding dovetails well with findings from a number of other studies documenting shared environmental effects on conduct disorder and childhood antisocial behavior (Jacobson, Prescott, & Kendler, 2000; Lyons et al., 1995; Miles & Carey, 1997; Thapar & McGuffin, 1996; but see Slutske et al., 1997, for an exception). However, our findings show that the influence of the shared environment on conduct disorder is specific to this syndrome rather than a function of its comorbidity with other syndromes. Young et al. (2000) also found residual effects of the shared environment on conduct disorder, but in their study, these residual effects also influenced substance experimentation.

Thus, findings from both groups emphasize the utility of a hierarchical model in understanding both specific and general etiological factors in the externalizing disorders. Overall, the shared environment has little impact within the externalizing spectrum, but it does appear to impact conduct disorder and experimentation with substances. In addition, conduct disorder and substance experimentation refer to behaviors earlier in the life course (as opposed to adolescent antisocial behavior and substance dependence). Thus, shared environmental factors may be more important earlier in life (cf. Burt et al., 2001).

Unique Nonshared Environmental Effects on Each Externalizing Facet

Most of the unique variance in each externalizing syndrome was traced to nonshared environmental factors (i.e., factors that made our participants different, despite their shared genes and rearing within the same families; Turkheimer & Waldron, 2000). Indeed, each of the unique nonshared variance estimates in Figure 3.1 was significant (cf. Young et al., 2000).

One possible interpretation of these findings invokes unsystematic or random effects. Random and unsystematic effects mimic nonshared environmental effects because they create differences among relatives, such as twins. Thus, it may be that latent variables (which represent the systematic covariance among multiple indicators) are, in general, more heritable than measured variables (which are more saturated with the unsystematic or random effects specific to specific variables). The nonshared environment may represent such stochastic processes, rather than systematic linear relations between environmental events and phenotypes (Turkheimer & Waldron, 2000).

An alternative viewpoint on the finding of unique nonshared environmental contributions to each measured phenotype might be that nonshared environmental factors account for the differentiation of closely related disorders. That is, genetic factors may work in concert to influence the overall likelihood of developing a disorder in the externalizing spectrum, but what determines the way this liability is expressed are events whose impact is unique to a specific person at specific points in time. For example, nonshared environmental factors contribute more to the variance of mental disorders measured on single occasions, compared with aggregate estimates of disorder status when disorders are measured on multiple occasions (Foley, Neale, & Kendler, 1998; Kendler, Karkowski, & Prescott, 1999). Thus, future research might extend the approach taken here by studying the externalizing spectrum longitudinally, attempting to link specific, transient environmental events not shared by twins (e.g., unique peer groups; Harris, 1995) to differences in their phenotypic externalizing propensities over time. Such an approach would allow for separation between the effects of temporal instability and random or unsystematic effects and, hence, could extend our understanding of the meaning of the unique nonshared environmental variance in each externalizing phenotype. In addition, this approach takes full advantage of a hierarchical conception of the externalizing spectrum in attempting to identify specific, unique environmental experiences that account for differential manifestations of the broad externalizing factor in different persons, at different times.

Unique Genetic Effects on Disinhibitory Personality

The heritability of each externalizing phenotype we studied could be traced to the heritability of the overarching externalizing factor, with one exception: a disinhibitory personality style. Young et al. (2000) also found residual genetic effects on their index of disinhibitory personality, the trait of novelty seeking. One interpretation of this finding is substantive, that is, it may be the case that there are genetic factors that impact uniquely on personality but do not influence overall risk for externalizing psychopathology. Another interpretation of this finding is methodological. Specifically, we measured personality and psychopathology in distinctive ways, using a self-report instrument and an in-person clinical interview, respectively. Although these measurement strategies reflect distinctive traditions in personality and psychopathology research, there is nothing inherent in either construct that demands measurement by interview vs. self-report questionnaire. For example, interviews have been developed to assess normal-range personality traits such as the "big 5" (Trull et al., 1998) and self-report instruments have been developed to assess *DSM*-defined psychopathology (Zimmerman & Mattia, 2001). Thus, future research could disentangle methodological and substantive interpretations of our finding of unique genetic contributions to a disinhibitory personality style by measuring both constructs (personality and psychopathology) using both approaches (interview and self-report questionnaire).

Etiologic Bases for the Link Between a Disinhibitory Personality Style and Externalizing Disorders

Although we found unique genetic variance in our measure of disinhibited personality, this variable also had a significant loading on the broad externalizing factor (cf. Jang et al., 2000; Young et al., 2000). Thus, personality and psychopathology are linked at an etiologic level. Part of the heritability of a disinhibitory personality style can be traced to its role as an indicator of the highly heritable latent externalizing factor, a factor also indicated by psychopathological syndromes.

This finding extends the existing literature by documenting that the phenotypic association between disinhibited personality traits and externalizing disorders can be traced to etiologic factors in common between these phenotypes. Previous research in this area consists primarily of cross-sectional studies of unrelated persons (Sher & Trull, 1994), and such studies are open to multiple interpretations because they cannot establish the etiologic bases of the link between personality and psychopathology (cf. Nathan, 1988; Tarter, 1988). Our study, and the recent studies reported by Jang et al. (2000) and Young et al. (2000), are the first reports, to our knowledge, to document a genetic basis for the disinhibitory personality style–externalizing disorder link. Our study extends the work of Jang et al. (2000) to a population-based sample assessed with in-person interviews, and also extends the work of Young et al. (2000) to a larger, older sample showing more severe forms of externalizing disorder (such as substance dependence) assessed by multiple methods (both parent and child report). In addition, our study places the personality–externalizing disorder connection within the theoretical context of the externalizing spectrum. Disinhibitory personality, substance dependence, and antisocial behavior disorders are linked as indicators of the higher order, highly heritable externalizing factor that spans normal (personality) and abnormal (psychopathological) variation. These findings, now emerging from three independent research groups, thereby challenge the notion of a sharp dividing line between normal and abnormal variation.

In summary, we have presented evidence supporting a hierarchical model of the externalizing spectrum of disorder in late adolescence. Each phenotype we studied was significantly linked to a latent and highly heritable externalizing factor, yet each phenotype also contained unique variance traceable to etiologic factors impacting separately on each phenotype. Thus, our model accommodates evidence for both etiologic specificity and generality within the externalizing spectrum. Nevertheless, much work remains to be done in characterizing the specific genes and environments that account for shared and distinctive etiologic factors impacting on phenotypes in the externalizing spectrum. We hope our model serves a generative role in suggesting strategies for this next phase of research.

REFERENCES

Achenbach, T. M., & Edelbrock, C. S. (1978). The classification of child psychopathology: A review and analysis of empirical efforts. *Psychological Bulletin, 85*, 1275–1301.

Achenbach, T. M., & Edelbrock, C. S. (1984). Psychopathology of childhood. *Annual Review of Psychology, 35*, 227–256.

Achenbach, T. M., McConaughy, S. H., & Howell, C. T. (1987). Child/adolescent behavioral and emotional problems: Implications of cross-informant correlations for situational specificity. *Psychological Bulletin, 101*, 213–232.

Akaike, H. (1987). Factor analysis and AIC. *Psychometrika, 52*, 317–332.

American Psychiatric Association. (1987). *Diagnostic and statistical manual of mental disorders* (3rd ed., rev.). Washington, DC: Author.

Bock, G. R., & Goode, J. A. (Eds.). (1996). *Genetics of criminal and antisocial behavior*. New York: Wiley.

Bohman, M., Sigvardsson, S., & Cloninger, C. R. (1981). Maternal inheritance of alcohol abuse: Cross-fostering analysis of adopted women. *Archives of General Psychiatry, 38,* 965–969.

Browne, M. W., & Cudeck, R. (1993). Alternative ways of assessing model fit. In K. A. Bollen & J. S. Long (Eds.), *Testing structural equation models* (pp. 136–162). Newbury Park, CA: Sage.

Burt, S. A., Krueger, R. F., McGue, M., & Iacono, W. G. (2001). Sources of covariation among attention-deficit/hyperactivity disorder, oppositional defiant disorder, and conduct disorder: The importance of shared environment. *Journal of Abnormal Psychology, 110,* 516–525.

Cadoret, R. J., O'Gorman T. W., Troughton, E. & Heywood, E. (1985). Alcoholism and antisocial personality: Interrelationships, genetic and environmental factors. *Archives of General Psychiatry, 42,* 161–167.

Cadoret, R. J., Troughton, E., & O'Gorman, T. W. (1987). Genetic and environmental factors in alcohol abuse and antisocial personality. *Journal of Studies on Alcohol, 48,* 1–8.

Carey, G., & Goldman, D. (1997). The genetics of antisocial behavior. In D. M. Stoff & J. Breiling (Eds.), *Handbook of antisocial behavior* (pp. 243–254). New York: Wiley.

Caspi, A., Moffitt, T. E., Newman, D. L., & Silva, P. A. (1996). Behavioral observations at age 3 years predict adult psychiatric disorders: Longitudinal evidence from a birth cohort. *Archives of General Psychiatry, 53,* 1033–1039.

Caspi, A., Taylor, A., Moffitt, T. E., & Plomin, R. (2000). Neighborhood deprivation affects children's mental health: Environmental risks identified in a genetic design. *Psychological Science, 11,* 338–342.

Clark, L. A., Watson, D., & Reynolds, S. (1995). Diagnosis and classification of psychopathology: Challenges to the current system and future directions. *Annual Review of Psychology, 46,* 121–153.

Cloninger, C. R., Bohman, M., & Sigvardsson, S. (1981). Inheritance of alcohol abuse: Cross-fostering analysis of adopted men. *Archives of General Psychiatry, 38,* 861–868.

Cloninger, C. R., Sigvardsson, S., & Bohman, M. (1988). Childhood personality predicts alcohol abuse in young adults. *Alcoholism: Clinical and Experimental Research, 12,* 494–505.

Crowe, R. R. (1974). An adoption study of antisocial personality. *Archives of General Psychiatry, 31,* 785–791.

DiLalla, L. F., & Gottesman, I. I. (1989). Heterogeneity of causes for delinquency and criminality: Lifespan perspectives. *Development and Psychopathology, 1,* 339–349.

Doyle, A. E. (1998). *The familial transmission of antisocial behavior: Evidence from the Minnesota Twin Family Study.* Unpublished doctoral dissertation, University of Minnesota, Minneapolis.

Elkins, I. J., Iacono, W. G., Doyle, A. E., & McGue, M. (1997). Characteristics associated with the persistence of antisocial behavior: Results from recent longitudinal research. *Aggression and Violent Behavior, 2*, 101–124.

Foley, D. L., Neale, M. C., & Kendler, K. S. (1998). Reliability of a lifetime history of major depression: Implication for heritability and comorbidity. *Psychological Medicine, 28*, 857–870.

Goodwin, D. W., Schulsinger, F., Hermansen, L., Guze, S. B., & Winokur, G. (1973). Alcohol problems in adoptees raised apart from alcoholic biological parents. *Archives of General Psychiatry, 28*, 238–243.

Gorenstein, E. E., & Newman, J. P. (1980). Disinhibitory psychopathology: A new perspective and a model for research. *Psychological Review, 87*, 303–315.

Gottesman, I. I., & Goldsmith, H. H. (1994). Developmental psychopathology of antisocial behavior: Inserting genes into its ontogenesis and epigenesis. In C. A. Nelson (Ed.), *Minnesota Symposia on Child Psychology: Vol. 27. Threats to optimal development: Integrating biological, psychological, and social risk factors* (pp. 69–104). Hillsdale, NJ: Erlbaum.

Grove, W. M., Eckert, E. D., Heston, L., Bouchard, T. J., Jr., Segal, N., & Lykken, D. T. (1990). Heritability of substance abuse and antisocial behavior: A study of monozygotic twins reared apart. *Biological Psychiatry, 27*, 1293–1304.

Harris, J. R. (1995). Where is the child's environment? A group socialization theory of development. *Psychological Review, 102*, 458–489.

Heath, A. C., Bucholz, K. K., Madden, P. A. F., Dinwiddie, S. H., Slutske, W. S., Bierut, L. J., et al. (1997). Genetic and environmental contributions to alcohol dependence risk in a national twin sample: Consistency of findings in women and men. *Psychological Medicine, 27*, 1381–1396.

Holdcraft, L. C., Iacono, W. G., & McGue, M. K. (1998). Antisocial personality disorder and depression in relation to alcoholism: A community-based sample. *Journal of Studies on Alcohol, 59*, 222–226.

Howard, M. O., Kivlahan, D., & Walker, R. D. (1997). Cloninger's tridimensional theory of personality and psychopathology: Applications to substance use disorders. *Journal of Studies on Alcohol, 58*, 48–66.

Hur, Y.-M., McGue, M., & Iacono, W. G. (1995). Unequal rate of monozygotic and like-sex dizygotic twin birth: Evidence from the Minnesota Twin Family Study. *Behavior Genetics, 25*, 337–340.

Iacono, W. G., Carlson, S. R., Taylor, J., Elkins, I. J., & McGue, M. (1999). Behavioral disinhibition and the development of substance-use disorders: Findings from the Minnesota Twin Family Study. *Development and Psychopathology, 11*, 869–900.

Jacobson, K. C., Prescott, C. A., & Kendler, K. S. (2000). Genetic and environmental influences on juvenile antisocial behaviour assessed on two occasions. *Psychological Medicine, 30*, 1315–1325.

Jang, K. L., Vernon, P. A., & Livesley, W. J. (2000). Personality disorder traits, family environment, and alcohol misuse: A multivariate behavioral genetic analysis. *Addiction, 95*, 873–888.

Jensen, A. R. (1980). *Bias in mental testing*. New York: Free Press.

Kendler, K. S., Davis, C. G., & Kessler, R. C. (1997). The familial aggregation of common psychiatric and substance use disorders in the National Comorbidity Survey: A family history study. *British Journal of Psychiatry, 170*, 541–548.

Kendler, K. S., Karkowski, L. M., & Prescott, C. (1999). Fears and phobias: Reliability and heritability. *Psychological Medicine, 29*, 539–553.

Kendler, K. S., Neale, M. C., Kessler, R. C., Heath, A. C., & Eaves, L. J. (1993). A longitudinal twin study of personality and major depression in women. *Archives of General Psychiatry, 50*, 853–862.

Krueger, R. F. (1999a). Personality traits in late adolescence predict mental disorders in early adulthood: A prospective–epidemiological study. *Journal of Personality, 67*, 39–65.

Krueger, R. F. (1999b). The structure of common mental disorders. *Archives of General Psychiatry, 56*, 921–926.

Krueger, R. F. (2000). Phenotypic, genetic, and nonshared environmental parallels in the structure of personality: A view from the Multidimensional Personality Questionnaire. *Journal of Personality and Social Psychology, 79*, 1057–1067.

Krueger, R. F. (2002). Psychometric perspectives on comorbidity. In J. E. Helzer & J. J. Hudziak (Eds.), *Defining psychopathology in the 21st century: DSM–V and beyond* (pp. 41–54). Washington, DC: American Psychiatric Publishing.

Krueger, R. F., Caspi, A., Moffitt, T. E., & Silva, P. A. (1998). The structure and stability of common mental disorders (*DSM–III–R*): A longitudinal–epidemiological study. *Journal of Abnormal Psychology, 107*, 216–227.

Krueger, R. F., Caspi, A., Moffitt, T. E., Silva, P. A, & McGee, R. (1996). Personality traits are differentially linked to mental disorders: A multitrait–multidiagnosis study of an adolescent birth cohort. *Journal of Abnormal Psychology, 105*, 299–312.

Krueger, R. F., & Finger, M. S. (2001). Using item response theory to understand comorbidity among anxiety and unipolar mood disorders. *Psychological Assessment, 13*, 140–151.

Krueger, R. F., Hicks, B. M., & McGue, M. (2001). Altruism and antisocial behavior: Independent tendencies, unique personality correlates, distinct etiologies. *Psychological Science, 12*, 397–402.

Krueger, R. F., McGue, M., & Iacono, W. G. (2001). The higher-order structure of common DSM mental disorders: Internalization, externalization, and their connections to personality. *Personality and Individual Differences, 30*, 1245–1259.

Lahey, B. B., Loeber, R., Hart, E. L., Frick, P. J., Applegate, B., Zhang, Q., et al. (1995). Four-year longitudinal study of conduct disorder in boys: Patterns and predictors of persistence. *Journal of Abnormal Psychology, 104*, 83–93.

Lilienfeld, S. O., Waldman, I. D., & Israel A. C. (1994). A critical examination of the use of the term and concept of comorbidity in psychopathology research. *Clinical Psychology: Science and Practice, 1*, 71–83.

Livesley, W. J., Jang, K. L., Jackson, D. N., & Vernon, P. A. (1993). Genetic and environmental contributions to dimensions of personality disorder. *American Journal of Psychiatry, 150*, 1826–1831.

Lyons, M. J., True, W. R., Eisen, S. A., Goldberg, J., Meyer, J. M., Faraone, S. V., et al. (1995). Differential heritability of adult and juvenile antisocial traits. *Archives of General Psychiatry, 52*, 906–915.

Masse, L. C., & Tremblay, R. E. (1997). Behavior of boys in kindergarten and the onset of substance use during adolescence. *Archives of General Psychiatry, 54*, 62–68.

McGue, M., Pickens, R. W., & Svikis, D. S. (1992). Sex and age effects on the inheritance of alcohol problems: A twin study. *Journal of Abnormal Psychology, 101*, 3–17.

McGue, M., Slutske, W., & Iacono, W. G. (1999). Personality and substance use disorders: II. Alcoholism versus drug use disorders. *Journal of Consulting and Clinical Psychology, 67*, 394–404.

McGue, M., Slutske, W., Taylor, J., & Iacono, W. G. (1997). Personality and substance use disorders: I. Effects of gender and alcoholism subtype. *Alcoholism: Clinical and Experimental Research, 21*, 513–520.

Miles, D. R., & Carey, G. (1997). Genetic and environmental architecture of human aggression. *Journal of Personality and Social Psychology, 72*, 207–217.

Mineka, S., Watson, D., & Clark, L. A. (1998). Comorbidity of anxiety and unipolar mood disorders. *Annual Review of Psychology, 49*, 377–412.

Nathan, P. E. (1988). The addictive personality is the behavior of the addict. *Journal of Consulting and Clinical Psychology, 56*, 183–188.

Neale, M. C. (1997). Mx: Statistical modeling (4th ed.) [Computer software, Department of Psychiatry, Medical College of Virginia]. (Available from M. C. Neale, Box 126, Medical College of Virginia, Richmond, VA 23298)

Neale, M. C., & Cardon, L. R. (1992). *Methodology for genetic studies of twins and families.* Dordrecht, the Netherlands: Kluwer Academic.

Patrick, C. J., & Zempolich, K. A. (1998). Emotion and aggression in the psychopathic personality. *Aggression and Violent Behavior, 3*, 303–338.

Patterson, G. R., DeGarmo, D. S., & Knutson, N. (2000). Hyperactive and antisocial behaviors: Comorbid or two points in the same process? *Development and Psychopathology, 12*, 91–106.

Pickens, R. W., Svikis, D. S., McGue, M., & LaBuda, M. C. (1995). Common genetic mechanisms in alcohol, drug, and mental disorder comorbidity. *Drug and Alcohol Dependence, 39*, 129–138.

Pickens, R. W., Svikis, D. S., McGue, M., Lykken, D. T., Heston, L. L., & Clayton, P. J. (1991). Heterogeneity in the inheritance of alcoholism: A study of male and female twins. *Archives of General Psychiatry, 48*, 19–28.

Prescott, C. A., & Kendler, K. S. (1999). Genetic and environmental contributions to alcohol abuse and dependence in a population-based sample of male twins. *American Journal of Psychiatry, 156*, 34–40.

Raftery, A. E. (1995). Bayesian model selection in social research. *Sociological Methodology*, *25*, 111–163.

Roberts, S. B., & Kendler, K. S. (1999). Neuroticism and self-esteem as indices of the vulnerability to major depression in women. *Psychological Medicine*, *29*, 1101–1109.

Robins, L. M., Babor, T., & Cottler, L. B. (1987). *Composite International Diagnostic Interview: Expanded Substance Abuse Module*. Unpublished manuscript, Washington University, St. Louis.

Robins, L. N., & Price, R. (1991). Adult disorders predicted by childhood conduct problems: Results from the NIMH Epidemiological Catchment Area Project. *Psychiatry*, *54*, 116–132.

Rutter, M. L. (1997). Nature–nurture integration: The example of antisocial behavior. *American Psychologist*, *52*, 390–398.

Sher, K. J., & Trull, T. J. (1994). Personality and disinhibitory psychopathology: Alcoholism and antisocial personality disorder. *Journal of Abnormal Psychology*, *103*, 92–102.

Sher, K. J., & Trull, T. J. (1996). Methodological issues in psychopathology research. *Annual Review of Psychology*, *47*, 371–400.

Slutske, W. S., Heath, A. C., Dinwiddie, S. H., Madden, P., Bucholz, K. K., Dunne, M. P., et al. (1997). Modeling genetic and environmental influences in the etiology of conduct disorder: A study of 2,682 adult twin pairs. *Journal of Abnormal Psychology*, *106*, 266–279.

Slutske, W. S., Heath, A. C., Dinwiddie, S. H., Madden, P. A. F., Bucholz, K. K., Dunne, M. P., et al. (1998). Common genetic risk factors for conduct disorder and alcohol dependence. *Journal of Abnormal Psychology*, *107*, 363–374.

Tabachnick, B. G., & Fidell, L. S. (1996). *Using multivariate statistics* (3rd ed.). New York: HarperCollins.

Tarter, R. E. (1988). Are there inherited behavioral traits that predispose to substance abuse? *Journal of Consulting and Clinical Psychology*, *56*, 189–196.

Tellegen, A. (1985). Structures of mood and personality and their relevance to assessing anxiety with an emphasis on self-report. In A. H. Tuma & J. D. Maser (Eds.), *Anxiety and the anxiety disorders* (pp. 681–706). Hillsdale, NJ: Erlbaum.

Tellegen, A. (1992). *Exploring personality through test construction: Development of the Multidimensional Personality Questionnaire (MPQ)*. Unpublished manuscript, Department of Psychology, University of Minnesota, Minneapolis.

Thapar, A., & McGuffin, P. (1996). A twin study of antisocial and neurotic symptoms in childhood. *Psychological Medicine*, *26*, 1111–1118.

Tremblay, R. E., Pihl, R. O., Vitaro, F., & Dobkin, P. L. (1994). Predicting early onset of male antisocial behavior from preschool behavior. *Archives of General Psychiatry*, *51*, 732–739.

Trull, T. J., Widiger, T. A., Useda, J. D., Holcomb, J., Doan, B. T., Axelrod, S. R., et al. (1998). A structured interview for the assessment of the five-factor model of personality. *Psychological Assessment*, *10*, 229–240.

Tsuang, M. T., Lyons, M. J., Eisen, S. A., Goldberg, J., True, W., Lin, N., et al. (1996). Genetic influences on DSM–III–R drug abuse and dependence: A study of 3,372 twin pairs. *American Journal of Medical Genetics, 67*, 473–477.

Turkheimer, E., & Waldron, M. (2000). Nonshared environment: A theoretical, methodological, and quantitative review. *Psychological Bulletin, 126*, 78–108.

van den Bree, M. B. M., Svikis, D. S., & Pickens, R. W. (1998). Genetic influences in antisocial personality and drug use disorders. *Drug and Alcohol Dependence, 49*, 177–187.

van den Oord, E. J. C. G., Simonoff, E., Eaves, L. J., Pickles, A., Silberg, J., & Maes, H. (2000). An evaluation of different approaches for behavior genetic analyses with psychiatric symptom scores. *Behavior Genetics, 30*, 1–18.

Verona, E., & Patrick, C. J. (2000). Suicide risk in externalizing syndromes: Temperamental and neurobiological underpinnings. In T. E. Joiner (Ed.), *Suicide science: Expanding the boundaries*. (pp. 137–173). Boston: Kluwer Academic.

Waldman, I. D., & Slutske, W. S. (2000). Antisocial behavior and alcoholism: A behavioral genetic perspective on comorbidity. *Clinical Psychology Review, 20*, 255–287.

Watson, D., & Clark, L. A. (1993). Behavioral disinhibition versus constraint: A dispositional perspective. In D. M. Wegner & J. W. Pennebaker (Eds.), *Handbook of mental control* (pp. 506–527). New York: Prentice Hall.

Welner, Z., Reich, W., Herjanic, B., Jung, K., & Amado, H. (1987). Reliability, validity, and parent–child agreement studies of the Diagnostic Interview for Children and Adolescents (DICA). *Journal of the American Academy of Child and Adolescent Psychiatry, 26*, 649–653.

Widiger, T. A., & Clark, L. A. (2000). Toward *DSM–V* and the classification of psychopathology. *Psychological Bulletin, 126*, 946–963.

Widiger, T. A., & Sankis, L. (2000). Adult psychopathology: Issues and controversies. *Annual Review of Psychology, 51*, 377–404.

Young, S. E., Stallings, M. C., Corley, R. P., Krauter, K. S., & Hewitt, J. K. (2000). Genetic and environmental influences on behavioral disinhibition. *American Journal of Medical Genetics (Neuropsychiatric Genetics), 96*, 684–695.

Zimmerman, M., & Mattia, J. I. (2001). A self-report scale to help make psychiatric diagnoses: The Psychiatric Diagnostic Screening Questionnaire. *Archives of General Psychiatry, 58*, 787–794.

Zuckerman, M. (1979). Sensation seeking and risk taking. In C. E. Izard (Ed.), *Emotions in personality and psychopathology* (pp. 163–197). New York: Plenum Press.

4

ETIOLOGICAL CONTRIBUTIONS TO HEAVY DRINKING FROM LATE ADOLESCENCE TO YOUNG ADULTHOOD

SERENA M. KING, S. ALEXANDRA BURT, STEPHEN M. MALONE,
MATT McGUE, AND WILLIAM G. IACONO

Heavy drinking is a relatively common behavior during the transition from adolescence to adulthood (Arnett, 2000; Schulenberg et al., 2001). Of all age groups, underage drinkers (ages 18 to 20 years) and young adults (ages 21 to 25 years) consume the largest amount of alcohol in the United States and have the highest rates of heavy drinking (including "binge" drinking; i.e., the consumption of five or more drinks on one occasion; Foster, Vaughn, Foster, & Califano, 2003; Naimi et al., 2003). Heavy drinking is accompanied by serious short- and long-term negative behavioral consequences, including impaired judgment and coordination, reduced behavioral inhibition, risky sexual behavior, and traffic fatalities (Wechsler, Davenport, Dowdall, Moekens, & Castillo, 1994; Wechsler & Isaac, 1992). As a result of its deleterious effects on the individual and community, excessive alcohol consumption has drawn the attention of the U.S. Centers for Disease

An earlier version of this article was presented at the June 2003 annual meeting of the Research Society on Alcoholism, Ft. Lauderdale, Florida. This research was supported in part by National Institutes of Health Grants DA-05147 and AA-09367. Serena M. King was supported by the Eva O. Miller endowed fellowship of the graduate school of the University of Minnesota.

Control and Prevention, and the U.S. Surgeon General has indicated that reducing binge drinking is a goal of Healthy People 2010 (U.S. Department of Health & Human Services, 2001). Despite its public health significance, few studies have examined the origins of heavy alcohol consumption during the transition from adolescence to young adulthood.

Studies documenting the natural history of heavy drinking behaviors support the existence of at least two developmental pathways from adolescence to young adulthood: an earlier onset, heavy drinking group and a later onset, developmentally limited form of heavy drinking (Chassin, Pitts, & Prost, 2002; Schulenberg et al., 2001; Sher & Gotham, 1999). Earlier onset heavy drinking (emerging during the high school years) is associated with a poorer prognostic outcome, a history of conduct disorder, more alcohol problems in adulthood, and higher levels of externalizing symptomatology relative to later onset heavy drinking (Baer, Kivlahan, & Marlatt, 1995; Chassin et al., 2002; Sher & Gotham, 1999). Although the behavioral genetic literature is limited, twin studies on age of drinking onset (McGue, Iacono, Legrand, Malone, & Elkins, 2001) and quantity and frequency of drinking in adolescence suggest that genetic factors contribute in an important way to early onset heavy drinking (Viken, Kaprio, Koskenvuo, & Rose, 1999).

Later onset heavy drinking (e.g., during the college years) may be driven in part by a developmentally normative, culturally sanctioned rite of passage that involves getting drunk, drinking heavily, and learning to regulate alcohol use in young adulthood (Chassin et al., 2002; Schulenberg et al., 2001; Schulenberg, O'Malley, Bachman, Wadsworth, & Johnston, 1996). From this perspective, a later onset, developmentally limited form of heavy drinking is affected primarily by transient environmental factors, and genetic influences may be weaker than for early onset heavy drinking. Developmental theory provides a useful framework in explaining the emergence of an early onset, persistent type and a later onset, developmentally limited form of heavy drinking. In the alcoholism domain, developmental taxonomies have been used to describe etiologically diverse groups of alcoholics. Most notably, Zucker's (1994) theory outlined several developmental subtypes of alcoholism, including a chronic antisocial form and a developmentally limited form, driven by role transitions. Recently, investigators have theorized that a developmentally limited form of heavy drinking may be influenced in part by increased risk taking that comes along with greater autonomy and newly acquired freedom from adult sanctions (Schulenberg & Maggs, 2002; Schulenberg et al., 2001). Specifically, later onset heavy drinking may be driven by a complex interplay of developmentally appropriate environmental and contextual changes (i.e., the leaving home transition, entering college, changing living arrangements, greater access and availability of alcohol; Gotham, Sher, & Wood, 2003; Schulenberg & Maggs, 2002). These changing environmental conditions may introduce unique, time-limited environmental influences that promote or encourage heavy alcohol use (Clapp, Shillington, & Segars, 2000; Lange et al., 2002; Sher, Bartholow, & Nanda, 2001; Wechsler, Dowdall, Davenport, & Castillo, 1995).

Several community-based and collegiate studies have documented specific environmental correlates of heavy drinking during the transition to young adulthood (Chassin et al., 2002; Hussong & Chassin, 2002; Schulenberg & Maggs, 2002). However, epidemiological, genetically uninformative samples are limited by their reliance on family history data as proxies for genetically inherited risk and cannot distinguish environmental and genetic causal influences on drinking. Specifically, in genetically uninformative samples, it is difficult to distinguish truly environmental effects from person–environment correlations arising from selective *environment seeking* (i.e., when a person's temperament leads them to seek out a particular environment; Scarr & McCartney, 1983). Hence, a goal of our study was to examine the relative genetic and environmental influences on heavy drinking during the transition to young adulthood in the context of a genetically informative design.

As drinking behavior develops during the transition to young adulthood, gender differences in the etiology and developmental course of drinking become increasingly evident. On a phenotypic level, men are more likely to be heavy drinkers in young adulthood and less likely to transition out of large-effect drinking (or binge drinking) than women (Jackson, Sher, Gotham, & Wood, 2001). On an etiological level, some studies suggest weaker genetic effects on alcoholism in women than men (McGue, Pickens, & Svikis, 1992), even though the preponderance of evidence is consistent with no gender differences in heritability (Heath et al., 1997). Collectively, evidence indicates that the developmental course of alcohol use may differ in men and women, though it is unclear whether there are gender differences in the etiological bases of alcohol use.

Recently, researchers have suggested that intermediate phenotypes (or trait-like indicators) such as P3 amplitude reduction (P3-AR), may be useful indicators of the specific action of genes involved in alcoholism (Enoch, Schuckit, Johnson, & Goldman, 2003; Gunzerath & Goldman, 2003; Iacono, Malone, & McGue, 2003). P3-AR is a well-established (particularly in males) electrophysiological brain correlate found in affected and unaffected relatives of alcoholic probands (Iacono, Carlson, Malone, & McGue, 2002; Iacono et al., 2003; Polich, Pollack, & Bloom, 1994). The existence of a psychophysiological marker of genetic risk provides the opportunity to further substantiate our hypothesis that early onset heavy drinking is more biologically influenced than later onset heavy drinking, as we would expect greater P3 amplitude reduction in the former than the latter.

Current evidence thus suggests that biological factors interact with environmental factors to influence drinking during the transition from late adolescence to young adulthood. The genetic and environmental structure of heavy drinking during this transition, however, has been largely unexamined. Several unresolved questions are fundamental to understanding the causal roots of heavy drinking during this high-growth developmental period in alcohol use. Do the genetic and environmental influences on heavy drinking change in relative importance from adolescence to young adulthood? Are there overlapping genetic and environmental influences contributing to P3 amplitude and heavy drinking? Are the etiologic bases of heavy drinking different for men and women?

We examined the underlying genetic and environmental architecture of heavy drinking from adolescence to young adulthood. We also evaluated the extent to which correlated genetic and environmental factors influenced heavy drinking from ages 17 to 20 years, providing a significant advance in understanding both time-specific and time-independent sources of variation in heavy drinking. Given evidence that earlier onset heavy drinking may be under greater genetic influence relative to later onset heavy drinking, we expected that as adolescents entered young adulthood, environmental influences would become increasingly salient while biological factors would become less important in explaining variation in drinking patterns.

Using a community-based longitudinal design, we sought to explore the etiology of heavy drinking during the transition to young adulthood. Specifically, the following hypotheses were addressed:

Hypothesis 1. The transition to young adulthood is accompanied by a decreasing influence of genetic factors and increasing influence of time-specific environmental effects on heavy drinking.

Hypothesis 2. Early heavy drinking is associated with reduced P3 amplitude and this association is primarily genetically mediated.

Hypothesis 3. Biological influences on early heavy drinking, as indicated by heritability and reduced P3 amplitude, are more pronounced in men than women.

METHOD

Participants

Participants were 578 twin men and 674 twin women participating in the Minnesota Twin Family Study (MTFS). The MTFS is a population-based, longitudinal–epidemiological study of substance use disorders and related psychopathology in twins and their family members. Families were ascertained through public birth records in the state of Minnesota. Families who lived more than 1 day's drive from our laboratory and families where at least one twin had a physical or cognitive disability that interfered with the day-long assessment were excluded from participation. Approximately 17% of the eligible families refused participation. Of the families who declined participation, 80% completed a brief telephone or mail survey. Although there were some slight differences between participating and nonparticipating families (i.e., slightly higher educational and occupational attainment in participating families; an average of 0.3 years more education in fathers and 0.2 years more education in mothers), there were no significant differences between these two groups on mental health indexes (see Iacono, Carlson, Taylor, Elkins, & McGue, 1999, for a more thorough description). Participating families were generally representative of the population of Minnesota for the birth cohort sampled, with a large majority being Caucasian (98%).

At intake assessment, twins ranged in age from 16 to 18 years (in females M = 17.5, SD = 0.5; in males M = 17.5, SD = 0.4). Twins were reassessed at follow up, approximately 3 years later. At follow up, twins ranged in age from 19 to 22 years (in women, M = 20.7, SD = 0.6; in men M = 20.7, SD = 0.5). A total of 481 (83.2%) male and 630 (93.5%) female twins completed a follow-up assessment. All twins were assessed in person at intake, but 193 (17.3%) of the follow-up sample completed their follow-up assessment over the phone because they could not travel to our laboratories. Population sampling strategies were used to obtain the intake sample, which is demographically representative of the state of Minnesota and has rates of psychopathology and substance use that are generally commensurate with population-based epidemiological samples (see Costello, Mustillo, Erkanli, Keeler, & Angold, 2003; Grant, 1997). For a more detailed description, see Iacono et al. (1999).

Measures

Alcohol Use

Information on alcohol use behaviors was collected through semistructured interview (in person or by telephone) using a modified version of the Substance Abuse Module (SAM), a component of the Composite International Diagnostic Interview (CIDI; Robins, Babor, & Cottler, 1987) for the *Diagnostic and Statistical Manual of Mental Disorders, Third Edition, Revised* (*DSM–III–R*; American Psychiatric Association, 1987). As a part of a large, comprehensive interview for alcohol and drug use disorders, three questions were asked about past 12-month patterns of alcohol consumption.

To measure alcohol use, we constructed a quantitative measure of heavy drinking. Relative to diagnoses, quantitative phenotypes (or continuously measured observed behaviors) may better account for the substantial variation in alcohol use behaviors from adolescence to young adulthood. Moreover, quantitative alcohol phenotypes may be less susceptible to false negatives than diagnoses and may provide a better index of familial risk for alcoholism (Malone, Iacono, & McGue, 2002). We used three measures (frequency, typical drinks consumed, and proportion of times drunk) to index alcohol consumption during the previous 12 months. Combining subjective effects (drunkenness) and alcohol consumption measures reduces measurement error and results in a more reliable estimate of typical alcohol consumption patterns (Gotham, Sher, & Wood, 1997; Midanik, 1999; O'Neill, Parra, & Sher, 2001).

Participants reported their frequency of drinking in the past 12 months on a 10-point scale (1 = *less than once a year* to 10 = *three times a day*). To make this scale comparable with the scale used with the other items, responses were collapsed into a 5-point scale (0 = *never drank or drank less than once a month*, 1 = *about once a month*, 2 = *two to three times a month*, 3 = *one to two times a week*, 4 = *three times a week or more*). Second, we assessed the frequency of drunkenness during the past 12 months (an indicator of the subjective effects of alcohol): "What proportion of the time that you drank during the past 12 months did you drink enough to feel drunk?" Respondents indicated the proportion of times they became drunk when drinking in the past 12 months on a 5-point scale (responses ranged from 0 = *never or nearly never*, 1 = *less than half of the time I drank*, 2 = *about half of the time I drank*, 3 = *more than half of the time I drank*, 4 = *every time or nearly every time that I drank*). Third, typical past-12-month alcohol consumption was measured in drinks: "How much did you have on average each time you drank during the past 12 months?" The definition of a drink was presented in a visual exhibit (i.e., a drink was a glass of wine, bottle of beer, or a highball or shot glass of hard liquor). Equivalencies of large amounts of alcohol were provided to assist in the estimation of drinks (i.e., 1 pint of liquor = 12 drinks, 1 quart of liquor = 24 drinks). For all respondents, units were combined into a 5-point scale of typical drinks consumed: 0 = *0 to 1 drink*, 1 = *2 to 3 drinks*, 2 = *4 to 5 drinks*, 3 = *6 to 7 drinks*, and 4 = *8 or more drinks*. A heavy drinking score (HEAVY) was computed by summing the three 5-point items (typical number of drinks consumed, proportion of times drunk, and frequency of drinking) at intake and follow-up assessments (scores ranged from 0 to 12). Alpha reliability estimates for the three item scale were high (α = .82 at both Times 1 and 2). Standardized skewness coefficients indicated modest positive skewness of the HEAVY measure at intake (1.23 + 0.07) but no skewness at follow up (0.07 + 0.07). Because our longitudinal analyses required that our measure of heavy drinking be similarly scaled at the two assessment points and because there was no evidence of skewness at follow up, we elected to not transform the data prior to analysis.

Rates of alcohol abstention (no use of alcohol in the past 12 months; National Institute on Alcohol Abuse and Alcoholism [NIAAA], 2000) did not differ significantly by sex at either age 17 (40.3% of males; 44.5% of females), $\chi^2 = 2.21$, $p = ns$, or 20 (11.2% of men and 12.4% of women), $\chi^2 = 0.30$, $p = ns$. Attriters had higher scores on HEAVY at intake assessment than those who returned for follow-up assessment ($M_{returners} = 2.09$, $SD_{returners} = 3.03$ vs. $M_{attriters} = 2.96$, $SD_{attriters} = 3.50$; $p = .01$). However, this difference did not vary significantly by gender ($p = ns$). Attriters did not differ significantly from follow-up participants on age 17 P3 amplitude, $\chi^2 = 2.87$, $p = ns$.

Psychophysiological Assessment (Age 17)

Electroencephalographic (EEG) activity was recorded with a Grass Neurodata Acquisition System (Grass-Telefactor, West Warwick, RI) from a Pz electrode referenced to linked earlobes. Electrooculographic (EOG) activity was recorded from electrodes placed above the pupil and on the outer canthus of one eye. We used a visual oddball paradigm task designed after that of Begleiter, Porjesz, Bihari, and Kissin (1984) where a target stimulus was an oval representing the top view of a human head with a nose and one ear. Participants were instructed to press a button indicating on which side of the head the ear and nose appeared. Participants completed 240 trials: 160 neutral presentations with a simple oval and 80 target trials. Neutral trials did not require a response. The stimuli were each presented for 98 ms with inter-stimulus intervals distributed randomly between 1 and 2 seconds. Each trial consisted of a 500-millisecond baseline period before stimulus onset and a 1,500-millisecond poststimulus response window. EEG data were smoothed by means of a digital low-pass filter with a cutoff frequency of 7.5 Hz. A blink-correction procedure was used to reduce the contamination of EEG due to artifacts such as eyeblinks. Using a computer program, the largest peak amplitude between 200 and 800 ms after the stimulus presentation was identified. A trained scorer supervised the computer algorithm and overrode the algorithm's selection when it incorrectly identified the P3 wave. More complete details of the P3 assessment can be found in Iacono et al. (2002).

Zygosity Determination

Zygosity was determined by the agreement of several separate estimates: (a) parents reported physical resemblance between their twins; (b) MTFS staff evaluated visage, hair color, and face and ear shape for physical similarity; and (c) ponderal and cephalic indexes and fingerprint ridge counts were entered into an algorithm. A serological analysis was performed when these three estimates did not agree. A previous validation study ($n = 50$ adolescent twin pairs) found that when the three zygosity estimates agreed, the consensus determination was confirmed by the serological analysis in every case. This finding suggests that the method of zygosity determination used by the MTFS is accurate.

Statistical Analyses

Age and Sex Effects on Drinking Behavior

To statistically account for the correlated observations that were due to using a twin sample, we used a repeated measures, mixed-effects analysis of variance (ANOVA), including age (age 17 vs. age 20 assessment), sex, and the Age × Sex interaction for each drinking measure to determine if there were significant mean changes from ages 17 to 20 and whether changes were dependent on sex. Mixed models were used with the twin data to account for their correlated nature by statistically treating data from members of twin pairs as clustered within families. A fuller explanation of mixed-effects models can be found in Bryk and Raudenbush (1992). Standardized effect sizes were computed using the difference in estimated means as the numerator and the square root of residual variance as the denominator.

Biometric Modeling

Biometric modeling was used to examine the genetic and environmental influences on HEAVY from ages 17 to 20. Twin methodology uses the difference in the proportion of genes shared by monozygotic (MZ) and dizygotic (DZ) twins to estimate genetic and environmental contributions to variance in observed behaviors or characteristics (phenotypes). MZ or identical twins share 100% of their segregating genes, whereas DZ or fraternal twins share an average of 50% of their segregating genes. MZ and DZ correlations were compared with estimated additive genetic, shared, and nonshared environmental effects. The additive genetic component (a^2) refers to the average effect of individual alleles summed over loci. The shared environmental component (c^2) is that part of the environment that is common to both members of a twin pair and acts to make the twins within a pair (both MZ and DZ) similar to each other. The familial environment is often considered to be a primary component of c^2 (Burt, Krueger, McGue, & Iacono, 2003), although other related effects, such as neighborhood effects, have also been implicated (Caspi, Taylor, Moffitt, & Plomin, 2000). Nonshared environment (e^2) encompasses environmental factors unique to each twin within a pair. Nonshared environment differentiates each twin within a pair (both MZ and DZ), making them less similar. Measurement error, which similarly acts to reduce both MZ and DZ correlations, is also contained within e^2. (Interested readers are referred to Plomin, DeFries, McClearn, & McGuffin, 2001, for a more detailed explanation of twin study methodology.) Twin methodology relies on the *equal environments assumption*, which assumes that MZ twin pairs are no more likely to share the environmental factors that are etiologically relevant to the phenotype under study than are DZ twin pairs. The equal environments assumption has been repeatedly tested and supported for numerous phenotypes, including many mental disorders (Hettema, Neale, & Kendler, 1995; Kendler, Neale, Kessler, Heath, & Eaves, 1993; Morris-Yates, Andrews, Howie, & Henderson, 1990; Scarr & Carter-Saltzman, 1979).

Because not all of the twins who participated at intake completed a follow-up assessment, we made use of full-information maximum-likelihood (FIML) raw data techniques, which correct for statistical biases that are due to missing data while appropriately accounting for the statistical imprecision associated with missing data (Little & Rubin, 1987). Mx, a structural equation modeling program (Neale, 1997), was used to fit models to the raw data. When fitting models to raw data, variances, covariances, and means of those data are freely estimated by minimizing minus twice the log likelihood ($-2lnL$). The minimized value of $-2lnL$ of the data under unrestricted baseline model can then be compared with $-2lnL$ under a more restrictive biometric model. This comparison provides a likelihood-ratio chi-square test of goodness of fit of the more restrictive model relative to the baseline model. Statistically significant chi-square values reflect a poor fit. Akaike's information criterion (AIC; equals $\chi^2 - 2\ df$; Akaike, 1987), which measures model fit relative to parsimony, is also used to determine the best fitting model among a set of fitted models, with the lowest (or most negative) AIC considered best.

Twin data on HEAVY at the two time points were analyzed with Mx using a general bivariate decomposition model (see Figure 4.1). This model allows for age-specific genetic (A1, A2), shared environmental (C1, C2), and nonshared environmental (E1, E2) effects that are correlated over time (r_a, r_c, r_e). Specifically, the bivariate decomposition approach parses the phenotypic variance of each phenotype and the phenotypic covariance across time into that which is due to genetic, shared environmental, and nonshared environmental factors. These statistics reveal the extent to which a specific effect (e.g., the genetic effect) on one variable is correlated with the same effect on another variable. This allowed us to determine the extent to which stability in HEAVY is accounted for by common genetic, shared, and nonshared environmental factors by estimating the contribution of these three factors to the covariance in HEAVY over time. For example, if a1 is the additive genetic effect at Time 1, a^2 is the additive genetic effect at Time 2, and r_a is the genetic correlation over time, then the genetic contribution to stability is estimated by dividing $a_1 \times a_2 \times r_a$ by the phenotypic covariance. Similar calculations can be used to estimate the shared and nonshared environmental contributions to phenotypic stability. Finally, the longitudinal biometric model was used to estimate genetic and environmental contributions to change in HEAVY between ages 17 and 20. The genetic contribution to change is $(1 - r_a^2) \times a_2^2$, whereas the shared and nonshared environmental contributions can be obtained using similar calculations. In these ways, the

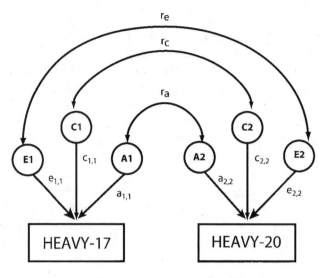

Figure 4.1. Path diagram of the bivariate decomposition model of HEAVY from ages 17 to 20. HEAVY = composite score of typical amount consumed, proportion of times drunk, and frequency of drinking. The variance in liability to variation in HEAVY at each time point is parsed into its additive genetic (A1, A2), shared (C1, C2), and nonshared environmental (E1, E2) effects. The cross paths (r_e, r_c, r_a) represent the correlated influences between ages 17 and 20.

bivariate model allowed us to make inferences regarding the etiology of HEAVY at each age, as well as the etiology of stability and change in HEAVY from ages 17 to 20 years.

Modeling the Association Between P3 Amplitude and Heavy Drinking at Age 17

We first determined whether P3 amplitude was associated with age of onset of heavy drinking. Three heavy drinking onset groups were created on the basis of the quantity and frequency of drinking reported at intake and follow-up assessments. At the age 17 intake assessment, all individuals who reported a typical (past 12-month) alcohol consumption level of five or more drinks at a time and drank at least once a month were considered early onset heavy drinkers. This level of consumption is in accordance with standard definitions of heavy alcohol use (NIAAA, 2000). Individuals who reported typical consumption levels of fewer than five drinks at age 17 but reported newly emergent consumption levels of five or more drinks at least once a month at age 20 were considered late heavy drinkers. Nondrinkers and individuals reporting a typical consumption level of less than five drinks at both intake and follow-up assessments were in the nonheavy group. Individuals who did not return for the follow-up assessment but met our criteria for being an early, heavy drinker by the Age 17 assessment were classified as early heavy drinkers. The three groups reflected the onset of heavier levels of drinking and so were coded numerically as 0 = *no onset*, 1 = *late onset*, and 2 = *early onset of heavy drinking*. Of the 1,252 individuals with complete intake data, 1,138 (91%) could be classified into one of the three onset groups, and of this group, 1,003 (86%; 438 males and 565 females) also had valid P3 data at intake and therefore could be used in the present analyses. Among male participants, 107 (24%) were classified as early onset heavy drinkers, 148 (34%) were classified as late onset, and 183 (42%) were classified as nonheavy drinkers. For female participants, the corresponding samples sizes are 72 (13%), 107 (19%), and 386 (68%). The effect of heavy drinking onset on P3 amplitude was evaluated using a two-way, mixed effects regression model with sex, heavy drinking onset group (treated as an ordinal variable), and the Sex × Heavy Drinking interaction as independent variables. Hierarchical linear modeling methods were used to account for the clustered nature of the twin data. Because our hypotheses were directional, one-tailed rather than two-tailed p values were used to assess statistical significance.

We next sought to determine whether the association of P3 amplitude and HEAVY is primarily genetically mediated, as hypothesized. Biometric methods of analysis were used to estimate genetic and environmental contributions to the phenotypic correlation between P3 amplitude and HEAVY. Specifically, we fit a bivariate model (similar to the model used in the longitudinal analysis) to estimate the contributions of genetic, shared, and nonshared environmental factors to both heavy drinking and P3 amplitude at age 17 as well as the covariance between these two phenotypes.

RESULTS

Age and Sex Effects on Drinking Behavior

To examine age and sex effects on all measures, we fit a repeated measures, mixed-effects ANOVA model including sex, age (age 17 vs. age 20), and the Sex × Age interaction as predictors for the drinking outcome measures included in this study. Estimated means, standard errors, effect sizes, and significance levels are presented in Table 4.1. Mean levels for all measures increased significantly from ages 17 to 20 (all $ps < .0001$; standardized effect sizes of 0.59 to 1.12). All effects of sex were significant and indicated that men reported higher overall mean levels than women ($ps < .01$; effect sizes of 0.26 to 0.55). Moreover, all Sex × Time interactions were significant, reflecting that mean increases from age 17 to 20 were larger for men than women (all interaction $ps < .05$; standardized mean increases were from 0.24 to 0.49 larger

TABLE 4.1
Age and Gender Effects on Drinking Behavior

Drinking measure	Males: Estimated M (SE)		Females: Estimated M (SE)		Effect size		
	Age 17 (n = 574)	Age 20 (n = 481)	Age 17 (n = 668)	Age 20 (n = 629)	Age	Sex	Age × Sex
Typical number of drinks consumed per drinking occasion[a]	0.95 (0.06)	2.14 (0.07)	0.60 (0.06)	1.31 (0.06)	0.88***	0.55***	0.44***
Frequency of drinking[b]	0.64 (0.06)	1.87 (0.06)	0.54 (0.05)	1.33 (0.05)	1.12***	0.35***	0.49***
Proportion of times drunk[c]	0.92 (0.06)	1.62 (0.06)	0.78 (0.05)	1.24 (0.06)	0.59***	0.26**	0.24**
HEAVY score (0 to 12)	2.52 (0.16)	5.63 (0.17)	1.92 (0.15)	3.89 (0.15)	1.05***	0.48***	0.47***

Note. For main effects, effect size is mean difference divided by square root of estimated residual variance. For the interaction effect sizes, the tabled values indicate the degree to which drinking increased disproportionately more for men than women from Ages 17 to 20. Numbers outside of parentheses represent mean estimates and numbers inside of parentheses represent standard errors. HEAVY = composite of typical number of drinks consumed (0 to 4) + frequency of drinking (0 to 4) + proportion of times drunk (0 to 4). [a]Expressed in the typical number of drinks consumed on a 0 to 4 scale. [b]Represents the average frequency of drinking on a 0 to 4 scale (0 = *never drank or drank less than once a month*, 1 = *about once a month*, 2 = *2 to 3 times a month*, 3 = *1 to 2 times a week*, 4 = *3 or 4 times a week or more*). [c]Expressed in the following terms: 0 = *never or nearly never*, 1 = *less than half of the time I drank*, 2 = *about half of the time I drank*, 3 = *more than half of the time I drank*, 4 = *every time or nearly every time that I drank*.
**p < .01.   ***p < .001.

in men than women). Estimates of the variance for HEAVY were 11.72 for male participants and 7.60 for female participants at intake assessment, and 12.46 for male participants and 9.27 for female participants at follow-up assessment.

Genetic and Environmental Influences on Heavy Drinking From Late Adolescence to Young Adulthood

We initially estimated variances, covariances, and means for the raw data to get a baseline index of fit ($-2\ln L$ = 11,435.637, df = 2292), which was used in turn to evaluate the fit of the biometric models. We tested a general ACE bivariate model, in which the variance attributable to genetic (A), shared environmental (C), and unique environmental plus measurement error (E) factors were all estimated. The model was fit both allowing for sex differences in variance parameter estimates, $\chi^2(30)$ = 30.91, AIC= -29.09, and constraining the parameter estimates to be equal across sex, $\chi^2(39)$ = 70.74, AIC = -7.26. The sex-differences model consequently fit better than the no-sex-differences model by both the AIC (-29.09 vs. -7.26) and the χ^2 difference test, $\Delta\chi^2(9)$ = 39.83, $p < .001$, indicating that parameter estimates varied significantly by gender. To determine the source of the overall significant gender difference, we fit a series of submodels where specific parameters were constrained to be equal in the male and female samples. The fit of these submodels relative to the baseline sex differences model is given in Table 4.2. We could constrain the C parameter at age 17 or age 20 and the A parameter at age 20 to be equal in male and female participants without a significant decrement in model fit. Equating the A parameter in males and females at age 17, however, led to a significant increase in χ^2, $\Delta\chi^2$ = 6.50, $p < .01$, and a larger AIC (ΔAIC = 4.50). Therefore, these analyses suggest that the major source of the gender differences is greater genetic effects on HEAVY at age 17 for males than females. Because a sex-differences model fit significantly better than a no-sex-differences model, all subsequent analyses were undertaken separately in the male and female samples.

Figure 4.2 presents the standardized path diagram for the male twins. Variance component estimates can be obtained by squaring the corresponding genetic and environmental path coefficients, and these estimates are presented along with their confidence intervals at the bottom of Figure 4.2. These results indicate that for males at both ages 17 and 20, HEAVY was significantly influenced by both genetic and nonshared environmental factors (age 17, a^2 = 57%, c^2 = 11%, e^2 = 32%; age 20, a^2 = 39%, c^2 = 23%, e^2 = 38%). Shared environmental factors were not statistically significant at either age. Although genetic factors appeared somewhat more salient at age 17 (a^2 = 57%) than at age 20 (a^2 = 39%), constraining these two estimates to be equal did not significantly increase the χ^2 statistic, $\Delta\chi^2(1)$ = 0.46, $p > .25$.

TABLE 4.2
Fit Statistics for Models Testing Gender Differences in Sources of Variance

Model	−2LL	df	No. of parameters in model	AIC	Change in model fit relative to base			
					$\Delta\chi^2$	Δdf	Δp	ΔAIC
Base: Sex differences in variance parameters	11,466.5	2322	26	6,822.5				
No sex differences in variance parameters	11,506.3	2331	17	6,844.3	39.8	9	<.001	21.8
No sex difference in A at 17	11,473.0	2323	25	6,827.0	6.5	1	.01	4.5
No sex difference in A at 20	11,467.3	2323	25	6,821.3	0.8	1	.37	−1.2
No sex difference in C at 17	11,467.1	2323	25	6,821.1	0.6	1	.44	−1.4
No sex difference in C at 20	11,466.7	2323	25	6,820.7	0.2	1	.66	−1.8

Note. All models involved constraining the designated parameters equal in the male and female samples and were compared with the base model in which parameters were allowed to vary in the male and female samples. AIC = Akaike information criteria; A = additive genetic factor; C = shared environmental factor.

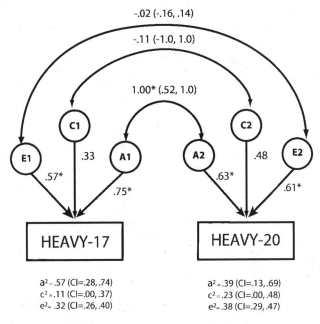

-.02 (-.16, .14)

-.11 (-1.0, 1.0)

1.00* (.52, 1.0)

C1   C2

E1   .33   A1   A2   .48   E2

.57*   .63*

.75*   .61*

HEAVY-17   HEAVY-20

$a^2 = .57$ (CI=.28, .74) $a^2 = .39$ (CI=.13, .69)
$c^2 = .11$ (CI=.00, .37) $c^2 = .23$ (CI=.00, .48)
$e^2 = .32$ (CI=.26, .40) $e^2 = .38$ (CI=.29, .47)

Figure 4.2. Genetic and environmental influences on heavy drinking in men from ages 17 to 20. HEAVY = composite score of typical amount consumed, proportion of times drunk, and frequency of drinking. Paths are squared to determine the percentage of variance accounted for by genetic (A), shared (C), and nonshared environmental (E) influences. These univariate estimates of HEAVY are presented below their respective variable, along with their 95% confidence intervals (CIs). Statistically significant (at $p < .05$) paths have CIs that do not overlap with zero. These paths are indicated by an asterisk.

Table 4.3 gives estimates of the genetic and environmental contributions to stability and change to HEAVY over time. For male participants, the phenotypic correlation between HEAVY at age 17 and age 20 was .45. As Figure 4.2 illustrates, the genetic and environmental correlations indicate that the stability of male heavy drinking over time was primarily a result of genetic factors. Specifically, the genetic correlation was estimated to be 1.0, which implies that the genetic factors influencing HEAVY at age 17 were the same as those influencing HEAVY at age 20. Furthermore, the shared and non-shared environmental correlations were nonsignificant and effectively zero, indicating that the shared and nonshared environmental factors that influenced HEAVY at age 17 were different from those influencing HEAVY at age 20. Consequently, essentially all of the phenotypic stability of HEAVY in male participants was attributable to genetic factors. Alternatively, as indicated in the right column of Table 4.3, a change in male heavy drinking over

TABLE 4.3

Percentage of Stability and Change in Heavy Drinking From Ages 17 to 20 Attributable to Additive Genetic (A), Shared (C), and Nonshared (E) Environmental Factors

Gender	Parameter	Stability (%)	Change (%)	Phenotypic stability in HEAVY over time (r)
Men	A	100	0	
	C	00	37.7	
	E		62.3	
				.45*
Women	A	0.5	37.9	
	C	69.5	3.8	
	E	30.0	58.3	
				.38*

Note. HEAVY = composite of typical number of drinks consumed (0 to 4) + frequency of drinking (0 to 4) + proportion of times drunk (0 to 4). A = additive genetic factor; C = shared environmental factor; E = nonshared environmental factor.
*$p < .05$.

time was attributable to both nonshared (62.3%) and shared environmental factors (37.7%).

Figure 4.3 presents the standardized path diagram for the female twins. Variance component estimates could once again be obtained by squaring the genetic and environmental path coefficients. As suggested by the above finding of significant gender differences in parameter estimates, the results for the female twins were quite different from those of the male twins. These results indicate that, at both ages 17 and 20, HEAVY was primarily influenced by shared and nonshared environmental factors (age 17, $a^2 = 18\%$, $c^2 = 37\%$, $e^2 = 46\%$; age 20, $a^2 = 30\%$, $c^2 = 22\%$, $e^2 = 49\%$). Genetic factors were not statistically significant at age 17, $\Delta\chi^2(1) = 0.76$ (see Figure 4.3), but approached being statistically significant at age 20, $\Delta\chi^2(1) = 3.27$, $p = .08$. Nonetheless, as was true with the male sample, the difference in heritability at ages 17 and 20 was not statistically significant, $\Delta\chi^2(1) = 0.5$, $p = .460$, $\Delta AIC = -1.50$.

For female participants, the phenotypic correlation between HEAVY at ages 17 and 20 was .38 (see Table 4.3), a value somewhat lower than the corresponding value in male participants. The genetic and environmental correlations suggest that the underlying genetic and environmental architectures in HEAVY over time differed substantially in female and male participants. Specifically, for women, the stability of HEAVY was primarily a result of the enduring effects of shared environmental factors. The shared environmental correlation was .92 (see Figure 4.3), suggesting that the shared environmental factors influencing HEAVY at age 17 were the same as those influencing HEAVY at age 20 and shared environmental factors accounted for nearly 70% of the stability in women's heavy drinking (see Table 4.3). The nonshared environmental correlation is also statistically significant, but is rather

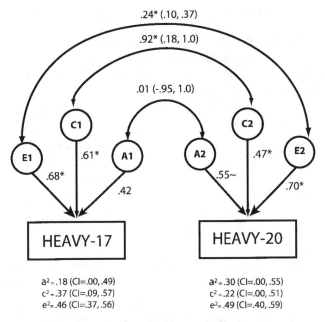

Figure 4.3. Genetic and environmental influences on heavy drinking in women from ages 17 to 20. HEAVY = composite score of typical amount consumed, proportion of times drunk, and frequency of drinking. Paths are squared to determine the percentage of variance accounted for by genetic (A), shared (C), and nonshared environmental (E) influences. These univariate estimates of HEAVY are presented below their respective variable, along with their 95% confidence intervals (CIs). Statistically significant (at $p < .05$) paths are indicated by an asterisk. Paths that are marginally significant ($p < .10$) are indexed with an approximation symbol (i.e., ~).

small and nonshared environmental factors account for only 30% of the stability of HEAVY. The genetic correlation is small, nonsignificant, and genetic factors contribute little to the stability of HEAVY in females. Change in HEAVY for females is largely attributable to additive genetic (38%) and nonshared (58%) environmental factors; shared environmental factors contributed little to change (4%). Thus, in females the stability of HEAVY is largely a function of shared environmental forces that continue to be important across time, while change is due primarily to genetic and nonshared environmental factors.[1]

---

[1]Our finding of gender differences in the heritability of heavy drinking cannot be attributed to differential rates of abstention at ages 17 or 20. Heavy drinking did not vary substantially by gender, and deleting individuals who were abstemious at age 20 resulted in the same general pattern of results as found in the full sample, namely, that heavy drinking was substantially more heritable in men than in women.

The Association of P3 Amplitude and Heavy Drinking

A two-way, mixed effects model was used to test the effect of sex, heavy drinking onset group, and the Sex × Group interaction on P3 amplitude. To test our a priori hypotheses (early < late < nonheavy on P3 amplitude for men), we treated the onset group variable as an ordinal variable (0 = *nonheavy drinking*, 1 = *late heavy drinking*, 2 = *early heavy drinking*). Consistent with our hypotheses, we found a significant main effect for onset group, $F(1, 445) = 12.95, p < .001$. The interaction between sex and onset group was statistically significant, $F(1, 445) = 2.95, p < .05$, however, indicating a significant relationship of heavy drinking onset to P3 amplitude was found for male participants but not female participants. No main effect of sex on P3 amplitude was found. In men, the early onset heavy drinking group had the lowest P3 amplitude relative to the late and nonheavy groups. Figure 4.4 depicts the means and standard errors for P3 amplitude by onset group and gender.

To determine whether P3 amplitude was associated with individual differences in heavy drinking at a given age in addition to its association with heavy drinking onset, we correlated P3 amplitude with the HEAVY drinking score as assessed at age 17 (i.e., the age at which P3 was assessed). Consistent with the observation that P3 amplitude was associated with onset of heavy drinking in male participants but not female participants, the phenotypic

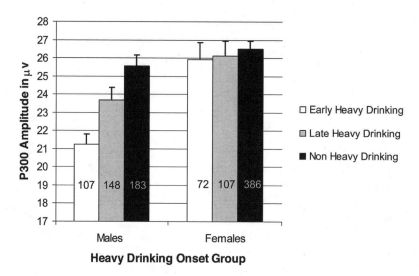

Figure 4.4. P3 amplitude by ONSET group and gender. Numbers in bars represent group *n*s. Early Heavy = at intake assessment (age 17), five or more drinks on average and drinking at least once a month during the past 12 months; Late Heavy = less than five drinks on average at intake, but at follow up (age 20) five or more drinks on average and drinking at least once a month during the past 12 months; Non Heavy = less than five drinks on average or abstention at ages 17 and 20.

correlation between HEAVY at age 17 and P3 amplitude was significant for males ($r = -.19$, $p = .01$) but not for females ($r = .00$), and the male and female correlations differed significantly from each other, $\chi^2(1) = 6.48$, $p = .01$. To determine whether the correlation between P3 amplitude and HEAVY in males was genetically mediated, we fit a bivariate biometric model (a similar model was not fit in the female sample because of the lack of any correlation between P3 amplitude and HEAVY in that sample). Before fitting a biometric model of P3 amplitude and HEAVY at age 17, we obtained a baseline index of model fit by estimating means and covariances ($-2\ln l = 6,295.80$, $df = 1051$), which was used subsequently to evaluate fit of the reduced models. A general ACE bivariate model fit the data well, $\Delta\chi^2(15) = 16.8$, $p = .33$, $\Delta AIC = -13.20$ ($-2\ln L = 13,565.0$, $df = 2311$). Consistent with earlier twin studies on P3 amplitude, the contribution of shared environmental effects to variance in P3 amplitude was near zero ($c^2 = .001$), so that this parameter along with the associated shared environmental correlation could be dropped from the model without reducing model fit, $\Delta\chi^2(2) = 0.02$, $p = .99$, $\Delta AIC = -3.98$. Standardized estimates for this model are given in Figure 4.5. As expected, P3 amplitude was strongly heritable. The genetic correlation was statistically significant and accounted for 84% of the phenotypic correlation between P3 and HEAVY. The nonshared environmental correlation was not statistically significant and accounted for only 16% of the phenotypic correlation.

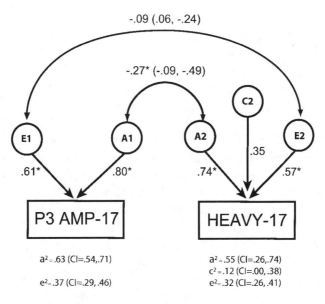

Figure 4.5. Biometric model of P3 amplitude (AMP) and heavy drinking in men at age 17. a^2 = additive genetic factors; c^2 = shared environmental factors; e^2 = nonshared environmental factors; CI = confidence interval.

DISCUSSION

The transition from late adolescence to early adulthood is associated with a substantial increase in heavy drinking. To identify and characterize genetic and environmental contributions to individual differences in heavy drinking during this developmental period, a large sample of male and female twins was assessed first in late adolescence (age 17) and second in early adulthood (age 20). Longitudinal analysis of the resulting data supports the following conclusions: (a) Biological factors appear to be more influential to heavy drinking in men versus women, (b) the magnitude of heritable influences on heavy drinking is not significantly greater at age 17 than at age 20, and (c) change in heavy drinking is predominantly due to nonshared environmental factors. We discuss each of these conclusions in turn. Our longitudinal phenotypic analysis indicated that there are significant increases in heavy drinking during the transition to early adulthood, and, although the increase was observed in both sexes, it was more marked in men than women. Our longitudinal behavioral genetic analysis allowed us to extend previous research by showing that the etiological basis for these changes may differ in men and women. Previous research has been somewhat inconsistent as to whether genetic factors differentially affect drinking behavior in men and women. In a sample of twins, McGue et al. (1992) reported significantly greater heritability of alcoholism in men than women, although subsequent and larger twin studies have failed to find a gender effect on alcoholism heritability (Heath et al., 1997; Kendler et al., 1992). Both Han, McGue, and Iacono (1999) and Heath and Martin (1988) reported greater heritability in men than women, although other studies have failed to find a similar gender difference (e.g., Maes et al., 1998). In the present study we not only found evidence for differential heritability but also a possible reason for the inconsistent findings on the effect of gender. Constraining parameter estimates in the general biometric model to be equal in the male and female samples resulted in a significant decrement in model fit. Follow-up analyses revealed that the only parameter estimate to differ significantly in the male and female samples was the genetic effect at age 17. The effect of this difference can be seen in the heritability estimates for heavy drinking, which differed markedly at age 17 (a^2s= .57 in males and .18 in females) but minimally at age 20 (a^2s= .40 and .30, respectively).

The gender difference in the heritability of heavy drinking is paralleled by a gender difference in the genetic determinants of stability and change in heavy drinking. For males, the stability of heavy drinking was due entirely to genetic factors, while for females the stability of heavy drinking was due entirely to shared and nonshared environmental factors. Alternatively, only in the female sample did genetic factors contribute to change in heavy drinking. These data thus suggest that whether gender moderates the heritability of problem drinking may depend on developmental stage, such that gender differences may be amplified in samples in which early onset cases predominate but minimized in samples with late onset cases.

Our analysis of P3 amplitude provides additional evidence for a differential influence of biological factors on heavy drinking in men and women. P3 amplitude is a well-known psychophysiological marker of alcoholism risk as well as an index of vulnerability to generalized externalizing psychopathology (Iacono et al., 2002). Previous research on P3 amplitude, however, suggests that it may be a less reliable marker of biological risk in women compared with men (Bauer, Costa, & Hesselbrock, 2001; Hill & Steinhauer, 1992; Justus, Finn, & Steinmetz, 2001; Polich, Burns, & Bloom, 1988; Van Beijsterveldt, van Baal, Molenaar, Boomsma, & de Geus, 2001). In the present study we found that P3 amplitude was associated with heavy drinking in males but not in females. Specifically, in males, reduced P3 amplitude was associated with both an early age of heavy drinking onset and, among those with an onset of heavy drinking by age 17, with greater involvement in heavy drinking. In contrast, in females, P3 amplitude was neither correlated with heavy drinking onset nor degree of heavy drinking at age 17. It is important that joint biometric analysis of P3 amplitude and heavy drinking at age 17 in the male sample revealed that the association between the two was primarily genetically mediated. Thus, we find that P3 amplitude is correlated with heavy drinking in males only and that the basis for this association is common genetic rather than common environmental factors.

What factors might account for a greater biological contribution to heavy drinking in males versus females during this developmental transition? Although not specifically addressed in our study, previous work has shown a strong relationship between behavioral indicators of impulsivity and the development of alcoholism. Externalizing disorders like conduct disorder and antisocial personality disorder play a critical role in the development of alcoholism (Disney, Elkins, McGue, & Iacono, 1999; King, Iacono, & McGue, 2004). Aggressivity and conduct disorder are less predictive of alcohol abuse in women than men and are influenced by gene–environment interactions in women (Cadoret, Riggins-Caspers, Yates, Troughton, & Stewart, 2000). Recent molecular genetic work has further suggested that specific serotonin polymorphisms related to aggressiveness and externalizing psychopathology may be differentially important for girls and boys (Cadoret et al., 2003). Gender differences in the relative contributions of genes associated with aggressivity and conduct disorder on alcoholism may partially explain our finding of less genetic influence on alcoholism in women relative to men.

Alternatively, it is useful to ask what factors might account for greater environmental contribution to heavy drinking in females versus males during this developmental transition? Donavan, Jessor, and Jessor (1983) have suggested that major life transitions and relationships have a stronger impact on women's than men's drinking. For example, Leonard and Mudar (2003) found that the drinking behavior of wives in newlywed couples changed to become more like that of their husbands' but that husbands did not change their drinking behavior to become more like that of their wives'. Although few of our female participants were likely to have married between ages 17 and 20, the findings of Leonard and Mudar demonstrated that environmental factors, and especially interpersonal relationships, may be particularly important during transitional phases in the development of alcohol use and abuse among women.

Researchers have suggested that an early onset form of heavy drinking emerging during adolescence may be etiologically distinct from a later form, which onsets during young adulthood. In particular, early onset problem drinking is thought to be more heritable than late onset problem drinking, leading us to predict that the heritability of heavy drinking would decrease from age 17 to age 20. Counter to expectation, we did not find significant differences in the heritability of heavy drinking between ages 17 and 20 in either the male or female sample. Several factors may account for our failure to support the hypothesis. First, the 3-year interval may not have been of sufficient duration to observe the hypothesized effect. Alternatively, failure to observe changes in heritability may reflect gene–environment correlational processes. As adolescents pass into young adulthood, they gain greater autonomy and control over their living arrangements (e.g., dorm vs. fraternity) and options for social activity (e.g., parties, bar attendance, nights out on the town; Bachman et al., 2002; Harford, Wechsler, & Seibring, 2002). As opportunities for selecting new relationships and social activities increase, individuals may seek out environments that were not previously available during the adolescent years but are compatible with their underlying genetic propensities. This process of niche picking has been called an *active* genotype–environment correlation (Scarr & McCartney, 1983) and can serve to either maintain or even enhance heritable effects. Recently, investigators have suggested that ample social opportunities for drinking during young adulthood may provide favorable conditions for this type of effect (Schulenberg & Maggs, 2002). Kahler, Read, Wood, and Palfai (2003) found support for the idea that individual differences among students prior to college may influence selection of social environments that promote heavier drinking behaviors. Alternatively, and consistent with recent theory and research emphasizing the importance of developmental role transitions in alcohol use (Sher & Gotham, 1999), our results indicate that nonshared environmental factors are the major contributor to change in heavy drinking in both men and women. In behavioral genetic models, estimates of nonshared environmental influence (e^2) represent environments that are unique to each member of a twin pair as well as measurement error. In this developmental context, prime candidates for nonshared environmental influence are deviant peers and other sibling-specific environmental contexts (i.e., unique college environments). Recent evidence suggests that deviant peer influence may be an environmental influence important to variation in substance use (Walden, McGue, Iacono, Burt, & Elkins, 2004). Such factors may act uniquely or interactively to promote heavy drinking. The influence of peer groups may become increasingly salient during this developmental transition as adolescents acquire new friendship groups (Jackson et al., 2001; Gotham et al., 1997; Schulenberg & Maggs, 2002). Moreover, in contrast to age 17, at age 20 men and women may share living arrangements with their same-age peers, providing greater opportunities to form close social bonds that may significantly impact social activities and interests. This conclusion is supported by recent research using a genetically informative design to demonstrate that college attendance per se may be a salient environmental influence on heavy drinking, at least in women (Slutske et al., 2004).

Despite the convergent evidence for gender differences found in the P300 and longitudinal biometric analyses, several limitations of this study warrant consideration. The results of our study need to be replicated in other large, population-based longitudinal designs. In addition, given that the sex differences in the influence of additive genetic factors were more pronounced at age 17 than age 20, etiological influences on heavy drinking may change with time so that it will be important to extend our findings to other developmental stages both prior and subsequent to the ages observed here. Last, our findings could have been affected by somewhat differential rates of attrition, such that those who failed to return at age 20 had higher levels of heavy drinking than those who returned. Given the overall high rate of participation, however, it is difficult to see how differential attrition could have had a major impact on our results.

In summary, our findings provide multimethod support for etiological differences in heavy drinking in men and women. Although both men and women show substantial increases in alcohol involvement from adolescence to young adulthood, the underlying causes of their drinking are notably different. Moreover, we found that emergent nonshared environmental forces are especially important to understanding changes in drinking behavior in early adulthood. A necessary next step in this program of research will be to identify the specific genetic (using molecular techniques) and environmental (with genetically informative designs) factors that influence transitions in drinking behavior.

REFERENCES

Akaike, H. (1987). Factor analysis and AIC. *Psychometrika, 52*, 317–332.

American Psychiatric Association. (1987). *Diagnostic and statistical manual of mental disorders* (3rd ed., rev.). Washington, DC. Author.

Arnett, P. J. (2000). Emerging adulthood: A theory of development from the late teens through the twenties. *American Psychologist, 55,* 469–480.

Bachman, J. G., O'Malley, P. M., Schulenberg, J. E., Johnston, L. D., Bryant, A. L., & Merline, A. C. (2002). *The decline of substance use in young adulthood: Changes in social activities, roles and beliefs.* Mahwah, NJ: Erlbaum.

Baer, J. S., Kivlahan, D. R., & Marlatt, G. A. (1995). High-risk drinking across the transition from high school to college. *Alcoholism: Clinical and Experimental Research, 19,* 54–61.

Bauer, L. O., Costa, L., & Hesselbrock, V. M. (2001). Effects of alcoholism, anxiety, and depression on P300 in women: A pilot study. *Journal of Studies on Alcohol, 62,* 571–579.

Begleiter, H., Porjesz, B., Bihari, B., & Kissin, B. (1984, September 28). Event-related brain potentials in boys at risk for alcoholism. *Science, 225,* 1493–1496.

Bryk, A. S., & Raudenbush, S. W. (1992). *Hierarchical linear models: Applications and data analysis methods.* Newbury Park, CA: Sage.

Burt, S. A., Krueger, R. F., McGue, M., & Iacono, W. G. (2003). Parent–child conflict and the comorbidity among childhood externalizing disorders. *Archives of General Psychiatry, 60,* 505–513.

Cadoret, R. J., Langbehn, D., Caspers, K., Troughton, E. P., Yucuis, R., Sandhu, H. K., & Philibert, R. (2003). Associations of the serotonin transporter promoter polymorphism with aggressivity, attention deficit, and conduct disorder in an adoptee population. *Comprehensive Psychiatry, 44,* 88–101.

Cadoret, R. J., Riggins-Caspers, K., Yates, W. R., Troughton, E. P., & Stewart, M. A. (2000). Gender effects in gene-environment interaction in substance abuse. In E. Frank (Ed.), *Gender and its effects on psychopathology* (pp. 253–279). Washington, DC: American Psychiatric Association.

Caspi, A., Taylor, A., Moffitt, T. E., & Plomin, R. (2000). Neighborhood deprivation affects children's mental health: Environmental risks identified in a genetic design. *Psychological Science, 11,* 338–342.

Chassin, L., Pitts, S. C., & Prost, J. (2002). Binge drinking trajectories from adolescence to emerging adulthood in a high-risk sample: Predictors and substance abuse outcomes. *Journal of Consulting and Clinical Psychology, 70,* 67–78.

Clapp, J. D., Shillington, A. M., & Segars, L. B. (2000). Deconstructing contexts of binge drinking among college students. *American Journal of Drug and Alcohol Abuse, 26,* 139–154.

Costello, E. J., Mustillo, S., Erkanli, A., Keeler, G., & Angold, A. (2003). Prevalence and development of psychiatric disorders in childhood and adolescence. *Archives of General Psychiatry, 60,* 837–844.

Disney, E. R., Elkins, I. J., McGue, M., & Iacono, W. G. (1999). Effects of ADHD, conduct disorder, and gender on substance use and abuse in adolescence. *American Journal of Psychiatry, 156,* 1515–1521.

Donavan, J. E., Jessor, R., & Jessor, L. (1983). Problem drinking in adolescence and young adulthood: A follow-up study. *Journal of Studies on Alcohol, 59,* 647–658.

Enoch, M., Schuckit, M., Johnson, B., & Goldman, D. (2003). Genetics of alcoholism using intermediate phenotypes. *Alcoholism: Clinical and Experimental Research, 27*, 169–175.

Foster, S. E., Vaughan, R. D., Foster, W. H., & Califano, J. A. (2003). Alcohol consumption and expenditures for underage drinking and adult excessive drinking. *Journal of the American Medical Association, 28*, 989–995.

Gotham, H. J., Sher, K. J., & Wood, P. K. (1997). Predicting stability and change in frequency of intoxication from the college years to beyond: Individual difference and role-transition variables. *Journal of Abnormal Psychology, 106*, 619–621.

Gotham, H. J., Sher, K. J., & Wood, P. K. (2003). Alcohol involvement and developmental task completion during young adulthood. *Journal of Studies on Alcohol, 64*, 32–42.

Grant, B. F. (1997). Prevalence and correlates of alcohol use and *DSM–IV* alcohol dependence in the United States: Results of the National Longitudinal Alcohol Epidemiologic Survey. *Journal of Studies on Alcohol, 58*, 464–473.

Gunzerath, L., & Goldman, D. (2003). G X E: A NIAAA workshop on gene–environment interactions. *Alcoholism: Clinical and Experimental Research, 27*, 540–562.

Han, C., McGue, M. K., & Iacono, W. G. (1999). Lifetime tobacco, alcohol, and other substance use in adolescent Minnesota twins: Univariate and multivariate behavioral genetic analyses. *Addiction, 94*, 981–993.

Harford, T. C., Wechsler, H., & Seibring, M. (2002). Attendance and alcohol use at parties and bars in college: A national survey of current drinkers. *Journal of Studies on Alcohol, 63*, 726–733.

Heath, A. C., Bucholz, K. K., Madden, P. A. F., Dinwiddie, S. H., Slutske, W. S., Bierut, L. J., et al. (1997). Genetic and environmental contributions to alcohol dependence risk in a national twin sample: Consistency of findings in women and men. *Psychological Medicine, 27*, 1381–1396.

Heath, A. C., & Martin, N. G. (1988). Teenage alcohol use in the Australian twin register: Genetic and social determinants of starting to drink. *Alcoholism: Clinical and Experimental Research, 12*, 735–741.

Hettema, J. M., Neale, M. C., & Kendler, K. S. (1995). Physical similarity and the equal environments assumption. *Behavior Genetics, 25*, 327–335.

Hill, S. Y., & Steinhauer, S. R. (1992). Assessment of prepubertal and postpubertal boys and girls at risk for developing alcoholism with P300 from a visual discrimination task. *Journal of Studies on Alcohol, 54*, 350–358.

Hussong, A., & Chassin, L. (2002). Parental alcoholism and the leaving home transition. *Development and Psychopathology, 14*, 139–157.

Iacono, W. G., Carlson, S. R., Malone, S. M., & McGue, M. (2002). P3 event-related potential amplitude and the risk for disinhibitory disorders in adolescent boys. *Archives of General Psychiatry, 59*, 750–757.

Iacono, W. G., Carlson, S. R., Taylor, J., Elkins, I. J., & McGue, M. (1999). Behavioral disinhibition and the development of substance-use disorders: Findings from the Minnesota Twin Family Study. *Development & Psychopathology, 11*, 869–900.

Iacono, W. G., Malone, S. M., & McGue, M. (2003). Substance use disorders, externalizing psychopathologies, and P300 event-related amplitude. *International Journal of Psychophysiology, 48*, 147–178.

Jackson, K. M., Sher, K. J., Gotham, H. J., & Wood, P. K. (2001). Transitioning into and out of large-effect drinking in young adulthood. *Journal of Abnormal Psychology, 110*, 378–391.

Justus, A. N., Finn, P. R., & Steinmetz, J. E. (2001). P300, disinhibited personality, and early-onset alcohol problems. *Alcoholism: Clinical and Experimental Research, 25*, 1457–1466.

Kahler, C. W., Read, J. P., Wood, M. D., & Palfai, T. P. (2003). Social environmental selection as a mediator of gender, ethnic and personality effects on college student drinking. *Psychology of Addictive Behaviors, 17*, 226–234.

Kendler, K. S., Heath, A. C., Neale, M. C., Kessler, R. C., & Eaves, L. J. (1992). A population based twin study of alcoholism in women. *Journal of the American Medical Association, 268*, 1877–1882.

Kendler, K. S., Neale, M. C., Kessler, R. C., Heath, A. C., & Eaves, L. J. (1993). The test of the equal-environment assumption in twin studies of psychiatric illness. *Behavior Genetics, 23*, 21–27.

King, S. M., Iacono, W. G., & McGue, M. (2004). Childhood externalizing and internalizing psychopathology in the prediction of early substance use. *Addiction, 99*, 1548–1559.

Lange, J. E., Clapp, J. D., Reavy, R., Jaccard, J., Johnson, M. B., Voas, R. B., et al. (2002). College binge drinking: What is it? Who does it? *Alcoholism: Clinical and Experimental Research, 26*, 723–730.

Leonard, K. E., & Mudar, P. (2003). Peer and partner drinking and the transition to marriage: A longitudinal examination of selection and influence processes. *Psychology of Addictive Behaviors, 17*, 115–125.

Little, R. J. A., & Rubin, D. B. (1987). *Statistical analysis with missing data*. New York: Wiley.

Maes, H. H., Woodward, C. E., Murrelle, L., Meyer, J. M., Silberg, J. L., Hewitt, J. K., et al. (1998). Tobacco, alcohol and drug use in 8–16 year old twins: The Virginia Twin Study of Adolescent Behavioral Development (VTSABD). *Journal of Studies on Alcohol, 60*, 293–305.

Malone, S. M., Iacono, W. G., & McGue, M. (2002). Drinks of the father: Father's maximum number of drinks consumed predicts externalizing disorders, substance use, and substance use disorders in preadolescent and adolescent offspring. *Alcoholism: Clinical and Experimental Research, 26*, 1823–1832.

McGue, M., Iacono, W. G., Legrand, L. N., Malone, S., & Elkins, I. (2001). The origins of age at first drink: I. Associations with substance-use disorders, disinhibitory behavior and psychopathology, and P3 amplitude. *Alcoholism: Clinical and Experimental Research, 25*, 1156–1165.

McGue, M. Pickens, R. W., & Svikis, D. S. (1992). Sex and age effects on the inheritance of alcohol problems: A twin study. *Journal of Abnormal Psychology, 101*, 3–17.

Midanik, L. T. (1999). Drunkenness, feeling the effects and 5+ measures. *Addiction, 94*, 887–897.

Morris-Yates, A., Andrews, G., Howie, P., & Henderson, S. (1990). Twins: A test of the equal environments assumption. *Acta Psychiatrica Scandinavica, 81*, 322–326.

Naimi, T. S., Brewer, R. D., Mokdad, A., Denny, C., Serdula, M. K., & Marks, J. S. (2003). Binge drinking among U.S. adults. *Journal of the American Medical Association, 289*, 70–75.

National Institute on Alcohol Abuse and Alcoholism. (2000). *The alcohol and other drug (AOD) thesaurus: A guide to concepts and terminology in substance abuse and addiction* (3rd ed.). Bethesda, MD: Author. Retrieved August 15, 2004, from http://etoh.niaaa.nih.gov/

Neale, M. C. (1997). *Mx: Statistical modeling* (4th ed.). Richmond, VA: Medical College of Virginia, Department of Psychiatry. (Send request for information to M. C. Neale, Medical College of Virginia, Box 710, Richmond, VA 23298.)

O'Neill, S. E., Parra, G. R., & Sher, K. J. (2001). Clinical relevance of heavy drinking during the college years: Cross-sectional and prospective perspectives. *Psychology of Addictive Behaviors, 15*, 350–359.

Plomin, R., DeFries, J. C., McClearn, G. E., & McGuffin, P. (2001). *Behavioral genetics* (4th ed.). New York: Worth.

Polich, J., Burns, T., & Bloom, F. E. (1988). P300 and the risk for alcoholism: Family history, task difficulty, and gender. *Alcoholism: Clinical and Experimental Research, 12*, 248–254.

Polich, J., Pollack, V. E., & Bloom, F. E. (1994). Meta-analysis of P300 amplitude from males at risk for alcoholism. *Psychological Bulletin, 115*, 55–73.

Robins, L. M., Babor, T., & Cottler, L. B. (1987). *Composite International Diagnostic Interview: Expanded substance abuse module*. Unpublished manuscript, Washington University, St. Louis, MO.

Scarr, S., & Carter-Saltzman, L. (1979). Twin method: Defense of a critical assumption. *Behavior Genetics, 9*, 527–542.

Scarr, S., & McCartney, K. (1983). How people make their own environments: A theory of genotype→environment effects. *Child Development, 54*, 424–435.

Schulenberg, J., Maggs, J. L., Long, S. W., Sher, K. J., Gotham, H. J., Baer, J. S., et al. (2001). The problem of college drinking: Insights from a developmental perspective. *Alcoholism: Clinical and Experimental Research, 25*, 473–477.

Schulenberg, J., O'Malley, P. M., Bachman, J. G., Wadsworth, K. N., & Johnston, L. D. (1996). Getting drunk and growing up: Trajectories of frequent binge drinking during the transition to young adulthood. *Journal of Studies on Alcohol, 57*, 289–304.

Schulenberg, J. E., & Maggs, J. L. (2002). A developmental perspective on alcohol use and heavy drinking during adolescence and the transition to young adulthood. *Journal of Studies on Alcohol, 14*(Suppl.), 54–70.

Sher, K. J., Bartholow, B. D., & Nanda, S. (2001). Short- and long-term effects of fraternity and sorority membership on heavy drinking: A social norms perspective. *Psychology of Addictive Behaviors, 15*, 42–51.

Sher, K. J., & Gotham, H. J. (1999). Pathological alcohol involvement: A developmental disorder of young adulthood. *Development and Psychopathology, 11*, 933–956.

Slutske, W. S., Hunt-Carter, E. E., Nabors-Oberg, R. E., Sher, K. J., Bucholz, K. K., Madden, P. F., Anokhin, A., & Heath, A. C. (2004). Do college students drink more than their non-college-attending peers? Evidence from a population-based longitudinal female twin study. *Journal of Abnormal Psychology, 113*, 530–540.

U.S. Department of Health and Human Services (2001). *Healthy people 2010* (Vol. 1, 2nd ed.). Washington, DC: U.S. Government Printing Office.

Van Beijsterveldt, C. E. M., van Baal, G. C. M., Molenaar, P. C. M., Boomsma, D. I., & de Geus, E. J. C. (2001). Stability of genetic and environmental influences on P300 amplitude: A longitudinal study of adolescent twins. *Behavior Genetics, 31*, 533–543.

Viken, R. J., Kaprio, J., Koskenvuo, M., & Rose, R. J. (1999). Longitudinal analyses of the determinants of drinking and of drinking to intoxication in adolescent twins. *Behavior Genetics, 29*, 455–461.

Walden, B., McGue, M., Iacono, W. G., Burt, S. A., & Elkins, I. (2004). Identifying shared environmental contributions to early adolescent substance use: The respective roles of parents and peers. *Journal of Abnormal Psychology, 113*, 440–450.

Wechsler, H., Davenport, A., Dowdall, G., Moekens, B., & Castillo, S. (1994). Health and behavioral consequences of binge drinking in college. *Journal of the American Medical Association, 272*, 1672–1677.

Wechsler, H., Dowdall, G. W., Davenport, A., & Castillo, S. (1995). Correlates of college student binge drinking. *American Journal of Public Health, 85*, 921–926.

Wechsler, H., & Isaac, N. (1992). "Binge" drinkers at Massachusetts colleges: Prevalence, drinking style, time trends, and associated problems. *Journal of the American Medical Association, 267*, 2929–2931.

Zucker, R. A. (1994). Pathways to alcohol problems and alcoholism: A developmental account of the evidence for multiple alcoholisms and for contextual contributions to risk. In R. A. Zucker, K. Howard, & G. M. Boyd (Eds.), *The development of alcohol problems: Exploring the biopsychosocial matrix of risk* (pp. 255–289). Rockville, MD: National Institute on Alcohol Abuse and Alcoholism.

5

TRENDS IN ECSTASY USE IN THE UNITED STATES FROM 1995 TO 2001: COMPARISON WITH MARIJUANA USERS AND ASSOCIATION WITH OTHER DRUG USE

SILVIA S. MARTINS, GUIDO MAZZOTTI,
AND HOWARD D. CHILCOAT

Ecstasy (3,4-methylenedioxy-methamphetamine; MDMA) is a drug that is often associated with dance music clubs and rave movements, which represent part of the "youth culture" of the last decade. Although there has been increased interest in the use of this drug in recent years, little is known about the co-occurrence of ecstasy use with other drug use. Few clinical and epidemiologic studies have focused specifically on the issue of ecstasy use in relation to other drug use (Degenhardt, Barker, & Topp, 2004; Gross, Barrett, Shestowsky, & Pihl, 2002; Pedersen & Skrondal, 1999; Topp, Hando, Dillon, & Solowij, 1999). Other drug use among ecstasy users is an issue that is understudied and still needs to be addressed. By examining the co-occurrence of ecstasy and other drug use as ecstasy spreads in the population it is possible to further understanding of the dynamics of the ecstasy "epidemic."

Ecstasy use became more widespread throughout the world during the 1990s. The drug was introduced to the general population in Western

This research was supported in part by Grant DA11952 from the National Institute on Drug Abuse to Howard D. Chilcoat. Silvia S. Martins received a postdoctoral scholarship from the National Council of Research (CNPq-Brazil).

Reprinted from *Experimental and Clinical Psychopharmacology*, 13, 244–252 (2005). Copyright 2005 by the American Psychological Association.

European countries during the late 1980s (Pedersen & Skrondal, 1999) and then spread to North America (Landry, 2002), South America (de Almeida & Silva, 2003), Australia and New Zealand (Topp et al., 1999; Wilkins, Bhatta, Pledger, & Casswell, 2003), South-East Asia (Wilkins et al., 2003), the Near East (Çorapçioglu & Ogel, 2004), and the Middle East (United Nations Office for Drug Control and Drug Prevention, 2001). Epidemiological studies show that ecstasy use is increasing in many countries (von Sydow, Lieb, Pfister, Höfler, & Wittchen, 2002), including the United States (Landry, 2002). For example, in European countries ecstasy use increased during the 1990s, and recent available data show that lifetime prevalence in the general population was higher than 3% in countries such as Spain, Ireland, the Netherlands, and the United Kingdom (European Monitoring Centre for Drugs and Drug Addiction, 2003). In Australia, 6.1% of the general population aged 14 years or older reported lifetime ecstasy use (Degenhardt et al., 2004). The Monitoring the Future Study has already shown that lifetime ecstasy use steadily increased in the United States from 1991 to 2001 in college students (from 2.0% to 13.1%) and young adults (from 3.2% to 11.6%), and from 1996 to 2001 in 8th (from 2.3% to 3.5%), 10th (from 4.6% to 6.2%), and 12th (from 4.6% to 9.2%) grade students (Johnston, O'Malley, & Bachman, 2001a, 2001b, 2002; Johnston, O'Malley, Bachman, & Schulenberg, 2003). According to the same researchers, past-year ecstasy use fell from 2001 to 2003 in 8th (from 3.5% to 2.1%), 10th (from 6.2% to 3%), and 12th (from 9.2% to 4.5%) grade students, and in recent years there was an increase in the proportion of students who see ecstasy as a dangerous drug, but past year prevalence of ecstasy use in these students was still high in 2003 (Johnston et al., 2003). The Drug Abuse Warning Network has reported that there was an increase in emergency room visits associated with ecstasy from 1994 to 2001 (253 visits in 1994 and 5,542 visits in 2001); from 2001 to 2002 (4,026 visits) ecstasy-related emergency visits remained stable (Substance Abuse and Mental Health Services Administration [SAMHSA], 2003).

Regardless of the possibility of occurrence of a wide range of harmful effects (Baggott, 2002; Parrott, Sisk, & Turner, 2000), until recently, ecstasy has been viewed as a relatively benign substance by its consumers and by the lay population (Topp et al., 1999). Ecstasy users often describe positive effects when they use the drug, saying they feel "euphoric," "blissful," and "more attached to other people" (Walters, Foy, & Castro, 2002). Clinical research has demonstrated that ecstasy can cause acute side effects that include difficulty concentrating, anxiety, depressed mood, dissociation feelings, dry mouth, nausea, insomnia, loss of appetite, and sweating (Baggott, 2002; Liechti, Gamma, & Vollenweider, 2001; Morland, 2000). It is also well established that ecstasy use can cause hyperthermic syndromes, which might lead to death (Baggott, 2002). Long-term ecstasy use might lead to neurotoxic consequences (Montoya, Sorrentino, Lukas, & Price, 2002; Morland, 2000).

Most of the studies about ecstasy users conducted in North America have focused on specific subpopulations, such as college students (Boyd et al., 2003) and club and rave attendees (Fendrich, Wislar, Johnson, & Hubbell, 2003; Gross et al., 2002). At first, ecstasy was only used by specific subpopulations, especially those initially associated with rave movements (Pedersen & Skrondal, 2002). During the past decade, rave movements became more popular, and ecstasy use spread into other venues, including at home or at the homes of friends (Degenhardt et al., 2004). The perception of ecstasy as a relatively benign drug might have accelerated the diffusion process of this drug in the population (Ferrence, 2001). Lenton et al. (1997) have hypothesized that, as the rave–dance drug culture became more popular, the risk of ecstasy-related harmful effects might increase. After analyzing the drug use habits of 83 rave attendees (76% of them were ecstasy users), these researchers concluded that new ecstasy users have less drug-use experience and have less knowledge about the possible side effects of the drug (Lenton et al., 1997). Assuming Lenton et al.'s conclusion is valid for the general population, then, when the prevalence of ecstasy use increases in a country, new ecstasy users should be more drug naive than more experienced ecstasy users and the association between ecstasy and other drug use would decrease over time as the prevalence of ecstasy use increases.

Despite the fact that ecstasy use is increasing in North America, little is known about its relationship with other drugs of abuse in the general population. For instance, Gross et al. (2002) described 210 rave attendees in Montreal, Quebec, Canada, and found that first use of ecstasy was mostly preceded by alcohol use, nicotine use, marijuana use, LSD use, psilocybin use, amphetamine use, and cocaine use. Because this was a sample of rave attendees, we cannot generalize these findings to the general population. To our knowledge, no epidemiological study in the United States has addressed co-occurrence of other drug use in ecstasy users. A Norwegian epidemiological study investigated the association of ecstasy use with other drug use. The researchers surveyed 10,812 adolescents living in the city of Oslo (ages 14 to 17) and concluded that ecstasy use was often intermingled with the use of marijuana, amphetamines, and heroin. According to their study, first ecstasy use occurred after first use of alcohol, cigarettes, marijuana, and amphetamines, whereas it preceded first heroin use (Pedersen & Skrondal, 1999). In an Australian national representative sample of adolescents and young adults, ecstasy was most commonly used with alcohol, marijuana, and amphetamines (Degenhardt et al., 2004).

Studies throughout the world have shown that ecstasy use is increasing and that ecstasy use can occur concurrently with other drug use. However, none of these studies have investigated the patterns of other drug use among ecstasy users across a period of time. We hypothesized that adolescents who started to use ecstasy later in the "epidemic" (i.e., early 2000s) might be more drug naive compared with their counterparts who started using ecstasy early in the "epidemic" (early 1990s). In order to fill this gap in understanding about the use of ecstasy, we set out to (a) estimate changes in ecstasy prevalence over time, (b) estimate the overlap of ecstasy use and other drug use in the United States, (c) test whether these associations between ecstasy and other drugs change as prevalence of ecstasy use increases in the U.S. population, and (d) compare other drug use in ecstasy users versus marijuana users.

To analyze the patterns and prevalence of polydrug use among ecstasy users, we found it useful to compare the co-occurrence of other drug use in ecstasy users with that of another group of illegal drug users, for example, marijuana users. This approach has advantages over the comparison of ecstasy users with a population that does not use drugs because marijuana users might share more similarities with ecstasy users than nonusers in the general population. Virtually all ecstasy users have used marijuana. Marijuana is generally considered a gateway drug, and its users have made the transition to other drug use. Prevalence of marijuana use in the general population is relatively high, providing a large comparison group and strengthening power. Because power is a function of the sample sizes of both groups that are being compared, having a large comparison group such as marijuana users strengthens the ability to detect differences between groups of drug users. For these reasons, marijuana users are a suitable comparison group for ecstasy users. The comparison of other drug use in ecstasy and marijuana users should help achieve better understanding of the extent of other drug involvement among ecstasy users. It is important to stress that we compared ecstasy users with marijuana users who do not use ecstasy, so that ecstasy use among marijuana users would not act as a confounder in the analysis.

METHOD

Sample and Measures

We analyzed data from the 1995, 1997, 1999, and 2001 National Household Survey on Drug Abuse (NHSDA), which was renamed the National Survey on Drug Use and Health in 2002. The NHSDA is sponsored by SAMHSA and is designed to provide estimates of the prevalence of legal and illegal drug use in the household population (aged 12 and over) of the United States. Surveys have been conducted on a regular basis since 1971. African American, Hispanic American, and young people were oversampled to increase the precision estimates for these groups. Overall response rates were similar across each year and ranged from 80.6% to 92% for household screening (percentage of eligible occupied households among the selected addresses) and 69% to 85.3% for completed interviews. More detailed information about the sampling and survey methodology in the NHSDA can be obtained elsewhere (SAMHSA, 2002). To assess lifetime ecstasy use, a question on the NHSDA questionnaire (part of the hallucinogen section) asks, "Have you ever, even once, used 'Ecstasy,' also known as MDMA?" To assess lifetime marijuana use, a question asks, "Have you ever, even once, used marijuana or hashish?" Similar questions are included to assess other drug use. Binge drinking is defined in the NHSDA questionnaire as drinking five or more drinks on the same occasion on at least 1 day in the past 30 days. The following question, related to age of first ecstasy use, was available only on the 2001 NHSDA: "Now think only about Ecstasy. How old were you the first time you used 'Ecstasy,' also known as MDMA?" Until 2001, the NHSDA questions about ecstasy use only addressed lifetime use of the drug; however, past year and past month indicators of ecstasy use were included in the 2001 NHSDA.

In 1999, the surveys underwent a major redesign, changing from a paper-printed questionnaire to a computer-assisted questionnaire. In 1999, a subsample of the interviews was conducted with the paper-printed questionnaire in order to compare both instruments; this comparison showed that lifetime prevalence estimates of drug use tended to be slightly higher with the computer-assisted interview (Chromy, Davis, Packer, & Gfroerer, 2002). Although it is not possible to determine whether increases in prevalence of ecstasy use from 1998 to 1999 were due to an actual increase in prevalence in the population or were the result of changes in survey methods, there are a number of indications suggesting that the increase is real. The increases are consistent with trends observed in the Monitoring the Future Study (in which surveys did not undergo any changes) during 1998 and 1999 (Johnston et al., 2000, 2001a, 2001b, 2002, 2003). Also, changes in prevalence of ecstasy use from 1998 to 1999 in the NHSDA are consistent with general trends observed through 2001. It should be noted that the focus of this chapter is the associations of ecstasy use with other drug use and demographic characteristics over time. We expect these associations would be less sensitive to changes in survey methodology than would estimates of prevalence (Chilcoat, Lucia, & Breslau, 1999).

Statistical Analysis

We analyzed demographic data (age, gender, race–ethnicity, and total family income) and drug use variables (lifetime ecstasy and other drug use) for all NHSDA surveys cited above. We performed statistical analysis with STATA 8.0 software (Stata Corporation, 2003) and used its survey commands to account for sample weighting and complex survey design. We analyzed association with demographic characteristics and other drug use associations by using weighted chi-square tests and weighted logistic regression models.

RESULTS

Demographic Characteristics of Ecstasy Users

Lifetime ecstasy use increased from 1995 (1.6%) through 2001 (3.6%) in the overall sample, with prevalence twice as high in 2001 compared with 1995 (odds ratio [OR] = 2.2, 95% confidence interval [CI] = 1.8–2.8). The comparison showed increases from 1995 to 2001 across almost all age categories (ages 12 to 17: from 1.2% to 3.13%, OR = 2.7, CI = 1.7–4.0; ages 18 to 25: from 3.45% to 13.09%, OR = 4.2, CI = 3.2–5.5; ages 26 to 34: from 2.8% to 5.99%, OR = 2.2, CI = 1.7–2.9), with the exception of those older than 35 (Figure 5.1A). Analyses of ecstasy use by race–ethnicity from years 1995 to 2001 showed that prevalence was higher for Whites compared with African Americans (1995: OR = 8.1, CI = 4.4–15.0; 2001: OR = 3.3, CI = 2.6–4.3) and Hispanic Americans (1995: OR = 2.3, CI = 1.5–3.6; 2001: OR = 1.4, CI = 1.2–1.7); however, prevalence of ecstasy use for Whites was not statistically significantly higher than that for "Others" (includes Native Americans, Native Hawaiians, Pacific Islanders, and Asian Americans). However, ecstasy use has increased in all races–ethnicities (Figure 1B). Across all years, ecstasy use was higher for males compared with females; for example, in 1997 males were 2 times more likely to be ecstasy users than were females (OR = 2.1, CI = 1.5–2.9). However, for females, prevalence of ecstasy use in 2001 was almost 3 times higher than it was in 1995 (OR = 2.6, CI = 2.0–3.4), whereas it was

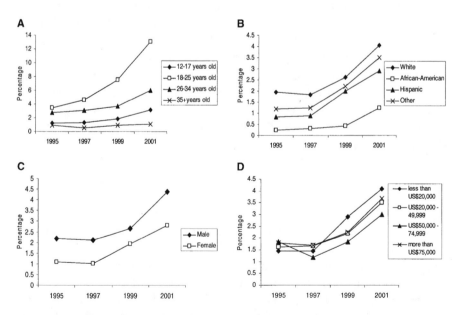

Figure 5.1. Lifetime ecstasy use from 1995 to 2001 by (A) age, (B) race–ethnicity, (C) gender, and (D) income.

only twice as high in males in 2001 compared with 1995 (OR = 2.0, CI = 1.6–2.6; Figure 1C). Comparisons of data from 2001 versus those from 1995 show that lifetime ecstasy use significantly increased in almost all family income classes (less than US$20,000: OR = 2.9, CI = 1.9–4.4; US$20,000–US$49,999: OR = 2.2, CI = 1.7–3.0; more than US$75,000: OR = 2.1, CI = 1.1–4.0), with a trend toward increase in those with annual family income of US$50,000–US$74,999 (OR = 1.6, CI = 1.0–2.8; Figure 1D).

Other Drug Use Among Ecstasy Users

To test the hypothesis that the association of ecstasy use with other drug use would become weaker (especially in the younger age groups) as ecstasy use increased over time, we estimated the prevalence of lifetime other drug use in ecstasy users in 1995, 1997, 1999, and 2001 and compared the prevalence of other drug use among ecstasy users in 2001 versus in 1995 (see Table 5.1). Our hypothesis was confirmed for several of the drug use associations: The comparison of data from 2001 with those of 1995 showed an overall decrease among ecstasy users in cocaine use (OR = 0.6, CI = 0.4–0.9), LSD use (OR = 0.5, CI = 0.3–0.8), stimulant use (OR = 0.7, CI = 0.5–0.9), and sedative use (from 27.5% in 1995 to 15.0% in 2001, OR = 0.5, CI = 0.3–0.7; not shown in Table 5.1). There was a trend toward decrease in overall heroin use in ecstasy users that was not statistically significant (OR = 0.7, CI = 0.4–1.1). Overall, prevalence of crack use, inhalant use (50% of ecstasy users in all years; not shown in Table 5.1), and pain killer use (50% of ecstasy users in all years; not shown in Table 5.1) remained stable over time, and the overall prevalence of tranquilizer use was 35% in ecstasy users in 1995, 1997, and 2001, with a slight increase in use in 1999 compared with 1995 (46%, OR = 1.6, CI = 1.1–2.5; not shown in Table 5.1). Adolescent and young adult ecstasy users in 2001 tended to be more drug naive as compared with their 1995 counterparts: There was a steep decrease in heroin use in adolescent ecstasy users, dropping from 38.9% in 1995 to 7.1% in 2001 (OR = 0.1, CI = 0.04–0.3), there were decreases in crack use in adolescents (OR = 0.1, CI = 0.04–0.4) and young adults (OR = 0.5, CI = 0.3–0.9), there were decreases in LSD use in adolescents (OR = 0.1, CI = 0.04–0.4) and young adults (OR = 0.4, CI = 0.2–0.7), and there was a decrease in sedative use in young adults (from 17.6% in 1995 to 8.6% in 2001, OR = 0.4, CI = 0.2–0.8; not shown in Table 5.1). Comparisons of data from 2001 versus those from 1995 show that there were trends toward decreases in cocaine use in adolescents (OR = 0.5, CI = 0.2–1.2) and young adults (OR = 0.8, CI = 0.5–1.2), but they were not statistically significant. Contrary to our hypothesis, tranquilizer use (not shown in Table 5.1) increased in adolescents (from 11.4% in 1995 to 33.2% in 2001; OR = 3.8, CI = 1.4–10.9). Almost all ecstasy users used alcohol (from 98.81% in 1999 to 100% in 1995; not shown in Table 5.1) and marijuana from 1995 to 2001 (see Table 5.1).

TABLE 5.1
Prevalence (in Percentages) of Lifetime Other Drug Use in Ecstasy Users Versus Marijuana Users

Drug and age group	Prevalence							
	1995		1997		1999		2001	
	Ecstasy (n=298)	Marijuana (n=5,583)	Ecstasy (n=485)	Marijuana (n=7,298)	Ecstasy (n=1,850)	Marijuana (n=16,756)	Ecstasy (n=3,169)	Marijuana (n=17,714)
Marijuana								
Overall	98.09	—	98.53	—	96.11	—	96.79	—
12–17	91.69	—	94.62	—	92.52	—	90.83	—
18–25	97.34	—	99.55	—	96.91	—	96.91	—
26–34	99.75	—	97.49	—	96.24	—	97.41	—
35 +	98.73	—	100.00	—	95.85	—	98.60	—
Cocaine								
Overall	73.41	30.30	68.88	29.20	71.10	29.78	61.82	29.32
12–17	52.13	8.77	60.22	11.75	46.82	8.24	33.88	6.75
18–25	61.54	19.29	57.27	16.26	60.64	18.08	54.44	14.90
26–34	83.04	38.50	71.46	35.00	77.45	32.36	66.70	26.86
35 +	79.57	31.75	90.27	32.10	90.95	34.10	88.18	35.33
Crack								
Overall	18.45	5.12	23.46	4.90	21.58	6.64	17.64	6.24
12–17	35.23	2.56	20.53	5.94	14.72	1.83	6.91	2.30
18–25	24.27	5.19	21.94	4.88	18.20	4.82	14.69	3.85
26–34	23.48	7.18	16.88	6.39	25.11	9.24	20.95	7.33
35 +	5.84	4.19	38.14	4.17	26.19	6.65	26.21	6.81

Heroin								
Overall	17.43	2.76	17.80	2.00	15.81	3.06	12.23	2.66
12–17	38.88	1.04	13.27	1.38	15.58	0.92	7.10	0.47
18–25	11.29	0.92	12.41	1.11	15.23	1.41	9.59	0.91
26–34	17.98	1.93	9.88	1.50	12.74	1.70	11.45	1.42
35+	17.11	4.05	42.54	2.51	19.94	4.22	22.56	3.61
LSD								
Overall	80.10	20.64	86.75	20.07	74.28	21.17	66.95	19.27
12–17	90.06	19.26	89.42	21.67	67.04	14.26	53.32	8.48
18–25	83.47	23.62	87.85	23.81	75.73	21.85	66.00	17.35
26–34	76.39	19.07	83.01	20.42	67.43	21.64	67.53	19.76
35+	78.31	20.68	89.50	18.75	81.17	21.48	75.35	20.49
Stimulants								
Overall	47.47	12.20	36.22	10.95	45.84	17.03	38.41	15.63
12–17	28.92	7.66	30.37	8.91	41.15	12.13	37.13	10.68
18–25	28.00	6.63	27.66	5.49	43.06	12.68	36.38	11.47
26–34	40.08	11.58	23.65	9.03	34.18	14.08	25.51	11.17
35+	73.40	14.98	74.94	13.45	63.84	19.76	61.09	18.34

Note. Percentages are weighted.

The data from Table 5.1 enable comparisons of the prevalence of other drug use among ecstasy users within a particular cohort as it ages. For example, the cohort of individuals who were 12 to 17 years old in 1995 would have been 18 to 23 years old in 2001, which overlaps with the 18- to 25-year-old age category in both Table 5.1 and Figure 5.1. Within this cohort, lifetime prevalence of ecstasy use increased 10-fold between 1995 and 2001 (from 1.2% for 12- to 17-year-olds in 1995 to 13.1% for 18- to 25-year-olds in 2001, as shown in Figure 5.1). The lifetime prevalence of heroin use among 12- to 17-year-old ecstasy users in 1995 was 38.9% but decreased to 9.6% when this cohort was 18 to 25 years old in 2001 (see Table 5.1). It appears that the reduction in heroin use among ecstasy users was due to the addition of ecstasy users since 1995 who were much less likely to be heroin users than at the start of this interval. Similar patterns were observed for crack use among ecstasy users, supporting the hypothesis that ecstasy users in this age group who started using ecstasy after 1995 tended to be more drug naive and used less crack and heroin compared with those who started to use ecstasy earlier.

Other Drug Use in Ecstasy Users Versus Marijuana Users

Given the high degree of co-occurrence of other drug use among ecstasy users, we compared the prevalence of other drug use in ecstasy users with the prevalence of other drug use in marijuana users (who never used ecstasy). Almost all (98%; not shown in Table 5.1) marijuana users also used alcohol. The prevalence of other lifetime drug use was much higher for ecstasy users versus marijuana users (see Table 5.1). In contrast to marijuana users, ecstasy users as a whole were more than 4 times more likely to use cocaine (1995: $OR = 6.4$, 1997: $OR = 5.4$, 1999: $OR = 5.8$, 2001: $OR = 3.9$), were more than three times more likely to use crack (1995: $OR = 4.2$, 1997: $OR = 5.9$, 1999: $OR = 3.9$, 2001: $OR = 3.2$), were 7 times more likely to use heroin in 1995 ($OR = 7.5$), and were 5 times more likely to use heroin in 2001 ($OR = 5.1$). Comparisons of data from 2001 to 1995 showed that there were decreases in prevalence of LSD use and cocaine use in adolescent (LSD: $OR = 0.4$, $CI = 0.3–0.5$; cocaine: $OR = 0.7$, $CI = 0.6–0.9$) and young adult marijuana users (LSD: $OR = 0.7$, $CI = 0.6–0.8$; cocaine: $OR = 0.6$, $CI = 0.5–0.7$), which is similar to what occurred in ecstasy users. Although there was a decrease in crack use in adolescent ecstasy users, there was an overall increase in crack use in adolescent marijuana users in 2001 compared with in 1995, mainly because of an increase in crack use among adolescent marijuana users in 1997 ($OR = 2.4$, $CI = 1.2–4.7$). Although heroin use decreased in adolescent ecstasy users, it remained stable in marijuana users across all age groups. Sedative use remained stable in marijuana users (prevalence around 6% in all years; not shown in Table 5.1). Dissimilar to the decrease in stimulant use in ecstasy users, overall stimulant use slightly increased in marijuana users in comparisons of data from 2001 versus 1995 (OR = 1.3, CI = 1.1–1.6) and across all age groups. Comparisons of data from 2001 versus 1995 showed that inhalant use (15.8% vs. 14%, OR = 1.2, CI = 1.1–1.3), tranquilizer use (11.9% vs. 9.6%, OR = 1.3, CI = 1.2–1.7), and pain reliever use (16.9% vs. 12.5%, OR = 1.4, CI = 1.6–2.4) also increased in marijuana users as a whole (results not shown in Table 5.1). Similar to adolescent ecstasy users, there were trends toward tranquilizer use increase in adolescent marijuana users (6.8% in 2001 vs. 3.85% in 1995, OR = 1.9, CI = 0.9–3.6) as well as in young adult marijuana users (8.9% in 2001 vs. 7.5% in 1995, OR = 1.2, CI = 0.9–1.6), but they were not statistically significant (not shown in Table 5.1).

Binge Drinking Among Ecstasy Users Versus Marijuana Users

Although co-occurrence of many other drugs decreased in ecstasy users, binge drinking increased across ecstasy users of all age ranges from 1995 to 2001 (overall from 45.8% in 1995 to 64.0% in 2001, OR = 2.1, CI = 1.5–3.0; see Figure 5.2), a pattern similar to that observed among marijuana users (overall from 29.7% to 33.4%, OR = 1.2, CI = 1.1–1.3; see Figure 5.3). However, considerably more ecstasy users had binge drinking episodes compared with marijuana users in 1999 and 2001. For example, in 1999, 60.3% of the ecstasy users had episodes of binge drinking compared with 35.7% of the marijuana users (OR = 2.7, CI = 2.3–3.3); these numbers in 2001 were 64.0% and 33.4% (OR = 3.5, CI = 3.1–4.0), respectively.

Age of First Ecstasy Use and Other Drug Use

The addition of age of onset of ecstasy use in the 2001 NHSDA enabled a determination of order of onset of ecstasy relative to other drugs (see Table 5.2). Most ecstasy users initiated ecstasy use after they had already tried alcohol and marijuana (94.8% and 88.3%, respectively). Forty-five percent of ecstasy users

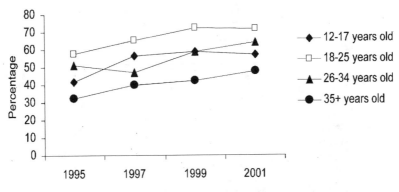

Figure 5.2. Binge drinking in ecstasy users from 1995 to 2001 by age.

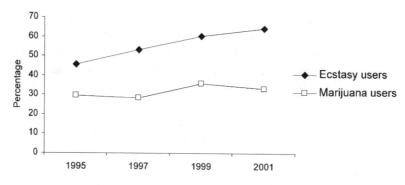

Figure 5.3. Binge drinking in ecstasy users versus marijuana users from 1995 to 2001.

had initiated LSD use before starting to use ecstasy; 17.4% initiated ecstasy and LSD use in the same year, and 37.4% initiated ecstasy use before LSD use. On the other hand, most ecstasy users had first used ecstasy at a younger age than they first initiated cocaine, crack, heroin, stimulants, inhalants, painkillers (61.3%), tranquilizers (71.1%), and sedatives (87.8%; the last three drug classes are not shown in Table 5.2).

Other Drug Use in Past Year and Past Month Ecstasy Use

Both past year and past month ecstasy use are only available in the 2001 data file. It is interesting to note that overall other lifetime drug use was similar among past year ecstasy users and lifetime ecstasy users. For instance, 61.8% of lifetime ecstasy users used cocaine and 62.9% of past year ecstasy users used this drug. Analogous results were found when we compared crack use (17.6% of lifetime ecstasy users and 15.3% of past year ecstasy users), heroin use (12.2% of lifetime ecstasy users and 10.0% of past year ecstasy

TABLE 5.2
Age at Onset of Other Drug Use Compared With
Age at Onset of Ecstasy Use (in Percentages)

Drug	Younger	Same age	Older
Alcohol	94.81	3.26	1.93
Marijuana	88.31	6.49	5.20
LSD	37.35	17.41	45.24
Cocaine	35.92	12.39	51.69
Crack	8.74	3.11	88.15
Heroin	4.51	2.86	92.63
Inhalants	34.41	7.65	57.94
Stimulants	24.67	8.63	67.00

Note. From 2001 National Household Survey on Drug Abuse data for lifetime ecstasy users.

users), LSD use (67.0% of lifetime ecstasy users and 60.4% of past year ecstasy users), and stimulant use (38.4% of lifetime ecstasy users and 36.7% of past year ecstasy users). We obtained similar results when we compared lifetime and past year ecstasy users by age group. Overall past month ecstasy users also did not differ from lifetime ecstasy users in other lifetime drug use. However, adolescent (ages 12 to 17) past month ecstasy users used more cocaine compared with adolescent lifetime ecstasy users (cocaine: 49.02% vs. 33.9%, OR = 2.2, CI = 1.3–3.8).

DISCUSSION

The main findings of our study can be summarized as follows: (a) Ecstasy use increased in the U.S. general population from 1995 to 2001 for all age groups, race–ethnicities, genders, and socioeconomic classes; (b) the rate of increase was higher in the younger age groups (especially ages 18 to 25) compared with older age groups; (c) ecstasy users were likely to use many other drugs, including alcohol, marijuana, cocaine, crack, heroin, LSD, and stimulants than were marijuana users; and (d) association of ecstasy use with other drug use was strongest early in the "epidemic" and diminished in magnitude as the number of new users increased (e.g., decrease in crack, heroin, and LSD use in adolescent ecstasy users).

Because the focus is on demographic and drug use associations with ecstasy use, it is unlikely that the changes implemented in the NHSDA in 1999 would bias the results of this study. If an increase in the lifetime use of two drugs, such as ecstasy and cocaine, occurred solely as the result of the changes in the NHSDA in 1999, it does not necessarily mean that this would affect the association of these two drugs. If there was a bias, it would likely be in the direction of increasing the association between these drugs. However, in this study, there was a decrease in reporting the use of cocaine, heroin, and LSD among ecstasy users and a decrease in the associations of these drugs with ecstasy use. Therefore, it is unlikely that changes in the NHSDA would have biased the results of this study.

It is noteworthy that the lifetime prevalence of ecstasy use for young adults (ages 18 to 25) in 2001 was extremely high (13.09%) and was 4 times higher than it was in 1995. Although the prevalence of ecstasy use was highest among Whites and males, researchers and clinicians should keep in mind that its use has increased in other races–ethnicities and in females in the past few years. It is interesting to note that ecstasy use among Hispanic Americans was nearly nonexistent during the 1990s but that there was an increase in the prevalence of use for this group in 1999 and 2001. Future research will determine whether the increase is maintained for this group. Contrary to the belief that ecstasy use is confined to higher social classes (Beck & Rosenbaum, 1994;

Peroutka, Newman, & Harris, 1988), our results show that ecstasy users belong to all social classes, as defined by annual family income.

According to our results, lifetime ecstasy users tend to be polydrug users; however, the pattern of other drug use among ecstasy users seems to have changed during the years. Even though the prevalence of binge drinking was already high in this specific group in 1995, this drinking pattern seems to have become even more common among ecstasy users in recent years, suggesting that ecstasy users, particularly those with a more recent onset, might have a higher risk of developing alcohol disorders. It is not possible to determine whether ecstasy and alcohol use occurred on the same occasions by using the NHSDA data because until 2001 data were collected only for lifetime prevalence of ecstasy use. Our results are similar to those of the Degenhardt et al. (2004) epidemiological study conducted in Australia, in which ecstasy users tended to use alcohol, marijuana, and amphetamines in the same time period. These authors also investigated what kind of drugs ecstasy users used concurrently with ecstasy: 74.7% of the young adults and 54.4% of the adolescents had used alcohol together with ecstasy at least once in the year preceding the interview (Degenhardt et al., 2004). Topp et al. (1999) analyzed other drug use in a sample of 329 Australian ecstasy users and stated that polydrug use was the norm among their sample, with at least two thirds of their participants using other drugs (including alcohol) either in combination with ecstasy or on the days following ecstasy use. Clinical studies have already shown that the consumption of both alcohol and ecstasy can increase the risk of development of psychopathological problems such as depression, psychotic disorders, cognitive impairment, bulimia, impulse control disorders, and panic attacks (Schifano, DiFuria, Forza, Minicuci, & Bricolo, 1998).

It is interesting to note that in adolescent ecstasy users, there was a significant decrease in lifetime heroin, crack, and LSD use from 1995 through 2001. A similar pattern of decrease in crack and LSD use was observed in young adult ecstasy users. As we hypothesized, those ecstasy users who began using later in the "epidemic" appeared to be more drug naive than those who started using ecstasy early in the "epidemic." This phenomenon could simply be related to the fact that during the 1990s, ecstasy use became more easily accepted by conventional adolescents and, as such, is not restricted to adolescents who have already tried a variety of other drugs and engage in more deviant behaviors (Baggott, 2002; Parker, Aldridge, & Measham, 1998). On the other hand, the information about adolescents in our sample could be censored. For example, many of these ecstasy users might have recently started using ecstasy and might not have accumulated enough time to initiate use of other drugs, such as cocaine and heroin, subsequent to ecstasy use. According to Lenton et al. (1997), ecstasy users who have less drug-using experience (i.e., who are more drug naive) are prone to a higher risk of drug-related harmful effects because they tend to have less knowledge about the possibility of ecstasy side effects when compared with more experienced users. This should be taken into account when developing prevention and harm reduction strategies for this population. Although our study focuses on trends in ecstasy use from 1995 to 2001, data from the Monitoring the Future Study show that past year ecstasy use decreased among youth from 2001 to 2003 (Johnston et al., 2003). If this decreasing pattern of ecstasy use remains in future population surveys (not only in youth, but also in young adults), it will be necessary to investigate whether the adolescents and young adults who will continue to use ecstasy will be polydrug users, thus resembling those who used ecstasy early in the "epidemic." In addition, the factors that determine the maintenance of ecstasy use in a subpopulation of adolescents and young adults while its use decreases need to be addressed in future studies.

In the data files analyzed, we only have information on age of first ecstasy use in the 2001 sample and not in previous years. Our results show that ecstasy users have usually tried this drug after having already tried alcohol and marijuana, and, in some cases, first ecstasy use occurred in the same time period as LSD initiation. In a typical "drug use sequence," initial ecstasy use usually preceded the use of cocaine, inhalants, pain killers, stimulants, tranquilizers, sedatives, crack, and heroin. These results are consistent with epidemiological and clinical studies conducted in other countries (Gross et al., 2002; Pedersen & Skrondal, 1999).

Past year and past month ecstasy use data are available only in the 2001 file. Prevalence of other drug use among these groups of ecstasy users were similar to prevalence of other drug use in lifetime ecstasy users, with the exception of adolescent past month ecstasy users who used more cocaine as compared with adolescent lifetime ecstasy users. Past year and past month indicators of ecstasy use include both chronic and recent onset ecstasy users who need to be further investigated in future studies.

Despite the fact that ecstasy is seen as a benign substance (Topp et al., 1999), when we compared other drug use in ecstasy users versus marijuana users who had never tried ecstasy (at least until they were interviewed), there were striking differences: Across all years, the prevalence of all other drug use was much higher among ecstasy users compared with marijuana users. These results lead us to the following important considerations: (a) Ecstasy users in the United States are predominantly polydrug users, which is similar to what was found in epidemiological studies conducted in Europe and Australia (Degenhardt et al., 2004; Pedersen & Skrondal, 1999; Topp et al., 1998); (b) ecstasy use is introduced after alcohol and marijuana and before other drugs in a typical drug use sequence; (c) young ecstasy users tend to be more drug naive and, as such, they are more vulnerable to the harmful interactions of ecstasy with other drugs; and (d) public health strategies should address the possibility of harmful interactions between ecstasy and other drug use.

Some limitations of our study include the following. (a) Our participants, especially adolescents, might be underreporting their drug use; however, some authors have stated that underreporting probably remains constant over time (Morral, McCaffrey, & Chien, 2003) and thus should not yield differential patterns of reported co-occurrence over time. If the participants were underreporting their drug use, then the ecstasy and other drug use prevalence would be even higher than the prevalence we obtained. (b) We analyzed ecstasy users as a group; however, there are possible within-group differences that need to be addressed in future studies, and drug use characteristics might be different for chronic and recent onset ecstasy users. (c) Data that would help to determine whether ecstasy users are using other drugs on the same occasions they use ecstasy are unavailable. (d) We relied on lifetime prevalence of ecstasy use to conduct our analysis, which is based on participant recall. (e) The methods of administration of the NHSDA were different in the years analyzed, although we suspect that these changes would have little impact on the inference of this study.

Prevention and harm reduction strategies that target ecstasy users are still in their infancy. It is necessary to invest in educational programs in order to prevent adolescents and young adults from using ecstasy, as well as to explain to current ecstasy users both the side effects of the drug and the harmful interactions it has with other drugs. Future studies are needed to identify subgroups among ecstasy users, specifically regular and more problematic ecstasy users.

REFERENCES

Baggott, M. (2002). Preventing problems in ecstasy users: Reduce use to reduce harm. *Journal of Psychoactive Drugs, 34,* 145–162.

Beck, J., & Rosenbaum, M. (1994). *Pursuit of ecstasy: The MDMA experience.* Albany: State University of New York Press.

Boyd, C. J., McCabe, S. E., & d'Arcy, H. (2003). Ecstasy use among college undergraduates: Gender, race, and sexual identity. *Journal of Substance Abuse Treatment, 24,* 209–215.

Chilcoat, H. D., Lucia, V. C., & Breslau, N. (1999). Level of agreement between DIS and UM–CIDI substance use disorders: Implications for research. *International Journal of Methods in Psychiatric Research, 8,* 83–101.

Chromy, J., Davis, T., Packer, L., & Gfroerer, J. (2002). *Mode effects on substance use measures: Comparison of the 1999 CAI and PAPI data.* In J. Gfroerer, J. Eyerman, & J. Chromy (Eds.), Redesigning an ongoing National Household Survey: Methodological issues (DHHS Publication No. SMA 03-3768, pp. 135–157). Rockville, MD: Substance Abuse and Mental Health Services Administration.

Çorapçioglu, A., & Ogel, K. (2004). Factors associated with ecstasy use in Turkish students. *Addiction, 99,* 67–76.

de Almeida, S. P., & Silva, M. T. A. (2003). Ecstasy (MDMA): Effects and patterns of use reported by users in Sao Paulo. *Revista Brasileira de Psiquiatria, 25,* 11–17.

Degenhardt, L., Barker, B., & Topp, L. (2004). Patterns of ecstasy use in Australia: Findings from a National Household Survey. *Addiction, 99,* 187–193.

European Monitoring Centre for Drugs and Drug Addiction. (2003). *Annual Report 2003: The state of the drugs problems in the European Union and Norway.* Lisbon, Portugal: European Monitoring Centre for Drugs and Drug Addiction.

Fendrich, M., Wislar, J. S., Johnson, T. P., & Hubbell, A. (2003). A contextual profile of club drug use among adults in Chicago. *Addiction, 98,* 1693–1703.

Ferrence, R. (2001). Diffusion theory and drug use. *Addiction, 96,* 165–173.

Gross, S. R., Barrett, S. P., Shestowsky, J. S., & Pihl, R. O. (2002). Ecstasy and drug consumption patterns: A Canadian rave population study. *Canadian Journal of Psychiatry, 47,* 546–551.

Johnston, L. D., O'Malley, P. M., & Bachman, J. G. (2000). *Monitoring the Future: National Survey results on adolescent drug use: Overview of key findings, 1999* (NIH Publication No. 00-4690). Bethesda, MD: National Institute on Drug Abuse.

Johnston, L. D., O'Malley, P. M., & Bachman, J. G. (2001a). *Monitoring the Future: National survey results on drug use, 1975–2000: Vol. I. Secondary school students* (NIH Publication No. 02-5106). Bethesda, MD: National Institute on Drug Abuse.

Johnston, L. D., O'Malley, P. M., & Bachman, J. G. (2001b). *Monitoring the Future: National survey results on drug use, 1975–2000: Vol. II. College students and young adults ages 19–40* (NIH Publication No. 02-5107). Bethesda, MD: National Institute on Drug Abuse.

Johnston, L. D., O'Malley, P. M., & Bachman, J. G. (2002). *Monitoring the Future: National results on adolescent drug use. Overview of key findings, 2001* (NIH Publication No. 02-5105). Bethesda, MD: National Institute on Drug Abuse.

Johnston, L. D., O'Malley, P. M., Bachman, J. G., & Schulenberg, J. E. (2003, December). *Ecstasy use falls for second year in a row, overall teen drug use drops.* Retrieved February 12, 2004, from http://www.monitoringthefuture.org

Landry, M. J. (2002). MDMA: A review of epidemiologic data. *Journal of Psychoactive Drugs, 34,* 163–169.

Lenton, S., Boys, A., & Norcross, K. (1997). Raves, drugs, and experience: Drug use by a sample of people who attend raves in Western Australia. *Addiction, 92,* 1327–1337.

Liechti, M. E., Gamma, A., & Vollenweider, F. X. (2001). Gender differences in the subjective effects of MDMA. *Psychopharmacology, 154,* 161–168.

Montoya, A. G., Sorrentino, R., Lukas, S. E., & Price, B. H. (2002). Long-term neuropsychiatric consequences of "ecstasy" (MDMA): A review. *Harvard Review of Psychiatry, 10,* 212–220.

Morland, J. (2000). Toxicity of drug abuse—Amphetamine designer drugs (ecstasy): Mental effects and consequences of a single dose. *Toxicology Letters, 112–113,* 147–152.

Morral, A. R., McCaffrey, D. F., & Chien, S. (2003). Measurement of adolescent drug use. *Journal of Psychoactive Drugs, 35*, 301–309.

Parker, H., Aldridge, J., & Measham, F. (1998). *Illegal leisure: The normalization of adolescent recreational drug use*. London: Routledge.

Parrott, A. C., Sisk, E., & Turner, J. J. D. (2000). Psychobiological problems in heavy "ecstasy" (MDMA) polydrug users. *Drug and Alcohol Dependence, 60*, 105–110.

Pedersen, W., & Skrondal, A. (1999). Ecstasy and new patterns of drug use: A normal population study. *Addiction, 94*, 1695–1706.

Peroutka, S. J., Newman, J. H., & Harris, H. (1988). Recreational use of 3,4 methylenedioxymethamphetamine (MDMA, ecstasy). *Neuropsychopharmacology, 1*, 273–277.

Schifano, F., DiFuria, L., Forza, G., Minicuci, N., & Bricolo, R. (1998). MDMA ("ecstasy") consumption in the context of polydrug abuse: A report on 150 patients. *Drug and Alcohol Dependence, 52*, 85–90.

Stata Corporation. (2003). STATA Statistical Software: Release 8.0 [Computer software]. College Station, TX: Author.

Substance Abuse and Mental Health Services Administration. (2002). *Results from the 2001 National Household Survey on Drug Abuse: Vol. I. Summary of national findings* (DHHS Publication No. SMA 02-3758, NHSDA Series H-17). Rockville, MD: Author.

Substance Abuse and Mental Health Services Administration (2003). *Emergency department trends from Drug Abuse Warning Network, final estimates: 1995–2002* (DHHS Publication No. SMA 03-3780, DAWN Series D-24). Rockville, MD: Author.

Topp, L., Hando, J., Dillon, P., Roche, A., & Solowij, N. (1999). Ecstasy use in Australia: Patterns of use and associated harm. *Drug and Alcohol Dependence, 55*, 105–115.

United Nations Office for Drug Control and Drug Prevention. (2001). *The 2001 Lebanon RSA report. Substance use and misuse in Lebanon*. Beirut, Lebanon: Institute for Development Research and Applied Care.

von Sydow, K., Lieb, R., Pfister, H., Höfler, M., & Wittchen, H. U. (2002). Use, abuse, and dependence of ecstasy and related drugs in adolescents and young adults: A transient phenomenon? Results from a longitudinal community study. *Drug and Alcohol Dependence, 66*, 147–159.

Walters, S. T., Foy, B. D., & Castro, R. J. (2002). The agony of ecstasy: Responding to growing MDMA use among college students. *Journal of American College Health, 51*, 139–141.

Wilkins, C., Bhatta, K., Pledger, M., & Casswell, S. (2003). Ecstasy use in New Zealand: Findings from the 1998 and 2001 National Drug Surveys [Electronic version]. *The New Zealand Medical Journal, 116*, 1–10.

III

PREVENTION AND HARM REDUCTION

6

TOWARD A PSYCHOLOGY
OF HARM REDUCTION

ROBERT J. MacCOUN

During the 1980s, a grassroots movement called *harm reduction* (or *harm minimization*) emerged in Amsterdam, Rotterdam, and Liverpool as a response to pervasive drug-related public health problems (Heather, Wodak, Nadelmann, & O'Hare, 1993). The movement gradually spread to many other European cities, eventually influencing the policies of several nations (MacCoun, Saiger, Kahan, & Reuter, 1993). Harm reduction is not yet a well-developed approach. Rather, it is a set of programs that share certain public health goals and assumptions. Central among them is the belief that it is possible to modify the behavior of drug users, and the conditions in which they use, in order to reduce many of the most serious risks that drugs pose to public health and safety. Examples of specific harm reduction interventions for drug use include needle and syringe exchange, low-threshold methadone maintenance, "safe-use" edu-

Preparation of this chapter was supported by grants from the California Wellness Foundation/University of California Wellness Lectures Program and the Alfred P. Sloan Foundation. An earlier version of this chapter was presented as part of the California Wellness Foundation/ University of California Wellness Lecture Series during October 1996. Many of the ideas presented here were developed in collaboration with Peter Reuter. I thank Chung Han Lee for research assistance, and Phil Tetlock, Julie Goldberg, Geno Smolensky, Suzanne Scotchmer, and Tom Schelling for helpful discussions.

Reprinted from *American Psychologist, 53*, 1199–1208 (1998). Copyright 1998 by the American Psychological Association.

cational campaigns, and the use of treatment as an alternative to incarceration for convicted drug offenders.

THE ENDS OF DRUG CONTROL

Table 6.1 lists and briefly defines six overlapping drug control strategies. The first two have dominated the American drug policy debate, centered on the appropriate balance between *supply reduction* (interdiction, source country control, domestic drug law enforcement) and *demand reduction* (treatment, prevention) in the federal budget. But despite their disagreements, demand-side and supply-side advocates share a common allegiance to what might be called the use reduction paradigm—the view that the highest, if not the exclusive, goal of drug policy should be to reduce (and hopefully eliminate) psychoactive drug use. In both practice and rhetoric, use reduction usually means *prevalence reduction*. That is, the goal has been to reduce the total number of users by discouraging initiation on the part of nonusers, and by promoting abstinence for current users. Table 6.1 introduces three newer terms—*quantity reduction, micro harm reduction,* and *macro harm reduction*— that are described in more detail below. These terms add more jargon to an already jargon-laden domain, but I hope to show that they make it possible to think more strategically about options for effective drug control.

The harm reduction critique of the enforcement-oriented U.S. drug strategy is twofold. First, prevalence-reduction policies have failed to eliminate drug use, leaving its harms largely intact. Second, these harsh enforcement policies are themselves a *source* of many drug-related harms, either directly or by exacerbating the harmful consequences of drug use (Nadelmann, 1989). Although many drug-related harms result from the psychopharmacologic effects of drug consumption, many others are mostly attributable to drug prohibition and its enforcement (MacCoun, Reuter, & Schelling, 1996). These harms would be greatly reduced, if not eliminated, under a regime of legal availability. The acknowledgment that prohibition is a source of harm does not imply that legalizing drugs would necessarily lead to a net reduction

TABLE 6.1
Overlapping Drug Control Strategies

Strategy	Goal
Supply reduction	Reduce total supply of drugs
Demand reduction	Reduce total demand for drugs
Prevalence reduction	Reduce total number of drug users
Quantity reduction	Reduce total quantity consumed
Micro harm reduction	Reduce average harm per use of drugs
Macro harm reduction	Reduce total drug-related harm

in harm; as we shall see, much depends on the effects of legal change on levels of drug use (MacCoun, 1993; MacCoun & Reuter, 1997). But by almost exclusively relying on use reduction—especially drug law enforcement—as an indirect means of reducing harm, we are forgoing opportunities to reduce harm directly. We are even increasing some harms in the process.

AMERICAN RESISTANCE TO HARM REDUCTION

With remarkable consistency, the U.S. government has aggressively resisted harm reduction (Kirp & Bayer, 1993; Reuter & MacCoun, 1995). For example, there are probably more than 1 million injecting drug users in this country, and injection drug use accounts for about one third of all AIDS cases. Though the evidence is not unanimous, a considerable body of evidence demonstrates that needle exchange programs can bring about significant reductions in HIV transmission (Des Jarlais, Friedman, & Ward, 1993; General Accounting Office, 1993; Hurley, Jolley, & Kaldor, 1997; Lurie & Reingold, 1993).[1] Lurie and Drucker (1997) recently estimated that between 4,394 and 9,666 HIV infections could have been prevented in the United States between 1987 and 1995 if a national needle exchange program had been in place. Yet there are fewer than 100 needle exchange programs operating in the United States. Why? Because prescription laws, paraphernalia laws, and local "drug-free zone" ordinances ban needle exchange programs in most of the country. Indeed, almost half of the existing programs are operating under an illicit or quasi-legal status. Despite the fact that these programs have been endorsed by the Centers for Disease Control, the National Academy of Sciences, and various leading medical journals and health organizations, drug policy officials in the federal government and most state governments have actively opposed needle exchange. In 1998, Department of Health and Human Services (DHHS) Secretary Donna Shalala publicly endorsed needle exchange on scientific grounds but subsequently announced that the administration had decided that federal funding of needle exchanges would be unwise. A *Washington Post* story claimed that DHHS officials had arranged her press conference in the mistaken belief that the President would support needle exchange funding; Secretary Shalala's memo of talking points announcing his support was reported to say "the evidence is airtight" and "from the beginning of this effort, it has been about science, science, science" (J. F. Harris & Goldstein, 1998).

---

[1]This finding is not universal; participation in needle exchanges was associated with elevated HIV risk in recent studies in Vancouver (Strathdee et al., 1997) and Montreal (Bruneau et al., 1997), though the authors caution that this association might reflect features that distinguish these evaluations from others in the literature; for example, they were conducted at the peak of the HIV epidemic, their clients were heavily involved in cocaine injection, and the number of needles dispersed fell well short of the amount needed to prevent needle sharing (Bruneau & Schechter, 1998). A broader comparison of 81 U.S. cities estimated a 5.9% increase in HIV seroprevalence in 52 cities without needle exchange, and a 5.8% decrease in 29 cities with needle exchange during the period 1988 to 1993 (Hurley, Jolley, & Kaldor, 1997).

Our almost exclusive emphasis on use reduction rather than harm reduction probably has many causes (Reuter & MacCoun, 1995). One is the fear that harm reduction is a Trojan horse for the drug legalization movement (e.g., McCaffrey, 1998). Another factor might be that whereas harm reduction focuses on harms to users, drug-related violence and other harms to *nonusers* are more salient in the United States than in Europe. In addition, prevalence is more readily measurable than harms, and few harm-reduction programs, with the notable exception of needle exchange, have been rigorously evaluated—though political opposition to harm reduction is itself a major cause of the lack of relevant data. But other objections involve beliefs about behavior. For example, it may seem only logical that reducing use is the best way to reduce harm. But this logic holds only if the elimination of drug use is nearly complete, and if efforts to reduce use do not themselves cause harm. Unfortunately, many prevalence-reduction policies often fail on one or both counts. Although it is true that abstinence from drugs (or teenage sex, or drinking among alcoholics) is "100% effective" at reducing harm, the key policy question is whether we are 100% effective at convincing people to *become* abstinent. Finally, the most frequent objection to harm reduction is the claim that harm reduction programs will "send the wrong message." The logic by which harm reduction "sends the wrong message" is rarely articulated in any detail, suggesting that for its proponents, the proposition is self-evident. It seems likely that harm-reduction advocates will continue to face opposition in the United States until they successfully address this concern.

HARM REDUCTION IN OTHER POLICY DOMAINS

The tension between preventing a behavior and reducing the harmfulness of that behavior is not unique to the debate about illicit drugs. Table 6.2 lists some intriguing parallels in other contemporary American policy debates. Despite many superficial differences, each domain involves a behavior that poses risks to both the actor and others. And each raises the question about the relative efficacy of policies that aim to reduce the harmful consequences of a risky behavior (harm reduction) versus policies designed to discourage the behavior itself (prevalence or quantity reduction).

The first row of Table 6.2—safety standards for consumer products—is notable for its relative lack of controversy outside of the halls of Congress. Even though these safety regulations clearly have a harm-reduction rationale—albeit one generally not recognized as such—recent Congressional efforts to scale them back have received a remarkably lukewarm public response. But in the other domains listed in Table 6.2, a debate centers on the fear that an intervention to reduce harm—harm reduction in spirit if not in name—will in some way "send the wrong message," encouraging the risky behavior. The parallels to drugs are

TABLE 6.2
Policies Aimed at Reducing Harms Associated With Risky Behaviors

Policy	Risky behavior	Harms that policy tries to reduce
Mandated safety standards for motor vehicles, toys, sports equipment, food, pharmaceuticals, and so on	Driving, participation in sports, consumption of products, and so on	Physical injury, illness, death
Needle exchange	Intravenous drug use	HIV transmission
Teaching of controlled drinking skills	Drinking by diagnosed alcoholics	Social, psychological, and physical harms of alcohol abuse
School condom programs	Unprotected sexual contact among teens	Sexually transmitted diseases, unwanted pregnancies
Welfare	Becoming or remaining unemployed	Poor quality of life (housing, health, education), especially for children
Provision of benefits for illegal immigrants	Illegal immigration to the United States	Poor quality of life (housing, health, education), especially for children

particularly striking for the topic of condom distribution in schools (and to a lesser degree, sex education). Advocates argue that condom distribution is needed to reduce the risks of unplanned pregnancies and sexually transmitted diseases, whereas opponents vociferously argue that distribution programs and other safe sex interventions actually promote sexual activity (Mauldon & Luker, 1996). On the other hand, recent U.S. debates about welfare and immigration benefits may seem to have little to do with concepts like risk regulation or harm reduction. But at an abstract level, the issues are similar. Assertions are made that policies designed to mitigate the harmful consequences of being unemployed, or of immigrating to the United States, actually encourage people to become (or remain) unemployed, or to immigrate to the United States. Aside from brief excursions into the lessons of motor vehicle safety standards and tobacco and alcohol policy, this chapter focuses almost exclusively on harm reduction for illicit drugs. But it seems possible that the analysis might provide insights for other domains of risk reduction—in part because my arguments were often informed by those literatures but also because it seems unlikely that the underlying behavioral questions are unique to the drug domain.

OVERVIEW

The remainder of this chapter explores critics' concerns about harm reduction. This chapter does not attempt a comprehensive review of the evaluation literature on harm reduction or on the specifics of interventions at the clinical level (see Des Jarlais, Friedman, & Ward, 1993; Heather et al., 1993). Instead, the chapter has four goals: (a) to demonstrate the value of distinguishing microlevel harm from macrolevel harm and prevalence of a behavior from the quantity or frequency of that behavior; (b) to identify potential trade-offs between prevalence reduction, quantity reduction, and micro harm reduction; (c) to explore some nonconsequentialist psychological bases for opposition to harm reduction; and (d) to offer some tentative suggestions for successfully integrating harm reduction into our national drug control strategy. The next section examines two different senses in which harm reduction might "send the wrong message," either directly through its rhetorical effects or indirectly by making drug use less risky. I offer a theoretical framework for integrating prevalence-reduction and harm-reduction policies. I believe it offers a way of thinking about harm reduction that might reduce some of the barriers to a more flexible public health orientation to U.S. drug policy. But not necessarily. The tone of the harm-reduction debate suggests that attitudes toward drug policies—on both sides—are influenced by deeply rooted and strongly felt symbolic factors that are largely independent of concerns about policy effectiveness per se. These factors are explored in a later section.

USE REDUCTION AND HARM REDUCTION: AN INTEGRATIVE FRAMEWORK

Micro Versus Macro Harm Reduction

The efficacy of harm reduction depends on behavioral responses to policy interventions. In explaining this point, it is important to make a distinction between levels of analysis that is sometimes obscured in the harm-reduction literature. Let me begin with a truism that is largely overlooked in the harm-reduction debate: *Total Harm = Average Harm per Use × Total Use*, where total use is a function of the number of users and the quantity each user consumes and average harm per use is a function of two vectors of specific drug-related harms, one involving harms to users (e.g., overdoses, addiction, AIDS) and the other involving harms to nonusers (e.g., HIV transmission, criminal victimization; MacCoun & Caulkins, 1996; Reuter & MacCoun, 1995).

Figure 6.1 depicts this relationship graphically using a causal path diagram. Links a and b depict the intended effects of harm-reduction and use-reduction policies, respectively. Links c, d, and e depict the ancillary harmful effects—unintended and often unanticipated—these policies might have. Link c denotes the unintended harms caused by prohibiting a risky behavior (e.g., the lack of clean needles, lack of drug quality control, violence associated with

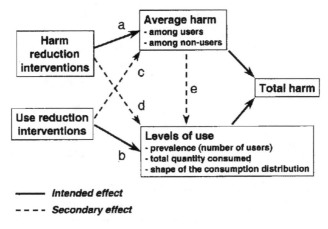

Figure 6.1. Use reduction and harm reduction: an integrative framework.

illicit markets, inflated prices that encourage income-generating crime, and so on; Nadelmann, 1989). This category of unintended harms is of central concern to any assessment of alternative legal regimes for drug control (MacCoun, Reuter, & Schelling, 1996). But here I focus on a second set of unintended consequences, those resulting from harm-reduction policies, to see whether objections to harm reduction have merit. If a harm-reduction strategy reduces harm per incident but leads to increases in drug use (links d and e), the policy might still achieve *net* harm reduction; on the other hand, a sufficiently large increase in use could actually result in an *increase* in total harm. There are two potential mechanisms for such an unintended consequence, one direct and one indirect. For reasons to be explained, link d can be conceptualized as the direct *rhetorical* effect (if any) of harm reduction on total use; link e is an indirect *compensatory behavior* effect. Either might be interpreted as "sending the wrong message."

Direct Version: Does Harm Reduction Literally Send the Wrong Message?

The rhetorical hypothesis is that irrespective of their effectiveness in reducing harms, harm-reduction programs literally communicate messages that encourage drug use. As noted earlier, those who espouse this rhetorical hypothesis rarely explain how it is supposed to work. The most plausible interpretation is that without intending to do so, harm reduction sends tacit messages that are construed as approval or at least the absence of strong disapproval—of drug consumption.

If harm reduction service providers *intend* to send a message, it is something like this: "We view drugs as harmful. We discourage you from using them, and we are eager to help you to quit if you've started. But if you will not quit using drugs, we can help you to use them less harmfully." Is that the only message? Psycholinguistic theory and research do suggest that people readily draw additional inferences that are *pragmatically implied* by an actor's conduct, regardless of whether those inferences were intended, or even endorsed, by the actor (R. J. Harris & Monaco, 1978; Wyer & Gruenfeld, 1995). Thus if we provide heroin users with clean needles, they might infer that we don't expect them to quit using heroin—if we did, why give them needles? Arguably, this perception could undermine their motivation to quit.

But would users infer that we believe heroin use is *good*, or at least "not bad"? It is not obvious how harm reduction might actually imply *endorsement* of drug use. Ultimately, whether any such rhetorical effects occur is an empirical question. It would be useful to assess the kinds of unintended inferences that users and nonusers draw from harm-reduction messages, and from the mere existence of harm-reduction programs. But in the absence of such evidence, the rhetorical hypothesis that harm reduction conveys approval of drug use is purely speculative.

Moreover, it is difficult to reconcile this notion with the secondary prevention and treatment efforts that frequently accompany actual harm-reduction interventions. Through such efforts, users are informed that their behavior is dangerous to themselves and others and that assistance and support are available to help them if they wish to quit drug use. Braithwaite's (1989) research on *reintegrative shaming* indicates that it is possible simultaneously to send a social message that certain acts are socially unacceptable while still helping the actors to repair their lives. Braithwaite suggests that this approach is integral to Japanese culture, but it is also reflected in the Christian tradition of "hating the sin but loving the sinner."

Indirect Version: Does a Reduction in Harm Make Drugs More Attractive?

Even if no one took harm reduction to imply government endorsement of drugs, harm reduction might still influence levels of drug use *indirectly* through its intended effect, that is, by reducing the riskiness of drug use. This is a second interpretation of "sending the wrong message." Though there are ample grounds for being skeptical of a pure "rational-choice" analysis of drug use (MacCoun, 1993), the notion that reductions in risk might influence drug use is certainly plausible and would be consistent with a growing body of evidence of compensatory behavioral responses to safety interventions. Thus we should be mindful of potential trade-offs between harm reduction and use reduction.

Risk assessors have known for some time that engineers tend to overestimate the benefits of technological improvements in the safety of traffic signals, automobiles, cigarettes, and other products. The reason is that engineers often fail to anticipate that technological improvements lead to changes in behavior. When technological innovations successfully reduce the probability of harm given unsafe conduct, they make that conduct less risky. And if the perceived risks were motivating actors to behave somewhat self-protectively, a reduction in risk should lead them to take fewer precautions than before, raising the probability of their unsafe conduct to a higher level. This notion has been variously labeled *compensatory behavior, risk compensation, offsetting behavior*, or in its most extreme form, *risk homeostasis*—a term that implies efforts to maintain a constant level of risk (Wilde, 1982). Although some find this general idea counterintuitive, one economist has noted that, on reflection, it is hardly surprising that "soldiers walk more gingerly when crossing minefields than when crossing wheat fields," and "circus performers take fewer chances when practicing without nets" (Hemenway, 1988).

Compensatory behavioral responses to risk reduction have been identified in a variety of settings. For example, everything else being equal, drivers have responded to seat belts and other improvements in the safety of automobiles by driving faster and more recklessly than they would in a less safe vehicle (Chirinko & Harper, 1993). Similarly, filters and low-tar tobacco each reduce the harmfulness per unit of tobacco, yet numerous studies have demonstrated that smokers compensate by smoking more cigarettes, inhaling more deeply, or blocking the filter vents (Hughes, 1995). In both domains, some of the safety gains brought about by a reduction in the probability of harm given unsafe conduct have been offset by increases in the probability of that conduct. Though early correlational studies were criticized on methodological grounds, the compensatory behavioral hypothesis has received important support from recent controlled laboratory experiments (Stetzer & Hofman, 1996).

The compensatory behavioral mechanism suggests that if reductions in average drug-related harm were to motivate sufficiently large increases in drug use, micro harm reduction would actually increase macro harm. Blower and McLean (1994) offer a similar argument based on epidemiological simulations that suggest that an HIV vaccine, unless perfectly prophylactic, could actually exacerbate the San Francisco AIDS epidemic, provided that individuals behaved less cautiously in response to their increased sense of safety. But to date, research on compensatory responses to risk reduction provides little evidence that behavioral responses produce net increases in harm, or even the constant level of harm predicted by the "homeostatic" version of the theory. Instead, most studies find that when programs reduce the probability of harm given unsafe conduct, any increases in the probability of that conduct are slight, reducing but not eliminating the gains in safety (Chirinko & Harper, 1993; Hughes, 1995; Stetzer & Hofman, 1996). As a result, in our terms, micro harm reduction produces macro harm reduction.

Do Drug Interventions Achieve Macro Harm Reduction?

It is impossible to calculate total drug harm in any literal fashion, or to rigorously compare total harm across alternative policy regimes (MacCoun, Reuter, & Schelling, 1996). Many of the harms are difficult to quantify, and observers will differ in their weighting of the various types of harm. Thus at the strategic level of national policy formation, macro harm reduction is not a rigid analytical test but rather a heuristic principle: Are we reducing drug harms, and reducing drug use in ways that do not increase drug harm? But at the level of specific interventions, macro reduction of *specific* harms is a realistic evaluation criterion, as illustrated by the compensatory behavioral research just cited. Unfortunately, few drug policy programs are evaluated with respect to both use reduction and harm reduction. Prevention and treatment programs are generally evaluated with respect to changes in abstinence or relapse rates, whereas harm reduction evaluators tend to assess changes in crime, morbidity, and mortality rates. As a result, researchers are unable to determine whether many programs achieve macro harm reduction.

The empirical literature on needle exchange is a notable and exemplary exception. There is now a fairly sizable body of evidence that needle exchange programs produce little or no measurable increase in injecting drug use (Lurie & Reingold, 1993; Watters, Estilo, Clark, & Lorvick, 1994). Because it significantly reduces average harm, needle exchange provides both micro and macro harm reduction. But the empirical success record for needle exchange does not constitute blanket support for the harm reduction movement. Each intervention must be assessed empirically on its own terms.

Let me offer a few cautionary tales. One harm reduction intervention that has been tried and rejected is the "zone of tolerance" approach tried by Zurich officials in the Platzspitz—or, as the American press labeled it, "Needle Park." By allowing injecting drug users to congregate openly in this public park and to shoot up without police interference, city officials were able to make clean needles and other health interventions readily available at the time and place of drug use. Even sympathetic observers agree that these benefits were ultimately offset by increases in local crime rates and in the prevalence of hard drug use in the city (Grob, 1992). Another example involves bongs and water pipes. Though these devices have been touted as a means of reducing the health risks of marijuana smoking, a recent test found that they actually increase the quantity of tars ingested. The apparent reason harkens back to the compensatory behavioral mechanism. Water pipes filter out more THC than tar, so users smoke more to achieve the same high, thereby increasing their risk (Gieringer, 1996). The Zurich case and the bong study suggest that harm-reduction strategies can fail, but it is important to note that neither failure resulted from increasing rates of *initiation* to drug use. In the Zurich case, the prevalence of drug use rose because the park attracted users from other

Swiss cities and neighboring countries. Arguably, the program might have been successful had other European cities adopted the idea simultaneously. In the bong case, the filtering benefits were offset by increases in consumption levels among users, but I am unaware of any evidence that bongs and water pipes have ever encouraged nonusers to start smoking marijuana.

One can imagine hypothetical examples of how a harm-reduction strategy might plausibly attract new users. For example, from a public health perspective, we are better off if current heroin injectors switch to smoking their drug. Imagine a public information campaign designed to highlight the relative health benefits of smoking. If some fraction of nonusers have resisted heroin because of an aversion to needles (for anecdotal evidence, see Bennetto, 1998), our campaign might indeed end up encouraging some of them to take up heroin smoking, despite our best intentions. Of course, no one has seriously proposed such a campaign. But the example demonstrates that concerns about increased use are plausible in principle.

Quantity Reduction as a Middle Ground?

As noted earlier, American drug policy rhetoric is dominated by concerns about the number of users, drawing a bright line between "users" and "nonusers." This is illustrated by our national drug indicator data. Most available measures of drug use are *prevalence* oriented: rates of lifetime use, use in the past year, or use in the past month. But drug-related harms may well be more sensitive to changes in the *total quantity consumed* than to changes in the total number of users. One million occasional drug users may pose fewer crime and health problems than 100,000 frequent users. Our nation's recent cocaine problems provide an illustration. After significant reductions in casual use in the 1980s, total consumption has become increasingly concentrated among a smaller number of heavy users. At an individual level, these heavy users are at much greater risk than casual users with respect to acute and chronic illness, accidents, job- and family-related problems, and participation in criminal activities. Thus although cocaine prevalence has declined, total cocaine consumption and its related harms have remained relatively stable (Everingham & Rydell, 1994).

This suggests that *quantity reduction* (reducing consumption levels) holds particular promise as a macro harm reduction strategy. Quantity reduction occupies a point halfway between prevalence reduction and micro harm reduction. Like prevalence reduction, quantity reduction targets use levels rather than harm levels. But like harm reduction, quantity reduction is based on the premise that when use cannot be prevented, we might at least be able to mitigate its harms.

What is less clear is the optimal targeting strategy for quantity reduction. Consider the distribution of users across consumption levels, which for most psychoactive drugs (licit and illicit) is positively skewed, with a long right tail indicating a small fraction of very heavy users. One strategy is to target those heaviest users—to "pull in" the right tail of the distribution. The marginal gains in risk reduction should be greatest at the right tail, and only a small fraction of users need be targeted.

This approach has received considerable attention—and notoriety—in the alcohol field under the rubric "controlled drinking." Few public health experts dispute the notion that problem drinkers are better off drinking lightly than drinking heavily. But there has been an extraordinary furor surrounding the notion of controlled drinking as a treatment goal. The evidence suggests that (a) although abstinence-based treatment programs experience high relapse rates, many of the relapsing clients successfully reduce their drinking to relatively problem-free levels; (b) it is possible to *teach* controlled drinking skills to many, but not all, problem drinkers; (c) we cannot yet predict which problem drinkers will be able to control their drinking at moderate levels; and (d) most treated problem drinkers fail to achieve either abstinence or controlled levels of drinking (Marlatt, Larimer, Baer, & Quigley, 1993). But opponents assert that irrespective of any benefits to be derived from controlled drinking, the very notion undermines the goal of abstinence and discourages drinkers from achieving it. The small-scale studies conducted to date do not support that claim, but the evidence is not yet decisive.

In addition to the abstinence-moderation debate, a second quantity-reduction debate has emerged among alcohol experts. Are problem drinkers even the appropriate intervention target? An alternative quantity-reduction strategy targets the middle of the alcohol consumption distribution. For some years, many experts have argued that the total social costs of alcohol might be better reduced by lowering average consumption levels rather than concentrating on the most problematic drinkers at the right tail (Rose, 1992; Skog, 1993). If so—and this is a matter of ongoing debate in the pages of *Addiction* and other journals—broad-based efforts to reduce total drug use might indeed be the best way to achieve total harm reduction, at least for alcohol consumption. The controversy here has been more purely technical and less emotional than the controlled drinking debate, in part because few people still champion the notion of abstinence for casual drinkers. Many Americans seem quite willing to accept the notion of "nonproblem" alcohol consumption yet reject the notion of "nonproblem" marijuana or cocaine consumption.

In fact, the viability of "lower-risk" drug consumption, and the relative efficacy of the "pull in the tail" and the "lower the average" strategies, will depend on a variety of factors. One factor is the degree of skew of the consumption distribution: The greater the probability mass in the right tail, the greater the efficacy of targeting heavy users. A second is the dose-response curve for risks, which is usually S-shaped for those drug-risk combinations that have been studied. (We know a great deal more about dose-response functions for health and public safety risks involving licit drugs than for comparable risks involving illicit drugs.) When this function is very steep, even moderate consumption levels are very risky, making the "shift-the-distribution" strategy more efficacious. A third factor involves the possibility that individuals with a higher propensity for danger self-select higher consumption levels. The latter effect will spuriously inflate the quantity-risk relationship. To the extent that this effect predominates, convincing right-tail users to cut back may yield fewer benefits than anticipated.

THE PUBLIC ACCEPTABILITY OF HARM REDUCTION

Whereas American citizens and policymakers have embraced drug strategies that promote prevalence reduction, harm reduction and some forms of quantity reduction are often greeted with considerable hostility—when they are not ignored altogether. In this section, I offer a number of hypotheses about this negative reaction. The opposition to harm reduction surely has multiple causes, so these explanations are not mutually exclusive. They vary along a continuum ranging from *consequentialist* to *symbolic* grounds for opposition. Many people probably hold both kinds of views. Harm reduction opponents might be placed along this continuum based on their responses to the following hypothetical questions:

1. If new evidence suggested that needle exchange (or some other harm-reduction strategy) reduced total harm, would you still be opposed?
2. If the answer is "yes": If new evidence suggested a reduction in harm, *with no increase in use*, would you still be opposed?
3. If the answer is "yes": Would you be opposed to drug use even if it were made *completely* harmless?

Those who would say "no" to the first question are pragmatic or consequentialist in their opposition to harm reduction. Those who say "yes" to the third question are at the other extreme; for them, drug use is intrinsically immoral, irrespective of its consequences—what philosophers call a *deontological* stance. Those who would support harm reduction only if there were no increase in drug use fall somewhere in between. Their views might reflect a complex mix of instrumental and symbolic concerns.

Consequentialist Grounds

The consequentialist grounds for opposing harm reduction are the easiest to describe. They are characterized primarily by the belief that harm reduction will be counterproductive, either by failing to reduce average harm or by increasing drug use enough to increase total harm. Those who oppose harm reduction on truly consequentialist grounds should change their mind and support it if the best available facts suggest that an intervention reduces harm without producing offsetting increases in use. In recent years, the favorable evidence for needle exchange has received increasing publicity in the mass media. This media coverage may explain why a 1996 poll found that 66% of Americans endorsed needle exchange as a means of preventing AIDS—a dramatic increase over earlier surveys (The Henry J. Kaiser Family Foundation, 1996). Of course, this may be an over-optimistic reading of the impact of empirical research (MacCoun, 1998). Program evaluations rarely yield unequivocal verdicts; even when effects are statistically reliable, they are usually open to multiple interpretations. Expert consensus on the effects of high-profile policy interventions is rare, even when the accumulated body of research is large. And the vehemence of the opposition to harm reduction suggests that attitudes toward these interventions are based on something more than purely instrumental beliefs about the effectiveness of alternative drug policies.

Attitudes toward the death penalty are instructive in this regard. Attitude research indicates that many citizens overtly endorse a *deterrence* rationale for the death penalty, believing that "it will prevent crimes." Yet most do not change their views when asked how they would feel if there were unequivocal evidence that execution provided no marginal deterrence above and beyond life imprisonment. The evidence suggests that ostensibly instrumental views are actually masking deeper retributive motives (Ellsworth & Gross, 1994). As a result, support for capital punishment is relatively impervious to research findings (Lord, Ross, & Lepper, 1979). The nonconsequentialist grounds for opposing harm reduction are more complex than the consequentialist grounds. There are a number of distinct psychological processes that might play a role in shaping these views.[2]

The Need for Predictability and Control

Harmonious social relations require a minimal level of predictability because we must routinely relinquish control to other people—automobile drivers, surgeons, airline pilots, our children's teachers, and so on. The notion that others are using drugs can be threatening because it suggests that they've lost some self-control. Although harm reduction can minimize the consequences of diminished control, it may be more reassuring to believe that others are completely abstinent. When we are unable to control aversive

---

[2] Note that these psychological accounts by themselves do not constitute evidence for or against the wisdom of opposition to harm reduction, nor are they meant to imply that such views are somehow pathological.

stimuli, any signal that helps us to anticipate danger will significantly reduce our anxiety (Miller, 1980). Perhaps the belief that others are abstinent from drugs works like a "safety signal" to free us from worrying about their conduct.

Our fears about others are augmented by a robust bias in risk perceptions. Most people—adults as well as adolescents—perceive themselves to be less vulnerable than the average person to risks of injury or harm (e.g., Weinstein & Klein, 1995). An apparent corollary is that most of us believe we are surrounded by people less cautious or skillful than ourselves. We may think we can control our own use of intoxicants (most of us feel that way about alcohol), but we find it harder to believe that others will do the same. Indeed, this might explain why a sizable minority of regular cannabis users opposes the complete legalization of that drug (Erickson, 1989).

Aversion to Making Value Trade-Offs

Our attitudes toward public policy involve more than simple judgments about effectiveness and outcomes. They are symbolic expressions of our core values. Unfortunately, most difficult social problems bring core values into conflict. Drug problems are no exception; they bring personal liberty into conflict with public safety, compassion into conflict with moral accountability. Contemplating harm reduction brings these conflicts into strong relief. According to Tetlock's *value pluralism model* acknowledging such conflicts is psychologically aversive, and so many people avoid explicit trade-off reasoning, preferring simpler mental strategies (Tetlock, Peterson, & Lerner, 1996). The easiest is to deny that there is a conflict, by ignoring one value or the other. If that doesn't work, we may adopt a simple "lexicographic" ranking. Many of us engage in complex multidimensional tradeoff reasoning only when we can't avoid it, as when the conflicting values are each too salient to dismiss or ignore.

In a recent content analysis of op-ed essays debating the reform of drug laws, my colleagues and I found that legalizers and decriminalizers (all of whom were harm-reduction advocates, though the converse is not necessarily true) used significantly more complex arguments than prohibitionists (MacCoun, Kahan, Gillespie, & Rhee, 1993). The reform advocates were less likely to view the drug problem in terms of a simple good-bad dichotomy; they identified multiple dimensions to the problem and were more likely to acknowledge trade-offs and counterarguments to their own position. It may be hard to persuade others to acknowledge the full complexity of harm-reduction logic unless the values that support it become more salient in drug policy discourse.

The Propriety of Helping Drug Users

Of course, there is little basis for value conflict if one feels that drug users *should* suffer harm when they use drugs. There are a number of reasons why some people might hold this view. One is authoritarianism, a complex trait defined as a chronic tendency to cope with anxiety by expressing hostility toward outgroup members; intolerance of unconventional behavior; and submissive, unquestioning support of authority figures. Authoritarianism is strongly correlated with support for punitive drug policies (Peterson, Doty, & Winter, 1993). Indeed, several items from the Right Wing Authoritarianism Scale—a leading research instrument for measuring this trait—seem to equate authoritarianism with opposition to harm-reduction interventions almost by definition (Christie, 1991). According to Item 7, "The facts on crime, sexual immorality, and the recent public disorders all show we have to crack down harder on deviant groups and troublemakers if we are going to save our moral standards and preserve law and order." Item 12 states, "Being kind to loafers or criminals will only encourage them to take advantage of your weakness, so it's best to use a firm, tough hand when dealing with them." And authoritarians are more likely to disagree with Item 19: "The courts are right in being easy on drug offenders. Punishment would not do any good in cases like these."

But scoring high in authoritarianism is probably not a prerequisite for hostility toward drug users. There is a general antagonism to hard drug users among U.S. citizens, partly stemming from the strong association between drugs and street violence in American cities. It is much easier to see harshness as the appropriate response in the United States than in Europe, where drug use is more likely to be perceived as a health problem. Race and social distance may play a role here as well; arguably, Americans were more tolerant of drug users in the 1970s, when the mass media's prototypical drug user was an Anglo-American student in a college dorm instead of a young African American man on a city street corner (Kirp & Bayer, 1993). As a result, Americans have supported (or at least tolerated) sentencing policies that tend to disproportionately burden minority and poor offenders relative to those who are Anglo-American or middle class (Tonry, 1995).

But irrespective of race and class, the mere fact that someone uses drugs will often be sufficient to categorize them as "the other," particularly if we don't already know them. Citizens with a friend or family member who is an addict may embrace micro harm reduction, whatever its aggregate consequences, but those who don't know any addicts may prefer a strategy of isolation and containment.

Even in the absence of malice, many people may feel that addicts should suffer the consequences of their actions. Addiction is widely viewed as a voluntary state, regardless of many experts' views to the contrary (Weiner, Perry, & Magnusson, 1988). Many Americans, especially conservatives, are unwilling to extend help to actors who are responsible for their own suffering; such actors are seen as undeserving (Skitka & Tetlock, 1993). The retributive view that bad acts require punishment is deeply rooted in the Judeo-Christian tradition, particularly in Protestant fundamentalist traditions. In light of the possibility that opposition to harm reduction traces back to our nation's strong Puritan and Calvinist roots, it is quite ironic that the Dutch and the Swiss have championed such an approach in Europe.

Disgust and Impurity

A final ground for opposing harm reduction might be the vague, spontaneous, and nonrational sense that drug use defiles the purity of the body and hence that anything that comes in contact with drug users becomes disgusting through a process of contagion. Stated so bluntly, this may sound utterly implausible; such concepts are quite alien to Western moral discourse. Nevertheless, this kind of thinking is quite explicit in other cultures, and anthropologists argue that it often lurks below the surface of our own moral judgments (Douglas, 1966; Haidt, Koller, & Dias, 1993). I know of no direct evidence that such reactions influence attitudes toward drug policy, but the hypothesis is testable in principle and worthy of further investigation.

CONCLUSION

In this chapter, I have tried to take a frank look at the arguments against harm reduction, and I have suggested that, like most policy interventions, the approach has potential pitfalls. Not every harm-reduction intervention will be successful, and some might even increase aggregate harm. We are still woefully ignorant about the complex interplay between formal drug policies and informal social and self-control factors (MacCoun, 1993). Still, the evidence to date on harm reduction is encouraging (as the success of needle exchange programs makes clear), and I believe that we have much to gain by integrating harm-reduction interventions and goals into our national drug control strategy. I conclude by offering five hypotheses about how harm reduction might be more successful—successful both in reducing aggregate harm and in attracting and retaining a viable level of political support.

1. Harm-reduction interventions should have the greatest political viability when they can demonstrate a reduction in average harm—especially harms that affect nonusers—without increasing drug use levels. Interventions that lead to increases in drug use are likely to encounter stiff opposition, even if they yield demonstrable net reductions in aggregate harm. Thus, harm-reduction interventions need to be rigorously evaluated with respect to four types of outcome: effects on targeted harms, "side

effects" on untargeted harms (especially harms to nonusers), effects on participants' subsequent use levels, and effects on local nonparticipants' use levels.

2. Because the compensatory behavioral mechanism is triggered by perceived changes in risk, harm-reduction efforts seem least likely to increase drug use when those harms being reduced were already significantly underestimated, discounted, or ignored by users and potential users (see Wilde, 1982). At one extreme, if perceptions of risk are serious enough, few people will use the drug in the first place. (Witness the almost complete disappearance of absinthe after its dangers became apparent in the late 19th century.) At the other extreme, those who are either ignorant of, or indifferent to, a drug's risks, seem unlikely to escalate their use when an intervention lowers those risks.

3. Similarly, interventions involving safe-use information or risk-reducing paraphernalia should be less likely to increase total use, and hence be more politically viable, when they are highly salient for heavy users but largely invisible to potential initiates to drug use. Maintenance interventions, which provide drugs or drug substitutes for addicts, should be less likely to encourage use if the program has few barriers to entry for heavy users but high barriers to entry for casual users. (The risk of these targeting strategies is that new initiates may fail to obtain the benefits of the interventions.)

4. Reducing users' consumption levels should generally provide harm reduction, an important strategy for achieving use reduction when heavy users refuse to become abstinent.

5. Whenever feasible, harm-reduction interventions should be coupled with credible primary and secondary prevention efforts, as well as low-threshold access to treatment.

This last point is a truism among many harm-reduction providers. Still, a few in the harm-reduction movement are uncomfortable with the notion that harm-reduction programs should urge users to stop their drug use. Some take that position on libertarian grounds, but others associate traditional use-reduction efforts with dishonesty ("reefer madness"), hypocrisy ("what about alcohol and tobacco?"), or an apparent willingness to jeopardize user health (e.g., the U.S. decision to spray Mexican marijuana crops with paraquat in the 1970s). But harm-reduction advocates who categorically reject the opposition risk undermining their own cause. Americans who oppose harm reduction are unlikely to change their views until they feel their fears have been taken seriously.

REFERENCES

Bennetto, A. (1998, July 13). Epidemic of heroin sweeps Britain. *The Independent* [On line]. Available at http:/www.mapinc.org/drugnews/ v98/n571/aol.html

Blower, S. M., & McLean, A. R. (1994, September 2). Prophylactic vaccines, risk behavior change, and the probability of eradicating HIV in San Francisco. *Science, 265*, 1451–1454.

Braithwaite, J. (1989). *Crime, shame, and reintegration.* Cambridge, England: Cambridge University Press.

Bruneau, J., Lamoth, E, Franco, E., Lachance, N., Désy, M., Soto, J., & Vincelette, J. (1997). High rates of HIV infection among injection drug users participating in needle exchange programs in Montreal: Results of a cohort study. *American Journal of Epidemiology, 146*, 994–1002.

Bruneau, J., & Schechter, M. T. (1998, April 9). The politics of needles and AIDS. *New York Times*, p. A11.

Chirinko, R. S., & Harper, E. P. (1993). Buckle up or slow down? New estimates of offsetting behavior and their implications for automobile safety regulation. *Journal of Policy Analysis and Management, 12*, 270–296.

Christie, R. (1991). Authoritarianism and related constructs. In J. P. Robinson, P. R. Shaver, & L. S. Wrightsman (Eds.), *Measures of personality and social psychological attitudes* (pp. 501–571). New York: Academic Press.

Des Jarlais, D. C., Friedman, S. R., & Ward, T. P. (1993). Harm reduction: A public health response to the AIDS epidemic among injecting drug users. *Annual Review of Public Health, 14*, 413–450.

Douglas, M. (1966). *Purity and danger: An analysis of concepts of pollution and taboo.* London: Routledge.

Ellsworth, P.C., & Gross, S.R. (1994). Hardening of the attitudes: Americans' views on the death penalty. *Journal of Social Issues, 50*, 19–52.

Erickson, P. G. (1989). Living with prohibition: Regular cannabis users, legal sanctions, and informal controls. *International Journal of the Addictions, 24*, 175–188.

Everingham, S. S., & Rydell, C. P. (1994). *Modelling the demand for cocaine.* Santa Monica, CA: RAND.

General Accounting Office. (1993). *Needle exchange programs: Research suggests promise as an AIDS prevention strategy* (GAO/HRD-93-60). Washington, DC: U.S. General Accounting Office.

Gieringer D. (1996). Marijuana research: Waterpipe study. *Multidisciplinary Association for Psychedelic Studies, 6*, 59–63.

Grob, P. J. (1992). The Needle Park in Zurich: The story and the lessons to be learned. *European Journal on Criminal Policy and Research, 1*, 48–60.

Haidt, J., Koller, S. H., & Dias, M. G. (1993). Affect, culture, and morality, or is it wrong to eat your dog? *Journal of Personality and Social Psychology, 65*, 613–628.

Harris, J. F., & Goldstein, A. (1998, April 23). Puncturing an AIDS initiative. *Washington Post*, p. A01.

Harris, R. J., & Monaco, G. E. (1978). Psychology of pragmatic implication: Information processing between the lines. *Journal of Experimental Psychology: General 107*, 1–22.

Heather, N., Wodak, A., Nadelmann, E., & O'Hare, P. (Eds.). (1993). *Psychoactive drugs and harm reduction: From faith to science.* London: Whurr.

Hemenway, D. (1988). *Prices and choices: Microeconomic vignettes* (2nd ed.). Cambridge, MA: Bellinger.

The Henry J. Kaiser Family Foundation. (1996, March). *The Kaiser survey on Americans and AIDS/HIV.* Menlo Park, CA: Author.

Hughes, J. R. (1995). Applying harm reduction to smoking. *Tobacco Control, 4*, S33–S38.

Hurley, S. E, Jolley, D. J., & Kaldor, J. M. (1997). Effectiveness of needle-exchange programmes for prevention of HIV infection. *The Lancet, 349,* 1797–1800.

Kirp, D. L., & Bayer, R. (1993). The politics. In J. Stryker & M. D. Smith (Eds.), *Dimensions of HIV prevention: Needle exchange* (pp. 77–98). Menlo Park, CA: The Henry J. Kaiser Foundation.

Lord, C. G., Ross, L., & Lepper, M. R. (1979). Biased assimilation and attitude polarization: The effects of prior theories on subsequently considered evidence. *Journal of Personality and Social Psychology, 37,* 2098–2109.

Lurie, P., & Drucker, E. (1997). An opportunity lost: HIV infections associated with lack of a national needle-exchange programme in the USA. *The Lancet, 349,* 604–608.

Lurie, P., & Reingold, A. L. (Eds.). (1993). *The public health impact of needle exchange programs in the United States and abroad.* Berkeley, CA: School of Public Health, University of California, Berkeley and San Francisco; Institute for Health Policy Studies, University of California San Francisco.

MacCoun, R. J. (1993). Drugs and the law: A psychological analysis of drug prohibition. *Psychological Bulletin, 113,* 497–512.

MacCoun, R. (1998). Biases in the interpretation and use of research results. *Annual Review of Psychology, 49,* 259–287.

MacCoun, R. J., & Caulkins, J. (1996). Examining the behavioral assumptions of the national drug control strategy. In W. K. Bickel & R. J. DeGrandpre (Eds.), *Drug policy and human nature: Psychological perspectives on the prevention, management, and treatment of illicit drug use* (pp. 177–197). New York: Plenum Press.

MacCoun, R. J., Kahan, J., Gillespie, J., & Rhee, J. (1993). A content analysis of the drug legalization debate. *Journal of Drug Issues, 23,* 615–629.

MacCoun, R., & Reuter, P. (1997, October 3). Interpreting Dutch cannabis policy: Reasoning by analogy in the legalization debate. *Science, 278,* 47–52.

MacCoun, R. J., Reuter, P., & Schelling, T. (1996). Assessing alternative drug control regimes. *Journal of Policy Analysis and Management, 15,* 330–352.

MacCoun, R., Saiger, A., Kahan, J., & Reuter, P. (1993). Drug policies and problems: The promise and pitfalls of cross-national comparisons. In N. Heather, A. Wodak,

E. Nadelmann, & P. O'Hare (Eds.), *Psychoactive drugs and harm reduction: From faith to science* (pp. 103–117). London: Whurr.

Marlatt, G. A., Larimer, M.E., Baer, J. S., & Quigley, L.A. (1993). Harm reduction for alcohol problems: Moving beyond the controlled drinking controversy. *Behavior Therapy, 24*, 461–504.

Mauldon, J., & Luker, K. (1996, Winter). Does liberalism cause sex? *The American Prospect, 24*, 80–85.

McCaffrey, B. (1998, July 27). Legalization would be the wrong direction. *Los Angeles Times*.

Miller, S. M. (1980). Why having control reduces stress: If I can stop the roller coaster I don't want to get off. In J. Garber & M. E. P. Seligman (Eds.), *Human helplessness: Theory and applications* (pp. 71–95). New York: Academic Press.

Nadelmann, E. (1989, December 1). Drug prohibition in the United States: Costs, consequences, and alternatives. *Science, 245*, 939–947.

Peterson, B. E., Doty, R. M., & Winter, D. G. (1993). Authoritarianism and attitudes toward contemporary social issues. *Personality and Social Psychology Bulletin, 19*, 174–184.

Reuter, P., & MacCoun, R. (1995). Drawing lessons from the absence of harm reduction in American drug policy. *Tobacco Control, 4*, S28–S32.

Rose, G. (1992). *The strategy of preventive medicine*. Oxford, England: Oxford University Press.

Skitka, L. J., & Tetlock, P.E. (1993). Of ants and grasshoppers: The political psychology of allocating public assistance. In B. Mellers & J. Baron (Eds.), *Psychological perspectives on justice* (pp. 205–233). Cambridge, England: Cambridge University Press.

Skog, O. J. (1993). The tail of the alcohol consumption distribution. *Addiction, 88*, 601–610.

Stetzer, A., & Hofman, D. A. (1996). Risk compensation: Implications for safety interventions. *Organizational Behavior and Human Decision Processes, 66*, 73–88.

Strathdee, S. A., Patrick, D. M., Currie, S. L., Cornelisse, P. G. A., Rekart, M. L., Montaner, J. S. G., Schechter, M. T., & O'Shaughnessy, M. V. (1997). Needle exchange is not enough: Lessons from the Vancouver injecting drug use study. *AIDS, 11*, F59–F65.

Tetlock, P.E., Peterson, R., & Lerner, J. (1996). Revising the value pluralism model: Incorporating social content and context postulates. In C. Seligman, J. Olson, & M. Zanna (Eds.), *The psychology of values: The Ontario symposium* (pp. 25–51). Mahwah, NJ: Erlbaum.

Tonry, M. H. (1995). *Malign neglect: Race, crime, and punishment in America*. New York: Oxford University Press.

Watters, J. K., Estilo, M. J., Clark, G. L., & Lorvick, J. (1994). Syringe and needle exchange as HIV/AIDS prevention for injection drug users. *Journal of the American Medical Association, 271*, 115–120.

Weiner, B., Perry, R. B., & Magnusson, J. (1988). An attributional analysis of reactions to stigma. *Journal of Personality and Social Psychology, 55*, 738–748.

Weinstein, N. D., & Klein, W. M. (1995). Resistance of personal risk perceptions to debiasing interventions. *Health Psychology, 14*, 132–140.

Wilde, G. (1982). The theory of risk homeostasis: Implications for safety and health. *Risk Analysis, 2*, 209–225.

Wyer, R. S., & Gruenfeld, D. H. (1995). Information processing in interpersonal communication. In D. E. Hewes (Ed.), *The cognitive bases of interpersonal communication* (pp. 7–47). Hillsdale, NJ: Erlbaum.

7

ADOLESCENT SUBSTANCE USE OUTCOMES IN THE RAISING HEALTHY CHILDREN PROJECT: A TWO-PART LATENT GROWTH CURVE ANALYSIS

ERIC C. BROWN, RICHARD F. CATALANO, CHARLES B. FLEMING,
KEVIN P. HAGGERTY, AND ROBERT D. ABBOTT

Public health research suggests that reducing risks and enhancing promotive and protective factors are promising strategies for the prevention of substance abuse and other related problems (Coie et al., 1993; Mrazek & Haggerty, 1994; Stouthamer-Loeber, Loeber, Wei, Farrington, & Wikstroem, 2002). Risk factors are conditions in the individual or environment that predict greater likelihood of developing a problem such as substance abuse. Research has shown that multiple risk factors in the individual, family, and environment predict early adolescent substance use, which is itself a strong predictor of later substance abuse (Hawkins et al., 1997; Pedersen & Skrondal, 1998). Examples of risk factors for early substance use include the following: (a) being a male adolescent (Hops, Davis, & Lewin, 1999), (b) antisocial behavior (Ellickson, Tucker, Klein, & McGuigan, 2001), (c) low commitment to school (Williams, Ayers, Abbott, Hawkins, & Catalano, 1999), and

Work on this chapter was supported by National Institute on Drug Abuse Grant R01-DA08093. We gratefully acknowledge the assistance provided by Bengt Muthén and helpful comments by C. Hendricks Brown and members of the Prevention Science Methodology Group (Designs and Analyses for Mental Health Preventive Trials, R01-MH40859). Additionally, we thank the staff, families, and students of the participating schools in Edmonds School District 15 for their support and cooperation.

(d) associating with peers who use substances (Griffin, Botvin, Scheier, & Nichols, 2002; for a review of additional risk factors, see Hawkins, Catalano, & Miller, 1992).

In addition to risk factors, researchers have identified promotive factors that counterbalance the effects of risk as well as protective factors that moderate the effects of risk (for the remainder of this chapter, we include promotive factors as part of the term *protective factors*). Examples of protective factors include the following: (a) affiliation with prosocial peers (Spoth, Redmond, Hockaday, & Yoo, 1996), (b) parental supervision and support (Marshal & Chassin, 2000), and (c) psychosocial composite indices of protection (Jessor, Van Den Bos, Vanderryn, Costa, & Turbin, 1995). Many risk and protective factors for early substance use also are factors for other problem behaviors, including delinquency, school dropout, and teen pregnancy (Howell, Krisberg, Hawkins, & Wilson, 1995).

Only a few adolescent interventions that address multiple risk and protective factors at appropriate developmental periods have been tested. Most interventions have been brief (e.g., Kellam, Rebok, Ialongo, & Mayer, 1994; Spoth, Redmond, & Shin, 2001), have addressed a narrow range of risk and protective factors (e.g., Botvin & Griffin, 2002; Eddy, Reid, & Fetrow, 2000), or have focused on a single social domain (e.g., Ellickson, Bell, & Harrison, 1993). Two projects, the Fast Track project (Conduct Problems Prevention Research Group, 1992) and the Seattle Social Development Project (SSDP; Hawkins, Catalano, Kosterman, Abbott, & Hill, 1999) addressed a broad range of developmentally salient risk and protective factors in school, family, peer, and individual domains. These interventions targeted risk and protective factors in early childhood to prevent initiation and escalation of problem behaviors in adolescence. To date, these *social development* interventions have demonstrated positive effects in reducing substance use, violent behavior, conduct problems, and risky sexual behavior, as well as improving academic performance, commitment to school, and social–cognitive skills (Catalano et al., 2003; Conduct Problems Prevention Research Group, 2002; Lonczak, Abbott, Hawkins, Kosterman, & Catalano, 2002).

In this study, we examined the efficacy of the Raising Healthy Children (RHC) project. Modeled after SSDP, RHC is a comprehensive, multicomponent preventive intervention designed to promote positive youth development by targeting developmentally appropriate risk and protective factors. However, unlike SSDP, the intervention extends beyond the elementary-school period to include universal and selective components in middle and high school years. As a theory-based intervention, RHC is guided by the social development model (SDM; Catalano & Hawkins, 1996; Hawkins & Weis, 1985), which integrates empirically supported aspects of social control (Hirschi, 1969), social learning (Bandura, 1973), and differential association theories (Matsueda, 1988) into a framework for strengthening prosocial bonds and beliefs. Within this framework, the SDM emphasizes that prevention should (a) begin before the formation of antisocial beliefs and behaviors; (b) recognize the importance of individual and family characteristics as well as larger social contexts of community, school, and peer influences; and (c) identify and address the changing needs of its target population with regard to risk and protective factors that change in influence during the course of development. Specifically, the SDM organizes risk and protective factors into a causal model that explicates the mechanisms leading toward antisocial behavior. These mechanisms are specified as a sequence of mediated effects influenced by both prosocial and antisocial processes.

Following the SDM, four distinct points of intervention were targeted by RHC: (a) opportunities for involvement with prosocial others (e.g., family, teachers, and peers who did not use substances); (b) students' academic, cognitive, and social skills; (c) positive reinforcements and rewards for prosocial involvement; and (d) healthy beliefs and clear standards regarding substance use avoidance. According to theory underlying the intervention, increased opportunities for prosocial involvement, coupled with both positive reinforcements for that involvement and better skills on the part of the student, are theorized to lead to stronger bonds to prosocial others. After strong bonds are established, individuals will tend to behave in a manner consistent with the norms and values of the individuals and groups with whom they associate. In turn, stronger prosocial bonds support positive belief formation against antisocial behaviors (e.g., adolescent substance use).

As the primary domains of social influence during elementary school years are theorized within the SDM to be the family and school, RHC intervention components during this period focused on these domains. Evaluation of early intervention effects found that teachers reported less disruptive and aggressive behavior and stronger effort on schoolwork for intervention students compared with controls (Catalano et al., 2003). As students approach adolescence, peer influences become more important and bonds to family and school may become strained (Hawkins, Guo, Hill, Battin-Pearson, & Abbott, 2001). Preventive interventions that target norms and teach skills for resisting negative social influences during this period have been shown to be effective in reducing substance use (e.g., Griffin et al., 2002; Hansen & Graham, 1991). Thus, the constellation of intervention components within RHC gradually shifted from early risk and protective factors in the social domains of school and family (e.g., academic performance, bonding, and parental monitoring) toward individual- and peer-related risk and protective factors (e.g., refusal skills, healthy beliefs, and associations with peers who use substances).

A social development perspective to intervention also suggests that the goals of the intervention need to be flexible as well. Whereas preventive interventions for early adolescent substance use often center around abstinence themes, after adolescents begin to use substances, messages related to the prevention of escalating or problematic substance use become increasingly important. Furthermore, recent data have shown that some degree of experimentation with substances is normative (e.g., Johnston, O'Malley, & Bachman, 2003). Noting this, an increasing number of researchers have suggested that a concomitant goal of prevention should be the reduction in the amount of use (quantity or frequency) among users (e.g., Maggs & Schulenberg, 1998; McBride, Midford, Farringdon, & Phillips, 2000). As the prevalence of substance use increases typically during adolescence, a corresponding increase in the frequency of use is likely. Thus, social development approaches to the prevention of substance use address risk and protective factors not only for initial and experimental use but for heavy or problematic use as well.

The purpose of this study was to test the efficacy of the RHC intervention on rates of substance use during early-to-middle adolescence. As a social development intervention, RHC was designed to be flexible in addressing both the developmental needs and the particular goals of its target population of students and their families. Whereas a primary aim of RHC was to deter students from using illicit substances in earlier developmental periods, increasing emphasis also was placed on avoiding escalation of use. In light of this, this study addressed two related questions: First, has the intervention been efficacious in reducing students' likelihood to use alcohol, marijuana, or cigarettes? Second, has the intervention been efficacious in altering the frequency at which students use alcohol, marijuana, or cigarettes?

METHOD

Participants

Participants consisted of a longitudinal panel of first- and second-grade students originally enrolled in 1 of 10 public elementary schools in a suburban school district north of Seattle, Washington (substance use outcomes were assessed when these students were in Grades 6 to 10). The school district consisted of five different municipalities and surrounding areas with fairly high standards of living and others that were primarily working class; in addition, the school district ranked as the third largest in Washington. Of the 25 elementary schools in the district, the 10 schools that ranked the highest on aggregate measures of risk (e.g., low income status, low standardized achievement test scores, high absenteeism, high mobility) were selected into the study. Schools were matched on these risk factors, and one school from each matched pair was assigned randomly to either an intervention ($n = 5$) or control ($n = 5$) condition. Families of first- and second-grade students from within these schools were recruited into the longitudinal study. To be included in the RHC sample, students had to remain in their school throughout the entire 1st year of their participation in the study and have a parent who spoke English, Spanish, Korean, or Vietnamese.

In Year 1, 938 parents of 1,239 eligible students provided written consent to participate in the study. In Year 2, the sample was augmented with an additional 102 students from a second eligible pool of 131 students who newly entered 1 of the 10 schools during second grade, thus yielding a total sample of 1,040 students. For the analysis sample, 77 students were excluded because they were missing data for all substance use outcome measures during Grades 6 to 10. Inspection of casewise patterns of self-reported substance use indicated questionable validity for an additional 4 students who reported maximal levels of substance use for almost all types of substances during all measurement occasions, which prompted their exclusion from the analysis. Because of the small percentage (5%) of siblings in the sample, siblings were not excluded from the analysis. These criteria resulted in a final sample of 959 students (92% of the total sample) for analysis. Of the analysis sample, 54% were male students and 46% were female students; 82% were European American, 7% were Asian/ Pacific Islander, 4% were African American, 4% were Hispanic, and 3% were Native American. Mean age of students at the beginning of the study was 7.7 years ($SD = 0.6$), selected from both first- (52%) and second-grade (48%) classrooms. Of the sample, 28% were from low-income households, defined as having received Aid to Families with Dependent Children, Temporary Assistance for Needy Families, food stamps, or free/reduced lunch programs during the first 2 years of the project.

Intervention Implementation, Fidelity, and Exposure

RHC consisted of prevention strategies that addressed risk and protective factors in four key domains (for details, see Catalano et al., 2003; Haggerty, Catalano, Harachi, & Abbott, 1998). *School intervention strategies* consisted of a series of teacher and staff development workshops that included proactive classroom management techniques; cooperative learning methods; and strategies to promote student motivation, participation, reading, and interpersonal and problem-solving skills. Workshops were conducted with teachers in intervention schools while students were in elementary grades and in the 1st year of middle school. Additionally, one-on-one classroom-based coaching sessions with teachers were conducted monthly throughout the school year to monitor and enhance fidelity of school intervention strategies. After the 1st year of the project, teachers participated in monthly booster sessions to further reinforce RHC school intervention strategies. Teachers also were provided with a substitute teacher for a half day so that they could observe other project teachers using RHC teaching strategies in their classrooms. School intervention strategies were designed to enhance students' learning, interpersonal, and problem-solving skills, as well as increase their academic performance and bonding to school.

Individual *student intervention strategies* consisted of volunteer student participation in after school tutoring sessions and study clubs during Grades 4 to 6 and individualized booster sessions and group-based workshops during middle and high school years. These strategies were designed to (a) improve academic achievement, (b) increase students' bonding to school, (c) teach refusal skills, and (d) develop prosocial beliefs regarding healthy behaviors. Additionally, through classroom instruction and annual summer camps during elementary school, and social skills booster retreats in middle school, RHC provided universal *peer intervention strategies* for students to learn and practice social, emotional, and problem-solving skills in the classroom and in other social situations.

Family intervention strategies consisted of multiple-session parenting workshops (e.g., "Raising Healthy Children," "How to Help Your Child Succeed in School," and "Preparing for the Drug Free Years") and in-home services for selected families. Family intervention strategies were delivered to families in group and individual sessions during Grades 1 to 8. Parents of intervention students were invited and encouraged to attend the schoolwide workshops offered at the school. During high school, booster sessions were delivered through in-home visits in which both parents and students completed assessments that covered specific developmental risk areas (e.g., transition to high school, peer influences, family expectations, family conflict). These sessions were individualized to target the specific skills identified through the assessment process. Families who had moved outside the local geographic area had all intervention materials mailed to them with assessments completed through phone consultation. Family intervention strategies were designed to (a) enhance parents' skills in child rearing and educational support, (b) decrease family management problems and conflict, (c) identify and clarify family standards and rules regarding student behaviors (e.g., substance use, dating, and sex), and (d) practice peer resistance skills. All individualized intervention strategies included specified protocols for both assessment and intervention goals. Through the combined use of school, student, peer, and family intervention strategies, RHC sought to reduce risk factors of poor family management, family conflict, early antisocial behavior, academic failure, low commitment to school, associations with peers who use substances, and favorable attitudes toward drug use. RHC also sought to enhance protective factors of bonding to family and school, set healthy beliefs and expectations, and teach social and emotional skills. Whereas all four intervention strategies were designed to deter substance use in earlier developmental periods, family and student booster sessions in middle and high school additionally targeted problematic use in later adolescence.

Implementation of the intervention was coordinated by RHC-employed school–home coordinators (SHCs) who were former elementary school teachers or education specialists with experience in providing services to parents and families. The SHCs were responsible for all aspects of coordinating and implementing the intervention—including hiring, supporting, and training teachers and parents to administer school and family intervention strategies—coordinating parent and student workshops, soliciting feedback from students and parents for intervention refinement, and conducting periodic one-on-one follow-up visits with intervention students and their families. SHCs met weekly with the project director to review progress with individual cases. All intervention curricula were manualized with intervention training sessions monitored by the project director to ensure fidelity to curricula materials.

The RHC study design called for teachers in Grades 1 to 7 to receive at least six staff development workshop sessions and to begin the workshops during the year prior to receiving the students in the study. Workshops were delivered by a staff development coordinator who was an experienced educational trainer with a doctoral-level degree in curriculum and instruction. Each year, teachers were observed repeatedly in the classroom (three times in the fall and three times in the spring) by independent raters to ensure fidelity to school intervention strategies. Over 94% ($n = 140$) of eligible teachers and staff in intervention schools attended development workshops, with a mean attendance of 5.7 sessions ($SD = 3.1$, range = 0–15). While intervention students were in elementary school, more than 1,700 classroom coaching visits were made, which resulted in more than 684 reinforcement notes to teachers; 41 videotapes; 1,225 conferences with teachers; and 210 modeling sessions.

The number of intervention contacts (lasting 30 minutes or more for students, or 60 minutes or more for families) received by students and families were recorded to monitor intervention exposure. For student and peer intervention strategies, 27% of intervention students attended at least one study club (offered twice a week during Grades 4 to 6), 40% attended at least one of the middle school retreats or workshops (out of five that were offered during Grades 7 to 8), and 51% attended at least one summer camp (out of the four that were offered during Grades 2 to 5). Typically, three family intervention workshop series were offered per year. Over half (51%) of the intervention students' families voluntarily attended at least one group workshop; 35% received individual contacts that included home-based services; and 77% received at least one middle or high school period booster workshop. All intervention students and their families received at least one intervention component with overall means of 28.3 contacts ($SD = 44.5$) received by students and 12.6 contacts ($SD = 12.3$) received by their families.

Procedure

Student data collection in Years 6 to 8 (i.e., Grades 6 to 9) consisted of both group and one-on-one survey administration in students' schools during regular school hours. Trained interviewers read aloud survey questions to students who were instructed to confidentially record their responses on a response sheet and return it to the interviewer at the end of the interview. Students who were not at school at time of data collection (e.g., who were absent, were home schooled, or had dropped out of school) were contacted at home and individually administered an in-person, telephone, or mail-in survey. In Year 9 (i.e., Grades 9 and 10), a one-on-one, computer-assisted personal interviewing mode of data collection was used in which interviewers read survey questions aloud to students and recorded their verbal responses directly into a data-collection program on a laptop computer. Retention rates for student surveys during project Years 6 to 10 were all greater than 88%. To maintain confidentiality, students' parents, teachers, and other school personnel were not present and did not participate in any student data-collection activities. All students were informed that their responses would not be shared with their parents or other school personnel. A small yearly gift (e.g., disposable camera, clock radio) or monetary compensation (e.g., $10 gift certificate) was given to students for their participation in each wave of the study.

Measures

Substance Use Outcomes

Annual substance use measures were constructed from student self-reports of frequency of alcohol, marijuana, and cigarette use during both previous year and previous month time periods. Consistent with previous adolescent alcohol use research (e.g., Bryant, Schulenberg, O'Malley, Bachman, & Johnston, 2003), a 6-point scale ranging from 0 (*no use in the previous year*) to 5 (*20 or more times within the past month*) was created for alcohol and marijuana use. For cigarette use, a similar 6-point scale was created ranging from 0 (*no use in previous year*) to 5 (*more than 40 cigarettes per day*).

Intervention Status and Background Variables

We assigned intervention status as an intent-to-treat analysis using students' original school assignment; that is, students from the five program schools were coded 1 and students from the five control schools were coded 0. Background variables consisted of the following: students' grade-cohort status (coded 0 for students from the first-grade cohort with substance use data from Grades 6 to 9 and 1 for students from the second-grade cohort with data from Grades 7 to 10) and gender (coded 0 for female students and 1 for male students). Although it was not possible to test for equivalency in preintervention rates of substance use (i.e., the intervention began before initiation of substance use for both intervention and control groups), it was possible for the groups to be different in their latent propensity to use substances. Therefore, two additional measures theorized to be related to adolescent substance use were included as covariates. First, a measure of classroom antisocial behavior was constructed that consisted of the average of 10 items taken from either (a) the Teacher Report Form/4–18 (Achenbach, 1991) Aggressive Syndrome Behavior Scale or (b) the Teacher Observation of Classroom Adaptation—Revised (Werthamer-Larsson, Kellam, & Wheeler, 1991), completed by teachers at baseline (i.e., students' 1st year of entry into the study). Response options for the items consisted of a 3-point scale ranging from 1 (*rarely or never true*) to 3 (*often true*). Alpha reliability coefficient for the Year 1 antisocial behavior measure scale was .91 ($M = 1.24$, $SD = 0.38$). Second, a baseline measure of low income status was constructed to identify families that received Aid to Families with Dependent Children, Temporary Assistance for Needy Families, food stamps, or free-lunch school programs (coded 1 for receipt of service and 0 otherwise). Intervention status and all background variables were mean centered for analysis.

Data Analysis

Two-Part Latent Growth Model

To address the research questions posed in this study, we used a two-part latent growth model (LGM) strategy (B. Muthén, 2001; Olsen & Schafer, 2001). As a longitudinal adaptation to two-part (or two-equation) multiple regression models (e.g., Ellickson et al., 2001; Manning, 1997), this strategy decomposed the original distribution of substance use outcomes into two parts, each modeled by separate, but correlated, growth functions (see Figure 7.1). In Part 1 of the model, nonuse was separated from the rest of the distribution by creation of binary indicator variables that distinguished any positive level of use within the previous year (coded 1) from nonuse (coded 0). Use-versus-nonuse outcome variables for each substance were analyzed as a random-effects logistic growth model with the log odds of use regressed on growth factors. Intervention status and background variables were included as covariates for examination of interindividual differences in growth trajectories. Detailed specifications for this part of the model are described in the following studies: B. Muthén (2001) and B. Muthén and Asparouhov (2002).

Part 2 of the model consisted of continuous indicator variables that represented the frequency of substance use, given that some use had taken place. Here, each frequency-of-use outcome was modeled as an LGM with growth factors of nonzero substance use regressed on intervention status and

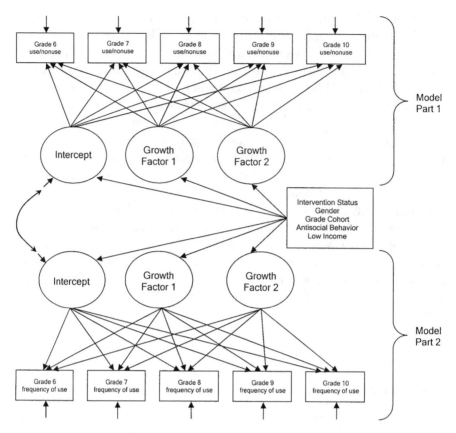

Figure 7.1. Path diagram for two-part latent growth model. Top portion of diagram depicts Part 1 of the model (i.e., substance use vs. nonuse); bottom portion depicts Part 2 of the model (i.e., frequency of substance use). Growth Factors 1 and 2 correspond to piecewise or linear and quadratic growth factors (correlations between growth factors within each model part are omitted for clarity).

background variables following traditional latent growth modeling techniques for normally distributed substance use measures (e.g., Curran, 2000; Duncan & Duncan, 1996; Taylor, Graham, Cumsille, & Hansen, 2000). However, in this part of the model, substance nonuse within each time period was treated as missing data for frequency of use, following standard assumptions of data missing at random (MAR; Little & Rubin, 1987). Thus, students who reported nonuse of a particular substance throughout the study contributed little information to growth parameter estimates (i.e., means, variances, and covariances) of frequency-of-use trajectories; however, any and all information related to positive substance use was incorporated in the derivation of growth parameters.

The procedure for constructing the two-part LGMs consisted of first identifying the unconditional (i.e., without intervention status or background variables) functional form of each part of the model separately. Change in use-versus-nonuse and frequency-of-use outcomes was modeled as linear, quadratic, or piecewise growth. Loadings for linear and quadratic growth factors were specified as orthogonal polynomial contrasts, with intercepts centered at the middle of the time points (Raudenbush & Xiao-Feng, 2001). Loadings for piecewise growth functions were specified as segmented linear growth functions (Raudenbush & Bryk, 2002), again with intercepts centered at the midpoint. These different parameterizations were selected to model change in substance use (a) as a constant process (i.e., using linear growth), (b) with gradual acceleration or deceleration in use (i.e., using quadratic growth), or (c) as a discontinuous process (i.e., using piecewise growth) typically characterized by a transitional event, for example, entry into high school. An additional rationale for examining segmented piecewise growth was to account for potentially differential impact of covariates on growth between middle and high school periods (Li, Duncan, & Hops, 2001). As model Parts 1 and 2 were free to follow different functional forms, it also was possible for intervention status and background variables to have differential effects on growth factors between each model part. To represent the potential conditionality of the frequency-of-use outcome on the initial decision whether to engage in substance use, we allowed growth factors between model Parts 1 and 2 to be correlated. We analyzed all models using Mplus 3.0 (L. K. Muthén & Muthén, 2004), which provided maximum-likelihood parameter estimates with robust standard errors under MAR via numerical integration.[1]

We assessed model fit for each part of the two-part LGMs using chi-square difference tests based on model log-likelihood values and by plotting observed rates against model-predicted values and visually inspecting for misfit. Additionally, standardized residuals (i.e., observed minus model-predicted values) were plotted for each time point and assessed for potential outliers. For frequency-of-use outcomes, we also assessed model fit using the comparative fit index (CFI; Bentler, 1990), Tucker–Lewis fit index (TLI; Tucker & Lewis, 1973), and root-mean-square error of approximation (RMSEA; Browne & Cudeck, 1993; Steiger & Lind, 1980). These indices were not available to evaluate fit in Part 1 of the models.

We conducted analysis of intervention effects and background variables in conditional models using two-tailed tests of significance, with $p < .05$ as the criterion for statistical significance. All analyses were conducted at the individual (i.e., student) level, with standard errors for intervention effects adjusted by outcome-specific design effects (Dielman, 1994) to account for potential clustering of students from their original school assignments.

---

[1] Mplus scripts used in the analyses can be obtained from the Mplus Web site (http://www.statmodel.com).

Missing Data

To determine whether there was differential attrition among students excluded from the analysis because of missing outcome data ($n = 81$), we examined proportions of missingness for intervention status and background variables. Results indicated no significant difference in the proportion of students with missing outcome data for intervention versus control groups, first- versus second-grade cohorts, low income status, or level of student antisocial behavior. However, a significantly greater proportion of female students had missing outcome data (9.8%) than male students (6.0%), $\chi^2(1, N = 1,040) = 5.03$, $p < .05$; therefore, a follow-up logistic regression was conducted to examine the difference in proportions of missingness between intervention and control groups by gender. Results indicated no significant Intervention Status × Gender interaction, Wald's $\chi^2(1, N = 1,040) = 1.05$, $p < .05$. Given these results and the small degree of missing outcome data, we relied on full information maximum likelihood estimation under the assumption of data MAR.

RESULTS

Prevalence and Frequency of Substance Use

Prevalence rates for alcohol, marijuana, and cigarette use for the measured time periods are presented in Table 7.1. For marijuana and cigarette use, extremely low prevalence rates in Grade 6 precluded the use of this time point in the analysis and are not shown in the table. Prevalence rates for all three substances increased generally during Grades 6 to 10. For example, 29% of all students in Grade 6 had used alcohol at least once in the previous 12 months. By Grade 10, the percentage of students who had tried alcohol in the previous 12 months had increased to 51%. The percentage of students who used marijuana increased from 8% in Grade 7 to 31% in Grade 10. Additionally, prevalence of cigarette use doubled from 9% in Grade 7 to 18% in Grade 10. Rates of substance use in the RHC sample during Grade 10 were similar to population-based rates for students in the state of Washington (Washington State Department of Health, 2003).

As shown in Table 7.1, apparent differences in rates of alcohol and marijuana use between male and female students are notable. Female students engaged in lower rates of sixth-grade alcohol and seventh-grade marijuana use (24% and 5%, respectively) than male students (34% and 11%, respectively). However, by ninth grade, rates of alcohol and marijuana use by female students (50% and 27%, respectively) had reached or surpassed rates of use by male students (44% and 27%, respectively). For those students having positive use within a grade (independent of use in other grades), descriptive statistics for frequency of alcohol, marijuana, and cigarette use are presented

TABLE 7.1
Annual Substance Use Prevalence Rates by Intervention Status
and Gender

Grade	Intervention	Controls	Female students	Male students	Total sample
		Alcohol			
6[a]	.29	.30	.24	.34	.29
7	.33	.29	.29	.33	.31
8	.37	.40	.43	.34	.38
9	.46	.48	.50	.44	.47
10[b]	.52	.50	.52	.50	.51
		Marijuana			
7	.08	.09	.05	.11	.08
8	.16	.18	.16	.18	.17
9	.25	.28	.27	.27	.27
10[b]	.30	.31	.27	.33	.31
		Cigarettes			
7	.09	.08	.10	.08	.09
8	.14	.13	.17	.11	.14
9	.16	.17	.18	.15	.16
10[b]	.16	.20	.20	.16	.18

Note. Prevalence rates denote the proportion of students having used each substance within the previous 12 months.
[a]Represents first-grade cohort only.   [b]Represents second-grade cohort only.

in Table 7.2. Longitudinal patterns of growth in frequency of alcohol and marijuana use were different from patterns of growth in prevalence rates for these two substances. Whereas the prevalence of alcohol and marijuana use increased each year during Grades 6 to 10, mean frequency of alcohol and marijuana use peaked at eighth grade and declined thereafter. However, mean frequency of cigarette use increased throughout Grades 7 to 10.

Two-Part Latent Growth Model of Alcohol Use

Unconditional Model

As the first step in modeling alcohol use, we examined the functional form of growth for each part of the two-part LGM separately, excluding intervention status and background variables (recall that Part 1 of the model refers to growth in substance use vs. nonuse, and Part 2 refers to the frequency of use, given that some use had taken place). Comparison of intercept-only, linear, quadratic, and piecewise growth functions for Part 2 of the alcohol use model indicated that frequency of alcohol use was best modeled as a two-segment piecewise model consisting of separate linear growth functions for

TABLE 7.2
Descriptive Statistics for Frequency of Substance Use

Grade	n	M	SD	Skewness	Kurtosis
			Alcohol		
6[a]	143	1.57	0.88	1.97	4.32
7	297	1.85	0.99	1.31	1.37
8	361	2.05	1.07	0.91	0.03
9	430	1.98	1.08	1.02	0.24
10[b]	227	1.81	1.06	1.34	1.04
			Marijuana		
7	79	2.41	1.33	0.60	−0.87
8	158	2.58	1.44	0.53	−1.10
9	245	2.29	1.31	0.72	−0.77
10[b]	136	2.21	1.39	0.77	−0.87
			Cigarettes		
7	82	1.68	0.95	1.99	3.45
8	128	2.02	1.29	1.32	1.30
9	149	2.03	1.16	1.25	1.49
10[b]	80	2.09	1.06	0.88	0.91

Note. Scale ranges from 1 (*some use within the past year*) to 5 (*20 or more times within the past month*).
[a]Represents first-grade cohort only.   [b]Represents second-grade cohort only.

Grades 6 to 8 and Grades 8 to 10, $\chi^2(8, N = 628) = 13.52$, $p < .10$, CFI = .944, TLI = .937, and RMSEA = .033.[2] In Part 1 of the model, a linear growth model demonstrated better fit to alcohol use (vs. nonuse) than an intercept-only model, $\Delta\chi^2(1, N = 959) = 89.66$, $p < .01$. Inclusion of a quadratic growth factor did not improve model fit, $\Delta\chi^2(1, N = 959) = 0.28$, $p < .05$. Because the segmented piecewise model allowed us to examine the same linear pattern of growth in the data as well as account for the possibility of differential covariate effects between middle and high school periods, we chose to model growth in this part of the model in a similar piecewise fashion.

Examination of growth factor variances and covariances indicated significant variation in intercept growth factors for both model Parts 1 and 2 (variances = 5.105 and 0.341; SEs = 0.567 and 0.060; $ps < .001$; respectively), indicating significant individual heterogeneity around mean levels of alcohol use (vs. nonuse) and frequency of use at Grade 8. Intercept growth factors between model Parts 1 and 2 also exhibited significant positive covariation ($r = .686, p < .001$), suggesting that students with lower propensities to engage in alcohol use (at Grade 8) had correspondingly less frequent use. For both model parts, minimal heterogeneity in linear growth during Grades 6 to 8

---

[2] Fit indices were based on n = 628 students with nonzero frequency of alcohol use.

resulted in nonsignificant slope variances; these variances were required to be fixed at zero for model convergence. Although variances for linear growth factors during Grades 8 to 10 also were nonsignificant (variances = 0.576 and 0.048; SEs = 0.306 and 0.041; ps > .05; for model Parts 1 and 2, respectively), these parameters were estimable and retained for subsequent analysis of intervention status and background variables. All other covariances among growth parameters, both within and between model parts, were nonsignificant and subsequently fixed at zero.

Intervention Status and Background Variables

Next, intervention status and background variables were added to both parts of the model and regressed on intercept and piecewise growth segments. Parameter coefficients (i.e., growth factor means) and standard errors for the final two-part LGM are shown in Table 7.3. Results of the alcohol use-versus-nonuse part of the model indicated a significant gender effect with female students being more likely to use alcohol at Grade 8 and having a significantly greater rate of increase in their likelihood to use alcohol during Grades 6 to 8 relative to male students. Higher baseline classroom antisocial behavior was associated with both a greater likelihood to use alcohol at

TABLE 7.3
Parameter Estimates and Standard Errors
for Alcohol Use Growth Factors and Covariates

Variable	Grade 8 status		Linear growth Grades 6–8[a]		Linear growth Grades 8–10	
	Estimate	SE	Estimate	SE	Estimate	SE
Part 1: Use versus nonuse						
Growth factor mean	0.821***	0.117	.440***	.106	.452***	.099
Intervention group	0.013	0.556	−.005	.198	.047	.190
Gender (male students)	−0.687**	0.232	−.815***	.178	.092	.171
Grade cohort (older)	0.398	0.230	.274	.215	.069	.196
Antisocial behavior	0.838**	0.312	.191	.235	.567*	.264
Low income	0.674**	0.238	.495**	.179	−.131	.180
Part 2: Frequency of use						
Growth factor mean	1.774***	0.061	.297***	.050	−.207***	.046
Intervention group	−0.031	0.412	−.029	.095	−.199*	.096
Gender (male students)	0.076	0.098	−.081	.071	−.045	.077
Grade cohort (older)	0.054	0.099	.075	.100	.242**	.093
Antisocial behavior	0.287*	0.123	.005	.078	−.056	.105
Low income	0.056	0.102	.028	.078	.072	.087

Note. Standard errors for intervention effects adjusted by corresponding design effects.
[a]Growth factor variance and associated covariances set to zero in model Parts 1 and 2.
*p < .05. **p < .01. ***p < .001.

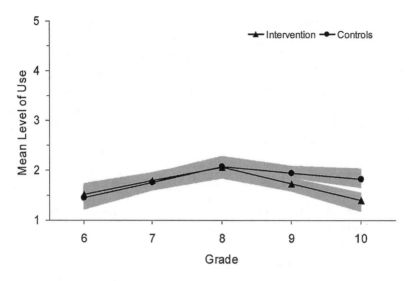

Figure 7.2. Adjusted mean trajectories for frequency of alcohol use (excluding nonuse) during Grades 6 to 10 by intervention status. Shaded regions represent 95% confidence bands for mean trajectories. Scale ranges from 1 (*some use within the past year*) to 5 (*20 or more times within the past month*).

Grade 8 and growth in the likelihood to use alcohol during Grades 8 to 10. Additionally, students from low socioeconomic status (SES) households were at greater likelihood of using alcohol at Grade 8 and had greater growth in use during Grades 6 to 8. No significant difference was found between students in the intervention group and controls for change in alcohol use versus nonuse.

Results of the frequency-of-alcohol use part of the model show a significant intervention effect, indicating a greater rate of linear decline in the frequency of alcohol use during Grades 8 to 10 for the intervention group relative to controls.[3] Model-implied mean trajectories for intervention and control groups (adjusted by covariates) are shown in Figure 7.2. Shaded regions in the figure denote 95% confidence bands around each group's mean trajectory (Curran, Bauer, & Willoughby, 2004). The standardized effect size for the difference in mean trajectories was $\delta = .91$.[4] In terms of an adjusted

---

[3] To determine whether intervention effects for frequency of alcohol use and marijuana use were caused by students in the control condition having earlier onset of use (and consequently having higher frequency of use in latter grades), we constructed a covariate that represented the grade at which students first used each respective substance. This covariate and its interaction with intervention status were included in the final conditional models as predictors of linear growth during Grades 8 to 10 (for frequency of alcohol use) and Grades 7 to 10 (for frequency of marijuana use). Results of these analyses indicated nonsignificant main effects and interaction terms ($ps > .05$) for both outcomes, suggesting that the declines in these outcomes by intervention students were not associated with the timing of initial use.
[4] Delta is defined as the group difference in a growth factor divided by the population standard deviation of that growth factor (see Raudenbush & Xiao-Feng, 2001, Equation 13).

mean difference in frequency-of-use rates at Grade 10, the corresponding effect size was $d = .40$. Additionally, a significant grade-cohort effect was present for growth in frequency of alcohol use during Grades 8 to 10, with a greater decline for the first-grade cohort than the second-grade cohort. To determine whether the intervention effect was consistent for both grade cohorts, we added an Intervention Status × Grade Cohort interaction term to the Grades 8 to 10 segment of the model. Results indicated that the interaction term had no significant effect on growth in frequency of alcohol use during this period ($\beta = -.089$, $SE = .139$, $p < .05$), indicating that grade-cohort status did not moderate the effects of the intervention on frequency of alcohol use.

Two-Part Latent Growth Model of Marijuana Use

Unconditional Model

Given the apparent nonlinear growth in marijuana use during Grades 7 to 10, a curvilinear growth model for the Part 1 use-versus-nonuse outcome that contained intercept, linear, and quadratic growth factors was compared with an intercept-and-linear-only growth model (because only four time points were available to model marijuana use, the two-segment piecewise model was not considered). Results indicated better fit for the curvilinear model than the linear model, $\Delta\chi^2(1, N = 959) = 5.40$, $p < .01$. The unconditional curvilinear model for the Part 2 frequency of marijuana use exhibited marginal negative linear growth ($\beta = -.047$, $SE = .030$, $p = .058$) and nonsignificant quadratic growth ($\beta = -.057$, $SE = .047$, $p > .05$). However, fit of the intercept-only model was poor, $\chi^2(8, N = 340) = 15.75$, $p = .046$, CFI = .718, TLI = .789, and RMSEA = .053.[5] Inclusion of a linear growth factor substantially improved model fit, $\chi^2(5, N = 340) = 8.46$, $p = .133$, CFI = .890, TLI = .890, and RMSEA = .038; therefore, the linear growth term was retained in the final unconditional model for frequency of marijuana use.

Significant variation existed in intercept growth factors (i.e., Grade 8.5 status) for both model Parts 1 and 2 (variances = 9.113 and 0.691; $SEs = 1.251$ and 0.154; $ps < .001$; respectively). Growth factor intercepts between outcomes were significantly correlated ($r = .796$, $p < .001$). In Part 1 of the model, variances for both linear and quadratic growth factors were nonsignificant and were required to be fixed at zero for model convergence. In Part 2 of the model, the variance for the linear growth factor also was nonsignificant (variance = 0.024, $SE = 0.017$, $p > .05$) but was retained as a freely estimated parameter for analysis of intervention status and background variables. All

---

[5]Fit indices were based on $n = 340$ students with nonzero frequency of marijuana use.

other covariances among growth parameters, both within and between model parts, were nonsignificant and subsequently fixed at zero.

Intervention Status and Background Variables

Results of the final two-part growth latent model for marijuana use, including intervention status and background variables, are shown in Table 7.4. Significant gender, grade cohort, baseline antisocial behavior, and income effects were found for the intercept growth factor in Part 1 of the model, indicating that female students, second-grade-cohort students, students with high baseline antisocial behavior, and students from low SES households had significantly higher rates of marijuana use (vs. nonuse) at Grade 8.5 than their respective counterparts. Additionally, female students demonstrated a significantly greater increase in marijuana use during Grades 7 to 10 than male students, with female students reaching male students' prevalence of marijuana use by ninth grade and declining thereafter. No significant differences were found in marijuana use growth rates between intervention students and controls. However, for frequency of marijuana use, results indicated a significant intervention effect, with students in the intervention group exhibiting greater linear decline in the

TABLE 7.4
Parameter Estimates and Standard Errors for Marijuana
Use Growth Factors and Covariates

Variable	Grade 8.5 status		Linear growth		Quadratic growth[a]	
	Estimate	*SE*	Estimate	*SE*	Estimate	*SE*
Part 1: Use versus nonuse						
Growth factor mean	3.233***	0.212	.475***	.065	−.463***	.112
Intervention group	−0.178	0.498	.055	.104	−.008	.143
Gender (male students)	−0.388	0.274	−.170*	.088	.514***	.146
Grade cohort (older)	0.888**	0.311	.071	.120	.175	.217
Antisocial behavior	1.306***	0.351	.203	.106	−.133	.214
Low income	0.878*	0.283	.030	.083	−.138	.149
Part 2: Frequency of use						
Growth factor mean	1.511***	0.139	−.005	.037	—	—
Intervention group	0.103	0.132	−.223***	.052	—	—
Gender (male students)	−0.100	0.128	.088	.053	—	—
Grade cohort (older)	0.160	0.134	.001	.068	—	—
Antisocial behavior	0.221	0.148	.003	.082	—	—
Low income	0.006	0.121	.005	.053	—	—

Note. Standard errors for intervention effects adjusted by corresponding design effects. Dashes indicate that values were not applicable because quadratic growth factor was not included in Part 2 model.
[a]Quadratic growth factor variance and associated covariances in model Part 1 set to zero.
*$p < .05$. **$p < .01$. ***$p < .001$.

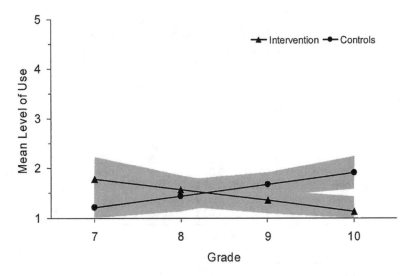

Figure 7.3. Adjusted mean trajectories for frequency of marijuana use (excluding nonuse) during Grades 7 to 10 by intervention status. Shaded regions represent 95% confidence bands for mean trajectories. Scale ranges from 1 (*some use within the past year*) to 5 (*20 or more times within the past month*).

frequency of marijuana use than students in the control group (see Figure 7.3). Intervention effect sizes were $\delta = 1.44$ for the standardized difference in mean trajectories and $d = .57$ for the adjusted mean difference in frequency-of-use rates at Grade 10.

Two-Part Latent Growth Model of Cigarette Use

Unconditional Model

For the unconditional cigarette use-versus-nonuse outcome, results of the unconditional model indicated better fit with intercept, linear, and quadratic growth factors than the intercept-and-linear-only model, $\Delta\chi^2(1, N = 959) = 6.31, p < .01$. For the frequency-of-use outcome, a quadratic growth model similarly provided optimal fit to the data, $\chi^2(1, N = 239) = 6.93, p = .33$, CFI = .953, TLI = .953, and RMSEA = .026.[6] Among all growth factors in both Parts 1 and 2 of the model, significant variation existed only for intercept growth factors (i.e., Grade 8.5 status; variances = 10.342 and 0.865; SEs = 1.531 and 0.190; ps < .001; respectively). Again, growth factor intercepts between model Parts 1 and 2 were highly correlated ($r = .856, p < .001$). All other variances and covariances in the model were fixed at zero.

---

[6] Fit indices were based on $n = 239$ students with nonzero frequency of cigarette use.

TABLE 7.5
Parameter Estimates and Standard Errors
for Cigarette Use Growth Factors and Covariates

Variable	Grade 8.5 status		Linear growth[a]		Quadratic growth[a]	
	Estimate	SE	Estimate	SE	Estimate	SE
Part 1: Use versus nonuse						
Growth factor mean	4.245***	0.280	.146*	.074	−.395**	.133
Intervention group	0.164	0.741	−.153	.105	−.123	.155
Gender (male students)	−0.795**	0.306	.051	.089	.149	.161
Grade cohort (older)	1.118**	0.374	.183	.143	.249	.255
Antisocial behavior	1.030**	0.374	−.105	.101	−.074	.206
Low income	0.916**	0.318	.094	.090	.029	.156
Part 2: Frequency of use						
Growth factor mean	0.833***	0.187	.133**	.044	−.048	.094
Intervention group	0.017	0.150	−.008	.042	−.033	.092
Gender (male students)	−0.112	0.132	−.066	.048	−.055	.108
Grade cohort (older)	0.022	0.193	−.057	.086	−.271	.167
Antisocial behavior	0.431*	0.172	.000	.061	.205	.118
Low income	0.108	0.132	−.013	.040	−.010	.090

Note. Standard errors for intervention effects adjusted by corresponding design effects.
[a]Growth factor variance and associated covariances set to zero in model Parts 1 and 2.
*$p < .05$. **$p < .01$. ***$p < .001$.

Intervention Status and Background Variables

Results of the final two-part LGM of cigarette use, including intervention status and background variables, are shown in Table 7.5.[7] Similar to marijuana use, significant effects for background variables indicated that female students, second-grade-cohort students, students with high baseline antisocial behavior, and students from low SES households had higher rates of cigarette use (vs. nonuse) at Grade 8.5. The only significant effect for frequency of cigarette use was for baseline antisocial behavior, with higher levels related significantly to more cigarette smoking at Grade 8.5. No other variables were associated with change in either cigarette use-versus-nonuse or frequency-of-use outcomes.

DISCUSSION

In this study, we examined the efficacy of the RHC intervention on trajectories of alcohol, marijuana, and cigarette use during early-to-middle

---

[7]Given the high degree of skewness and kurtosis for Grade 7 frequency of cigarette use, parallel analyses were conducted with log-transformed outcome data. Results indicated no substantive differences between analyses with log-transformed and untransformed outcomes; therefore, for consistency, we report results from analysis of cigarette use in the original metric.

adolescence. Using the SDM as a theoretical framework for the intervention, RHC targeted a broad set of empirically supported risk and protective factors through the multiple contexts of school, family, peers, and the individual student. As the aims of the intervention were designed to be both developmentally appropriate and consistent with the goals of its participating families, we investigated students' substance use in terms of the likelihood to abstain from use as well as the frequency of use for those who did not abstain from use.

We analyzed these related outcomes using a two-part LGM strategy. Similar to standard LGM techniques, this method allows for the examination of both intra- and interindividual patterns of change in substance use trajectories. However, the two-part LGM decomposes the original semicontinuous outcome measures into dichotomous use-versus-nonuse and continuous frequency-of-use parts. In addition to providing a more detailed examination of the effects of the intervention, this approach substantially improved the normality of the frequency-of-use outcomes—a fundamental assumption underlying the appropriateness of LGMs in general. Consequently, we recommend this approach to other researchers faced with similarly distributed outcomes.

Results of this study provide evidence for the efficacy of the RHC intervention in reducing the frequency of alcohol and marijuana use. Between-group examination of alcohol and marijuana frequency-of-use trajectories shows greater decreases for intervention students relative to controls during middle to high school periods. Standardized effect sizes associated with mean trajectory differences are substantial (0.91 and 1.44, respectively), representing almost a full standard deviation unit difference in mean alcohol frequency-of-use trajectories and almost a 1.5 standard deviation unit difference in mean marijuana frequency-of-use trajectories between intervention students and controls. In terms of adjusted mean differences in frequency-of-use rates at Grade 10, corresponding effects sizes represent medium intervention effects (0.40 and 0.57, respectively). Although these findings support the intervention's goal of reducing frequent use, the lack of significant intervention effects on students' decision to engage in alcohol or marijuana use demonstrates a lack of support for the intervention's abstinence-oriented goals regarding these two substances.

The differential impact of the RHC intervention on alcohol and marijuana use outcomes is noteworthy. From a social development perspective, intervention students' bonding with those with prosocial beliefs and standards is keeping them from more frequent alcohol and marijuana use, which would disappoint those they are bonded to and threaten their investment in school or family relations if they were to do otherwise. However, experimentation with alcohol and marijuana, perhaps because of low risk of detection or general acceptance as a rite of passage, may not pose as great a threat to bond disruption. Consequently, experimental use may not be as amenable to social development interventions. Findings by Ellickson et al. (2001) note the distinction between experimental and problematic use, suggesting that "prevention programs that target alcohol misuse may be more successful than those that advocate abstinence" (p. 773). In contrast, the addictive nature of cigarette smoking and increased public information campaigns regarding youth smoking may account for its nonsignificant relationships with the intervention. Experimental cigarette use appears to be less normative, as evidenced by its low prevalence in our sample compared with alcohol and marijuana use. Furthermore, the greater potential for cigarette addiction may make escalating (i.e., more frequent) use less susceptible to social development intervention. From a prevention perspective, more research is needed to disentangle the mediating processes leading toward adolescents' decisions to engage in experimental and escalating substance use.

Differences in the longitudinal patterns of substance use between model Parts 1 and 2 (within each type of substance) are noteworthy as well. Results of this study show that, whereas prevalence rates for alcohol and marijuana use increased during the middle to early high school period, frequency-of-use patterns for these substances were either nonlinear (for alcohol) or remained relatively unchanged (for marijuana). Conversely, although the prevalence of cigarette use changed very little during Grades 8 to 10, frequency of cigarette use increased steadily during the same period. Although different longitudinal patterns are apparent between use-versus-nonuse and frequency-of-use outcomes within each substance, we note that growth processes between outcomes are related nonetheless. The large correlation ($r = .69$) between intercept growth factors for alcohol use is consistent with findings from similar research that has used this methodology (Olsen & Schafer, 2001). This, and the large correlations between intercepts within marijuana- and cigarette-use models ($rs = .80$ and $.86$, respectively) can be interpreted as strong positive relationships between a student's latent propensity to engage in use and the ensuing conditional decision on how often to use. In other words, students who are less likely to use are less likely to use often if they do use. As failure to model this "could introduce substantial bias into the estimated coefficients" (Olsen & Schafer, 2001, p. 738), we advise researchers using two-part models to consider such relationships in their analysis. Results of this study also demonstrate that predictor variables can have differential effects on patterns of substance use depending on level of use. Gender, for example, was related to patterns of alcohol and marijuana use with female prevalence rates catching up to male students' rates by 10th grade. This increase in prevalence rates of alcohol and marijuana use by gender is consistent with reported national trends (Johnston et al., 2003). However, in this study, gender was not associated with patterns of frequency of alcohol or marijuana use. These findings are consistent with results from other studies that have found differential effects of risk factors on level-dependent substance use outcomes (Colder & Chassin, 1999; Gutierres, Molof, & Ungerleider, 1994; Olsen & Schafer, 2001). The implication for substance abuse prevention programs is that they recognize students' developmentally related levels of substance use (e.g., experimental or heavy) and tailor their interventions to that level.

Although this study addresses several methodological deficits that often characterize prevention studies of adolescent substance use (e.g., nonexperimental design, lack of theoretical or empirical basis, no long-term follow-up, differential attrition), generalizability of results from this study are limited by relying solely on adolescent self-reported substance use, the predominantly European American composition of the sample (reflective of the suburban school district from which students were sampled), and the exclusion criteria incorporated into the study design (e.g., students who did not remain in their original schools throughout the 1st entire year of the study were excluded). Additionally, this study did not exhaustively examine other explanatory variables (i.e., risk and protective factors) with regard to their potential prediction of substance use. As the focus of the study was to test the efficacy of the RHC intervention, covariates were limited to those variables that had well-established predictive relationships with substance use (e.g., antisocial behavior and low SES) and could statistically control for pretest differences between intervention and control students.

As a comprehensive, longitudinal preventive intervention with universal and selective components, the RHC project incorporates principles of effective prevention programs (Nation et al., 2003) to address empirically identified and developmentally appropriate risk and protective factors for adolescent substance use. Although the effects of the intervention presented in this study are limited, they support the efficacy of the intervention in reducing the frequency of early alcohol and marijuana use, which are known risk factors for later substance abuse. It will be important to see whether these effects demonstrated in middle and early high school are maintained and are associated with outcomes related to heavy or problematic use as students reach the ages of peak use.

REFERENCES

Achenbach, T. M. (1991). *Manual for the Teacher's Report Form and 1991 Profile*. Burlington: University of Vermont, Department of Psychiatry.

Bandura, A. (1973). *Aggression: A social learning analysis*. Englewood Cliffs, NJ: Prentice Hall.

Bentler, P. M. (1990). Comparative fix indexes in structural models. *Psychological Bulletin, 107*, 238–246.

Botvin, G. J., & Griffin, K. W. (2002). Life skills training as a primary prevention approach for adolescent drug abuse and other problem behaviors. *International Journal of Emergency Mental Health, 4*, 41–48.

Browne, M. W., & Cudeck, R. (1993). Alternative ways of assessing model fit. In K. A. Bollen & J. S. Long (Eds.), *Testing structural equation models* (pp. 136–162). Newbury Park, CA: Sage.

Bryant, A. L., Schulenberg, J. E., O'Malley, P. M., Bachman, J. G., & Johnston, L. D. (2003). How academic achievement, attitudes, and behaviors relate to the course of substance use during adolescence: A 6-year, multiwave national longitudinal study. *Journal of Research on Adolescence, 13,* 361–397.

Catalano, R. F., & Hawkins, J. D. (1996). The social development model: A theory of antisocial behavior. In J. D. Hawkins (Ed.), *Delinquency and crime: Current theories* (pp. 149–197). New York: Cambridge University Press.

Catalano, R. F., Mazza, J. J., Harachi, T. W., Abbott, R. D., Haggerty, K. P., & Fleming, C. B. (2003). Raising healthy children through enhancing social development in elementary school: Results after 1.5 years. *Journal of School Psychology, 41,* 143–164.

Coie, J. D., Watt, N. F., West, S. G., Hawkins, J. D., Asarnow, J. R., Markman, H. J., et al. (1993). The science of prevention: A conceptual framework and some directions for a national research program. *American Psychologist, 48,* 1013–1022.

Colder, C. R., & Chassin, L. (1999). The psychosocial characteristics of alcohol users versus problem users: Data from a study of adolescents at risk. *Development and Psychopathology, 11,* 321–348.

Conduct Problems Prevention Research Group. (1992). A developmental and clinical model for the prevention of conduct disorders: The FAST Track Program. *Development and Psychopathology, 4,* 509–527.

Conduct Problems Prevention Research Group. (2002). Predictor variables associated with positive Fast Track outcomes at the end of third grade. *Journal of Abnormal Child Psychology, 30,* 37–52.

Curran, P. J. (2000). A latent curve framework for the study of developmental trajectories in adolescent substance use. In J. S. Rose, L. Chassin, C. C. Presson, & S. J. Sherman (Eds.), *Multivariate applications in substance use research: New methods for new questions* (pp. 1–42). Mahwah, NJ: Erlbaum.

Curran, P. J., Bauer, D. J., & Willoughby, M. T. (2004). Testing main effects and interactions in latent curve analysis. *Psychological Methods, 9,* 220–237.

Dielman, T. E. (1994). Correction for the design effect in school-based substance use and abuse prevention research: Sample size requirements and analysis considerations. In A. Cázares & L. A. Beatty (Eds.), *NIDA Research Monograph: Scientific methods for prevention intervention research* (Vol. 139, pp. 115–126). Rockville, MD: National Institute on Drug Abuse.

Duncan, S. C., & Duncan, T. E. (1996). A multivariate latent growth curve analysis of adolescent substance use. *Structural Equation Modeling, 3,* 323–347.

Eddy, J., Reid, J. B., & Fetrow, R. A. (2000). An elementary school-based prevention program targeting modifiable antecedents of youth delinquency and violence: Linking the Interests of Families and Teachers (LIFT). *Journal of Emotional and Behavioral Disorders, 8,* 165–176.

Ellickson, P. L., Bell, R. M., & Harrison, E. R. (1993). Changing adolescent propensities to use drugs: Results from Project ALERT. *Health Education Quarterly, 20*, 227–242.

Ellickson, P. L., Tucker, J. S., Klein, D. J., & McGuigan, K. A. (2001). Prospective risk factors for alcohol misuse in late adolescence. *Journal of Studies on Alcohol, 62*, 773–782.

Griffin, K. W., Botvin, G. J., Scheier, L. M., & Nichols, T. R. (2002). Factors associated with regular marijuana use among high school students: A long-term follow-up study. *Substance Use and Misuse, 37*, 225–238.

Gutierres, S. E., Molof, M., & Ungerleider, S. (1994). Relationship of "risk" factors to teen substance use: A comparison of abstainers, infrequent users, and frequent users. *International Journal of the Addictions, 29*, 1559–1579.

Haggerty, K. P., Catalano, R. F., Harachi, T. W., & Abbott, R. D. (1998). Description de l'implementation d'un programme de prévention des problèmes de comportement à l'adolescence [Preventing adolescent problem behaviors: A comprehensive intervention description]. *Criminologie, 31*, 25–47.

Hansen, W. B., & Graham, J. W. (1991). Preventing alcohol, marijuana, and cigarette use among adolescents: Peer pressure resistance training versus establishing conservative norms. *Preventive Medicine, 20*, 414–430.

Hawkins, J. D., Catalano, R. F., Kosterman, R., Abbott, R., & Hill, K. G. (1999). Preventing adolescent health-risk behaviors by strengthening protection during childhood. *Archives of Pediatrics and Adolescent Medicine, 153*, 226–234.

Hawkins, J. D., Catalano, R. F., & Miller, J. Y. (1992). Risk and protective factors for alcohol and other drug problems in adolescence and early adulthood: Implications for substance-abuse prevention. *Psychological Bulletin, 112*, 64–105.

Hawkins, J. D., Graham, J. W., Maguin, E., Abbott, R. D., Hill, K. G., & Catalano, R. F. (1997). Exploring the effects of age of alcohol use initiation and psychosocial risk factors on subsequent alcohol misuse. *Journal of Studies on Alcohol, 58*, 280–290.

Hawkins, J. D., Guo, J., Hill, K. G., Battin-Pearson, S., & Abbott, R. D. (2001). Long term effects of the Seattle Social Development Intervention on school bonding trajectories. *Applied Developmental Science, 5*, 225–236.

Hawkins, J. D., & Weis, J. G. (1985). The social development model: An integrated approach to delinquency prevention. *Journal of Primary Prevention, 6*, 73–97.

Hirschi, T. (1969). *Causes of delinquency*. Berkeley: University of California Press.

Hops, H., Davis, B., & Lewin, L. M. (1999). The development of alcohol and other substance use: A gender study of family and peer context. *Journal of Studies on Alcohol, Suppl. 13*, 22–31.

Howell, J. C., Krisberg, B., Hawkins, J. D., & Wilson, J. J. (Eds.). (1995). *A sourcebook: Serious, violent, and chronic juvenile offenders*. Thousand Oaks, CA: Sage.

Jessor, R., Van Den Bos, J., Vanderryn, J., Costa, F. M., & Turbin, M. S. (1995). Protective factors in adolescent problem behavior: Moderator effects and developmental change. *Developmental Psychology, 31*, 923–933.

Johnston, L. D., O'Malley, P. M., & Bachman, J. G. (2003). *Monitoring the Future national survey results on drug use, 1975–2002: I. Secondary school students* (NIH Publication No. 03-5375). Washington, DC: National Institute on Drug Abuse.

Kellam, S. G., Rebok, G. W., Ialongo, N. S., & Mayer, L. S. (1994). The course and malleability of aggressive behavior from early first grade into middle school: Results of a developmental epidemiology-based preventive trial. *Journal of Child Psychology & Psychiatry, 35,* 259–281.

Li, F., Duncan, T. E., & Hops, H. (2001). Examining developmental trajectories in adolescent alcohol use using piecewise growth mixture modeling analysis. *Journal of Studies on Alcohol, 62,* 199–210.

Little, R. J. A., & Rubin, D. B. (1987). *Statistical analysis with missing data.* New York: Wiley.

Lonczak, H. S., Abbott, R. D., Hawkins, J. D., Kosterman, R., & Catalano, R. F. (2002). Effects of the Seattle Social Development Project on sexual behavior, pregnancy, birth, and sexually transmitted disease outcomes by age 21 years. *Archives of Pediatrics and Adolescent Medicine, 156,* 438–447.

Maggs, J. L., & Schulenberg, J. (1998). Reasons to drink and not to drink: Altering trajectories of drinking through an alcohol misuse prevention program. *Applied Developmental Science, 2,* 48–60.

Manning, W. (1997). Alternative econometric models of alcohol demand. In K. J. Bryant & M. Windle (Eds.), *The science of prevention: Methodological advances from alcohol and substance abuse research* (pp. 101–121). Washington, DC: American Psychological Association.

Marshal, M. P., & Chassin, L. (2000). Peer influence on adolescent alcohol use: The moderating role of parental support and discipline. *Applied Developmental Science, 4,* 80–88.

Matsueda, R. L. (1988). The current state of differential association theory. *Crime and Delinquency, 34,* 277–306.

McBride, N., Midford, R., Farringdon, F., & Phillips, M. (2000). Early results from a school alcohol harm minimization study: The School Health and Alcohol Harm Reduction Project. *Addiction, 95,* 1021–1042.

Mrazek, P. J., & Haggerty, R. J. (Eds.). (1994). *Reducing risks for mental disorders: Frontiers for prevention intervention research.* Washington, DC: National Academy Press.

Muthén, B. (2001). *Two-part growth mixture modeling.* Unpublished manuscript.

Muthén, B., & Asparouhov, T. (2002, December 9). *Latent variable analysis with categorical outcomes: Multiple-group and growth modeling in Mplus* (No. 4, Version 5). Retrieved January 27, 2004, from http://www.statmodel.com/mplus/examples/webnote.html

Muthén, L. K., & Muthén, B. O. (2004). *Mplus user's guide* (3rd ed.). Los Angeles: Author.

Nation, M., Crusto, C., Wandersman, A., Kumpfer, K. L., Seybolt, D., Morrissey-Kane, E., et al. (2003). What works in prevention: Principles of effective prevention programs. *American Psychologist, 58,* 449–456.

Olsen, M. K., & Schafer, J. L. (2001). A two-part random-effects model for semicontinuous longitudinal data. *Journal of the American Statistical Association, 96,* 730–745.

Pedersen, W., & Skrondal, A. (1998). Alcohol consumption debut: Predictors and consequences. *Journal of Studies on Alcohol, 59,* 32–42.

Raudenbush, S. W., & Bryk, A. S. (2002). *Hierarchical linear models: Applications and data analysis methods* (2nd ed.). Newbury Park, CA: Sage.

Raudenbush, S. W., & Xiao-Feng, L. (2001). Effects of study duration, frequency of observation, and sample size on power in studies of group differences in polynomial change. *Psychological Methods, 6,* 387–401.

Spoth, R. L., Redmond, C., Hockaday, C., & Yoo, S. (1996). Protective factors and young adolescent tendency to abstain from alcohol use: A model using two waves of intervention study data. *American Journal of Community Psychology, 24,* 749–770.

Spoth, R. L., Redmond, C., & Shin, C. (2001). Randomized trial of brief family interventions for general populations: Adolescent substance use outcomes 4 years following baseline. *Journal of Consulting and Clinical Psychology, 69,* 627–642.

Steiger, J. H., & Lind, J. C. (1980, May). *Statistically based tests for the number of common factors.* Paper presented at the annual meeting of the Psychometric Society, Iowa City, IA.

Stouthamer-Loeber, M., Loeber, R., Wei, E., Farrington, D. P., & Wikstroem, P.-O. H. (2002). Risk and promotive effects in the explanation of persistent serious delinquency in boys. *Journal of Consulting and Clinical Psychology, 70,* 111–123.

Taylor, B. J., Graham, J. W., Cumsille, P., & Hansen, W. B. (2000). Modeling prevention program effects on growth in substance use: Analysis of five years of data from the Adolescent Alcohol Prevention Trial. *Prevention Science, 1,* 183–197.

Tucker, L. R., & Lewis, C. (1973). A reliability coefficient for maximum likelihood factor analysis. *Psychometrika, 38,* 1–10.

Washington State Department of Health. (2003). *2002 Healthy Youth Survey.* Retrieved September 15, 2003, from http://www3.doh.wa.gov/ HYS

Werthamer-Larsson, L., Kellam, S. G., & Wheeler, L. (1991). Effect of first-grade classroom environment on shy behavior, aggressive behavior, and concentration problems. *American Journal of Community Psychology, 19,* 585–602.

Williams, J. H., Ayers, C. D., Abbott, R. D., Hawkins, J. D., & Catalano, R. F. (1999). Racial differences in risk factors for delinquency and substance use among adolescents. *Social Work Review, 23,* 241–256.

8

PROJECT DARE: NO EFFECTS AT 10-YEAR FOLLOW-UP

DONALD R. LYNAM, RICHARD MILICH, RICK ZIMMERMAN,
SCOTT P. NOVAK, TK LOGAN, CATHERINE MARTIN,
CARL LEUKEFELD, AND RICHARD CLAYTON

The use of illegal substances in childhood and adolescence occurs at an alarming rate. In response to this problem, there has been a widespread proliferation of schoolwide intervention programs designed to curb, if not eliminate, substance use in this population. Project DARE (Drug Abuse Resistance Education) is one of the most widely disseminated of these programs (Clayton, Cattarello, & Johnstone, 1996).

The widespread popularity of DARE is especially noteworthy, given the lack of evidence for its efficacy. Although few long-term studies have been conducted, the preponderance of evidence suggests that DARE has no long-term effect on drug use (Dukes, Ullman, & Stein, 1996; McNeal & Hansen, 1995; Rosenbaum, Flewelling, Bailey, Ringwalt, & Wilkinson, 1994). For example, Clayton et al. (1996) examined the efficacy of DARE among over 2,000 6th-grade students in a city school system. The students' attitudes toward drugs, as well as actual use, were assessed before and after the intervention and then for the next 4 years through 10th grade. Although the

This research was supported by Grant DA05312-10 from the National Institute on Drug Abuse and by General Clinical Research Center Grant M01 RR026202 from the National Institutes of Health.

Reprinted from *Journal of Consulting and Clinical Psychology*, 67, 590–593 (1999). Copyright 1999 by the American Psychological Association.

DARE intervention produced a few initial improvements in the students' attitudes toward drug use, these changes did not persist over time. More importantly, there were no effects in actual drug use initially or during the follow-up period. Further, results from shorter term studies are no more encouraging; these studies suggest that the short-term effects of DARE on drug use are, at best, small. In a meta-analysis of eight evaluations of the short-term efficacy of DARE, Ennett, Tobler, Ringwalt, and Flewelling (1994) found that the average effect size produced by DARE on drug use was .06, an effect size that does not differ significantly from zero.

Given the continued popularity of DARE, the limited number of long-term follow-ups, and the possibility of "sleeper effects" (effects showing up years after program participation), it seems important to continue to evaluate the long-term outcomes of DARE. The present study followed up the Clayton et al. (1996) sample through the age of 20. As far as we know, this 10-year follow-up is the longest reported on the efficacy of DARE. The original study, although presenting 5-year follow-up data, assessed adolescents during a developmental period when experimentation with drugs is quite prevalent and even considered normative by some authors (Moffitt, 1993; Shedler & Block, 1990). The prevalence of minor drug use during this period may suppress the effects of DARE. However, by the age of 20, experimentation with drugs has reached its peak and begun to decline; it may be during this period that the effects of DARE will become evident. In fact, Dukes, Stein, and Ullman (1997) reported a 6-year follow-up that demonstrated an effect for DARE on the use of harder drugs when participants were in the 12th grade; this effect was not present 3 years earlier.

METHOD

Participants

The initial sample for this study consisted of sixth graders in the 1987–1988 academic year in a Midwestern metropolitan area of 230,000. An overwhelming majority of the sample came from urban or suburban areas. With regard to socioeconomic status (SES), the area is considered one of the more prosperous counties in a state known for its pockets of extreme poverty. Although actual SES measures were not collected, given the size and inclusiveness of the sample, the sample can be assumed to represent all economic strata. Of the initial sample, 51% were male and 75% were White.

Data were collected before and after the administration of DARE. Follow-up questionnaire data were collected from the students over a 5-year period from 6th through 10th grade. Of the original participants, completed questionnaires were obtained on at least three occasions (once in 6th grade, once in 7th or 8th grade, and once in 9th or 10th grade) for 1,429 students. This became the sample targeted for the present young adult follow-up study. Completed mailed surveys were received from 1,002 participants between the ages of 19 and 21.

The final sample of 1,002 consisted of 431 (43%) men and 571 (57%) women. The average age of the participants was 20.1 ($SD = 0.78$). The racial composition of the sample was as follows: 748 (75.1%) were White, 204 (20.4%) were African American, and 44 (0.4%) were of other race or ethnicity. Seventy-six percent of the final sample had received DARE, which corresponds almost exactly to the 75% of sixth graders who were originally exposed to DARE.

We conducted attrition analyses to determine whether the 1,002 participants differed from those 427 individuals who were eligible for the mailed survey study but from whom no survey was obtained. A dummy variable representing present-missing status was simultaneously regressed using a pairwise correlation matrix onto 15 variables from the original assessment: sex; ethnicity; age; DARE status; peer-pressure resistance; self-esteem, and use of, and positive and negative expectancies toward, cigarettes, alcohol, and marijuana. Missing status accounted for a small but significant proportion of the variance in the linear combination of the 15 study measures ($R^2 = .06$), $F(15, 1339) = 6.08$, $p < .001$, but only 3 variables were independently linked to missing status. Participants who were missing completed surveys tended to be older males who reported using cigarettes in the sixth grade. In general, attrition seemed to have little effect on the results that are reported here.

Procedures

Those individuals who could be located were sent a letter and a consent form requesting their participation in a follow-up to their earlier participation in the DARE evaluation. Those individuals who returned the signed consent form were mailed a questionnaire that took approximately 30 to 45 minutes to complete. Of the available sample, 5 had died, 176 refused to participate, 83 could not be located, and 163 were contacted but did not return the survey. For their time and effort, participants were paid $15 to $50.

Measures

Similar to the earlier data collection, participants were asked questions about their use of alcohol, tobacco, marijuana, and other illegal drugs. For each drug category, participants were asked to report how often they had used the substance in their lifetime, during the past year, and during the past month. In addition, participants were asked a variety of questions concerning their expectancies about drug use. For each drug, respondents reported

how likely they believed using that drug would lead to five negative consequences (e.g., "get in trouble with the law" and "do poorly at school or work")
as well as how likely they believed using that drug would lead to eight positive consequences (e.g., "feel good" and "get away from problems"). Negative
and positive expectancy scores were formed for each drug at each age. Two
potential mediators of the DARE intervention, peer-pressure resistance and
self-esteem, were also assessed. Participants responded to nine items designed
to assess the ability to resist negative peer pressure (e.g., "If one of your best
friends is skipping class or calling in sick to work, would you skip too?").
Finally, participants responded to the 10-item Rosenberg Self-Esteem Scale
(Rosenberg, 1965). All scale scores had acceptable reliabilities (alphas ranged
from .73 to .93, with an average of .84).

Initial DARE Intervention

A complete description of the experimental and comparison interventions is contained in the Clayton et al. (1996) study. Twenty-three elementary
schools were randomly assigned to receive the DARE intervention, whereas the
remaining 8 schools received a standard drug-education curriculum. The
DARE intervention was delivered by police officers in 1-hour sessions over
17 weeks. The focus of the DARE curriculum is on teaching students the skills
needed to recognize and resist social pressures to use drugs. Additionally, the
curriculum focuses on providing information about drugs, teaching decision-
making skills, building self-esteem, and choosing healthy alternatives to drug
use. The control condition was not a strict no-treatment condition but instead
consisted of whatever the health teachers decided to cover concerning drug
education in their classes. The drug education received by students in the control condition cannot be described in detail because of the considerable latitude
on the part of teachers and schools in what was taught. Nonetheless, in many
instances, emphasis was placed on the identification and harmful effects of
drugs, peer pressure was frequently discussed, and videos using scare tactics were
often shown. These drug education units lasted approximately 30 to 45 minutes over a period of 2 to 4 weeks.

RESULTS AND DISCUSSION

Because the school, and not the individual, was the unit of randomization
in the present study, we used hierarchical linear modeling, with its ability to
model the effect of organizational context on individual outcomes. For each of
the substances (cigarettes, alcohol, and marijuana), we constructed three hierarchical linear models (HLMs) that examined amount of use, positive
expectancies, and negative expectancies. We conducted additional analyses on

peer-pressure resistance, self-esteem, and the variety of past-year illicit drug use. An HLM was used to model the effect of DARE on the school mean of each dependent variable (drug use and expectancies) while controlling for pre-DARE factors. This allowed for the comparison of how each school mean varied with the effect of DARE. We conducted preliminary analyses in which the effect of DARE was also modeled on the relationship between pre-DARE baseline and the substantive outcomes. Significant effects would suggest that DARE affected the relation between pre- and post-DARE outcomes. These effects were not significant and were thus fixed across schools. Respondents' sixth-grade reports of lifetime use served as baseline measures, whereas age-20 reports of past-month use of cigarettes, alcohol, and marijuana served as outcome measures.[1] The results of the full HLMs are presented in Table 8.1.

Cigarettes

Pre-DARE levels of use and negative expectancies about cigarette use were significantly related to their counterparts 10 years later. There were no relations between DARE status and cigarette use and expectancies, suggesting that DARE had no effect on either student behavior or expectancies.

Alcohol

Pre-DARE levels of lifetime alcohol use and positive and negative expectancies about alcohol use were significantly related to their counterparts 10 years later. DARE status was unrelated to alcohol use or either kind of alcohol expectancy at age 20.

Marijuana

Pre-DARE levels of past-month marijuana use and negative expectancies about use were significantly related to their counterparts 10 years later. Similar to the findings for cigarettes, respondents' sixth-grade positive expectancies about marijuana use were not significantly related to marijuana expectancies at age 20. DARE status was unrelated to marijuana use or either kind of marijuana expectancy at age 20.

Illicit Drug Use

Finally, the number of illicit drugs (except marijuana) used in the past year was examined. Because no measures for these items were obtained

---

[1] Results were unchanged when prevalence of use or heavy use, rather than frequency of use, was used as the outcome variable.

TABLE 8.1

Hierarchical Linear Models Examining the Influence of Project DARE on Age-20 Levels of Drug Use, Drug Expectancies, Peer-Pressure Resistance, and Self-Esteem

Variable	Fixed effect[a]
Frequency of past-month cigarette use	
Intercept (γ_0)	−.076
Level 1: Pre-DARE lifetime cigarette use (β_1)	.240***
Level 2: DARE status (γ_1)	.101
Negative expectancies toward cigarettes	
Intercept (γ_0)	.108
Level 1: Pre-DARE expectancies (β_1)	.145***
Level 2: DARE status (γ_1)	−.152
Positive expectancies toward cigarettes	
Intercept (γ_0)	−.071
Level 1: Pre-DARE expectancies (β_1)	.009
Level 2: DARE status (γ_1)	.053
Frequency of past-month alcohol use	
Intercept (γ_0)	−.034
Level 1: Pre-DARE lifetime alcohol use (β_1)	.115**
Level 2: DARE status (γ_1)	−.018
Negative expectancies toward alcohol	
Intercept (γ_0)	.075
Level 1: Pre-DARE expectancies (β_1)	.105**
Level 2: DARE status (γ_1)	−.034
Positive expectancies toward alcohol	
Intercept (γ_0)	−.052
Level 1: Pre-DARE expectancies (β_1)	.085*
Level 2: DARE status (γ_1)	.048
Frequency of past-month marijuana use	
Intercept (γ_0)	.033
Level 1: Pre-DARE lifetime marijuana use (β_1)	.098**
Level 2: DARE status (γ_1)	−.044
Negative expectancies toward marijuana	
Intercept (γ_0)	−.013
Level 1: Pre-DARE expectancies (β_1)	.123***
Level 2: DARE status (γ_1)	.039
Positive expectancies toward marijuana	
Intercept (γ_0)	−.021
Level 1: Pre-DARE expectancies (β_1)	.045
Level 2: DARE status (γ_1)	.011
Variety of illegal drugs used in past year[b]	
Intercept (γ_0)	−.081
Level 2: DARE status (γ_1)	.080
Peer-pressure resistance	
Intercept (γ_0)	.058
Level 1: Pre-DARE peer-pressure resistance (β_1)	.118**
Level 2: DARE status (γ_1)	−.139
Self-esteem	
Intercept (γ_0)	.133
Level 1: Pre-DARE self-esteem (β_1)	.129**
Level 2: DARE status (γ_1)	−.181*

Note. DARE status is coded 0 = control, 1 = DARE intervention.
[a]All beta coefficients presented are group-mean-centered, standardized effect sizes. [b]There were no baseline measures for this model; thus, a means-as-outcomes model was estimated.
*$p < .05$;   **$p < .01$;   ***$p < .001$.

during the initial baseline measurement, we estimated a means-as-outcomes HLM using no Level 1 predictors and only DARE status as a predictor at Level 2. The results show that DARE had no statistically significant effect on the variety of illicit drugs used.

Peer-Pressure Resistance

The results for peer-pressure resistance were similar to previous results. Pre-DARE levels of peer-pressure resistance were significantly related to peer-pressure resistance levels 10 years later, whereas DARE status was unrelated to peer-pressure resistance levels.

Self-Esteem

Finally, pre-DARE levels of self-esteem were significantly related to self-esteem levels at age 20. Surprisingly, DARE status in the sixth grade was negatively related to self-esteem at age 20, indicating that individuals who were exposed to DARE in the sixth grade had lower levels of self-esteem 10 years later. This result was clearly unexpected and cannot be accounted for theoretically; as such, it would seem best to regard this as a chance finding that is unlikely to be replicated.

Our results are consistent in documenting the absence of beneficial effects associated with the DARE program. This was true whether the outcome consisted of actual drug use or merely attitudes toward drug use. In addition, we examined processes that are the focus of intervention and purportedly mediate the impact of DARE (e.g., self-esteem and peer resistance), and these also failed to differentiate DARE participants from nonparticipants. Thus, consistent with the earlier Clayton et al. (1996) study, there appear to be no reliable short-term, long-term, early adolescent, or young adult positive outcomes associated with receiving the DARE intervention.

Although one can never prove the null hypothesis, the present study appears to overcome some troublesome threats to internal validity (i.e., unreliable measures and low power). Specifically, the outcome measures collected exhibited good internal consistencies at each age and significant stability over the 10-year follow-up period. For all but two measures (positive expectancies for cigarettes and marijuana), measurements taken in sixth grade, before the administration of DARE, were significantly related to measurements taken 10 years later, with coefficients ranging from small ($\beta = 0.09$ for positive expectancies about alcohol) to moderate ($\beta = 0.24$ for cigarette use). Second, it is extremely unlikely that we failed to find effects for DARE that actually existed because of a lack of power. Thus, it appears that one can be fairly confident that DARE created no lasting changes in the outcomes examined here.

Advocates of DARE may argue against our findings. First, they may argue that we have evaluated an out-of-date version of the program and that a newer version would have fared better. Admittedly, we evaluated the original DARE curriculum, which was created 3 years before the beginning of this study. This is an unavoidable difficulty in any long-term follow-up study; the important question becomes, How much change has there been? To the best of our knowledge, the goals (i.e., "to keep kids off drugs") and foci of DARE (e.g., resisting peer pressure) have remained the same across time as has the method of delivery (e.g., police officers). We believe that any changes in DARE have been more cosmetic than substantive, but this is difficult to evaluate until DARE America shares the current content of the curriculum with the broader prevention community.

One could also argue that the officers responsible for delivering DARE in the present study failed to execute the program as intended. This alternative seems unlikely. DARE officers receive a structured, 80-hour training course that covers a number of topics, including specific knowledge about drug use and consequences of drug use, as well as teaching techniques and classroom-management skills. Considerable emphasis is given to practice teaching and to following the lesson plans. Although we did not collect systematic data on treatment fidelity in the present study, a process evaluation by Clayton, Cattarello, Day, and Walden (1991) attested to the fidelity to the curriculum and to the quality of teaching by the DARE officers.

Finally, advocates of DARE might correctly point out that the present study did not compare DARE with a no-intervention condition but rather with a control condition in which health teachers did their usual drug-education programs. Thus, technically, we cannot say that DARE was not efficacious but instead that it was no more efficacious than whatever the teachers had been doing previously. Although this is a valid point, it is unreasonable to argue that a more expensive and longer running treatment (DARE) should be preferred over a less expensive and less time-consuming one (health education) in the absence of differential effectiveness (Kazdin & Wilson, 1978).

This report adds to the accumulating literature on DARE's lack of efficacy in preventing or reducing substance use. This lack of efficacy has been noted by other investigators in other samples (e.g., Dukes et al., 1996; Ennett et al., 1994; Wysong, Aniskiewicz, & Wright, 1994). Yet DARE continues to be offered in a majority of the nation's public schools at great cost to the public (Clayton et al., 1996). This raises the obvious question, why does DARE continue to be valued by parents and school personnel (Donnermeyer & Wurschmidt, 1997) despite its lack of demonstrated efficacy? There appear to be at least two possible answers to this question. First, teaching children to refrain from drug use is a widely accepted approach with which few individuals would argue. Thus, similar to other such interventions, such as the "good touch/bad touch" programs to prevent sexual abuse (Reppucci & Haugaard,

1989), these "feel-good" programs are ones that everyone can support, and critical examination of their effectiveness may not be perceived as necessary.

A second possible explanation for the popularity of programs such as DARE is that they *appear* to work. Parents and supporters of DARE may be engaging in an odd kind of normative comparison (Kendall & Grove, 1988), comparing children who go through DARE with children who do not. The adults rightly perceive that most children who go through DARE do not engage in problematic drug use. Unfortunately, these individuals may not realize that the vast majority of children, even without any intervention, do not engage in problematic drug use. In fact, even given the somewhat alarming rates of marijuana experimentation in high school (e.g., 40%; Johnston, O'Malley, & Bachman, 1996), the *majority* of students do not engage in any drug use. That is, adults may believe that drug use among adolescents is much more frequent than it actually is. When the children who go through DARE are compared with this "normative" group of drug-using teens, DARE appears effective.

REFERENCES

Clayton, R. R., Cattarello, A. M., Day, L. E., & Walden, K. P. (1991). Persuasive communication and drug abuse prevention: An evaluation of the DARE program. In L. Donohew, H. Sypher, & W. Bukowski (Eds.), *Persuasive communication and drug abuse prevention* (pp. 295–313). Hillsdale, NJ: Erlbaum.

Clayton, R. R., Cattarello, A. M., & Johnstone, B. M. (1996). The effectiveness of Drug Abuse Resistance Education (Project DARE): 5-year follow-up results. *Preventive Medicine, 25*, 307–318.

Donnermeyer, J. F., & Wurschmidt, T. N. (1997). Educators' perceptions of the D.A.R.E. program. *Journal of Drug Education, 27*, 259–276.

Dukes, R. L., Stein, J. A., & Ullman, J. B. (1997). Long-term impact of Drug Abuse Resistance Education (D.A.R.E.). *Evaluation Review, 21*, 483–500.

Dukes, R. L., Ullman, J. B., & Stein, J. A. (1996). A three-year follow-up of Drug Abuse Resistance Education (D.A.R.E.). *Evaluation Review, 20*, 49–66.

Ennett, S. T., Tobler, N. S., Ringwalt, C. L., & Flewelling, R. L. (1994). How effective is drug abuse resistance education? A meta-analysis of Project DARE outcome evaluations. *American Journal of Public Health, 84*, 1394–1401.

Johnston, L. D., O'Malley, P. M., & Bachman, J. G. (1996). *National survey results on drug use from the Monitoring the Future Study, 1975–1994*. Rockville, MD: National Institute on Drug Abuse.

Kazdin, A. E., & Wilson, G. T. (1978). Criteria for evaluating psychotherapy. *Archives of General Psychiatry, 35*, 407–416.

Kendall, P. C., & Grove, W. M. (1988). Normative comparisons in therapy outcomes. *Behavioral Assessment, 10*, 147–158.

McNeal, R. B., & Hansen, W. B. (1995). An examination of strategies for gaining convergent validity in natural experiments. *Evaluation Review, 19,* 141–158.

Moffitt, T. E. (1993). Adolescence-limited and life-course persistent antisocial behavior: A developmental taxonomy. *Psychological Review, 100,* 674–701.

Reppucci, N. D., & Haugaard, J. J. (1989). Prevention of child sexual abuse: Myth or reality. *American Psychologist, 44,* 1266–1275.

Rosenbaum, D. P., Flewelling, R. P., Bailey, S. L., Ringwalt, C. L., & Wilkinson, D. L. (1994). Cops in the classroom: A longitudinal evaluation of Drug Abuse Resistance Education (D.A.R.E.). *Journal of Research in Crime and Delinquency, 31,* 3–31.

Rosenberg, M. (1965). *Society and the adolescent self-image.* Princeton, NJ: Princeton University Press.

Shedler, J., & Block, J. (1990). Adolescent drug use and psychological health: A longitudinal inquiry. *American Psychologist, 45,* 612–630.

Wysong, E., Aniskiewicz, R., & Wright, D. (1994). Truth and DARE: Tracking drug education to graduation and as symbolic politics. *Social Problems, 41,* 448–472.

IV

INITIATION
AND PROGRESSION
IN ADOLESCENCE

9

A LONGITUDINAL ANALYSIS OF FRIENDSHIPS AND SUBSTANCE USE: BIDIRECTIONAL INFLUENCE FROM ADOLESCENCE TO ADULTHOOD

THOMAS J. DISHION AND LEE D. OWEN

Drug use initiation in middle adolescence is associated with long-term adjustment problems such as drug and alcohol abuse (Robins & Przybeck, 1985), dropping out of school (Kaplan & Liu, 1994; Newcomb & Bentler, 1988), marital instability (Kandel, Davies, Karus, & Yamaguchi, 1986; Yamaguchi & Kandel, 1985), mental health problems (Johnson & Kaplan, 1990), and poor job performance (Stein, Smith, Guy, & Bentler, 1993). These adjustment outcomes occur even after controlling for a history of behavior problems, which tend to precede adolescent drug use (Block, Block, & Keyes, 1988; Kellam, Brown, Rubin, & Ensminger, 1983; McCord, 1981; Pulkkinen, 1983; Robins & McEvoy, 1990; Smith & Fogg, 1979; Windle, 1990).

Often co-occurring with adolescent substance use are delinquency and precocious sexuality (Dishion & Loeber, 1985; Elliott, Huizinga, & Ageton, 1985; Jessor, 1976; Jessor & Jessor, 1977). These problem behaviors are highly intercorrelated but tend to emerge as a developmental sequence (Loeber,

This project was supported by Grant DA 07031 from the National Institute on Drug Abuse at the National Institutes of Health to Thomas J. Dishion and by Grant MH 37940 from the National Institute of Mental Health to Deborah Capaldi. Thanks to Ann Simas for editing and graphics preparation on the manuscript.

Reprinted from *Developmental Psychology*, 38, 480–491 (2002). Copyright 2002 by the American Psychological Association.

1988). For example, substance use predicts male sexual precocity, which in turn predicts parenting out of wedlock and unsafe sexual practices (Capaldi, Crosby, & Stoolmiller, 1996). Despite the rather high covariation among various forms of problem behavior, studying the processes associated specifically with each is necessary for unraveling unique and shared etiologies (Loeber, 1988). For example, in research on the childhood antecedents of adolescent tobacco, alcohol, and marijuana use, peer rejection in elementary school was found to be associated expressly with the early use of tobacco but not with alcohol and marijuana use (Dishion, Capaldi, & Yoerger, 1999).

A common factor leading to all forms of substance use is involvement in a substance-using peer group (Chassin, Presson, Sherman, Montello, & McGrew, 1986; Duncan, Duncan, & Hops, 1994; Elliott et al., 1985; Hawkins, Catalano, & Miller, 1992). Peer-clustering theory, therefore, is probably the most broadly supported model of early-onset substance use (Oetting & Beauvais, 1990; O'Malley, Bachman, & Johnston, 1988). The strength of the covariation between peer clustering and substance use is quite high: Association with deviant peers at age 13–14 accounted for 49% of the variance in substance use by age 15–16 (Dishion, Capaldi, Spracklen, & Li, 1995). Peer influence is also critical to both early initiation and progressions from legal to illegal substances (Graham, Collins, Wugalter, Chung, & Hansen, 1991).

The study of peer influence naturally includes an analysis of friendships. It is hypothesized that friends can influence drug use and, conversely, that drug use impacts the selection of friends. Some research focuses on friendships and drug use over relatively short temporal intervals that support a bidirectional effect. For example, examination of the covariation between monthly substance use "bursts" and contact with substance-using friends has revealed statistically reliable effects (Dishion & Medici Skaggs, 2000). The months in which young, high-risk adolescents increased their drug use were those months in which they increased contact with substance-using friends. In addition, in the course of the school year, bidirectional effects among high school students were found between drug use attitudes and the formation of friendship cliques. Research by Kandel (1986) revealed that drug use attitudes contributed to the formation of friendship cliques, and over the year, friendship cliques changed drug use attitudes over time.

Simply driving by almost any public secondary school in the United States would reveal groups of youngsters standing outside in circles smoking cigarettes. Such casual observations suggest that adolescent drug use may serve a secondary function: enhancing peer interaction. Evidence indicates that some youth are vulnerable to the peer-enhancing function of substance use by virtue of their social standing. Ennett and Bauman (1994) found that marginality in the peer network in early adolescence predicts initiation of smoking. As discussed earlier, a history of peer rejection uniquely predicts early-onset smoking in boys (Dishion, Capaldi, & Yoerger, 1999) after controlling for antisocial behavior, family management, and family context and substance use. Moreover, boys with a history of poor peer relationships (isolated and rejected) were most likely to increase smoking at high school entry (Dishion, Capaldi, et al., 1995). The transition to high school represents two dynamics: (a) The age between 13 and 14 is a time of rapid biological change associated with pubertal growth, and (b) the transition to high school is a social change in which peer groups are often reorganized.

The majority of initial smoking episodes, however, occur after school, in the company of friends in unsupervised households and community settings (Friedman, Lichtenstein, & Biglan, 1985). Friends seem to covary on the substances they prefer (Dinges & Oetting, 1993), suggesting that friendships are organized around activities that involve the use of specific substances. Not surprisingly, these activities are highly social, include males and females, and involve high levels of positive affect (i.e., "partying"). Indeed, partying is one of the major "routine activities" of adolescent drug users (Osgood, Wilson, O'Malley, Bachman, & Johnston, 1996).

From a social interaction perspective, the fabric of peer influence is formulated from the momentary action–reaction patterns that occur within specific friendships. These patterns have a training function that is difficult for even the participants to track cognitively (Dishion & Patterson, 1999; Patterson, Reid, & Dishion, 1992). Examination of 30-minute videotapes of friendship interactions revealed a deviant friendship process, which is defined by contingent positive reactions to deviant talk within a friendship dyad.

The construct of the deviant friendship process was found to uniquely predict several adolescent problem behavior outcomes, as summarized in Figure 9.1. Deviant friendship process accounted for escalations in tobacco, alcohol, and marijuana use from age 13–14 to age 15–16 after controlling for prior use of each substance (Dishion, Capaldi, et al., 1995). In addition, deviant friendship process accounted for escalations in serious delinquency (Dishion, Spracklen, Andrews, & Patterson, 1996) and adolescent violence (Dishion, Eddy, Haas, Li, & Spracklen, 1997).

More recently, Patterson, Dishion, and Yoerger (2000) established a construct of deviant friendship process that included direct observations of deviant talk within the dyad, coder impressions of deviant talk, and time spent with peers. Peer influence was assumed to be proportional to the process within the friendship and the amount of unsupervised time spent together. This construct mediated the relation between early adjustment problems in boys and multiple forms of adjustment problems in young adulthood.

The present study builds on this work by examining the bidirectional influence between deviant friendships and substance use over the course of adolescence. To address these questions, we focused on the measurement of deviant friendship process at the beginning (age 13–14) and end (age 17–18) of adolescence. The influence of friendships was considered at the transition

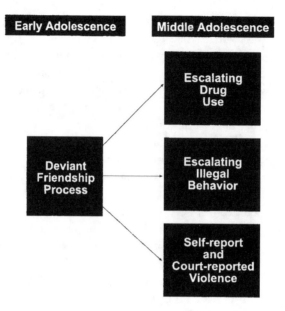

Early Adolescence	Middle Adolescence

Escalating Drug Use

Deviant Friendship Process

Escalating Illegal Behavior

Self-report and Court-reported Violence

Figure 9.1. Deviancy training in adolescent friendships and problem behavior outcomes in the Oregon Youth Study.

into high school (age 13–14), as well as into young adulthood, often corresponding to the transition out of school (age 17–18). Substance use was measured in middle adolescence (age 15–16) and young adulthood (age 21–23). Middle adolescence is a developmental milestone for substance use. Use by this age is prognostic of later substance abuse (Robins & Przybeck, 1985). In young adulthood, substance use is at its peak (Yamaguchi & Kandel, 1985), defining potentially persistent lifetime patterns.

Consistent with earlier work, the reciprocal influence of deviant friendship process was examined separately for tobacco, alcohol, and marijuana use. Epidemiological research suggests these as the three major substances of use and abuse in young adulthood (Anthony, Warner, & Kessler, 1997). Over time, the joint influence of deviant friendship process and substance use is considered in relation to alcohol and marijuana abuse, dangerous drug use, and intravenous drug use in young adulthood.

The following hypotheses were tested:

1. Deviant friendship process contributes to the development and progression of substance use from adolescence to young adulthood. Specifically, deviant friendship process predicts tobacco, alcohol, and marijuana use at age 15–16 and uniquely predicts the use and abuse of these substances in young adulthood.
2. Early-onset substance use has a secondary function of promoting friendships with substance-using friends. Specifically, substance

use in middle adolescence will predict deviant friendship process in late adolescence, after controlling for deviant friendship in early adolescence.

3. Progressions to alcohol abuse, marijuana abuse, use of addictive substances, and intravenous substance use are predicted by early-onset substance use and a persistent tendency to develop friendships with substance-using peers.

The Oregon Youth Study (OYS) boys ($N = 206$) and their friends were used to test the bidirectional hypotheses. The OYS is an ongoing longitudinal study of the contribution of family and peers to social adjustment (see Patterson et al., 1992). The methodology used for the OYS boys relevant to this study is detailed here as well as in other reports (Capaldi & Patterson, 1987; Patterson et al., 1992).

METHOD

Sample

The OYS boys consist of two successive fourth-grade cohorts from neighborhood schools with the highest crime rates within a medium-sized metropolitan area in the Pacific Northwest. All fourth-grade boys were invited to participate; a recruitment rate of 74.4% resulted in a sample size of 206 (Capaldi & Patterson, 1987). Comparisons of participants with anonymous teacher reports showed that nonparticipants (24.6%) were slightly less problematic in school than were participants. Recruitment for the OYS sample began in the 1983–1984 school year (Cohort 1, Wave 1, mean age = 10 years). The resulting sample was primarily of lower socioeconomic status, with an ethnic distribution of 90% European American. There was an economic recession at that time, which was particularly pronounced in the Pacific Northwest. Over 20% of the parents were unemployed, and 20% of all families received some form of welfare or financial assistance in the 1st year of the study (Capaldi & Patterson, 1987; Patterson et al., 1992). At recruitment (age 9–10), 42% of the families had two biological parents, 32% were single, biological-parent families, and 26% were step-parent families.

Procedure

Yearly assessments consisted of parent and son interviews, videotaped interaction tasks, school data, and court record searches. The main interview and most questionnaires pertained to behavior over the previous year. Peers were asked to engage in an interaction task with the adolescent participants three times during assessment (ages 13–14, 15–16, and 17–18). The primary focus of the present research was to understand the relative influence of friends on progressions in substance use from early adolescence to young adulthood; therefore, early- and late-adolescent friendship processes were studied.

Youth Interviews

Yearly face-to-face interviews were conducted by the assessment staff. The interviews covered a wide range of topics, including self-reported substance use, delinquency, peer antisocial behavior, parent and child relationships, employment, and parenting. For the present research, focus was on youth self-reported substance use in middle adolescence and young adulthood. Data from when the boys were age 15–16 represented the midadolescent development period. To assess substance use in young adulthood, data were drawn from the interviews between the ages of 20 and 23 years. Substance-use indicators from the three young adult waves were averaged to arrive at a global score in young adulthood. Substance use was considered separately by tobacco, alcohol, and marijuana.

Peer Interaction Task

The Peer Interaction Task (PIT) included interviews, questionnaires, and a videotaped discussion task between the participant and his chosen male friend. During the family interview, the boys were asked to nominate "three kids with whom you spend the most time" and then to choose the one with whom they would most like to participate in an observed assessment. Parent and child nominations were compared, and peers were selected on the basis of nomination by the study participant and confirmation by the parent. As in the work of Panella and Henggeler (1986) and Forgatch, Fetrow, and Lathrop (1985), the PIT was designed to elicit a wide range of responses between the boy and his friend. The dyads were videotaped during a 25-minute session involving five segments, during which the boys were asked to plan an activity together and then to discuss and solve four current problems. Each boy selected a problem he was having with his parents as well as a problem he had getting along with peers. The sequence of the tasks after the activity planning was counterbalanced to prevent order effects.

Topic Code

The Topic Code (Poe, Dishion, Griesler, & Andrews, 1990), developed to assess the process in which peers influence problem behavior, consists of two topic categories and two classes of interpersonal reaction. All symbolic content (verbal and nonverbal) was organized into the broadband topics, which were referred to as *normative* and *deviant* talk. Upon examination of the listener's impact on the organization of the discourse, most breaks in the discourse topics were found to contain positive reactions (laughs) or pauses in the conversation. Therefore, "laugh" and "pause" were the codes given to the listener reactions. The codes were entered into a hand-held electronic data collection device and were changed only when the interactant changed, the topic changed, or a pause or laugh by the interactant was entered. Once the data were gathered, the codes were summarized by dyad. In this analysis, the code was not considered changed until the topic changed or until a pause or laugh was entered. Interactant changes were ignored when coding topic, as a discourse unit, was considered to be dyadic.

Deviant Talk

Verbal behavior and gestures in this category displayed some element of a violation of conventional norms, or rule breaking. The code category of "rule-break" was coded for both verbal and nonverbal norm violation. Behavior coded as rule breaking included inappropriate activities (e.g., disrobing for the camera), vandalism, drug use, victimization, stealing, obscene gestures, getting into trouble at school, and any behavior that was contrary to instructions given for the task.

Normative Talk

All verbal and nonverbal behavior that did not fall into the rule-breaking category was coded as normative. The most common topics concerned recreation, school, family, money, and social- and peer-related issues.

Laugh

Positive affective reactions by the listener were coded as "laugh." Much of this behavior was actual laughter in reaction to the topics under discussion. "Laugh" was also coded for other nonverbal affective endorsements (e.g., thumbs up, smiles, "high five," and so forth). Other affective reactions such as fear and anger were not coded. Because of the general quality of the recordings, other emotions could not be measured reliably, so a wider range of reactions was not defined for the Topic Code.

Pause

Three seconds or more of silence were coded as "pause." In designing the Topic Code, "pause" was originally conceptualized as a negative event. Cohorts 1 and 2 were coded separately by two groups of coders who were unaware of any other data related to the participants. Reliability scores for a randomly selected

12% of Cohort 1 in Study Year 5 (age 13–14) showed a mean coder agreement of 90% and a kappa of .74; 15% of Cohort 2 was randomly selected for reliability, yielding a mean agreement of 94% and a kappa of .67.

Construct Formation

In building scales and constructs, two criteria were used (see Patterson et al., 1992). First, items included in the scale had to show internal consistency, an alpha of .6 or higher, and an item–total correlation of .2 ($p < .05$) or higher (see Table 9.1). Second, a scale had to converge with other indicators designed to assess the same construct (i.e., the factor loading for a one-factor solution had to be .3 or higher).

Deviant Friendship Process

The first indicator for this construct came from interviewer impressions. The interviewers responded to four questions concerning their sense that (a) the dyad engaged in antisocial behavior or prosocial behavior (reversed) and (b) the peer tended to encourage antisocial or prosocial (reversed) behavior. The mean across the four items was used for the peer interviewer impression score. An independent group of videotape coders also responded to six impression questions on the boys' use of alcohol, tobacco, marijuana, cocaine, hallucinogens, and speed or methamphetamine use. The mean of the items was computed for each boy and his friend; then the average of each was used to represent dyadic drug talk. The third indicator reflects the amount of time each boy and his friend spent together. In the interview, the boys were simply asked, "How many hours in the average week do you spend together?" The mean of the two reports was taken to represent a dyadic estimate of the amount of time the target and peer spent together. Finally, the direct observation measure of deviant talk within the friendship was used. Past research has used a rate-per-minute score and the binomial z score, representing the contingency between deviant talk and "laugh" (Dishion, Capaldi, et al., 1995; Dishion, French, & Patterson, 1995; Dishion et al., 1996, 1997; Patterson et al., 2000). The distributions on these "deviancy training" scores were skewed. The average duration of a bout of deviant talk, however, was less skewed in distribution. Thus, the average duration of bouts of deviant talk served as an excellent indicator of the boys' tendency to engage in deviancy training with friends (Dishion, 2000).

Self-Reported Tobacco Use

When the boys were 15–16 years old, they were asked the frequency with which they had used tobacco over the past year. The frequency of tobacco use was recoded across waves into an 8-level scale to provide consistency across

TABLE 9.1
The Psychometrics of the Deviant Friendship Process Construct

Dyadic antisocial indicators	Early adolescence (age 13–14)			Late adolescence (age 17–18)		
	Item–total correlation	Adjusted α	Dyad correlation	Item–total correlation	Adjusted α	Dyad correlation
Interviewer impressions, dyadic antisocial		.82			.85	
"How often do you think these two engage in						
delinquent or antisocial behavior?"	.62			.68		
prosocial behavior together?"	.65			.70		
"How often do you think this peer actively encourages						
antisocial or delinquent behavior of the target child?"	.60			.69		
prosocial or competent behavior of the target child?	.68			.71		
Coder impressions, dyadic drug talk						
Peer drug talk		.71	.89		.78	.92
Peer made specific references to						
Alcohol use	.41			.34		
Tobacco use	.36			.39		
Marijuana use	.63			.57		
Cocaine use	.47			.53		
Hallucinogen use	.31			.52		
Speed (methamphetamine) use	.33			.56		
Target drug talk		.72			.75	
Target made specific references to						
Alcohol use	.38			.26		
Tobacco use	.47			.40		
Marijuana use	.51			.62		
Cocaine use	.46			.49		
Hallucinogen use	.46			.46		
Speed (methamphetamine) use	.25			.53		
Hours peer and target child spend together ("How many hours in the average week do you spend. . .?")			.65			.65

waves and to reduce skewness. To recode, we divided the frequency counts by 12, and the result was recoded as follows: 0.01–0.17 = 1 (*once or twice*), 0.18–0.99 = 2 (*every 2–3 months*), 1.00–1.40 = 3 (*once a month*), 1.50–3.90 = 4 (*every 2–3 weeks*), 4.00– 7.90 = 5 (*once a week*), 8.00–29.90 = 6 (*2–3 times a week*), 30.00– 59.90 = 7 (*once a day*), and 60.00–Highest = 8 (*2–3 times a day*). In young adulthood (at ages 20–21, 21–22, and 22–23), the young men were asked how many times they had used tobacco in the past year. These counts were also recoded to an ordinal frequency scale (as above). For all substance use measures, the indicator for young adulthood was represented by taking the average of the 3 years (age 20–23) as a robust estimate of substance use in young adulthood.

Self-Reported Alcohol Use

At each assessment wave, the boys were asked about the frequency, volume, and level of intoxication resulting from alcohol. The following strategy was used to compute an estimate of alcohol use in middle adolescence and young adulthood. In the latter stage, alcohol use was averaged across three waves of assessment, as described above.

At each wave, the boys were asked to recall the number of times they had used beer, wine, and spirits during the previous year. As with tobacco, these frequency counts were recoded to the 8-point scale. The average frequency of beer, wine, and spirits use served as an indicator of alcohol use.

If the boys reported alcohol use, they were then asked to rate the volume they consumed on a 7-point scale ranging from *less than one drink (can of beer, glass of wine, shot of liquor)* to *six drinks or more*. The mean volume of the three types of alcohol was used as another indicator.

Again, those boys reporting alcohol use were asked a series of questions that assessed alcohol intoxication. The average score for the following items was taken as the indicator in adolescence and young adulthood: (a) "Over the last two weeks, how many times have you had five drinks in a row?" (b) "Over the past two weeks, how many times have you had three to four drinks in a row?" (c) "When you drink alcoholic beverages, do you usually get high?" (d) "If yes, how high do you get?" (e) "Have you ever tried to stop using alcoholic beverages and found you couldn't stop?" (f) "Have you ever been drunk?" (g) "Have you ever been drunk in a public place?" (h) "Have you ever passed out from drinking?" (i) "Have you ever thrown up from drinking?" (j) "Have you ever lost or broken things when drinking?"

Self-Reported Marijuana Use

Marijuana use was indicated by both frequency and patterns of use. As with tobacco and alcohol frequency, the boys were asked to recall the number of times they used marijuana. The counts were recoded to the frequency scale in both adolescence and young adulthood, as described previously.

If the boys had used marijuana at least once a month, they were asked a series of questions regarding their pattern of use. As with the other substances, the mean of the following scores was used for adolescence and young adulthood: (a) "Have you ever tried to stop using marijuana and found you could not?" (b) "Have you found that you can't get as high on marijuana as you used to?" (c) "Have you ever gone to school while high on marijuana?" (d) "Have you had any problems related to school, such as not doing schoolwork or forgetting things, because of marijuana?"

In young adulthood, the young men were asked the following: (a) "When you use marijuana, how high do you get?" (b) "Have you ever tried to stop using marijuana and found you could not?" (c) "Have you found that you can't get as high on marijuana as you used to?" (d) "Have you ever gone to school or work while high on marijuana?" (e) "Have you had any problems related to school or work, such as not doing schoolwork or forgetting things, because of marijuana?" (f) "Have you had any problems with relationships with others because of marijuana?" (g) "Has there been a week in the past year when you haven't smoked marijuana at all?"

Adolescent Substance Use

An adolescent substance use composite score was formed for use as an independent variable in regression analyses on young adult drug abuse. First, the specific indicators from each substance were standardized and combined to form specific scores for tobacco (frequency), alcohol (frequency, volume, and intoxication), and marijuana (frequency and intoxication) use. These substance scores were then standardized and combined by taking the mean to represent a composite substance use score for age 15–16.

Self-Reported Dangerous Drug Use

During the three assessments covering age 20–23, young men were asked if they had used any of a wide range of other drug types (labeled as *dangerous* because of the potential for lethal overdose or addiction) including cocaine, crack, PCP, speed, crank, methamphetamine, and heroin. The dangerous drug-use variable was calculated at each wave by counting the number of dangerous drugs used in the previous year. The mean of the number used in each of the three waves was then used to represent dangerous drug use in young adulthood.

Self-Reported Drug Injection

During the three young adult assessments, the young men were asked how many times they had injected drugs in the previous year. For each assessment, their report was dichotomized as either injection (1) or no injection (0). A summary score was then created to indicate whether or not the participants had reported injecting drugs in any of the 3 years during young adulthood. Seven young men out of the 205 (3.4%) reported injecting drugs during the 3-year period.

Data Analytic Strategy

To examine longitudinal trends, we computed multivariate analyses of variance on comparable indicators across waves. Structural equation modeling (SEM) was used to examine longitudinal, bidirectional effects using the AMOS program (Arbuckle, 1997). The full information maximum likelihood (FIML) algorithm was used (Arbuckle, 1996, 1997), which has been demonstrated to provide unbiased estimates when the data are missing at random. For the FIML model estimation, $N = 201$, because 5 targets did not participate in either wave because of missing data on the friendship assessment. Fortunately, the OYS has few missing data (95% retention across waves), and models correcting for missing data and those using listwise deletion were nearly identical.

To predict young adult substance use, we computed multiple regressions using composite measures for the independent and dependent constructs. These models also evaluated interaction effects between adolescent substance use and deviant friendships on adult substance abuse.

Data on substance use are plagued by skewness and kurtosis. These data were examined for outliers and skewed distributions. In the data set, the alcohol use construct in adulthood was normally distributed, yet all other substance-use constructs were skewed and kurtotic. The main strategy for handling these disparate distributions was to examine models by transforming the data ($\log = 1$) to improve the distributions. In addition, all models were analyzed with the asymptotically distribution free (ADF) estimation algorithm available in the AMOS program. The effect coefficients are noted in the results for the tobacco and marijuana use models. Again, the effect coefficients are quite similar using both the maximum likelihood and ADF procedure.

Controlling for boys' history of antisocial behavior allows for the analysis of a third factor explanation for the link between deviant friendship process and substance use across adolescence. Thus, the models were run while controlling for the boys' antisocial behavior with a multimethod, multi-agent indicator for the boys at age 12 (Dishion et al., 1997).

RESULTS

Initially, the longitudinal trends were analyzed for deviant friendship process and substance use. Table 9.2 provides the mean level for each of the

TABLE 9.2
Means and Standard Deviations of Model Indicators

Indicator	N	Year 5 (age 13–14)		Year 7 (age 15–16)		Year 9 (age 17–18)		Year 12 (age 20–21)		Year 13 (age 21–22)		Year 14 (age 22–23)	
		M	SD	M	SD	M	SD	M	SD	M	SD	M	SD
Target and peer interview, hours together per week	167	17.30	16.87			20.68	21.89						
Coder impressions, dyadic drug talk	165	1.10	0.24			1.49	0.45						
Interviewer impressions, dyadic antisocial behavior	167	2.31	0.67			2.33	0.77						
Topic code, duration of rule-break talk (in seconds)	166	227.77	250.69			226.78	278.96						
Target interview													
Frequency of													
Tobacco use	195			2.52	3.38			4.46	3.65	4.33	3.69	4.48	3.66
Alcohol use	195			0.90	1.12			1.94	1.25	2.43	1.38	2.39	1.32
Marijuana use	194			0.74	1.77			1.99	2.53	2.04	2.63	2.00	2.52
Volume of alcohol use	195			1.38	1.62			2.76	1.47	2.91	1.44	2.77	1.50
Patterns of													
Alcohol use	193			0.40	0.61			1.08	0.75	1.07	0.76	0.98	0.66
Marijuana use	194			0.13	0.45			0.42	0.58	0.38	0.57	0.31	0.45

indicators on both constructs. When the boys were compared at ages 13–14 and 17–18, observed deviant friendship process was equivalent across time on two of the four measures. In early adolescence, the mean duration of bouts of deviant talk was 227 seconds (almost 4 minutes), and in late adolescence it was 226 seconds. Observers rated the boys as somewhat more encouraging of deviant behavior and drug use in late adolescence than in early adolescence, and the boys themselves reported spending more time together (17.3 vs. 20.7 hours per week).

Trends in substance use were as expected: The boys' frequency, volume, and pattern of substance use increased dramatically from adolescence to young adulthood. On all indices of substance use, there was at least a twofold (100%) increase in usage patterns, and the differences between adolescence and adulthood were statistically reliable. Consistent with other research (Kandel, Yamaguchi, & Chen, 1992), however, increases in substance use from age 20–23 were negligible.

It is interesting to consider the stability in the boys' selection of friends and their relationship patterns. SEM was used to examine the stability in the deviant friendship process construct. Over a 5-year period, the stability coefficient was .53, which is statistically reliable ($p < .01$). Therefore, even though only 22 of 180 boys assessed at both times brought in the same friend at ages 13–14 and 17–18, the tendency to connect, spend time, and encourage deviant behavior with a friend was highly stable over this period of development. Table 9.3 provides the convergent validity and individual stabilities for each of the indicators in the deviant friendship process construct. The stability was highest for the duration of deviant talk and the coder impressions of drug use talk ($r = .30$ and $r = .30$, respectively). This was a surprising finding, given that the boys were observed for only 30 min in highly contrived circumstances (e.g., videotaping). In this sense, deviant friendship process is an interaction style that is relatively consistent over time.

Reciprocal covariation was also examined between smoking, alcohol consumption, and marijuana use, beginning with an SEM describing the

TABLE 9.3
Convergent Validity and Stability of the Deviant Friendship Process
Indicators at Ages 13–14 and 17–18

Indicator	1	2	3	4
1. Hours per week	.14 (167)	.38** (178)	.24** (178)	.15* (175)
2. Coder impressions, drug talk	.18* (186)	.30** (165)	.52** (178)	.46** (175)
3. Interviewer impressions, dyadic antisocial	.26** (189)	.37** (186)	.20** (167)	.37** (175)
4. Average duration of rule-break talk	.28** (190)	.51** (188)	.43** (190)	.30** (166)

Note. The ns appear in parentheses. Correlation coefficients below the diagonal are convergent validities at age 13–14. Correlation coefficients above the diagonal are convergent validities at age 17–18. Correlation coefficients on the diagonal are stability estimates from age 13–14 to age 17–18.
* $p < .05$. ** $p < .01$.

reciprocal covariation between tobacco use and deviant friendship process (as shown in Figure 9.2). Clearly, early adolescent friendships are associated with early smoking, as well as the reverse. Smoking at age 13–14 predicts deviant friendship process at age 17–18 after controlling for the influence of earlier friendship patterns. It is interesting that friendship patterns at age 17–18 also predict the use of tobacco in young adulthood ($\beta = .25$) when smoking at age 15–16 is included in the multivariate analysis.

The overall model shown in Figure 9.2 fits the data, as reflected in the chi-square goodness-of-fit test, $\chi^2(32, N = 201) = 31.6, p = .49$. Of the variation in young adult tobacco use, 32% was accounted for primarily by tobacco use in middle adolescence. In contrast, 47% of the variation in deviant friendship process at age 17–18 was accounted for by adolescent tobacco use and early associations with deviant peers. The distribution of tobacco use was highly skewed and kurtotic. Using the ADF estimation procedure yielded results quite similar to those in Figure 9.2 and also showed an adequate fit between the model and the data (comparative fit index = .99, $p = .39$). The model for alcohol use was less compelling, as shown in Figure 9.3. By and large, the model accounted for little variation (4%) in young adult alcohol use. However, early deviant friendship process was associated with adolescent alcohol use ($\beta = .52$), and reciprocally, adolescent alcohol use accounted for unique variance in later selection of a deviant friend ($\beta = .35$) after controlling for stability. Forty-four percent of the variation in deviant friendship process at age 17–18 was accounted for by both constructs. This model fit the data reasonably well, $\chi^2(72, N = 201) = 84.6, p = .15$. An ADF estimation approach to this model did not improve the fit, nor did it change the conclusions regarding the low predictability of young adult alcohol use.

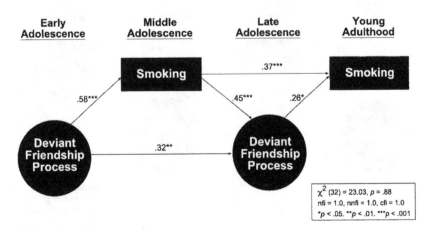

Figure 9.2. Deviant friendship process and the development of tobacco abuse. nfi = normed fit index; nnfi = nonnormed fit index; cfi = comparative fit index.

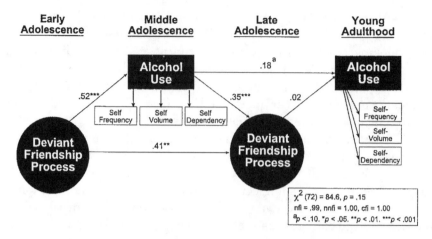

Figure 9.3. Deviant friendship process and the development of alcohol abuse. nfi = normed fit index; nnfi = nonnormed fit index; cfi = comparative fit index.

Finally, the model describing the reciprocal link between marijuana use and friendships is summarized in Figure 9.4. Again, we find that deviant friendship process predicts adolescent marijuana use (β = .57, p < .01), and in turn, early marijuana use predicts deviance in friendships in late adolescence (β = .44, p < .01) after controlling for the stability in the friendship characteristics. Again, stability of deviant friendship process was reduced (β = .34) but remained statistically reliable when marijuana use was entered into the model.

Marijuana use in adolescence and late adolescent deviant friendships predicted young adult marijuana use at about the same level (β = .28, p < .01). The model accounts for 25% of the variance in marijuana use in young

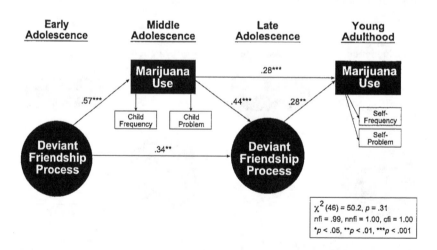

Figure 9.4. Deviant friendship process and the development of marijuana abuse. nfi = normed fit index; nnfi = nonnormed fit index; cfi = comparative fit index.

adulthood and 49% of the variation in late adolescent deviant friendship process. The ADF estimation procedure also produced an adequate fit between the model and the data and did not change the general pattern of multivariate results shown in Figure 9.4.

Quite possibly, the covariation between substance use and peer deviance is merely a function of the boys' general tendency to engage in antisocial behavior. To address this issue, we ran three models, controlling for the antisocial behavior construct as assessed at age 12. Consistent with earlier research (Dishion, Capaldi, et al., 1995, 1999), antisocial behavior predicted both early deviant friendship process (minimum $\beta = .51$) and substance use in middle adolescence (tobacco, $\beta = .25$; alcohol, $\beta = .20$; marijuana, $\beta = .09$) after controlling for deviant friendships. Inclusion of the boys' antisocial construct at age 12, however, did not change the pattern of findings for deviant friendships in late adolescence or substance use in young adulthood. That is, the pattern of reciprocal covariation between deviant friendship process and substance use from early adolescence to young adulthood remained unchanged, controlling for antisocial behavior at age 12. Thus, antisocial boys, indeed, tend to select deviant friends in early adolescence and are more likely to initiate substance use early.

Finally, multiple regression was used to predict young adult substance use from adolescent substance use and deviant friendships. A regression format was used for these analyses to provide a basis for testing interaction effects (Aiken & West, 1991). As described above, the dependent variables in young adulthood included alcohol abuse, marijuana abuse, dangerous substances, and drug injection.

Adolescent substance use predicted three of the four dependent variables (see Table 9.4). The effect of adolescent substance use on adult alcohol abuse was not statistically reliable, and deviant friendship process was predictive only

TABLE 9.4
Predicting Young Adult Substance Abuse From Adolescent Adaptation

Independent variable	Dependent variables from age 20–23			
	Alcohol abuse	Marijuana abuse	Dangerous drugs	Drug injection[a]
Deviant friendship process (ages 13–14 and 17–18)	.18	.29**	.19	3.49†
Substance use (tobacco, marijuana, alcohol)	.21	.29**	.36**	2.99†
Deviant Friendship Process × Substance Use	−.26*	−.12	−.21*	.51
Adjusted R^2	.06	.20	.14	.21[b]

[a]Exponentiated β. [b]Nagelkerke R^2.
†$p < .10$. *$p < .05$. **$p < .01$.

of marijuana abuse. The Deviant Friendship Process × Substance Use interaction was statistically reliable for alcohol abuse and dangerous drug use in young adulthood.

The statistically reliable interactions are plotted in Figure 9.5 with terciles as cutoff points for examining trends (Aiken & West, 1991). Inspection of Figure 9.5 reveals that for alcohol abuse, youth with very low substance use and nondeviant friends are quite unlikely to abuse alcohol in adulthood. The trend for dangerous drug use is more challenging to interpret with respect to existing models of substance abuse. Apparently, a subset of adolescent boys used substances in adolescence but had low involvement with deviant peers. This subset is likely to escalate to dangerous drug use by young adulthood, as revealed by the plots in Figure 9.5.

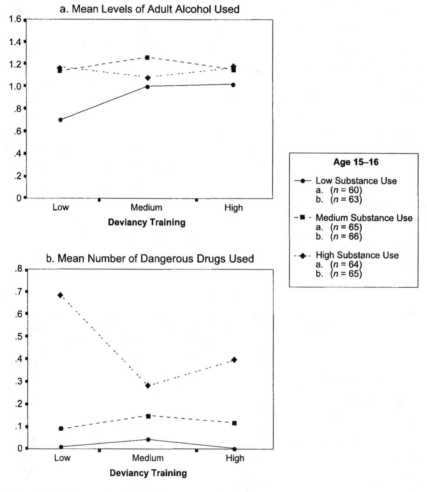

Figure 9.5. Interaction effects for young adult substance abuse and adolescent social and behavioral history.

In general, the regression models accounted for modest variation in adult substance use, ranging from 6% for alcohol abuse to 20% for dangerous drug use. Logistic regressions were used to predict the binomial drug injection score. Early substance use and deviant friendship process marginally ($p < .10$) predicted drug injection; however, only 6 of the boys reported such behavior.

DISCUSSION

The OYS affords both advantages and disadvantages with respect to understanding the bidirectional relation between friendship and substance use from adolescence to adulthood. Advantages include the availability of high-quality repeated measures of constructs related to this question. Another advantage is the high level of initial recruitment and retention across 15 years of research. The limitations include the sample size ($N = 206$) and the inclusion of only European American males. The limitations restrict the researcher's ability to explore both gender and ethnic variation within the reported findings.

Despite such limitations, these findings are consistent with previous research on peer influence on adolescent substance use. In support of the first hypothesis, the strongest proximal correlate of adolescent substance use is the tendency to cluster into peer groups that use substances (Dinges & Oetting, 1993; Dishion & Loeber, 1985; Elliott et al., 1985; Jessor & Jessor, 1977; Kandel, 1973; Oetting & Beauvais, 1987, 1990). These data extend this research by including a measure of peer influence on friendship, including direct observations of deviant talk, a self-report index of time spent together, and staff impressions.

Improving the measurement of deviant peer involvement in this way is more than a psychometric improvement. Philosophers of behavioral science often guide researchers to more carefully attend to "method issues" in developmental theory.

The present study has two such noteworthy issues. The first is the use of multiple measurement methods, thus avoiding problems of monomethod bias (e.g., Cook & Campbell, 1979). The second methodological advancement is the measurement of the friendship as a relationship process, which enables the translation of an abstract construct to real-time behavior (see Fiske, 1986). Indeed, direct observations of friendship have enriched understanding of the dark side of friendships (see Hartup, 1996), revealing a process of interchange that appears salient to the development of problem behavior.

Consistent with the second hypothesis, these data suggest that an important secondary function of substance use may be the power of drugs to connect individuals within peer groups. Lifestyle, as reflected in drug attitudes and behaviors, may be the currency with which a person shops for relationships

(Patterson et al., 1992). Unbeknownst to most people, those relationships then shape their attitudes and behavior. Deviance, in particular, seems to be a rather salient sorting feature in the friendship selection process. The extent to which two adolescent males organize their friendships on deviance, as seen here, seems to be relevant to a variety of problem behaviors and developmental outcomes. Selection and influence, therefore, go hand and fist. This finding is consistent with ecological perspectives on social development, which emphasize the primary role of relationships (Bronfenbrenner, 1989; Dishion, French, & Patterson, 1995; Hinde, 1989; Patterson & Reid, 1984).

This research captures a developmentally significant transition. Substance use by age 15 has been shown to be prognostic of substance abuse by young adulthood when other factors such as problem behavior are controlled (Robins & Przybeck, 1985). However, it appears that not all substances are equal with respect to risk. The most unique finding is that alcohol use in adolescence is not a good predictor of young adult alcohol use or abuse in adulthood. This finding is in agreement with those of other investigators (e.g., Donovan, Jessor, & Costa, 1991). The general assumption is that alcohol use in adolescence is practically normative (Hops, Davis, & Lewin, 1999), and certainly it is by young adulthood (i.e., normally distributed). Perhaps because alcohol use is a normative behavior in this culture in late adolescence to adulthood, the dynamics associated with its emergence do not fit the developmental pattern characteristic of other problem behaviors.

Heterogeneity in developmental trends also emerged in the longitudinal analysis of young adult drug abuse, providing partial support for the third hypothesis of this study. In general, overall levels of substance use predicted marijuana abuse, dangerous drug use, and drug injection. Deviant friendship process, however, accounted for only marijuana use and drug injection. It is also important to note that these models account for relatively low levels of variation in adult drug abuse (6% to 20%), suggesting that there is much to be learned about the ecology and dynamics of young adult substance abuse.

Unexpected findings were those showing an interaction between deviant friendships and substance use in the prediction of dangerous drug use. Visual inspection of the data suggests a subgroup of adolescents who used substances, and did not seem to have deviant friends, but nonetheless escalated to high levels of dangerous drug use as young adults. These youth seem to be on a trajectory that is not only unique but alarming, a path difficult to interpret from a problem behavior perspective. Loeber (1988) identified a pure substance use group (i.e., not accompanied by other problem behaviors) in his formulation of adolescent developmental trajectories; however, follow-up data were unavailable at that time to discern the developmental pathway into adulthood. A larger sample is needed for more careful analysis of adolescent subgroups in order to understand diverse influences on their substance-using patterns. It is possible that sibling or parent drug use promotes early onset in youth otherwise on a normative developmental path (Brook, Brook, & Whiteman, 1999).

The implication of the present research for prevention is relatively straightforward: Prevention efforts must focus on both the individual and the peer ecology. Research by Botvin (2000) suggests that promoting social influence skills in schools can prevent early-onset substance use. This research suggests that, in addition, emphasis on how peer environments are structured needs attention within prevention programs. A current prevention trial focuses exclusively on parenting practices in the middle school years (Dishion & Kavanagh, 2000). Initial findings show that engaging parents in services that support parenting are producing reduced growth in deviant peer involvement and substance use (Dishion, Bullock, & Granic, 2002; Dishion, Kavanagh, Nelson, Schneiger, & Kaufman, 2002). In addition, randomly assigning high-risk youth to interventions that aggregate peers can actually increase problem behavior and drug use (Dishion et al., 1999). Clearly, both studies suggest that adults can and do structure environments that are highly relevant to the formation of peer ecologies, which are conducive to progressions in problem behavior.

These findings also suggest that the task of treatment programs for drug abuse is both complex and formidable. In young adolescence, use of substances may have two functions, the most obvious being the function of changing affective states and inducing euphoria. The second, perhaps as pernicious, is the function of providing a form of commerce with the social world for the drug user. Inasmuch as substance use plays a central role in a young person's relationship organization, alternative interpersonal settings and strategies are critical to emphasize in the endeavor to promote abstinence and well-being in the young adult years. The young adult years are a critical transition point for many individuals, when selection of partners, formation of families, and the foundation for the next generation are established. Thus, prevention and treatment in adolescence and young adulthood are very important for optimizing life-course development.

REFERENCES

Aiken, L. S., & West, S. G. (1991). *Multiple regression: Testing and interpreting interactions*. Thousand Oaks, CA: Sage.

Anthony, J., Warner, L. A., & Kessler, R. C. (1997). Comparative epidemiology of dependence on tobacco, alcohol, controlled substances and inhalants: Basic findings from the National Comorbidity Survey. In G. A. Malatt & G. R. VandenBos (Eds.), *Addictive behaviors: Readings on etiology, prevention and treatment* (pp. 3–39). Washington, DC: American Psychological Association.

Arbuckle, J. L. (1996). Full information estimation in the presence of incomplete data. In G. A. Marcoulides & R. E. Schumacker (Eds.), *Advanced structural equation modeling: Issues and techniques* (pp. 243–277). Mahwah, NJ: Erlbaum.

Arbuckle, J. L. (1997). AMOS Users' Guide (Version 3.6) [Computer software]. Chicago: SmallWaters Corporation.

Block, J., Block, J. H., & Keyes, S. (1988). Longitudinally foretelling drug usage in adolescence: Early childhood personality and environmental precursors. *Child Development, 59,* 336–355.

Botvin, G. J. (2000). Preventing drug use in schools: Social and competence enhancement approaches targeting individual-level etiological factors. *Addictive Behaviors, 25,* 887–897.

Bronfenbrenner, U. (1989). Ecological systems theory. In P. Vasta (Ed.), *Annals of child development, Vol. 6. Six theories of child development: Revised formulations and current issues* (pp. 187–249). London: JAI Press.

Brook, J. S., Brook, D. W., & Whiteman, M. (1999). Older sibling correlates of younger sibling drug use in the context of parent–child relations. *Genetic, Social, and General Psychology Monographs, 125*(4), 451–468.

Capaldi, D. M., Crosby, L., & Stoolmiller, M. (1996). Predicting the timing of first sexual intercourse for at-risk adolescent males. *Child Development, 67,* 344–359.

Capaldi, D. M., & Patterson, G. R. (1987). An approach to the problem of recruitment and retention rates for longitudinal research. *Behavioral Assessment, 9,* 169–177.

Chassin, L., Presson, C. C., Sherman, S. J., Montello, D., & McGrew, J. (1986). Changes in peer and parent influence during adolescence: Longitudinal versus cross-sectional perspectives on smoking initiation. *Developmental Psychology, 22,* 327–334.

Cook, T. D., & Campbell, D. T. (1979). *Quasi-experimentation: Design and analysis issues for field settings.* Boston: Houghton Mifflin.

Dinges, M. N., & Oetting, E. R. (1993). Similarity in drug use patterns between adolescents and their friends. *Adolescence, 28,* 253–266.

Dishion, T. J. (2000). Cross-setting consistency in early adolescent psychopathology: Deviant friendships and problem behavior sequelae. *Journal of Personality, 68*(6), 1109–1126.

Dishion, T. J., Bullock, B. M., & Granic, I. (2002). Pragmatism in modeling peer influence: Dynamics, outcomes, and change processes. *Development and Psychopathology, 14,* 969–981.

Dishion, T. J., Capaldi, D. M., Spracklen, K. M., & Li, F. (1995). Peer ecology of male adolescent drug use. *Development and Psychopathology, 7,* 803–824.

Dishion, T. J., Capaldi, D. M., & Yoerger, K. (1999). Middle childhood antecedents to progression in male adolescent substance use: An ecological analysis of risk and protection. *Journal of Adolescent Research, 14,* 175–206.

Dishion, T. J., Eddy, J. M., Haas, E., Li, F., & Spracklen, K. (1997). Friendships and violent behavior during adolescence. *Social Development, 6,* 207–223.

Dishion, T. J., French, D. C., & Patterson, G. R. (1995). The development and ecology of antisocial behavior. In D. Cicchetti & D. J. Cohen (Eds.), *Developmental psychopathology: Vol. 2. Risk, disorder, and adaptation* (pp. 421–471). New York: Wiley.

Dishion, T. J., & Kavanagh, K. (2000). A multilevel approach to family-centered prevention in schools: Process and outcome. *Addictive Behaviors, 25,* 899–911.

Dishion, T. J., Kavanagh, K., Nelson, S., Schneiger, A., & Kaufman, N. (2002). Preventing early adolescent substance use: A family-centered strategy for the public middle school. *Prevention Science, 3,* 191–201.

Dishion, T. J., & Loeber, R. (1985). Male adolescent marijuana and alcohol use: The role of parents and peers revisited. *American Journal of Drug and Alcohol Abuse, 11,* 11–25.

Dishion, T. J., & Medici Skaggs, N. (2000). An ecological analysis of monthly "bursts" in early adolescent substance use. *Applied Developmental Science, 4,* 89–97.

Dishion, T. J., & Patterson, G. R. (1999). Model-building in developmental psychopathology: A pragmatic approach to understanding and intervention. *Journal of Clinical Child Psychology, 28,* 502–512.

Dishion, T. J., Spracklen, K. M., Andrews, D. M., & Patterson, G. R. (1996). Deviancy training in male adolescent friendships. *Behavior Therapy, 27,* 373–390.

Donovan, J. E., Jessor, R., & Costa, F. M. (1991). Adolescent health behavior and conventionality–unconventionality: An extension of problem behavior theory. *Health Psychology, 10,* 52–61.

Duncan, T. E., Duncan, S. C., & Hops, H. (1994). The effects of family cohesiveness and peer encouragement on the development of adolescent alcohol use: A cohort sequential approach to the analysis of longitudinal data. *Journal of Studies on Alcohol, 55,* 588–599.

Elliott, D., Huizinga, D., & Ageton, S. (1985). *Explaining delinquency and drug use.* Beverly Hills, CA: Sage.

Ennett, S. T., & Bauman, K. E. (1994). The contribution of influence and selection to adolescent peer group homogeneity: The case of adolescent cigarette smoking. *Journal of Personality and Social Psychology, 67,* 653–663.

Fiske, D. W. (1986). Specificity of method and knowledge in social science. In D. W. Fiske & R. A. Shweder (Eds.), *Metatheory in social science* (pp. 61–82). Chicago: University of Chicago Press.

Forgatch, M. S., Fetrow, B., & Lathrop, M. (1985). *Solving problems in family interactions.* Unpublished training manual. (Available from Oregon Social Learning Center, 160 East 4th Avenue, Eugene, OR 97401-2426.)

Friedman, L. S., Lichtenstein, E., & Biglan, A. (1985). Smoking onset among teens: An empirical analysis of initial situations. *Addictive Behaviors, 10,* 1–13.

Graham, J. W., Collins, L. M., Wugalter, S. E., Chung, N. K., & Hansen, W. B. (1991). Modeling transitions in latent-stage sequential processes: A substance use prevention example. *Journal of Consulting and Clinical Psychology, 59,* 48–57.

Hartup, W. W. (1996). The company they keep: Friendships and their developmental significance. *Child Development, 67*, 1–13.

Hawkins, J. D., Catalano, R. F., & Miller, J. Y. (1992). Risk and protective factors for alcohol and other drug problems in adolescence and early adulthood: Implications for substance abuse prevention. *Psychological Bulletin, 112*, 64–105.

Hinde, R. A. (1989). Ethological and relationship approaches. In R. Vasta (Ed.), *Annals of child development: Vol. 6. Six theories of child development: Revised formulations and current issues* (pp. 251–285). Hillsdale, NJ: Erlbaum.

Hops, H., Davis, B., & Lewin, L. M. (1999, March). The development of alcohol and other substance use: A gender study of family and peer context. *Journal of Studies on Alcohol, 13*(Suppl.), 22–31.

Jessor, R. (1976). Predicting time of onset of marijuana use: A developmental study of high school youth. *Journal of Consulting and Clinical Psychology, 44*, 125–134.

Jessor, R., & Jessor, S. L. (1977). *Problem behavior and psychosocial development*. New York: Academic Press.

Johnson, R. J., & Kaplan, H. B. (1990). Stability of psychological symptoms: Drug use consequences and intervening processes. *Journal of Health and Social Behavior, 31*, 277–291.

Kandel, D. (1973, September 14). Adolescent marijuana use: Role of parents and peers. *Science, 181*, 1067–1081.

Kandel, D. B. (1986). Process of peer influence on adolescence. In R. K. Silbereisen (Ed.), *Development as action in context* (pp. 33–52). Berlin, Germany: Springer-Verlag.

Kandel, D. B., Davies, M., Karus, D., & Yamaguchi, K. (1986). The consequences in young adulthood of adolescent drug involvement. *Archives of General Psychiatry, 43*, 746–754.

Kandel, D. B., Yamaguchi, K., & Chen, K. (1992). Stages of progression in drug involvement from adolescence to adulthood: Further evidence for the gateway theory. *Journal of Studies on Alcohol, 53*, 447–457.

Kaplan, H. B., & Liu, X. (1994). A longitudinal analysis of mediating variables in the drug use–dropping out relationship. *Criminology, 32*, 415–439.

Kellam, S. G., Brown, C. H., Rubin, B. R., & Ensminger, M. E. (1983). Paths leading to teenage psychiatric symptoms and substance use: Developmental epidemiological studies in Woodlawn. In S. R. Guze, F. J. Earns, & J. E. Barrett (Eds.), *Childhood psychopathology and development* (pp. 17–51). New York: Raven Press.

Loeber, R. (1988). Natural histories of conduct problems, delinquency, and associated substance use: Evidence for developmental progressions. In B. B. Lahey & A. E. Casdin (Eds.), *Advances in clinical child psychopathology* (Vol. 2, pp. 73–124). New York: Plenum Press.

McCord, J. (1981). Consideration of some effects of a counseling program. In S. E. Martin, L. B. Sechrest, & R. Redner (Eds.), *New directions in the rehabilitation of criminal offenders* (pp. 394–405). Washington, DC: National Academy of Sciences.

Newcomb, M., & Bentler, P. (1988). *Consequences of adolescent drug use.* Newbury Park, CA: Sage.

Oetting, E. R., & Beauvais, F. (1987). Peer cluster theory, socialization characteristics, and adolescent drug use: A path analysis. *Journal of Consulting and Clinical Psychology, 34,* 205–213.

Oetting E. R., & Beauvais, F. (1990). Adolescent drug use: Findings of national and local surveys. *Journal of Consulting and Clinical Psychology, 58,* 385–394.

O'Malley, P. M., Bachman, J. G., & Johnston, L. D. (1988). Period, age, and cohort effects on substance use among young Americans: A decade of change, 1976–86. *American Journal of Public Health, 78,* 1315–1321.

Osgood, D. W., Wilson, J. K., O'Malley, P. M., Bachman, J. G., & Johnston, L. D. (1996). Routine activities and individual deviant behavior. *American Sociological Review, 61,* 635–655.

Panella, D., & Henggeler, S. W. (1986). Peer interactions of conduct-disordered, anxious-withdrawn, and well-adjusted black adolescents. *Journal of Abnormal Child Psychology, 14,* 1–11.

Patterson, G. R., Dishion, T. J., & Yoerger, K. (2000). Adolescent growth in new forms of problem behavior: Macro- and micro-peer dynamics. *Prevention Science, 1,* 3–13.

Patterson, G. R., & Reid, J. B. (1984). Social interactional processes within the family: The study of moment-by-moment family transactions in which human social development is imbedded. *Journal of Applied Developmental Psychology, 5,* 237–262.

Patterson, G. R., Reid, J. B., & Dishion, T. J. (1992). *A social learning approach: IV. Antisocial boys.* Eugene, OR: Castalia.

Poe, J., Dishion, T. J., Griesler, P., & Andrews, D. W. (1990). *Topic code.* Unpublished coding manual. (Available from Oregon Social Learning Center, 160 East Fourth Avenue, Eugene, OR 97401-2426)

Pulkkinen, L. (1983). Youthful smoking and drinking in a longitudinal perspective. *Journal of Youth and Adolescence, 12,* 253–283.

Robins, L. N., & McEvoy, L. (1990). Conduct problems as predictors of abuse. In L. N. Robins & M. Rutter (Eds.), *Straight and devious pathways from childhood to adulthood* (pp. 182–204). New York: Cambridge University Press.

Robins, L. N., & Przybeck, T. R. (1985). Age of onset of drug use as a factor in drug and other disorders. In C. L. Jones & R. J. Battjes (Eds.), *Etiology of drug abuse: Implications for prevention* (Research Monograph No. 56, pp. 178–193). Rockville, MD: National Institute on Drug Abuse.

Smith, G. M., & Fogg, C. P. (1979). Psychological antecedents of teenage drug use. *Research in Community Mental Health, 1,* 87–102.

Stein, J. A., Smith, G. M., Guy, S. M., & Bentler, P. M. (1993). Consequences of adolescent drug use on young adult job behavior and job satisfaction. *Journal of Applied Psychology, 78,* 463–474.

Windle, M. (1990). A longitudinal study of antisocial behaviors in early adolescence as predictors of late adolescence substance use: Gender and ethnic group differences. *Journal of Abnormal Psychology*, 99, 86–91.

Yamaguchi, K., & Kandel, D. B. (1985). On resolution of role incompatibility: A life event history analysis of family roles and marijuana use. *American Journal of Sociology*, 90, 1284–1325.

10

CONJOINT DEVELOPMENTAL TRAJECTORIES OF YOUNG ADULT ALCOHOL AND TOBACCO USE

KRISTINA M. JACKSON, KENNETH J. SHER, AND JOHN E. SCHULENBERG

In the past decade, much research has been focused on modeling age trends in substance use and on examining both predictors and outcomes of such trends. Such research on the natural history of substance use has demonstrated that, on average, substance use tends to increase throughout adolescence, decline over young adulthood, and level off by the fourth decade of life (Bachman, Wadsworth, O'Malley, Johnston, & Schulenberg, 1997; Chen & Kandel, 1995). Despite the importance of identifying these normative age trends, however, the emphasis on average change belies the growing evidence that the developmental course of substance use is systematically heterogeneous across the life course with distinct variation in the timing and degree of escalation and duration. Identifying and modeling distinct courses of substance use can reveal the extent to which different risk and protective factors

Preparation of this chapter was supported by National Institute on Alcohol Abuse and Alcoholism Grants R21 AA12383 and K01 AA13938 to Kristina M. Jackson; the Monitoring the Future Project, from which the data were obtained, is funded by the National Institute on Drug Abuse Grant DA01411 to Lloyd D. Johnston. We thank Tammy Chung, Jennifer Krull, Denis McCarthy, Bengt Muthén, Linda Muthén, Patrick O'Malley, Gilbert Parra, Lance Swenson, and Phillip Wood for their assistance in analyses and helpful comments on previous drafts of this chapter.

Reprinted from *Journal of Abnormal Psychology, 114,* 612–626 (2005). Copyright 2005 by the American Psychological Association.

contribute to divergent developmental courses, and may have implications for intervention and treatment utilization, content, timing, and outcome (Schulenberg, Maggs, Steinman, & Zucker, 2001). This "person-centered" or "pattern-centered" emphasis (as opposed to a more "variable-centered" emphasis) has recently gained popularity and is based on understanding individual trajectories over time, rather than understanding average growth over time (Bates, 2000). More broadly, this reflects the growing understanding about the heterogeneity in the course of psychopathologies across the life course (Cicchetti & Rogosch, 2002). A key assumption of these "developmental typology" groupings is that the experience of those within a given group is distinctive; for example, those in the heavy chronic use groups use substances (and engage in related behaviors) in distinctive ways compared to those in low substance use groups.

DEVELOPMENTAL COURSE OF ALCOHOL USE AND TOBACCO USE

During recent years, theoretical and empirical research has begun to chart the longitudinal course of alcohol involvement during adolescence and young adulthood. Theoretical (Zucker, 1987, 1994; Zucker, Fitzgerald, & Moses, 1995) and empirical (e.g., Bennett, McCrady, Johnson, & Pandina, 1999; Chassin, Pitts, & Prost, 2002; Colder, Campbell, Ruel, Richardson, & Flay, 2002; Schulenberg, O'Malley, Bachman, Wadsworth, & Johnston, 1996; Schulenberg, Wadsworth, O'Malley, Bachman, & Johnston, 1996; Tucker, Orlando, & Ellickson, 2003) work suggests that although clearly there is some variation in course, several prototypical courses have emerged, including a nonuser/stable-low-user course, a chronic or high use course, a "developmentally limited" course (transitioning or maturing out of drinking), and some evidence for a late-onset (increasing) course. Trajectories derived from adolescent samples tend to include more late-onset courses, whereas samples that include young adults tend to show more courses that remit (developmentally limited).

Although there is considerably less research examining developmental course of smoking, there is evidence for developmental pathways of smoking that are similar to these drinking courses. In addition, some researchers have identified a stable light- or moderate-smoking group (which may comprise "chippers," i.e., those who indulge only occasionally). Colder et al. (2001) identified five patterns of use over six waves (as well as an a priori nonsmoking group): early rapid escalators, low moderate escalators, late slow escalators, stable light smokers, and stable puffers. Chassin, Presson, Pitts, and Sherman (2000) characterized six smoking trajectories over six waves: a nonsmoking group and an erratic group were identified a priori; and then an early-onset stable group, a late-onset stable group, a quitter group, and an experimenter group were empirically identified. Finally, White, Pandina, and Chen (2002) identified three trajectories of smoking over five waves: a heavy–regular smoking group, an occasional–maturing out group, and a nonsmoking–experimental group; however, the two trajectories of smokers were indistinguishable based on risk factors. Note that although these studies generally span late adolescence through early adulthood, the definition and meaning of the trajectory groups tend to vary by ages included.

DEVELOPMENTAL COURSE
OF ALCOHOL–TOBACCO COMORBIDITY

One of the fundamental aspects of alcohol involvement is its high co-occurrence with other substances, particularly the strong association between alcohol involvement and tobacco use (henceforth termed *comorbidity*). Alcoholics are more likely to smoke than nonalcoholics (Bien & Burge, 1990; Gulliver et al., 1995; Kozlowski et al., 1993; Martin, Kaczynski, Maisto, & Tarter, 1996; York & Hirsch, 1995), and social drinkers are also more likely to smoke than nondrinkers (Istvan & Matarazzo, 1984). In a similar manner, individuals with a diagnosable tobacco use disorder exhibit greater risk for an alcohol use disorder (Breslau, 1995), and smokers are more likely to drink than nonsmokers (Bien & Burge, 1990; Breslau, 1995; DiFranza & Guerrera, 1990; Torabi, Bailey, & Majd-Jabbari, 1993; Zacny, 1990). Concurrent alcohol and tobacco use interact synergistically to produce greater health risks than expected from use of either substance alone (Bien & Burge, 1990), including elevated rates of esophageal (Munoz & Day, 1996), laryngeal (Flanders & Rothman, 1982), and oral cancers (Blot et al., 1988).

Comorbidity has traditionally been viewed as a cross-sectional phenomenon; that is, the existence of two or more conditions occurring at a single point in time. Implicit in this approach is that each comorbid condition is adequately characterized as a static entity. Recent data, however, emphasize the importance of course of single disorders or conditions, suggesting that comorbidity should be viewed in the context of the longitudinal course of each co-occurring condition. Despite the recent surge of longitudinal research on comorbidity, however, "too little attention has been given to the implications of diagnostic course, both singly and across related disorders" (Widiger & Clark, 2000, p. 956). Correspondingly, empirical research in the area of alcohol–tobacco comorbidity has generally failed to consider both course and comorbidity, with no research to date examining the concurrent relation between trajectories of smoking and drinking. White, Johnson, and Buyske (2000) used growth mixture modeling to extract univariate trajectories of drinking and smoking of 15- to 28-year-olds, and they examined the predictive utility of parental modeling and parenting behaviors on these patterns of substance use. However, consistent with the emphasis of their study, trajectories of alcohol and tobacco use were independently derived, and there was no discussion of the association between the two. Using five waves of data from a mixed-gender young adult sample ($N = 449$), we examined in our previous work trajectories of combined alcohol use disorders and tobacco dependence using latent class analysis (Jackson, Sher, & Wood, 2000b). We extracted five longitudinal types of alcohol–tobacco use disorder over time: (a) nondiagnosing, (b) developmentally limited alcohol use disorder, (c) chronic alcohol use disorder, (d) chronic tobacco use disorder, and (e) comorbid alcohol and tobacco use disorder. This procedure, however, did not explicitly model the temporal ordering of the manifest variables. There exists the potential for correlated errors between an alcohol use disorder and a tobacco use disorder at a given measurement occasion. B. Muthén (2001) reanalyzed the same data with a mixture modeling approach and identified three classes of alcohol use disorders (AUD) and three classes of tobacco dependence (TD). Next, he estimated joint probabilities between the classes. Although most AUD classes had low TD, nearly a third of chronic and decreasing AUD were increasing in TD; 12% of decreasing AUD and 5% of chronic AUD had chronic TD. The results of these analyses mapped onto what was done by Jackson et al. (2000a)—the five trajectory groups were represented by the five most prevalent cells in B. Muthén (2001).

This earlier work has demonstrated the feasibility and promise of jointly considering course of multiple disorders but has been limited by both relatively small samples that may be inadequate for detecting relatively rare but clinically important classes and data that are not nationally representative. Also, in contrast to our earlier work focusing on substance use disorders, identification of subtypes based on longitudinal profiles of continuous alcohol and tobacco use can more clearly resolve intensity of substance use than profiles based on dichotomous variables with a relatively high threshold. This resolution may lead to the identification of additional subtypes that better permit us to distinguish between those who are experiencing a "developmental disturbance" (Schulenberg, Maggs, Long, et al., 2001; Schulenberg & Zarrett, 2006) versus those who are at risk for continued heavy use, or problems—for example, distinguishing between Zucker's (1987, 1994) developmentally limited and life-course persistent courses. Nationally representative data are more characteristic of the general population, which is particularly important when examining certain forms of substance use because college students are more likely to binge drink and less likely to smoke than their noncollege peers (Johnston, O'Malley, Bachman, & Schulenberg, 2004a, 2004b; O'Malley & Johnston, 2002). Moreover, large samples permit detection of relatively rare classes that may be important from a clinical standpoint.

In addition, extant literature on trajectories of alcohol and tobacco involvement fails to consider more than a single cohort.[1] Monitoring the Future (MTF) panel data (Johnston et al., 2004a, 2004b) show secular changes in drinking and smoking over the past 3 decades such that drinking has become less prevalent, whereas smoking, which decreased in prevalence over the 1980s, has in recent years become more prevalent (particularly among women). Data from the National Household Survey on Drug Abuse suggest that the recent increase in smoking has been due to cigars, but also to a lesser extent, to cigarettes (Department of Health & Human Services, 2000). When considering courses of substance use, it is important to isolate cohort and historical differences from actual developmental trends.

THIRD-VARIABLE ANALYSES

Determining the extent to which risk factors distinguish among courses of comorbidity can provide construct validity for the trajectories and can not only illuminate the nature of comorbidity but can provide a better understanding of alcohol use and smoking in general. We explored three general questions, subsequently described.

The first question concerns the extent to which heavy drinking and smoking possess common risk factors, that is, whether alcohol and tobacco use have *common versus unique correlates*. To do this, we compared risk factors for courses that have comparable trajectories of substance use but are discriminated by the specific substance (e.g., courses with relatively chronic high drinking and persistent low smoking vs. relatively persistent low drinking and chronic high smoking). For example, we might expect alcohol expectancies to be substance-specific and predict only drinking, or alcohol expectancies may reflect a general expectation about the effects of all substances and would predict smoking to the same degree as drinking.

Our second question concerns whether variables associated with comorbid classes are similar to or different from classes characterized by use of a single substance. To address this question, we examined the extent to which predictors of comorbid trajectories are similar or distinct from those of single-substance trajectories. Several patterns of association are possible that are associated with additive effects, synergistic effects, or comorbid-specific correlates. This type of analysis permits the discovery of "masked effects" attributable to confounding. For example, an effect for smoking may exist by virtue of smoking's relation with drinking, or vice versa. To test this comparison, we compared the prediction of comorbidity with the prediction of single substance courses.

---

[1] Although data used by White et al. (2000) contained three cohorts, analyses were restricted to the middle cohort.

Our third question concerns the extent to which it is possible to distinguish among comorbid classes characterized by similar trajectories of the same substance but by different trajectories of the second substance. Our approach was to examine correlates of temporal patterns of comorbidity with constant levels of a target substance. Controlling for the comorbid substance permits examination of different levels of a given substance and provides better resolution of risk factors for a given substance. For example, if two trajectories have similar smoking course but are differentiated by drinking course, we can compare these trajectories to examine risk factors for drinking. Given the high comorbidity between drinking and smoking, this is a much more illustrative approach than simply comparing risk factors for univariate drinking courses and univariate smoking courses.

THE CURRENT STUDY

The goal of the current study was to describe the concurrent course of heavy alcohol use and tobacco use during early adulthood (ages 19 to 26), the time of transition from the high school environment to college, military service, and/or part- or full-time occupation. We used a longitudinal developmental framework and validated these courses using available etiologically relevant predictors. We examined heavy alcohol use rather than alcohol quantity or frequency because heavy drinking increases risk for onset (or continuation) of alcohol problems and alcohol use disorders (Wechsler & Austin, 1998) and is common in this developmental period of life (Bachman et al., 1997; Wechsler, Lee, Kuo, & Lee, 2000). A full 41% of college students and 34% to 42% of those aged 21 to 26 binge drank at least once in the past 2 weeks (Johnston et al., 2004a, 2004b). We chose smoking quantity because "regular smoking" is inconsistently defined (White et al., 2002) and because smoking frequency data were not available in this sample.

We used a mixture modeling procedure (Jones, Nagin, & Roeder, 2001; B. Muthén, 2001; B. Muthén et al., 2002; B. Muthén & Muthén, 2000; Nagin, 1999; for applications of this technique in the substance use area, see Colder et al., 2001, 2002; Li, Barrera, Hops, & Fisher, 2002). General growth mixture modeling is a form of latent growth modeling, but with the addition of an unobserved categorical variable that models variability via discrete homogeneous classes of individuals (rather than via a parameter measuring variability around the latent growth factors). This technique has some important advantages over other techniques used to derive developmental courses of substance use (e.g., cluster analysis), because it treats group membership as a latent (error-free) variable, and accounts for the temporal ordering of prospective data. In the current study, we examined alcohol–tobacco comorbidity by using a dual-trajectory model, in which we explicitly modeled comorbidity. Prior to deriving these trajectories of comorbidity, however, we first examined alcohol and tobacco use individually, in line with prior research, and we examined the association between the two substances. This allowed us to compare the two approaches to simultaneously studying developmental course and comorbidity of different forms of substance use. Finally, we examined the extent to which the courses of drinking, smoking, and comorbidity were associated with six etiologically relevant risk factors: sex, race, alcohol expectancies, delinquency, religiosity (reflecting, to some extent, conventionalism), and parent education.

Panel data were drawn from the MTF study, a large national data set ($N = 32,087$) that allows fairly broad generalizability to young adults in the United States. In addition, the data enabled us to avoid potential confounds between developmental change and secular change, because MTF is a multiple-cohort study collected over a long historical period, with cohorts beginning in 1976 (and ongoing today). Previously, Schulenberg, O'Malley, et al. (1996) and Schulenberg, Wadsworth, et al. (1996) identified trajectories of heavy drinking with MTF panel data using conceptual groupings and cluster analysis;[2] the current study extends this work by focusing on the course of comorbid heavy drinking and smoking, using mixture modeling which models growth as a process.

METHOD

Respondents and Procedure

The MTF project (e.g., Bachman et al., 1997; Johnston et al., 2004a, 2004b), funded by the National Institute on Drug Abuse (NIDA), is an ongoing national study of adolescents and young adults, particularly focusing on substance use. Beginning in 1975, approximately 17,000 12th-grade students have completed self-administered questionnaires each year in their classrooms (national samples of 8th and 10th graders were added in 1991). A multistage random sampling procedure is used, in which particular geographic areas were selected, followed by the selection (with probability proportionate to size) of schools in each area. In the third stage, classes within each school were randomly selected, within which up to 350 students were selected. Beginning with the class of 1976, approximately 2,400 respondents were randomly selected for biennial follow-up from each cohort through mail surveys,

---

[2] A number of our heavy drinking classes are consistent with those found in Schulenberg, O'Malley, et al. (1996) and Schulenberg, Wadsworth, et al. (1996), including the nonheavy drinking class, the late-onset (increase) class, the developmentally limited (decrease) class, and the chronic class.

with about half being surveyed 1 year later and the other half being surveyed 2 years later (and each half followed biennially thereafter). Respondents who reported heavy drug use at baseline were oversampled for follow-up.[3] Panel data are based on the follow-up data for senior-year cohorts 1976 to 1997: Waves 2 to 5 (henceforth termed *Times 1 to 4*). Respondents were, on average, 18 years old at Wave 1, 19 to 20 years old at Wave 2, 21 to 22 years old at Wave 3, 23 to 24 years old at Wave 4, and 25 to 26 years old at Wave 5. However, there was variability around these ages. Given the current study's focus on developmental trajectories, we sought to retain homogeneity in age (age at Time 1 ranged from 17 to 23 years, resulting in greater age range within a year than between years). Therefore, we restricted the sample to the modal ages (subsequently described in greater detail)—that is, those who were 18 to 20 years old at Time 1 (N = 32,087; M = 19.31; 44% male; 82% Caucasian).

Retention rates for any one follow-up survey averaged 75% to 80%. Previous attrition analyses with similar MTF panel samples have shown that, compared with those excluded, those retained in the longitudinal sample were more likely to be female, White, higher on high school grade point average and parental education level, and lower on high school truancy and senior year substance use (e.g., Schulenberg, O'Malley, Bachman, & Johnston, 2000; Schulenberg, O'Malley, et al., 1996; Schulenberg, Wadsworth, et al., 1996). Fortunately, relatively new missing data techniques in Mplus have removed the necessity to restrict the sample to respondents present at all waves. This technique, which assumes that data are missing at random, estimates the model using full information maximum likelihood.

Measures

Substance use measures for these analyses included heavy (binge) drinking and current tobacco use. The MTF substance use items have been used for decades in both the project's surveys and by other researchers. They have been shown to demonstrate excellent psychometric properties, and their reliability and validity have been reported and discussed extensively (e.g., Johnston & O'Malley, 1985; O'Malley, Bachman, & Johnston, 1983). Although alcohol and tobacco use as well as sex, race, age, parent education, and religion were assessed on all participants, some psychosocial scales (alcohol expectancies and delinquency) were systematically given to random

---

[3] To account for this selective probability of retention, we reestimated our primary analyses (i.e., the mixture models for heavy drinking, smoking, and drinking/smoking) with a weight statement, downweighting the heavy drug users. The pattern of trajectories was virtually identical, but the weighted results showed more individuals in the nondrinker–nonsmoker categories (i.e., 68% vs. 64% for nonheavy drinkers; 74% vs. 69% for nonsmokers; 62% vs. 57% for nonheavy drinkers–nonsmokers), which is consistent with the oversampling of the heavy drug users.

subsamples of the full respondent sample; analyses using these variables reflect this reduced sample size.

Heavy Alcohol Use

A single ordinal item assessed frequency of "binge" drinking (operationalized as five or more drinks in a row) in the past 2 weeks. Item responses included 1 (*never drink*), 2 (*once*), 3 (*twice*), 4 (*3–5 times*), 5 (*6–9 times*), and 6 (*10 or more times*); Time 1 $M = 1.96$.

Tobacco Use

A single ordinal item assessing the quantity of cigarettes smoked per day in the past 30 days was assessed. Item response categories included 1 (*not at all*), 2 (*less than one cigarette per day*), 3 (*one to five cigarettes per day*), 4 (*about one half pack per day*), 5 (*about one pack per day*), 6 (*about one and one half packs per day*), and 7 (*two packs or more per day*); Time 1 $M = 1.94$.[4]

Background Variables

Age, sex (recoded 1 = male, 0 = female), and race were assessed at baseline. We coded race broadly into five categories: White, Black, Hispanic, Asian, and Other (including Native American and other ethnic minorities) and created four dummy codes with White as the reference group.

Alcohol expectancies were assessed using 15 items, including items assessing drinking to get drunk (similar to Wechsler & Isaac, 1992), drinking to cope (similar to Jessor & Jessor, 1977), and drinking for tension reduction and social facilitation (Goldman, Brown, & Christiansen, 1987; Goldman, Del Boca, & Darkes, 1999; $\alpha = .58$). The binary items included "to relax or relieve tension," "to feel good or get high," and "because it tastes good." We did not have a measure of smoking expectancies. Past-year delinquency was the mean of scores ranging from 1 (*not at all*) to 5 (*5 or more times*) for 15 items, including such items as "got in a serious fight in school or at work" and "been arrested and taken to a police station." Internal consistency was good ($\alpha = .79$). Religiosity (a proxy for conventionalism) was assessed with 2 items: "importance of religion" and "attendance at religious services" (interitem $r = .62$). Ratings for "importance of religion" ranged from 1 (*not important*) to 4 (*very important*), and ratings for "attendance at religious services" ranged from 1 (*never*) to 4 (*about once a week or more*).

---

[4] These values differ slightly from other work using MTF panel data (e.g., Bachman et al., 1996; Schulenberg et al., 2000; Schulenberg, O'Malley, et al., 1996) because of differences in sample definition and cohorts involved.

Last, parent education was computed by taking the mean of ratings for maternal and paternal education (interitem $r = .55$), which ranged from 1 (*completed grade school or less*) to 6 (*graduate or professional school after college*).

Analytic Procedure

We used general growth mixture modeling (GGMM), using Mplus 3.01 (L. K. Muthén & Muthén, 1998–2004). GGMM is based on a latent growth model (LGM) context. Like LGM, growth is represented by latent growth factors (usually an intercept and one or more slope factors). However, in GGMM, homogeneous clusters (or "mixtures") of individual trajectories are identified and are represented by a categorical latent variable. The extent to which LGM parameters differ across mixtures or classes is modeled. In addition, class prevalence is given, and each participant receives a probability of class membership for each class, ranging from 0 to 1.0. Finally, the influence of external predictors can be explored in a latent variable context in Mplus, by using a multinomial logistic regression procedure. Note that although drinking and smoking are ordinal in nature, they are approximated as continuous variables and thus are appropriate for the GGMM technique.

We identified classes based on the mean of the growth factors alone (i.e., we did not allow the growth factor variances to differ across classes) because freeing the variances across classes typically resulted in model nonconvergence. Other applications of GGMM have also distinguished classes based on growth factor means only (e.g., Colder et al., 2002; Tucker et al., 2003). Although Li et al. (2002) were able to model growth factor variances across class, their model was limited to two classes, which is a relatively simple analytic model. We allowed variances to be nonzero and constrained to be equal to each other, which still allowed us to consider minor variations within class (rather than assuming more "pure" classes and setting variances to zero). We used the (accelerated) expectation maximization (EM) algorithm and ROBUST maximum likelihood estimation, which gives (full-information) maximum likelihood parameter estimates and robust standard errors (L. K. Muthén & Muthén, 1998–2004).

RESULTS

First, we examine our two outcome variables, frequency of heavy drinking and smoking quantity, and we discuss the effects of birth cohort. Following, we briefly present the results of the mixture models for both heavy alcohol use and smoking, and we examine comorbidity between the two. Then, we present the mixture model for comorbidity. Finally, we explore prediction of alcohol–tobacco comorbidity courses by six etiologically relevant variables.

Preliminary Analyses

On average, heavy drinking frequency slightly decreased over the course of the study when respondents were between ages 18 and 26: Time 1 M = 1.96 (SD = 1.34); Time 2 M = 1.98 (SD = 1.32); Time 3 M = 1.83 (SD = 1.24); Time 4 M = 1.71 (SD = 1.17).[5] Although average growth was negative, the standard deviations suggest that individuals did not have the same pattern of growth, and graphs of heavy drinking (not shown) indicated great heterogeneity in the data. Average smoking quantity did not change over the course of the study, with substantial variability in smoking scores; Time 1 M = 1.97 (SD = 1.52); Time 2 M = 1.99 (SD = 1.57); Time 3 M = 1.97 (SD = 1.59); Time 4 M = 1.93 (SD = 1.59).

Cohort Effects

Prior to discussion of our models, we briefly discuss the nature of our sample. Data were collected using a multicohort design (see Table 10.1); within each cohort, there was significant age heterogeneity (in part because of the process of collecting follow-up data at biennial intervals). As a consequence, respondents were born in years ranging from 1955 through 1978, creating potential birth cohort effects. Using Cohort × Time repeated measures analyses of variance, we examined the effect of cohort on heavy drinking and smoking. Cohort had a significant linear effect on heavy drinking, $F(1, 19103) = 28.62$, $p < .001$, $\eta^2 = .002$, but no quadratic or cubic effect (see Figure 10.1, top panel). Likewise, cohort had a significant linear effect on smoking $F(1, 19276) = 85.95$, $p < .001$, $\eta^2 = .005$, and a significant quadratic effect, $F(1, 19276) = 33.70$, $p < .001$, $\eta^2 = .001$, but no cubic effect (see Figure 10.1, bottom panel).

In addition, Figure 10.1 shows that consistent with preliminary analyses, there was a decrease in heavy drinking but not smoking as respondents age. Given the clear linear effect for cohort (birth year, ranging from 1957 to 1976) on both heavy drinking and smoking, we modeled cohort in all analyses.

---

[5] To make the trajectories more interpretable with respect to drinking unit, heavy drinking was recoded to range from 0 to 10 episodes of binge drinking in the past 2 weeks by taking the midpoint of an item (e.g., 3 to 5 times in the past 2 weeks would be recoded to 4 M = 1.31, M = 1.31, M = 1.10, M = 0.93 for Times 1 to 4, respectively). Analogous to the binge-drinking item, smoking quantity was recoded to range from 0 to 2 packs per day, or 40 cigarettes (M = 3.71, M = 3.98, M = 4.01, M = 3.95 for Times 1 to 4, respectively). However, the distribution of these variables were much more skewed than the original variable and resulted in poorer model convergence (skew ranged from 2.03 to 2.63 for heavy drinking and from 2.12 to 2.23 for smoking; kurtosis ranged from 4.07 to 7.67 for heavy drinking and from 3.65 to 4.32 for smoking). Transformations such as taking the logarithm (Neter, Wasserman, & Kutner, 1990) did not remedy the problem sufficiently. Hence, we retained the original variables (skew ranged from 1.12 to 1.57 for heavy drinking and from 1.34 to 1.47 for smoking; kurtosis ranged from 0.08 to 1.53 for heavy drinking and from 0.37 to 0.72 for smoking).

TABLE 10.1
Year Assessed as a Function of Birth-Year Cohort and Age
(at Time of Assessment)

Birth-year cohort	Age									
	18	19	20	21	22	23	24	25	26	27
1955					77		79		81	
1956				77	78	79	80	81	82	83
1957			77	78	79	80	81	82	83	84
1958		77	78	79	80	81	82	83	84	85
1959	77	78	79	80	81	82	83	84	85	86
1960	78	79	80	81	82	83	84	85	86	87
1961	79	80	81	82	83	84	85	86	87	88
1962	80	81	82	83	84	85	86	87	88	89
1963	81	82	83	84	85	86	87	88	89	90
1964	82	83	84	85	86	87	88	89	90	91
1965	83	84	85	86	87	88	89	90	91	92
1966	84	85	86	87	88	89	90	91	92	93
1967	85	86	87	88	89	90	91	92	93	94
1968	86	87	88	89	90	91	92	93	94	95
1969	87	88	89	90	91	92	93	94	95	96
1970	88	89	90	91	92	93	94	95	96	97
1971	89	90	91	92	93	94	95	96	97	98
1972	90	91	92	93	94	95	96	97	98	99
1973	91	92	93	94	95	96	97	98	99	00
1974	92	93	94	95	96	97	98	99	00	
1975	93	94	95	96	97	98	99	00		
1976	94	95	96	97	98	99	00			
1977	95	96	97	98	99	00				
1978	96	97	98	99	00					

Note. In the table cells, years do not contain the first two digits (i.e., 19 for all except the year 2000).

As discussed earlier, we restricted our sample to those who were aged 18 to 20 (66% of the sample, $N = 32,087$) at Time 1 to remove the age heterogeneity, and we controlled for birth cohort (i.e., birth year) by treating it as an exogenous variable predicting Times 1 to 4 drinking and smoking. In all subsequent models, the cohort effect is significant for all time points for both drinking and smoking models.[6]

---

[6] We further probed cohort effects by examining them at the level of the intercept and slope factors. The only significant cohort effects were on intercept; that is, cohort did not predict linear or quadratic slope for either heavy drinking or smoking. This analysis assumes that all of the cohort effect was transferred through the intercept (i.e., Time 1), which we believe is less tenable than cohort having an effect through Times 1 to 4 heavy alcohol use and Times 1 to 4 smoking. To further examine time trends, we explored whether cohort had a nonlinear effect on these assessments. We created quadratic (cohort²) and cubic (cohort³) variables and tested the extent to which these variables predicted Times 1 to 4 heavy alcohol use and Times 1 to 4 smoking. None of the cubic trends were significant and the quadratic trend was significant for tobacco use only (standardized $\beta = .03$). Given our goal of parsimony, as well as identification problems in including the quadratic and cubic cohort variables (given limited degrees of freedom, inclusion of these variables as well as the linear cohort variable necessitated that their values be constrained to be equal across Times 1 to 4), we freely estimated the parameters between cohort (linear trend only) and each of the manifest variables.

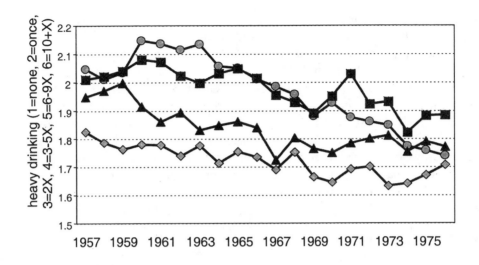

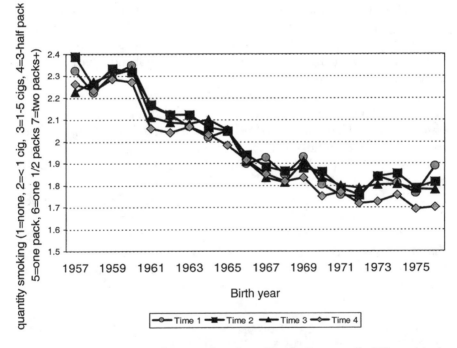

Figure 10.1. Heavy drinking (top panel) and smoking (bottom panel) at Times 1 to 4 as a function of birth cohort. Item responses for heavy or binge drinking were 1 (*never drink*), 2 (*once*), 3 (*twice*), 4 (*3–5 times*), 5 (*6–9 times*), and 6 (*10 or more times*). Item responses for quantity of smoking were 1 (*not at all*), 2 (*less than 1 cigarette per day*), 3 (*1–5 cigarettes per day*), 4 (*about ½ pack per day*), 5 (*about one pack per day*), 6 (*about 1½ packs per day*), and 7 (*2 packs or more per day*).

Mixture Modeling: Extracting Trajectories

We based the general growth mixture models on a basic latent growth model with an intercept and linear and quadratic slopes.[7] Model fit was evaluated using information criteria fit indices (Bayesian information criterion, BIC; Schwartz, 1978; and Akaike's information criterion, AIC; Akaike, 1987), as well as using the Vuong–Lo–Mendell–Rubin likelihood ratio test for k versus $k − 1$ classes (Lo, Mendell, & Rubin, 2001; B. Muthén et al., 2002), which is significant if k classes show improvement over $k − 1$ classes. In addition, given the large sample size (which affects values of AIC and BIC), we considered three other criteria: class prevalence (we tended not to consider classes that included less than 5% of the sample as they were unlikely to be replicable), class interpretability (the extent to which an additional class provided unique information), and stability (the extent to which the nature and prevalence of the classes changed when demographic variables were controlled). See Colder et al. (2002) for a more extended explanation of these criteria. We noted significant variability around the mean for the intercept and slope factors, suggesting individual differences and the likelihood of distinct classes of heavy drinkers and smokers over the observation period.

Prior to fitting the dual trajectory model for alcohol and tobacco use, we estimated separate (single-domain) models for alcohol and tobacco use. We identified four trajectories of frequency of heavy drinking, including non-heavy drinkers (including nondrinkers) (64%), chronic heavy drinkers (12%), developmentally limited (decrease) heavy drinkers (16%), and late-onset (increase) heavy drinkers (8%), and five trajectories of smoking quantity, including nonsmokers (69%), chronic smokers (12%), late-onset (increase) smokers (6%), developmentally limited (decrease) smokers (6%), and moderate smokers (7%). A cross-tabulation of group membership for heavy drinking by smoking revealed that heavy drinking and smoking were associated, $\chi^2(12, N = 31{,}853) = 2{,}449.78$, $p < .001$; $\Phi = .28$; Cramér's $V = .16$.[8] A first-order configural frequency analysis technique (von Eye, 2002)[9] that tested observed versus expected cell frequencies revealed that, although there were 20 (4×5) different potential trajectories of smoking and drinking,

---

[7] The intercept was centered at Time 1 which corresponds to modal ages 19-20. Based on our previous work looking at (negative) growth in substance use (Parra, Sher, Krull, & Jackson, 2003), we modeled the negative relation between the intercept and the slope factors as a directional relation, rather than as a covariance, in order to address the phenomenon that when modeling negative growth, the higher an individual is at Time 1, the greater he or she falls over time (suggesting perhaps a floor effect for those low at Time 1).

[8] For this analysis, we determined group membership by assigning an individual to the class to which he or she was most likely to belong. We also examined comorbidity using weighted estimates (weighted by probability of group membership in both groups). As might be expected by high entropy in our models, weighted estimates and corresponding tests of association were very similar to those using unweighted estimates.

[9] We used Lehmacher's approximation to the binomial probability (with Küchenhof's correction for continuity; cf. von Eye, 2002).

some of these particular combinations of smoking and drinking were less likely to occur than chance (antitypes) (e.g., nonheavy drinkers with smoking classes; nonsmokers with drinking classes), and correspondingly, some combinations were more expected to occur than chance (types; e.g., cells along the diagonal; chronic heavy drinkers with chronic high smokers and moderate smokers; chronic smokers with developmentally limited drinkers). On the basis of these findings, we examined prospective comorbidity by modeling both substances simultaneously to determine which of these conjoint types were most clearly represented in our sample, expecting that some of these "types" would have increased likelihood of being identified as a conjoint trajectory.

Identification of Trajectories

We tested two- through eight-group solutions (the nine-group model would not converge on a solution; see Table 10.2). According to BIC and AIC, we observed significant improvements in model fit up to eight classes, although according to the Vuong–Lo–Mendell–Rubin likelihood ratio test, the six-class model best fit the data. However, the seven-class model contained the moderate–moderate class (6% of the sample) that we believed added additional information. In addition, based on stability of the models in the presence of different exogenous covariates, class prevalences, and interpretability, the seven-class model appeared to be the best model. As such, we chose the seven-class model; Figure 10.2 presents mean growth from Times 1 to 4 in frequency of heavy alcohol use and smoking quantity by class, weighted by estimated class probabilities. Classes were as follows: a nonheavy drinking–nonsmoking class (56%), a chronic heavy drinking and chronic heavy smoking class (6%), a low drinking but heavy smoking class (8%), a heavy drinking but low smoking (perhaps chippers; Shiffman, 1989) class (14%), a moderate-drinker, late-onset heavy smoking class (5%), a moderate-drinker, developmentally limited heavy

TABLE 10.2
Goodness of Fit for the Dual Trajectory
Comorbidity Model

No. classes	AIC	BIC	Entropy
2	612,134.79	612,536.77	.94
3	608,195.36	608,655.97	.89
4	596,215.21	596,751.19	.90
5	588,369.40	588,964.00	.93
6	581,357.43	581,993.90	.92
7	577,348.87	578,035.59	.92
8	573,837.80	574,583.14	.92

Note. AIC = Akaike's (1987) information criterion; BIC = Bayesian information criterion (Schwartz, 1978).

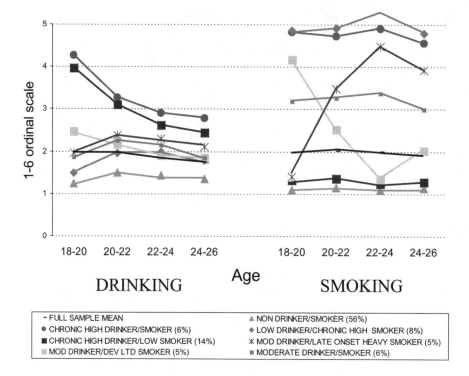

Figure 10.2. Mixture model for frequency of heavy drinking (left) and smoking quantity (right) at Times 1–4 weighted by estimated class probabilities. Akaike's (1987) information criterion = 577,348.87; Bayesian information criterion (Schwartz, 1978) = 578,035.59; Entropy = .92.

smoking class (5%), and a moderate drinking–smoking class (6%). There appears to be more variability in smoking—moderate drinking is accompanied by three types of smokers (moderate, late-onset, and developmentally limited smokers). Yet, there were four heavy smoking groups—two developmentally graded, two chronic; the chronic smoking classes were distinguishable by drinking (low heavy drinking vs. heavy drinking).

Prediction of Trajectory Group Membership

Next, also within the Mplus framework, we examined the extent to which the trajectory groups differed on several etiologically relevant predictors taken from baseline (Time 1). Zero-order correlations between drinking, smoking, and our six predictors (sex, race, alcohol expectancies, delinquency, religiosity, and parent education) are shown in Table 10.3. Table 10.4 presents means and proportions on the predictors for each of the trajectory groups. To test group differences, we conducted a series of multinomial logistic regressions. Predictors, which were tested univariately because of the

TABLE 10.3
Zero-Order Correlations Between Heavy Drinking, Smoking, and Predictors

Variable	Frequency of heavy drinking				Smoking quantity			
	Time 1	Time 2	Time 3	Time 4	Time 1	Time 2	Time 3	Time 4
Alcohol expectancies (N = 2,309)	.24	.19	.19	.18	.19	.17	.17	.15
Delinquency (N = 3,554)	.35	.25	.25	.24	.16	.12	.12	.10
Religiosity/conservatism (N = 15,092)	-.20	-.17	-.16	-.16	-.19	-.17	-.16	-.16
Parent education (N = 14,820)	.06	.08	.04	.04	-.09	-.07	-.09	-.10
Sex (% male) (N = 15,162)	.21	.25	.27	.27	-.02	-.00	.01	.01
Race (N = 15,162)								
% Black	-.11	-.11	-.09	-.08	-.08	-.07	-.06	-.05
% Other	-.01	-.01	.00	.00	.03	.03	.03	.03
% Hispanic	-.03	-.03	-.01	-.01	-.04	-.05	-.05	-.05
% Asian	-.05	-.04	-.04	-.04	-.04	-.04	-.04	-.03

TABLE 10.4

Means and Proportions of External Predictors Across Dual Trajectories of Heavy Drinking–Smoking Quantity

	Dual drinking–smoking						
Predictor	Nonsmoke, nondrink 57%	Chronic drink, chronic smoke 6%	Low drink, chronic smoke 9%	Chronic drink, low smoke 14%	Moderate drink, late onset smoke 4%	Moderate drink, dv ltd smoke 5%	Moderate drink, moderate smoke 6%
Alcohol expectancies (N = 2,309)	0.20[a]	0.31[b,c]	0.26[c]	0.28[b,c]	0.26[b,c]	0.28[b,c]	0.27[c]
Delinquency (N = 3,554)	1.09[a]	1.36[b]	1.17[c]	1.33[a,b]	1.20[c]	1.25[b,c]	1.17[c]
Religiosity (N = 15,092)	2.85[a]	2.24[b]	2.39[c]	2.44[c]	2.54[d]	2.40[c,d]	2.55[d]
Parent education (N = 14,820)	3.65[a]	3.56[a]	3.31[b]	3.89[c]	3.57[a]	3.64[a]	3.68[a]
Sex (% male) (N = 15,162)	61[a]	40[b]	65[a,b]	30[c]	48[d]	62[a,b]	70[b]
Race (N = 15,162)							
% Black	12[a]	2[b]	3[b]	2[b]	8[c]	3[b]	12[a]
% Other	3[a]	5[a]	5[a]	2[b]	4[a,b]	3[a,b]	4[a]
% Hispanic	6[a]	1[b]	1[b]	4[c]	2[b,c]	4[c,d]	6[a,d]
% Asian	3[a]	1[b]	0.2[b]	1[b]	1[a,b]	1[b,c]	2[a,c]

Note. Means that share at least one superscript (within a row) are not significantly different at $p < .001$ according to pairwise odds ratios taken from multinomial logistic regressions (with different reference groups). Means are presented for continuous variables (alcohol expectancies, delinquency, religiosity, and parent education); proportions are presented for categorical variables (sex, race). Although continuous variables were standardized for the multinomial logistic regressions, raw means are presented here. Variables were assessed at Time 1. Note that despite multiple start values, the models that included alcohol expectancies as a predictor failed to converge. The estimates shown herein are for models with the latent class part of the model constrained to equal the values in the full model (with no exogenous risk factors; see Footnote 10). dv ltd = developmentally limited.

differing number of participants and nonoverlapping samples (discussed previously) for each, were modeled as exogenous to the class membership variable in the context of the general growth mixture model. Prior to analysis, these variables were standardized to increase interpretability of coefficients (odds ratios [ORs]). Note that these coefficients are not (derived from) partial regression coefficients, as would be obtained in a multivariate regression procedure. Means and proportions with the same subscript (within a row) in Table 10.4 were not significantly different using a pairwise odds ratio (drawing from a method used by Tucker et al., 2003), according to the multinomial logistic regressions (changing the reference group accordingly). Although there exists a large number of possible pairwise contrasts, we were specifically interested in three sets of contrasts based on our research questions using a priori comparisons. To illustrate these contrasts, we focused primarily on the courses that show chronic drinking and/or smoking, because these are highly clinically relevant and have less ambiguity than some of the other drinking and smoking courses, although we did consider additional courses for our third question. To reduce possibility of Type I error, especially given our large sample size, we applied a Bonferroni correction and reported tests that were significant at $p < .001$ ($\alpha = .05/48$, the total number of tests; 8 comparisons $\times$ 6 variables = 48).

For our first set of contrasts, *common versus unique correlates*, we compared trajectories that had similar course (level and slope) of a given substance but were discriminated by the specific substance. That is, to what extent is prediction of a given substance due to that particular substance versus to the course of substance use in general? More specifically, we tested a set of three comparisons. In our first two comparisons, we examined prediction of single chronic substances (chronic high drinking–low smoking and low drinking–chronic high smoking) to the nonusing reference group (nondrinking–nonsmoking) to examine whether risk factors differ for prediction of chronic alcohol use than for the prediction of chronic tobacco use. If correlates were *common*, we would expect to find similar results for the two comparisons. If correlates were *unique*, we would observe some differential prediction. Analyses revealed that relative to the nondrinker–nonsmoker group, higher alcohol expectancies (OR = 1.89),[10] higher delinquency (OR = 2.54), lower religiosity (OR = 0.62), higher parent education (OR = 1.22), being male (OR = 3.70), and not being Black (OR = 0.18), Asian (OR = 0.22), Hispanic (OR = 0.58), or Other ethnicity (OR = 0.67) increased the odds of being in the chronic drinker–low smoker group, and higher alcohol expectancies (OR = 1.62), higher

---

[10] Despite multiple start values, the models that included alcohol expectancies as a predictor failed to converge. The estimates shown herein are for models with the latent class part of the model constrained to equal the values in the full model (with no exogenous risk factors). Note that when delinquency was modeled this way, estimates were extremely similar to those from the fully estimated model (presented herein), with no substantive differences.

delinquency (OR = 1.73), lower religiosity (OR = 0.59), lower parent education (OR = 0.74), being Other ethnicity (OR = 1.53) and not being Black (OR = 0.24), Asian (OR = 0.06), or Hispanic (OR = 0.17) significantly increased the odds of being in the low drinker–chronic smoker group. The different direction of effect for parent education between the two comparisons as well as the similar risk factors (alcohol expectancies, delinquency, religiosity, not being Asian or Hispanic) for the two suggests that there are some general similarities as well as some specific differences in prediction of the two substances.

Although the greater magnitude of some of the effects in one substance versus the other (i.e., alcohol expectancies, delinquency) in the above comparisons suggests differential prediction of the two substances, it does not explicitly test this issue. This led us to make a third comparison, in which we compared the chronic high heavy drinking–low smoking trajectory with the low drinking–chronic high smoking trajectory. Findings revealed that higher delinquency (OR = 1.47), higher parent education (OR = 1.65), being male (OR = 4.34), not being in the Other ethnic group (OR = 0.53), and being Hispanic (OR = 3.42) significantly increased the odds of being in the chronic high drinker–low smoker group relative to the low drinker–chronic high smoker group, indicating that delinquency, parent education, being male, and being Hispanic or Caucasian are associated with chronic high drinking more so than chronic high smoking. This provides further support that the risk factors are more unique than they are common.

In sum, this comparison revealed that, despite most predictors' being associated with both drinking and smoking (see Table 10.3), trajectory analyses suggested that most predictors were differentially related to the use of one substance versus the other. Higher delinquency, higher parent education, being male, being Hispanic, and not being in the Black or Other ethnic groups were associated with greater drinking and less smoking. Alcohol expectancies had limited support as a unique risk factor, because they were more highly associated with chronic high drinking than chronic high smoking but the explicit comparison failed to reach significance. Religiosity, however, did not differentiate between trajectories that were characterized by similar course but different substances, suggesting that this factor is more common than unique.

In our second set of contrasts, *comorbidity versus single substance correlates*, we performed three contrasts. In the first, we predicted the comorbidity trajectory (chronic drinking–chronic smoking) by using the nondrinker–nonsmoker group as reference group. Higher expectancies (OR = 2.20); higher delinquency (OR = 2.64); lower religiosity (OR = 0.49); being male (OR = 2.35); and not being Black (OR = 0.16), Hispanic (OR = 0.20), or Asian (OR = 0.24) significantly increased the odds of being in the chronic drinker–chronic smoker group relative to the nondrinker–nonsmoker group. For alcohol expectancies, delinquency, religiosity, and being Black, this was a similar pattern of findings as the single-substance comparisons but with parameters generally greater in magnitude (although the extent to which this is true cannot be explicitly tested), which suggests that their prediction of comorbidity is additive or perhaps even synergistic. Next, we examined alcohol use with versus without comorbid tobacco use and we examined tobacco use with versus without comorbid alcohol use. Specifically, we examined prediction of the comorbid course (chronic drinking–chronic smoking) to the single chronic substance courses (chronic drinking–low smoking and low drinking–chronic smoking). Analyses revealed that lower religiosity (OR = 0.79), lower parent education (OR = 0.76), being female (OR = 0.64), not being Hispanic (OR = 0.34), and being in the Other ethnic group (OR = 1.89) increased the odds of being in the chronic drinker–chronic smoker group relative to the chronic drinker–low smoker group, and higher alcohol expectancies (OR = 1.36), higher delinquency (OR = 1.53), lower religiosity (OR = 0.83), higher parent education (OR = 1.25), and being male (OR = 2.76) significantly increased the odds of being in the chronic drinker–chronic smoker group relative to the low drinker–chronic smoker group.

In sum, some risk factors predicted comorbidity above and beyond a single substance, suggesting perhaps an additive effect. Certain risk factors predicted comorbidity relative to the chronic drinking course (low parent education, being female, not being Hispanic, and being in the Other ethnic group), suggesting that drinking with smoking is different from drinking alone. Still others predicted comorbidity relative to the chronic smoking course (alcohol expectancies, delinquency, lower religiosity, high parent education, and being male), suggesting that smoking with drinking is different from smoking alone.

Finally, in our third contrast, *correlates of patterns of comorbidity with constant levels of a single substance*, we explored prediction of a given substance while controlling for the other. Although our empirical trajectories did not allow for a comparison of smoking course while holding drinking constant, we were able to examine divergent alcohol trajectories while holding smoking constant. Specifically, we compared the moderate drinking–moderate smoking group with two groups: moderate drinking–late onset (increase) smoking and moderate drinking–developmentally limited (decrease) smoking. Findings revealed that being female (OR = 0.40) and being Black (OR = 1.61) or Hispanic (OR = 4.00) significantly increased the odds of being in the moderate drinker–moderate smoker group relative to the moderate drinker–late onset smoker group; and having high religiosity (OR = 1.20) and being Black (OR = 4.17) significantly increased the odds of being in the moderate drinker–moderate smoker group relative to the moderate drinker–developmentally limited smoker group. In sum, being female, being of high religiosity, and being Black or Hispanic increased risk for stable moderate smoking, as opposed to time-delimited smoking that remits after early young adulthood (ages 18 to 22) or escalates during late young adulthood (ages 22 to 26).

DISCUSSION

Substance use tends to peak during the transition to adulthood. Yet, this normative trend does not apply to all, or even most, young people. Especially during this transition time, when diversity in life paths increases and changes in contexts are often pervasive and simultaneous, it is essential to identify distinct courses of substance use (Schulenberg & Maggs, 2002). In turn, these distinct courses can assist in advances in the understanding of the causes, correlates, and consequences of substance use during the transition to adulthood. Our findings have implications regarding the etiology of substance use and of psychopathology in general.

To characterize the nature of comorbidity over the course of development, we took the approach of modeling conjoint trajectories using nationally representative, prospective, multiwave data.[11] We identified seven co-occurring trajectories of alcohol and tobacco use, controlling for secular changes occurring over 2 decades. In addition, we examined the extent to which available covariates (specifically, sex, race, alcohol expectancies, delinquency, religiosity, and parent education) predicted course of alcohol–tobacco comorbidity.

Implications for Studying Comorbidity

The present study demonstrates both the importance and empirical feasibility of considering both developmental course and comorbidity in the characterization of alcohol–tobacco comorbidity during early young adulthood. Our findings extend to problems of clinical concern, and our techniques generalize to (multiple) psychiatric disorders in general. Although the explicit diagnostic criteria sets introduced in the third edition of the *Diagnostic and Statistical Manual of Mental Disorders* and subsequent revisions (e.g., American Psychiatric Association, 1980, 1987, 1994) signify a major leap forward in psychiatric phenotype definition by rejuvenating the Kraepelinian approach to diagnosis, they represent only a partial embrace of a Kraepelinian approach that equally emphasized syndrome description by using specific behavioral

---

[11] The dilemma in modeling prospective comorbidity of two substances is whether to model the univariate course of each substance separately and to then examine the association between the two, or whether to examine multiple courses of comorbidity itself. Although both approaches have intuitive appeal to the study of course of comorbidity, the dual trajectory approach is a more parsimonious, pragmatic approach, especially when it comes to exploring the relation of comorbidity to etiological predictors of interest. If external predictors were explored in the context of the single-domain trajectories, it would be necessary to examine 20 combinations of drinking and smoking, rather than simply seven, and perhaps reify dual substance use trajectories that are unlikely to exist.

indicators and longitudinal course (Widiger & Clark, 2000). To a large extent, formal diagnostic nosology has not kept up with either theory or data that highlight the importance of considering both longitudinal course and co-occurring comorbidity as critical phenotypes. Our approach could be applied to the study of any set of problem behaviors that exhibits a developmental time course and tends to be comorbid with other co-occurring conditions or symptoms. Additionally, by extension, more than two disorders or behaviors theoretically could be studied using this approach (e.g., alcohol, depression, and marital discord), although at the present time, practical constraints (especially sample size and number of longitudinal measurement occasions) limit the number of domains that can be modeled simultaneously.

Alcohol–Tobacco Comorbidity

This is the first study to explicitly identify such trajectories of concurrent drinking and smoking. Although the majority of respondents tended to be nonheavy drinker–nonsmoker, nearly half were either moderate-to-high chronic drinkers or smokers, or some combination thereof. Identification of common drinking and smoking groups might provide information for targeted prevention or treatment initiatives. For example, a full two fifths of individuals who smoke chronically also binge drink chronically, suggesting that chronic smoking could be an index for other addictive syndromes. In addition, individuals who binge drank moderately tended to belong to one of three smoking groups: moderate, late-onset, or developmentally limited. Although research has long since established that heavy drinkers tend to smoke, it is relatively silent about the extent to which moderate drinkers smoke, other than noting a dose-dependent association between drinking and smoking (Madden, Bucholz, Martin, & Heath, 2000). Although the present work suggests that moderate drinking could be an antecedent (perhaps even a cause), a consequence, or simply a co-occurring condition with smoking, the present study is limited in its ability to resolve this issue. Rather than using more variable-centered approaches such as cross-lagged panel models, multivariate latent growth curve models, or state-trait models (Sher & Wood, 1997), which resolve the extent to which comorbidity is attributable to uni- or bidirectional relations between alcohol and tobacco involvement versus a function of common third variables, we selected our approach to explore the developmental courses of co-occurring drinking and smoking and to identify correlates of these courses. This approach of modeling "developmental comorbidity" is in some ways a more fundamental portrayal of comorbidity than variable-centered alternatives which fail to resolve observable comorbid "types" and provide prevalence estimates for these. We do note that prior work suggests reciprocal causation between alcohol use disorders and tobacco dependence (Sher et al., 1996), suggesting that both directions of influence occur, although common third-variable influences are also likely (Jackson et al., 2000b). However, such "third variables" would need to be differentially expressed as a function of development in order to explain the range of comorbid types revealed by the current set of analyses.

Our model also revealed the extent to which comorbidity changed over time. For example, the most chronic group reported less heavy drinking over time, tracking the decline in drinking following adolescence (Johnston et al., 2004a, 2004b; B. Muthén & Muthén, 2000), presumably due to the adoption of a more conventional lifestyle (Bachman et al., 1997; Fillmore, 1988; Jessor, Donovan, & Costa, 1991). Despite considerable cross-sectional comorbidity, patterns of use can diverge over time and there is some degree of functional independence, in a developmental sense, of tobacco and alcohol use, at least in a subset of the population.

Prediction of Courses of Alcohol–Tobacco Comorbidity

Although our data set was somewhat limited in its assessment of etiologically relevant covariables, consideration of patterns of prediction is nonetheless informative. There is some evidence that parent education, gender, and race were unique risk factors that may have exhibited an "additive" effect in associations with co-occurring drinking and smoking (by virtue of larger estimates for comorbid vs. single substance comparisons). Also consistent with a unique, additive effect is that prediction of comorbidity (a) showed low parent education and being female to be associated with drinking only when accompanied by smoking and (b) showed high parent education and being male to be associated with smoking only when accompanied by drinking. Consistent with findings for chronic smoking, being female, being of high religiosity, and being Black or Hispanic were associated with increased risk of stable moderate smoking, whereas being male, being of low religiosity, and being White were associated with time-delimited courses of smoking (drinking held constant). This suggests that these risk factors are also specific to *course* within a substance.

Low religiosity, reflecting to some extent low conservatism, appeared to be a relatively *common* risk factor for substance use that exhibited an additive effect when considering alcohol–tobacco comorbidity. It was negatively associated with both drinking and smoking, but it did not differentiate between drinking and smoking trajectories with similar course, suggesting that it was more common than unique. In addition, it predicted a course of comorbidity above and beyond a single substance course, suggesting that it has an additive effect. In sum, sex, race, parent education, and religiosity tended to be additive in nature, suggesting that comorbidity may simply be a sign of severity for this particular set of predictors.

Perhaps of greatest interest, although alcohol expectancies and delinquency seemed to be relatively unique risk factors, these risk factors actually had a "masked" effect whereby their association with smoking could be attributed to a relation with drinking via smoking's association with drinking—that is, when we controlled for drinking, smoking no longer showed an effect; its effect existed only by virtue of its comorbidity with drinking. The opposite was not true: When we controlled for smoking, alcohol expectancies and delinquency still predicted drinking. Specifically, alcohol expectancies and delinquency were each positively bivariately associated with drinking and smoking, as well as with drinking trajectories and smoking trajectories; however, when we examined drinking and smoking in a comorbidity framework, these risk factors were associated with smoking only if there was comorbid drinking.

Given (a) that previous research has shown similar expectancies across substances (Stacy, Galaif, Sussman, & Dent, 1996) and similarity between motivations for drinking and motivations for smoking (Johnson & Jennison, 1992), and (b) that work in our own laboratory (using different data) has shown a robust relation between alcohol expectancies and tobacco dependence (Jackson et al., 2000b), it might be tempting to conclude that expectancies are relatively common across substance. However, the present findings suggest that any observed association between alcohol expectancies and smoking is most likely due to smoking's comorbidity with drinking. Likewise, although work has shown that conduct disorder and delinquency predict tobacco use, dependence, or both (Bardone et al., 1998; Bryant, Schulenberg, Bachman, O'Malley, & Johnston, 2000; Windle, 1990), our findings suggest that these latter relations may be due in part to smoking's association with drinking. Masked effects such as those observed for alcohol expectancies and delinquency permit us to learn new information that cannot be obtained by separately examining predictors of drinking and predictors of smoking. We note that these masked effects are consistent with previous findings in alcohol–tobacco comorbidity (Jackson et al., 2000a) that revealed informative associations in the context of comorbidity that were not apparent from considering the single-domain relations alone. Specifically, Jackson et al. showed childhood stressors to be associated with an increased likelihood of belonging to the comorbid class. However, in the absence of a co-occurring AUD, childhood stressors were not a risk factor for TD. This conditional effect was not detected from a single-domain approach. Univariate substance-specific (alcohol-only or tobacco-only) approaches may obscure specific relations that can only be observed when explicitly modeling comorbidity, and future research exploring risk factors for a behavior or disorder that is highly comorbid with another behavior or disorder must consider the risk factors in the context of the co-occurring behavior.

Strengths and Limitations

Data for the current study were taken from a large, nationally representative sample with multiple cohorts, allowing us to control for secular effects; in a single-cohort study, it is unclear how generalizable the findings are to other historic periods. However, characteristics of the data set also somewhat limited our study. Our participants were age 18 or older at the first assessment, and we certainly may have missed important developmental changes because much of the onset of substance use (particularly smoking) occurs in early-to-middle adolescence. Retention rates (65%) were acceptable (especially given that data were collected through low-cost mail surveys over a 6-year period), but attrition was somewhat differential with respect to variables important in this analysis. This suggests that our findings reflect a more conservative population in terms of substance use. Furthermore, we did not have syndromal diagnostic data. Although the heavy or "binge" drinking criteria of five or more drinks per occasion (or four or more for women) has been the topic of much debate, the association between binge drinking and alcohol consequences, problems, and dependence is robust, and data suggest that the five-drink measure is indeed a meaningful threshold (Wechsler & Austin, 1998).[12] Also, we believe that the limitations of using consumption measures are offset by their consistent assessment over four waves, and the present study complements previous findings on alcohol–tobacco comorbidity that used structured interviews but were limited with respect to generalizability, sample size, and multiple cohorts (Jackson et al., 2000b). We note that we have found using other data (Jackson & Sher, 2004) moderate agreement between classification of heavy drinking and alternate measures of alcohol consumption, including alcohol use disorders. We also were limited to examining a set of risk factors that were relatively demographic in nature or were administered to a small random subgroup of participants. Presumably, work in behavioral genetics or prevention–treatment outcome studies can further establish the construct validity of the trajectory groups. However, multiple cohorts over 2 decades, multiple waves with consistent assessment of drinking and smoking, and a large representative sample provide a unique opportunity to characterize joint trajectories of behaviors that are closely related to clinical problems, and these strengths outweigh any of the limitations discussed above.

Although we used a state-of-the-art modeling technique to identify ordered trajectories of substance use, we note that this technique is not without its drawbacks. In mixture modeling analyses, mixtures can be extracted

---

[12] We note that in other work in our lab, using a prospective (six-wave) sample of young adults (Sher, Walitzer, Wood, & Brent, 1991), trajectories of heavy drinking showed a moderate degree of overlap (percent agreement ranged from 60% to 69%; kappas ranged from .28 to .38) with trajectories of interview-based alcohol use disorder diagnoses and questionnaire-based measures of alcohol consequences and alcohol dependence (Sher & Jackson, 2003) as well as with alcohol consumption ($\kappa = .50$).

even when none exist, if the data are non-normal but contain only a single population (Bauer & Curran, 2003; but see B. O. Muthén, 2003). Although our findings from the single-domain approach were consistent with both theory and extant empirical research on trajectories of drinking and smoking, we still exercise caution in drawing conclusions about comorbidity from these data until the replicability of these comorbid groups is established. Regardless of replicability of the current work, the general approach represents an important step forward in psychiatric epidemiology by demonstrating the feasibility of modeling comorbidity and course within a person-centered approach to data analysis.

REFERENCES

Akaike, H. (1987). Factor analysis and AIC. *Psychometrika, 52,* 317–332.

American Psychiatric Association. (1980). *Diagnostic and statistical manual of mental disorders* (3rd ed.). Washington, DC: Author.

American Psychiatric Association. (1987). *Diagnostic and statistical manual of mental disorders* (3rd ed., rev.). Washington, DC: Author.

American Psychiatric Association. (1994). *Diagnostic and statistical manual of mental disorders* (4th ed.). Washington, DC: Author.

Bachman, J. G., O'Malley, P. M., Johnston, L. D., Rodgers, W. L., Schulenberg, J., Lim, J., & Wadsworth, K. N. (1996). *Changes in drug use during ages 18–32* (Monitoring the Future Occasional Paper No. 39). Ann Arbor, MI: Institute for Social Research.

Bachman, J. G., Wadsworth, K. N., O'Malley, P. M., Johnston, L. D., & Schulenberg, J. E. (1997). *Smoking, drinking, and drug use in young adulthood: The impacts of new freedoms and new responsibilities.* Mahwah, NJ: Erlbaum.

Bardone, A. M., Moffitt, T. E., Caspi, A., Dickson, N., Stanton, W. R., & Silva, P. A. (1998). Adult physical health outcomes of adolescent girls with conduct disorder, depression, and anxiety. *Journal of the American Academy of Child & Adolescent Psychiatry, 37,* 594–601.

Bates, M. E. (2000). Integrating person-centered and variable-centered approaches in the study of developmental courses and transitions in alcohol use: Introduction to the special section. *Alcoholism: Clinical & Experimental Research, 24,* 878–881.

Bauer, D. J., & Curran, P. J. (2003). Distributional assumptions of growth mixture models: Implications for over-extraction of latent trajectory classes. *Psychological Methods, 8,* 338–363.

Bennett, M. E., McCrady, B. S., Johnson, V., & Pandina, R. J. (1999). Problem drinking from young adulthood to adulthood: Patterns, predictors and outcomes. *Journal of Studies on Alcohol, 60,* 605–614.

Bien, T. H., & Burge, J. (1990). Smoking and drinking: A review of the literature. *International Journal of Addiction, 25,* 1429–1454.

Blot, W. J., McLaughlin, J. K., Winn, D. M., Austin, D. F., Greenberg, R. S., Preston-Martin, S., et al. (1988). Smoking and drinking in relation to oral and pharyngeal cancer. *Cancer Research, 48,* 3282–3287.

Breslau, N. (1995). Psychiatric comorbidity of smoking and nicotine dependence. *Behavior Genetics, 25,* 95–101.

Bryant, A. L., Schulenberg, J., Bachman, J. G., O'Malley, P. M., & Johnston, L. D. (2000). Understanding the links among school misbehavior, academic achievement, and cigarette use: A national panel study of adolescents. *Prevention Science, 1,* 71–87.

Chassin, L., Pitts, S. C., & Prost, J. (2002). Binge drinking trajectories from adolescence to emerging adulthood in a high-risk sample: Predictors and substance abuse outcomes. *Journal of Consulting and Clinical Psychology, 70,* 67–78.

Chassin, L., Presson, C. C., Pitts, S. C., & Sherman, S. J. (2000). The natural history of cigarette smoking from adolescence to adulthood in a Midwestern community sample: Multiple trajectories and their psychosocial correlates. *Health Psychology, 19,* 223–231.

Chen, K., & Kandel, D. B. (1995). The natural history of drug use from adolescence to the mid-thirties in a general population sample. *American Journal of Public Health, 85,* 41–47.

Cicchetti, D., & Rogosch, F. A. (2002). A developmental psychopathology perspective on adolescence. *Journal of Consulting and Clinical Psychology, 70,* 6–20.

Colder, C. R., Campbell, R. T., Ruel, E., Richardson, J. L., & Flay, B. R. (2002). A finite mixture model of growth trajectories of adolescent alcohol use: Predictors and consequences. *Journal of Consulting and Clinical Psychology, 70,* 976–985.

Colder, C. R., Mehta, P., Balanda, K., Campbell, R. T., Mayhew, K. P., Stanton, W. R., et al. (2001). Identifying trajectories of adolescent smoking: An application of latent growth mixture modeling. *Health Psychology, 20,* 127–135.

Department of Health and Human Services (2000). *Summary of findings from the 1999 National Household Survey on Drug Abuse.* Rockville, MD: Author.

DiFranza, J. R., & Guerrera, M. P. (1990). Alcoholism and smoking. *Journal of Studies on Alcohol, 51,* 130–135.

Fillmore, K. M. (1988). *Alcohol use across the life course.* Toronto, Ontario, Canada: Addiction Research Foundation.

Flanders, W. D., & Rothman, K. J. (1982). Interaction of alcohol and tobacco in laryngeal cancer. *American Journal of Epidemiology, 115,* 371–379.

Goldman, M. S., Brown, S. A., & Christiansen, B. A. (1987). Expectancy theory: Thinking about drinking. In H. T. Blane & K. E. Leonard (Eds.) *Psychological theories of drinking and alcoholism* (pp. 181–266). New York: Guilford Press.

Goldman, M. S., Del Boca, F. K., & Darkes, J. (1999). Alcohol expectancy theory: The application of cognitive neuroscience. In K. E. Leonard & H. T. Blane (Eds.), *Psychological theories of drinking and alcoholism* (2nd ed., pp. 203–246). New York: Guilford Press.

Gulliver, S. B., Rohsenow, D. J., Colby, S. M., Dey, A. N., Abrams, D. B., Niaura, R. S., & Monti, P. M. (1995). Interrelationship of smoking and alcohol dependence, use, and urges to use. *Journal of Studies on Alcohol, 56,* 202–206.

Istvan, J., & Matarazzo, J. D. (1984). Tobacco, alcohol, and caffeine use: A review of their relationships. *Psychological Bulletin, 95,* 301–326.

Jackson, K. M., & Sher, K. J. (2004). *Similarities and differences of longitudinal phenotypes across alternate measures of alcohol involvement.* Manuscript submitted for publication.

Jackson, K. M., Sher, K. J., & Wood, P. K. (2000a). Trajectories of conjoint substance use disorders: A developmental, typological approach to comorbidity. *Alcoholism: Clinical and Experimental Research, 24,* 902–913.

Jackson, K. M., Sher, K. J., & Wood, P. K. (2000b). Prospective analyses of comorbidity: Tobacco and alcohol use disorders. *Journal of Abnormal Psychology, 109,* 679–694.

Jessor, R., Donovan, J. E., & Costa, F. M. (1991). *Beyond adolescence: Problem behavior and young adult development.* New York: Cambridge University Press.

Jessor, R., & Jessor, S. (1977). *Problem behavior and psychosocial development.* New York: Academic Press.

Johnson, K. A., & Jennison, K. M. (1992). The drinking–smoking syndrome and social context. *International Journal of the Addictions, 27,* 749–792.

Johnston, L. D., & O'Malley, P. M. (1985). Issues of validity and population coverage in student surveys of drug use. In B. A. Rouse, N. J. Kozel, & L. G. Richards (Eds.), *Self-report methods of estimating drug use: Meeting current challenges to validity* (NIDA Research Monograph No. 57, pp. 31–54). Washington, DC: National Institute on Drug Abuse.

Johnston, L. D., O'Malley, P. M., Bachman, J. G., & Schulenberg, J. E. (2004a). *National survey results on drug use from the Monitoring the Future study, 1975–2003: Volume I: Secondary school students.* Bethesda, MD: National Institute on Drug Abuse.

Johnston, L. D., O'Malley, P. M., Bachman, J. G., & Schulenberg, J. E. (2004b). *National survey results on drug use from the Monitoring the Future study, 1975–2003: Volume II: College students and young adults.* Bethesda, MD: National Institute on Drug Abuse.

Jones, B. L., Nagin, D. S., & Roeder, K. (2001). A SAS procedure based on mixture models for estimating developmental trajectories. *Sociological Methods & Research, 29,* 374–393.

Kozlowski, L. T., Henningfield, J. E., Keenan, R. M., Lei, H., Leigh, G., Jelinek, L. C., et al. (1993). Patterns of alcohol, cigarette, and caffeine and other drug use in two drug abusing populations. *Journal of Substance Abuse Treatment, 10,* 171–179.

Li, F., Barrera, M., Jr., Hops, H., & Fisher, K. J. (2002). The longitudinal influence of peers on the development of alcohol use in late adolescence: A growth mixture analysis. *Journal of Behavioral Medicine, 25,* 293–315.

Lo, Y., Mendell, N. R., & Rubin, D. (1991). Testing the number of components in a normal mixture. *Biometrika, 88,* 767–778.

Madden, P. A. F., Bucholz, K. K., Martin, N. G., & Heath, A. C. (2000). Smoking and the genetic contribution to alcohol-dependence risk. *Alcohol Health & Research World, 24,* 209–214.

Martin, C. S., Kaczynski, N. A., Maisto, S. A., & Tarter, R. E. (1996). Polydrug use in adolescent drinkers with and without *DSM–IV* alcohol abuse and dependence. *Alcoholism: Clinical and Experimental Research, 20,* 1099–1108.

Munoz, N., & Day, N. E. (1996). Esophageal cancer. In D. Schoffenfield & J. F. Fraumani Jr. (Eds.), *Cancer epidemiology and prevention* (pp. 681–706). New York: Oxford University Press.

Muthén, B. (2001). Latent variable mixture modeling. In G. A. Marcoulides & R. E. Schumacker (Eds.), *New Developments and techniques in structural equation modeling* (pp. 1–33). Mahwah, NJ: Erlbaum.

Muthén, B. O. (2003). Statistical and substantive checking in growth mixture modeling: Comment on Bauer and Curran. *Psychological Methods, 8,* 369–377.

Muthén, B., Brown, C. H., Masyn, K., Jo, B., Khoo, S. T., Yang, C.-C., et al. (2002). General growth mixture modeling for randomized preventive interventions. *Biostatistics, 3,* 459–475.

Muthén, B., & Muthén, L. K. (2000). Integrating person-centered and variable-centered analyses: Growth mixture modeling with latent trajectory classes. *Alcoholism: Clinical & Experimental Research, 24,* 882–891.

Muthén, L. K., & Muthén, B. O. (1998 –2004). *Mplus user's guide* (3rd ed.). Los Angeles: Authors.

Nagin, D. S. (1999). Analyzing developmental trajectories: A semiparametric, group-based approach. *Psychological Methods, 4,* 139–157.

Neter, J., Wasserman, W., & Kutner, M. H. (1990). *Applied linear statistical models: Regression, analysis of variance, and experimental designs.* Homewood, IL: Irwin.

O'Malley, P. M., Bachman, J. G., & Johnston, L. D. (1983). Reliability and consistency of self-reports of drug use. *International Journal of the Addictions, 18,* 805–824.

O'Malley, P. M., & Johnston, L. D. (2002). Epidemiology of alcohol and other drug use among American college students. *Journal of Studies on Alcohol,* Suppl. 14, 23–29.

Parra, G. R., Sher, K. J., Krull, J. L., & Jackson, K. M. (2003). *Heavy drinking occasions and peer alcohol involvement: A latent growth analysis over 11 years.* Manuscript submitted for publication.

Schulenberg, J. E., & Maggs, J. L. (2002). A developmental perspective on alcohol use and heavy drinking during adolescence and the transition to young adulthood. *Journal of Studies on Alcohol, S14,* 54–70.

Schulenberg, J., Maggs, J. L., Long, S. W., Sher, K. J., Gotham, H. J., Baer, J. S., et al. (2001). The problem of college drinking: Insights from a developmental perspective. *Alcoholism: Clinical & Experimental Research, 25,* 473–477.

Schulenberg, J., Maggs, J. L., Steinman, K., & Zucker, R. A. (2001). Development matters: Taking the long view on substance abuse etiology and intervention during adolescence. In P. M. Monti, S. M. Colby, & T. A. O'Leary (Eds.), *Adolescents, alcohol, and substance abuse: Reaching teens through brief intervention.* (pp. 19–57). New York: Guilford Press.

Schulenberg, J., O'Malley, P. M., Bachman, J. G., & Johnston. L. D. (2000). "Spread your wings and fly": The course of health and well-being during the transition to young adulthood. In L. Crockett & R. Silbereisen (Eds.), *Negotiating adolescence in times of social change* (pp. 224–255). New York: Cambridge University Press.

Schulenberg, J., O'Malley, P. M., Bachman, J. G., Wadsworth, K. N., & Johnston, L. D. (1996). Getting drunk and growing up: Trajectories of frequent binge drinking during the transition to young adulthood. *Journal of Studies on Alcohol, 57,* 289–304.

Schulenberg, J., Wadsworth, K. N., O'Malley, P. M., Bachman, J. G., & Johnston, L. D. (1996). Adolescent risk factors for binge drinking during the transition to young adulthood: Variable- and pattern-centered approaches to change. *Developmental Psychology, 32,* 659–674.

Schulenberg, J. E., & Zarrett, N. R. (2006). Mental health during emerging adulthood: Continuity and discontinuity in courses, causes, and functions. In J. J. Arnett & J. Tanner (Eds.), *Emerging adults in America: Coming of age in the 21st century* (pp. 135–172). Washington DC: American Psychological Association.

Schwartz, G. (1978). Estimating the dimension of a model. *Annals of Statistics, 6,* 461–464.

Sher, K. J., Gotham, H. J., Erickson, D. J., & Wood, P. K. (1996). A prospective high-risk study of the relationship between tobacco dependence and alcohol use disorders. *Alcoholism: Clinical and Experimental Research, 20,* 485–491.

Sher, K. J., & Jackson, K. M. (2003, June). Similarities and differences of longitudinal phenotypes across alternate measures of alcohol involvement. In M. Russell (Chair), *Connecting the dots: Drinking patterns and alcohol problems from a life course perspective.* Symposium conducted at the meeting of the Research Society on Alcoholism, Fort Lauderdale, FL.

Sher, K. J., Walitzer, K. S., Wood, P. K., & Brent, E. E. (1991). Characteristics of children of alcoholics: Putative risk factors, substance use and abuse, and psychopathology. *Journal of Abnormal Psychology, 100,* 427–448.

Sher, K. J., & Wood, P. K. (1997). Methodological issues in conducting prospective research on alcohol-related behavior: A report from the field. In K. J. Bryant, S. G. West, & M. Windle (Eds.), *The science of prevention: Methodological advances from alcohol and substance abuse research* (pp. 3–41). Washington, DC: American Psychological Association.

Shiffman, S. (1989). Tobacco "chippers": Individual differences in tobacco dependence. *Psychopharmacology, 97,* 539–547.

Stacy, A. W., Galaif, E. R., Sussman, S., & Dent, C. W. (1996). Self-generated drug outcomes in high-risk adolescents. *Psychology of Addictive Behaviors, 10,* 18–27.

Torabi, M. R., Bailey, W. J., & Majd-Jabbari, M. (1993). Cigarette smoking as a predictor of alcohol and other drug use by children and adolescents: Evidence of the "gateway drug effect." *Journal of School Health, 63,* 302–306.

Tucker, J. S., Orlando, M., & Ellickson, P. L. (2003). Patterns and correlates of binge drinking trajectories from early adolescence to young adulthood. *Health Psychology, 22,* 79–87.

von Eye, A. (2002). *Configural frequency analysis: Methods, models, and applications.* Mahwah, NJ: Erlbaum.

Wechsler, H., & Austin, S. B. (1998). Binge drinking: The five/four measure. *Journal of Studies on Alcohol, 59,* 122–124.

Wechsler, H., & Isaac, N. (1992). "Binge" drinkers at Massachusetts colleges. *Journal of the American Medical Association, 267,* 2929–2931.

Wechsler, H., Lee, J. E., Kuo, M., & Lee, H. (2000). College binge drinking in the 1990s: A continuing problem: Results of the Harvard School of Public Health 1999 College Alcohol Study. *Journal of American College Health, 48,* 199–210.

White, H. R., Johnson, V., & Buyske, S. (2000). Parental modeling and parenting behavior effects on offspring alcohol and cigarette use: A growth curve analysis. *Journal of Substance Abuse, 12,* 287–310.

White, H. R., Pandina, R. J., & Chen, P. (2002). Developmental trajectories of cigarette use from early adolescence into young adulthood. *Drug and Alcohol Dependence, 65,* 167–178.

Widiger, T. A., & Clark, L. A. (2000). Toward *DSM–V* and the classification of psychopathology. *Psychological Bulletin, 126,* 946–963.

Windle, M. (1990). A longitudinal study of antisocial behaviors in early adolescence as predictors of late adolescent substance use: Gender and ethnic group differences. *Journal of Abnormal Psychology, 99,* 86–91.

York, J. L., & Hirsch, J. A. (1995). Drinking patterns and health status in smoking and nonsmoking alcoholics. *Alcoholism: Clinical and Experimental Research, 19,* 666–673.

Zacny, J. P. (1990). Behavioral aspects of alcohol–tobacco interactions. In M. Galanter (Ed.), *Recent developments in alcoholism Vol. 8: Combined alcohol and other drug dependence* (pp. 205–219). New York: Plenum Press.

Zucker, R. A. (1987). The four alcoholisms: A developmental account of the etiologic process. In P. C. Rivers (Ed.), *Nebraska Symposium on Motivation: Vol. 34. Alcohol and addictive behavior* (pp. 27–83). Lincoln: University of Nebraska Press.

Zucker, R. A. (1994). Pathways to alcohol problems and alcoholism: A developmental account of the evidence for multiple alcoholisms and for contextual contributions to risk. In R. A. Zucker, J. Howard, & G. M. Boyd (Eds.), *The development of alcohol problems: Exploring the biopsychosocial matrix of risk* (NIH Publication No. 94-3495, pp. 255–289). Rockville, MD: National Institute on Alcohol Abuse and Alcoholism.

Zucker, R. A., Fitzgerald, H. E., & Moses, H. D. (1995). Emergence of alcohol problems and the several alcoholisms: A developmental perspective on etiologic theory and life course trajectory. In D. Cicchetti & D. J. Cohen (Eds.), *Developmental psychopathology: Vol. 2. Risk, disorder, and adaptation* (pp. 677–711). New York: Wiley.

V

FAMILY DYNAMICS AND FAMILY IMPACT

11

THE ROLES OF FAMILIAL ALCOHOLISM AND ADOLESCENT FAMILY HARMONY IN YOUNG ADULTS' SUBSTANCE DEPENDENCE DISORDERS: MEDIATED AND MODERATED RELATIONS

QING ZHOU, KEVIN M. KING, AND LAURIE CHASSIN

The high prevalence of substance use disorders (SUDs) that occur in young adulthood (Newman et al., 1996) makes this an important developmental period for studying the etiology of substance dependence. Although previous research indicates that characteristics of the family in childhood and adolescence can elevate or reduce risk for later SUDs (see reviews by Chassin, Ritter, Trim, & King, 2003; Hawkins, Catalano, & Miller, 1992), few studies have examined the mediational and moderational mechanisms underlying these links. Moreover, despite the importance of distinguishing between alcohol and drug use outcomes (Chassin, Flora, & King, 2004; McGue, Slutske, & Iacono, 1999), few studies have examined differential etiological pathways to alcohol versus drug use disorders or their combination. The present study tested whether family harmony in adolescence mediated the relation between familial alcoholism and young adults' alcohol and drug dependence disorders, and whether the relation between adolescent family

This work was supported by NIDA Grant DA05227 from the National Institute on Drug Abuse to Laurie Chassin. The authors thank Kate Morse and Pam Schwartz for coordinating the data collection and David B. Flora and Jenn-Yun Tein for consultation on these analyses.

Reprinted from *Journal of Abnormal Psychology, 115*, 320–331 (2006). Copyright 2006 by the American Psychological Association.

harmony and later substance dependence was moderated by the density of familial alcoholism.

FAMILIAL ALCOHOLISM AND YOUNG ADULTS' SUBSTANCE DEPENDENCE DISORDERS

Longitudinal studies have shown that having alcoholic parent(s) creates significant risk for substance use problems among offspring (e.g., Chassin, Pitts, DeLucia, & Todd, 1999; Sher, Walitzer, Wood, & Brent, 1991). Moreover, individuals with high family history density (FHD) of alcoholism are at especially high risk for substance use problems (Curran et al., 1999; Johnson & Pickens, 2001; Stoltenberg, Mudd, Blow, & Hill, 1998; Windle, 1996). However, despite relatively strong evidence for parental and familial alcoholism as a risk factor for SUDs, there is still much to know about the processes underlying this risk, which may include genetic and environmental pathways (McGue, 1999). Recently, Walden, McGue, Iacono, Burt, and Elkins (2004) found that two environmental factors—parent–child relationships and peer deviance—accounted for more than 70% of the variance in early substance use, which increases risk for later SUDs (Hawkins et al., 1992). Therefore, environmental liabilities associated with growing up in families with alcoholic members may increase risk for SUDs (Jacob et al., 2003), and thus mediate the associations between familial alcoholism and offspring substance use.

ADOLESCENT FAMILY HARMONY AS A MEDIATOR IN THE RELATION BETWEEN FAMILIAL ALCOHOLISM AND YOUNG ADULTS' SUBSTANCE DEPENDENCE DISORDERS

Family environmental factors that have been linked to offspring's substance use-related problems include parental social support (Wills, Resko, Ainette, & Mendoza, 2004), parental monitoring or discipline (Chassin, Curran, Hussong, & Colder, 1996; King & Chassin, 2004), and family structure (Eitle, 2005). Several family environment factors have also been found to mediate the effect of parental or familial alcoholism on offspring's substance use problems, including parental monitoring (Chassin et al., 1996) and parental discipline (King & Chassin, 2004). Family disharmony, characterized by high levels of conflict (including interparental and parent–child conflict, or family conflict in general), may be an additional environmental mechanism by which familial alcoholism influences SUDs in offspring. Family disharmony may promote children's aggressive or disruptive behaviors and deficits in emotion regulation (Cummings & Davies, 1996). Family conflict may also interfere with effective parenting, which affects risk for later substance abuse and dependence

(Cummings & Davies, 1996; Patterson, DeBaryshe, & Ramsey, 1989; Sher, 1991). Consistent with these theories, both concurrent and prospective relations have been found between family disharmony and substance use problems among offspring (e.g., Guo, Hill, Hawkins, Catalano, & Abbott, 2002; Sher, Gershuny, Peterson, & Raskin, 1997; Wills, Sandy, Yaeger, & Shinar, 2001). Moreover, the link between familial alcoholism and family disharmony has also been supported. Familial alcoholism is related to marital conflict (Heyman, O'Leary, & Jouriles, 1995), negative communications among family members (Jacob, Leonard, & Haber, 2001), and parent–child conflict (El-Sheikh & Flanagan, 2001). Therefore, we posited a mediational pathway in which familial alcoholism lowers family harmony, which in turn increases risk for SUDs.

Only a few researchers have directly examined the mediating role of family disharmony in the link between familial alcoholism and developmental outcomes in childhood through young adulthood, and they have not studied SUDs as an outcome. For example, family disharmony mediated risk for difficulty in leaving home for children of alcoholics in the transition from adolescence to young adulthood (Hussong & Chassin, 2002). Family cohesion and adaptability mediated the link between parental problem drinking and school-age children's adjustment problems (El-Sheikh & Buckhalt, 2003; El-Sheikh & Flanagan, 2001). Family disharmony in toddlerhood mediated the link between parent antisocial behavior (but not parent alcohol problems) and boys' later externalizing problems (Loukas, Fitzgerald, Zucker, & von Eye, 2001). Thus, family disharmony mediates familial alcoholism effects on a range of negative offspring outcomes, but this has not been tested for young adult SUDs. The current study provides the first prospective test of this mediating relation.

DIFFERENTIAL PREDICTION OF ALCOHOL DEPENDENCE, DRUG DEPENDENCE, AND THEIR COMBINATION

Most research on young adults' SUDs either examines alcohol or drug use outcomes in isolation or aggregates them into an overall index of "substance use disorder." However, recent work suggests that alcohol and drug use disorders and their combination may have distinct antecedents. For example, drug disorders, with or without alcohol disorders, have been associated with the externalizing-spectrum problems including conduct problems and antisocial behavior (Krueger et al., 2002; Taylor, Iacono, & McGue, 2000; Taylor, Malone, Iacono, & McGue, 2002). Compared with alcohol disorders, drug disorders tend to be more strongly related to behavioral undercontrol (disinhibition [McGue et al., 1999]; impulsivity and low agreeableness [Chassin et al., 2004]), whereas alcohol disorders in the absence of drug disorder tend to be more strongly related to negative emotionality (McGue et al., 1999) and neuroticism (Chassin et al., 2004). Moreover, Chassin et al. (2004) found that impulsivity mediated the links between parental alcoholism and drug dependence with or without alcohol dependence, but not the link between parental alcoholism and alcohol dependence alone.

Thus, previous research suggests that drug problems (compared to alcohol problems in the absence of drug problems) are more closely tied to behavioral undercontrol and externalizing-spectrum problems such as conduct disorder and aggression. Given these findings, the family factors that are thought to produce behavioral undercontrol and externalizing behaviors may also be more closely related to drug problems than to alcohol problems in the absence of drug problems. Sher (1991) described a deviance proneness pathway to SUDs by which dysfunctional family environments interact with difficult temperament to produce behavioral undercontrol, externalizing behaviors, school failure, and deviant peer affiliations. Similarly, Patterson's (Patterson, 1982; Patterson et al., 1989) developmental model of antisocial behavior suggests that dysfunctional family processes, including family conflict, produce children's conduct problems, which in turn lead to rejection by normal peers, school failure, and involvement in deviant peer groups whose norms promote antisocial behaviors. Given these theories, and the link between family conflict and offspring's behavioral undercontrol and conduct problems (Grych & Fincham, 1990), we hypothesized that family conflict would be more predictive of young adults' drug dependence with or without alcohol dependence than of alcohol dependence in the absence of drug dependence, and that the mediational role of family harmony would be specific to the link between familial alcoholism and drug dependence disorders (with or without alcohol dependence).

To our knowledge, the current study is the first to examine the differential prediction of alcohol versus drug dependence and their combination from family environment characteristics. Moreover, because personality has been shown to be an important predictor of these differential diagnoses, we also adjusted for the effects of personality when testing for these relations. Finally, because developmental pathways to substance use may be moderated by gender or ethnicity (e.g., Baker & Yardley, 2002; Chassin & Ritter, 2001; Mahaddian, Newcomb, & Bentler, 1988), we included gender and ethnicity as covariates in the models, and tested the interactions between gender and ethnicity and our predictors.

IS THE RELATION BETWEEN ADOLESCENT FAMILY HARMONY AND YOUNG ADULTS' SUBSTANCE DEPENDENCE DISORDER MODERATED BY FAMILY HISTORY DENSITY OF ALCOHOLISM?

It is also possible that the same environmental characteristic (e.g., family harmony) may have a different impact on the offspring's SUDs depending on the density of familial alcoholism. Several studies have found that familial

SUD interacts with environmental factors in predicting children's and adolescents' adjustment (El-Sheikh & Buckhalt, 2003; El-Sheikh & Flanagan, 2001) or substance use problems (Legrand, McGue, & Iacono, 1999). However, it is unclear whether these interactions differentially affect alcohol versus drug disorder. Moreover, there are important differences in the forms of the interactions that have been found. In a classic stress-buffering interaction (Rutter, 1990), a protective factor (e.g., family harmony) buffers the response to risk such that in the presence of a risk factor (e.g., familial alcoholism) individuals with higher levels of a protective factor exhibit better outcomes than do individuals with lower levels of the protective factor. Consistent with this type of interaction, El-Sheikh and Buckhalt (2003) found that the positive effect of high family cohesion and adaptability on children's adjustment problems was stronger among families with more rather than fewer parental drinking problems. Similarly, Legrand et al. (1999) found that the positive effect of a low-risk peer environment on male adolescents' substance use was stronger at higher than at lower levels of familial SUD. Assuming that the protective factor is modifiable, classic stress-buffering interactions support the importance of interventions that increase levels of the protective factor.

In contrast, findings from other studies (including findings based on the current sample) suggest a different pattern of interaction, which has been termed "protective but reactive" (Luthar, Cicchetti, & Becker, 2000). In these cases, although the protective factor buffers against risk, the effect of the protective factor becomes *weaker* at higher levels of risk (compared to lower levels of risk). For example, King and Chassin (2004) found that the positive effect of parental support on drug disorder was weaker among individuals with higher rather than lower levels of behavioral undercontrol. Similarly, El-Sheikh and Flanagan (2001) found that the positive effect of low parent–child conflict on children's internalizing problems was weaker in families with higher rather than lower parental problem drinking. For preventive interventions, protective but reactive interactions point to potential limitations of interventions aimed at increasing protective factors, because their effectiveness may be reduced at high levels of risk. Thus, the present study tested whether the relation between adolescent family harmony and young adults' substance dependence disorder was moderated by FHD of alcoholism, showing either classic stress buffering or a protective but reactive interaction.

METHOD

Participants

Participants were from an ongoing study of parental alcoholism (Chassin et al., 2004; Chassin, Rogosch, & Barrera, 1991). At Time 1, there were 454 adolescents (M age = 13.2 years, range = 10.5–15.5), 246 of whom had at least one biological alcoholic parent who was also a custodial parent (children of alcoholics [COAs]) and 208 demographically matched adolescents with no biological or custodial alcoholic parents (control participants). At a young adult follow-up (Time 4), full biological siblings were included if they were in the age range of 18 to 26 (and all of these siblings were again invited to participate at Time 5, five years later). A total of 327 siblings (78% of eligible participants) were interviewed at Time 4, and 350 siblings (83%) were interviewed at Time 5 (n = 378 interviewed at either wave). The combined sample of original targets and their siblings was n = 734 at Time 4 (M age = 21.1), n = 762 at Time 5 (M age = 26.6), and n = 817 with at least one wave of measurement. Retention in young adulthood was excellent, with 407 (90%) of the original target sample interviewed at Time 4 and 411 (91%) interviewed at Time 5 (96% had data at either time point). We use parent report data from the three annual adolescent assessments (Time 1 to Time 3), and self-report data from the two 5-year young adult follow-ups (Times 4 and 5).

Details of sample recruitment are reported elsewhere (Chassin, Barrera, Bech, & Kossak-Fuller, 1992). COA families were recruited using court records of DUI arrests, health maintenance organization wellness questionnaires, and community telephone screening. Parental lifetime *Diagnostic and Statistical Manual of Mental Disorders* (3rd ed.; *DSM–III*; American Psychiatric Association, 1980) alcohol abuse or dependence was confirmed with a structured interview. Demographically matched control families were recruited using telephone interviews. When a COA was recruited, reverse directories were used to locate families in the same neighborhood. Families were screened to match the COA participant in ethnicity, family structure, target child's age (within 1 year), and socioeconomic status, using the property value code from the reverse directory. Structured interviews were used to confirm that neither parent met lifetime *DSM–III* criteria for alcohol abuse or dependence.

A complete description of sample representativeness is reported elsewhere (Chassin et al., 1991). The sample was unbiased with respect to alcoholism indicators available in archival records (e.g., blood alcohol levels recorded at the time of the arrest; see Chassin et al., 1992, for details). Moreover, the alcoholic sample had rates of other psychopathology similar to those that were reported for a community-dwelling alcoholic sample (Helzer & Pryzbeck, 1988). However, those who refused participation were more likely to be Hispanic, suggesting some caution in generalization to more diverse samples.

Procedure

Data were collected with computer-assisted interviews either at families' homes or on campus, or by telephone for out-of-state participants.

Interviewers were unaware of the family's group membership. Interviews required one to three hours, and participants were paid up to $70 over the waves. To encourage honest responding, we reinforced confidentiality with a Department of Health and Human Services Certificate of Confidentiality.

Selection of the Current Subsample

A total of 732 participants from 393 families (84% of total sample; 90% of Time 4 to 5 sample) had complete data on parental and grandparental alcoholism, at least partial family harmony data from Times 1 to 3, and substance dependence diagnosis information at Waves 4 or 5. Because some research has shown that DSM–III–R diagnoses of substance abuse are more ambiguous and less reliable than those of substance dependence (Pollock, Martin, & Langenbucher, 2000), participants who had a lifetime diagnosis of alcohol or drug abuse (but not dependence) were dropped from analyses, which resulted in a final sample of 678 young adults (see Table 11.1 for the descriptive data). Compared with the original targets, the siblings were older and more likely to be married at Time 5, but no other differences were found. Compared with control participants, the COAs had a lower proportion of non-Hispanic Caucasians, were less likely to be married at Time 5, and were less likely to receive higher education.

We next compared those who were retained for analysis ($n = 678$) with those who were dropped because of missing data or an abuse-only diagnosis ($n = 99$). The two groups did not differ in gender, ethnicity, or familial alcoholism. However, those who were dropped were more likely to have a parent with antisocial personality disorder (16% of those dropped vs. 6% of those retained, $\chi^2 = 8.93$, $p < .01$), and had mothers with slightly less education (high school graduates vs. some postsecondary education, $t = 2.48$, $p < .05$). Because these differences are small, some caution is warranted in generalization.

Measures

The measures used in the current study were part of the larger interview battery.

Adolescent Family Harmony

At Times 1, 2, and 3, mothers and fathers reported on their perception of family harmony during the past 3 months using the five-item family conflict scale from Bloom's Family Processes Scale (Bloom, 1985). The items assess the extent to which family members fought a lot, got angry, threw

TABLE 11.1
Demographic Characteristics of the Young Adult Sample

	Total (N = 678)	Original targets vs. siblings		COAs vs. Non-COAs	
		Original targets (n = 354)	Siblings (n = 324)	COAs (n = 332)	Non-COAs (n = 346)
Demographics					
% Females	46.6	45.8	47.5	45.8	47.4
% Non-Hispanic Caucasian	27.6	25.7	29.6	32.5*	22.8*
% COA	49.0	52.0	45.7	—	—
Mean age at T5	26.6	25.6*	27.6*	26.5	26.6
% Married at T5	41.0	31.9*	43.5*	34.1*	47.4*
% Employed	91.1	93.2	88.8	92.2	90.2
% Completed a college degree	30.5	31.1	29.9	26.5*	34.4*
% Attended some college	61.2	61.3	61.0	55.4*	66.8*
Mean (SD) of FHD	0.45 (0.39)	0.46 (0.40)	0.43 (0.39)	0.77 (0.28)*	0.13 (0.18)*
Mean (SD) of family harmony	3.43 (0.57)	3.46 (0.57)	3.40 (0.58)	3.26 (0.58)*	3.61 (0.53)*
Ns for substance dependence diagnosis groups					
ALC group	137	68	69	87*	50*
DRUG group	44	25	19	25	19
ALC + DRUG group	102	55	47	72*	30*
NON group	395	206	189	148*	247*

Note. The * indicates significant difference between groups. COA = children of alcoholics; FHD = family history density of alcoholism; ALC = alcohol dependence only; DRUG = drug dependence only; NON = no diagnoses.

things, lost their tempers, hit each other, and criticized each other ($\alpha = .68$, .68, and .69 for fathers' reports at Times 1, 2, and 3, and .69, .73, and .70 for mothers' reports). The items were reverse-scored such that a high score reflected greater family harmony. Bloom's Family Processes Scale has been widely used in research and its psychometric properties (including factor integrity) have been well established (for a review, see Bloom & Naar, 1994). In two previous studies of the current sample (Hussong & Chassin, 1997, 2002), this measure was related to lowered likelihood of adolescent substance use initiation, better young adult psychological adjustment (i.e., fewer externalizing and internalizing symptoms), and fewer difficulties in the leaving-home transition.

We examined the factor structure of the measure using Mplus Version 2.12 (Muthén & Muthén, 2003) to estimate a confirmatory factor model with three correlated latent factors: Family Harmony at Time 1, Time 2, and Time 3, each indicated by fathers' and mothers' reports of harmony at each time point. The measurement model fit the data well, $\Delta\chi^2(df = 3, n = 454$ families) = .24, $p = .97$, comparative fit index (CFI) = 1.00, root-mean-square error of approximation (RMSEA) = .000, standardized root-mean-square residual (SRMR) = .004. All the model-estimated loadings were significant in a positive direction (the standardized loadings ranged from .50 to .91). Moreover, the three latent factors (i.e., Family Harmony at Time 1, Time 2, and Time 3) were highly correlated (rs ranged from .69 to .83). On the basis of these results, we created a composite score of family harmony by first averaging across fathers' and mothers' reports of family harmony within time, and then averaging the computed scores across the three time points. We also tested for invariance of this measurement model across the COA versus non-COA groups in a two-group structural equation model that constrained the loadings, correlations among latent factors, and correlations among error terms to be invariant across the two groups. This constrained two-group model fit the data well, $\chi^2(df = 18, n = 246$ and 208 for COA and non-COA families) = 22.57, $p = .21$, CFI = .99, RMSEA = .033, SRMR = .073, indicating that the measurement model was invariant across the COA versus non-COA groups.

Parental Alcoholism, Parental Psychopathology, and Family History Density of Alcoholism

At Times 1 and 4, parent's lifetime *DSM–III* diagnoses of parent alcoholism (abuse or dependence), affective disorder (major depression or dysthymia), and antisocial personality disorder were assessed by direct interview using the Diagnostic Interview Schedule (DIS, Version III; Robins, Helzer, Croughan, & Ratcliff, 1981). For noninterviewed parents (24% of fathers, 13% of mothers), lifetime alcoholism diagnoses were established using

Family History–Research Diagnostic Criteria (FH-RDC, Version 3; Endicott, Andreason, & Spitzer, 1975) based on spouse's report.[1, 2]

Diagnoses of grandparental alcoholism were established using FH-RDC (Version 3, Endicott et al., 1975) based on parent report at Times 2 and 4. Parents reported on each of the child's four biological grandparents, with acceptable agreement across reporters (pooled $\kappa = .56$). A grandparent was considered to have a positive diagnosis of alcoholism if he or she met the FH-RDC criterion based on reports from either parent; a grandparent had a negative diagnosis if he or she did not meet FH-RDC criteria according to reports from both parents (unless only one reporter was available). FHD scores were created by considering alcoholism in both parents and all four grandparents and assigning weights to alcoholic relatives based on their familial relatedness (Stoltenberg et al., 1998; Zucker, Ellis, & Fitzgerald, 1994). Each nonalcoholic relative was given a score of 0. Each alcoholic parent scored .50, and each alcoholic grandparent scored .25. These scores were then summed (possible range = 0–2). The overall mean of .45 ($SD = .39$) indicated that participants averaged one alcoholic relative, but they varied from zero ($N = 195$, FHD score = 0) to six alcoholic relatives ($N = 3$, FHD score = 2).

As expected, COAs had higher FHD scores than did non-COAs ($t = -35.17$, $p < .001$, $df = 558.27$, see Table 11.1), and COAs also had greater variation in FHD scores ($SD_{COA} = .28$, $SD_{non-COA} = .18$, Levene's test for equality of variances, $p < .05$). Moreover, there was minimal overlap between COAs and non-COAs in their FHD scores. By definition, the minimum FHD score for COAs was .50, and only 10.6% of non-COAs had scores that reached or exceeded this level. Thus, the FHD score largely maintained the distinction between COAs and non-COAs, but provided additional variation within the COA group in terms of density of familial alcoholism.

---

[1] Noninterviewed parents were considered not to meet criteria (except for alcoholism, where FH–RDC criteria were used for diagnosis based on spousal reports). This allowed us to include single-parent families, but it underestimates the prevalence of parental psychopathologies other than alcoholism, which could produce negatively biased estimates of their effects. Note that such underestimates could not occur when the interviewed parent met diagnostic criteria because in those cases parent psychopathology was coded as present. Thus, these errors could occur only in cases where the interviewed parent did not meet criteria and the noninterviewed parent would have. Given our high interview rates for parents, this occurrence was not frequent. On the basis of data from our two-interviewed-parent families, estimates of potential misclassification errors were only 1% for antisocial personality diagnoses and 3% for depression. Thus, misclassification error should not substantially affect the findings.

[2] Because parental affective disorder and antisocial personality disorder are also possible risk factors for offspring's SUD (e.g., Chassin et al., 2003; Hawkins et al., 1992), we also tested our mediation and moderation models by adding Time 1 measures of parental affective disorder and antisocial personality disorder as covariates. We also tested the current models without FHD in the model to examine the specific effect of parental affective disorder and antisociality. Results indicated that parental affective disorder and antisocial personality disorder did not predict young adults' substance dependence contrasts adjusting for the effects of other predictors in the models, either with or without FHD in the models. Moreover, the results of the mediational and moderational analyses were unchanged. Therefore, parental antisocial personality and affective disorder were not considered further.

Young Adults' Alcohol and Drug Dependence Diagnoses

At Times 4 and 5, participants' lifetime *DSM–III–R* alcohol and drug dependence diagnoses were obtained with a computerized version of the DIS (Robins et al., 1981). Rates of lifetime dependence were 35.2% for alcohol and 21.6% for drugs. As expected in a study that oversamples individuals at high risk, these prevalences are higher than national data. For example, National Comorbidity Survey participants aged 18 to 25 showed 17.5% lifetime alcohol dependence and 9% lifetime drug dependence (Kessler, 2002). For the current analyses, the outcome was a four-category nominal variable: no diagnoses at either wave (henceforth called "NON"; $n = 395$, 58.3%), alcohol dependence only at either wave (henceforth called "ALC"; $n = 137$, 20.2%), drug dependence only at either wave (henceforth called "DRUG"; $n = 44$, 6.5%), and both alcohol and drug dependence disorders diagnosed at either wave (henceforth called "ALC + DRUG"; $n = 102$, 15.0%).[3]

To examine variation in severity of disorders as well as the possibility of subclinical problems within the nondiagnosed group, we compared the groups on their alcohol and drug dependence symptoms (the maximum number of lifetime dependence symptoms at Time 4 or 5) using an analysis of variance. The ALC + DRUG group reported the most alcohol ($M = 3.59$, $SD = 1.94$) and drug dependence ($M = 4.31$, $SD = 2.14$) symptoms, significantly more alcohol symptoms than the ALC group but not significantly more drug symptoms than the DRUG group ($p > .05$). The ALC group had more alcohol dependence symptoms than did the DRUG group (1.22 vs. .69, $p < .05$), and the DRUG group had more drug dependence symptoms than did the ALC group (2.61 vs. .45, $p < .05$). Thus, the ALC + DRUG group had somewhat more severe alcohol dependence than did the ALC group, but not more severe drug disorder than did the DRUG group.

Moreover, supporting the distinctiveness among the groups, the ALC group averaged less than one drug symptom (.45) and did not significantly differ from the NON group in their drug symptoms (.13, $p > .05$). Conversely, the DRUG group averaged less than one alcohol symptom (.69) and did not significantly differ from the NON group in their alcohol symptoms (.26, $p > .05$). Finally, alcohol and drug symptoms in the NON group did not significantly differ from zero (.26 for alcohol and .13 for drugs), suggesting that they did not have subclinical levels of disorder.

---

[3] Because the siblings were not assessed in adolescence, there is a possibility that some SUDs already existed in adolescence and did not precede the measurement of adolescent family environment. However, for the original target sample, there were only 8 participants who met criteria for alcohol or drug disorders in adolescence (using the Diagnostic Interview for Children and Adolescents, Parent Version; Herjanic & Reich, 1982) and removing these participants did not influence the findings. Thus, it is likely that the rates of SUDs for all participants in adolescence was low, and it is unlikely that preexisting adolescent SUDs could explain the current results.

Young Adult Personality

At Times 4 and 5, young adults self-reported their personality characteristics (neuroticism, extraversion, agreeableness, openness, conscientiousness) using the NEO Five-Factor Inventory (NEO–FFI; Costa & McCrae, 1992). Self-reported personality was relatively consistent over the two occasions (correlations from .53 to .63). Thus, scores from the two waves were averaged unless one score was missing. In that case the available wave of measurement was used. Internal consistencies ranged from .72 to .86 across the scales and measurement waves.

Data Analytic Strategy

We used multilevel modeling with MIXNO software (Hedeker, 1999) because of the nonindependence of the sibling data. To ensure that the effects of the predictors were independent of gender and ethnicity as covariates, we also tested the two-way and three-way interactions involving these covariates. However, because none of these interactions was significant, they were dropped from the final regression models.

Mediated effects occur when, in the context of a theoretical rationale, the relation between two variables can be explained at least in part by a path through an intervening variable. This effect can be tested in two ways: by testing the significance of the difference between the coefficients of the predictor to the outcome with and without the mediator in the model (Baron & Kenny, 1986) and by testing the significance of the product of the coefficients for paths from the predictor to the mediator and the mediator to the outcome. Recent work has shown that the Baron and Kenny method is seriously underpowered compared to the product of coefficients method (Mackinnon, Lockwood, Hoffman, West, & Sheets, 2002; Shrout & Bolger, 2002). Thus, we used the regression coefficients from ordinary least squares (OLS) regression (predicting family harmony from FHD) and mixed effects multinomial logistic regressions (predicting substance dependence diagnoses from harmony and FHD) to calculate the significance of the indirect effect (FHD → family harmony → substance dependence) using the techniques of MacKinnon and colleagues (MacKinnon & Dwyer, 1993; MacKinnon, Lockwood, & Williams, 2004).[4,5]

---

[4] Although each coefficient can be assumed to be normally distributed, their product is not. Rather, the product tends to be skewed and highly kurtotic (MacKinnon et al., 2004), which suggests that critical values from the standard normal table will be incorrect. Thus traditional tests (e.g., Sobel, 1982) of the significance of the mediated effect are underpowered. However, confidence limits and thus a test of significance can be obtained from this asymmetric distribution by a method which has been shown to have better power and Type I error rates than the Sobel approach to significance testing (MacKinnon et al., 2004). Critical values from an asymptotic distribution based on the product of two coefficients can be obtained from Meeker, Cornwell, and Aroian (1981), and based on these values, confidence

We examined moderation by testing the significance of the FHD × Family Harmony interaction when added to our base model. When a significant interaction was found, we probed the nature of the interactions using simple slope analyses (Aiken & West, 1991). Furthermore, we tested whether the mediated path (FHD → family harmony → substance dependence) varied as a function of FHD level (high, medium, and low) by conducting the simple mediational analyses using the methods of Tein, Sandler, McKinnon, and Wolchik (2004).

RESULTS

Sibling Correlations

To examine the effects of the nestedness due to sibling data, we tested a mixed multinomial logistic regression model predicting alcohol and drug dependence with a single predictor (gender) and examined the intraclass correlation (ICC). There was a significant effect of sibling relationship (ICC = 0.33) such that siblings were more similar than were nonsiblings. This supports our use of a data analytic procedure that accounted for the nestedness of the data.

Family Harmony as a Mediator of Familial Alcoholism's Effects

We first tested the relation of FHD to family harmony using OLS regression. After adjusting for ethnicity and gender, higher FHD significantly predicted lower family harmony during adolescence ($\beta = -.41$, $p < .001$, $\Delta R^2 = .11$). Next, we estimated a mixed-effects multinomial logistic regression predicting SUD diagnostic group from gender, ethnicity, FHD, and family harmony. Results are shown in Table 11.2. Gender (but not ethnicity) predicted substance dependence. Males had higher odds of being in the ALC group or the ALC + DRUG group versus the NON group and males had lower odds of being in the DRUG group or the ALC + DRUG group versus the ALC group. Family harmony significantly decreased the odds of being in the DRUG group or the ALC + DRUG group versus the NON group. Moreover, compared to the ALC group, family harmony significantly decreased the odds of being in

---

intervals can be constructed. Significant mediated effects are indicated by confidence intervals not containing zero. Thus, for the present analyses we tested the significance of the indirect effect using this method, and we report asymmetric confidence intervals.

[5] Because multinomial logistic regression uses maximum likelihood estimation to produce estimates of coefficients, the scale of the outcome across analyses differs and thus coefficients are not directly comparable. Using coefficients from different analyses to compute the coefficient for the indirect effect would incorrectly estimate the magnitude of the effect. MacKinnon and Dwyer (1993) describe a method for standardizing coefficients from logistic regression equations that allows the comparison of coefficients across equations and thus properly computes the coefficient for an indirect effect.

TABLE 11.2

Mixed-Effects Multinomial Logistic Regressions Predicting the Contrasts Among Substance Dependence Diagnosis Groups From the Covariates, FHD, and Adolescent Family Harmony

Independent variables	ALC vs. NON		DRUG vs. NON		ALC + DRUG vs. NON	
	B	Adjusted OR[a]	B	Adjusted OR[a]	B	Adjusted OR[a]
Intercept	−1.23	0.29	0.63	1.88	0.85	2.34
Gender	1.47***	4.35	0.30	1.35	0.70*	2.01
Ethnicity	−0.39	0.68	−0.54	0.58	−0.18	0.84
FHD	1.85***	6.36	1.00†	2.72	1.94***	6.96
Family harmony	−0.45	0.64	−0.99**	0.37	−1.05***	0.35

Independent variables	DRUG vs. ALC		ALC + DRUG vs. ALC		ALC + DRUG vs. DRUG	
	B	Adjusted OR[a]	B	Adjusted OR[a]	B	Adjusted OR[a]
Intercept	2.32†	10.18	2.43*	11.36	0.20	1.22
Gender	−1.27**	0.28	−0.88**	0.41	0.45	1.57
Ethnicity	−0.15	0.86	0.22	1.25	0.42	1.52
FHD	−0.92†	0.40	0.02	1.02	0.93†	2.53
Family harmony	−0.60†	0.55	−0.63*	0.53	0.03	1.03

Note. FHD = family history density of alcoholism; ALC = alcohol dependence only; NON = no diagnoses; DRUG = drug dependence only.
[a]Adjusted OR = adjusted odds ratio, or the odds ratio adjusted for the effects of other predictors in the regression model.
† $p < .10$. * $p < .05$. ** $p < .01$. *** $p < .001$.

the ALC + DRUG group and marginally decreased the odds of being in the DRUG group.

In the same model (after adjusting for the effects of family harmony), FHD remained a significant predictor of substance dependence,[6] increasing the odds of being in the ALC group or the ALC + DRUG group versus the NON group, and the odds of being in the ALC + DRUG group versus the DRUG group. Moreover, FHD marginally increased the odds of being in the DRUG versus NON group and the ALC group (see Table 11.2).

We then used the coefficients from the OLS regression and multinomial regression to test the significance of the indirect (mediated) effects (i.e., FHD → family harmony → SUDs), for each pairwise diagnostic group comparison. To test the significance of the indirect effects, the logistic coefficients were standardized. Then, for each indirect effect, asymmetric upper and lower confidence intervals were constructed (MacKinnon et al., 2004). We also calculated the proportion of the total effect of FHD on the outcome that was indirect through family harmony (MacKinnon, Warsi, & Dwyer, 1995; see Figure 11.1, in which significant indirect effects are represented by bold lines).

There was a significant indirect effect of FHD through family harmony for the contrasts of DRUG versus NON (upper confidence limit [UCL] = .84, lower confidence limit [LCL] = .15, 32% mediated) and ALC + DRUG versus NON (UCL = .81, LCL = .25, 20% mediated). The indirect effect of FHD through harmony was also significant for the contrast between ALC + DRUG and ALC (UCL = .57, LCL = .07, 91% mediated), but not between ALC and DRUG.

In summary, a denser family history of alcoholism was associated with lower family harmony in adolescence, which in turn increased young adults' risk for drug dependence (with and without alcohol dependence) compared to having no diagnosis, as well as increased the risk for having both alcohol and drug dependence diagnoses compared to alcohol dependence only.

To ensure that these findings were robust to different operationalizations of familial alcoholism and not an artifact of combining the COA and control groups, we repeated the analyses using parental alcoholism (COA vs. non-COA) in place of FHD scores and obtained the same pattern of results. Specifically, adolescent family harmony significantly mediated the relations between parental alcoholism and contrasts between the DRUG and the NON groups (UCL = .71, LCL = .05, $p < .01$, 27% mediated), between the ALC + DRUG and the NON groups (UCL = .69, LCL = .15, $p < .01$, 21%

---

[6] Because parental drug problems may also account for the prediction of offspring's SUDs, it is important to consider their effects on the present models. However, previous analyses of the same sample have shown that parental drug problems in predicting patterns of alcohol and drug dependence were nonsignificant over and above the effects of FHD (Chassin et al., 2004). Therefore, parental drug problems were not included in the regression models.

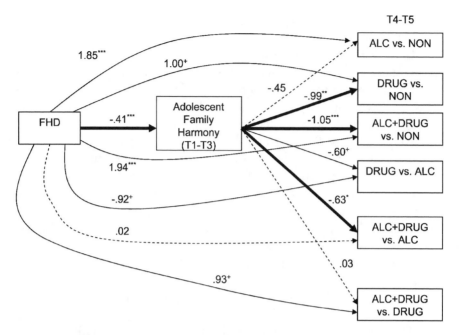

Figure 11.1. Adolescent family harmony as a mediator in the relations between family history density of alcoholism (FHD) and young adults' substance dependence. The numbers presented are the unstandardized regression coefficients obtained from the ordinary least squares regression predicting family harmony from FHD and the multinomial logistic regressions predicting the contrasts among young adults' substance dependence categories from FHD and family harmony (gender and ethnicity were controlled in both regressions). The thick lines represent significant mediational pathways. ALC = alcohol dependence only; NON = no diagnoses; DRUG = drug dependence only; T = time point. *$p < .05$. **$p < .01$. ***$p < .001$.

mediated), and between the ALC + DRUG and the ALC groups (UCL = .48, LCL = .01, $p < .01$, 86% mediated). Compared with the control participants, COA families had lower harmony, which in turn increased young adults' risk for drug dependence disorders with or without alcohol dependence compared with no diagnoses, as well as increased the risk for developing both alcohol and drug dependence compared with alcohol dependence only.

Personality as a Competitive Mediator

Although the present study focused on family harmony, personality has also been shown to mediate the effect of family history on diagnosis (Chassin et al., 2004). Accordingly, we repeated the above models including personality factors as competitive mediators to test whether the effects of family harmony were robust to the effects of personality. To do this, we used a subsample of participants ($N = 647$) with personality (NEO–FFI) data. As Chassin et al. (2004) found, NEO–FFI agreeableness and neuroticism predicted substance dependence diagnoses (both $ps < .01$) and mediated the effect of FHD on dependence diagnoses (all $p < .05$, mediated effect ranged from 11% to 28%). After including personality, the main effects of harmony on diagnosis were generally unchanged, reducing the magnitude but not the direction of the mediational effects of adolescent family harmony. Family harmony remained a significant mediator of the effects of FHD in differentiating ALC + DRUG from NON ($p < .05$, 16% mediated). The effect of family harmony became marginally significant in differentiating ALC + DRUG from ALC ($p < .10$) and DRUG from NON ($p < .10$). Correspondingly, the indirect (mediated) effect of harmony became marginally significant in distinguishing ALC + DRUG from ALC ($p < .10$, 41% mediated) and DRUG from NON ($p < .10$, 31% mediated).

The Interaction Between Family History Density and Adolescent Family Harmony in Predicting Later Substance Use Disorders

To examine whether the effect of family harmony on SUDs was moderated by FHD, we added the two-way interaction (FHD × Family Harmony) to the multinomial regression models. FHD and family harmony were mean centered (Aiken & West, 1991) to reduce collinearity among the predictors (for results, see Table 11.3). The FHD × Family Harmony interaction was significant in the contrasts between DRUG and NON ($p < .05$), and between ALC + DRUG and NON ($p < .01$, see Table 11.3). The form of these interactions is shown in Figure 11.2. Adolescent family harmony was significantly associated with decreased odds of being in the DRUG group versus the NON group at both low (-1 SD) and medium (mean) levels of FHD (simple slopes $= -1.98$ and -1.04, $p < .001$ and $.004$, adjusted odds ratio (OR) $= .14$ and $.35$ for low and mean levels of FHD, respectively). However, as the density of familial alcoholism increased, this relation weakened such that family harmony was unrelated to the odds of DRUG versus NON for those from families with high ($+1$ SD) FHD. The same pattern was seen for the contrast between the ALC + DRUG group versus the NON group. Family harmony significantly reduced the odds of being in the ALC + DRUG group versus the NON group at low (-1 SD) and medium (mean) levels of FHD (simple slopes $= -2.00$ and -1.20, $p < .001$, adjusted OR $= .14$ and $.30$). However, as the density of familial alcoholism increased, this relation weakened and became nonsignificant at high ($+1$ SD) levels of FHD. To ensure that the lack of association between family harmony and substance dependence at high FHD was not due to the restricted variability in family harmony, we compared the variance in family harmony among those with high versus low FHD and found no significant differences (F for Levene's test for equality of variances $= .54$, $p = .46$).

Because these interactions suggested that the effects of family harmony on the DRUG versus NON and the ALC + DRUG versus NON contrasts differed by levels of FHD, it is likely that the strength of the indirect effect

TABLE 11.3

Mixed-Effects Multinomial Logistic Regressions Predicting the Contrasts Among Substance Dependence Diagnosis Groups From the Covariates, FHD, Adolescent Family Harmony, and FHD × Family Harmony Interaction

Independent variables	ALC vs. NON		DRUG vs. NON		ALC + DRUG vs. NON	
	B	Adjusted OR[a]	B	Adjusted OR[a]	B	Adjusted OR[a]
Gender	1.46***	4.31	0.32	1.38	0.70	2.01
Ethnicity	-0.41	0.66	-0.59	1.80	-0.22	0.80
FHD	1.92***	6.82	1.34*	3.82	2.25***	9.49
Family harmony	-0.42	0.66	-1.03**	2.80	-1.20***	0.30
FHD × Family Harmony	1.01	2.75	2.38**	10.80	2.03**	7.61

Independent variables	DRUG vs. ALC		ALC + DRUG vs. ALC		ALC + DRUG vs. DRUG	
	B	Adjusted OR[a]	B	Adjusted OR[a]	B	Adjusted OR[a]
Gender	-1.25**	0.29	-0.87**	0.42	1.82**	6.17
Ethnicity	-0.18	0.83	0.21	1.23	-0.11	1.12
FHD	-0.61	0.54	0.29	1.34	0.49	1.63
Family harmony	-0.65†	0.52	-0.80**	0.45	1.27†	3.56
FHD × Family Harmony	1.35	3.86	0.95	1.16	-2.56	0.08

Note. FHD = family history density of alcoholism; ALC = alcohol dependence only; NON = no diagnoses; DRUG = drug dependence only.
[a]Adjusted OR = adjusted odds ratio, or the odds ratio adjusted for the effects of other predictors in the regression model. FHD = family history density of alcoholism.
† $p < .10$. * $p < .05$. ** $p < .01$. *** $p < .001$.

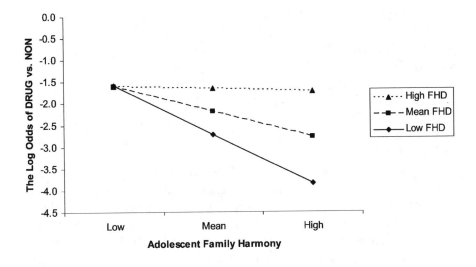

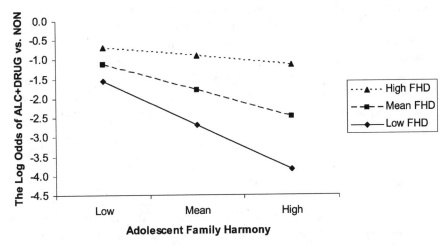

Figure 11.2. The interactions between family history density of alcoholism (FHD) and family harmony in predicting the drug dependence only (DRUG) versus no diagnoses (NON) and the alcohol dependence only (ALC) + DRUG versus NON contrasts.

(FHD → family harmony → substance dependence) also differed as a function of FHD. To examine this hypothesis, we tested the simple mediated and indirect effects at low (−1 SD), medium (mean), and high (+1 SD) FHD using the methods of Tein et al. (2004).[7]

---

[7] In this method, the FHD variable was rescaled so that the zero point corresponded to 1 SD below the mean, that is, rescaled FHD = (FHD centered at mean) − (−1 SD of FHD) and created the FHD × Family Harmony interaction term with the rescaled FHD. The models were then reestimated with the covariates, family harmony, the rescaled FHD, and the interaction term, and the main effect of family harmony (above and beyond other predictors in the model) now corresponds to the simple effect of family harmony at low (−1 SD) FHD. We then tested the significance of the simple indirect effect. The above steps were then repeated with FHD centered at the mean and at 1 SD above the mean.

The indirect effect of FHD on the DRUG versus NON contrast through family harmony was significant at low (−1 SD) FHD (UCL = 1.79, LCL = .31, $p < .01$, 42% mediated) and medium (mean) FHD (UCL = 1.03, LCL = .08, $p < .01$, 27% mediated). However, the indirect effect became nonsignificant at high (+1 SD) FHD. Similarly, the indirect effect of FHD on the ALC + DRUG versus NON contrast through family harmony was significant at low (−1 SD) FHD (UCL = 1.66, LCL = .43, $p < .01$, 42% mediated) and mean FHD (UCL = 1.03, LCL = .24, $p < .01$, 20% mediated), but nonsignificant at high (+1 SD) FHD.

As above, we repeated these moderational analyses with COA status rather than FHD score as a predictor. Parental alcoholism significantly interacted with family harmony in predicting the contrast between the ALC + DRUG and NON group ($B = 1.29, p < .05$). The simple slope analyses showed that family harmony was more strongly associated with decreased odds of developing both alcohol and drug dependence versus having no diagnosis in nonalcoholic families (simple slope = −1.88, $p < .001$) than in alcoholic families (simple slope = −.59, $p = .09$). The Parental Alcoholism × Family Harmony interaction was marginally significant for the DRUG versus NON contrast ($b = 1.28, p < .10$). Family harmony was significantly associated with decreased odds of developing drug dependence disorder only versus having no diagnosis in nonalcoholic families (simple slope = −1.69, $p < .001$), but it was unrelated to the DRUG versus NON contrast in alcoholic families (simple slope = −.40, $p = .41$).

DISCUSSION

The present study examined family harmony as a mediator of familial alcoholism effects on the development of drug versus alcohol disorders in young adulthood. We tested the mediational role of family harmony with and without adjusting for personality, and we tested whether the relation between family harmony and young adults' SUDs was moderated by FHD.

Family Harmony as a Mediator

The first finding of note was that a higher density of familial alcoholism was associated with lower family harmony during adolescence, which in turn increased risk for substance dependence disorders in young adulthood. Thus, the effects of familial alcoholism on young adults' SUDS can be accounted for, in part, by their earlier exposure to high conflict in their families. Importantly, this mediational path (i.e., FHD → family harmony → alcohol + drug dependence) remained significant after adjusting for the effects of personality (although the mediational path to drug dependence became only slightly weaker). This suggests that the risks conferred by personality and family environment are unique and additive so that both personality and family environment serve to account for familial alcoholism effects on the development of SUDs. These results are consistent with previous studies on the mediating role of family harmony in the link between familial alcoholism and adjustment (e.g., El-Sheikh & Buckhalt, 2003; El-Sheikh & Flanagan, 2001; Hussong & Chassin, 2002; Loukas et al., 2001) and extend these studies by demonstrating the effect of family harmony on young adults' substance dependence diagnoses. However, because family harmony only partially mediated familial alcoholism effects, other mechanisms are also necessary to fully explain the relation between familial alcoholism and SUDs.

Differential Pathways From Familial Alcoholism to Alcohol, Drug, and Combined Dependence

An important contribution of the present study is the distinction between alcohol and drug dependence disorders and their combination in examining the mediational pathways. We found that family harmony during adolescence decreased the risk of drug dependence with or without alcohol dependence compared to either alcohol dependence only or no diagnosis. However, family harmony did not differentiate young adults with alcohol dependence only from those with no diagnoses. These results support the suggestions by McGue et al. (1999), Taylor et al. (2000, 2002), and Chassin et al. (2004) that separate mechanisms may be involved in the development of drug dependence (with and without alcohol dependence) compared with alcohol dependence in the absence of drug dependence. The current findings extend those studies by identifying family harmony as an additional differentiating predictor.

Why should family harmony be more specifically linked to drug dependence than to alcohol dependence in the absence of drug dependence? One possibility rests with the illegal nature of drug use and its link to behavioral undercontrol. Because young adults with drug dependence (with or without alcohol dependence) necessarily engage in illegal behavior, they may be more behaviorally undercontrolled (i.e., more "deviance prone") than individuals with alcohol disorders alone. This is consistent with previous findings that behavioral undercontrol was more strongly related to drug use disorders than to alcohol use disorders alone (Chassin et al., 2004; McGue et al., 1999). Given the large literature that connects behavioral undercontrol and externalizing problems to family conflict and dysfunctional family processes (Grych & Fincham, 1990; Patterson et al., 1989), the results of the current study further suggest that family processes may be especially important to the development of drug use disorders with or without alcohol use disorders because highly conflictual families are likely to produce adolescents with higher levels of undercontrol and externalizing problems. An alternative interpretation focuses not on the illegal and deviance prone nature of drug use compared with alcohol use but rather on the relative severity of disorder in the different diagnostic subgroups. Because those with both alcohol and drug dependence tended to have the more severe disorders than those with alcohol dependence alone, it may also be that individuals who are behaviorally undercontrolled and who live in conflictual families develop both a broader spectrum of SUDs and more severe disorders.

In contrast, although familial alcoholism was associated with heightened risk for alcohol dependence only compared with no diagnoses, this relation was not mediated through family harmony (see Figure 11.1). This suggests that those from alcoholic families who develop alcohol dependence in the absence of drug dependence may follow a different pathway—a pathway that is less comorbid with externalizing or behavioral undercontrol, that is less related to family harmony, and that leads to less severe alcoholism. The pathway to alcohol dependence in the absence of drug disorder only may be more alcohol specific and may involve other mediators, such as a heritable sensitivity to alcohol effects.

The Interaction Between Family History Density and Family Harmony

Another important contribution of the current study is the demonstration that the effects of family harmony on SUDs varied with the density of familial alcoholism. Specifically, family harmony decreased risk for developing drug dependence with or without alcohol dependence only at low to moderate (but not high) levels of FHD. Moreover, the mediated effects of FHD on drug dependence (with or without alcohol dependence) through family harmony also disappeared at high levels of FHD.

The form of this interaction is what Luthar, Cicchetti, and Becker (2000) called "protective but reactive" in that a protective factor (such as a favorable family environment) generally provides benefits, but the protective effect turns weaker at higher levels of risk (such as FHD). A similar protective but reactive interaction was found between parenting and offspring temperament in another study based on the same sample (King & Chassin, 2004), where the protective effects of parental support on the risk for drug use disorder disappeared at high levels of behavioral undercontrol. Individuals with a strong diathesis for SUD (indicated either by dense familial alcoholism or high levels of behavioral undercontrol) may be less influenced by qualities of the family environment (e.g., parenting and family conflict) because that diathesis inhibits bonding with the family, because other pathways may override familial influences, or both.

It is interesting to speculate about why the current findings (and other findings from this data set; King & Chassin, 2004) produce interactions that are protective but reactive whereas some other studies find classic buffering effects (e.g., El-Sheikh & Buckhalt, 2003; Legrand et al., 1999). The different findings may reflect differing degrees of risk across samples. That is, samples with greater representation of the highest risk levels (e.g., denser alcoholic pedigrees, more undercontrolled participants) may produce protective but reactive interactions whereas lower-risk samples may produce classic buffering effects. Consistent with this interpretation, using a clinical sample of young children, Wootton, Frick, Shelton, and Silverthorn (1997) found a protective but reactive interaction such that the protective effects of effective parenting against conduct problems diminished among children with high personality risk. In contrast, studies that did not oversample high-risk individuals (Legrand et al., 1999; Stice & Gonzales, 1998) have found classic buffering interactions. Interestingly, studies of a sample in which COAs were selected using a less strict criterion for parental alcoholism (i.e., the Michigan Alcoholism Screening Test) than the current DSM diagnoses have reported both the classic buffering and protective but reactive interactions (El-Sheikh & Buckhalt, 2003; El-Sheikh & Flanagan, 2001). However, the sampling difference interpretation is speculative, and other method or design differences (e.g., differing ages of the participants, differing outcome variables, and differing protective factors) may be responsible for differences in findings across studies.

Finally, although the current study makes an important contribution by providing the first prospective test of the role of family harmony as a differential mediator of familial alcoholism effects on drug and alcohol dependence, it is also necessary to consider some of its limitations. First, our measure of FHD included only grandparents and parents, and future research could expand the measure to include more relatives. Second, different diagnostic criteria might produce different findings, and our use of RDC criteria might underestimate rates of grandparental disorder, whereas DSM–III–R criteria may overdiagnose SUDs. Third, our community sample of alcoholic families had low rates of comorbid antisocial personality disorder, and different findings might be produced in samples with more familial antisociality. Fourth, our findings may be specific to SUDs, and not necessarily similar for other mental health problems. Finally, we assessed SUDs in young adulthood, and the relations among family harmony, FHD, and substance dependence diagnoses may differ at different ages. For example, at younger ages when alcohol use is more uncommon and thus more "deviant," it might be more difficult to detect unique predictors of alcohol compared to drug outcomes. At ages when alcohol use becomes statistically common and therefore less deviant than drug use (as in young adulthood), it might be easier to detect a difference between alcohol and drug use disorders.

In sum, the current study found that adolescent family harmony decreased young adults' risk for drug dependence but did not predict alcohol dependence in the absence of drug dependence. Family harmony partially mediated the effect of familial alcoholism on young adults' combined alcohol and drug dependence, and this effect was unique, after adjusting for the effects of personality. However, this mediated effect varied with the density of familial alcoholism, such that protective benefits of family harmony were lost at high levels of familial alcoholism density. These findings suggest both the importance of distinguishing between alcohol and drug outcomes and that interventions designed to improve adolescent family environment may be insufficient for COAs with a high density of familial alcoholism.

REFERENCES

Aiken, L. S., & West, S. G. (1991). *Multiple regression: Testing and interpreting interactions.* Newbury Park, CA: Sage.

American Psychiatric Association. (1980). *Diagnostic and statistical manual of mental disorders* (3rd ed.). Washington, DC: Author.

Baker, J. R., & Yardley, J. K. (2002). Moderating effect of gender on the relationship between sensation seeking-impulsivity and substance use in adolescence. *Journal of Child and Adolescent Substance Abuse, 12,* 27–43.

Baron, R. M., & Kenny, D. A. (1986). The moderator-mediator variable distinction in social psychological research: Conceptual, strategic, and statistical considerations. *Journal of Personality and Social Psychology, 51,* 1173–1182.

Bloom, B. L. (1985). A factor analysis of self-report measures of family functioning. *Family Process, 24,* 225–239.

Bloom, B. L., & Naar, S. (1994). Self-report measures of family functioning: Extensions of a factorial analysis. *Family Process, 33,* 203–216.

Chassin, L., Barrera, M., Bech, K., & Kossak-Fuller, J. (1992). Recruiting a community sample of adolescent children of alcoholics: A comparison of three subject sources. *Journal of Studies on Alcohol, 53,* 316–319.

Chassin, L., Curran, P. J., Hussong, A. M., & Colder, C. R. (1996). The relation of parent alcoholism to adolescent substance use: A longitudinal follow-up study. *Journal of Abnormal Psychology, 105,* 70–80.

Chassin, L., Flora, D., & King, K. M. (2004). Trajectories of alcohol and drug use and dependence from adolescence to adulthood: The effects of familial alcoholism and personality. *Journal of Abnormal Psychology, 113,* 483–498.

Chassin, L., Pitts, S. C., DeLucia, C., & Todd, M. (1999). A longitudinal study of children of alcoholics: Predicting young adult substance use disorders, anxiety, and depression. *Journal of Abnormal Psychology, 108,* 106–119.

Chassin, L., & Ritter, J. (2001). Vulnerability to substance use disorders in childhood and adolescence. In R. E. Ingram & J. M. Price (Eds.), *Vulnerability to psychopathology: Risk across the life span* (pp. 107–134). New York: Guilford Press.

Chassin, L., Ritter, J., Trim, R., & King, K. (2003). Adolescent substance use. In R. Barkley & E. Mash (Eds.), *Handbook of child psychopathology* (pp. 119–232). New York: Plenum Press.

Chassin, L., Rogosch, F., & Barrera, M. (1991). Substance use and symptomatology among adolescent children of alcoholics. *Journal of Abnormal Psychology, 100,* 449–463.

Costa, P., & McCrae, R. (1992). *Revised NEO Personality Inventory (NEO-PI–R) and NEO Five-Factor Inventory (NEO–FFI) professional manual.* Odessa, FL: Psychological Assessment Resources.

Cummings, M. E., & Davies, P. (1996). Emotional security as a regulatory process in normal development and the development of psychopathology. *Development and Psychopathology, 8,* 123–139.

Curran, G. M., Stoltenberg, S. F., Hill, E. M., Mudd, S. A., Blow, F. C., & Zucker, R. A. (1999). Gender differences in the relationships among SES, family history of alcohol disorders and alcohol dependence. *Journal of Studies on Alcohol, 60,* 825–832.

Eitle, D. (2005). The moderating effects of peer substance use on the family-structure–adolescent substance use association: Quantity versus quality of parenting. *Addictive Behaviors, 30,* 963–980.

El-Sheikh, M., & Buckhalt, J. A. (2003). Parental problem drinking and children's adjustment: Attachment and family functioning as moderators and mediators of risk. *Journal of Family Psychology, 17,* 510–520.

El-Sheikh, M., & Flanagan, E. (2001). Parental problem drinking and children's adjustment: Family conflict and parental depression as mediators and moderators of risk. *Journal of Abnormal Child Psychology, 29,* 417–432.

Endicott, J., Andreason, N., & Spitzer, R. (1975). *Family history diagnosis criteria.* New York: Biometrics Research, New York Psychiatric Institute.

Grych, J. H., & Fincham, F. D. (1990). Marital conflict and children's adjustment: A cognitive–contextual framework. *Psychological Bulletin, 108,* 267–290.

Guo, J., Hill, K. G., Hawkins, J. D., Catalano, R. F., & Abbott, R. D. (2002). A developmental analysis of sociodemographic, family, and peer effects on adolescent illicit drug initiation. *Journal of American Academy of Child and Adolescent Psychiatry, 41,* 838–845.

Hawkins, J. D., Catalano, R. F., & Miller, J. Y. (1992). Risk and protective factors for alcohol and other drug problems in adolescence and early adulthood: Implications for substance abuse prevention. *Psychological Bulletin, 112,* 64–105.

Hedeker, D. (1999). MIXNO: A computer program for mixed-effects nominal logistic regression. *Journal of Statistical Software, 4,* 1–92.

Helzer, J. E., & Pryzbeck, T. R. (1988). The co-occurrence of alcoholism with other psychiatric disorders in the general population and its impact on treatment. *Journal of Studies on Alcohol, 49,* 219–224.

Herjanic, B., & Reich, W. (1982). Development of a structured psychiatric interview for children: Agreement between parent and child on individual symptoms. *Journal of Abnormal Child Psychology, 10,* 307–324.

Heyman, R. E., O'Leary, K. D., & Jouriles, E. N. (1995). Alcohol and aggressive personality styles: Potentiators of serious physical aggression against wives? *Journal of Family Psychology, 9,* 44–57.

Hussong, A. M., & Chassin, L. (1997). Substance use initiation among adolescent children of alcoholics: Testing protective factors. *Journal of Studies on Alcohol, 58*, 272–279.

Hussong, A. M., & Chassin, L. (2002). Parent alcoholism and the leaving home transition. *Development and Psychopathology, 14*, 139–157.

Jacob, T., Leonard, K. E., & Haber, J. R. (2001). Family interactions of alcoholics as related to alcoholism type and drinking condition. *Alcoholism: Clinical and Experimental Research, 25*, 835–843.

Jacob, T., Waterman, B., Heath, A., True, W., Bucholz, K. K., Haber, R., et al. (2003). Genetic and environmental effects on offspring alcoholism. *Archives of General Psychiatry, 60*, 1265–1272.

Johnson, E. O., & Pickens, R. W. (2001). Familial transmission of alcoholism among nonalcoholics and mild, severe, and dyssocial subtypes of alcoholism. *Alcoholism: Clinical and Experimental Research, 25*, 661–666.

Kessler, R. C. (2002). *National Comorbidity Study, 1990–1992.* Available at the University of Michigan Survey Research Center, Inter-University Consortium for Political and Social Science Research Web site: http://www.icpsr.umich.edu

King, K. M., & Chassin, L. (2004). Mediating and moderated effects of adolescent behavioral undercontrol and parenting in the prediction of drug use disorders in emerging adulthood. *Journal of Addictive Behaviors, 18*, 239–249.

Krueger, R. F., Hicks, B. M., Patrick, C. J., Carlson, S. R., Iacono, W. G., & McGue, M. (2002). Etiologic connections among substance dependence, antisocial behavior and personality: Modeling the externalizing spectrum. *Journal of Abnormal Psychology, 111*, 411–424.

Legrand, L. N., McGue, M., & Iacono, W. G. (1999). Searching for interactive effects in the etiology of early-onset substance use. *Behavior Genetics, 29*, 433–443.

Loukas, A., Fitzgerald, H. E., Zucker, R. A., & von Eye, A. (2001). Parental alcoholism and co-occurring antisocial behavior: Prospective relationships to externalizing behavior problems in their young sons. *Journal of Abnormal Child Psychology, 29*, 91–106.

Luthar, S. S., Cicchetti, D., & Becker, B. (2000). The construct of resilience: A critical evaluation and guidelines for future work. *Child Development, 71*, 543–562.

MacKinnon, D. P., & Dwyer, J. H. (1993). Estimating mediated effects in prevention studies. *Evaluation Review, 17*, 144–158.

MacKinnon, D. P., Lockwood, C. M., Hoffman, J. M., West, S. G., & Sheets, V. (2002). A comparison of methods to test mediation and other intervening variable effects. *Psychological Methods, 7*, 83–104.

MacKinnon, D. P., Lockwood, C. M., & Williams, J. (2004). Confidence limits for the indirect effect: Distribution of the product and resampling methods. *Multivariate Behavioral Research, 39*, 99–128.

MacKinnon, D. P., Warsi, G., & Dwyer, J. H. (1995). A simulation study of mediated effect measures. *Multivariate Behavioral Research, 30*, 41–62.

Mahaddian, E., Newcomb, M. D., & Bentler, P. M. (1988). Risk factors for substance use: Ethnic differences among adolescents. *Journal of Substance Abuse, 1*, 11–23.

McGue, M. (1999). The behavioral genetics of alcoholism. *Current Directions in Psychological Science, 8*, 109–115.

McGue, M., Slutske, W., & Iacono, W. G. (1999). Personality and substance use disorders: II. Alcoholism versus drug use disorders. *Journal of Consulting and Clinical Psychology, 67*, 394–404.

Meeker, W. Q., Cornwell, L. W., & Aroian, L. A. (1981). *Selected tables in mathematical statistics: Vol. VII. The product of two normally distributed random variables.* Providence, RI: American Mathematical Society.

Muthén, L. K., & Muthén, B. O. (2003). Mplus (Version 2.12) [Computer software]. Los Angeles: Author.

Newman, D. L., Moffitt, T. E., Caspi, A., Magdol, L., Silva, P. A., & Stanton, W. R. (1996). Psychiatric disorder in a birth cohort of young adults: Prevalence, comorbidity, clinical significance, and new case incidence from ages 11 to 21. *Journal of Consulting and Clinical Psychology, 64*, 552–562.

Patterson, G. R. (1982). *Coercive family process.* Eugene, OR: Castalia.

Patterson, G. R., DeBaryshe, B. D., & Ramsey, E. (1989). A developmental perspective on antisocial behavior. *American Psychologist, 44*, 329–335.

Pollock, N. K., Martin, C. S., & Langenbucher, J. W. (2000). Diagnostic concordance of *DSM–III, DSM–III–R, DSM–IV* and *ICD–10* alcohol diagnoses in adolescents. *Journal of Studies on Alcohol, 61*, 439–446.

Robins, L. N., Helzer, J. E., Croughan, J., & Ratcliff, K. S. (1981). National Institute of Mental Health Diagnostic Interview Schedule: Its history, characteristics, and validity. *Archives of General Psychiatry, 38*, 381–389.

Rutter, M. (1990). Psychological resilience and protective mechanisms. In J. Rolf, A. S. Masten, D. Cicchetti, K. H. Nuechterlein, & S. Weintraub (Eds.), *Risk and protective factors in the development of psychopathology* (pp. 181–214). New York: Cambridge University Press.

Sher, K. J. (1991). *Children of alcoholics: A critical appraisal of theory and research.* Chicago: University of Chicago Press.

Sher, K. J., Gershuny, B. S., Peterson, L., & Raskin, G. (1997). The role of childhood stressors in the intergenerational transmission of alcohol use disorders. *Journal of Studies on Alcohol, 58*, 414–427.

Sher, K. J., Walitzer, K. S., Wood, P. K., & Brent, E. E. (1991). Characteristics of children of alcoholics: Putative risk factors, substance use and abuse, and psychopathology. *Journal of Abnormal Psychology, 100*, 427–448.

Shrout, P. E., & Bolger, N. (2002). Mediation in experimental and nonexperimental studies: New procedures and recommendations. *Psychological Methods, 7*, 422–445.

Sobel, M. E. (1982). Asymptotic confidence intervals for indirect effects in structural equation models. In S. Leinhard (Ed.), *Sociological methodology 1982* (pp. 290–312). Washington, DC: American Sociological Association.

Stice, E., & Gonzales, N. (1998). Adolescent temperament moderates the relation of parenting to antisocial behavior and substance use. *Journal of Adolescent Research, 13*, 5–31.

Stoltenberg, S. F., Mudd, S. A., Blow, F. C., & Hill, E. M. (1998). Evaluating measures of family history of alcoholism: Density versus dichotomy. *Addiction, 93*, 1511–1520.

Taylor, J., Iacono, W. G., & McGue, M. (2000). Evidence for a genetic etiology of early-onset delinquency. *Journal of Abnormal Psychology, 109*, 634–643.

Taylor, J., Malone, S., Iacono, W. G., & McGue, M. (2002). Development of substance dependence in two delinquency subgroups and nondelinquents from a male twin sample. *Journal of the American Academy of Child and Adolescent Psychiatry, 41*, 386–393.

Tein, J., Sandler, I. N., MacKinnon, D. P., & Wolchik, S. A. (2004). How did it work? Who did it work for? Mediation in the context of a moderated prevention effect for children of divorce. *Journal of Consulting and Clinical Psychology, 72*, 617–624.

Walden, B., McGue, M., Iacono, W. G., Burt, S. A., & Elkins, I. (2004). Identifying shared environmental contributions to early substance use: The respective roles of peers and parents. *Journal of Abnormal Psychology, 113*, 440–450.

Wills, T. A., Resko, J. A., Ainette, M. G., & Mendoza, D. (2004). Role of parental social support and peer support in adolescent substance use: A test of mediated effects. *Psychology of Addictive Behaviors, 18*, 122–134.

Wills, T. A., Sandy, J. M., Yaeger, A., & Shinar, O. (2001). Family risk factors and adolescent substance use: Moderation effects for temperament dimensions. *Developmental Psychology, 37*, 283–297.

Windle, M. (1996). On the discriminative validity of a family history of problem drinking index with a national sample of young adults. *Journal of Studies on Alcohol, 57*, 378–386.

Wootton, J. M., Frick, P. J., Shelton, K. K., & Silverthorn, P. (1997). Ineffective parenting and childhood conduct problems: The moderating role of callous-unemotional traits. *Journal of Consulting and Clinical Psychology, 65*, 301–308.

Zucker, R. A., Ellis, D. A., & Fitzgerald, H. E. (1994). Developmental evidence for at least two alcoholisms: I. Biopsychosocial variation among pathways into symptomatic difficulty. In T. F. Babor, V. Hesselbrock, R. E. Meyer, & W. Shoemaker (Eds.), *Types of alcoholics: Evidence from clinical, experimental and genetic research* (pp. 134–146). New York: New York Academy of Sciences.

12

FAMILY RISK FACTORS AND ADOLESCENT SUBSTANCE USE: MODERATION EFFECTS FOR TEMPERAMENT DIMENSIONS

THOMAS ASHBY WILLS, JAMES M. SANDY, ALISON YAEGER, AND ORI SHINAR

In recent years, research has linked temperament to the potential for development of problem behavior. Temperament dimensions are characteristics that are early appearing, show reasonable stability over time, and have a constitutional basis (Pedlow, Sanson, Prior, & Oberklaid, 1993; Rothbart & Bates, 1998; Rothbart, Derryberry, & Posner, 1994). Temperament dimensions have been related to substance use in early adolescence (Masse & Tremblay, 1997; Wills, DuHamel, & Vaccaro, 1995) and to substance abuse and behavior problems in early adulthood (Caspi, Henry, McGee, Moffitt, & Silva, 1995; Pulkkinen & Pitkanen, 1994). With this evidence, a growing body of epigenetic theory has addressed questions about the role of temperament characteristics in the development of problem behavior (Rothbart & Ahadi, 1994; Tarter & Vanyukov, 1994; Wills, Sandy, & Yaeger, 2000).

This research was supported by Research Scientist Development Award K02-DA00252 and Grant R01-DA08880 from the National Institute on Drug Abuse. We thank the superintendents of the school districts for their support; the parents and participating students for their cooperation; Sean Cleary, Marnie Filer, and John Mariani for assistance with the research; and Mike Stoolmiller for statistical consultation.

Reprinted from *Developmental Psychology, 37,* 283–297 (2001). Copyright 2001 by the American Psychological Association.

In this research, we investigated predictions about moderation effects in the relationship of family risk factors to early-onset substance use, which is known to be of particular prognostic significance (Hawkins et al., 1997; Kandel & Davies, 1992; Robins & Przybeck, 1985). It has been posited that temperament characteristics can make children differentially susceptible to the impact of experiences (Wachs, 1992; Wachs & Gandour, 1983), and theoretical work has suggested that development of problem behavior occurs through transactions between a child's temperament and the family environment (Brody & Flor, 1996; Rothbart & Bates, 1998; Rutter et al., 1997). However, as Bates, Pettit, Dodge, and Ridge (1998) noted, there is relatively little evidence showing replicated moderation effects involving temperament dimensions.

A focus on moderation is suggested by findings from resiliency research (Garmezy, 1993; Glantz & Johnson, 1999; Luthar, Cicchetti, & Becker, 2000). A noteworthy example is a study by Werner (1986) of high-risk youth from a cohort study conducted on Kauai, Hawaii. A subsample of 49 participants who were the offspring of alcoholic parents was identified, and variables were analyzed that differentiated persons showing relatively good adjustment in young adulthood (i.e., resilient group) from those showing poor adjustment. Werner reported that the primary caretaker's perception of the infant's temperament was a significant predictor of resilience, with 58% of participants rated as "cuddly and affectionate" at age 1 showing good adjustment at follow-up, compared with 14% for those not so rated. This prospective finding is notable in theoretical terms because it suggests that temperament served to moderate the impact of family risk factors on children's development of substance abuse and mental health problems. However, there have been few attempts to replicate or extend the finding. The present research considered parent-child conflict, parental substance use, and family life events because these have been related to adolescent substance use (e.g., Chassin, Pillow, Curran, Molina, & Barrera, 1993; Wills, Vaccaro, & McNamara, 1992). We studied several types of temperament dimensions because, in principle, moderation effects may occur through either decreasing or increasing the impact of a risk factor (Rutter et al., 1997; Wills, Cleary, & Shinar, 2002). The following section describes the theoretical basis for the predictions and outlines issues in investigating moderation effects.

PREVIOUS RESEARCH ON MODERATION

Previous studies have tested several types of interactional models for temperament characteristics (Wachs, 1992, chap. 8). For example, studies have found that infants with difficult temperament showed more extreme cognitive reactions to stressors such as noise, crowding, or family structure (Henry, Caspi, Moffitt, & Silva, 1996; Wachs & Gandour, 1983). Barron and

Earls (1984) found that the relation between family stress and behavior problems in 3-year-olds was greater among children characterized as temperamentally inflexible; Crockenberg (1987) reported that infants with difficult temperament showed more extreme behavioral reactions to family stressors. Maziade et al. (1990) found psychiatric disorders in adolescence particularly prevalent among individuals rated at age 7 as temperamentally difficult and as having parents with relatively poor discipline practices; this finding was obtained at age 12 and at age 16.[1]

Research by Bates et al. (1998) tested moderation effects between parental discipline practices and a temperamental construct of *resistance to control* (i.e., being socially unresponsive, dominating, or impulsive), using data from two studies in which participants were initially assessed in early childhood and were followed through middle childhood. Results indicated an interaction between temperament and parental discipline such that the relationship between temperament and externalizing problems was greater among families with low restrictive control. Stice and Gonzales (1998) used a high school sample to study moderation for two parenting measures (parental support and parental control) in relation to two composite indices termed *undercontrol* (including impulsivity, sensation seeking, disorganization, irresponsibility, unconventionality, and low delay of gratification) and *negative affectivity* (including dysphoria, anxiety, irritation, anger, and stress). These investigators found some significant interactions, such that the relation of parenting factors to antisocial behavior was greater among students with high undercontrol. Smith and Prior (1995) studied a sample of families selected for severe psychosocial stress on the basis of a composite stress measure. They examined predictors of children doing relatively better or worse on outcomes such as social competence and behavior problems. An index of *easy-going temperament* (e.g., low emotionality, ability to engage others) had higher levels among the resilient group. This study showed differential outcomes according to temperament profiles among a group of children all exposed to a comparable level of family stressors.

THEORETICAL BASIS FOR MODERATION EFFECTS

Although there is a credible basis for hypothesizing moderation effects, there has been relatively little longitudinal research focusing on moderation effects for family risk factors, as suggested by Werner (1986). The present

---

[1] Tschann, Kaiser, Chesney, Alkon, and Boyce (1996) reported an interaction effect in a preschool sample such that family conflict was positively related to behavior problems among children with difficult temperament but inversely related to behavior problems among children with easy temperament. This interaction, different in form from those found in other studies, may be attributable to the relatively young age of the participants.

research addressed this question from the perspective of epigenetic theory, which posits that behavioral patterns become more complex over time with cognitive and social maturation and that temperament characteristics may influence the organization of behavior (Goldsmith, Gottesman, & Lemery, 1997; Rothbart & Ahadi, 1994; Scarr, 1992). For substance use, epigenetic models suggest that temperament phenotypes will not have a direct relationship to growth over time in a complex behavior pattern such as tobacco and alcohol use, but rather will affect patterns of social relationships that represent more proximal risk factors for substance use, such as affiliation with deviance-prone peers (Tarter & Vanyukov, 1994; Zucker, 1994).

The present study assessed several dimensions of temperament that have been replicated across studies and have been linked theoretically to substance-use liability (Rothbart & Ahadi, 1994; Tarter & Vanyukov, 1994). *Task attentional orientation* is the ability to focus attention on performing and completing tasks. *Positive emotionality* is the tendency to frequently experience positive mood. *Activity level* is the tendency to be physically active and exploratory and to become restless when sitting still. *Negative emotionality* is the tendency to be easily irritated and intensely upset. These dimensions have been shown to have moderate heritability (Buss & Plomin, 1984; Rothbart & Bates, 1998) and to exhibit stability of core attributes over time (Hagekull, 1989; Pedlow et al., 1993). Research has indicated task attentional orientation and positive emotionality to be protective factors with respect to adolescent substance use, whereas activity level and negative emotionality are risk factors (e.g., Wills et al., 1995; Wills, Windle, & Cleary, 1998; Windle, 1991).

Hypotheses about moderation were derived from the proposition in epigenetic models that temperament characteristics may serve to promote adaptation through reducing reactivity to aversive stimuli or, alternatively, may detract from adaptation if they serve to amplify negative reactions to environmental influences (Rothbart & Ahadi, 1994; Tarter, Moss, & Vanyukov, 1995). We hypothesized that the dimensions of task attentional orientation and positive emotionality would have buffer effects, that is, that they would reduce the impact of family risk factors. Attentional orientation is the precursor of what Rutter et al. (1997) termed *planfulness*, that is, the ability to anticipate problem situations and consider alternative courses of action, and it has been suggested as relevant for reducing the impact of risk-promoting circumstances (Giancola, Martin, Tarter, Pelham, & Moss, 1996; Quinton, Pickles, Maughan, & Rutter, 1993; Wills et al., 1998). For positive emotionality, it has been shown that high levels of positive affect reduce the impact of negative experiences on substance use (Wills, Sandy, Shinar, & Yaeger, 1999). Individuals with positive mood may be less reactive to conflicts with parents, for example, and positive mood may also help to promote the development of problem-solving approaches to situations (Rothbart & Ahadi,

1994). Thus, task orientation and positive emotionality were predicted to have protective moderation effects in relation to family risk factors. Vulnerability interactions (i.e., increasing the impact of risk factors) were hypothesized for activity level and negative emotionality. Negative emotionality can make individuals more reactive to family conflicts or negative life events, and high activity level is implicated in greater susceptibility to influences for substance use, such as parental modeling of tobacco or alcohol use (Tarter et al., 1995). Thus, activity level and negative emotionality were predicted to show vulnerability interactions in relation to family risk factors.

For studying growth over time in substance use it is important to inquire about the locus where moderation effects occur. Although there is evidence of individual differences in susceptibility to environmental factors (Rutter, Champion, Quinton, Maughan, & Pickles, 1995; Wachs, 1992), most studies have dealt with variables that are fairly distal to the processes that produce adverse outcomes. Rutter et al. (1997) suggested that researchers give attention to proximal processes to provide more understanding about the locus in the etiological process where moderation effects operate. In addressing this issue we drew on a proposition from epigenetic models suggesting that an important locus for temperament-environment interactions is in effects on peer relationships. For example, Scarr and McCartney (1983) originally suggested that temperament characteristics may exert a systematic influence on the nature and impact of peer relationships. Moffitt (1993) also suggested that some temperamental dimensions predispose individuals toward more affiliation with, and being affected to a greater extent by, deviant peers; she proposed that such a process might be involved in the interaction between individual characteristics and social contexts. In addition, the epigenetic analysis by Tarter et al. (1995) proposed that substance-use outcomes depend on an interaction between a temperament phenotype and the social context of development, with the peer environment being increasingly important as individuals enter adolescence. These propositions suggest predictions about the relevance of peer variables for moderation effects.

In addressing this question, we focused on peer substance use and employed latent growth analysis, which has advantages for studying change in behavior over time because it models both the intercept (i.e., initial level) and the slope (i.e., rate of change over time) for a construct (Stoolmiller, 1995; Windle, 1997). Use of tobacco and alcohol among friends has been identified as a proximal risk factor for adolescent substance use (see Hawkins, Catalano, & Miller, 1992), and studies have linked change in peer use to increases in adolescents' tobacco and alcohol use (e.g., Curran, Stice, & Chassin, 1997). In the latent growth approach, moderation effects for temperament could be represented as differences in the paths from family risk factors to intercept or slope constructs or as differences in the relation between peer and adolescent substance-use constructs. Epigenetic models suggest also that temperament characteristics could affect the impact of the peer group (Scarr & McCartney, 1983), so we tested for this type of effect.

SUMMARY OF THE PRESENT RESEARCH

The present research tested for moderation effects in a multiethnic sample of participants assessed on three occasions over the age range from 11 to 14 years. We obtained measures of several temperament dimensions and used specific measures of three family characteristics, as suggested by Wachs (1992, chap. 8). The present study provided a relatively large sample size, which has been discussed as a relevant methodological characteristic for detecting moderation effects (Aiken & West, 1991, chap. 8; McClelland & Judd, 1993; Plomin & Daniels, 1984; Plomin & Hershberger, 1991). Temperament dimensions were assessed through two sources, self-reports and teacher ratings, to determine whether observed effects could be attributable to method variance (Rothbart & Bates, 1998).

We hypothesized that protective moderation (i.e., a lower relationship between family risk factors and proximal factors) would be found for the temperament dimensions of task attentional orientation and positive emotionality, whereas risk-enhancing moderation (i.e., a higher relationship between family risk factors and proximal factors) would be found for activity level and negative emotionality. Moderation effects were analyzed in latent growth modeling, with the anticipation that effects of family risk factors on intercept constructs, and relationships between initial peer substance use and growth in adolescent substance use, would differ across subgroups that were based on temperament characteristics. Multiple-group analyses with structural equation modeling were used to test differences in coefficients across temperament subgroups.

METHOD

Participants

The participants were students from public school districts in a metropolitan area. The districts are in mixed urban–suburban communities that are socioeconomically representative of the state population (U.S. Department of Commerce, 1992). At study outset, participants were in sixth-grade classes in a total of 18 elementary schools; the sample was resurveyed two times at yearly intervals, when students were in seventh grade and eighth grade in a total of six junior high schools. At study outset, the mean age of the participants was

11.5 years ($SD = 0.6$). The sample was 50% female and 50% male. Ethnic background was 27% African American, 23% Hispanic, 3% Asian American, 36% Caucasian, 7% other ethnicity, and 5% mixed ethnicity. An item on family structure indicated that 56% of the participants were living with two biological parents, 34% were living with a single parent, and 10% were in a blended family (one biological parent and one stepparent). The mean parental education on a scale ranging from 1 to 6 was 3.9 ($SD = 1.4$), a level just above high school graduate.

Procedure

A self-report questionnaire was administered to students in classrooms by trained research staff using a standardized protocol. The questionnaire took approximately 40 minutes to administer. After giving standardized instructions to students, staff members circulated in the classroom to answer any individual questions about particular items. The survey was administered under confidential conditions, and a Certificate of Confidentiality protecting the data was obtained from the Public Health Service. Students were instructed that they should not write their names on the survey and were assured that their answers were strictly confidential and would not be shown to their parents or teachers. Methodological research has shown that when participants are assured of confidentiality, self-reports of substance use have good validity (Murray & Perry, 1987).

Students participated under a procedure in which parents were informed about the nature and methods of the study through a notice sent by direct mail. The parent was informed that he or she could have the child excluded from the research by contacting either the researcher or a designated administrator at the school. Students were informed about the nature and methods of the research through a written description at the time of questionnaire administration and were informed that they could refuse or discontinue participation.

The sampling frame for the study consisted of all English-speaking students in the sixth-grade school population. The initial survey was conducted in the spring of 1994. The size of the sample in the sixth grade was 1,810 participants; the completion rate (number of participating students divided by total school enrollment from class lists) was 94%, with nonparticipation occurring because of parental exclusion (1%), student refusal (1%), or absenteeism or unavailability because of other school activities (4%). In seventh grade the completion rate was 88%, with parental exclusion of 4%, student refusal of 3%, and student absenteeism of 5%. In eighth grade the completion rate was 86%, with parental exclusion of 3%, student refusal of 6%, and student absenteeism of 6%. Longitudinal tracking of participants was accomplished through a procedure in which students were given a questionnaire with the same numerical code number each year, based on name matching from class lists and teacher verification of students at the time of question-naire administration. A total of 1,269 students provided usable data over all three waves of the study, for a retention rate of 70%.

Self-Report Measures

Demographic

Demographic items asked about age and gender. An item on ethnicity listed five response options (African American, Asian American, Hispanic, White, and Other) with multiple responding allowed; in addition to single-option responses, codes were assigned for persons who checked African American and White, Hispanic and White, or African American and His-panic. An item on family composition asked what adult(s) the participant currently lived with (eight options, with multiple responding allowed); this item was recoded for analysis to three categories (intact family, single-parent family, or blended family). Items about education for father and mother, respectively, had response options of grade school, some high school, high school graduate, some college, college graduate, and postcollege (master's or doctoral degree or other professional education). Participants were instructed that if they were uncertain about their fathers' or mothers' education, they should leave that item blank.

Temperament Dimensions

Temperament dimensions were assessed with a 25-item inventory con-sisting of scales from the Revised Dimensions of Temperament Survey (DOTS-R; Windle & Lerner, 1986) and the Emotionality, Activity, and Sociability Inventory (EAS; Buss & Plomin, 1984). A 6-item scale on task attentional orientation (DOTS-R, Cronbach's α over waves = .70–.83) con-tained items about focusing on tasks and persisting until finished. A 5-item scale on positive emotionality (DOTS-R, αs = .74–.86) included items about generally being in a cheerful mood and smiling frequently. A 6-item scale on physical activity level (DOTS-R, αs = .82–.89) had items about moving around frequently and being restless when having to sit still. A 5-item scale on negative emotionality (EAS, αs = .74–.81) contained items about getting easily and intensely upset.[2]

---

[2] This study also assessed sociability, the tendency to enjoy being around people, which has an uncertain theoretical status as a predictive factor (Sher & Trull, 1994; Tarter, 1988; Wills, Mariani, & Filer, 1996). Our results showed generally nonsignificant results for sociability, suggesting that it increased some paths but decreased other paths. Because of the complex theory and data, we do not discuss sociability in detail.

Parent–Child Conflict

An inventory on the parent–child relationship included a 3-item scale for parent–child conflict (αs = .75–.82) derived from research by Barerra, Chassin, and Rogosch (1993). The scale contained the items "I have a lot of arguments with my parent," "I often feel my parent is giving me a 'hard time'," and "I feel my parent doesn't understand me." Participants were instructed in answering the items to think about the one parent they talked to the most; this instruction was given because of the substantial proportion of single-parent families anticipated in the sample.

Family Life Events

A checklist of negative life events, based on a previous inventory (Wills, McNamara, Vaccaro, & Hirky, 1996), asked the participant to indicate whether each event had occurred during the previous year, using a dichotomous (yes/no) response scale. The inventory had an 11-item scale for Family Life Events (αs = .61–.63), which included those that could have occurred to a family member and were unlikely to have been caused by the adolescent himself or herself (e.g., "My father/mother was unemployed").

Parental Tobacco or Alcohol Use

Questions about regular substance use by parents (defined as weekly or more often) included items for cigarette smoking, alcohol use (beer or wine), and liquor (whiskey, scotch, rum). Measures for parental smoking, beer or wine drinking, and liquor drinking were coded on 3-point scales (1 = neither uses, 2 = one uses, and 3 = two use); a 3-item composite score produced alphas of .65 to .69.

Friends' Substance Use

Items asked the participant whether any of his or her friends smoked cigarettes, drank beer or wine, or smoked marijuana. Responses were on 0-to-4 scales with response points of none, one, two, three, and four or more. A 3-item composite score yielded alphas of .75 to .87 over assessments.

Participant's Substance Use

Substance use by the participant was measured with three items that asked about the typical frequency of his or her cigarette, alcohol, and marijuana use. Items were introduced to participants with the following stem: "How often do you [smoke cigarettes/drink alcohol/smoke marijuana]?"

Responses were on 0-to-5 scales with scale points of *never used, tried once-twice, used four–five times, usually use a few times a month, usually use a few times a week*, and *usually use every day*. Reliabilities for a 3-item composite score were .60, .75, and .79 for sixth, seventh, and eighth grades, respectively.

Teacher-Report Measures

To report on temperament, teachers used the same items completed by the participants except that the items were worded in a third-party format. The teacher ratings were obtained at approximately the same time as the student questionnaire was administered; ratings were made outside of school hours, and teachers were compensated for making them. Teachers were instructed to rate only students they were familiar with and to rate items as they observed them in the school setting. Completion rates for the teacher ratings were 98%, 97%, and 94% for the first, second, and third waves, respectively. Internal consistencies were as follows: task attentional orientation, αs = .97–.98; positive emotionality, αs = .95–.96; activity level, αs = .98–.99; negative emotionality, αs = .93–.95. It should be noted that teachers did not know what students said about themselves on the self-report questionnaires; hence, the teacher ratings represent an independent source of data.

RESULTS

Descriptive Statistics for Substance Use

Data on substance use showed that levels of use were relatively low at the initial assessment but increased thereafter. The percentage of participants who had smoked cigarettes four times or more often was 7% in sixth grade, 19% in seventh grade, and 28% in eighth grade; the percentage who had used alcohol four times or more often was 8% in sixth grade, 20% in seventh grade, and 30% in eighth grade. Prevalence rates for marijuana were lower, with the percentage using four times or more often being less than 1% in sixth grade, 5% in seventh grade, and 11% in eighth grade. These prevalence rates are generally comparable to data for this age range from other studies (Johnston, O'Malley, & Bachman, 1995; Oetting & Beauvais, 1990), although rates of marijuana use are somewhat lower.

The substance-use indices were intercorrelated, and the correlations increased with age. Correlations among indices for adolescents' tobacco, alcohol, and marijuana use were mostly in the range from .40 to .60. For peer substance use, correlations among indices of friends' tobacco, alcohol, and marijuana use were mostly in the range from .50 to .70. These intercorrelations are consistent with other data for this age range (Hays, Widaman,

DiMatteo, & Stacy, 1987; Wills & Cleary, 1995). Because of the intercorrelations, the indices of tobacco, alcohol, and marijuana use were combined for analysis in a composite score (Needle, Su, & Lavee, 1989; Newcomb & Bentler, 1988).

Descriptive Statistics for Temperament and Family Variables

Descriptive statistics for self-report and teacher-report data are presented in Table 12.1. In self-report data, distributions for the temperament dimensions were normal for the most part, with skewness values in the range from 0.00 to 0.28. The exception was positive emotionality, which was skewed toward more favorable values (skewness value is negative by convention) because participants tended to rate themselves as having fairly positive mood. In teacher reports a similar pattern was found, with zero or negative skewness for protective dimensions; activity level and negative emotionality had greater positive skewness because of a halo effect, with teachers tending to rate more students at the top or bottom on these dimensions. Thus, the patterning of distributions was similar for self-reports and teacher reports. In self-reports there was a slight decline in means over time for all dimensions; mean levels for teacher reports were more erratic, probably reflecting the fact that ratings were done by different groups of teachers, who had different anchor points.

The three family risk factors had moderate positive skewness because distributions were shifted somewhat toward lower values of conflict, negative events, and parental tobacco or alcohol use. There was no obvious temporal trend for family life events or parental substance use, but there was an increase over time in parent-child conflict. This appears to be a typical pattern in adolescence and has been observed in other studies (e.g., Wills & Cleary, 1996).[3]

Relationships Among Predictor Variables

Zero-order correlations of predictors with peer substance use and adolescent substance use for self- and teacher-reports for sixth- and seventh-grade data are presented in Table 12.2. (Data for the eighth-grade assessments were similar and are not reported here.) Correlations of temperament dimensions with substance use for self-reports were significant ($p < .0001$) for all four dimensions; significant correlations with peer substance use ($p < .0001$ with two exceptions) were also noted. Correlations of temperament dimensions

---

[3] Attrition tests compared baseline data for persons in all three waves of the study (stayers) versus those leaving after the first wave (dropouts). Dropout status was not related to initial levels of tobacco, alcohol, or marijuana use. For temperament, dropouts had higher levels at sixth grade only on negative emotionality (M = 13.20, compared with 12.31 for the stayers). Thus there was minimal evidence of differential attrition, as in other longitudinal studies (e.g., Kandel & Davies, 1992; Newcomb & Bentler, 1988).

TABLE 12.1
Descriptive Statistics for Temperament Dimensions and Family Variables, for Self-Report and Teacher-Report Data, for Three Assessments

Variable (no. of items)	6th grade			7th grade			8th grade		
	M	SD	Skew	M	SD	Skew	M	SD	Skew
Self-reports									
Task orientation (6)	19.15	4.90	0.00	18.39	5.54	0.01	18.30	5.43	0.08
Positive emotionality (5)	20.75	3.95	−1.06	20.33	4.38	−0.99	19.99	4.60	−0.93
Activity level (6)	17.87	6.38	0.09	16.59	6.85	0.27	16.51	6.81	0.28
Negative emotionality (5)	15.70	4.64	0.09	14.50	5.07	0.24	14.58	5.10	0.23
Parent-child conflict (3)	6.61	3.45	0.88	7.01	3.48	0.73	7.51	3.60	0.57
Family events (10)	12.42	1.98	0.88	12.17	1.84	0.90	12.12	1.81	0.93
Parental tobacco/alcohol use (3)	4.47	1.44	0.95	4.47	1.47	0.93	4.45	1.48	0.95
Teacher reports									
Task orientation (6)	18.03	7.74	−0.01	16.93	7.33	0.16	18.16	7.13	0.00
Positive emotionality (5)	18.47	5.06	−0.58	17.33	4.86	−0.39	17.72	4.56	−0.42
Activity level (6)	12.05	7.50	1.06	12.88	7.62	0.86	11.76	6.94	1.09
Negative emotionality (5)	11.60	5.66	0.71	11.92	5.60	0.66	11.60	5.43	0.56

Note. Response scales ranged from 1 to 5 for each item except for family events (from 1 to 2) and parental tobacco/alcohol use (from 1 to 3). Positive skewness values indicate the distribution shifted toward the lower end of the scale; negative values indicate the distribution shifted toward the higher end of the scale. Note that family variables were assessed only through self-reports.

TABLE 12.2

Correlations for Temperament Dimensions and Family Variables and Peer and Adolescent Substance Use, for Self-Reports and Teacher Reports, for Two Assessments

Variable	1	2	3	4	5	6	7	8	9
			Self-reports						
1. Task orientation	—	.31	-.01	-.20	-.18	-.12	-.11	-.14	-.16
2. Positive emotionality	.29	—	.07	-.23	-.15	-.10	-.09	-.12	-.14
3. Activity level	-.01	.03	—	.36	.27	.16	.14	.17	.17
4. Negative emotionality	-.11	-.19	.41	—	.43	.24	.17	.23	.20
5. Parent–child conflict	-.07	-.19	.28	.41	—	.27	.19	.29	.29
6. Family life events	-.05	-.10	.18	.29	.24	—	.27	.30	.23
7. Parental tobacco/alcohol use	-.07	-.09	.18	.16	.20	.27	—	.27	.35
8. Peer substance use	-.08	-.10	.20	.23	.18	.27	.25	—	.63
9. Adolescent substance use	-.12	-.17	.15	.19	.25	.15	.35	.57	—
			Teacher reports						
1. Task orientation	—	.29	-.60	-.59	-.20	-.17			
2. Positive emotionality	.30	—	-.01	-.21	-.05	-.05			
3. Activity level	-.53	.05	—	.67	.15	.14			
4. Negative emotionality	-.51	-.29	.61	—	.16	.14			
5. Peer substance use	-.17	-.03	.20	.22	—	.60			
6. Adolescent substance use	-.14	-.04	.12	.16	.57	—			

Note. Correlations for the sixth grade are below the diagonal; correlations for the seventh grade are above the diagonal. (Family variables and peer and adolescent substance use were assessed only in self-reports.) Approximate significance levels are as follows: $r = |.09|$, $p < .01$; $r = |.11|$, $p < .001$; $r = |.12|$, $p < .0001$.

with family variables were consistent with previous data; for example, task attentional orientation was related to more favorable parent–child relationships, and activity level was related to less favorable parent–child relationships (Blackson, Tarter, Martin, & Moss, 1994; Rothbart & Ahadi, 1994; Wills et al., 1998). The average correlation between the protective temperament dimensions (task attentional orientation and positive emotionality) and the risk-promoting dimensions (activity level and negative emotionality) was –.08, indicating that these are distinct domains.

Correlations of teacher-reported temperament with peer substance use and adolescent substance use mostly paralleled the patterns observed in the self-report data, with significant relationships ($p < .0001$) observed for task attentional orientation, activity level, and negative emotionality. The exceptions were the correlations of teacher ratings of positive emotionality with peer and adolescent substance use, which were nonsignificant. The general corroboration of predictive relationships for substance use from an independent source of evidence indicates that the relationships observed for self-reports are not attributable to method variance.[4] A difference in correlation patterns for teacher-report data was evidence for a halo effect, with larger correlations between activity level and negative emotionality and substantial inverse correlations between risk and protective dimensions.

Effects for the family risk factors showed all three variables positively related ($p < .0001$) to both peer and adolescent substance use. These findings are consistent with previous research (Hawkins et al., 1992; Wills, McNamara, et al., 1996). It is noteworthy that significant relationships to substance use were observed at around 11 years of age.

Analyses of Moderation Effects

Attention to moderation effects was suggested by cross-sectional multiple regression analyses that showed significant interactions between temperament and family risk factors for predicting concurrent level of substance use. These interactions (found for self-reports and teacher reports) are not reported in detail here because the focus of this research was on addressing moderation in a longitudinal context using latent growth modeling (Willett & Sayer, 1994; Windle, 1997). A latent growth model approaches the analysis of repeated measures from the perspective of an individual growth curve for each participant; each growth curve has a certain starting point (intercept) and a certain growth over time (slope). The basic measurement model

---

[4] The ranges of correlations between self-reports of temperament and teacher ratings of temperament over grade assessments were .12–.20 for activity level, .13–.24 for negative emotionality, .08–.10 for task attentional orientation, and .10–.14 for positive emotionality (cf. Achenbach et al., 1987; Smith & Prior, 1995). Because of the level of intercorrelation, we conducted separate analyses for self-reports and teacher reports.

has two latent constructs, one representing the intercept (i.e., initial level) for the construct, the other representing the slope (i.e., rate of change) for the construct. To test effects on a proximal factor—peer substance use—we analyzed what is termed an *associative* model (Duncan, Duncan, Strycker, Li, & Alpert, 1999), including intercept and slope constructs for both peers' substance use and adolescents' substance use. In this approach, the family factors measured at Grade 6 are considered as exogenous to the model; they may be related to intercepts for peer or adolescent substance use or to rate of growth for peer or adolescent substance use over the period from 11 to 14 years of age. These constructs meet the assumptions for latent growth modeling (Curran et al., 1997; Wills & Cleary, 1999), so we do not present the measurement-model analyses for the constructs in detail here.

The analytic procedure involves first estimating a model for the total sample. The measurement model was based on three indicators for peer substance use, the sum of scores for friends using tobacco, alcohol, and marijuana at a given time point (sixth grade, seventh grade, or eighth grade); correspondingly, three indicators for adolescent substance use were based on the sum of scores for the participant's use of tobacco, alcohol, and marijuana at a given time point. The intercept constructs for peer use and adolescent use were specified by setting factor loadings for each of the observed values to 1. The slope constructs for peer use and adolescent use were specified by setting the loadings for the observed values to 0, 1, and 2, reflecting the equal spacing of assessments over time. In the structural model, the family measures from sixth grade (conflict, events, and substance use) were specified as exogenous constructs, with each measured by a single indicator. Demographic controls were also specified as exogenous, including one binary index for gender, two binary indices for ethnicity (Black vs. Hispanic or White and Hispanic vs. Black or White), two binary indices for family structure (single vs. blended or intact and blended vs. single or intact), and one 6-point scale for parental education. Peer and adolescent substance use intercept and slope constructs were specified as endogenous, with covariances specified between intercept constructs and between slope constructs and covariances specified between intercept and slope for each of the peer and adolescent constructs. Aside from these basic specifications, structural coefficients were introduced only if they had modification indices corresponding to $p < .01$, and correlated errors were introduced only if they had modification indices corresponding to $p < .0001$. The model was estimated following the procedures of Willett and Sayer (1994), using LISREL 8 with the maximum-likelihood method (Jöreskog & Sörbom, 1996).[5]

---

[5] From an analytic sample of 1,102 cases with complete longitudinal data on predictor and criterion variables, there was shrinkage in sample size through exclusion of small or mixed-race groups (180 cases) and missing data on parental education (160 cases).

A model with seven exogenous paths, one endogenous path, and one correlated error term had reasonable fit: $\chi^2(62, N = 762) = 135.59$; comparative fit index (CFI) = .98. The model is presented in Figure 12.1. The results discussed here are all independent effects and are significant at $p < .0001$ unless otherwise noted. There were substantial covariances between the intercept constructs and between the slope constructs, but there was little relationship between intercept and slope for peer substance use, $t(760) = 0.76$, ns, or adolescent substance use, $t(760) = 0.27$, ns. There were independent effects from parent-child conflict to the peer use intercept, the adolescent use intercept, the peer use slope, $t(760) = 3.55$, $p < .001$, and the adolescent use slope, $t(760) = 2.88$, $p < .01$; participants with more conflict had higher initial levels of peer use and own use and showed a greater rate of growth for both constructs. Participants whose families experienced more negative events had a higher initial level of peer substance use. Participants in families with more parental tobacco or alcohol use had higher initial levels for peer use and own

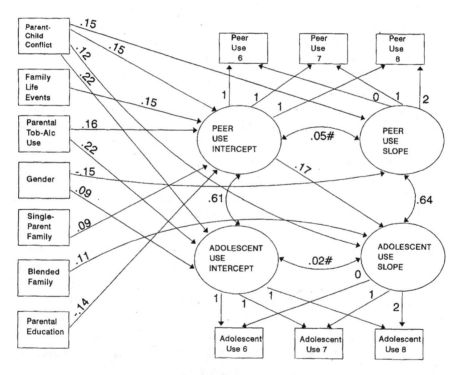

Figure 12.1. Latent growth model with sixth-grade family variables and demographic variables related to intercept and slope constructs for peer substance use and adolescent substance use, for the total sample. Coefficients are standardized values, except for factor loadings, which are fixed. All coefficients are significant ($p < .01$) unless otherwise noted (# = ns). Curved double-headed arrows indicate covariances; single-headed arrows indicate path effects. Ethnicity indices and covariances among exogenous variables were included in the model but are excluded from the figure for graphic simplicity. Tob-Alc = tobacco/alcohol.

use. The effect from the peer use intercept to the adolescent use slope indicated that participants with a higher initial level of peer use showed a larger rate of increase in their own substance use; this path is consistent with previous research (Curran et al., 1997). Demographic effects indicated that male gender was related to more initial adolescent substance use, $t(760) = 2.94$, $p < .01$, but to a lower rate of growth in peer use. Indices for African American ethnicity and Hispanic ethnicity were included in the model, but both had nonsignificant effects. Other demographic effects (with ethnicity controlled for) indicated that single-parent family structure was related to more initial peer substance use, $t(760) = 2.76$, $p < .01$, that blended family structure was related to a greater rate of growth in adolescent substance use, $t(760) = 3.22$, $p < .001$, and that parental education was related to a lower initial level of peer substance use. We note that exogenous and endogenous effects in the model without demographic controls were quite similar to those in the model with demographic controls.

Multiple-Group Analysis

Multiple-group analyses were conducted for temperament subgroups as defined from self-reports and from teacher reports. The sample was divided by a median split on a score for protective temperament (task attentional orientation + positive emotionality) or a score for difficult temperament (activity level + negative emotionality), derived in each case from data aggregated over the three waves from self-reports or teacher reports.[6] These analyses were performed without demographic controls in order to maximize statistical power (Plomin & Hershberger, 1991), and there were approximately 525 cases in each subgroup. A base model was determined through inputting covariance matrices and mean vectors for the subgroups and estimating the model in Figure 12.1 simultaneously in both subgroups with no constraints (Jaccard & Wan, 1996; Jöreskog & Sörbom, 1996, chap. 9). Equality constraints were then imposed to determine whether specified coefficients differed across subgroups.

An initial analysis was performed to determine whether latent growth parameters differed across temperament subgroups. Table 12.3 presents parameters for intercept and slope constructs for the temperament subgroups in a base model with no exogenous variables (because intercept coefficients in a model with exogenous variables are conditional means and can be influenced by group differences in the exogenous variables). These parameters were compared in a multiple-group analysis in which one coefficient was constrained to be equal across the subgroups, and the chi-square difference

---

[6] The stability correlations for individual temperament dimensions ranged from .40 to .60 for 1-year lags and were between .36 and .50 for the 2-year lag.

TABLE 12.3
Means and Variances (Var.) for Intercept and Slope Parameters for Latent Growth Models for Temperament Subgroups

Subgroup	Peer use intercept		Peer use slope		Adolescent use intercept		Adolescent use slope	
	M	Var.	M	Var.	M	Var.	M	Var.
Self-report								
Low protective	1.69***	4.73*	2.20	3.55	0.99***	1.50***	0.87*	1.42*
High protective	1.31	3.22	1.99	3.35	0.64	0.89	0.65	1.00
Teacher report								
Low protective	1.96***	3.70***	2.24*	3.11	0.98***	1.60***	0.73	1.48*
High protective	1.19	3.58	1.90	3.52	0.68	0.87	0.73	1.03
Self-report								
Low difficult	1.10***	2.37***	1.84***	3.03	0.61***	1.01*	0.62**	1.14
High difficult	1.94	5.16	2.32	3.59	1.01	1.51	0.91	1.34
Teacher report								
Low difficult	1.09***	3.12	1.84***	3.36	0.65***	0.73***	0.68	0.88***
High difficult	2.06	4.19	2.31	3.26	1.01	1.71	0.83	1.66

Note. Tabled values are means and variances for alphas, the intercept and slope parameters, in a model with no exogenous variables. Significance levels are from a multiple-group test in which one parameter was constrained to be equal across two temperament subgroups.
*Parameters differ at $p < .05$. **Parameters differ at $p < .01$. ***Parameters differ at $p < .001$.

for model fit was obtained. The subgroup with higher protective temperament had significantly lower intercepts for peer substance use and adolescent substance use; lower slope was also noted for peer use (for teacher reports) and for adolescent use (for self-reports). The subgroup with higher difficult temperament had significantly higher intercepts for peer use and adolescent use and greater slopes for peer use (for both sources) and adolescent use (for self-reports). In several cases, the variances of the intercept and slope parameters differed across temperament subgroups, typically with greater variance among subgroups with low protective temperament or higher difficult temperament. These differences in latent growth parameters demonstrate that temperament is related to substance use in the latent growth context.

Multiple-Group Tests for Protective-Temperament Dimensions

Multiple-group analyses were performed to test the hypotheses about moderation effects. Using the model in Figure 12.1 and subgroups divided on temperament characteristics, we imposed equality constraints on specified sets of parameters to determine whether constraining these coefficients to be equal across temperament subgroups would degrade the fit of the multiple-group model, as indicated by an increase in the chi-square compared with that of the base model.[7] A significant difference in chi-square derived from this test (constrained model − base model, with df = number of parameters constrained) would provide evidence that effects in the latent growth model differ significantly across temperament groups, that is, there is a moderation effect. We tested hypotheses that paths from family risk factors to endogenous constructs and the path from initial peer substance use to growth in adolescent substance use differed across subgroups.

Covariances between latent growth constructs (e.g., between peer and adolescent substance use intercepts) were tested in a separate procedure that compared the factor correlations rather than the covariances. This was done because there were variance differences across subgroups, and the magnitude of covariances is sensitive to the variance of the variables analyzed; hence observed differences in covariances may be attributable to variance differences across groups. To compare factor correlations, we specified a second-order factor analysis with four intercept and slope constructs, with the second-order factor variances fixed at 1 and with loadings of the first-order factors on the second-order factors freely estimated. Constraints were then imposed to test equality of the correlations among the second-order constructs.

---

[7] An issue in multisample analysis is that the definition used to block the subgroups may not correspond with the parts of the sample in which the interaction is occurring (Rigdon, Schumacker, & Wothke, 1998). To address this issue, we performed multisample analyses with temperament subgroups based on median splits, tertiles, and quartiles. Results for these analyses indicated that the median split was the most appropriate blocking procedure.

For a conservative omnibus test, all coefficients to intercepts and slopes were constrained to be equal across temperament subgroups. This test was not significant for self-report data, difference $\chi^2(8) = 10.77$, $p > .10$, but was significant for teacher-report data, difference $\chi^2(8) = 21.60$, $p < .01$. To characterize the moderation, coefficients in the base model for temperament subgroups, analyzed with no constraints, are presented in Figure 12.2; the figure indicates when coefficients differ by > 3 SE (approximately $p < .05$). The pattern of results was similar across sources, with four paths substantially lower in the high-protective subgroup: the two paths from parent-child conflict to the adolescent use intercept and the peer use slope, the path from parental tobacco or alcohol use to the adolescent use intercept, and the path from the peer use intercept to the adolescent use slope. A multiple-group test constraining these coefficients to be equal across groups in the self-report data resulted in a difference chi-square ($df = 4$) of 7.82 ($p < .10$), suggesting that these paths differed across temperament subgroups. A test for teacher reports of temperament (see Figure 12.2B) resulted in a difference chi-square ($df = 4$) of 16.12 ($p < .001$), showing that these paths differed significantly across subgroups. In some instances, the moderation consisted of a relative reduction of the coefficient for the high-protective subgroup, with the coefficient remaining significant in both subgroups. In other cases, there was complete buffering. For example, the path from parent-child conflict to the peer use slope was significant in the low-protective subgroup for self-reports, $t = 3.61$, $p < .001$, and for teacher reports, $t = 3.93$, $p < .0001$, but nonsignificant in the high-protective subgroup, $ts = 1.61$ (self-reports) and 0.98 (teacher reports), both ns. (The t tests have approximately 500 df.) Teacher reports indicated that the path from the peer use intercept to the peer use slope was approximately three times as large in the low-protective subgroup, $t = 3.94$, $p < .0001$, as in the high-protective subgroup, $t = 2.01$, $p < .05$. In the model with teacher reports, the factor correlation for the peer use intercept and the adolescent use intercept differed significantly across subgroups, difference $\chi^2(1) = 12.37$, $p < .001$, with a lower correlation in the high-protective subgroup. Other factor correlations in models for self-reports and teacher reports did not differ significantly.

These analyses indicated similar findings for models based on self-reports and teacher reports of temperament, though the effects were stronger for the teacher-report data. Moderation for protective temperament was attributable to three types of effects. One was that paths from parental risk factors to intercepts were lower among participants in the high-protective subgroup; across analyses, these effects were noted for the paths from parent-child conflict and parental substance use to the adolescent use intercept. Second, the effect of parent-child conflict on growth in peer substance use was lower among participants in the high-protective subgroup. Third, the impact of peers was reduced, as reflected in a lower correlation between intercepts for

(A)

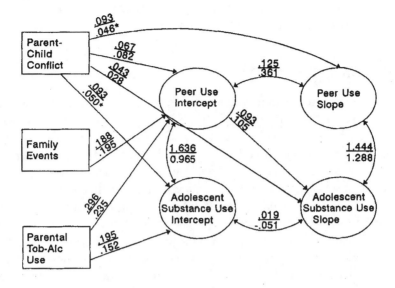

(B)

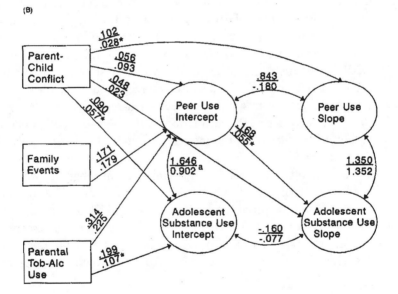

Figure 12.2. Parameters in a latent growth model for subgroups defined by a median split on protective temperament for self-report data (A) and teacher-report data (B). Values given are unstandardized coefficients. Values above the line are for the subgroup with low-protective temperament; values below the line are for the subgroup with high-protective temperament. Tob-Alc = tobacco/alcohol. *Coefficient differs across subgroups by > 3 *SE* (*p* < .05). ªFactor correlations differ significantly (*p* < .01) across subgroups.

peer use and adolescent use and a lower path from initial peer use to growth in adolescents' use, though these effects were significant only for the temperament subgrouping based on teacher reports.[8]

Multiple-Group Tests for Difficult-Temperament Dimensions

For difficult-temperament dimensions, the omnibus test was not significant for self-reports, difference $\chi^2(8) = 8.42$, ns, but was marginally significant for teacher reports, difference $\chi^2(8) = 13.73$, $p < .10$. Coefficients from the base models are presented in Figures 12.3A and 12.3B. The pattern was similar across sources and indicated four paths were substantially larger in the high-difficult subgroup: the paths from parent-child conflict and parental substance use to the adolescent substance use intercept, the path from parental substance use to the peer use intercept, and the path from the peer use intercept to the adolescent use slope. A multiple-group test constraining these paths for self-report data resulted in a difference chi-square ($df = 4$) of 2.65, which is nonsignificant. For the models based on teacher reports of temperament (see Figure 12.3B), the test constraining these four paths resulted in a difference chi-square ($df = 4$) of 10.56 ($p < .05$), showing that these paths differed significantly across temperament subgroups. For most paths, the moderation effect consisted of a relative reduction of the coefficients across subgroups. For the path from the peer use intercept to the adolescent use slope in the teacher reports, the t was 1.66 (ns) in the low-difficult subgroup and 3.56 ($p < .001$) in the high-difficult subgroup (dfs for t tests are approximately 500). The factor correlation for the peer use intercept and the adolescent use intercept differed across groups in the model for self-reports, difference $\chi^2(1)$ = 11.29, $p < .001$, with a greater correlation in the high-difficult subgroup. The other factor correlations in the models for self- and teacher reports did not differ significantly.

The observed differences for difficult-temperament subgroups were similar in form but primarily significant for teacher-report data. The impact of parental substance use on initial levels of both peer and adolescent substance use and the impact of parent-child conflict on initial level of adolescent use were greater among participants who were higher on difficult-temperament dimensions. The impact of initial peer substance use on growth in adolescents'

---

[8] We note that the substance-use scale included some responses that indicated experimental use (*used 1–2 times* and *used 4–5 times*) and some responses that indicated higher rates of use (*used in the past month, week,* or *day*). We used these response categories because of previous research indicating that nonusers, experimenters, and regular users were discriminated on a. number of measures and that the typical pattern of early onset and escalation is one of movement upward from experimental use to regular use (Wills, McNamara, et al., 1996). We replicated the present latent growth analyses with a modified substance-use scale in which the two experimenter categories were recoded into a single group. The results were significant and similar to those reported here, indicating that the observed moderation effects are not attributable simply to effects on minimal levels of substance use.

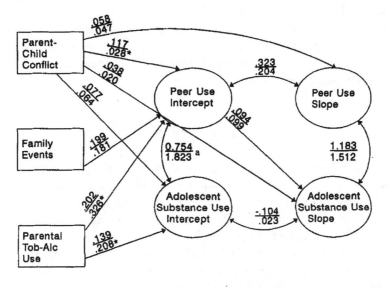

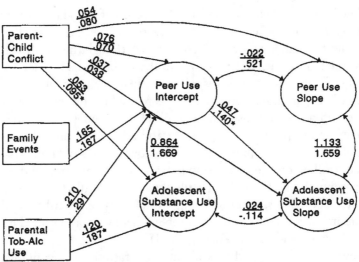

Figure 12.3. Parameters in a latent growth model for subgroups defined by a median split on difficult temperament for self-report data (A) and teacher-report data (B). Values given are unstandardized coefficients. Values above the line are for the subgroup with low-difficult temperament; values below the line are for the subgroup with high-difficult temperament. Tob-Alc = tobacco/alcohol. *Coefficient differs across subgroups by > 3 *SE* (*p* < .05). [a]Factor correlations differ significantly (*p* < .01) across subgroups.

substance use was greater in the high-difficult subgroup as defined by teacher reports, and the correlation of initial levels of peer substance use and adolescent substance use differed for subgroups defined by self-reports. Differences in the impact of parent-child conflict on growth in peer substance use, as observed for protective-temperament dimensions, were not observed for difficult-temperament dimensions.

DISCUSSION

In this research we tested hypotheses about moderation effects for substance use in a representative sample followed from late childhood through middle adolescence. The study addressed methodological issues noted in several sources: There were specific measures of several family risk factors (Wachs, 1992), the sample size provided reasonable power for detecting interactions (Plomin & Hershberger, 1991), and temperament dimensions were assessed with standardized measures obtained from two different sources (Rothbart & Bates, 1998). The relation of family factors to outcomes was addressed in a latent growth context that considered the relation of risk factors to the intercept and the slope for peer substance use and adolescent substance use (Rutter et al., 1997).

The basic latent growth model indicated that family factors were significantly related to intercept and slope constructs and that these effects were independent of demographic characteristics. Although the family risk factors were correlated (see Table 12.2), each of the variables had somewhat different effects. Family life events was related only to a higher intercept for peer substance use; parental substance use was related to the intercepts for both peer use and adolescent use; and parent–child conflict was related to the intercepts and slopes for both peer use and adolescent use. Other studies, using different analytic approaches, have shown effects of family risk factors while controlling for the correlation between temperament and the warmth of the parent–child relationship (Wills et al., 1995; Wills, Gibbons, Gerrard, & Brody, 2000). Thus, effects deriving from family relationships and family stress are important contributors to problem behavior, as outlined in several models (Conger et al., 1992; Zucker, 1994).

Several of the hypotheses about moderation were confirmed. The impact of parent–child conflict and parental substance use on intercept and slope constructs and the impact of peer substance use on growth in adolescent substance use were reduced among participants with a higher level of task attentional orientation and positive emotionality. Conversely, the impact of parental risk factors and peer substance use was greater among participants with a higher activity level and higher negative emotionality. There was some corroboration across reporters, because patterns of moderation results were similar in self-report and teacher-report data, though the results tended to be stronger for teacher reports. No moderation was noted for the effect of family life events, and this (null) finding also was consistent across sources. The moderation effects for family factors provide a conceptual replication of findings from Werner (1986), and moderation effects linked to the peer context are consistent with suggestions by Scarr and McCartney (1983) and Rutter et al. (1997).[9]

Locus and Magnitude of Moderation Effects

The present research investigated the locus of moderation effects in a longitudinal context. The findings indicated that in this multivariate system, moderation was attributable to several types of effects. There were altered paths from family risk factors to initial levels for peer substance use and adolescent substance use, and there was an altered impact of initial peer use on growth in adolescent use. Some evidence also suggested altered covariance between initial levels of peer use and adolescent use. The finding of multiple loci for moderation is analogous to findings from research on social support, which has shown that buffering effects for social support occur through the alteration of several types of pathways, including reducing the effect of risk factors and increasing the effect of protective factors (Wills & Cleary, 1996; Wills & Filer, 2001). Thus, the present results show moderation as a process involving more than one locus and including effects on more distal factors and more proximal factors. This perspective is consistent with transactional models of relations between simple temperament dimensions and complex problem behaviors (Brody, Stoneman, & Gauger, 1996; Wills, Sandy, & Yaeger, 2000).

Given the existence of significant moderation effects, it is relevant to inquire about the magnitude of these effects (Chaplin, 1991). One index of effect size is the comparative magnitude of coefficients (Jaccard & Wan, 1996). In the multiple-group models, the typical effect size was shown by the coefficient in the unfavorable (low protective or high difficult) temperament group being approximately twice as large as the coefficient in the favorable (high protective or low difficult) temperament group. There were two instances of complete buffering: for the paths from parent–child conflict to growth in peer substance use and from the peer use intercept to growth in

---

[9] Later, Werner and Smith (1992) reported that a variable labeled *activity at age 1 year* was a resilience factor. It is possible that very early measures of activity are protective, but it is not clear how this variable was measured. Several authors have noted that disorganized active behavior (as measured here) is often confused with the kind of energetic self-confidence referred to as vigor or surgency, which is focused and goal-directed (Tarter, Alterman, & Edwards, 1985; Zaparniuk & Taylor, 1997) and is sometimes indicated as a protective factor (see, e.g., Caspi, Moffitt, Newman, & Silva, 1996). Because many studies have indicated physical activity level as a risk factor (Wills et al., 1995, 1998; Wills, Sandy, & Yaeger, 2000; Windle, 1991), we think that Werner's study may have measured a different construct.

adolescent use. The magnitude of these moderation effects seems meaningful and is comparable to the impact of effective prevention programs (e.g., Donaldson, Graham, Piccinin, & Hansen, 1995; Pentz et al., 1989).

We found that moderation effects for temperament based on self-report data were generally corroborated across analyses by teacher reports of temperament. The patterning of coefficient differences for parent-child conflict and parental substance use was consistent across sources, and significant coefficient differences noted for one source were corroborated in the majority of instances with a significant difference for the other source. The corroboration is noteworthy because, as in other research (Achenbach, McConaughy, & Howell, 1987), self-reports and teacher reports were not highly correlated. Some differences between sources could be noted. For example, the path from the peer use intercept to the adolescent use slope differed significantly across temperament subgroups based on teacher data, whereas this difference was not found in self-reports; and several path differences were significant in teacher reports while being in the same direction but nonsignificant for self-reports. Although this finding could suggest that teacher reports have greater validity, this conclusion would not necessarily be warranted because the teacher reports were derived from different groups of teachers at each time point and hence seem likely to increase the amount of independent information in the data compared with self-reports. This question remains a topic of interest for the field (Achenbach et al., 1987), and further research on the relative predictive value of information from different sources is warranted.

When one considers moderation, the question arises whether the observed effects represent the child's characteristics modifying the impact of parental characteristics or the parental environment altering the expression of temperament. It is possible that either aspect of moderation may predominantly occur for some combination of variables. For example, parental discipline may alter the relationship between resistance to control and problem behavior (Bates et al., 1998; Kochanska, 1995), consistent with the latter model. However, other studies have found differences in outcomes according to children's temperament characteristics while controlling for family risk (Smith & Prior, 1995; Werner, 1986); these findings are consistent with the former model of moderation. Transactional models might caution against assuming a simple unidirectional process and instead suggest research aimed at understanding the dynamic relations between child and parent characteristics over time (Tarter et al., 1995; Wills, Sandy, & Yaeger, 2000). Providing a complete understanding of this issue is beyond the scope of any single study, and further research may help to clarify these issues.

There are some aspects of the present research that could be noted as possible limitations. The measures of temperament were relatively simple ones and did not represent all conceivable dimensions that have been discussed under the rubric of temperament. Further research may assess more dimensions of temperament, over a wider range of ages, and may include alternative assessment procedures such as interviews or observational measures. The present research used predictors from one time point as covariates, and further research could employ time-varying covariates when appropriate. The substance use measures focused on frequency of use and did not index diagnosable substance abuse; with older samples it may be appropriate to test moderation hypotheses in relation to diagnostic indices of substance abuse or dependence (Newcomb, 1992).

The Nature of Moderation Effects

The present findings from a multivariate context provide suggestive evidence for several mechanisms through which moderation effects can occur. The most distal mechanism, that is, that temperament directly alters the effect of family factors on initial levels of adolescent substance use or affiliation with peer users, received mixed support. There was no observed moderation for the impact of family life events on the intercepts for peer use or adolescent use, but significant differences were observed for the impact of parent-child conflict and parental substance use on both the peer use intercept and the adolescent use intercept. The observed effects are suggestive of an emotional mechanism, in which positive emotionality, for example, could serve to dampen adverse emotional reactions to conflict and thus decrease risk for substance use or risk-prone associations produced by an elevated level of negative affect (Castro, Maddahian, Newcomb, & Bentler, 1987; Chassin et al., 1993; Wills, Sandy, Shinar, & Yaeger, 1999). The lack of moderation for family life events may be attributable to the fact that this variable primarily involves the parents, and temperament characteristics of the child may be less relevant for buffering this aspect of family experiences. Another type of mechanism is suggested for the path from parental tobacco or alcohol use to the adolescent use intercept; here, difficult temperament characteristics could make individuals more susceptible to parental modeling or could exacerbate the effect of a shared vulnerability (Rutter et al., 1997).

A different type of mechanism could relate to growth processes. Path differences were noted for the impact of parent-child conflict on growth in peer substance use and the impact of peer substance use on growth in adolescent substance use. These findings together are interpretable as indicating a greater susceptibility to adverse peer influences among individuals with certain temperament characteristics and are consistent with some findings of greater covariance of peer substance use with adolescent substance use. This may be attributable in part to social perception, such that some individuals perceive deviance-prone peers as more socially desirable and are more inclined to view them as positive models (Blanton, Gibbons, Gerrard, Conger, & Smith, 1997; Gibbons & Gerrard, 1995). It may also reflect greater susceptibility to situational influences for substance use. Individuals with higher problem-solving ability are likely to be better at anticipating potential problem situations and better at responding with a well-controlled approach to problem situations that may arise, such as, for example, being offered cigarettes in a group setting and declining in a nonprovocative manner (Wills & Cleary, 1999; Wills, Sandy, & Shinar, 1999). In contrast, individuals with difficult temperament characteristics may tend to affiliate with deviance-prone peers (Scarr & McCartney, 1983) and be more likely to respond in an uncontrolled manner in some situations, such as continuing to escalate problem behavior in a situation in which others would stop (Patterson, DeBaryshe, & Ramsey, 1989; Wills, McNamara, et al., 1996). Thus, moderation effects of temperament could occur through processes that involve both situational anticipation and situational reactions.

A theoretical question about the observed temperament effects for peer variables is whether they primarily represent a process of (a) selecting different types of peers (i.e., reactive covariance) or (b) being more vulnerable to influences for deviance that could arise from a peer group (i.e., moderation). These processes are distinguishable theoretically, but the current evidence in the area does not provide a clear resolution of this issue. The available evidence shows temperament characteristics related from early ages to greater affiliation with deviance-prone peers (Wills & Cleary, 1999; Wills, Sandy, & Yeager, 2000), but the moderation observed for the impact of peer substance use (i.e., the path from the peer use intercept to the adolescent use slope) seems more consistent with a susceptibility mechanism. Both types of processes may be operative: Dispositional characteristics can shape decisions persons make so that some individuals inhabit a social world with substantially different types of peers. At the same time, temperament characteristics can make some individuals more susceptible to the impact of both parental behavior and peer behavior. Research focused on such questions may help to provide a better understanding of the relations among dispositional characteristics, peer behavior, and problem behavior.

REFERENCES

Achenbach, T. M., McConaughy, S. H., & Howell, C. T. (1987). Child/adolescent behavioral and emotional problems: Implications of cross-informant correlations for situational specificity. *Psychological Bulletin, 101*, 213–232.

Aiken, L. S., & West, S. G. (1991). *Multiple regression: Testing and interpreting interactions.* Newbury Park, CA: Sage.

Barrera, M., Jr., Chassin, L., & Rogosch, F. (1993). Effects of social support and conflict on adolescent children. *Journal of Personality and Social Psychology, 64*, 602–612.

Barron, A., & Earls, F. (1984). Relation of temperament and social factors to behavior problems in 3-year-old children. *Journal of Child Psychology and Psychiatry, 25,* 23–33.

Bates, J. E., Pettit, G. S., Dodge, K. A., & Ridge, B. (1998). Interaction of temperamental resistance to control and restrictive parenting in the development of externalizing behavior. *Developmental Psychology, 34,* 982–995.

Blackson, T. C., Tarter, R. E., Martin, C. S., & Moss, H. M. (1994), Temperament-induced father–son family dysfunction. *American Journal of Orthopsychiatry, 64,* 280–292.

Blanton, H., Gibbons, F. X., Gerrard, M., Conger, K. J., & Smith, G. E. (1997). The role of family and peers in the development of prototypes associated with health risks. *Journal of Family Psychology, 11,* 1–18.

Brody, G. H., & Flor, D. L. (1996). Family processes and youth competence in rural, two-parent African American families. *Developmental Psychology, 33,* 1000–1011.

Brody, G. H., Stoneman, Z., & Gauger, K. (1996). Parent–child relationships, family problem-solving behavior, and sibling relationship quality: The moderating role of sibling temperaments. *Child Development, 67,* 1289–1300.

Buss, A., & Plomin, R. (1984). *Temperament: Early developing personality traits.* Hillsdale, NJ: Erlbaum.

Caspi, A., Henry, B., McGee, R. O., Moffitt, T. E., & Silva, P. A. (1995). Temperamental origins of child and adolescent behavior problems: From age three to age fifteen. *Child Development, 66,* 55–68.

Caspi, A., Moffitt, T., Newman, D., & Silva, P. (1996). Behavioral observations at age 3 years predict adult psychiatric disorders. *Archives of General Psychiatry, 53,* 1033–1039.

Castro, F. G., Maddahian, E., Newcomb, M. D., & Bentler, P. M. (1987). A multivariate model of the determinants of cigarette smoking among adolescents. *Journal of Health and Social Behavior, 28,* 273–289.

Chaplin, W. F. (1991). The next generation of moderator research in personality psychology. *Journal of Personality, 59,* 143–178.

Chassin, L. A., Pillow, D. R., Curran, P. J., Molina, B., & Barrera, M. (1993). Relation of parental alcoholism to early adolescent substance use: A test of three mediating mechanisms. *Journal of Abnormal Psychology, 102,* 3–19.

Conger, R. D., Conger, K. J., Elder, G. H., Lorenz, F. O., Simons, R. L., & Whitbeck, L. B. (1992). A family process model of economic hardship and adjustment of early adolescent boys. *Child Development, 63,* 526–541.

Crockenberg, S. (1987). Predictors and correlates of anger toward and punitive control of toddlers by adolescent mothers. *Child Development, 58,* 964–975.

Curran, P. J., Stice, E., & Chassin, L. (1997). The relation between adolescent alcohol use and peer alcohol use: A longitudinal random coefficients model. *Journal of Consulting and Clinical Psychology, 65,* 130–140.

Donaldson, S. I., Graham, J. W., Piccinin, A. M., & Hansen, W. B. (1995). Resistance skills training and the onset of alcohol use. *Health Psychology, 14,* 291–300.

Duncan, T. E., Duncan, S. C., Strycker, L. A., Li, F., & Alpert, A. (1999). *An introduction to latent growth curve modeling*. Mahwah, NJ: Erlbaum.

Garmezy, N. (1993). Vulnerability and resilience. In D. C. Funder, R. D. Parke, C. Tomlinson-Keasey, & K. Widaman (Eds.), *Studying lives through time: Personality and development* (pp. 377–398). Washington, DC: American Psychological Association.

Giancola, P. R., Martin, C. S., Tarter, R. E., Pelham, W. E., & Moss, H. B. (1996). Executive cognitive functioning and aggressive behavior in preadolescent boys at risk for substance abuse. *Journal of Studies on Alcohol, 57*, 352–359.

Gibbons, F. X., & Gerrard, M. (1995). Predicting young adults' health risk behavior. *Journal of Personality and Social Psychology, 69*, 505–517.

Glantz, M. D., & Johnson, J. L. (Eds.). (1999). *Resilience and development: Positive life adaptations*. New York: Kluwer Academic/Plenum Press.

Goldsmith, H. H., Gottesman, I. I., & Lemery, K. S. (1997). Epigenetic approaches to developmental psychopathology. *Development and Psychopathology, 9*, 365–387.

Hagekull, B. (1989). Longitudinal stability of temperament within a behavioral style framework. In G. A. Kohnstamm, J. E. Bates, & M. K. Rothbart (Eds.), *Temperament in childhood* (pp. 283–297). New York: Wiley.

Hawkins, J. D., Catalano, R. F., & Miller, J. Y. (1992). Risk and protective factors for alcohol and other drug problems in adolescence and early adulthood. *Psychological Bulletin, 112*, 64–105.

Hawkins, J. D., Graham, J. W., Maguin, E., Abbott, R., Hill, K. G., & Catalano, R. F. (1997). Exploring the effects of age of alcohol use initiation and psychosocial risk factors on subsequent alcohol misuse. *Journal of Studies on Alcohol, 58*, 280–290.

Hays, R. D., Widaman, K. F., DiMatteo, M. R., & Stacy, A. W. (1987). Structural equation models of drug use. *Journal of Personality and Social Psychology, 52*, 134–144.

Henry, B., Caspi, A., Moffitt, T. E., & Silva, P. A. (1996). Temperamental and familial predictors of violent and nonviolent criminal convictions: From age 3 to age 18. *Developmental Psychology, 32*, 614–623.

Jaccard, J., & Wan, C. K. (1996). *LISREL approaches to interaction effects in multiple regression*. Thousand Oaks, CA: Sage.

Johnston, L. D., O'Malley, P. M., & Bachman, J. G. (1995). *National survey results on drug use from the Monitoring the Future study, 1975–1994: Vol. 1. Secondary school students*. Rockville, MD: National Institute on Drug Abuse.

Jöreskog, K. G., & Sörbom, D. (1996). *LISREL 8: User's guide*. Chicago: Scientific Software International.

Kandel, D., & Davies, M. (1992). Progression to regular marijuana involvement: Phenomenology and risk factors for near-daily use. In M. Glantz & R. Pickens (Eds.), *Vulnerability to drug abuse* (pp. 211–253). Washington, DC: American Psychological Association.

Kochanska, G. (1995). Children's temperament, mother's discipline, and security of attachment: Multiple pathways to emerging internalization. *Child Development, 66*, 597–615.

Luthar, S. S., Cicchetti, D., & Becker, B. (2000). The construct of resilience: A critical evaluation and guidelines for future work. *Child Development, 71*, 543–562.

Masse, L. C., & Tremblay, R. E. (1997). Behavior of boys in kindergarten and the onset of substance use during adolescence. *Archives of General Psychiatry, 54*, 62–68.

Maziade, M., Caron, C., Cote, R., Merette, C., Bernier, H., Laplante, B., Boutin, P., & Thivierge, J. (1990). Psychiatric status of adolescents who had extreme temperaments at age 7. *American Journal of Psychiatry, 147*, 1531–1536.

McClelland, G. H., & Judd, C. M. (1993). Statistical difficulties of detecting interactions and moderator effects. *Psychological Bulletin, 114*, 376–390.

Moffitt, T. E. (1993). The neuropsychology of conduct disorder. *Development and Psychopathology, 5*, 135–151.

Murray, D. M., & Perry, C. L. (1987). The measurement of substance use among adolescents. *Addictive Behaviors, 12*, 225–233.

Needle, R., Su, S., & Lavee, Y. (1989). A comparison of the empirical utility of three composite measures of adolescent drug involvement. *Addictive Behaviors, 14*, 429–441.

Newcomb, M. D. (1992). Understanding the multidimensional nature of drug use and abuse. In M. Glantz & R. Pickens (Eds.), *Vulnerability to drug abuse* (pp. 255–297). Washington, DC: American Psychological Association.

Newcomb, M. D., & Bentler, P. M. (1988). Impact of adolescent drug use and social support on problems of young adults. *Journal of Abnormal Psychology, 97*, 64–75.

Oetting, E. R., & Beauvais, F. (1990). Adolescent drug use: Findings of national and local surveys. *Journal of Consulting and Clinical Psychology, 58*, 385–394.

Patterson, G. R., DeBaryshe, B. D., & Ramsey, E. (1989). A developmental perspective on antisocial behavior. *American Psychologist, 44*, 329–335.

Pedlow, R., Sanson, A., Prior, M., & Oberklaid, F. (1993). Stability of maternally reported temperament from infancy to 8 years. *Developmental Psychology, 29*, 998–1007.

Pentz, M. A., Dwyer, J. H., MacKinnon, D., Flay, B., Hansen, W., Wang, E., & Johnson, C. A. (1989). A multi-community trial for primary prevention of adolescent drug abuse. *Journal of the American Medical Association, 261*, 3259–3266.

Plomin, R., & Daniels, D. (1984). The interaction between temperament and environment: Methodological considerations. *Merrill-Palmer Quarterly, 30*, 149–162.

Plomin, R., & Hershberger, S. (1991). Genotype–environment interaction. In T. D. Wachs & R. Plomin (Eds.), *Conceptualization and measurement of organism–environment interaction* (pp. 29–43). Washington, DC: American Psychological Association.

Pulkkinen, L., & Pitkanen, T. (1994). A prospective study of the precursors to problem drinking in young adulthood. *Journal of Studies on Alcohol, 55*, 578–587.

Quinton, D., Pickles, A., Maughan, B., & Rutter, M. (1993). Partners, peers, and pathways: Assortative pairing and continuities in conduct disorder. *Development and Psychopathology, 5,* 763–783.

Rigdon, E. E., Schumacker, R. E., & Wothke, W. (1998). A comparative review of interaction and nonlinear modeling. In R. E. Schumacker & G. A. Marcoulides (Eds.), *Interaction and nonlinear effects in structural equation modeling* (pp. 1–16). Mahwah, NJ: Erlbaum.

Robins, L. N., & Przybeck, T. R. (1985). Age of onset of drug use as a factor in drug and other disorders. In C. L. Jones & R. J. Battjes (Eds.), *Etiology of drug abuse* (pp. 178–192). Rockville, MD: National Institute on Drug Abuse.

Rothbart, M. K., & Ahadi, S. A. (1994). Temperament and the development of personality. *Journal of Abnormal Psychology, 103,* 55–66.

Rothbart, M. K., & Bates, J. E. (1998). Temperament. In W. Damon (Series Ed.) & N. Eisenberg (Vol. Ed.), *Handbook of child psychology: Vol. 3. Social, emotional, and personality development* (5th ed., pp. 105–176). New York: Wiley.

Rothbart, M. K., Derryberry, D., & Posner, M. J. (1994). A psychobiological approach to the development of temperament. In J. E. Bates & T. D. Wachs (Eds.), *Temperament: Individual differences at the interface of biology and behavior* (pp. 83–116). Washington, DC: American Psychological Association.

Rutter, M., Champion, L., Quinton, D., Maughan, B., & Pickles, A. (1995). Understanding individual differences in environmental risk exposure. In P. Moen, G. Elder, & K. Luscher (Eds.), *Examining lives in context: Perspectives on the ecology of human development* (pp. 61–93). Washington, DC: American Psychological Association.

Rutter, M., Dunn, J., Plomin, R., Simonoff, E., Pickles, A., Maughan, B., et al. (1997). Integrating nature and nurture: Implications of person–environment correlations and interactions for developmental psychopathology. *Development and Psychopathology, 9,* 335–364.

Scarr, S. (1992). Developmental theories for the 1990s: Development and individual differences. *Child Development, 63,* 1–19.

Scarr, S., & McCartney, K. (1983). How people make their own environments: A theory of genotype → environment effects. *Child Development, 54,* 424–435.

Sher, K. J., & Trull, T. (1994). Personality and disinhibitory psychopathology: Alcoholism and antisocial personality disorder. *Journal of Abnormal Psychology, 103,* 92–102.

Smith, J., & Prior, M. (1995). Temperament and stress resilience in school-age children: A within-families study. *Journal of the American Academy of Child and Adolescent Psychiatry, 34,* 168–179.

Stice, E., & Gonzales, N. (1998). Adolescent temperament moderates the relation of parenting to antisocial behavior. *Journal of Adolescent Research, 13,* 5–31.

Stoolmiller, M. (1995). Using latent growth models to study developmental processes. In J. Gottman (Ed.), *The analysis of change* (pp. 103–138). Mahwah, NJ: Erlbaum.

Tarter, R. E. (1988). Are there inherited behavioral traits that predispose to substance abuse? *Journal of Consulting and Clinical Psychology, 56*, 189–196.

Tarter, R. E., Alterman, A., & Edwards, K. (1985). Vulnerability to alcoholism in men: A behavior–genetic perspective. *Journal of Studies on Alcohol, 46*, 329–356.

Tarter, R. E., Moss, H. B., & Vanyukov, M. M. (1995). Behavior genetic perspective of alcoholism etiology. In H. Begleiter & B. Kissin (Eds.), *The genetics of alcoholism* (pp. 294–326). New York: Oxford University Press.

Tarter, R. E., & Vanyukov, M. (1994). Alcoholism as a developmental disorder. *Journal of Consulting and Clinical Psychology, 62*, 1096–1107.

Tschann, J. M., Kaiser, P., Chesney, M. A., Alkon, A., & Boyce, W. T. (1996). Resilience and vulnerability among preschool children: Family functioning, temperament, and behavior problems. *Journal of the American Academy of Child and Adolescent Psychiatry, 35*, 184–192.

U. S. Department of Commerce. (1992). *1990 Census of the population: General population characteristics (New York)*. Washington, DC: U.S. Government Printing Office.

Wachs, T. D. (1992). *The nature of nurture*. Newbury Park, CA: Sage.

Wachs, T. D., & Gandour, M. J. (1983). Temperament, environment and cognitive–intellectual development. *International Journal of Behavioral Development, 6*, 135–152.

Werner, E. E. (1986). Resilient offspring of alcoholics: A longitudinal study from birth to age 18. *Journal of Studies on Alcohol, 47*, 34–40.

Werner, E. E., & Smith, R. S. (1992). *Overcoming the odds: High risk children from birth to adulthood*. Ithaca, NY: Cornell University Press.

Willett, J. B., & Sayer, A. G. (1994). Using covariance structure analysis to detect correlates and predictors of change over time. *Psychological Bulletin, 116*, 363–381.

Wills, T. A., & Cleary, S. D. (1995). Stress-coping model for alcohol–tobacco interactions in adolescence. In J. Fertig & J. Allen (Eds.), *Alcohol and tobacco: From basic science to clinical practice* (pp. 107–128). Bethesda, MD: National Institute on Alcohol Abuse and Alcoholism.

Wills, T. A., & Cleary, S. D. (1996). How are social support effects mediated? A test for parental support and adolescent substance use. *Journal of Personality and Social Psychology, 71*, 937–952.

Wills, T. A., & Cleary, S. D. (1999). Peer and adolescent substance use among 6th–9th graders: Latent growth analyses of influence versus selection mechanisms. *Health Psychology, 18*, 453–463.

Wills, T. A., Cleary, S. D., & Shinar, O. (2002). Temperament dimensions and health behavior: A developmental model. In L. Hayman, J. R. Turner, & M. Mahon (Eds.), *Health and behavior in childhood and adolescence* (pp. 3–36). New York: Springer Publishing Company.

Wills, T. A., DuHamel, K., & Vaccaro, D. (1995). Activity and mood temperament as predictors of adolescent substance use. *Journal of Personality and Social Psychology, 68*, 901–916.

Wills, T. A., & Filer, M. (2001). Social networks and social support. In A. Baum, T. A. Revenson & J. E. Singer (Eds.), *Handbook of health psychology* (pp. 209–234). Mahwah, NJ: Erlbaum.

Wills, T. A., Gibbons, F. X., Gerrard, M., & Brody, G. (2000). Protection and vulnerability processes for early onset of substance use: A test among African American children. *Health Psychology, 19*, 253–263.

Wills, T. A., Mariani, J., & Filer, M. (1996). The role of family and peer relationships in adolescent substance use. In G. R. Pierce, B. R. Sarason, & I. G. Sarason (Eds.), *Handbook of social support and the family* (pp. 521–549). New York: Plenum Press.

Wills, T. A., McNamara, G., Vaccaro, D., & Hirky, A. E. (1996). Escalated substance use: A longitudinal grouping analysis. *Journal of Abnormal Psychology, 105*, 166–180.

Wills, T. A., Sandy, J. M., & Shinar, O. (1999). Cloninger's constructs related to substance use level and problems in late adolescence: A mediational model based on self-control and coping motives. *Experimental and Clinical Psychopharmacology, 7*, 122–134.

Wills, T. A., Sandy, J. M., Shinar, O., & Yaeger, A. (1999). Contributions of positive and negative affect to adolescent substance use: Test of a bidimensional model in a longitudinal study. *Psychology of Addictive Behaviors, 13*, 327–338.

Wills, T. A., Sandy, J. M., & Yaeger, A. (2000). Temperament and early onset of substance use: An epigenetic approach to risk and protection. *Journal of Personality, 68*, 1127–1152.

Wills, T. A., Vaccaro, D., & McNamara, G. (1992). The role of life events, family support, and competence in adolescent substance use: A test of vulnerability and protective factors. *American Journal of Community Psychology, 20*, 349–374.

Wills, T. A., Windle, M., & Cleary, S. D. (1998). Temperament and novelty-seeking in adolescent substance use: Convergence of dimensions of temperament with constructs from Cloninger's theory. *Journal of Personality and Social Psychology, 74*, 387–406.

Windle, M. (1991). Difficult temperament: Associations with substance use, family support, and problem behaviors. *Journal of Clinical Psychology, 47*, 310–315.

Windle, M. (1997). Alternative latent variable approaches to modeling change in adolescent alcohol involvement. In K. J. Bryant, M. Windle, & S. G. West (Eds.), *The science of prevention: Methodological advances from alcohol and substance abuse research* (pp. 43–78). Washington, DC: American Psychological Association.

Windle, M., & Lerner, R. M. (1986). The Revised Dimensions of Temperament Survey. *Journal of Adolescent Research, 1*, 213–229.

Zaparniuk, J., & Taylor, S. (1997). Impulsivity in children and adolescents. In C. D. Webster & M. A. Jackson (Eds.), *Impulsivity: Theory, assessment, and treatment* (pp. 158–179). New York: Guilford Press.

Zucker, R. A. (1994). Pathways to alcohol problems: A developmental account of the evidence for contextual contributions to risk. In R. A. Zucker, G. M. Boyd, & J. Howard (Eds.), *The development of alcohol problems* (pp. 255–289). Rockville, MD: National Institute on Alcohol Abuse and Alcoholism.

VI

SCREENING AND ASSESSMENT

13

TEST–RETEST RELIABILITY OF ALCOHOL MEASURES: IS THERE A DIFFERENCE BETWEEN INTERNET-BASED ASSESSMENT AND TRADITIONAL METHODS?

ELIZABETH T. MILLER, DAN J. NEAL, LISA J. ROBERTS, JOHN S. BAER, SALLY O. CRESSLER, JANE METRIK, AND G. ALAN MARLATT

The use of emergent Web-based computer technology offers an unprecedented opportunity to conduct cross-sectional and longitudinal research studies in a cost-efficient manner while increasing survey accessibility to study participants and providing a more accurate data collection alternative to researchers (Miller, 1997). Costs associated with traditional assessment methods, such as publishing and distributing paper surveys, mailing materials to and telephoning study participant reminders, and data collection and entry are eliminated. The estimated costs to develop, publish, and maintain Web-based surveys are significantly lower (Schmidt, 1997). In addition, the data retrieved from Web-based surveys are potentially more accurate and more complete, and they provide essentially clean data moments after the survey is completed. The Web may prove superior to paper because it potentially provides increased accessibility; capability for dynamic and interactive forms, which eliminate the

This research was supported by Grant AA05591 from the National Institute on Alcohol Abuse and Alcoholism, awarded to G. Alan Marlatt. We gratefully acknowledge the support and assistance of George Dittmeier, Sally Weatherford, Mary Larimer, Leah Era, Jill Carlsen, and Nina Mauritzen; manuscript review by Dan Kivlahan, Thad Leffingwell, and Aaron Turner; and editing by Jessica Cronce.

Reprinted from *Psychology of Addictive Behaviors, 16*, 56–63 (2002). Copyright 2002 by the American Psychological Association.

viewing of irrelevant questions; and customized feedback tailored to the content of the responses.

Given all of the aforementioned benefits of Web-based research, there are concomitant concerns about the reliability and validity of the data collected by means of this technology. Previous research indicates that the psychometric properties of computerized psychological assessments are not compromised (Skinner & Pakula, 1986) and that disclosure of high-risk sexual behaviors, HIV infection, and alcohol and tobacco misuse may in fact be enhanced (Gerbert et al., 1999; Turner et al., 1998). Web-based assessments of personality constructs do not appear to compromise the psychometric properties of the measures used (Buchanan & Smith, 1999; Pasveer & Ellard, 1998; Smith & Leigh, 1997). It is unfortunate that within the field of alcohol research there are limited data available on the psychometric properties of measures of rates of alcohol use, symptoms, and problems (Del Boca & Brown, 1996) and a "troubling omission" of test–retest reliability data for alcohol screening measures (Allen, Litten, Fertig, & Babor, 1997). For example, previous reports provide psychometric data regarding internal consistency of a commonly used measure of alcohol problems, the Alcohol Dependence Scale (ADS; Skinner & Allen, 1982), and a commonly used alcohol problem screen, the Alcohol Use Disorders Identification Test (AUDIT; Allen et al., 1997). However, to our knowledge there is no current published information on test–retest reliabilities for the AUDIT or the ADS. Neither are we aware of test–retest reliabilities for other frequently used measures, such as the Rutgers Alcohol Problem Index (RAPI; White & Labouvie, 1989), a problem screen for adolescents, or measures of stages of change (i.e., the University of Rhode Island Change Assessment [URICA]; Prochaska & DiClemente, 1986). Test–retest reliability data are available for measures of alcohol consumption (quantity: $r = .93$, frequency: $r = .87$, and peak: $r = .94$) with a 30-day interval between assessments (L. C. Sobell, Sobell, Leo, & Cancilla, 1988; M. B. Sobell, Sobell, Klajner, Pavan, & Basian, 1986). Virtually no data exist comparing the psychometric properties of established measures on the basis of means of administration: Web or paper and pencil.

Our primary goal was to compare traditional test administration methods (paper-based) with the use of innovative Web-based assessment techniques. A secondary benefit of the study was to provide reliability data for measures commonly used in research on alcohol use. We chose to study college students not only because of national concerns about the risks of heavy drinking on college campuses (Johnston, O'Malley, & Bachman, 1996) but also because college students present a range of drinking habits (from abstinence to heavy problem use) and a range of experience with the Web (from those who never use the Internet to those who use the Internet on a regular daily basis).

METHOD

Participants

The participants were 255 undergraduate students (aged 18 to 29) at a large West coast university recruited by means of on-campus newspaper advertisements and flyers. Members of the fraternity and sorority system and graduate students were excluded from the study because of potential conflict with other ongoing research projects. The average age of the sample was 20.9 years ($SD = 1.95$), with 25 individuals (10%) between the ages of 24 and 29. Participants were primarily female (64%), with a range of ethnic groups represented (60% Caucasian, 26% Asian/Pacific Islander, 4% Hispanic, 3% African American, and 7% Other). The majority of participants (62%) lived off campus; 26% lived on campus, 11% lived at home with family, and 1% indicated "other" living arrangements. This sample included a range of self-reported levels of alcohol use: light users (45%), moderate users (37%), heavy users (5%), abstainers (11%), and those who had never tried alcohol (3%). There were no significant differences in drinking rates as a function of any demographic variables. Regardless of drinking status, the median number of drinks consumed per week by all students was 2. Wechsler, Molnar, Davenport, and Baer (1999) similarly reported a median of 1.5 drinks per week among a representative national sample of college students.

The first 300 participants who returned a signed consent form were randomly assigned to one of three conditions: paper-based (P&P, $N = 100$), Web-based (Web, $N = 100$), or Web-based with interruption (Web-I, $N = 100$). We included the final condition to determine whether taking a break (for a minimum of 1 hour and a maximum of 48 hours) would affect the psychometric properties of the data. Having an interruption provided a proxy of real world interruptions (e.g., participant fatigue, lack of time to initiate or complete the survey) that may be common with self-paced and home-based assessments and may lower a test's reliability (Babor, 1996). A total of 280 participants (93% of those randomized) completed the assessment at Time 1 (P&P, $n = 94$; Web, $n = 93$; Web-I, $n = 93$), resulting in an attrition rate of 7% for the Time 1 assessment. At Time 2, 255 of the participants completed the assessment (P&P, $n = 88$; Web, $n = 83$; Web-I, $n = 84$), resulting in an overall attrition rate of 15% (P&P: 12%, Web: 17%, Web-I: 16%), $\chi^2(3, N = 280) = 0.165$, $p = .92$. Comparisons of demographic variables and drinking measures assessed at baseline made with analysis of variance (ANOVA) and chi-square procedures between participants with complete data and those lost to attrition at Time 2 revealed no significant differences in age, sex, ethnicity, residence, drinking rates (quantity and frequency), alcohol-related problems (RAPI scores), or alcohol dependence (AUDIT and ADS scores).

Assessment Format and Incentives

Participants were randomly assigned to one of three conditions (see following sections). Communication was conducted primarily through e-mail, although a telephone number was also provided in the event of problems or questions. E-mail reminders were sent out before each assessment along with instructions on how to access and complete the Web-based assessments for participants assigned to Web conditions and where to pick up and return the paper-and-pencil packet. The measures were identical in terms of questions and possible responses. The only difference between the P&P and Web conditions was the method of data collection. Participants completed Web-based assessments by accessing a designated secure Web site.[1] Participants received $15 payment for each completed assessment. Payments were mailed to all participants on the last day of each of the data collection periods.

P&P Condition

Participants ($N = 88$) picked up each of the Time 1 and Time 2 packets of paper-based self-report measures at the Addictive Behaviors Research Center (ABRC). On completion, at each time period, they deposited their completed packet in a secure drop box at the ABRC.

Web Condition

For the purpose of security and data integrity, participants ($N = 83$) were instructed to access a secure Web site for the study and enter a personal identification number composed of the student identification number and birth date. Internet or survey-related problems were addressed via e-mail and telephone. Participants who did not have access to the Internet ($n = 1$) were provided access to computers at the ABRC. Participants were also reminded that some of the departmental locations would be public, thus possibly minimizing privacy. On completion of the survey, participants were prompted to submit their data. On submission, the data were automatically entered into a tab-delimited format file and were no longer available to participants.

Web-I Condition

The Web-I condition was identical to the Web condition, with one exception: Participants ($n = 84$) were asked to take a break from their survey by quitting the browser at any point during the survey and reconnecting to the secure study Web site when they were ready to resume. Once

---

[1]Web-based data collection and management services for this project were provided by DatStat Inc.

logged back into the survey, participants automatically returned to the page, which they had bookmarked, where previously entered data were saved. The interruption period was not predetermined and could range from a minimum of 1 hour to a maximum of 48 hours. This experimental condition was included to test for the reliability of results with a break during the assessment procedure.

Measures

Measures assessed in this study included screening for hazardous use of alcohol, dependence, alcohol-related negative consequences, and measures of consumption (quantity, frequency, and peak). Motivation to change and stage of change were also assessed. All participants were assessed on two separate occasions during the same timeframe. Data collection was conducted over two 48-hour periods 1 week apart.

Demographics

Demographic information included age, sex, ethnicity, height, weight, and resident status. Weight was included in these analyses for purposes of estimating blood alcohol level.

Screening for Hazardous Alcohol Use

The AUDIT (Babor et al., 1992; Saunders, Aasland, Babor, de la Fuente, & Grant, 1993) is a measure used to identify individuals at risk for developing alcohol use disorders. It is a 10-item questionnaire related to dependence criteria.

Assessment of Alcohol Dependence

Participants also completed the ADS (Skinner & Allen, 1982), a widely used assessment of severity of physical dependence symptoms.

Alcohol-Related Problems

Participants completed the RAPI (White & Labouvie, 1989), which asks respondents to rate the frequency of occurrence of 23 items reflecting alcohol's impact on social and health functioning over the past 6 months. Sample items include "not able to work or study for a test," "caused shame or embarrassment," "was told by a friend or neighbor to stop or cut down on drinking."

Drinking Rates

We assessed drinking rates using three different measures of alcohol use at each assessment. Participants reported their typical drinking quantity, frequency, and the single greatest amount of alcohol consumption (peak consumption) over the past month. For the assessment of typical drinking quantity and most recent peak consumption, response options ranged from 0 to *15 or more drinks*. Participants also reported their average drinking quantity and peak consumption for each day of a "typical" week (Collins, Parks, & Marlatt, 1985). Response options and associated labels for the assessment of number of drinks ranged from 0 to *15 or more drinks*. To assess the number of hours over which the drinks were consumed, response options and associated labels ranged from *0 to 1 hr* (0) to *10 or more hr* (10). We used this to compute a weekly average of alcohol consumption. These quantity–frequency–peak indexes have been effective in documenting reductions in drinking in previous studies with college student drinkers (Baer, 1993; Kivlahan, Marlatt, Fromme, Coppel, & Williams, 1990; Marlatt, Baer, & Larimer, 1995).

Readiness to Change

We used a modified version of the URICA (Prochaska & DiClemente, 1986) to measure participants' increases in precontemplation, contemplation, action, and maintenance scores as well as readiness-to-change behavior. We adapted the URICA to reflect stages of change for alcohol use, rather than problem smoking, and shortened it to include only items relevant for college-age students, a 20-item version. Sample items include "As far as I'm concerned, my drinking does not need changing," "Sometimes I think I should cut down on my drinking," and "I have a problem with alcohol and I really think I should work on it."

Assessment Format Preferences

We measured assessment format *preferences* by comparing three self-report items: perceived accuracy of responses, convenience of assessment method, and future format preference. The accuracy of responses was captured in the single item "How accurate were your responses to this survey?" with response options ranging from 0%, *completely inaccurate* (0) to 100%, *completely accurate* (100) in 10% increments. The convenience-of-assessment-method item read "How convenient was it to complete this survey on paper/Web?" (depending on format). Response options included *not at all* (0), *slightly* (1), *moderately* (2), *very* (3), or *extremely* (4). We assessed future format preference with the following item: "In the future, how would you prefer to complete a survey?" Response options included *on the Web* (0), *on paper* (1), or *either way* (2).

RESULTS

Preliminary Analyses

We first compared assessment format groups with respect to demographic variables, including age, gender, ethnicity, residence, and level of alcohol use. No significant differences were observed. Next, with a series of one-way ANOVAs we examined mean differences in responses by assessment format at Time 1 and 1 week later, at Time 2 (see Table 13.1). Overall there were no significant mean differences among the three assessment groups on any measures of alcohol use at Time 1 or Time 2. It should be noted that, given our sample size, we had power of .80 to detect only moderate effect sizes (i.e., $F = 0.22$). However, given such power one would expect significant results for approximately one quarter of the tests at random, which was not the case. In addition, a multivariate analysis of variance of repeated measures over time revealed no significant patterns of change as a function of method of assessment, multivariate $F(30, 392) = 1.32$, $p = .12$, ns.

Of the Web and Web-I participants, 78 (47%) reported completing the Web-based survey at a campus computer cluster, 60 (36%) reported completing it at home, 14 (9%) said they completed it at work, 6 (4%) completed it at a friend's home, 3 (2%) completed it at a parent's home, and 3 (2%) completed it at another university. On average, participants in the Web-I condition took close to a 3-hour break ($M = 2.89$, $SD = 6.31$), with 9 participants extending the break beyond a 12-hour period.

Analytic Approach

Because of the heavily skewed distributions of our data, and the need to provide confidence intervals for tests of differences between reliability estimates, we adopted a bootstrap approach to test for differences in reliabilities among groups (Efron & Tibshirani, 1993). Bootstrapping is a nonparametric technique that involves repeatedly resampling with replacement from the data set to approximate the distribution function of the statistic. Unlike the Fisher R-to-Z method, which is a traditional approach to comparing independent correlation coefficients, bootstrapping assumes not that the underlying distribution of the data is bivariate normal but only that the empirical distribution is representative of the population. Confidence intervals constructed by means of a bootstrapping method are more likely, probabilistically speaking, to contain the more accurate parameter estimates as compared with the confidence intervals constructed by means of traditional normal-distribution based formulas. Using bootstrap analyses, we made pairwise comparisons between the P&P versus Web groups, the P&P versus Web-I groups, and the Web versus Web-I groups, for each of 16 measures. Therefore, a total of 48 comparisons were

TABLE 13.1
Means, Standard Deviations, and Significance by Group and Measure at Time 1 and Time 2

Measure	Paper and pencil				Web				Web-interrupted					
	Time 1		Time 2		Time 1		Time 2		Time 1		Time 2		F(2)	p
	M	SD	M	SD	M	SD	M	SD	M	SD	M	SD		
ADS	7.2	-4.8	6.7	4.3	6.3	3.8	5.5	3.6	7.3	5.3	6.5	5.2	1.03	.36
AUDIT														
Total	4.4	3.4	4.5	3.3	4.6	3.6	4.2	3.2	4.8	3.7	4.6	3.8	0.18	.83
Q–F	3.4	2.0	3.3	2.0	3.3	2.3	3.2	2.1	3.1	1.8	3.0	1.8	0.33	.72
Dependence	0.3	0.6	0.4	0.7	0.4	0.7	0.4	0.9	0.6	0.9	0.6	1.0	2.49	.09
Problems	0.8	1.3	0.8	1.2	0.8	1.3	0.8	1.1	1.1	1.6	1.0	1.5	1.23	.29
RAPI														
1 month	1.5	2.9	1.4	2.8	1.6	2.8	1.4	2.7	1.5	5.4	1.7	4.9	0.01	.99
6 month	4.1	5.4	4.2	5.1	3.9	6.2	3.8	5.3	3.9	9.3	4.2	8.6	0.02	.98
1 year	7.8	8.8	6.9	7.1	6.2	8.4	5.5	7.2	7.7	11.3	7.3	11.2	0.69	.50
URICA														
Readiness	-3.4	1.6	-3.7	1.6	-3.3	2.2	-3.7	2.0	-3.0	1.7	-3.1	1.9	0.73	.48
Precontemplation	-2.2	2.9	-1.3	2.8	-1.7	3.0	-1.2	2.7	-1.6	2.5	-1.3	2.7	1.26	.29
Contemplation	-5.2	3.5	-5.2	3.8	-4.9	3.8	-5.3	3.8	-4.3	3.6	-4.4	3.8	0.95	.39
Action	-7.1	3.2	-7.4	3.0	-7.0	3.6	-7.3	3.3	-6.2	3.8	-6.4	3.7	1.40	.25
Maintenance	-7.0	2.8	-7.1	3.1	-6.6	3.6	-7.2	3.3	-6.3	3.2	-6.6	3.1	0.72	.49
Peak quant.	3.9	3.4	4.1	3.4	3.7	3.2	3.1	3.1	3.9	3.0	3.7	2.5	0.05	.96
Peak BAL	.079	.77	.078	.074	.067	.063	.064	.056	.083	.08	.075	.068	1.04	.36
Weekly avg. quant.	0.43	0.64	0.54	0.74	0.64	0.83	0.63	0.77	0.59	0.77	0.66	0.87	1.64	.20

Note. N = 255. There were no significant differences among groups on any measure at the .05 level. ADS = Alcohol Dependence Scale; AUDIT = Alcohol Use Disorders Identification Test; Q–F = Quantity–Frequency; RAPI = Rutgers Alcohol Problem Index; URICA = University of Rhode Island Change Assessment; Peak quant. = peak quantity of alcohol consumption; Peak BAL = peak blood alcohol level; Weekly avg. quant. = average weekly alcohol consumption.

made. For each correlation coefficient we created 1,000 bootstrap samples, yielding 1,000 estimates for the parameter. We then estimated means and standard errors for each group. We then applied a two-sample Z test using the means and standard errors from the bootstrap replications.

Test–Retest Reliability

We assessed in two ways the overall test–retest reliabilities for all the measures, collapsed across groups: Pearson's product–moment correlation coefficients and intraclass correlations. The intraclass correlation coefficient, which measures agreement, is a more stringent assessment of test–retest reliability than Pearson's r, which measures association (Cicchetti, 1994). According to the guidelines described by Cicchetti (1994), when the reliability is below .70, the level of clinical significance is unacceptable; when it is between .70 and .79, it is fair; when it is between .80 and .89, it is good; and when it is .90 or above it is excellent. Table 13.2 shows Pearson's reliability coefficients and the intraclass correlation coefficients for the test and retest ratings of each of the alcohol measures with their associated subscales when appropriate. The test–retest reliabilities ranged from .59 to .93. All of the correlation coefficients observed were significant at the .01 level (two-tailed). Thus, these measures have sufficient reliability for both scientific research and clinical applications.

With the bootstrap technique, only 3 significant differences out of 48 comparisons emerged when group comparisons were conducted with alpha set at .05. On the AUDIT Quantity–Frequency subscale, there were significant differences between the P&P and Web groups ($z = 2.22, p = .03$) and the Web and Web-I groups ($z = 2.35, p = .02$). On the AUDIT Dependence subscale there was a significant difference between the Web and Web-I groups ($z = 2.04, p = .04$). As shown in Table 13.2, when alpha is relaxed to .10 and .25, 5 and 12 significant differences emerge, respectively.

Given the large number of analyses needed to compare each measure between each group and the alpha used in the tests, it is not unrealistic to expect to find statistically significant results; in fact, it would be more surprising if there had been no statistically significant differences. The problem arises from an overinflated simultaneous error rate. The more tests that are run, the more likely it becomes to find a significant result even when the null hypothesis is true (cf. Moore & McCabe, 1993). Given that at each level of significance the percentage of "significant" tests is approximately equal to alpha, we interpreted these significant results as simple random deviations that could occur in probability testing. This conclusion is further strengthened by the fact that the pattern of "significant" effects appears to be random; if small effect sizes were present, one would expect that the pattern of results would at least partially indicate that one condition is showing higher test–retest reliabilities compared with the other two conditions.

TABLE 13.2
Pearson Product–Moment and Intraclass Correlation (ICC) Test–Retest Reliabilities

	Group						Significance testing (z)			Overall	
	P&P		Web		Web-I						
Measure	Pearson's r	95% CI	Pearson's r	95% CI	Pearson's r	95% CI	P&P/Web	P&P/Web-I	Web/Web-I	Pearson's r	ICC
ADS	.88	.80, .93	.84	.74, .91	.93	.82, .97	0.57	−0.93	−1.31*	.90	.89
AUDIT											
Total	.92	.86, .96	.92	.85, .96	.95	.91, .97	−0.03	−0.92	−0.83	.93	.93
Q–F	.90	.83, .95	.96	.93, .98	.90	.83, .94	−2.22***	0.10	2.35***	.92	.92
Dependence	.55	.33, .75	.41	.24, .62	.81	.51, .92	0.82	−1.40*	−2.04***	.64	.63
Problems	.88	.74, .94	.84	.75, .92	.92	.77, .97	0.34	−0.55	−0.89	.89	.89
RAPI											
1 month	.83	.57, .93	.78	.61, .88	.94	.27, .99	0.38	−0.50	−0.71	.89	.89
6 month	.86	.71, .93	.89	.79, .94	.96	.79, .99	−0.56	−1.33*	−1.03	.92	.92
1 year	.88	.79, .93	.88	.79, .94	.96	.89, .98	−0.06	−1.85**	−1.82**	.92	.91
URICA											
Readiness	.76	.58, .89	.85	.74, .92	.87	.77, .93	−1.03	−1.40*	−0.36	.83	.83
Precontemplation	.65	.52, .76	.54	.37, .68	.64	.48, .75	1.08	0.17	−0.88	.60	.59
Contemplation	.72	.57, .83	.84	.72, .92	.81	.70, .89	−1.47*	−1.11	0.50	.79	.79
Action	.72	.53, .85	.76	.57, .87	.84	.72, .92	−0.26	−1.29*	−1.04	.78	.77
Maintenance	.65	.45, .79	.78	.63, .87	.70	.59, .80	−1.19*	−0.54	0.84	.71	.71
Peak quant.	.89	.81, .94	.88	.77, .94	.85	.71, .94	0.20	0.53	0.31	.87	.87
Peak BAL	.89	.82, .94	.83	.73, .90	.85	.70, .94	1.13	0.46	0.39	.86	.86
Weekly avg. quant.	.86	.63, .95	.93	.86, .96	.93	.79, .98	−0.98	−0.82	0.00	.90	.90

Note. N = 255. P&P = paper and pencil; Web-I = Web-interrupted; CI = confidence interval; ADS = Alcohol Dependence Scale; AUDIT = Alcohol Use Disorders Identification Test; Q–F = Quantity–Frequency; RAPI = Rutgers Alcohol Problem Index; URICA = University of Rhode Island Change Assessment; Peak quant. = peak quantity of alcohol consumption; Peak BAL = peak blood alcohol level; Weekly avg. quant. = average weekly alcohol consumption.
* p < .05. ** p < .01. *** p < .001.

Validity

An examination of all pairwise correlations across three groups was prohibitively large for bootstrap analyses. We used two techniques to test issues of validity across experimental conditions: Box's M test (Box, 1949) and comparison of a subset of correlations between variables. Box's M test is a test of the equality of covariance matrices. Box's M was computed on the covariance matrices of the three groups, and each covariance matrix included both the Time 1 and Time 2 total scores for each measure (i.e., each matrix included the ADS; AUDIT; RAPI 1 month, 6 months, and 1 year; URICA; peak quantity, peak blood alcohol concentration) and average quantity at Time 1 and Time 2. (To simplify analyses, subscales were not included.) Box's M test indicated significant differences among the three covariance matrices, $M = 721.6$, $F(342, 50390) = 1.74$, $p < .001$.

We examined validity by comparing selected correlations across groups. First, we chose three measures to reduce the overall number of tests conducted and therefore reduce the probability of Type I errors. We used the three measures of average quantity/week, ADS, and AUDIT, because they best represent standard measures of alcohol-related use, abuse, and negative consequences. The intercorrelations for each group were calculated (i.e., for average quantity and ADS, average quantity and AUDIT, and ADS and AUDIT we calculated three correlation coefficients for every assessment method: P&P, Web, and Web-I) for both assessment periods and are presented in Table 13.3.

Next, we made a series of pairwise comparisons of the intercorrelations. We again computed standard errors for the intercorrelations using bootstrap estimates with 1,000 replications. For each group, pairwise comparisons were made against the other two groups for each correlation between the same measures, leading to three significance tests (P&P vs. Web, P&P vs. Web-I, and Web vs. Web-I) at each assessment for each pair of measures. We computed a total of 18 comparisons. At the .05 level, there were no significant differences in any of the intercorrelations at either assessment period; there were two significant differences when alpha was relaxed to .10. The results of these analyses, and the confidence intervals for the intercorrelations, are presented in Table 13.3.

Thus, although Box's M indicates some significant differences among the covariance matrices of the three groups, few differences were found with inspection. Box's M could also be inflated on the basis of the non-normality of the variables that were selected for the analyses. In either case, the magnitude of the Box's M is quite small, suggesting that differences in validity across experimental conditions, if replicable, are likely small. Our selective examination of pairwise correlations suggests possible differences in the relationship between drinking quantity and ADS scores based on methods of

TABLE 13.3
Intercorrelations of Measures by Group at Time 1 and Time 2

Measure	Time 1 Paper and pencil		Time 1 Web		Time 1 Web-interrupted		Time 2 Paper and pencil		Time 2 Web		Time 2 Web-interrupted	
	r	95% CI	r	95% CI	r	95% CI	r	95% CI	r	95% CI	r	95% CI
Avg./ADS	.38$_a$	.17, .61	.56	.40, .70	.73$_a$	.47, .88	.57	.35, .72	.45$_b$	.21, .62	.76$_b$	.47, .89
Avg./AUDIT	.67	.44, .84	.82	.73, .88	.86	.67, .93	.83	.71, .91	.78	.71, .90	.82	.56, .91
ADS/AUDIT	.74	.65, .83	.63	.43, .80	.77	.59, .89	.78	.66, .86	.70	.55, .82	.82	.64, .91

Note. $N = 255$. Correlations in rows within time periods with the same subscripts are significantly different from each other at $p < .10$. CI = confidence interval; Avg. = average weekly alcohol consumption; ADS = Alcohol Dependence Scale; AUDIT = Alcohol Use Disorders Identification Test.

administration ($p < .10$), although patterns of differences were not consistent when examined at Time 1 and Time 2.

Subjective Convenience and Preferences

We conducted analyses to test for differences among subjective ratings of accuracy, convenience, and assessment format preference between participants completing Web-based versus paper-based assessments. An ANOVA revealed no significant differences between self-reported accuracy of response reporting, $F(2, 250) = 1.64$, $p = .20$, ns. Highly significant differences were detected among groups in terms of convenience of use, with 26% of P&P participants reporting survey completion as being "slightly" to "not at all" convenient, compared with only 7% of Web and 7% of Web-I participants, whereas more than 80% of Web and 80% of the Web-I participants reported that completing the Web survey was "very" to "extremely" convenient, compared with only 56% of the P&P participants, $F(2, 207) = 13.42$, $p < .001$.

Significant differences were also found among groups in terms of assessment preference in the event of a future survey. More than 40% of P&P participants indicated a preference to complete a Web survey, and 63% of Web and 55% of Web-I participants indicated a preference for the same method. Only 16% of the P&P participants said they would rather complete another paper survey, and close to 40% reported no preference. Moreover, only 6% of Web and 2% of Web-I participants reported a preference for a paper compared with a Web survey, and slightly more than 30% reported no preference, $F(2, 250) = 12.79$, $p < .001$.

DISCUSSION

In this study we compared Web-based assessment techniques with traditional paper-based methods and obtained test–retest reliabilities of measures commonly used in research on alcohol use. Our results provide evidence for the test–retest reliability of the total scores for the ADS, AUDIT, RAPI, URICA, and quantity–frequency items for research and clinical applications. However, we caution against reliance on the AUDIT Dependence subscales and the URICA subscales.

Our data generally demonstrate that completing a survey on the Web did not result in moderate to large differences in response sets of participants compared with those of participants who completed a paper survey. No significant differences were found between assessment techniques on test–retest reliability, suggesting that Web-based modes of data collection do not compromise the integrity of the data and are a suitable alternative to more traditional methods. Our data, as currently analyzed, appear encouraging yet equivocal with respect to differences in validity of scales as a result of method of test administration. Some differences likely exist, although they appear small. We found that allowing breaks during a lengthy Web-based assessment battery did not compromise the reliability or validity of the measures. Students preferred the Web-based assessment to the paper-and-pencil assessment.

It should also be noted that although we failed to find many significant differences, this could be a function of our analytic technique. Because of the non-normality inherent in the type of data we collected, we chose to use a bootstrapping method that does not rely on any assumptions regarding the marginal or joint distributions of the data. A different approach (i.e., Fisher's r to Z), which requires an assumption of bivariate normality, produces some significant differences between the paper-and-pencil and Web-interrupted versions in the intercorrelations between weekly quantity and other measures.[2] We believe, however, that in this case the bootstrapped standard errors do yield results that are more accurate with regard to the variability of the estimates of reliability and intercorrelation.

With regard to the analyses reported here, it should be noted further that the power to detect small differences was relatively poor. For example, with our ANOVAs, although the power to detect medium to large effects was quite adequate (for medium $F = 0.25$, power = .95, and large $F = 0.4$, power = .99), for quite small ($F = 0.10$) effect sizes, the corresponding power estimate was only .28. Thus, it is ultimately impossible to determine whether the non-significant differences observed herein were a result of a true null hypothesis or a lack of statistical power. Yet, given the results reported, it is also reasonable to conclude that if group differences existed that were in fact different from zero, they would be very small. As previously noted, the lack of significant findings beyond what would be expected by chance provides further support for the null hypothesis. The testing of differences in validity among many measures posed additional challenges. Our analyses suggest that some small differences are likely as a function of assessment method, yet we do not have more specific clues for which among many intercorrelations are most affected. It is possible, of course, that we simply did not select variables where differences exist. Studies with larger samples with greater power might detect differences not observed herein.

Most participants (80%) found the Web-based survey very convenient to use, and only 8% indicated a preference to use a paper-based survey in the future, if given a choice. Because participants were randomly assigned to conditions, and thus required to complete the survey on the Web (regardless of previous Internet experience), they were obliged to learn how to access the Internet for purposes other than e-mail. If study participants had been given

[2]At Time 1, differences between P&P and Web-I were evident between weekly quantity and ADS ($z = 3.10$) and weekly quantity and AUDIT ($z = 2.93$). At Time 2, differences between P&P and Web-I were evident between weekly quantity and ADS ($z = 2.01$).

the option to complete the survey on the Web or on paper, these results may have been different. Anecdotal evidence, including open-ended survey comment sections, suggests that this opportunity increased some participants' sense of empowerment in their general use of the Internet and increased the likelihood of future Internet use for coursework and other activities. Previous Web-based assessment studies suggest that students with no previous Internet experience are willing and able to successfully complete a Web-based assessment (e.g., Miller, 2000).

Unlike Gerbert et al. (1999) and Turner et al. (1998), who found that technologically advanced assessment methods (audio, computer, and video) produced higher rates of risk disclosure, our participants' responses did not differ with more advanced technology. Our findings suggest that Web-based data collection does not statistically enhance or diminish the consistency of responses. Moreover, our results address concerns about the impact of computerization on the psychometric properties of instruments raised by Skinner and Pakula (1986). Given the findings from this study, the application of these Web-based assessment measures offers advantages to both researchers and study participants without compromising the reliability of the results drawn from the data. Using the Internet for data collection is a cost-efficient alternative to traditional techniques and has the potential to minimize data collection and entry errors while increasing accessibility.

This study had several limitations related to the use of a primarily computer literate non-high-risk drinking college student sample. Because the measures tested in this study are frequently used as outcome markers in prevention effectiveness trials—which, by their very nature, include participants with varied levels of use—we chose to cast a broad net and not limit the sample to high-risk users. An additional important question not investigated in this study was whether high-risk students, those frequently targeted for prevention and treatment research, are likely to differ with respect to computer literacy and access. It is unclear whether high-risk populations are likely to differ from this sample with respect to accessibility to, literacy regarding, and comfort with computers. The limited research on this topic suggests there are no significant differences and in fact suggests that there are benefits associated with the use of a computer when questions of a sensitive nature are asked, including a sense of privacy, cost efficiency, and the application of skip patterns (Gerbert et al., 1999; Turner et al., 1998). Finally, the perceived convenience of assessment format may have been affected in both conditions by unfamiliar procedures. Web participants who were inexperienced with the Internet were obliged to learn how to access the Web-based survey, and the P&P participants were required to pick up and deliver their paper-based surveys to a specific location on campus or complete them on site. Although returning a paper-based survey by mail is typically experienced as inconvenient, the additional physical requirements for pickup and delivery or on-site completion may have lowered the perceived convenience for the paper-and-pencil format.

Additional studies thus should be conducted with different samples—in particular, adult samples and clinical populations—to determine whether significant differences exist between both the method of data collection as well as the reliability and validity of responses. Furthermore, although Web-based assessment may be a cost-effective alternative and offer increased accessibility to researchers and participants, conducting Web-based data collection may not be a practical option for every population because of limited economic resources (i.e., access) and physical or mental–cognitive impairments. It is important that the practical and technical considerations, such as Internet accessibility, computer literacy of participants, validity of responses, multiple submissions, security and data integrity violations, browser incompatibility, and modem speed be addressed prior to the initiation of a Web-based project. Furthermore, confidentiality of participants and participant responses is an important issue and not unique to Web-based assessment techniques. We obviated these obstacles by using a Web-based research consulting service provider (see footnote 1). We did not ask participants how private or not private the environment in which they completed their surveys was; however, this may be an important variable and should be included in future Web-based research. To our knowledge, no studies have examined the effect of private versus nonprivate settings on Web-based assessment item response.

The questions explored in this research study were of a nature such that we tried to support, as opposed to reject, the null hypothesis. Yet our statistical techniques were designed to measure differences, not similarities. With the more conservative bootstrap estimates, we observed only three statistically significant results over 48 tests when testing reliability estimates and only four statistically significant results over 80 tests when testing reliability and validity estimates, which does not rise above what one would expect on the basis of chance alone. In our case, increasing alpha increased our power to detect significant differences but revealed a number of differences consistent with increased Type I error. A better approach is to increase sample size in repeated studies. Nevertheless, it is with caution that we conclude that there are no significant differences in method of assessment of the aforementioned measures. We may lack power to detect all possible effects, and we may not have measured all domains where differences could exist. Although the heavily skewed distributions of our data were unexpected, this fact was not surprising given our population. In fact, the nature of high-risk user populations suggests that the data will be skewed, and therefore reliable analytic techniques should be addressed with this fact in mind.

Repeated studies of Web-based assessment techniques with various populations and divergent topics over time are highly recommended in order to fully understand whether these findings are a true representation of a lack of differences in assessment technique or response sets. It is our hope that researchers will continue to keep pace with technology by conducting these comparative studies in parallel with increased use of maximizing the benefits that Web-based data collection offers.

REFERENCES

Allen, J. P., Litten, R. Z., Fertig, J. B., & Babor, T. (1997). A review of research on the Alcohol Use Disorders Identification Test (AUDIT). *Alcoholism: Clinical and Experimental Research, 21*, 613–619.

Babor, T. F. (1996). Reliability of the Ethanol Dependence Syndrome Scale. *Psychology of Addictive Behaviors, 10*, 97–103.

Babor, T. F., Hofmann, M., Del Boca, F. K., Hesselbrock, V., Meyer, R. E., Dolinsky, Z. S., & Rounsaville, B. (1992). Types of alcoholics: I. Evidence for an empirically derived typology based on indicators of vulnerability and severity. *Archives of General Psychiatry, 49*, 599–608.

Baer, J. S. (1993). Etiology and secondary prevention of alcohol problems with young adults. In J. S. Baer, G. A. Marlatt, & R. J. McMahon (Eds.), *Addictive behaviors across the life span: Prevention, treatment, and policy issues* (pp. 111–137). Newbury Park, CA: Sage.

Box, G. E. P. (1949). A general distribution theory for a class of likelihood criteria. *Biometrika, 36*, 317–346.

Buchanan, T., & Smith, J. L. (1999). Using the Internet for psychological research: Personality testing on the World Wide Web. *British Journal of Psychology, 90*, 125–144.

Cicchetti, D. V. (1994). Guidelines, criteria and rules of thumb for evaluating normed and standardized assessment instruments in psychology. *Psychological Assessment, 6*, 284–290.

Collins, R. L., Parks, G. A., & Marlatt, G. A. (1985). Social determinants of alcohol consumption: The effects of social interaction and model status on the self-administration of alcohol. *Journal of Consulting and Clinical Psychology, 53*, 189–200.

Del Boca, F. K., & Brown, J. M. (1996). Issues in the development of reliable measures in addictions research: Introduction to Project MATCH assessment strategies. *Psychology of Addictive Behaviors, 10*, 67–74.

Efron, B., & Tibshirani, R. J. (1993). *An introduction to the bootstrap.* London: Chapman & Hall.

Gerbert, B., Bronstone, A., Pantilat, S., McPhee, S., Allerton, M., & Moe, J. (1999). When asked, patients tell: Disclosure of sensitive health-risk behaviors. *Medical Care, 37*, 104–111.

Johnston, L. D., O'Malley, P. M., & Bachman, J. G. (1996). *National survey results on drug use from the Monitoring the Future Study, 1975–1994: Vol. 2. College students and young adults.* Rockville, MD: U.S. Department of Health and Human Services, Public Health Service, National Institutes of Health.

Kivlahan, D. R., Marlatt, G. A., Fromme, K., Coppel, D. B., & Williams, E. (1990). Secondary prevention with college drinkers: Evaluation of an alcohol skills training program. *Journal of Consulting and Clinical Psychology, 58,* 805–810.

Marlatt, G. A., Baer, J. S., & Larimer, M. E. (1995). Preventing alcohol abuse in college students: A harm-reduction approach. In G. Boyd, J. Howard, & R. Zucker (Eds.), *Alcohol problems among adolescents: Current directions in prevention research* (pp. 147–172). Hillsdale, NJ: Erlbaum.

Miller, E. T. (1997). *Predicting successful self-initiated health-related behavior change in the context of New Year's resolutions: Utilizing the Internet for survey research.* Unpublished master's thesis, University of Washington.

Miller, E. T. (2000). Preventing alcohol abuse and alcohol-related negative consequences among freshmen college students: Using emerging computer technology to deliver and evaluate the effectiveness of brief intervention efforts (Doctoral dissertation, University of Washington, 2000). *Dissertation Abstracts International, 61,* 8.

Moore, D. S., & McCabe, G. P. (1993). *Introduction to the practice of statistics* (2nd ed.). New York: Freeman.

Pasveer, K. A., & Ellard, J. H. (1998). The making of a personality inventory: Help from the WWW. *Behavior Research Methods, Instruments, & Computers, 30,* 309–313.

Prochaska, J. O., & DiClemente, C. C. (1986). Toward a comprehensive model of change. In W. R. Miller & N. Heather (Eds.), *Treating addictive behaviors: Processes of change. Applied clinical psychology* (pp. 3–27). New York: Plenum Press.

Saunders, J. B., Aasland, O. G., Babor, T. F., de la Fuente, J. R., & Grant, M. (1993). Development of the Alcohol Use Disorders Identification Test (AUDIT): WHO collaborative project on early detection of persons with harmful alcohol consumption: II. *Addiction, 88,* 791–804.

Schmidt, W. C. (1997). World-Wide Web survey research: Benefits, potential problems, and solutions. *Behavior Research Methods, Instruments and Computers, 29,* 274–279.

Skinner, H. A., & Allen, B. A. (1982). Alcohol dependence syndrome: Measurement and validation. *Journal of Abnormal Psychology, 91,* 199–209.

Skinner, H. A., & Pakula, A. (1986). Challenge of computers in psychological assessment. *Professional Psychology: Research and Practice, 17,* 44–50.

Smith, M. A., & Leigh, B. (1997). Virtual subjects: Using the Internet as an alternative source of subjects and research environment. *Behavior Research Methods, Instruments, and Computers, 29,* 496–505.

Sobell, L. C., Sobell, M. B., Leo, G. I., & Cancilla, A. (1988). Reliability of a timeline method: Assessing normal drinkers' reports of recent drinking and a comparative evaluation across several populations. *British Journal of Addiction, 83,* 393–402.

Sobell, M. B., Sobell, L. C., Klajner, F., Pavan, D., & Basian, E. (1986). The reliability of a timeline method for assessing normal drinker college students' recent drinking history: Utility for alcohol research. *Addictive Behaviors, 11*, 149–161.

Turner, C. F., Ku, L., Rogers, S. M., Lindberg, L. D., Pleck, J. H., & Sonenstein, F. L. (1998, May 8). Adolescent sexual behavior, drug use, and violence: Increased reporting with computer survey technology. *Science, 280*, 867–873.

Wechsler, H., Molnar, B. E., Davenport, A. E., & Baer, J. S. (1999). College alcohol use: A full or empty glass? *Journal of American College Health, 47*, 247–252.

White, H. R., & Labouvie, E. W. (1989). Toward the assessment of adolescent problem drinking. *Journal of Studies on Alcohol, 50*, 30–37.

14

THE NEUROPSYCHOLOGICAL TEST PERFORMANCE OF DRUG-ABUSING PATIENTS: AN EXAMINATION OF LATENT COGNITIVE ABILITIES AND ASSOCIATED RISK FACTORS

WILLIAM FALS-STEWART AND MARSHA E. BATES

There is now ample evidence from multiple lines of research that chronic ingestion of alcohol and other psychoactive substances is associated with neuroanatomical changes that appear to give rise to discernable cognitive impairments. Among different populations of patients with long-term histories of substance dependence, particularly chronic alcohol misuse, neuroimaging techniques typically reveal general cortical shrinkage (e.g., Pfefferbaum et al., 1993), enlarged ventricles (e.g., Wang et al., 1992), increased space between the gyri of the cerebral cortex (Lilliquist & Bigler, 1992), and reduced glucose utilization (Volkow et al., 1994).

Changes in neurobehavioral performance are also evident on neuropsychological tests. For instance, aside from permanent neurological damage in the subset of alcohol-dependent patients who develop Korsakoff's syndrome or alcoholic dementia, there is a general profile of cognitive impairment observed among individuals with extended histories of alcohol dependence.

This study was supported by Grants P50 AA 08747 and AA 11594 from the National Institute of Alcohol Abuse and Alcoholism; Grants DA/AA 03395, DA12189, and DA14402 from the National Institute on Drug Abuse; and a grant from the Alpha Foundation.

Typically, such individuals have relatively preserved vocabulary and verbal learning skills but have measurable deficits on tests of verbal problem solving, conceptual shifting, perceptual–spatial and abstracting abilities, motor speed, information-processing speed, and memory (Errico, Parsons, & King, 1991; Grant, 1987).

Research examining the cognitive functioning of patients who abuse psychoactive substances other than alcohol has thus far been less developed and has reached fewer definitive conclusions. However, many of the available neuropsychological studies have found cognitive decrements among detoxified patients who have histories of abusing cocaine (O'Malley, Adamse, Heaton, & Gawin, 1992), sedative-hypnotics (Bergman, Borg, Engelbrecktson, & Vikander, 1989), and solvents (Allison & Jerrom, 1984); polysubstance-abusing patients also display neurocognitive deficits (Grant et al., 1978; Grant & Judd, 1976). Although estimates of the prevalence of mild to moderate neuropsychological impairment vary depending on the neuropsychological tests administered, performance criteria against which the presence of the impairment is determined, and the sample that is evaluated, findings from several different investigations suggest that between one third and three fourths of individuals who chronically abuse alcohol or other drugs have measurable cognitive deficits (e.g., Bates & Convit, 1999; Rourke & Loberg, 1996).

RISK FACTORS ASSOCIATED WITH IMPAIRED COGNITIVE PERFORMANCE IN SUBSTANCE-ABUSING PATIENTS

The etiology of these neuropsychological decrements remains a source of considerable debate. A significant body of research indicates that ethanol and other psychoactive drugs are neurotoxic to structures that are associated with cognitive performance (e.g., Freund, 1982; Lilliquist & Bigler, 1992). In turn, some investigators have found that quantity and frequency of alcohol use (Schaeffer & Parsons, 1986) and other drug abuse (Freitas & Fals-Stewart, 1999) are associated with neuropsychological test performance (Schaeffer & Parsons, 1986). Age of onset of heavy alcohol use may also be predictive of performance on cognitive tests, with those who begin at an early age showing more deficits (Portnoff, 1982). A pattern of prolonged polydrug abuse also appears to be associated with impaired cognitive performance (Lilliquist & Bigler, 1992).

However, many investigators have contended that other factors may also contribute to the deficits observed in substance-abusing patients, including (a) sociodemographic characteristics, (b) psychiatric functioning, (c) physical health, (d) family history of alcoholism, and (e) premorbid cognitive functioning. For example, several studies suggest that compared with their younger counterparts, older substance-abusing patients do not perform as well on neuropsychological tests (e.g., Eckardt, Stapleton, Rawlings, Davis, &

Grodin, 1995). Grant, Adams, and Reed (1984) found that alcoholics with lower levels of education were more often impaired than those patients with higher levels of education.

In terms of psychiatric comorbidity, affective dysfunction, particularly elevated levels of depression and anxiety, appears to be negatively related to neuropsychological test performance (e.g., Sinha, Parsons, & Glenn, 1989). In addition, some studies have found that alcoholic patients diagnosed with antisocial personality disorder (ASPD) perform worse on neuropsychological tests than patients who do not have this disorder (e.g., Malloy, Noel, Rogers, Longabaugh, & Beattie, 1989); however, other studies have not found this particular link (e.g., Sutker & Allain, 1987).

Physical functioning also appears to be related to cognitive functioning among substance-abusing patients. For example, hepatic dysfunction, as measured by high levels of gamma-glutamine transferase (GGT), may be negatively related to cognitive performance (Irwin et al., 1989). In addition, an increased number of head injuries, particularly those marked by loss of consciousness and posttraumatic amnesia, is associated with poorer performance on neuropsychological tests (Grant, Adams, & Reed, 1984).

Family history of alcoholism also appears to be associated with impaired neuropsychological performance. Alcoholic patients with a positive family history of alcoholism performed worse on tests of abstract reasoning, learning, and memory when compared with alcoholic patients without such histories (Schaeffer, Parsons, & Errico, 1988; Schaeffer, Parsons, & Yohman, 1984). Moreover, some studies have found that children of alcoholic patients display impaired performance on neuropsychological tests before the onset of alcohol or other substance use (e.g., Poon, Ellis, Fitzgerald, & Zucker, 2000).

Investigators have explored the relationship between premorbid functioning and neuropsychological deficits observed in alcoholics. For example, several studies have found that levels of cognitive functioning in alcoholic patients are associated with test scores that provide estimates of premorbid functioning, such as the Vocabulary subtest of the Wechsler Adult Intelligence Scale (e.g., Cutting, 1988; Draper & Manning, 1982).

LIMITATIONS OF PREVIOUS STUDIES

It should be noted that patients who had primarily or exclusively misused alcohol were used in the studies that identified many of these neurocognitive risk factors. It is not clear which of these risk factors would be identified among patients who primarily abuse psychoactive substances other than alcohol or have a polydrug abuse pattern.

Another limitation shared by many of these studies is that patients are often classified as cognitively impaired or intact on the basis of scores on single tests or use of a single cutoff score on a battery of tests. Even in studies that have used multidimensional neuropsychological assessment batteries that were designed to evaluate a broad range of abilities, a single summary score is often used to categorize examinees as impaired or intact. Obviously, such classifications of cognitive status grossly oversimplify the multidimensional nature of neuropsychological functioning and ability. Moreover, most neuropsychological studies of individuals who chronically abuse alcohol or other psychoactive substances have used relatively small sample sizes which, in turn, have precluded rigorous examination of multiple neurobehavioral constructs that might underlie neuropsychological test performance (because of low statistical power). The risk factors associated with the presence of impairment previously noted may be related to performance in certain domains of neurocognitive functioning and not others, versus a general association with impaired overall cognitive performance. For example, Bates, Labouvie, and Voelbel (2002) found familial alcoholism was associated only with decreased verbal ability, whereas childhood learning problems were uniquely associated with lower executive functioning. If the neurobehavioral constructs are not adequately identified, it is not possible to discern the association of possible risk factors to the appropriate cognitive ability area. As previously noted, it is also unclear whether the risk factors identified with primarily alcoholic patients would be found with drug-abusing patients.

The purpose of the present investigation was to model quantitatively the underlying neuropsychological ability domains of a relatively large sample of drug-abusing patients entering substance abuse treatment by using a broad array of tests designed to assess vulnerable areas of cognitive functioning. Furthermore, we also examined the relationship of different cognitive risk factors to the different domains of cognitive functioning identified.

METHOD

Participants

Participants were drawn from patients admitted to one of two substance abuse treatment programs, both of which were located in the northeastern United States. More specifically, participants ($N = 329$) were recruited from an outpatient treatment program; a separate sample of participants ($N = 258$) was recruited from an 8-to-12-month residential therapeutic community (TC). Potential participants were excluded if they (a) had a history of organic brain disorder; (b) met the *Diagnostic and Statistical Manual of Mental Disorders* (3rd ed., rev.; American Psychiatric Association, 1987) criteria for schizophrenia, delusional (paranoid) disorder, or other psychotic disorders; (c) had medical problems that precluded testing (e.g., color blindness, paralysis); or

TABLE 14.1
Sociodemographic and Background Characteristics of Patients From the Outpatient and Therapeutic Community Treatment Programs

Characteristic	Outpatient program (N = 329)				Therapeutic community (N = 258)			
	M	SD	n	%	M	SD	n	%
Age	30.4	5.2			31.6	6.3		
Years of education	12.1	1.3			12.2	2.1		
Male			240	73			190	74
Racial/ethnic composition								
White			222	67			189	73
African American			90	27			60	23
Hispanic			7	2			5	2
Other			10	3			4	2
Primary drug of abuse								
Cocaine			190	58			134	52
Opiates			78	24			70	27
Amphetamines			34	10			39	15
Sedative/hypnotics			20	7			12	5
Cannabis			7	2			3	1
Met DSM–III–R diagnostic criteria for								
Alcohol dependence			241	73			190	74
Cocaine dependence			198	60			160	62
Opiate dependence			104	32			89	34
Cannabis dependence			31	9			17	7
Dependence on another drug			57	17			49	19

Note. DSM–III–R = Diagnostic and Statistical Manual of Mental Disorders (3rd ed., rev.).

(d) were unable to read testing materials. Both programs were certified to treat, and therefore only accepted, patients who primarily abused drugs other than alcohol; thus, patients whose primary drug of abuse was alcohol were referred to other treatment programs and were not included in the investigation.[1] The sociodemographic and background characteristics of participants from the two programs are shown in Table 14.1.

In the outpatient program, 362 consecutive admissions were approached to be in the study. Seventeen of those admitted (5%) refused to participate; an additional 16 admissions (4%) who agreed to participate met one or more of the exclusion criteria and were thus not included, resulting in a sample of 329 from that program. From the TC, 275 consecutive admissions were approached to participate in the investigation; 14 admissions (5%) refused to participate, and an additional 3 patients (1%) who agreed to participate met one or more of the exclusion criteria, resulting in a final sample of 258 participants from that program.

---

[1]We used a decision tree algorithm, described in Fals-Stewart (1996), to determine the primary drug of abuse for each patient, with determinations based on unweighted combinations of patients' self-report data, diagnostic information, prior treatment information, and frequency of use for each drug over the 90 days and the 12 months prior to evaluation.

Measures

The Neuropsychological Screening Battery (NSB; Heaton, Thompson, Nelson, Filley, & Franklin, 1990) is a compilation and adaptation of a number of widely used neuropsychological tests. The NSB was designed to provide a standardized assessment of a broad range of neurocognitive abilities, including psychomotor speed, sequencing efficiency, visual attention, verbal and nonverbal learning, delayed recall, visuoconstructional skills, expressive and receptive language functions, and reading comprehension. The battery consists of (a) the Symbol Digit Modalities Test (SDMT; Smith, 1973); (b) the Trail Making Test, Parts A and B (TMT; Armitage, 1946); (c) time and errors from the Numerical Attention Test (NAT; Rennick, Keiser, Rodin, Rim, & Lennox, 1974); (d) learning and memory scores from the Wechsler Memory Scale (WMS; Wechsler, 1945); (e) copy, learning, and memory scores from the Rey–Osterrieth Complex Figure (ROCF; Osterrieth, 1944); and (f) written fluency (WF), oral fluency (OF), commands with auditory sequencing (CAS), visual naming (VN), and sentence repetition (SR) from an abbreviated version of the Benton Multilingual Aphasia Exam (MAE; Benton & Hamsher, 1976). Tests of aural comprehension (AC) and reading comprehension (RC) are also included in the battery.

This battery has been shown to discriminate reliably between substance-abusing patients and demographically matched non-substance-abusing participants (Fals-Stewart, 1996; O'Malley et al., 1992). Another investigation found there was high agreement between the NSB and another well-validated neuropsychological testing battery in identifying cognitively impaired substance-abusing patients (Fals-Stewart, 1996).

The NSB was supplemented with selected neuropsychological tests found in other studies to be sensitive to the types of cognitive impairments observed among substance-abusing patients (e.g., Fals-Stewart, 1992; Walker, Donovan, Kivlahan, & O'Leary, 1983). These included the Category Test (CT; Halstead, 1947), the Block Design (BD) test (Wechsler, 1955), and the Tactual Performance Test—Time and Location scores (TPT; Arthur, 1947).

Risk Factors

On the basis of the extensive neuropsychology of alcoholism literature, we assessed a variety of factors that may be associated with cognitive performance in these substance-abusing patients. Substance use risk factors assessed were (a) quantity and frequency of alcohol and drug use, (b) years of regular alcohol use, (c) years of regular drug use, (d) substance use diagnoses, and (e) extent of polydrug abuse by a count of the number of different current substance use dependence diagnoses. To assess the frequency of alcohol and other substance use, the Timeline Followback Interview (TLFB; Sobell & Sobell, 1996) was administered to participants, with frequency of use for the past year being the target time interval. The TLFB has excellent psychometric properties for the evaluation of alcohol use (e.g., Sobell, Toneatto, & Sobell, 1994) and other drug use (e.g., Fals-Stewart, O'Farrell, Freitas, McFarlin, & Rutigliano, 2000). Percentage days abstinent (PDA) from drugs and alcohol; percentage days drinking (PDD); percentage days heavy drinking (PDHD), defined as six or more standard drinks; and percentage days any drug use (PDDU) were derived from the TLFB.

Participants also were asked as part of their intake assessment when they began drinking alcohol regularly and when they began using other drugs regularly. From these responses, years of alcohol use and years of drug use were determined. All participants were also interviewed with the substance use disorders module of the Structured Clinical Interview for *DSM–III–R* (SCID; Spitzer, Williams, Gibbon, & First, 1990) to determine substances for which they met current dependence criteria.

Sociodemographic Characteristics

Age and education were the primary sociodemographic risk factors evaluated. Information about participants' sociodemographic and background characteristics were obtained from a standard demographic interview.

Psychiatric Functioning

Three aspects of participants' psychiatric function were evaluated: (a) level of depression, (b) level of anxiety, and (c) the presence of ASPD. Depression was evaluated using the Beck Depression Inventory (BDI; Beck & Beamesderfer, 1974), a widely used self-report measure of depressive symptoms. Scores on the BDI range from 0 to 63, with higher scores indicating greater levels of depression. The Clinical Anxiety Scale (CAS; Westhuis & Thyer, 1986) is a self-report inventory used to measure general anxiety, with higher scores indicating greater anxiety. The presence of ASPD was determined using the Axis II ASPD module of the Structured Clinical Interview for *DSM–III–R* (SCID–II; Spitzer, Williams, Gibbon, & First, 1990).

Physical Health

Liver functioning was determined by levels of the enzyme GGT, with higher levels indicating poorer liver functioning. The extent of the severity of past head injuries was rated on a 5-point scale developed and used by Grant et al. (1984). Scores on the rating scale were based on affirmative responses to questions concerning the number of head injuries with loss of consciousness and duration of posttraumatic amnesia; higher scores indicated a larger number and more severe past head injuries.

Family History

Family history for alcoholism was considered positive if any first-degree family member (i.e., biological parent or sibling) had a history of alcoholism, as reported by participants.

Premorbid Functioning

The North American Adult Reading Test (NAART; Blair & Spreen, 1989) is a reading test of 61 irregularly spelled words (e.g., *debris, psalm, caveat*), printed in two columns on both sides of an 8.5 in. × 11 in. card, which is given to the examinee to read aloud. Each pronunciation error is counted as one point; the cumulative number of errors is entered into an equation to provide a lower limit estimate of an examinee's premorbid intelligence quotient (IQ; Stebbins, Wilson, Gilley, Bernard, & Fox, 1990).

Procedure

Within a week of admission to the treatment programs, patients completed a psychosocial intake interview, which included a sociodemographic questionnaire, and were administered the TLFB and the SCID by one of two trained research assistants. The neuropsychological tests were administered between 14 and 21 days after patients were admitted to the programs. All of these tests were administered on the same day in one assessment session, which lasted roughly 90 minutes. These examinations were conducted by one of two trained master's-level psychometricians. Patients also completed the BDI, the CAS, the NAART, and the head injury rating scale interview at that time and submitted urine and breath samples. Analysis of urine and breath samples taken from patients at the time of the neuropsychological assessments revealed no recent alcohol or other drug use. The mean reported number of days between last use of any psychoactive substance and the testing session was 27.6 days (SD = 5.3), with a range of 12 to 58 days.

Only patients in the TC were required to provide blood as part of their physical examination. Blood was drawn within 36 hours of admission and was collected in the morning after an overnight fast; GGT levels were determined using standard laboratory testing procedures.

Analyses

A three-step analytic plan was used to examine the latent structure of the participants' neuropsychological subtest scores and to explore the relationship of these factors to the identified risk covariates. An exploratory factor analysis (EFA) was used on the neuropsychological test scores from the participants from the outpatient treatment program. This EFA was done within a confirmatory factor analysis (CFA) framework (Jöreskog, 1978) and is often referred to as a confirmatory maximum-likelihood approach to EFA (Gorsuch, 1983). This method has the advantage of calculating factor loadings with their standard errors, thus allowing for calculation of t ratios to determine their significance. Starting with a one-factor solution, a factor was added successively to each model until a nonsignificant chi-square was found, indicating acceptable model fit. The final solution was retained for subsequent analysis. The factors were allowed to correlate, analogous to a promax rotation in standard EFA. No risk factors were incorporated into the EFA.

Using the results from the EFA of the neuropsychological subtest scores from the outpatient sample, a CFA was conducted using the neuropsychological subtest scores of participants from the TC. More specifically, a model was developed and tested in the CFA, using the factors identified in the EFA, with significant factor loadings from the EFA used to identify and test path coefficients in the initial CFA for each measure. The CFA model assumed correlated latent factors and uncorrelated errors. The CFA did not assume simple structure. However, each measure could have loadings on any given factor, depending on the number of factors for which the measure had significant loadings in the EFA. The need for model respecification in the initial CFA model was determined by indicators of overall model fit. These included (a) the chi-square test, with nonsignificant values indicating adequate model fit; (b) the root-mean-square error of approximation (RMSEA; Browne & Cudeck, 1993), with values less than .06 indicating acceptable fit; and (c) the comparative fit index (CFI; Bentler, 1990) and the Tucker–Lewis Index (TLI; Tucker & Lewis, 1973), with values of greater than .95 on each of these indices indicating acceptable fit (Hu & Bentler, 1998). Information from modification indices guided changes made to the initial and subsequent models to improve fit.

A starting model composed of direct paths from each risk factor to the retained latent factors in the final CFA was sequentially simplified by eliminating small and nonsignificant paths. At each step in the test of the hierarchical models, the trimmed model was compared by the chi-square difference test with the preceding model (Kline, 1998). The model was no longer trimmed when elimination of the smallest path caused a significant increment in the chi-square. The amount of variance in the latent abilities that was associated with the retained risk factors was calculated.

This analytic strategy was useful in controlling for the multiple associations of potential risk correlates. It allowed tests of the associative strength of risk factors with underlying abilities that influence performance on neuropsychological tests, rather than with observed test scores. Thus, because of the control of measurement error and test-specific variance in performance, results may generalize beyond the specific neuropsychological tests that were used in this study and be compared with other findings in the literature. MPlus (Muthén & Muthén, 1998) was used to estimate model parameters for the EFA and the CFA from raw data using maximum likelihood.

RESULTS

Neuropsychological Subtest Scores

The neuropsychological subtest scores of participants from the outpatient treatment program and the therapeutic community are located in Table 14.2. These scores are similar to results obtained on these neuropsychological tests by substance-abusing patients who have participated in previous investigations (e.g., Fals-Stewart, 1996; O'Malley et al., 1992).

TABLE 14.2
Means and Standard Deviations of Neuropsychological Subtest Scores

Subtest	Outpatient (N = 329)		Therapeutic community (N = 258)	
	M	SD	M	SD
Symbol Digit Modalities Test[b]	51.3	11.4	48.3	10.8
Trail Making Test				
Part A[a]	25.1	6.0	26.3	5.8
Part B[a]	81.3	25.6	84.2	27.1
Numerical Attention Test				
Time[a]	155.3	33.8	157.2	34.2
Errors[a]	3.6	2.8	3.9	2.9
Wechsler Memory Scale Story				
Story Learning[b]	13.6	2.4	13.9	3.1
Story Memory[a]	11.2	5.3	10.9	4.9
Rey–Osterrieth Complex Figure				
Figure Copy[b]	16.4	2.4	16.6	2.8
Figure Learning[b]	14.4	4.3	14.9	5.2
Figure Memory[a]	4.8	7.6	5.1	5.3
Visual Naming[b]	17.8	2.1	17.1	3.0
Aural Comprehension[b]	11.3	0.5	11.9	0.5
Reading Comprehension[b]	11.8	0.6	11.8	0.7
Written Fluency[b]	12.2	3.0	12.0	2.8
Oral Fluency[b]	12.9	5.2	12.6	5.0
Commands With Auditory				
Sequencing[b]	22.6	2.8	22.0	3.0
Sentence Repetition[b]	4.8	0.7	4.7	0.8
Block Design[b]	8.8	4.9	8.0	4.0
Category Test (errors)[a]	47.6	19.2	46.9	17.2
Tactual Performance Test				
Time[a]	0.6	0.2	0.7	0.3
Location[b]	3.1	0.4	3.3	0.5

[a]Higher scores indicate poorer performance. [b]Lower scores indicate poorer performance.

Exploratory Factor Analysis of Neuropsychological Test Scores of Substance-Abusing Patients From the Outpatient Clinic

As noted, the results of successive EFA solutions were evaluated, starting with a one-factor model. The first solution that had acceptable fit to the data was the four-factor solution, $\chi^2(123, N = 329) = 143.1$, $p < .05$, RMSEA = .02, CFI = .99, TLI = .95; thus, this solution was retained for examination and used to develop the CFA model. The factor loadings for each neuropsychological subtest on each of the retained factors in the EFA are shown in Table 14.3. The resulting solution did not achieve simple structure; most test scores had significant loadings on multiple factors. We labeled Factor 1, which had highest loadings on the SDMT, the TMT–Part B, the BD test, and the CT, *Executive Functioning*. Factor 2 was marked by high loadings on several expressive and receptive language and verbal subtests (e.g., Aural Comprehension, Reading Comprehension, Written Fluency) and was named

TABLE 14.3

Factor Loadings for the Neuropsychological Subtest Scores
of the Outpatient Sample

Subtest	Factor				Communality
	1	2	3	4	
Symbol Digit Modalities Test	.44*	.21	.36*	.14	.39
Trail Making Test					
Part A	−.38*	−.17	−.53*	.09	.46
Part B	−.52*	−.12	−.38*	−.11	.44
Numerical Attention Test					
Time	−.13	−.24	−.44*	−.19	.40
Errors	.04	−.09	−.39*	−.13	.18
Wechsler Memory Scale Story					
Story Learning	.19	.54*	−.07	.40*	.49
Story Memory	.21	−.24	−.09	−.60*	.47
Rey–Osterrieth Complex Figure					
Figure Copy	.14	−.09	−.36*	.20	.20
Figure Learning	.39*	.08	.15	.52*	.45
Figure Memory	.19	−.20	−.24	−.45*	.34
Visual Naming	.14	.37*	.12	.19	.21
Aural Comprehension	.22	.44*	−.06	.21	.29
Reading Comprehension	.09	.51*	−.14	.11	.30
Written Fluency	.24	.49*	.18	.14	.35
Oral Fluency	.18	.54*	.15	−.04	.34
Commands With Auditory Sequencing	.20	.24	−.13	.30*	.20
Sentence Repetition	.19	.32*	.19	.20	.21
Block Design	.51*	.20	.22	.13	.37
Category Test (errors)	−.46*	−.18	−.29	−.18	.36
Tactual Performance Test					
Time	.09	−.11	−.48*	−.21	.29
Location	.14	.13	.12	.41*	.22

*$p < .05$.

Verbal Ability. Factor 3 was most strongly associated with tests involving psychomotor and information-processing speed (e.g., TMT–Part A, NAT) and was thus labeled *Speed*. Subtests designed to assess memory (e.g., Figure Memory from the ROCF, Story Memory from the WMS Story, Location score from the TPT) loaded on Factor 4, which we named *Memory*.

Confirmatory Factor Analysis of Neuropsychological Subtest Scores of Substance-Abusing Patients From the Therapeutic Community

Confirmatory Factor Analysis Results

We used the resulting model derived from the EFA and tested it using a CFA with NSB test results from patients in the TC. More specifically, we tested a model with four latent variables, which corresponded to each of the four factors identified in the EFA. For each latent variable, we tested path coefficients to the neuropsychological subtest score that corresponded to the significant factor loadings from the EFA. For example, the first latent variable in the CFA corresponded to the Executive Functioning factor from the EFA. The significance of the path coefficient for each subtest that had significant loadings for the Executive Functioning factor from the EFA (i.e., SDMT, TMT–Part A, TMT–Part B, Figure Learning from the ROCF, the BD test, and the CT) to the latent variable in the CFA model was tested.

The test of the four-factor model yielded the following fit indices: $\chi^2(178, N = 329) = 227.31$, $p < .01$, RMSEA = .03, CFI = .94, TLI = .91. Although the chi-square value was significant, the RMSEA, CFI, and TLI were nearly acceptable, suggesting the model was relatively close to providing an acceptable fit to the data, but perhaps could be modified to improve overall fit. Examination of the modification indices suggested the addition of a path from the Commands With Auditory Sequencing to the Verbal Ability factor would improve model fit; adding this path resulted in acceptable fit indices, $\chi^2(177, N = 258) = 200.42$, *ns*, RMSEA = .02, CFI = .94, TLI = .91. This final model is shown on the right side of Figure 14.1.

Risk Factor Correlates of Latent Neuropsychological Abilities

The scores on the risk factor measures for patients from the TC are located in Table 14.4. Before examining the relationship of different risk factors on the four latent constructs, we examined the intercorrelations among the risk factor measures to determine whether there might be a problem with multicollinearity. The four variables derived from the TLFB had correlations greater than .50 with each other: (a) PDA, (b) PDHD, (c) PDDU, and (d) PDD. From this set, PDHD was retained because, when tested with no other

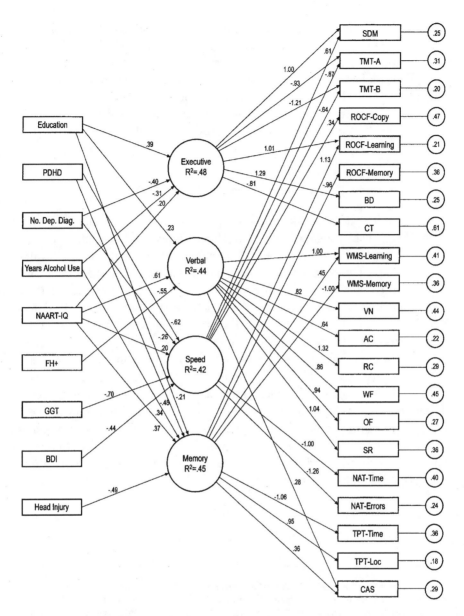

Figure 14.1. Measurement model of 15 neuropsychological test scores and path model of risk factor correlates. The right-hand portion of the figure shows the measurement model. Unstandardized factor loadings are shown on the arrows. Residual variances of the indicators are shown as proportions in the small circles. The large center circles show latent factor labels. R^2 values refer to the proportion of true variance in latent abilities accounted for by the risk factor correlates. Higher scores on the latent factors mean higher ability levels. The left-hand portion of the figure shows the path model of risk factor correlates. Significant unstandardized path coefficients are shown on the arrows. SDM = Symbol Digit Modalities; TMT–A = Trail Making Test—Part A; TMT–B = Trail Making Test—Part B; ROCF–Copy = Rey–Osterrieth Complex Figure—Figure Copy; ROCF–Learning = Rey–Osterrieth

risk factors in the model, it had the highest average association with the latent constructs. The correlations among the risk factors to be tested (after elimination of PDA, PDDU, and PDD) ranged from .03 to .42.

The risk factors that were retained in the final model are shown on the left side of Figure 14.1. The final path model yielded a significant chi-square; however, the other fit indices suggested a reasonably good fit to the data, $\chi^2(439, N = 258) = 494.52, p < .05$, RMSEA = .02, CFI = .98, TLI = .95.[2]

DISCUSSION

In their review, Rourke and Loberg (1996) noted a primary limitation shared by many investigations exploring the neuropsychological functioning of alcoholic patients is that these studies often fail to use multiple tests to evaluate a cognitive ability area; this limitation is also shared by most studies examining cognitive performance of drug-abusing patients. Moreover, because most studies have recruited relatively small sample sizes, the power to identify different ability areas represented by several tests was often low. The purpose of the present study was to identify latent neuropsychological abilities of substance-abusing patients using a comprehensive battery of tests and to explore neurocognitive risk factors that may be associated with these performance areas.

An EFA on the subtest scores of substance-abusing patients entering outpatient treatment identified four latent neuropsychological ability areas: executive functioning, verbal ability, psychomotor and information-processing speed, and memory. This solution, with only slight modification, was cross-validated using a CFA with a different sample of drug-abusing patients entering a TC. This four-factor model of neuropsychological abilities is consistent

---

[2]The correlations and covariances among the measures used in the EFA and the CFA are available from William Fals-Stewart on request.

Complex Figure—Figure Learning; ROCF–Memory = Rey–Osterrieth Complex Figure—Figure Memory; BD = Block Design test; CT = Category Test (errors); WMS–Learning = Wechsler Memory Scale Story—Story Learning; WMS–Memory = Wechsler Memory Scale Story—Story Memory; VN = Visual Naming; AC = Aural Comprehension; RC = Reading Comprehension; WF = Written Fluency; OF = Oral Fluency; SR = Sentence Repetition; NAT–Time = Numerical Attention Test—Time; NAT–Errors = Numerical Attention Test—Errors; TPT–Time = Tactual Performance Test—Time; TPT–Loc = Tactual Performance Test—Location; CAS = Commands With Auditory Sequencing; Education = Years of education; PDHD = percentage of days of heavy drinking during the previous year; No. Dep. Diag.= Number of diagnoses of current substance use diagnoses; NAART–IQ = North American Adult Reading Test—Intelligence Quotient; FH+ = positive family history for alcoholism; GGT = gamma-glutamine transferase; BDI = Beck Depression Inventory; Head Injury = Score on 5-point head injury scale.

TABLE 14.4

Scores on Risk Factor Measures for Participants
From the Therapeutic Community

Domain	n	%	M	SD
Sociodemographic				
Age			31.6	6.3
Education			12.2	2.1
Substance use				
Years of regular alcohol use			8.8	5.3
Years of regular drug use			6.5	6.1
No. of drugs for which participants met *DSM–III–R* dependence criteria			2.4	1.2
PDA			27.3	29.4
PDD			63.1	21.3
PDHD			45.6	38.4
PDDU			69.4	21.3
Psychiatric functioning				
BDI			11.6	6.2
CAS			15.8	14.1
Current ASPD diagnosis	78	30		
Physical functioning				
GGT level			39.8	29.3
Head injury index			2.1	1.3
Family history				
FH+	165	64		
Premorbid functioning				
NAART-estimated IQ			103.4	11.6

Note. DSM–III–R = Diagnostic and Statistical Manual of Mental Disorders (3rd ed., rev.); PDA = percentage of days abstinent in the past year; PDD = percentage of days drinking in the past year; PDHD = percentage of days of heavy drinking in the past year; PDDU = percentage of days of drug use in the past year; BDI = Beck Depression Inventory; CAS = Clinical Anxiety Scale; ASPD = antisocial personality disorder; GGT = gamma-glutamine transferase; FH+ = positive family history for alcoholism; NAART = North American Adult Reading Test.

with theoretical and empirical evidence that neuropsychological test performances are factorially complex and are supported by multiple brain regions and information-processing operations (e.g., Cummings, 1995; Hill, Lewis, Dean, & Woodcock, 2000; Reitan & Wolfson, 1994).

The latent Executive Functioning factor supported behavior on tests of abilities subserved by the dorsolateral prefrontal–subcortical circuit (Chow & Cummings, 1999), such as verbal fluency, perseveration, mental flexibility and control, abstraction, and response inhibition. That executive functioning also appears to influence performances on visuospatial tests is consistent with recent findings that measures, such as digit symbol tests, assess higher level cognitive processes in addition to perceptual speed (Parkin & Java, 1999) and that sensory motor tasks factor along the lines of cognitive complexity (Hill et al., 2000). Factor loadings for the Verbal Ability factor indicated that this latent ability influenced tasks involving comprehension, receptive and expressive language, and general auditory information processing. The Speed factor had a straightforward structure; the tests involved timed performances and had scores involving errors loaded on this factor. The Memory factor supported tests that were designed largely to evaluate this cognitive ability domain.

Our findings also indicate the retained risk factors accounted for a substantial proportion of the true variance of latent abilities that underlie neuropsychological test performances. The two most generalized and robust predictors of ability in our sample were the estimate of premorbid functioning and years of education. As suggested by some authors (e.g., Loberg, 1989; Rhodes & Jasinski, 1990), poor premorbid cognitive functioning may be indicative of learning problems in school, and childhood learning disorders may be related to the etiology of substance abuse (e.g., a compromised central nervous system may lead to less resilience in the presence of familial and social risk factors, thus leading to unhealthy responses to these stressors, including substance use). Education also influenced most of the latent neuropsychological abilities, which is consistent with a large body of evidence indicating that education influences neuropsychological test performances in general (e.g., for a review, see Heaton, Ryan, Grant, & Matthews, 1996).

Although the participants in the sample consisted of patients who primarily abused drugs other than alcohol, indicators of alcohol career length and recent drinking quantity nonetheless appeared to be significant risk factors. More specifically, participants' years of regular alcohol use influenced both memory and executive functioning, and frequency of heavy drinking over the past year influenced psychomotor speed and memory. The relationship between neuropsychological test performance and years of regular drinking and extent of excessive drinking is consistent with other studies, although not all investigations have found this link (for a review, see Parsons & Stevens, 1986).

It was also interesting that although no single substance use diagnosis was retained in the final model as a risk factor, the number of substances for which participants' met current criteria for dependence appeared to influence both executive functioning and speed. This provides some support for the hypothesis put forth by Lilliquist and Bigler (1992) that abuse of any single drug may result in little to no impairment because of the brain's capacity to compensate for deficits in one area by relying on intact functioning in other areas. However, polydrug abuse, by affecting the central nervous system in multiple areas, may circumvent the brain's power to compensate for losses.

Certainly, it is also plausible that premorbid executive deficits may place individuals at high risk for abusing multiple psychoactive substances. It is also important to highlight that in general, it is problematic to discern whether any single psychoactive substance (other than alcohol) is a risk factor, primarily because drug-abusing patients typically use multiple substances on a regular basis (e.g. Fals- Stewart, Schafer, Lucente, Rustine, & Brown, 1994). Thus, isolating the effects of a single substance on cognitive performance is difficult.

Family history of alcoholism loaded on only the Verbal Ability factor, which was somewhat surprising given that some previous studies suggest that patients with positive family histories have deficits in learning and memory (e.g., Schaeffer et al., 1984). High GGT levels in alcoholic patients have been linked to neuropsychological decrements in visuoperceptual and visuoconceptual abilities (Irwin et al., 1989). In turn, deficits in these areas may have resulted in some slowing on certain tests in our battery that rely to a certain degree on these ability areas, such as the TMT and components of the ROCF, perhaps accounting for the influence of GGT on the Speed factor. Head injuries are fairly common among alcohol- and drug-abusing patients (Hillbom & Holm, 1989) and, consistent with prior studies, we found lifetime head injury severity is associated with memory deficits (e.g., Solomon & Malloy, 1992). Depression was associated with slower syntactic processing speed. Previous findings of slowed response speed in depressed samples have been attributed to a slowing of response processing, rather than perceptual or motor slowing (Veiel, 1997).

The findings of the present investigation are, in many respects, very similar to the results of a recently completed study by Bates et al. (2002), in which these authors identified, through CFA, a similar four-factor structure of latent neuropsychological abilities (i.e., executive, verbal, speed, and memory) among a relatively large sample of patients who primarily abused alcohol. Although the present study and the one completed by Bates and colleagues used several of the same neuropsychological tests, the batteries were not largely overlapping, suggesting that this structure of latent abilities may be somewhat robust across samples and across tests sensitive to the types of impairments observed among substance-abusing patients.

The present study was marked by several important strengths. Perhaps most important, we not only used a large sample of substance-abusing patients to conduct the EFA, but we were able to cross-validate those findings using a CFA on a separate, but similar sample of substance-abusing patients. Certainly, the availability of sufficient samples to both explore latent domains of functioning in a structural equation modeling framework and to test that structure on a separate sample are rare, not only in the neuropsychology of substance abuse literature, but also in neuropsychology research in general. We also administered widely used and well-established neuropsychological test measures to the participants. In addition, we examined a relatively comprehensive array of commonly reported neuropsychological risk factors for substance-abusing populations and measured these with psychometrically sound measures. It is also important to highlight that the participants consisted of individuals who primarily abused drugs other than alcohol; as already noted, neuropsychological studies of drug abuse are far less common than neuropsychological studies of alcoholism, and more of these studies are clearly needed to determine this population's profile of cognitive impairment, possible cognitive risk factors, and so forth.

However, certain limitations of this study should also be noted. The patient samples used in this study were very heterogeneous in terms of the nature and severity of their substance use disorders. In addition, particularly in comparison with studies that have examined patients who primarily abuse alcohol, participants in the present study varied in terms of primary drug of choice. This heterogeneity certainly added error variance to the models tested, and the results may not generalize to other polydrug-abusing patient populations among which the patterns of substance use are dissimilar to those of patients participating in this study. It is also difficult to determine the effect of any recent alcohol use on neuropsychological test performances. Although patients reported no recent alcohol consumption (i.e., the most recent self-reported drinking by any examinee was 14 days before testing) and were given breath tests before testing, results of which indicated none of the participants had consumed alcohol directly prior to testing, breath tests have a fairly small time frame in which they can accurately detect drinking. Thus, patients could have engaged in unreported heavy drinking a few days before testing, which could have influenced test performances. This was far more of a concern in the outpatient treatment sample; patients in the TC were in a drug- and alcohol-free residential program, did not have any contact with individuals from outside the TC between the time they entered the program and the testing session, and were carefully monitored by staff members.

Although we examined single risk factors using a carefully considered analytic strategy, these analyses are best viewed as exploratory. The risk factor variables that were chosen for analysis were selected based primarily on the neuropsychology of alcoholism; other neurocognitive sources of risk not identified in that literature may be important in polydrug-abusing patients.

It is plausible that the presence of neurocognitive deficits in different ability areas would have a negative impact on treatment outcomes. If we view treatment as a learning situation, impaired ability to receive, encode, and integrate newly presented information would likely interfere with the treatment process. However, the relationship between cognitive status and substance abuse treatment response has been mixed, with selected studies finding a relationship between cognitive status and various indicators of treatment outcome (e.g., Gregson & Taylor, 1977; Parsons, 1983) and others not finding this association (e.g., Macciocchi, Ranseen, & Schmitt, 1989). Generally, studies examining these relationships have done so using a summary indicator of cognitive status, often based on a small number of tests, and have generally considered only its direct relationship to outcome. Given the multidimensional nature of neuropsychological functioning found in the present study, it is perhaps not surprising that there has been such disparity in the findings in investigations that have examined neuropsychological status unidimensionally. Future studies need to examine the associations of the multiple dimensions of cognitive functioning, such as those identified in the present investigation, to different treatment outcome indicators. Considered within a framework of other biopsychosocial factors that may influence outcome, the direct, moderating, and mediating role of different aspects of cognitive performance can then be more fully delineated.

REFERENCES

Allison, W. M., & Jerrom, D. W. A. (1984). Glue sniffing: A pilot study of the cognitive effects of long-term use. *International Journal of Addiction, 19*, 453–458.

American Psychiatric Association. (1987). *Diagnostic and statistical manual of mental disorders* (3rd ed., rev.). Washington, DC: Author.

Armitage, S. G. (1946). An analysis of certain psychological tests used for evaluation of brain injury. *Psychological Monographs, 60*(Whole No. 277).

Arthur, G. A. (1947). *A point scale of performance test* (Revised Form II). New York: Psychological Corporation.

Bates, M. E., & Convit, A. (1999). Neuropsychology and neuroimaging of alcohol and drug abuse. In A. Calev (Ed.), *Neuropsychological functions in psychiatric disorders* (pp. 342–375). Washington, DC: American Psychiatric Press.

Bates, M. E., Labouvie, E. W., & Voelbel, G. T. (2002). Individual differences in latent neuropsychological abilities at addictions treatment entry. *Psychology of Addictive Behaviors, 16*, 35–46.

Beck, A. T., & Beamesderfer, A. (1974). Assessment of depression: The Beck Depression Inventory. In P. Pichot (Ed.), *Psychological measurements in psychopharmacology* (pp. 151–169). Basel, Switzerland: Karger.

Bentler, P. M. (1990). Comparative fit indexes in structural models. *Psychological Bulletin, 107*, 238–246.

Benton, A. L., & Hamsher, K. (1976). *Multilingual aphasia examination*. Iowa City, IA: University Hospitals, Department of Neurology.

Bergman, H., Borg, S., Engelbrecktson, K., & Vikander, B. (1989). Dependence on sedative hypnotics: Neuropsychological impact, field dependence and clinical consequences in a five year follow-up study. *British Journal of Addiction, 81*, 547–553.

Blair, J. R., & Spreen, O. (1989). Predicting premorbid IQ: A revision of the National Adult Reading Test. *Clinical Neuropsychologist, 3*, 129–136.

Browne, M. W., & Cudeck, R. (1993). Alternative ways of assessing model fit. In K. Bollen & K. Long (Eds.), *Testing structural equations models* (pp. 136–162). Newbury Park, CA: Sage.

Chow, T. W., & Cummings, J. L. (1999). Frontal–subcortical circuits. In B. L. Miller & J. L. Cummings (Eds.), *The human frontal lobes: Functions and disorders* (pp. 3–26). New York: Guilford Press.

Cummings, J. L. (1995). Anatomic and behavioral aspects of frontal–subcortical circuits. In J. Grafman, K. J. Holyoak, & F. Boller (Eds.), *Annals of the New York Academy of Sciences: Vol. 769. Structure and functions of the human prefrontal cortex* (pp. 1–13). New York: New York Academy of Sciences.

Cutting, J. C. (1988). Alcohol cognitive impairment and aging: Still an uncertain relationship. *British Journal of Addiction, 83,* 995–997.

Draper, R. J., & Manning, A. (1982). Vocabulary deficits and abstraction impairment in hospitalized alcoholics. *Psychological Medicine, 12,* 341–347.

Eckardt, M. J., Stapleton, J. M., Rawlings, R. R., Davis, E. Z., & Grodin, D. M. (1995). Neuropsychological functioning of detoxified alcoholics between the ages of 18 and 35. *American Journal of Psychiatry, 152,* 53–59.

Errico, A. L., Parsons, O. A., & King, A. C. (1991). Assessment of verbosequential and visuospatial cognitive abilities in chronic alcoholics. *Psychological Assessment, 3,* 693–696.

Fals-Stewart, W. (1992). Using the subtests of the Brain Age Quotient to screen for cognitive deficits among substance abusers. *Perceptual and Motor Skills, 75,* 244–246.

Fals-Stewart, W. (1996). Intermediate length screening of impairment among psychoactive substance-abusing patients: A comparison of two batteries. *Journal of Substance Abuse, 8,* 1–17.

Fals-Stewart, W., O'Farrell, T. J., Freitas, T. T., McFarlin, S. K., & Rutigliano, P. (2000). The Timeline Followback reports of psychoactive substance use by drug-abusing patients: Psychometric properties. *Journal of Consulting and Clinical Psychology, 68,* 134–144.

Fals-Stewart, W., Schafer, J., Lucente, S., Rustine, T., & Brown, L. (1994). Neurobehavioral consequences of prolonged alcohol and substance abuse: A review of findings and treatment implications. *Clinical Psychology Review, 14,* 775–788.

Freitas, T. T., & Fals-Stewart, W. (1999, August). *Effects of drug use intensity on cognitive functioning.* Poster presented at the 107th Annual Convention of the American Psychological Association, Boston.

Freund, G. (1982). The interaction of chronic alcohol consumption and aging on brain structures and function. *Alcoholism: Clinical and Experimental Research, 6,* 13–21.

Gorsuch, R. (1983). *Factor analysis* (2nd ed.). Hillsdale, NJ: Erlbaum.

Grant, I. (1987). Alcohol and the brain: Neuropsychological correlates. *Journal of Consulting and Clinical Psychology, 55,* 310–324.

Grant, I., Adams, K. M., Carlin, A. S., Rennick, P. M., Judd, L. L., & Schoof, K. (1978). The collaborative neuropsychological study of polydrug users. *Archives of General Psychiatry, 35,* 1063–1074.

Grant, I., Adams, K. M., & Reed, R. (1984). Aging, abstinence, and medical risk factors in the prediction of neuropsychological deficit among long-term alcoholics. *Archives of General Psychiatry, 41,* 710–718.

Grant, I., & Judd, L. L. (1976). Neuropsychological and EEG disturbances in poly-drug users. *American Journal of Psychiatry, 133,* 1039–1042.

Gregson, R. A. M., & Taylor, G. M. (1977). Prediction of relapse in men alcoholics. *Journal of Studies on Alcohol, 38,* 1749–1759.

Halstead, W. C. (1947). *Brain and intelligence: A quantitative study of the frontal lobes.* Chicago: University of Chicago Press.

Heaton, R. K., Ryan, L., Grant, I., & Matthews, C. G. (1996). Demographic influences on neuropsychological test performance. In I. Grant & K. M. Adams (Eds.), *Neuropsychological assessment of neuropsychiatric disorders* (pp. 141–163). New York: Oxford University Press.

Heaton, R. K., Thompson, L. L., Nelson, L. M., Filley, C. M., & Franklin, G. M. (1990). Brief and intermediate length screening of neuropsychological impairment in multiple sclerosis. In S. M. Rao (Ed.), *Multiple sclerosis: A neuropsychological perspective* (pp. 149–160). New York: Oxford University Press.

Hill, S. K., Lewis, M. N., Jr., Dean, R. S., & Woodcock, R. W. (2000). Constructs underlying measures of sensory-motor functions. *Archives of Clinical Neuropsychology, 15,* 631–641.

Hillbom, M., & Holm, L. (1989). Contribution of traumatic brain injury to neuropsychological deficits in alcoholics. *Journal of Neurology, Neurosurgery and Psychiatry, 49,* 1348–1353.

Hu, L., & Bentler, P. M. (1998). Fit indices in covariance structure analysis: Sensitivity to underparametized model misspecification. *Psychological Methods, 3,* 424–453.

Irwin, M., Smith, T. L., Butters, N., Brown, S., Baird, S., Grant, I., & Schuckit, M. A. (1989). Graded neuropsychological impairment and elevated gamma-glutamyl transferase in chronic alcoholic men. *Alcoholism: Clinical and Experimental Research, 13,* 99–103.

Jöreskog, K. G. (1978). Structural analysis of covariance and correlation matrices. *Psychometrica, 43,* 443–477.

Kline, R. (1998). *Principles and practice of structural equation modeling.* New York: Guilford Press.

Lilliquist, M. W., & Bigler, E. D. (1992). Neurological and neuropsychological consequences of drug abuse. In D. I. Templer, L. C. Hartladge, & W. G. Cannon (Eds.), *Preventable brain damage: Brain vulnerability and brain health* (pp. 161–192). New York: Springer Publishing Company.

Loberg, T. (1989). The role of neuropsychology in secondary prevention. In T. Loberg, W. R. Miller, P. E. Nathan, & G. A. Marlatt (Eds.), *Addictive behaviors: Prevention and early intervention* (pp. 69–86). Amsterdam: Swets & Zeitlinger.

Macciocchi, S. N., Ranseen, J. D., & Schmitt, F. A. (1989). The relationship between neuropsychological impairment in alcoholics and treatment outcome at one year. *Archives of Clinical Neuropsychology, 4,* 365–370.

Malloy, P., Noel, N., Rogers, S., Longabaugh, R., & Beattie, M. (1989). Risk factors for neuropsychological impairment in alcoholics: Antisocial personality, age, years of drinking and gender. *Journal of Studies on Alcohol, 50,* 422–426.

Muthén, L., & Muthén, B. (1998). *Mplus: The comprehensive modeling program for applied researchers: User's guide*. Los Angeles: Authors.

O'Malley, S., Adamse, M., Heaton, R. K., & Gawin, F. H. (1992). Neuropsychological impairment in chronic cocaine abusers. *American Journal of Drug and Alcohol Abuse, 18,* 131–144.

Osterrieth, P. A. (1944). Le teste de copie d'une figure complexe [The test of copying a complex figure]. *Archives de Psychologie, 30,* 206–356.

Parkin, A. J., & Java, R. I. (1999). Deterioration of frontal lobe function in normal aging: Influences of fluid intelligence versus perceptual speed. *Neuropsychology, 13,* 539–545.

Parsons, O. A. (1983). Cognitive dysfunction and recovery in alcoholics. *Substance and Alcohol Actions/Misuse, 4,* 175–190.

Parsons, O. A., & Stevens, L. (1986). Previous alcohol intake and residual cognitive deficits in detoxified alcoholics and animals. *Alcohol and Alcoholism, 21,* 137–157.

Pfefferbaum, A., Sullivan, E., Rosenbaum, M., Shear, P., Mathalon, D., & Lim, K. (1993). Increase in brain cerebrospinal fluid volume is greater in older than in younger alcoholic patients: A replication study and CT/MRI comparison. *Psychiatry Research Neuroimaging, 50,* 257–274.

Poon, E., Ellis, D. A., Fitzgerald, H. E., & Zucker, R. A. (2000). Intellectual, cognitive, and academic performance among sons of alcoholics during the early school years: Differences related to subtypes of familial alcoholism. *Alcoholism: Clinical and Experimental Research, 24,* 1020–1027.

Portnoff, L. A. (1982). Halstead–Reitan impairment in chronic alcoholics as a function of age of drinking onset. *Clinical Neuropsychology, 4,* 115–119.

Reitan, R. M., & Wolfson, D. (1994). A selective and critical review of neuropsychological deficits and the frontal lobes. *Neuropsychology Review, 4,* 161–198.

Rennick, P. M., Keiser, T., Rodin, E., Rim, L., & Lennox, K. (1974, December). *Carbamazepine: Behavioral side effects in temporal lobe epilepsy during short-term comparison with placebo*. Paper presented at the annual meeting of the American Epilepsy Society, New York.

Rhodes, S. S., & Jasinski, D. R. (1990). Learning disabilities in alcohol-dependent adults: A preliminary study. *Journal of Learning Disabilities, 23,* 551–556.

Rourke, S. B., & Loberg, T. (1996). The neurobehavioral correlates of alcoholism. In I. Grant & K. M. Adams (Eds.), *Neuropsychological assessment of neuropsychiatric disorders* (pp. 423–485). New York: Oxford University Press.

Schaeffer, K. W., & Parsons, O. A. (1986). Drinking practices and neuropsychological test performance in sober male alcoholics and social drinkers. *Alcohol, 3,* 175–179.

Schaeffer, K. W., Parsons, O. A., & Errico, A. L. (1988). Abstracting deficits and childhood conduct disorder as a function of familial alcoholism. *Alcoholism: Clinical and Experimental Research, 12,* 617–618.

Schaeffer, K. W., Parsons, O. A., & Yohman, J. R. (1984). Neuropsychological differences between male familial and nonfamilial alcoholics and nonalcoholics. *Alcoholism: Clinical and Experimental Research, 8,* 347–351.

Sinha, R., Parsons, O. A., & Glenn, S. W. (1989). Drinking variables, affective measures and neuropsychological performance: Familial alcoholism and gender correlates. *Alcohol, 6,* 77–85.

Smith, A. (1973). *Digit Symbol Modalities Test.* Los Angeles: Western Psychological Services.

Sobell, L. C., & Sobell, M. B. (1996). *Timeline followback user's guide: A calendar method for assessing alcohol and drug use.* Toronto, Ontario, Canada: Addiction Research Foundation.

Sobell, L. C., Toneatto, R., & Sobell, M. B. (1994). Behavioral assessment and treatment planning for alcohol, tobacco, and other drug problems: Current status with an emphasis on clinical applications. *Behavior Therapy, 25,* 533–580.

Solomon, D. A., & Malloy, P. F. (1992). Alcohol, head injury, and neuropsychological function. *Neuropsychology Review, 3,* 249–280.

Spitzer, R., Williams, J., Gibbon, M., & First, M. (1990). *Structured Clinical Interview for DSM–III–R—Patient edition (Version 1.0).* Washington, DC: American Psychiatric Press.

Stebbins, G. T., Wilson, R. S., Gilley, D. W., Bernard, B. A., & Fox, J. H. (1990). Use of the National Adult Reading Test to estimate premorbid IQ in dementia. *Clinical Neuropsychologist, 4,* 64–68.

Sutker, P. A., & Allain, A. N. (1987). Cognitive abstraction, shifting, and control: Clinical sample comparisons of psychopaths and nonpsychopaths. *Journal of Abnormal Psychology, 96,* 73–75.

Tucker, L. R., & Lewis, C. (1973). The reliability coefficient for maximum likelihood factor analysis. *Psychometrica, 38,* 1–10.

Veiel, H. O. F. (1997). A preliminary profile of neuropsychological deficits associated with major depression. *Journal of Clinical and Experimental Neuropsychology, 19,* 587–603.

Volkow, N. D., Wang, G. J., Hitzemann, R., Fowler, J., Wolf, A., Overall, J., et al. (1994). Recovery of brain glucose metabolism in detoxified alcoholics. *American Journal of Psychiatry, 151,* 178–183.

Walker, R. D., Donovan, D. M., Kivlahan, D. R., & O'Leary, M. R. (1983). Length of stay, neuropsychological performance, and aftercare: Influences on alcoholism treatment outcome. *Journal of Consulting and Clinical Psychology, 51,* 900–911.

Wang, G., Volkow, N., Hitzman, R., Oster, Z., Roque, C., & Cestaro, V. (1992). Brain imaging of an alcoholic with MRI, SPECT, and PET. *American Journal of Physiologic Imaging, 7,* 194–198.

Wechsler, D. (1945). A standardized memory scale for clinical use. *Journal of Psychology, 19,* 87–95.

Wechsler, D. (1955). *Manual for the Wechsler Adult Intelligence Scale.* New York: Psychological Corporation.

Westhuis, D., & Thyer, B. A. (1986). *Development and validation of the Clinical Anxiety Scale: A rapid assessment instrument for empirical practice.* Unpublished manuscript.

15

IMMEDIATE ANTECEDENTS OF CIGARETTE SMOKING: AN ANALYSIS FROM ECOLOGICAL MOMENTARY ASSESSMENT

SAUL SHIFFMAN, CHAD J. GWALTNEY, MARK H. BALABANIS, KENNETH S. LIU, JEAN A. PATY, JON D. KASSEL, MARY HICKCOX, AND MARYANN GNYS

It is clear that nicotine dependence is a driving motive behind tobacco use and cigarette smoking (U.S. Department of Health and Human Services, 1988). Nevertheless, deeper understanding of motivation for smoking continues to propel theoretical speculation and empirical research. In particular, a notable feature of the nicotine-dependence or nicotine-regulation model is that it does not readily account for the situational variability in smoking. Researchers have focused on the immediate motives or triggers for smoking, in part because falling nicotine blood levels, per se, which would dictate regularly spaced smoking, do not seem to adequately explain variations in daily smoking rate and timing (Hatsukami, Morgan, Pickens, & Champagne, 1990; Pomerleau & Pomerleau, 1987). Some evidence suggests that smoking follows discernable patterns and is particularly likely to occur in certain situations or

Saul Shiffman has undertaken research and consultancy for manufacturers of smoking cessation products, including nicotine replacement products and bupropion, and at the time this chapter was written was consulting exclusively for Glaxo-SmithKline. Saul Shiffman and Jean A. Paty are also founders of invivodata, inc., which provides electronic diaries for clinical trials. This research was supported by Grant DA06084 from the National Institute on Drug Abuse. We are grateful to David Abrams and Michael Sayette for providing useful comments on a draft of this chapter.

Reprinted from *Journal of Abnormal Psychology*, *111*, 531–545 (2002). Copyright 2002 by the American Psychological Association.

contexts, such as emotional distress or alcohol consumption (e.g., Gilbert, Sharpe, Ramanaiah, Detwiler, & Anderson, 2000; Ikard, Green, & Horn, 1969; McKennell, 1970; Russell, Peto, & Patel, 1974; Shiffman & Balabanis, 1995). (As a shorthand, we call these linkages between smoking and situational antecedents the "situational associations" of smoking.) Under most models, such associations cannot be explained by the need to maintain steady-state nicotine levels. Thus, the associations provide hints about other motivational and behavioral processes that control smoking. The question of "why people smoke" is closely intertwined with that of "when people smoke." Indeed, the prompting of smoking by situational stimuli is part of almost every theoretical account of smoking.

AFFECT AND SMOKING

Perhaps the most prominent and theoretically important situational association with smoking is that between smoking and mood. Both negative and positive affect have been proposed as important triggers for smoking, and most theories of smoking emphasize the role of affect in driving smoking. The starting point for many theoretical speculations about affect and smoking is smokers' consistent reports that both negative and positive affect influence their smoking. Almost every self-report survey of smoking patterns or motives has generated factors representing negative affect and positive affect as antecedents of smoking (Gilbert et al., 2000; Ikard et al., 1969; McKennell & Thomas, 1967; though see Russell et al., 1974). Furthermore, affective motives for smoking are typically the most strongly and universally endorsed (Gilbert et al., 2000; Ikard et al., 1969; McKennell, 1970). Negative affect is also the most commonly attributed cause of smoking relapse (Cummings, Gordon, & Marlatt, 1980; Shiffman, 1982), further highlighting negative affect's apparent contribution.

Other observational data and some laboratory data also link smoking and affect. On a population level, smokers tend to report more negative affect than nonsmokers (e.g., Anda et al., 1990; Breslau, Kilbey, & Andreski, 1994; Kirkcaldy, Cooper, Brown, & Athanasou, 1994; Naquin & Gilbert, 1996), and smokers under high stress tend to smoke more (Creson, Schmitz, & Arnoutovic, 1996). In addition, controlled laboratory studies suggest that experimentally induced increases in stress lead to increased desire to smoke (Payne, Schare, Levis, & Colletti, 1991; Perkins & Grobe, 1992; Tiffany & Drobes, 1990) and smoking intensity (e.g., Payne et al., 1991; Pomerleau & Pomerleau, 1987; Rose, Ananda, & Jarvik, 1983; Schachter, Silverstein, & Perlick, 1977).

Because smokers' self-reports of negative affect cuing smoking are so consistent and compelling, almost every theory of smoking, dating back to Tomkins (1966, 1968), predicts or accommodates a relationship between mood and smoking. The influential integrative accounts of Leventhal and Cleary (1980) and Pomerleau and Pomerleau (1984, 1987) both put mood and mood regulation at the center of their accounts of smoking.

A simple physical dependence model posits that decreases in nicotine levels lead to symptoms of nicotine withdrawal, prompting smoking to relieve those symptoms. Because nicotine withdrawal is primarily marked by disturbances of affect (dysphoria, irritability, anxiety, and restlessness; *Diagnostic and Statistical Manual of Mental Disorders* [4th ed.; *DSM–IV*]; American Psychiatric Association, 1994), such negative affect states become the cues for smoking. Furthermore, because nicotine relieves withdrawal, these negative affect states become discriminative stimuli signaling that negative reinforcement can be obtained by self-administering nicotine. Thus, withdrawal-related negative affect becomes a strong cue for smoking. Other withdrawal symptoms such as difficulty concentrating (American Psychiatric Association, 1994; Shiffman, Paty, Gnys, Kassel, & Elash, 1995; Snyder & Henningfield, 1989) would similarly become cues for smoking. Although pure withdrawal-based models are challenged to explain why smoking does not always occur at regular intervals, Kozlowski and Herman (1984) have suggested that nicotine regulation only controls nicotine levels (and thus smoking) within broad bounds, leaving room for other environmental and affective cues to influence smoking.

Several models propose links between smoking and affect that are not mediated by withdrawal relief, but by direct "therapeutic" effects of nicotine on negative affect (Balfour & Ridley, 2000; Pomerleau & Pomerleau, 1987; Wise, 1988). The evidence that nicotine reduces negative affect other than withdrawal is mixed (Kassel, Stroud, & Paronis, 2001). Some models suggest that it is nicotine's ability to either increase or decrease arousal (rather than negative affect) that motivates smoking under conditions of either low- or high-arousal states, implying a curvilinear relationship with arousal (Eysenck, 1973; Frith, 1971). Still other models suggest that stress or negative affect may cue or prime smoking, even though smoking itself may have no effect on negative affect (Robinson & Berridge, 1993; Stewart, de Wit, & Eikelboom, 1984). In any case, multiple models predict that negative affect or arousal is associated with smoking even if the smoker is not in withdrawal.

Starting with Wikler's (1948) account of conditioned withdrawal effects, most accounts of drug use and affect also invoke secondary effects that are due to learning and conditioning (e.g., Grunberg & Baum, 1985; Leventhal & Cleary, 1979). Other theorists (e.g., Poulos, Hinson, & Siegel, 1981; Robinson & Berridge, 1993; Stewart et al., 1984) have suggested that the contexts of drug use itself (rather than drug withdrawal) might come to elicit craving and consequently drug use, in this case smoking. Niaura et al. (1988) proposed an account of how conditioning and social learning processes may underlie the role of affect in smoking.

Although most models emphasize the link between negative affect and smoking, links to positive affect have also been proposed, perhaps through activation of the incentive system (Baker, Morse, & Sherman, 1987; Robinson & Berridge, 1993; Stewart et al., 1984). Baker et al. (1987) have suggested that smoking (or at least craving) would be linked to positive affect under conditions of availability but to negative affect under deprivation. Some of these models essentially predict a curvilinear relationship between affect and smoking.

Finally, even models that do not emphasize the role of affect may predict that affective experience will cue smoking. In Tiffany's (1990) model, smoking is controlled by automatic processes. By consuming cognitive resources, affective experience may detract from nonautomatic processing, thus promoting automatic processing and thus cuing smoking. Emotions and other cues could also become releasing stimuli for automatic smoking. Thus, a very diverse range of theoretical models predict that smoking will be cued and prompted by negative and/or positive affect. In this study, we evaluate the association between affect and smoking, using real-world data about ad lib smoking episodes. We do not evaluate the effect of smoking on mood (cf. Parrott, 1999; Perkins, Grobe, Fonte, & Breus, 1992). Rather, we examine the role of affective experience as an antecedent or cue for smoking.

OTHER CUES

Although affect has been a major focus of theoretical accounts, other stimuli may also cue smoking. As with affect, the points of departure for these theories are observations that link smoking to various antecedent stimuli. Some of these stimuli (notably alcohol and caffeine) are pharmacological and, thus, susceptible to pharmacological explanations. Others (e.g., smoking-related stimuli) have no known pharmacological effects, and their associations with smoking are typically explained through conditioning mechanisms. Below, we briefly review the associations between smoking and alcohol and caffeine consumption and its association with smoking cues.

Alcohol

It has been observed that drinkers smoke and smokers drink (reviewed in Shiffman & Balabanis, 1995). In addition to this between-persons linkage, evidence suggests a situational linkage (see Shiffman & Balabanis, 1995) whereby drinking cues smoking. This has been observed both in smokers' self-reports (McKennell & Thomas, 1967) and in laboratory studies (Griffiths, Bigelow, & Liebson, 1976; Mello & Mendelson, 1986; Mintz et al., 1985; Nil, Buzzi, & Battig, 1984). This association may have a pharmacological basis, and several possible mechanisms have been proposed (Burch, de Fiebre,

Marks, & Collins, 1988; Collins, Burch, de Fiebre, & Marks, 1988; Lyon, Tong, Leigh, & Clare, 1975; Michel & Battig, 1989; see review in Shiffman & Balabanis, 1995).

Coffee

Within populations, smoking and coffee drinking are correlated (e.g., Carmody, Brischetto, Matarazzo, O'Donnell, & Connor, 1985). Situationally, smokers report smoking when they have coffee (Lane, 1996), and this has been observed in laboratory experiments (Marshall, Epstein, & Green, 1980; Marshall, Green, Epstein, Rogers, & McCoy, 1980). It is not clear whether caffeine, per se, is responsible (Chait & Griffiths, 1983; Kozlowski, 1976; Lane & Rose, 1995). Both pharmacological and behavioral explanations have been proposed (Lane, 1996; Marshall, Epstein, & Green, 1980; Marshall, Green, et al., 1980; Orlikov & Ryzov, 1991; Sawyer, Julia, & Turin, 1982; Shoaib, Swanner, Yasar, & Goldberg, 1999; Tanda & Goldberg, 2000).

Smoking Cues

The influence of conditioning processes is most evident in the link between smoking and smoking stimuli—cues specific to smoking, such as cigarettes themselves. In laboratory studies, cigarette cues can prompt smoking (Herman, 1974; Payne et al., 1991; cf. Niaura, Abrams, Pedraza, Monti, & Rohsenow, 1992) and craving (e.g., Carter & Tiffany, 1999; Niaura et al., 1988). Because these stimuli have no special pharmacological or biological meaning, their influence must be due to conditioning or cuing mechanisms.

Urge to Smoke

Although not an independent stimulus, urge to smoke has also been studied as an antecedent or trigger of smoking. Despite the intuitive link between urges and smoking and the central role of urges in some theories of smoking and drug use (e.g., Baker et al., 1987; Marlatt & Gordon, 1985; Wise, 1988), the empirical data linking urges to subsequent smoking have been surprisingly weak and inconsistent, leading some to question the role of craving in prompting smoking (Tiffany, 1990).

Methods for Studying Antecedents of Smoking

Despite the longstanding interest in these stimulus associations, they have rarely been studied in the real world. Laboratory studies do suggest that affect, smoking cues, and consumption of alcohol and caffeine can elicit craving or smoking, but it has never been established whether these cues actually do influence smoking in the smoker's everyday environment. Almost all the evidence cited in support of situational associations comes from smokers' global self-reports of smoking patterns, as reported on smoking typology questionnaires (Ikard et al., 1969; McKennell, 1970; Russell et al., 1974). Unfortunately, these assessments are fraught with psychometric problems (Shiffman, 1993), and these global, retrospective self-reports apparently do not accurately reflect actual smoking patterns (Shiffman, 1993; Shiffman & Prange, 1988; Tate, Schmitz, & Stanton, 1991). When smokers are asked to recall and summarize their smoking experience, the limits of autobiographical memory limit their accuracy and introduce bias (Hammersley, 1994; Shiffman, Hufford, et al., 1997).

We have described an alternative assessment approach that avoids the problems of global recall by assessing behavior in real time and in real-world contexts, thus avoiding problems of recall and ensuring ecological validity (Shiffman, 1993; Stone & Shiffman, 1994). In an ecological momentary assessment (EMA) approach to assessing smoking contexts, we have recorded smoking in real time, cigarette by cigarette. A substantial body of research supports the validity of self-monitoring (e.g., Epstein & Collins, 1977; Follick, Ahern, & Laser-Wolston, 1984; McFall, 1977; Montgomery & Reynolds, 1990) in both research (Shiffman, 1993; Stone & Shiffman, 1994) and clinical assessment (e.g., Beck, 1995; Craske & Barlow, 1993).

Unfortunately, by itself, self-monitoring data about when smoking occurs cannot address the association between these antecedents and smoking. Having such data provides information about the frequency of these antecedents in smoking occasions, which cannot be evaluated without information about the base rate of the antecedents (Epstein & Collins, 1977; Paty, Kassel, & Shiffman, 1992). For example, even if 50% of a smoker's cigarettes were preceded by depressed affect, we would not know whether smoking is actually associated with depression (and thus possibly triggered by it) unless we also know how often the smoker felt depressed when not smoking. By analogy to the case–control design used to establish epidemiological associations, smoking situational associations can only be established by including as case controls instances of nonsmoking.[1]

In the present study, we assessed smoking situational associations by contrasting data on the contexts of smoking and nonsmoking occasions. Smokers carried a small hand-held computer, the Electronic Diary (ED; PSION Organizer II LZ 64; PSION, Ltd., London), on which they were to record every cigarette. On a sample of smoking occasions, ED administered an assessment of the context. To sample nonsmoking contexts, we adapted the experience sampling method (see Csikszentmihalyi & Larson, 1987;

---

[1] As in case–control studies, we seem to reverse the role of cause and effect, assessing the putative causes conditional on the effects, rather than the other way around. Also, as in case–control designs, we have constrained the observations to equally represent smoking and nonsmoking occasions.

Shiffman et al., 1994; Shiffman, Paty, et al., 1996): ED "beeped" participants at random (nonsmoking) times to administer a similar situational assessment. Comparison of the smoking and nonsmoking contexts estimated the associations between smoking and situational variables such as mood, activities, smoking cues, and consumption of alcohol and caffeine.

The use of a computer to elicit and record data was an important aspect of the method (e.g., Shiffman et al., 2000; Shiffman, Engberg, et al., 1997; Shiffman, Hufford, et al., 1997; Shiffman, Paty, et al., 1996). Research shows that written diaries are often completed retrospectively and often faked (Litt, Cooney, & Morse, 1998; Shiffman et al., 1994; Stone, Shiffman, Schwartz, Broderick, & Hufford, 2002), which negates the advantage of real-time data capture. The use of palmtop computers to capture and time-tag records ensures real-time recording (Shiffman, Paty, et al., 1996; Shiffman & Stone, 1998; Stone et al., 2002).

METHOD

Participants

Participants were 304 smokers who enrolled in a smoking cessation research study. Data from some of these participants have been used in other publications (e.g., Shiffman, Engberg, et al., 1997; Shiffman et al., 1994, 2000).[2] Participants were recruited through advertisements for smoking cessation treatment and paid $50 for participating. To qualify, participants had to smoke at least 10 cigarettes per day, to have been smoking for at least 2 years, and to report high motivation and overall efficacy to quit during a screening interview (combined score of 150 on the sum of two 0–100 scales).

On a smoking history questionnaire, participants reported smoking an average of 27.6 ± 11.9 cigarettes per day and smoking for 23.1 ± 9.8 years. On average, the sample participants smoked their first cigarette of the day 16.1 ± 25.6 minutes after waking. The mean age of the sample was 44.1 ± 10 years. The sample was predominantly female (57%) and Caucasian (93%). Ninety-eight percent of the participants had completed high school, and 71% had some college experience.

Procedure

On enrollment, participants were trained to use a hand-held computer designed to allow data collection in near real time: the ED (for a complete

---

[2] This sample also includes 33 participants who were not part of the main study reported in prior publications but who participated in a pilot study of nicotine replacement whose baseline protocol was similar to that of the base study. Participants in this study abstained for a half day during baseline, but this day was not used in the analysis.

description of the ED system, see Shiffman, Paty, et al., 1996). Participants monitored ad lib smoking for 16 days prior to a designated quit date; they were instructed not to change their smoking during this time. The first 3 days of monitoring were designed to allow the participant to become familiar with the ED; data from these days were not used in analysis. We used data from the 1st week after this period (Days 4 to 11) to avoid any changes in smoking behavior that might occur as the quit date approached.

During the monitoring period, participants were instructed to record each cigarette on the ED immediately before smoking. On most of these occasions, participants had only to push a single key; ED simply recorded the smoking event. On about 4 to 5 smoking occasions per day ($M = 4.4$, $SD = 2.6$), selected at random by ED, ED administered an assessment. Participants were also prompted audibly by the ED 4 to 5 times daily ($M = 4.8$, $SD = 2.3$) at random times to complete a similar assessment while they were not smoking ("nonsmoking assessments"). The timing of the prompts was random, with the constraint that no prompts were issued for 10 minutes after a cigarette entry. Prompting covered all waking hours.

We have analyzed several measures of compliance and validity for the ED measures (Shiffman & Paty, 2002). The most direct measure of compliance was participants' response when prompted by ED. Participants responded to 91% of all prompts within the 2 minutes allowed. In 10.6% of these occasions, they responded to the prompt but requested a delay ($M = 12.4$ min, $SD = 7.1$ minutes) in completing the assessment. Participants used an ED option to suspend random prompting (e.g., when driving, to avoid intruding on important meetings) an average of once every 2.5 days, for an average of 24.2 minutes per day. Participants used a similar feature for naps once every 5 days, for a daily average duration of 18.4 minutes. Thus, although participants had access to features that allowed for some time-out from observation, the features were sparingly used and likely did not substantially bias the data.

We also examined the number of cigarette entries each participant made on ED and compared it with the number of cigarettes participants reported smoking in a timeline follow-back (TLFB) assessment of those days, with retrospection over a period of less than 1 week. The average smoking rate from the two methods correlated highly ($r = .84$). On average, participants recalled smoking 2.5 cigarettes more per day than they recorded on ED ($M = 22.4$, $SD = 9.1$ vs. $M = 24.9$, $SD = 10.0$ cigarettes per day), but on 34% of days, their TLFB recall of smoking included fewer cigarettes than they had actually recorded on ED. ED cigarette counts correlated with biochemical measures (cotinine and CO) as well as TLFB measures, but in a multivariate equation, they actually accounted for more incremental variance in biochemical measures. Participants reported on a follow-up questionnaire that they had entered the vast majority (95.2 ± 8.5%) of the cigarettes that they smoked. Thus, compliance, although not perfect, appears to have been excellent. We saw evidence of possible reactivity: Daily smoking frequency dropped an average of 0.30 cigarettes per day over the study period ($p < .0001$).

Assessments

Cigarette and nonsmoking assessments incorporated identical assessments of situation, activity, and mood, lasting approximately 1 to 3 minutes. Participants responded to one item at a time on screen, without being able to see prior responses.

Affect

Participants rated mood adjectives derived from the circumplex model of affect (Larsen & Diener, 1992; Russell, 1980), which specifies that affect consists of two bipolar dimensions: positive–negative affect and arousal. These items were scored on a 4-point scale (1 = NO!!, 2 = no??, 3 = yes??, 4 = YES!!; see Meddis, 1972). We also included bipolar items on affect and arousal to directly tap these key circumplex dimensions, as well as affect items drawn from the DSM–IV criteria for tobacco withdrawal.

Factor analyses of the mood data (based on 66,230 assessments from the pre- and postquit period) yielded three orthogonal factors (see Shiffman, Paty, et al., 1996). The first two replicated those expected under the circumplex model: Negative Affect ($\alpha = .87$), a bipolar valence factor (items were happy [had negative factor coefficient], irritable, miserable, tense, contented [had negative factor coefficient], frustrated/angry, sad, and overall feeling [had negative factor coefficient]); Arousal ($\alpha = .79$; items included tired, energetic [had negative factor coefficient], overall arousal level [had negative factor coefficient]). Nicotine withdrawal items did not factor separately but loaded cleanly on the Negative Affect factor. However, a single item regarding "restlessness" did not load heavily on Negative Affect but seemed to tap unique, nicotine-withdrawal-syndrome–related variance and was independently associated with relapse (Shiffman, Paty, et al., 1996); therefore, we retained this as a separate item for analysis. A third factor, Attention Disturbance ($\alpha = .64$), captured reports of difficulty concentrating (composed of feeling spacey and difficulty concentrating).

Smoking Urge

Participants separately rated smoking urge and smoking craving, each on 0-to-10 scales (0 = *no urge*, 10 = *maximum urge*). In a previous study (Shiffman, Engberg, et al., 1997), we determined that urge and craving ratings were largely redundant; only urge to smoke is included in these analyses.

Setting

Participants reported their location (see Table 15.1), whether smoking was permitted, whether they were in the company of others, and whether others were smoking in view of the participant ("no"; "yes, in my social group"; "yes, in view only"). We also assessed whether the participant moved locations to smoke. This allowed us to differentiate between the contexts in which the cigarette was smoked and the contexts associated with deciding to smoke. Because the contexts associated with deciding to smoke are more relevant to the questions of this chapter, they were selected for analysis (although these observations were excluded from some analyses; see Data Reduction and Analysis section in this chapter).

Activity

Participants reported whether they were engaged in a variety of activities, as listed in Table 15.1. Results from analyses of coffee/tea and alcohol could be distorted by individuals who never consume either beverage. Therefore, analyses of these variables were restricted to individuals who reported drinking coffee or tea ($n = 286$) or alcohol ($n = 147$) at least once during the monitoring period.

Validation

These assessments have demonstrated validity in other analyses. For example, the measures of affect, urge, activity, and setting were able to distinguish situations associated with smoking lapses from those associated with temptations and from control situations experienced around the same time (e.g., Shiffman, Engberg, et al., 1997; Shiffman, Paty, et al., 1996).[3] The measures were also validated by examining expected associations. For example, affect and arousal showed orderly and expected patterns over time of day, by weekday–weekend, and in relation to concomitant activities. The measures also conformed to expected patterns for individual differences: For example, women were more engaged in household chores, unemployed participants engaged in greater leisure, and so forth.

Data Reduction and Analysis

The unit of analysis was the individual observation, but accounted for the nesting of multiple observations within subjects, using generalized

---

[3] We additionally validated the ratings in the subset of the present sample that was asked to abstain for about 5 hours on one morning during monitoring (these data were excluded from the main analyses; see Footnote 2). Compared with scores on surrounding mornings, scores during abstinence were significantly higher on negative affect, attention disturbance, restlessness, and urge. These data demonstrate that these measures and assessment methods are sensitive to deprivation effects.

TABLE 15.1
Environmental Contexts: Percentage of Observations in Which Contexts Are Endorsed, Odds Ratios (OR), and 95% Confidence Intervals (CI) From GEE Analyses

Environmental items (all binary scales)	Including all observations				Excluding restricted observations			
	r	NS (%)	Cig (%)	OR (95% CI)	r	NS (%)	Cig (%)	OR (95% CI)
Location								
Home	.10	48	59	1.53 (1.41–1.67)****	.04	59	65	1.25 (1.11–1.41)***
Work	−.11	29	20	0.61 (0.56–0.68)****	−.03	18	15	0.85 (0.71–1.00)
Other's home	−.02	5	5	0.89 (0.77–1.04)	−.03	6	4	0.84 (0.70–1.01)
Bar or restaurant	.05	3	4	1.71 (1.45–2.01)****	.04	3	4	1.54 (1.27–1.86)****
Controlling for drinking alcohol, other smokers, eating, engaged in leisure				1.00 (0.84–1.20)				1.05 (0.86–1.29)
Car	−.03	8	6	0.76 (0.66–0.88)***	−.06	9	6	0.58 (0.49–0.69)****
Outside	.03	3	4	1.37 (1.09–1.74)**	.01	3	4	1.01 (0.78–1.31)
Other location	−.07	4	2	0.51 (0.42–0.62)****	−.03	2	2	0.97 (0.74–1.27)
Activity								
Working/chores	−.08	47	39	0.70 (0.65–0.76)****	−.04	41	36	0.82 (0.74–0.90)****
Job vs. all other	−.12	30	20	0.60 (0.55–0.67)****	−.05	20	17	0.76 (0.66–0.87)***
Controlling for other smokers interacting for business								
House/personal vs. all other	.01	16	17	1.09 (1.00–1.20)	−.01	19	18	0.90 (0.76–1.06)
Leisure	.05	43	48	1.22 (1.12–1.32)****	.01	49	50	0.99 (0.89–1.09)
Telephone	.00	9	9	0.97 (0.86–1.11)	.01	9	9	1.02 (0.87–1.19)
Interacting with others	−.06	54	48	0.79 (0.73–0.85)****	−.06	51	45	0.83 (0.75–0.91)***
Socializing vs. all other	.03	23	25	1.11 (1.03–1.20)**	.00	25	25	1.01 (0.91–1.11)
Business vs. all other	−.11	17	10	0.53 (0.47–0.59)****	−.07	11	7	0.65 (0.55–0.77)****
House issues vs. all other	.00	8	8	1.03 (0.91–1.16)	−.03	9	8	0.88 (0.76–1.03)
Arguing vs. all other	.01	1	1	1.32 (0.96–1.83)	.01	1	1	1.05 (0.71–1.56)
Other vs. all other	−.04	5	4	0.81 (0.68–0.96)*	−.04	5	4	0.85 (0.68–1.05)
Inactive	.08	23	30	1.42 (1.31–1.55)****	.07	26	31	1.21 (1.08–1.35)***
Waiting vs. all other	.04	5	6	1.26 (1.09–1.45)**	.05	5	6	1.12 (0.94–1.34)
Between activities vs. all other	.07	9	12	1.51 (1.34–1.71)****	.06	9	13	1.28 (1.11–1.48)***
Doing nothing vs. all other	.02	10	12	1.22 (1.10–1.34)***	.01	12	12	1.07 (0.93–1.23)
Other activity	−.03	18	16	0.84 (0.75–0.94)**	−.04	18	15	0.76 (0.67–0.87)****

(continues)

TABLE 15.1

Environmental Contexts: Percentage of Observations in Which Contexts Are Endorsed, Odds Ratios (OR), and 95% Confidence Intervals (CI) From GEE Analyses   (Continued)

Environmental items (all binary scales)	Including all observations				Excluding restricted observations			
	r	NS (%)	Cig (%)	OR (95% CI)	r	NS (%)	Cig (%)	OR (95% CI)
Food and drink								
Any eating or drinking	.13	36	49	1.67 (1.56–1.78)****	.13	38	50	1.68 (1.54–1.82)****
Coffee or tea vs. all others	.10	20	28	1.57 (1.45–1.71)****	.10	20	29	1.55 (1.39–1.72)****
Controlling for bar or restaurant, others smoking, eating, engaged in leisure				1.20 (1.08–1.34)**				1.19 (1.04–1.36)**
Alcohol vs. all others	.08	6	11	2.10 (1.80–2.45)****	.08	7	12	1.94 (1.62–2.33)****
Controlling for bar or restaurant, others smoking, eating, engaged in leisure				1.38 (1.14–1.67)***				1.30 (1.06–1.60)
Eating (meal or snack)	.06	18	22	1.32 (1.23–1.43)****	.05	19	23	1.32 (1.21–1.44)****
Meal vs. all others	.05	10	13	1.37 (1.26–1.50)****	.04	10	13	1.33 (1.20–1.47)****
Snack vs. all others	.03	8	10	1.18 (1.06–1.31)**	.03	8	9	1.23 (1.08–1.39)**
Meal vs. snack (snack is reference)	−.01	45	42	0.88 (0.77–1.00)*	.01	44	42	0.96 (0.82–1.11)
Smoking environment								
Smoking is forbidden	−.20	26	11	0.36 (0.32–0.42)****				
Smoking is discouraged	−.03	13	11	0.85 (0.76–0.96)*				
Smoking is allowed	−.19	61	78	2.19 (1.96–2.45)****				
Smoking allowed[a]	.20	2.34 ± 0.87[b]	2.66 ± 0.67[b]	1.68 (1.57–1.79)****				
Others smoking	.11	10	17	1.78 (1.58–2.01)****	.06	14	17	1.34 (1.18–1.54)****
Controlling for bar or restaurant, alcohol, eating, engaged in leisure				1.63 (1.44–1.85)****				1.23 (1.07–1.41)**
Smokers in group vs. in view (view is reference)	.06	74	74	0.97 (0.77–1.23)	.07	74	73	1.03 (0.81–1.32)
Other								
Alone	.06	39	45	1.27 (1.18–1.37)****	.05	44	49	1.19 (1.09–1.31)***

Note. GEE = generalized estimating equations; NS = nonsmoking assessments; Cig = cigarette.
[a] Response scale: 1 = *smoking is forbidden*, 2 = *smoking is discouraged*, 3 = *smoking is allowed*. [b] For this variable only, values indicate means and standard deviations.
*p < .05. **p < .01. ***p < .001. ****p < .0001.

estimating equations (GEE; Zeger, Liang, & Albert, 1988).[4] The analysis treated assessment type (cigarette vs. nonsmoking) as a categorical dependent variable to be modeled as a function of independent situational variables (mood, activity, situation). Some situational variables provided for subcoding (e.g., activity = work, job related vs. home-related). Where this applied, we analyzed the subcategories by contrasting each one against the aggregate of all others, to test for differences among subcategories. Because the dependent variable (smoking or not) was binary, the GEE models the log odds of smoking in a particular context (i.e., ratio of the odds that a participant smokes in a context to the odds that a participant smokes in the absence of a context). We report the odds ratios (Rudas, 1998) and their 95% confidence intervals. To provide some control of Type I error, even though these analyses were considered somewhat exploratory, we emphasized interpretation only when $p < .01$.

Another way to think of these data is that one can estimate for each participant the degree of association between smoking as an antecedent, expressed as a correlation coefficient. The average of these coefficients summarizes the association within the sample. For descriptive purposes, to convey effect sizes, we display these averaged within-subject correlation coefficients (point-biserial or phi coefficients, depending on the variable type).

Analysis proceeded in four steps:[5]

1. We analyzed data from all cigarette ($n = 10,084$) and nonsmoking ($n = 11,155$) observations.
2. We controlled for externally imposed smoking restrictions by excluding nonsmoking observations where smoking was "forbidden" and cigarette observations where the participant changed location to smoke. We implemented this control because smoking regulations could mask some associations (by suppressing smoking when it might otherwise occur) or result in artifactual associations (when smoking restrictions covary with the situational variable). We present this as a parallel analysis in the tables.[6]

---

[4] AR(1) and exchangeable autocorrelation structures yielded similar results. Only results from analyses using an AR(1) structure are reported.

[5] We also performed two additional sets of analyses: (a) We adjusted for time of day prior to assessing target contexts, and (b) we excluded cigarette entries occurring close together in time because the second cigarette in a back-to-back sequence might be prompted by the first cigarette rather than by situational antecedents. Results from these variant analyses were virtually identical to the analysis presented.

[6] We also performed analyses in which we statistically controlled for smoking restrictions rather than excluding observations. In these analyses, responses to the "smoking permitted" item were transformed into dummy variables and entered in the GEE equations prior to the target variables. Results from these analyses were similar to results from the presented analyses that were based on excluding observations.

3. We controlled for potential confounders or mediators of significant relationships. For example, a relationship between smoking and being at a bar or restaurant may be due to other variables, such as alcohol consumption or presence of other smokers in these settings. In these analyses, we reevaluated the link between smoking and the situational context while controlling for the influence of such confounds or potential mediators.

4. Finally, we summarize analyses in which we analyzed subsets of observations where the time lags between cigarette entries and nonsmoking assessments fell within certain limits.

RESULTS

Descriptive Statistics

On average, participants contributed 7.85 ± 0.36 days of data for analysis. All participants provided at least 7 days. During this interval, participants had recorded 51,109 cigarette entries (168.1 ± 70.2 per participant). The data set included 2,386 days of data, encompassing 10,084 cigarette and 11,155 nonsmoking assessments. The proportion of observations in which each environmental context was present is displayed in Table 15.1, by observation type (i.e., cigarette or nonsmoking assessment). Means and standard deviations for continuous affect variables are presented in Table 15.2, by observation type.

Smoking Regulations

Smoking restrictions were commonly reported. Smoking was forbidden in 26% of nonsmoking observations and 11% of cigarette assessments (Table 15.1). These reported smoking restrictions influenced smoking. The odds of smoking were reduced by 64% when smoking was forbidden. Conversely, the odds were increased 119% when smoking was allowed (neither forbidden nor discouraged). Participants also frequently reported changing locations to smoke. Participants changed locations prior to 21% of cigarette assessments. As expected, changing location was much more likely when participants reported that smoking was forbidden in the original environment, $\chi^2(2, N = 8111) = 2,644.5, p < .0001$. Because smoking restrictions had the potential to perturb the normal associations between smoking and context, a subsequent set of analyses controlled for the effect of smoking prohibitions, by eliminating nonsmoking observations in which smoking was said to be forbidden (because the person might otherwise have smoked) and cigarette observations where the participant changed location to smoke (because changing locations muddled the context data; see "Excluding restricted observations" column in Tables 15.1 and 15.2).

TABLE 15.2
Affect Variables: Means, Standard Deviations, Odds Ratios (OR), and 95% Confidence Intervals (CI) From GEE Analyses

| | Including all observations | | | | Excluding restricted observations | | | |
| | | M ± SD | | | | M ± SD | | |
Variable	r	NS	Cig	OR (95% CI)	r	NS	Cig	OR (95% CI)
Urge to smoke (0–10)	.45	4.10 ± 3.08	6.25 ± 2.39		.43	4.23 ± 3.02	6.25 ± 2.40	
Linear								
Range 0–6				1.33 (1.29–1.37)****				1.36 (1.31–1.41)****
Range 7–10				1.64 (1.56–1.72)****				1.65 (1.56–1.74)****
Quadratic				1.08 (1.00–1.16)*				1.10 (1.01–1.20)*
				0.96 (0.95–0.96)****				0.96 (0.95–0.97)****
Affect: Factor								
Negative affect (factor score)	.02	−0.08 ± 0.95	−0.06 ± 0.96		.03	−0.13 ± 0.94	−0.07 ± 0.96	
Linear				1.02 (0.98–1.07)				1.07 (1.01–1.13)*
Quadratic				1.00 (0.98–1.02)				0.98 (0.95–1.01)
Attention deficit (factor score)	.01	−0.06 ± 0.87	−0.04 ± 0.89		−.01	−0.03 ± 0.88	−0.05 ± 0.89	
Linear				1.03 (0.98–1.07)				0.98 (0.91–1.05)
Arousal (factor score)	−.01	0.08 ± 0.99	0.06 ± 0.98		.01	0.05 ± 0.99	0.05 ± 0.99	
Linear				0.98 (0.95–1.02)				1.02 (0.97–1.07)
Quadratic				1.00 (0.97–1.03)				1.00 (0.96–1.04)
Affect: Individual summary items[a]								
Overall affect (1–5)[b]	−.03	3.55 ± 0.84	3.52 ± 0.84		−.02	3.56 ± 0.83	3.52 ± 0.84	
Linear				0.96 (0.92–1.01)				0.97 (0.91–1.03)
Quadratic				0.98 (0.94–1.01)				1.01 (0.97–1.07)
Overall arousal (1–5)[c]	−.02	2.88 ± 0.97	2.86 ± 0.97		.00	2.86 ± 0.97	2.85 ± 0.97	
Linear				0.98 (0.94–1.01)				1.01 (0.96–1.07)
Quadratic				1.00 (0.97–1.03)				1.01 (0.97–1.05)
Restlessness (1–4)[d]	.10	1.50 ± 0.79	1.62 ± 0.86		.08	1.50 ± 0.78	1.59 ± 0.84	
Linear				1.18 (1.12–1.24)****				1.15 (1.08–1.24)****
Quadratic				1.00 (0.94–1.06)				1.06 (0.98–1.15)
Negative affect residual				1.21 (1.15–1.28)****				1.14 (1.06–1.22)***
Hunger (1–4)	−.04	1.69 ± 0.99	1.59 ± 0.94		−.04	1.69 ± 0.99	1.57 ± 0.93	
Linear				0.90 (0.87–0.94)****				0.88 (0.84–0.92)****
Quadratic				1.03 (0.99–1.09)				1.02 (0.96–1.09)
Control for eating				0.92 (0.88–0.95)****				0.89 (0.85–0.93)****

Note. GEE = generalized estimating equations; NS = nonsmoking assessments; Cig = cigarette.
[a]These items were used in computing the factor scores above. They are included separately to provide the reader with data on affect summaries with a simple scale. [b]Item text: "Overall feeling?" 1 = *very bad*, 2 = *bad*, 3 = *neutral*, 4 = *good*, 5 = *very good.* [c]Item text: "Your arousal/energy level?" 1 = *very low*, 2 = *low*, 3 = *moderate*, 4 = *high*, 5 = *very high.* [d]Restlessness was not included in the scoring of the affect factors but kept separate, as described in the Method section.
*p < .05. ***p < .001. ****p < .0001.

Environmental Contexts and Smoking

Location

Table 15.1 shows analyses assessing the relationship between location–activity and smoking. Smokers were more likely to smoke at home, even after controlling for smoking restrictions. Conversely, smokers were less likely to smoke when in vehicles. Smoking was also less likely in workplaces. However, this effect was eliminated when smoking-restricted observations were removed. The biggest promoter of smoking was being in bars and restaurants: Being in those locations increased the odds of smoking by 54%, even when smoking restrictions were accounted for. However, when we controlled for alcohol and food consumption, the presence of other smokers, and leisure activity, bars and restaurants were no longer associated with increased odds of smoking, indicating that these other variables completely mediate the influence of these locations. Similarly, it appeared that differential distribution of smoking restrictions accounted for the univariate association of smoking with outdoor locations and other locations (inverse), as these associations disappeared when restrictions were controlled.

Activity

Several activities showed robust associations with smoking. Most prominently, smokers were less likely to be smoking when they were working. This held true (though somewhat diminished) even when we controlled for smoking restrictions. Subanalyses of different kinds of work activities suggested that job-related work accounted for much of the effect. (This was in turn accounted for by the presence of other smokers and work-related social interactions, as demonstrated by the disappearance of the effect when these variables were controlled.) After controlling for smoking restrictions, smoking was also less likely when participants engaged in an unassessed ("other") type of work. Conversely, engaging in leisure activities was associated with more smoking, but this effect was attributable to the fact that leisure tended to occur where smoking was not restricted. Smokers were more likely to smoke when they were inactive, particularly when they were "between activities," even when smoking restrictions were controlled.

People were less likely to smoke when engaged in interaction with others (see also "alone" variable in Table 15.1), even when smoking restrictions were considered. Subanalyses of interactions suggest that the effect was largely due to business-related interactions, which were associated with a 35% reduction in the odds of smoking, even when smoking restrictions were controlled. Smokers smoked more when socializing, but this was accounted for by smoking restrictions.

Food, Coffee/Tea, and Alcohol Consumption

Smokers were more likely to be smoking if they had recently eaten food, regardless of whether they ate a meal or a snack. This effect was not substantially diminished when smoking restrictions were controlled.

Consumption of coffee or tea was associated with a 55% increase in the odds of smoking, even when smoking restrictions were controlled. The effect was diminished, but not eliminated, when we accounted for possible confounding variables (being at a bar or restaurant, the presence of others smoking, consumption of food, and engaging in leisure).

Consumption of alcohol doubled the odds of smoking. This was somewhat diminished when smoking restrictions were accounted for and even further diminished to trend level when other correlated variables such as being in a bar, the presence of others smoking, consumption of food, and leisure activity were accounted for.

Smoking Cues

When others were smoking in the participant's presence, the odds of smoking were significantly increased by 78%. This was diminished to an odds ratio of 1.34 when smoking restrictions were accounted for, and the effect was maintained when we controlled for drinking, location at a bar or restaurant, and leisure activity. Subanalyses broke out others' smoking according to whether the smoker was part of the participant's immediate social group or just a stranger who could be seen smoking. Both contexts equally increased the odds of smoking, and there was no reliable difference between them, suggesting that the effect is not mediated by social bonds.

Internal States and Smoking

Urge to Smoke

Means and standard deviations for urge scores from cigarette and nonsmoking observations are listed in Table 15.2. The urge to smoke variable demonstrated a substantial association with smoking. There was a linear effect of urge to smoke such that the odds of smoking were increased by 33% for every 1-point increase in urge to smoke (on a 0-to-10 scale). There was also a curvilinear effect, reflecting a flattening of the relationship near the top of the craving scale (see Figure 15.1). These effects were not attenuated when the effect of smoking restrictions was controlled.

Affect

In the full data set, smoking was unrelated to Negative Affect, Arousal, or Attention Disturbance. The odds ratios were all close to 1.0, and the average

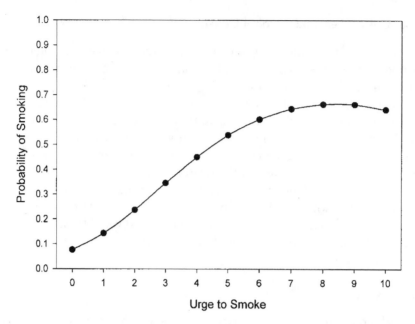

Figure 15.1. The relationship between urge ratings and the probability of smoking. Note that the design of the study artificially constrained the probability of smoking to be approximately .50 (because we collected equal numbers of smoking and nonsmoking observations, in a case–control design). The analysis of these data was based on the odds ratio, which is insensitive to these base rates (Rudas, 1998).

correlations were close to 0. The affect scores are bipolar (e.g., a high score on Negative Affect represents distress, and a low score represents contentment or happiness).[7] Thus, if smoking occurred when smokers were at either extreme—say, either unhappy or happy—a linear effect might not be observed, but the data would show curvilinear effects. These effects also were not observed.

The results change modestly when we control for smoking restrictions. Negative Affect now demonstrates a trend toward modest association with smoking. For every 1-point (i.e., 1 standard deviation) increase in Negative Affect, the odds of smoking are increased by 7%. (To supplement analysis of the factor scores for Negative Affect and Arousal, we also analyzed each individual affect item, with similar results; we present two items in Table 15.2.) There was no curvilinear relationship between Negative Affect and smoking.

Restlessness was evaluated as a separate single-item score. Participants were more likely to smoke when they were more restless, even when Negative Affect scores were controlled.

The odds of smoking were increased about 20% for every 1-point increase in Restlessness (1-to-4 scale). Controlling for smoking restrictions

---

[7] To test whether there might be effects that were due to extreme affect, we dichotomized affect ratings; the conclusion was unchanged.

did not diminish the effect. The odds of smoking were decreased when smokers were more hungry, even after controlling for eating and for situational smoking restrictions.

Lags Between Observations and Sensitivity Testing

To better understand the dynamics of the data, we analyzed the time lags between the smoking and nonsmoking observations in the dataset. The lag between a recorded smoking episode and a subsequent nonsmoking prompt was constrained by the ED's program to be at least 10 minutes. The mean interval between a smoking entry and a nonsmoking assessment was 46.5 ± 34.4 minutes. Two thirds of prompt assessments (67.0%) were completed between 20 and 60 minutes after a cigarette entry, and 96.7% fell within 120 minutes of a cigarette entry.

Similarly, we examined the lags between randomly scheduled nonsmoking prompts and subsequent smoking assessments. These lags averaged 32.4 ± 33.8 min. In all, 97.5% of smoking assessments fell within 120 minutes. The distribution of intervals was skewed toward shorter intervals: 21.7% of the smoking assessments fell within 5 minutes after a prompt, suggesting that the prompts may have prompted smoking, or recording of smoking.

We conducted sensitivity tests to see how our findings may have been influenced by particularly short or long lags. For example, analyzing nonsmoking observations that fell soon after a smoking occasion may underestimate the difference between smoking and nonsmoking contexts, because of their proximity in time. Similarly, cigarettes smoked soon after a prompt may underestimate the distinction of smoking occasions. In this case, if ED prompts actually prompted the smoking, the prompting would be the driving variable, and the influence of more natural variables would be masked. Conversely, because nicotine withdrawal symptoms start to emerge after about 120 minutes, nonsmoking assessments that fall a long time after the last cigarettes could be picking up nicotine withdrawal symptoms and confounding the comparison of smoking and nonsmoking occasions.

To test whether our findings were influenced by the extreme lag times, we recomputed the analyses after removing observations with extreme lags. In four reanalyses, we dropped observations with cigarette-to-prompt lags ≥ 120 minutes or lags ≤ 20 minutes and prompt-to-cigarette lags ≥ 120 minutes or lags ≤ 5 minutes. Dropping these observations did not substantially alter the findings. The possible exception is that when cigarettes recorded within 5 minutes of an ED-issued prompt (and which may have been prompted by the ED assessment prompt) were dropped, the observed associations between smoking and antecedents were slightly enhanced. However, the effects were small, the patterns did not change, and there was no change in the associations between smoking and affect.

DISCUSSION

Stimulus-control models of smoking have been influential in shaping our thinking about nicotine self-administration (and, indeed, about all drug use and abuse). According to these models, particular environmental or affect cues, after repeated associations with smoking, can prompt smoking. Most accounts of smoking have emphasized the role of affect as an important antecedent and driver of smoking. However, these relationships have never been evaluated in real-world settings. This is, to our knowledge, the first detailed study of smoking antecedents in naturalistic settings, based on a substantial dataset (21,239 observations) from a large sample of smokers ($N = 304$). The results support the hypothesis that smoking is under partial control of situational antecedents: Certain locations and activities were associated with enhanced likelihood of smoking. However, the analyses largely contradicted the hypothesis that smoking is under substantial control of affective antecedents. In general, and contrary to theory and some prior data, our data suggest that the association between smoking and situational factors is weak. Although urge to smoke, alcohol consumption, smoking restrictions, and a few other setting variables were significantly associated with smoking, many hypothesized relationships failed to materialize or were weaker than expected.

The most striking finding is the near absence of a relationship between affect and smoking. When all data points were considered, there was no reliable association between smoking and negative affect. When we excluded situations where smoking was restricted, a trend emerged (findings at .05 were not considered significant), but the effect was very small: Just before smoking, mood was only 0.06 standard deviation more negative than in nonsmoking situations, and the average within-subject correlation between smoking and negative affect was only .03. Our affect assessment was based on a bipolar factor score for affective valence, rooted in the circumplex model of affect (Larsen & Diener, 1992; Russell, 1980), with high scores indicating negative affect and low scores indicating positive affect. To test whether smoking might be associated with both positive and negative mood (i.e., the extremes), we tested for curvilinear effects and found that there were none. We also found no relationship at all between arousal and smoking. In short, smoking was largely unrelated to affective state.

This finding may seem at odds with literature suggesting that smoking is driven by negative affect, but the link is in fact not firmly established in the literature.[8] The lion's share of the evidence that negative affect prompts

---

[8] Although several studies have reported epidemiological correlations, such as that heavy smoking is associated with stress (Anda et al., 1990; Breslau et al., 1994; Kirkcaldy et al., 1994; Naquin & Gilbert, 1996), this could be because smoking causes stress (see Cohen & Lichtenstein, 1990; Parrott, 1999) or because some third factor is associated with both stress and heavy smoking.

smoking comes from smokers' self-reports on questionnaires, which are subject to question on multiple grounds (Shiffman, 1993). The few laboratory studies that observed increased smoking after manipulating negative affect (e.g., Dobbs, Strickler, & Maxwell, 1981; Payne et al., 1991; Pomerleau & Pomerleau, 1987; Rose et al., 1983; Schachter et al., 1977) did not actually examine whether negative affect caused smokers to initiate smoking; rather, the studies directed smokers to smoke and assessed how much they smoked. Different processes may control initiation of smoking and the intensity of smoking once it is initiated.

Laboratory studies also use uncharacteristic stressors to generate levels and kinds of affect not typically seen in real life. The laboratory studies can only establish that negative affect could, in principle, influence smoking intensity, not that it actually does so under real-world conditions. Laboratory studies' poor ecological validity and problems controlling for withdrawal effects limit the generalizability of the results. The present study suggests that during a week of ad-lib smoking in the real world, momentary affect plays little role in prompting smoking.

In contrast to ad lib smoking, there is strong evidence, including real-time data using the methods and samples of this study, showing a strong link between affect and relapse (Baer & Lichtenstein, 1988; Cummings et al., 1980; Shiffman, 1982; Shiffman, Paty, et al., 1996). However, this effect may be mediated by entirely different mechanisms. For example, emotional upset may disrupt smokers' attempts at self-control and thus lead to smoking (Muraven & Baumeister, 2000; Shiffman & Jarvik, 1987). The experience of a strong link between affect and smoking in highly salient relapse situations may help develop smokers' beliefs that they smoke when they are upset.

It is also possible that smoking might initially be responsive to affect but that these associations disappear with long-term smoking. Over a long period and hundreds of thousands of repetitions (our sample had smoked an average of 23 years), smoking may come to be functionally autonomous and driven primarily by nicotine regulation. Indeed, the development of stereotypic and automatized patterns of use and the loosening of environmental control have been described as a hallmark of dependence (Edwards & Gross, 1976; see also Tiffany, 1990). However, smokers' experience of affective influence at salient times—early in their smoking careers and in relapse episodes—may inculcate strong and persistent beliefs that smoking is affect driven even when these circumstances are not relevant: Cognitive research suggests that such impressions of self may be long-lasting and resistant to change that is based on new experience.

The lack of a relationship among smoking and withdrawal-relevant mood states and difficulty concentrating damages the hypothesis that withdrawal symptoms prompt the smoking of most cigarettes. This is consistent with the boundary model (Kozlowski & Herman, 1984), which posits that smokers spend much of their time in a zone of comfort, wherein their smoking is prompted by other factors. Consistent with the boundary model, smokers may also anticipate their need to smoke and smoke in advance to maintain themselves within the comfort zone. This would tend to blur the immediate influences analyzed in this study. However, our study should have detected even a small number of affect-driven smoking episodes and, thus, presents a challenge to withdrawal-based models of acute smoking regulation.

Whereas overall affective valence was not associated with smoking, restlessness showed a modest association (average $r = .08$), which was independent of overall affective valence. Restlessness is a distinct symptom of nicotine withdrawal (*DSM–IV*; American Psychiatric Association, 1994), and also distinguishes relapse situations independent of negative affect (Shiffman, Paty, et al., 1996). Perceived restlessness could reflect some sort of unchanneled activation of the appetitive "go" system or the incentive salience system (Baker et al., 1987; Robinson & Berridge, 1993), which is activated when nicotine seeking is triggered. More research on restlessness may be useful.

Although associations with subjective states were modest or absent, our study documented a number of associations between smoking and other setting variables. The smoking environment substantially influenced smoking. Smoking was less likely when smoking was forbidden or discouraged. Smoking policies exercise control over smoking, but it is far from perfect: 11% of cigarettes included in this analysis were smoked in situations where smoking was forbidden and 11% when it was discouraged.

The influence of smoking restrictions posed a challenge in assessing the associations between smoking and contextual variables. By artificially constraining when and where smokers can light up, such restrictions could potentially have disrupted the natural associations between situational stimuli and smoking. Smokers may sometimes wish or need to smoke, but cannot. At other times, smokers may smoke when they do not really want to in order to capitalize on a fleeting opportunity to smoke. This could potentially blunt associations with contextual variables or introduce artifactual associations. We controlled for this by analyzing only those observations where the influence of restrictions should be minimized (i.e., nonsmoking observations where smoking was not forbidden and smoking occasions where the smoker did not have to escape a restricted environment). However, prolonged imposition of external constraints could have so disrupted normal patterns of smoking that the "native" associations have become difficult to observe. For example, smokers may smoke even in the absence of triggering stimuli in anticipation of being unable to smoke later. Analyses of smoking patterns in situations that are less restrictive (e.g., other countries) may be revealing.

Social and sensory smoking cues also influenced smoking. Smoking was more likely when others were smoking, even when other contextual factors were controlled. Others' smoking could influence the smoker either by providing visual and olfactory cues or by providing social cues for smoking (including offers of cigarettes): Social influences would be strongest when the other smokers are part of one's immediate social group rather than strangers glimpsed across a room. We found that smoking by others in one's group and that by others just in view of the smoker exercised similar influence on smoking, suggesting that sensory cuing, rather than social influence, is responsible. (It is interesting to note that a similar analysis of influences on relapse concluded that in that setting, the effect of others' smoking was mediated by social rather than sensory factors; Shiffman, Paty, et al., 1996.) This is consistent with the laboratory findings that both the sight and smell of cigarettes (Sayette & Hufford, 1994) and the sight of someone smoking (McDermut & Haaga, 1998; Warren & McDonough, 1999) elicit craving.

Smokers were generally more likely to smoke when they had been eating or drinking. However, the relationship between consumption of alcohol and smoking was reduced to a statistical trend after controlling for smoking restrictions and other correlated contexts (e.g., presence in a bar and others' smoking). This was unexpected because alcohol has demonstrated robust relationships with smoking in laboratory studies (Shiffman & Balabanis, 1995) and indeed, in a previous report on ad lib smoking correlates from this laboratory (Shiffman et al., 1994). Because alcohol consumption was so strongly tied to place, activity, smoking regulations, and others' smoking, our analysis may have overcontrolled for these situational variables, making the effect of alcohol difficult to discern. In any case, the analysis at least suggests that much of the association between drinking and smoking may be under the control of situational stimuli that typically accompany real-world alcohol consumption. In any case, because most people smoke far more frequently than they drink, alcohol consumption can have only a modest impact on smoking.

Coffee (and tea) drinking was also associated with smoking. The data do not allow a clear attribution to caffeine, per se, because they do not distinguish between caffeinated and decaffeinated beverages. Smoking was also more likely when participants had been eating. The link between eating and smoking and smokers' preference for a postprandial cigarette have long been known, but the mechanism has yet to be elucidated (Gritz et al., 1988; Lee, Jacob, Jarvik, & Benowitz, 1989). Strikingly, smokers were also somewhat less likely to smoke when they were hungry, even when statistically adjusting for recent eating. This again suggests complex interactions among smoking, eating, and hunger (Perkins, Epstein, Fonte, Mitchell, & Grobe, 1995) that remain to be adequately described.

Smokers' current activity influenced smoking behavior. Smokers were significantly less likely to smoke when working, particularly on job-related activities, even after controlling for smoking restrictions. However, this relationship was accounted for by the presence of other smokers and interacting with others for business. Anecdotally, people seem to not smoke when occupied but to smoke during breaks in activity. Indeed, being between activities was associated with smoking and also with relapse (Shiffman, 1982).

Smoking was particularly likely to occur in bars, restaurants, and at home and particularly unlikely to occur in vehicles. Of course, a physical location is often just a marker for a collection of other contextual variables, such as smoking regulations, the behavior of others, and so on. For example, the excess smoking observed in bars and restaurants could be entirely accounted for by the presence of others smoking, food and alcohol consumption, and leisure activity. In other words, the setting, cues, and behavior, not the location per se, drive smoking.

The single strongest association observed in this study was between urge and smoking. This effect was most evident for low to moderate ranges of urge. We found a curvilinear relationship between urge and smoking: Increases in urge intensity between 0 and 6 (on a 0–10 scale) resulted in steeply increasing likelihood of smoking. Further increases beyond an urge of 6 did not much increase the already high likelihood of smoking, perhaps because an urge of this level is adequate to cue smoking when it is not otherwise constrained. Thus, urge appears to exert effects on smoking through a threshold effect, such that urges 7 or greater do not increase the chance of smoking. This suggests one reason why a relationship between urge and smoking sometimes may not be observed (Tiffany, 1990): It is only evident at low to moderate urge levels. Many studies, particularly laboratory studies with deprived smokers, may be conducted with smokers at higher urge levels, where the relationship is flat. In any case, the relatively strong relationship observed contradicts skepticism about whether urge is associated with smoking (Tiffany, 1990). However, the data do not directly contradict Tiffany's model of urges, which suggests that urges become evident when automatic processes supporting smoking are interrupted, precisely what would happen as a participant remembered to make a data entry in this study. In any case, the data suggest that urges are associated with ad-lib smoking in real-world settings. This should not be surprising: Urges have long been described as a subjective read-out of the drive to smoke, and are likely important subjective prompts to initiate smoking.

This study had several limitations. Our observations were correlational, rather than experimentally controlled. Indeed, participants decided when to smoke and, at the time they completed the smoking assessments, knew they were about to smoke. Anticipation of smoking may have blunted some effects that might have been observed otherwise. We also cannot rule out confounding influences of unobserved variables in this correlational design, although we controlled for some of the more obvious confounds.

The study's validity depends heavily on participant compliance. We achieved excellent verifiable compliance with response to randomly issued beeps: Participants responded to 91% within 2 minutes. Although participants appear to have recorded the vast majority of their cigarettes, we could not objectively confirm that they did so in a timely way. If participants were noncompliant, this could bias the results. For example, if participants particularly failed to record cigarettes when they were emotionally distraught, this would blunt the relationship between affect and smoking. The number of cigarettes recorded on ED was sometimes fewer than those reported in timeline follow-back, which could indicate some noncompliance (or poor estimation in global self-report; see Klesges, Debon, & Ray, 1993). Although subjects were instructed to record cigarettes before they smoked them, it was impossible to verify when subjects made the recordings. We also observed small decreases in reported smoking over the study period (0.30 cigarettes per day), consistent with prior findings on self-monitoring (Abrams & Wilson, 1979). It is not known whether method-related reactivity might affect smoking patterns as well as rate.

Our study relied solely on self-report. Other measures of affect (e.g., facial coding: Ekman & Friesen, 1978) and/or objective observations of smoking could potentially lead to different conclusions. We also cannot directly assess what reactive impact the beeping or the rating task itself may have had on affect ratings. However, we note that the affect ratings were validated in connection to other outcomes, including smoking relapse. Our study also focused solely on momentary affect immediately before smoking. It is possible that more pervasive or enduring mood states have some influence that would not be seen in these data. For example, when participants are having "a bad day" or experiencing accumulating stress, negative mood might pervade both their smoking and nonsmoking observations. However, our focus was on understanding what might immediately cue or motivate smoking within a day.

Our sample—heavy smokers seeking smoking cessation treatment—may not be representative. Heavy, frequent smokers may not have much room to moderate their smoking according to the situation. Also, as nicotine dependence climbs, smoking may break loose of situational controls and come to be controlled primarily by the need to maintain nicotine levels. However, heavy smokers are particularly likely to report negative affect smoking (U.S. Department of Health and Human Services, 1988), so links between affect and smoking should nevertheless have been evident in this sample. It is also possible that smokers who are quitting are more aware of their smoking or change their smoking pattern in some way. A study of smoking patterns among representative samples of lighter smokers and among those not seeking treatment may be warranted.

The analyses reported here do not exhaust questions about situational antecedents of smoking, particularly as regards affect and smoking. For example, it has been suggested that smoking is linked to positive affect during smoking and to negative affect during deprivation (Baker et al., 1987). Smokers in this study were smoking ad lib but may nevertheless have experienced transient deprivation. Further analyses might explore its effects on the affect–smoking relationship. It may also be useful to analyze certain subsets of smoking occasions, such as the first few cigarettes of the day, or those later in the day; there may be differences in situational associations. Further analyses could also explore individual differences in the situational distribution of smoking; for example, it has been suggested that women are more likely to smoke in response to negative affect (U.S. Department of Health and Human Services, 1988), and other individual differences have been suggested (e.g., Gilbert et al., 2000; Ikard et al., 1969). Such individual differences, if they cancel each other out, might result in a null association in the aggregate, as observed here. This chapter also focused exclusively on smoking itself as an outcome; it may be useful to analyze craving as a product of situational factors and to explore the impact of smoking on affect.

The study also offers substantial strengths. The study used EMA methods and computer technology to collect data in real time, thus avoiding the biases that plague retrospective data. We did not ask participants to recall or summarize their smoking patterns: Participants had only to appreciate and report their current state, and associations were determined statistically. This is the first study to use nonsmoking situations as controls (see Epstein & Collins, 1977; Paty et al., 1992) to properly compute associations between smoking and situational antecedents. The study analyzed a substantial sample of smoking behavior. We examined smoking as it occurred in the natural environment over a period of 1 week, at all hours of the day and night, during which participants recorded an average of about 170 cigarettes. Smoking observations were sampled at random from these recorded smoking episodes, and control observations were sampled randomly from non-smoking occasions, likely resulting in a representative sampling of experience. We analyzed a large sample of smoking and control observations, over 10,000 each, from a relatively large sample of over 300 smokers. This allowed for powerful statistical tests of study hypotheses. Finally, the context measures used in the study were based on theory (e.g., Larsen & Diener, 1992; Russell, 1980), derived from prior research (e.g., Shiffman et al., 1995), and demonstrated to reliably distinguish smoking lapses from tempting situations and random-control situations in this very sample (Shiffman, Paty, et al., 1996).

We conclude that real-world smoking is under only modest control of situational stimuli. In this analysis, affect had little association with smoking: At the time participants were moved to smoke, they felt neither better nor worse than they did when they were not smoking. As the link between affect and smoking has played such a dominant role in theories about smoking, it is time to empirically test the association, and to revise theory in light of new evidence.

REFERENCES

Abrams, D. B., & Wilson, G. T. (1979). Self-monitoring and reactivity in the modification of cigarette smoking. *Journal of Consulting and Clinical Psychology, 47*, 243–251.

American Psychiatric Association. (1994). *Diagnostic and statistical manual of mental disorders* (4th ed.). Washington, DC: Author.

Anda, R. F., Williamson, D. F., Escobedo, L. G., Mast, E. E., Giovino, G. A., & Remington, P. L. (1990). Depression and the dynamics of smoking. *Journal of the American Medical Association, 264*, 1541–1543.

Baer, J., & Lichtenstein, E. (1988). Classification and prediction of smoking relapse episodes: An exploration of individual differences. *Journal of Consulting and Clinical Psychology, 56*, 104–110.

Baker, T. B., Morse, E., & Sherman, J. E. (1987). The motivation to use drugs: A psychobiological analysis of urges. In P. C. Rivers (Ed.), *The Nebraska Symposium on Motivation: Alcohol use and abuse* (pp. 257–323). Lincoln: University of Nebraska Press.

Balfour, D. J. K., & Ridley, D. L. (2000). The effects of nicotine on neural pathways implicated in depression: A factor in nicotine addiction? *Pharmacology Biochemistry and Behavior, 66*, 79–85.

Beck, S. J. (1995). Behavioral assessment. In M. Hersen & R. T. Ammerman (Eds.), *Advanced abnormal child psychology* (pp. 157–170). Hillsdale, NJ: Erlbaum.

Breslau, N., Kilbey, M. M., & Andreski, P. (1994). *DSM–III–R* nicotine dependence in young adults: Prevalence, correlates, and associated psychiatric disorders. *Addiction, 89*, 743–754.

Burch, J. B., de Fiebre, C. M., Marks, M. J., & Collins, A. C. (1988). Chronic ethanol or nicotine treatment results in partial cross-tolerance between these agents. *Psychopharmacology, 95*, 452–458.

Carmody, T. P., Brischetto, C. S., Matarazzo, J. D., O'Donnell, R. P., & Connor, W. E. (1985). Co-occurrent use of cigarettes, alcohol, and coffee in healthy, community-living men and women. *Health Psychology, 4*, 323–335.

Carter, B. L., & Tiffany, S. T. (1999). Meta-analysis of cue-reactivity in addiction research. *Addiction, 94*, 327–340.

Chait, L. D., & Griffiths, R. R. (1983). Effects of caffeine on cigarette smoking and subjective response. *Clinical Pharmacology and Therapeutics, 34*, 612–622.

Cohen, S., & Lichtenstein, E. (1990). Perceived stress, quitting smoking, and smoking relapse. *Health Psychology, 9*, 466–478.

Collins, A. C., Burch, J. B., de Fiebre, C. M., & Marks, M. J. (1988). Tolerance to and cross tolerance between ethanol and nicotine. *Pharmacology Biochemistry & Behavior, 29*, 365–373.

Craske, M. G., & Barlow, D. H. (1993). Panic disorder and agoraphobia. In D. H. Barlow (Ed.), *Clinical handbook of psychological disorders: A step-by-step treatment manual* (pp. 1–47). New York: Guilford Press.

Creson, D., Schmitz, J. M., & Arnoutovic, A. (1996). War-related changes in cigarette smoking: A survey study of health professionals in Sarajevo. *Substance Use and Misuse, 31*, 639–646.

Csikszentmihalyi, M., & Larson, R. (1987). Validity and reliability of the experience-sampling method. *Journal of Nervous and Mental Disease, 175*, 509–513.

Cummings, C., Gordon, J. R., & Marlatt, G. A. (1980). Relapse: Prevention and prediction. In W. R. Miller (Ed.), *The addictive behaviors* (pp. 291–322). Oxford, England: Pergamon.

Dobbs, S. D., Strickler, D. P., & Maxwell, W. A. (1981). The effects of stress and relaxation in the presence of stress on urinary pH and smoking behaviors. *Addictive Behaviors, 6*, 345–353.

Edwards, G., & Gross, M. M. (1976). Alcohol dependence: Provisional description of a clinical syndrome. *British Medical Journal, 1*, 1058–1061.

Ekman, P., & Friesen, W. V. (1978). *Facial action coding system.* Palo Alto, CA: Consulting Psychologists Press.

Epstein, L. H., & Collins, F. L. (1977). The measurement of situational influences of smoking. *Addictive Behaviors, 2*, 47–53.

Eysenck, H. J. (1973). Personality and the maintenance of the smoking habit. In W. L. Dunn (Ed.), *Smoking behavior: Motives and incentives* (pp. 113–146). Washington, DC: Winston.

Follick, M. J., Ahern, D. K., & Laser-Wolston, N. (1984). Evaluation of a daily activity diary for chronic pain patients. *Pain, 19*, 373–382.

Frith, C. D. (1971). Smoking behaviour and its relation to the smoker's immediate experience. *British Journal of Social and Clinical Psychology, 10*, 73–78.

Gilbert, D. G., Sharpe, J. P., Ramanaiah, N. V., Detwiler, F. R., & Anderson, A. E. (2000). Development of a situation × trait adaptive response (STAR) model-based smoking motivation questionnaire. *Personality and Individual Differences, 29*, 65–84.

Griffiths, R. R., Bigelow, G. E., & Liebson, I. (1976). Facilitation of human tobacco self-administration by ethanol: A behavioral analysis. *Journal of the Experimental Analysis of Behavior, 25*, 279–292.

Gritz, E. R., Ippoliti, A., Jarvik, M. E., Rose, J. E., Shiffman, S., Harrison, A., & Van Vunakis, H. (1988). The effect of nicotine on the delay of gastric emptying. *Alimentary Pharmacology and Therapeutics, 2*, 173–188.

Grunberg, N. E., & Baum, A. (1985). Biological commonalities of stress and substance abuse. In S. Shiffman & T. A. Wills (Eds.), *Coping and substance abuse* (pp. 25–62). New York: Academic Press.

Hammersley, R. (1994). A digest of memory phenomena for addiction research. *Addiction, 89*, 283–293.

Hatsukami, D. K., Morgan, S. F., Pickens, R. W., & Champagne, S. E. (1990). Situational factors in cigarette smoking. *Addictive Behaviors, 15*, 1–12.

Herman, C. P. (1974). External and internal cues as determinants of the smoking behavior of light and heavy smokers. *Journal of Personality and Social Psychology, 30*, 664–672.

Ikard, F. F., Green, D., & Horn, D. (1969). A scale to differentiate between types of smoking as related to the management of affect. *International Journal of the Addictions, 4,* 649–659.

Kassel, J. D., Stroud, L. R., & Paronis, C. A. (2001). *Smoking, stress, and negative affect: Associations and mechanisms across stages of smoking.* Manuscript submitted for publication.

Kirkcaldy, B. D., Cooper, C. L., Brown, J. M., & Athanasou, J. A. (1994). Job stress and health profiles of smokers, ex-smokers and non-smokers. *Stress Medicine, 10,* 159–166.

Klesges, R. C., Debon, M., & Ray, J. W. (1993). *Are self-reports of smoking biased? Evidence from the Second National Health and Nutrition Examination Survey.* Unpublished manuscript.

Kozlowski, L. T. (1976). Effects of caffeine consumption on nicotine consumption. *Psychopharmacology, 47,* 165–168.

Kozlowski, L. T., & Herman, C. P. (1984). The interaction of psychosocial and biological determinants of tobacco use: More on the boundary model. *Journal of Applied Social Psychology, 14,* 244–256.

Lane, J. D. (1996). Association of coffee drinking with cigarette smoking in the natural environment. *Experimental and Clinical Psychopharmacology, 4,* 409–412.

Lane, J. D., & Rose, J. E. (1995). Effects of daily caffeine intake on smoking behavior in the natural environment. *Experimental and Clinical Psychopharmacology, 3,* 49–55.

Larsen, R. J., & Diener, E. (1992). Promises and problems with the circumplex model of emotion. In M. Clark (Ed.), *Review of personality and social psychology* (pp. 25–59). Newbury Park, CA: Sage.

Lee, B. L., Jacob, P., Jarvik, M. E., & Benowitz, N. L. (1989). Food and nicotine metabolism. *Pharmacology Biochemistry and Behavior, 33,* 621–625.

Leventhal, H., & Cleary, P. D. (1979). Behavioral modification of risk factors: Technology or science? In M. L. Pollock & D. Schmidt (Eds.), *Heart disease and rehabilitation* (pp. 297–313). New York: Houghton Mifflin.

Leventhal, H., & Cleary, P. D. (1980). The smoking problem: A review of the research and theory in behavioral risk modification. *Psychological Bulletin, 88,* 370–405.

Litt, M. D., Cooney, N. L., & Morse, P. (1998). Ecological momentary assessment (EMA) with treated alcoholics: Methodological problems and potential solutions. *Health Psychology, 17,* 48–52.

Lyon, R. J., Tong, J. E., Leigh, G., & Clare, G. (1975). The influence of alcohol and tobacco on the components of choice reaction time. *Journal of Studies on Alcohol, 36,* 587–596.

Marlatt, G. A., & Gordon, J. R. (1985). *Relapse prevention.* New York: Guilford Press.

Marshall, W. R., Epstein, L. H., & Green, S. B. (1980). Coffee drinking and cigarette smoking: I. Coffee, caffeine and cigarette smoking behavior. *Addictive Behaviors, 5,* 389–394.

Marshall, W. R., Green, S. B., Epstein, L. H., Rogers, C. M., & McCoy, J. F. (1980). Coffee drinking and cigarette smoking: II. Coffee, urinary pH and cigarette smoking behavior. *Addictive Behaviors, 5,* 395–400.

McDermut, W., & Haaga, D. A. F. (1998). Effect of stage of change on cue reactivity in continuing smokers. *Experimental and Clinical Psychopharmacology, 6,* 316–324.

McFall, R. M. (1977). Parameters of self-monitoring. In R. B. Stuart (Ed.), *Behavioral self-management: Strategies, techniques, and outcome* (pp. 196–214). New York: Brunner/Mazel.

McKennell, A. C. (1970). Smoking motivation factors. *British Journal of Social and Clinical Psychology, 9,* 8–22.

McKennell, A. C., & Thomas, R. K. (1967). *Adults' and adolescents' smoking habits and attitudes.* London: British Ministry of Health.

Meddis, R. (1972). Bipolar factors in mood adjective checklists. *British Journal of Social and Clinical Psychology, 11,* 178–184.

Mello, N. K., & Mendelson, J. H. (1986). Cigarette smoking: Interactions with alcohol, opiates, and marijuana. In M. C. Braide & H. M. Ginsburg (Eds.), *Strategies for research on the interactions of drug abuse* (National Institute on Drug Abuse Research Monograph No. 68, pp. 154–180). Washington, DC: U.S. Government Printing Office.

Michel, C., & Battig, K. (1989). Separate and combined psychophysiological effects of cigarette smoking and alcohol consumption. *Psychopharmacology, 97,* 65–73.

Mintz, J., Boyd, G., Rose, J. E., Charuvastra, V. C., & Jarvik, M. E. (1985). Alcohol increases cigarette smoking: A laboratory demonstration. *Journal of Addictive Behaviors, 10,* 203–207.

Montgomery, G. K., & Reynolds, N. C. (1990). Compliance, reliability, and validity of self-monitoring for physical disturbances of Parkinson's disease. *Journal of Nervous and Mental Disease, 178,* 636–641.

Muraven, M., & Baumeister, R. F. (2000). Self-regulation and depletion of limited resources: Does self-control resemble a muscle? *Psychological Bulletin, 126,* 247–259.

Naquin, M. R., & Gilbert, G. G. (1996). College students' smoking behavior, perceived stress, and coping styles. *Journal of Drug Education, 26,* 367–376.

Niaura, R., Abrams, D. B., Pedraza, M., Monti, P. M., & Rohsenow, D. J. (1992). Smokers' reactions to interpersonal interaction and presentation of smoking cues. *Addictive Behaviors, 17,* 557–566.

Niaura, R. S., Rohsenow, D. J., Binkoff, J. A., Monti, P. M., Pedraza, M., & Abrams, D. B. (1988). Relevance of cue reactivity to understanding alcohol and smoking relapse. *Journal of Abnormal Psychology, 97,* 133–152.

Nil, R., Buzzi, R., & Battig, K. (1984). Effects of single doses of alcohol and caffeine on cigarette smoke puffing behavior. *Pharmacology Biochemistry & Behavior, 20,* 583–590.

Orlikov, A., & Ryzov, I. (1991). Caffeine-induced anxiety and increase of kynurenine concentration in plasma of healthy subjects: A pilot study. *Biological Psychiatry, 29,* 391–396.

Parrott, A. C. (1999). Does cigarette smoking cause stress? *American Psychologist, 54,* 817–820.

Paty, J. A., Kassel, J. D., & Shiffman, S. (1992). The importance of assessing base rates for clinical studies: An example of stimulus control of smoking. In M. DeVries (Ed.), *The experience of psychopathology* (pp. 347–352). Cambridge, England: Cambridge University Press.

Payne, T. J., Schare, M. L., Levis, D. J., & Colletti, G. (1991). Exposure to smoking-relevant cues: Effects on desire to smoke and topographical components of smoking behavior. *Addictive Behaviors, 16,* 467–479.

Perkins, K. A., Epstein, L. H., Fonte, C., Mitchell, S. L., & Grobe, J. E. (1995). Gender, dietary restraint, and smoking's influence on hunger and the reinforcing value of food. *Physiology & Behavior, 57,* 675–680.

Perkins, K. A., & Grobe, J. E. (1992). Increased desire to smoke during acute stress. *British Journal of Addiction, 87,* 1037–1040.

Perkins, K. A., Grobe, J. E., Fonte, C., & Breus, M. (1992). "Paradoxical" effects of smoking on subjective stress versus cardiovascular arousal in males and females. *Pharmacology Biochemistry & Behavior, 42,* 301–311.

Pomerleau, O. F., & Pomerleau, C. S. (1984). Neuroregulators and the reinforcement of smoking: Towards a behavioral explanation. *Neuroscience and Biobehavioral Reviews, 8,* 503–513.

Pomerleau, O. F., & Pomerleau, C. S. (1987). A biobehavioral view of substance abuse and addiction. *Journal of Drug Issues, 17,* 111–131.

Poulos, C. X., Hinson, R. E., & Siegel, S. (1981). The role of Pavlovian processes in drug tolerance and dependence: Implications for treatment. *Addictive Behaviors, 6,* 205–211.

Robinson, T. E., & Berridge, K. C. (1993). The neural basis of drug craving: An incentive-sensitization theory of addiction. *Brain Research Reviews, 18,* 247–291.

Rose, J., Ananda, R., & Jarvik, M. E. (1983). Cigarette smoking during anxiety-provoking and monotonous tasks. *Addictive Behaviors, 8,* 353–359.

Rudas, T. (1998). *Odds ratios in the analysis of contingency tables* (Sage University Papers Series 119: Quantitative applications in the social sciences). Thousand Oaks, CA: Sage.

Russell, J. (1980). A circumplex model of affect. *Journal of Personality and Social Psychology, 37,* 345–356.

Russell, M. A. H., Peto, J., & Patel, U. A. (1974). The classification of smoking by factorial structure of motives. *Journal of the Royal Statistical Society, 137,* 313–346.

Sawyer, D. A., Julia, H. L., & Turin, A. C. (1982). Caffeine and human behavior: Arousal, anxiety, and performance effects. *Journal of Behavioral Medicine, 5,* 415–439.

Sayette, M., & Hufford, M. (1994). Effects of cue exposure and deprivation on cognitive resources in smokers. *Journal of Abnormal Psychology, 103,* 812–818.

Schachter, S., Silverstein, B., & Perlick, D. (1977). Psychological and pharmacological explanations of smoking under stress. *Journal of Experimental Psychology: General, 106,* 31–40.

Shiffman, S. (1982). Relapse following smoking cessation: A situational analysis. *Journal of Consulting and Clinical Psychology, 50,* 71–86.

Shiffman, S. (1993). Assessing smoking patterns and motives. *Journal of Consulting and Clinical Psychology, 61,* 732–742.

Shiffman, S., & Balabanis, M. (1995). Associations between alcohol and tobacco. In J. B. Fertig & J. P. Allen (Eds.), *Alcohol and tobacco: From basic science to clinical practice* (Research Monograph No. 30, pp. 17–36). Bethesda, MD: National Institutes of Health.

Shiffman, S., Balabanis, M. H., Paty, J. A., Engberg, J., Gwaltney, C. J., Liu, K., et al. (2000). Dynamic effects of self-efficacy on smoking lapse and relapse. *Health Psychology, 19,* 315–323.

Shiffman, S., Engberg, J., Paty, J. A., Perz, W., Gnys, M., Kassel, J. D., & Hickcox, M. (1997). A day at a time: Predicting smoking lapse from daily urge. *Journal of Abnormal Psychology, 106,* 104–116.

Shiffman, S., Fischer, L. A., Paty, J. A., Gnys, M., Kassel, J. D., Hickcox, M., & Perz, W. (1994). Drinking and smoking: A field study of their association. *Annals of Behavioral Medicine, 16,* 203–209.

Shiffman, S., Hufford, M., Hickcox, M., Paty, J. A., Gnys, M., & Kassel, J. D. (1997). Remember that? A comparison of real-time versus retrospective recall of smoking lapses. *Journal of Consulting and Clinical Psychology, 65,* 292–300.

Shiffman, S., & Jarvik, M. E. (1987). Situational determinants of coping in smoking relapse crises. *Journal of Applied Social Psychology, 17,* 3–15.

Shiffman, S., & Paty, J. A. (2002, February). *Electronic diary methods for assessing smoking: Compliance and validity.* Poster presented at the Eighth Annual Meeting of the Society for Research on Nicotine and Tobacco, Savannah, GA.

Shiffman, S., Paty, J. A., Gnys, M., Kassel, J. D., & Elash, C. (1995). Nicotine withdrawal in chippers and regular smokers: Subjective and cognitive effects. *Health Psychology, 14,* 301–309.

Shiffman, S., Paty, J. A., Gnys, M., Kassel, J. D., & Hickcox, M. (1996). First lapses to smoking: Within subjects analysis of real time reports. *Journal of Consulting and Clinical Psychology, 64,* 366–379.

Shiffman, S., & Prange, M. (1988). Self-reported and self-monitored smoking patterns. *Addictive Behaviors, 13,* 201–204.

Shiffman, S., & Stone, A. A. (1998). Ecological momentary assessment: A new tool for behavioral medicine research. In D. Krantz & A. Baum (Eds.), *Technology and methods in behavioral medicine* (pp. 117–131). Mahwah, NJ: Erlbaum.

Shoaib, M., Swanner, L. S., Yasar, S., & Goldberg, S. R. (1999). Chronic caffeine exposure potentiates nicotine self-administration in rats. *Psychopharmacology, 142,* 327–333.

Snyder, F. R., & Henningfield, J. E. (1989). Effects of nicotine administration following 12h of tobacco deprivation: Assessment on computerized performance tasks. *Psychopharmacology*, *97*, 17–22.

Stewart, J., de Wit, H., & Eikelboom, R. (1984). Role of unconditioned and conditioned drug effects in the self-administration of opiates and stimulants. *Psychological Review*, *91*, 251–268.

Stone, A. A., & Shiffman, S. (1994). Ecological momentary assessment (EMA) in behavioral medicine. *Annals of Behavioral Medicine*, *16*, 199–202.

Stone, A. A., Shiffman, S., Schwartz, J. E., Broderick, J. E., & Hufford, M. R. (2002). Patient non-compliance with paper diaries. *British Medical Journal*, *324*, 1193–1194.

Tanda, G., & Goldberg, S. R. (2000). Alteration of the behavioral effects of nicotine by chronic caffeine exposure. *Pharmacology Biochemistry & Behavior*, *66*, 47–64.

Tate, J. C., Schmitz, J. M., & Stanton, A. L. (1991). A critical review of the reasons for smoking scale. *Journal of Substance Abuse*, *3*, 441–445.

Tiffany, S. T. (1990). A cognitive model of drug urges and drug use behavior: Role of automatic and non-automatic processes. *Psychological Review*, *97*, 147–168.

Tiffany, S. T., & Drobes, D. J. (1990). Imagery and smoking urges: The manipulation of affective content. *Addictive Behaviors*, *15*, 531–539.

Tomkins, S. S. (1966). Psychological model for smoking behavior. *American Journal of Public Health*, *56*, 17–26.

Tomkins, S. (1968). A modified model of smoking behavior. In E. F. Borgatta & R. R. Evans (Eds.), *Smoking, health, and behavior* (pp. 165–186). Chicago: Aldine.

U.S. Department of Health and Human Services. (1988). *The health consequences of smoking: Nicotine addiction, a report of the Surgeon General.* Washington, DC: Author.

Warren, C. A., & McDonough, B. E. (1999). Event-related brain potentials as indicators of smoking cue-reactivity. *Clinical Neurophysiology*, *110*, 1570–1584.

Wikler, A. (1948). Recent progress in research on the neurophysiologic basis of morphine addiction. *American Journal of Psychiatry*, *105*, 329–338.

Wise, R. A. (1988). The neurobiology of craving: Implications for the understanding and treatment of addiction. *Journal of Abnormal Psychology*, *97*, 118–132.

Zeger, S. L., Liang, K., & Albert, P. S. (1988). Models for longitudinal data: A generalized estimating equation approach. *Biometrics*, *44*, 1049–1060.

VII

TREATMENT APPROACHES AND MODELS

16

RELAPSE PREVENTION FOR ALCOHOL AND DRUG PROBLEMS: THAT WAS ZEN, THIS IS TAO

KATIE WITKIEWITZ AND G. ALAN MARLATT

Relapse prevention (RP) is a cognitive–behavioral approach with the goal of identifying and preventing high-risk situations for relapse. In this article we summarize the major tenets of RP and the cognitive–behavioral model of relapse, including recent empirical support for hypothesized determinants of relapse. We also provide a brief discussion of meta-analyses and reviews of controlled trials incorporating RP techniques. Finally, we describe a reconceptualization of the relapse process and propose future directions for clinical applications and research initiatives.

RELAPSE: THAT WAS THEN

In 1986, Brownell, Marlatt, Lichtenstein, and Wilson published an extensive, seminal review on the problem of relapse in addictive behaviors. Relapse

This research was supported by National Institute of Alcohol Abuse and Alcoholism Grant R21 AA013942-01. We thank Alan Shields, Denise Walker, and Ursula Whiteside for thorough reviews of a draft of this chapter. The phrase "That was Zen, this is Tao" is attributed to Peter da Silva. Zen has been defined as the art of seeing into the nature of one's own being, whereas *Tao* (according to the *Oxford English Dictionary Online*, 2004) is defined as "the way to be followed, the right conduct, doctrine or method."

Reprinted from *American Psychologist, 59*, 224–235 (2004). Copyright 2004 by the American Psychological Association.

has been described as both an outcome—the dichotomous view that the person is either ill or well—and a process, encompassing any transgression in the process of behavior change. Essentially, when individuals attempt to change a problematic behavior, an initial setback (lapse) is highly probable. One possible outcome, following the initial setback, is a return to the previous problematic behavior pattern (relapse). Another possible outcome is the individual's getting back on track in the direction of positive change (prolapse). Regardless of how relapse is defined, a general reading of case studies and research literature demonstrates that most individuals who attempt to change their behavior in a certain direction (e.g., lose weight, reduce hypertension, stop smoking, etc.) will experience lapses that often lead to relapse (Polivy & Herman, 2002).

Twenty-five years ago, Marlatt (1978) obtained qualitative information from 70 male alcoholics regarding the primary situations that led them to initiate drinking during the first 90 days following inpatient treatment. On the basis of their responses, Marlatt (1985) proposed a cognitive–behavioral model of the relapse process, shown in Figure 16.1, which centers on the high-risk situation and the individual's response in that situation. If the individual lacks an effective coping response and/or confidence to deal with the situation (low self-efficacy; Bandura, 1977), the tendency is to give in to temptation. The decision to use or not use is then mediated by the individual's outcome expectancies for the initial effects of using the substance (Jones, Corbin, & Fromme, 2001). Individuals who decide to use the substance may be vulnerable to the "abstinence violation effect," which is the self-blame and loss of perceived control that individuals often experience after the violation of self-imposed rules (Curry, Marlatt, & Gordon, 1987).

RELAPSE PREVENTION

The cognitive–behavioral model forms the basis for RP, an intervention designed to prevent and manage relapse in individuals who have received, or

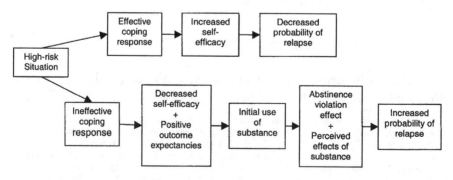

Figure 16.1. Cognitive–behavioral model of relapse.

are receiving, treatment for addictive behavior problems (Carroll, 1996). Treatment approaches based on RP begin with the assessment of potentially high-risk situations for relapse. A high-risk situation is defined as a circumstance in which an individual's attempt to refrain from a particular behavior (ranging from any use of a substance to heavy or harmful use) is threatened. The circumstances that are high-risk people (e.g., drug dealers), places (e.g., favorite bars), and events (e.g., parties) often vary from person to person and within each individual. Challenging an individual's expectations for the perceived positive effects of a substance and discussing the psychological components of substance use (e.g., placebo effects) help the client make more informed choices in threatening situations. Likewise, discussing the abstinence violation effect and preparing clients for lapses may help prevent a major relapse. High-risk situations often arise without warning (R. C. Hawkins & Hawkins, 1998). Marlatt and Gordon (1985, p. 49) described the problem of "apparently irrelevant decisions," which are decisions that a person makes without realizing the implications of the decision leading to the possibility of a lapse. For example, a man who is trying to abstain from drinking takes a shortcut that entails walking past his favorite bar. Although he had no intention of drinking or stopping at his favorite bar, the decision to take that particular route could present a risky situation (Marlatt, 1985). In the assessment of high-risk situations, a role-play measure, such as the Alcohol-Specific Role Play Test (Monti et al., 1993), can be used to assess observable responses in high-risk and seemingly non-high-risk situations. Education about the relapse process, the likelihood of a lapse occurring, and lifestyle imbalance may better equip clients to navigate the rough terrain of cessation attempts.

Effectiveness and Efficacy of Relapse Prevention

Several studies have evaluated the effectiveness and efficacy of RP approaches for substance use disorders (Carroll, 1996; Irvin, Bowers, Dunn, & Wang, 1999), and there is evidence supporting RP for depression (Katon et al., 2001), sexual offending (Laws, Hudson, & Ward, 2000), obesity (Brownell & Wadden, 1992; Perry et al., 2001), obsessive–compulsive disorder (Hiss, Foa, & Kozak, 1994), schizophrenia (Herz et al., 2000), bipolar disorder (Lam et al., 2003), and panic disorder (Bruce, Spiegel, & Hegel, 1999). Carroll (1996) conducted a narrative review of 24 randomized, controlled trials, including studies of RP for smoking, alcohol, marijuana, and cocaine addiction. Carroll concluded that RP was more effective than no treatment and was equally effective as other active treatments (e.g., supportive therapy, interpersonal therapy) in improving substance use outcomes.

Several studies have shown sustained main effects for RP, suggesting that RP may provide continued improvement over a longer period of time (indicating a "delayed emergence effect"), whereas other treatments may only be effective over a shorter duration (Carroll, Rounsaville, Nich, & Gordon, 1994; J. D. Hawkins, Catalano, Gillmore, & Wells, 1989; Rawson et al., 2002). These findings suggest a lapse–relapse learning curve, in which there is a higher likelihood of a lapse immediately following treatment, but incremental changes in coping skills lead to a decreased probability of relapse over time. Polivy and Herman (2002) candidly described the problem of learning new behaviors—as many as 90% of individuals do not achieve behavior change on their first attempt.

Irvin et al. (1999) conducted a meta-analysis of RP techniques in the treatment of alcohol, tobacco, cocaine, and polysubstance use. On the basis of 26 studies, representing a sample of 9,504 participants, the overall treatment effects demonstrated that RP was a successful intervention for reducing substance use and improving psychosocial adjustment. Relapse prevention was most effective for individuals with alcohol problems, suggesting that certain characteristics of alcohol use are particularly amenable to the current RP model. Scientist-practitioners should continue to modify RP procedures to incorporate the idiosyncrasies of other substances (e.g., cocaine, cigarettes, and heroin) and nonsubstance (e.g., depression, anxiety) relapse. For example, Roffman, Stephens, Simpson, and Whitaker (1990) have developed a marijuana-specific RP intervention that has produced greater reductions in marijuana use than a comparison social support treatment.

Relapse Replication and Extension Project

The wide clinical application of RP led the National Institute of Alcohol Abuse and Alcoholism to sponsor a replication of Marlatt's original taxonomy (Marlatt, 1978) for classifying relapse episodes. Collaborators at three research centers (Brown University; the Research Institute on Addictions in Buffalo, NY; and the University of New Mexico) recruited 563 participants from 15 treatment sites that represented a number of different treatment approaches and settings (e.g., cognitive–behavioral treatment [CBT] and 12-step, and including both outpatient and inpatient treatment). The Relapse Replication and Extension Project (RREP) focused on the identification of high-risk situations and examined the reliability and validity of the taxonomic system for classifying alcohol relapse episodes (Lowman, Allen, Stout, & the Relapse Research Group, 1996).

The data and research questions used in the RREP raised significant methodological issues concerning the predictive validity of Marlatt's (1978) relapse taxonomy and coding system (Longabaugh, Rubin, Stout, Zywiak, & Lowman, 1996; Stout, Longabaugh, & Rubin, 1996). On the basis of the findings, a major reconceptualization of the relapse taxonomy was recommended (Donovan, 1996; Kadden, 1996). Longabaugh et al. (1996) suggested a revision of the taxonomy categories to include greater distinction between the inter- and intrapersonal determinants, more emphasis on craving, and less focus on hierarchically defined relapse codes. In contrast, Donovan concluded that the RREP did not adequately test the assumptions of the broader cognitive–behavioral model of relapse, on which several RP intervention strategies are based. Many of the RREP findings, including the influence of negative affect, the abstinence violation effect, and the importance of coping in predicting relapse, are in fact quite supportive of the original RP model (Marlatt, 1996).

In response to the criticisms provided by the researchers in the RREP (Donovan, 1996; Kadden, 1996; Longabaugh et al., 1996), as well as to other critiques of RP and the cognitive–behavioral model of relapse (Allsop & Saunders, 1989; Heather & Stallard, 1989), we have devoted the remainder of this article to a review of relapse risk factors and the relapse process. Although no single model of relapse could ever encompass all individuals attempting all types of behavior change, a more thorough understanding of the critical determinants of relapse and underlying processes may provide added insight into the treatment and prevention of disorders susceptible to relapse.

DETERMINANTS OF RELAPSE: THIS IS NOW

Intrapersonal Determinants

Self-Efficacy

Self-efficacy is defined as the degree to which an individual feels confident and capable of performing a certain behavior in a specific situational context (Bandura, 1977). As described in the cognitive–behavioral model of relapse, higher levels of self-efficacy are predictive of improved alcohol treatment outcomes in both males and females, for inpatient and outpatient treatment, and for short (1 year) and long-term (3 year) follow-ups (Burling, Reilly, Moltzen, & Ziff, 1989; Greenfield et al., 2000; Project MATCH Research Group, 1997; Rychtarik, Prue, Rapp, & King, 1992). In general, self-efficacy is a predictor of outcomes across all types of addictive behaviors, including gambling (Sylvain, Ladouceur, & Boisvert, 1997), smoking (e.g., Baer, Holt, & Lichtenstein, 1986), and drug use (e.g., Sklar, Annis, & Turner, 1999). Yet despite the preponderance of evidence demonstrating a strong relationship between self-efficacy and treatment outcomes, the mechanism by which self-efficacy influences outcome has not been determined (Maisto, Connors, & Zywiak, 2000; Sklar et al., 1999).

The measurement of self-efficacy continues to be a challenge, especially considering the context-specific nature of the construct. Although several self-report instruments have been developed to measure past and current self-efficacy in relation to alcohol and drug use (e.g., Annis, 1982; DiClemente, Carbonari, Montgomery, & Hughes, 1994), these measures are limited to assessing self-efficacy within circumscribed contexts rather than in individualized high-risk situations. One promising assessment strategy, Ecological Momentary Assessment (EMA), is the use of personal digital assistants to collect data in real time (Stone & Shiffman, 1994). On the basis of data collected with EMA, Shiffman and colleagues (2000) found that baseline self-efficacy was as predictive of the first smoking lapse as were daily self-efficacy measurements, demonstrating the stability of self-efficacy during abstinence. However, daily variation in self-efficacy was a significant predictor of smoking relapse progression following the first lapse, above and beyond baseline self-efficacy and pretreatment smoking behavior. Using the same methodology, Gwaltney and colleagues (2002) showed that individuals who experience a smoking lapse as well as those who abstain from smoking following treatment are capable of discriminating nonrisk from high-risk situations, with situations that are rated as high-risk (e.g., negative affect contexts) receiving the lowest self-efficacy ratings.

Outcome Expectancies

Outcome expectancies are typically described as an individual's anticipation of the effects of a future experience (S. A. Brown, Goldman, & Christiansen, 1985). These expectancies influence behavioral responding, depending on the strength and valence (whether the person anticipates either a positive or a negative experience) of the expectancy, and the previous effects of a substance. Experimental studies (using placebo designs) have demonstrated that an individual's expectancies play a major role in the subjective experience of a substance, regardless of whether the substance is a placebo or the actual drug (Juliano & Brandon, 2002; Marlatt & Rohsenow, 1980).

Treatment outcome studies have demonstrated that positive reinforcement outcome expectancies (e.g., "A cigarette would be relaxing") are associated with poorer treatment outcomes (Connors, Tarbox, & Faillace, 1993) and that negative outcome expectancies (e.g., "I will have a hangover") are related to improved outcomes (Jones & McMahon, 1996). Jones and colleagues (2001) concluded that although expectancies are strongly related to outcomes, there is very little evidence that targeting expectancies in treatment leads to changes in posttreatment consumption. One possible explanation for these findings is that expectancies influence outcome via their relationship with other predictors of relapse. For example, Cohen, McCarthy, Brown, and Myers (2002) demonstrated that expectations partially mediate the relationship between negative affect and smoking behavior.

Craving

The maintenance of positive expectancies in the anticipation of consumption has been shown to be significantly related to increased subjective reports of craving (Palfai, Davidson, & Swift, 1999). Craving is possibly the most widely studied and poorly understood concept in the study of drug addiction (Lowman, Hunt, Litten, & Drummond, 2000). One common finding is that craving is a poor predictor of relapse (e.g., Kassel & Shiffman, 1992; Tiffany, Carter, & Singleton, 2000). Drummond, Litten, Lowman, and Hunt (2000) proposed that the subjective experience of craving may not directly predict substance use, but relapse may be predicted from the correlates and underlying mechanisms of craving. For example, Sayette, Martin, Hull, Wertz, and Perrott (2003) experimentally demonstrated that cue exposure was predictive of nicotine craving, but only for smokers who were deprived of nicotine. These findings are consistent with previous research demonstrating that during abstinence, the perceived availability of a substance plays a large role in craving responses (for a review, see Wertz & Sayette, 2001).

Siegel, Baptista, Kim, McDonald, and Weise (2000) proposed that both craving and symptoms of withdrawal may act as drug-compensatory responses, which are conditioned by several exposures to drug-related stimuli (e.g., seeing an advertisement for a desired brand of cigarettes) paired with the physical effects of a drug. Therefore drug cues elicit a physiological response to prepare the individual for the drug effects. On the basis of this model, withdrawal and craving may be limited to situations in which preparatory responses to drug effects have been learned (Siegel et al., 2000; Wenger & Woods, 1984).

Studies on the role of cue reactivity in addiction have demonstrated that drug-related stimuli elicit self-reported craving and increased physiological responding, but cue reactivity has not been shown to be a consistent predictor of relapse (Carter & Tiffany, 1999; Rohsenow, Niaura, Childress, Abrams, & Monti, 1990). Niaura (2000) presented a dynamic regulatory model of drug relapse in which cues are proposed to activate attentional processes, craving, positive outcome expectancies, and physiological responses. Efficacy and coping are described as "the braking mechanisms for the affective/urge circuits" (Niaura, 2000, p. 159), whereby high self-efficacy and/or an effective coping response can prevent the escalation of preparatory drug responding. Taken out of the laboratory, cue reactivity could have an impact on the treatment and assessment of addictive behavior (Carter & Tiffany, 1999). For example, measures of cue reactivity could be used to identify an individual's high-risk situations for relapse.

Motivation

Motivation may relate to the relapse process in two distinct ways: the motivation for positive behavior change and the motivation to engage in the problematic behavior. This distinction captures the ambivalence that is experienced by individuals attempting to change an addictive behavior (Miller & Rollnick, 2002). The hesitancy toward change is often highly related to both self-efficacy (e.g., "I really want to quit shooting up, but I don't think that I'll be able to say no") and outcome expectancies (e.g., "I would quit drinking, but then I would have a hard time meeting people"). Prochaska and DiClemente (1984) proposed a transtheoretical model of motivation, incorporating five stages of readiness to change: precontemplation, contemplation, preparation, action, and maintenance. Each stage characterizes a different level of motivational readiness, with precontemplation representing the lowest level of readiness (DiClemente & Hughes, 1990).

According to the tenets of operant conditioning, the motivation to use in a particular situation is based on the positive or negative reinforcement value of a specific outcome in that situation (Bolles, 1972). For example, if an individual is in a highly stressful situation and holds the positive outcome expectancy that smoking a cigarette will reduce his or her level of stress, then the incentive of smoking a single cigarette has high reinforcement value. Baker, Piper, McCarthy, Majeskie, and Fiore (2004) have demonstrated that perceived or expected reductions in negative affect and withdrawal symptoms (Piasecki et al., 2000) provide negative reinforcement value for smoking behavior and may be described as motivation to use. These findings highlight the feedback mechanism that may be operating in motivational circuits, whereby consumption is influenced both by expectations derived from previous experience and by the perceived effects of a substance in the moment. If these expectations provide reinforcement, then the individual will more likely be motivated to continue using.

Coping

Several types of coping have been proposed, including stress, temptation, cognitive, and behavioral coping (Shiffman, 1984), as well as approach and avoidance coping (Moos, 1993). Recently, Chung, Langenbucher, Labouvie, Pandina, and Moos (2001) demonstrated that increased behavioral approach coping (e.g., meditation and/or deep breathing exercises) was predictive of fewer alcohol problems (i.e., alcohol problem severity and alcohol dependence symptoms) and reduced interpersonal and psychological problems 12-months following treatment. Gossop, Steward, Browne, and Marsden (2002) found that patients who used more cognitive coping strategies (e.g., "urge-surfing"; Marlatt, 1985) had lower rates of relapse to heroin use.

Litt, Kadden, Cooney, and Kabela (2003) demonstrated that self-efficacy and coping independently predicted successful outcomes and that higher levels of readiness to change enhanced the use of coping skills. In this study the availability of coping skills following treatment was a significant predictor of outcome, regardless of the treatment received. Both CBT and interpersonal psychotherapy led to substantially greater increases in coping skills. These results are consistent with a recent review conducted by Morgenstern and Longabaugh (2000), who concluded that changes in coping skills following cognitive–behavioral interventions do not uniquely mediate substance abuse outcomes, compared with other active treatments. On the contrary, using a participant-generated role-play measure of coping called the Cocaine Risk Response Test, Carroll, Nich, Frankforter, and Bisighini (1999) found significant improvements on CBT-type coping skills in those individuals assigned to CBT but not in those assigned to comparative treatments.

To date, very little is known about the cognitive–behavioral processes that underlie current definitions of coping. E. A. Skinner, Edge, Altman, and Sherwood (2003) have suggested the use of hierarchical structures of coping "families" based on functional classes of behavior. One coping family, self-reliance, may be a potential predictor of outcome following treatment for addictive behavior. Self-reliance, which incorporates emotional and behavioral regulation, emotional expression, and emotional approach coping, resonates with the notion of self-regulation (defined as the monitoring and altering of one's behavior), which has been shown to be associated with substance abuse, impulsivity, and risk taking (J. M. Brown, Miller, & Lawendowski, 1999).

A recent analogy provided by Baumeister, Heatherton, and Tice (1994) described self-regulation as a type of muscle, which may be strengthened and which may also become fatigued. The "fatigue" of self-regulation, or loss of self-control associated with repeated use of self-control resources, provides an explanation for why individuals are more likely to use an ineffective coping strategy when they are experiencing stress and/or negative affect. Consistent with this explanation is the finding of Muraven, Collins, and Neinhaus (2002) that individuals who experienced self-regulation fatigue tended to consume more alcohol and reach higher blood alcohol levels than those whose ability to self-regulate was not depleted. These data suggest that considering previous definitions of coping as well as current research on self-regulation may help elucidate the functional relationship between coping processes and treatment outcomes.

Emotional States

Several studies have reported a strong link between negative affect and relapse to substance use (e.g., Hodgins, el Guebaly, & Armstrong, 1995; Shiffman, Paty, Gnys, Kassel, & Hickcox, 1996). Baker et al. (2004) have recently identified negative affect as the primary motive for drug use. According to this model, excessive substance use is motivated by positive and negative affective regulation such that substances provide negative reinforcement when they provide relief from negative affective states (Khantzian, 1974; Tennen, Affleck, Armeli, & Carney, 2000). A recent study using EMA provided support for this model, with alcohol consumption being prospectively predicted from nervous mood states and cross-sectionally associated with reduced levels of nervousness (Swendsen et al., 2000).

In Marlatt's (1978) original study of relapse precipitants, negative affect was an unambiguous predictor of lapses following treatment. Today, advancements in technology and methodologies have complicated an understanding of the affect–relapse relationship (Kassel, Stroud, & Paronis, 2003). Cohen et al. (2002) demonstrated, as mentioned earlier, that negative affect is mediated by outcome expectancies in the prediction of smoking behavior, and Gwaltney et al. (2001) found abstinence self-efficacy to be lowest in negative affect contexts. Baker et al. (2004) have provided evidence for the association between postcessation negative affect and relapse; however, the interdependence of negative affect and withdrawal severity remains unclear (Kenford et al., 2002). Furthermore, precessation negative affect, including comorbid major depression, is not consistently related to increased relapse risk (Burgess et al., 2002).

Interpersonal Determinants

Functional social support, or the level of emotional support, is highly predictive of long-term abstinence rates across several addictive behaviors (e.g., Beattie & Longabaugh, 1999; Dobkin, Civita, Paraherakis, & Gill, 2002; Havassy, Hall, & Wasserman, 1991; McMahon, 2001). The quality of social support, or the level of support from nonsubstance abusers (Dobkin et al., 2002), has also been related to relapse. For example, low levels of high-quality support (i.e., support for abstinence), including interpersonal conflict (Cummings, Gordon, & Marlatt, 1980) and high levels of low-quality support (social pressure to use substances), are predictive of lapse episodes (S. A. Brown, Vik, & Craemer, 1989).

The structural dimension of social support, or the availability of support, has been shown to moderate the relationship between social support and relapse. Beattie and Longabaugh (1999) found that the presence of a support system of people who encouraged abstinence mediated the relationship between general support and outcomes. Unfortunately, increased substance use may increase alienation from non-substance-abusing friends and family members. This restructuring of social networks may involve a feedback mechanism whereby increased use is associated with a decrease in support from nonsubstance abusers, which may lead to more substance use (Peirce, Frone, Russell, Cooper, & Mudar, 2000).

FUTURE DIRECTIONS IN THE DEFINITION, MEASUREMENT, AND TREATMENT OF RELAPSE: THIS IS NOW

Conceptualizing the Relapse Process

Synthesizing recent empirical findings into a unified theory involves reconceptualizing relapse as a multidimensional, complex system. The proposed model is similar to dynamic developmental models (e.g., Courage & Howe, 2002; Dodge & Pettit, 2003; van der Maas & Molenaar, 1992) in that the focus is on the interrelationships between dispositions, contexts, and past and current experiences. However, unlike previous models, the proposed model of relapse focuses on situational dynamics rather than on developmental changes. In our research and clinical work, we have observed seemingly insignificant changes in levels of risk (e.g., slight decreases in mood ratings) kindle a lapse episode, often initiated by a minor cue. For example, increased stress level may trigger a high-risk situation in which a slight reduction in coping efficacy (McKay, Alterman, Mulvaney, & Koppenhaver, 1999) greatly increases the likelihood of the person's using an ineffective coping response, thereby increasing the probability of a lapse (Rabois & Haaga, 2003).

At any moment, individuals who are attempting to maintain new health behaviors (e.g., sticking with a diet, abstaining from drinking or drug use) are often faced with the challenge of balancing contextual cues and potential consequences. We propose that multiple influences trigger and operate within high-risk situations and influence the global functioning of the system, a process that embodies principles of self-organization (Barton, 1994; Kauffman, 1995).[1] This self-organizing process incorporates the interaction between background factors (e.g., years of dependence, family history, social support, and comorbid psychopathology), physiological states (e.g., physical withdrawal), cognitive processes (e.g., self-efficacy, outcome expectancies, craving, the abstinence violation effect, motivation), and coping skills. These factors were also included in the original model of relapse proposed by Marlatt and colleagues (Brownell et al., 1986; Marlatt & Gordon, 1985). Unlike Marlatt's earlier model, which has been criticized for the hierarchical classification of relapse factors (Longabaugh et al., 1996), the current model does not presume that certain factors are more influential than others.

---

[1] Although there is no agreed upon definition of *self-organization*, many authors describe self-organization by the characteristics of emerging systems—namely, systems in which small changes in parameters within a system result in large, qualitative changes at the global level. The following is a definition of self-organization provided by Camazine et al. (2003): "Self-organization is a process in which patterns at the global level of a system emerge solely from numerous interactions among the lower-level components of the system. Moreover, the rules specifying interactions among the system's components are executed using only local information, without reference to the global pattern" (p. 8). For a more psychologically minded description of self-organization, we recommend the book *Clinical Chaos*, edited by Chamberlain and Butz (1998).

As shown in Figure 16.2, the reconceptualized dynamic model of relapse allows for several configurations of distal and proximal relapse risks. Distal risks (solid lines) are defined as stable predispositions that increase an individual's vulnerability to lapse, whereas proximal risks (dotted lines) are immediate precipitants that actualize the statistical probability of a lapse (Shiffman, 1989). Connected boxes are hypothesized to be nonrecursive—that is, there is a reciprocal causation between them (e.g., coping skills influence drinking behavior, and in turn, drinking influences coping; Gossop et al., 2002). These *feedback loops* allow for the interaction between coping skills, cognitions, craving, affect, and substance use behavior (Niaura, 2000). The role of contextual factors is indicated by the large striped circle in Figure 16.2, with substance cues (e.g., walking by the liquor store) moderating the relationship between risk factors and substance use behavior (Litt, Cooney, & Morse, 2000).

The timing of risk factors is also inherent in the proposed system, whereby temporal relationships between distal risk determinants and hypothesized proximal relapse precipitants play an important role in relapse proneness (Piasecki, Fiore, McCarthy, & Baker, 2002). We have illustrated time-dependent interactions with light gray circles in Figure 16.2. The white and gray circles represent tonic and phasic processes (the phasic circle is contained within the high-risk situation circle). The circle on the far left (solid border) represents tonic processes, indicating an individual's chronic vulnerability for relapse. Tonic processes often accumulate and lead to the instigation of a high-risk situation, providing the foundation for the possibility of a

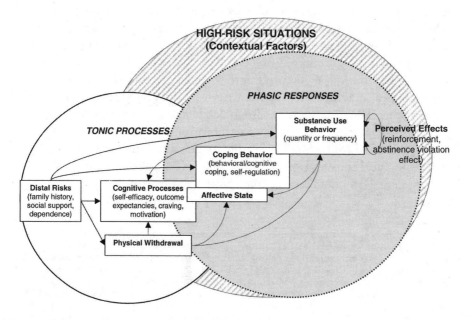

Figure 16.2. Dynamic model of relapse.

lapse. The phasic response (dotted border) incorporates situational cognitive, affective and physical states, and coping skills utilization. The phasic response is conceptualized as the cusp, or turning point, of the system, where behavioral responding may lead to a sudden change in substance use behavior. Alternatively, an individual may promptly use an effective coping strategy (e.g., self-regulation) and experience a de-escalation of relapse risk.

The interrelationship between tonic and phasic processes in the prediction of lapses and relapse has been demonstrated in several recent studies on the dynamics of posttreatment outcomes. Shiffman and colleagues (2000) demonstrated that baseline self-efficacy (tonic) predicts lapses, and daily variation in self-efficacy (phasic) predicts the progression from a lapse to relapse. The self-reported experience of craving (e.g., "urges"; Rohsenow & Monti, 1999) appears to be an acute risk for relapse, as urge ratings are increasing (phasic process), but stable levels of urge (tonic process) do not necessarily add predictive power above and beyond that predicted by the initial increase in urge ratings (Shiffman et al., 2000).

Litt et al. (2003) demonstrated that baseline readiness to change (tonic process) was not directly related to drinking outcomes, but it did influence outcome through its effect on coping (phasic process). Hedeker and Mermelstein (1996), however, showed that a decline in momentary motivation (phasic process) was a significant predictor of relapse in individuals who were attempting to quit smoking. Also, they found that the experience of a lapse led to further reductions in motivation, a finding that is consistent with the abstinence violation effect (Curry et al., 1987). It has been demonstrated that the relationship between postcessation negative affect and outcomes is mediated by self-efficacy (Cinciripini et al., 2003) and outcome expectancies (Cohen et al., 2002); however, precessation negative affect and/or comorbid major depression are not significantly related to outcome (Burgess et al., 2002), demonstrating that affect may be operating within both tonic and phasic processes.

Together these empirical findings demonstrate that responding in a high-risk situation is related to both distal and proximal risk factors operating within both tonic and phasic processes. Recognizing this complexity may provide clinicians with an edge in the treatment of addictive behaviors and the prevention of relapse (R. C. Hawkins & Hawkins, 1998). The clinical utility of the proposed model depends on clinicians' ability to gather detailed information about an individual's background, substance use history, personality, coping skills, self-efficacy, and affective state. The consideration of how these factors may interact within a high-risk situation (which could be assessed in treatment using cue reactivity or client-generated role-play exercises) and how changes in proximal risks can alter behavior leading up to high-risk situations will enable clients to continually assess their own relapse vulnerability. As Kauffman (1990), one of the pioneers in the study of complex systems, stated, "The internal portrait, condensed image, of the external world carried by the individual and used to guide its interactions, must be tuned, just so, to the ever evolving complexity of the world it helped create" (p. 320).

Future Research Strategies

The theoretical conceptualization of relapse presented in this article is not new to the study of addictive behaviors; substance abuse treatment outcomes have consistently been described as dynamic and complex (Brownell et al., 1986; Donovan, 1996; Niaura, 2000). Methodological limitations, however, have prevented these researchers from testing dynamic models of relapse. Recent innovations in computing technology afford researchers the opportunity to develop testable theories of relapse as a dynamic system. For example, Piasecki et al. (2000) have provided interesting findings on the withdrawal dynamics of smoking cessation, demonstrating that relapse vulnerability is indexed by the severity, trajectory, and variability of withdrawal symptoms. Boker and Graham (1998) investigated dynamic instability and self-regulation in the development of adolescent substance abuse, demonstrating that relatively small changes feed back into the system and lead to large changes in substance abuse over a relatively short period of time. Warren, Hawkins, and Sprott (2003) used nonlinear time series analysis to successfully model an individual's daily alcohol intake; this method provided a fit to the data that was superior to that of a comparable linear model and more accurately described the idiosyncrasies of drinking dynamics. R. C. Hawkins and Hawkins (1998) also presented a case study of an individual's alcohol intake over a 6-year period. Based on more than 2,000 data points, their analyses revealed a periodic cycle in which sudden shifts in drinking behavior were observed after periods of stability.

The utility of nonlinear dynamical systems, such as models based on chaos and/or catastrophe theory,[2] in the prediction and explanation of substance abuse has been described by several authors (Ehlers, 1992; R. C. Hawkins & Hawkins, 1998; H. A. Skinner, 1989; Warren et al., 2003). In general, many of the tenets of these theories are consistent with the hypotheses of the reconceptualized dynamic model of relapse (e.g., feedback loops, rapid changes in behavior, self-organization). Hufford, Witkiewitz, Shields, Kodya, and Caruso (2003) evaluated a catastrophe model of 6-month posttreatment alcohol consumption, incorporating alcohol dependence,

---

[2] Catastrophe and chaos theories are special cases of dynamical systems theory, an area of mathematics in which differential and difference equations are used to describe the behavior of complex systems. Catastrophe theory applies to the modeling of abrupt changes in the behavior of a system, determined by small changes in system parameters; chaos theory refers to the modeling of unstable, nonrepeating (aperiodic) behavior in deterministic systems.

self-efficacy, depression, family history, and stress as predictors. The results demonstrated that a catastrophe model provided a better fit to the data than a linear model. Witkiewitz, Hufford, Caruso, and Shields (2002) replicated these findings with data from Project MATCH (Project MATCH Research Group, 1997), showing that negative affect, self-efficacy, and distal risks were predictors of relapse in a catastrophe model but not in a comparable linear model.

Catastrophe models are just one class of nonlinear models, and many alternative nonlinear and dynamic models may also provide a good fit to the data (Davidian & Giltinan, 1995). Furthermore, a variety of modeling techniques can provide valuable information about the unique contributions of risk factors at various time points (van der Maas & Molenaar, 1992). Currently we are using parameter estimates from catastrophe models to examine the relationship between relapse risk factors and drinking outcomes in the Relapse Replication and Extension Project (RREP), described previously.

Assessing Relapse

Progress in the area of quantitative modeling procedures will only inform an understanding of the relapse process to the extent that operational definitions of relapse are improved. Advancements in the assessment of lapses may provide the impetus for a more comprehensive definition of relapse and exhaustive understanding of this complex process (Haynes, 1995). A few of the recent developments that may increase the ability to accurately measure addictive behavior include EMA (Stone & Shiffman, 1994), interactive voice response technology (Mundt, Bohn, Drebus, & Hartley, 2001), physiological measures (Niaura, Shadel, Britt, & Abrams, 2002), and brain imaging techniques (Bauer, 2001).

Although certain hypothesized precipitants of relapse cannot be ethically demonstrated in an experimental setting, investigations have demonstrated that some aspects of stress, cue reactivity, and craving have been shown to predict "relapse" in animals (Littleton, 2000; Shaham, Erb, & Stewart, 2000). Shaham et al. (2000) reported that foot shock stress causes reinstatement of heroin and cocaine seeking in rats, and several researchers have demonstrated environment-dependent tolerance and place preferences for cages previously associated with alcohol administration (e.g., Kalant, 1998).

Leri and Stewart (2002) tested whether a group of rats that self-administered heroin experienced different relapse rates than did rats that received an investigator-administered lapse (called "priming"). The results demonstrated that self-initiated heroin use paired with heroin-related stimuli led to heroin seeking during the relapse test. Exposure to a priming dose of heroin and heroin-related stimuli had little or no effect on subsequent heroin-seeking behavior, suggesting a dynamic interplay between internal system processes, cues, and positive reinforcement.

Relapse Prevention Treatment in the 21st Century

We view RP as having an important role in the continuous development of brief interventions for alcohol and drug problems, such as motivational interviewing (Miller & Rollnick, 2002), brief physician advice (Fleming, Barry, Manwell, Johnson, & London, 1997), and brief assessment and feedback (Dimeff, Baer, Kivlahan, & Marlatt, 1999; Monti, Colby, & O'Leary, 2001). Incorporating the cognitive–behavioral model of relapse and RP techniques, either within the brief intervention or as a booster session, will provide additional help for individuals who are attempting to abstain or moderate their use following treatment. Relapse prevention techniques may also be supplemented by other treatments for addictive behaviors, such as pharmacotherapy (Schmitz, Stotts, Rhoades, & Grabowski, 2001) or mindfulness meditation (Marlatt 2002). Currently a treatment is being developed that will integrate RP techniques with mindfulness training into a cohesive treatment package for addictive behaviors (for an introduction to this treatment, see Witkiewitz, Marlatt, & Walker, 2005).

Medication and meditation have already been used successfully as adjuncts to RP (Schmitz et al., 2001; Taub, Steiner, Weingarten, & Walton, 1994), but in some ways researchers may be getting ahead of the data. Relapse prevention techniques need to be studied in more diverse samples of individuals, including ethnic minority groups (De La Rosa, Segal, & Lopez, 1999) and adolescents who receive formal treatment (McCarthy, Tomlinson, Anderson, Marlatt, & Brown, 2003). The dynamic model of relapse presented in this article needs to be empirically tested and replicated across drug classes and with a variety of distinct substance-using populations (e.g., individuals with co-occurring disorders, polydrug users).

CONCLUSIONS

Relapse is a formidable challenge in the treatment of all behavior disorders. Individuals engaging in behavior change are confronted with urges, cues, and automatic thoughts regarding the maladaptive behaviors they are attempting to modify. Several authors have described relapse as complex, dynamic, and unpredictable (Buhringer, 2000; Donovan, 1996; Marlatt, 1996; Shiffman, 1989), but previous conceptualizations have proposed static models of relapse risk factors (e.g., Marlatt & Gordon, 1985; Stout et al., 1996). The reconceptualization of relapse proposed in this article acknowledges the complexity and unpredictable nature of substance use behavior following the commitment to abstinence or a moderation goal. Future research should continue to focus on refining measurement devices and developing better data analytic strategies for assessing behavior change. Empirical testing of the proposed dynamic model of relapse and further refinements of this new model will add to the understanding of relapse and how to prevent it.

REFERENCES

Allsop, S., & Saunders, B. (1989). Relapse and alcohol problems. In M. Gossop (Ed.), *Relapse and addictive behavior* (pp. 11–40). London: Routledge.

Annis, H. M. (1982). *Situational Confidence Questionnaire*. Toronto, Ontario, Canada: Addiction Research Foundation.

Baer, J. S., Holt, C. S., & Lichtenstein, E. (1986). Self-efficacy and smoking reexamined: Construct validity and clinical utility. *Journal of Consulting and Clinical Psychology, 54*, 846–852.

Baker, T. B., Piper, M. E., McCarthy, D. E., Majeskie, M. R., & Fiore, M. C. (2004). Addiction motivation reformulated: An affective processing model of negative reinforcement. *Psychological Review, 111*, 33–51.

Bandura, A. (1977). Self-efficacy: Toward a unifying theory of behavioral change. *Psychological Review, 84*, 191–215.

Barton, S. (1994). Chaos, self-organization, and psychology. *American Psychologist, 49*, 5–14.

Bauer, L. O. (2001). Predicting relapse to alcohol and drug abuse via quantitative electroencephalography. *Neuropsychopharmacology, 25*, 332–340.

Baumeister, R. F., Heatherton, T. F., & Tice, D. M. (1994). *Losing control: How and why people fail at self-regulation*. San Diego, CA: Academic Press.

Beattie, M. C., & Longabaugh, R. (1999). General and alcohol-specific social support following treatment. *Addictive Behaviors, 24*, 593–606.

Boker, S. M., & Graham, J. (1998). A dynamical systems analysis of adolescent substance abuse. *Multivariate Behavioral Research, 33*, 479–507.

Bolles, R. (1972). Reinforcement, expectancy, and learning. *Psychological Review, 79*, 394–409.

Brown, J. M., Miller, W. R., & Lawendowski, L. A. (1999). The self-regulation questionnaire. In L. VandeCreek & T. L. Jackson (Eds.), *Innovations in clinical practice: A source book* (Vol. 17, pp. 281–292). Sarasota, FL: Professional Resource Press.

Brown, S. A., Goldman, M. S., & Christiansen, B. A. (1985). Do alcohol expectancies mediate drinking patterns of adults? *Journal of Consulting and Clinical Psychology, 53*, 512–519.

Brown, S. A., Vik, P. W., & Craemer, V. A. (1989). Characteristics of relapse following adolescent substance abuse treatment. *Addictive Behaviors, 14*, 291–300.

Brownell, K. D., Marlatt, G. A., Lichtenstein, E., & Wilson, G. T. (1986). Understanding and preventing relapse. *American Psychologist, 41*, 765–782.

Brownell, K. D., & Wadden, T. A. (1992). Etiology and treatment of obesity: Understanding a serious, prevalent, and refractory disorder. *Journal of Consulting and Clinical Psychology, 60*, 505–517.

Bruce, T. J., Spiegel, D. A., & Hegel, M. T. (1999). Cognitive–behavioral therapy helps prevent relapse and recurrence of panic disorder following alprazolam discontinuation: A long-term follow-up of the Peoria and Dartmouth studies. *Journal of Consulting and Clinical Psychology, 67*, 151–156.

Buhringer, G. (2000). Testing CBT mechanisms of action: Humans behave in a more complex way than our treatment studies would predict. *Addiction, 95*, 1715–1716.

Burgess, E. S., Brown, R. A., Kahler, C. W., Niaura, R., Abrams, D. B., Goldstein, M. G., & Miller, I. W. (2002). Patterns of change in depressive symptoms during smoking cessation: Who's at risk for relapse? *Journal of Consulting and Clinical Psychology, 70*, 356–361.

Burling, T. A., Reilly, P. M., Moltzen, J. O., & Ziff, D. C. (1989). Self-efficacy and relapse among inpatient drug and alcohol abusers: A predictor of outcome. *Journal of Studies on Alcohol, 50*, 354–360.

Camazine, S., Deneubourg, J., Franks, N., Sneyd, J., Theraulaz, G., & Bonabeau, E. (2003). *Self-organization in biological systems.* Princeton, NJ: Princeton University Press.

Carroll, K. M. (1996). Relapse prevention as a psychosocial treatment: A review of controlled clinical trials. *Experimental and Clinical Psychopharmacology, 4*, 46–54.

Carroll, K. M., Nich, C., Frankforter, T. L., & Bisighini, R. M. (1999). Do patients change in the ways we intend? Assessing acquisition of coping skills among cocaine-dependent patients. *Psychological Assessment, 11*, 77–85.

Carroll, K. M., Rounsaville, B. J., Nich, C., & Gordon, L. T. (1994). One-year follow-up of psychotherapy and pharmacotherapy for cocaine dependence: Delayed emergence of psychotherapy effects. *Archives of General Psychiatry, 51*, 989–997.

Carter, B. L., & Tiffany, S. T. (1999). Meta-analysis of cue-reactivity in addiction research. *Addiction, 94*, 327–340.

Chamberlain, L. L., & Butz, M. R. (1998). *Clinical chaos: A therapist's guide to nonlinear dynamics and therapeutic change.* Philadelphia: Brunner/Mazel.

Chung, T., Langenbucher, J., Labouvie, E., Pandina, R. J., & Moos, R. H. (2001). Changes in alcoholic patients' coping responses predict 12-month treatment outcomes. *Journal of Consulting and Clinical Psychology, 69*, 92–100.

Cinciripini, P. M., Wetter, D. W., Fouladi, R. T., Blalock, J. A., Carter, B. L., Cinciripini, L. G., et al. (2003). The effects of depressed mood on smoking cessation: Mediation by postcessation self-efficacy. *Journal of Consulting and Clinical Psychology, 71*, 292–301.

Cohen, L. M., McCarthy, D. M., Brown, S. A., & Myers, M. G. (2002). Negative affect combines with smoking outcome expectancies to predict smoking behavior over time. *Psychology of Addictive Behaviors, 16*, 91–97.

Connors, G., Tarbox, A., & Faillace, L. (1993). Changes in alcohol expectancies and drinking behavior among treated problem drinkers. *Journal of Studies on Alcohol*, *54*, 676–683.

Courage, M. L., & Howe, M. L. (2002). From infant to child: The dynamics of cognitive change in the second year of life. *Psychological Bulletin*, *128*, 250–277.

Cummings, C., Gordon, J. R., & Marlatt, G. A. (1980). Relapse: Strategies of prevention and prediction. In W. R. Miller (Ed.), *The addictive behaviors* (pp. 291–321). Oxford, England: Pergamon Press.

Curry, S., Marlatt, G. A., & Gordon, J. R. (1987). Abstinence violation effect: Validation of an attributional construct with smoking cessation. *Journal of Consulting and Clinical Psychology*, *55*, 145–149.

Davidian, M., & Giltinan, D. M. (1995). *Nonlinear models for repeated measurement data*. New York: Chapman & Hall.

De La Rosa, M. R., Segal, B., & Lopez, R. E. (1999). *Conducting drug abuse research with minority populations: Advances and issues*. Binghamton, NY: Haworth Press.

DiClemente, C. C., Carbonari, J. P., Montgomery, R. P. G., & Hughes, S. O. (1994). The Alcohol Abstinence Self-Efficacy Scale. *Journal of Studies on Alcohol*, *55*, 141–148.

DiClemente, C. C., & Hughes, S. O. (1990). Stages of change profiles in outpatient alcoholism treatment. *Journal of Substance Abuse*, *2*, 217–235.

Dimeff, L. A., Baer, J. S., Kivlahan, D. R., & Marlatt, G. A. (1999). *Brief Alcohol Screening and Intervention for College Students (BASICS): A harm reduction approach*. New York: Guilford Press.

Dobkin, P. L., Civita, M., Paraherakis, A., & Gill, K. (2002). The role of functional social support in treatment retention and outcomes among outpatient adult substance abusers. *Addiction*, *97*, 347–356.

Dodge, K. A., & Pettit, G. S. (2003). A biopsychosocial model of the development of chronic conduct problems in adolescence. *Developmental Psychology*, *39*, 349–371.

Donovan, D. M. (1996). Marlatt's classification of relapse precipitants: Is the Emperor still wearing clothes? *Addiction*, *91*(Suppl.), 131–137.

Drummond, D. C., Litten, R. Z., Lowman, C., & Hunt, W. A. (2000). Craving research: Future directions. *Addiction*, *95*(Suppl. 2), 247–255.

Ehlers, C. L. (1992). The new physics of chaos: Can it help us understand the effects of alcohol? *Alcohol Health and Research World*, *16*, 169–176.

Fleming, M. F., Barry, K. L., Manwell, L. B., Johnson, K., & London, R. (1997). Brief physician advice for problem alcohol drinkers: A randomized controlled trial in community-based primary care practices. *JAMA*, *277*, 1039–1045.

Gossop, M., Stewart, D., Browne, N., & Marsden, J. (2002). Factors associated with abstinence, lapse or relapse to heroin use after residential treatment: Protective effect of coping responses. *Addiction*, *97*, 1259–1267.

Greenfield, S., Hufford, M., Vagge, L., Muenz, L., Costello, M., & Weiss, R. (2000). The relationship of self-efficacy expectancies to relapse among alcohol dependent men and women: A prospective study. *Journal of Studies on Alcohol*, *61*, 345–351.

Gwaltney, C. J., Shiffman, S., Norman, G. J., Paty, J. A., Kassel, J. D., Gnys, M., et al. (2001). Does smoking abstinence self-efficacy vary across situations? Identifying context-specificity within the Relapse Situation Efficacy Questionnaire. *Journal of Consulting and Clinical Psychology, 69,* 516–527.

Gwaltney, C. J., Shiffman, S., Paty, J. A., Liu, K. S., Kassel, J. D., Gnys, M., et al. (2002). Using self-efficacy judgments to predict characteristics of lapses to smoking. *Journal of Consulting and Clinical Psychology, 70,* 1140–1149.

Havassy, B. E., Hall, S. M., & Wasserman, D. A. (1991). Social support and relapse: Commonalities among alcoholics, opiate users, and cigarette smokers. *Addictive Behaviors, 16,* 235–246.

Hawkins, J. D., Catalano, R. F., Gillmore, M. R., & Wells, E. A. (1989). Skills training for drug abusers: Generalization, maintenance, and effects on drug use. *Journal of Consulting and Clinical Psychology, 75,* 559–563.

Hawkins, R. C., & Hawkins, C. A. (1998). Dynamics of substance abuse: Implications of chaos theory for clinical research. In L. Chamberlain & M. R. Butz (Eds.), *Clinical chaos: A therapist's guide to nonlinear dynamics and therapeutic change* (pp. 89–101). Philadelphia: Brunner/Mazel.

Haynes, S. N. (Ed.). (1995). Introduction to the special section on chaos theory and psychological assessment. *Psychological Assessment, 7,* 3–4.

Heather, N., & Stallard, A. (1989). Does the Marlatt model underestimate the importance of conditioned craving in the relapse process? In M. Gossop (Ed.), *Relapse and addictive behavior* (pp. 180–208). London: Routledge.

Hedeker, D., & Mermelstein, R. (1996). Random-effects regression models in relapse research. *Addictions, 91,* S211–S229.

Herz, M. I., Lamberti, J. S., Mintz, J., Scott, R., O'Dell, S., McCartan, L., et al. (2000). A program for relapse prevention in schizophrenia: A controlled study. *Archives of General Psychiatry, 57,* 277–283.

Hiss, H., Foa, E., & Kozak, M. J. (1994). Relapse prevention for treatment of obsessive-compulsive disorder. *Journal of Consulting and Clinical Psychology, 62,* 801–808.

Hodgins, D. C., el Guebaly, N., & Armstrong, S. (1995). Prospective and retrospective reports of mood states before relapse to substance use. *Journal of Consulting and Clinical Psychology, 63,* 400–407.

Hufford, M. R., Witkiewitz, K., Shields, A. L., Kodya, S., & Caruso, J. C. (2003). Applying nonlinear dynamics to the prediction of alcohol use disorder treatment outcomes. *Journal of Abnormal Psychology, 112,* 219–227.

Irvin, J. E., Bowers, C. A., Dunn, M. E., & Wang, M. C. (1999). Efficacy of relapse prevention: A meta-analytic review. *Journal of Consulting and Clinical Psychology, 67,* 563–570.

Jones, B. T., Corbin, W., & Fromme, K. (2001). A review of expectancy theory and alcohol consumption. *Addiction, 96,* 57–72.

Jones, B. T., & McMahon, J. (1996). A comparison of positive and negative alcohol expectancy value and their multiplicative composite as predictors of post-treatment abstinence survivorship. *Addiction, 91,* 89–99.

Juliano, L. M., & Brandon, T. H. (2002). Effects of nicotine dose, instructional set, and outcome expectancies on the subjective effects of smoking in the presence of a stressor. *Journal of Abnormal Psychology, 111*, 88–97.

Kadden, R. (1996). Is Marlatt's taxonomy reliable or valid? *Addiction, 91*(Suppl.), 139–146.

Kalant, H. (1998). Research on tolerance: What can we learn from history? *Alcoholism: Clinical and Experimental Research, 22*, 67–76.

Kassel, J. D., & Shiffman, S. (1992). What can hunger tell us about drug craving? A comparative analysis of the two constructs. *Advances in Behavior Therapy and Research, 14*, 141–167.

Kassel, J. D., Stroud, L. R., & Paronis, C. A. (2003). Smoking, stress, and negative affect: Correlation, causation, and context across stages of smoking. *Psychological Bulletin, 129*, 270–304.

Katon, W., Rutter, C., Ludman, E. J., Von Korff, M., Lin, E., Simon, G., et al. (2001). A randomized trial of relapse prevention of depression in primary care. *Archives of General Psychiatry, 58*, 241–247.

Kauffman, S. (1990). The sciences of complexity and "origins of order." *PSA: Proceedings of the Biennial Meeting of the Philosophy of Science Association, 2*, 299–322.

Kauffman, S. (1995). *At home in the universe: The search for laws of self-organization and complexity.* Oxford, England: Oxford University Press.

Kenford, S. L., Smith, S. S., Wetter, D. W., Jorenby, D. E., Fiore, M. C., & Baker, T. B. (2002). Predicting relapse back to smoking: Contrasting affective and physical models of dependence. *Journal of Consulting and Clinical Psychology, 70*, 216–227.

Khantzian, E. J. (1974). Opiate addiction: A critique of theory and some implications for treatment. *American Journal of Psychotherapy, 28*, 59–70.

Lam, D. H., Watkins, E. R., Hayward, P., Bright, J., Wright, K., & Kerr, N. (2003). A randomized controlled study of cognitive therapy for relapse prevention for bipolar affective disorder. *Archives of General Psychiatry, 60*, 145–152.

Laws, D., Hudson, S., & Ward, T. (2000). *Remaking relapse prevention with sex offenders: A sourcebook.* Thousand Oaks, CA: Sage.

Leri, F., & Stewart, J. (2002). The consequences of different "lapses" on relapse to heroin seeking in rats. *Experimental and Clinical Psychopharmacology, 10*, 339–349.

Litt, M. D., Cooney, N. L., & Morse, P. (2000). Reactivity to alcohol-related stimuli in the laboratory and in the field: Predictors of craving in treated alcoholics. *Addiction, 95*, 889–900.

Litt, M. D., Kadden, R. M., Cooney, N. L., & Kabela, E. (2003). Coping skills and treatment outcomes in cognitive–behavioral and interactional group therapy for alcoholism. *Journal of Consulting and Clinical Psychology, 71*, 118–128.

Littleton, J. (2000). Can craving be modeled in animals? The relapse prevention perspective. *Addiction, 95*, 83–90.

Longabaugh, R., Rubin, A., Stout, R. L., Zywiak, W. H., & Lowman, C. (1996). The reliability of Marlatt's taxonomy for classifying relapses. *Addiction, 91*(Suppl.), 73–88.

Lowman, C., Allen, J., Stout, R. L., & the Relapse Research Group. (1996). Replication and extension of Marlatt's taxonomy of relapse precipitants: Overview of procedures and results. *Addiction, 91*(Suppl.), 51–71.

Lowman, C., Hunt, W. A., Litten, R. Z., & Drummond, D. C. (2000). Research perspectives on alcohol craving: An overview. *Addiction, 95*(Suppl. 2), 45–54.

Maisto, S. A., Connors, G. J., & Zywiak, W. H. (2000). Alcohol treatment, changes in coping skills, self-efficacy, and levels of alcohol use and related problems 1 year following treatment initiation. *Psychology of Addictive Behaviors, 14,* 257–266.

Marlatt, G. A. (1978). Craving for alcohol, loss of control, and relapse: A cognitive–behavioral analysis. In P. E. Nathan, G. A. Marlatt, & T. Loberg (Eds.), *New directions in behavioral research and treatment* (pp. 271–314). New York: Plenum Press.

Marlatt, G. A. (1985). Relapse prevention: Theoretical rationale and overview of the model. In G. A. Marlatt & J. R. Gordon (Eds.), *Relapse prevention* (pp. 250–280). New York: Guilford Press.

Marlatt, G. A. (1996). Lest taxonomy become taxidermy: A comment on the relapse replication and extension project. *Addiction, 91*(Suppl.), 147–153.

Marlatt, G. A. (2002). Buddhist psychology and the treatment of addictive behavior. *Cognitive and Behavioral Practice, 9,* 44–49.

Marlatt, G. A., & Gordon, J. R. (1985). *Relapse prevention: Maintenance strategies in the treatment of addictive behaviors.* New York: Guilford Press.

Marlatt, G. A., & Rohsenow, D. J. (1980). Cognitive processes in alcohol use: Expectancy and the balanced placebo design. In N. K. Mello (Ed.), *Advances in substance abuse: Behavioral and biological research* (pp. 159–199). Greenwich, CT: JAI Press.

McCarthy, D. M., Tomlinson, K. L., Anderson, K. G., Marlatt, G. A., & Brown, S. A. (2003). *Relapse in alcohol and drug disordered adolescents with comorbid psychopathology: Changes in psychiatric symptoms.* Manuscript submitted for publication.

McKay, J. R., Alterman, A. I., Mulvaney, F. D., & Koppenhaver, J. M. (1999). Predicting proximal factors in cocaine relapse and near miss episodes: Clinical and theoretical implications. *Drug and Alcohol Dependence, 56,* 67–78.

McMahon, R. C. (2001). Personality, stress, and social support in cocaine relapse prediction. *Journal of Substance Abuse Treatment, 21,* 77–87.

Miller, W. R., & Rollnick, S. (2002). *Motivational interviewing: Preparing people for change* (2nd ed.). New York: Guilford Press.

Monti, P. M., Colby, S. M., & O'Leary, T. (2001). *Adolescents, alcohol, and substance abuse: Reaching teens through brief interventions.* New York: Guilford Press.

Monti, P. M., Rohsenow, D. J., Abrams, D. B., Zwick, W. R., Binkoff, J. A., Munroe, S. M., et al. (1993). Development of a behavior analytically derived alcohol-specific role-play assessment instrument. *Journal of Studies on Alcohol, 54,* 710–721.

Moos, R. H. (1993). *Coping Responses Inventory* (Youth form manual). Odessa, FL: Psychological Assessment Resources.

Morgenstern, J., & Longabaugh, R. (2000). Cognitive–behavioral treatment for alcohol dependence: A review of evidence for its hypothesized mechanisms of action. *Addiction, 95,* 1475–1490.

Mundt, J. C., Bohn, M. J., Drebus, D. W., & Hartley, M. T. (2001). Development and validation of interactive voice response (IVR) alcohol use assessment instruments. *Alcoholism: Clinical and Experimental Research, 25*(5, Suppl.), 248.

Muraven, M., Collins, R. L., & Neinhaus, K. (2002). Self-control and alcohol restraint: An initial application of the self-control strength model. *Psychology of Addictive Behaviors, 16,* 113–120.

Niaura, R. (2000). Cognitive social learning and related perspectives on drug craving. *Addiction, 95,* 155–164.

Niaura, R., Shadel, W. G., Britt, D. M., & Abrams, D. B. (2002). Response to social stress, urge to smoke, and smoking cessation. *Addictive Behaviors, 27,* 241–250.

Oxford English Dictionary Online. (2004). Retrieved March 14, 2004, from http://dictionary.oed.com/cgi/entry/00246934

Palfai, T., Davidson, D., & Swift, R. (1999). Influence of naltrexone on cue-elicited craving among hazardous drinkers: The moderational role of positive outcome expectancies. *Experimental and Clinical Psychopharmacology, 7,* 266–273.

Peirce, R. S., Frone, M. R., Russell, M., Cooper, M. L., & Mudar, P. (2000). A longitudinal model of social contact, social support, depression, and alcohol use. *Health Psychology, 19,* 28–38.

Perry, M. G., Nezu, A. M., McKelvey, W. F., Shermer, R. L., Renjilian, D. A., & Viegener, B. J. (2001). Relapse prevention and problem-solving therapy in the long-term management of obesity. *Journal of Consulting and Clinical Psychology, 69,* 722–726.

Piasecki, T. M., Fiore, M. C., McCarthy, D., & Baker, T. B. (2002). Have we lost our way? The need for dynamic formulations of smoking relapse proneness. *Addictions, 97,* 1093–1108.

Piasecki, T. M., Niaura, R., Shadel, W. G., Abrams, D., Goldstein, M., Fiore, M. C., & Baker, T. B. (2000). Smoking withdrawal dynamics in unaided quitters. *Journal of Abnormal Psychology, 109,* 74–86.

Polivy, J., & Herman, C. P. (2002). If at first you don't succeed: False hopes of self-change. *American Psychologist, 57,* 677–689.

Prochaska, J. O., & DiClemente, C. C. (1984). *The transtheoretical approach: Crossing the traditional boundaries of therapy.* Malabar, FL: Krieger.

Project MATCH Research Group. (1997). Matching alcoholism treatment to client heterogeneity: Post-treatment drinking outcomes. *Journal of Studies on Alcohol, 58,* 7–29.

Rabois, D., & Haaga, D. A. (2003). The influence of cognitive coping and mood on smokers' self-efficacy and temptation. *Addictive Behaviors, 28,* 561–573.

Rawson, R. A., McCann, M., Flammino, F., Shoptaw, S., Miotto, K., Reiber, C., et al. (2002). A comparison of contingency management and cognitive–behavioral approaches for cocaine- and methamphetamine-dependent individuals. *Archives of General Psychiatry, 59,* 817–824.

Roffman, R. A., Stephens, R. S., Simpson, E. E., & Whitaker, D. (1990). Treatment of marijuana dependence: Preliminary results. *Journal of Psychoactive Drugs, 20,* 129–137.

Rohsenow, D. J., & Monti, P. M. (1999). Does urge to drink predict relapse after treatment? *Alcohol Research and Health, 23,* 225–232.

Rohsenow, D. J., Niaura, R. S., Childress, A. R., Abrams, D. B., & Monti, P. M. (1990). Cue reactivity in addictive behaviors: Theoretical and treatment implications. *International Journal of the Addictions, 25,* 957–993.

Rychtarik, R. G., Prue, D. M., Rapp, S., & King, A. (1992). Self-efficacy, aftercare and relapse in a treatment program for alcoholics. *Journal of Studies on Alcohol, 53,* 435–440.

Sayette, M. A., Martin, C. S., Hull, J. G., Wertz, J. M., & Perrott, M. A. (2003). The effects of nicotine deprivation on craving response covariation in smokers. *Journal of Abnormal Psychology, 112,* 110–118.

Schmitz, J., Stotts, A., Rhoades, H., & Grabowski, J. (2001). Naltrexone and relapse prevention treatment for cocaine-dependent patients. *Addictive Behaviors, 26,* 167–180.

Shaham, Y., Erb, S., & Stewart, J. (2000). Stress-induced relapse to heroin and cocaine seeking in rats: A review. *Brain Research Reviews, 33,* 13–33.

Shiffman, S. (1984). Coping with temptations to smoke. *Journal of Consulting and Clinical Psychology, 52,* 261–267.

Shiffman, S. (1989). Conceptual issues in the study of relapse. In M. Gossop (Ed.), *Relapse and addictive behavior* (pp. 149–179). London: Routledge.

Shiffman, S., Balabanis, M., Paty, J., Engberg, J., Gwaltney, C., Liu, K., et al. (2000). Dynamic effects of self-efficacy on smoking lapse and relapse. *Health Psychology, 19,* 315–323.

Shiffman, S., Paty, J. A., Gnys, M., Kassel, J. D., & Hickcox, M. (1996). First lapses to smoking: Within-subjects analysis of real-time reports. *Journal of Consulting and Clinical Psychology, 64,* 366–379.

Siegel, S., Baptista, M. A. S., Kim, J. A., McDonald, R. V., & Weise, K. L. (2000). Pavlovian psychopharmacology: The associate basis of tolerance. *Experimental and Clinical Psychopharmacology, 8,* 276–293.

Skinner, E. A., Edge, K., Altman, J., & Sherwood, H. (2003). Searching for the structure of coping: A review and critique of category systems for classifying ways of coping. *Psychological Bulletin, 129,* 216–269.

Skinner, H. A. (1989). Butterfly wings flapping: Do we need more "chaos" in understanding addictions? *British Journal of Addiction, 84,* 353–356.

Sklar, S. M., Annis, H. M., & Turner, N. E. (1999). Group comparisons of coping self-efficacy between alcohol and cocaine abusers seeking treatment. *Psychology of Addictive Behaviors, 13,* 123–133.

Stone, A. A., & Shiffman, S. (1994). Ecological momentary assessment (EMA) in behavioral medicine. *Annals of Behavioral Medicine, 16,* 199–202.

Stout, R. L., Longabaugh, R., & Rubin, A. (1996). Predictive validity of Marlatt's taxonomy versus a more general relapse code. *Addiction, 91*(Suppl.), 99–110.

Swendsen, J. D., Tennen, H., Carney, M. A., Affleck, G., Willard, A., & Hromi, A. (2000). Mood and alcohol consumption: An experience sampling test of the self-medication hypothesis. *Journal of Abnormal Psychology, 109,* 198–204.

Sylvain, C., Ladouceur, R., & Boisvert, J. M. (1997). Cognitive and behavioral treatment of pathological gambling: A controlled study. *Journal of Consulting and Clinical Psychology, 65,* 727–732.

Taub, E., Steiner, S. S., Weingarten, E., & Walton, K. G. (1994). Effectiveness of broad spectrum approaches to relapse prevention in severe alcoholism: A long-term, randomized, controlled trial of transcendental meditation, EMG biofeedback and electronic neurotherapy. *Alcoholism Treatment Quarterly, 11,* 122–187.

Tennen, H., Affleck, G., Armeli, S., & Carney, M. A. (2000). A daily process approach to coping: Linking theory, research, and practice. *American Psychologist, 55,* 626–636.

Tiffany, S., Carter, B., & Singleton, E. (2000). Challenges in the manipulation, assessment and interpretation of craving relevant variables. *Addiction, 95*(Suppl. 2), 177–187.

van der Maas, H., & Molenaar, P. (1992). A catastrophe–theoretical approach to cognitive development. *Psychological Review, 99,* 395–417.

Warren, K., Hawkins, R. C., & Sprott, J. C. (2003). Substance abuse as a dynamical disease: Evidence and clinical implications of nonlinearity in a time series of daily alcohol consumption. *Addictive Behaviors, 28,* 369–374.

Wenger, J. R., & Woods, S. C. (1984, May 4). Factors in ethanol tolerance. *Science, 224,* 524.

Wertz, J. M., & Sayette, M. A. (2001). A review of the effects of perceived drug use opportunity on self-reported urge. *Experimental and Clinical Psychopharmacology, 9,* 3–13.

Witkiewitz, K., Hufford, M. R., Caruso, J. C., & Shields, A. S. (2002, November). *Increasing the prediction of alcohol relapse using catastrophe theory: Findings from Project MATCH.* Poster session presented at the annual meeting of the Association for the Advancement of Behavior Therapy, Reno, NV.

Witkiewitz, K., Marlatt, G. A., & Walker, D. D. (2005). Mindfulness-based relapse prevention for alcohol and substance use disorders. *Journal of Cognitive Psychotherapy, 19,* 211–228.

17

BRIEF TREATMENTS
FOR CANNABIS DEPENDENCE:
FINDINGS FROM A RANDOMIZED
MULTISITE TRIAL

THE MARIJUANA TREATMENT PROJECT RESEARCH GROUP

Of the 15.9 million illicit drug users estimated from the 2001 National Household Survey on Drug Abuse, 76% were current (past month) users of marijuana, and the majority of these (56%) used marijuana exclusively (Substance Abuse and Mental Health Services Administration [SAMHSA], 2002). The proportion of the U.S. adult population who meet *Diagnostic and*

The participating investigators of The Marijuana Treatment Project Research Group, listed in alphabetical order, are as follows: Thomas F. Babor, Department of Community Medicine and Health Care, University of Connecticut School of Medicine; Kathleen Carroll, Department of Psychiatry, Yale University; Kenneth Christiansen, The Village South, Inc., Miami, Florida; Jean Donaldson and James Herrell, Center for Substance Abuse Treatment, Rockville, Maryland; Ronald Kadden and Mark Litt, Department of Psychiatry, University of Connecticut School of Medicine; Bonnie McRee, Department of Community Medicine and Health Care, University of Connecticut School of Medicine; Michael Miller, The Village South, Inc.; Roger Roffman, School of Social Work, University of Washington; Nadia Solowji, Department of Psychology, University of Wollongong, Wollongong, Australia; Karen Steinberg, Department of Psychiatry, University of Connecticut School of Medicine; Robert Stephens, Department of Psychology, Virginia Polytechnic Institute and State University; and Janice Vendetti, Department of Community Medicine and Health Care, University of Connecticut School of Medicine. Funding for this research was provided by Substance Abuse and Mental Health Services Administration, Center for Substance Abuse Treatment Grants UR4 TI11273, UR4 TI11310, UR4 TI11274, and UR4 TI11270. The opinions expressed are those of the authors. We thank Deborah Talamini for administrative support, Ron Jackson for facilitating the University of Washington and Evergreen Treatment Services collaboration, and the numerous therapists and research assistants who were responsible for the implementation of the study.

Reprinted from *Journal of Consulting and Clinical Psychology, 72,* 455–466 (2004). Copyright 2004 by the American Psychological Association.

Statistical Manual of Mental Disorders (4th ed.; *DSM–IV*; American Psychiatric Association, 1994) criteria for cannabis dependence has been estimated at 4.2% (Anthony, Warner, & Kessler, 1994), the highest prevalence for any substance other than alcohol. Cessation of marijuana use by some chronic marijuana users has been associated with a withdrawal syndrome characterized by anxiety, irritability, restlessness, sleep disturbance, and appetite change (Budney, Novy, & Hughes, 1999; Haney, Ward, Comer, Foltin, & Fischman, 1999; Kouri & Pope, 2000). Although marijuana dependence is often secondary to alcohol, cocaine, and opiate abuse, some marijuana users have begun to seek treatment for marijuana as their primary drug of abuse (Roffman & Barnhart, 1987; Stephens, Roffman, & Simpson, 1993). Findings from the SAMHSA Drug and Alcohol Services Information System indicate that marijuana was the primary substance of abuse for 14.1% of adult admissions reported to the Treatment Episode Data Set in 2000 (SAMHSA, 2003). The relatively low treatment utilization by persons with cannabis dependence might be due to lack of specific treatment for marijuana dependence and to the reluctance of many chronic marijuana users to seek treatment in programs dominated by alcoholics and people dependent on heroin and cocaine (Stephens et al., 1993).

Heavy marijuana users surveyed both in the community and in drug abuse treatment settings report a variety of medical and psychosocial problems related to their marijuana use (Budney, Radonovich, Higgins, & Wong, 1998; Roffman & Barnhart, 1987; Stephens, Roffman, & Curtin, 2000; Stephens, Roffman, & Simpson, 1994), and there is evidence that regular use is associated with pulmonary, reproductive, and immunologic consequences (Committee on Substance Abuse, 1999). Marijuana-dependent adults seeking treatment report that their use has persisted in the face of multiple forms of impairment, and most perceive themselves as being unable to stop (Stephens et al., 1994, 2000).

Recent studies have identified potentially effective interventions for marijuana-dependent adults (Budney, Higgins, Radonovich, & Novy, 2000; Stephens et al., 1994, 2000), but these studies also have raised questions about the optimal duration or intensity of treatment and the generalizability of treatment effects to more diverse populations. In a study of 212 daily marijuana smokers, Stephens et al. (1994) compared 10 sessions of cognitive–behavioral group therapy (CBT) with 10 sessions of group discussion. All treatment groups met weekly for the first 8 weeks and then every other week for the next 4 weeks for a total of ten 2-hour sessions. Both groups showed similar reductions in marijuana use and related problems. Continuous abstinence rates at 3, 6, and 12 month follow-ups were only 37%, 22%, and 14%, respectively. Nevertheless, significant and clinically meaningful reductions in the frequency of marijuana use and associated problems were observed at each follow-up. Contrary to predictions, the CBT group did not have a greater reduction in marijuana use. And the lack of differences between intervention conditions left open the possibility that change was due in part to high levels of motivation in this self-referred and high-functioning sample.

In a subsequent study, Stephens et al. (2000) extended the length of the CBT group intervention (i.e., 14 sessions over 4 months) and compared it with two individual sessions of motivational enhancement therapy (MET) and with a delayed treatment control (DTC) condition in a sample of 291 adult daily marijuana smokers. Both active treatments were associated with substantial reductions in marijuana use relative to the DTC condition. Frequency of use and related problems were reduced by more than 50% throughout the 16-month follow-up in both active treatments. The 2-session MET treatment produced outcomes comparable to the longer CBT treatment at all follow-up points, suggesting that brief interventions may be as effective as extended counseling for this population. The DTC condition helped rule out motivation for change as the sole explanation for the apparent effects of treatment. However, the lack of differences between treatments was difficult to interpret because length of treatment was confounded with treatment modality (group vs. individual) and therapist experience (MET had more experienced therapists). Again, the sample was relatively homogenous, with most participants being relatively high-functioning White males.

Budney et al. (2000) randomly assigned 60 marijuana-dependent adults to one of three treatments that varied in intensity and content: 4 sessions of MET, 14 sessions of combined MET/ CBT, or 14 sessions of MET/CBT plus the use of voucher-based incentives that were linked to weekly negative urinalysis results. The same therapists delivered all treatments individually. The voucher-based condition produced more weeks of continuous abstinence from marijuana during the 14-week treatment period and greater abstinence at the end of treatment (35%) than MET/CBT (10%) or MET (5%) conditions. There were no significant differences between the briefer MET treatment and longer MET/CBT without vouchers. However, the small sample size may have limited the study's ability to detect trends favoring the 14-session MET/CBT intervention.

Another recent study of brief interventions for treatment-seeking adult marijuana users in Australia compared six sessions of MET/CBT with one session of MET/CBT and with a DTC condition (Copeland, Swift, Roffman, & Stephens, 2001). Both treatments were delivered individually and produced greater reductions in marijuana use compared with the DTC condition at a 6-month follow-up. However, the few significant differences between the two active treatments were inconsistent and did not clearly favor the longer treatment. Again, continuous abstinence rates were low, but reductions in problems associated with use appeared to be substantial.

These studies indicate that many marijuana-dependent adults respond well to several types of interventions, even though continuous abstinence is a less common outcome than reduced marijuana use. The studies comparing different therapeutic modalities raise important questions about the optimal duration, intensity, and type of treatment. The generalizability of findings is also unknown because the studies have been conducted in a limited number of localities with fairly homogenous samples of treatment seekers. The present chapter describes a multisite randomized clinical trial designed to replicate and extend findings from previous studies. A two-session MET intervention was compared with a nine-session multicomponent intervention. The location of the study in three demographically distinct communities was intended to increase sample heterogeneity and to assess the generalizability of the outcomes. We hypothesized that both treatments would produce outcomes superior to untreated controls. Furthermore, we hypothesized that the nine-session treatment would result in better outcomes than the two-session intervention despite the relative lack of differences in previous studies. Trends in two of those studies suggest that somewhat longer MET/CBT treatments would fare better if therapist experience and modality were controlled.

METHOD

Participants

Recruitment took place between May 1997 and August 1998. Of the 450 randomized patients, 84% were referred to the project via specific advertising that offered free treatment; 8% were referred by a family member, friend, or relative; 5% were referred from a general advertisement for the agency or clinic; and the remainder were from social service agencies, medical doctors, private practitioners (nonmedical), or self-referrals. The advertisements targeted adults who were interested in receiving free outpatient treatment composed of individual therapy to help them quit their heavy marijuana use (see Steinberg et al., 2002). To attract minority and female participants, sites used gender-specific and minority-specific outreach strategies that made use of local media, public service announcements, and flyers. Interested individuals were invited to call or visit the treatment site for information.

The three collaborating sites collectively recruited 450 eligible participants, with a final sample of 308 men and 142 women. Participants were recruited through media advertisements and agency referrals. A total of 1,211 interested callers were screened by telephone during the 16-month recruitment period. Of these initial callers, 398 (33%) were ineligible because they met one or more of the following exclusion criteria: unwillingness to accept random assignment (21%), legal status that might have interfered with treatment (e.g., mandated treatment, pending jail sentencing; 16%), current

DSM–IV (American Psychiatric Association, 1994) diagnosis of dependence on another drug or alcohol (31%), need for immediate medical or psychiatric treatment that did not allow for randomization into the DTC group (16%), currently receiving therapy or attending a self-help group (20%), and inability to provide a contact person (20%).

As shown in Figure 17.1, 813 of those screened were eligible, but 363 callers declined to participate or did not attend the baseline interview. Participants were eligible if they were 18 years of age or older, had a *DSM–IV* (American Psychiatric Association, 1994) diagnosis of current marijuana dependence, and used marijuana on at least 40 of the 90 days prior to the study. Study participants ($N = 450$) were compared with eligible individuals who declined study participation ($n = 363$) on variables obtained during the screening interview. Nonparticipants were more likely to be African Americans, $\chi^2(3, N = 813) = 17.7, p < .01$; unmarried, $\chi^2(1, N = 813) = 10.6$, $p < .01$; less educated, $t(811) = 5.03, p < .001$, and unemployed, $\chi^2(2, N = 813) = 18.23, p < .001$, than those who participated (see Vendetti, McRee, Miller, Christiansen, Herrell, & The Marijuana Treatment Project Research Group, 2002, for more information on pretreatment dropouts).

As shown in Table 17.1, participants were primarily men (68.0%) who had an average of 14 years of education. Sixty-nine percent were White, whereas 12.0% were African American and 17.1% were Hispanic. Approximately 60.0%

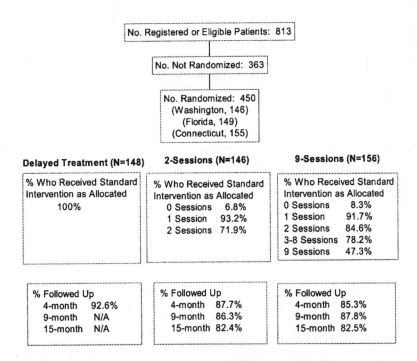

Figure 17.1. Profile of marijuana treatment project. N/A = not applicable.

TABLE 17.1
Baseline Characteristics of the Randomized Sample by Treatment Condition, With Means and Standard Deviations for Continuous Variables

Variable	Total N = 450	Delayed n = 148	2-session n = 146	9-session n = 156	χ^2	p	F	p
			Categorical					
Men (%)	68.4	70.9	63.7	70.5	2.26	.323		
Ethnicity (%)					8.95	.176		
White	69.3	76.4	65.1	66.7				
Hispanic	17.3	15.5	20.5	16.0				
African American	12.2	8.1	13.0	15.4				
Other	1.1	0.0	1.4	1.9				
Not married (%)	59.8	60.8	59.6	59.0	0.11	.947		
Residence (%)					0.85	.932		
Owns	45.8	48.6	43.8	44.9				
Rents	51.8	49.3	53.4	52.6				
Room/shelter	2.4	2.0	2.7	2.6				
Employment (%)					2.75	.840		
Full-time	69.1	70.3	65.8	71.2				
Part-time	14.0	13.5	16.4	12.2				
Unemployed	12.4	10.8	13.0	13.5				
Student/retired/homemaker	4.4	5.4	4.8	3.2				
			Continuous					
Age							0.90	.408
M	36.10	36.61	35.36	36.30				
SD	8.33	8.72	8.05	8.22				
Years of education							1.36	.257
M	14.17	14.39	13.95	14.18				
SD	2.32	2.43	2.37	2.18				
Years at present job							0.33	.720
M	5.21	5.30	4.71	5.08				
SD	5.66	5.92	5.45	5.87				

of the sample was currently unmarried. Sixty-nine percent worked full time, 14.0% worked part time, and 12.4% were unemployed. The average age of the sample was 36 years (range = 18–62). On average, participants reported using marijuana on 82 of the past 90 days, smoking 3.7 times a day, and being high more than 6 hours a day. Use of alcohol and other drugs was infrequent. The sample also reported a mean of 17.9 years of *regular marijuana use* (defined as 3 or more times per week) and 9.2 years of self-defined "problem use." Participants endorsed an average of 5.6 of the 7 DSM–IV (American Psychiatric Association, 1994) dependence criteria. Only 18% had ever received treatment for drug abuse, and 7% had been treated for alcohol abuse. There were no significant differences among participants assigned to the three study conditions on basic demographic or problem severity measures (see Stephens et al., 2002, for a detailed presentation of the success of randomization).

Research Design and Sites

The study was conducted at the University of Connecticut's Department of Psychiatry, Farmington (n = 155); The Village South, Inc., Miami, Florida (n = 149); and Evergreen Treatment Services, Seattle, Washington (n = 146). Two of the sites (Miami and Seattle) were outpatient substance abuse treatment facilities not affiliated with universities. Sites were chosen through a competitive process that took into account geographic representation, access to clinical facilities, and potential for recruiting a diverse group of chronic marijuana users. The participants recruited at the three sites were similar in age, marital status, and years employed in their current position, but they differed in ethnic distribution, education, and employment rates. Such differences were anticipated given the diversity in the demographic makeup of these regions. Small differences were also found across sites in the baseline frequency and quantity of marijuana, alcohol, and other drug use. Participants in Miami tended to use marijuana and other illicit drugs more frequently, whereas alcohol use and related problems were higher in Seattle (see Stephens et al., 2002, for more detail and discussion of site differences).

The three treatment conditions were (a) a two-session MET intervention lasting 5 weeks; (b) a nine-session, 3-month duration multicomponent treatment that added CBT and case management (CM) to MET sessions; and (c) a 4-month DTC group. Both active treatments were delivered individually. Participants were randomly assigned to conditions at each site using an urn randomization program (Stout, Wirtz, Carbonari, & Del Boca, 1994) to balance key variables (i.e., age, gender, ethnicity, employment status, education, and marijuana problem severity, as measured by the Marijuana Problem Scale described below) across treatment groups. The research design and sample size provided sufficient power to detect medium-sized effects between treatment conditions (see Stephens et al., 2002, for more information on the rationale and design of the study).

Assessment Procedures

Baseline Assessments

All participants completed a baseline assessment session conducted by trained research staff at each site. During the baseline session, participants signed an informed consent form and completed a series of structured interviews and self-report questionnaires. Diagnoses of alcohol and drug abuse or dependence were obtained using the Structured Clinical Interview (SCID; First, Spitzer, Gibbon, & Williams, 1996) for the *DSM–IV* (American Psychiatric Association, 1994), which has been shown to yield valid and reliable psychiatric diagnoses. The SCID was used to make a final determination of eligibility (presence of marijuana dependence) and to assess dependence severity. The total number of dependence and abuse symptoms (range = 0–11) was used to measure the severity of marijuana-related consequences. The Addiction Severity Index (ASI; McLellan et al., 1992), a structured interview, was used to measure the severity of medical, employment, legal, alcohol and drug, and psychiatric problems. The time line follow-back (TLFB; Sobell & Sobell, 1992) interview was used to measure the frequency and pattern of marijuana and other drug consumption. The TLFB used calendar prompts for the 90 days prior to the interview and was modified to identify the time periods of each day (i.e., 12:00 a.m.–6:00 a.m.; 6:00 a.m.–12:00 p.m.; 12:00 p.m.–6:00 p.m.; 6:00 p.m.–12:00 a.m.) during which the participant smoked marijuana to assess the extent of smoking across the day. Single-item summary measures of the quantities of marijuana (e.g., number of joints) and alcohol (i.e., standard drinks) consumed on a typical day of use were added to the TLFB interview, rather than assessing quantity consumed on each day of the period. An index of total number of standard alcoholic drinks consumed during the 90 days before assessment was constructed by multiplying the number of days of any use by the typical number of drinks per day.

Participants also completed several self-report questionnaires that served as secondary outcomes. The Beck Depression Inventory (BDI; Beck, Ward, & Mendelson, 1961) and the state portion of the State–Trait Anxiety Inventory (STAI; Spielberger, Gorsuch, Lushene, Vagg, & Jacobs, 1983) were used to measure common psychological states associated with substance abuse. The Marijuana Problem Scale (MPS; Stephens et al., 2000) was used to measure the occurrence of 19 recent (previous 90 days) problems (e.g., guilt, low energy, medical problems, sleep disturbance, legal problems) associated with cannabis use. The MPS was included to characterize the possible benefits of reducing marijuana use. Additional self-report measures of potential predictors of outcomes were included for exploratory purposes, but presentation of these data is beyond the scope of the present chapter.

Collateral Interviews

Collateral verification of substance use was obtained from a random sample of one third of the participants at the 4- and 9-month follow-up assessments. Collaterals were spouses or partners (56%), other relatives (15%), or friends (29%) of the participants. Collaterals were interviewed by phone and provided estimates of the frequency of marijuana, alcohol, and other drug use during the 90 days preceding the follow-up. At the 4- and 9-month follow-ups, the correlations between participant and collateral reports of days of marijuana use were .73 and .68, respectively, indicating a moderate to high level of agreement.

One hundred percent of those who reported complete abstinence during the 4-month follow-up were corroborated by their collateral informants, whereas 91% who reported smoking marijuana during this time period were in agreement with their informants. The 9% of disagreement occurred because the collateral reported abstinence when the participant reported smoking. The discrepancies for both indices occurred because participants reported more marijuana use than collaterals.

Urine Toxicology Tests

Urine toxicology tests were used to screen participants for exclusion criteria (e.g., unreported drug use) and to validate verbal report measures. Urine samples, collected at intake and at the 4- and 9-month follow-up points, were processed by a centralized laboratory to detect recent use of tetrahydrocannabinol and nine other psychoactive substances. Enzyme immunoassay tests were used as a first pass. Quantitative analysis was conducted on all positive screenings using gas chromatography/mass spectrometry. The screening results were compared with self-reported marijuana use during the 2-week period before the specimen was collected. Percentage of agreement was very high for each time point (94% at baseline, 91% at 4 months, 92% at 9 months). As with the collateral data, most discrepancies occurred because participants reported marijuana use when the urine screening indicated that the participant was abstinent. For example, approximately 5% of participants reported smoking during the 2-week time period when their urine results were negative. This discrepancy might be due to the participant reporting marijuana use that occurred earlier in the 2-week time period before the specimen collection, resulting in the marijuana metabolite being undetectable in the urine at the time of the test. Even smaller proportions of participants reported abstinence when their urine screens were positive (0.9% at baseline, 3.6% at

4 months, and 2.9% at 9 months). False positives can arise for a number of reasons, including procedural errors such as incorrect sample identification or clerical error. Both the urine specimen results and collateral informant interview data suggest that participants did not systematically underreport their use of marijuana.

Treatment Interventions

The two-session and nine-session interventions were similar to those used in previous studies (Budney et al., 2000; Stephens et al., 1994, 2000), with somewhat greater latitude given to therapists in the nine-session protocol to meet the needs of a more racially and socioeconomically diverse sample (see Steinberg et al., 2002, for a more detailed presentation of the treatments). Both treatments promoted complete abstinence from marijuana as the treatment goal but were not dogmatic in this regard. Therapists attempted to help participants who had a goal of moderate use to see the advantage of initiating a period of complete abstinence before attempting controlled use, but they continued to support attempts to reduce marijuana consumption if complete abstinence was rejected. The same therapists conducted both treatments at each site.

The primary models used in the study were MET and CBT. MET refers to an empathic therapeutic style designed to resolve ambivalence and elicit motivation to change (Dunn, DeRoo, & Rivara, 2001; Miller & Rollnick, 2002). MET intervention is based on the assumption that even if clients possess sufficient skills to curtail their marijuana use, they must first resolve their ambivalence about marijuana use and increase their motivation to change. Once they have decided that the costs of marijuana use outweigh the benefits, they are more likely to use their existing abilities and support systems to stop marijuana use. In studies with adult marijuana users, one (Copeland et al., 2001) or two sessions (Stephens et al., 2000) of motivational interviewing were found to be more efficacious than no treatment.

A CBT intervention was included in the present trial because motivation to change may not be sufficient by itself, especially for clients who began using marijuana in their early teens and who have been using it regularly ever since (Baer, Kivlahan, & Donovan, 1999). Regular use since adolescence may leave them with coping skills deficits that could handicap their efforts to curtail use, no matter how strong their motivation. Hence, cognitive restructuring and skills training may be required to develop the personal coping resources needed to achieve and maintain abstinence (Monti, Abrams, Kadden, & Cooney, 1989). Combining a motivational intervention with skills training is likely to result in enhanced engagement in treatment and better substance use outcomes. In support of this, a review of motivational intervention studies for substance use disorders (Dunn et al., 2001) found that the most change occurred when motivational sessions were added as an enhancement before more intensive treatment.

To a lesser extent, CM constructs were used to broaden the focus of CBT treatment beyond substance abuse alone. The CM component was suggested by research on the importance of identifying and reducing nonsubstance problems in the lives of drug users in order to achieve successful substance use outcomes (McLellan et al., 1997).

Two-Session Intervention

The two-session treatment involved MET sessions scheduled 1 week and 5 weeks after randomization. These 1-hour sessions were separated by 1 month to allow participants enough time to make changes that could be evaluated and discussed with the therapist at the second meeting. During the first session, the therapist reviewed and discussed a personal feedback report (PFR) to motivate the client and provide support for the selection of treatment goals and strategies for change. The PFR included summaries of the client's recent marijuana use, problems, concerns, attitudes favoring and opposing change in marijuana use, and ratings of self-confidence about change. At the second session, efforts to reduce marijuana use were reviewed and adjustments in strategy were made as necessary. MET was used to address ambivalence as needed. Participants had the option of involving a significant other (SO; e.g., spouse, partner, or friend) during the second session. When present (15% of the sessions), the SO was involved in identifying the pros and cons of change and in developing strategies for remaining abstinent.

Nine-Session Intervention

The nine-session therapy included elements of MET, CM, and CBT and was delivered over a 12-week period. It was designed to permit a tailoring of content to meet the needs of a diverse sample (see Steinberg et al., 2002). The first eight sessions were scheduled weekly, starting 1 week after baseline assessment. The ninth session was scheduled during Week 12, four weeks after the eighth session, in order to give participants the opportunity to review change strategies with their therapists after a period without weekly contact. The first two sessions involved the review of a PFR and the use of MET to bolster motivation for change. However, the treatment protocol allowed counselors to return to MET strategies throughout the nine sessions to acknowledge any ambivalence regarding change and to assist the client in making use of the upcoming sessions, given possible changes in goals (e.g., not motivated to quit, but wishing to become moderate in marijuana use; ambivalent about initiating any change) and current motivational levels. The

CM component was suggested by research on the importance of identifying and reducing nonsubstance problems in the lives of drug users in order to achieve successful substance use outcomes (McLellan et al., 1997). During the two CM sessions that typically followed MET sessions, therapists used data from the ASI (McLellan et al., 1992) and other instruments, as well as the participant's self-report, to identify potential obstacles to abstinence related to marijuana use (e.g., legal, housing, social support, vocational, psychiatric, transportation, parenting, and medical problems). They subsequently worked together to set goals, identify resources in the community, develop a plan, and monitor progress toward goal attainment for each targeted problem. In subsequent sessions, some time was devoted to a review and discussion of progress toward these goals. Although the protocol suggested two sessions of CM, it allowed therapists to devote more or less CM time in subsequent sessions, depending on participants' needs.

The CBT component of the treatment protocol offered the third opportunity for tailoring therapy to the needs of a diverse clientele. CBT identifies potential triggers or high-risk situations for drug use and helps the client develop coping skills to avoid drug use in those situations. The protocol included five core and five elective CBT modules adapted from prior treatment protocols for marijuana use (Stephens et al., 2000) and other drugs (e.g., Kadden et al., 1992). The core sessions were (a) Understanding Marijuana Use Patterns, (b) Coping with Cravings and Urges to Use, (c) Managing Thoughts about Re-Starting Marijuana Use, (d) Problem Solving, and (e) Marijuana Refusal Skills. Five elective modules covered the following areas: Planning for Emergencies/Coping with a Lapse, Seemingly Irrelevant Decisions, Managing Negative Moods and Depression, Assertiveness, and Anger Management. Although the remaining five sessions were designated primarily for CBT, therapists were given latitude in deciding along with the client whether to cover all CBT modules, modify the order in which they were covered, and/or substitute certain electives for core modules. Furthermore, the need for MET to address ambivalence or CM to address substantial nonsubstance problems altered the exact ratio of treatment components.

In the nine-session intervention, 29% of the participants involved an SO who could attend up to two sessions. The first session oriented the SO to the treatment and sought to foster the client's motivation by encouraging the SO and participant to discuss the impact of the participant's marijuana use on the relationship or family. The counselor helped the SO and client formulate a change plan that involved identifying areas in which the SO could help the participant with their treatment goals. The second SO session focused on how the SO and client had worked with each other, allowing the therapist to work on communication skills. Future support for the achievement and maintenance of behavior change was also considered.

Delayed Treatment Control Condition

Participants assigned to the DTC condition waited 4 months and then completed a second assessment. The DTC group also was assessed briefly by phone at 4 and 12 weeks postrandomization to check for possible clinical deterioration during the waiting period. No participants were referred to treatment or withdrawn from the trial because of clinical deterioration. At the completion of the 4-month waiting period, participants in the DTC group were allowed to initiate either of the two treatment protocols. We found that 23.7% chose the two-session intervention, 63.5% chose the nine-session intervention, and 12.8% entered neither treatment. We also compared DTC participants who chose the two-session treatment with participants randomized to the same brief treatment in terms of number of sessions completed. It is interesting that those who could choose the brief treatment attended significantly fewer sessions ($M = 1.23$) than those who were assigned to it ($M = 1.65$), $t(179) = 3.29$, $p = .01$. There were no differences between groups that chose or were assigned to the extended treatment.

Therapist Training and Treatment Fidelity

Therapists ($N = 13$) were primarily psychologists and master's-level therapists with previous experience in behavioral therapies. They were trained to follow detailed therapy manuals developed by investigators for each of the three treatments. The manuals prescribed the content and technique of each therapy session. Following an initial 2-day training at the project's Coordinating Center, therapists returned to their respective sites. They were certified to begin conducting the treatments only after a review of several videotaped therapy sessions with pilot participants to demonstrate that they were competently following the treatment protocols. The training supervisor at the Coordinating Center continued the supervision of each therapist throughout the study period by reviewing randomly selected therapy videotapes.

Independent evaluators blind to treatment assignments reviewed 633 treatment sessions for therapist competency, adherence to protocol, and other indicators of therapy process. Therapists were found to closely adhere to the manuals throughout treatment. There were no significant differences across sites in treatment adherence, competence, and other process measures.

Follow-Up Procedures

Participants in both of the active treatment conditions were assessed at 4, 9, and 15 months after the start of treatment using relevant baseline assessment instruments. The primary assessment for the DTC group was conducted at 4 months postrandomization. DTC participants were not assessed after the 4-month follow-up. Research assistants were not blinded to the participant's experimental condition. The TLFB (Sobell & Sobell, 1992), ASI (McLellan et al., 1992), and SCID (First et al., 1996, Cannabis Use Disorders section) were repeated at the 4- and 9-month in-person follow-ups, as were questionnaires assessing marijuana-related problems and potential mediators of treatment effects. Participants were paid $50 for each of the 4- and 9-month follow-ups. At 15 months, participants received $25 for completing telephone interviews that assessed only frequency of marijuana use and negative consequences via the MPS (Stephens et al., 2000).

Data Analysis

General linear model (GLM) analyses were performed on outcome measures from each follow-up. Treatment condition and research site were between-participants factors, and the follow-up assessment points formed a within-participants factor labeled *time*. Initial outcomes at the 4-month follow-up were evaluated with 3 (treatment) × 2 (site) × 2 (time) GLM analyses because the DTC condition was only available at this follow-up. Significant interactions were followed by planned contrasts comparing means of the treatment conditions or sites while controlling for the baseline value of the dependent variable. A Bonferroni-corrected alpha of .016 (.05/3) indicated treatment differences. Change over time and maintenance of treatment gains for the two active treatments were evaluated across the baseline, 4-month follow-up, and 9-month follow-up assessments with 2 (treatment) × 2 (site) × 3 (time) GLM analyses. The 15-month follow-up data were analyzed separately, with 2 (treatment) × 2 (time) GLM analyses comparing baseline and follow-up measures. Comparisons with baseline data are provided for descriptive purposes along with appropriate cautions in their interpretation. Initially, analyses included only participants completing the respective follow-up assessments. Additional analyses were performed to assess the impact of missing data on the primary outcomes. The primary outcome measure was the proportion of days of marijuana use during the preceding 90 days, which reflected the degree of success in achieving abstinence. Secondary outcome measures included the mean number of quarterly periods during which marijuana was used per day of use (0–4), the number of joints smoked per day, number of problems related to use (i.e., total score from the MPS [Stephens et al., 2000] scale; 0–19), number of SCID (First et al., 1996) dependence symptoms (0–7), number of SCID abuse symptoms (0–4), ASI (McLellan et al., 1992) composite scores, and measures of depression (BDI; Beck et al., 1961) and anxiety (STAI; Spielberger et al., 1983).

RESULTS

Treatment Attendance

The mean number of sessions attended by MET clients was 1.6, with 71.9% receiving both sessions (see Figure 17.1). For the nine-session treatment, the mean number of sessions attended was 6.5. Over 47.0% of the sample attended all nine sessions, whereas 8.3% failed to attend any sessions.

Cannabis Use and Related Problems

Table 17.2 presents the baseline, 4-, and 9-month follow-up means (and standard deviations) for the primary and secondary cannabis-related outcome measures for each treatment condition. At the 4-month follow-up, we observed consistent differences between groups on measures of marijuana use and related consequences during the previous 90 days. Significant effects of time on all measures were qualified by significant Treatment × Time interactions (see Table 17.2). There were no significant Treatment × Site × Time interactions. We found a main effect of site, $F(2, 388) = 16.90$, $p < .001$, and a significant Site × Time interaction, $F(2, 388) = 7.63$, $p < .001$, on the measure of joints smoked per day. At baseline, mean number of joints smoked per day was highest at the Farmington site and lowest at the Seattle site, with all three sites differing significantly from each other. At the 4-month follow-up, after controlling for baseline use, there were no significant differences between sites in the mean number of joints smoked per day.

The percentages of reductions in days smoked from baseline were 15.9%, 35.7%, and 58.8% for the DTC, two-session, and nine-session treatment conditions, respectively. The planned contrasts indicated that both the two-session and nine-session treatments resulted in greater reductions in the percentage of days of marijuana smoking compared with the DTC condition. Between-group effect sizes (d; Cohen, 1988) for the two-session and nine-session treatments compared with the DTC condition were .59 and 1.14, respectively. Furthermore, the nine-session treatment produced significantly greater reductions than the two-session treatment ($d = .52$). Figure 17.2 illustrates the results for the percentage of days when marijuana was used in the previous 90 days.

A similar pattern of results was evident in the GLM analyses for other measures of marijuana use and related problems at the 4-month follow-up. Both the two-session ($d = .60$) and nine-session ($d = .91$) treatments resulted in significantly fewer periods of marijuana use per day relative to the DTC condition, and the nine-session participants reported fewer periods of marijuana use than the two-session participants ($d = .40$). There were fewer dependence symptoms in the two-session ($d = .33$) and nine-session ($d = .90$) conditions

TABLE 17.2

Measures of Marijuana Use and Related Problems Assessed at Treatment Intake (Baseline) and at 4-Month and 9-Month Follow-Up According to Three Study Conditions

Variable	Delayed treatment[a]			2-session treatment[a]			9-session treatment[b]			Treatment × Time Effect	
	M	SD	95% CI	M	SD	95% CI	M	SD	95% CI	F	p
Percentage of days smoking											
Baseline	89.88	14.11	87.2; 92.6	86.92	17.15	84.1; 89.7	87.56	17.24	84.8; 90.3		
4 months	75.59	30.69	69.7; 81.5	55.86	36.18	49.7; 62.0	36.17	38.83	30.0; 42.1	41.83	<.001
9 months				59.76	36.78	53.4; 66.6	43.87	37.48	39.8; 52.5	10.16	<.001
Periods smoked per day											
Baseline	2.35	0.83	2.2; 2.5	2.24	0.73	2.1; 2.4	2.32	0.81	2.2; 2.4		
4 months	1.95	1.05	1.8; 2.1	1.35	0.89	1.2; 1.5	1.02	1.07	0.9; 1.2	29.80	<.001
9 months				1.39	0.92	1.2; 1.6	1.19	1.02	1.1; 1.4	4.96	<.01
Joints per day											
Baseline	2.77	2.19	2.4; 3.2	3.02	2.80	2.6; 3.4	2.79	2.35	2.3; 3.2		
4 months	2.03	1.94	1.7; 2.3	1.50	1.62	1.2; 1.8	1.00	1.71	0.9; 1.5	3.91	<.05
9 months				1.59	2.28	1.4; 2.4	1.48	2.53	1.6; 2.6	0.12	>.05

	Delayed[a]			2-session			9-session			F	p
	M	SD	95% CI	M	SD	95% CI	M	SD	95% CI		
Dependence symptoms											
Baseline	5.56	1.33	5.74; 5.80	5.70	1.20	5.5; 5.6	5.62	1.17	5.4; 5.8		
4 months	4.36	1.92	4.0; 4.68	3.70	2.26	3.3; 4.1	2.47	2.34	2.1; 2.8	23.78	<.001
9 months				3.63	2.08	3.2; 4.0	2.81	2.40	2.5; 3.3	6.11	<.01
Abuse symptoms											
Baseline	2.11	0.84	2.0; 2.2	2.10	0.87	2.0; 2.2	2.06	0.77	1.9; 2.2		
4 months	1.63	0.91	1.5; 1.8	1.38	1.10	1.2; 1.6	1.03	1.02	1.9; 1.2	7.38	<.001
9 months				1.59	1.04	1.4; 1.8	1.11	1.07	0.9; 1.3	4.94	<.01
Marijuana problems											
Baseline	9.07	3.53	8.5; 9.7	10.18	3.47	9.5; 10.8	9.47	3.51	8.9; 10.1		
4 months	7.77	3.90	7.0; 8.5	8.35	4.06	7.6; 9.1	6.02	4.85	5.3; 6.8	9.99	<.001
9 months				7.22	4.21	6.3; 7.9	5.43	4.31	4.8; 6.2	2.79	>.05

Note. The delayed-treatment group was not assessed at the 9-month follow-up. CI = confidence interval.
[a]Data for the baseline and 4-month follow-up are based on those participants with complete data at both assessments (delayed = 137; 2-session = 128; 9-session = 133). [b]Data for the 9-month follow-up are based on those participants with complete data at all three assessments (2-session = 120; 9-session = 126).

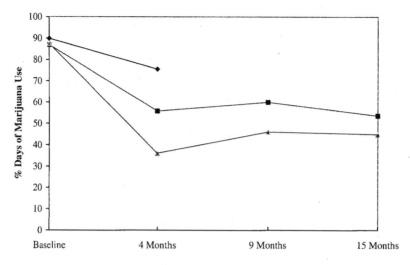

Figure 17.2. Percentage of days of marijuana use. Solid diamonds = delayed treatment; solid squares = two-session treatment; solid triangles = nine-session treatment.

relative to the DTC condition, with the nine-session condition differing significantly from the two-session condition (d = .52). The number of joints smoked per day was significantly lower in both active treatment groups compared with the DTC group (ds = .29 and .43), but did not differ significantly between active treatments. On measures of marijuana abuse symptoms and marijuana-related problems, the nine-session treatment showed greater reductions than both the two-session treatment and the DTC condition, which did not differ significantly from each other (abuse symptoms ds = .38 and .63, respectively; marijuana problem ds = .53 and .41, respectively).

When the analyses were restricted to the two active treatments across the baseline, 4-month, and 9-month follow-ups, significant effects of time remained on all measures. Planned comparisons confirmed that all marijuana use measures were significantly reduced from baseline. We found significant Treatment × Time interactions on measures of percentage of days smoking, periods smoked per day, as well as dependence and abuse symptoms (see Table 17.2). Comparisons of means at the 9-month follow-up controlling for baseline values of the same measures indicated that there were greater reductions in the nine-session treatment compared with the two-session treatment for the percentage of days of marijuana use (d = .37), dependence symptoms (d = .31), and abuse symptoms (d = .45). Again, we found a main effect of site, $F(2, 242)$ = 10.83, $p < .001$, and a Site × Time interaction, $F(1, 242)$ = 3.28, $p < .05$, on the measure of joints smoked per day that reflected only the baseline differences between sites. A significant Site × Time interaction on the measure of joints per day was similar to that found for 4-month analyses.

The GLM analyses performed on summary measures of percentage of days of marijuana use, joints smoked per day, and the MPS (Stephens et al., 2000) at the 15-month telephone follow-up showed significant effects of time on all variables and reflected reductions in marijuana use relative to baseline values. A significant Treatment × Time interaction, $F(1, 242) = 4.41, p < .05$, revealed that participants in the nine-session treatment had a lower percentage of days of marijuana use ($M = 44.86, SD = 40.52$) compared with the two-session treatment ($M = 53.65, SD = 38.57$), although the between-groups effect size was small ($d = .22$). However, reductions in the percentage of days of use relative to baseline were still substantial in both conditions (48% and 33%, respectively). There was no differential effect of treatments for joints per day or marijuana-related problems.

Effects of Missing Data

The overall 4-month, 9-month, and 15-month follow-up rates were 89%, 87%, and 83%, respectively. Attrition from follow-up did not differ as a function of treatment assignment at any follow-up (see Figure 17.1). Comparisons of those lost to follow-up with those interviewed revealed no significant differences for gender, age, education, marijuana use, or dependence severity measures. Thus, follow-up samples appeared to be representative of the randomized sample.

To further explore the effect of missing data, we repeated the analyses of the primary outcome variable by using the participant's baseline value if follow-up data were missing. The same pattern of significant time and Treatment × Time interactions was found for percentage of days of marijuana use at the 4-month, $F(2, 441) = 30.56, p < .001$, 9-month, $F(4, 882) = 28.01$, $p < .001$, and 15-month, $F(1, 296) = 3.71, p < .06$, follow-ups, although the latter effect did not quite reach conventional levels of significance. There were no significant effects of site in these analyses.

Abstinence and Improvement Outcomes

At the 4-month follow-up, there were significant differences in rates of complete abstinence for the preceding 90 days, $\chi^2(N = 398) = 25.22, p < .001$. The nine-session condition showed higher rates of complete abstinence (22.6%) compared with the two-session (8.6%) and DTC (3.6%) conditions. Abstinence rates for the nine-session (15.6%) and two-session (9.5%) treatments did not differ significantly at the 9-month follow-up, $\chi^2(N = 261) = 2.15, p < .05$. At the 15-month follow-up, more nine-session participants reported 90 days of abstinence (22.7%) compared with two-session participants (12.5%), $\chi^2(N = 248) = 4.38, p < .001$. To investigate whether a subset of participants could be considered improved despite continued use, we classified users as improved if they did not report any symptoms of dependence or abuse in the SCID (First et al., 1996) interviews. Table 17.3 shows the percentages of participants who were abstinent, improved, or not improved at the 4- and 9-month follow-ups by treatment condition, as well as their rates of marijuana use. Improvement could not be calculated for the 15-month follow-up because the SCID was not administered. An additional 4%–9% of participants could be categorized as improved, depending on the treatment group and follow-up. Rates of improvement were generally comparable in the two active treatments and larger than in the DTC condition. As can be seen, users without problems had reduced their marijuana use substantially more than continuing users, who were still experiencing dependence or abuse symptoms.

Secondary Outcomes

Table 17.4 shows outcomes on measures of psychosocial functioning. In these analyses, there were main effects of site on several variables previously noted to have differed at baseline, but no interactions of site with time and treatment. There were significant effects of time on the BDI (Beck et al., 1961), STAI-S (Spielberger et al., 1983), and ASI (McLellan et al., 1992) psychiatric composite scores in both the 4-month and 9-month analyses that indicated reduced levels of psychological distress at both follow-ups. However, only the STAI-S at the 4-month follow-up showed a significant Treatment × Time interaction. Anxiety was lower in the nine-session treatment than in the other treatment conditions. This difference was no longer significant at the 9-month follow-up. There were no significant time effects in the analyses of ASI employment and medical composite scores, suggesting

TABLE 17.3
Abstinent, Improved, and Not Improved Outcomes

	Treatment condition			Percentage of days used marijuana	
Follow-up	Delayed	2-session	9-session	M	SD
4 months	n = 137	n = 127	n = 132		
Abstinent	3.6%	8.7%	22.7%	0.0	0.0
Improved	3.6%	8.7%	7.6%	12.0	16.6
Not improved	92.7%	82.7%	69.7%	67.6	33.0
9 months		n = 125	n = 137		
Abstinent		9.6%	15.3%	0.0	0.0
Improved		5.6%	9.5%	19.5	20.1
Not improved		84.8%	75.2%	64.3	33.1

Note. Participants were classified as improved if they reported marijuana use but did not report any *DSM–IV* symptoms of dependence or abuse in the 90-day period prior to the follow-up.

TABLE 17.4

Measures of Medical, Psychiatric, Other Secondary Outcomes Assessed at Treatment Intake (Baseline), and at 4-Month and 9-Month Follow-Up According to Three Study Conditions

Variable	Delayed treatment[a]			2-session treatment[a]			9-session treatment[b]			Treatment × Time Effect	
	M	SD	95% CI	M	SD	95% CI	M	SD	95% CI	F	p
BDI											
Baseline	10.09	7.35	8.8; 11.4	13.21	8.60	11.8; 14.6	11.39	7.00	10.0; 12.8		
4 months	7.87	6.78	6.5; 9.2	10.35	8.50	8.9; 11.8	7.71	7.76	6.3; 9.1	1.41	>.05
9 months				10.16	9.36	7.4; 11.6	7.34	8.29	5.3; 9.5	0.09	>.05
STAI-S											
Baseline	37.29	11.53	35.3; 39.3	41.61	12.19	39.5; 43.7	39.87	11.62	37.8; 41.9		
4 months	35.50	11.21	33.6; 37.4	37.50	11.61	35.5; 39.5	33.35	10.13	31.4; 35.3	5.24	<.01
9 months				38.85	12.66	36.2; 40.4	33.61	11.32	31.7; 35.9	1.68	>.05
ASI medical composite											
Baseline	0.16	0.25	0.1; 0.2	0.28	0.31	0.2; 0.3	0.26	0.30	0.2; 0.3		
4 months	0.15	0.26	0.1; 0.2	0.29	0.35	0.2; 0.3	0.22	0.30	0.2; 0.3	1.35	>.05
9 months				0.26	0.32	0.2; 0.3	0.25	0.32	0.2; 0.3	1.58	>.05
ASI employment composite											
Baseline	0.18	0.16	0.1; 0.2	0.24	0.25	0.2; 0.3	0.23	0.21	0.2; 0.3		
4 months	0.20	0.17	0.2; 0.2	0.22	0.22	0.2; 0.3	0.20	0.19	0.2; 0.2	3.41	<.05
9 months				0.21	0.24	0.2; 0.2	0.22	0.20	0.2; 0.3	3.37	<.05

(continues)

TABLE 17.4

Measures of Medical, Psychiatric, Other Secondary Outcomes Assessed at Treatment Intake (Baseline), and at 4-Month and 9-Month Follow-Up According to Three Study Conditions   *(Continued)*

Variable	Delayed treatment[a]			2-session treatment[a]			9-session treatment[b]			Treatment × Time Effect	
	M	SD	95% CI	M	SD	95% CI	M	SD	95% CI	F	p
ASI psychiatric composite											
Baseline	0.14	0.17	0.1; 0.2	0.16	0.19	0.1; 0.2	0.15	0.19	0.1; 0.2		
4 months	0.13	0.18	0.1; 0.2	0.15	0.19	0.1; 0.2	0.13	0.18	0.1; 0.2	0.11	>.05
9 months				0.19	0.20	0.1; 0.2	0.14	0.19	0.1; 0.2	0.67	>.05
ASI alcohol composite											
Baseline	0.11	0.12	0.1; 0.1	0.12	0.13	0.1; 0.1	0.11	0.13	0.1; 0.1		
4 months	0.11	0.12	0.1; 0.1	0.11	0.11	0.1; 0.1	0.10	0.11	0.1; 0.1	0.54	>.05
9 months				0.12	0.13	0.1; 0.1	0.10	0.11	0.1; 0.1	0.16	>.05
Total drinks											
Baseline	46.57	85.48		59.41	84.56		48.79	79.10			
4 months	42.92	62.48		46.00	72.63		34.81	71.49		0.82	>.05
9 months				45.56	76.62		46.12	106.70		4.37	<.05

Note. The delayed-treatment group was not assessed at the 9-month follow-up. BDI = Beck Depression Inventory; STAI-S = State-Trait Anxiety Inventory, State Version; ASI = Addiction Severity Index composite scores.
[a]Data for the baseline and 4-month follow-up are based on those participants with complete data at both assessments (delayed = 137; 2-session = 128; 9-session = 133). [b]Data for the 9-month follow-up are based on those participants with complete data at all three assessments (2-session = 120; 9-session = 126).

that little change occurred. Contrasts following significant Treatment × Time effects on the measure of employment functioning at both follow-ups failed to show any significant differences between treatment conditions after controlling for baseline values.

The ASI (McLellan et al., 1992) Alcohol Composite score showed a significant effect of time at the 4-month follow-up, indicating an overall reduction in alcohol problem severity, but there was no time effect in the 9-month analyses, and Treatment × Time interactions were not evident at either follow-up. However, the analyses of total drinks consumed showed significant time effects at both follow-ups generally indicative of reduced drinking. In the 9-month analyses, we found both a significant Treatment × Time effect (see Table 17.4) and a significant Treatment × Site × Time effect, $F(4, 478) = 3.75$, $p < .01$. Subsequent 2 (treatment) × 3 (time) GLM analyses performed separately for each site revealed that a significant Treatment × Time interaction was present only at the Miami site. At this site, two-session participants reported significant reductions in alcohol use at the 4-month follow-up and further reductions at the 9-month follow-up. In contrast, nine-session participants decreased their alcohol use somewhat at 4 months but had increased their use relative to baseline at the 9-month follow-up. This pattern was not found at either of the other sites, and there was no evidence of a similar pattern of change at the Miami site on any other measures of drug use. Therefore, we urge caution in its interpretation.

To further explore whether changes in alcohol use were related to changes in marijuana use, we computed partial correlations between the percentage of days of marijuana use and each of the two measures of alcohol use (i.e., ASI [McLellan et al., 1992] composite and total drinks) at each follow-up. We controlled for the baseline value of each measure in computing the correlations to examine the relationship between change in marijuana use and change in alcohol use (i.e., residualized change scores). None of the partial correlations were significant, and all were less than .10. Taken together, these analyses suggest a tendency for alcohol use to decline somewhat over time and that change was not related to changes in marijuana use.

Generalizability of Outcomes

To explore whether outcomes were generalizable across gender, ethnicity (White, non-White), and employment status (employed full time, employed part time, unemployed), we included each of these potential moderators in sets of exploratory analyses. For each set, we included one of the moderators as a between-participants factor in GLM analyses. We then repeated analyses for all outcome measures at all follow-ups. There were no significant three-way interactions between treatment condition, moderator status, and time in any of the sets. Thus, there was no indication that these characteristics influenced the pattern of outcomes.

DISCUSSION

The results of this randomized trial suggest that both a two-session motivational treatment and a nine-session multicomponent treatment were effective in reducing marijuana use compared with a DTC condition. The nine-session intervention produced superior outcomes compared with the two-session treatment in terms of reductions in marijuana use up to 12 months following treatment termination. Reductions in marijuana use were accompanied by reductions in symptoms of marijuana dependence and abuse. Treatment effects were robust across sites and a number of participant characteristics, including gender and ethnicity. The findings relating to follow-up rates, validity of self-reports, and treatment fidelity suggest that the study was executed with a high degree of internal validity. Overall, the findings suggest that treatment for marijuana dependence could have a significant impact on chronic marijuana use and that both substance abuse treatment programs and behavioral health care providers should consider making marijuana-specific treatment more available and accessible.

The very modest reductions in marijuana use for participants assigned to the DTC condition underline the significance of the changes among those assigned to the two active treatment conditions. The findings from the DTC group suggest that marijuana-focused treatments may be necessary for this population to achieve abstinence or to significantly reduce marijuana use. It is of note that many participants reported some difficulty in finding help for their marijuana-related problems through the current drug abuse treatment system. The findings are generally consistent with prior studies (Budney et al., 1998; Stephens et al., 1994, 2000) in suggesting that well-defined behavioral treatments for marijuana dependence produce encouraging levels of improvement, and that treatment is associated with clinically meaningful benefits even for those who do not achieve complete abstinence.

There are also some important differences between the outcomes observed in this study and those reported in previous research. Stephens et al. (2000) found no differences between 2-session and 14-session treatments. Although the research designs and treatments evaluated in the two studies were similar, the Stephens et al. study delivered the longer treatment in a group format, used more experienced therapists for the brief treatment, and recruited a less diverse and possibly more motivated sample. In contrast, our findings are more similar to two more recent studies that compared treatments of different lengths (Budney et al., 2000; Copeland et al., 2001) and uncovered some evidence that longer treatments produced better outcomes. In those studies, the same therapists delivered the treatments individually, but relatively small samples may have prevented definitive conclusions regarding differences between treatment conditions.

In addition to the reductions observed in the frequency and daily intensity of marijuana smoking, there were parallel reductions in marijuana-dependence symptoms and marijuana-related problems. In each of these measures, the nine-session group showed the greatest improvements, the two-session group showed intermediate reductions, and the DTC group showed little change. Although the magnitudes of change in the nine-session treatment are large and clinically meaningful, we cannot draw the same conclusion for the two-session condition. Although we observed statistically significant reductions in frequency of marijuana use and dependence symptoms relative to no treatment, other measures of problems related to marijuana use were not consistently different. Thus, it may be that small reductions in marijuana use do not result in meaningful changes on clinical indices. To further explore the meaning of reduced use, we categorized participants as abstinent, improved, or not improved for the 90-day period preceding follow-up. Abstinence rates were relatively small overall but clearly favored the nine-session condition. Improvement occurred about equally in both the two-session and nine-session conditions, and less frequently in the DTC condition. Improved participants were using marijuana on 12% to 20% of days on average, whereas the not improved participants were using on only 64% to 68% of the days. These findings support the notion that complete abstinence is not the only clinically meaningful outcome of treatment. It is important to note that our definition of improvement was very conservative and required participants to be without any symptoms of abuse or dependence. These improvement rates should be thought of only as illustrations of the impact of reduced use. It is likely that many additional participants experienced meaningful reductions in problems associated with marijuana use without achieving abstinence.

Effects of treatment on depression, psychiatric severity, medical problems, and alcohol use severity over time were not significant. These findings are consistent with other studies (Budney et al., 2000; Copeland et al., 2001) and may be a function of low initial problem severity in these areas. We have argued that the constellation of concerns that bring marijuana users to treatment may not manifest themselves in major socioeconomic or psychosocial problems (Stephens, Babor, Kadden, Miller, & The Marijuana Treatment Project Research Group, 2002). Instead, it may be a more subtle dissatisfaction with multiple areas of functioning and concerns about future health problems that motivate the desire to quit or reduce use.

Consistent with prior studies focused solely on the treatment of marijuana use (Stephens et al., 2000, 1994), there was no evidence that reductions in marijuana use led to an increase in alcohol use. Although primary marijuana users without significant other drug involvement may be underrepresented in existing treatment agencies, this finding, along with our general success in recruiting large samples of such users, supports the development, dissemination, and marketing of treatment programs for this population of users.

Several limitations of the study should be noted. First, many participants sought help in response to specific advertisements for treatment of primary marijuana dependence. Thus, the results may not generalize to persons whose marijuana dependence is secondary to other types of substance dependence, who are referred to treatment under legal mandate, or who are unmotivated to seek treatment. Second, the design does not allow for conclusions regarding the "active ingredients" in the treatments, only that more treatment was better than less treatment. Numbers of sessions were confounded with differential content and process such that it is impossible to know whether the CBT and CM were specifically active in the improved outcomes in the nine-session condition. Future analyses of therapy session process ratings in relation to outcomes may shed some light on important aspects of the interventions but are beyond the scope of this chapter. Future studies should consider dismantling designs in which hypothesized active components of the interventions are offered individually or in specific combinations and are compared with appropriate attention-placebo interventions to control for number of sessions of contact. Third, we were unable to conduct a full in-person assessment 12 months after treatment because of funding limitations. Although results at the 15-month follow-up suggest the maintenance of marijuana use outcomes, future studies should address longer term outcomes. Finally, outcomes may have been influenced by different expectancies of success created by the treatments of different lengths. Participants were told that neither active treatment was known to be superior to the other, but assessment of differential treatment efficacy expectancies was not conducted.

Unlike the historical portrayal of marijuana as a benign drug, this study as well as previous research suggest that individuals can develop a chronic use pattern that is associated with dependence symptoms and recurrent psychosocial problems. Individuals who use marijuana chronically as their primary drug tend not to seek treatment in traditional drug treatment settings. It appears from this and other studies that when given the opportunity, many respond to treatment primarily by cutting back rather than quitting entirely. There is thus ample reason to explore ways to improve outcomes, evaluate the economic costs and benefits of the treatments, and study the effect of brief treatments for marijuana dependence in nontraditional settings such as primary care practices. The evidence for treatment efficacy presented in this chapter should also prompt efforts toward screening and early intervention in emergency departments, correctional facilities, and other settings.

REFERENCES

American Psychiatric Association. (1994). *Diagnostic and statistical manual of mental disorders* (4th ed.). Washington, DC: Author.

Anthony, J. C., Warner, L. A., & Kessler, R. C. (1994). Comparative epidemiology of dependence on tobacco, alcohol, controlled substances, and inhalants: Basic findings from the National Comorbidity Survey. *Experimental and Clinical Psychopharmacology, 2,* 244–268.

Baer, J. S., Kivlahan, D. R., & Donovan, D. M. (1999). Integrating skills training and motivational therapies. *Journal of Substance Abuse Treatment, 17,* 15–23.

Beck, A. T., Ward, C. H., & Mendelson, M. (1961). An inventory for measuring depression. *Archives of General Psychiatry, 4,* 461–471.

Budney, A. J., Higgins, S. T., Radonovich, K. J., & Novy, P. L. (2000). Adding voucher-based incentives to coping skills and motivational enhancement improves outcomes during treatment for marijuana dependence. *Journal of Consulting and Clinical Psychology, 68,* 1051–1061.

Budney, A. J., Novy, P. L., & Hughes, J. R. (1999). Marijuana withdrawal among adults seeking treatment for marijuana dependence. *Addiction, 94,* 1311–1321.

Budney, A. J., Radonovich, K. J., Higgins, S. T., & Wong, C. J. (1998). Adults seeking treatment for marijuana dependence: A comparison to cocaine-dependent treatment seekers. *Experimental and Clinical Psychopharmacology, 6,* 1–8.

Cohen, J. (1988). *Statistical power analysis for the behavioral sciences* (2nd ed.). Hillsdale, NJ: Erlbaum.

Committee on Substance Abuse. (1999). Marijuana: A continuing concern for pediatricians. *Pediatrics, 104,* 982–985.

Copeland, J., Swift, W., Roffman, R., & Stephens, R. (2001). A randomized controlled trial of brief cognitive–behavioral interventions for cannabis use disorder. *Journal of Substance Abuse Treatment, 21,* 55–64.

Dunn, C., DeRoo, L., & Rivara, F. P. (2001). The use of brief interventions adapted from motivational interviewing across behavioral domains: A systematic review. *Addiction, 96,* 1725–1742.

First, M. B., Spitzer, R. L., Gibbon, M., & Williams, J. B. (1996). *Structured Clinical Interview for DSM–IV, Axis I Disorders–Patient Edition (SCID-I/P, Version 2.0).* New York: Biometrics Research Department, New York State Psychiatric Institute.

Haney, M., Ward, A. S., Comer, S. D., Foltin, R. W., & Fischman, M. W. (1999). Abstinence symptoms following smoked marijuana in humans. *Psychopharmacology, 141,* 395–404.

Kadden, R., Carroll, K., Donovan, D., Cooney, N., Monti, P., Abrams, D., et al. (1992). *Cognitive–behavioral coping skills therapy manual: A clinical research guide for therapists treating individuals with alcohol abuse and dependence* (DHHS Publication No. ADM 92-1895). Washington, DC: U. S. Government Printing Office.

Kouri, E. M., & Pope, H. G., Jr. (2000). Abstinence symptoms during withdrawal from chronic marijuana use. *Experimental and Clinical Psychopharmacology, 8,* 483–492.

McLellan, A. T., Grisson, G. R., Zanis, D., Randall, M., Brill, P., & O'Brien, C. (1997). Problem-service "matching" in addiction treatment: A prospective study in 4 programs. *Archives of General Psychiatry, 54,* 730–735.

McLellan, A., Kushner, H., Metzger, D., Peters, R., Smith, I., Grissom, G., et al. (1992). The fifth edition of the Addiction Severity Index. *Journal of Substance Abuse Treatment, 9,* 199–213.

Miller, W. R., & Rollnick, S. (2002). *Motivational interviewing: Preparing people to change addictive behavior* (2nd ed.). New York: Guilford Press.

Monti, P. M., Abrams, D. B., Kadden, R. M., & Cooney, N. L. (1989). *Treating alcohol dependence: A coping skills training guide.* New York: Guilford Press.

Roffman, R. A., & Barnhart, R. (1987). Assessing need for marijuana dependence treatment through an anonymous telephone interview. *International Journal of the Addictions, 22,* 639–651.

Sobell, L. C., & Sobell, M. B. (1992). Time line follow-back: A technique for assessing self-reported alcohol consumption. In R. Litten & J. Allen (Eds.), *Measuring alcohol consumption* (pp. 41–72). Totowa, NJ: Humana Press.

Spielberger, C. D., Gorsuch, R. L., Lushene, R., Vagg, P. R., & Jacobs, G. A. (1983). *Manual for the State–Trait Anxiety Inventory (Form Y).* Palo Alto, CA: Consulting Psychologists Press.

Steinberg, K. L., Roffman, R. A., Carroll, K. M., Kabela, E., Kadden, R., Miller, M., et al. (2002). Tailoring cannabis dependence treatment for a diverse population. *Addiction, 97,* 135–142.

Stephens, R. S., Babor, T. F., Kadden, R., Miller, M., & The Marijuana Treatment Project Research Group. (2002). The Marijuana Treatment Project: Rationale, design and participant characteristics. *Addiction, 97,* 109–124.

Stephens, R. S., Roffman, R. A., & Curtin, L. (2000). Comparison of extended versus brief treatments for marijuana use. *Journal of Consulting and Clinical Psychology, 68,* 898–908.

Stephens, R. S., Roffman, R. A., & Simpson, E. E. (1993). Adult marijuana users seeking treatment. *Journal of Consulting and Clinical Psychology, 61,* 1100–1104.

Stephens, R. S., Roffman, R. A., & Simpson, E. E. (1994). Treating adult marijuana dependence: A test of the relapse prevention model. *Journal of Consulting and Clinical Psychology, 62,* 92–99.

Stout, R. L., Wirtz, P. W., Carbonari, J. P., & Del Boca, F. K. (1994). Ensuring balanced distribution of prognostic factors in treatment outcome research. *Journal of Studies on Alcohol, 12,* 70–75.

Substance Abuse and Mental Health Services Administration. (2002). *Results from the 2001 National Household Survey on Drug Abuse: Vol. I. Summary of national findings* (NHSDA Series H-17, DHHS Publication No. SMA 02-3758). Rockville, MD: Author.

Substance Abuse and Mental Health Services Administration Office of Applied Studies. (2003). *Treatment Episode Data Set (TEDS): 1992– 2001* (National Admissions to Substance Abuse Treatment Services, DASIS Series S-20, DHHS Publication No. SMA 03-3778). Rockville, MD: Author.

Vendetti, J., McRee, B., Miller, M., Christiansen, K., Herrell, J., & The Marijuana Treatment Project Research Group. (2002). Correlates of pre-treatment drop-out among persons with marijuana dependence. *Addiction, 97,* 125–134.

18

SMOKING CESSATION: PROGRESS, PRIORITIES, AND PROSPECTUS

RAYMOND NIAURA AND DAVID B. ABRAMS

This chapter is intended to provide an update on the current status of research on, and issues pertaining to, smoking and smoking cessation and was originally third in a series of articles on the subject (Lichtenstein, 1982; Lichtenstein & Glasgow, 1992). We begin by reviewing information on population incidence and prevalence of smoking, followed by an examination of key issues and predictions raised by the prior reviews—most of which remain salient and unresolved. We then give our perspective on the myriad developments in smoking cessation clinical research over the past decade, focusing especially on systematic development of evidence-based guidelines for treatment, contrasting pharmacologic and behavioral approaches, and raising yet again more questions regarding the future of smoking cessation in the decade to come. By necessity, this review is exclusive; we follow the example of our predecessors in focusing mostly on cessation rather than prevention efforts—a topic that requires its own review—and we must, reluctantly, be selective even in reviewing recent developments because of the explosion of treatment-related research.

Reprinted from *Journal of Consulting and Clinical Psychology, 70*, 494–509 (2002). Copyright 2002 by the American Psychological Association.

TRENDS IN SMOKING INCIDENCE AND PREVALENCE

Tobacco use contributes to over 450,000 deaths annually and is the leading cause of preventable morbidity, mortality, and health expense in the United States (Centers for Disease Control and Prevention [CDC], 1994c, 1994d). Recent surveys reported increases in youth smoking and slowing in adult prevalence reduction (CDC, 1998a, 1998b). For example, in 1997, 35.8% of high school students reported lifetime prevalence of having smoked at least one cigarette every day for the past 30 days. Despite a steady yearly decrease in smoking prevalence, and an increase in the quit ratio (the ratio of former smokers to ever-smokers in the population) since 1965, for the first time ever in 1991 smoking prevalence failed to decrease and the quit ratio failed to increase (CDC, 1994a). In the year 2000, 23.2% of U.S. adults were current smokers (CDC Behavioral Risk Factor Surveillance System Web site: http://apps.nccd.cdc.gov/brfss/). More disturbing, perhaps, are the disparities in smoking prevalence along sociodemographic dimensions: that is, 17.0% versus 34.0% for Asian Pacific islanders compared with Alaskan American natives; 11.6 % versus 35.4% for those with more than 16 years of education compared with those who attended but did not complete high school; 12.0% versus 29.0% for those older than 65 years compared with those 44 years of age or younger (CDC, 1999). (The latter statistic, however, may owe as much to premature-smoking-related mortality as to older individuals' ability to finally quit smoking.) Smoking prevalence is also significantly and positively associated with factors such as poverty and comorbid psychiatric disorders, most notably, depression, alcoholism, substance abuse, and schizophrenia (Dalack, Healy, & Meador-Woodruff, 1998; Glassman, 1993; Lasser et al., 2000). Thus, smoking prevalence is largely a function of increases in smoking initiation and failure to quit among established smokers.

The selection hypothesis of smoking prevalence argues that smokers able to quit successfully are those who are relatively unfettered by characteristics that make it difficult to quit, that is, they are less nicotine dependent, and they are less likely to suffer from psychiatric comorbidity (Fagerström et al., 1996; Hughes, 1993). Following this logic, continuing smokers will consist mostly of those who will be unable to quit, for example, because of problems with nicotine dependence, psychiatric comorbidity, and other factors associated with increased rates of smoking. As a result, smoking prevalence should begin to stabilize as fewer smokers overall are able to quit. If the selection hypothesis holds true, we will be faced increasingly with issues surrounding the development of more effective treatments that target the needs of the special, hard-core-smoking populations and with the challenge of disseminating existing and new treatments so that they reach, motivate, and are utilized by these smokers. At the same time, segments of the young adult population, such as college students, are taking up smoking at higher rates than previously (Rigotti, Lee, & Wechsler, 2000; Wechsler, Rigotti, Gledhill-Hoyt, & Lee, 1998), and it is unclear whether existing treatments will work for these younger smokers. So we are faced with at least the double challenge of motivating and treating what may be a recalcitrant group of older smokers and a group of younger smokers whose reasons for smoking remain largely unknown, as does their ultimate trajectory toward entrenched tobacco dependence.

THE CONTINUUM OF CARE:
WHERE HAVE WE BEEN AND WHERE ARE WE GOING?

Perhaps the single most important issue highlighted by our predecessors in this series was the tension in shifting from the predominantly intensive clinical approach to smoking cessation, on the one hand, to the public-health-based, broad dissemination perspective, on the other, which they dubbed the "clinical-public health continuum" (Lichtenstein & Glasgow, 1992). The argument for a public-health-based model of treatment dissemination is reinforced, in part, by what we know about smokers' motivation to quit and the means by which smokers try to quit. For example, in 1994 most smokers (70%) reported wanting to quit completely (CDC, 1996). The majority, however, are not ready to quit within the next 6 months, and motivation is lowest among low socioeconomic-status (SES) groups (Abrams & Biener, 1992; Velicer et al., 1995). The vast majority of smokers (97%) quit on their own or with minimal assistance; very few utilize formal treatment services (Fiore, Novotny, & Pierce, 1990). Moreover, although intensive treatment programs are efficacious (i.e., they have demonstrated efficacy in tightly controlled research settings), their effectiveness (i.e., how they work and can be disseminated in real-world settings and populations) is likely to remain low. Barriers include inability to reach the broadest segment of the smoking population; desire of most smokers to quit on their own; low utilization; high dropout; high cost; and lack of third-party reimbursement for treatment expenses. In addition, these programs do not reach underserved smokers, who often cannot afford or do not seek expensive smoking cessation clinic programs (U.S. Department of Health and Human Services, 1992).

Thus, there remains an acute need to provide the motivated smokers with the means to quit and to reach, in addition, the less motivated smokers in ways that guarantee contact. The challenge from the public health perspective, therefore, is to disseminate widely accepted, low-cost, efficacious treatments to the greatest number of smokers. By contrast, expensive and more efficacious treatments (e.g., combined pharmacologic and behavioral interventions delivered by smoking cessation specialists) are by definition less able to be disseminated widely and are less likely to appeal to most smokers.

As a result, a compelling argument was made that so-called alternative service delivery methods, such as physician or health care provider interventions, work site interventions, and community-wide approaches, should take center stage largely because of their promise of increased efficiency, which is defined as Population × Reach × Efficacy (Abrams et al., 1996). That is, even if the absolute efficacy of an intervention delivered is moderate or even small, its efficiency will be large if it reaches enough smokers.

To be fair, Lichtenstein and Glasgow (1992) did not suggest abandoning research on more intensive treatments. Rather, they questioned whether an asymptote had been reached in the search for effective ingredients in intensive clinical research designs and whether, in fact, most of the efficacy of intensive treatments could be accounted for by increased contact as compared with the effects of specific treatment components. They also questioned the cost-effectiveness of intensive clinic-based treatments relative to those that could be more readily disseminated. However, they maintained that intensive treatments would find their niche in terms of offering hard-core or recalcitrant smokers (e.g., high-risk medical patients or heavy, dependent smokers who have been unable to quit) a (one hopes) cost-effective means of quitting.

Now, a decade later, we have the benefit of hindsight and considerable research to evaluate the ways in which the public health model has been embraced by the research and intervention delivery communities and the degree to which each of the alternative delivery service vehicles—health care providers, work sites, and communities—has performed.

Work Sites

Work-site health promotion interventions, including those with a smoking cessation component, have demonstrated some efficacy (Abrams, Emmons, Linnan, & Biener, 1994; Jeffrey et al., 1993; Pelletier, 1993). Unfortunately, most work-site trials have been plagued with significant methodological problems, such as low participation rates, employee self-selection bias, few work sites, and unit of randomization and analysis issues (e.g., using the work site and not the individual as the unit). Other problems have included highly structured, expensive interventions limiting dissemination, relatively short duration interventions, and the difficulty of separating intervention effects from secular trends and other macrolevel contextual influences on smoking rates (e.g., local and state policy changes).

Two recently completed work-site intervention trials (Glasgow, Terborg, Hollis, Severson, & Boles, 1995; Sorensen et al., 1996) overcame most of the aforementioned methodological problems, were the most statistically powered studies of their kind, and reached the same general conclusion: There is no evidence for differential efficacy of an intervention versus a comparison condition. Both studies targeted multiple behaviors for change (e.g., diet, physical activity, smoking), which may have diffused the focus on smoking, and one study demonstrated significant intervention effects on other behaviors (Sorensen et al., 1996). To be sure, the results for smoking are disappointing and require explanation. Among the most plausible are (a) smoking is such a difficult behavior to change that it requires a level of intervention intensity that is difficult if not impossible to realize because of inherent constraints in many work-site environments, and (b) there is considerable variability in individual work site response to intervention that precludes observing an intervention main effect. The latter explanation is particularly compelling because high variability in response to the intervention was observed in both studies—some work sites responded well to the interventions, whereas others responded poorly. This suggests that increased study is required to tailor interventions to the context of particular work sites—being able to understand what structural, cultural, and other work-site-specific factors enhance or impede behavior change at the level of the individual smoker. In our opinion, the negative results for work-site studies should serve as a challenge, rather than as an indictment of the approach, because the problem of variability in intervention response can in theory be addressed and because work sites retain tremendous potential for reaching a majority of smokers.

Community-Level Interventions

Similar to work-site studies, despite some promising early results (Farquhar et al., 1990), large, methodologically sound studies have failed to provide convincing evidence that community approaches produce significant reductions in the population prevalence of smoking, at least in North America (cf. Puska et al., 1983). The Community Intervention Trial for Smoking Cessation (COMMIT) matched 11 pairs of communities, representing over 20,000 smokers, and randomly assigned one of each pair to a 4-year intervention or comparison condition (COMMIT Research Group, 1995a, 1995b). The intervention, carried out by community volunteers, local agencies, and staff, was implemented through four community task forces representing each of four channels: public education through media and community-wide events, health care providers, work sites and other organizations, and cessation resources. Process measures indicated that nearly all mandated activities were implemented in a timely fashion. Notably, the trial targeted heavy smokers. Prevalence data among the study population aged 25 to 64 years showed no intervention effect on heavy smoking prevalence (COMMIT Research Group, 1995a). Cohort data similarly showed no effect on heavy smokers, but there was a significant intervention effect (3%) for light to moderate smokers (COMMIT Research Group, 1995b). Arguably, extrapolating from the cohort results, the public health impact of the COMMIT intervention was an additional 3,000 light to moderate smokers quit in the 11 communities that participated in the study.

Other large-scale community-level intervention studies have yielded similarly disappointing results. The Minnesota Heart Health study, a 5-year, community-level, multicomponent, and delivery channel intervention, which targeted multiple risk factors including smoking, failed to show a significant intervention effect on smoking in their cohort sample, although cross-sectional analyses showed a modest effect for quitting among women (Lando et al., 1995). The Stanford Five City Project reported a small treatment effect for quitting but no effect on smoking prevalence (Fortmann, Taylor, Flora, & Jatulis, 1993). The Pawtucket Heart Health Program failed to demonstrate any intervention effect (Carlton, Lasater, Assaf, Feldman, & McKinlay, 1994). The successor to COMMIT, the National Cancer Institute's (NCI) American Stop Smoking Intervention Trial for Cancer Prevention (ASSIST) was not so much a controlled intervention trial as it was a dissemination of strategies with periodic surveillance used in COMMIT but implemented at the statewide level, with state health departments and other agencies heading up broad coalitions. There has been to date no clear evidence that ASSIST has had a significant population impact on smoking cessation per se. However, a 7% reduction in per capita cigarette consumption was attributable to the ASSIST program (Manley et al., 1997).

The cynical view of results of community-level intervention studies is that these efforts are disappointing at best and a total waste of effort and money at worst. We view the latter opinion as too harsh. For example, despite its limited effectiveness, the COMMIT intervention was still cost-effective, comparing favorably with a number of other preventive interventions (Shipley, Hartwell, Austin, Clayton, & Stanley, 1995). It is possible that some of the component parts of the intervention were effective for subgroups of smokers. Moreover, we echo some of Cummings's (1999) conclusions regarding whether community interventions are a good investment. It is perhaps unrealistic to expect a community-level intervention to exert its effects when not even a decade has passed (cf. Puska et al., 1983). This is, in part, because this sort of intervention should be working on changing societal norms and policies regarding tobacco, and this requires sustained effort.

Community-level interventions should, to the extent possible, strive to implement intervention strategies that have been proven effective in efficacy trials or that have the benefit of inferred causality through other established epidemiologic and econometric evaluation methods (e.g., effects of pricing and policy changes on tobacco consumption). We strongly advocate that any community-level intervention be tied closely to a formal evaluation of its effectiveness in terms of smoking cessation, if not in the setting of a controlled trial, then at least in terms of surveillance to allow comparisons in cessation trends among communities that differ in terms of community-level intervention activities. To do otherwise, we believe, would be a waste of our precious resources. There is also a need for community-level interventions to move away from thinking about reaching entire populations. As we have seen, reach is an important factor in the public health equation for smoking cessation, but the intervention needs to reach those most in need: smokers who are heavy dependent, smokers with comorbid psychiatric conditions, and smokers who for whatever reason are unable to quit with minimal assistance. Finally, community-level interventions may be quite good at setting the stage for cessation efforts by increasing motivation to quit, boosting awareness of the benefits of quitting, and increasing awareness of treatment resources. However, we venture that these interventions have been hobbled by the inability to provide effective tools for smokers, especially heavy dependent smokers, to help them quit. For example, self-help materials, as they are currently configured, are minimally effective (Fiore et al., 1996, 2000). Nicotine replacement therapy (NRT), by contrast, has been proven efficacious and safe for virtually all smokers (Fiore et al., 1996, 2000). Community-level interventions may therefore need to work to increase access to proven efficacious treatments such as NRT (especially because patch and gum products are available over the counter; OTC) and to focus not only on motivating the smoker to seek out such treatment but also on working at the policy level to change health insurance reimbursement and payment practices so that underserved smokers can afford to use the most efficacious treatments. One strategy may be to mainstream NRT, once considered an expensive, intensive treatment, into community-level interventions to increase efficiency by addressing the efficacy part of the equation (Shiffman, Mason, & Henningfield, 1998).

Health Care Provider Interventions

There are two compelling reasons to suppose that cessation interventions delivered by health care providers can and should be widely promulgated: Smokers come into contact with the health care system on a frequent basis, providing the opportunity for intervention, and interventions delivered by health care providers are efficacious. More than 70% of smokers have contact with a physician each year (Davis, 1988), and health care providers have multiple occasions to provide personalized cessation interventions to patients who smoke. Smokers who receive even brief clinical interventions demonstrate significantly increased cessation rates compared with those who receive no advice, and there is a dose-dependent relationship between the intensity of person-to-person contact and successful cessation outcome (Fiore et al., 1996, 2000). Moreover, smokers often cite the importance of physicians' advice in influencing their decision to quit smoking (S. Burns, Cohen, Gritz, & Kottke, 1994).

Primary care clinicians, however, are not taking full advantage of opportunities to intervene with their patients who smoke. Only about half of current smokers report that their physicians have either asked them about smoking or advised them to quit (Goldstein et al., 1997). In one recent survey (Thorndike, Rigotti, Stafford, & Singer, 1998), cessation counseling rates by physicians were found to have increased from 16.0% of smokers in 1991 to 29.0% in 1993 and then to have decreased to 21.0% in 1995. Among a population-based sample of smokers who had seen a physician during the previous year, only 51.0% reported that they were talked to about their smoking, 45.5% were advised to quit, 14.9% were offered specific assistance, and 3.0% had a follow-up appointment arranged (Goldstein et al., 1997).

Although most physicians believe in the importance of addressing smoking with their patients (Wechsler, Levine, Idelson, & Coakley, 1996), incorporating counseling into routine practice remains a challenge. Barriers include time demands; provider uncertainty about how to provide counseling; skepticism about the efficacy of counseling; insufficient reimbursement; and lack of office resources, systems, and support (Orleans, Glynn, Manley, & Slade, 1993; Walsh & McPhee, 1992). These barriers influence physician readiness to adopt smoking cessation interventions into their routine office practice (Main, Cohen, & DiClemente, 1995).

Previous controlled trials have demonstrated the efficacy of intervention strategies designed to increase physicians' adoption of components of the National Cancer Institute's "4As" smoking cessation strategy: Ask about smoking at every visit, Advise all smokers to quit, Assist the patient to stop smoking, and Arrange follow-up to reinforce the cessation messages and to address relapse (Manley, Epps, Husten, Glynn, & Shopland, 1991). Efficacious strategies for increasing the frequency and intensity of clinician-delivered smoking cessation interventions include linking identification of smoking status with the use of a vital-sign stamp, using other reminders to prompt physicians to intervene, training physicians in counseling skills, and providing patients with access to nicotine replacement and educational materials in the medical office setting (Fiore et al., 1995; Kottke et al., 1992; McPhee & Detmer, 1993). One recent study demonstrated that a brief multicomponent intervention including NRT, when appropriate, tailored to smokers' level of motivation, and performed by general practitioners and office staff outperformed usual care (brief advice to quit; Pieterse, Seydel, DeVries, Mudde, & Kok, 2001).

However, most previous studies were efficacy trials that used the practices of physicians who chose to participate in smoking cessation studies or resident clinics rather than representative samples of community physicians. Moreover, many of the experimental interventions that were found to be effective (e.g., assessment of smokers, chart reminders, treatment algorithms, patient educational materials) were implemented in clinical settings by research staff rather than by the physicians or office staff. Recently, a large, multicommunity dissemination trial tested an intervention that included medical office staff training, office systems to support counseling, and physicians' continuing medical education. At the patient level of reporting, smokers in the physician intervention communities were more likely to report receiving material about smoking from their doctors than smokers in comparison communities, but differences in other smoker-reported physician activities, such as setting a quit date, were not detected (Ockene et al., 1997). Thus, effective strategies are needed to enhance the adoption of efficacious smoking cessation interventions within a population of primary care physicians and practices. Moreover, the impact of such an intervention at the level of the population of smokers must also be formally evaluated. Sufficient evidence also exists to suggest that interventions delivered by other health care providers (e.g., nurses, physician assistants, dentists, pharmacists) are efficacious and that there are additive effects with multiple providers (S. Burns et al., 1994; Severson, Andrews, Lichtenstein, Gordon, & Barckley, 1998). Moreover, there is good evidence now to suggest that interventions among smokers hospitalized as a result of smoking-related illnesses can be efficacious, although these interventions are not yet widely adopted or disseminated (France, Glasgow, & Marcus, 2001). Medicaid now offers prescription benefits for pharmacologic smoking cessation aids in several states (CDC, 2001). More research is needed on how best to exact and institutionalize structural changes in policies and practices to facilitate delivery of smoking cessation messages and resources in various health care settings (Lichtenstein, 1997).

Other Public Health Approaches

Although space limitations preclude comprehensive discussion, we would be remiss not to mention important efforts in the arena of media, policy and legislation, health care benefit, and other societal-level interventions. Several states and communities have directed campaigns of multimedia counter-tobacco advertising, proscription of advertising to minors, legislation to ban smoking in public and other areas, increased tobacco taxes, and so forth. Noteworthy examples are efforts by states such as California, Massachusetts, Oregon, Arizona, and Florida, which have witnessed steeper declines in smoking prevalence than most other states, which can reasonably be attributed to these multipronged efforts (Kessler & Myers, 2001). Remarkably, these efforts have also been directly linked to declines in the incidence of cardiovascular diseases at the population level (Fichtenberg & Glantz, 2000). Medicaid can provide prescription benefits for pharmacologic smoking cessation aids, and since 1998, the three major health care plans in Minnesota have provided coverage for NRT and bupropion (Solberg et al., 2001). It remains to be seen whether these changes in prescription coverage will result in significantly increased cessation rates, but we have every reason to be optimistic. Consequently, we enjoin all those who identify with the behavioral medicine perspective to embrace the public health perspective in thinking about creative ways in which policy, legislative, and treatment efforts can be combined to maximize motivation and resources necessary for tobacco users to quit.

Current Status of Public Health Interventions

Has the public health model with its emphasis on effectiveness research taken center stage? Not quite, but it certainly shares the limelight with efficacy research, in particular studies of pharmacologic interventions for smoking cessation, which have burgeoned in the past decade (see What's New Since 1992? section). Efficacy and effectiveness models of research must share the same stage and act in harmony, for the results of one set of studies fuel the other. Only when a sufficient evidence base exists for a given treatment approach, whether it is pharmacologic, behavioral, or other, can it serve as a potential treatment tool for widespread dissemination. So what works to help smokers quit?

WHAT'S NEW SINCE 1992?

Evidence, Meta-Analyses, and Guidelines

In our opinion, among the most important developments in smoking cessation research and practice in the past decade are the evidence-based guidelines and reports documenting the efficacy of particular pharmacologic and nonpharmacologic interventions for smoking cessation and the rapid growth of pharmacologic intervention studies, particularly those involving NRT.

In 1996, the U.S. Agency for Health Care Policy and Research (AHCPR) issued their "Clinical Practice Guideline for Smoking Cessation" (Fiore et al., 1996). The British Health Education Authority sponsored a similar effort, entitled "Smoking Cessation Guidelines for Health Professionals" (Raw, McNeill, & West, 1998). Both guidelines are evidence-based and relied heavily on meta-analyses of published research studies to formulate conclusions and recommendations. The British Guidelines used meta-analyses performed by the AHCPR authors, as well as those performed as part of the Cochrane Library, an online, regularly updated database of smoking cessation clinical trials (see http://www.cochrane.org/). Both the United States and British guidelines focused on interventions provided by health professionals, in particular primary care physicians. The American Psychiatric Association also published smoking cessation guidelines that presented more of a focus on dealing with the problem of smoking among those for whom primary care treatment has failed, patients with psychiatric difficulties, and patients in smoke-free facilities (Hughes et al., 1996). The respective guidelines are quite similar in their conclusions regarding effective interventions for smoking cessation. Most recently, the AHCPR guideline was updated (Fiore et al., 2000; http://www.surgeongeneral.gov/tobacco/) as part of a collaboration between the Agency for Health Research and Quality (formerly AHCPR); the NCI; the National Heart, Lung, and Blood Institute; the National Institute on Drug Abuse; the CDC; the Robert Wood Johnson Foundation; and the University of Wisconsin Center for Tobacco Research and Intervention. Here we focus briefly on the results presented in the updated Guideline and selectively review what we believe are particularly noteworthy findings and conclusions.

The reader is referred to the source (Fiore et al., 1996) for details concerning how the Guideline was constructed, criteria for inclusion of studies in the meta-analyses, and so forth. It is worth noting, however, that the original Guideline identified 3,000 research articles published between 1975 and 1994, and the update (Fiore et al., 2000) identified an additional 3,000 articles published between 1994 and 1999, a testament to the rapid increase in clinical trials efficacy research emphasis upon smoking cessation. It is also noteworthy that more than 1 million copies of the 1996 Guideline and its affiliated products have been disseminated. However, the public health impact of this dissemination is difficult to evaluate, and implementation of the Guideline in various treatment settings, and evaluation of the efficacy of its use, remains a challenge (Sippel, Osborne, Bjornson, Goldberg, & Buist, 1999).

Structural and Psychosocial Aspects of Treatment

Most of the conclusions reached in the initial Guideline remained true in the update. In 1992 Lichtenstein and Glasgow speculated that "more is better, usually" (p. 521) asserting that personal contacts distributed over time, and not necessarily number of intervention components, are probably most important in determining successful quitting. As usual, our predecessors were mostly right. In meta-analyses, efficacy was strongly and positively associated with time spent in counseling, defined either as session length, total contact time, or number of treatment sessions. Analysis of format types (e.g., self-help, proactive telephone counseling, group counseling, and individual psychotherapy) also showed that more was better, with number of combined formats demonstrating a positive relationship with outcome. Of all format types, individual counseling was superior in terms of its effect (odds ratio [OR] = 1.7), although proactive telephone counseling and group counseling were also found to be efficacious (ORs = 1.2 and 1.3, respectively). The effect for self-help was inconsistent and weak compared with other formats, and it did not appear that combining different types of self-help approaches conferred any advantage in terms of quitting.

The meta-analyses also addressed the efficacy of particular types of psychosocial content. No evidence for efficacy could be detected for the following content categories: relaxation/breathing exercises, contingency contracting, weight and/or diet issues, cigarette fading, acupuncture, and negative affect. The categories of content areas that enjoyed statistically significant associations with cessation included (a) in-treatment social support; (b) extra-treatment social support (i.e., providing direction or support to increase support in the smoker's environment); (c) problem solving (providing practical information such as skills training, relapse prevention, and stress management); and (d) aversive smoking procedures such as rapid smoking, rapid puffing, and other smoke exposure.

The analyses of content should be viewed with caution because intervention studies rarely use a particular content in isolation; content tends to be correlated with other aspects of treatment (e.g., more sessions = more content), and studies often tailor content to the needs of the smokers being studied. Nevertheless, in future cessation studies, researchers should take some guidance in focusing on, including, and improving content that is supported by evidence. Future researchers should neither abandon research on other content areas that do not currently enjoy the benefit of evidence-based support, although our recommendation is to use with caution. These content categories or treatment components may benefit particular subgroups of smokers (e.g., negative affect treatments may benefit smokers predisposed toward depression when quitting smoking).

Despite the apparent strengths of meta-analysis, it is important to remain critical of general findings and recommendations. For example, whereas the Guideline (Fiore et al., 1996, 2000) suggests that social support and problem solving are important, active ingredients of effective behavioral treatments, the devil still lies in the details.

A Research Agenda for Behavioral Interventions

In 1993, Shiffman threw down the gauntlet, claiming that behavioral smoking cessation is in a rut. This claim was based in part on the observation that innovations in behavioral techniques or approaches for cessation had dwindled in the late 1980s compared with the 1960s and 1970s. He also correctly observed that most of the techniques found to be efficacious had been combined in favor of multicomponent cessation programs and delivered by means of various modalities. Moreover, researchers have confirmed that multicomponent programs enjoy greater efficacy compared with single component programs (Fiore et al., 2000). To move us out of a rut, Shiffman further recommended, among other things, that more attention needs to be paid to how developments in theory or basic science are implemented in treatment, with a rededication to basic research on smoking behavior and nicotine dependence; that we need to pay attention to treatment process; and that more work needs to be done to explore the unrealized promise of patient–treatment matching.

With perhaps a few exceptions, it does not seem that there has been much innovation in developing new behavioral cessation treatments since Shiffman's (1993) review (but contrast this with the proliferation of modalities for delivery of treatments and patient–treatment matching strategies). Cognitive–behavioral mood management techniques have been developed and evaluated, focusing on managing depressed mood postcessation (Hall, Munoz, & Reus, 1994; Hall et al., 1996). It is does not appear, though, that this added treatment component boosts efficacy beyond more traditional cognitive–behavioral multicomponent treatment packages (Fiore et al., 2000). However, there may be insufficient research on this topic to do it justice with meta-analysis. Moreover, it remains to be determined whether this approach is differentially effective for smokers who are at high risk for cessation-induced exacerbation of depressive symptoms. Another approach, motivational interviewing (MI) or motivational enhancement (Rollnick, Butler, & Stott, 1997), emphasizes motivating less-than-ready individuals to begin to make changes in thoughts and behaviors that will eventually propel them toward control of their addiction. The advantage of this approach is that it targets the low range of motivation, whereas typical treatments are better matched to more highly motivated individuals. Preliminary studies with smokers indicate some efficacy (Butler et al., 1999; Colby et al., 1998), but more studies are needed (and are currently underway) to fully evaluate MI's potential. Another quasibehavioral treatment is biomarker feedback, which is designed ostensibly to motivate or reinforce behavior change. Biomarkers include indices of smoke and nicotine intake/exposure, such as carbon monoxide or cotinine, and measures of tobacco-related tissue cell/tissue damage and toxicity, such as pulmonary function, precancerous lesions, and evidence of genetic damage. More systematic research is needed to evaluate the full potential of this sort of feedback in motivating smokers to make a quit attempt and to reinforce maintenance of cessation, for example, if biomarkers show reversibility of risk or damage on cessation.

Despite the relative paucity of new behavioral treatments, it is our sense that there has been a return to basic science issues and to theory. The lag between translation of the results of basic science into therapeutic applications is long, so it may be some time before new behavioral treatments are developed. We are, however, optimistic. Two areas that we believe deserve increased and more immediate research emphasis are intra- and extra-treatment social support and problem-solving/relapse prevention, both of which are associated with favorable outcomes (Fiore et al., 2000). Researchers still do not understand exactly the process by which these treatment components work and, with few exceptions (Piasecki & Baker, 2001; West, Edwards, & Hajek, 1998), little has been done in the way of forging interventions to maximize the potential influence of social support. One should also look to recent developments in theoretical understanding of the process of relapse and its converse, the maintenance of cessation, to help guide development of more effective interventions in this regard (Ockene et al., 2000).

Finally, we urge readers to consult the individual articles that constitute the evidence for the Guideline meta-analyses (http://www.surgeongeneral.gov/tobacco/) and come to their own interpretation of what constitutes the active (or inactive) ingredients of behavioral treatments. Indeed, this should be the starting point for research on enhancing existing treatments and even on developing new ones. Researchers must not fall into the trap of expecting the meta-analyses to be the last word on the subject.

Match Making, High Stepping, and Master Tailoring

Other issues that deserve comment have to do not so much with behavioral treatment components or content as with how and to whom intervention elements are delivered. Treatment matching and stepped care models have been discussed but have received scant research attention (Abrams et al., 1996; Orleans, 1993). The major theoretical advantage of matching is that smokers can be assessed according to some relevant, predictive dimension prior to treatment, be assigned to receive the treatment that is appropriate and adequate for them, and can avoid thereby the cumulative burdens of trial and failure. Treatment matching should also improve cost-effectiveness. Preliminary evidence suggests that matching treatments to degree of nicotine dependence (e.g., dose of nicotine gum, nicotine nasal spray) and to level of motivation to quit (e.g., with tailored self-help materials or expert systems feedback) improves efficacy (Herrera et al., 1995; Velicer, Prochaska, Fava, Laforge, & Rossi, 1999).

Stepped care models of treatment usually include a matching component, but then step up the intensity of treatment at the point of failure. Some models step up treatment according to various algorithms that take into account the reasons for failure (Abrams et al., 1996; Hughes, 1994). Stepped care models for smoking cessation have not yet been systematically evaluated (cf. S. S. Smith et al., 2001). Their unrealized promise lies in recycling treatment failures (perhaps very quickly after an initial slip; e.g., S. S. Smith et al., 2001), maintaining motivation to quit, and recognizing that nicotine dependence is a chronic relapsing condition that may require sustained treatment to improve efficacy compared with short-term static treatments.

Promising developments that may help address problems in treatment matching and stepped care are tailored communications and computer and information technologies, such as the World Wide Web, telephone interactive voice recognition, and interactive video (Robinson, Patrick, Eng, & Gustafson, 1998). Tailoring smoking cessation communication and information has largely focused on print communications, but this is rapidly changing (Abrams, Mills, & Bulger, 1999). With the aid of computer technology, smoking cessation resources could be tailored quite specifically to the individual smokers, and tailoring could be dynamic and close to real time, with communications changing and adapting to the smokers' experience as they progress through the process of quitting (Kreuter, Strecher, & Glassman, 1999; Velicer & Prochaska, 1999). (See also Aveyard et al., 1999.) More research is needed to see how rapidly developing communication technologies can be best leveraged to reach especially the smokers who are least motivated to quit or who have been recalcitrant to previous treatments (Robinson et al., 1998). One should not ignore, however, developments in interpersonal delivery of interventions and information such as by means of telephone counseling (Lichtenstein, Glasgow, Lando, Ossip-Klein, & Boles, 1996; Zhu et al., 1996).

Pharmacologic Interventions

The Guideline (Fiore et al., 2000) makes it clear that several forms of NRT are efficacious: nicotine gum, the transdermal nicotine patch, the nicotine inhaler, and nicotine nasal spray. Two non-nicotine pharmacologic treatments, bupropion hydrochloride, an atypical antidepressant with noradrenergic and dopaminergic activity, and clonidine, a centrally acting antihypertensive agent, have also demonstrated efficacy since the 1996 Guideline and are recommended treatment options (Fiore et al., 2000; Hurt et al., 1997). Bupropion has received Food and Drug Administration (FDA) approval for smoking cessation, whereas clonidine has not. Table 18.1 depicts the 6-month abstinence estimated ORs and 95% confidence intervals for the different treatments relative to placebo. Overlapping confidence intervals indicate that the treatments have statistically nondistinguishable effects. A recent head-to-head comparison of the nicotine patch, gum, inhaler, and spray showed no differential efficacy (Hajek et al., 1999).

TABLE 18.1
Odds Ratios (95% Confidence Intervals)
for Efficacious Smoking Treatments Relative to Placebo

Gum	Patch	Spray	Inhaler	Bupropion	Clonidine
1.5 (1.3–1.8)	1.9 (1.7–2.2)	2.7 (1.8–4.1)	2.5 (1.7–3.6)	2.1 (1.5–3.0)	2.1 (1.4–3.2)

Despite some evidence that high-nicotine-dependence smokers may benefit more from nicotine gum (especially 4 mg gum) and nasal spray (Herrera et al., 1995; Sutherland et al., 1992), the majority of the evidence suggests that smokers in general benefit from all forms of demonstrated efficacious pharmacotherapies. Therefore, the choice of treatment should depend to a large degree on factors such as patient and provider preference, affordability, and side effects. For example, clonidine is considered a second-line pharmacologic agent partly because of increased likelihood of side effects and rebound blood pressure problems on discontinuation of the drug. It is also clear that NRT works with little or no adjunctive behavioral treatment. This is not to say, however, that behavioral treatment is not important. Rather, it appears that the amount of behavioral treatment sets the base rate for quitting and that adding NRT doubles this quit rate (Hughes, 1995; Hughes, Goldstein, Hurt, & Shiffman, 1999).

The FDA granted approval for OTC sales of the gum in 1995 and the patch in 1996. This decision was based on extensive clinical and safety experience (Shiffman, Pinney, Gitchell, Burton, & Lara, 1997), trials demonstrating efficacy in OTC-like environments, and the desire to increase smokers' access to proven effective therapies and thereby increase the likelihood that motivated smokers would use NRT and quit (Hughes et al., 1999). Some studies have suggested that the public health benefit of OTC has been considerable (Shiffman et al., 1998). However, the efficacy of the gum and patch in this environment is less than that observed in controlled clinical trials and probably depends to a significant degree on factors such as underdosing, ceasing use prematurely, using inappropriately, and having an (un)availability of supplemental behavioral treatment. For example, use of a program consisting of telephone support and tailored cessation materials boosted quit rates significantly for those OTC patch and gum users who availed themselves of this resource compared with patch users who did not (Shiffman, Paty, Rohay, DiMarino, & Gitchell, 2000; Shiffman, Paty, Rohay, DiMarino, & Strecher, 2001).

A Research Agenda for Pharmacologic Treatments

One obvious but largely neglected area of study is determining mechanisms of action. For example, NRT works to alleviate withdrawal distress, yet it is unclear how much of its efficacy can be attributed to relief of withdrawal symptoms (West, 1992). It is also unclear to what extent NRT products replace the primary reinforcing effects derived from tobacco use. Therapeutic effects may differ for different NRT products. Nicotine nasal spray, with its relatively rapid onset, may more closely mimic the effects of smoking in terms of central nervous system stimulation and other factors. Products such as the gum and the inhaler may capitalize on behavioral aspects such as replacement of behaviors related to smoking and self-control of administration. NRT may also exert its effects through other mechanisms including having instructional or expectancy factors; making cigarettes less reinforcing, possibly preventing a slip from becoming a relapse; or disrupting the pairing of nicotine intake and environmental cues for smoking (Hughes, 1993). Surprisingly little is known about mechanisms of efficacy for bupropion and other antidepressants such as nortriptyline. These compounds exert small effects on symptoms of withdrawal (Hall et al., 1998; Prochazka et al., 1998; Shiffman, Johnson, et al., 2000), and there is some evidence for mood modulation, but it is unclear whether these effects are responsible for cessation efficacy. The emphasis of pharmacologic randomized clinical trial research is on demonstrating a main effect for the active versus the placebo drug. Unfortunately, this often begets a one-size-fits-all approach to use of the medication and belies considerable variability in treatment response. A significant main effect usually does not mean significant benefit for every smoker in the active drug condition; rather, there is likely to be a continuum of responders to nonresponders. Focusing on the extreme groups may prove to be an interesting strategy in determining what individual factors are responsible for treatment response. Some studies have attempted to understand which smokers respond differentially to pharmacologic intervention, notably the patch (Kenford et al., 1994; Swan, Jack, & Ward, 1997) and fluoxetine (Hitsman et al., 1999; Niaura et al., 2002). The latter studies found that elevated pretreatment symptoms of depression predicted positive response to fluoxetine versus placebo. Understanding mechanisms of action not only is theoretically important but also should help guide development of new therapeutic compounds and may aid in tailoring of pharmacologic treatments to the particular needs of individual smokers.

Should pharmacologic treatments be seen as adjuncts to behavioral treatments or stand-alone therapies? At least for NRT, it appears that the two work additively (Hughes et al., 1999), although formal tests of this proposition are lacking, especially for combinations of behavioral treatments with the patch and behavioral treatments with non-NRT compounds. It is important, therefore, to know what kind of behavioral treatment components work best with pharmacologic agents and what format and delivery systems are best suited to each product and situation. Is there dose-related incremental efficacy when intensity of behavioral treatment (components and/or contact) is increased and overlaid, for example, on use of the patch? Stated more simply, how much more can behavioral treatment add to patch efficacy? Hughes (1995) also posed several hypotheses concerning the mechanisms by which behavioral and pharmacologic treatments might combine to increase treatment efficacy: (a) Behavioral treatments improve skills necessary to achieve and maintain abstinence, whereas pharmacologic treatment improves withdrawal; (b) pharmacologic treatment provides relief of withdrawal early on and provides the necessary bridge through the most difficult period, whereas behavioral treatment provides skills necessary to prevent relapse subsequently; (c) behavioral skills may be specifically helpful for a subset of smokers, whereas pharmacologic treatment helps another subset; and (d) one treatment may increase compliance with the other (Hughes, 1995). There have been no systematic investigations of these or other proposed mechanisms whereby behavioral and pharmacologic treatments may potentiate one another.

The issue of combining pharmacotherapies deserves additional attention. There is mixed evidence that combinations of NRT products boost efficacy compared with use of individual products (Blondal, Gudmundsson, Olasfsdottir, Gustavsson, & Westin, 1999; Bohandana, Nilsson, & Martinet, 1999; Sutherland, 1999). However, combined use of the patch and gum appears to alleviate withdrawal symptoms more than either product alone (Fagerström, 1994), and there is no evidence for increased toxicity (Kornitzer, Boutsen, Dramaix, Thijs, & Gustavsson, 1995). The combination of bupropion and the patch was also found to be efficacious, at least in the short term, with no evidence of increased adverse events for the combination (Jorenby et al., 1999). So the question remains: For which smokers are combinations of particular products helpful, that is, those with breakthrough withdrawal symptoms, those with a need for additional behavioral replacement, those whose level of nicotine replacement is insufficient, those who need additional support during high risk for relapse situations, those who need different agents to address different withdrawal symptoms (e.g., depression vs. anxiety), or those for whom treatment of comorbidity (e.g., major depression) is also required?

Two other issues deserve comment: (a) Continued development of pharmacologic approaches to smoking cessation (what's in the product-development pipeline) and (b) the potential for long-term use of pharmacologic treatments to sustain cessation. New forms of NRT continue to be developed and evaluated. The nicotine lozenge and sublingual tablet are approved for use in Europe (Britton et al., 2000) and will probably be introduced to the U.S. consumer as prescription products in the near future. It is unclear whether these products confer a significant advantage over other NRT products. More exciting, perhaps, are treatments that target other potential mechanisms of action for cessation. Cigarette smoking inhibits monoamine oxidase (MAO A and B) in the brain (Berlin & Anthenelli, 2001; Fowler et al., 2000) This increases levels of dopamine and breaks down acetylcholine so smoking increases cholinergic and adrenergic transmission. One study found short-term efficacy for smoking cessation using moclobemide, a MAO A inhibitor (Berlin et al., 1995). What is intriguing about this research is that the effects of smoking on MAO inhibition in the brain are quite large and diffuse and do not appear to be attributable to the effects of nicotine per se but rather to some other aspects of smoking that exert psychoactive effects (Fowler et al., 1998). It remains to be seen what precise role MAO plays in the expression of tobacco dependence and whether MAO inhibitors will prove efficacious for smoking cessation.

The revised Guideline (Fiore et al., 2000) also drew attention to recent studies demonstrating the efficacy of nortriptyline for cessation (Hall et al., 1998; Prochazka et al., 1998). It is not clear how these medications could be used except perhaps as second-line agents, contingent on bupropion failure. There is no strong evidence to support the use of other antidepressants at this time, although as new and atypical antidepressants are developed it may be worth testing their efficacy for smoking cessation at least in small, "proof of concept" pilot studies. There has also been some promising work using combined agonist/antagonists (e.g., nicotine patch with mecamylamine) demonstrating good effects (Rose, Behm, & Westman, 1998), but it remains to be demonstrated how viable this approach may be for widespread use, given the possibility of significant side effects. Another avenue of exploration concerns developing antagonist or agonist/antagonist drugs that target specific subtypes of nicotinic receptors in the brain that are thought to be primarily responsible for mediating the reinforcing properties of nicotine (Picciotto, Caldarone, King, & Zachariou, 2000). Finally, work is being conducted on immunologically mediated approaches to reductions in self-administration of nicotine-containing products. One example is a nicotine vaccine that may "innoculate" the smoker, preventing nicotine from reaching regions in the brain that govern reinforcement and reward (Pentel et al., 2000). Whether any of these new approaches will prove fruitful remains to be seen. However, we predict research will continue in the pharmaceutical arena for some time to come, and it will be conducted quickly and efficiently by the pharmaceutical industry if there is sufficient promise of financial return on the research investment. Toward this end, strategic private/government/industry partnerships should be forged and rapid disclosure of study results, both positive and negative, should be encouraged to move the field along at a rapid pace. Should the pipeline for new drug products dry up, however, we will need to focus more on how efficacious pharmacologic treatments can best be used and perhaps targeted to subgroups of smokers to maximize therapeutic efficacy.

One final issue deserves comment—whether it may be feasible and safe for smokers to use pharmacotherapy for long periods of time to sustain abstinence. NRT products are typically indicated for use for 8 to 12 weeks. Some smokers, though, will use NRT products for even up to several years (Hughes, 1998), and it appears that safety and abuse potential are within tolerable limits (Benowitz, 1998). There are, however, to our knowledge no randomized controlled trials of long-term use of NRT products. One recent industry-sponsored trial evaluated the efficacy of using bupropion versus placebo for 1 year among smokers who had successfully quit smoking during a 7-week open-label treatment phase with bupropion (Hays et al., 2001). Brief behavioral counseling was provided at each treatment visit throughout the open label and double-blind phases of the study. Participants were followed for an additional year after long-term treatment. Results supported the efficacy of treatment for all intervals except for the final follow-up. Long-term pharmacologic treatment may be worth pursuing, but several issues arise. Among these are the additional benefit derived from drug treatment beyond supportive behavioral counseling and whether ex-smokers need to be maintained continuously on a drug or whether they could use it as needed (e.g., to prevent a slip or prevent a slip from becoming a relapse). Cost-effectiveness issues also loom with long-term treatment. In light of cost, safety, and abuse-liability issues with certain drugs, perhaps the most important question is determining who really will benefit from long-term treatment.

COST-EFFECTIVENESS, DISSEMINATION, ADOPTION, AND IMPLEMENTATION

There is now no doubt that smoking cessation treatment is both cost-effective and cost-beneficial (Cromwell, Bartosch, Fiore, Hasselblad, & Baker, 1997; Curry, Grothaus, McAfee, & Pabiniak, 1998; Warner, 1997). Indeed, smoking cessation interventions are arguably the most cost-effective of any preventive or other medical interventions (Tengs et al., 1995). Moreover, interventions are cost-effective across a range of intensity, for example, from clinician advice to pharmacotherapy to specialized clinics, as well as across populations such as pregnant women, hospitalized smokers, and smokers who have suffered a myocardial infarction (Parrott, Godfrey, Raw, West, & McNeill, 1998). So one potential limitation identified as a concern 10 years ago (Lichtenstein & Glasgow, 1992) turns out to be not a concern but a strength.

Why, then, if cessation interventions are cost-effective and cost-beneficial, are they not being more widely disseminated and adopted, especially by health care systems (McPhillips-Tangum, 1998; Warner, 1998)? There are myriad structural issues and barriers that are described elsewhere (Eisenberg, 1997; Jeddeloh, 1996). More important, perhaps, is that interventions still cost something, and this cost must be borne by the consumer or by third-party payers, such as health insurance companies, governments, and employers. Third-party payers want to see short-term return on investment, and this has been hard to demonstrate with cessation interventions despite evidence that smokers tend to use health care services disproportionately (Pronk, Goodman, O'Connor, & Martinson, 1999). Rapid turnover within health care plans also makes it difficult to realize concrete financial gains as a result of smoking cessation, the benefits of which may not accrue for some years (Goldstein & Niaura, 1998). Some have also argued that, although short-term medical expenditures related to smoking cessation might decrease, long-term expenditures might increase, in part, because of increased longevity (Barendregt, Bonneux, & Van De Mass, 1997). How are we to respond to this dilemma? Paying for smoking cessation may be more salable if short-term return on investment can be demonstrated for subgroups of smokers. This appears to be the case, for example, with pregnant smokers (Adams & Young, 1999). In addition, it may be possible to show short-term benefits of cessation among subgroups of smokers who are high users of health care services, such as post-MI and stroke patients (Lightwood & Glantz, 1997). Another way to respond to the dilemma would be to ignore the economic arguments for the moment and simply insist that providing maximum access to resources at no or reduced cost to the smokers who want to quit is a societal priority because it is the right thing to do in terms of preserving and improving the public health. Will this argument auger well with those who decide how public and private monies are spent? Time and politics will tell.

We would be remiss if we did not at least mention the tobacco settlement in which over 200 billion dollars will be distributed by the tobacco industry to 46 state governments (4 other states settled separately for 40 billion dollars) over a period of 25 years (for the full Attorneys General report on the Master Settlement Agreement, see http://www.naag.org/tobacco public/library.cfm). Proper use of these funds represents tremendous potential to address enormous public health issues, such as prevention of tobacco use among youth and providing access to smoking cessation resources for current smokers. Surely, the settlement presents the opportunity to disseminate what we know are efficacious and cost-effective treatments, as codified in the Guideline, to motivated smokers. At this juncture, volumes have been written about the settlement, mostly as editorial comments in the scientific and popular press, and we will not review the range of opinions on how this money should be used (Lima & Siegel, 1999). We predict, though, that with the exception of a handful of long-sighted, well-organized states, most of it will be squandered on politically expedient concerns other than tobacco and that the overall impact of the settlement on prevalence of smoking in the United States will be minimal. Indeed, recent reports have suggested that a small fraction of funds is currently being spent on tobacco prevention, treatment, and research (Kessler & Myers, 2001).

OTHER ISSUES

Harm Reduction

Considerable interest has been generated recently by the consideration of alternatives to complete abstinence as desirable outcomes of tobacco-use intervention efforts. This approach has been referred to as harm reduction, and is predicated on data suggesting a strong dose-dependent relationship between exposure to tobacco toxins and subsequent morbidity and mortality (D. M. Burns, 1997). Moreover, some unknown proportion of smokers who may be unable or unwilling to quit may find the prospect of reducing exposure to reduce harm an acceptable alternative to total abstinence. To some unknown degree, normative influences may also be shifting attention away from the notion that smoking is deadly and that abstinence is the only safe alternative to smoking.

Research is only now being proposed and conducted on methods to reduce toxin exposure, so it is too early to render judgment on the empirical merits of this approach. (Readers should not confuse harm reduction with efforts by the tobacco industry in either the past or the future to develop a "safe cigarette." *Harm reduction* here refers to reducing exposure to tobacco toxins through behavioral and/or pharmacologic means.) One of the interesting consequences of adopting a harm reduction philosophy is that there is a shift in focus away from abstinence (although this is not necessarily abandoned as the most desirable outcome) to other outcomes such as reduction in smoke exposure and, most important, exposure to biologically relevant toxins related to mechanisms of disease (Stratton, Shetty, Wallace, & Bondurant, 2001). Moreover, reduction, theoretically, can be achieved in a variety of ways; that is, not only in sustained reductions in the amount of tobacco ingested but also in changed patterns of tobacco use, such as in achieving periods of temporary abstinence. An exemplar would be to encourage pregnant women to abstain at least during their pregnancies.

Shiffman et al. (1998) have outlined principles that should guide a harm reduction philosophy and approach to tobacco control. Among these principles are the assumptions that (a) the purpose of reducing exposure to tobacco toxins is to reduce the death and disease caused by tobacco; (b) the long-range goal should be to leave smokers both tobacco and nicotine free and should not reduce the likelihood of eventual cessation; (c) any method used to reduce exposure, especially pharmacologic agents such as NRT products, should pose no added safety risks; (d) exposure reduction therapies should not worsen an individual's level of nicotine dependence and should not lead to increased population prevalence of nicotine dependence or expansion of use beyond the smoking population; and (e) pharmacologic means, if used to reduce tobacco toxin exposure, should not appeal to adolescents. The degree to which pharmacologic interventions, and in particular NRT products, can result in acceptable, safe, and verifiable reductions in toxin exposure will be the target of considerable research and intervention efforts for some time to come.

Individual Differences and Special Populations

Interest in individual characteristics of smokers that might predict treatment response has been abundant, but a few areas stand out as particularly deserving of attention: genetic influences, gender differences, psychiatric comorbidities, and adolescent smoking and prevention.

Numerous studies of twins have confirmed what appears to be moderate to large genetic influences on various aspects of smoking behavior (Kendler, 1998). In general, genetic influence tends to be stronger for persistent smoking, inability to quit smoking, and transition to regular smoking than it is for smoking initiation and early stages of smoking (Carmelli, Swan, Robinette, & Fabsitz, 1992; Heath & Martin, 1993). However, environmental effects are also prepotent, and studies to date have not been able to effectively examine Gene × Environment interactions. Lacking in particular are family studies of smoking and nicotine dependence phenotypes (Cheng, Swan, & Carmelli, 2000). Such studies are necessary to determine what are the heritable forms of smoking behaviors and aspects of nicotine dependence that may or may not portend response to different tobacco dependence treatments. At the same time, genetic association studies have pointed to specific candidate genes, such as the dopamine transporter gene polymorphism SLC6A3-9, that may be linked to smoking status, age of smoking initiation, and length of prior quit attempts (Lerman et al., 1999; Sabol et al., 1999). Other genes have been identified that regulate, in part, metabolism of nicotine (Pianezza, Sellers, & Tyndale, 1998) and may influence development of nicotine dependence. Increasingly, we shall see studies that examine whether such candidate genes moderate the effects of smoking cessation treatments, particularly pharmacologic treatments. However, studies such as these should be guided by theoretical and practical understanding of how genes and treatments operate at molecular biologic and other levels (Gelernter, 1997), so that we have, a priori, some idea of how genes and treatments ought to interact to decrease the possibility of Type I errors in searching for Gene × Treatment interaction effects (Pomerleau & Kardia, 1999).

Possible gender differences in ability to quit smoking, with and without treatment, have come under increasing scrutiny (Wetter, Fiore et al., 1999). Several studies suggest that women as compared with men have more difficulty quitting smoking, despite evidencing less nicotine dependence (Wetter, Kenford, et al., 1999). Moreover, women in particular may be less responsive to NRT. Some evidence exists to suggest that women smokers may be influenced more by non-nicotine-related stimuli related to smoking, which may explain in part decreased responsivity to NRT (for reviews, see Perkins, 2001; Perkins, Donny, & Caggiula, 1999). However, very little is known regarding the array of factors, ranging from drug sensitivity to sociocultural influences, that may ultimately explain potential gender differences in smoking initiation, prevalence, risk for relapse, and response to treatment. Understanding gender differences in smoking cessation, including possibly smoking for weight control, responding to nicotine, and responding to treatments, may lead to improved interventions for smoking cessation for both women and men (Perkins et al., 2001; U.S. Department of Health and Human Services, 2001).

The past decade has seen numerous studies document strong relationships between smoking and psychiatric comorbidities, including especially mood disorders, alcohol and other substance abuse and dependence, attention-deficit and hyperactivity disorder, and schizophrenia. One recent population-based study estimated that 41% of persons suffering from current mental illness were smokers and that over 40% of the tobacco in the United States is consumed by persons with a comorbid psychiatric disorder (Lasser et al., 2000). Particularly relevant for the population of smokers are high lifetime prevalence rates of depression and alcohol/substance abuse (Glassman, 1993) compared with the nonsmoking general population. Moreover, psychiatric comorbidities, whether historical or current, appear to significantly impede efforts at smoking cessation (Hughes et al., 1996), and conversely, quitting smoking may significantly increase risk of relapse to major depressive disorder, at least among those with such a prior history (Glassman, Covey, Stetner, & Rivelli, 2001). At issue, therefore, is understanding reasons that comorbid psychiatric conditions increase the likelihood of smoking and decrease the likelihood of quitting and using this understanding to adapt existing or develop new interventions targeted to the needs of these subgroups. For example, if history or current symptoms of depression portend treatment failure, will treatments that target increases in symptoms of depression precipitated by cessation be efficacious for this subgroup of smokers? More generally, if smokers with certain psychiatric disorders smoke to redress associated symptoms, can treatments, either pharmacologic or behavioral, be developed that serve a function similar to the effects of smoking, thereby decreasing dependence on tobacco and nicotine and increasing the likelihood of cessation? NRT products should theoretically show good efficacy in this regard, but there is as of yet little evidence to suggest they are differentially effective for smokers with and without psychiatric comorbid conditions.

The Guideline (Fiore et al., 2000) has also pointed to the importance of considering how treatments may be best developed and adapted for special populations, including, for example, racial and ethnic minorities, pregnant women, adolescents, those suffering from smoking-related illnesses and who may be hospitalized or receiving health care in a variety of treatment settings, smokers with psychiatric comorbidity/chemical dependency, and older smokers. We refer the reader to the Guideline for a more comprehensive discussion of these issues, but we wish to highlight recent developments with regard to adolescent prevention and treatment efforts.

A recent study presented the results of what is arguably the largest school-based prevention intervention of its kind (Peterson, Kealey, Mann, Marek, & Sarason, 2000). The Hutchinson Smoking Prevention Project determined the long-term impact of a theory-based, social influences model of intervention beginning at Grade 3 and progressing through Grade 12. The intervention was implemented in 20 schools, with 20 control schools matched on prevalence of tobacco use, school district size, and location. The intervention was grounded soundly in behavioral theory and contained all of the essential ingredients for school-based tobacco prevention as recommended by a national expert panel convened by the NCI (Glynn, 1989), as well as implementing all of the elements for school-based tobacco prevention efforts as recommended by the CDC (CDC, 1994b). This study is a model in terms of study design, intervention implementation with sustained fidelity, follow-up rates that are unprecedented, assessment of long-term outcomes, statistical power that is more than adequate, and data analysis with sophisticated methods. No significant intervention effects were observed.

The results are disappointingly negative but arguably quite real. We do not believe that an exercise in trying to determine how the study was flawed would be productive, but the results suggest that, perhaps, researchers should abandon the social influences model of prevention, at least as it is currently conceived and implemented (Clayton, Scutchfield, & Wyatt, 2000). It is also worth noting that some successes in school-based prevention have been reported (e.g., Botvin, Baker, Dusenbury, Botvin, & Diaz, 1995). These latter studies focused on a broader life-skills perspective and targeted multiple problem behaviors, so there may be some lessons to be learned from this perspective. It is also important to note that some states that have implemented the CDC school-based guidelines for tobacco prevention have witnessed declines in smoking prevalence (Bauer, Johnson, Hopkins, & Brooks, 2000; Rohde et al., 2001). Prevention efforts that have also incorporated a family based intervention component also show promise (Spoth, Redmond, & Shin, 2001). However sobering the results of the Hutchinson Smoking Prevention Project may appear, they nonetheless compel investigators to pursue with even greater vigor research into what will actually constitute effective prevention strategies.

Although prevention efforts are being challenged, so are smoking cessation treatments for the adolescent smoker. Reviews suggest that 3- to 6-month outcomes of behaviorally based cessation programs achieve abstinence rates of about 13% (Sussman, Lichtman, Ritt, & Pallonen, 1998). This coupled with evidence that adolescent regular smokers are similar to adult smokers in terms of reasons for smoking, difficulty quitting, and other criteria for tobacco dependence (Hurt et al., 2000) has led to efforts to treat these smokers with NRT. Yet, despite evidence of safety, tolerability, and decreased withdrawal symptoms among adolescents treated with the nicotine patch, efficacy has not been demonstrated (Hurt et al., 2000; T. A. Smith et al., 1996). However disappointing, it must be recognized that treatment of the adolescent smoker is still in its infancy. Numerous issues remain to be addressed, including variability in motivation, trust, and the therapeutic relationship with authority figures; the need to actively participate in decisions regarding treatment; confidentiality of treatment; and the need for additional behavioral supportive treatments, to name a few. We expect that, however daunting, research will continue to proliferate in this area because of the health-related importance of cessation early on in the life course.

CONCLUDING COMMENTS

This is an exciting and challenging time for smoking cessation research and clinical practice. The attention now focused on tobacco-related research is unprecedented. We have witnessed the formation of the Society for Research on Nicotine and Tobacco, the first scientific organization whose sole focus is on tobacco-related research. Major funding initiatives devoted to tobacco research have been sponsored by the NCI, the National Institute on Drug Abuse, and philanthropic organizations such as the Robert Wood Johnson Foundation. In 1999, these organizations funded several Transdisciplinary Tobacco Use Research Centers (TTURC). The TTURCs represent an effort to bridge the gap among disciplines, from molecular genetic to epidemiologic to clinical applications to policy implications of the scientific findings, to better understand the etiology of tobacco use and nicotine dependence and to translate this knowledge into practical interventions. The transdisciplinary focus is particularly important, as it is a means for disciplinary experts to learn each others' scientific language, methods, and paradigms from which ideally will spring entirely novel ways to think about tobacco use, dependence, and treatment. Whoever reviews the field in 10 years will be able to evaluate whether the TTURCs were a success in terms of significantly advancing our knowledge of tobacco dependence and its management. In our opinion, however, it is only through sincere yet difficult efforts to cross traditional disciplinary scientific boundaries that the research community will be able to forge innovations in interventions that will truly meet the needs of all smokers and will have a significant impact on the public health.

Finally, we should not ignore the global burden of disease, of which tobacco use remains a significant and growing cause (Murray & Lopez, 1996). Although we in developed countries such as the United States have witnessed an abundance of scientifically based efforts to reduce tobacco use with considerable success, in the global context we are a minority. Prevalence of smoking and tobacco use in many developed and developing countries is high and continues to rise (for World Health Organization statistics on prevalence of tobacco use worldwide, see http://tobacco.who.int/). We must look beyond our own borders to disseminate our knowledge of what works to help combat the global tobacco-use epidemic.

REFERENCES

Abrams, D. B., & Biener, L. (1992). Motivational characteristics of smokers at the worksite: A public health challenge. *Preventive Medicine, 21,* 679–687.

Abrams, D. B., Emmons, K. E., Linnan, L., & Biener, L. (1994). Smoking cessation at the workplace: Conceptual and practical considerations. In R. Richmond (Ed.), *Interventions for smokers: An international perspective* (pp. 137–169). New York: Williams & Wilkins.

Abrams, D. B., Mills, S., & Bulger, D. (1999). Challenges and future directions for tailored communication research. *Annals of Behavioral Medicine, 21,* 299–306.

Abrams, D. B., Orleans, C. T., Niaura, R. S., Goldstein, M. G., Prochaska, J. O., & Velicer, W. (1996). Integrating individual and public health perspectives for treatment of tobacco dependence under managed health care: A combined stepped care and matching model. *Annals of Behavioral Medicine, 18,* 290–304.

Adams, E. K., & Young, T. L. (1999). Costs of smoking: A focus on maternal, childhood, and other short-run costs. *Medical Care Research and Review, 56,* 3–29.

Aveyard, P., Cheng, K. K., Almond, J., Sherratt, E., Lancashire, R., Lawrence, T., et al. (1999). Cluster randomised controlled trial of expert system based on the transtheoretical ("stages of change") model for smoking prevention and cessation in schools. *British Medical Journal, 319,* 948–953.

Barendregt, J. J., Bonneux, L., & Van De Mass, P. J. (1997). The health care costs of smoking. *New England Journal of Medicine, 337,* 1052–1057.

Bauer, U. E., Johnson, T. M., Hopkins, R. S., & Brooks, R. G. (2000). Changes in youth cigarette use and intentions following implementation of a tobacco control program: Findings from the Florida Youth Tobacco Survey. *Journal of the American Medical Association, 284,* 723–728.

Benowitz, N. L. (Ed.). (1998). *Nicotine safety and toxicity.* New York: Oxford University Press.

Berlin, I., & Anthenelli, R. M. (2001). Monoamine oxidases and tobacco smoking. *International Journal of Neuropsychopharmacology, 4,* 33–42.

Berlin, I., Said, S., Spreux-Varoquaux, O., Olivares, R., Launay, J. M., & Puech, A. J. (1995). Monoamine oxidase A and B activities in heavy smokers. *Biological Psychiatry, 38,* 756–761.

Blondal, T., Gudmundsson, J., Olasfsdottir, I., Gustavsson, G., & Westin, A. (1999). Nicotine nasal spray with nicotine patch for smoking cessation: Randomised trial with six year follow-up. *British Medical Journal, 318,* 285–288.

Bohandana, A., Nilsson, F., & Martinet, Y. (1999). Nicotine inhaler and nicotine patch: A combination therapy for smoking cessation. *Nicotine and Tobacco Research, 1,* 189.

Botvin, G. J., Baker, E., Dusenbury, L., Botvin, E. M., & Diaz, T. (1995). Long-term follow-up results of a randomized drug abuse prevention trial in a white middle class population. *Journal of the American Medical Association, 273,* 1106–1112.

Britton, J., Bates, C., Channer, K., Cuthbertson, L., Godfrey, C., Jarvis, M., & McNeil, A. (2000). *Nicotine addiction in Britain: A report of the Tobacco Advisory Group of the Royal College of Physicians.* Sudbury, England: Lavenham Press.

Burns, D. M. (1997, March). *Estimating the benefits of a risk reduction strategy.* Paper presented at the Society for Research on Nicotine and Tobacco, Nashville, Tennessee.

Burns, S., Cohen, S., Gritz, E., & Kottke, T. (1994). *Tobacco and the Clinician: Interventions for medical and dental practice* (Vol. 5). Bethesda, MD: U.S. Department of Health and Human Services.

Butler, C. C., Rollnick, S., Cohen, D., Bachmann, M., Russell, I., & Stott, N. (1999). Motivational consulting versus brief advice for smokers in general practice: A randomized trial. *British Journal of General Practice, 49,* 611–616.

Carlton, R. A., Lasater, T. M., Assaf, A. R., Feldman, H. A., & McKinlay, S. M. (1994, March). *The Pawtucket Heart Health Program: Cross-sectional results from a community intervention trial.* Paper presented at the 34th Annual Conference on Cardiovascular Disease Epidemiology and Prevention, Tampa, FL.

Carmelli, D., Swan, G. E., Robinette, D., & Fabsitz, R. (1992). Genetic influence on smoking: A study of male twins. *New England Journal of Medicine, 327,* 829–833.

Centers for Disease Control and Prevention. (1994a, May 20). Cigarette smoking among adults—United States, 1992, and changes in the definition of current cigarette smoking. *Morbidity and Mortality Weekly Report, 43,* 342–346.

Centers for Disease Control and Prevention. (1994b, February 25). Guidelines for school health programs to prevent tobacco use and addiction. *Morbidity and Mortality Weekly Report, 43,* 1–18.

Centers for Disease Control and Prevention. (1994c, July 8). Medical-care expenditures attributable to cigarette smoking—United States, 1993. *Morbidity and Mortality Weekly Report, 43,* 469–472.

Centers for Disease Control and Prevention. (1994d, June 10). Surveillance for smoking-attributable mortality and years of potential life lost, by state—United States, 1990. *Morbidity and Mortality Weekly Report, 43,* 1–8.

Centers for Disease Control and Prevention. (1996, July 12). Cigarette smoking among adults—United States, 1994. *Morbidity and Mortality Weekly Report, 45,* 588–590.

Centers for Disease Control and Prevention. (1998a, October 9). Incidence of initiation of cigarette smoking—United States, 1965–1996. *Morbidity and Mortality Weekly Report, 47,* 837–840.

Centers for Disease Control and Prevention. (1998b, May 22). Selected cigarette smoking initiation and quitting behaviors among high school students—United States, 1997. *Morbidity and Mortality Weekly Report, 47,* 386–389.

Centers for Disease Control and Prevention. (1999, November 5). Cigarette smoking among adults—United States, 1997. *Morbidity and Mortality Weekly Report, 48,* 993–996.

Centers for Disease Control and Prevention. (2001, November 9). State Medicaid coverage for tobacco dependence treatments—United States, 1998 and 2000. *Morbidity and Mortality Weekly Report, 50,* 979–982.

Cheng, L. S., Swan, G. E., & Carmelli, D. (2000). A genetic analysis of smoking behavior in family members of older adult males. *Addiction, 95,* 426–436.

Clayton, R. R., Scutchfield, F. D., & Wyatt, S. W. (2000). Hutchinson Smoking Prevention Project: A new gold standard in prevention science requires new transdisciplinary thinking. *Journal of the National Cancer Institute, 92,* 1964–1965.

Colby, S. M., Monti, P. M., Barnett, N. P., Rohsenow, D. J., Weissman, K., Spirito, A., et al. (1998). Brief motivational interviewing in a hospital setting for adolescent smoking: A preliminary study. *Journal of Consulting and Clinical Psychology, 66,* 574–578.

COMMIT Research Group. (1995a). Community Intervention Trial for Smoking Cessation (COMMIT): I. Cohort results from a four-year community intervention. *American Journal of Public Health, 85,* 183–192.

COMMIT Research Group. (1995b). Community Intervention Trial for Smoking Cessation (COMMIT): II. Changes in adult cigarette smoking prevalence. *American Journal of Public Health, 85,* 193–200.

Cromwell, J., Bartosch, W. J., Fiore, M. C., Hasselblad, V., & Baker, T. (1997). Cost-effectiveness of the clinical practice recommendations in the AHCPR guideline for smoking cessation. Agency for Health Care Policy and Research. *Journal of the American Medical Association, 278,* 1759–1766.

Cummings, K. M. (1999). Community-wide interventions for tobacco control. *Nicotine and Tobacco Research, 1*(Suppl. 1), 113-116.

Curry, S. J., Grothaus, L. C., McAfee, T., & Pabiniak, C. (1998). Use and cost effectiveness of smoking-cessation services under four insurance plans in a health maintenance organization. *New England Journal of Medicine, 339,* 673–679.

Dalack, G. W., Healy, D. J., & Meador-Woodruff, J. H. (1998). Nicotine dependence in schizophrenia: Clinical phenomena and laboratory findings. *American Journal of Psychiatry, 155,* 1490–1501.

Davis, R. M. (1988). Editorial: Uniting physicians against smoking: The need for a coordinated national strategy. *Journal of the American Medical Association, 259,* 2900–2901.

Eisenberg, J. M. (1997). Changing physicians' practices. *Tobacco Control, 6*(Suppl. 1), 68–70.

Fagerström, K. O. (1994). Combined use of nicotine replacement products. *Health Values, 18,* 15–20.

Fagerström, K. O., Kunze, M., Schoberberger, J. C., Breslau, N., Hughes, J. R., Puska, P., et al. (1996). Nicotine dependence versus smoking prevalence. *Tobacco Control, 5,* 52–56.

Farquhar, J. W., Fortmann, S. P., Flora, J. A., Taylor, C. B., Haskell, W. L., Williams, P. T., et al. (1990). Effects of community-wide education on cardiovascular disease risk factors: The Stanford Five-City Project. *Journal of the American Medical Association, 264,* 359–365.

Fichtenberg, C. M., & Glantz, S. A. (2000). Association of the California Tobacco Control Program with declines in cigarette consumption and mortality from heart disease. *New England Journal of Medicine, 343,* 1772–1777.

Fiore, M., Bailey, W., Cohen, S., Dorfman, S. F., Goldstein, M. G., Gritz, E. R., et al. (1996). *Smoking cessation: Clinical practice guideline No. 18*. (DHHS Publication No. ADM 96-0692). Rockville, MD: Agency for Health Care Policy and Research, Public Health Service.

Fiore, M., Bailey, W., Cohen, S., Dorfman, S. F., Goldstein, M. G., Gritz, E. R., et al. (2000). *Treating tobacco use and dependence: A clinical practical guideline*. Rockville, MD: U.S. Department of Health and Human Services, Public Health Service.

Fiore, M. C., Jorenby, D. E., Schensky, A. E., Smith, S. S., Bauer, R. R., & Baker, T. B. (1995). Smoking status as the new vital sign: Effect on assessment and intervention in patients who smoke. *Mayo Clinic Proceedings, 70*, 209–213.

Fiore, M. C., Novotny, T. E., & Pierce, J. P. (1990). Methods used to quit smoking in the United States: Do cessation programs help? *Journal of the American Medical Association, 263*, 2760–2765.

Fortmann, S. P., Taylor, C. B., Flora, J. A., & Jatulis, D. E. (1993). Changes in adult cigarette smoking prevalence after 5 years of community health education: The Stanford Five-City Project. *American Journal of Epidemiology, 137*, 82–96.

Fowler, J. S., Volkow, N. D., Wang, G. J., Pappas, N., Logan, J., MacGregor, R., et al. (1998). Neuropharmacological actions of cigarette smoke: Brain monoamine oxidase B (MAO B) inhibition. *Journal of Addictive Diseases, 17*, 23–24.

Fowler, J. S., Wang, G. J., Volkow, N. D., Franceschi, D., Logan, J., Pappas, N., et al. (2000). Maintenance of brain monoamine oxidase B inhibition in smokers after overnight cigarette abstinence. *American Journal of Psychiatry, 157*, 1864–1866.

France, E. K., Glasgow, R. E., & Marcus, A. C. (2001). Smoking cessation interventions among hospitalized patients: What have we learned? *Preventive Medicine, 32*, 376–388.

Gelernter, J. (1997). Genetic association studies in psychiatry: Recent history. In K. Blum & E. P. Nobel (Eds.), *Handbook of psychiatric genetics* (pp. 25–46). New York: CRC.

Glasgow, R. E., Terborg, J. R., Hollis, J. F., Severson, H. H., & Boles, S. M. (1995). Take heart: Results from the initial phase of a work-site wellness program. *American Journal of Public Health, 85*, 209–216.

Glassman, A. H. (1993). Cigarette smoking: Implications for psychiatric illness. *American Journal of Psychiatry, 150*, 546–553.

Glassman, A. H., Covey, L. S., Stetner, F., & Rivelli, S. (2001). Smoking cessation and the course of major depression: A follow-up study. *Lancet, 357*, 1929–1932.

Glynn, T. J. (1989). Essential elements of school-based smoking prevention programs. *Journal of School Health, 59*, 181–188.

Goldstein, M., Niaura, R., Willey-Lessne, C., DePue, J., Eaton, C., Rakowski, W., & Dube, C. (1997). Physicians counseling smokers. A population-based survey of patients' perceptions of health care provider-delivered smoking cessation interventions. *Archives of Internal Medicine, 157*, 1313–1319.

Goldstein, M. G., & Niaura, R. (1998). Smoking. In E. Topol, R. M. Califf, J. M. Isner, E. N. Prystowsky, P. W. Serruys, J. L. Swain, et al. (Eds.), *Textbook of cardiovascular medicine* (pp. 145–169). Philadelphia: Lippincott-Raven.

Hajek, P., West, R., Foulds, J., Nilsson, F., Burrows, S., & Meadow, A. (1999). Randomized comparative trial of nicotine polacrilex, a transdermal patch, nasal spray, and an inhaler. *Archives of Internal Medicine, 159*, 2033–2038.

Hall, S. M., Munoz, R. F., & Reus, V. I. (1994). Cognitive–behavioral intervention increases abstinence rates for depressive-history smokers. *Journal of Consulting and Clinical Psychology, 62*, 141–146.

Hall, S. M., Munoz, R. F., Reus, V. I., Sees, K. L., Duncan, C., Humfleet, G. L., & Hartz, D. T. (1996). Mood management and nicotine gum in smoking treatment: A therapeutic contact and placebo-controlled study. *Journal of Consulting and Clinical Psychology, 64*, 1003–1009.

Hall, S. M., Reus, V. I., Munoz, R. F., Sees, K. L., Humfleet, G., Hartz, D. T., et al. (1998). Nortriptyline and cognitive–behavioral therapy in the treatment of cigarette smoking. *Archives of General Psychiatry, 55*, 683–690.

Hays, J. T., Hurt, R. D., Rigotti, N. A., Niaura, R., Gonzales, D., Durcan, M. J., et al. (2001). Sustained-release bupropion for pharmacologic relapse prevention after smoking cessation: A randomized controlled trial. *Annals of Internal Medicine, 135*, 423–433.

Heath, A., & Martin, N. (1993). Genetic models for natural history of smoking: Evidence for a genetic influence on smoking persistence. *Journal of Addictive Behaviors, 18*, 19–34.

Herrera, N., Franco, R., Herrera, L., Partidas, A., Rolando, R., & Fagerström, K. O. (1995). Nicotine gum, 2 and 4 mg., for nicotine dependence. A double-blind placebo-controlled trial within a behavior modification support program. *Chest, 108*, 447–451.

Hitsman, B., Pingitore, R., Spring, B., Mahableshwarkar, A., Mizes, J. S., Segraves, K. A., et al. (1999). Antidepressant pharmacotherapy helps some cigarette smokers more than others. *Journal of Consulting and Clinical Psychology, 67*, 547–554.

Hughes, J. R. (1993). Pharmacotherapy for smoking cessation: Unvalidated assumptions, anomalies, and suggestions for further research. *Journal of Consulting and Clinical Psychology, 61*, 751–760.

Hughes, J. R. (1994). An algorithm for smoking cessation. *Archives of Family Medicine, 3*, 280–285.

Hughes, J. R. (1995). Combining behavioral therapy and pharmacotherapy for smoking cessation: An update. In L. S. Onken, J. D. Blaine, & J. J. Boren (Eds.), *Integrating behavior therapies with medication in the treatment of drug dependence* (Monograph 150, pp. 92–109). Washington, DC: National Institute on Drug Abuse.

Hughes, J. R. (1998). Dependence on and abuse of nicotine replacement medications: An update. In N. L. Benowitz (Ed.), *Nicotine safety and toxicity* (pp. 147–157). New York: Oxford University Press.

Hughes, J. R., Fiester, S., Goldstein, M. G., Resnick, M. P., Rock, N., & Ziedonis, D. (1996). American Psychiatric Association practice guideline for the treatment of patients with nicotine dependence. *American Journal of Psychiatry, 153*(Suppl. 1), 1-31.

Hughes, J. R., Goldstein, M. G., Hurt, R. D., & Shiffman, S. (1999). Recent advances in the pharmacotherapy of smoking. *Journal of the American Medical Association, 281*, 72–76.

Hurt, R. D., Croghan, G. A., Beede, S., Wolter, T. D., Croghan, I. T., & Patten, C. A. (2000). Nicotine patch therapy in 101 adolescent smokers: Efficacy, withdrawal symptom relief, and carbon monoxide and plasma cotinine levels. *Archives of Pediatric & Adolescent Medicine, 154*, 31–37.

Hurt, R. D., Sachs, D. P., Glover, E. D., Offord, K. P., Johnston, J. A., Dale, L. C., et al. (1997). A comparison of sustained-release bupropion and placebo for smoking cessation. *New England Journal of Medicine, 337*, 1195–1202.

Jeddeloh, R. J. (1996). A managed-care perspective on the AHCPR guideline. *Tobacco Control, 6*(Suppl. 1), 91–93.

Jeffrey, R. W., Forster, J. L., French, S. A., Kelder, S. H., Lando, H. A., McGovern, P. G., et al. (1993). The Healthy Worker Project: A worksite intervention for weight control and smoking cessation. *American Journal of Public Health, 83*, 395–401.

Jorenby, D. E., Leischow, S. J., Nides, M. A., Rennard, S. I., Johnston, J. A., Hughes, A. R., et al. (1999). A controlled trial of sustained-release bupropion, a nicotine patch, or both for smoking cessation. *New England Journal of Medicine, 340*, 685–691.

Kendler, K. (1998, July). *The genetic epidemiology of smoking.* Paper presented at the conference, Addicted to Nicotine: A National Research Forum, National Institutes of Health, Bethesda, MD.

Kenford, S. L., Fiore, M. C., Jorenby, D. E., Smith, S. S., Wetter, D., & Baker, T. B. (1994). Predicting smoking cessation: Who will quit with and without the nicotine patch. *Journal of the American Medical Association, 271*, 589–594.

Kessler, D. A., & Myers, M. L. (2001). Editorial: Beyond the tobacco settlement. *New England Journal of Medicine, 345*, 535–537.

Kornitzer, M., Boutsen, M., Dramaix, M., Thijs, J., & Gustavsson, G. (1995). Combined use of nicotine patch and gum in smoking cessation. *Preventive Medicine, 24*, 41–47.

Kottke, T. E., Solberg, L. I., Brekke, M. L., Conn, S. A., Maxwell, P., & Brekke, M. J. (1992). A controlled trial to integrate smoking cessation advice into primary care practice: Doctors Helping Smokers, Round III. *Journal of Family Practice, 34*, 701–708.

Kreuter, M. W., Strecher, V. J., & Glassman, B. (1999). One size does not fit all: The case for tailoring print materials. *Annals of Behavioral Medicine, 21*, 276–283.

Lando, H. A., Pechacek, T. F., Pirie, P. L., Murray, D. M., Mittlemark, M. B., Lichtenstein, E., et al. (1995). Changes in adult cigarette smoking in the Minnesota Heart Health Program. *American Journal of Public Health, 85*, 201–208.

Lasser, K., Boyd, J. W., Woolhandler, S., Himmelstein, D., McCormick, D., & Bor, D. H. (2000). Smoking and mental illness: A population-based prevalence study. *Journal of the American Medical Association, 284*, 2606–2610.

Lerman, C., Caporaso, N. E., Audrain, J., Main, D., Bowman, E. D., Lockshin, B., et al. (1999). Evidence suggesting the role of specific genetic factors in cigarette smoking. *Health Psychology, 18*, 14–20.

Lichtenstein, E. (1982). The smoking problem: A behavioral perspective. *Journal of Consulting and Clinical Psychology, 50*, 804–819.

Lichtenstein, E. (1997). Behavioral research contributions and needs in cancer prevention and control: Tobacco use prevention and cessation. *Preventive Medicine, 26*, S57–S63.

Lichtenstein, E., & Glasgow, R. E. (1992). Smoking cessation: What have we learned over the past decade? *Journal of Consulting and Clinical Psychology, 60*, 518–527.

Lichtenstein, E., Glasgow, R. E., Lando, H. A., Ossip-Klein, D. J., & Boles, S. M. (1996). Telephone counseling for smoking cessation: Rationales and meta-analytic review of evidence. *Health Education Research, 11*, 243–257.

Lightwood, J. M., & Glantz, S. A. (1997). Short-term economic and health benefits of smoking cessation: Myocardial infarction and stroke. *Circulation, 96*, 1089–1096.

Lima, J. C., & Siegel, M. (1999). The tobacco settlement: An analysis of newspaper coverage of a national policy debate, 1997–98. *Tobacco Control, 8*, 247–253.

Main, D. S., Cohen, S. J., & DiClemente, C. C. (1995). Measuring physician readiness to change cancer screening: Preliminary results. *American Journal of Preventive Medicine, 11*, 54–58.

Manley, M., Epps, R. P., Husten, C., Glynn, T., & Shopland, D. (1991). Clinical interventions in tobacco control: A National Cancer Institute training program for physicians. *Journal of the American Medical Association, 266*, 3172–3173.

Manley, M., Pierce, J. P., Gilpin, E. A., Rosbrook, B., Berry, C., & Wun, L. M. (1997). Impact of the American Stop Smoking Intervention Study on cigarette consumption. *Tobacco Control, 6*(Suppl. 2), 12–16.

McPhee, S. J., & Detmer, W. M. (1993). Office-based interventions to improve delivery of cancer prevention services by primary care physicians. *Cancer, 72*, 1100–1112.

McPhillips-Tangum, C. (1998). Results from the first annual survey on Addressing Tobacco in Managed Care. *Tobacco Control, 7*(Suppl. 1), 11–13.

Murray, C. J. L., & Lopez, A. D. (1996). Quantifying the burden of disease and injury attributable to ten major risk factors. In C. J. L. Murray & A. D. Lopez (Eds.), *The global burden of disease* (Vol. 1, pp. 295–324). Cambridge, MA: Harvard University Press.

Niaura, R., Spring, B., Borrelli, B., Hedeker, D., Goldstein, M., Keuthen, N., et al. (2002). Multicenter trial of fluoxetine as adjunct to behavioral smoking cessation treatment. *Journal of Consulting and Clinical Psychology, 70*, 887–896.

Ockene, J. K., Lindsay, E. A., Hymowitz, N., Giffen, C., Purcell, T., Pomrehn, P., & Pechacek, T. (1997). Tobacco control activities of primary-care physicians in the Community Intervention Trial for Smoking Cessation: COMMIT Research Group. *Tobacco Control, 6*(Suppl.), 49–56.

Ockene, J. K., Mermelstein, R. J., Bonollo, D. S., Emmons, K. M., Perkins, K. A., & Voorhees, C. C. (2000). Relapse and maintenance issues for smoking cessation. *Health Psychology, 19*(Suppl. 1), 17–31.

Orleans, C. T. (1993). Treating nicotine dependence in medical settings: A stepped-care model. In C. T. Orleans & J. Slade (Eds.), *Nicotine addiction: Principles and management* (pp. 145–162). New York: Oxford University Press.

Orleans, C. T., Glynn, T. J., Manley, M. W., & Slade, J. (1993). Minimal-contact quit smoking strategies for medical settings. In C. T. Orleans & J. Slade (Eds.), *Nicotine addiction: Principles and management* (pp. 181–220). New York: Oxford University Press.

Parrott, S., Godfrey, C., Raw, M., West, R., & McNeill, A. (1998). Guidance for commissioners on the cost effectiveness of smoking cessation interventions. *Thorax, 53*(Suppl.), 1–38.

Pelletier, K. R. (1993). A review and analysis of the health and cost-effective outcome studies of comprehensive health promotion and disease prevention programs at the work-site: 1991–1993 update. *American Journal of Health Promotion, 8,* 50–62.

Pentel, P. R., Malin, D. H., Ennifar, S., Hieda, Y., Keyler, D. E., Lake, J. R., et al. (2000). A nicotine conjugate vaccine reduces nicotine distribution to brain and attenuates its behavioral and cardiovascular effects in rats. *Pharmacology, Biochemistry, and Behavior, 65,* 191–198.

Perkins, K. A. (2001). Smoking cessation in women: Special considerations. *CNS Drugs, 15,* 391–411.

Perkins, K. A., Donny, E., & Caggiula, A. R. (1999). Sex differences in nicotine effects and self-administration: Review of human and animal evidence. *Nicotine & Tobacco Research, 1,* 301–315.

Perkins, K. A., Marcus, M. D., Levine, M. D., D'Amico, D., Miller, A., Broge, M., et al. (2001). Cognitive–behavioral therapy to reduce weight concerns improves smoking cessation outcome in weight-concerned women. *Journal of Consulting and Clinical Psychology, 69,* 604–613.

Peterson, A. V., Kealey, K. A., Mann, S. L., Marek, P. M., & Sarason, I. G. (2000). Hutchinson Smoking Prevention Project: Long-term randomized trial in school-based tobacco use prevention—Results on smoking. *Journal of the National Cancer Institute, 92,* 1979–1991.

Pianezza, M. L., Sellers, E. M., & Tyndale, R. F. (1998, June 25). Nicotine metabolism defect reduces smoking. *Nature, 393,* 750.

Piasecki, T. M., & Baker, T. B. (2001). Any further progress in smoking cessation treatment? *Nicotine and Tobacco Research, 4,* 311–323.

Picciotto, M. R., Caldarone, B. J., King, S. L., & Zachariou, V. (2000). Nicotinic receptors in the brain: Links between molecular biology and behavior. *Neuropsychopharmacology, 22,* 451–465.

Pieterse, M. E., Seydel, E. R., DeVries, H., Mudde, A. N., & Kok, G. J. (2001). Effectiveness of a minimal contact smoking cessation program for Dutch general practitioners: A randomized controlled trial. *Preventive Medicine, 32,* 182–190.

Pomerleau, O. F., & Kardia, S. L. R. (1999). Introduction to the featured section: Genetic research on smoking. *Health Psychology, 18,* 3–6.

Prochazka, A. V., Weaver, M. J., Keller, R. T., Fryer, G. E., Licari, P. A., & Lofaso, D. (1998). A randomized trial of nortriptyline for smoking cessation. *Archives of Internal Medicine, 158,* 2035–2039.

Pronk, N. P., Goodman, M. J., O'Connor, P. J., & Martinson, B. C. (1999). Relationship between modifiable health risks and short-term health care charges. *Journal of the American Medical Association, 282,* 2235–2239.

Puska, P., Salonen, J., Nissinen, A., Tuomilehto, J., Vartiainin, E., Korhonen, H., et al. (1983). Change in risk factors for coronary heart disease during 10 years of a community intervention programme (North Karelia Project). *British Medical Journal, 287,* 1840–1844.

Raw, M., McNeill, A., & West, R. (1998). Smoking cessation guidelines for health professionals. *Thorax, 53*(Suppl. 5), 1–19.

Rigotti, N. A., Lee, J. E., & Wechsler, H. (2000). U.S. college students use of tobacco products: Results of a national survey. *Journal of the American Medical Association, 284,* 699–705.

Robinson, T. N., Patrick, K., Eng, T. R., & Gustafson, D. (1998). An evidence-based approach to interactive health communication: A challenge to medicine in the information age. *Journal of the American Medical Association, 280,* 1264–1269.

Rohde, K., Pizacani, B., Stark, M., Pietrukowicz, M., Mosback, C., Romoli, C., et al. (2001, August 10). Effectiveness of school-based programs as a component of a statewide tobacco control initiative—Oregon, 1999–2000. *Morbidity and Mortality Weekly Report, 50,* 663–666.

Rollnick, S., Butler, C. C., & Stott, N. (1997). Helping smokers make decisions: The enhancement of brief intervention for general medical practice. *Patient Education and Counseling, 31,* 191–203.

Rose, J. E., Behm, F. M., & Westman, E. C. (1998). Nicotine-mecamylamine treatment for smoking cessation: The role of pre-cessation therapy. *Experimental and Clinical Psychopharmacology, 6,* 331–343.

Sabol, S. Z., Nelson, M. L., Fisher, C., Gunzerath, L., Brody, C. L., Hu, S., et al. (1999). A genetic association for cigarette smoking behavior. *Health Psychology, 18,* 7–13.

Severson, H. H., Andrews, J. A., Lichtenstein, E., Gordon, J. S., & Barckley, M. F. (1998). Using the hygiene visit to deliver a tobacco cessation program: Results of a randomized clinical trial. *Journal of the American Dental Association, 129,* 993–999.

Shiffman, S. (1993). Smoking cessation treatment: Any progress? *Journal of Consulting and Clinical Psychology*, *61*, 718–722.

Shiffman, S., Johnson, J. A., Khayrallah, M., Elash, C. A., Gwaltney, C. J., Paty, J. A., et al. (2000). The effect of bupropion on nicotine craving and withdrawal. *Psychopharmacology*, *148*, 33–40.

Shiffman, S., Mason, K. M., & Henningfield, J. E. (1998). Tobacco dependence treatments: Review and prospectus. *Annual Review of Public Health*, *19*, 335–358.

Shiffman, S., Paty, J. A., Rohay, J. M., DiMarino, M. E., & Gitchell, J. (2000). The efficacy of computer-tailored smoking cessation material as a supplement to nicotine polacrilex gum therapy. *Archives of Internal Medicine*, *160*, 1675–1681.

Shiffman, S., Paty, J., Rohay, J., DiMarino, M., & Strecher, V. (2001). The efficacy of computer-tailored smoking cessation material as a supplement to nicotine patch therapy. *Drug & Alcohol Dependence*, *64*, 35–46.

Shiffman, S., Pinney, J., Gitchell, J., Burton, S. L., & Lara, E. A. (1997). Public health benefit of over-the-counter nicotine medications. *Tobacco Control*, *6*, 306–310.

Shipley, R. H., Hartwell, T. W., Austin, W. D., Clayton, A. C., & Stanley, L. C. (1995). Community stop-smoking contests in the COMMIT trial: Relationship of participation to costs. *Preventive Medicine*, *24*, 286–292.

Sippel, J. M., Osborne, M. L., Bjornson, W., Goldberg, B., & Buist, A. S. (1999). Smoking cessation in primary care clinics. *Journal of General Internal Medicine*, *14*, 670–676.

Smith, S. S., Jorenby, D. E., Piasecki, T. M., Baker, T. B., Fiore, M. C., Anderson, J. E., et al. (2001). Strike while the iron is hot: Can stepped-care treatments resurrect relapsing smokers? *Journal of Consulting and Clinical Psychology*, *69*, 429–439.

Smith, T. A., House, R. F., Croghan, I. T., Gauvin, T. R., Colligan, R. C., Offord, K. P., et al. (1996). Nicotine patch therapy in adolescent smokers. *Pediatrics*, *98*, 659–667.

Solberg, L. I., Boyle, R. G., Davidson, G., Magnan, S., Carlson, C. L., & Alesci, N. L. (2001). Aids to quitting tobacco use: How important are they outside controlled trials? *Preventive Medicine*, *33*, 53–58.

Sorensen, G., Thompson, B., Glanz, K., Feng, Z., Kinne, S., DiClemente, C., et al. (1996). Work site-based cancer prevention: Primary results from the Working Well Trial. *American Journal of Public Health*, *86*, 939–947.

Spoth, R. L., Redmond, C., & Shin, C. (2001). Randomized trial of brief family interventions for general populations: Adolescent substance use outcomes 4 years following baseline. *Journal of Consulting and Clinical Psychology*, *69*, 627–642.

Stratton, K., Shetty, P., Wallace, R., & Bondurant, S. (Eds.). (2001). *Clearing the smoke: Assessing the science base for harm reduction*. Washington, DC: Institute of Medicine, National Academy Press.

Sussman, S., Lichtman, K., Ritt, A., & Pallonen, U. (1998). Effects of thirty-four adolescent tobacco use cessation and prevention trials on regular users of tobacco products. *Substance Use and Misuse*, *33*, 2703–2720.

Sutherland, G. (1999). A placebo-controlled double-blind combination trial of nicotine patch and spray. *Nicotine and Tobacco Research, 1*, 186– 187.

Sutherland, G., Stapelton, J. A., Russell, M. A. H., Jarvis, M. J., Hajek, P., Belcher, M., & Feyerabend, C. (1992). Randomised controlled trial of nasal nicotine spray in smoking cessation. *Lancet, 340*, 324–329.

Swan, G., Jack, L. M., & Ward, M. M. (1997). Subgroups of smokers with different success rates after use of transdermal nicotine. *Addiction, 92*, 207–217.

Tengs, T. O., Adams, M. E., Pilskin, J. S., Safran, D. G., Siegel, J. E., Weinstein, M. C., & Graham, J. D. (1995). Five hundred life saving interventions and their cost effectiveness. *Risk Analysis, 15*, 369–390.

Thorndike, A. N., Rigotti, N. A., Stafford, R. S., & Singer, D. E. (1998). National patterns in the treatment of smokers by physicians. *Journal of the American Medical Association, 279*, 604–608.

U.S. Department of Health and Human Services. (1992). *Health behavior research in minority populations: Access, design, and implementation* (DHHS Publication No. 92-2965). Washington, DC: Public Health Service.

U.S. Department of Health and Human Services. (2001). *Women and smoking: A Report of the Surgeon General.* Atlanta: National Center for Chronic Disease Prevention and Health Promotion, Office on Smoking and Health.

Velicer, W. F., Fava, J. L., Prochaska, J. O., Abrams, D. B., Emmons, K. M., & Pierce, J. P. (1995). Distribution of smokers by stage in three representative samples. *Preventive Medicine, 24*, 401–411.

Velicer, W. F., & Prochaska, J. O. (1999). An expert system intervention for smoking cessation. *Patient Education and Counseling, 36*, 119–129.

Velicer, W. F., Prochaska, J. O., Fava, J. L., Laforge, R. G., & Rossi, J. S. (1999). Interactive versus noninteractive interventions and dose-response relationships for stage-matched smoking cessation programs in a managed care setting. *Health Psychology, 18*, 21–28.

Walsh, J. M., & McPhee, S. J. (1992). A systems model of clinical preventive care: An analysis of factors influencing patient and physician. *Health Education Quarterly, 19*, 157–175.

Warner, K. E. (1997). Cost effectiveness of smoking cessation therapies: Interpretation of the evidence and implications for coverage. *Pharmacoeconomics, 11*, 538–549.

Warner, K. E. (1998). Smoking out the incentives for tobacco control in managed care settings. *Tobacco Control, 7*(Suppl.), 50–54.

Wechsler, H., Levine, S., Idelson, R. K., & Coakley, E. (1996). The physician's role in health promotion revisited—A survey of primary care practitioners. *New England Journal of Medicine, 334*, 996–998.

Wechsler, H., Rigotti, N. A., Gledhill-Hoyt, J., & Lee, H. (1998). Increased levels of cigarette use among college students: A cause for national concern. *Journal of the American Medical Association, 280*, 1673–1678.

West, R. (1992). The nicotine replacement paradox in smoking cessation: How does nicotine gum really work? *British Journal of Addiction, 87*, 165–167.

West, R., Edwards, M., & Hajek, P. (1998). A randomised controlled trial of a "buddy" system to improve success at giving up smoking in general practice. *Addiction, 93*, 1007–1011.

Wetter, D., Fiore, M. C., Young, T. B., McClure, J., DeMoor, C. A., & Baker, T. B. (1999). Gender differences in response to nicotine replacement therapy: Objective and subjective indices of tobacco withdrawal. *Experimental and Clinical Psychopharmacology, 7*, 135–144.

Wetter, D., Kenford, S. L., Smith, S. S., Fiore, M. C., Jorenby, D. E., & Baker, T. B. (1999). Gender differences in smoking cessation. *Journal of Consulting and Clinical Psychology, 67*, 555–562.

Zhu, S. H., Stretch, V., Balabanis, M., Rosbrook, B., Sadler, G., & Pierce, J. P. (1996). Telephone counseling for smoking cessation: Effects of single-session and multiple-session interventions. *Journal of Consulting and Clinical Psychology, 64*, 202–211.

19

RISK FACTORS AND NEUROPSYCHOLOGICAL RECOVERY IN CLIENTS WITH ALCOHOL USE DISORDERS WHO WERE EXPOSED TO DIFFERENT TREATMENTS

MARSHA E. BATES, DANIELLE BARRY, ERICH W. LABOUVIE,
WILLIAM FALS-STEWART, GERALD VOELBEL,
AND JENNIFER F. BUCKMAN

About 50% to 80% of persons diagnosed with alcohol use disorders display deficits on neuropsychological tests, indicating subtle to profound impairment of attention, cognitive flexibility, episodic and working memory, abstract reasoning, and other cognitive abilities (Bates & Convit, 1999; Rourke & Løberg, 1996). A sizable minority of these adults display impairments as clinically severe as those seen in persons with traumatic brain injury (Bates, 1997; Donovan, Kivlahan, Kadden, & Hill, 2001; Victor & Adams, 1985). More severely impaired clients may benefit from cognitive rehabilitation in addition to addiction treatment (Allen, Goldstein, & Seaton, 1997). Yet, deficit severity may be underestimated by treatment providers because of its insidious onset (Knight & Longmore, 1994) and the difficulty in detecting impairments in conversation or structured interviews (Fals-Stewart,

Preliminary results of this study were presented at the 24th Annual Scientific Meeting of the Research Society on Alcoholism, Montreal, Quebec, Canada, June 2001, and at the 25th Annual Scientific Meeting of the Research Society on Alcoholism, San Francisco, California, June 2002. This study was supported by National Institute of Alcohol Abuse and Alcoholism Grants P50 AA 08747, AA 11594, and K02 AA 00325. We thank Frances Del Boca for her help with the medical test and neuropsychological data sets and J. Scott Tonigan for his assistance with the risk covariate data sets from Project MATCH.

Reprinted from *Journal of Consulting and Clinical Psychology, 72,* 1073–1080 (2004). Copyright 2004 by the American Psychological Association.

1997). Evidence suggests that negative characteristics often attributed to clients, such as inattention, low motivation, and minimization or denial of problem severity, may arise from cognitive deficits that are distinct from other psychological or psychosocial disruptions that are attributable to the primary use disorder (Fals-Stewart, Shanahan, & Brown, 1995; Goldman, 1995).

Although thorough neuropsychological assessment of all clients entering addiction treatment may not be feasible, risk factors have been identified that account for up to 57% of the true variance in executive function, memory, verbal ability, and information-processing speed of clients with substance use disorders at treatment entry (Bates, Labouvie, & Voelbel, 2002; Fals-Stewart & Bates, 2003; Hesselbrock, Weidenman, & Reed, 1985; Malloy, Noel, Rogers, Longabaugh, & Beattie, 1989). Older age, lower education, health problems, psychiatric diagnoses, familial alcoholism, and duration of heavy drinking, for example, have been inversely related to neuropsychological ability. Treatment providers can use information about risk factors in their initial functional analysis of client strengths and weaknesses to help identify those clients most at risk for cognitive compromise and in need of neuropsychological assessment.

Following the planning phase of addiction treatment, however, it is not clear whether risk covariates are informative about meaningful individual differences in neuropsychological recovery over time. This is an important question in view of evidence that alcohol-related impairment is often not permanent and that spontaneous, time-dependent neuropsychological recovery may follow abstinence or greatly reduced drinking (Parsons, 1998; Rourke & Grant, 1999). Questions concerning the need for cognitive rehabilitation, long-term employment options, and other psychosocial outcomes could be more adequately addressed if the likelihood and extent of expected cognitive improvement were more predictable. There is some evidence that age, severity of depressive symptoms, and chronicity of use are negatively associated with neuropsychological recovery (Rourke & Grant, 1999; Schafer et al., 1991). Yet, the literature is not straightforward, and interpretation is problematic because of methodological difficulties in controlling for practice effects and inconsistencies in the neuropsychological tests and time points used in different studies. Moreover, applied questions regarding clinically significant versus statistically significant improvements in neuropsychological functioning, and whether spontaneous recovery of function varies in clients exposed to different addiction treatment approaches, have received very little attention.

In this study, we used data from Project MATCH, a clinical trial of three alcohol treatments, to examine hypotheses about whether risk factors associated with cognitive deficits at treatment entry predict cognitive recovery over 15 months. A structural equation modeling approach to hypothesis testing was used, and the magnitude and prediction of recovery over time was considered in relation to the effect size (ES) of statistically significant mean changes and path coefficients. We predicted that risk factors for impairment identified in the previous literature would be associated with poorer neuropsychological ability in clients at treatment entry and with less cognitive recovery at 15 months. Improvement over time in depressive symptoms and medical test results, in addition to decreases in alcohol consumption, were expected to facilitate greater recovery. We also examined whether changes in depressive symptoms and medical problems mediated the influence of alcohol consumption on recovery of cognitive ability. Finally, we explored differential changes in cognitive status in clients exposed to cognitive–behavioral coping skills therapy (CBT; Kadden et al., 1995), motivational enhancement therapy (MET; Miller, Zweben, DiClemente, & Rychtarik, 1995), and twelve-step facilitation (TSF; Nowinski, Baker, & Carroll, 1992) treatment approaches.

METHOD

Participants

Data were from 1,726 participants (952 outpatient, 774 aftercare clients) of Project MATCH, a large, national multisite clinical trial that assessed differences in treatment outcomes between three alcohol treatments: CBT, MET, and TSF. Two separate populations of clients were included: 952 outpatient participants who were actively seeking treatment for an ongoing use disorder and 774 aftercare participants who were enrolled in the study after completion of an inpatient or intensive day treatment (Project MATCH Research Group, 1997). Details of the inclusion and exclusion criteria are available in many publications (e.g., Project MATCH Research Group, 1997). In summary, participants were required to (a) have a *Diagnostic and Statistical Manual of Mental Disorders* (3rd ed., rev.; American Psychiatric Association, 1987) diagnosis of alcohol abuse or dependence; (b) indicate alcohol as the primary drug of abuse; (c) have maintained active drinking during the 3 months prior to treatment entry; (d) be 18 years of age or older; (e) have a minimum of a sixth-grade reading level; and (f) have an absence of legal, probation, or parole requirements. Exclusion criteria were current drug dependence other than alcohol, intravenous drug use during the 6 months prior to the study, and symptoms of acute psychosis and severe organic impairment. If necessary, participants were detoxified prior to treatment entry. Demographic characteristics are described in Table 19.1.

Measures

Neuropsychological Tests

Assessments included the Vocabulary and Abstraction subtests of the Shipley Institute of Living Scale (SILS; Zachary, 1986), Parts A and B of the

TABLE 19.1
Demographic Characteristics of the Project MATCH Participants

Variable	Outpatient (n = 952)	Aftercare (n = 774)	Total sample (N = 1,726)
Age (years)	38.88 ± 10.72	41.91 ± 11.11	40.24 ± 10.99
Education (years)	13.44 ± 2.15	13.08 ± 2.05	13.28 ± 2.11
Gender (%)			
Men	72	80	76
Women	28	20	24
Race–ethnicity (%)			
White	82	81	82
African American	6	15	10
Hispanic–Latino	12	4	8

Note. Age and education values are *M*s ± *SD*s.

Trail Making Test (TMT-A, TMT-B; Reitan & Wolfson, 1985), and the Symbol Digit Modalities Test (SDMT; Smith, 1982). Although the battery was brief, the tests are reliable, valid, and sensitive to cerebral dysfunction and brain damage (Lezak, 1995; Spreen & Strauss, 1998). These tests assess the following important areas of functioning impaired in samples with substance use disorders: abstraction, cognitive flexibility, working memory, and psychomotor processing speed (Knight & Longmore, 1994; Nixon, 1995). Raw SILS and SDMT accuracy scores and TMT time (in seconds) scores were analyzed.

Psychopathology

Diagnoses of mood, anxiety, and antisocial personality disorder (ASPD) were obtained with the Computerized Diagnostic Interview Schedule (Robins, Helzer, Cottler, & Goldring, 1989) and coded as 0 or 1 to indicate absence or presence of disorder, respectively. The psychiatric severity composite score was from the Addiction Severity Index (McLellan, Luborski, Woody, & O'Brien, 1980). Depression symptoms were assessed with the Beck Depression Inventory (BDI; Beck, Rush, Shaw, & Emery, 1979).

Medical Problems

A composite score was constructed on the basis of the sum of abnormal results from five blood and urine tests used to detect signs of liver, blood, kidney, and connective tissue disease (1 for each abnormal test result, 0 for each normal result). Abnormal test results suggest physiological dysfunction or medical illness that may interfere with cognitive ability and recovery of ability (Lehman, Pilich, & Andrews, 1993; Marsano, 1994).

Family History of Alcoholism

Familial alcoholism history was determined from the family history section of the Addiction Severity Index (McLellan et al., 1992) and coded as 1 for a positive family history and 0 for a negative family history in all first-degree relatives.

Quantity of Alcohol Consumed

Drinking data were collected using the Form 90 (Miller, 1996; Miller & Del Boca, 1994). The total number of alcoholic drinks consumed in the 3 months prior to treatment entry was the baseline measure, and the total number of alcoholic drinks consumed between baseline and the 15-month evaluation was the follow-up measure.

Procedure

Participants who met all screening criteria and provided informed consent were scheduled for three intake assessments during which neuropsychological tests and risk covariate measures were administered. Participants then were randomly assigned to enter one of three 12-week treatments for alcohol use disorders. The Form 90 data were administered at all five follow-up assessments. Neuropsychological test, medical test, and BDI data were used from the 15-month follow-up (see Project MATCH Research Group, 1997, for detailed procedures).

Data Analysis

Mplus (Muthén & Muthén, 1998) was used to simultaneously estimate model parameters in both outpatient and aftercare samples from raw data with a maximum likelihood approach with missing data assumed to be missing at random (Little & Rubin, 1987). A full information covariance matrix, in which all participants were included, was analyzed to minimize bias (Allison, 2002; Kline, 1998; Naehri, Laaksonen, Hietala, Ahonen, & Lyyti, 2001). All outpatients and all but 1 aftercare participant completed the initial neuropsychological assessment; 827 (87%) outpatient and 663 (86%) aftercare participants also completed the follow-up assessment. Comparison of participants who did and did not complete the follow-up assessment revealed no significant differences on the intake neuropsychological measures or selected demographic variables. The largest source of missing data was a medical test result, which was missing for 392 and 357 participants at treatment entry and 15 months, respectively.

Confirmatory factor analysis was used to examine three alternative measurement models of neuropsychological ability on the basis of conceptual models and a consideration of the common measures in this and earlier studies (Bates et al., 2002; Fals-Stewart & Bates, 2003). The fit of an inclusive one-factor model of general cognitive ability (SILS Vocabulary, SILS Abstraction, SDMT, TMT-A, and TMT-B) was contrasted with the fit of a one-factor model of executive cognitive ability (SILS Abstraction, SDMT, and TMT-B), and a two-factor model of executive ability (SILS Abstraction, TMT-B) and psychomotor speed (SDMT, TMT-A).

We examined whether the neuropsychological measurement model was invariant over time (treatment entry, 15 months) and across outpatient and aftercare samples. Because increases in performance due to practice are test specific, practice effects were reflected in the model as changes in the intercepts of individual tests over time. Therefore, the contribution of practice to increased performance at 15 months was examined by testing for significant decreases in model fit when intercepts were constrained to be equal across time. Changes in performance due to recovery of underlying ability were reflected in changes in means of the latent ability factors. Cognitive recovery was thus defined by significant changes (increases) in the mean of the latent ability factors across time while constraining factor loadings and intercepts to be equal across time.

Structural equation path modeling was then used to determine the amount of true variance in neuropsychological ability at treatment entry and in change in ability over time that was associated with risk factors. Taking individual differences in risk covariates into account, we explored differences in initial cognitive ability and changes in ability over time in the three treatment approaches. Treatments (TSF, CBT, and MET) were dummy coded, with TSF designated as the reference group to which initial ability and recovery in CBT and MET were compared. Thus, by controlling for the associations of multiple risk correlates and by accounting for measurement error and test-specific variance in performance, the structural equation modeling approach potentially allows results to generalize beyond the specific tests that are used to assess ability within a given neuropsychological domain (e.g., executive function).

RESULTS AND DISCUSSION

Table 19.2 shows mean scores and standard deviations for each neuropsychological test. Mean scores, standard deviations, and frequencies for the other measures are provided in Tables 19.3 and 19.4.

502 *BATES ET AL.*

TABLE 19.2
Means and Standard Deviations of Raw Neuropsychological Test Scores

Test	Outpatient		Aftercare		Total sample	
	M	*SD*	*M*	*SD*	*M*	*SD*
Treatment entry	(*n* = 952)		(*n* = 773)		(*N* = 1,725)	
SILS–Abstraction	26.40	8.63	23.60	9.25	25.15	9.02
SILS–Vocabulary	30.72	5.25	29.63	5.25	30.23	5.27
Trail Making, Part A	30.79	11.50	37.21	19.15	33.67	15.73
Trail Making, Part B	72.53	33.39	87.86	47.73	79.42	41.17
SDMT	50.56	9.70	45.99	10.78	48.52	10.45
15 Months	(*n* = 827)		(*n* = 660)		(*N* = 1,487)	
SILS–Abstraction	27.59	8.53	24.29	9.72	26.13	9.22
SILS–Vocabulary	30.94	5.48	29.61	5.56	30.35	5.56
Trail Making, Part A	27.97	10.39	36.01	17.02	31.54	14.30
Trail Making, Part B	68.08	31.12	83.74	41.76	75.05	37.06
SDMT	51.91	10.05	46.23	11.00	49.39	10.85

Note. SILS = Shipley Institute of Living Scale; SDMT = Symbol Digit Modalities Test.

Neuropsychological Measurement Model

As can be seen from the model fit statistics in Table 19.5, both the one-factor general ability model that included all five tests and the two-factor model (executive, psychomotor speed) fit the data poorly. The alternative one-factor model of executive cognitive ability that included SILS Abstraction, TMT-B, and the SDMT provided a close fit to the data across time and samples. The chi-square statistic was significant, likely due to the large sample size, in view of all other fit indices that exceeded the cutoffs recommended as indicating close fit (Hu & Bentler, 1999; Yu & Muthén, 2002). Figure 19.1 shows the measurement model for outpatient and aftercare samples at baseline and 15 months. The latent executive function factor can be interpreted as supporting abstract reasoning, working memory, set shifting, cognitive flexibility, and the initiation and regulation of action. Executive functions are necessary for abstraction and novel problem solving in the intellectual arena and are also crucial to self-regulation and social problem solving (Damasio & Anderson, 2003; Stuss & Benson, 1986).

Constraining the test intercepts to be equal across time did not cause a significant decrease in model fit ($p < .05$), suggesting the absence of practice effects on performance across 15 months. Yet, within this constrained model, the outpatient sample had significantly higher latent ability levels than the aftercare sample at both assessment times (treatment entry: 0.000 [outpatient], −0.952 [aftercare]; 15 months: 0.342 [outpatient], −0.784 [aftercare]; $p < .05$). This finding replicates and extends the greater severity of deficit previously noted in the aftercare sample at treatment entry (Donovan et al., 2001).

TABLE 19.3

Risk Factor Predictors of Neuropsychological Ability

Predictor	Outpatient			Aftercare		
	n	*M*	*SD*	*n*	*M*	*SD*
No. of standard drinks consumed						
3 months before treatment entry	952	1,056.87	815.86	774	1,845.72	1,434.72
Treatment entry to 15 months	830	989.42	1,318.18	618	916.17	1,707.74
Medical test results						
At treatment entry	943	1.81	1.02	391	1.92	1.05
At 15 months	745	0.71	1.03	624	0.89	1.16
BDI score						
At treatment entry	896	9.84	7.97	722	10.57	8.56
At 15 months	825	7.09	7.65	680	8.97	9.13

Note. The number of standard drinks consumed was derived from the Form 90. Medical test results are the sum of abnormal results from five tests used to detect signs of liver, blood, kidney, and connective tissue disease. BDI = Beck Depression Inventory.

TABLE 19.4
Baseline Prevalence of Psychiatric Disorders and Family History of Alcohol Use Disorders

Variable (%)	Outpatient ($n = 882$)	Aftercare ($n = 750$)	Total sample ($N = 1,632$)
Mood disorder	30.57	36.05	33.02
Anxiety disorder	34.14	45.61	39.28
ASPD	9.56	15.76	12.34
Positive family history[a]	78.89	74.29	76.83

Note. Mood, anxiety, and antisocial personality disorder (ASPD) diagnoses were obtained with the Computerized Diagnostic Interview Schedule. Positive history of familial alcoholism (first-degree relatives) was obtained from the family history section of the Addiction Severity Index.
[a]Outpatient group, $n = 939$; aftercare group, $n = 761$; total sample, $N = 1,700$.

The increase in the latent means across 15 months is statistically significant in both samples ($p < .05$). These significant latent mean increases, combined with the lack of significant change in each test's intercept, support the idea that temporal improvements in executive ability were due to recovery of function, not practice effects. At the same time, the ESs for recovery are small. Although there is significant debate within the field as to how to best derive clinical significance of neuropsychological data (e.g., Jacobson, Roberts, Berns, & McGlinchey, 1999), researchers commonly use approaches such as measuring ES or using cutoff values based on confidence intervals. Unfortunately, established measures of clinical significance use manifest, rather than latent, variables. Despite this complication, the small ESs found here suggest that at the level of the group mean, changes in the latent executive ability factor do not represent clinically significant increases over time.

TABLE 19.5
Goodness-of-Fit Statistics for Three Measurement Models and One Structural Model

Model	One factor: General cognitive	Two factor: Executive function and speed	One factor: Executive function	Risk-factor path model
χ^2	420.611	1,183.303	54.459	559.966
df	18	36	22	246
p	.00	.00	<.01	.00
RMSEA	.16	.19	.04	.04
CI	.15–.18	.18–.20	.03–.06	.03–.04
SRMR	.08	.09	.05	.04
CFI	.86	.85	.99	.96
TLI	.84	.78	.99	.95

Note. RMSEA = root-mean-square error of approximation; CI = 90% confidence interval of the RMSEA; SRMR = standardized root-mean-square residual; CFI = comparative fit index; TLI = Tucker–Lewis Index.

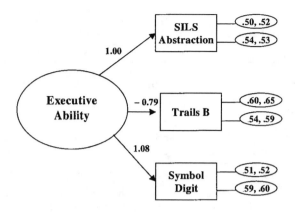

Figure 19.1. Measurement model: baseline and 15 months. Residuals for outpatient sample (baseline, 15 months) are in the top ovals connected to each test on the right side of the diagram; aftercare-sample residuals are in the bottom ovals. Unstandardized factor loadings are shown on the arrows. SILS = Shipley Institute of Living Scale; Trails B = Trail Making Test, Part B; Symbol Digit = Symbol Digit Modalities Test.

Risk Factor Correlates of Latent Neuropsychological Abilities

The initial model included hypothesized direct and indirect paths from the risk covariates to the latent neuropsychological ability factor at baseline and 15-month follow-up, and then nonsignificant and small paths were sequentially eliminated until there was a significant decrease in model fit according to the chi-square difference test. As shown in Table 19.5, the final path model yielded a significant chi-square, but other fit indices suggest a close agreement to the data, with the entire 90% confidence interval for the root-mean-square error of approximation falling below recommended cutoffs for close fit. Figure 19.2 shows the final path model, including unstandardized path coefficients and an indication of the magnitude of estimated ESs (expressed as proportion of variance) for all significant paths. Standard deviations of the latent factors and continuous manifest variables are provided because the effect sizes of unstandardized path coefficients need to be interpreted with respect to the standard deviations of the variables. For ease of interpretation, ESs = .10 were coded as small, ESs = .10 to .24 were coded as medium, and ESs = .25 and greater were coded as large (Murphy & Myors, 2004). With one exception (gender effect on standard drinks following treatment entry in aftercare), all paths were replicated across samples. With three exceptions (paths with dual coefficients), the absolute magnitude of the coefficients was replicated across samples (constraining the path coefficients to be equal across samples did not cause a significant increase in chi-square). Replication of the pattern and magnitude of the paths across independent samples supports the reliability of the results.

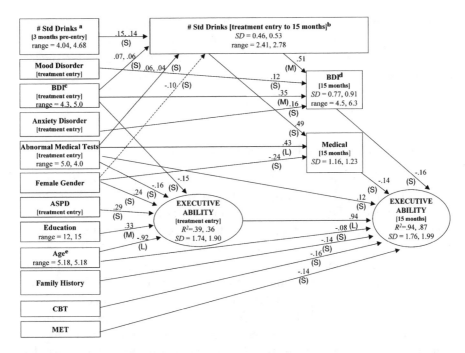

Figure 19.2. Risk factor path model. All significant paths were replicated across outpatient (OP) and aftercare (AC) samples with the exception of the path from female gender to alcohol consumption (dashed line). When unstandardized OP and AC path coefficients or standard deviations differed, the OP value is listed first. For dichotomous variables, the unstandardized path coefficients represent the difference between the ability means of the two groups. The point ranges of continuous variables are shown in parentheses (OP, AC). Paths in which the effect sizes (ESs) < .10 were coded as small (S), ESs = .10 –.24 were coded as medium (M), and ESs = .25 and greater were coded as large (L). Note that several continuous variables were rescaled to facilitate iterative estimation: The number of standard drinks consumed (# Std Drinks)[a] = square root (# Std Drinks/300); # Std Drinks[b] =square root (# Std Drinks [treatment entry to 15 months]/1,800); Beck Depression Inventory (BDI)[c] = BDI/10; BDI[d] = BDI/10; and Age[e] = Age/11. ASPD = antisocial personality disorder; CBT = cognitive–behavioral coping skills therapy; MET = motivational enhancement therapy.

Executive Ability at Baseline

Younger age and higher education were the strongest predictors of executive ability. Depression symptoms, abnormal medical test results, male gender, and the absence of ASPD[1] were associated with poorer ability in both groups, although their unique ESs were much smaller. As anticipated, because of random assignment, no differences in initial level of executive ability were

---

[1] The positive association between ASPD and baseline cognitive ability (ES = small) was unanticipated and may have been due to differential ASPD-subtype representation (Gorton, Swirsky-Sacchetti, Sobel, Samuel, & Gordon, 1999) or concurrent control of risk covariates (Waldstein, Malloy, Stout, & Longabaugh, 1996).

observed between participants in the three alcohol treatments. The present results generally replicate, in a sample of persons with primary alcohol use disorders, previous research using clients with primary drug use disorders or alcohol and drug use disorders that has shown that similar risk covariates account for a notable proportion of true variance in executive ability at addiction treatment entry (e.g., Bates et al., 2002; Fals-Stewart & Bates, 2003).

Mediators and Executive Recovery at 15 Months

Baseline medical test results,[2] older age, and a positive family history status directly predicted less neuropsychological recovery, although their unique ESs were modest. The influence of several other of the risk covariates on recovery was mediated through their influence on cognitive status at treatment entry. Intensity of alcohol consumption between baseline and 15 months in both groups was predicted by alcohol use in the 3 months prior to treatment, depression symptoms at baseline, and abnormal baseline medical test results. This suggests that severity of alcohol dependence, depressive symptoms, and physical health problems are associated with a poorer drinking prognosis for individuals entering alcohol treatment. Greater alcohol consumption across 15 months was a moderately strong predictor of less improvement in medical problems and depressive symptoms, and the influence of alcohol consumption on cognitive recovery was fully mediated by these effects. These findings underscore the importance of treating comorbid health problems and depression in alcohol-treatment clients.

Finally, participants assigned to MET and CBT showed significantly less improvement in latent executive ability compared with those assigned to TSF. Our aim in including treatment modality in the model was exploratory, as the three treatments were neither designed nor modified to affect cognitive recovery. Given the higher rate of abstinence among those in the TSF condition relative to the other treatments (Project MATCH Research Group, 1998), the techniques of TSF may have potentially contributed to cognitive recovery by increasing the likelihood of sustained abstinence and/or by providing a social environment conducive to cognitive rehabilitation. TSF incorporated the principles of Alcoholics Anonymous (AA) and encouraged clients to attend daily AA meetings, reinforcing the inherent structure of AA with additional guidance tailored to an individual client's specific needs and challenges. One may speculate that aspects of TSF have a subtle yet positive effect on cognition because TSF attempts to enhance motivation by breaking complex, long-term goals into small manageable subgoals, allowing

---

[2] A nonpredicted positive path between abnormal baseline medical tests and higher cognitive ability at 15 months was significant (ES = small). The emergence of this path in the model most likely indicates that changes in medical test results over time had more influence on executive ability than either baseline or 15-month values alone.

clients to accumulate a history of successes. This technique has been recommended in enhancing treatment adherence among cognitively impaired individuals who may have motivational deficits related to their organic cognitive deficits (Heinssen, 1996; Jeffrey, 1981). The ESs of the statistically significant negative paths from CBT and MET to cognitive ability at 15 months were small, however, suggesting that enhancement of cognitive recovery directly related to participation in TSF was modest at best.

Baseline ability and risk factors together predicted 94% of the variance in executive ability at the 15-month follow-up in the outpatient sample and 87% in the aftercare sample. Baseline ability uniquely accounted for 62% of the variance in executive ability at 15 months. As noted above, the ESs for individual risk covariates and treatments were small (each accounting uniquely for <1% of the variance), yet collectively they accounted for large proportions of the variance in executive ability at 15 months (32% in outpatient group, 25% in aftercare group). Thus, the overall pattern of findings suggests that although the average level of change in executive functioning in the samples was small, multiple risk factors in combination contributed to individual differences in cognitive recovery. That is, risk factors for impairment assessed at treatment entry were indirectly informative about the likelihood of cognitive improvement via relations to baseline ability. Over time, the influence of these factors combined with familial alcoholism history, age, treatment approach, and less than normative improvement in depression and medical problems to influence differential recovery.

It is important to note that these results are limited to executive cognitive ability and may not generalize to other cognitive domains such as memory or verbal abilities. Additional limitations include missing data at follow-up and assessed risk covariates that are not comprehensive. In addition, speculations regarding the advantages of TSF should be considered very cautiously. In view of the small ES of increases in the latent ability mean, the present findings question the extent of normative cognitive recovery that might be expected to occur in a spontaneous fashion following alcohol treatment without cognitive rehabilitation. It is possible that some previous studies overestimated the extent of spontaneous recovery in substance use disordered samples by focusing primarily on the statistical significance of increases in test performance. The modest average recovery found here and the small size of unique treatment effects on recovery point to the need for addiction treatments that are specifically modified or designed to promote cognitive recovery in clients with moderate to severe cognitive impairment. In an earlier study, Fals-Stewart and Lucente (1994) found that patients who received cognitive rehabilitation while in long-term residential substance abuse treatment exhibited an accelerated rate of cognitive recovery early in treatment and better long-term outcomes, suggesting that cognitive rehabilitation may enhance this important aspect of recovery from alcohol and other drug use disorders.

REFERENCES

Allen, D. N., Goldstein, G., & Seaton, B. E. (1997). Cognitive rehabilitation of chronic alcohol abusers. *Neuropsychology Review, 7*, 21–39.

Allison, P. D. (2002). *Missing data.* Thousand Oaks, CA: Sage.

American Psychiatric Association. (1987). *Diagnostic and statistical manual of mental disorders* (3rd ed., rev.). Washington, DC: Author.

Bates, M. E. (1997). Stability of neuropsychological assessments early in alcoholism treatment. *Journal of Studies on Alcohol, 58*, 617–621.

Bates, M. E., & Convit, A. (1999). Neuropsychology and neuroimaging of alcohol and illicit drug abuse. In A. Calev (Ed.), *The assessment of neuropsychological functions in psychiatric disorders* (pp. 373–445). Washington, DC: American Psychiatric Publishing.

Bates, M. E., Labouvie, E. W., & Voelbel, G. T. (2002). Individual differences in latent neuropsychological abilities at addictions treatment entry. *Psychology of Addictive Behaviors, 16*, 35–46.

Beck, A. T., Rush, A. J., Shaw, B. F., & Emery, G. (1979). *Cognitive therapy of depression.* New York: Guilford Press.

Damasio, A. R., & Anderson, S. W. (2003). The frontal lobes. In K. Heilman & E. Valenstein (Eds.), *Clinical neuropsychology* (4th ed., pp. 404–446). New York: Oxford University Press.

Donovan, D. M., Kivlahan, D. R., Kadden, R. M., & Hill, D. (2001). Cognitive impairment as a patient-treatment matching hypothesis. In R. Longabaugh & P. W. Wirtz (Eds.), *Project MATCH monograph series: Vol. 8. Project MATCH hypotheses: Results and causal chain analyses* (pp. 62–81). Rockville, MD: National Institute on Alcohol Abuse and Alcoholism.

Fals-Stewart, W. (1997). Ability of counselors to detect cognitive impairment among substance-abusing patients: An examination of diagnostic efficiency. *Experimental and Clinical Psychopharmacology, 5*, 39–50.

Fals-Stewart, W., & Bates, M. E. (2003). The neuropsychological test performance of drug-abusing patients: An examination of latent cognitive abilities and associated risk factors. *Experimental and Clinical Psychopharmacology, 11*, 34–45.

Fals-Stewart, W., & Lucente, S. (1994). The effect of cognitive rehabilitation on the neuropsychological status of patients in drug abuse treatment who display neurocognitive impairment. *Rehabilitation Psychology, 39*, 75–94.

Fals-Stewart, W., Shanahan, T., & Brown, L. (1995). Treating alcoholism and substance abuse: A neuropsychiatric perspective. *Psychotherapy in Private Practice, 14*, 1–21.

Goldman, M. (1995). Recovery of cognitive functioning in alcoholics—The relationship to treatment. *Alcohol Health & Research World, 19*, 148–154.

Gorton, G. E., Swirsky-Sacchetti, T., Sobel, R., Samuel, S., & Gordon, A. (1999). Neuropsychological functions in personality disorder. In A. Calev (Ed.),

Assessment of neuropsychological functions in psychiatric disorders (pp. 233–280). Washington, DC: American Psychiatric Publishing.

Heinssen, R. K. (1996). The cognitive exoskeleton: Environmental interventions. In P. W. Corrigan & S. C. Yudofsky (Eds.), *Cognitive rehabilitation for neuropsychiatric disorders* (pp. 395–423). Washington, DC: American Psychiatric Publishing.

Hesselbrock, M. N., Weidenman, M. A., & Reed, H. B. (1985). Effect of age, sex, drinking history, and antisocial personality on neuropsychology of alcoholics. *Journal of Studies on Alcohol, 46*, 313–320.

Hu, L.-T., & Bentler, P. M. (1999). Cutoff criteria for fit indexes in covariance structure analysis: Conventional criteria versus new alternatives. *Structural Equation Modeling, 6*, 1–55.

Jacobson, N. S., Roberts, L. J., Berns, S. B., & McGlinchey, J. B. (1999). Methods for defining and determining the clinical significance of treatment effects: Description, application, and alternatives. *Journal of Consulting and Clinical Psychology, 67*, 300–307.

Jeffrey, D. L. (1981). Cognitive clarity: Key to motivation in rehabilitation. *Journal of Rehabilitation, 47*, 33–35.

Kadden, R., Carroll, K., Donovan, D., Cooney, N., Monti, P., Abrams, D., et al. (1995). *Project MATCH monograph series: Vol. 3. Cognitive–behavioral coping skills therapy manual: A clinical research guide for therapists treating individuals with alcohol abuse and dependence*. Rockville, MD: National Institute on Alcohol Abuse and Alcoholism.

Kline, R. B. (1998). *Principles and practices of structural equation modeling*. New York: Guilford Press.

Knight, R. G., & Longmore, B. E. (1994). *Clinical neuropsychology of alcoholism*. Hillsdale, NJ: Erlbaum.

Lehman, L. B., Pilich, A., & Andrews, N. (1993). Neurological disorders resulting from alcoholism. *Alcohol Health and Research World, 17*(4), 305–309.

Lezak, M. D. (1995). *Neuropsychological assessment* (3rd ed.). New York: Oxford University Press.

Little, R., & Rubin, D. (1987). *Statistical analysis with missing data*. New York: Wiley.

Malloy, P., Noel, N., Rogers, S., Longabaugh, R., & Beattie, M. (1989). Risk factors for neuropsychological impairment in alcoholics: Antisocial personality, age, years of drinking, and gender. *Journal of Studies on Alcohol, 50*, 422–426.

Marsano, L. (1994). Alcohol and malnutrition. *Addictions Nursing, 6*, 62–71.

McLellan, A. T., Kushner, H., Metzger, D., Peters, R., Smith, I., Grissom, G., et al. (1992). The fifth edition of the Addiction Severity Index. *Journal of Substance Abuse Treatment, 9*, 199–213.

McLellan, A. T., Luborski, L., Woody, G. E., & O'Brien, C. P. (1980). An improved diagnostic evaluation instrument for substance abuse patients: The Addiction Severity Index. *The Journal of Nervous and Mental Disease, 168*, 26–33.

Miller, W. R. (1996). *Project MATCH monograph series: Vol. 5. Manual for Form 90: A structured assessment interview for drinking and related behaviors*. Rockville, MD: National Institute on Alcohol Abuse and Alcoholism.

Miller, W. R., & Del Boca, F. K. (1994). Measurement of drinking behavior using the Form 90 family of instruments. *Journal of Studies on Alcohol Supplement, 12,* 112–118.

Miller, W. R., Zweben, A., DiClemente, C. C., & Rychtarik, R. G. (1995). *Project MATCH monograph series: Vol. 2. Motivational enhancement therapy manual: A clinical research guide for therapists treating individuals with alcohol abuse and dependence*. Rockville, MD: National Institute on Alcohol Abuse and Alcoholism.

Murphy, K. R., & Myors, B. (2004). *Statistical power analysis* (2nd ed.). Mahwah, NJ: Erlbaum.

Muthén, L., & Muthén, B. (1998). *Mplus: The comprehensive modeling program for applied researchers: User's guide*. Los Angeles: Authors.

Naehri, V., Laaksonen, S., Hietala, R., Ahonen, T., & Lyyti, H. (2001). Treating missing data in a clinical neuropsychological dataset—Data imputation. *Clinical Neuropsychologist, 15,* 380–392.

Nixon, S. J. (1995). Assessing cognitive impairment. *Alcohol Health and Research World, 19,* 97–103.

Nowinski, J., Baker, S., & Carroll, K. (1992). *Project MATCH monograph series: Vol. 1. Twelve-step facilitation therapy manual: A clinical research guide for therapists treating individuals with alcohol abuse and dependence*. Rockville, MD: National Institute on Alcohol Abuse and Alcoholism.

Parsons, O. A. (1998). Neurocognitive deficits in alcoholics and social drinkers: A continuum? *Alcoholism: Clinical and Experimental Research, 22,* 954–961.

Project MATCH Research Group. (1997). Matching alcoholism treatments to client heterogeneity: Project MATCH posttreatment drinking outcomes. *Journal of Studies on Alcohol, 58,* 7–29.

Project MATCH Research Group. (1998). Matching alcoholism treatments to client heterogeneity: Project MATCH three-year drinking outcomes. *Alcoholism: Clinical and Experimental Research, 22,* 1300–1311.

Reitan, R. M., & Wolfson, D. (1985). *The Halstead–Reitan Neuropsychological Battery: Theory and clinical implications*. Tucson, AZ: Neuropsychology Press.

Robins, L., Helzer, J., Cottler, L., & Goldring, E. (1989). *NIMH Diagnostic Interview Schedule: Version III Revised (DIS–III–R), question by question specifications*. St. Louis, MO: Washington University.

Rourke, S. B., & Grant, I. (1999). The interactive effects of age and length of abstinence on the recovery of neuropsychological functioning in chronic male alcoholics: A 2-year follow-up study. *Journal of the International Neuropsychological Society, 5,* 234–246.

Rourke, S. B., & Løberg, T. (1996). The neurobehavioral correlates of alcoholism. In I. Grant & K. M. Adams (Eds.), *Neuropsychological assessment of neuropsychi-*

atric disorders (pp. 423–485). New York: Oxford University Press.

Schafer, K., Butters, N., Smith, T., Irwin, M., Brown, S., Hanger, P., et al. (1991). Cognitive performance of alcoholics: A longitudinal evaluation of the role of drinking history, depression, liver function, nutrition, and family history. *Alcoholism: Clinical and Experimental Research, 15,* 653–660.

Smith, A. (1982). *Symbol Digit Modalities Test (SDMT) manual (revised).* Los Angeles: Western Psychological Services.

Spreen, O., & Strauss, E. (1998). *A compendium of neuropsychological tests: Administration, norms, and commentary* (2nd ed.). New York: Oxford University Press.

Stuss, D. T., & Benson, D. F. (1986). *The frontal lobes.* New York: Raven Press.

Victor, M., & Adams, R. A. (1985). The alcoholic dementias. In J. A. M. Frederiks (Ed.), *Handbook of clinical neurology: Neurobehavioural disorders* (Rev. Series 2, Vol. 46, pp. 335–352). Amsterdam: Elsevier.

Waldstein, S. R., Malloy, P. F., Stout, R., & Longabaugh, R. (1996). Predictors of neuropsychological impairment in alcoholics: Antisocial versus nonantisocial subtypes. *Addictive Behaviors, 21,* 21–27.

Yu, C.-Y., & Muthén, B. (2002). *Evaluation of model fit indices for latent variable models with categorical and continuous variables.* Unpublished manuscript.

Zachary, R. A. (1986). *Shipley Institute of Living Scale: Revised manual.* Los Angeles: Western Psychological Services.

20

ALCOHOL AND TOBACCO CESSATION IN ALCOHOL-DEPENDENT SMOKERS: ANALYSIS OF REAL-TIME REPORTS

NED L. COONEY, MARK D. LITT, JUDITH L. COONEY,
DAVID T. PILKEY, HOWARD R. STEINBERG,
AND CHERYL A. ONCKEN

Many individuals with alcohol problems also smoke cigarettes. Hughes (1995) reviewed 11 studies that examined the prevalence of smoking in alcoholics and found that a median of 83% of alcoholics in these studies were current smokers, compared with 30% in the general population. The negative health consequences of smoking among alcohol and drug abusers are substantial. One longitudinal study has indicated that smoking killed more alcoholics than did alcohol (Hurt et al., 1996).

Studies have examined the efficacy of providing smoking cessation treatment concurrent with initial treatment for alcohol and drug problems. The impact of concurrent smoking treatment on alcohol and drug outcomes was not consistent across studies. Researchers have reported that smoking cessation treatment either did not affect alcohol and drug outcomes (Burling, Burling, & Latini, 2001; Burling, Marshall, & Seidner, 1991; Hurt et al., 1994) or served to improve these outcomes (Bobo, McIlvain, Lando, Walker, &

This research was supported by Grant R01 AA11197 from the National Institute on Alcohol Abuse and Alcoholism, Grant P50 DA13334 from the National Institute on Drug Abuse, and the U.S. Department of Veterans Affairs.

Reprinted from *Psychology of Addictive Behaviors, 21*, 277–286 (2007). Copyright 2007 by the American Psychological Association.

Leed-Kelly, 1998). However, a mandatory smoking ban (Joseph, Nichol, & Anderson, 1993) was associated with worse drug use outcomes, and a recent study comparing concurrent versus delayed smoking intervention found worse drinking outcomes in the concurrent treatment group (Joseph, Willenbring, Nugent, & Nelson, 2004). The lack of consistency among outcome studies suggests a need to focus more carefully on the processes involved in smoking and smoking cessation among treated alcohol dependent smokers.

A number of theories have been advanced to explain the association between smoking and alcohol dependence (Cooney, Cooney, Patten, & George, 2004; Kalman, 1998), including behavioral theories that focus on factors that may underlie relapse after cessation of alcohol and tobacco use. The cross-substance coping response hypothesis (Monti, Rohsenow, Colby, & Abrams, 1995), which is based on a social learning model, postulates that smoking may be used to cope with cravings for alcohol, or drinking may be used to cope with craving for cigarettes. Research on cross-substance coping has yielded mixed results. This theory is supported by questionnaire data from detoxified alcoholics showing that many expected that they would smoke to cope with urges to drink (Monti et al., 1995). Laboratory data contrary to this theory were reported by our research group (Cooney, Cooney, Pilkey, Kranzler, & Oncken, 2003). We examined alcohol-dependent smokers enrolled in alcohol treatment and found that acute cigarette deprivation led to high levels of cigarette craving but no increase in alcohol urges. However, a similar laboratory study conducted with a hazardous drinking, nontreatment seeking sample found that cigarette deprivation was associated with an increased urge to drink (Palfai, Monti, Ostafin, & Hutchison, 2000). Cross-substance coping response theory leads to the testable prediction that, among abstinent alcoholics, smoking occasions are associated with increased alcohol urges prior to smoking and with decreased alcohol urges immediately after smoking.

An alternative theory—cross-substance cue reactivity—is based on classical conditioning principles. Alcohol and tobacco are often consumed together, and thus, repeated pairings of smoking cues with drinking behavior and vice versa are thought to result in these cues acquiring conditioned stimulus properties (Istvan & Matarazzo, 1984). Thus, smoking may come to elicit urges to drink, and drinking may elicit urges to smoke. Laboratory-based studies of alcohol-dependent smokers have supported this theory, with findings that alcohol cue exposure elicits smoking urges (Cooney et al., 2003; Drobes, 2002; Gulliver et al., 1995; Rohsenow et al., 1997). One study also demonstrated that smoking cues elicit alcohol urges (Drobes, 2002). Cross-substance cue reactivity theory would predict that concurrent treatment of smoking and drinking would lead to better alcohol outcomes than would alcohol treatment alone because ex-smokers have less exposure than do continuing smokers to cues that elicit alcohol craving. Another prediction is that continuing smokers experience increased alcohol craving after smoking a cigarette. Note that the cross-substance coping theory and the cross-substance cue reactivity theory lead to opposite predictions for alcoholics concurrently treated for smoking. Cross-substance coping theory predicts that cessation of smoking among abstinent alcoholics would increase alcohol cravings and relapse, whereas the cross-substance cue reactivity theory predicts that smoking cessation would decrease alcohol cravings and relapse.

An additional behavioral theory—the limited strength model (Muraven & Baumeister, 2000)—has relevance for treating alcohol-dependent smokers. This theory postulates that self-control is a limited resource and that exerting self-control may consume self-control strength, thereby reducing the amount of strength available for subsequent self-control efforts. This theory has not been tested in alcohol-dependent smokers, but it was supported in studies of alcohol consumption among moderate drinkers, both in the laboratory (Muraven, Collins, & Nienhaus, 2002) and in the natural environment (Muraven, Collins, Shiffman, & Paty, 2005). This theory leads to the prediction that abstinent alcohol-dependent individuals who have quit smoking and are fighting cigarette cravings may be at greater risk for alcohol relapse.

The present study used Ecological Momentary Assessment (EMA; Shiffman & Stone, 1998) methodology, which is well suited to examine alcohol–tobacco interactions as they occur in the natural environment. Data are collected in real time, avoiding bias introduced with retrospective recall (Shiffman et al., 1997). Participants carry an electronic diary (ED) throughout the day, enhancing ecological validity as data are collected in the natural environment. Problems of faked compliance (Litt, Cooney, & Morse, 1998; Stone, Shiffman, Schwartz, Broderick, & Hufford, 2003) are avoided because each record is electronically date and time stamped by the ED. EMA studies of smokers have demonstrated a strong link between negative affect and smoking relapse (Shiffman, Paty, Gnys, Kassel, & Hickcox, 1996). Alcohol consumption has also been linked with smoking relapse in nonalcoholic smokers (Shiffman et al., 1996).

A cognitive–behavioral model of lapse and relapse (Marlatt & Gordon, 1985) focuses on negative affect, low self-efficacy, and craving as important proximal intrapersonal determinants of first use. Negative affect is often cited as a primary relapse trigger. Low self-efficacy reduces the likelihood that an individual will make an effort to cope with temptation. Craving is a complex construct with physiological, learning, and cognitive determinants (see Supplement 2 of the journal *Addiction*, Volume 95, 2000). Although there is much research on these predictors of relapse (Marlatt & Witkiewitz, 2005), few studies have examined them by using EMA methods.

The present study used EMA methods to investigate alcohol–tobacco interaction processes in the context of a randomized clinical trial of brief versus intensive smoking cessation treatment delivered concurrently with alcohol treatment. The outcomes of this clinical trial will be presented in a subsequent report. This report focuses on the following process questions, which were formulated to test the above-mentioned behavioral theories of alcohol–tobacco interactions: What is the effect of smoking treatment intensity and smoking quit status on the frequency and intensity of alcohol urges? Among continued smokers, are alcohol urges associated with the onset of smoking occasions? Among continued smokers, what is the immediate effect of a smoking episode on alcohol urges? EMA methodology was also used to examine proximal antecedents to the alcohol and tobacco relapses that occurred soon after treatment, comparing the predictive power of smoking and drinking urges with other potential predictors, including negative affect and self-efficacy ratings. These analyses allowed a test of cross-substance relapse predictions, that is, whether smoking urges are predictive of alcohol relapse and whether alcohol urges are predictive of smoking relapse.

METHOD

Participants

This study was approved by the Human Studies Subcommittee of the Veterans Affairs (VA) Connecticut Healthcare System. Participants were recruited from two intensive outpatient substance abuse programs at the VA Connecticut Healthcare System. Nonveteran women recruited from the community were included in the sample to obtain a more representative sample. After beginning treatment in the substance abuse program, individuals were asked whether they would be interested in participating in a research study that would provide them with smoking treatment concurrent with their substance abuse treatment. To be included in the study, participants had to be at least 18 years old, meet *Diagnostic and Statistical Manual of Mental Disorders* (4th ed.; *DSM–IV*; American Psychiatric Association, 1994) criteria for alcohol and nicotine dependence during the past 3 months, be interested in receiving treatment for both alcohol and cigarette use, and smoke at least 10 cigarettes per day.

Exclusion criteria were diagnosis of current opioid dependence, current cannabis abuse or dependence, current intravenous drug use, acute medical or psychiatric disorder requiring treatment, use of medications known to influence alcohol or cigarette urges (naltrexone, disulfiram, bupropion), medical problems or conditions that would contraindicate nicotine patch use, impaired vision or hearing that would interfere with using a hand-held computer, reading ability below the fifth-grade level (Slosson Oral Reading Test; Slosson, 1963), lack of reliable transportation to treatment or excessive commuting distance, unstable housing during the 14 days following treatment, and inability to provide a name of an individual who could be contacted to help locate the participant if he or she was missing at follow-up.

After obtaining written informed consent, 133 individuals enrolled and were randomized to smoking cessation treatment, but 15 dropped out of the study by leaving the substance abuse treatment program early ($n = 12$) or for other reasons ($n = 3$). Thus, 118 individuals were asked to participate in the EMA protocol during the 2 weeks after treatment. Of these, 102 (86%) provided EMA data for analyses, with 16 individuals excluded due to failure to complete any EMA recording.

Measures and Instruments

Baseline Assessment and Sample Characteristics

Recruited individuals were given a screening interview to identify those who were likely to meet criteria for inclusion in the study and to collect basic demographic and clinical information. The substance-related disorders and psychotic screening sections of the Structured Clinical Interview for DSM–IV Axis I Disorders, Patient Edition, Version 2.0 (SCID-I/P; First, Spitzer, Gibbon, & Williams, 1996) were used to determine whether participants met inclusion/exclusion criteria for alcohol dependence, drug dependence, and psychotic disorders. The six-item Fagerström Test for Nicotine Dependence was used to characterize the sample. This scale has an internal consistency reliability of $\alpha = .61$, and its total score has been shown to be closely related to biochemical measures of intensity of smoking (Heatherton, Kozlowski, Frecker, & Fagerström, 1991).

Retrospective Measures of Alcohol and Tobacco Use

Alcohol and cigarette consumption was measured with Form 90 (Miller & Del Boca, 1994), a structured interview that combines the calendar prompts of the Timeline Followback method (Sobell & Sobell, 1992) and the drinking pattern estimation procedures of the Comprehensive Drinker Profile (Marlatt & Miller, 1984). Form 90 was administered at baseline, and a 14-day version (Form 14) was administered at the end of the 14-day EMA data collection period. Participants' self-reports were verified by means of biochemical assessments. Breath tests were used to detect recent alcohol use at baseline and at the post-EMA time points. Expired breath carbon monoxide readings ≤ 10 ppm were considered corroboration of cigarette abstinence. Participants were paid $15 for participation in the baseline and post-EMA interviews.

Design and Procedure

All participants were enrolled in a 3-week intensive outpatient substance abuse treatment program located at one of two VA sites in Connecticut.

Within 1 week of program admission, participants completed baseline assessment measures and then were randomized either to intensive smoking cessation treatment, consisting of behavioral counseling and transdermal nicotine replacement, or to brief smoking cessation advice without nicotine replacement. These interventions were delivered concurrent with the 3-week intensive outpatient program.

Alcohol and Tobacco Treatment

As a platform for the smoking cessation intervention trial, the substance abuse intensive outpatient program provided an initial rehabilitation treatment, utilizing a cognitive–behavioral coping skills approach. Length of stay in the program was 3 weeks, with required program meetings 5 days per week and 5 hours per day. Urine and breath were monitored for drug and alcohol use throughout participation in the program.

The intensive smoking cessation intervention was administered in three 60-minute individual sessions. On the scheduled quit date, participants were provided a 4-week supply of 21-milligram Nicoderm transdermal nicotine patches, followed by prescriptions for 2 weeks at 14 milligrams and 2 weeks at 7 milligrams. The brief smoking cessation advice intervention was based on the recommendations of the Agency for Healthcare Policy and Research (Smoking Cessation Clinical Guideline Panel and Staff, 1996). The smoking cessation therapist saw participants for one 15-min session, followed by a brief 5-minute follow-up appointment within 3 days of the quit date. Nicotine replacement was not offered to participants in this condition.

Ecological Momentary Assessment Protocol

During the 14 days immediately after discharge from the intensive outpatient program, all participants were asked to participate in an EMA protocol, which involved computerized self-monitoring of alcohol urges, smoking urges, smoking behavior, mood state, and alcohol abstinence self-efficacy. Data were recorded on handheld computers that were configured to sample these variables under the following three conditions: (a) immediately prior to cigarette smoking, (b) 5 minutes after the onset of cigarette smoking, and (c) at random time points unrelated to smoking. This EMA sampling strategy thus gathered data on background conditions that change slowly and are assessed using the random time-based strategy and also gathered data on momentary states that change rapidly and are assessed using the event-based strategy linked to before and after smoking episodes (for a discussion of these sampling strategies, see Shiffman, 2005). The 14-day monitoring period was selected to assess processes occurring outside the intensive substance abuse treatment environment, at a time when most participants were expected to be abstinent from alcohol and some participants were expected to be abstinent from cigarettes.

The ED used was a hand-held Psion LZ-64 computer with 32K RAM; a 4-line, 20-character LCD screen; a real-time clock-calendar; an audio speaker; and data-recording capability. Signal-contingent recording occurred by programming the ED to prompt participants on a quasirandom basis four times per day, with one randomly scheduled prompt in each of four 3.5-hour recording time periods (i.e., 8:00 a.m. to 11:30 a.m., 11:30 a.m. to 3:00 p.m., 3:00 p.m. to 6:30 p.m., and 6:30 p.m. to 10:00 p.m.). When recording was inconvenient, participants had the option of delaying responding to the ED signals for either 5 or 15 minutes. Participants met with research staff at the end of each week to upload ED data and to complete other assessments. As an incentive to adhere to the EMA protocol, participants were paid $5.00 for each completed ED assessment day.

Event-contingent recording occurred by instructing participants to initiate an ED recording immediately prior to smoking each cigarette. Only the first cigarette-initiated recording within each of the four recording time periods triggered the full computerized event recording questionnaire; the rest of the cigarette-initiated recordings within a recording time period caused the ED to record the date and time of smoking and then shut off. This was done to minimize burden on the participant. The result of this programming was that participants completed the ED questionnaire on up to four cigarettes per day. Interval-contingent recording was made possible by programming the ED such that for each of those first cigarette-initiated recordings within the four time periods, the computer displayed the full event recording questionnaire and prompted the individual to complete a second full questionnaire 5 min later. This was intended to assess self-report processes during or shortly after a period of smoking. Therefore, up to four occasions per day, full questionnaires were recorded immediately prior to smoking and 5 minutes after the onset of smoking. These event- and interval-contingent recordings provided the before-cigarette and after-cigarette ratings of urge to smoke and urge to drink, which were the basis of our examination of the function of tobacco smoking on alcohol urges. The protocol did not include alcohol-contingent recordings because few drinking episodes were expected to occur during the 2 weeks immediately following intensive alcohol treatment.

For every recording, whether initiated by the participant or by the ED, the participant was prompted to report any occurrence of smoking or drinking behavior within the day and to rate how he or she was feeling "right now" on a series of items on an 11-point Likert-type scale ranging from 0 (*not at all*) to 10 (*very much*). Desire to drink was assessed with the item "Alcohol urge." Alcohol abstinence self-efficacy was assessed with the item "Can resist drinking." Mood state was recorded as a potential antecedent to alcohol and tobacco relapse with 12 items derived from a semantic space analysis of mood adjectives in the circumplex model of mood experience (Larsen & Diener, 1992; Russell, 1980). Mood states were classed along two major dimensions: pleasantness (negative vs. positive) and arousal (high arousal vs. low arousal). Four quadrants of moods were thus created: positive–high arousal items (active, peppy), positive–low arousal (quiet, relaxed), negative–high arousal (nervous, angry) and negative–low arousal (bored, sad). The items were combined by quadrant to yield four reliable mood composites (internal reliability αs = .80). Intercorrelations of mood scores revealed that the four scores were moderately correlated with each other but were not redundant. Negative–high arousal scores and negative–low arousal scores were correlated ($r = .50$), and positive–high arousal scores and positive–low arousal scores were correlated ($r = .41$). As expected, positive and negative moods were modestly and negatively correlated with each other. Given these levels of correlations, in our analyses of the mood data, we regarded problems of multicollinearity as minimal.

RESULTS

The sample ($N = 102$) was 87% male and 13% female. The mean age was 45.9 years (±7.3 years). Race was 66.7% White, 25.5% Black, 2.0% Hispanic, and 2.9% other. Seventy-two percent of the participants were unemployed, and 29.3% were married or were living with a spouse or partner. All met DSM–IV criteria for alcohol and nicotine dependence, drank a mean of 64% of the days during the 3 months prior to seeking treatment at the VA sites, and consumed a mean of 17.4 ($SD = 11.3$) alcoholic drinks per day. They reported a mean of 3.9 prior treatments for alcohol problems ($SD = 6.3$). Participants smoked a mean of 99% of days and a mean of 26.6 cigarettes ($SD = 10.3$) per day during the 3 months prior to seeking treatment. The mean Fagerström Test for Nicotine Dependence score was 5.3 ($SD = 2.2$). They reported smoking for a mean of 28.4 years ($SD = 9.6$) and attempted to quit a mean of 4.0 times ($SD = 5.1$). Participants met lifetime criteria for other substance dependence as follows: cocaine (32.8%), opioid (9.6%), cannabis (4.0%), stimulant (8.0%), hallucinogen (1.6%), and sedative/hypnotic/anxiolytic (5.8%).

Posttreatment Abstinence Rates by Treatment Condition: Drinking and Smoking

Short-term drinking and smoking abstinence was examined with retrospective reports from the 2-week, post-ED assessment. Drinking data were obtained for 98% of cases, and missing cases were treated as nonabstinent. At the post-ED assessment, the 14-day point prevalence alcohol abstinence rate was 90.2% across smoking treatment conditions. Logistic regression analysis, conducted with pretreatment drinking level as a continuous covariate, revealed that alcohol abstinence rates did not differ significantly by smoking treatment condition.

Fourteen-day point prevalence cigarette abstinence was also examined at the post-ED time point, with abstinence verified by carbon monoxide levels of < 10 ppm. Missing cases were treated as nonabstinent. The abstinence rate was 5.8% (3/52) for the brief treatment and 24.0% (12/50) for the intensive treatment (12/50). Logistic regression analysis indicated that this was a significant treatment effect ($b = 1.65$, $SE = 0.68$, $OR = 5.63$, $CI = 1.36–19.74$).

Influence of Smoking Treatment on Urge to Drink

Participants who provided EMA data responded to 73% of the random prompts by the ED. Those who reported cigarette smoking during the EMA assessment period initiated a mean of 15.7 ($SD = 16.1$) precigarette assessments and 15.7 ($SD = 16.0$) postcigarette assessments. Examination of the distribution of urge-to-drink ratings revealed that this variable was not normally distributed but, rather, was highly skewed (skewness = 3.63), with a mode and median of 0 and scattered recordings above 0. To accommodate this distribution, urge to drink was recomputed as a dichotomous variable (positive urge rating) in which any urge recording above 0 was coded as 1 and scores of 0 were coded as 0.

A random effects logistic regression, or generalized estimating equations analysis (GEE; Proc Genmod, SAS Institute), was conducted to determine whether smoking cessation treatment condition influenced occurrence of any positive alcohol urge (i.e., any urge to drink recording = 0). Time was modeled as three fixed factors: Week number, Day number crossed with Week, and Recording Number crossed with Day. An autoregressive covariance structure (AR 1) was adopted for the repeated measures model. Results indicate that smoking treatment condition did not influence likelihood of randomly prompted ED ratings of positive alcohol urges ($Z = 0.46$, $p > .60$).

Association of Smoking Status With Urge to Drink

A GEE model was conducted as described above, with the exception that smoking status during the 2-week monitoring period (smoking [$n = 83$] vs. abstinent [$n = 19$]) was substituted in the models for the treatment condition variable. Results indicate that smoking status was not associated with occurrence of randomly prompted ED ratings of positive drinking urges ($Z = -0.75$, $p > .40$).

Influence of Cigarette Smoking Episode on Urge to Drink

Alcohol-dependent individuals who stop drinking may use cigarettes to help control urges to drink. This hypothesis was tested by selecting those records in which a participant initiated a recording at the onset of smoking and in which the person was subsequently prompted and responded 5 minutes after the onset of smoking. A total of 79 participants provided pre- and postcigarette ED recordings. A logistic regression analysis was conducted, in which occurrence of positive alcohol urge recording was examined as a function of recording type (onset of smoking vs. 5 minutes after onset of smoking), treatment condition, and Recording Type × Treatment Condition. Number of records completed by a participant was used as a covariate. Results indicate a significant main effect for recording type ($B = .39$; $SE = .22$; Wald $\chi^2 = 4.18$; $OR = 1.64$; $CI = 1.02–2.27$; $p < .05$) and a significant effect for number of recordings made ($B = .007$; $SE = .001$; Wald $\chi^2 = 49.64$; $OR = 1.10$; $CI = 1.00 –1.11$; $p < .01$) but no main effect for smoking cessation treatment condition or for Recording Type × Treatment Condition. Examination of predicted probabilities indicated that probability of positive urge to drink was higher after smoking a cigarette than it was before smoking (see Figure 20.1). The absolute probability of urge to drink, however, was low both before and after smoking. The analysis was repeated with only those records in which participants rated the situation as one in which it was socially acceptable to drink. The results were comparable to those presented for the entire sample of records.

To ensure that effects on drinking urges were not due to passage of time, we conducted an analysis that examined the effects of time of day within recording day on probability of reporting positive drinking urges. Time of day had no effect on probability of positive urges ($B = 0.01$; $SE = 0.02$; $Z = 0.74$).

A similar analysis was used to compare probability of positive urge to drink during random (computer-prompted) recordings versus cigarette-onset

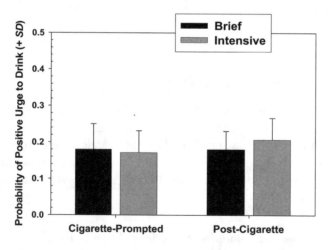

Figure 20.1. Mean probability of positive urge to drink at smoking onset and after smoking episodes by treatment condition.

recordings. Records were selected such that the random recording and the cigarette-onset recording had to occur during the same time period on the same day (to control for variation attributable to time of day). The number of random recordings was comparable for the two treatment conditions (1,975 among brief treatment participants and 1,965 among intensive treatment participants). However, the number of cigarette-onset recordings differed greatly by condition (1,665 for brief treatment participants vs. 664 for intensive treatment participants), $\chi^2(1) = 274.54$, $p < .001$. The logistic regression analysis showed no effect on the likelihood of positive urge to drink attributable to recording type (random vs. cigarette onset) and no effect for smoking treatment condition. There was, however, a significant Recording Type × Treatment Condition interaction ($B = .65$; $SE = .21$; Wald $\chi^2 = 9.23$; $OR = 1.91$; $CI = 1.26 –1.90$; $p < .01$). The nature of this interaction is shown in Figure 20.2. Chi-square analysis of simple effects indicated that, for those in the brief treatment, the likelihood of positive urge to drink was not significantly higher during the random prompts than during the cigarette-onset records. For those in the intensive treatment, however, the likelihood of positive urge to drink was significantly higher during the cigarette-onset records than during the random records, $\chi^2(1) = 15.84$, $p < .001$. As in the previous analysis, the mean probability of positive urge to drink assessed at random or cigarette-prompted recordings was fairly low (no higher than 18%). This analysis was repeated by selecting only those records in which participants rated the situation as one in which it was socially acceptable to drink, and the results were comparable to those presented for the entire sample of situations.

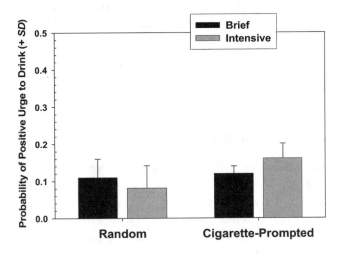

Figure 20.2. Mean rated urge to drink at smoking onset and at random, nonsmoking time points by treatment condition.

Momentary Predictors of First Drink

The design of the present study allowed us to examine the momentary predictors of both the first drink and the first cigarette reported by participants during the 14-day EMA monitoring period, using procedures similar to those described by O'Connell, Schwartz, Gerkovich, Bott, and Shiffman (2004). Of the 102 participants who received smoking treatment and provided EMA data, 13 reported their first posttreatment drink as occurring during the EMA monitoring period. These participants reported a mean of 28 days ($SD = 10.4$) abstinent from alcohol prior to the start of EMA data collection. A random effects logistic regression analysis was conducted for these 13 participants, using the first ED record in which alcohol use was reported as the index case. Those records from the ED recording period immediately preceding the recording period in which a first drink was reported provided the momentary predictor variables. These lead recordings were completed up to 3.5 hours prior to the recordings that reported the first drink. Comparison records were all other signal-contingent records from the same 13 participants, except those in which any drinking was reported.

Momentary predictors included urge to smoke, urge to drink, alcohol abstinence self-efficacy, and the four mood composite measures: negative–high arousal mood, negative–low arousal mood, positive–high arousal mood, and positive–low arousal mood. In addition, some situational constraints on drinking were also tested, including time of day, weekend versus weekday recording, and social appropriateness of drinking ("Is drinking socially acceptable here?"). These recordings occurred within the same day, anywhere from 3 hours to 15 minutes prior to the occurrence of drinking. Between-subjects predictors were smoking treatment condition and baseline drinking level (percent days abstinent). Results of this analysis are shown in Table 20.1.

The results indicate that urge to smoke was predictive of occurrence of first drink and that alcohol abstinence self-efficacy was protective. Interestingly, prior ratings of positive urge to drink and negative affect were not predictive of occurrence of first drink.

Momentary Predictors of First Cigarette

To detect antecedents of the first cigarette smoked, it was necessary to select those participants who first had stopped smoking. Of the 102 persons who received smoking treatment and provided EMA data, 31 patients reported being abstinent from smoking for at least 2 days prior to EMA monitoring, and of those, 12 reported onset of smoking during the EMA monitoring period. These participants reported a mean of 5.4 days ($SD = 4.5$) abstinent from cigarettes prior to the beginning of the EMA period. The first-cigarette records from these 12 participants served as the index cases.

TABLE 20.1
Analysis of Logistic Regression Parameter Estimates

Predictor	Estimate	Odds ratio	SE	95% confidence limits	Z
Baseline Drinking	−0.46	0.63	1.23	0.06–7.10	0.14
Time of Day 1	−0.79	2.28	1.15	0.23–22.36	0.49
Time of Day 2	−1.62	—	0.96	—	0.09
Time of Day 3	−0.63	—	0.91	—	0.49
Time of Day 4	0.00	—	—	—	—
Day of recording	0.09	1.09	0.03	0.91–1.16	1.50
Weekday	−0.08	0.92	0.79	0.20–4.33	−0.10
Weekend	0.00	—	—	—	—
Condition 1 (brief)	0.71	2.03	0.79	0.43–9.59	0.79
Condition 2 (intensive)	0.00	—	—	—	—
Urge to drink	−1.54	1.22	1.15	0.23–2.04	1.79
Urge to smoke	0.22	1.24	0.12	1.19–1.58	3.18*
Alcohol abstinence self–efficacy	−0.18	0.83	0.10	0.69–0.98	−3.54*
Socially acceptable to drink (no)	−0.51	0.60	0.58	0.19–1.87	−0.88
Socially acceptable to drink (yes)	0.00	—	—	—	—
Negative–high arousal mood	0.19	1.22	0.18	0.86–1.73	1.10
Negative–low arousal mood	−0.06	0.94	0.30	0.52–1.70	−0.20
Positive–high arousal mood	0.11	1.12	0.22	0.72–1.75	0.50
Positive–low arousal mood	−0.05	0.95	0.11	0.77–1.17	−0.51

Note. Dependent variable = lag of occurrence of first drink in EMA monitoring period (N_{events} = 13). Reference records = all other nondrinking records from the same participants ($N_{reference}$ = 779).
*p < .05.

Comparison records were all other signal-contingent records from the same 12 participants, except for those records in which smoking was recorded. As with the analysis of antecedents to first drink, this analysis was a within-person comparison.

Logistic regression was used to evaluate the momentary predictors of occurrence of the first cigarette of the EMA monitoring period using assessments obtained in the recording prior to that in which the first cigarette was reported. These recordings occurred within the same day, anywhere from 3 hours to 15 minutes prior to the occurrence of smoking. Momentary predictors included urge to smoke, urge to drink, alcohol abstinence self-efficacy, and the four mood composite measures: negative–high arousal mood, negative–low arousal mood, positive–high arousal mood, and positive–low arousal mood. As with the analyses of predictors of first drink, potential situational constraints on smoking were also examined, including time of day, day of recording period, weekend versus weekday, and social acceptability of drinking in that situation. Between-subjects (Level 2) predictors were smoking treatment condition and baseline drinking level (percentage of days abstinent).

Because of the small number of events (first cigarettes), the predictors were evaluated in sets. First, the between-subjects predictors were tested: smoking cessation treatment condition and baseline drinking level. Second, the continuous, motivation-related variables were tested: urge to smoke, urge to drink, and alcohol abstinence self-efficacy. The third set consisted of the affective variables, negative–high arousal mood, negative–low arousal mood, positive–high arousal mood, and positive–low arousal mood. The fourth set consisted of the situational constraint variables.

As shown in Table 20.2, baseline drinking level (percent days abstinent) and smoking cessation treatment condition emerged as predictors of first cigarette such that less baseline drinking and assignment to the more intensive smoking treatment were protective against lapsing. Urge to smoke and negative–high arousal affect also emerged as predictors of first cigarette. A final analysis was conducted in which only baseline drinking, treatment condition, smoking urge, and negative–high arousal mood were included. In this analysis, only urge to smoke emerged as a significant predictor of smoking. Treatment condition, negative–high arousal mood, and baseline drinking dropped out. Situational variables such as time of day did not emerge as significant in the prediction of first cigarette.

DISCUSSION

This study examined alcohol–tobacco interaction processes immediately after concurrent alcohol and tobacco treatment. Analyses of alcohol craving across the 2-week posttreatment ED recording period revealed that

TABLE 20.2

Analyses of Logistic Regression Parameter Estimates

Predictor	Estimate	Odds ratio	SE	95% confidence limits	Z
Set 1					
Baseline percent days abstinent	-0.13	0.88	0.06	0.78–0.98	-2.26*
Treatment Condition 1 (brief)	0.13	0.88	0.02	0.84–0.92	5.87***
Treatment Condition 2 (intensive)	0.00	—	—	—	—
Set 2					
Urge to drink	0.09	1.14	1.65	0.71–2.89	0.98
Urge to smoke	0.17	1.19	0.05	1.08–1.30	3.75***
Alcohol abstinence self–efficacy	0.63	1.88	0.72	0.89–3.97	1.65
Set 3					
Negative–high arousal	0.47	1.60	0.15	1.18–2.16	3.03***
Negative–low arousal	-0.19	0.82	0.16	0.60–1.13	-1.21
Positive–high arousal	-0.32	0.72	0.20	0.49–1.07	-1.64
Positive–low arousal	0.09	1.09	0.11	0.87–1.37	0.79
Set 4					
Time of Day 1	-0.74	0.24	1.15	0.03–1.79	-0.65
Time of Day 2	0.68	—	0.78	—	0.87
Time of Day 3	-0.81	—	1.31	—	-0.62
Time of Day 4	0.00	—	—	—	—
Day number of period	-0.04	0.96	0.08	0.83–1.12	-0.48
Weekday	0.21	1.23	0.82	0.25–6.13	0.26
Weekend	0.00	—	—	—	—
Socially acceptable to drink (no)	0.07	1.08	0.80	0.22–5.15	0.09
Socially acceptable to drink (yes)	0.00	—	—	—	—
Set 5					
Percent days abstinent	2.37	10.67	1.43	0.65–175.40	1.66
Treatment condition (brief)	0.51	1.67	0.79	0.35–7.92	0.65
Treatment condition (intensive)	0.00	—	—	—	—
Negative–high arousal	0.28	1.22	0.21	0.82–1.83	0.98
Urge to smoke	1.10	1.19	0.10	1.17–1.35	2.30*

Note. Dependent variable = lag of occurrence of first cigarette in EMA monitoring period (N_{events} = 12). Reference records = all other non-smoking records from the same participants ($N_{reference}$ = 1,762).

*$p < .05$.   ***$p < .001$.

the frequency of alcohol craving was low, with no significant differences between smokers and nonsmokers or between those in brief or intensive smoking treatment. Other researchers have also reported low levels of reported alcohol craving on EMA measures obtained from treated alcohol-dependent individuals (Krahn, Bohn, Henk, Grossman, & Gosnell, 2005; Litt, Cooney, & Morse, 2000). Floor effects may have been operating to reduce the sensitivity of an alcohol-craving measure to smoking cessation treatment or tobacco abstinence effects in a sample of intensively treated alcohol-dependent individuals. However, hypotheses that smoking cessation would raise the level of alcohol craving, as predicted by cross-substance coping response theory, or lower the level of alcohol craving, as predicted by cross-substance cue reactivity theory, were not supported. This finding is consistent with the results of a laboratory study in this population (Cooney et al., 2003), which looked for, but did not find, evidence that acute cigarette deprivation elicited changes in alcohol urges.

One strength of EMA methodology is its ability to examine proximal antecedents and consequences of important events. We hypothesized that smoking a cigarette might have an immediate impact on alcohol urges. Results reveal a modest increase in the occurrence of alcohol urges from pre- to postsmoking. This finding was replicated when we selected only ED records that were made in situations in which it was socially acceptable to drink. This subanalysis provided a stronger test of hypotheses than did the analysis conducted across all situations because drinking was not constrained by the environment. A possible limitation of this analysis is that we were unable to determine whether an increase in drinking urge occurred simply as a result of repeated recording (5 minutes apart) and regardless of whether a cigarette was smoked in the interim. However, we consider this possibility unlikely. The finding of increased alcohol urge after smoking does not support the notion of smoking as an effective cross-substance coping response in which smoking is an effective way to cope with craving for alcohol. However, results are consistent with findings from laboratory studies of cross-substance cue reactivity in which smoking cues elicit urges to drink in alcohol-dependent smokers (Drobes, 2002) or urges to use drugs in drug dependent smokers (Taylor, Harris, Singleton, Moolchan, & Heishman, 2000). These results strengthen the rationale for recommending smoking cessation for individuals during an early phase of alcohol recovery.

EMA methodology was also used to examine the antecedents to smoking episodes, comparing ratings obtained at the onset of multiple smoking episodes with ratings obtained at randomly sampled nonsmoking occasions. Overall, there was no significant difference between the frequency of alcohol urge reports obtained at the onset of smoking occasions compared with nonsmoking occasions, and this finding was replicated in a subanalysis using only recordings obtained from situations that were rated as socially acceptable for drinking. This is another set of findings that failed to support the cross-substance coping hypothesis, which predicted that smoking onset would be associated with alcohol urges. An unpredicted, statistically significant interaction effect was found, indicating that those in the intensive smoking treatment reported higher alcohol urges at the onset of smoking compared with random, nonsmoking occasions. This suggests that alcohol urges were prompting smoking behavior, which is consistent with the cross-substance coping model, but it is not clear why this process would be limited to those who received intensive smoking treatment.

Another strength of EMA methodology is its ability to examine the predictors of relapse episodes using randomly sampled assessments obtained in the hours prior to the reported first use. Note that these assessments reflect background changes in subjective states preceding drinking lapse but not the momentary state immediately proximal to the lapse. High ratings of confidence in one's ability to resist drinking predicted lower likelihood of subsequent drinking lapse and, surprisingly, high ratings of urge to smoke predicted higher likelihood of drinking lapse. Both high urge to smoke and low confidence in ability to resist drinking can be viewed as markers of depleted self-control strength, so this finding could be seen as supporting the limited strength theory that exercising self-control over cigarette smoking consumes self-control strength, thereby reducing the amount of strength available for subsequent efforts to exercise control over alcohol craving (Muraven & Baumeister, 2000). However, this interpretation is complicated by the fact that 10 of the 13 participants who reported drinking lapses also reported smoking prior to the drinking lapse. Future research would need to follow a larger sample of alcohol- and cigarette-abstinent individuals to provide a stronger test of how alcohol–tobacco interactions influence the relapse process.

Also unexpected was the finding that background changes in alcohol urge and negative affect recorded in the hours preceding a relapse did not predict drinking relapse episodes. Krahn et al. (2005) also found that background levels of alcohol craving and negative affect assessed with EMA did not predict alcohol relapse. One possibility is that these states do increase immediately prior to alcohol relapse but that the changes are too short lived to be detected hours before the onset of drinking. Another possibility is that automatic processes, rather than conscious alcohol craving, are determining initial alcohol relapse (Tiffany, 1990).

Smoking lapse episodes also were predicted by higher ED-recorded urge to smoke as well as by higher negative, high–arousal mood (nervous, angry) recorded in the hours before the lapse. Studies of nonalcoholic smokers attempting smoking cessation also found that smoking relapse was predicted by smoking urge (Killen & Fortmann, 1997; Shiffman et al., 1996; West, Hajek, & Belcher, 1989) and by negative affect (Shiffman et al., 1996). The mechanism underlying these findings cannot be determined from the present study but may involve a conditioned association of negative affect and smoking, efforts by individuals to use smoking to cope with negative affect, or affective disruption leading to a reduction in self-control strength (Muraven & Baumeister, 2000).

Regarding clinical implications, there appears to be no effect of concurrent intensive smoking cessation treatment on alcohol craving in the weeks soon after treatment. Real-time, in vivo assessment found a modest increase in alcohol craving immediately after smoking episodes. These process findings suggest no evidence of harmful effects of adding concurrent smoking cessation to alcohol treatment. On the other hand, smoking urges reported at randomly timed in vivo assessments were predictive of imminent alcohol relapse. Taken together, these results suggest that practitioners can recommend concurrent smoking cessation for alcohol-dependent smokers but should use intensive pharmacological and/or behavioral interventions to maximally control smoking urges in the early phase of tobacco abstinence. Relatively fast-acting nicotine medications such as nicotine gum or nicotine nasal spray may be useful because they can provide a pharmacological coping strategy when alcohol-dependent smokers are confronted with intense cravings, perhaps warding off both alcohol and tobacco relapse.

EMA methods were used only during a 2-week period after discharge from the intensive outpatient program. Thus, our findings are relevant to understanding only early craving and relapse. Future studies are needed to examine momentary process measures of later relapse. Such studies will be difficult, however, because the risk of relapse declines over time.

Although participants were instructed to complete cigarette-initiated recording at the onset of smoking, their ratings may have been affected by the smoking episode itself. Even the random EMA recordings may have been affected by the participants' reactions to being prompted by the EMA device alarm. These reactions may be positive (reminder to keep on coping) or negative (irritation at the interruption). However, short-term EMA monitoring was not found to have significant reactive effects on drinking behavior in a study using electronic diaries (Hufford, Shields, Shiffman, Paty, & Balabanis, 2002) or in a study using programmable wrist watches (Litt et al., 1998). Strengths of this methodology include the use of real-time reports rather than retrospective reports, the examination of proximal, momentary states surrounding smoking episodes, and the prospective examination of antecedents to both smoking and drinking relapse in a sample that recently completed concurrent alcohol and tobacco treatment.

Although EMA methodology allows one to examine large numbers of observations within subjects, the sample size for analyses of the proximal predictors of alcohol and tobacco relapse was small. These results should be considered preliminary and in need of further study. Future research on alcohol-dependent smokers might need to use a more intensive smoking cessation intervention that would generate higher cigarette abstinence rates, allowing data collection from a larger sample of patients who are abstinent from cigarettes. Theories of alcohol–tobacco interactions can be examined by using both EMA studies in clinical samples and human laboratory studies that experimentally manipulate tobacco abstinence followed by assessments of alcohol craving and/or consumption (e.g., Mckee, Krishnan-Sarin, Shi, Mase, & O'Malley, 2006).

The very low urge-to-drink ratings obtained in this sample of treated alcohol-dependent individuals made it difficult to find significant relationships with this variable. Other EMA studies with this population also found that the frequency and intensity of alcohol craving was low (Litt et al., 2000; Lukasiewicz, Benyamina, Reynaud, & Falissard, 2005). Nevertheless, some significant effects were observed for the alcohol urge variable in the present study. Findings with urge to drink may differ in samples that have not been recently treated in intensive, abstinence-oriented programs or for those who have high levels of alcohol dependence (Litt et al., 2000; Steinberg et al., 2006).

REFERENCES

American Psychiatric Association. (1994). *Diagnostic and statistical manual of mental disorders* (4th ed.). Washington, DC: Author.

Bobo, J. K., McIlvain, H. E., Lando, H. A., Walker, R. D., & Leed-Kelly, A. (1998). Effect of smoking cessation counseling on recovery from alcoholism: Findings from a randomized community intervention trial. *Addiction, 93,* 877–887.

Burling, T. A., Burling, A. S., & Latini, D. (2001). A controlled smoking cessation trial for substance-dependent inpatients. *Journal of Consulting and Clinical Psychology, 69,* 295–304.

Burling, T. A. Marshall, G. D., & Seidner, A. L. (1991). Smoking cessation for substance abuse inpatients. *Journal of Substance Abuse, 3,* 269–276.

Cooney, J. L., Cooney, N. L., Patten, C. A., & George, T. P. (2004). Comorbidity of nicotine dependence with affective, psychotic and substance use disorders. In H. R. Kranzler & J. A. Tinsley (Eds.), *Dual diagnosis and psychiatric treatment: Substance abuse and comorbid disorders* (2nd ed., pp. 211–259). New York: Marcel Dekker.

Cooney, J. L., Cooney, N. L., Pilkey, D. T., Kranzler, H. R., & Oncken, C. A. (2003). Effects of nicotine deprivation on urges to drink and smoke in alcoholic smokers. *Addiction, 98,* 913–921.

Drobes, D. J. (2002). Cue reactivity in alcohol and tobacco dependence. *Alcoholism: Clinical and Experimental Research, 26,* 1928–1929.

First, M. B., Spitzer, R. L., Gibbon, M., & Williams, J. B. W. (1996). *Structured Clinical Interview for DSM–IV Axis I Disorders–Patient Edition (SCID-I/P Version 2.0).*

New York: New York State Psychiatric Institute, Biometrics Research Department.

Gulliver, S. B., Rohsenow, D. J., Colby, S. M., Dey, A. N., Abrams, D. B., Niaura, R. S., et al. (1995). Interrelationship of smoking and alcohol dependence, use, and urges to use. *Journal of Studies on Alcohol, 56*, 202–206.

Heatherton, T. F., Kozlowski, L. T., Frecker, R. C., & Fagerström, K. O. (1991). The Fagerström Test for Nicotine Dependence: A revision of the Fagerström Tolerance Questionnaire. *British Journal of Addiction, 86*, 1119–1127.

Hufford, M. R., Shields, A. L., Shiffman, S., Paty, J., & Balabanis, M. (2002). Reactivity to ecological momentary assessment: An example using undergraduate problem drinkers. *Psychology of Addictive Behaviors, 16*, 205–211.

Hughes, J. R. (1995). Clinical implications of the association between smoking and alcoholism. In J. Fertig & J. P. Allen (Eds.), *Alcohol and tobacco: From basic science to clinical practice* (NIAAA Research Monograph No. 95–3931). Washington, DC: U.S. Government Printing Office.

Hurt, R. D., Eberman, K. M., Croghan, I. T., Offord, K. P., Davis, L. J. Jr., Morse, R. M., et al. (1994). Nicotine dependence treatment during inpatient treatment for other addictions: A prospective intervention trial. *Alcoholism: Clinical and Experimental Research, 18*, 867–872.

Hurt, R. D., Offord, K. P., Croghan, I. T., Gomez-Dahl, L., Kottke, T. E., Morse, R. M., et al. (1996). Mortality following inpatient addictions treatment: Role of tobacco use in a community-based cohort. *Journal of the American Medical Association, 275*, 1097–1103.

Istvan, J., & Matarazzo, J. D. (1984). Tobacco, alcohol and caffeine use: A review of their interrelationships. *Psychological Bulletin, 95*, 301–326.

Joseph, A. M., Nichol, K. L., & Anderson, H. (1993). Effect of treatment for nicotine dependence on alcohol and drug treatment outcomes. *Addictive Behaviors, 18*, 635–644.

Joseph, A. M., Willenbring, M. L., Nugent, S. M., & Nelson, D. B. (2004). A randomized trial of concurrent versus delayed smoking intervention for patients in alcohol dependence treatment. *Journal of Studies on Alcohol, 65*, 681–691.

Kalman, D. (1998). Smoking cessation treatment for substance misusers in early recovery: A review of the literature and recommendations for practice. *Substance Use & Misuse, 33*, 2021–2047.

Killen, J. D., & Fortmann, S. P. (1997). Craving is associated with smoking relapse: Findings from three prospective studies. *Experimental and Clinical Psychopharmacology, 5*, 137–142.

Krahn, D. D., Bohn, M. J., Henk, H. J., Grossman, J. L., & Gosnell, B. (2005). Patterns of urges during early abstinence in alcohol-dependent subjects. *The American Journal on Addiction, 14*, 248–255.

Larsen, R. J., & Diener, E. (1992). Promises and problems with the circumplex model of emotion. In M. S. Clark (Ed.), *Review of personality and social psychology: Vol. 13. Emotion* (pp. 25–59). Newbury Park, CA: Sage.

Litt, M. D., Cooney, N. L., & Morse, P. M. (1998). Ecological momentary assessment (EMA) with alcoholics: Methodological problems and potential solutions. *Health Psychology, 17,* 48–52.

Litt, M. D., Cooney, N. L., & Morse, P. M. (2000). Reactivity to alcohol-related stimuli in the laboratory and in the field: Predictors of craving in treated alcoholics. *Addiction, 95,* 889–900.

Lukasiewicz, M., Benyamina, A., Reynaud, M., & Falissard, B. (2005). An in vivo study of the relationship between craving and reaction time during alcohol detoxification using the ecological momentary assessment. *Alcoholism: Clinical and Experimental Research, 29,* 2135–2143.

Marlatt, G. A., & Gordon, J. R. (Eds.). (1985). *Relapse prevention: Maintenance strategies in the treatment of addictive behaviors.* New York: Guilford Press.

Marlatt, G. A., & Miller, W. R. (1984). *Comprehensive drinker profile.* Odessa, FL: Psychological Assessment Resources.

Marlatt, G. A., & Witkiewitz, K. (2005). Relapse prevention for alcohol and drug problems. In G. A. Marlatt & D. M. Donovan (Eds.), *Relapse prevention: Maintenance strategies in the treatment of addictive behaviors* (2nd ed., pp. 1–44). New York: Guilford Press.

Mckee, S. A., Krishnan-Sarin, S., Shi, J., Mase, T., & O'Malley, S. S. (2006). Modeling the effect of alcohol on smoking lapse behavior. *Psychopharmacology, 189,* 201–210.

Miller, W. R., & Del Boca, F. K. (1994). Measurement of drinking behavior using the Form-90 family of instruments. *Journal of Studies on Alcohol, 12,* 112–118.

Monti, P. M., Rohsenow, D. J., Colby, S. M., & Abrams, D. B. (1995). Smoking among alcoholics during and after treatment: Implications for models, treatment strategies, and policy. In J. B. Fertig & J. P. Allen (Eds.), *Alcohol and tobacco: From basic science to clinical practice* (NIAAA Research Monograph 30, pp. 187–206). Washington, DC: U.S. Government Printing Office.

Muraven, M., & Baumeister, R. F. (2000). Self-regulation and depletion of limited resources: Does self-control resemble a muscle? *Psychological Bulletin, 126,* 247–259.

Muraven, M., Collins, R. L., & Nienhaus, K. (2002). Self-control and alcohol restraint: An initial application of the self-control strength model. *Psychology of Addictive Behaviors, 16,* 113–120.

Muraven, M., Collins, R. L., Shiffman, S., & Paty, J. A. (2005). Daily fluctuations on self-control demands and alcohol intake. *Psychology of Addictive Behaviors, 19,* 140–147.

O'Connell, K., Schwartz, J., Gerkovich, M., Bott, M., & Shiffman, S. (2004). Playful and rebellious states vs. negative affect in explaining the occurrence of temptations and lapses during smoking cessation. *Nicotine & Tobacco Research, 6,* 661–674.

Palfai, T. P., Monti, P. M., Ostafin, B., & Hutchison, K. (2000). Effects of nicotine deprivation on alcohol-related information processing and drinking behavior. *Journal of Abnormal Psychology, 109,* 96–106.

Rohsenow, D. J., Monti, P. M., Colby, S. M., Gulliver, S. B., Sirota, A. D., Niaura, R. S., et al. (1997). Effects of alcohol cues on smoking urges and topography among alcoholic men. *Alcoholism Clinical & Experimental Research, 21*, 101–107.

Russell, J. A. (1980). A circumplex model of affect. *Journal of Personality and Social Psychology, 39*, 1161–1178.

Shiffman, S. (2005). Dynamic influences on smoking relapse process. *Journal of Personality, 73*, 1715–1748.

Shiffman, S., Hufford, M., Hickcox, M., Paty, J. A., Gnys, M., & Kassel, J. D. (1997). Remember that? A comparison of real-time versus retrospective recall of smoking lapses. *Journal of Consulting and Clinical Psychology, 65*, 292–300.

Shiffman, S., Paty, J. A., Gnys, M., Kassel, J. A., & Hickcox, M. (1996). First lapses to smoking: Within-subjects analysis of real-time reports. *Journal of Consulting and Clinical Psychology, 64*, 366–379.

Shiffman, S., & Stone, A. A. (1998). Ecological momentary assessment: A new tool for behavioral medicine research. In D. Krantz & A. Baum (Eds.), *Technology and methods in behavioral medicine* (pp. 117–131). Mahwah, NJ: Erlbaum.

Slosson, R. L. (1963). *Slosson Oral Reading Test manual.* East Aurora, NY: Slosson Educational Publications.

Smoking Cessation Clinical Guideline Panel and Staff. (1996). The Agency for Health Care Policy and Research smoking cessation clinical practice guideline. *Journal of the American Medical Association, 275*, 1270–1280.

Sobell, L. C., & Sobell, M. B. (1992). Timeline follow-back: A technique for assessing self-reported alcohol consumption. In R. Litten & J. Allen (Eds.), *Measuring alcohol consumption* (pp. 41–71). Totowa, NJ: Humana Press.

Steinberg, H. R., Cooney, N. L., Pilkey, D. T., Litt, M. D., Cooney, J. L., & Oncken, C. A. (2006, February). *Predictors of momentary smoking and drinking urges in alcohol dependent smokers.* Poster presented at the annual meeting of the Society for Research on Nicotine and Tobacco, Orlando, FL.

Stone, A. A., Shiffman, S., Schwartz, J. E., Broderick, J. E., & Hufford, M. R. (2003). Patient compliance with paper and electronic diaries. *Controlled Clinical Trials, 24*, 182–199.

Taylor, R. C., Harris, N. A., Singleton, E. G., Moolchan, E. T., & Heishman, S. J. (2000). Tobacco craving: Intensity-related effects of imagery scripts in drug abusers. *Experimental and Clinical Psychopharmacology, 8*, 75–87.

Tiffany, S. T. (1990). A cognitive model of drug urges and drug-use behavior: Role of automatic and nonautomatic processes. *Psychological Review, 97*, 147–168.

West, R. J., Hajek, P., & Belcher, M. (1989). Severity of withdrawal symptoms as a predictor of outcome of an attempt to quit smoking. *Psychological Medicine, 19*, 981–985.

21

ADDICTIVE DISORDERS IN CONTEXT: PRINCIPLES AND PUZZLES OF EFFECTIVE TREATMENT AND RECOVERY

RUDOLF H. MOOS

There has been an expanding cornucopia of research on addictive behaviors in the past 30 years. We have formulated conceptual models, measured key constructs, examined salient theoretical issues, and made substantial progress in understanding the ebb and flow of addictive disorders. An integrated biopsychosocial orientation and a theoretical paradigm of evaluation research have supplanted earlier adherence to an oversimplified biomedical model and reliance on a restrictive methodological approach to treatment evaluation. And yet, in an ironic way, more remains to be done than before, in part because of our increased knowledge and in part because of new clinical perspectives and treatment procedures and the evolving social context in which we ply our trade. Here, I set out seven principles that exemplify

Preparation of this chapter was supported by the Department of Veterans Affairs Health Services Research and Development Service and by National Institute on Alcohol Abuse and Alcoholism Grant AA12718. The work was conducted in part under the auspices of the Substance Use Disorders Module of the Veterans Affairs Quality Enhancement Research Initiative. Penny Brennan, John Finney, John Kelly, Jennifer Ritsher, Kathleen Schutte, and Christine Timko made helpful comments on a draft of the chapter. An adapted version of this chapter was presented as an invited address at the 110th Annual Convention of the American Psychological Association, Chicago, August 2002. The views expressed here are the author's and do not necessarily represent the views of the Department of Veterans Affairs.

Reprinted from *Psychology of Addictive Disorders*, 17, 3–12 (2003). In the public domain.

advances in our effort to understand the processes involved in effective treatment and recovery. I then describe some unresolved puzzles and important questions for future research.

PRINCIPLES: WHAT WE KNOW OR THINK WE KNOW

The first two principles of effective treatment and recovery address the context of addictive disorders, the next two principles focus on the structure of treatment, and the following two principles consider the process and content of treatment. The final principle addresses treatment outcome.

Principle 1: Treated or Untreated, an Addiction Is Not an Island Unto Itself

People with addictive disorders exist in a complex web of social forces, not on an island unto themselves, free of social context. Formal treatment can be a compelling force for change, but it typically has only an ephemeral influence. In contrast, relatively stable factors in people's lives, such as informal help and ongoing social resources, tend to play a more enduring role. Moreover, a recovery that is sustained after treatment is not due simply to treatment; it is nurtured by the same sets of factors that maintain the resolution of problems without treatment (Biernacki, 1986; Moos, Finney, & Cronkite, 1990; Vaillant, 1995). This contextual perspective highlights the need for a fundamental shift in thinking about intervention programs and evaluating their effects. Many of the hard-won gains of intervention programs fade away over time. This is precisely as expected on the basis of our knowledge about environmental impact and the diversity of contexts to which individuals are exposed. An intervention program is but one of multiple life contexts. Other powerful environments also shape mood and behavior; ongoing environmental factors can augment or nullify the short-term influence of an intervention. The fact that the evolving conditions of life play an essential role in the process of remission from addictive disorders is a hopeful sign. It implies that these disorders need not become chronic, that individuals who are able to establish and maintain relatively positive social contexts are likely to recover, and that treatment directed toward improving individuals' life circumstances is likely to be helpful.

Principle 2: Common Dynamics Underlie the Process of Problem Resolution That Occurs in Formal Treatment, Informal Care, and "Natural" Recovery

Individuals trying to resolve substance abuse problems usually begin by using one or more sources of informal help, such as a family member or friend, a physician or member of the clergy, or Alcoholics Anonymous (AA) or another self-help group. If such attempts fail repeatedly, some individuals enter formal treatment. On average, these individuals have more severe problems and more difficult life contexts, and are more impaired than individuals who resolve problems on their own or with informal help; outside help may be especially needed when an individual has few personal or social resources on which to base a recovery (Finney & Moos, 1995).

Nevertheless, it may not be important or fruitful to distinguish between problem resolution that occurs with or without treatment. There is no compelling conceptual reason to distinguish between the influence of an AA sponsor, a spouse or partner, and a relative or friend, versus that of a counselor or psychotherapist on an addicted individual. The cognitive and social processes that underlie the resolution of addictive problems are common to formal treatment and informal help, and the other dynamics of change are likely to be similar, regardless of the context in which they occur.

In addition, any distinction between life context and informal help or formal treatment is arbitrary: When individuals enter an intervention program it becomes part of their life context. Ongoing life settings and intervention programs are comparable in that both establish a context for individual development or dysfunction, both involve person–environment matching processes, and both may be altered by the participants they seek to alter. Moreover, both are environmental conditions that can be characterized by common social processes, as embodied by the quality of interpersonal relationships, the goals, and the structure of the setting (Moos, 2002).

Principle 3: The Duration and Continuity of Care Are More Closely Related to Treatment Outcome Than Is the Amount or Intensity of Care

Although patients with substance use disorders who receive more outpatient mental health care tend to have better short-term outcomes (Brochu, Landry, Bergeron, & Chiocchio, 1997; Fiorentine & Anglin, 1996; Jerrell & Ridgely, 1999), there is growing evidence that the duration of care is more important than the amount of care. In a sample of more than 20,000 patients who participated in a nationwide program to monitor the quality of care in the Department of Veterans Affairs, Moos, Finney, Federman, and Suchinsky (2000) found that patients who had a longer episode of mental health care had better risk-adjusted substance use, family, and legal outcomes than did those who had a shorter episode. These findings held after the intensity of care was controlled. Drug-dependent patients with longer episodes of residential or outpatient care experience better substance use and crime-related outcomes than do patients with shorter episodes (Crits-Christoph & Siqueland, 1996; Prendergast, Podus, & Chang, 2000; Simpson, Joe, & Brown, 1997).

In other studies, patients who obtained outpatient mental health care over a longer interval had better 1-year substance use outcomes (Ouimette, Moos, & Finney, 1998) and were more likely to be remitted at 2 years (Ritsher, Finney, & Moos, 2002) than were patients who had outpatient care for a shorter interval. The findings were comparable among patients from community-based residential settings; moreover, after the duration of outpatient mental health care was controlled, the amount of care did not independently predict 1-year outcomes (Moos, Schaefer, Andrassy, & Moos, 2001).

The finding that the duration of treatment for alcohol and drug use disorders is more closely related to outcome than is the sheer amount of treatment is consistent with the fact that the enduring aspects of individuals' life contexts are associated with the recurrent course of remission and relapse. Thus, low-intensity, telephone-based case monitoring delivered by paraprofessional personnel may be an effective long-term treatment strategy for many patients (Stout, Rubin, Zwick, Zywiak, & Bellino, 1999). If taken seriously, these findings could impel an additional shift in resources from intensive to extensive care (Humphreys & Tucker, 2002).

Principle 4: Patients Treated by Substance Abuse or Mental Health Specialists Experience Better Outcomes Than Do Patients Treated by Primary Care or Nonspecialty Providers

There is considerable controversy about whether individuals with substance use disorders need to receive specialty substance abuse or mental health care, or whether brief treatment by nonspecialty providers is sufficient. Studies of interventions in primary care and general medical clinics show that advice and brief counseling are effective in reducing alcohol consumption (Fleming et al., 2002; Moyer, Finney, Swearingen, & Vergun, 2002). However, these studies have focused mainly on problem drinkers rather than on alcohol dependent individuals.

Moos et al. (2000) examined the association between the type of provider and treatment outcomes in the Veterans Affairs quality monitoring program. Among more than 20,000 patients with substance use disorders, 25% obtained little or no outpatient substance abuse or psychiatric care. Compared with patients treated by primary care or other nonspecialty providers, patients who received substance abuse or psychiatric specialty care had longer and more comprehensive care and better risk-adjusted 1-year outcomes. They were more likely to be abstinent and free of substance use problems, less likely to have psychiatric symptoms, and more likely to be employed (Moos et al., 2000).

In conjunction with prior studies, these findings show that patients with substance use disorders who obtain specialty care receive more services and more appropriate care, are more satisfied with their care, and have better treatment outcomes than do comparable patients seen only in the general medical sector (Ettner, Hermann, & Tang, 1999; Mechanic, 1990; Rogers, Wells, Meredith, Sturm, & Burnam, 1993). Such specialty care can be provided by addictions counselors, or by social workers and nurses trained as addiction counselors, rather than by doctoral-level staff. Accordingly, health care policymakers need to reevaluate the desirability of shifting these patients' care from specialty to nonspecialty providers.

Principle 5: Treatment Settings and Counselors Who Establish a Therapeutic Alliance, Are Oriented Toward Personal Growth Goals, and Are Moderately Structured Tend to Promote Positive Outcomes

Common aspects of treatment may have as much or more of an impact on clients than does the specific content or type of treatment (Hubble, Duncan, & Miller, 1999). In general, counselors who are more empathic and able to establish a therapeutic alliance enhance their clients' involvement in treatment and treatment outcomes (Norcross, 2002). Clients of counselors who are confrontational or use confrontational interventions consistently do poorly, probably because criticism and lack of support elicit resistance and withdrawal (Miller & Wilbourne, 2002). Similarly, supportive group and residential treatment settings tend to enhance patients' participation in treatment, strengthen their self-confidence, and contribute to a reduction in symptoms and substance use (Moos, 1997).

A positive treatment alliance and a cohesive treatment setting may be helpful and perhaps even necessary conditions for change, but they are not sufficient conditions. To motivate clients to improve, counselors also need to set specific performance goals and to maintain an appropriate level of structure. Similarly, group and residential treatment settings that emphasize self-direction and work and social skills, and are clear and well organized, tend to engage clients in treatment, to reduce clients' symptoms, and to enhance clients' social functioning and community adaptation (Moos, 1997).

From a broader perspective, clients help to create the context of treatment, and counselors direct clients toward specific goals. As a case in point, Carl Rogers believed that counselors should offer noncontingent empathy and warmth in therapy. Nonetheless, Rogers responded with varying levels of empathy and warmth that were contingent on the content of clients' problems (Truax, 1966). Cohesion and support are not just interpersonal constructs but always involve an orientation toward specific goals and structure. Accordingly, the finding that a positive treatment alliance predicts good treatment outcome may be due in part to a relatively structured focus on clients' real life social contexts and coping skills. When a positive alliance is not associated with good outcome, it may be due to a lack of goal direction and clarity in treatment.

Principle 6: The Common Component of Effective Psychosocial Interventions Is the Focus on Helping Clients Shape and Adapt to Their Life Circumstances

According to recent reviews, the most effective psychosocial modalities for the treatment of addictive disorders are cognitive–behavioral interventions, social skills training, a community reinforcement approach, motivational interviewing, behavioral contracting, stress management and relapse prevention training, and behavioral marital therapy (Crits-Christoph & Siqueland, 1996; Finney & Monahan, 1996; Miller & Wilbourne, 2002). These types of interventions focus primarily on enhancing clients' competence in coping with daily life, developing clients' social skills, improving the match between clients' abilities and environmental demands, and altering reinforcement patterns in clients' community settings.

There is considerable evidence for the effectiveness of 12-step treatment (Ouimette, Finney, & Moos, 1997; Project MATCH Research Group, 1997, 1998) and therapeutic communities (De Leon, 1997); these approaches also emphasize patients' community living skills and adaptation to ongoing life contexts. Moreover, in standard substance abuse treatment programs, services that are focused on patients' community contexts and coping, such as life skills training and enhanced social services, are associated with better outcomes (Connors & Walitzer, 2001; McLellan et al., 1998).

Consistent with the conclusion Luborsky, Singer, and Luborsky (1975) reached more than 25 years ago, treatment programs with diverse ideologies are effective in reducing substance use and improving psychosocial outcomes. These effective programs engage clients in a common focus, which is to help them understand, adapt to, and alter their life circumstances.

Principle 7: Among Individuals Who Recognize a Problem and Are Willing or Motivated to Receive Help, Formal Intervention or Treatment Leads to Better Outcomes Than Does Remaining Untreated

Although clients in treatment seem to benefit, one nagging question is whether individuals who obtain treatment experience better outcomes than those who do not. In this vein, a recurring criticism of Project MATCH is that it lacked an untreated comparison group, and thus, although patients generally had good outcomes, they might have had comparable outcomes had they remained untreated.

A growing number of studies have addressed this issue. Among individuals with less severe drinking problems, those who receive a brief intervention have better alcohol-related outcomes than do nonintervention comparison groups (Moyer et al., 2002). In a study of individuals who sought help for their alcohol use disorders and had never received formal treatment,

Timko, Moos, Finney, and Lesar (2000) found that individuals who entered formal treatment relatively quickly had better 1-year and 8-year alcohol-related outcomes than did individuals who obtained no help. Individuals who stayed in treatment longer had the best outcomes (Moos & Moos, 2003).

With respect to individuals with more severe alcohol use disorders, Emrick (1975) concluded that entry into formal treatment raised the likelihood of improved drinking outcomes. More recent evidence shows that persons who have been in treatment are more likely to be abstinent (Armor & Meshkoff, 1983; Dawson, 1996) and experience less distress (Bovasso, Eaton, & Armenian, 1999) at follow-up than do untreated individuals. Similarly, compared with no treatment, treatment reduces drug use and criminal behavior and improves social functioning among drug-dependent individuals (Anglin, Speckart, Booth, & Ryan, 1989; McLellan et al., 1996).

These findings are not an artifact of self-selection, because individuals who enter treatment typically have more severe substance abuse problems than do untreated individuals, but they have better long-term outcomes. In addition, recovery without treatment is less common among individuals with more severe alcohol problems (Cunningham, 1999). Moreover, individuals who follow a course of stable remission can attain relatively normal functioning and life contexts (Finney, Moos, & Timko, 1999).

UNRESOLVED PUZZLES: WHAT WE NEED TO KNOW

I have set out seven principles about effective treatment and recovery. Although substantial progress has been made, a number of questions remain to be resolved. After commenting on the diversity of the samples of individuals on which the above principles are based, I focus on three puzzles about the structure and process of treatment. I then consider two puzzles about the content of treatment and one about treatment outcome. The final puzzle addresses the context of addictive disorders.

Several studies of substance abuse treatment have involved nationwide samples of treatment programs and patients who vary widely in demographic and diagnostic characteristics and in the severity and chronicity of their disorder. More broadly, in a review of 700 alcohol treatment outcome studies, Swearingen, Moyer, and Finney (2003) noted that more than 15% of the patients in these studies were women and about 20% were Black, almost 50% were married, about 60% were high school graduates and 15% were college graduates, about 60% were employed, and almost half had not been in treatment before.

Individuals included in studies of brief interventions, and those who are untreated or are early in their help-seeking career, also span a broad range of demographic and substance use characteristics. Thus, the above principles should apply to a diverse population of substance-using individuals. Nevertheless, there are likely to be exceptional groups of individuals characterized by distinctive motivations, life contexts, and coping skills. Addiction researchers should continue to search for ethnic, social, and genetic subgroups in which new principles or alternative processes of recovery and relapse may apply.

Puzzle 1: How Can We Best Conceptualize and Examine Service Episodes and Treatment Careers?

Comparative studies of treatment outcome typically consider only one delimited segment of care, such as a specific course of residential or outpatient treatment. In reality, however, almost all clients obtain packages of services, or episodes of care, that encompass more than one setting, modality, and orientation.

In an attempt to focus on this issue, Moos et al. (2000) specified an episode of mental health care for a sample of almost 21,000 patients with substance use disorders (Moos et al., 2000). On average, these episodes lasted about 9 months, much longer than the time span of treatment examined in most outcome studies. Many of these patients had inpatient/residential care and outpatient care, and the majority had both substance abuse and psychiatric care. These patients also had a mixture of individual, group, and day treatment, and most probably experienced diverse orientations of treatment.

The fact that patients with substance use disorders typically receive a diverse array of services over an extended interval raises several questions. For clients who use services intermittently, when does a new episode begin, and when does it end? Given the presumed match between patients' acuity and the allocation of services, how can one validly compare the outcomes of widely varying types of episodes? How can one evaluate the effects of specific treatment modalities in the context of episodes in which patients are exposed to more than one modality of care?

Over time, multiple service episodes merge and become treatment careers (Hser, Anglin, Grella, Longshore, & Prendergast, 1997). How do initial treatment experiences affect the likelihood of seeking subsequent treatment and the progression of different types of episodes? Do individuals who seek treatment early in the course of the disorder eventually need less treatment than individuals who delay seeking treatment? Are longer treatment careers associated with an increased duration of subsequent treatment and better outcomes, as Hser and colleagues (Hser, Grella, Chou, & Anglin, 1998) suggested? How can we identify the family, peer, and community forces that shape the characteristics of service episodes and treatment careers?

Puzzle 2: What Is the Role of the Health Care Work Environment in Treatment Process and Outcome and in Enhancing Clinicians' Morale and Openness to Innovations in Treatment Delivery?

The health care work environment is an important and relatively neglected component of the substance abuse treatment system. We know that an involving and cohesive workplace that emphasizes task orientation and clarity is associated with provider satisfaction and performance in health care settings in general (Moos, 1994b). However, very little is known about the connections between the quality of the workplace, staff members' beliefs about addictive disorders, and the quality of treatment for patients with substance use disorders.

In a study that addressed these issues, Moos and Moos (1998) found that staff members in supportive and goal-directed work environments were more likely to espouse disease model beliefs and a 12-step orientation toward substance abuse treatment. These work environments were associated with more supportive and goal-directed treatment settings. Patients in these settings received more services, were more involved in self-help groups, were more satisfied with treatment, improved more during treatment, and were more likely to participate in continuing outpatient care (Moos & Moos, 1998).

These findings raise intriguing questions. Do organizational factors, such as team structure and challenging leadership, enhance staff morale and therapeutic behavior because they promote a cohesive and goal-directed workplace (Schulz, Greenley, & Brown, 1995)? More specifically, does a 12-step philosophy provide a more coherent and sustainable belief system, and thus more goal congruence and clarity, than does a cognitive–behavioral orientation, which is based more on scientific evidence and technical expertise? Is it true that an ideology based only on empirical support cannot sustain service providers (Cherniss & Krantz, 1983)?

Many substance abuse treatment providers experience conditions that impede innovation and the adoption of new clinical practices, such as high work pressure and ambiguity, conflicts with other providers, and demoralization. How can organizational development programs improve the quality of substance abuse staff teams, the work setting, and ultimately the quality of treatment? Is it best to introduce total quality improvement processes or to use a simpler assessment and feedback method that empowers providers to identify and alter problematic aspects of the work milieu (Berwick, Godfrey, & Roessner, 1991; Shortell et al., 1995)?

Puzzle 3: How Can We Better Understand the Connections Among the Theory, Process, and Outcome of Treatment?

Although studies of the comparative effectiveness of substance abuse treatment are commonplace, relatively few have examined the processes underlying the effects of different treatment modalities. Comparative evaluations rarely provide information about how treatment works, for whom treatment works or does not work, or how treatment can work better or be allocated more effectively. In an attempt to address this issue, Finney, Noyes, Coutts, and Moos (1998) found that patients in 12-step programs improved more than did patients in cognitive–behavioral programs on proximal outcomes assumed to be specific to 12-step treatment, such as attending 12-step meetings and taking the steps. In contrast, patients in cognitive–behavioral programs showed no greater change than did 12-step patients on proximal outcomes assumed to underlie cognitive–behavioral treatment, such as self-efficacy and coping skills (Finney, Noyes, Coutts, & Moos, 1998). The associations between cognitive–behavioral proximal outcomes and 1-year outcomes were as strong for patients from 12-step programs as for patients from cognitive–behavioral programs (Finney, Moos, & Humphreys, 1999).

Similarly, cognitive–behavioral treatment in Project MATCH did not enhance clients' social skills more than did 12-step facilitation treatment (Longabaugh, Wirtz, & Rice, 2001). Thus, the proximal outcomes thought to be specific to cognitive–behavioral treatment may be a function of common conditions in both 12-step and cognitive–behavioral treatment. More broadly, we do not know why cognitive–behavioral treatment is effective, because there is relatively little support for the idea that the treatment works by enhancing clients' coping skills (Morgenstern & Longabaugh, 2000).

These findings raise quite basic questions. Do the theories underlying 12-step, cognitive–behavioral, and other treatments overemphasize the content as compared with the common aspects of treatment, such as the alliance, goals, and duration of care? Can we develop theories about these common aspects, such as how a specific combination of conditions enhances clients' engagement in treatment and self-efficacy? Can "logic models" that specify providers' beliefs about how treatment works (Conrad, Matters, Hanrahan, & Luchins, 1999) guide the development of better theories and the identification of proximal outcomes that are more predictive of long-term change?

Puzzle 4: How Can We Identify Effective Patient–Treatment Matching Strategies?

Many clinicians believe that patient–treatment matching can enhance treatment outcomes, but the key variables involved have eluded us. The majority of matching studies has tried to identify stable patient characteristics that are associated with differential outcomes of varying models or theories of treatment. Despite an extensive search, however, there is little or no evidence that patients' personality characteristics interact with models of treatment to affect outcomes (Longabaugh & Wirtz, 2001; Mattson et al., 1994).

A promising alternative involves matching clients' cognitive and psychosocial functioning with common aspects of treatment, such as the level of support, performance expectations, and structure. This approach focuses more on clients' changing characteristics and the common conditions in which treatment is delivered than on stable personal factors and the content of treatment. Functionally able clients tend to respond well to self-directed treatment that involves high performance expectations and relatively little structure, whereas impaired clients need more support and structure. As clients' cognitive and psychosocial skills improve, they should be able to adapt to a more demanding and self-directed setting (Litt, Babor, DelBoca, Kadden, & Cooney, 1992; Timko, Moos, & Finney, 2000).

Another matching approach is to target services more precisely to address patients' specific problems. In recent tests of this model, clients in matched care conditions, who received counseling sessions focused on target problem areas, stayed in treatment longer and had better 6-month outcomes than usual care patients did (Hser, Polinsky, Maglione, & Anglin, 1999; McLellan et al., 1997). Even with such matching, however, the question remains of how demanding and structured counseling should be for different patients.

One way to pursue problem–service matching is to encompass patients' life contexts. In this vein, Zywiak, Longabaugh, and Wirtz (2002) found that Project MATCH outpatients with networks supportive of drinking had better 3-year outcomes in 12- step treatment than in motivational enhancement treatment, apparently because they were more likely to attend AA and develop substitute networks. I mentioned earlier that treatments that focus on patients' life contexts tend to be effective; accordingly, targeting services more specifically to address life context problems should enhance treatment outcome.

Puzzle 5: How Should We Organize and Sequence Treatment for Patients With Dual Disorders, Such as Patients With Substance Use Disorders and Major Depression or Posttraumatic Stress Disorder?

Between 30% and 60% of individuals who have substance use disorders also have one or more psychiatric disorders. These dually diagnosed individuals have more severe medical, financial, housing, and legal problems; seek treatment services more often; and, on average, have poorer overall outcomes than do individuals with only substance use disorders (Regier et al., 1990; Rosenthal & Westreich, 1999). There are treatment guidelines for patients with substance use disorders (American Psychiatric Association, 1995) and for patients with prevalent psychiatric disorders, such as depression and posttraumatic stress disorder (American Psychiatric Association, 1993; Foa, Keane, & Friedman, 2000), but much less is known about effective treatment for dually diagnosed patients.

Clinicians have espoused three models of dual diagnosis care: (a) serial treatment, in which one disorder is treated after the other; (b) parallel treatment, in which the two disorders are treated at the same time by different providers; and (c) integrated treatment, in which coordinated care is provided for both disorders. Integrated models that combine substance abuse and psychiatric care tailored for clients with comorbid disorders appear to be most effective (Barrowclough et al., 2001; Drake, Mercer-McFadden, Mueser, McHugo, & Bond, 1998; Herman et al., 2000). In this regard, Moggi, Ouimette, Finney, and Moos (1999) found that dually diagnosed patients treated in substance abuse programs with a stronger dual diagnosis orientation (as defined by high support and structure; enhanced services for housing, legal, and family problems; and a focus on psychotropic medication) had better 1-year symptom and employment outcomes (Moggi, Ouimette, Finney, & Moos, 1999).

These and related findings are useful, but more specific information is needed about best practices in this area. What are the critical components of dual-diagnosis programs and, given their complexity and cost, how can they be implemented in an integrated system of care? How can we shape therapeutic communities that are structured enough to control impulsive behavior and yet permissive enough to encourage self-direction? Can a single clinician effectively manage both disorders? If not, how can we best coordinate substance abuse counseling, supportive group psychotherapy, medical management, and community-based case management?

Puzzle 6: How Can We Integrate Formal Substance Abuse Treatment and Patients' Involvement and Participation in Self-Help Groups?

When individuals with substance use disorders participate in recovery-focused self-help groups, they experience better substance use and social functioning outcomes. These findings hold for individuals who receive formal treatment (Humphreys & Moos, 2001; Morgenstern, Labouvie, McCrady, Kahler, & Frey, 1997; Tonigan, Toscova, & Miller, 1996) as well as for those who do not (Humphreys & Moos, 1996; Timko, Moos, Finney, & Lesar, 2000). Moreover, the positive outcomes of 12-step facilitation treatment, as well as those of other treatment modalities, may reflect how much they encourage involvement in self-help groups during the follow-up period (Humphreys, Huebsch, Finney, & Moos, 1999; Tonigan, Connors, & Miller, 2002).

Given these findings, a number of questions need to be addressed. Does a consistent orientation in treatment and self-help amplify the effects of each of these modalities? In this regard, patients in 12-step facilitation treatment may benefit more from participation in AA than do patients in cognitive–behavioral treatment (Humphreys, Huebsch, et al., 1999), whereas participation in AA may not add to the benefit of behavioral treatment (McCrady, Epstein, & Hirsch, 1999). When there is no expected booster effect of "orientation congruence," how can one reconcile this finding with the idea that congruent settings should enhance each other's impact?

A related set of questions involves how self-help groups work. Potential mechanisms include the maintenance of motivation and self-efficacy to avoid drinking, enhanced friendship networks, and reliance on approach coping (Connors, Tonigan, & Miller, 2001; Humphreys, Mankowski, Moos, & Finney, 1999; Morgenstern et al., 1997). An intriguing question is whether the benefits of self-help groups wane as quickly as do the benefits of treatment when individuals stop going to meetings. In fact, because self-help groups do not explicitly teach coping skills, as typically occurs in treatment, does their influence taper off more quickly than does the influence of treatment?

Other important questions abound: Is the intensity of participation in self-help groups associated with better outcomes, as suggested by the principle of "90 meetings in 90 days," or is the duration of participation more important, as seems to be the case with formal treatment? Are the common factors in AA groups, such as the strength of one's relationship with a sponsor, more essential than participation in the group itself? How often do cohesive and powerful groups lead to progressive conformity and subservience or to isolation and extrusion of individuals with incongruent beliefs?

Puzzle 7: How Can We Develop More Unified Models of the Role of Life Context Factors and Formal and Informal Care in the Recovery Process?

To grasp the essence of the process of recovery, we need to place ongoing life context factors, formal treatment, and self-help groups into a unified model and understand these apparently disparate contexts in terms of their underlying dimensions and dynamics. As noted earlier, these diverse settings can be conceptualized in terms of three domains: (a) quality of interpersonal relationships, (b) personal growth goals, and (c) level of structure. Moreover, there are consistent linkages between these domains and outcomes. Thus, when intervention programs, self-help groups, or families are cohesive and expressive, individuals tend to experience high morale and to feel bonded to the setting. When intervention programs, self-help groups, or families emphasize independence and task orientation, individuals tend to become more assertive and self-confident (Moos, 1994a, 2002).

Because the influence of any one of these domains depends on the context in which it is embedded, it is important to recognize their interconnections. With respect to treatment, researchers tend to focus on alliance (a relationship dimension), or on skills development (a personal growth goal), or on directedness (an index of structure), when they know that the power of any one of these characteristics depends on the relative emphasis on the others. In the context of the family, cohesion in the service of independence promotes initiative and self-confidence; cohesion in the service of conformity spawns passivity and enmeshment (Moos & Moos, 1994).

At present, we have only a dim vision of how the influence of treatment or self-help groups varies depending on clients' life contexts. Unmarried patients may benefit more from community reinforcement because it provides a compensatory source of support for individuals with few social resources (Azrin, Sisson, Meyers, & Godley, 1982). Patients with high network support for drinking may benefit more from 12-step facilitation treatment because it enhances participation in AA and provides a new abstinence-oriented support system (Zywiak et al., 2002). We need to learn more about how formal treatment and self-help groups substitute for, amplify, or diminish the influence of other contexts.

How does treatment or a self-help group compensate for a lack of family and friend resources, counteract the influence of detrimental peers, or amplify the power of a supportive partner? How do enhanced services, such as housing assistance, parenting classes, and employment counseling, affect clients' life context and substance use outcomes? Most fundamentally, how can we maximize positive carryover from substance abuse intervention programs to clients' ongoing life contexts?

EVIDENCE-BASED PRACTICES AND PARADIGM TRANSFORMATION

An underlying issue in our research endeavor involves the scientific paradigm we use to accrue new knowledge and how we apply that knowledge. In this respect, clinicians and researchers alike face a fundamental question: Will the movement toward empirically supported treatments and practice guidelines ultimately transform our most cherished assumptions about how treatment should be delivered and evaluated?

The newest panacea in health care involves empirically supported treatments, evidence-based guidelines, and accountability systems to enhance the process and outcome of care. Total quality improvement enthusiasts initially expected a relatively painless process whereby expert consensus panels formulate guidelines, professional organizations and health care systems disseminate them, and providers adopt new clinical practices in light of empirical evidence about their efficacy. However, a storm of resistance and two main sets of barriers have arisen: (a) lack of an adequate evidence base and (b) providers' collegially validated concerns about whether current guidelines have value in clinical practice (Chambless & Ollendick, 2001; Norcross, 1999).

One set of issues is that the findings of tightly controlled efficacy trials may not generalize to real-life clinical settings with more heterogeneous patient populations and less well-trained clinicians (Nathan, 1998). In this vein, the exclusion criteria used in efficacy studies result in an underrepresentation of African American and low-income individuals and of individuals with severe substance abuse and psychiatric problems (Humphreys & Weisner, 2000). Additional issues involve the lack of standard comparative information on patients and of a standard condition against which alternative treatments can be compared (Donovan, 1999; Finney, 2000). More broadly, we should recognize that efficacy trials provide only one specific context for observation and are not necessarily the royal road to a divine blueprint of revealed truth.

Providers' concerns about practice guidelines include the possibility that clients' needs may be subjugated to technique-focused treatment, that fidelity may take priority over flexibility, and that the training and intensity of care needed to deliver evidence-based treatments reduce their feasibility (Addis, Wade, & Hatgis, 1999). These concerns raise researchable issues: Does the application of practice guidelines compromise treatment alliance and innovation and, if so, how can these effects be counteracted? Can we develop a set of "acceptable deviations" from apparent best practices by allowing clinicians to espouse a rationale for following alternative standards of care for specific patients? More generally, how can clinicians and researchers collaborate to develop an evidence-based approach to evaluating the dissemination, implementation, maintenance, and outcomes of evidence-based clinical practices (Corrigan, Steiner, McCracken, Blaser, & Barr, 2001; Rosenheck, 2001)?

Another key question is whether an emphasis on evidence-based practice can be integrated with the reemerging humanitarian, recovery-based model that values clients' personal experiences, responsibility, choice, and empowerment (Frese, Stanley, Kress, & Vogel-Scibilia, 2001). Given the advocacy principle of "nothing about us without us," what are providers to do when their clients prefer an emphasis on personal growth and quality of life over an evidence-based symptom reduction approach? As clients improve, how can we provide them with more autonomy and choice about the type of treatment and services they receive? Finally, how can we implement evidence-based practices and yet fully incorporate clients' preferences into clinical decision making?

Quality improvement efforts that rely on evidence-based practice guidelines enable us to broaden the prevailing paradigm about how to advance substance abuse and psychiatric care (Wells, 1999). This paradigm bases existing guidelines primarily on syntheses of findings from efficacy trials, which focus on the impact of manual-guided interventions administered by closely monitored treatment providers to carefully selected patient samples. We need to find out how effective and acceptable ensuing best practices are when they are disseminated in quality-improvement programs and applied to a diversity of patients under normal conditions of treatment delivery. If the prevailing paradigm on the advancement of clinical practice is valid, then these efforts should lead to better quality care and improved client outcomes.

If the prevailing paradigm is found wanting, we may see the emergence of a new perspective that emphasizes naturalistic longitudinal observation, the epidemiology and social manifestations of a disorder, community-based participatory research, and the value of interventions in improving the health of communities instead of just individuals (Hohmann & Shear, 2002; McLellan et al., 1996). Such a fundamental shift in the foci of our research would enable us to grasp the full implications of the essential role of social context in the ebb and flow of addictive disorders.

REFERENCES

Addis, M. E., Wade, W. A., & Hatgis, C. (1999). Barriers to dissemination of evidence-based practices: Addressing practitioners' concerns about manual-based psychotherapies. *Clinical Psychology Science and Practice, 6*, 430–441.

American Psychiatric Association. (1993). Practice guidelines for major depressive disorders in adults. *American Journal of Psychiatry, 150*(Suppl. 4), 1–26.

American Psychiatric Association. (1995). Practice guidelines for the treatment of patients with substance use disorders: Alcohol, cocaine, opioids. *American Journal of Psychiatry, 152*(Suppl. 11), 1–80.

Anglin, M. D., Speckart, G. R., Booth, M. W., & Ryan, T. M. (1989). Consequences and costs of shutting off methadone. *Addictive Behaviors, 14*, 307–326.

Armor, D. J., & Meshkoff, J. E. (1983). Remission among treated and untreated alcoholics. *Advances in Substance Abuse, 3*, 239–269.

Azrin, N. H., Sisson, R. W., Meyers, R., & Godley, M. (1982). Alcoholism treatment by disulfiram and community reinforcement therapy. *Journal of Behavior Therapy and Experimental Psychiatry, 13*, 105–112.

Barrowclough, C., Haddock, G., Tarrier, N., Lewis, S. W., Moring, J., O'Brien, R., et al. (2001). Randomized controlled trial of motivational interviewing, cognitive behavior therapy, and family intervention for patients with comorbid schizophrenia and substance use disorders. *American Journal of Psychiatry, 158*, 1706–1713.

Berwick, D. M., Godfrey, A. B., & Roessner, J. (1991). *Curing health care*. San Francisco: Jossey-Bass.

Biernacki, P. (1986). *Pathways from heroin addiction: Recovery without treatment*. Philadelphia: Temple University Press.

Bovasso, G. B., Eaton, W. W., & Armenian, H. K. (1999). The long-term outcomes of mental health treatment in a population-based study. *Journal of Consulting and Clinical Psychology, 67*, 529–538.

Brochu, S., Landry, M., Bergeron, J., & Chiocchio, F. (1997). The impact of a treatment process for substance users as a function of their degree of exposure to treatment. *Substance Use and Misuse, 32*, 1993–2011.

Chambless, D. L., & Ollendick, T. H. (2001). Empirically supported psychological interventions: Controversies and evidence. *Annual Review of Psychology, 52*, 685–716.

Cherniss, C., & Krantz, D. L. (1983). The ideological community as an antidote to burnout in the human services. In B. A. Farber (Ed.), *Stress and burnout in the human service professions* (pp. 198–212). Elmsford, NY: Pergamon Press.

Connors, G. J., Tonigan, J. S., & Miller, W. R. (2001). A longitudinal model of intake symptomatology, AA participation, and outcome: Retrospective study of the Project MATCH outpatient and aftercare samples. *Journal of Studies on Alcohol, 62,* 817–825.

Connors, G. J., & Walitzer, K. S. (2001). Reducing alcohol consumption among heavily drinking women: Evaluating the contributions of life-skills training and booster sessions. *Journal of Consulting and Clinical Psychology, 69,* 447–456.

Conrad, K. J., Matters, M. D., Hanrahan, P., & Luchins, D. J. (Eds.). (1999). *Homelessness prevention in treatment of substance abuse and mental illness: Logic models and implementation of eight American projects.* New York: Haworth Press.

Corrigan, P. W., Steiner, L., McCracken, S. G., Blaser, B., & Barr, M. (2001). Strategies for disseminating evidence-based practices to staff who treat people with serious mental illness. *Psychiatric Services, 52,* 1598–1606.

Crits-Christoph, P., & Siqueland, L. (1996). Psychosocial treatment for drug abuse: Selected review and recommendations for national health care. *Archives of General Psychiatry, 53,* 749–756.

Cunningham, J. A. (1999). Resolving alcohol-related problems with and without treatment: The effects of different problem criteria. *Journal of Studies on Alcohol, 60,* 463–466.

Dawson, D. A. (1996). Correlates of past-year status among treated and untreated persons with formal alcohol dependence: United States, 1992. *Alcoholism: Clinical and Experimental Research, 20,* 771–779.

De Leon, G. (Ed.). (1997). *Community as method: Therapeutic communities for special populations and special settings.* Westport, CT: Praeger.

Donovan, D. (1999). Efficacy and effectiveness: Complementary findings from two multisite trials evaluating outcomes of alcohol treatments differing in theoretical orientations. *Alcoholism: Clinical and Experimental Research, 23,* 564–572.

Drake, E. E., Mercer-McFadden, C., Mueser, K. T., McHugo, G. J., & Bond, G. R. (1998). Review of integrated mental health and substance abuse treatment for patients with dual disorders. *Schizophrenia Bulletin, 24,* 589–608.

Emrick, C. D. (1975). A review of psychologically oriented treatment of alcoholism: II. The relative effectiveness of different treatment approaches and the effectiveness of treatment versus no treatment. *Journal of Studies on Alcohol, 36,* 88–108.

Ettner, S. L., Hermann, R. C., & Tang, H. (1999). Differences between generalists and mental health specialists in the psychiatric treatment of Medicare beneficiaries. *Health Services Research, 34,* 737–760.

Finney, J. (2000). Limitations in using existing alcohol treatment trials to develop practice guidelines. *Addiction, 95,* 1491–1500.

Finney, J., & Monahan, S. (1996). The cost effectiveness of treatment for alcoholism: A second approximation. *Journal of Studies on Alcohol, 57,* 229–243.

Finney, J., & Moos, R. (1995). Entering treatment for alcohol abuse: A stress and coping model. *Addiction, 90,* 1223–1240.

Finney, J. W., Moos, R. H., & Humphreys, K. (1999). A comparative evaluation of substance abuse treatment: II. Linking proximal outcomes of 12-step and cognitive–behavioral treatment to substance use outcomes. *Alcoholism: Clinical and Experimental Research, 23,* 537–544.

Finney, J., Moos, R., & Timko, C. (1999). The course of treated and untreated substance use disorders: Remission and resolution, relapse and mortality. In B. McCrady & E. Epstein (Eds.), *Addictions: A comprehensive guidebook* (pp. 30–49). New York: Oxford University Press.

Finney, J. W., Noyes, C., Coutts, A., & Moos, R. (1998). Evaluating substance abuse treatment process models: I. Changes on proximal outcome variables during 12-step and cognitive–behavioral treatment. *Journal of Studies on Alcohol, 59,* 371–380.

Fiorentine, R., & Anglin, D. (1996). More is better: Counseling participation and the effectiveness of outpatient drug treatment. *Journal of Substance Abuse Treatment, 13,* 341–348.

Fleming, M. F., Mundt, M. P., French, M. T., Manwell, L. B., Stauffacher, E. A., & Barry, K. L. (2002). Brief physician advice for problem drinkers: Long-term efficacy and benefit-cost analysis. *Alcoholism: Clinical and Experimental Research, 26,* 36–43.

Foa, E. B., Keane, T. M., & Friedman, M. J. (Eds.). (2000). *Effective treatments for PTSD: Practice guidelines from the International Society for Traumatic Stress Studies.* New York: Guilford Press.

Frese, F. J., Stanley, J., Kress, K., & Vogel-Scibilia, S. (2001). Integrating evidence-based practices and the recovery model. *Psychiatric Services, 52,* 1462–1468.

Herman, S. E., Frank, K. A., Mowbray, C. T., Ribisi, K. M., Davidson, W. S., II, BootsMiller, B., et al. (2000). Longitudinal effects of integrated treatment on alcohol use for persons with serious mental illness and substance use disorders. *Journal of Behavioral Health Services and Research, 27,* 286–302.

Hohmann, A. A., & Shear, M. K. (2002). Community-based intervention research: Coping with the "noise" of real life in study design. *American Journal of Psychiatry, 159,* 201–207.

Hser, Y., Anglin, M. D., Grella, C., Longshore, D., & Prendergast, M. L. (1997). Drug treatment careers: A conceptual framework and existing research findings. *Journal of Substance Abuse Treatment, 14,* 543–558.

Hser, Y., Grella, C., Chou, C., & Anglin, M. D. (1998). Relationships between drug treatment careers and outcomes: Findings from the National Drug Abuse Treatment Outcome Study. *Evaluation Review, 22,* 496–519.

Hser, Y., Polinsky, M. L., Maglione, M., & Anglin, M. D. (1999). Matching clients' needs with drug treatment services. *Journal of Substance Abuse Treatment, 16,* 299–305.

Hubble, M. A., Duncan, B. L., & Miller, S. D. (Eds.). (1999). *The heart and soul of change.* Washington, DC: American Psychological Association.

Humphreys, K., Huebsch, P., Finney, J., & Moos, R. (1999). A comparative evaluation of substance abuse treatment: V. Substance abuse treatment can enhance the effectiveness of self-help groups. *Alcoholism: Clinical and Experimental Research, 23,* 558–563.

Humphreys, K., Mankowski, E., Moos, R., & Finney, J. (1999). Enhanced friendship networks and active coping mediate the effect of self-help groups on substance abuse. *Annals of Behavioral Medicine, 21,* 54–60.

Humphreys, K., & Moos, R. (1996). Reduced substance abuse related health care costs among voluntary participants in Alcoholics Anonymous. *Psychiatric Services, 47,* 709–713.

Humphreys, K., & Moos, R. (2001). Can encouraging substance abuse patients to participate in self-help groups reduce the demand for continuing outpatient care? A quasi-experimental study. *Alcoholism: Clinical and Experimental Research, 25,* 711–716.

Humphreys, K., & Tucker, J. (2002). Toward more responsive and effective systems for alcohol-related problems. *Addiction, 97,* 126–132.

Humphreys, K., & Weisner, C. (2000). Use of exclusion criteria in selecting research subjects and its effect on the generalizability of alcohol treatment outcome studies. *American Journal of Psychiatry, 157,* 588–594.

Jerrell, J. M., & Ridgely, M. S. (1999). The relative impact of treatment program "robustness" and "dosage" on client outcomes. *Evaluation and Program Planning, 22,* 323–330.

Litt, M. D., Babor, R. F., DelBoca, F. K., Kadden, R. M., & Cooney, N. (1992). Types of alcoholics: II. Applications of an empirically derived typology to treatment matching. *Archives of General Psychiatry, 49,* 609–614.

Longabaugh, R., & Wirtz, P. W. (Eds.). (2001). *Project MATCH hypotheses: Results and causal chain analyses* (NIH Publication No. 01-4238). Bethesda, MD: National Institute on Alcohol Abuse and Alcoholism.

Longabaugh, R., Wirtz, P., & Rice, C. (2001). Social functioning. In R. Longabaugh & P. W. Wirtz (Eds.), *Project MATCH hypotheses: Results and causal chain analyses* (NIH Publication No. 01-4238, pp. 285–294). Bethesda, MD: National Institute on Alcohol Abuse and Alcoholism.

Luborsky, L., Singer, B., & Luborsky, L. (1975). Comparative studies of psychotherapies: Is it true that "Everyone has won and all must have prizes?" *Archives of General Psychiatry, 32,* 995–1008.

Mattson, M. E., Allen, J. P., Longabaugh, R., Nickless, C. J., Connors, G. J., & Kadden, R. M. (1994). A chronological review of empirical studies of matching alcoholic clients to treatment. *Journal of Studies on Alcohol, 12*(Suppl.), 16–29.

McCrady, B. S., Epstein, E. E., & Hirsch, L. S. (1999). Maintaining change after conjoint behavioral alcohol treatment for men: Outcomes at 6 months. *Addiction, 94,* 1381–1396.

McLellan, A. T., Grissom, G. R., Zanis, D., Randall, M., Brill, P., & O'Brien, C. P. (1997). Problem–service "matching" in addiction treatment: A prospective study in four programs. *Archives of General Psychiatry, 54,* 730–735.

McLellan, A. T., Hagan, T. A., Levine, M., Gould, F., Meyers, K., Bencivengo, M., & Durell, J. (1998). Supplemental social services improve outcomes in public addiction treatment. *Addiction, 93,* 1489–1499.

McLellan, A. T., Woody, G. E., Metzger, D., McKay, J., Durell, J., Alterman, A. I., & O'Brien, C. P. (1996). Evaluating the effectiveness of addiction treatments: Reasonable expectations, appropriate comparisons. *Millbank Quarterly, 74,* 51–85.

Mechanic, D. (1990). Treating mental illness: Generalist versus specialist. *Health Affairs, 9,* 61–75.

Miller, W. R., & Wilbourne, P. L. (2002). Mesa Grande: A methodological analysis of clinical trials of treatments for alcohol use disorders. *Addiction, 97,* 265–277.

Moggi, F., Ouimette, P., Finney, J., & Moos, R. (1999). Effectiveness of substance abuse treatment for dual diagnosis patients: A model of treatment factors associated with one-year outcomes. *Journal of Studies on Alcohol, 60,* 856–866.

Moos, R. (1994a). *The Social Climate Scales: A user's guide* (2nd ed.). Palo Alto, CA: Consulting Psychologists Press.

Moos, R. (1994b). *Work Environment Scale manual* (3rd ed.). Palo Alto, CA: Consulting Psychologists Press.

Moos, R. (1997). *Evaluating treatment environments: The quality of psychiatric and substance abuse programs.* New Brunswick, NJ: Transaction.

Moos, R. (2002). The mystery of human context and coping: An unraveling of clues. *American Journal of Community Psychology, 30,* 67–88.

Moos, R., Finney, J., & Cronkite, R. (1990). *Alcoholism treatment: Context, process, and outcome.* New York: Oxford University Press.

Moos, R., Finney, J. W., Federman, B., & Suchinsky, R. (2000). Specialty mental health care improves patients' outcomes: Findings from a nationwide program to monitor the quality of care for patients with substance use disorders. *Journal of Studies on Alcohol, 61,* 704–713.

Moos, R., & Moos, B. (1994). *Family Environment Scale manual* (3rd ed.). Palo Alto, CA: Consulting Psychologists Press.

Moos, R., & Moos, B. (1998). The staff workplace and the quality and outcome of substance abuse treatment. *Journal of Studies on Alcohol, 59,* 43–51.

Moos, R., & Moos, B. (2003). Long-term influence of duration and intensity of treatment on previously untreated individuals with alcohol use disorders. *Addiction, 98,* 325–337.

Moos, R., Schaefer, J., Andrassy, J., & Moos, B. (2001). Outpatient mental health care, self-help groups, and patients' 1-year treatment outcomes. *Journal of Clinical Psychology, 57,* 1–15.

Morgenstern, J., Labouvie, E., McCrady, B. S., Kahler, C. W., & Frey, R. M. (1997). Affiliation with Alcoholics Anonymous after treatment: A study of its therapeutic effects and mechanisms of action. *Journal of Consulting and Clinical Psychology, 65,* 768–777.

Morgenstern, J., & Longabaugh, R. (2000). Cognitive–behavioral treatment for alcohol dependence: A review of evidence for its hypothesized mechanisms of action. *Addiction, 95,* 1475–1490.

Moyer, A., Finney, J. W., Swearingen, C. E., & Vergun, P. (2002). Brief interventions for alcohol problems: A meta-analytic review of controlled investigations in treatment-seeking and non-treatment-seeking populations. *Addiction, 97,* 279–292.

Nathan, P. E. (1998). Practice guidelines: Not yet ideal. *American Psychologist, 53,* 290–299.

Norcross, J. C. (1999). Collegially validated limitations of empirically validated treatments. *Clinical Psychology Science and Practice, 6,* 472–476.

Norcross, J. C. (Ed.). (2002). *Psychotherapy relationships that work: Therapist contributions and responsiveness to patient needs.* New York: Oxford University Press.

Ouimette, P. C., Finney, J. W., & Moos, R. (1997). Twelve-step and cognitive–behavioral treatment for substance abuse: A comparison of treatment effectiveness. *Journal of Consulting and Clinical Psychology, 65,* 220–234.

Ouimette, P. C., Moos, R., & Finney, J. (1998). Influence of outpatient treatment and 12-step group involvement on one-year substance abuse treatment outcomes. *Journal of Studies on Alcohol, 59,* 513–522.

Prendergast, M. L., Podus, D., & Chang, E. (2000). Program factors and treatment outcomes in drug dependence treatment: An examination using meta-analysis. *Substance Use & Misuse, 35,* 1931–1965.

Project MATCH Research Group. (1997). Matching alcoholism treatment to client heterogeneity: Project MATCH posttreatment drinking outcomes. *Journal of Studies on Alcohol, 58,* 7–29.

Project MATCH Research Group. (1998). Matching alcoholism treatments to client heterogeneity: Project MATCH three-year drinking outcomes. *Alcoholism: Clinical and Experimental Research, 22,* 1300–1311.

Regier, D. A., Farmer, M. E., Rae, D. S., Locke, B. Z., Keith, S. J., Judd, L. L., & Goodwin, F. K. (1990). Comorbidity of mental disorders with alcohol and other drug abuse. *Journal of the American Medical Association, 264,* 2511–2518.

Ritsher, J., Finney, J., & Moos, R. (2002). The influence of treatment orientation and continuing care on substance abuse patients' two-year remission. *Psychiatric Services, 53,* 595–601.

Rogers, W. H., Wells, K. B., Meredith, L. S., Sturm, R., & Burnam, A. (1993). Outcomes for adult outpatients with depression under prepaid or fee-for-service financing. *Archives of General Psychiatry, 50,* 517–525.

Rosenheck, R. A. (2001). Organizational process: A missing link between research and practice. *Psychiatric Services, 52,* 1607–1612.

Rosenthal, R. N., & Westreich, L. (1999). Treatment of persons with dual diagnoses of substance use disorder and other psychological problems. In B. S. McCrady & E. E. Epstein (Eds.), *Addictions: A comprehensive guidebook* (pp. 439–476). New York: Oxford University Press.

Schulz, R., Greenley, J. R., & Brown, R. (1995). Organization, management, and client effects on staff burnout. *Journal of Health and Social Behavior, 36,* 333–345.

Shortell, S. M., O'Brien, J. L., Carman, J. M., Foster, R. W., Hughes, E. F., Boerstler, H., & O'Conner, E. J. (1995). Assessing the impact of continuous quality improvement/total quality management: Concept versus implementation. *Health Service Research, 30,* 377–401.

Simpson, D. D., Joe, G. W., & Brown, B. S. (1997). Treatment retention and follow-up outcomes in the Drug Abuse Treatment Outcome Study (DATOS). *Psychology of Addictive Behaviors, 11,* 294–307.

Stout, R. L., Rubin, A., Zwick, W., Zywiak, W., & Bellino, L. (1999). Optimizing the cost-effectiveness of alcohol treatment: A rationale for extended case monitoring. *Addictive Behaviors, 24,* 17–35.

Swearingen, C. E., Moyer, A., & Finney, J. W. (2003). Alcoholism treatment outcome studies, 1970–1998: An expanded look at the nature of the research. *Addictive Behaviors, 28,* 415–436.

Timko, C., Moos, R., & Finney, J. (2000). Models of matching patients and treatment programs. In K. Craik, R. Price, & W. B. Walsh (Eds.), *Person–environment psychology: New directions and perspectives* (2nd ed., pp. 169–196). Mahwah, NJ: Erlbaum.

Timko, C., Moos, R., Finney, J. W., & Lesar, M. D. (2000). Long-term outcomes of alcohol use disorders: Comparing untreated individuals with those in Alcoholics Anonymous and formal treatment. *Journal of Studies on Alcohol, 61,* 529–540.

Tonigan, J. S., Connors, G. J., & Miller, W. R. (2002). Participation and involvement in Alcoholics Anonymous. In T. F. Babor & F. K. Del Boca (Eds.), *Treatment matching in alcoholism* (International Research Monographs in the Addictions, pp. 184–204). New York: Cambridge University Press.

Tonigan, J. S., Toscova, R., & Miller, W. R. (1996). Meta-analysis of the literature on Alcoholics Anonymous: Sample and study characteristics moderate findings. *Journal of Studies on Alcohol, 57,* 65–72.

Truax, C. B. (1966). Reinforcement and non-reinforcement in Rogerian psychotherapy. *Journal of Abnormal Psychology, 71,* 1–9.

Vaillant, G. E. (1995). *The natural history of alcoholism revisited.* Cambridge, MA: Harvard University Press.

Wells, K. B. (1999). Treatment research at the crossroads: The scientific interface of clinical trials and effectiveness research. *American Journal of Psychiatry, 156,* 5–10.

Zywiak, W. H., Longabaugh, R., & Wirtz, P. W. (2002). Decomposing the relationships between pretreatment social network characteristics and alcohol treatment outcomes. *Journal of Studies on Alcohol, 63,* 114–121.

22

ABSTINENCE-BASED INCENTIVES IN METHADONE MAINTENANCE: INTERACTION WITH INTAKE STIMULANT TEST RESULTS

MAXINE L. STITZER, JESSICA PEIRCE, NANCY M. PETRY, KIMBERLY KIRBY, JOHN ROLL, JOSEPH KRASNANSKY, ALLAN COHEN, JACK BLAINE, RYAN VANDREY, KEN KOLODNER, AND RUI LI

Previous research, much of it conducted with stimulant abusers entering outpatient psychosocial counseling treatment, has documented the importance of drug use at treatment entry, defined by submission of a drug-positive urine, as a predictor of treatment outcome (Alterman et al., 1997; Alterman, McKay, Mulvaney, & McLellan, 1996; Ehrman, Robbins, & Cornish, 2001; Kampman et al., 2001; Petry et al., 2006; Petry, Alessi, Marx, Austin, & Tardif, 2005; Petry et al., 2004; Reiber, Ramirez, Parent, & Rawson, 2002). Similar findings about the importance of early treatment drug use as a predictor of later outcome have also emerged from research conducted with patients enrolled in opioid substitution therapy. Morral, Belding, and Iguchi (1999), for example, found that submission of opiate-negative urine samples during Treatment Week 2 was associated with positive 6-month treatment outcome based on retention and limited or no drug use in methadone maintenance patients. Strain, Stitzer, Liebson, and Bigelow (1998) found that the percentage of cocaine-positive urines submitted during the first 2 weeks of treatment

This research was supported with funding from the National Drug Abuse Treatment Clinical Trials Network (Grant U10 DA13034).

predicted 29% of the variance in cocaine test results during the next 5 months. Petry, Martin, and Simcic (2005) found that urinalysis test result at study intake was the only pretreatment variable that predicted submission of a cocaine-negative sample at 6-month follow-up in a contingency management study with stabilized methadone maintenance patients. Similarly, Sofuoglu, Gonzalez, Poling, and Kosten (2003) found that a cocaine-negative urine at study start predicted better outcomes (more cocaine-negative urines submitted) during a 24-week trial that tested both a medication (desipramine vs. placebo) and an abstinence-based contingency management intervention in buprenorphine-maintained patients.

Whereas the above studies have reported on the association between drug use and overall treatment outcome, other studies have shown that drug use severity, as revealed by percentage of drug-positive tests observed during a prestudy baseline evaluation, is specifically associated with response versus nonresponse to abstinence-based contingency management treatment interventions in methadone maintenance patients. Specifically, studies have shown that patients with fewer baseline drug-positive urines are overrepresented among those who respond well to abstinence incentive interventions. In an early study, Stitzer, Iguchi, and Felch (1992) noted that the ability to achieve a sustained period of abstinence during an abstinence-contingent methadone take-home intervention was associated with a lower percentage of baseline drug-positive urines and fewer different drugs detected in the urine. Similarly, Kidorf, Stitzer, and Brooner (1994) observed that submission of fewer urine samples positive for any drug during the first month of methadone maintenance treatment was strongly associated with later ability to earn methadone take-home privileges in usual care based on absence of detected drug use. Silverman et al. (1998) noted that patients who maintained long periods of sustained abstinence in a voucher incentive program submitted more opiate- and cocaine-negative samples during baseline than did nonresponders. Similarly, Preston et al. (1998) found that less drug use as detected in quantitative urinalysis testing was a significant predictor of sustained abstinence versus nonresponse during a voucher-based contingency management intervention. However, in the study by Sofuoglu et al. (2003), significant effects of desipramine but not contingency management were mediated by drug use severity. That is, effects of contingency management were seen irrespective of baseline drug use, but a desipramine versus placebo difference was seen only in those testing stimulant negative at study entry.

Although this research shows that individuals with less severe drug use are likely to be overrepresented among treatment responders in an abstinence-focused contingency management program, it is not clear whether treatment response is restricted to those with less severe drug use or whether patients with both higher and lower rates of drug use can benefit from these interventions. In the present chapter, we examine the interaction between incentive effects and baseline urinalysis test results of methadone maintenance patients who enrolled in a large multisite study of abstinence-based contingency management conducted within the National Drug Abuse Treatment Clinical Trials Network (Peirce et al., 2006). This study, which showed a significant main effect of the incentive procedure in reducing overall rates of stimulant drug use, was ideal for investigating the relationship between baseline urine test results and treatment outcome in a large and regionally diverse sample of methadone maintenance patients who use stimulants during treatment. Thus, the present study's purpose was to confirm the previously observed association between intake urine test results and overall treatment outcome and to determine whether intake stimulant test result was a mediator of treatment response—that is, whether incentives were differentially effective depending on participants' testing stimulant negative versus positive at study entry.

METHOD

Participants

Study participants included in the current analysis were 386 methadone maintenance patients enrolled in six different clinics who met the following study eligibility criteria: (a) They had been enrolled in treatment for between 30 and 1,095 days (3 years), and (b) they had submitted a stimulant- (cocaine, amphetamine, or methamphetamine) positive clinical urine within 2 weeks of study entry. The only exclusion criterion was self-report of being in remission from a gambling problem, for which no one was excluded. Two participants from the original sample were omitted because they did not have a study intake urine test result recorded. Participants assigned to incentive versus control conditions did not differ on any demographic or drug use characteristics (Peirce et al., 2006).

Procedure

The first study urine was collected following completion of a study intake battery, for which participants were compensated with a prize item of their choice worth about $20. The urine was tested on-site using the OnTrack TesTcup 5 (Roche Diagnostics, Indianapolis, IN), which detected cocaine, amphetamine, methamphetamine, cannabinoids, and morphine. Because stimulant drug abstinence was the primary target for intervention, the first urine test result (stimulant positive vs. negative) was used to stratify participants prior to randomization into incentive versus control treatments. The same urine test result formed the basis for stratified group analyses in the present study. Although urine test data collected over a more extended time frame might have provided a more complete and accurate picture of prestudy drug use severity, baseline urine test data were not collected as part of the study, nor were they available to the study from the clinical records.

Participants who submitted samples twice per week testing negative for stimulants (urinalysis testing for cocaine, amphetamine, and methamphetamine) and alcohol (breath alcohol level = .01 g/dL) could earn draws from an abstinence bowl containing 500 chips. The number of draws awarded escalated by one per week during the 12-week study provided that consecutive samples tested stimulant and alcohol negative. If a positive sample or an unexcused absence occurred, the number reset to a single draw, after which draws could again escalate for consecutive negative tests. Those testing stimulant and alcohol negative could earn two bonus draws at each visit if they were also negative for opiates (urines were tested for cannabinoids, but these results had no programmed consequences). The draws resulted in prize winnings under a probability schedule with overall possible earnings of $400 for those who remained continuously abstinent for all target drugs over the 12-week study. It should be noted that the overall incidence of positive breath alcohol readings was very low (1%) throughout the study so that outcomes represent primarily stimulant use and that the preponderance (91%) of stimulant-positive samples were for cocaine, with the remainder being amphetamine or methamphetamine.

Data Analysis

Participants testing stimulant positive ($n = 292$) versus negative ($n = 94$) on their first study urine were first compared on a variety of demographic and drug use variables, using t test for continuous and chi-square for categorical variables.

For the outcome, time to study dropout, Cox proportional hazards regression was used. Study dropout was defined as occurring after 30 consecutive days with no urinalysis sample submitted at a study visit. The dropout "event" was defined on the day of the last submitted urine sample. Time to dropout was calculated from the first day of the study. If dropout did not occur during the 12-week period, data were censored at Day 84. Retention analyses are reported using hazard ratios and 95% confidence intervals (CIs).

General estimating equation analysis was used to determine whether result of the first study urine was related to subsequent likelihood of submitting stimulant (cocaine, amphetamine, or methamphetamine) negative versus positive urines at each of 24 consecutively scheduled twice-weekly study visits. Results are reported as adjusted odds ratios (ORs) with 95% CIs indicating the likelihood that participants in one subgroup or study condition had different outcomes than participants in another subgroup or study condition.

Two sets of analyses were conducted, with missing samples coded either as missing or as positive. This strategy allows for a comparison of outcomes when two very different assumptions are made concerning the meaning of missing data. The incidence of missing urines for the intent-to-treat sample ranged from 37% to 40% in all study subgroups except for those testing stimulant negative at intake and subsequently assigned to the incentive condition, where only 21% of samples were missing.

An identical modeling strategy was used for both retention (survival analysis) and urinalysis (general estimating equation) data. The first model tested for main effects of incentives versus control interventions and of stimulant-positive versus stimulant-negative initial urinalysis test result. A second model was run that included the same main effects plus an Incentive Condition × Initial Urine Test Result interaction. Finally, the effect of incentive versus control intervention was examined separately in stratified models for those who tested stimulant positive versus negative on their first study urine. This planned analysis was conducted to determine whether beneficial effects of the incentive intervention were apparent in both participants testing stimulant positive and those testing stimulant negative at study intake.

Both retention and drug use analyses were rerun with the nine demographic and drug dependence variables shown in Table 22.1 entered as covariates. Statistical outcomes for the urine-positive versus urine-negative variable were not substantially different with these covariates included, and data are reported for the unadjusted analyses.

TABLE 22.1
Sample Demographic and Drug Dependence Variables

Variable	Stimulant positive ($n = 292$)	Stimulant negative ($n = 94$)
Demographics		
Gender (% female)	47.3	34.0*
Race (% White)	23.7	34.0†
Age (% > 40 years)	61.6	54.3*
Employed[a] (%)	30.6	33.3
Criminal justice referral[b] (%)	5.8	6.4
Entered from controlled environment (%)	0.3	0.0
Drug dependence		
Stimulant dependent[c] (%)	87.7	66.0**
Alcohol dependent[c] (%)	15.1	22.3
Cannabis dependent[c] (%)	9.8	3.4
Methadone dose (mg; $M \pm SD$)	85.5 (25.5)	86.5 (29.4)
Months of treatment prior to study start	9.2 (9.8)	8.4 (8.6)

[a]Usual employment status in past 3 years is full-time work. [b]Intake was prompted, suggested, or required by the criminal justice system. [c]Assessed using *DSM–IV* Checklist (Forman, Svikis, Montoya, & Blaine, 2004; Hudziak et al., 1993).
†$p < .06$. *$p \leq .05$. **$p < .01$.

RESULTS

Table 22.1 shows demographic data for stimulant-positive versus stimulus-negative participants. Those testing stimulant positive at study entry were older (greater percentage above the age of 40; $p < .05$) compared with stimulant-negative participants, more likely to be female ($p < .05$), and marginally less likely to be a member of a minority ethnic group ($p < .06$). Participants testing stimulant positive at study entry were also more likely to meet criteria for stimulant dependence (88% vs. 66%, $p < .01$) as described in the *Diagnostic and Statistical Manual of Mental Disorders* (4th ed.; American Psychiatric Association, 1994).

Study retention data are shown in Figure 22.1. Although there was a trend for less dropout among those testing negative at intake and assigned to the incentive treatment, Cox proportional hazards analysis revealed no significant main effect of intake urinalysis result on study retention (hazard ratio [HR] = 1.25; 0.82–1.91), nor was the effect on retention significant for the stimulant-negative subgroup (HR = 1.55; 0.72–3.32). At the end of the 12-week intervention, 70% of those testing stimulant negative at baseline versus 64% of those testing stimulant positive at baseline were still attending study visits. Note that those coded as study dropouts may have continued in treatment at the clinic.

Figure 22.2 shows results for urinalysis data with missing samples coded as missing. There was a large and statistically significant effect of intake urine test result on overall submission of stimulant-negative samples during the

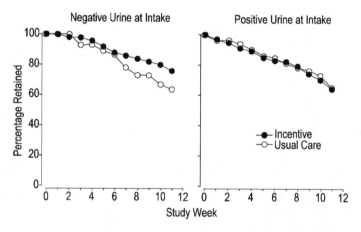

Figure 22.1. Study retention for participants who tested stimulant negative (left panel; $n = 94$) versus stimulant positive (right panel; $n = 292$) at study intake. Data in each panel are shown separately for participants exposed to usual care psychosocial counseling treatment with (closed symbols) or without (open symbols) an added stimulant abstinence incentive procedure.

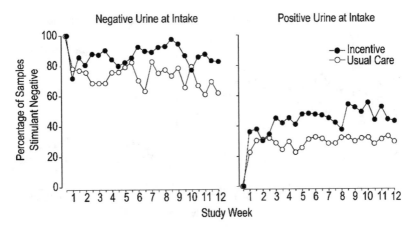

Figure 22.2. Percentage of stimulant- and alcohol-negative samples submitted for each of 24 study visits during the 12-week intervention with missing samples coded as missing. Data are shown separately for participants who tested stimulant negative (left panel; *n* = 94) versus stimulant positive (right panel; *n* = 292) at study intake. Data in each panel are shown separately for participants exposed to usual care psychosocial counseling treatment with (closed symbols) or without (open symbols) an added stimulant abstinence incentive procedure.

study (OR = 8.67; CI = 5.81–12.94). Overall percentage of samples testing stimulant and alcohol negative during the 12-week study was 82% in those who entered stimulant negative versus 34% in those entering stimulant positive. When missing urines were coded as missing, there was no interaction between baseline urine test result and incentive intervention (*p* = .60). In the stratified analysis, abstinence incentives had a significant effect on percentage of negative samples submitted during the study both for those testing negative at study entry (OR = 2.27; CI = 1.13– 4.75) and for those testing positive at study entry (OR = 1.84; CI = 1.25–2.71). Figure 22.3 shows urinalysis data with missing samples coded as positive, a measure that encompasses incentive effects on retention, compliance with urine testing schedules, and submission of positive urines. Results were very similar to those obtained with urines coded as missing. There was a large and significant effect of intake urine test result on submission of stimulant-negative samples during the study (OR = 5.30; CI = 3.78–7.45), with overall percentage of samples testing stimulant and alcohol negative being 58% in those who entered stimulant negative versus 21% in those entering stimulant positive. The interaction between urine test result and incentive effects was nonsignificant (*p* = .27), and a significant increase in submission of stimulant-negative urines was associated with the incentive intervention both for those testing negative (OR = 2.49; CI = 1.42–4.37) and for those testing positive (OR = 1.70; CI = 1.17–2.47) at study entry.

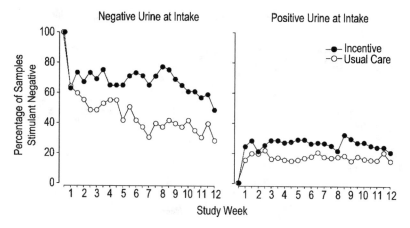

Figure 22.3. Percentage of stimulant- and alcohol-negative samples submitted for each of 24 study visits during the 12-week intervention with missing samples coded as positive. Data are shown separately for participants who tested stimulant negative (left panel; $n = 94$) versus stimulant positive (right panel; $n = 292$) at study intake. Data in each panel are shown separately for participants exposed to usual care psychosocial counseling treatment with (closed symbols) or without (open symbols) an added stimulant abstinence incentive procedure.

In the original study report (Peirce et al., 2006), individual differences in overall treatment outcome were characterized by classifying participants according to the total number of stimulant- and alcohol-negative samples they delivered during the study, a measure that reflects both retention and any during-treatment drug use. Table 22.2 shows the percentage of study participants testing stimulant negative at study entry as a function of this treatment outcome measure. The data show that those with better outcomes were more likely to have been stimulant negative at study entry.

DISCUSSION

This secondary analysis of data from the National Drug Abuse Treatment Clinical Trials Network multisite study of abstinence incentives in methadone maintenance patients replicates and extends previous observations about the poor treatment outcome prognosis conferred by drug-positive urine tests during an early treatment baseline (Kidorf et al., 1994; Morral et al., 1999; Preston et al., 1998; Silverman et al., 1998; Stitzer et al., 1992) or at the start of a study (Petry, Martin, et al., 2005; Sofuoglu et al., 2003). Overall, those in the present study who tested stimulant positive at study entry were 5 to 8 times more likely to deliver drug-positive urines during the study (depending on assumptions made about missing urines) independent of

TABLE 22.2
Intake Urine Test and Study Outcome

Number of negative urines	n	Stimulant negative at study intake (%)
0	110	0
1–6	124	22
7–18	95	33
19–24	57	63

Note. Numbers reflect the total number of negative samples submitted during the 12-week study. Negative urine categories are those reported in the main outcome article (Peirce et al., 2006). However, two intermediate intervals (7–12 and 13–18) were collapsed here to increase sample size.

specific treatment conditions to which they were exposed. This is consistent with the lower prevalence of stimulant dependence in the group testing negative at study entry (Table 22.1).

The novel information provided by this study comes from examination of the interaction between intake urine test result and treatment interventions. Methadone-maintained patients were selected for this study on the basis of submission of a stimulant-positive urine during the 2 weeks prior to the start of their participation, and the majority of participants (76%) started the study with submission of a stimulant-positive urine. Nevertheless, there was a sufficient sample of stimulant-negative participants to permit evaluation of the impact of this variable on outcomes in subgroups that were very similar on demographic and drug use variables except for the higher likelihood of a stimulant dependence diagnosis in the urine-positive-at-intake group (Table 22.1).

Consistent with previous reports, patients who submitted a stimulant-negative urine at study entry, indicating a less regular or consistent pattern of drug use, were overrepresented among those who had very good outcomes under an abstinence incentive procedure (see Table 22.2). This imbalance in absolute number of treatment responders might suggest to clinicians that incentives should be offered only to patients with less severe baseline drug use. However, when data were analyzed separately for those submitting a positive versus negative sample at entry, the stratified analysis demonstrated that the abstinence incentives reduced during-treatment drug use relative to use seen under control conditions, both in patients who tested stimulant positive and in those who tested stimulant negative at study entry (Figures 22.2 and 22.3). This type of analysis has not generally been conducted in previous studies of abstinence incentives (but see Petry et al., 2004).

The ORs obtained in stratified analysis were only slightly higher (2.3 and 2.5, depending on missing data assumptions) for those testing stimulant negative at study entry as compared with those testing stimulant positive (1.7 and 1.8). This suggests that size of the incentive effect was similar in magnitude for these two groups. It is nevertheless notable that the absolute magnitude of effect in the two subgroups was very different (Figures 22.2 and 22.3), such that the percentage of negative urines submitted during treatment with abstinence incentives by those with positive urines at intake did not even reach the level of negative urines observed under usual care conditions among those testing stimulant negative at intake. This relatively low absolute level of negative urines makes it more difficult for clinicians to appreciate the impact of incentive effects in patients with relatively more severe profiles of stimulant drug use. Nevertheless, results of the stratified analysis are important from a clinical perspective because they suggest that incentives can beneficially be offered to all methadone patients, irrespective of their baseline drug use severity, as a strategy for improving treatment outcome.

The finding that abstinence incentives were effective in those testing stimulant negative at study start is important, as it is possible that there would be little room for improvement in this group, thus making abstinence incentives unnecessary. This was not the case, however, as there was still considerable room for improvement in the usual care treatment sample, even when missing samples were coded as missing rather than as stimulant positive (Figure 22.2). Thus, the abstinence incentive intervention was appropriate and clinically useful for this group.

With regard to the group testing stimulant positive at study start, it is impressive that abstinence incentives were demonstrably effective, as these individuals may have difficulty earning incentives early in the program and thus may not be exposed to the benefits of the abstinence incentive procedure (Preston, Umbricht, Wong, & Epstein, 2001). It may be important in this regard to note that a free (priming) gift was given in the parent study to all participants following the intake interview so that they could come in contact with and appreciate the available rewards. Nevertheless, the relatively low representation of stimulant-positive participants among those with excellent treatment outcomes (Table 22.2) suggests that additional intervention tailoring may be needed to improve response rates in patients with heavier during-treatment drug use. One strategy that has been successful in addressing this problem is to increase the magnitude of reinforcement offered (Dallery, Silverman, Chutuape, Bigelow, & Stitzer, 2001), but other strategies may also be useful, especially because cost is usually considered a barrier to use of incentive therapies in community treatment programs.

The large and diverse sample that included methadone maintenance patients from six different clinics with regionally diverse locations within the United States strengthens the generality of findings from this study. One potential weakness is that outcome prediction was based on results of a single urine test obtained at the start of the study and thus may not be representative of overall prestudy rates and patterns of drug use among participants. It is nevertheless impressive to note how well this single urine test result was able to differentiate among those with higher versus lower overall rates of stimulant drug use during the study (Figures 22.2 and 22.3) as well as those who had relatively better versus worse outcomes during an abstinence incentive intervention (Table 22.2).

In summary, this study found that an abstinence incentive targeting stimulant and alcohol use was effective in lowering during-treatment stimulant drug use independent of prestudy levels of drug use. This finding is consistent with previous observations indicating that those with lower levels of drug use are more likely to be overrepresented among responders to an abstinence incentive intervention, but it makes the important point that incentives are effective in stimulant-abusing methadone patients regardless of their baseline levels of drug use. These findings suggest that abstinence incentives have significant clinical benefits independent of initial drug use severity among methadone maintenance patients with ongoing stimulant drug use. Thus, abstinence incentives may be offered to all methadone maintenance patients who evidence ongoing stimulant drug use during treatment as a strategy to improve overall treatment outcomes for this difficult to treat group of patients.

REFERENCES

Alterman, A. I., Kampman, K., Boardman, C. R., Cacciola, J. S., Rutherford, M. J., McKay, J. R., & Maany, I. (1997). A cocaine-positive baseline urine predicts outpatient treatment attrition and failure to attain initial abstinence. *Drug and Alcohol Dependence, 46*, 79–85.

Alterman, A. I., McKay, J. R., Mulvaney, F. D., & McLellan, A. T. (1996). Prediction of attrition from day hospital treatment in lower socioeconomic cocaine-dependent men. *Drug and Alcohol Dependence, 40*, 227–233.

American Psychiatric Association. (1994). *Diagnostic and statistical manual of mental disorders* (4th ed.). Washington, DC: Author.

Dallery, J., Silverman, K., Chutuape, M. A., Bigelow, G. E., & Stitzer, M. L. (2001). Voucher-based reinforcement of opiate plus cocaine abstinence in treatment-resistant methadone patients: Effects of reinforcer magnitude. *Experimental and Clinical Psychopharmacology, 9*, 317–325.

Ehrman, R. N., Robbins, S. J., & Cornish, J. W. (2001). Results of a baseline urine test predict levels of cocaine use during treatment. *Drug and Alcohol Dependence, 62*, 1–7.

Forman, R. F., Svikis, D., Montoya, I. D., & Blaine, J. (2004). Selection of a substance use disorder diagnostic instrument by the National Drug Abuse Treatment Clinical Trials Network. *Journal of Substance Abuse Treatment, 27*, 1–8.

Hudziak, J. J., Helzer, J. E., Wetzel, W. W., Kessel, K. B., McGee, B., Janca, A., & Przybeck, T. (1993). Use of the DSM–III–R Checklist for initial diagnostic assessment. *Comprehensive Psychiatry, 34*, 375–383.

Kampman, K. M., Alterman, A. I., Volpicelli, J. R., Maany, I., Muller, E. S., Luce, D. D., et al. (2001). Cocaine withdrawal symptoms and initial urine toxicology results predict treatment attrition in outpatient cocaine dependence treatment. *Psychology of Addictive Behaviors, 15*, 52–59.

Kidorf, M., Stitzer, M. L., & Brooner, R. K. (1994). Characteristics of methadone patients responding to take-home incentives. *Behavior Therapy, 25*, 109–121.

Morral, A. R., Belding, M. A., & Iguchi, M. Y. (1999). Identifying methadone maintenance clients at risk for poor treatment response: Pretreatment and early progress indicators. *Drug and Alcohol Dependence, 55*, 25–33.

Peirce, J. M., Petry, N. M., Stitzer, M. L., Blaine, J., Kolodner, K., Li, R., et al. (2006). Lower-cost incentives increase stimulant abstinence in methadone maintenance community treatment: Results of the National Drug Abuse Treatment Clinical Trials Network Multi-Site Study. *Archives of General Psychiatry, 63*, 201–208.

Petry, N. M., Alessi, S. M., Carroll, K. M., Hanson, T., MacKinnon, S., Rounsaville, B., & Sierra, S. (2006). Contingency management treatments: Reinforcing abstinence versus adherence with goal-related activities. *Journal of Consulting and Clinical Psychology, 74*, 592–601.

Petry, N. M., Alessi, S. M., Marx, J., Austin, M., & Tardif, M. (2005). Vouchers versus prizes: Contingency management treatment of substance abusers in community settings. *Journal of Consulting and Clinical Psychology, 73*, 1005–1014.

Petry, N. M., Martin, B., & Simcic, F. (2005). Prize reinforcement contingency management for cocaine dependence: Integration with group therapy in a methadone clinic. *Journal of Consulting and Clinical Psychology, 73*, 354–359.

Petry, N. M., Tedford, J., Austin, M., Nich, C., Carroll, K. M., & Rounsaville, B. J. (2004). Prize reinforcement contingency management for treating cocaine users: How low can we go, and with whom? *Addiction, 99*, 349–360.

Preston, K. L., Silverman, K., Higgins, S. T., Brooner, R. K., Montoya, I., Schuster, C. R., & Cone, E. J. (1998). Cocaine use early in treatment predicts outcome in a behavioral treatment program. *Journal of Consulting and Clinical Psychology, 66*, 691–696.

Preston, K. L., Umbricht, A., Wong, C. J., & Epstein, D. H. (2001). Shaping cocaine abstinence by successive approximations. *Journal of Consulting and Clinical Psychology, 69*, 643–654.

Reiber, C., Ramirez, A., Parent, D., & Rawson, R. A. (2002). Predicting treatment success at multiple timepoints in diverse patient populations of cocaine-dependent individuals. *Drug and Alcohol Dependence, 68*, 35–48.

Silverman, K., Wong, C. J., Umbricht-Schneiter, A., Montoya, I. D., Schuster, C. R., & Preston, K. L. (1998). Broad beneficial effects of cocaine abstinence reinforcement among methadone patients. *Journal of Consulting and Clinical Psychology, 66*, 811–824.

Sofuoglu, M., Gonzalez, G., Poling, J., & Kosten, T. R. (2003). Prediction of treatment outcome by baseline urine cocaine results and self-reported cocaine use for cocaine and opioid dependence. *American Journal of Drug and Alcohol Abuse, 29*, 713–727.

Stitzer, M. L., Iguchi, M. Y., & Felch, L. J. (1992). Contingent take-home incentive: Effects on drug use of methadone maintenance patients. *Journal of Consulting and Clinical Psychology, 60,* 927–934.

Strain, E. C., Stitzer, M. L., Liebson, I. A., & Bigelow, G. E. (1998). Useful predictors of outcome in methadone-treated patients: Results from a controlled clinical trial with three doses of methadone. *Journal of Maintenance in the Addictions, 1,* 15–28.

VIII

ISSUES IN SPECIFIC POPULATIONS

23

PREVENTING SUBSTANCE ABUSE IN AMERICAN INDIAN AND ALASKA NATIVE YOUTH: PROMISING STRATEGIES FOR HEALTHIER COMMUNITIES

ELIZABETH H. HAWKINS, LILLIAN H. CUMMINS,
AND G. ALAN MARLATT

Substance abuse, particularly alcohol misuse, is consistently cited as one of the most critical health concerns facing American Indian and Alaska Native communities (Beauvais, 1996; French, 2000; Indian Health Service, 1977; King, Beals, Manson, & Trimble, 1992; Mail, Heurtin-Roberts, Martin, & Howard, 2002; U.S. Department of Health and Human Services, 2001; Young, 1988). It has had profoundly harmful consequences on both individual and societal levels, and it is widely believed that few Indian families remain unaffected, either directly or indirectly. The historical and political context surrounding alcohol use among American Indians and Alaska Natives is far too complex to address in the scope of this chapter (for a more in-depth discussion of this topic, see E. H. Hawkins & Blume, 2002). Although many communities have experienced social and cultural devastation that can be directly attributed to alcohol use, it

Preparation of this chapter was supported in part by the National Institute on Alcohol Abuse and Alcoholism (NIAAA) Grant 1 R0 1 AA12321-02, *Intervention for Adolescent Indian Drinking*, and NIAAA Institutional Research Training Grant T32AA07455. We wish to acknowledge our colleagues at the Seattle Indian Health Board and the Addictive Behaviors Research Center for their support and encouragement and to thank the participants of the Journeys of the Circle project for the inspiration and motivation they provided us. This chapter is humbly offered in support of Native youth everywhere as they strive to make healthy lifestyle choices.

is essential to note the large variance in actual rates of alcohol use and related problems experienced in Indian Country. Alcohol has and continues to be damaging to Native communities, yet there is a sizeable population of Native Americans who do not drink or who are nonproblem drinkers (Mail & Johnson, 1993; Myers, Kagawa-Singer, Kumanyika, Lex, & Markides, 1995). Although some degree of alcohol use is extremely common among American Indian youth, often it is not the first substance used or the primary drug of choice (Beauvais, Oetting, Wolf, & Edwards, 1989; Novins, Beals, & Mitchell, 2001).

This chapter is intended as an overview of the published literature on substance use prevention among American Indian adolescents, focusing on the most widely used drugs: tobacco, inhalants, alcohol, and marijuana. Because research focusing on Native Americans has had relatively little representation in mainstream psychological journals, the field as a whole is largely unaware of many salient issues. For this reason, this chapter focuses exclusively on this underserved and often at-risk population. Information on other ethnic groups is presented when it is useful for making relevant comparisons or providing context in terms of the general alcohol and substance use literature. It may appear that some of the research focusing on Native populations presented in this review is outdated or lacks comprehensiveness. However, it is important to bear in mind that this reflects the current state of the published research literature, emphasizing the need for more attention and resources to be directed toward the Native community.

The chapter is organized into three sections. The first section provides an introduction to the American Indian/Alaska Native population and background information on prevalence rates, patterns and consequences of use, and risk and protective factors for the substances most commonly used by Indian youth. In the second section, the published prevention outcome research literature found in the MEDLINE and PsycINFO databases is reviewed, and selected programs that were developed specifically to reduce substance use among Indian adolescents are described. In the last section, recommendations are offered for the most promising prevention strategies currently in practice, and a recently developed substance abuse prevention program for urban Indian adolescents that incorporates these recommendations is introduced.

SUBSTANCE USE AND ABUSE AMONG AMERICAN INDIAN AND ALASKA NATIVE ADOLESCENTS

Brief Introduction to Native Populations

According to U.S. population estimates, there are 2.5 million people who report their sole race to be American Indian/Alaska Native, and 4.1 million people who report being American Indian/Alaska Native in combination with one or more other races (U.S. Census Bureau, 2001b). American Indians are an incredibly diverse group, currently representing 562 federally recognized tribal nations and Alaska Native villages and corporations that range in membership from less than 100 to more than 350,000 (Bureau of Indian Affairs, 2002). There are additional tribes recognized only by individual states, and numerous tribes, bands, and American Indian villages that are not formally recognized by the federal government for political reasons. Federally recognized Native American tribes are located in 35 states within 10 distinct cultural areas. More than 200 tribal languages are currently spoken (Fleming, 1992).

A common stereotype depicts Native Americans as residing on remote reservations, well removed from the rest of America. In reality, the majority (63%) live in urban areas, and only 22% of Native Americans live on reservations and tribal trust lands (U.S. Census Bureau, 1993). The American Indian population is a young one, with a median age of 28.0, 34% being under 18 years old. In contrast, the median age for the overall U.S. population is 35.3, with 26% younger than 18 (U.S. Census Bureau, 2001a). About 10,000 American Indian and Alaska Native children today attend federal boarding schools. First started in the 1870s as a method of forcibly assimilating Indians into American society, the aim of boarding schools was to systematically "kill the Indian, save the man" (Richard Pratt, founder of the first off-reservation boarding school in 1879, as cited in Kelley, 1999, section 3, para. 1). Intergenerational historical trauma and grief has been the result. The mission of federal Indian boarding schools has greatly changed, and 52 remain open today (44 on reservations and 8 in off-reservation locations).

Although some similarities and commonalities among Native American groups do exist, there is significant heterogeneity among communities and individuals according to tribal-specific factors; degree of Indian ancestry or blood quantum; residential pattern; and cultural affiliation, identity, and participation. When considering the issue of substance use and misuse, it is important to take into consideration the diversity of American Indians and Alaska Natives and the implications it has for the development and implementation of prevention efforts.

Although the official terminology as set by the federal government's Office of Management and Budget dictates that this collective group be referred to as *American Indian/Alaska Native* (Robbin, 2000), it is common practice to also use the terms *American Indian, Indian, Native American,* and *Native*. Most generally, these terms are used to identify American Indians and/or Alaska Natives. In contrast, when *Alaska Native* is used alone, it generally refers only to Indians of that region. In this chapter, these terms are used interchangeably, but every effort is made to distinguish between regional and cultural groups when appropriate. In working with Indians, community confidentiality is often considered equal in importance to the protection provided to individuals. Therefore, in most instances individual tribes and communities are not specifically referenced, and instead more general terms are used.

Prevalence of Substance Use

Large-scale national surveys provide comprehensive epidemiological data on alcohol, tobacco, and illicit drug use trends among youth. However, because of small sample sizes, they often do not include analyses of substance use patterns for American Indians. Fortunately, though, much is known about trends in Indian adolescent drug use because of research from three main sources. The first is school-based surveys conducted by the Tri-Ethnic Center for Prevention Research at Colorado State University (http://triethniccenter.colostate.edu). For more than 25 years, these anonymous surveys have been administered annually to a nationally representative sample of 7th through 12th graders living on or near reservations. Each year more than 2,000 youth respond to questions about their drug use, risk and protective factors, violence, and victimization. The second source of information comes from an examination of data from the Monitoring the Future (MTF) project, which has been in existence since 1975 (http://www.monitoringthefuture. org). Almost 45,000 adolescents and young adults from more than 400 schools across the country annually complete a survey about their substance use and related attitudes and beliefs. Wallace et al. (2002) analyzed data collected between 1996 and 2000 from approximately 64,000 high school seniors, thus sufficiently increasing the sample size of Native Americans to perform analyses of substance use trends. The last source includes reports that combine multiple years of data from the Substance Abuse and Mental Health Services Administration's (SAMHSA) National Household Survey on Drug Abuse (NHSDA; http://www.drugabusestatistics.samhsa. gov). The NHSDA is designed to provide drug use estimates for all 50 states plus the District of Columbia over a 5-year sampling period. Every year the NHSDA is administered as an in-person interview to more than 68,000 people who are representative of the civilian, noninstitutionalized U.S. population age 12 or older.

Using these three national databases, plus supplementary research where available, prevalence data are reviewed for the substances most commonly used by American Indian and Alaska Native youth across the country, namely tobacco, inhalants, alcohol, and marijuana.

Tobacco

Tobacco is one of the most frequently used drugs by Native youth. According to data for 12- to 17-year-olds from the last available NHSDA, 27.5% of American Indians/Alaska Natives were current smokers, compared with 16.0% of Whites, 10.2% of Latinos, 8.4% of Asian Americans, and 6.1%

of African Americans (SAMHSA, Office of Applied Studies, 2002). A study using MTF data (Wallace et al., 2002) reported that among 12th graders, the 30-day prevalence of cigarette smoking for American Indians is 46.1%, as compared to 34.3% for the overall population. Native American 12th graders also have the highest rate of smoking half a pack or more of cigarettes a day, at 17.1% versus an overall total rate of 12.7% (Wallace et al., 2002).

LeMaster, Connell, Mitchell, and Manson (2002) used data from the Voices of Indian Teens Project to determine the prevalence of cigarette and smokeless tobacco use among Native adolescents. Their sample consisted of 2,390 youth ages 13 to 20 attending high schools in five Indian communities west of the Mississippi. Approximately 50% of the youth reported having smoked cigarettes, with 30% smoking "once in a while." Slightly less than 3% (2.8%) reported smoking 11 or more cigarettes a week, and only 1.2% said that they smoked a pack or more a day. The lifetime prevalence of smokeless tobacco use was 21%, with 3.6% reporting use 4 to 6 days a week and 6.7% reporting use every day.

Inhalants

Inhalants are commonly among the first substances used by Indian youth, often preceding the use of alcohol (Beauvais et al., 1989). Beauvais (1992a) reported that Indian youth living on reservations had higher lifetime inhalant use rates than did Indian youth not living on reservations or White youth. Among 8th graders, 34% of reservation Indians reported lifetime inhalant use, compared with 20% for nonreservation Indians and 13% for Whites. The 12th graders surveyed reported lifetime use rates of 20% for reservation Indians, 15% for nonreservation Indians, and 10% for Whites. Reservation Indians in the 8th grade also had the highest rates of 30-day inhalant use (15%), followed by nonreservation Indians (8%), and Whites (5%). Among 12th graders, nonreservation Indians had the highest rate (3%), with reservation Indian and White students using at the same rate (2%).

Native youth living apart from their families in boarding schools were also found to have extremely high prevalence rates, with 44% of students reporting that they had used inhalants (Okwumabua & Duryea, 1987). In contrast, a study conducted with urban American Indian adolescents found that 12.3% of the youth surveyed reported some lifetime inhalant use (Howard, Walker, Silk Walker, Cottler, & Compton, 1999).

MTF survey data reviewed by Wallace et al. (2002) revealed that American Indian 12th graders had the highest past-year prevalence rate for inhalant use at 9.4%, as compared with 12th graders of all other ethnic groups combined at 6.6%. The 30-day prevalence rate was also higher than all but one other ethnic group at 4.3%, in contrast to an all-ethnic groups rate of

2.4% (Cuban Americans were the only group with a higher 30-day prevalence, at 6.6%).

Alcohol

Estimates of the prevalence of alcohol use among American Indian adolescents vary significantly. On the basis of national data of American Indian students collected from 1975 to 1994, Beauvais (1996) reported that 15% of Native youth had consumed alcohol or used drugs at least once by the age of 12, 62% had been intoxicated at least once by age 15, and 71% of 7th through 12th graders had used alcohol during their lifetime. May (1986) reported that approximately one third of Native Americans had tried alcohol by 11 years of age. This latter rate is substantiated by another study, which found that 44% of 4th and 5th graders surveyed in the Pacific Northwest and Oklahoma (mean age = 10.3 years) had tried alcohol (Moncher, Holden, & Trimble, 1990). Among American Indian boarding school students, the lifetime prevalence rate of alcohol use was found to be 93%, with 53% of these considered to be at risk for serious alcohol abuse (Dinges & Duong-Tran, 1993). A longitudinal study following urban American Indian adolescents in Seattle showed that at Year 5 (mean age = 15.8 years) 41.5% of the youth reported having drunk alcohol to the point of intoxication (Walker et al., 1996).

Beauvais (1992a) compared drinking rates for reservation Indians, nonreservation Indians, and White students in the 8th and 12th grades. Nonreservation Indian 8th graders were more likely to report lifetime alcohol use (80%) than reservation Indian (70%) or White (73%) 8th graders. However, lifetime prevalence rates for 12th graders were highly comparable among these three groups. Reservation Indians in both the 8th and 12th grades were most likely to report having been drunk in their lifetime (49% of 8th graders, 87% of 12th graders), followed by nonreservation Indians (42% and 76%) and Whites (27% and 73%). A similar pattern was found for the 30-day prevalence of having been drunk, with 8th and 12th graders on reservations having the highest rate, followed by nonreservation Indians, and then Whites.

In 1998 the National Institute on Drug Abuse reported slightly higher rates of alcohol use for American Indian youth as compared with youth from other ethnic groups. They reported that 93% of American Indian and 87% of non-American Indian high school seniors had tried alcohol during their lifetime. The rates for past-month use were 56% and 51%, respectively. More recently, Wallace et al. (2002) reported a past-year alcohol use prevalence of 76.5% and a 30-day prevalence of 55.1% for American Indian 12th graders, rates similar to other ethnic groups. In comparison to all other ethnic groups combined, however, American Indian students had the highest rate of daily alcohol use (6.1% vs. 3.5%) and were the group most likely to have consumed five drinks or more in a row in the previous 2 weeks (37.0% vs. 30.8%).

Marijuana

Marijuana use is also significantly higher among American Indian and Alaska Native adolescents than other groups. Beauvais (1996) found that nearly 50% of Indian students in the 7th through 12th grades reported having used marijuana on at least one occasion. In another study (Beauvais, 1992a) he found that of the 8th graders surveyed, 47% of reservation Indians, 26% of nonreservation Indians, and 13% of Whites reported lifetime marijuana use. For 8th graders, 30-day prevalence was also highest for reservation youth (23%), followed by nonreservation (10%) and White youth (5%). Twelfth-grade adolescents living on reservations had higher lifetime (77%) and 30-day (33%) rates of use than did nonreservation Indian (58% and 21%) and White students (38% and 13%).

Data from the MTF surveys (Wallace et al., 2002) also show that American Indian teens had the highest annual (45.3%) and 30-day (29.6%) marijuana prevalence rates compared with teens of other ethnic groups. In addition, they were more likely than teens of other ethnic groups to use on a regular basis. Almost 10% of Indian 12th graders said that they used marijuana daily, compared with 5.4% of the total 12th grade population.

A study using data from the Voices of Indian Teens Project sampled 9th to 12th graders in seven predominantly American Indian schools in four western communities. Using a total sample size of 1,464 youth, Novins and Mitchell (1998) found that 55.7% of Native teens reported using marijuana at least once during their lifetime, and 40.0% had used marijuana in the past month. Among those adolescents who had used marijuana in the past month, 42.5% reported using 1 to 3 times, 27.5% reported using 4 to 10 times, and 30.0% said that they had used 11 or more times.

Summary

Epidemiological research indicates a high level of normative adolescent substance use. However, it suggests that much of this use is experimental or episodic in nature, with only a small minority of adolescents qualifying as heavy users. Within the Native American population, youth tend to initiate substance use at a younger age, continue use after initial experimentation, and have higher rates of polysubstance use (Beauvais, 1992a; U.S. Congress, Office of Technology Assessment [OTA], 1990). Substance initiation in Indian communities typically occurs between the ages of 10 and 13, with the onset for some individuals beginning as early as 5 or 6 years of age (Beauvais, 1996; Okwumabua & Duryea, 1987).

The stage, or gateway, theory has been proposed to explain the progression of adolescent drug involvement (Golub & Johnson, 1994; Kandel & Faust, 1975; Kandel & Yamaguchi, 1993; Kandel, Yamaguchi, & Chen, 1992;

Weinberg, Radhert, Colliver, & Glantz, 1998). This theory postulates that for most individuals, initiation of drug use follows a specific sequence: (a) legal substances, such as tobacco and alcohol; (b) marijuana; (c) other illicit drugs; (d) cocaine; and (e) crack. However, an adolescent's use of substances at one stage does not necessarily mean that he or she will move on to the next stage. The applicability of stage theory to American Indian and Alaska Native adolescents has been questioned. One study found that among American Indian youth (ages 9 to 15) living in South Carolina, the use of alcohol predicted subsequent use of tobacco and illicit drugs, similar to what might be expected given the stage theory (Federman, Costello, Angold, Farmer, & Erkanli, 1997). However, Novins et al. (2001) found that among users of both alcohol and marijuana, approximately 35% reported using alcohol first, whereas 35% reported using marijuana first. Further, these researchers found that 75% of adolescents using substances from three or more classes reported patterns of use inconsistent with stage theory. They recommend that a modification which categorizes substances as *initiating* (tobacco, alcohol, inhalants, marijuana) or *heavy* (other illicit drugs) more accurately and appropriately captures the drug use trends of Indian youth.

Patterns of Substance Use

According to the *Diagnostic and Statistical Manual of Mental Disorders* (American Psychiatric Association, 2000), substance abuse is characterized by a maladaptive pattern of use leading to recurrent and significant impairment or distress. For example, criteria for alcohol abuse include problems at work or school due to drinking, or repeatedly driving while intoxicated. Substance dependence is a more severe disorder and is additionally marked by the development of tolerance or withdrawal symptomatology (American Psychiatric Association, 2000). Terms such as *addiction* or *alcoholism* generally refer to substance dependence disorders.

Whereas diagnostic criteria for adults are clearly defined, there is less standardization for the diagnosis of substance use disorders in adolescents. To a large extent, this is the result of significant developmental, physiological, and social differences between adult and adolescent substance use and misuse. For example, research indicates that young people drink less frequently than adults but that they tend to consume larger amounts when they do drink (Oetting & Beauvais, 1989; White & Labouvie, 1989). Among youth, drinking and drug use is more likely to be associated with "partying." This pattern decreases the likelihood that substance-abusing youth will experience tolerance or withdrawal symptoms, which are necessary criteria for a diagnosis of substance dependence.

May (1996) reported that both American Indian youth and adults frequently consume large amounts of alcohol in a short period of time, a style often referred to as *binge drinking* (commonly defined as five or more drinks in a row for males and four or more drinks in a row for females; Wechsler, Lee, Kuo, & Lee, 2000). Beauvais (1992c) has observed two distinct types of drinkers among American Indian adolescents. He reported that approximately 20% of American Indian youth in the 7th through 12th grades begin heavily using alcohol and other drugs at an early age and continue this use into adulthood. These adolescents are at high risk for lifelong problems with alcohol abuse and dependence. The second type of drinker, which is also estimated to account for 20% of American Indian youth, uses alcohol socially and recreationally. Drinking for this group is often experimental in nature and highly dependent on the environment. This pattern is less likely to lead to long-term problems.

It has been noted that in addition to using alcohol and other drugs at high rates, American Indian and Alaska Native youth often tend to use in ways different from other adolescent groups. Numerous studies have examined gender and regional or cultural differences. However, research findings often contradict one another, highlighting the complexities of making general statements about this very heterogeneous group.

Gender Differences

Within the general adolescent population, boys usually have higher rates of drug use, particularly higher rates of frequent use, than do girls. In particular, they tend to have higher rates of heavy drinking, smokeless tobacco use, and steroid use (Johnston, O'Malley, & Bachman, 2002). From his research using school-based surveys, Beauvais (1992c) reported that there does not appear to be a significant difference in alcohol use rates between American Indian adolescent boys and girls. Furthermore, it has been reported that American Indian male and female adolescents experience drinking problems at equally high rates (Beauvais, 1992c; Cockerham, 1975; Oetting & Beauvais, 1989), and in a sample of urban Native youth, gender may not have influenced which youth abused alcohol (Walker, 1992).

The NHSDA found no significant gender differences in cigarette smoking rates for American Indians and Alaska Natives, in contrast to data for other ethnic/racial groups which indicated that smoking rates were higher for female than male adolescents (SAMHSA, Office of Applied Studies, 2002). Similarly, LeMaster et al. (2002) found no gender differences in the rate of cigarette use but did find a significant difference in the use of smokeless tobacco between American Indian male and female adolescents (27% and 15%, respectively).

Inhalant use was roughly equal among boys and girls surveyed in the Voices of Indian Teens project (May & Del Vecchio, 1997). However, it was suggested that this might differ on the basis of the age of the participants sampled. A survey conducted with boarding school students showed that boys tended to begin experimenting with inhalants earlier than did girls. The peak period of risk for inhalant use for boys was between 10 and 11 years of age, whereas for girls it was between 12 and 13 years (Okwumabua & Duryea, 1987).

Novins and Mitchell (1998) reported that although there were no gender differences at low frequency of marijuana use, defined as using one to three times in the past month, boys were significantly more likely to use marijuana at a high frequency, defined as using 11 or more times in the past month (odds ratio = 2.37, 99% confidence interval = 1.52, 3.69). Further, it was found that low frequency marijuana use among girls was indicative of a more severe pattern of substance use than was low frequency use among boys. For both boys and girls, more frequent marijuana use was associated with the increased use of other illicit drugs as well (Novins & Mitchell, 1998).

Regional and Tribal Differences

Although tribal differences have been noted in rates of adult drinking (Levy & Kunitz, 1971; May, 1996; Silk-Walker, Walker, & Kivlahan, 1988), Indian adolescents appear to use alcohol at similar levels regardless of tribe (Beauvais, 1998). However, other factors do appear to affect drinking patterns. Higher levels of alcohol use have been found among youth who live on reservations (Beauvais, 1992a), youth who attend boarding schools (Dick, Manson, & Beals, 1993), and youth who drop out of school (Beauvais, Chavez, Oetting, Deffenbacher, & Cornell, 1996). Similarly, inhalant use seems to be more prevalent among youth living on reservations or in other rural areas due to the low cost, easy availability, and the difficulties of obtaining other substances.

A study that compared Alaska Native and American Indian youth found that Native adolescents living in Alaska were almost twice as likely to smoke on a daily basis (Blum, Harmon, Harris, Bergeisen, & Resnick, 1992). SAMHSA's Office of Applied Studies (2002) reported a regional difference in cigarette smoking rates: For other racial/ethnic groups, adolescents living in the South are more likely to smoke than their peers in the western United States. This difference is nonexistent among American Indians, with youth in the southern and western regions of the United States smoking at approximately the same rate (SAMHSA, Office of Applied Studies, 2002). On the other hand, a study that surveyed students in seven predominantly American Indian high schools west of the Mississippi River found differences in the prevalence of marijuana use based on tribe; however, tribal membership stopped being a predictor when other covariates (such as past month alcohol use and report of having peers that encouraged alcohol use) were entered into the regression equations (Novins & Mitchell, 1998).

Consequences and Correlates of Substance Use

Research shows that although American Indian teens may have lifetime alcohol use rates similar to non-American Indian teens, they tend to drink more frequently and to consume alcohol in larger quantities when they do drink. In addition, they are more likely to have tried tobacco, inhalants, and marijuana, and to use these substances on a regular basis. Furthermore, the age at which American Indian youth initiate substance use tends to be younger than what is found in other groups. These trends are likely to significantly impact the development of American Indian adolescents by interfering with the learning of age-appropriate behaviors and skills (Bentler, 1992). In addition, these trends place them at increased risk for participating in potentially dangerous behaviors and for experiencing acute negative consequences of use (May, 1982). Substance-abusing youth have a greater likelihood of suffering social and interpersonal consequences because of their violation of parental, societal, and legal norms.

Although most teenage substance use is believed to "mature out" (Kandel & Logan, 1984; Mitchell, Novins, & Holmes, 1999), early onset of substance use and problem drinking has been linked to a multitude of negative outcomes. Adolescent alcohol use is associated with a wide range of high-risk behaviors, such as driving while drinking (Beauvais, 1992b), delinquency and running away (U.S. Congress, OTA, 1990; Zitzow, 1990), and unprotected sexual activity (Rolf, Nansel, Baldwin, Johnson, & Benally, 2002). It is also associated with psychiatric distress, including concerns such as depression, conduct disorder, and suicide (Dinges & Duong-Tran, 1993; Grossman, Milligan, & Deyo, 1991; Manson, Shore, & Bloom, 1985; May, 1987; Nelson, McCoy, Stetter, & Vanderwagen, 1992; O'Nell, 1992–1993; U.S. Congress, OTA, 1990); academic difficulties (Beauvais, 1996; U.S. Congress, OTA, 1990); and later problems with substance abuse (J. D. Hawkins et al., 1997; May & Moran, 1995).

Substance misuse is directly implicated in the disproportionately high morbidity and mortality rates found among American Indian teens. American Indian youth (ages 15 to 24 years) have an all-cause mortality rate 2.1 times higher than that of the general population (196.5 vs. 95.3 per 100,000 population) and 2.3 times higher than that of Whites, the group with the lowest rate (196.5 vs. 84.3 per 100,000 population; Indian Health Service, Office of Public Health, Program Statistics Team, 1999). Of the 10 leading causes of death for American Indian adolescents, at least 3 are related to heavy use of alcohol: accidents, suicide, and homicide (Indian Health Service, Office of Public Health, Program Statistics Team, 1999). In addition, the alcoholism death rate for Native youth served by Indian Health Services was 11.3 times higher than the combined all-races rate (Indian Health Service, Office of Public Health, Program Statistics Team, 1999). This statistic does not include alcohol-related deaths due to accidents, suicide, or homicide.

Risk Factors

Research suggests that the etiologic influences of American Indian adolescent substance use are similar to those found for other ethnic groups. Higher levels of alcohol and drug use among American Indian youth can be attributed to poverty and extremely poor social conditions that have exposed them to significantly more risk factors, which may directly or indirectly lead to more alcohol and drug use (Beauvais & LaBoueff, 1985). Life stress is a demonstrated risk factor for substance use (Dick et al., 1993; King et al., 1992; King & Thayer, 1993; LeMaster et al., 2002; Wills, McNamara, Vaccaro, & Hirky, 1997), and adolescence is a period of time when stress pertaining to social, physical, cognitive, and academic growth is enhanced (Dick et al., 1993). As a result, youth are particularly vulnerable to developing potentially harmful methods of coping with stressors that arise within themselves, their immediate environment, or their cultural milieu.

Intrapersonal Variables

Factors rooted within an individual, such as beliefs and attitudes, tendency to engage in risk behaviors, and psychological distress, contribute to increased rates of adolescent substance use. Among American Indian teens, the perception that substance use is an indicator of adulthood has been suggested as an explanation for an increased tendency to use (Schinke et al., 1985). Similarly, positive expectancies of alcohol's effects were predictive of higher rates of alcohol problems among urban American Indian teens (E. H. Hawkins, 2002).

High-risk behaviors and psychological distress potentially serve as both risk factors for and consequences of substance use. Inhalant users in a sample of urban American Indian youth exhibited higher rates of lifetime conduct disorder and alcohol dependence, more aggressive behavior, more sensation seeking, greater negative emotionality, and lower perceived self-worth than did nonusers (Howard et al., 1999). In another study, distressing life events of death and loss were linked to increased use of cigarettes and smokeless tobacco (LeMaster et al., 2002).

Environmental Influences

Environmental contexts (including community, family, and peer variables) have great impact on the development of substance use and misuse among American Indian and Alaska Native adolescents. These sources of primary socialization directly and indirectly communicate social norms and values. The community, which includes elders, schools, law enforcement, and health agencies, among other institutions, plays a vital role in the transmission of what is considered acceptable substance use behavior (Oetting & Donnermeyer, 1998). Youth learn which actions are tolerated or even sanctioned, as well as the consequences for engaging in behavior that falls outside the community's norms.

Likewise, the family conveys powerful messages to youth regarding substance use. Adult models of substance abuse (LeMaster et al., 2002; Weibel-Orlando, 1984) and lack of clear-cut familial sanctions against substance abuse (Oetting, Beauvais, & Edwards, 1988) are associated with increased rates of use among youth. Some researchers have noted that drinking within families may be one way of maintaining a sense of cohesion and solidarity (O'Nell, 1992–1993; Spicer, 1997). Studies have also suggested that a lack of stability in the home (Garcia-Mason, 1985) and disorientation within family relationships (Albaugh & Albaugh, 1979) are risk factors for substance use.

During adolescence, peer influences may be as or more important than family variables in the development of substance use problems. Participation in positive peer clusters is less likely to lead to deviant behaviors, whereas antisocial peer associations and pressures can serve as risk factors for substance use (Oetting, Swaim, Edwards, & Beauvais, 1989).

Cultural Factors

Cultural epidemiologists have suggested that the stresses of forced acculturation, urbanization, and cultural disruption have increased the vulnerability of American Indian youth for developing psychological problems (Beauvais & LaBoueff, 1985; Kemnitzer, 1973; Spindler & Spindler, 1978). Among American Indians and Alaska Natives there is a historical and generational trauma that underlies this risk (for a comprehensive discussion of historical trauma and grief, see Brave Heart & DeBruyn, 1998). Many Indian communities share similar experiences of warfare and colonization, coercive methods of assimilation, loss of traditional land and customs, boarding school educations and abuses, longstanding struggles to maintain treaty rights, poverty, and high rates of unemployment and disease. These factors, plus many more that are tribe or community specific, are often viewed as risk factors for substance use, as tobacco, alcohol, and other drug use may offer a method of coping with these stressors.

Specific cultural factors that have been associated with increased substance use include ethnic dislocation (May, 1982; Oetting, Beauvais, & Velarde, 1982; Trimble, Padilla, & Bell-Bolek, 1987), acculturation stress (LaFromboise, 1988), alienation from the larger culture (Moncher et al., 1990), and an excessive amount of unstructured time on reservations, during which drinking is often a response to boredom (E. D. Edwards & Edwards, 1988). In addition, Whitbeck, Hoyt, McMorris, Chen, and Stubben (2001) have found perceived discrimination to be a risk factor for alcohol and drug use. In their study, 49% of fifth- through eighth-grade students from three reservations in the upper Midwest reported experiencing significant discrimination. This was strongly associated with early onset substance abuse, a relationship that was mediated by adolescent anger and delinquent behaviors.

Protective Factors

Although risk is a widely understood and agreed upon concept, protection is not, and there has been little consensus on the definition and operationalization of protective factors (see Jessor, VandenBos, Vanderryn, Costa, & Turbin, 1995). Some define risk and protection as opposite ends of a single dimension. A protective factor, then, is the absence of or a low level of risk. Others argue that the concept of protection is orthogonal and extends beyond the mere absence of risk. These scholars contend that a protective factor is an independent variable that can have a direct effect on behavior and can also moderate the relationship between a risk factor and behavior (J. D. Hawkins, Catalano, & Miller, 1992; Rutter, 1987). Both definitions of protection are represented in the studies presented here.

Universal Factors

Among adolescents in the general population, protective factors include stable and supportive relationships with parents and prosocial adults, self-efficacy in social relations, bonding to conventional society, community resources, cultural involvement, participation in organized group activities, and involvement in religious activities (Barrett, Simpson, & Lehman, 1988; Elder, Leaver-Dunn, Wang, Nagy, & Green, 2000; J. D. Hawkins et al., 1992; Newcomb & Felix-Ortiz, 1992; Tyler & Lichtenstein, 1997). Comparatively little is known about factors that serve to protect Indian youth against the development of substance use problems. There is no compelling reason to believe that the factors listed here would not also be protective for Indian adolescents. Indeed, strong bonds with the family and school are believed to serve as protective factors against deviance, whereas peer associations can serve as sources for either prosocial or deviant norms (Oetting, Donnermeyer, Trimble, & Beauvais, 1998). In one of the few published studies of protective factors among American Indian youth, LeMaster et al. (2002) found that academic orientation served to lower the risk for cigarette smoking.

Culture-Specific Factors

Much is unknown about protective factors that are specific to the cultural and community context of Native Americans. Despite the strongly held belief in the positive power of Indian cultural identity and participation, research has yielded conflicting findings. For example, one study demonstrated that inhalant abuse rates were lower for youth who participated in structured activities such as traditional tribal activities and ceremonies (Thurman & Green, 1997). Similarly, Mason (1995) found that a positive culturally oriented self-concept was associated with lower rates of substance use. However, attendance at cultural events has also been linked to marijuana and cigarette use (Petoskey, Van Stelle, & De Jong, 1998), and in one study traditional orientation was highly correlated with problem behaviors such as getting drunk or high (Mail, 1997). In a sample of urban Native youth, increased report of alcohol-related problems was associated with identification with the "Indian way of life" (E. H. Hawkins, 2002). Still other studies have found no relationship between cultural identity and substance use (Bates, Beauvais, & Trimble, 1997).

There remains strong support for the idea that bicultural competence serves to decrease risk for substance misuse. *Bicultural competence* has been defined as the ability to alternate between one's ethnic and White identities in response to contextual cultural cues (LaFromboise, Coleman, & Gerton, 1993). This capability is widely believed to be instrumental in helping Indian youth successfully negotiate potentially harmful situations by increasing positive coping skills, self-efficacy, and social support, factors that have been linked to positive outcomes in substance abuse treatment (Annis & Davis, 1991; Marlatt & Gordon, 1985; Rychtarik, Prue, Rapp, & King, 1992). A similar model is stake theory, which holds that identifying with, or having a stake in, both Native and mainstream cultures can serve as a protective factor against substance abuse (Ferguson, 1976; Honigmann & Honigmann, 1968).

Among many ethnic groups, positive outcomes in issues of health and adjustment, including addictive behaviors, are associated with higher levels of bicultural competence (LaFromboise et al., 1993). For Native adolescents living on reservations or tribal land, having a bicultural identity has been associated with increased social competencies, personal mastery, self-esteem, and social support (Moran, Fleming, Somervell, & Manson, 1999). However, it is clear that further research is needed to clarify the role culture plays as a source of risk or protection for substance use problems in this population.

SUBSTANCE MISUSE PREVENTION

The recognition that substance use among American Indian youth often begins at an early age has resulted in a growing emphasis on prevention rather than treatment efforts. Research detailing epidemiology, etiology, and domains of risk and protection can provide the basis for developing prevention programs and identifying intervention targets. These preventive interventions are designed to reach children early and limit the initiation of substance use and/or the later development of substance abuse and related consequences.

An Overview of Prevention Concepts

Prevention services are widely characterized as primary, secondary, or tertiary (Caplan, 1964). Within the health field, primary prevention programs are aimed at reducing the incidence of a particular disorder or risk factor. Secondary prevention programs target early identification and treatment to reduce the prevalence of a particular problem. Tertiary prevention programs focus on reducing the severity or impact of an established condition. Because this framework assumes dichotomous categorization (i.e., present and absent), using this classification system often makes it difficult to distinguish between primary and secondary prevention. Instead, mental health and substance abuse problems tend to be conceptualized as spectrum disorders, with attention focused on the level and severity of functional impairment rather than the strict presence or absence of a disorder.

In 1994, the Institute of Medicine proposed a new model that divides the continuum of care into three categories: prevention, treatment, and maintenance. The prevention category distinguishes between three classifications of prevention programs: universal, selective, and indicated. In a universal program, specific individuals are not singled out for an intervention; rather, all individuals within a defined area or population are offered the service. Examples of this include high school health education classes and anti-smoking media campaigns. Selective prevention targets groups of individuals considered at higher than average risk because of the presence of one or more risk factors. A program designed for children of alcoholics or an after-school mentoring program for youth experiencing behavioral problems are examples of selective prevention. Indicated prevention programs are aimed at specific individuals who have already begun engaging in high-risk behaviors but who do not meet criteria for a substance use disorder. Examples of this kind of intervention might include adolescents screened for problems at school or a physician's office, or those mandated to treatment. Selective and indicated preventions are also often referred to as forms of *targeted prevention*.

Universal and targeted prevention programs both have their advantages and disadvantages (Offord, 2000). Universal programs tend to cast a wider net and can, therefore, potentially influence more people. They also tend to be less stigmatizing, as no one individual is singled out for attention. However, they are often expensive, usually have a smaller effect on any one person, and may have the greatest effect on those at lowest risk. Targeted programs have the potential advantage of efficiency, as available resources are directed only at the high-risk group. In addition, they tend to be more intensive and may have greater impact on an individual level. A common difficulty in indicated interventions, though, is the cost and commitment necessary to screen individuals to determine risk status. Furthermore, risk factors are usually fairly weak predictors of future pathology, so screening may not accurately target individuals in the most need. Finding the balance between sensitivity (the ability to accurately detect those who are at risk) and specificity (the ability to correctly identify those who are not at risk) often presents a challenge for clinicians and researchers.

Prevention for American Indian Youth

Universal, selective, and indicated substance abuse prevention programs are all commonly found in American Indian communities. Distinctions between different types of prevention are often blurred, however, as commonly the entire community is considered at risk and is the focus of intervention. Unfortunately, the majority of prevention efforts in Indian Country have not been rigorously evaluated for efficacy. In addition, specific details of these programs often are not published or available in a manner that allows them to be easily shared with other communities. Moran and Reaman (2002) provided information on prevention programs that have not been published in the mainstream literature. Limited program information can also be found through SAMHSA's Center for Substance Abuse Prevention (2003; see also Western Center for the Application of Prevention Technologies, 2002). While many of these programs have the potential for success in combating Indian adolescent substance abuse and for making valuable contributions to the development of prevention efforts in other communities, this chapter focuses on reviewing those studies that have been evaluated and published in peer-refereed journals.

The principal source of information in this chapter comes from searches of the MEDLINE and PsycINFO databases. Information on qualitative findings has been included where relevant, although the emphasis here is on presenting quantitative outcome data. The programs reviewed tend to fall into two categories: those that target entire communities for change and those that focus their efforts primarily on individual behavior change.

Community-Oriented Approaches

Several researchers have suggested that programs that target an entire community rather than specific individuals may be more effective for the prevention and treatment of substance abuse in American Indian and Alaska Native adolescents (Beauvais & LaBoueff, 1985; E. D. Edwards & Edwards, 1988; Gutierres, Russo, & Urbanski, 1994; LaFromboise, Trimble, & Mohatt, 1990; Petoskey et al., 1998; Wiebe & Huebert, 1996). A community-based approach may be preferred for a variety of reasons. Some authors have described the inclusion of an entire community in the intervention as consistent with Native values and traditions, which stress collective decision making in resolving community or tribal concerns (E. D. Edwards & Edwards, 1988; LaFromboise et al., 1990). Others have emphasized the role that sociocultural factors play in the development of drug and alcohol abuse and argued that a more comprehensive approach is necessary to address risk factors at familial and community levels (Gutierres et al., 1994). Most authors agree that whether a curriculum is intended to serve primarily individuals or larger groups, community support for the intervention is vital to the success of any treatment or prevention program (Beauvais & LaBoueff, 1985; E. D. Edwards & Edwards, 1988; LaFromboise et al., 1990; Wiebe & Huebert, 1996).

Community empowerment is one approach that is community based in its theoretical underpinnings and has been used to develop substance abuse prevention for Native American youth (Petoskey et al., 1998; Rowe, 1997). Generally, this method utilizes multiple strategies to increase knowledge about drugs and alcohol throughout a community and to change community norms regarding use. Often the initial step in the community empowerment approach is the development of a core group composed of community members who serve as leaders, role models, and decision-makers regarding the implementation of prevention strategies.

Petoskey et al. (1998) described the Parent, School and Community Partnership Program, a project that aimed to reduce alcohol, tobacco, and other drug (ATOD) use among Native American youth living on or near three reservations in northern Wisconsin and Minnesota. A major component of this program was the Red Cliff Wellness School Curriculum, a culturally focused, skills-based substance abuse curriculum that was designed to be implemented by classroom teachers in Grades 4 through 12. In addition, the project involved the following: (a) the training of a small group of community members to be leaders and facilitators regarding community health, (b) a community curriculum offered to all members and designed to increase community involvement and problem solving around ATOD issues, and (c) teacher training in the implementation of the school-based curriculum. Outcome variables such as past-month substance use; attitudes toward use and perceptions of harmfulness; and attitudes toward school, academic achievement, absenteeism, and cultural involvement were assessed prior to curriculum implementation, at the end of the program year, and at 1-year follow-up. Comparison data were provided by similar schools that had agreed to collect data during Years 1 and 2 in order to receive the curriculum in Year 3. Although past-month alcohol use increased for both groups at follow-up, the authors reported a significant two-way interaction of site and time, indicating some slowing in the rise in alcohol use for participants in the intervention group. At all three data collection points, students who received the intervention reported lower levels of past-month marijuana use. Past-month cigarette use increased for both groups over time; however, this outcome was not a specific target of the intervention. Although there were no significant differences in likelihood to accept alcohol from friends between groups, students from the intervention group were less likely to accept marijuana at 1-year follow-up. It is interesting that these authors also found that increased frequency of attendance at powwows was associated with increased use of substances. Cultural affiliation has often been perceived as a protective factor, yet this study found a sex difference in the relationship between Indian identity and substance use: Increased Indian identity was associated with decreased use in girls and increased use in boys.

Rowe (1997) described the Target Community Partnership Project, an effort that utilized the community empowerment approach to address substance abuse with a Native American tribe in Washington State. Strategies used in this project included (a) creating partnerships among community members, professional services staff, and tribal departments; (b) implementing a process of ongoing training for the community around ATOD issues; (c) organizing community-wide alcohol- and drug-free events; (d) enhancing health, welfare, and youth services for those individuals with substance abuse or children affected by substance-abusing parents; and (e) advocating for new tribal policies restricting the use and abuse of drugs and alcohol. Several types of quantitative and qualitative outcomes were assessed over the course of approximately 4 years with adult and youth surveys conducted in the first and last years. Some of these included adult perception of harm from drugs and alcohol (as measured by an anonymous community survey), youth perception of harm from alcohol (as measured by a school survey), number of individuals referred to substance abuse treatment, number of families receiving services for alcohol and drug-related parenting problems, community perceptions of improvements in drug and alcohol use and drug dealing, community perception of social changes, tribal staff perception of changes in community norms, tribal policies related to ATOD, number of sober adults in the community, current youth alcohol use, current peer alcohol use, and number of alcohol and drug-related juvenile and adult arrests. Although the author described many positive overall changes in the community, including improved social conditions, a shift in social norms regarding drugs and alcohol, the creation of new policies and laws around substance use, and increased collaboration among tribal organizations, no significant change was found in adults' perceived harmfulness of ATOD use. Because the sample of youth surveyed for quantitative data was likely too small to discern significant change over time, the only significant outcome was an increase in the number of friends that youth reported did not expect them to drink. In addition, Rowe indicated an increase in the number of individuals reportedly seeking abstinence. Although the numbers of drug- and alcohol-related arrests, substance-related referrals, and referrals of families for services all increased, the author suggested that this was an indication of improved awareness among community members rather than an indication of rising use.

Dorpat (1994) described a multi-arm prevention program implemented by the Puyallup Tribe of Indians, a tribe that inhabits a primarily urban reservation located in Tacoma, Washington. Although a description of the program does not indicate that its format was intentionally based on any particular community-based theory, the nature of the program's development and content appears similar to other community-based interventions reported here. PRIDE (Positive Reinforcement in Drug Education) was a prevention program conceived and developed through the guidance of the Puyallup Tribal Council and local school administration. Its four components included (a) development of students' cultural identity through both curricular and extracurricular instruction and activities in the schools; (b) implementation of a school-based prevention curriculum dealing with health awareness, drug and alcohol awareness, refusal skills, and life skills; (c) enforcement of a security policy for reducing in-school drug use and development of a drug-free environment on school campuses; and (d) coordinated counseling, referral, and/or case management services for those students identified as drug users. Although the author reported that a formal process evaluation supported program efficacy, only one postintervention student survey was described in terms of outcome evaluation. This survey demonstrated high rates of expected school completion and positive attitudes about health among students. The survey also indicated 22% of high school students reported drinking to get drunk. The author compared this with a public school survey conducted separately from the study in which 46% of local high school juniors reported drinking to get drunk once per month. Although these outcomes appear positive, efficacy is difficult to establish without baseline or comparison group data.

In general, it appears that community-based approaches, and specifically community empowerment, may provide promising ways of developing culturally relevant substance abuse prevention programs for Native American adolescents. Further investigation and outcome data are necessary to better document the efficacy of community-based interventions and to better understand which aspects of these programs are most helpful.

Individual-Oriented Approaches

The majority of programs that have focused prevention at the individual level have utilized the approach of adolescent skills-training interventions. As an extension of social learning theory (Bandura, 1986), primary socialization theory has been used as a method to explain American Indian adolescent alcohol use (Oetting & Donnermeyer, 1998). According to this model, socialization is the process of learning social norms and behaviors and is an active interaction between the individual and the primary socialization sources (namely, the family, school, and peer clusters). The goal of socialization is the development of the abilities and competencies needed to function successfully within a culture. Drinking among adolescents, then, reflects this process of socialization, and the norms and expectations of the family, community, and mainstream society.

The link between social–cognitive factors and alcohol problems is appealing from a prevention perspective because attitudes, beliefs, and behavior are subject to modification. Skills training is a vehicle commonly used for motivating and effecting change in substance use patterns. As a result, it is perhaps the most widely researched approach and provides the richest literature on intervention outcomes for the American Indian population.

Peer-Led Interventions

Skills-training programs are often enhanced by using peers as a component of the intervention. Research has shown that peer leaders can be at least as, and sometimes more, effective than adult health educators when working with adolescent populations (Mellanby, Rees, & Tripp, 2000), especially in effecting change in attitudes and behaviors (Bangert-Drowns, 1988; Tobler, 1986).

Theories of social learning (Bandura, 1986), social inoculation (McGuire, 1964), and social norms (Fishbein & Azjen, 1975) underlie the rationale for this approach by predicting that individual behaviors are influenced by the attitudes and behaviors of the social group to which that individual belongs. More specifically, these theories hold that people are more likely to take on the attitudes and behaviors of those members of their social group whom they perceive as similar to themselves. This may be especially true during adolescence, a time when individuals may be more influenced by peer-group norms (Bangert-Drowns, 1988; Covert & Wangberg, 1992). Researchers have applied these theories to Native American populations specifically by observing that drinking patterns among American Indian adolescents can be both shaped and maintained by peer-group expectations (Carpenter, Lyons, & Miller, 1985; Curley, 1967).

Only one published study thus far has evaluated the usefulness of incorporating a peer-counseling component into an alcohol abuse prevention program for American Indian adolescents (Carpenter et al., 1985). The overall approach of this program was to teach responsible drinking utilizing self-control training. Thirty students, from 16 tribes, attending a residential high school were identified as at risk for problem drinking and were randomly assigned to one of three interventions: (a) self-monitoring alone, (b) self-monitoring with peer counseling, or (c) self-monitoring with peer counseling in addition to an alcohol education class. The participants represented tribes from across the United States and had an average age of 16 years (range = 14–20 years).

Participants were assessed prior to the intervention, postintervention, and at follow-ups of 4 months, 9 months, and 12 months postintervention. Quantity of weekly drinking, frequency of drinking, and peak blood alcohol concentration in the past 3 months decreased significantly in all groups over time. However, no differences between groups were observed, indicating effects were similar regardless of minimal or full program participation. Carpenter et al. (1985) concluded that these findings are consistent with previous research that has "found only modest differences between extensive self-control training programs and more minimal interventions, as long as the latter have included self-monitoring and basic self-help guidelines" (p. 307).

Bicultural Competence Interventions

Skills-training-based programs designed for American Indian and Alaska Native youth often incorporate a bicultural competence approach in order to increase relevancy and effectiveness. A critical component of bicultural competence is learning important coping skills for negotiating both mainstream and Native cultures. This experience can be empowering, increasing a sense of self-efficacy and leading adolescents to be more functional navigators of their often complex environments.

A study conducted among American Indian youth living on two western Washington reservations shows modest support for a bicultural competence skills intervention for preventing substance abuse (Schinke et al., 1988). Participants included 137 youth (mean age = 11.8 years) who after pretesting were randomly assigned by reservation site into prevention and control conditions. Participants in the bicultural competence condition were instructed in and practiced communication, coping, and discrimination skills using behavioral and cognitive methods. For example, youth were introduced to culturally relevant examples of verbal and nonverbal influences on substance use, were guided in self-instruction and relaxation techniques to help cope with the pressure of substance use situations, and were taught techniques to anticipate temptations and explore healthier alternatives to substance use. Youth in the control condition received no intervention. Adolescents in the bicultural competence group showed greater posttest and 6-month follow-up improvements than those in the control group on measures of substance-related knowledge, attitudes, and interactive abilities and on self-reported rates of tobacco, alcohol, and drug use (Schinke et al., 1988).

Another study involved 1,396 Native youth from 10 reservations in Idaho, Montana, North Dakota, Oklahoma, and South Dakota (Schinke, Tepavac, & Cole, 2000). Participants were randomly assigned by school to one of three experimental conditions. Two of the three conditions involved 15- to 50-minute weekly sessions focusing on cognitive–behavioral life skills training. Youth learned problem-solving, coping, and communication skills for preventing substance abuse. However, the standard life skills training techniques and content were expanded and adapted to fit the bicultural world of the Native American adolescents. One of these intervention conditions also included a community involvement component, in which multiple community systems worked together to plan activities to raise awareness of substance abuse prevention. The third condition consisted of a control group that did not receive any intervention.

The authors found that except for cigarette use, follow-up rates of smokeless tobacco, alcohol, and marijuana use were lower for youth who had received the skills intervention than for those who were in the control group (Schinke et al., 2000). At the 30-month follow-up, smokeless tobacco use, defined as seven or more instances of use in the past week, was approximately 7% for the skills intervention groups and a little less than 11% for the control group. At the 42-month follow-up, the rates were 10% and 18%, respectively. Alcohol consumption, defined as four or more drinks in the week prior to measurement, was also significantly lower at the 30- and 42-month follow-ups for the two intervention groups (23% vs. 30% and 16% vs. 19%, respectively). Although the youth who participated in the skills plus community involvement condition had lower rates of alcohol use than the control group, their rates were higher than those youth in the skills-only group. Although these results did not reach statistical significance, this trend was present at the 18-, 30-, and 42-month follow-ups. At the final follow-up (42 months), marijuana use rates were significantly lower for Native American youth who had participated in the skills intervention (7%) than for those in the control group (15%). Moran and Reaman (2002) described initial outcomes from the Seventh Generation project, which involved urban American Indian fourth through seventh graders in Denver. This after-school alcohol prevention program utilized a life skills approach with the following content areas: correcting misperceptions of alcohol use norms, enhancing values that conflict with alcohol use, improving self-esteem, learning structured decision making, increasing refusal skills, and making a personal commitment to sobriety (Moran, 1998). Local community-based focus groups determined seven culturally specific core values, which were emphasized throughout the curriculum. These included harmony, respect, generosity, courage, wisdom, humility, and honesty. In this way, cultural relevance of the material was established without the use of traditional Native activities or artifacts. The intervention consisted of 13 weekly 2-hr sessions with a 5-week booster after 6 months. This quasi-experimental design compared 257 intervention youth with 121 nonintervention youth at pretest, posttest, and 1-year follow-up. The intervention and control groups were not significantly different at pretest or posttest, except that the intervention youth who completed the 1-year follow-up had significantly better decision making and greater Indian identity at pretest than did control group youth. At 1-year follow-up, the intervention group also displayed less positive beliefs about alcohol consequences, less depression, greater school bonding, more positive self-concept, and higher levels of perceived social support. In addition, a significant difference in reported drinking in the past 30 days (5.6% of intervention youth vs. 19.7% of comparison youth) was demonstrated.

The prevention programs reviewed here provide strong support for the use of a skills-training approach in reducing substance misuse among American Indian and Alaska Native adolescents. Collectively, the youth who participated in these programs symbolize the diversity found within the greater American Indian population. Tribes from across the country were represented, as were both reservation-based and urban youth and those attending public, tribal, and boarding schools. Further research is needed to determine the relative contributions made by the various dimensions of a specific program and to identify whether there are differential outcomes based on participant variables such as gender, age, residential, or cultural differences.

Limitations of Current Approaches

This chapter reviews prevention programs that have been evaluated and have demonstrated some degree of efficacy in reducing the prevalence of substance abuse and related consequences. However, the number of such programs is too few considering the magnitude of substance use problems experienced by American Indian and Alaska Native adolescents. It is vital that an evaluation component be established in the development and implementation of all prevention efforts. Critical aspects of effective evaluation include formulating a research design that allows for a comparison or control group while respecting a community's expectation of universal inclusion (Parker-Langley, 2002), recruiting a large enough sample size to perform more sophisticated statistical analyses, maintaining a follow-up period of suitable duration to ascertain the long-term effects of an intervention, and assessing both process and outcome variables. Only by doing this can the effectiveness of prevention programs be determined and, thus, resources be directed more competently toward addressing issues of substance misuse.

It has been said before, but it bears repeating: American Indians and Alaska Natives are an extremely culturally diverse group. Programs developed for one segment of the Indian population may not be generalizable to another. This may be due to actual geographical or cultural differences that render prevention efforts incompatible between certain groups, or it may reflect a long-standing desire on the part of some communities to assert and maintain a unique and independent identity. Regardless of reason, programs developed in one community may not work in or be accepted by others. Problems of generalizability are often mentioned in limitations sections, but the discussion ends there. Often, there is no additional dialogue nor recommendations offered regarding how to adapt interventions for use with other groups. This situation is extremely unfortunate, as information of this sort would likely benefit and guide the efforts of other communities struggling with these same concerns. Given the extensive need for effective substance abuse prevention among Indian adolescents, researchers need to address this very important issue.

Of all the programs reviewed here, only one specifically targeted multi-tribal urban youth (Moran, 1998; Moran & Reaman, 2002). This reflects a critical gap in prevention services and research. Although approximately two thirds of all American Indians and Alaska Natives now live in urban areas (U.S. Census Bureau, 1993), the vast majority of studies that are reported use a reservation-based sample. One reason for this may be that individuals in these communities tend to be easier to identify and are presumed to be more culturally homogenous. In addition, research-funding mechanisms often specifically target tribal populations rather than urban groups. These factors greatly impact the development and implementation of prevention programs. However, substance abuse prevention efforts for Native adolescents are critically limited by the lack of published accounts of culturally and developmentally appropriate strength-based urban programs. Urban youth are likely to have a much different relationship with their local and tribal community than do rural or reservation-based youth. In contrast to reservation-based adolescents who are likely to be more similar, urban youth represent a diverse spectrum of tribal nations, cultural knowledge, and traditional cultural participation. As a consequence, prevention research conducted with reservation samples may not transfer easily to adolescents living in metropolitan areas. More attention clearly needs to be focused on this overlooked and poorly understood group.

The body of literature regarding Indian adolescent substance use and abuse would benefit further from an expansion of current research efforts. Published studies tend to revolve around prevalence data and cross-sectional reports of risk factors. Very few published studies have explored risk prospectively and longitudinally (e.g., Federman et al., 1997; Walker et al., 1996). In addition, there are few published accounts of protective factors or avenues of resiliency for substance abuse problems among American Indian youth. Further exploration of these factors is essential to the development of effective interventions.

Developing prevention programs that are meaningful and relevant for American Indian youth is of critical importance. It is clear that simply applying adult and majority culture definitions and conceptualizations of problem drinking to Indian adolescents is neither appropriate nor useful. Instead, there needs to be a recognition that different developmental trajectories exist, with important individual differences in causes, course, and consequences of substance abuse (Baer, McLean, & Marlatt, 1998). Prevention programs that are culturally relevant and matched to the unique needs of Native adolescents are strongly indicated (Bobo, 1986; LaFromboise & Rowe, 1983; Schinke et al., 1988; Stone, 1981).

One method of assuring that programs are appropriate for their target population is extensive collaboration with and involvement of community members. Often this means going beyond the boundaries of traditional academic research and grant funding. It requires making a significant commitment of time and resources toward developing the trust and respect of community members and learning from them the best methods of designing and implementing a local program. In addition, such involvement entails providing community members with information, training, and technical assistance to maintain a program once it has been established. Most Indian communities are wary of researchers, and rightfully so. There has been a long history of "parachute" academics who "drop in" to a community with prevention program in hand, collect data, and then leave to move on to other projects. The time has come to make a long-term commitment to the Native American population by working with communities to develop and sustain effective prevention programs.

Although Indian communities are marshalling their resources to address substance-related harm and to find solutions that work for their community, these endeavors are not well evaluated or documented. Across the country there are innovative programs that are likely helping to reduce the negative consequences associated with alcohol and drug use. However, within the scientific literature there is a paucity of studies that offer both qualitative findings and quantitative data on efficacy. Nor has there been much discussion of attempts to culturally adapt prevention programs found to be effective with mainstream youth or with other segments of the Indian adolescent population. In general, available research often lacks the more sophisticated methodologies seen in mainstream research. To truly ameliorate the problems of alcohol misuse among Indians, these limitations need to be addressed and new, more inclusive models advanced.

PREVENTION STRATEGIES FOR HEALTHIER COMMUNITIES

Despite countless efforts to reduce substance abuse in Indian Country, alcohol- and drug-related problems continue to be the number one concern of most communities. Indian children and adolescents are using tobacco, inhalants, alcohol, and marijuana at disturbing rates. Perhaps more alarming is the age at which they begin using and the quantity and frequency of their use. The trends in substance use and misuse discussed earlier reinforce the need for effective prevention programs to stem the tide of harmful consequences.

Promising Prevention Approaches

In reviewing the research literature, several best-practice approaches for substance abuse prevention among American Indian and Alaska Native youth emerge. These include principles and strategies that have demonstrated the potential and promise to help reduce the severity of problems caused by alcohol and drug use. They include (a) conceptualizing prevention and behavior change as part of a continuum, (b) using a stepped-care approach, (c) utilizing a biculturally focused life skills curriculum, and (d) establishing community involvement and collaboration throughout the development and implementation of prevention efforts.

A Continuum of Prevention and Individual Behavior Change

Recent work in the development of cognitive–behavioral programs for the prevention and treatment of addictive behaviors has focused on a continuum of prevention and intervention approaches. To deter Native youth from experimenting with substances and to maintain abstinence, universal prevention programs are appropriate. Once experimentation and initial substance use has occurred, however, targeted prevention is called for so as to reduce the risk of harm and the potential for addiction. To prevent the escalation from alcohol and drug use to alcoholism or drug addiction, an early intervention approach that targets specific risk and protective factors is often recommended. For those who have already developed alcohol or drug dependency, participation in active treatment interventions and the prevention of relapse become the focus.

Contemporary approaches to individual intervention and treatment in mainstream populations have been greatly influenced by the stages of change model first described by Prochaska and DiClemente (1983). The four major stages designated in the model include precontemplation (no consideration or contemplation of changing the target behavior), contemplation (characterized by motivational ambivalence about the prospects of change), action (the individual commits to a plan of action), and maintenance (coping with the risk of relapse following successful action). A primary advantage of this model is that intervention strategies can be matched to an individual's particular stage of change (Marlatt, 1992), including motivational enhancement strategies for those in the precontemplation or contemplation stages (Miller & Rollnick, 2002) and relapse prevention skills (Marlatt & Gordon, 1985) to enhance the maintenance of change initiated in the action stage.

Clearly, the stages of change model can help address the issue of how to design prevention along a continuum of need, and it has important implications for developing promising new approaches for reducing the prevalence of alcohol problems among Native youth. In particular, the development of prevention programs may benefit from conceptualizing a range of behavior change options and strategies. American Indian and Alaska Native youth participating in prevention programs will likely already have experimented with alcohol and drugs to some degree but are not yet experiencing the adverse consequences associated with abuse or dependency. As such, targeted prevention offers a critical opportunity to provide an intervention that decreases the likelihood that their substance use will lead to abuse or dependence. For those who are unable or unwilling to stop drinking or using drugs altogether, a harm reduction approach may be helpful (Marlatt, 1998). For Indian communities, a harm reduction prevention model may be a viable alternative to traditional options because of its pragmatic emphasis on the acceptance of people at where they are in the process of substance use, abuse, and recovery (Daisy, Thomas, & Worley, 1998). Harm reduction attempts to broaden the availability of prevention and treatment services by lowering the threshold necessary for entry into such services (Larimer et al., 1998). With its emphasis on community outreach, self-determination, and learning appropriate ways to cope in the presence of high-risk environmental conditions, harm reduction has been reported as a promising model of intervention in a few First Nation communities in Canada (Landau, 1996).

A Stepped-Care Model

A stepped-care approach is integral in conceptualizing prevention and treatment along a continuum. According to the stepped-care treatment model (Sobell & Sobell, 1999), one begins with the first step, usually defined as an initial effort to quit or cut down on substance use without outside support or treatment. At this point, little is known about the process of self-initiated change or the natural history of recovery in the American Indian population, although a study is currently underway to document this process among Alaska Natives (Mohatt, Hazel, Allen, & Geist, 1999).

If self-change does not occur or is unsuccessful in terms of resolving substance problems, the stepped-care approach recommends "stepping up" the intensity of interventions by engaging the individual in a brief intervention, such as participation in a motivational interviewing session designed to enhance motivation for change and a commitment to taking action or getting assistance from others (Miller & Rollnick, 2002). If the brief intervention is not effective, the stepped-care approach calls for a more intensive intervention, such as participation in a self-help or professional treatment group. Finally, if the group intervention is not successful, the next step up might include intensive outpatient therapy, or even the possibility of residential or inpatient treatment as a last resort. Overall, the stepped-care model provides a series of cost-effective strategies that can be tailored to the individual's needs and resources.

A stepped-care approach may be useful for designing and implementing prevention efforts with Indian youth. The use of universal prevention programs, in which everyone in a certain environment receives the intervention and high-risk individuals or groups of individuals are not singled out, is similar to first step approaches that rely on self-initiated change. Targeted prevention programs, on the other hand, can provide more customized prevention by first assessing for adolescents' experiences with substance use and associated problems when they enter the program. In doing this sort of evaluation, youth who have already begun to experience problems with their alcohol and drug use can be identified and referred for a more intensive intervention or treatment as needed. In addition, certain guidelines or procedures to monitor the adolescents' use throughout the program could help to detect changes in functioning. If problems begin to occur that suggest a higher level of intervention is indicated, an individual youth's level of care can be stepped up. In this way, a stepped-care model allows the level and intensity of prevention or intervention to be matched to the adolescent's needs.

Bicultural Life Skills Approaches

Research with college student binge drinkers (Baer, Kivlahan, Blume, McKnight, & Marlatt, 2001; Baer et al., 1992; Kivlahan, Marlatt, Fromme, Coppel, & Williams, 1990; Marlatt et al., 1998) provides a foundation for integrating high-risk behaviors as potential targets for prevention programs, a strategy that may be efficacious for Native adolescents. In these approaches, an attempt is made to integrate multiple risk behaviors and to develop a lifestyle-coping skills prevention approach. Adolescents are provided with education regarding substance use and its effects, and are taught skills to prevent problems with alcohol, smoking, substance abuse, high-risk sexual behavior, and eating disorders (including risk for obesity and diabetes). As such, the overarching theme is one stressing health promotion and disease prevention, with an emphasis on developing skills for lifestyle balance (Marlatt, 1985). By addressing healthy lifestyles, a skills-based prevention program provides a good match for adolescent development, including a focus on growth, personal responsibility, and enhanced self-efficacy. By avoiding diagnostic labels, lifestyle skills training programs reduce the stigma and shame associated with seeking help for substance abuse or dependency. Adolescents are more likely to be attracted to programs that encourage new learning about how to cope with the challenges of life. Behavior change is viewed from this perspective as a "journey of discovery" rather than a process of "recovery."

Research has already begun to show the effectiveness of life skills training programs for both urban and reservation-based Native American adolescents, as they can potentially be used as a more developmentally and culturally appropriate prevention method than other programs (Moran & Reaman, 2002; Schinke et al., 1988, 2000). The majority of skills-based prevention programs reviewed here incorporated a bicultural component to make the program more relevant for Indian youth. The application of bicultural competence to interventions relies on learning and practicing communication, coping, and discrimination skills (LaFromboise & Rowe, 1983). It has been suggested that demonstrating the following six factors for both Indian and White cultures indicates bicultural competence: knowledge of cultural beliefs and values, positive group attitudes, bicultural efficacy, communication competency, role repertoires, and groundedness (LaFromboise et al., 1993). Cognitive and behavioral principles drawn from social learning theory appear to be an effective mechanism for transmitting bicultural competence skills. The positive outcomes of skills training programs presented here emphasize that adapting life skills training curricula to reflect the bicultural world in which Native youth live and stressing the adoption of bicultural competencies appear to be promising prevention approaches.

Community Involvement

Effective substance abuse prevention in Indian Country requires the involvement of community members in all stages of program development and implementation. This includes partnering with elders, parents, families, schools, juvenile justice, and mental health, chemical dependency, and medical professionals, as well as representatives from other relevant tribal and/or urban Indian organizations. Without a high level of collaboration, prevention efforts are likely to fail. In most instances, researchers are from outside the community, and there is an initial amount of distrust and skepticism expressed toward them. Nevertheless, overcoming these barriers and establishing good working relationships is essential to develop culturally relevant and sensitive programs. Although researchers and academics might bring with them a certain degree of scientific knowledge and technical skill, it is important to remember that community members are the experts on their community and culture. Their input not only needs to be solicited but also needs to be used to direct the project at every stage from initial planning through implementation and evaluation.

In many communities, a universal prevention approach that targets the entire community, rather than an individual or group, may be most appropriate. Involving multiple systems in the effort to change substance use behavior can be an effective mode of intervention. For many reasons, this may be especially true in smaller communities. First, in a smaller community there is likely to be less individual privacy and confidentiality. Community-wide interventions can reduce the stigma that might otherwise be associated with only targeting high-risk individuals. In addition, social institutions and agencies may work more closely with one another than those in larger cities, increasing the likelihood of making and maintaining systemic changes. Forming community partnerships when designing this kind of intervention is vital to it being accepted and successful.

The community readiness model advanced by the Tri-Ethnic Center for Prevention Research at Colorado State University provides a useful framework for communities that are seeking ways to reduce the degree of substance use and related problems among their youth (R. W. Edwards, Jumper-Thurman, Plested, Oetting, & Swanson, 2000). A community readiness model can help guide prevention efforts by assessing how ready a community is to accept and support a program. The idea of community readiness emphasizes that unless a community is ready to initiate a prevention program, it is likely to not happen at all, or to fail. The Tri-Ethnic Center developed the idea of community readiness into a comprehensive model that includes methods of measuring readiness, suggestions for interventions appropriate for each level, and strategies for increasing a community's level of readiness.

The theory of community readiness is very loosely based on the stages of change model described previously (Prochaska & DiClemente, 1983). However, because of the added complexities of dealing with group organizations and processes, a multidimensional nine-stage model was advanced. The nine stages of community awareness are as follows: no awareness, denial, vague awareness, preplanning, preparation, initiation, stabilization, confirmation/expansion, and professionalization. R. W. Edwards and colleagues (2000) from the Tri-Ethnic Center offer a method of assessing a community's readiness for implementing programs, using key informants (people who are involved in community affairs and knowledgeable about the issues at hand, although not necessarily leaders or decision makers). In addition, they present practical suggestions for ways to increase community readiness at each stage. As such, this model provides a valuable vehicle to gauge and increase a community's readiness and desire for prevention programs.

The Cultural Challenge

Both anthropologists and cross-cultural psychologists have described the importance of developing cultural, folk, or emic models to more accurately represent how certain behaviors, attitudes, or constructs may be understood within a particular sociocultural group (Quinn & Holland, 1987; Triandis, 1980). The expectation is that the application of cultural models to the design of prevention programs will enable them to be more culturally relevant and, therefore, effective. Many questions remain, though, regarding the best way to develop and promote a life skills prevention program for Native adolescents in a culturally appropriate manner.

In their discussion of cross-cultural issues, Moran and Reaman (2002) discussed the difference between emic and etic approaches to prevention. *Emic* approaches are those that are highly specific and meaningful to members of a particular culture, whereas *etic* approaches are based on cross-cultural behavior and models. Many would argue that given the great diversity of Native American cultures, emic approaches are necessary for effectively combating problems of substance abuse. In other words, "one size does not fit all" when it comes to developing successful prevention programs for Indian adolescents. Taken to the extreme, however, does this mean that every individual or group requires its own special program, or that any one method cannot be used successfully with others?

The dilemma at hand is whether culturally specific programs must be developed as a local model or whether a global model can be developed that has pan-tribal commonalities. This issue becomes vitally important when developing prevention efforts for urban Indian youth, as they often represent the full spectrum of tribal cultures, customs, and identities. In addition, reservation-based adolescents are exposed increasingly more frequently to the traditions and beliefs of other tribal nations, as well as to the lifestyles of mainstream America. It is essential that researchers begin to critically examine their prevention programs to identify core components that may be adapted for use in other communities.

The literature reviewed in this chapter provides strong support for one such commonality: Programs that train youth in bicultural competency appear to be more successful. Adolescents who are able to demonstrate their ability to function successfully in both Native and mainstream cultures may be less likely to develop problems with alcohol or drugs (LaFromboise et al., 1993; Moran et al., 1999). Although it may not be necessary to develop one's identity with both cultures, the capacity to cope with the demands of life in both Native and mainstream American societies is critical to successful prevention outcomes. Training in bicultural coping skills is essential to survival for both urban and reservation-based Native youth.

Coping skills training has been shown to be effective for both the prevention of alcohol abuse in adolescents and young adults (Baer et al., 2001; Dimeff, Baer, Kivlahan, & Marlatt, 1999) and in the treatment of alcohol dependence (Monti, Colby, & O'Leary, 2001). Because skills training is based on basic behavioral principles and is evidence based, it could be considered an etic approach to prevention. But how can this etic approach be incorporated into culturally appropriate emic programs, and how can these basic behavioral strategies be translated or integrated in diverse Indian communities? By drawing upon the rich resources of Native cultures in terms of myths, stories, legends, songs, and dances, it may be possible to transfer etic components into emic prevention programs.

Navigating Life's Challenges: The Canoe Journey

In the Pacific Northwest, a team of researchers from the University of Washington has been working with the Seattle Indian Health Board to develop a prevention program that addresses these issues in ways that are culturally congruent with the urban community and based on empirically validated principles. This project, named Journeys of the Circle, began with a series of focus groups with urban Native youth (Mail et al., 2003). These youth described a cultural experience unique to Northwest Coastal tribes: the Canoe Family. Throughout the year, youth who belong to the Canoe Family participate in a wide range of activities designed to prepare them for annual canoe journeys to visit other tribes both in British Columbia and the Pacific Northwest. Such activities include participation in "talking circles" with elders and respected community members, the construction of large ocean-going canoes that can carry groups of paddlers from one community to another, and learning how to navigate the waters of Puget Sound. When visiting canoes arrive at a particular destination, the event is celebrated with cultural protocols that include feasting on local specialties, singing, dancing, and participation in potlatches (gift-giving ceremonies). The only requirement for involvement in the Canoe Family is that youth make a commitment to being clean and sober throughout all activities. Participation in the Canoe Family is clearly a desirable and prestigious alternative to being involved in activities associated with drinking and taking drugs.

Using this information, researchers partnered with the Seattle Indian community to develop a prevention program based on the principles of the Canoe Family. Community members have been involved in every aspect of the program's development and evaluation, providing input and feedback through community meetings, focus groups, and an advisory board. The curriculum, entitled "Canoe Journey, Life's Journey," (La Marr & Abab, 2003) was recently pilot tested with urban Native youth who are at risk for alcohol and drug problems. The program consists of eight lessons and is administered in small co-ed groups to teens between the ages of 13 and 19. The course adopts the *medicine wheel* as a metaphorical image to organize the Canoe journey itself. The medicine wheel is divided into quadrants, each representing one of the four cardinal directions (as on a compass). Two lessons are devoted to each of these quadrants: north (mental or cognitive skills), west (emotional coping skills), south (physical skills) and east (spiritual coping). Group didactics, discussion, role-playing, and completion of homework assignments are used to train youth in goal setting, decision making, effective communication, coping with negative emotions, protecting the physical body, and enhancing spiritual values.

The overall goal of the course is the same as the Canoe Family: learning how to cope successfully with various life challenges and risks, so as to complete the journey safely and to enhance the value of a clean and sober lifestyle. One advantage of the canoe journey metaphor is that it emphasizes both the value of personal skills and the community values of the canoe team as a whole. Each canoeist must master basic skills ranging from navigation to survival. At the same time, each individual contributes to the overall success of the team effort. More than 120 Indian adolescents participated in the prevention program, and data evaluation is underway. Although it is too early to report findings, preliminary analyses suggest positive outcome trends at the 3-month follow-up (Cummins, Burns, Hawkins, & Marlatt, 2003; Marlatt et al., 2003).

Next Steps

The purpose of this chapter was to review the field of substance use prevention for American Indian and Alaska Native adolescents. Epidemiological data indicate that the level of substance use problems experienced by this population is endemic. Indian youth are using alcohol and drugs at high frequencies and quantities and are at great risk for a wide variety of associated negative consequences. The need for effective prevention and treatment services is paramount. Unfortunately, the majority of interventions currently underway are not being rigorously evaluated or disseminated for use in other communities.

On the basis of our review of the published outcome literature, we offer in this chapter a set of best-practice approaches to help guide the development and implementation of prevention programs for Native American youth. These include conceptualizing prevention along a continuum, using a stepped-care model to match interventions to the adolescent's needs, incorporating biculturally adapted life skills training into programs, and maintaining extensive community involvement and collaboration in every stage of the process. These are similar to the strategies for model prevention programs outlined by the Division of Knowledge Development and Evaluation at SAMHSA's Center for Substance Abuse Prevention (1999). SAMHSA suggests six approaches that can be used alone or in combination with each other. The first is *information dissemination*, which entails increasing knowledge and altering attitudes by providing information about the nature, prevalence, and consequences of substance abuse and addiction. The second strategy is *prevention education*, or teaching life and social skills. Third is *alternatives*, or providing drug-free activities to meet the developmental needs of youth and decrease their participation in events where substances are likely to be used. The fourth strategy is *problem identification and referral*; this suggests that prevention programs should have a method of identifying youth who have already begun experiencing substance-related problems in order to refer them to more intensive services or treatment as needed. Fifth is *community-based process*, or building interagency coalitions and providing community members and agencies with training in substance use education and prevention. The last strategy is an *environmental approach*, or altering policies that can reduce risk factors or increase protective factors.

These six strategies are highly consistent with the best-practice approaches recommended here, as well as with Native American community values and needs. Contemporary prevention efforts within Native communities often emphasize a holistic approach to health and thus resonate with Native American community values (Vanderwagen, 1999). Programs have begun to incorporate spiritual components with increasing frequency in hopes of instilling traditional values and a respect for sobriety before young people begin experiencing substance-related problems (Mail & Johnson, 1993). The development of effective prevention programs requires an understanding of the strengths and values inherent in Indian communities. Incorporating these cultural factors into prevention efforts will enhance the acquisition of culturally relevant coping skills and, ultimately, lead to a reduction in substance misuse.

The Journeys of the Circle project described earlier was developed to incorporate these best-practice approaches and strategies and to address the need for prevention efforts that are both etic and emic in their approach. Through a partnership with the local American Indian community, researchers created a prevention program that incorporates substance abuse education, bicultural life skills training, and after-school alternative activities. All participants were screened for alcohol and drug problems prior to entering the program and were referred for more intensive services where indicated. Although developed specifically for urban American Indian youth in Seattle, it may be relevant and useful for tribal communities as well. The core etic components can be modified and delivered using relevant emic cultural traditions and metaphors. In the Pacific Northwest, the canoe journey symbolism was a culturally congruent mode of delivering the curriculum. In other geographic and cultural regions, local stories, myths, and resources can be used to adapt the course to be more relevant and effective. Further research will lend information critically necessary to guide efforts to transfer and adapt the Journeys of the Circle program for use in other urban and reservation communities.

This review suggests that programs that utilize Indian strengths, values, and beliefs to promote healthy behavior and reduce the harm associated with high-risk behaviors, including substance misuse, are strongly indicated. The discriminating and thoughtful use of pan-tribal commonalities to adapt approaches found to be effective in mainstream populations is perhaps the most promising and cost-effective practice currently available. These programs can then be customized for implementation in individual community settings. Such interventions provide the foundation for programs that are both scientifically validated and culturally sensitive. By building on the recommendations outlined here and evaluating their results, the field of psychology can continue advancing the knowledge base concerning substance use prevention in Indian communities and thereby more effectively help Indian adolescents create and maintain healthier lifestyles.

REFERENCES

Albaugh, B., & Albaugh, P. (1979). Alcohol and substance sniffing among Cheyenne and Arapaho Indians of Oklahoma. *International Journal of the Addictions, 14,* 1001–1007.

American Psychiatric Association. (2000). *Diagnostic and statistical manual of mental disorders* (4th ed., text revision). Washington, DC: Author.

Annis, H. M., & Davis, C. S. (1991). Relapse prevention. *Alcohol Health and Research World, 15,* 204–212.

Baer, J. S., Kivlahan, D. R., Blume, A. W., McKnight, P., & Marlatt, G. A. (2001). Brief intervention for heavy drinking college students: Four-year follow-up and natural history. *American Journal of Public Health, 91,* 1310–1316.

Baer, J. S., Marlatt, G. A., Kivlahan, D. R., Fromme, K., Larimer, M., & Williams, E. (1992). An experimental test of three methods of alcohol risk reduction with young adults. *Journal of Consulting and Clinical Psychology, 60,* 974–979.

Baer, J. S., McLean, M. G., & Marlatt, G. A. (1998). Linking etiology and treatment for adolescent substance abuse: Towards a better match. In R. Jessor (Ed.), *New perspectives on adolescent risk behaviors* (pp. 182–220). Cambridge, England: Cambridge University Press.

Bandura, A. (1986). *Social foundations of thought and action: A social cognitive theory.* Englewood, NJ: Prentice-Hall.

Bangert-Drowns, R. L. (1988). The effects of school-based substance abuse education: A meta-analysis. *Journal of Drug Education, 18,* 243–265.

Barrett, M. E., Simpson, D. D., & Lehman, W. E. (1988). Behavioral changes of adolescents in drug abuse intervention programs. *Journal of Clinical Psychology, 44,* 461–473.

Bates, S. C., Beauvais, F., & Trimble, J. E. (1997). American Indian adolescent alcohol involvement and ethnic identification. *Substance Use & Misuse, 32,* 2013–2031.

Beauvais, F. (1992a). Comparison of drug use rates for reservation Indian, nonreservation Indian and Anglo youth. *American Indian and Alaska Native Mental Health Research, 5,* 13–31.

Beauvais, F. (1992b). The consequences of drug and alcohol use for Indian youth. *American Indian and Alaska Native Mental Health Research, 5,* 32–37.

Beauvais, F. (1992c). Trends in Indian adolescent drug and alcohol use. *American Indian and Alaska Native Mental Health Research, 5,* 1–12.

Beauvais, F. (1996). Trends in drug use among American Indian students and dropouts, 1975 to 1994. *American Journal of Public Health, 8,* 1594–1598.

Beauvais, F. (1998). American Indians and alcohol. *Alcohol Health & Research World, 22,* 253–259. Retrieved from http://pubs.niaaa. nih.gov/publications/arh22-4/253.pdf

Beauvais, F., Chavez, E., Oetting, E. R., Deffenbacher, J., & Cornell, G. (1996). Drug use, violence, and victimization among White American, Mexican American, and American Indian dropouts, students with academic difficulties, and students in good academic standing. *Journal of Consulting Psychology, 41,* 292–299.

Beauvais, F., & LaBoueff, S. (1985). Drug and alcohol abuse intervention in American Indian communities. *International Journal of the Addictions, 20,* 139–171.

Beauvais, F., Oetting, E. R., Wolf, W., & Edwards, R. W. (1989). American Indian youth and drugs, 1976–1987: A continuing problem. *American Journal of Public Health, 79,* 634–636.

Bentler, P. M. (1992). Etiologies and consequences of adolescent drug use: Implications for prevention. *Journal of Addictive Disorders, 11*(3), 47–61.

Blum, R. W., Harmon, B., Harris, L., Bergeisen, L., & Resnick, M. D. (1992). American Indian–Alaska Native youth health. *Journal of the American Medical Association, 267,* 1637–1644.

Bobo, J. K. (1986). Preventing drug abuse among American Indian adolescents. In L. D. Gilchrist & S. P. Schinke (Eds.), *Preventing social and health problems through life skills training* (pp. 43–54). Seattle: University of Washington, School of Social Work, Center for Social Welfare Research.

Brave Heart, M. Y., & DeBruyn, L. M. (1998). The American Indian holocaust: Healing historical unresolved grief. *American Indian and Alaska Native Mental Health Research, 8,* 56–78.

Bureau of Indian Affairs. (2002, July 12). Indian entities recognized and eligible to receive services from the United States Bureau of Indian Affairs. *Federal Register, 67.*

Caplan, G. (1964). *Principles of preventive psychiatry.* New York: Basic Books.

Carpenter, R. A., Lyons, C. A., & Miller, W. R. (1985). Peer-managed self-control program for prevention of alcohol abuse in American Indian high school students: A pilot evaluation study. *International Journal of the Addictions, 20,* 299–310.

Cockerham, W. C. (1975). Drinking attitudes and practices among Wind River reservation Indian youth. *Journal of Studies on Alcohol, 36,* 321–326.

Covert, J., & Wangberg, D. (1992). Peer counseling: Positive peer pressure. In G. W. Lawson & A. W. Lawson (Eds.), *Adolescent substance abuse: Etiology, treatment, and prevention* (pp. 131–139). Gaithersburg, MD: Aspen.

Cummins, L. H., Burns, K. M., Hawkins, E. H., & Marlatt, G. A. (2003, November). Skills for life: Outcomes of a substance abuse prevention program for urban American Indian and Alaska Native adolescents. In T. W. Lostutter (Chair), *Prevention research in alcohol and substance use/abuse in at-risk populations*. Symposium conducted at the meeting for the Advancement of Behavior Therapy, Boston.

Curley, R. T. (1967). Drinking patterns of the Mescalero Apache. *Quarterly Journal of Studies on Alcohol, 28,* 116–131.

Daisy, F., Thomas, L., & Worley, C. (1998). Alcohol abuse and harm reduction within the Native community. In G. A. Marlatt (Ed.), *Harm reduction: Pragmatic strategies for managing high-risk behaviors* (pp. 327–350). New York: Guilford Press.

Dick, R. W., Manson, S. M., & Beals, J. (1993). Alcohol use among male and female Native American adolescents: Patterns and correlates of student drinking in a boarding school. *Journal of Studies on Alcohol, 54,* 172–177.

Dimeff, L. A., Baer, J. S., Kivlahan, D. R., & Marlatt, G. A. (1999). *Brief alcohol screening and intervention for college students (BASICS): A harm reduction approach.* New York: Guilford Press.

Dinges, N. G., & Duong-Tran, Q. (1993). Stressful life events and co-occurring depression, substance abuse and suicidality among American Indian and Alaska Native adolescents. *Culture, Medicine and Psychiatry, 16,* 487–502.

Dorpat, N. (1994). PRIDE: Substance abuse education/intervention program. *American Indian and Alaska Native Mental Health Research, 4,* 122–133.

Edwards, E. D., & Edwards, M. E. (1988). Alcoholism prevention treatment and Native American youth: A community approach. *Journal of Drug Issues, 18,* 103–115.

Edwards, R. W., Jumper-Thurman, P., Plested, B. A., Oetting, E. R., & Swanson, L. (2000). Community readiness: Research to practice. *Journal of Community Psychology, 28,* 291–307.

Elder, C., Leaver-Dunn, D., Wang, M. Q., Nagy, S., & Green, L. (2000). Organized group activity as a protective factor against adolescent substance use. *American Journal of Health Behavior, 24,* 108–113.

Federman, E. B., Costello, E. J., Angold, A., Farmer, E. M. Z., & Erkanli, A. (1997). Development of substance use and psychiatric comorbidity in an epidemiologic study of White and American Indian young adolescents: The Great Smoky Mountain study. *Drug and Alcohol Dependence, 44,* 69–78.

Ferguson, F. N. (1976). Stake theory as an explanatory device in Navajo alcoholism treatment response. *Human Organization, 35,* 65–78.

Fishbein, M., & Azjen, I. (1975). *Belief, attitude, intention, and behavior: An introduction to theory and research.* Reading, MA: Addison-Wesley.

Fleming, C. M. (1992). The next twenty years of prevention in Indian country: Visionary, complex, and practical. *American Indian and Alaska Native Mental Health Research, 4,* 85–88.

French, L. A. (2000). *Addictions and Native Americans.* Westport, CT: Praeger.

Garcia-Mason, V. (1985). *Relationship of drug use & self-concept among American Indian youth.* Unpublished doctoral dissertation, University of New Mexico, Albuquerque.

Golub, A., & Johnson, B. D. (1994). The shifting importance of alcohol and marijuana as gateway substances among serious drug abusers. *Journal of Studies on Alcohol, 55,* 607–614.

Grossman, D. C., Milligan, B. C., & Deyo, R. A. (1991). Risk factors for suicide attempts among Navajo adolescents. *American Journal of Public Health, 81,* 870–874.

Gutierres, S. E., Russo, N. F., & Urbanski, L. (1994). Sociocultural and psychological factors in American Indian drug use: Implications for treatment. *International Journal of the Addictions, 29,* 1761–1786.

Hawkins, E. H. (2002). Navigating between two worlds: A sociocultural examination of alcohol problems among urban American Indian youth (Doctoral dissertation, University of Washington, 2002). *Dissertation Abstracts International, 63*(5), 2584B.

Hawkins, E. H., & Blume, A. W. (2002). Loss of sacredness: Historical contexts of health policies for indigenous people in the United States. In P. D. Mail, S. Heurtin-Roberts, S. E. Martin, & J. Howard (Eds.), *Alcohol use among American Indians: Multiple perspectives on a complex problem* (NIAAA Research Monograph No. 37, pp. 25–46). Bethesda, MD: National Institutes of Health, National Institute on Alcohol Abuse and Alcoholism.

Hawkins, J. D., Catalano, R. F., & Miller, J. Y. (1992). Risk and protective factors for alcohol and other drug problems in adolescence and early adulthood: Implications for substance abuse prevention. *Psychological Bulletin, 112,* 64–105.

Hawkins, J. D., Graham, J. W., Maguin, E., Abbott, R., Hill, K. G., & Catalano, R. F. (1997). Exploring the effects of age of alcohol use initiation and psychosocial risk factors on subsequent alcohol misuse. *Journal of Studies on Alcohol, 58,* 280–290.

Honigmann, J., & Honigmann, I. (1968). *Alcohol in a Canadian northern town.* Unpublished report, University of North Carolina at Chapel Hill, Institute for Research in Social Science.

Howard, M. O., Walker, R. D., Silk Walker, P., Cottler, L. B., & Compton, W. M. (1999). Inhalant use among urban American Indian youth. *Addiction, 94,* 83–95.

Indian Health Service. (1977). *Alcoholism: A high priority health problem* (DHEW Publication No. HAS 77-1001). Washington, DC: U.S. Government Printing Office.

Indian Health Service, Office of Public Health, Program Statistics Team. (1999). *Trends in Indian health: 1998–99.* Rockville, MD: U.S. Department of Health and Human Services.

Institute of Medicine. (1994). *Reducing risks for mental disorders: Frontiers for preventive intervention research.* Washington, DC: National Academy Press.

Jessor, R., Van Den Bos, J., Vanderryn, J., Costa, F. M., & Turbin, M. S. (1995). Protective factors in adolescent problem behavior: Moderator effects and developmental change. *Developmental Psychology, 31,* 923–933.

Johnston, L. D., O'Malley, P. M., & Bachman, J. G. (2002). *The Monitoring the Future National Survey results on adolescent drug use: Overview of key findings, 2001* (NIH Publication No. 02-5105). Rockville, MD: National Institute on Drug Abuse.

Kandel, D., & Faust, R. (1975). Sequence and stages in patterns of adolescent drug use. *Archives of General Psychiatry, 32,* 923–932.

Kandel, D., & Logan, J. A. (1984). Patterns of drug use from adolescence to young adulthood: I. Periods of risk for initiation, continued use, and discontinuation. *American Journal of Public Health, 74,* 660–666.

Kandel, D., & Yamaguchi, K. (1993). From beer to crack: Developmental patterns of drug involvement. *American Journal of Public Health, 83,* 851–855.

Kandel, D. B., Yamaguchi, K., & Chen, K. (1992). Stages of progression in drug involvement from adolescence to adulthood: Further evidence for the gateway theory. *Journal of Studies on Alcohol, 53,* 447–457.

Kelley, M. (1999, April 28). American Indian boarding schools: "That hurt never goes away." *CNEWS Features.* Retrieved May 3, 2003, from http://www.canoe.ca/ CNEWSFeatures9904/28_indians.html

Kemnitzer, L. S. (1973). Adjustment and value conflict in urbanizing Dakota Indians measured by Q-sort technique. *American Anthropologist, 75,* 687–707.

King, J., Beals, J., Manson, S. M., & Trimble, J. E. (1992). A structural equation model of factors related to substance use among American Indian adolescents. *Drugs and Society, 6,* 253–268.

King, J., & Thayer, J. F. (1993). Examining conceptual models for understanding drug use behavior among American Indian youth. In M. R. De La Rosa & J. R. Adrados (Eds.), *Drug abuse among minority youth: Advances in research and methodology* (NIDA Research Monograph No. 130, NIH Publication No. 93-3479, pp. 125–143). Rockville, MD: National Institute on Drug Abuse.

Kivlahan, D. R., Marlatt, G. A., Fromme, K., Coppel, D. B., & Williams, E. (1990). Secondary prevention with college drinkers: Evaluation of an alcohol skills training program. *Journal of Consulting and Clinical Psychology, 58,* 805–810.

LaFromboise, T. D. (1988). American Indian mental health policy. *American Psychologist, 43,* 388–397.

LaFromboise, T. D., Coleman, H. L. K., & Gerton, J. (1993). Psychological impact of biculturalism: Evidence and theory. *Psychological Bulletin, 114,* 395–412.

LaFromboise, T. D., & Rowe, W. (1983). Skills training for bicultural competence: Rationale and application. *Journal of Counseling Psychology, 30,* 589–595.

LaFromboise, T. D., Trimble, J. E., & Mohatt, G. (1990). Counseling intervention and American Indian tradition: An integrative approach. *Counseling Psychologist, 18,* 628–654.

La Marr, J. C., & Abab, T. (Eds.). (2003). *Canoe journey, life's journey: A life skills manual for Native adolescents.* Seattle: University of Washington, Seattle Indian Health Board and Addictive Behaviors Research Center.

Landau, T. C. (1996). The prospects of a harm reduction approach among indigenous people in Canada. *Drug and Alcohol Review, 15,* 393–401.

Larimer, M. E., Marlatt, G. A., Baer, J. S., Quigley, L. A., Blume, A. W., & Hawkins, E. H. (1998). Harm reduction for alcohol problems: Expanding access to and acceptability of prevention and treatment services. In G. A. Marlatt (Ed.), *Harm reduction: Pragmatic strategies for managing high-risk behaviors* (pp. 69–121). New York: Guilford Press.

LeMaster, P. L., Connell, C. M., Mitchell, C. M., & Manson, S. M. (2002). Tobacco use among American Indian adolescents: Protective and risk factors. *Journal of Adolescent Health, 30,* 426–432.

Levy, J. E., & Kunitz, S. J. (1971). Indian reservations, anomie, and social pathologies. *Southwestern Journal of Anthropology, 27,* 97–128.

Mail, P. D. (1997). Cultural orientation and positive psychological status as protective factors against problem behaviors in southwestern American Indian adolescents (Doctoral dissertation, University of Maryland at College Park, 1996). *Dissertation Abstracts International, 58*(1), 0204A.

Mail, P. D., Hawkins, E. H., La Marr, J., Blume, A. W., Radin, S., Goines M. A., & Chastain, C. (2003). *Ask the consumer: Focus groups with urban Indian adolescents.* Manuscript in preparation, University of Washington, Seattle.

Mail, P. D., Heurtin-Roberts, S., Martin, S. E., & Howard, J. (Eds.). (2002). *Alcohol use among American Indians: Multiple perspectives on a complex problem* (NIAAA Research Monograph No. 37). Bethesda, MD: National Institutes of Health, National Institute on Alcohol Abuse and Alcoholism.

Mail, P. D., & Johnson, S. (1993). Boozing, sniffing, and toking: An overview of the past, present, and future of substance use by American Indians. *American Indian and Alaska Native Mental Health Research, 5,* 1–33.

Manson, S., Shore, J., & Bloom, J. (1985). The depressive experience in American Indian communities: A challenge for psychiatric theory and diagnosis. In A. Kleinman & B. Good (Eds.), *Culture and depression: Studies in anthropology and cross-cultural psychiatry of affect and disorder* (pp. 331–368). Berkeley: University of California Press.

Marlatt, G. A. (1985). Lifestyle modification. In G. A. Marlatt & J. R. Gordon (Eds.), *Relapse prevention* (pp. 280–348). New York: Guilford Press.

Marlatt, G. A. (1992). Substance abuse: Implications of a biopsychosocial model for prevention, treatment, and relapse prevention. In J. Grabowski & G. R. VandenBos (Eds.), *Psychopharmacology: Basic mechanisms and applied intervention* (pp. 127–162). Washington, DC: American Psychological Association.

Marlatt, G. A. (1998). Highlights of harm reduction: A personal report from the First National Harm Reduction Conference in the United States. In G. A. Marlatt (Ed.), *Harm reduction: Pragmatic strategies for managing high-risk behaviors* (pp. 3–29). New York: Guilford Press.

Marlatt, G. A., Baer, J. S., Kivlahan, D. R., Dimeff, L. A., Larimer, M. E., Quigley, L. A., et al. (1998). Screening and brief intervention for high-risk college student drinkers: Results from a 2-year follow-up assessment. *Journal of Consulting and Clinical Psychology, 66,* 604–615.

Marlatt, G. A., & Gordon, J. R. (1985). *Relapse prevention: Maintenance strategies in the treatment of addictive behaviors*. New York: Guilford Press.

Marlatt, G. A., Larimer, M., Mail, P. D., Hawkins, E. H., Cummins, L. H., Blume, A. W., et al. (2003). Journeys of the circle: A culturally congruent life skills intervention for adolescent Indian drinking. *Alcoholism: Clinical & Experimental Research, 27*, 1327–1329.

Mason, V. G. (1995). *Relationship of drug use and self-concept among American Indian youth*. Unpublished doctoral dissertation, University of New Mexico, Albuquerque.

May, P. A. (1982). Substance abuse and American Indians: Prevalence and susceptibility. *International Journal of the Addictions, 17*, 1185–1209.

May, P. A. (1986). Alcohol and drug misuse prevention programs for American Indians: Needs and opportunities. *Journal of Studies on Alcohol, 47*, 187–195.

May, P. A. (1987). Suicide and self-destruction among American Indian youths. *American Indian and Alaska Native Mental Health, 1*, 52–69.

May, P. A. (1996). Overview of alcohol abuse epidemiology for American Indian populations. In G. D. Sandefur, R. R. Rindfuss, & B. Cohen (Eds.), *Changing numbers, changing needs: American Indian demography and public health* (pp. 235–261). Washington, DC: National Academy Press.

May, P. A., & Del Vecchio, A. M. (1997). The three common behavioral patterns of inhalant/solvent abuse: Selected findings and research issues. *Drugs and Society, 10*, 3–37.

May, P. A., & Moran, J. R. (1995). Prevention of alcohol misuse: A review of health promotion efforts among American Indians. *American Journal of Health Promotion, 9*, 288–299.

McGuire, W. J. (1964). Inducing resistance to persuasion: Some contemporary approaches. In L. Berkowitz (Ed.), *Advances in experimental social psychology* (Vol. 1, pp. 191–229). New York: Academic Press.

Mellanby, A. R., Rees, J. B., & Tripp, J. H. (2000). Peer-led and adult-led school health education: A critical review of available comparative research. *Health Education Research, 15*, 533–545.

Miller, W. R., & Rollnick, S. (2002). *Motivational interviewing: Preparing people for change* (2nd ed.). New York: Guilford Press.

Mitchell, C. M., Novins, D. K., & Holmes, T. (1999). Marijuana use among American Indian adolescents: A growth curve analysis from ages 14 through 20. *Journal of the American Academy of Child & Adolescent Psychiatry, 38*, 72–78.

Mohatt, G., Hazel, K., Allen, J., & Geist, C. (1999). *People Awakening Project: Discovering Alaska Natives' pathways to sobriety* (NIAAA Grant No. 1 R01 AA11446). Bethesda, MD: National Institute on Alcohol Abuse and Alcoholism.

Moncher, M. S., Holden, G. W., & Trimble, J. E. (1990). Substance abuse among Native-American youth. *Journal of Consulting and Clinical Psychology, 58*, 408–415.

Monti, P., Colby, S. M., & O'Leary, T. (Eds.). (2001). *Adolescents, alcohol, and substance abuse: Reaching teens through brief interventions.* New York: Guilford Press.

Moran, J. (1998). Alcohol prevention among urban American Indian youth. *Journal of Human Behavior in the Social Environment, 2,* 51–68.

Moran, J. R., Fleming, C. M., Somervell, P., & Manson, S. M. (1999). Measuring bicultural identity among American Indian adolescents: A factor analytic study. *Journal of Adolescent Research, 14,* 405–426.

Moran, J. R., & Reaman, J. A. (2002). Critical issues for substance abuse prevention targeting American Indian youth. *Journal of Primary Prevention, 22,* 201–233.

Myers, H. F., Kagawa-Singer, M., Kumanyika, S. K., Lex, B. W., & Markides, K. S. (1995). Panel III: Behavioral risk factors related to chronic diseases in ethnic minorities. *Health Psychology, 14,* 613–621.

National Institute on Drug Abuse. (1998). *Drug use among racial/ethnic minorities.* Rockville, MD: Author.

Nelson, S., McCoy, G., Stetter, M., & Vanderwagen, W. (1992). An overview of mental health services for American Indians and Alaska Natives in the 1990's. *Hospital and Community Psychiatry, 43,* 257–261.

Newcomb, M. D., & Felix-Ortiz, M. (1992). Multiple protective and risk factors for drug use and abuse: Cross-sectional and prospective findings. *Journal of Personality and Social Psychology, 63,* 280–296.

Novins, D. K., Beals, J., & Mitchell, C. M. (2001). Sequences of substance use among American Indian adolescents. *Journal of the American Academy of Child & Adolescent Psychiatry, 40,* 1168–1174.

Novins, D. K., & Mitchell, C. M. (1998). Factors associated with marijuana use among American Indian adolescents. *Addiction, 93,* 1693–1702.

Oetting, E. R., & Beauvais, F. (1989). Epidemiology and correlates of alcohol use among Indian adolescents living on reservations. In D. Spiegler, D. Tate, S. Aitken, & C. Christian (Eds.), *Alcohol use among U.S. ethnic minorities* (NIAAA Research Monograph No. 18, pp. 239–267). Rockville, MD: National Institute on Alcohol Abuse and Alcoholism.

Oetting, E. R., Beauvais, F., & Edwards, R. (1988). Alcohol and Indian youth: Social and psychological correlates and prevention. *Journal of Drug Issues, 18,* 87–101.

Oetting, E. R., Beauvais, F., & Velarde, J. (1982). Marijuana use by reservation Native American youth. *Listening Post Indian Health Services, 4,* 25–28.

Oetting, E. R., & Donnermeyer, J. F. (1998). Primary socialization theory: The etiology of drug use and deviance: I. *Substance Use & Misuse, 33,* 995–1026.

Oetting, E. R., Donnermeyer, J. F., Trimble, J. E., & Beauvais, F. (1998). Primary socialization theory: Culture, ethnicity, and cultural identification. The links between culture and substance use: IV. *Substance Use & Misuse, 33,* 2075–2107.

Oetting, E. R., Swaim, R. C., Edwards, R. S., & Beauvais, F. (1989). Indian and Anglo adolescent alcohol use and emotional distress: Path models. *American Journal of Drug and Alcohol Abuse, 15,* 153–172.

Offord, D. R. (2000). Selection of levels of prevention. *Addictive Behaviors, 25,* 833–842.

Okwumabua, J. O., & Duryea, E. J. (1987). Age of onset, periods of risk, and patterns of progression in drug use among American Indian high school students. *International Journal of the Addictions, 22,* 1269–1276.

O'Nell, T. D. (1992–1993). "Feeling worthless": An ethnographic investigation of depression and problem drinking at the Flathead Reservation. *Cultural Medicine & Psychiatry, 16,* 447–469.

Parker-Langley, L. (2002). Alcohol prevention programs among American Indians: Research findings and issues. In P. D. Mail, S. Heurtin-Roberts, S. E. Martin, & J. Howard (Eds.), *Alcohol use among American Indians: Multiple perspectives on a complex problem* (NIAAA Research Monograph No. 37, pp. 111–140). Bethesda, MD: National Institutes of Health, National Institute on Alcohol Abuse and Alcoholism.

Petoskey, E. L., Van Stelle, K. R., & De Jong, J. A. (1998). Prevention through empowerment in a Native American community. *Drugs and Society, 12,* 147–162.

Prochaska, J. O., & DiClemente, C. C. (1983). Stages and processes of self-change of smoking: Toward an integrative model of change. *Journal of Consulting and Clinical Psychology, 51,* 390–395.

Quinn, N., & Holland, D. (1987). Culture and cognition. In D. Holland & N. Dorothy (Eds.), *Cultural models in language and thought* (pp. 1–40). New York: Cambridge University Press.

Robbin, A. (2000). Classifying racial and ethnic group data in the United States: The politics of negotiation and accommodation. *Journal of Government Information, 27,* 129–156.

Rolf, J. E., Nansel, T. R., Baldwin, J. A., Johnson, J. L., & Benally, C. C. (2002). HIV/AIDS and alcohol and other drug abuse prevention in American Indian communities: Behavioral and community effects. In P. D. Mail, S. Heurtin-Roberts, S. E. Martin, & J. Howard (Eds.), *Alcohol use among American Indians: Multiple perspectives on a complex problem* (NIAAA Research Monograph No. 37, pp. 295–319). Bethesda, MD: National Institutes of Health, National Institute on Alcohol Abuse and Alcoholism.

Rowe, W. E. (1997). Changing ATOD norms and behaviors: A Native American community commitment to wellness. *Evaluation and Program Planning, 20,* 323–333.

Rutter, M. (1987). Psychological resilience and protective mechanisms. *American Journal of Orthopsychiatry, 57,* 316–331.

Rychtarik, R. G., Prue, D. M., Rapp, S., & King, A. C. (1992). Self-efficacy, aftercare, and relapse in a treatment program for alcoholics. *Journal of Studies on Alcohol, 53,* 435–440.

Schinke, S. P., Botvin, G. J., Trimble, J. E., Orlandi, M. A., Gilchrist, L. D., & Locklear, V. S. (1988). Preventing substance abuse among American Indian adolescents: A bicultural competence skills approach. *Journal of Counseling Psychology, 35,* 87–90.

Schinke, S. P., Shilling, R. F., Gilchrist, L. D., Barth, R. P., Bobo, J. K., Trimble, J., & Cvetkovivh, G. T. (1985). Preventing substance abuse with American Indian youth. *Social Casework, 66,* 213–217.

Schinke, S. P., Tepavac, L., & Cole, K. C. (2000). Preventing substance use among Native American youth: Three-year results. *Addictive Behaviors, 25,* 387–397.

Silk-Walker, P., Walker, D., & Kivlahan, D. (1988). Alcoholism, alcohol abuse, and health in American Indians and Alaska Natives. *American Indian and Alaska Native Mental Health Research, 1,* 65–83.

Sobell, M. B., & Sobell, L. C. (1999). Stepped care for alcohol problems: An efficient method for planning and delivering clinical services. In J. A. Tucker, D. M. Donovan, & G. A. Marlatt (Eds.), *Changing addictive behaviors: Bridging clinical and public health strategies* (pp. 331–343). New York: Guilford Press.

Spicer, P. (1997). Toward a (dys)functional anthropology of drinking: Ambivalence and the American Indian experience with drinking. *Medical Anthropology Quarterly, 11,* 306–323.

Spindler, G. D., & Spindler, L. S. (1978). Identity, militancy, and cultural congruence: The Menomonee and Kainai. *Annals of the American Academy of Political and Social Science, 436,* 73–85.

Stone, S. A. (1981). Cultural program for alcoholism. In J. S. Putnam (Ed.), *Indian and Alaskan Native mental health seminars* (pp. 411–432). Seattle, WA: Seattle Indian Health Board.

Substance Abuse and Mental Health Services Administration, Center for Substance Abuse Prevention. (2003). *Science-based prevention programs and principles 2002: Effective substance abuse and mental health programs for every community* (DHHS Publication No. SMA 03-3764). Rockville, MD: Author.

Substance Abuse and Mental Health Services Administration, Center for Substance Abuse Prevention, Division of Knowledge Development and Evaluation. (1999). *Understanding substance abuse prevention: Toward the 21st century: A primer on effective programs* (DHHS Publication No. SMA 99-3301). Rockville, MD: Author.

Substance Abuse and Mental Health Services Administration, Office of Applied Studies. (2002, January 25). *The National Household Survey on Drug Abuse (NHSDA) Report: Cigarette use among American Indian/Alaska Native youths.* Rockville, MD: U.S. Department of Health and Human Services.

Thurman, P. J., & Green, V. A. (1997). American Indian inhalant use. *American Indian and Alaska Native Mental Health Research, 8,* 24–40.

Tobler, N. S. (1986). Meta-analysis of 143 adolescent drug prevention programs: Quantitative outcome results of program participants compared to control or comparison group. *Journal of Drug Issues, 16,* 537–567.

Triandis, H. C. (1980). Introduction to *Handbook of Cross-Cultural Psychology.* In H. C. Triandis & W. W. Lambert (Eds.), *Handbook of cross-cultural psychology: Vol. 1. Perspectives* (pp. 1–14). Boston: Allyn & Bacon.

Trimble, J. E., Padilla, A., & Bell-Bolek, C. (1987). *Drug abuse among ethnic minorities* (NIDA Office of Science Monograph, DHHS Publication No. ADM 87-1474). Washington, DC: U.S. Government Printing Office.

Tyler, J., & Lichtenstein, C. (1997). Risk, protective, AOD knowledge, attitude, and AOD behavior. Factors associated with characteristics of high-risk youth. *Evaluation and Program Planning, 20,* 27–45.

U.S. Census Bureau. (1993). *We the first Americans.* Washington, DC: Author.

U.S. Census Bureau. (2001a, October 3). *Population by age, sex, race, and Hispanic or Latino origin for the United States: 2000 (PHC-T-9)* [Electronic version]. Retrieved October 9, 2002, from http://www.census.gov/population/www/cen2000/phc-t9.html

U.S. Census Bureau. (2001b, April 2). *Population by race only, race in combination only, race alone or in combination, and Hispanic or Latino origin, for the United States: 2000* [Data table]. Retrieved October 22, 2002, from the Population Division, Population Estimates Program: http://www.census.gov/population/cen2000/phc-t1/tab03.pdf

U.S. Congress, Office of Technology Assessment. (1990). *Indian adolescent mental health.* Washington, DC: U.S. Government Printing Office.

U.S. Department of Health and Human Services. (2001). *Mental health, culture, race, and ethnicity—A supplement to mental health: A report of the Surgeon General.* Rockville, MD: U.S. Department of Health and Human Services, Substance Abuse and Mental Health Services Administration, Center for Mental Health Services.

Vanderwagen, W. C. (1999). Public health, prevention, and primary care in American Indian and Alaska Native communities. In J. M. Galloway, B. W. Goldberg, & J. S. Alpert (Eds.), *Primary care of Native American patients: Diagnosis, therapy, and epidemiology* (pp. 27–29). Boston: Butterworth-Heinemann.

Walker, R. D. (1992). *Preliminary results: Alcohol abuse in urban Indian adolescents and women, R01-AA07103.* Seattle: University of Washington.

Walker, R. D., Lambert, M. D., Walker, P. S., Kivlahan, D. R., Donovan, D. M., & Howard, M. O. (1996). Alcohol abuse in urban Indian adolescents and women: A longitudinal study for assessment and risk evaluation. *American Indian and Alaska Native Mental Health Research, 7,* 1–47.

Wallace, J. M., Bachman, J. G., O'Malley, P. M., Johnston, J. D., Schulenberg, J. E., & Cooper, S. M. (2002). Tobacco, alcohol, and illicit drug use: Racial and ethnic differences among U.S. high school seniors, 1976–2000. *Public Health Reports, 117*(Suppl. 1), S67–S75.

Wechsler, H., Lee, J. E., Kuo, M., & Lee, H. (2000). College binge drinking in the 1990s: A continuing problem: Results of the Harvard School of Public Health College Alcohol Study. *Journal of American College Health, 48,* 199–210.

Weibel-Orlando, J. (1984). Indian alcoholism treatment programs as flawed rites of passage. *Medical Anthropology Quarterly, 15,* 62–67.

Weinberg, N., Radhert, E., Colliver, J., & Glantz, M. (1998). Adolescent substance abuse: A review of the past 10 years. *Journal of the American Academy of Child & Adolescent Psychiatry, 37,* 252–261.

Western Center for the Application of Prevention Technologies. (2002). *Building a successful prevention program.* Available at http://casat.unr.edu/westcapt/bestpractices/

Whitbeck, L. B., Hoyt, D. R., McMorris, B. J., Chen, A., & Stubben, J. D. (2001). Perceived discrimination and early substance abuse among American Indian children. *Journal of Health and Social Behavior, 42,* 405–424.

White, H. R., & Labouvie, E. W. (1989). Towards the assessment of adolescent problem drinking. *Journal of Studies on Alcohol, 50,* 30–37.

Wiebe, J., & Huebert, K. M. (1996). Community mobile treatment: What it is and how it works. *Journal of Substance Abuse Treatment, 13,* 23–31.

Wills, T. A., McNamara, G., Vaccaro, D., & Hirky, A. E. (1997). Escalated substance use: A longitudinal grouping analysis from early to middle adolescence. In G. A. Marlatt & G. R. VandenBos (Eds.), *Addictive behaviors: Readings on etiology, prevention, and treatment* (pp. 97–128). Washington, DC: American Psychological Association.

Young, T. J. (1988). Substance use and abuse among Native Americans. *Clinical Psychology Review, 8,* 125–138.

Zitzow, D. A. (1990). A comparison of time Ojibway adolescents spend with parents/elders in the 1930's and 1980's. *American Indian and Alaska Native Mental Health Research, 3,* 7–16.

24

EXAMINATION OF ETHNICITY IN CONTROLLED TREATMENT OUTCOME STUDIES INVOLVING ADOLESCENT SUBSTANCE ABUSERS: A COMPREHENSIVE LITERATURE REVIEW

MARILYN J. STRADA, BRAD DONOHUE, AND NOELLE L. LEFFORGE

It is well established that adolescent substance abusers evidence severe behavioral and emotional problems (Waldron, 1997). Although some sources have reported stabilizing trends in the relatively high prevalence of adolescent substance use (Substance Abuse and Mental Health Services Administration [SAMHSA], 2003), the number of adolescents entering substance abuse treatment has increased in the past few years (U.S. Department of Health and Human Services [HHS], 2003). Commensurate with the demand for adolescent drug abuse treatment, there has been a trend in substance abuse providers and funding agencies to use empirically supported therapies (ESTs), derived primarily from studies in which randomized clinical trial methodology is implemented. In support of these initiatives, the National Institute on Drug Abuse (NIDA; 1999) published a listing of scientifically based approaches that have been found to be effective in randomized clinical trials involving substance abusers, and the American Psychological Association (APA) Division

A summarized, poster version of this chapter was presented at the 112th Annual Convention of the American Psychological Association and the Minority Fellowship Program 1st Poster Session, both in Honolulu, HI, August 2004. Marilyn J. Strada wishes to thank the American Psychological Association Minority Fellowship Program, whose support indirectly funded the preparation of this article.

Reprinted from *Psychology of Addictive Behaviors*, 20, 11–27 (2006). Copyright 2006 by the American Psychological Association.

12 Task Force on Promotion and Dissemination of Psychological Procedures (1995; Chambless & Hollon, 1998; Chambless et al., 1996) delineated criteria for the evaluation of treatments prior to their utilization. Unfortunately, the extent to which treatments can be generalized to ethnic minority substance-abusing youths has not received the same degree of attention in the development and evaluation of ESTs (e.g., Bernal & Scharron-del-Rio, 2001; Clay, Mordhorst, & Lehn, 2002; Hall, 2001; Sue, 1998). This is particularly troubling as ethnic minorities are expected to represent 50% of the overall population in the United States by the year 2050 (U.S. Census Bureau, 1996) and as substance use rates among many of these populations are increasing relative to Caucasian youths (SAMHSA, 2003). Furthermore, as was highlighted in a U.S. Surgeon General's (HHS, 2001) supplemental report, consideration of ethnic culture in treatment is generally important, as it may influence, among several other factors, individuals' presentation of symptomatology, health-seeking behaviors, views about mental illness, and motivation to seek and stay in treatment. Additionally, studies have found that some aspects of ethnic culture, such as ethnic identity, tend to be more salient for members of ethnic minority cultures than for Caucasian individuals (Phinney, 1996). Indeed, ethnic identity has been positively associated with measures of psychological health in ethnic minorities as well as Caucasians when these individuals are in settings in which they represent a numerical minority (Greig, 2003). Moreover, Caucasian individuals report significantly fewer problems due to their ethnic culture and perceive their ethnic culture to be less important than do ethnic minority individuals (Donohue et al., 2006).

Relevant specifically to substance use, prevalence rates and patterns of substance use among some ethnic minority youths tend to differ from those rates and patterns observed among Caucasian youths (Centers for Disease Control & Prevention [CDCP], 2002), which may be indicative of a need to incorporate culture-related treatment components that clinicians do not typically include when treating members of the majority culture (e.g., psychoeducation). Consequently, although some researchers have recommended ESTs for use with ethnic minority individuals (Chambless et al., 1996), others have questioned the validity of ESTs in these populations (e.g., Bernal & Scharron-del-Rio, 2001; Clay et al., 2002; Hall, 2001; Sue, 1998). Indeed, some have reasoned that the unique characteristics and culture-related factors associated with substance use prevalence rates and use patterns may result in differential responses to treatment (Bernal & Scharron-del-Rio, 2001; Hall, 2001). Nevertheless, differences in response to treatment have not been thoroughly investigated because of inadequate representation of ethnic minority diverse individuals in study samples and lack of effect size reports specified separately for each ethnic minority group, which may otherwise permit meta-analytic examinations. Therefore, a starting point may be to examine this topic in a qualitative manner. Thus, the purpose of the present chapter is to (a) conduct a content analysis of the extent to which investigators of adolescent substance use treatment outcome studies have considered ethnicity-related factors in the design, implementation, and evaluation of treatments; (b) report issues that have restricted research in this area; and (c) provide clinical and research recommendations in the treatment of adolescent drug abusers who are of ethnic minority backgrounds.

METHOD

Search Method

We obtained treatment outcome studies for adolescent substance use through several sources. First, we identified treatment outcome review articles published in peer-reviewed journals and examined their reference sections to locate other relevant studies. We conducted computerized literature searches in the PsycINFO and Cited Reference engines using the names of each author of the studies selected. Next, we performed a PsycINFO search using a list of keywords specified in the abstracts of both review and treatment articles identified thus far. Finally, we also sought treatment outcome studies by searching the Web sites of the following substance abuse–related organizations: NIDA, SAMHSA, CDCP, and Center for Substance Abuse Treatment (CSAT).

Study Inclusion Criteria

In determining studies to be included in this review, we used the following criteria:

1. The study was published in peer-reviewed journal or scholarly book.
2. The study focused on substance-abusing adolescents with a maximum age of 21 years.
3. The study included random assignment of participants to experimental conditions.
4. The study included an outcome measure directly indicative of substance use.

Search Reliability

An independent rater blind to the purpose of the study examined all treatment outcome studies that were determined in the search to meet the aforementioned criteria (i.e., 18 studies). We obtained an interrater reliability coefficient by dividing the total number of agreements (i.e., the independent rater concurred that the article met the specified selection criteria) by the total number of agreements plus disagreements (i.e., the independent rater did not agree that the article met all of the aforementioned criteria) and multiplying the quotient by 100 (Uebersax, 1987). We obtained an interrater reliability coefficient of 94% for the 18 studies identified, which suggests that the selected articles were consistent with the aforementioned study inclusion criteria. The blind rater disagreed on one study (Henggeler et al., 1991) about whether the outcome measure directly indicated substance use. In that study, the principal measure was the number of arrests for substance use–related offenses.

Criteria Used to Determine the Consideration of Ethnicity in Controlled Outcome Studies

We examined the 18 articles that met study inclusion criteria to identify the extent to which these studies addressed ethnicity. That is, we coded each of the 18 articles for the presence or absence of the following criteria and computed the percentage of articles meeting each criterion:

1. There was consideration of ethnicity in any manner throughout the article (94% of articles).
2. Consideration of ethnicity in the design of the study was reported, such as considering ethnicity in block or stratified random assignment to experimental conditions, translating assessment measures, using translators, or using culture-specific assessment measures (28%).
3. The study reported representation of ethnicity to some extent (89%).
4. The authors examined ethnicity in pretreatment preliminary statistical analyses to determine the equivalence of various ethnic minority groups across experimental conditions (61%; we did not examine this criterion for studies that included only one ethnic minority group).
5. The authors conducted statistical analyses regarding differential response to treatment or moderating effects of ethnicity with a sufficient number (Cohen, 1992) of ethnic minority participants (5.6%).
6. Data were presented regarding attrition rates of ethnic minority groups or the influence of ethnicity on attrition was examined in statistical analyses (28%).

Reliability of Criteria Used to Examine the Consideration of Ethnicity

We obtained an interrater reliability coefficient for the aforementioned consideration of ethnicity criteria by dividing the total number of agreements (i.e., the independent rater blind to purpose of the study agreed that the criterion was met or not met) by the total number of agreements plus disagreements (i.e., the independent rater did not agree that the criterion was met or unmet) and multiplying the quotient by 100. For each criterion, we determined the interrater reliability coefficient to be 100%, which suggests that the independent rater completely agreed with Marilyn J. Strada's assessment of the percentage of articles meeting each of the aforementioned criteria.

RESULTS

As indicated above, the search procedure resulted in the identification of 18 adolescent substance abuse treatment outcome studies. These studies are presented in Table 24.1, which includes, for assessments used, treatments implemented, overall outcomes, and methods of considering ethnicity (if addressed). A synthesis of the information included in Table 24.1 is provided in this section.

Number of Studies

One notable finding was the relatively small number of studies identified for review in this article ($N = 18$), as compared with the literature on adult substance abuse treatment. However, there were noteworthy differences in the number of adolescent substance abuse treatment outcome studies published during the past 3 decades, with a considerable increase in the number of studies during the past few years (i.e., 1980s = 5 studies, 1990s = 7 studies, 2000 to 2004 = 6 studies). Although prior reviews of adolescent substance abuse treatment have identified a slightly larger number of studies than were identified in this review (e.g., Williams, Chang, & Addiction Centre Adolescent Research Group, Foothills Medical Centre, 2000), this review was limited to controlled outcome studies that used random assignment to treatment conditions and assessed levels of substance use pre- and posttreatment. Additionally, we excluded a study in which researchers included both adolescents and adults in their samples without reporting specific outcomes for each group separately (i.e., Azrin, McMahon, et al., 1994). Also excluded was a follow-up study specific to an adolescent sample in which no new participants were added, given that culture-related variables were already addressed in the initial study (i.e., Kaminer & Burleson, 1999).

The small number of studies identified, relative to the number of studies on adult populations, is unfortunate, given that the need for more studies with adolescent populations has been indicated by several researchers in the field (e.g., Shillington & Clapp, 2003; Williams et al., 2000). Although high-quality treatment outcome studies are complex and costly, which may explain

TABLE 24.1

Examination of Ethnicity in Adolescent Drug Abuse Treatment Outcome Studies

Article	Population description	Substances targeted	Outcome measure/instruments	Treatment (type, duration, and frequency)	Consideration of ethnicity in study design, implementation, and interpretation	Overall results	Consideration of ethnicity in discussion, conclusion, or recommendation sections
Amini et al. (1982)	Outpatient and inpatient $N = 87$ 52% Caucasian 22% Spanish surname 16% African American 10% Native Americans, Asians and other 69% male Age $M = 16$	Not specified	Social functioning scales (Indications of Disturbance in Peer Contacts, School Disturbance, Anti-Social Behavior, Drug Use, Problem Drug Use, Alcohol Use, Problem Alcohol Use, Global Change) MMPI	Inpatient Psychodynamically oriented individual, group, family, occupational, and recreational therapies, psychodrama, on-ward school program, outpatient aftercare Stay in tx $M = 132$ days; range 8 to 379 days Outpatient tx as usual Reporting to probation officers regularly, community resources typically available, but rarely psychotherapy No. participants assigned to each tx group not specified	Described ethnicity of sample Considered ethnicity in tx groups equivalence analysis Considered ethnicity in attrition effects examination	Group equivalence analysis showed no significant group differences on ethnicity. Attrition effects examination showed no significant differences between tx completers and noncompleters on ethnicity.	None specified
Azrin, Donohue, et al. (1994)	Outpatient $N = 26$ 81% Caucasian 19% African American or Hispanic (how many participants of each ethnicity not specified) 77% male Age $M = 16$	Mostly marijuana; also cocaine/ crack, hallucinogens	Parent Satisfaction Scale Youth Satisfaction Scale Beck Depression Inventory Quay Problem Behavior Checklist Urinalysis Parent/youth report of youth drug use, school attendance, employment, institutionalization, and arrests	Behavioral therapy One-hour sessions, twice per week; later reduced with progress Tx duration $M = 15.1$ sessions $n = 15$ Supportive therapy Two-hour session, once per week Tx duration $M = 14.9$ sessions $n = 11$	Described ethnic breakdown of sample Considered ethnicity in tx groups equivalence analysis	Group equivalence analysis showed no significant group differences on ethnicity	None specified
Azrin et al. (2001)	Outpatient $N = 56$ 79% Caucasian 16% Hispanic 2% African American 3% other 82% male Age $M = 15$	Marijuana, alcohol, hard drugs	Urinalysis Time-Line Follow-Back Interview Arrest history records Child Behavior Checklist Youth Self-Report Eyberg Child Behavior Inventory Sutter–Eyberg Student Behavior Inventory	Family behavior therapy Tx duration $M = 13.5$ sessions $n = 29$ Individual cognitive problem solving Tx duration $M = 13.7$ sessions $n = 27$ Both conditions: initial 6 sessions of 90 min, 7th to 15th sessions were 60 to 75 min; weekly sessions during first 3 months, decreased to biweekly	Described ethnic breakdown of sample Considered ethnicity in tx groups equivalence analysis Considered ethnicity in	Group equivalence analysis showed no significant group differences on ethnicity Attrition effects examination showed no significant	None specified

Study	Sample	Substances	Measures	Treatment	Ethnicity consideration	Results relevant to ethnicity	Cultural modifications
Friedman (1989)	Outpatient N = 135 90% Caucasian Ethnicity of remaining sample not specified 60% male Age M = 18	Alcohol, marijuana, amphetamines, other (cocaine, PCP, halluc., tranq.)	Social Problem-Solving Inventory—Revised Parent Happiness With Youth Scale Youth Happiness With Parent Scale Life Satisfaction Scale for Adolescents Beck Depression Inventory Client Interview Form Parent Interview Form Rosenberg Self-Esteem Scale Brief Symptom Inventory Family Role Task Inventory Parent–Adolescent Communication Form Family Environment Scale Parent–Child Relationship Problems Scale Emotional/Psychological Problems Inventory Drug Severity Index	sessions and then to monthly sessions by end of 6th month. Functional family therapy Tx duration 24 weeks n = 85 Parent training + youth individual counseling Tx duration 24 weeks n = 50	attrition effects examination	differences between tx completers and noncompleters on ethnicity	None specified
Henggeler et al. (1991) FANS study	Outpatient N = 47 74% African American 26% Caucasian 72% male Age M = 15	Alcohol, marijuana, hard drugs	National Youth Survey Soft Drug Use and Hard Drug Use subscales	Multisystemic therapy (MST) Home-based therapy Tx duration: 36 hr over 4-month period n = 28 Department of Youth Services—Usual Services Court ordered curfew, school attendance, probation officer supervision once per month n = 19	Considered ethnicity in tx groups equivalence analysis Considered ethnicity as moderating variable Described ethnic breakdown of sample	Group equivalence analysis showed no significant group differences on ethnicity Attrition effects examination showed no significant differences between tx completers and noncompleters on ethnicity No results relevant to ethnicity were reported	None specified
Henggeler et al. (1991) MDP study	Outpatient N = 200 70% Caucasian 30% African American 67% male Age M = 14	Not specified	Number of arrests for substance-related offenses (i.e., possession, selling)	MST n = 100 Individual counseling n = 100 No. sessions not specified	Described ethnic breakdown of sample Considered ethnicity in tx groups equivalence analysis Considered ethnicity in attrition effects examination	Group equivalence analysis showed no significant group differences on ethnicity Attrition effects examination showed no significant differences between tx completers and noncompleters on ethnicity	None specified

(continues)

TABLE 24.1
Examination of Ethnicity in Adolescent Drug Abuse Treatment Outcome Studies *(Continued)*

Article	Population description	Substances targeted	Outcome measure/instruments	Treatment (type, duration, and frequency)	Consideration of ethnicity in study design, implementation, and interpretation	Overall results	Consideration of ethnicity in discussion, conclusion, or recommendation sections
Henggeler et al. (1999)	Outpatient $N = 118$ 50% African American 47% Caucasian 1% Asian American 1% Hispanic 1% Native American 79% male Age $M = 16$	Alcohol, marijuana, other (hard drugs, prescription drugs, narcotics, inhalants)	Personal Experience Inventory Urinalysis Self-Report Delinquency Scale Arrest and out-of-home placement records from Department of Juvenile Justice	MST Home-based sessions Direct therapist contact hours $M = 40$ $n = 58$ Usual community services Probation officer ordered outpatient or inpatient substance abuse services from local clinic, 12-step program Average direct therapist contact hours not specified $n = 60$	Examined ethnic differences between study participants and refusers Described ethnic breakdown of sample Described ethnicity of therapists Considered ethnicity in tx groups equivalence analysis Considered ethnicity as moderating variable	No differences on ethnicity found between participants and refusers Group equivalence analysis showed no significant group differences on ethnicity No significant overall Tx × Time effects No significant moderating effects on account of ethnicity	None specified
Joanning et al. (1992)	Outpatient $N = 134$ Ethnicity of adolescents not specified (i.e., indicated ethnicity of parents) Gender not specified Age $M = 15$	Marijuana, hard drugs	Dyadic Adjustment Scale Parent–Adolescent Communication Questionnaire Family Coping Strategies Self-Report Family Inventory Urinalysis Drug involvement survey Legal involvement School performance Collateral reports of youth drug use from parents and therapists	Family systems therapy Seven to 15 weekly, 60 to 90-min sessions $n = 40$ Adolescent group therapy (AGT) Twelve weekly, 90-min sessions $n = 52$ Family drug education Six biweekly, 150-min sessions $n = 42$	Described ethnic breakdown of youths' parents Considered parents' ethnicity in tx groups equivalence analysis Considered parents' ethnicity in attrition effects examination	Group equivalence analysis showed no significant group differences on ethnicity Attrition effects examination showed no significant differences between tx completers and noncompleters on ethnicity	None specified

Study	Sample	Substance	Measures	Treatment conditions	Ethnicity consideration	Group equivalence	Limitations
Kaminer et al. (1998)	Outpatient $N = 32$ 88% Caucasian Ethnicity for remaining sample not specified Gender not specified Age $M = 16$	Not specified	Urinalysis Time-Line Follow-Back Diagnostic Interview Schedule for Children Child Behavior Checklist Youth Self-Report Teen Addiction Severity Index Situational Confidence Questionnaire Teen Tx Services Review	Cognitive–behavioral therapy (CBT) $n = 16$ Interactional therapy $n = 16$ Both conditions were 12 weekly, 90-min sessions	Described ethnic breakdown of sample Considered ethnicity in tx groups equivalence analysis	Group equivalence analysis showed no significant group differences on ethnicity	None specified
Kaminer et al. (2002)	Outpatient $N = 88$ 90% Caucasian Ethnicity of remaining sample not specified 79% male Age $M = 15$	Alcohol, marijuana	Urinalysis Self-report of substance use Teen Addiction Severity Index Diagnostic Interview Schedule for Children Structural Clinical Interview for the DSM Revised Dimensions of Temperament Survey	CBT $n = 51$ Psychoeducational therapy $n = 37$ Both conditions were 75- to 90-min weekly sessions for 8-week period	Mentioned ethnicity, but no breakdown of sample specified Examined tx by ethnicity effects	Group equivalence analysis showed no significant group differences on ethnicity	Mentioned lack of ethnic diversity in sample as a limitation of this study
Latimer et al. (2003)	Outpatient $N = 43$ 86% Caucasian 4.6% Hispanic 7% Native American 2.4% Asian American 76.7% male Age $M = 16$	Marijuana, alcohol, other drugs	Diagnostic Interview for Children and Adolescents (youth and parent versions) Adolescent Diagnostic Interview—Revised Personal Experience Inventory Urinalyses Family Assessment Measure Rational Thinking Questionnaire Social Problem Solving Inventory Motivated Strategies for Learning Questionnaire Client Personal History Questionnaire	Integrated family and CBT Sixteen weekly, 60-min individual family therapy sessions and 32 90-min cognitive–behavioral group sessions twice weekly $n = 21$ Drugs harm psychoeducation Sixteen weekly, 90-min sessions $n = 22$	Described ethnic breakdown of sample	No results relevant to ethnicity were reported	Acknowledged limitation of study's generalization because of under-representation of minorities

(continues)

TABLE 24.1

Examination of Ethnicity in Adolescent Drug Abuse Treatment Outcome Studies   (Continued)

Article	Population description	Substances targeted	Outcome measure/instruments	Treatment (type, duration, and frequency)	Consideration of ethnicity in study design, implementation, and interpretation	Overall results	Consideration of ethnicity in discussion, conclusion, or recommendation sections
Lewis et al. (1990)	Outpatient N = 84 Ethnicity not specified 80% male Age M = 16	Alcohol, marijuana, hard drugs	Family Adaptability and Cohesion Evaluation Scales Parent–Adolescent Communication Inventory Family Problem Assessment Scale Kveback Family Sculpture Test Dyadic Formation Inventory Poly-Drug Use History Questionnaire	Purdue brief family therapy n = 44 Training in parenting skills program n = 40 Length of tx in both conditions was 12 weeks	No considerations with regard to ethnicity specified	No results relevant to ethnicity were reported	Concluded this intervention can be implemented with ethnically diverse groups
Liddle et al. (2001)	Outpatient N = 182 51% Caucasian 18% African American 15% Hispanic 10% Native American 6% Asian American 80% male Age M = 16	Alcohol, marijuana, others	Index of Drug Severity Youth drug use self-report Parent collateral reports of youth drug use Urinalysis Acting Out Behaviors scale from Devereux Adolescent Behavior Rating Scale School performance based on GPA Global Health Pathology scale of the Beavers Interactional Competence Scales	Multidimensional family therapy Sixteen sessions over 5-month period n = 47 Multifamily education intervention Nine 90-min sessions over 16-week period n = 52 AGT No. sessions not specified n = 53 (30 cases refused to participate)	Described ethnic breakdown of sample Partially described ethnicity of therapists Considered ethnicity in tx groups equivalence analysis	Group equivalence analysis showed no significant group differences on ethnicity	Acknowledged inability to examine Tx × Ethnicity effects because of small sample of ethnic minority participants, which limits generalization
Santisteban et al. (2003)	Outpatient N = 126 100% Hispanics (51% Cuban, 14% Nicaraguan, 10% Colombian, 6% Puerto Rican, 3% Peruvian, 1% Mexican, 15% other Hispanic nationality)	Alcohol, marijuana, other drugs	Revised Behavior Problem Checklist Addiction Severity Index Family Environment Scale Structural Family Systems Rating Urinalysis Youth self-report of drug use	Brief strategic family therapy (BSFT) Four to 20 weekly, 60-min sessions Tx duration M = 11.2 sessions Group counseling Six to 16 weekly, 90-min sessions Tx duration M = 8.8 No. participants in each condition not specified	Described need for evaluating tx with this population Translated measures Described ethnic breakdown of sample Considered ethnicity in tx	Group equivalence analysis showed no significant group differences on ethnicity Attrition effects examination showed no significant	Indicated BSFT may be appropriate for non-Hispanic samples as well

Study	Sample	Drug type	Measures	Treatment conditions	Ethnicity considerations	Results	Limitations
	75% male Age M = 17				groups equivalence analysis Considered ethnicity in attrition effects examination (Cuban vs. non-Cuban)	differences between tx completers and noncompleters on ethnicity	None specified
Szapocznik et al. (1988)	Outpatient N = 108 100% Hispanic (82% Cuban) Gender not specified 60% male Age M = 16	Marijuana, cocaine	Psychiatric Status Schedule (includes drug abuse score) Client Oriented Data Acquisition Process	Strategic structural systems engagement n = 56 Engagement as usual n = 52	Described ethnic breakdown of sample Measured no. years participants lived in the United States Therapy was conducted bilingually in English and Spanish	No results relevant to ethnicity were reported	
Szapocznik et al. (1983)	Outpatient N = 37 100% Hispanic (84.4% Cuban) 78.3% male Age M = 15	Not specified	Psychiatric Status Schedule (includes drug abuse score) Behavior Problem Checklist Structural Family Tasks Ratings Family Environment Scale	One-person family therapy (OPFT) Eight or more sessions n = 19 Cojoint family therapy (CFT) Four to 7 sessions n = 18	Described ethnic breakdown of sample Measured no. years participants lived in the United States Translated measures to Spanish	No results relevant to ethnicity were reported	Acknowledge limited generalizability because of homogeneity of study sample
Szapocznik et al. (1986)	Population type not specified N = 35 100% Hispanic (77% Cuban) Gender not specified Age M = 17	Marijuana, barbiturates, alcohol	Psychiatric Status Schedule (includes drug abuse score) Behavior Problem Checklist Structural Family Tasks Ratings	OPFT n = 18 CFT n = 17 Both conditions allowed for a maximum of 12 to 15 sessions	Described ethnic breakdown of sample Measured no. years participants lived in the United States Described ethnicity of therapists Translated measures to Spanish	No results relevant to ethnicity were reported	None specified

(continues)

TABLE 24.1

Examination of Ethnicity in Adolescent Drug Abuse Treatment Outcome Studies   *(Continued)*

Article	Population description	Substances targeted	Outcome measure/instruments	Treatment (type, duration, and frequency)	Consideration of ethnicity in study design, implementation, and interpretation	Overall results	Consideration of ethnicity in discussion, conclusion, or recommendation sections
Waldron et al. (2001)	Outpatient $N = 120$ 38% Caucasian 46% Hispanic 8% Native American 8% other 80% male Age $M = 16$	Marijuana	Form 90D of Time-Line Follow-Back Parents' collateral reports of youth drug use Urinalysis Problem Oriented Screening Instrument Child Behavior Checklist	Functional family therapy (FFT) Tx duration 12 hr $n = 30$ CBT Tx duration 12 hr $n = 31$ Joint FFT + CBT Tx duration 24 hr $n = 29$ Psychoeducational group Eight secondary prevention format, 90-min sessions $n = 30$	Described ethnic breakdown of sample Considered ethnicity in random assignment Considered ethnicity in tx groups Considered equivalence analysis Described ethnicity of therapists Considered ethnicity in therapist assignment	Group equivalence analysis showed no significant group differences on ethnicity.	Acknowledged results may not generalize to other ethnic minority populations because sample consisted mostly of Caucasian and highly acculturated, English-speaking Hispanics

Note. Tx = treatment; MMPI = Minnesota Multiphasic Personality Inventory; halluc. = hallucinogens; tranq. = tranquilizers; FANS = Family and Neighborfood Services Project; MDP = Missouri Delinquency Project; GPA = grade point average.

the small number of studies conducted, the increasing number of adolescents in need of substance abuse treatment (HHS, 2003) warrants more research of this type, particularly in ethnic minority samples, as we discuss later.

Treatment Characteristics

Treatment settings

As presented in Table 24.1, most of the studies (94%) were reported to take place in outpatient settings. One of the studies focused on both outpatient and inpatient populations by comparing outcome between the two settings (Amini, Zilberg, Burke, & Salasnek, 1982), and the setting was unclear in another study (Szapocznik, Kurtines, Foote, Perez-Vidal, & Hervis, 1986). The predominant emphasis on outpatient settings in the studies reviewed seems somewhat representative of the type of settings in which treatment is provided in the general population. As reported by HHS (2003), the number of individuals receiving outpatient services is three times as many as that of individuals in residential and inpatient settings.

Substances Targeted

With the exception of 4 studies, most reported the substances targeted in treatment. Marijuana was the most common substance targeted (i.e., targeted in all 14 studies that reported this information), hard drugs were the second most commonly reported substance (e.g., amphetamines, cocaine; reported in 10 of the studies), and alcohol was targeted in 50% of these 14 studies. There were no instances in which hard drugs or alcohol were exclusively targeted. Treatment typically focused on reduction of marijuana by itself or in combination with hard drugs, alcohol, or both.

It is interesting that hard drugs were more commonly targeted for treatment in controlled studies than was alcohol consumption, even though national survey reports (e.g., CDCP, 2002; SAMHSA, 2003) have estimated youths' consumption of alcohol to be at least 10 times greater than their use of hard drugs. In most cases, researchers predetermined the emphasis of treatment to be on a particular substance. For instance, the participant inclusion criteria in Waldron, Slesnick, Brody, Turner, and Peterson's (2001) study excluded youths who abused only alcohol or tobacco, and Azrin, Donohue, Besalel, Kogan, and Acierno (1994) included participants who abused either illicit drugs only or illicit drugs in addition to alcohol. In general, researchers did not specify the rationale to focus on drugs as opposed to alcohol (e.g., differences in severity of behavior problems associated with one or the other substance, differences in treatment components required to treat the use of a particular substance, youths' propensity to simultaneously abuse multiple drugs). However, funding sources may, to some extent, influence these decisions. Indeed, the majority of studies were funded by NIDA, and only a few studies received financial support from other sources, such as the National Institute of Mental Health. The greater emphasis of treatment research on certain substances may have implications for members of ethnic minority populations. For instance, given that substance use prevalence rates vary across ethnic minority groups, limiting the substances targeted in treatment research may result in a lack of interest for or exclusion of some ethnic minority groups (SAMHSA, 2003). In this case, youths of some ethnic minority groups, such as African Americans, whose primary substance of abuse is alcohol and not hard drugs (SAMHSA, 2003), may not meet the study inclusion criteria. The studies reviewed provide some support for this theory, as the 2 studies with significant African American representation (i.e., 74% in the Henggeler et al., 1991, Family and Neighborhood Services Project study; 50% in Henggeler et al., 1999) predominately focused on alcohol and marijuana use. However, it should be mentioned that other factors, such as geographic location of the study sites, may influence sample composition as well. Indeed, there were several studies that focused on marijuana and alcohol (i.e., substances commonly abused across youths of ethnic minority background) in which the majority of participants were Caucasian. Thus, further exploration of factors that tend to influence the participation of ethnic minority youths in outcome research studies is warranted.

Another factor influencing the focus of treatment research may be the referral sources used to recruit participants. Several of the studies reviewed relied, at least partially, on referrals from juvenile justice agencies and courts for participant recruitment. According to Shillington and Clapp's (2003) study with a large group of youths mandated to treatment (i.e., over half of 4,733 adolescents), marijuana was the predominant substance abused, followed by methamphetamines and alcohol, which parallel the substances targeted in the studies reviewed in this article. However, the same study found that Caucasian youths tended to report significantly higher use of methamphetamines, as compared with African American and Hispanic/Latino youths. Furthermore, Shillington and Clapp (2003) found that African American and Hispanic youths were significantly more likely than Caucasian youths to be referred or mandated to seek substance abuse treatment. Therefore, a higher proportion of ethnic minority youths referred and mandated to treatment, as compared with Caucasian youths, should lead to a larger participant pool of diverse youths from which to recruit participants for treatment studies. However, a relatively smaller proportion of ethnic minority youths are likely to be best suited for or meet the inclusion criteria of studies in which the primary focus is on hard drugs, such as methamphetamines. Thus, the selection of abused substances targeted in treatment may be assisting in the perpetuation of a lack of ethnic minority representation in controlled outcome studies involving substance-abusing youths, as we emphasize below.

Demographic Characteristics of Studies' Participants

Sample sizes ranged from 26 to 200 participants, with approximately 40% of the studies having sample sizes of over 100 participants. Participants' ages across studies ranged from 14 to 18 years old, with a mean age across studies of 15.80 years (SD = 0.88). With the exception of 3 studies, all studies reported the gender of the participants. Representation of boys in the samples of those studies ranged from 60% to 82%. The age and gender characteristics of the samples across studies were also consistent with those reported in national surveys (e.g., CDCP, 2002; SAMHSA, 2003) and other studies that have reported this information for large samples of adolescents (e.g., Shillington & Clapp, 2003).

Reporting of Participants' Ethnicity

Most of the studies (89%) reported the ethnicity of the participants to some extent. Approximately a third of those studies provided detailed descriptions of the participants' ethnicity (i.e., every participant's ethnicity was accounted for), whereas the remaining two thirds of those studies reported partial descriptions. For example, Amini et al. (1982) identified participants' ethnicity by surname, 7 studies reported the ethnicity of some participants as "other," 2 studies reported the participants' ethnicity as a combined percentage of various groups (e.g., 10% Native Americans, Asians, and other), and 3 studies reported only the percentage of Caucasian participants represented. Therefore, in the majority of studies, the participants' characteristics were not reported with the degree of specificity that would qualify the studies as ESTs, according to Chambless et al.'s (1996; Chambless & Hollon, 1998) criteria. Additionally, this trend in the reporting of ethnicity did not seem to change noticeably over time across the studies reviewed. However, the practice of reporting limited information regarding ethnicity appears to be common in psychological research. Indeed, Chambless et al.'s (1996; Chambless & Hollon, 1998) examination of possible ESTs for some disorders (i.e., anxiety and stress, depression, health problems, some childhood problems, marital discord, sexual dysfunction) found that most studies did not describe the ethnicity of the participants. In addition, researchers in areas other than substance abuse (e.g., pediatric psychology) have also brought attention to the limited information provided in studies about participants' descriptions (Clay et al., 2002). Nevertheless, the extent to which participants' ethnicity was reported in adolescent substance abuse treatment studies was much greater (89%) than Clay et al. (2002) found in pediatric psychology studies (27%). The greater degree of specificity regarding participants' ethnicity in substance abuse treatment research may also be related to the finding that most studies were funded by government agencies (e.g., NIDA, National Institute of Mental Health), which often require specification of sample characteristics.

Of the studies that reported ethnicity to some extent, Caucasian youths were represented in 75%. Caucasian youths composed between 26% and 90% of the samples, with most of these studies (67%) reporting that Caucasian participants represented over 70% of the sample. The second largest group represented across studies was Hispanic/Latino participants. Sixty-three percent of the studies that reported participants' ethnicity included youths from Hispanic/Latino backgrounds. However, it was not possible to determine the exact representation of Hispanic/Latino participants in 2 of these studies. In 1 study, the researchers used Spanish surname to identify participants (Amini et al., 1982). Spanish surname was an acceptable method to identify individuals of Hispanic origin, according to U.S. Census Bureau standards, during the 1970s. However, this method may not be as accurate as self-identification. Indeed, there is a large degree of intermixing (e.g., colonization, immigration, interracial marriage) between Hispanics/Latinos and individuals of other ethnicities (Freeman, Lewis, & Colon, 2002), which may result in Hispanics/Latinos having European surnames or individuals with Spanish surnames identifying with other ethnicities. The 2nd study combined the number of Hispanic/Latino and African American participants (Azrin, Donohue, et al., 1994). In the studies that provided detailed sample descriptions, Hispanic/Latino youths were represented in 50% of the cases. Their representation ranged from 1% to 100%, with 5 of the 8 studies ranging from 1% to 46% and 4 studies focusing exclusively on Hispanic/Latino youths. The latter studies (Santisteban et al., 2003; Szapocznik, Kurtines, Foote, Perez-Vidal, & Hervis, 1983; Szapocznik et al., 1986, 1988) provided sample descriptions broken down by Hispanic/Latino subgroups (e.g., Mexican, Cuban). Across these 4 studies, Cuban youths made up the majority of the samples (range = 51% to 82%). Hispanic/Latino was the only ethnic minority group for which we identified studies that focused exclusively on one ethnic minority group. Emphasis of treatment research on specific ethnic minority groups has been proposed as the form of research that permits the evaluation of treatment components that are particularly effective with the specific ethnic minority group (Bernal & Scharron-Del-Rio, 2001).

Thirty-eight percent of the studies reported inclusion of African American participants. Representation of African American youth across these studies ranged from 2% to 74%, with half of the studies reporting 16% or less African American representation. African American youth made up the majority of the sample in two studies conducted by the same researchers (Henggeler et al., 1991; Henggeler, Pickrel, & Brondino, 1999). As mentioned above, one study (Azrin, Donohue, et al., 1994) reported a combined number of African American and Hispanic/Latino participants. Therefore, it was not possible to determine the exact representation of each group.

Compared with the other ethnic minority groups mentioned above, Native Americans and Asian Americans were represented to a lesser extent across studies. Twenty-five percent of the studies that reported ethnicity included Native American participants (range = 1% to 10%), whereas 19% included Asian American participants (range = 1% to 6%). One study (Amini et al., 1982) combined participants of Native American, Asian American, and "other" ethnicities into one group. In addition, because of the small number of Native American and/or Asian American participants in the samples, it is possible that the researchers might have placed these youths in an "other" category without specifying that members of these ethnicities were represented within that category. Thus, it was not possible to determine the exact degree of representation for these groups in that study. Consequently, it was not feasible to evaluate the external validity of the treatments implemented in Native American and Asian American populations on the basis of their representation in the studies. The small representation of individuals in these ethnicities is consistent with reports of underutilization of mental health services by some members of Native American and Asian American populations (CSAT, 2001), which would indicate a need to develop patient recruitment strategies in these ethnic minority groups. However, it should also be emphasized that poor representation of ethnic minority participants in some studies may simply be a function of the number of minority youths in a given geographic area. In any event, investigators should begin to report the representativeness of sample demographics to the geographic area from which study participants are drawn, thus providing a proper context in which to interpret results.

Overall, the general tendency across studies was to report participants' ethnicity according to the definitions established by some of the national funding agencies, such as the National Institutes of Health (i.e., American Indian/Alaska Native, Asian/Pacific Islander, Black/African American, Hispanic), without specifying subgroups within each ethnic minority group. This approach does not acknowledge the heterogeneity that exists within each of the ethnic minority groups (Hall, 2001).

The practice of reporting combined totals that include members of more than one ethnic minority group was also apparent, as was the tendency to create an "other" category that included those participants who did not fit within any of the ethnic minority groups listed. One notable study (Santisteban et al., 2003) provided an extensive description of the participants' ethnicity, detailing subgroups within a larger ethnic minority group (i.e., for Hispanics/Latinos, percentages of Cubans, Mexicans, etc., were reported). These findings largely support the criticism that most studies do not provide sufficient details about the ethnicity of the participants to allow conclusions as to the effectiveness of treatment among members of specific groups (Bernal & Scharron-del-Rio, 2001; Chambless & Hollon, 1998; Chambless et al., 1996; Clay et al., 2002).

When one considers that ethnic minority populations represent over 33% of the general population in the United States (U.S. Census Bureau, 2002), it appears that some members of ethnic minority groups (i.e., African Americans, Hispanics/Latinos) were represented in many of the samples across studies. That is, in some studies, ethnic minority youths made up more than 50% of the participants, and some studies focused specifically on ethnic minority youths (i.e., Hispanic/Latino youths). However, the representation of each ethnic minority group (i.e., Hispanic/Latino, African American, Asian American, Native American), in proportion to its individual degree of representation in the general population, varied across studies. For instance, both African American and Hispanic/Latino youths were proportionally represented in only a few studies, with the exception of, in the case of the latter population, those studies that focused exclusively on Hispanic/Latino populations. Nevertheless, African American and Hispanic/Latino youths had much greater representation than Native American and Asian American youths.

Some researchers (e.g., Bernal & Scharron-Del-Rio, 2001; Hall, 2001) have underscored the importance of considering treatment outcome separately for individuals of ethnic minority backgrounds. This is particularly the case because of the extensive heterogeneity that has been found in some domains, such as interdependence, experience of discrimination, and language (Hall, 2001), which are thought to impact various aspects of treatment (e.g., treatment services utilization, treatment preferences, and health beliefs; Bernal & Scharron-Del-Rio, 2001). Thus, some researchers have advocated the importance of including the number of ethnic minority participants that would permit examination of Ethnicity × Treatment effects, independent of proportional representation (Bernal, Bonillo, & Bellido, 1995), particularly given the small sample sizes in many of the studies. In addition, Hall (2001) proposed that "simple inclusion [of ethnic minority participants] is unlikely to yield much information on the cultural relevance of theories or interventions" (p. 504).

Outcome Measures

The majority of the studies reviewed incorporated outcome measures for various domains related to substance use, including use frequency, conduct problems, school performance, social functioning, and family relationships. In addition, a few studies included measures of other variables related to psychological functioning, such as depression, self-esteem, self-confidence, and temperament. Because the focus of the present article is on substance use, we do not discuss measures used to assess other functioning domains. However, to provide a comprehensive overview of measures used in adolescent substance abuse treatment outcome studies, in Table 24.1 we list all instruments used in the studies.

Relevant to substance use measures, a large portion of the studies (55%) used biological markers (i.e., urinalysis) in addition to self-report measures of substance use. Several studies (67%) obtained self-reports of substance use through questionnaires and/or subscales from large scales for related areas (e.g., Social Functioning Scales, Minnesota Multiphasic Personality Inventory; Amini et al., 1982), whereas other studies (72%) used structured methods to obtain estimates of substance use, such as the Time-Line Follow-Back (TLFB; Sobell & Sobell, 1992) and/or diagnostic-oriented instruments (e.g., Diagnostic Interview Schedule for Children, cited in Kaminer, Burleson, & Goldberger, 2002). A few studies (22%) obtained collateral reports about the youths' substance use from parents in addition to urinalysis and youth self-report. We examined the outcome measures in the studies for the extent to which the researchers considered validity and appropriateness of these measures for use with ethnic minority youths. Of interest was whether there were indications that the researchers (a) acknowledged the importance and/or relevance of using culturally appropriate measures in studies that included ethnic minority participants, (b) mentioned psychometric properties of the instruments and their validity for use in ethnic minority populations, and (c) specified caveats on interpretation of findings when measures were not found culturally appropriate. There were no studies found that addressed any of these three issues. However, 3 of the studies that focused exclusively on Hispanic/Latino youths (Santisteban et al., 2003; Szapocznik et al., 1983, 1986) indicated that the measures were translated to Spanish. Nevertheless, we do not know whether the researchers made translations following the transliteration and cross-cultural validation procedures that have been recommended in the literature for assessment instruments (e.g., Butcher, 1996). This is important given that translation of instruments is not equated with cultural appropriateness. Unfortunately, results obtained from outcome measures were not reported separately by ethnic minority group in any study, which might have permitted some evaluation about the cross-cultural validity of the measures. The lack of consideration of the cultural appropriateness of outcome measures that was evident in this group of studies is consistent with what has been apparent in other areas of psychological research (Clay et al., 2002). Although most of the studies reviewed did not meet Sue's (1998) criterion for ESTs of incorporating multiple, culturally appropriate measures, one can argue that some measures of substance use are inherently valid across cultures (e.g., biological markers).

Lack of consideration of an instrument's cultural suitability is an unfortunate oversight, particularly given that culturally appropriate versions of some of the instruments used may be available from the test's developers for some ethnic minority populations. For instance, the TLFB (Sobell & Sobell, 1992), which was used in some of the studies, has been translated into Spanish. The Spanish version of the TLFB incorporates events and holidays pertinent to Hispanic/Latino culture to trigger recall of substance use on special occasions, which may be viewed as a step toward cultural relevance. In addition to the omission of information about and/or acknowledgment of the importance of use of culturally appropriate measures, there was no mention in the studies about any limitations and/or caveats for interpretation related to the psychometric properties of the instruments.

Explicit Consideration of Ethnicity

With the exception of two studies (Kaminer, Burleson, Blitz, Sussman, & Rounsaville, 1998; Kaminer et al., 2002), most studies (89%) compared some form of family-oriented therapy with an individually, group-, and/or psychoeducationally oriented treatment approach. Some of those studies also compared family-oriented therapies with treatment as usual conditions. The 2 studies that did not implement family-oriented approaches involved comparisons between cognitive–behavior therapy (CBT) and psychoeducational and interactional therapies. We do not provide additional details in this article about the treatments used in these studies, as they have been discussed at great length in several outstanding reviews of adolescent substance abuse treatment (e.g., Liddle & Dakof, 1995; Ozechowski & Liddle, 2000; Waldron, 1997; Williams et al., 2000).

We examined the extent to which race/ethnicity was considered in treatment within any section of each article (e.g., introduction, study rationale, design, implementation, results, discussion). Of the 18 studies reviewed, 1 study included a segment within the introduction section describing factors in substance use unique to Hispanic/Latino youths and underscored the need to evaluate existent ESTs with this population (Santisteban et al., 2003). This study was one of those that implemented treatment with a sample consisting of 100% Hispanic/Latino youths.

Within the methodology section, some studies considered ethnicity at various stages. For example, some examined differences in ethnicity between those who agreed to participate in the study and those who refused (Henggeler et al., 1999). One of the studies conducted with 100% Hispanic/Latino participants modified the delivery of therapy services to be bilingual, as needed by participants (Szapocznik et al., 1988). In addition, 3 of the studies implemented with Hispanic/Latino participants included a measure of the number of years the participants had resided in the United States (Szapocznik et al., 1983, 1986, 1988), which suggests that a measure of acculturation might have been considered relevant. Some studies provided descriptions of the therapists' race/ethnicity (Henggeler et al., 1999; Liddle et al., 2001; Waldron et al., 2001). One of these studies (Waldron et al., 2001) also considered participants' and therapists' ethnicity in the process of random assignment to ensure pretreatment group equivalence. However, effects on treatment related to therapists' ethnicity and bias were not examined in any study. The relevance of examining these two variables is bolstered by an ever-increasing literature supporting ethnic match and psychotherapy bias. For instance, Sue (1998) reported that Caucasian, Mexican American, African American, and Asian American patients tended to stay in treatment for longer periods of time when they were matched with a therapist of the same race/ethnicity, and length of stay in treatment, in turn, has been associated with more favorable outcomes. In addition, attention has been called to the need to become more aware about the common occurrence of automatic biases and stereotypic attitudes that can impact the therapist–client relationship (APA, 2003). There was also no mention in most of the studies reviewed of modifications made to treatment components to accommodate ethnicity-related variables. However, some components of family-oriented therapies have been found to be highly compatible with the cultural values and beliefs of members of some ethnic minority groups (Bernal et al., 1995). For instance, the emphasis of family-oriented therapies on the involvement of family members (or supporting members of the community) in the treatment of the designated patients (e.g., multisystemic therapy [MST] by Henggeler et al., 1991, 1999) is consistent with the concept of interdependence, which is highly valued in some cultures (Hall, 2001).

Accordingly, one could theorize that family-oriented therapies may be more culturally sensitive and, thus, more efficacious in the treatment of ethnic minority youths. However, an examination of this variable for studies that included at least somewhat proportionate representation of ethnic minority participants did not fully support this theory, as the findings were mixed. For example, in a study of multidimensional family therapy (MDFT) involving a large, diverse sample, Liddle et al. (2001) showed that the family-oriented therapy was indeed more effective than group therapy and psychoeducational intervention. When evaluated in a similar sample 4 months after treatment, functional family therapy (FFT) was found to be more efficacious than individual CBT, joint FFT and CBT, and psychoeducational group therapy. However, only joint FFT and CBT and group therapy maintained improvements at the 7-month follow-up (Waldron et al., 2001). In another example, 2 of Henggeler et al.'s (1991) studies on MST with a relatively large sample of African American youths showed that MST was more efficacious in the reduction of substance use–related arrests than were individual counseling and probation services as usual. However, another study on MST and probation services as usual by the same researchers, with a relatively large sample of African American youths, found no overall Treatment × Time effects. Szapocznik et al.'s (1983, 1986, 1988) family-oriented treatments evaluated with Hispanic/Latino youths also produced mixed results. Two comparisons of one-person family therapy (OPFT) and conjoint family therapy resulted in favorable findings for OPFT (Szapocznik et al., 1983, 1986). Although the

OPFT approach included components from family-oriented therapies, the focus was on the implementation of treatment by one person in the family, without the involvement of other family members. A 3rd study by the same researchers compared strategic structural systems engagement (SSSE) and engagement as usual (Szapocznik et al., 1988). The results showed that SSSE was more efficacious than the engagement as usual condition. Similarly, Santisteban et al.'s (2003) study with Hispanic/Latino youths also demonstrated higher efficaciousness for the family-oriented therapy, brief strategic family therapy (BSFT), than for group counseling. The remaining studies had samples with higher proportions of Caucasian youths or did not specify the participants' ethnicity. Overall, although these findings were mixed and in most cases the treatments did not seem to be selected particularly for their cultural sensitivity, there seems to be some support for the efficaciousness of therapies that include components congruent with the cultural values and beliefs of some ethnic minority youths, but more work is needed in this area. Within statistical analysis sections, more than half (61%) of the studies included ethnicity as one of the variables in analyses of treatment groups equivalence, whereas a smaller number of studies (28%) included this variable in the examinations of attrition effects. Results of these analyses suggest that ethnicity did not interact with treatment outcome or attrition. Three studies (17%) examined the effects of race/ethnicity as a moderating variable (Friedman, 1989; Henggeler et al., 1999; Kaminer et al., 2002). No significant differences were found in treatment effects as a function of ethnicity in any of these studies. However, 2 of the studies (Friedman, 1989; Kaminer et al., 2002) conducted this analysis with samples that included small numbers of ethnic minority participants (i.e., both studies had 90% Caucasian, 10% not specified, with sample sizes ranging from 88 to 135 participants). The 3rd study (Henggeler et al., 1999) included a significantly larger number of participants of some ethnic minority backgrounds (i.e., 50% African American, 47% Caucasian, 1% Asian American, 1% Hispanic, 1% Native American). However, it was not clear whether all participants from the various ethnicities represented were included in one group and then compared with Caucasians or whether the analysis represented the moderating effects of ethnicity considering only Caucasian and African American youths. Only 1 study acknowledged the unfeasibility of conducting this analysis because of the small sample size of ethnic minority participants and emphasized caution in the interpretation of the results (Liddle et al., 2001).

A review of the discussion and conclusion sections revealed that most studies (61%) did not include stipulations or acknowledgments regarding possible limitations concerning ethnicity. Five of the 18 studies (22%) included acknowledgments regarding limited generalizability due to sample homogeneity (Kaminer et al., 2002; Latimer, Winters, D'Zurilla, & Nichols, 2003; Liddle et al., 2001; Szapocznik et al., 1983; Waldron et al., 2001). One study explicitly indicated that the treatment evaluated was appropriate for use with ethnic minority individuals, but the ethnicity of the participants was not specified in the sample description (Lewis, Piercy, & Sprenkle, 1990). In another study, in which all participants were Hispanic/Latino, the investigators suggested the treatment evaluated was appropriate for use with non-Hispanic individuals (Santisteban et al., 2003).

We also examined the studies to determine the extent to which they met Chambless et al.'s (1996; Chambless & Hollon, 1998) criteria for ESTs. Because the inclusion criteria used in the selection of these studies focused on controlled research procedures, we assumed that all studies met some of these criteria (i.e., implemented random assignment, assessed substance use before and after treatment). In addition, Chambless et al.'s criteria for ESTs required providing evidence demonstrating (a) the superiority of the treatment to the alternative treatment and (b) replication by at least one group of independent researchers. The following studies met the first criterion, as they demonstrated superior results compared with alternative treatments: behavior therapy (Azrin, Donohue, et al., 1994), MST (Henggeler et al., 1991), family systems therapy (Joanning, Thomas, Quinn, & Mullen, 1992), CBT (Kaminer et al., 1998), integrated family and cognitive behavior therapy (Latimer et al., 2003), Purdue brief family therapy (Lewis et al., 1990), MDFT (Liddle et al., 2001), BSFT (Santisteban et al., 2003), OPFT (Szapocznik et al., 1983), and FFT (Waldron et al., 2001). However, none of the studies listed above met the second criterion (i.e., replicated by at least one group of independent researchers). Although 2 studies evaluated FFT independently (Friedman, 1989; Waldron et al., 2001), their findings were mixed. However, Chambless and Hollon (1998) also delineated a slightly modified criterion that specifies that when the second criterion is not met, a study conducted that meets all other criteria can be considered "possibly efficacious" (p. 18) if there is no contradicting evidence. On the basis of this criterion, all treatments (mentioned above) that were more effective than the alternative treatments with which they were compared would be considered possibly efficacious.

We also examined the studies according to Sue's (1998) criteria for evaluation of ESTs' appropriateness in the treatment of ethnic minority populations. Aside from the criteria specified earlier, Sue (1998) suggested that participants should be assigned to treatment conditions in a blocked random order according to ethnicity and that researchers should use multiple, culturally cross-validated measures. On the basis of these criteria, none of the studies reviewed in the present article would be considered culturally appropriate. However, it is important to emphasize that lack of consideration of culture- or ethnicity-related variables may not be tantamount to lack of efficaciousness in ethnic minority populations. Indeed, none of the treatment modalities evaluated in the studies reviewed revealed counteractive effects or seemed to be ineffective in ethnic minority populations, with some including large groups of ethnic minority youths. Furthermore, it is plausible that investigators might have encountered issues related to culture and ethnicity while implementing these studies but did not report their methods of managing these issues in the published articles because of space constraints or lack of awareness about their relevance or importance to external validity. Thus, an investigation of the effects of considering and incorporating culture- and ethnicity-related variables seems warranted in adolescent drug treatment outcome research, but it is not our conclusion that its absence thus far indicates that existing treatments lack efficaciousness in ethnic minority populations.

DISCUSSION

Research Implications

The findings of this content analysis have several implications for both research and clinical practice. Relevant to research, investigators should incorporate several essential procedures into treatment outcome research to help increase the degree of interpretation that can be made about treatment generalizability to diverse populations. Some of these recommendations resonate with those already made by others (e.g., Bernal & Scharron-Del- Rio, 2001; Chambless et al., 1996; Hall, 2001; Sue, 1998). First, researchers should specify detailed descriptions about participants' characteristics that may potentially moderate treatment effects (e.g., ethnicity, gender, age, acculturation level, socioeconomic status). For instance, none of the studies reviewed appropriately reported the family income of youth participants. Such information would allow comparisons between low- and high-income ethnic minority groups rather than examinations of ethnicity in homogenous subgroups alone. Indeed, an affluent African American woman may share more variance in treatment outcome with an affluent Caucasian woman than with an impoverished African American woman. Along these lines, descriptions of ethnicity should reflect the heterogeneity of the populations with which the treatment is likely to be implemented, whenever possible. For instance, information regarding participants' identification with ethnic minority subgroups (e.g., Japanese, Korean) should be made available to the reader when sample size is appropriately large (Sue, 1998). Moreover, given that power may be insufficient to conduct statistical analyses of particular ethnic minority subgroups ex post facto, we recommend that outcome studies be planned to occur in geographic areas that are likely to be represented by ethnic minority subgroups of interest. Furthermore, investigators should provide sufficient detail regarding the characteristics of participants who are likely to benefit from the respective treatments that are evaluated to be effective (Chambless & Hollon, 1998). Although the focus of this review is on the consideration of ethnicity, consideration of other variables, such as gender and socioeconomic status, has been limited and also seems warranted. Along these lines, knowing whether the study samples are representative of the geographic areas in which the studies take place would also be useful to determine the generalizability of studies' results. Therefore, we encourage investigators to include this information along with their descriptions of study participants. In addition, although the reporting of therapists' ethnicity contributes to external validity, examinations of the effects of therapist–client ethnic match as well as therapist bias would also enhance internal and external validity.

Second, as specified in APA's (2002, 2003) ethical guidelines, researchers should consider the psychometric properties and cultural equivalence of assessment instruments prior to using them in studies. Indeed, as indicated earlier, some of the measures commonly implemented in substance abuse research have been culturally validated but remain largely unused. Although some substance use measures may seem intuitively unbiased because they consist of simple self-report formats, the effects of cultural bias have not been examined in controlled studies (Sue, Zane, & Young, 1994). In addition, the translation of measures should follow transliteration procedures so that cultural equivalence is maintained (Butcher, 1996). Researchers should also disclose whether culturally valid measures were unavailable, in which case they should present the possible limitations and caveats for interpretation. Finally, measures of constructs (e.g., interdependence, acculturation level) that have been associated with treatment outcome should be included (Hall, 2001).

Another methodological procedure that may assist in the interpretation of external validity is the implementation of block random assignment by ethnicity (Sue, 1998). Some of the procedures implemented in some of the treatments reviewed in this chapter were valuable to external validity. These included providing a description of therapists' characteristics and considering these characteristics in assignment to treatment conditions; examining differences between those who agreed to participate and those who refused; and examining effects of moderating variables, such as ethnicity, on attrition and treatment outcomes. In addition, reporting effect sizes by ethnicity may permit authors of future meta-analyses to conduct quantitative evaluations of differential response to treatment (Chambless et al., 1996).

The importance of incorporating ethnicity-related variables in treatment development is a recurrent theme throughout this chapter. However, before one takes this step, it is important to first evaluate the theoretical foundations of the treatment to identify components that may conflict with ethnic minority participants' cultural philosophies and values (Hall, 2001). Other components may be incorporated into the early stages of the study design. For instance, we encourage researchers to consider focusing studies on the types of substances that are abused by those who need the treatments. Additionally, investigators must be careful not to make generalizations of study results to ethnic minority populations that they did not evaluate in the outcome study. Indeed, few studies cautioned about making generalizations based on small, homogenous samples.

Finally, as we mentioned earlier, given that the samples of some of the studies reviewed in the present article included ethnic minority participants, it is reasonable to believe that some issues related to culture and ethnicity might have been encountered and addressed (e.g., by modifying study design or treatment protocol) but not reported because of space constraints or lack of awareness about their relevance or importance. It would be beneficial if investigators included in their dissemination of outcome study results a section depicting diversity issues that they encountered or addressed during the implementation of treatment or supervision of cases. Along these lines, it is common in preliminary and/or pilot studies to systematically examine clinical anecdotes that appear to be consistent across cases during the implementation of experimental treatments (e.g., noncompliance with prescribed treatment components). In this endeavor, if a Hispanic father with traditional values, for example, reported that contingency contracting is not accepted within the Hispanic culture, the research group would likely brainstorm, implement, and examine potential revisions to protocol to make the intervention more palatable to his family while maintaining the integrity of contingency contracting for use with other families. Clinical anecdotes such as this are often included within problem and solution sections in developed therapist treatment manuals but rarely disseminated in published treatment outcome studies.

Clinical Implications

Clinicians who conduct psychological evaluations and diagnose individuals of ethnic minority backgrounds should consider the cultural appropriateness of drug use assessment measures, particularly given that culturally validated versions of some of these measures have been developed. Clinicians who anticipate working with ethnic minority populations should make efforts to obtain and use these measures. When they do not use culturally appropriate measures, they should interpret test scores with caution in conjunction with other methods of evaluation (e.g., clinical interviews) and document these procedures (APA, 2003). Furthermore, the assessment process may incorporate semistructured interviews that elicit information from the client about the degree to which it is important for the client to address culture-related factors in therapy. In this manner, clinicians can formulate treatments that are tailored to the client's unique level of cultural orientation. In the absence of culturally validated psychological treatments, we recommend that clinicians use empirically derived treatments that have not been evaluated specifically with ethnic minority populations (APA Division 12 Task Force on Promotion and Dissemination of Psychological Procedures, 1995). However, it is important to consider that the aforementioned task force evaluations were not focused on adolescent substance abuse treatment outcome studies. Thus, we urge clinicians to use first those studies that have had some support in their evaluation with ethnic minority youths. As we mentioned earlier, some of the studies reviewed in this article were evaluated in Hispanic/Latino samples, and a few other studies included large samples of African American youths. In addition, clinicians should consider whether any treatment components are incongruent with a particular culture's philosophy. Other, less apparent clinical implications include the possible benefits of incorporating culture-related components into treatment protocols. For instance, because some components of family-oriented therapies seem to be compatible with the beliefs and values of some members of various ethnic minority groups (Bernal et al., 1995), members of these populations may be more receptive to treatment modalities that emphasize interdependence and family involvement. In implementing family-oriented therapies, it may be important that clinicians consider familial differences among members of diverse ethnic minority backgrounds. For some ethnic minority groups, extended family members as well as members of the church or community may be central in the individual's primary support system. However, it should be mentioned that none of the reviewed treatment outcome studies has empirically demonstrated the differential effectiveness of family-based interventions for use in ethnic minority samples, as compared with Caucasian youths.

Although none of the reviewed studies examined the influence of acculturation on treatment outcome, it makes intuitive sense that clinicians should examine the level of acculturation of the adolescent as well as the adolescent's family when providing treatments to members of ethnic minorities. Indeed, unacculturated ethnic minority youths and their family may require services that are focused on cultural adaptation (e.g., assist family members in obtaining social services, vocational and educational assistance) prior to initiation or during provision of treatments that are specific to substance abuse.

Future Directions

It is important to clarify that none of the studies selected for review was designed expressly to evaluate treatment response differential as a function of ethnicity. Therefore, our review is not intended to highlight the lack of consideration of this variable as an oversight on the part of the investigators. Instead, our hope is that, through retrospective examination of available treatments and their potential palatability to members of diverse cultures, we may facilitate the process of incorporating culture-related variables in future studies. Thus, in this section we offer some suggestions that may help enhance the generalizability of future treatment outcome studies. One of the reasons for contesting the external validity of ESTs in the treatment of members of ethnic minority populations has been the lack of utilization of multiple, cross-culturally validated measures. However, the dearth of these measures has been recognized (Chambless et al., 1996). Therefore, future research should focus on initiating the process of making these measures available for researchers' use by conducting cross-cultural validation studies on the measures most commonly used in adolescent substance abuse research. An important stage in the cross-cultural validation process is to review these measures for components that may be in conflict with culture-related concepts, values, or beliefs of individuals of ethnic minority backgrounds. In addition, cross-cultural validation involves ensuring that the content of the measures is equivalent in both cultures and that transliteration procedures are followed (e.g., use of independent translators, back-translation procedures), as opposed to simply translating the measures (see Butcher, 1996).

Another area of consideration in future research is the development of enlistment strategies to increase the number of ethnic minority youths who participate in treatment outcome studies. As we mentioned earlier, members of some ethnic minority groups tend to abuse substances at greater rates than youths in the general population, and they tend to be overrepresented among those who are mandated to treatment because of legal involvement. However, members of these populations continue to be underrepresented in most treatment outcome studies. Therefore, research efforts are needed to identify and understand the barriers that prevent ethnic minority youths and their family from participating in treatment outcome research as well as how to overcome such barriers. We identified several other possible areas of future research relevant to treatment. First, because of the limited data on effect sizes provided in published studies, it was not possible to determine quantitatively whether members of ethnic minority groups respond differentially to treatment. Thus, a first step might be to attempt to gather these data from researchers to permit meta-analytic studies. Combining effect sizes obtained across studies, separated by ethnicity, may provide further understanding about whether treatments that are developed without consideration of culture-related variables are indeed effective across ethnic minority populations. In addition, this procedure would help clarify whether those treatments thought to be congruent with ethnic cultures' values and beliefs (e.g., family-oriented therapies) are more effective than other alternatives (e.g., individual therapy) for adolescent ethnic minority drug abusers. Second, other long-term alternatives that may permit the examination of differential response to treatment might include the evaluation of ESTs with members of specific ethnic minority groups in sufficient sample sizes.

Concluding Remarks

Given the rapid growth of ethnic minority populations in the United States, researchers and therapists face greater demands to create and provide adequate treatments for substance-abusing youths. Furthermore, drug treatment needs of ethnic minority youths are disproportionately high. As we reviewed earlier, more ethnic minority youths are being referred to treatment than Caucasian youths, but these youths are experiencing higher rates of treatment dropout and unsatisfactory release from treatment (Shillington & Clapp, 2003). In addition, researchers and clinicians have been urged to avoid making assumptions about the effectiveness of treatments for specified populations until empirical evidence demonstrates success in the respective population (Chambless et al., 1996).

Given some of the limitations associated with qualitative research, it is a complex process to draw concrete conclusions about the extent to which ESTs generalize to ethnic minority populations, particularly given the small sample sizes and small representation of ethnic minority youths in most of the studies. Indeed, whether ESTs have external validity in ethnic minority populations may vary depending on which point of view one adopts. On the basis of the stringent criteria established in APA committees (e.g., Chambless et al., 1996), few treatments are considered efficacious for the general population. When the same treatments are evaluated for ethnic minority populations, the number of efficacious treatments is even smaller. In contrast, all studies reviewed appeared to meet the criteria for ESTs used by government substance abuse organizations that are a primary source of financial support (e.g., NIDA). For instance, regarding ethnic diversity, the main requirement in government-funded research tends to be that researchers should make efforts to include members of traditionally underrepresented groups (Hall, 2001) and that participants' ethnicity should be specified. Thus, funding agencies encourage investigators to have samples with representation of ethnic minority participants in proportion to their representation in the general population. However, advocates for the development of culturally sensitive treatments (e.g., Bernal & Scharron-del-Rio, 2001; Hall, 2001; Sue, 1998) appear to focus instead on the dearth of consideration of ethnicity-related variables across treatments (i.e., study design, assessment, treatment theoretical foundation, formulation, delivery, and the interpretation of findings). Optimal results are accomplished when relevant ethnic specific variables are incorporated into treatment. Thus, from this perspective, extant ESTs do not generalize to ethnic minority populations.

Although the suggestion is speculative, we propose that culture-specific treatment accommodations may be implicitly imbedded within treatment protocol and therapist supervision and clinical training but not explicitly disseminated in professional reports. Of course, if this information is available, we strongly urge these investigators to underscore it when reporting treatment outcome results. In any event, this review indicates that much work in this area is needed to demonstrate definitive conclusions regarding efficacy of ESTs in ethnic minority populations.

Last, it is important to emphasize that members within particular ethnic minority groups may be identified to share common characteristics. However, treatment outcome is complex, with multiple determinants. Thus, the study of ethnic groupings viewed in isolation will inevitably lead to overly simplistic conclusions that will probably be of little clinical utility.

REFERENCES

American Psychological Association. (2002). Ethical principles of psychologists and code of conduct. *American Psychologist, 57,* 1060–1073.

American Psychological Association. (2003). Guidelines on multicultural education, training, research, practice, and organizational change for psychologists. *American Psychologist, 58,* 377–402.

American Psychological Association Division 12 Task Force on Promotion and Dissemination of Psychological Procedures. (1995). Training in and dissemination of empirically-validated psychological treatments: Report and recommendations. *Clinical Psychologist, 48,* 3–23.

Amini, F., Zilberg, N. J., Burke, E. L., & Salasnek, S. (1982). A controlled study of inpatient vs. outpatient treatment of delinquent drug abusing adolescents: One year results. *Comprehensive Psychiatry, 23,* 436–444.

Azrin, N. H., Donohue, B., Besalel, V. A., Kogan, E. S., & Acierno, R. (1994). Youth drug abuse treatment: A controlled outcome study. *Journal of Child and Adolescent Substance Abuse, 3,* 1–16.

Azrin, N. H., Donohue, B., Teichner, G. A., Crum, T., Howell, J., & DeCato, L. A. (2001). A controlled evaluation and description of individual-cognitive problem solving and family-behavior therapies in dually-diagnosed conduct disordered and substance-dependent youth. *Journal of Child and Adolescent Substance Abuse, 11,* 1–43.

Azrin, N. H., McMahon, P. T., Donohue, B., Besalel, V. A., Lapinski, K. J., Kogan, E. S., et al. (1994). Behavior therapy for drug abuse: A controlled treatment outcome study. *Behavior Research and Therapy, 32,* 857–866.

Bernal, G., Bonillo, J., & Bellido, C. (1995). Ecological validity and cultural sensitivity for outcome research: Issues for the cultural adaptation and development of psychosocial treatments with Hispanics. *Journal of Abnormal Child Psychology, 23,* 67–82.

Bernal, G., & Scharron-del-Rio, M. R. (2001). Are empirically supported treatments valid for ethnic minorities?: Toward an alternative approach for treatment research. *Cultural Diversity & Ethnic Minority Psychology, 7,* 328–342.

Butcher, J. N. (1996). Translation and adaptation of the MMPI-2 for international use. In J. N. Butcher (Ed.), *International adaptations of the MMPI-2* (pp. 26–43). Minneapolis: University of Minnesota Press.

Center for Substance Abuse Treatment. (2001). *Cultural issues in substance abuse treatment* (DHHS Publication No. SMA 01-3612. NCADI Publication No. BKD323). Rockville, MD: Author.

Centers for Disease Control and Prevention. (2002, June 28). Youth risk behavior surveillance—United States, 2001. *Morbidity and Mortality Weekly Report, 51,* 1–64.

Chambless, D. L., & Hollon, S. D. (1998). Defining empirically supported therapies. *Journal of Consulting and Clinical Psychology, 66,* 7–18.

Chambless, D. L., Sanderson, W. C., Shoham, V., Johnson, S. B., Pople, K. S., Crits-Cristoph, P., et al. (1996). An update on empirically validated therapies. *Clinical Psychologist, 49,* 5–18.

Clay, D. L., Mordhorst, M. J., & Lehn, L. (2002). Empirically supported treatments in pediatric psychology: Where is the diversity? *Journal of Pediatric Psychology, 27,* 325–337.

Cohen, J. (1992). A power primer. *Psychological Bulletin, 112,* 155–159.

Donohue, B., Strada, M. J., Rosales, R., Taylor-Caldwell, A., Ingham, D., Ahmad, S., et al. (2006). The Semistructured Interview for Consideration of Ethnic Culture in Therapy Scale: Initial psychometric and outcome support. *Behavior Modification, 30,* 867–891.

Freeman, R. C., Lewis, Y. P., & Colon, H. M. (2002). *Handbook for conducting drug abuse research with Hispanic populations.* Westport, CT: Praeger.

Friedman, A. S. (1989). Family therapy vs. parent groups: Effects on adolescent drug abusers. *American Journal of Family Therapy, 17,* 335–347.

Greig, R. (2003). Ethnic identity development: Implications for mental health in African-American and Hispanic adolescents. *Issues in Mental Health Nursing, 24,* 317–331.

Hall, N. G. C. (2001). Psychotherapy research with ethnic minorities: Empirical, ethical, and conceptual issues. *Journal of Consulting and Clinical Psychology, 69,* 502–510.

Henggeler, S. W., Borduin, C. M., Melton, G. B., Mann, B. J., Smith, L. A., Hall, J., et al. (1991). Effects of multisystemic therapy on drug use and abuse in serious juvenile offenders: A progress report from two outcome studies. *Family Dynamics Addiction Quarterly, 1,* 40–51.

Henggeler, S. W., Pickrel, S. G., & Brondino, M. J. (1999). Multi-systemic treatment of substance abusing and dependent delinquents: Outcomes, treatment fidelity, and transportability. *Mental Health Services Research, 1,* 171–184.

Joanning, H., Thomas, F., Quinn, W., & Mullen, R. (1992). Treating adolescent drug abuse: A comparison of family systems therapy, group therapy, and family drug education. *Journal of Marital and Family Therapy, 18,* 345–356.

Kaminer, Y., & Burleson, J. A. (1999). Psychotherapies for adolescent substance abusers: 15-month follow-up of a pilot study. *American Journal of Addictions, 8,* 114–119.

Kaminer, Y., Burleson, J. A., Blitz, C., Sussman, J., & Rounsaville, B. J. (1998). Psychotherapies for adolescent substance abusers: A pilot study. *Journal of Nervous and Mental Disease, 186,* 684–690.

Kaminer, Y., Burleson, J. A., & Goldberger, R. (2002). Cognitive–behavioral coping skills and psychoeducation therapies for adolescent substance abuse. *Journal of Nervous and Mental Disease, 190,* 737–745.

Latimer, W. W., Winters, K. C., D'Zurilla, T., & Nichols, M. (2003). Integrated family and cognitive–behavioral therapy for adolescent substance abusers: A Stage I efficacy study. *Drug and Alcohol Dependence, 71,* 303–317.

Lewis, R. A., Piercy, F. P., & Sprenkle, D. H. (1990). Family-based interventions for helping drug-abusing adolescents. *Journal of Adolescent Research, 5,* 82–95.

Liddle, H. A., & Dakof, G. A. (1995). Efficacy of family therapy for drug abuse: Promising but not definitive. *Journal of Marital and Family Therapy, 21,* 511–544.

Liddle, H. A., Dakof, G. A., Parker, K., Diamond, G. S., Barrett, K., & Tejeda, M. (2001). Multidimensional family therapy for adolescent drug abuse: Results of a randomized clinical trial. *American Journal of Alcohol Abuse, 27,* 651–688.

National Institute on Drug Abuse. (1999). *Principles of drug addiction treatment: A research-based guide* (NIH Publication No. 99–4180). Rockville, MD: Author.

Ozechowski, T. J., & Liddle, H. A. (2000). Family-based therapy for adolescent drug abuse: Knowns and unknowns. *Clinical Child and Family Psychology Review, 3,* 269–298.

Phinney, J. S. (1996). When we talk about American ethnic groups, what do we mean? *American Psychologist, 51,* 918–927.

Santisteban, D. A., Coatsworth, J. D., Perez-Vidal, A., Kurtines, W. M., Schwartz, S. J., LaPerriere, A., & Szapocznik, J. (2003). Efficacy of brief strategic family therapy in modifying Hispanic adolescent behavior problems and substance use. *Journal of Family Psychology, 17,* 121–133.

Shillington, A. M., & Clapp, J. D. (2003). Adolescents in public substance abuse treatment programs: The impacts of sex and race on referrals and outcomes. *Journal of Child and Adolescent Substance Abuse, 12,* 69–91.

Sobell, L. C., & Sobell, M. B. (1992). Timeline follow-back: A technique for assessing self-reported alcohol consumption. In R. Z. Litten & J. P. Allen (Eds.), *Measuring alcohol consumption: Psychosocial and biochemical methods* (pp. 41–72). Totowa, NJ: Humana Press.

Substance Abuse and Mental Health Services Administration. (2003). *Results from the 2002 National Survey on Drug Use and Health: National findings* (Office of Applied Studies, NHSDA Series H-22, DHHS Publication No. SMA 03–3836). Rockville, MD: Author.

Sue, S. (1998). In search of cultural competence in psychotherapy and counseling. *American Psychologist, 53,* 440–448.

Sue, S., Zane, N., & Young, K. (1994). Research on psychotherapy with culturally diverse populations. In A. E. Bergin & S. L. Garfield (Eds.), *Handbook of psychotherapy and behavior change* (4th ed., pp. 783– 820). New York: Wiley.

Szapocznik, J., Kurtines, W. M., Foote, F. H., Perez-Vidal, A., & Hervis, O. (1983). Conjoint versus one-person family therapy: Some evidence for the effectiveness of conducting family therapy through one person. *Journal of Consulting and Clinical Psychology, 51,* 889–899.

Szapocznik, J., Kurtines, W. M., Foote, F. H., Perez-Vidal, A., & Hervis, O. (1986). Conjoint versus one-person family therapy: Further evidence for the effectiveness of conducting family therapy through one person with drug-abusing adolescents. *Journal of Consulting and Clinical Psychology, 54,* 395–397.

Szapocznik, J., Perez-Vidal, A., Brickman, A. L., Foote, F. H., Santisteban, D., Hervis, O., & Kurtines, W. M. (1988). Engaging adolescent drug abusers and their families in treatment: A strategic structural systems approach. *Journal of Consulting and Clinical Psychology, 56,* 552–557.

Uebersax, J. S. (1987). Diversity of decision-making models and the measurement of interrater agreement. *Psychological Bulletin, 101,* 140–146.

U.S. Census Bureau. (1996). *Statistical abstract of the United States: The national data book.* Washington, DC: U.S. Government Printing Offices.

U.S. Census Bureau. (2002). *American Community Survey profile, 2002.* Retrieved April 23, 2004, from http://www.census.gov/acs/www/Products/Profiles/Single/2002/ACS/Tabular/010/01000US1.htm

U.S. Department of Health and Human Services. (2001). *Mental health; Culture, race, and ethnicity—A supplement to mental health: A report of the surgeon general.* Rockville, MD: Author.

U.S. Department of Health and Human Services. (2003). *Treatment episode data set* [Data file]. Washington, DC: U.S. Department of Health and Human Services, Substance Abuse and Mental Health Services Administration, Office of Applied Studies.

Waldron, H. B. (1997). Adolescent substance abuse and family therapy outcome: A review of randomized trials. In T. H. Ollendick & R. J. Prinz (Eds.), *Advances in clinical psychology* (Vol. 19, pp. 199–234). New York: Plenum Press.

Waldron, H. B., Slesnick, N., Brody, J. L., Turner, C., & Peterson, T. (2001). Treatment outcomes for adolescent substance abuse at 4- and 7-month assessments. *Journal of Consulting and Clinical Psychology, 69,* 802–813.

Williams, R. J., Chang, S. Y., & Addiction Centre Adolescent Research Group, Foothills Medical Centre. (2000). A comprehensive and comparative review of adolescent substance abuse treatment outcome. *Clinical Psychology Science Practice, 7,* 138–166.

25

MEASURING ADOLESCENT DRUG ABUSE AND PSYCHOSOCIAL FACTORS IN FOUR ETHNIC GROUPS OF DRUG-ABUSING BOYS

KEN C. WINTERS, WILLIAM W. LATIMER, RANDY D. STINCHFIELD, AND ELIZABETH EGAN

Recent reviews of adolescent self-administered alcohol and other drug (AOD) abuse assessment instruments for use in treatment research concur that the field consists of numerous instruments, several of them characterized by favorable psychometric properties (Center for Substance Abuse Treatment, 1999; Leccese & Waldron, 1994). However, this body of literature predominately has focused on White youths and does not directly address the issue of instrument utility in non-White AOD-abusing youths (Weinberg, Rahdert, Colliver, & Glantz, 1998). A similar situation exists in the adult AOD abuse assessment field as well (Allen & Wilson, 2003). The lack of ethnic-specific psychometrically sound adolescent assessment measures is unfortunate in light of a growing body of literature regarding ethnicity and AOD behaviors among adolescents. Ethnicity has shown a significant association with drug use patterns (Johnston, O'Malley, & Bachman, 1999; Moon, Hecht, Jackson, & Spellers, 1999; Reardon & Buka, 2002). Wallace et al. (2002) summarized AOD use by

This research was supported in part by grants to Ken C. Winters (DA05104 and DA12995) and to William W. Latimer (DA00254) from the National Institute on Drug Abuse.

Reprinted from *Experimental and Clinical Psychopharmacology, 12,* 227–236 (2004). Copyright 2004 by the American Psychological Association.

ethnic groups among U.S. high school seniors during the 25 years from 1976 to 2000. With some exceptions, most ethnic differences are long-standing. On average, Native American seniors showed the highest level of AOD use, and African Americans and Asian Americans reported the lowest levels.

Ethnic differences are important for establishing that a tool is psychometrically unbiased across diverse ethnic/racial groups (Turner, DeMers, Fox, & Reed, 2001). Studies of ethnicity and measurement are subject to unique limitations and challenges, including the problem of assuming homogeneity of ethnic groups when race/ethnicity is defined on self-report measures that use very general categories, the accurate measurement of bi-ethnicity, and the challenge of designing measures that are cross-culturally valid (Okazaki & Sue, 1995). With respect to the latter challenge, instruments are typically developed so that they are conceptually similar and metrically equivalent across ethnic groups. Conceptual equivalence involves ensuring that the scale taps the same psychological construct for various cultural groups, whereas metric equivalence assumes that the value of the score achieved on a measure has similar meaning for different groups (Okazaki & Sue, 1995). To the extent that assessment measures are biased as a function of ethnicity, research on AOD patterns and substance use disorders are subject to interpretation problems (Martin & Winters, 1998).

The current study addresses the metric equivalence across ethnic groups of a multiscale self-administered questionnaire, the Personal Experience Inventory (PEI; Winters & Henly, 1989). The PEI's aim is to aid in the identification, referral, and treatment of adolescents suspected of drug involvement. In recognition of the limits of self-administered assessment, the PEI is one tool in an integrated battery that includes a structured diagnostic interview and a parent questionnaire (Winters, Latimer, & Stinchfield, 1999). The PEI consists of multiple scales that measure drug use problem severity and psychosocial risk. The instrument is listed as one of the suggested comprehensive assessment instruments in the Adolescent Assessment and Referral Treatment System of the National Institute on Drug Abuse (Rahdert, 1991). It has been reviewed in the 11th edition of the *Mental Measurement Yearbook* (Tucker, 1992), and its widespread use in research settings has been documented (Weinberg et al., 1998). Germane to the interests of this study, its use among non-White ethnic groups recently has risen considerably. According to a survey of service providers and researchers who evaluate youths with the PEI (Winters, 1997), the instrument was used 26% of the time to evaluate non-White youths.

Several studies with samples that were predominately White described reliability and validity evidence for the PEI scales. These psychometric studies included internal consistency reliability (problem severity scale αs = .84–.97; psychosocial risk scale αs = .72–.87) and test–retest reliability (1 week, summarizing across all scales = .40–.92; 1 month, summarizing across all scales = .44–.85) as well as evidence pertaining to criterion and concurrent validity (e.g., scales significantly related to diagnostic ratings, treatment referral recommendations, and alternative measures of similar constructs; Dembo, Schmeidler, Borden, Chin Sue, & Manning, 1997; Guthmann & Brenna, 1990; Henly & Winters, 1988, 1989; Jainchill, Yagelka, Hawke, & De Leon, 1999; Winters, Stinchfield, & Henly, 1996). This body of evidence demonstrates acceptable internal reliability evidence (e.g., αs > .70 based on standards discussed in Jacobson & Truax, 1991), validity evidence across a range of criterion and concurrent tests, and a mixed picture with respect to test–retest reliability (e.g., as reported in Winters & Henly, 1989, several scales have temporal stability estimates <.70).

Psychometric analyses of the PEI have not examined in a detailed manner the reliability and validity evidence for separate ethnic groups, however. The only published PEI study that attended to ethnicity in a meaningful way was a cross-sectional analysis that explored the association between the instrument's 12 Pychosocial Risk scales and drug use frequency over the prior 12 months in boys and girls evaluated at drug treatment programs (Winters, Latimer, Stinchfield, & Henly, 1999). The regression analysis showed that Peer Chemical Use and Deviant Behavior, and to a lesser degree, Psychological Disturbance, were consistently the most predictive psychosocial risk scales of drug use across African American, Native American, Hispanic, and White groups. The present study directly examines the psychometric properties of the PEI's problem severity and psychosocial risk scales across four ethnic groups of drug-abusing adolescents (African American, Native American, Hispanic, and White). The analysis is limited to boys because the database relevant to this does not contain large enough study samples of girls within each non-White ethnic group for adequate statistical power. Specifically we compare reliability (internal reliability and temporal stability) and various validity data among three non-White groups with prior data collected from a White sample.

METHOD

Measure

The PEI is a multiscale questionnaire of 278 items that address multiple areas pertaining to drug use involvement and psychosocial risk factors believed to either underlie or result from drug involvement. The questionnaire consists of two main parts (problem severity and psychosocial risk) that consist of scales, plus additional content that measures response distortion tendencies and drug use frequency.

Part 1: Problem Severity Scales

The problem severity part of the PEI consists of a core set of five drug abuse problem severity scales, considered the basic scales, which were developed from a combination of rational (e.g., literature review and consultation with experts) and empirical (factor-analytic) procedures (see Henly & Winters, 1988, for details). These scales cover a broad range of characteristics of youth drug involvement, including polydrug use, perceived social and psychological benefits, negative social and personal consequences, and loss of control. One basic scale, the Personal Involvement With Chemicals scale (PICS), consists of 29 items. The PICS was purposely assigned a large number of items given the dual intent to develop a scale that adequately measures a general drug abuse severity construct and outlier patterns of drug use experiences (for more details, see Henly & Winters, 1988; Winters & Henly, 1989). The other four basic scales consist of about 10 items each (range = 8–11 items). The items in this set are structured with a 4-point response option format (1 = *never*, 2 = *once or twice*, 3 = *sometimes*, 4 = *often*). In addition, the PEI consists of a secondary set of five Problem Severity scales, the clinical scales. Each scale in this set consists of 3 to 5 items from the PICS. The clinical scales were retained in the PEI because they offered drug use severity content that service providers during test development rated as highly desirable for treatment planning. However, the clinical scales do not add any substantive unique, reliable variance beyond the PICS (Henly & Winters, 1988). In the interest of brevity, and given the redundancy of the clinical scales, we limit the analysis of the Problem Severity scales to the basic set.

Part 2: Psychosocial Risk Scales

The other part of the PEI consists of 12 psychosocial risk scales (8 personal adjustment, 4 environmental risk) that measure risk factors reported to be related to the onset and maintenance of youth drug involvement (Brook, Whiteman, Cohen, & Tanaka, 1992; Kandel & Logan, 1984). Each scale consists of approximately eight items (range = 4–12 items) structured with either a 3-point response option format (1 = *never*, 2 = *once or twice*, 3 = *sometimes*) or a 4-point format (1 = *strongly agree*, 2 = *agree*, 3 = *disagree*, 4 = *strongly disagree*). As described in Henly and Winters (1989), scale development procedures were largely based on Jackson's (1967) procedure, which combines rational and empirical procedures. Briefly, 20 a priori scales identified from the extant literature were reduced to 12 scales after discarding redundant scales and retaining those that had acceptable levels of reliability ($\alpha > .70$) and independence (proportion of unique, reliable variance $> .25$). Undesirable items from resulting scales were pruned if they had a high correlation with the Marlowe–Crowne Social Desirability Scale (Crowne & Marlowe, 1960).

Other Content

In addition to problem severity and psychosocial risk scales, the PEI consists of measures of response distortion tendencies and drug use history items. With respect to response distortion, each part of the PEI contains Infrequency ("faking bad," inattention, random responding) and Defensiveness ("faking good") scales. Separate sets of response distortion scales were developed to accommodate those who wished to administer only one part of the test. The two Infrequency scales (7 and 11 items, respectively) refer to extremely unlikely behaviors and attitudes and, thus, are expected to show very low rates of endorsement. The two Defensiveness scales (11 and 12 items, respectively) are based on the Marlowe–Crowne Social Desirability Scale (Crowne & Marlowe, 1960), a frequently used measure of defensiveness or social desirability, and modified slightly for an adolescent population. Drug use history is measured with standard drug use frequency (items from the National Institutes of Health annual survey of drug use behavior of U.S. high school students (Johnston, Bachman, O'Malley, 1985). These items assess lifetime, prior year, and prior 3-month drug use frequency items for 12 drug categories. Items have a 7-point response option ($1 = never$; $7 = 40+ times$). As part of the concurrent validity analysis, we created an aggregate variable of prior year drug use frequency by summing across responses to the 12 drug categories for this time period ($\alpha = .89$; 1-week test–retest reliability $= .83$; data from Winters & Henly, 1989).

Participants

The drug clinic database consists of PEI scores and relevant sociodemographic and clinical data collected from 30 adolescent drug abuse evaluation and/or treatment programs (26 in the United States and 4 in Canada from 1994–2002). Participating programs were asked to contribute PEI scores for the purposes of assessment research, which included the updating of PEI norms and the provision of reliability and validity data not already collected during PEI development. In return for participation, programs received detailed PEI group summary reports and specific analyses on request (e.g., differences of PEI scores on the basis of a program's treatment referrals). The programs vary in type (private vs. public, evaluation only vs. assessment and treatment), modality (residential vs. outpatient), and intensity (short term vs. long term). A summary of characteristics for the drug clinic sample is provided in Table 25.1.

Participating programs were required to adhere to rigorous PEI test administration procedures (as described in the PEI research manual) and to mail completed test booklets to the investigator at the University of Minnesota—Twin Cities. No single program contributed more than 10% or less than 2% of the sample in the database. Consenting youths completed the PEI during the intake assessment process if they met the following

TABLE 25.1
Demographic Characteristics of the Drug Clinic Samples of Boys

Variable	Drug clinic (N = 3,191)	
	n	%
Teenage groups (13–18 years)		
White	2,052	64
African American	322	10
Native American	231	7
Hispanic	586	18
Monthly or greater use of any drug, prior year	2,949	92
Weekly or greater use of any drug, prior year	1,790	56
Used alcohol, prior year	3,116	98
Used marijuana, prior year	3,101	97
History of psychiatric problems	1,249	39
History of family drug abuse	2,147	67

Note. Drug use variables, psychiatric history, and family history are based on Personal Experience Inventory results.

criteria: (a) were capable of reading English at a fifth-grade reading level (as screened by procedures provided in the research PEI manual), (b) were not intoxicated or suffering from withdrawal symptoms, (c) were not acutely psychotic or mentally impaired, and (d) were specifically referred for an intake evaluation regarding suspected drug use problems.

Prior to data analysis, PEIs were excluded if the test protocol had a significant elevation on any of the four response distortion scales, that is, a T score >70. The standardization sample upon which the T scores were based was the drug clinic sample from the PEI clinic standardization study (described in Winters & Henly, 1989). T scores are computed separately for groups on the basis of gender and age (young = 12 to 15 years old; older = 16 to 18 years old). These exclusions reduced the sample by nearly 5%. We also excluded all cases in which scale scores could not be scored because of excessive unscorable responses. A scale with excessive unscorable responses occurred if at least 20% of the items were unscorable or omitted, which is a common rule for computer-scored scales. In none of the ethnic groups were more than 6 cases eliminated because of an unscorable scale, and a total of only 26 cases were dropped. Thus, the data analysis consisted of cases that included scores for all PEI scales.

We explored possible intraprogram cohort effects by computing mean PEI scale T scores for each calendar year for programs that contributed PEI data for at least a 3-year period (27 of the 30 programs). We then inspected each program's pattern of mean scores across participating years. Because no programs had PEI mean scale scores that varied appreciably across time (i.e., mean T scores based on the clinic standardization sample were consistently at or nearly at 50), we did not condition the data any further.

Procedure

Eligible participants were asked during the intake process to voluntarily participate in an assessment research project. PEI questionnaires were administered by a research staff member at the local programs and by program staff at nonlocal programs. All test administrators received detailed administration instructions, as provided by the PEI research manual. Except for three sites, confidentiality of PEI results was promised, which meant that clinical staff at the sites did not have access to individual test results. Staff did have access to individual PEI tests at the three sites noted above; these programs had purchased the computer software for producing PEI score reports. Consent forms for youths at these sites were appropriately adjusted. Signed consent was required from both the parent and adolescent client, except for participants older than 17 years, who did not require parental consent. Consenting clients at the residential programs were administered the PEI either the 2nd or 3rd day after admission to the program; clients at the outpatient assessment center were administered the PEI within the 2-hour appointment time. Client ethnicity was determined by their response to the question of ethnic/racial identity on the sociodemographic questionnaire.

Twelve sites were invited to participate in an additional validity investigation because of the high volume of non-White adolescents (i.e., program has a history of more non-White than White clientele). Among the 12 desirable programs, 10 agreed to participate. Those individuals who participated in additional data collection completed the regular intake procedure and (a) were readministered the PEI 1 week after initial administration and (b) were administered within 2 days of completing the initial PEI a highly structured and valid diagnostic interview (Adolescent Diagnostic Interview [ADI]; Winters & Henly, 1993) to measure substance use disorder diagnoses from the *Diagnostic and Statistical Manual of Mental Disorders* (4th ed.; *DSM–IV*; American Psychiatric Association, 1994). Readministration of the PEI was conducted by program staff at participating programs. Administration of the ADI, however, was conducted by trained research staff. ADI administrators were not allowed into the field until they had achieved at least a 90% agreement rate across all interview items against ratings from a standardized training tape. A random sample of tape-recorded interviews from the study ($n = 64$) was reviewed and rated for interrater reliability. Average percent agreement on item and diagnostic ratings was favorable (95% and 100%, respectively).

Data Analysis

Data analysis for reliability evidence involved computing Cronbach's coefficient alpha for internal reliability and Pearson product–moment correlation for test–retest reliability. Convergent validity evidence was evaluated by examining the association between PEI scales and drug use frequency; criterion validity evidence was examined using analyses of variance (ANOVAs) to test between-group differences on the PEI scales as a function of ethnic groups and diagnostic status. Construct validity analysis involved computing separate principal-components factor analyses for each ethnic group and comparing factor structures.

Pairwise ethnic comparisons for select analyses were structured around the primary aim of the study, that is, to evaluate White versus non-White groups. Thus, we computed the following pairwise comparisons: White versus African American, White versus Native American, and White versus Hispanic. The r-to-z transformation was used for pairwise comparisons involving correlational data (coefficient alpha, test–retest correlation, and PEI–drug use frequency correlation), and the Pearson chi-square statistic was used for pairwise comparisons involving the prevalence response bias rates. Sample sizes of 125 per group are needed to detect a medium effect at $p < .01$ of White vs. non-White pairwise differences with a .90 power level and to detect a small effect at .05 with a .70 power level (Cohen, 1977). The study's sample sizes are sufficient for all pairwise comparisons to meet these parameters of effect size and power level. Effect sizes of F ratios were compared between ethnic groups for the criterion validity analysis, and principal-components factor analysis was used to compare the factor structures of the PEI.

RESULTS

Reliability

Internal Consistency

Coefficient alpha data revealed a pattern of equivalence across the various groups (see Table 25.2). All pairwise ethnic comparisons were nonsignificant. No alphas among the basic scales across the non-White groups were below .81 (.81 to .97; $Mdn = .87$); the highest alphas (.96 to .97) were found with the primary basic scale, the Personal Involvement With Chemicals scale. No alphas among the psychosocial risk scales were below .70 (.70 to .87; $Mdn = .83$). Deviant Behavior, Uncontrolled, and Sibling Chemical Use consistently had the highest alphas; Rejecting Convention and Social Isolation consistently showed the lowest alphas.

Test–Retest Stability

The 1-week test–retest data revealed that scale stability coefficients, though quite variable, were comparable across ethnic groups. All correlations

TABLE 25.2

Internal Consistency (Coefficient Alpha) Reliability Estimates of Personal Experience Inventory (PEI) Scales Among the Participants by Ethnicity

PEI scale	White (*n* = 2,052)	African American (*n* = 322)	Native American (*n* = 231)	Hispanic (*n* = 586)
Basic problem severity				
Personal Involvement	.97	.97	.96	.96
Effects From Drug Use	.91	.87	.89	.87
Personal Consequences	.88	.84	.84	.82
Social Benefits	.90	.88	.86	.85
Polydrug Use	.87	.81	.87	.86
Psychosocial				
Negative Self-Image	.82	.70	.74	.77
Psychological Disturbance	.81	.75	.73	.80
Social Isolation	.78	.75	.73	.72
Uncontrolled	.87	.83	.85	.87
Rejecting Convention	.74	.70	.70	.75
Deviant Behavior	.85	.82	.86	.84
Absence of Goals	.82	.82	.81	.80
Spiritual Isolation	.87	.80	.83	.85
Peer Chemical Use	.82	.75	.71	.72
Sibling Chemical Use	.86	.86	.87	.85
Family Pathology	.82	.81	.73	.80
Family Estrangement	.81	.70	.72	.76

were significant at $p < .01$. As reported in Table 25.3, the estimates of temporal stability for the basic scales ranged from .69 to .91, with a median of .73; stability estimates for the psychosocial risk scales were generally lower than those for the basic scales, ranging from .51 to .91, with a median of .70. All pairwise ethnic comparisons were nonsignificant. The psychosocial risk scales that consistently showed the lowest temporal stability were Negative Self-Image, Psychological Disturbance, and Uncontrolled (cumulative range = .51 to .58). The psychosocial risk scales with the highest temporal stability coefficients were Sibling Chemical Use (.81 to .86) and Deviant Behavior (.86 to .91).

Validity

Convergent Validity

We computed correlations of PEI scale scores to prior year drug use frequency (see Table 25.4). For the basic scales, all correlations were statistically significant ($p < .01$). The magnitude of the correlations for this set of scales ranged from .38 to .83 (*Mdn* = .66). All pairwise difference tests of the correlations for the basic scales were nonsignificant. The magnitude of the correlations between drug use frequency and psychosocial risk scales were generally

TABLE 25.3
Test–Retest Stability (1 Week) of Personal Experience Inventory (PEI)
Scales Among the Participants by Ethnicity

PEI scale	White (n = 355)	African American (n = 132)	Native American (n = 141)	Hispanic (n = 166)
Basic problem severity				
Personal Involvement	.71	.73	.70	.72
Effects From Drug Use	.74	.71	.75	.72
Personal Consequences	.70	.69	.71	.72
Social Benefits	.82	.80	.82	.81
Polydrug Use	.91	.87	.90	.89
Psychosocial				
Negative Self-Image	.54	.56	.58	.51
Psychological Disturbance	.51	.52	.53	.54
Social Isolation	.68	.70	.72	.75
Uncontrolled	.53	.56	.55	.52
Rejecting Convention	.66	.65	.62	.69
Deviant Behavior	.89	.86	.91	.89
Absence of Goals	.72	.70	.60	.69
Spiritual Isolation	.71	.68	.72	.62
Peer Chemical Use	.67	.68	.72	.73
Sibling Chemical Use	.86	.83	.85	.81
Family Pathology	.83	.80	.81	.70
Family Estrangement	.73	.70	.75	.69

Note. All test–retest correlations were significant at the $p < .01$ level.

lower than observed with drug use frequency and basic scales (range $= -.01$ to .54; $Mdn = .31$). Among the 48 correlations, three were nonsignificant. Two of the nonsignificant correlations (.12 and .04 for Native American and Hispanic, respectively) were from the Absence of Goals scale, and the other nonsignificant correlation (for White participants) was from the Spiritual Isolation scale. In terms of ethnic comparisons, significantly lower correlations were observed on Absence of Goals for Native Americans ($r = .12$) than for Whites ($r = .21, p < .05$) and on Absence of Goals for Hispanics ($r = .04$) versus Whites ($r = .21, p < .01$). For the Spiritual Isolation scale, each non-White group had a significantly higher correlation ($rs = .34, .23,$ and $.21$, respectively, $ps < .01$) compared with the White group ($r = -.01$). All other pairwise comparisons were nonsignificant.

Criterion

Next, we evaluated the association of PEI basic scales and *DSM–IV* substance use disorder ratings across ethnic groups. These PEI scales are expected to reflect drug abuse severity, and prior validity studies with White samples have shown that mean scores on the basic scales differ significantly as a function of these mutually exclusive diagnostic groups: no diagnosis versus abuse only ver-

TABLE 25.4
Correlations of Personal Experience Inventory (PEI) Scales and Prior Year Drug Use Frequency Among the Participants by Ethnicity

PEI scale	White ($n = 2,052$)	African American ($n = 322$)	Native American ($n = 231$)	Hispanic ($n = 586$)
Basic problem severity				
Personal Involvement	.66**	.79**	.58**	.76**
Effects From Drug Use	.57**	.59**	.43**	.41**
Personal Consequences	.48**	.75**	.41**	.38**
Social Benefits	.62**	.69**	.44**	.60**
Polydrug Use	.77**	.78**	.77**	.83***
Psychosocial				
Negative Self-Image	.23*	.19*	.27**	.17*
Psychological Disturbance	.34**	.27**	.24*	.25**
Social Isolation	.12*	.12*	.13*	.16*
Uncontrolled	.35**	.43**	.47**	.36**
Rejecting Convention	.20*	.34**	.27**	.28**
Deviant Behavior	.46**	.45**	.40**	.37**
Absence of Goals	.21*	.33**	.12	.04
Spiritual Isolation	−.01	.34**	.23*	.21*
Peer Chemical Use	.43**	.54**	.49**	.32**
Sibling Chemical Use	.24*	.30*	.26**	.25**
Family Pathology	.21*	.22*	.37**	.12*
Family Estrangement	.19*	.20*	.31**	.27**

*$p < .05$. **$p < .01$.

sus one or more dependence diagnoses (Winters & Henly, 1989). Our interest was in comparing ethnic groups with respect to how basic scales vary as a function of diagnosis. We first computed a two-way ANOVA (Ethnicity × Diagnostic Group) for each basic scale. There were no significant interactions and no significant main effects for ethnicity on any of the basic scales. However, all main effects for diagnostic group were significant ($p < .01$). Next we computed separate one-way ANOVAs (diagnostic group) and post hoc comparisons within each ethnic group. All F ratios were statistically significant (F ratios ranged from 239 to 588; all $ps < .01$). All effect sizes (eta squared values) were large; none were less than .64, and the maximum was .82. The average effect size across F ratios was comparable: White, .71; African American, .81; Native American, .78; and Hispanic, .75. In addition, all Student–Newman–Keuls post hoc comparisons for all ethnic groups were significant ($p < .01$), indicating that the means were significantly different and ordered in the expected direction (no diagnosis < abuse only < one or more dependence diagnoses).

Principal-Components Factor Analysis

Because measures were collected from a clinical sample, the scales were skewed and the data were not multivariate normal. Consequently, confirmatory factor analysis was not considered an appropriate analytical approach. However, for each ethnic group, a principal-components factor analysis was extracted from the correlation matrix with factors allowed to covary (rotated obliquely). Four components with eigenvalues greater than 1 were extracted. However, an examination of the scree plot for each racial group supported only three components. As a result, the principal-components analysis was conducted again, this time for a three-components solution. The percentage of total variance explained by these three components for each racial group was 59, 57, 59, and 58 for White, African American, Native American, and Hispanic participants, respectively. Scales that loaded most highly on one component and that had a loading greater than or equal to .30 were retained on that component. The structure matrix and percentage of variance explained by each component for each racial group are reported in Table 25.5 (Whites and African Americans) and in Table 25.6 (Native Americans and Hispanics). The first component extracted was very similar across racial groups, with the following eight scales loading on this component across all four ethnic groups: Personal Involvement With Chemicals, Personal Consequences of Drug Use, Polydrug Use, Effects From Drug Use, Social Benefits of Drug Use, Deviant Behavior, Peer Chemical Environment, and Sibling Chemical Use. For White participants, however, Sibling Chemical Use did not load as highly (.39) as it did with the other ethnic groups, and it did not exhibit a high communality on extraction (.16). In addition, one scale, Uncontrolled, loaded on the first component for African Americans and Hispanics.

The following four scales were common across all ethnic groups for the second component: Negative Self-Image, Psychological Disturbance, Family Estrangement, and Family Pathology. Uncontrolled loaded on the second component for Whites and Native Americans. In addition, Social Isolation loaded on the second component for Whites and for Hispanics, whereas Absence of Goals loaded on this component only for Hispanics.

The third component, which accounted for the least amount of variance, consisted of two scales (Rejecting Convention and Spiritual Isolation) that loaded across all four racial groups, one scale (Absence of Goals) that loaded across Whites, African Americans, and Native Americans, and one scale (Social Isolation) that loaded on this component for African Americans and Native Americans.

Group Differences on Response Distortion

As noted in an earlier section, nearly 5% of cases were excluded from the analysis because of an elevation on at least one of the four PEI response distortion scales. We examined post hoc if there were any differences in the rate of exclusions as a function of group status (see Table 25.7). If we observed significantly higher rates of response distortion in the non-White

TABLE 25.5
Principal-Components Factor Analysis of Personal Experience Inventory
(PEI) Scales for White and African American Groups

PEI scale	Factor loading		

Structure matrix: White participants

	Component		
	1 (38%)	2 (13%)	3 (8%)
Personal Involvement with Chemicals	.919	.394	−.012
Personal Consequences of Drug Use	.896	.316	.024
Polydrug Use	.834	.289	.043
Effects From Drug Use	.802	.553	−.092
Social Benefits of Drug Use	.752	.427	−.093
Deviant Behavior	.725	.117	.195
Peer Chemical Environment	.680	.228	.179
Sibling Chemical Use	.385	.233	.077
Negative Self-Image	.347	.814	.069
Psychological Disturbance	.489	.776	−.051
Family Estrangement	.170	.712	.307
Family Pathology	.287	.628	.001
Uncontrolled	.588	.609	.220
Social Isolation	.229	.479	.585
Rejecting Convention	.341	.309	.778
Spiritual Isolation	−.039	−.003	.647
Absence of Goals	.254	.579	.601

Structure matrix: African American participants

	Component		
	1 (32%)	2 (16%)	3 (9%)
Personal Involvement with Chemicals	.901	.147	.013
Personal Consequences of Drug Use	.836	.208	.052
Effects From Drug Use	.810	.351	.030
Social Benefits of Drug Use	.768	.202	−.050
Polydrug Use	.726	.300	.051
Peer Chemical Environment	.614	.015	.005
Uncontrolled	.607	.468	−.129
Deviant Behavior	.576	−.133	−.168
Sibling Chemical Use	.475	.315	−.163
Family Estrangement	.105	.779	.196
Psychological Disturbance	.423	.772	−.133
Negative Self-Image	.092	.762	.150
Family Pathology	.330	.722	−.139
Social Isolation	−.084	.428	.668
Absence of Goals	−.015	.540	.642
Rejecting Convention	.217	.088	.629
Spiritual Isolation	−.096	−.211	.573

Note. The extraction method was principal-components analysis; the rotation method was Oblimin with Kaiser normalization.

TABLE 25.6
Principal-Components Factor Analysis of Personal Experience Inventory (PEI) Scales for Native American and Hispanic Groups

PEI scale	Factor loading		

Structure matrix: Native American

	Component		
	1 (35%)	2 (16%)	3 (8%)
Personal Involvement with Chemicals	.899	.396	.124
Personal Consequences of Drug Use	.886	.359	.042
Polydrug Use	.772	.317	.035
Deviant Behavior	.763	.163	−.015
Effects From Drug Use	.727	.566	.104
Social Benefits of Drug Use	.697	.308	.128
Peer Chemical Environment	.667	.095	−.005
Sibling Chemical Use	.419	.370	−.092
Psychological Disturbance	.325	.864	.018
Family Estrangement	.237	.796	.384
Negative Self-Image	.176	.756	.383
Family Pathology	.354	.720	.112
Uncontrolled	.474	.645	.073
Absence of Goals	−.021	.518	.742
Rejecting Convention	.173	.217	.727
Social Isolation	−.127	.326	.695
Spiritual Isolation	.128	−.011	.656

Structure matrix: Hispanic

	Component		
	1 (32%)	2 (16%)	3 (10%)
Personal Involvement with Chemicals	.907	.172	−.124
Personal Consequences of Drug Use	.865	.170	−.084
Polydrug Use	.820	.143	.013
Effects From Drug Use	.769	.369	−.212
Deviant Behavior	.725	−.064	.139
Social Benefits of Drug Use	.695	.273	−.193
Peer Chemical Environment	.652	.054	.081
Uncontrolled	.585	.496	.099
Sibling Chemical Use	.338	.305	.051
Family Estrangement	.170	.751	.178
Negative Self-Image	.101	.745	−.266
Psychological Disturbance	.409	.699	−.269
Family Pathology	.269	.659	.012
Absence of Goals	−.023	.655	.456
Social Isolation	−.024	.380	.568
Rejecting Convention	.232	.304	.772
Spiritual Isolation	−.086	−.036	.709

Note. The extraction method was principal-components analysis; the rotation method was Oblimin with Kaiser normalization.

TABLE 25.7
Prevalence (%) of Elevations on the Response Distortion Scales on the
Personal Experience Inventory (PEI) for the Participants by Ethnicity

Group	Infrequency-1 (%)	Infrequency-2 (%)	Defensiveness-1 (%)	Defensiveness-2 (%)
White	4.0	4.6	3.0	5.4
African American	4.1	9.8	4.2	4.1
Native American	4.2	8.9	5.0	6.7
Hispanic	3.3	5.2	3.8	6.1

Note. Each Infrequency scale measures "faking bad" and inattention; each Defensiveness scale measures "faking good." Each half of the PEI has a set of faking bad/inattention and faking good scales.

groups, the utility of the PEI would be compromised in such groups. All pairwise comparisons were nonsignificant on the response distortion scales for each half of the PEI (Infrequency-1, Infrequency-2, Defensiveness-1, and Defensiveness-2). However, two comparisons approached statistical significance. For Infrequency-2, the exclusion rate for African Americans (10%) and for Native Americans (9%) tended to be higher than the exclusion rate for Whites (5%), $\chi^2(1, N = 2,371) = 126, p > .08$, and $\chi^2(1, N = 2,279) = 131$, $p > .09$, respectively.

DISCUSSION

The present study provides a psychometric examination of the PEI as an instrument for measuring adolescent drug involvement and related problems among ethnic groups seen in a drug clinic setting. The findings can be summarized around five general themes. First, the internal consistency reliability data indicated that PEI scales are comparable across the four ethnic groups. Coefficient alphas exceeded .70 for all scales, with the basic scales consistently showing alphas in excess of .80. However, 1-week test–retest reliability estimates, though comparable across ethnic groups, were not adequate (<.70) for some of the psychosocial risk scales.

The second major study finding pertains to validity evidence across the ethnic groups. We found that validity coefficients of the PEI scales that are based on their association with drug use history do not vary appreciably as a function of ethnic group. The correlations of scale scores and prior 12-month drug use history were typically in the high-to-medium range for the basic scales and in the medium-to-low range for the psychosocial risk scales. In terms of criterion validity, basic scale scores varied in comparable ways across ethnic groups as a function of diagnostic ratings. That is, problem severity scales differentiated groups defined by no diagnosis, abuse only, and one or more dependence diagnoses in all ethnic samples.

The third major finding is that the principal-components factor analyses revealed more commonality than differences in terms of scale structure across ethnic groups. These data indicate that the pattern of interscale relationships conforms to common structures across ethnicity. All five basic scales and three psychosocial risk scales (Deviant Behavior, Peer Chemical Use, Sibling Chemical Use) loaded on the first component for all ethnic groups, and one scale, Uncontrolled, loaded on the first component for two ethnic groups (African American, Hispanic). A pattern of consistency was observed for the other two components as well. The second component consisted of the same four scales for all ethnic groups, a fifth scale (Uncontrolled) that was assigned to the White and Native American groups, and a sixth scale (Social Isolation) that was assigned to Whites and Hispanics. The third component was assigned the same two scales (Rejecting Convention and Spiritual Isolation) for all groups, and two other scales (Absence of Goals and Social Isolation) loaded on this third component for at least two ethnic groups. Thus, scale-factor assignments varied minimally across ethnic groups, and the rare instances of variability that were evident occurred mostly in the Hispanic and African American groups.

The fourth major conclusion from the data indicates that, generally speaking, response distortion elevations ("faking bad" and "faking good") were equivalent across the target groups. However, there was a tendency for the African American and Native American groups to show a slightly higher rate of "faking bad" on the Infrequency-2 scale.

Fifth, the data suggest that the psychometric properties of the PEI, although generally favorable and comparable across ethnic groups, are weak in some instances. Most notable is the lack of favorable test–retest coefficients for some of the psychosocial risk scales regardless of ethnicity, particularly in the case of Negative Self-Image, Psychological Disturbance, and Uncontrolled. Also, three psychosocial risk scales had internal consistency estimates among African Americans that were at the minimum of the favorable range, i.e., .70 (Negative Self- Image, Rejecting Convention, and Family Estrangement). These findings highlight the importance of appreciating that use of the full PEI should proceed with caution in light of evidence that some scales possess weak psychometric properties, and it reinforces the notion that the exclusion of the weaker scales may be advisable in clinical and research settings.

There are several study limitations to consider when interpreting the findings. The assessment of drug abuse in ethnically diverse populations requires the consideration of culturally relevant content. The PEI, as an instrument composed of scales that measure broadly defined constructs, may not contain scales considered vital in assessing drug use within a particular cultural context (e.g., role of poverty as a risk factor for drug use). Also, some of the scales revealed weak psychometric properties, particularly Spiritual Isolation, Absence of Goals, and Rejecting Convention, and 1-week test–retest data were poor for several psychosocial risk scales. These scales represent constructs identified from the adolescent drug abuse high-risk literature (Henly & Winters, 1989), but they should be further examined for their relevance in treatment-seeking populations. Youths with unique backgrounds that are reflected by differences in culture and socioeconomic status might require supplemental assessment (Center for Substance Abuse Treatment, 1999).

Also, we were not able to evaluate the adequacy of the PEI when administered to a non-English-speaking population, and it is important to keep in mind that this study investigated only one instrument. Finally, subject attrition occurred at intake. Although the rate of refusal to participate in the study was less than 5% for all participating programs, the attrited individuals may have produced findings quite different than those obtained with the study participants. However, a post hoc comparison of participants and nonparticipants revealed no significant differences on demographic and archival variables, such as number of previous treatments for a substance use disorder, number of treatments for a prior mental illness, and family history of a substance use disorder.

Several areas of future work are suggested by the present study. It will be important to repeat these psychometric comparisons with ethnic samples of girls once the PEI database has expanded. Another area for additional study pertains to the issue of how various ethnic groups differ in their knowledge of the mechanisms of testing (e.g., there are several choices but only one correct answer) and their belief in the legitimacy of the testing experience (Rodriquez, 1992). A drug clinic setting may elicit differential perceptions of the testing process that influence the validity of self-report. One convergent validity analysis used a measure of recent drug use frequency. This variable provides a limited perspective on drug use problem severity and it contributes to an inflated validity coefficient because of shared method variance with the PEI scales. It will be important for psychometric studies of the PEI to expand its use of criterion measures collected with a method different than self-report questionnaire (e.g., clinician rating) and to examine predictive validity as a function of ethnic groups. Also, sources of invalidity should be examined in future work, such as the time frame for which self-reports occur (e.g., short vs. longer time frames) and assessment method (e.g., interview vs. paper-and-pencil vs. computer administration). Indeed, there is a lack of research as to the optimal method for collecting data from youths suspected of drug abuse. Whether the more private methods of paper-and-pencil and computerized administration yield more self-disclosure compared with interview-administered procedures is worthy of further study. The issue of the appropriateness of the current drug clinic PEI norms for non-White youths needs to be considered as well. Future research will be needed to evaluate whether these PEI norms, which were collected from a largely White sample, provide an accurate calibration of drug abuse and psychosocial risk for other ethnic groups.

REFERENCES

Allen, J. P., & Wilson, V. B. (Eds.). (2003). *Assessing alcohol problems: A guide for clinicians and researchers* (2nd ed.). Bethesda, MD: National Institutes of Health.

American Psychiatric Association. (1994). *Diagnostic and statistical manual of mental disorders* (4th ed.). Washington, DC: Author.

Brook, J. S., Whiteman, M., Cohen, P., & Tanaka, J. S. (1992). Childhood precursors of adolescent drug use: A longitudinal analysis. *Genetic, Social, and General Psychology Monographs, 118,* 195–213.

Center for Substance Abuse Treatment. (1999). *Screening and assessing adolescents for substance use disorders* (Treatment Improvement Protocol Series No. 31). Rockville, MD: Substance Abuse Mental Health Services Administration.

Cohen, J. (1977). *Statistical power analysis for the behavioral sciences.* New York: Academic Press.

Crowne, D. P., & Marlowe, D. (1960). A new scale of social desirability independent of psychopathology. *Journal of Consulting Psychology, 24,* 349–354.

Dembo, R., Schmeidler, J., Borden, P., Chin Sue, C., & Manning, D. (1997). Use of the POSIT among arrested youths entering a juvenile assessment center: A replication and update. *Journal of Child and Adolescent Substance Abuse, 6,* 19–42.

Guthmann, D. R., & Brenna, D. C. (1990). The Personal Experience Inventory: An Assessment of the instrument's validity among a delinquent population in Washington state. *Journal of Adolescent Chemical Dependency, 1,* 15–24.

Henly, G. A., & Winters, K. C. (1988). Development of problem severity scales for the assessment of adolescent alcohol and drug abuse. *International Journal of the Addictions, 23,* 65–85.

Henly, G. A., & Winters, K. C. (1989). Development of psychosocial scales for the assessment of adolescent alcohol and drug involvement. *International Journal of the Addictions, 24,* 973– 1001.

Jackson, D. N. (1967). *Personality Research Form.* Goshen, NY: Research Psychologists Press.

Jacobson, N. S., & Truax, P. (1991). Clinical significance: A statistical approach to defining meaningful change in psychotherapy research. *Journal of Consulting and Clinical Psychology, 59,* 12–19.

Jainchill, N., Yagelka, J., Hawke, J., & De Leon, G. (1999). Adolescent admissions to residential drug treatment: HIV risk behaviors pre- and posttreatment. *Psychology of Addictive Behaviors, 13,* 163–173.

Johnston, L. D., Bachman, J. G., & O'Malley, P. M. (1985). *Monitoring the future: Questionnaire responses from the nation's high school seniors, 1984.* Ann Arbor, MI: Survey Research Center, Institute for Social Research.

Johnston, L. D., O'Malley, P. M., & Bachman, J. G. (1999). *National survey results on drug use from the monitoring the future study 1975–1998.* Rockville, MD: National Institute on Drug Abuse, U. S. Department. of Health and Human Services, Public Health Service, National Institutes of Health.

Kandel, D. B., & Logan, J. A. (1984). Patterns of drug use from adolescence to young adulthood: I. Periods of risk for initiation, continued use, and discontinuation. *American Journal of Public Health, 74,* 660–666.

Leccese, M., & Waldron, H. B. (1994). Assessing adolescent substance use: A critique of current measurement instruments. *Journal of Substance Abuse Treatment, 11,* 553–563.

Martin, C., & Winters, K. C. (1998). Diagnostic criteria for adolescent alcohol use disorders. *Alcohol Health and Research World, 22,* 95–106.

Moon, D. G., Hecht, M. L., Jackson, K. M., & Spellers, R. E. (1999). Ethnic and gender differences and similarities in adolescent drug use and refusals of drug offers. *Substance Use and Misuse, 34,* 1059–1083.

Okazaki, S., & Sue, S. (1995). Methodological issues in assessment research with ethnic minorities. *Psychological Assessment, 7,* 367–375.

Rahdert, E. (Ed.). (1991). *The Adolescent Assessment/Referral System manual* (DHHS Publication No. ADM 91–1735). Rockville, MD: U. S. Department of Health and Human Services; Alcohol, Drug Abuse, and Mental Health Administration; National Institute on Drug Abuse.

Reardon, S. F., & Buka, S. L. (2002). Differences in onset and resistance of substance abuse and dependence among Whites, Blacks, and Hispanics. *Public Health Reports, 117,* 51–59.

Rodriquez, O. (1992). Introduction to technical and societal issues in the psychological testing of Hispanics. In K. F. Geisinger (Ed.), *Psychological testing of Hispanics* (pp. 11–16). Washington, DC: American Psychological Association.

Tucker, J. A. (1992). Review of the Personal Experience Inventory. In J. J. Kramer & J. C. Conoley (Eds.), *The eleventh mental measurements yearbook* (pp. 661–663). Lincoln, NE: Buros Institute of Mental Measurements.

Turner, S., DeMers, S. T., Fox, H. R., & Reed, G. M. (2001). APA's guidelines for test user qualifications: An executive summary. *American Psychologist, 56,* 1099–1113.

Wallace, J. M., Bachman, J. G., O'Malley, P. M., Johnston, L. D., Schulenberg, J. E., & Cooper, S. M. (2002). Tobacco, alcohol, and illicit drug use. Racial and ethnic differences among U. S. high school seniors, 1976–2000. *Public Health Reports, 117,* 67–75.

Weinberg, N. Z., Rahdert, E., Colliver, J. D., & Glantz, M. D. (1998). Adolescent substance abuse: A review of the past 10 years. *Journal of the American Academy of Child and Adolescent Psychiatry, 37,* 252–261.

Winters, K. C. (1997). *Use of the PEI in clinic and juvenile offender settings.* Minneapolis: University of Minnesota, Center for Adolescent Substance Abuse Research.

Winters, K. C., & Henly, G. A. (1989). *Personal Experience Inventory and manual.* Los Angeles: Western Psychological Services.

Winters, K. C., & Henly, G. A. (1993). *Adolescent Diagnostic Interview and manual.* Los Angeles: Western Psychological Services.

Winters, K. C., Latimer, W. W., & Stinchfield, R. D. (1999). Clinical and research uses of the PEI in assessing adolescent drug abuse. In M. Maruish (Ed.), *The use of psychological testing for treatment planning and outcomes assessment* (2nd ed., pp. 599–630). Mahwah, NJ: Erlbaum.

Winters, K. C., Latimer, W. W., Stinchfield, R. D., & Henly, G. A. (1999). Examining psychosocial correlates of drug involvement among drug clinic-referred youth. *Journal of Child and Adolescent Substance Abuse, 9,* 1–17.

Winters, K. C., Stinchfield, R. D., & Henly, G. A. (1996). Convergent and predictive validity of scales measuring adolescent substance abuse. *Journal of Child and Adolescent Substance Abuse, 5,* 37–55.

26

META-ANALYSES OF *ALDH2* AND *ADH1B* WITH ALCOHOL DEPENDENCE IN ASIANS

SUSAN E. LUCZAK, STEPHEN J. GLATT, AND TAMARA L. WALL

Polymorphisms in two genes coding for alcohol-metabolizing enzymes, the aldehyde dehydrogenase gene *ALDH2* and the alcohol dehydrogenase gene *ADH1B* (formerly termed *ADH2*), have been associated with protection from alcohol dependence (Li, 2000). The variant *ALDH2*2* allele is prevalent in Northeast Asian individuals, but is rare in non-Asians. General population samples indicate that approximately 31% of Chinese, 45% of Japanese, 29% of Koreans, 10% of Thais, and 0% of Western and Central European Whites possess at least one *ALDH2*2* allele (Goedde et al., 1992). Asian alcoholics in treatment are less likely to be heterozygotes (*ALDH2*1/*2* genotype) compared with controls (C.-C. Chen et al., 1999; Y.-C. Chen et al., 1999; Higuchi, Matsushita, Murayama, Takagi, & Hayashida, 1995; Lee et al., 2001; Maezawa, Yamauchi, Toda, Suzuki, & Sakurai, 1995; Muramatsu et al., 1995; Nakamura et al., 1996; Tanaka et al., 1996; Thomasson et al., 1991). Possession of an *ALDH2*2* allele also has

This work was supported by National Institutes of Health Grants K02AA00269, K08AA14265, R01AA11257, R01DA012846, and R01DA018662. We gratefully acknowledge T.-K. Li for helpful comments on this chapter.

been associated with lower rates of alcohol dependence in general population studies (Assanangkornchai, Noi-pha, Saunders, & Ratanachaiyavong, 2003; W. J. Chen et al., 1996; W. J. Chen, Loh, Hsu, & Cheng, 1997; Luczak, Wall, Cook, Shea, & Carr, 2004; Shen et al., 1997; Thomasson et al., 1994). Even greater protection from alcohol dependence has been reported for individuals who are homozygous for the ALDH2*2 allele, with only three alcohol-dependent ALDH2*2 homozygotes reported to date (Y.-C. Chen et al., 1999; Luczak et al., 2004).

The ADH1B*2 allele has also been related to lower rates of alcohol dependence. ADH1B*2 is highly prevalent among Asian populations, moderately prevalent in Russian and Jewish Whites, and rare in Western and Central European Whites (Osier et al., 1999). General population samples indicate that approximately 92% of Chinese, 84% of Japanese, 96% of Koreans, 54% of Thais, and 1% to 8% of Western and Northern Europe Whites possess at least one ADH1B*2 allele (Goedde et al., 1992). ADH1B*2 has been related to lower rates of alcohol dependence in Asians, after controlling for the effects of ALDH2*2 in some (C.-C. Chen et al., 1999; W. J. Chen et al., 1996; Thomasson et al., 1991) but not all (Lee et al., 2001) reports. In a meta-analysis of five Han Chinese, four Japanese, and six White studies, Whitfield (2002) found that both Han Chinese and Japanese ADH1B*1/*2 individuals had approximately one fifth the risk of being alcohol dependent compared with ADH1B*1/*1 individuals, but White ADH1B*1/*2 individuals had approximately one half the risk. In Asians, ADH1B*2/*2 individuals had approximately one seventh (Han Chinese) to one tenth (Japanese) the risk of being alcohol dependent compared with ADH1B*1/*1 individuals. The prevalence of ADH1B*2/*2 was not high enough to determine its risk for alcohol dependence in Whites. Whitfield, however, did not control for ALDH2 genotype in his 2002 meta-analysis of Asians. It is common to stratify or statistically control for the ALDH2*2 allele to eliminate its influence as a possible confound in assessing the association of the ADH1B*2 allele with alcohol-related behavior in Asians (C.-C. Chen et al., 1999; Thomasson et al., 1991). In a prior meta-analysis, Whitfield (1997) did stratify for ALDH2 genotype. He found that the risk for alcohol dependence in ALDH2*1/*1 individuals with an ADH1B*2 allele was almost one third that in ADH1B*1 homozygotes and that the risk in ALDH2*1/*2 individuals with an ADH1B*2 allele was almost one fourth that in ADH1B*1 homozygotes, but he concluded that these risks were not significantly different from one another. Only one prior study has examined the influence of ADH1B*2 on alcohol dependence among Koreans, and it did not find a significant relationship above that of ALDH2*2 (Lee et al., 2001). Thus, the protection afforded by ADH1B*2 could differ across those with ALDH2 variations or across Asian ethnic groups.

PROPOSED MECHANISM OF INFLUENCE

One proposed mechanism for the effects of these genes on alcohol dependence is that they increase the level of acetaldehyde, an intermediary substance produced during the metabolism of alcohol (Eriksson, 2001; Quertemont, 2004). This increased level of acetaldehyde is then proposed to result in enhanced objective and subjective reactions to alcohol, which in turn reduce the likelihood of heavy drinking and alcohol-related problems, including alcohol dependence (Wall, Shea, Luczak, Cook, & Carr, 2005). ALDH2*2 has been consistently related to increased levels of acetaldehyde, heightened objective and subjective responses to alcohol, and decreased rates of heavy drinking and alcohol dependence (for review, see Wall et al., 2005). ADH1B*2, on the other hand, has not been associated with increased levels of acetaldehyde and has been inconsistently related to reactions to alcohol, measures of consumption, and alcohol dependence (for review, see Cook et al., 2005). Thus, the proposed mechanism appears to be supported for ALDH2, but requires further evidence for ADH1B.

GENETIC MODEL OF INFLUENCE

The relative effect of possessing one versus two ALDH2*2 or ADH1B*2 alleles on alcohol dependence is not clear. Each of these genes has two allelic forms in Asians, so there exist at least three possible models of influence: additive, *2 recessive, and *2 dominant. In an additive model, each *2 allele contributes a unique but equivalent level of protection. In a *2 recessive model, the protective effect of the *2 allele emerges only when two copies of the *2 allele are present. Finally, in a *2 dominant model, possessing one or two *2 alleles results in the same level of protection. A less strict form of the dominant model is the partial dominant model, in which the difference between the *1/*1 and *1/*2 genotypes is larger than the difference between the *1/*2 and *2/*2 genotypes (i.e., a nonlinear effect).

Researchers examining the effect of ALDH2*2 on ALDH2 enzyme activity have found evidence in support of both a partial dominant model of influence (Wang, Sheikh, Saigal, Robinson, & Weiner, 1996; Xiao, Weiner, & Crabb, 1996; Xiao, Weiner, Johnston, & Crabb, 1995) and a dominant model (Crabb, Edenberg, Bosron, & Li, 1989; Peng et al., 1999; Singh et al., 1989). In in vitro and in vivo studies, the ALDH2*1/*2 genotype resulted in 12% to 20% of the enzyme activity in the liver produced by the ALDH2*1/*1 genotype, and the ALDH2*2/*2 genotype resulted in no enzyme activity (Enomoto, Takase, Yasuhara, & Takada, 1991; Ferencz-Biro & Pietruszko, 1984; Ikawa, Impraim, Wang, & Yoshida, 1983; Xiao et al., 1996). In a low dose (0.2 g/kg) alcohol challenge study by Peng et al., substantial variation in acetaldehyde levels was found across each of the three *ALDH2* genotypes when controlling for *ADH1B*. Objective and subjective responses to alcohol also differed across genotypes, with stronger responses in *ALDH2*2* homozygotes compared with heterozygotes and in heterozygotes compared with *ALDH2*1* homozygotes. These data support a dominant or partial dominant model for *ALDH2*2* in relation to these objective and subjective endophenotypes. Which genetic model best describes the relationship between *ALDH2* and the alcohol dependence phenotype remains to be determined. The model of influence of *ADH1B* has also been examined previously. In his meta-analysis of *ADH1B*, Whitfield (2002) concluded that the effects of *ADH1B*2* alleles are not additive and that *ADH1B*1/*2* and *ADH1B*2/*2* individuals are more similar to one another in their risk for alcohol dependence than to *ADH1B*1/*1* individuals. This finding is suggestive of a dominant or partial dominant model of *ADH1B*2* for alcohol dependence. However, others have warned that this conclusion may be premature because it does not take into account the entire *ADH1* haplotype and the effects of linkage disequilibrium (i.e., proximity to another functional gene; Kidd, Osier, Pakstis, & Kidd, 2002).

POTENTIAL MODERATORS OF EFFECT

A variety of factors could potentially moderate the protective effects of *ALDH2*2* and *ADH1B*2* on alcohol dependence. For example, Higuchi et al. (1994) reported that rates of Japanese *ALDH2*1/*2* individuals seeking treatment for alcohol dependence increased from 2.5% in 1979 to 8% in 1986 to 13% in 1992. During this same time period, rates of per capita alcohol consumption in Japan also increased. The authors concluded that increased cultural acceptance of alcohol consumption may have reduced the protective effect of the *ALDH2*2* allele. This is an example of a gene–environment interaction, where the environment has presumably altered the protective effect of the gene. Other potential moderating factors, including sample characteristics (e.g., ethnicity, gender, and age of controls) and ascertainment procedures (e.g., diagnostic criteria and recruitment strategy), might also alter the *ALDH2* and *ADH1B* gene effects and will be taken into consideration in the present meta-analyses.

Ethnicity

The protective association of *ALDH2*2* with alcohol dependence appears consistent across reports, but it is not known if the level of protection is similar across Asian ethnicities that have different allele frequencies and varying cultural influences. The prevalence of alcohol dependence varies markedly across Chinese, Japanese, and Koreans (Helzer & Canino, 1992; Helzer et al., 1990), as does the prevalence of *ALDH2*2* and, to a lesser extent, *ADH1B*2* (Goedde et al., 1992). Both Chinese and Korean cultures are influenced by Confucian philosophy, which emphasizes drinking in moderation (Bond & Hwang, 1986; Cheng, 1980). Japanese and Korean cultures place importance on men socializing together and drinking heavily, which may result in greater acceptance of heavy alcohol consumption and alcohol-related problems (Cho & Faulkner, 1993; Higuchi, Matsushita, Muramatsu, Murayama, & Hayashida, 1996; J. Y. Park, Danko, Wong, Weatherspoon, & Johnson, 1998; S. C. Park, Oh, & Lee, 1998). It is possible that such differences in culture may interact with genetic variations and result in different levels of protection of *ALDH2* and *ADH1B* from alcohol dependence across Asian ethnic groups.

Gender

Gender discrepancies in rates of alcohol use and dependence are particularly pronounced in many Asian ethnicities (Helzer et al., 1990; World Health Organization, 2004). Men may be encouraged to drink in Asian cultures, but women are often strongly discouraged (Helzer et al., 1990; Higuchi et al., 1996). In the United States, men as a whole were 2.2 times more likely to have a lifetime *Diagnostic and Statistical Manual of Mental Disorders— Fourth Edition* (DSM–IV; American Psychiatric Association, 1994) diagnosis of alcohol dependence than women (17.2% vs. 7.8%), but Asian American men were 3.5 times more likely to be alcohol dependent than women (9.5% vs. 2.7%; Hasin & Grant, 2004). Rates of lifetime *Diagnostic and Statistical Manual of Mental Disorders—Third Edition* (DSM–III; American Psychiatric Association, 1980) alcohol dependence also markedly differed across gender in Asia, with alcohol dependence being diagnosed in 17% of Korean men but only 1% of Korean women and in 3% of Chinese men but only 0.1% of Chinese women (Helzer et al., 1990).

Several studies have evaluated gender-related differences in alcohol consumption associated with *ALDH2* (Higuchi et al., 1996; Muramatsu et al., 1995; Takeshita & Morimoto, 1999; Takeshita, Morimoto, Mao, Hashimoto, & Furuyama, 1994). The findings indicate that men drink significantly more than women, and differences in alcohol consumption associated with *ALDH2* are more evident in men compared with women. An alcohol challenge study of Asian American men and women found, however, comparable objective and subjective reactions across gender for *ALDH2* heterozygotes compared with *ALDH2*1* homozygotes (Luczak, Elvine-Kreis, Shea, Carr, & Wall, 2002), suggesting a similar mechanism of action for *ALDH2*2* for both men and women. Given that women may have a reduced likelihood of developing alcohol dependence regardless of their possession of these alleles, the protective effects of *ALDH2*2* and *ADH1B*2* against alcohol dependence could be less strong in women. Thus, studies using mixed-gender samples may yield different results than studies using samples composed of only men, especially if gender is mixed in only either case or control groups.

Age of Controls

Age of onset of alcohol dependence peaks in the United States in the early 20s (Schuckit, Anthenelli, Bucholz, Hesselbrock, & Tipp, 1995; Schuckit, Daeppen, Tipp, Hesselbrock, & Bucholz, 1998; U.S. Department of Health and Human Services, 1998), but in Asia, the peak age for alcohol dependence onset appears to be later (Helzer, Burnam, & McEvoy, 1991; Helzer et al., 1990; Yu, Liu, Xia, & Zhang, 1989). If a control sample is young, it is possible that some of these individuals will go on to later develop alcohol dependence. This may be particularly important in studies of Asians, where onset of alcohol abuse and dependence prevalence rates continue to increase into later life. Thus, studies that use older control samples could find greater effect sizes because the participants are more accurately categorized.

Diagnostic Criteria

Disorder severity in the case group could also influence the detection of genetic associations with alcohol dependence. Diagnostic criteria vary across studies, and different systems have been found to differ in their sensitivity for detecting genetic influences (van den Bree et al., 1998). Genetic linkage analyses from the Collaborative Study on the Genetics of Alcoholism have found different genetic markers and loadings for alcohol dependence depending on the diagnostic criteria used (Williams et al., 1999). *International Classification of Disease and Related Health Problems—Tenth Edition* (ICD–10; World Health Organization, 1993) dependence criteria have been shown to be more stringent than *DSM–IV* criteria, which in turn have been found to be more stringent than *Diagnostic and Statistical Manual of Mental Disorders—Third Edition—Revised* (DSM–III–R; American Psychiatric Association, 1987) criteria (Schuckit et al., 1994). Thus, fewer individuals (i.e., only those who have more severe problems) would be categorized as alcohol dependent using *ICD–10* criteria compared with *DSM–III–R* criteria. More stringent diagnostic criteria could differentiate the case and control groups to a greater extent, potentially increasing the effect sizes found for the genes.

Recruitment Strategy

Studies also vary in recruitment strategy. Many studies have compared cases in treatment with controls, but others have assessed alcohol dependence in general population samples. Individuals in treatment for alcohol dependence are likely to have a more severe form of alcohol dependence than those diagnosed in community samples. Studies comparing clinical and community samples of individuals with alcohol dependence support this contention, with a significantly greater number of alcohol-related symptoms being reported in treatment versus general population samples (Bucholz, Helzer, Shayka, & Lewis, 1994). General population samples include alcohol-dependent individuals who may not necessarily have sought treatment and have milder forms of alcohol dependence. Thus, the differences between cases and controls may be greater in treatment samples, thereby increasing the effect sizes found for the genes.

SUMMARY OF MODERATORS

In the present study, five study and sample characteristics will be tested as moderators of the effect sizes found for *ALDH2* and *ADH1B* in relation to alcohol dependence. Asian ethnic groups have varying rates of alcohol involvement and allele prevalences, both of which could alter the effect sizes found for the genes. Rates of alcohol consumption and dependence are also higher in men compared with women, so using samples of mixed gender might produce different findings compared with samples of only men. A young control group may miscategorize individuals who later develop alcohol dependence and thus is predicted to reduce the effect sizes found for the genes. A less severe case group, obtained either by using less stringent diagnostic criteria or by recruiting from general samples instead of treatment samples, may also reduce the effect sizes obtained.

PURPOSE

Despite the fact that, to date, *ALDH2* is the gene most strongly associated with alcohol involvement, no prior meta-analysis has specifically focused on the relationship of this gene with alcohol dependence per se (Brennan et al., 2004; Lewis & Smith, 2005). The effect size attributable to *ALDH2* has been calculated in individual studies, but never using all available data in the literature. In addition, the low prevalence of *ALDH2*2/*2* individuals makes it particularly difficult to determine the effect of possessing two *ALDH2*2* alleles compared with one or no *ALDH2*2* alleles without using a large amount of data. For *ADH1B* and alcohol dependence, two meta-analyses have been previously conducted (Whitfield, 1997, 2002), but neither focused on the effect of *ALDH2* on *ADH1B* in Asians, and they did not attempt to tease apart the influence of methodological variations on the effect sizes. The present study seeks to address these gaps in the literature by conducting a series of meta-analyses on *ALDH2* and *ADH1B* with alcohol dependence in Asians.

The present study has three specific aims. The first aim is to estimate the magnitude of protection provided by *ALDH2*2* and by *ADH1B*2*, after stratifying for *ALDH2*, against alcohol dependence in Asians. The second aim is to examine models of influence to determine the effects of possessing one versus two protective alleles of the *ALDH2* and *ADH1B* genes. The third aim is to test the relationships of several potential moderators, including ethnicity, gender, mean age of controls, diagnostic criteria for alcohol dependence, and recruitment method, of the obtained effect sizes for these genes.

METHOD

Literature Search and Gathering of Data Sets

To identify studies eligible for the meta-analyses, we surveyed Medline using the National Library of Medicine's PubMed (January 1966 to April 2005) online search engine. We conducted two searches with the following combinations of keywords: (alcoholism OR alcohol dependence) AND (aldehyde dehydrogenase OR *ALDH2*) and (alcoholism OR alcohol dependence) AND (alcohol dehydrogenase OR *ADH2* OR *ADH1B*). The retrieved abstracts were read to identify studies that examined associations of *ALDH2* and *ADH1B* gene polymorphisms with alcohol dependence in Asians. Studies of this type were then read in their entirety to assess their appropriateness for inclusion in the meta-analyses. All references cited in these works were also reviewed to identify additional works not indexed by this database.

Inclusion Criteria

Only those studies examining *ALDH2* polymorphisms and alcohol dependence were included in the meta-analyses. Studies that assessed both *ALDH2* and *ADH1B* polymorphisms so that *ALDH2–ADH1B* haplotypes could be determined were included in the *ADH1B* analyses. Furthermore, studies had to meet all of the following criteria: (a) be published in a peer-reviewed journal, (b) present original data, (c) be written in English, and (d) provide enough data to calculate an effect size. We also excluded studies, or samples within studies, that used cases with specific alcohol-related diseases such as alcohol liver disease, alcohol-related pancreatitis, and certain head and neck cancers. ALDH2*2 and ADH1B*2 genetic variations have been found to be risk factors for these diseases, perhaps due to their effect of increasing acetaldehyde accumulation (for reviews, see Brennan et al., 2004; Crabb, Matsumoto, Chang, & You, 2004; and Lewis & Smith, 2005), and thus, the genotypes of these cases may not be representative of a general sample of alcohol-dependent individuals. This approach is consistent with the rationale used by Whitfield (2002) in his meta-analysis of ADH1B.

The application of these criteria yielded 15 studies eligible for the ALDH2 meta-analyses. Two of these studies (W. J. Chen et al., 1997; Shen et al., 1997) could be divided into Chinese ethnic subgroups, including Ami, Atayal, Bunun, Elunchun, Han, Mongolian, and Paiwan, and one study (Luczak et al., 2004) could be divided into Chinese and Korean samples for a total of 22 ethnic group samples included in the meta-analyses. Chinese data were split into ethnic subgroups because these subgroups have different ALDH2 and ADH1B allele frequencies and cultures and thus may show differential influences of the polymorphisms. The ADH1B–ALDH2*1/*1 meta-analyses included eight studies with a total of 14 ethnic group data sets; the ADH1B–ALDH2*1/*2 meta-analyses included five studies with a total of six ethnic group samples. In this final database, the data from C.-C. Chen et al. (1999), Y.-C. Chen et al. (1999), and Thomasson et al. (1991) were combined and reported as described by Yin and Agarwal (2001, a review chapter that is the only report that presents the ADH1B–ALDH2 haplotype data from these publications). In addition, data from W. J. Chen et al., which were split into four ethnic subgroups in the ALDH2 and ADH1B–ALDH2*1/*1 databases, were combined into one due to the small ALDH2*1/*2 sample size (n = 9) and to be more consistent with the collapsed presentation of the Yin and Agarwal data.

We attempted to contact all corresponding authors of studies that reported ALDH2 and ADH1B data on Asians, but did not include ALDH2–ADH1B haplotypes to request this information. The laboratory of Dr. Andrew T. A. Cheng provided these data, including 43 more controls than reported by W. J. Chen et al. (1997). In the Tamara L. Wall laboratory data, we also eliminated 37 control individuals who met criteria for alcohol abuse and who had been included in our most recent publication to make our control group include only individuals without an alcohol use disorder (Luczak et al., 2004).

Coding of Sample Characteristics

Five sample characteristics were tested as potential moderating influences on the effect sizes: (a) ethnicity of the sample (Chinese, Japanese, or

Korean); (b) mean age of the control group; (c) gender index, calculated as (female cases/male cases)/(female controls/male controls); for all male samples, the gender index was set at 1.0 to represent no difference between the gender ratios of cases and controls; (d) diagnostic criteria for cases (*DSM–III–R* or *ICD–10*); and (e) recruitment strategy of the cases (treatment sample or general population sample). These descriptive characteristics of the studies are presented in Table 26.1.

Statistical Analyses

Data from each sample were used to construct three two-by-two tables in which participants were classified by diagnostic category (case or control) and by frequencies based on two-way genotype comparisons of all possible genotypes (*1/*2 vs. *1/*1, *2/*2 vs. *1/*1, and *2/*2 vs. *1/*2). These genotype comparisons were used to examine each gene's model of influence. As described above, an additive model of influence would be supported if a linear effect of the *2 allele was found, that is, the difference between the effect of *1/*1 and *1/*2 was the same as the difference between the effect of *1/*2 and *2/*2. A recessive *2 model of influence would be supported if the effects of *1/*1 and *1/*2 were the same and only *2/*2 was protective. A dominant *2 model would be supported if the protective effects of *1/*2 and *2/*2 were equivalent. Finally, a partial dominant *2 model of influence would be supported if there was a difference in effect between all genotypes, but the difference in the protective effect between *1/*1 and *1/*2 was greater than the difference between *1/*2 and *2/*2.

Tables 26.2, 26.3, and 26.4 present the genotypes and allele frequencies for cases and controls in each sample included in each of the three meta-analyses. The strength of associations in these tables was summarized using the odds ratio (OR), an estimate of relative risk, in which *2 was assigned as the protective allele for both *ALDH2* and *ADH1B*. Chi-square tests for deviation from Hardy Weinberg equilibrium were also calculated for each sample using the program HWSIM available at http://krunch.med.yale.edu/hwsim. Significance was calculated for a one-tailed test using a Monte Carlo permutation procedure with iterations set at 10,000 to adjust for the small sample size in some cells (e.g., *ALDH2*2/*2* and *ADH1B*1/*1*). The samples were analyzed by random-effects meta-analysis in Stata Version 8.0 (StataCorp LC, 2005). Type I error rate was set at .05. Five types of statistical analyses were conducted: (a) pooled effect size ORs and 95% confidence intervals (CIs), (b) influence of each individual sample on the pooled OR, (c) heterogeneity of ORs across the individual studies, (d) associations of moderator variables, and (e) publication bias. The pooled OR was calculated according to the methods of DerSimonian and Laird (1986), and its 95% CI was constructed using Woolf's (1955) method; significance of the pooled OR was

TABLE 26.1

Descriptive Characteristics of Studies Included in the *ALDH2* Meta-Analysis

Study and ethnicity (subsample)	Cases (n)	Controls (n)	Diagnostic system	Recruitment strategy	Mean age of controls	Gender index
Assanangkornchai et al. (2003) Thai	85	136	*ICD–10*	General and psychiatric	43	All men
C.-C. Chen et al. (1999) Han Chinese	219	495	*DSM–III–R*	Treatment	20	Male controls
W. J. Chen et al. (1996) Han Chinese	46	63	*DSM–III–R*	General and treatment	62	All men
W. J. Chen et al. (1997)						
Atayal Chinese	35	45	*DSM–III–R*	General	61 (55–66)	0.44
Ami Chinese	24	29	*DSM–III–R*	General	61 (55–66)	1.24
Bunun Chinese	60	72	*DSM–III–R*	General	61 (55–66)	0.66
Paiwan Chinese	30	44	*DSM–III–R*	General	61 (55–66)	0.81
Y.-C. Chen et al. (1999) Han Chinese	80	144	*DSM–III–R*	Treatment	20	Male controls
Higuchi et al. (1995) Japanese	655	461	*DSM–III–R*	Treatment	41	0.08
Lee et al. (2001) Korean	52	64	>80 g/d × 10 yr[a]	Treatment	50	All men
Luczak et al. (2004)						
Chinese American	10	203	*DSM–III–R*	General	22	0.24
Korean American	28	180	*DSM–III–R*	General	22	0.36
Maezawa et al. (1995) Japanese	96	60	*DSM–III–R*	Treatment	—	All men
Muramatsu et al. (1995) Han Chinese	32	105	*DSM–III–R*	Treatment	38	Male cases
Nakamura et al. (1996) Japanese	53	97	*DSM–III–R*	Treatment		

(continues)

TABLE 26.1
Descriptive Characteristics of Studies Included in the *ALDH2* Meta-Analysis *(Continued)*

Study and ethnicity (subsample)	Cases (*n*)	Controls (*n*)	Diagnostic system	Recruitment strategy	Mean age of controls	Gender index
Shen et al. (1997)						
Han Chinese	52	48	*ICD–10*	General	—	All men
Korean Chinese	55	50	*ICD–10*	General	—	All men
Mongolian Chinese	31	35	*ICD–10*	General	—	All men
Elunchun Chinese	31	37	*ICD–10*	General	—	All men
Tanaka et al. (1996)						
Japanese	90	66	*DSM–III–R*	Treatment	38	Male controls
Thomasson et al. (1994)						
Atayal Chinese	94	66	*DSM–III–R*	General	51	0.39
Thomasson et al. (1991)						
Han Chinese	50	50	*DSM–III*	Treatment	20	All men

Note. ICD–10 = International Classification of Disease and Related Health Problems—Tenth Edition; DSM–III–R = Diagnostic and Statistical Manual of Mental Disorders (3rd ed., rev.); DSM–III = Diagnostic and Statistical Manual of Mental Disorders (3rd ed.). d = days; yr = years. Values represent age in years. Dashes indicate that the data were not available.
^aConsuming > 80 grams of ethanol per day for > 10 years was the diagnosis for alcohol dependence.

determined by the z test. The influence of individual samples on the pooled OR was determined by sequentially removing each sample and recalculating the pooled OR and 95% CI. Heterogeneity of the ORs was assessed using a chi-square test of goodness of fit. Moderating influences of ethnicity, age of the control group, gender index, diagnostic criteria, and recruitment method on the pooled ORs were assessed using multiple regression.

Publication bias within the group of ORs was assessed by the method of Egger, Davey Smith, Schneider, & Minder (1997), in which the standard normal deviate of the OR (z) is regressed on the precision of the OR (POR, the inverse of the standard error of the OR). Because the POR increases with sample size, the regression of z on POR should run through the origin in the absence of bias (i.e., small samples with low precision have large standard errors and small standard normal deviates, whereas large samples with high precision have small standard errors and large standard normal deviates). The slope of the regression line indicates the size and direction of association, and in the presence of bias, the intercept of the regression will be significantly different from zero, as determined by the t test. Power calculations for differences between two proportions (relative genotype or allele frequency differences between cases and controls) were conducted using the sampsi procedure in the Stata software package. All power analyses were conducted as two-tailed tests with the type I error rates set at .05.

RESULTS

ALDH2 Meta-Analyses

Hardy–Weinberg equilibrium was found for all case and control samples with the exception of two control groups (see Table 26.2). Disequilibrium was found in the controls of the C.-C. Chen et al. (1999) study, $\chi^2(1, N = 495) = 7.04, p = .001$, and in the Korean Chinese controls of the Shen et al. (1997) study, $\chi^2(1, N = 50) = 4.56, p = .017$.

The pooled ORs and 95% CIs for the two-way genotype comparisons are shown in Table 26.5. For the total sample of 22 data sets included in the ALDH2 meta-analyses, the pooled OR derived from 1,980 cases and 2,550 controls was significant for the *1/*2 versus *1/*1 and *2/*2 versus *1/*1 analyses, but not for the *2/*2 versus *1/*2 analysis (shown in the first row of Table 26.5). The influence test for the *2/*2 versus *1/*2 analysis confirmed this lack of significance, with the sequential omission of any 1 of 19 individual samples resulting in 95% CIs that encompassed 1.0; influence tests in the total sample for the *1/*2 versus *1/*1 and *2/*2 versus *1/*1 analyses were robust and did not include 1.0 in the 95% CI with the omission of any sample.

TABLE 26.2

ALDH2 Genotypes and Allele Frequencies of Cases and Controls in Studies Included in the ALDH2 Meta-Analyses

Study and subsample	ALDH2 genotype			Allele frequency	
	*1/*1	*1/*2	*2/*2	*1	*2
Assanangkornchai et al. (2003)					
Case	81	4	0	0.98	0.02
Control	101	34	1	0.87	0.13
C.-C. Chen et al. (1999)					
Case	239	52	0	0.92	0.08
Control[a]	278	200	17	0.76	0.24
W. J. Chen et al. (1996)					
Case	38	8	0	0.91	0.09
Control	36	24	3	0.76	0.24
W. J. Chen et al. (1997)					
Atayal Chinese					
Case	35	0	0	1.00	0.00
Control	43	2	0	0.98	0.02
Ami Chinese					
Case	23	1	0	0.98	0.02
Control	28	1	0	0.98	0.02
Bunun Chinese					
Case	59	1	0	0.99	0.01
Control	70	2	0	0.99	0.01
Paiwan Chinese					
Case	30	0	0	1.00	0.00
Control	41	3	0	0.97	0.03
Korean American					
Case	21	5	1	0.87	0.13
Control	107	54	5	0.81	0.19
Maezawa et al. (1995)					
Case	76	20	0	0.90	0.10
Control	34	20	6	0.73	0.27
Muramatsu et al. (1995)					
Case	29	3	0	0.95	0.05
Control	57	43	5	0.73	0.27
Nakamura et al. (1996)					
Case	47	6	0	0.95	0.05
Control	58	29	10	0.75	0.25
Shen et al. (1997)					
Han Chinese					
Case	50	2	0	0.98	0.02
Control	28	18	2	0.77	0.23
Korean Chinese					
Case	49	6	0	0.95	0.05
Control[a]	17	30	3	0.64	0.38
Mongolian Chinese					
Case	29	2	0	0.97	0.03
Control	29	6	0	0.91	0.09

Study / Group					
Y.-C. Chen et al. (1999)					
Case	58	21	1	0.86	0.14
Control	79	56	9	0.74	0.26
Higuchi et al. (1995)					
Case	575	80	0	0.96	0.04
Control	268	162	31	0.73	0.27
Lee et al. (2001)					
Case	50	2	0	0.98	0.02
Control	35	25	4	0.74	0.26
Luczak et al. (2004) Chinese American					
Case	7	1	1	0.78	0.22
Control	81	80	14	0.69	0.31
Elunchun Chinese					
Case	31	0	0	1.00	0.00
Control	32	4	1	0.92	0.08
Tanaka et al. (1996)					
Case	86	4	0	0.98	0.02
Control	26	35	5	0.66	0.34
Thomasson et al. (1994)					
Case	91	3	0	0.98	0.02
Control	60	5	1	0.95	0.05
Thomasson et al. (1991)					
Case	44	6	0	0.94	0.06
Control	26	18	6	0.70	0.30

[a]Indicates that genotype frequencies significantly differed from Hardy–Weinberg equilibrium ($p < .05$).

In all samples combined, the pooled OR for the *1/*2 versus *1/*1 analysis was 0.22, 95% CI = 0.16, 0.30, z = 9.59, p = .000, and for the *2/*2 versus *1/*1 analysis was 0.12, 95% CI = 0.06, 0.24, z = 5.80, p = .000. This indicates that, compared with individuals with no ALDH2*2 alleles, those with one ALDH2*2 allele had approximately one fourth to one fifth the risk for alcohol dependence and those with two ALDH2*2 alleles had approximately one ninth the risk. The difference between having one or two ALDH2*2 alleles, however, as shown by the *2/*2 versus *1/*2 analysis, was not significant (OR = 0.49, CI = 0.24, 1.05, p = .066). It is important to note, however, that in all samples combined, there were only 3 (0.1%) ALDH2*2/*2 alcohol-dependent individuals and 129 (5.0%) ALDH2*2/*2 controls. Significant heterogeneity was observed within the total sample in the *1/*2 versus *1/*1 analysis, $\chi^2(21)$ = 40.6, p = .006, suggesting the presence of one or more moderating variables. Moderators were examined in all three genotype comparison models. The covariate diagnostic criteria was a significant moderator in the *1/*2 versus *1/*1 analysis (z = −2.17, p = .030). Studies that used ICD–10 criteria for alcohol dependence showed a greater protective effect of ALDH2*2 compared with studies that used DSM–III–R criteria; studies that used DSM–III criteria (Thomasson et al., 1991) and a quantity measure of 80 g of alcohol per day for 10 years (Lee et al., 2001) were omitted from these analyses. In addition, recruitment strategy and Japanese ethnicity were significant covariates in the *2/*2 versus *1/*1 analysis (recruitment strategy, z = 2.68, p = .007; and Japanese ethnicity, z = −2.46, p = .014) and *2/*2 versus *1/*2 analysis (recruitment strategy, z = 2.55, p = .011; and Japanese ethnicity, z = −2.04, p = .041). Samples that recruited cases from treatment settings showed a greater protective effect of ALDH2*2 compared with samples that recruited cases from general population samples. Japanese had lower ORs compared with the three other ethnicities combined in these analyses. This is consistent with two of the three identified alcohol-dependent ALDH2*2/*2 individuals being Chinese, one being Korean, and none being Japanese. The mean age of the control group, the gender index of the sample, Chinese ethnicity, and Korean ethnicity were not significantly related to the obtained pooled ORs.

The samples were next split into Chinese, Japanese, and Korean samples, and all models were retested to examine the protective effect of ALDH2*2 across ethnicity, even though only Japanese ethnicity was a significant covariate in the regression analyses. The relative pooled ORs across the models followed similar patterns across all three ethnicities. The pooled ORs were higher in the Chinese samples (n = 14) than in the total sample for all models, although Chinese ethnicity was not a significant covariate (see second row of Table 26.5). The protection of having one ALDH2*2 allele was about one third and the protection of having two ALDH2*2 alleles was about one sixth compared with having no ALDH2*2 alleles. As with the total sample combined, the OR for the *2/*2 versus *1/*2 analysis was not significant. Japanese samples ($n = 4$) had consistently lower pooled ORs compared with the total sample for all three models (see third row of Table 26.5). The protection of one ALDH2*2 allele was about one fifth and the protection of two ALDH2*2 alleles was nearly complete at 0.03, 95% CI = 0.01, 0.11, $z = 5.04$, $p = .000$, compared with no ALDH2*2 alleles. The pooled OR for the *2/*2 versus *1/*2 analysis appeared to be significant at 0.13, 95% CI = 0.03, 0.57, $z = 2.72$, $p = .007$, but the test of influence determined that this was not a robust finding, as exclusion of two of the four samples produced pooled ORs with 95% CIs that included 1.0. In Korean samples ($n = 3$), the pooled OR was only significant in the *1/*2 versus *1/*1 analysis, but the influence tests encompassed 1.0 for the Luczak et al. (2004) sample, indicating that the finding was not robust. Removing this sample reduced the 95% CI to below 1.0 for the *1/*2 versus *1/*1 analysis, but all three samples had 95% CIs encompassing 1.0 in the other two analyses. It is of interest to note that the ALDH2*2 allele frequency in the control groups of the three Korean samples varied substantially, from 0.19 in the Luczak et al. Korean American sample to 0.26 in the Lee et al. (2001) Korean sample to 0.38 in the Shen et al. (1997) Korean Chinese sample. While we acknowledge the lack of significance of the Korean pooled ORs, the patterns of the *1/*2 versus *1/*1 and *2/*2 versus *1/*1 results were fairly similar to those found in the other ethnicities and in the total sample (see fourth row of Table 26.5). The OR of the *2/*2 versus *1/*1 analysis was higher than expected, likely due to the fact that Luczak et al. had an alcohol-dependent Korean ALDH2*2/*2 individual in a relatively small sample. Despite this discrepancy, the findings appear consistent across ethnicities.

There was no evidence of publication bias in any of the ALDH2 models. The 95% CIs of the regressions of z on POR encompassed the origin for each group of samples.

ADH1B–ALDH2*1/*1 Meta-Analyses

Hardy–Weinberg equilibrium was found for all case and control samples with the exception of two case groups (see Table 26.3). Disequilibrium was found in the case group of Thomasson et al. (1991), $\chi^2(1, N = 43) = 8.38$, $p = .021$, and the case group of C.-C. Chen et al. (1999), $\chi^2(1, N = 240) = 29.97$, $p < .001$. The pooled ORs and 95% CIs for the meta-analyses of ADH1B in individuals with ALDH2*1/*1 are shown in Table 26.5. In the total sample of 12 data sets, the pooled OR derived from 685 cases and 890 controls was significant for the *1/*2 versus *1/*1 and *2/*2 versus *1/*1 analyses, but not for the *2/*2 versus *1/*2 analysis (shown in the sixth row of Table 26.5). The pooled ORs for the *1/*2 versus *1/*1 and *2/*2 versus *1/*1 analyses were robust; sequential omission of each of the 12 individual samples resulted in no 95% CIs that encompassed 1.0.

TABLE 26.3
ADH1B Genotypes of Cases and Controls in Studies Included in the ADH1B–ALDH2*1/*1 Meta-Analyses

Study and subsample	Participants with ADH1B genotype			Allele frequency	
	*1/*1	*1/*2	*2/*2	*1	*2
C.-C. Chen et al. (1999)					
Case[a]	92	77	71	0.54	0.46
Control	24	97	158	0.26	0.74
W. J. Chen et al. (1996)					
Case	9	14	15	0.42	0.58
Control	0	8	28	0.11	0.89
W. J. Chen et al. (1997)					
Atayal Chinese					
Case	0	5	30	0.07	0.93
Control	0	13	28	0.16	0.84
Ami Chinese					
Case	8	7	6	0.55	0.45
Control	2	11	13	0.29	0.71
Bunun Chinese					
Case	1	16	42	0.15	0.85
Control	1	27	41	0.10	0.90
Paiwan Chinese					
Case	0	9	21	0.15	0.85
Control	0	10	27	0.14	0.86
Y.-C. Chen et al. (1999)					
Case	15	19	24	0.42	0.58
Control	8	27	44	0.27	0.73
Luczak et al. (2004)					
Chinese American					
Case	0	3	4	0.21	0.79
Control	11	28	42	0.25	0.75
Korean American					
Case	1	8	12	0.24	0.76
Control	13	39	55	0.30	0.70
Nakamura et al. (1996)					
Case	16	19	12	0.54	0.46
Control	3	30	25	0.31	0.69
Tanaka et al. (1996)					
Case	26	40	20	0.53	0.47
Control	2	9	15	0.25	0.75
Thomasson et al. (1991)					
Case[a]	16	12	15	0.51	0.49
Control	2	12	11	0.32	0.68

Note. Numbers may not match exactly with *ALDH2* genotypes due to missing *ADH1B* genotype data.
[a]Indicates that genotype frequencies significantly differed from Hardy–Weinberg equilibrium ($p < .05$).

In all samples combined, individuals who possessed one $ADH1B*2$ allele were approximately one fourth (OR = 0.26, 95% CI = 0.16, 0.44, z = 5.15, p = .000) as likely to be alcohol dependent as individuals with no $ADH1B*2$ alleles, and individuals who possessed two $ADH1B*2$ alleles were approximately one fifth (OR = 0.20, 95% CI = 0.10, 0.39, z = 4.70, p = .000) as likely to be alcohol dependent as individuals with no $ADH1B*2$ alleles. The difference between possessing one and two $ADH1B*2$ alleles was not significant (OR = 0.81, 95% CI = 0.57, 1.16, z = 1.15, p = .248).

Significant heterogeneity was observed within the total sample in the $*2/*2$ versus $*1/*1$ analysis, $\chi^2(9)$ = 17.1, p = .047, suggesting the presence of one or more moderating variables. Moderators were examined in all three genotype comparison models. Both recruitment strategy and gender were significant moderators, with recruitment strategy being significant in the $*2/*2$ versus $*1/*1$ (z = 2.59, p = .010) and $*2/*2$ versus $*1/*2$ (z = 3.02, p = .003) analyses and gender being significant in the $*1/*2$ versus $*1/*1$ (z = −2.36, p = .018) and $*2/*2$ versus $*1/*1$ (z = −2.83, p = .005) analyses. As in the ALDH2 meta-analyses, samples that were recruited from treatment settings showed a greater protective effect of $ADH1B*2$. In addition, samples that included a greater proportion of men in the cases than in the controls also showed a greater protective effect of $ADH1B*2$. The mean age of the control group, Chinese ethnicity, and Japanese ethnicity did not moderate the obtained pooled ORs. One sample in this analysis used DSM–III criteria (Thomasson et al., 1991), and all others used DSM–III–R criteria, so diagnostic criteria were not tested as a moderator; only one sample was Korean, so this potential moderator also could not be tested. It is noteworthy, however, that all Japanese and Han Chinese samples were recruited from treatment settings, and no other ethnic groups were recruited from treatment settings. Therefore, it is possible that the moderation found for ethnicity is actually due to recruitment strategy. Japanese ethnicity was not a significant moderator when entered on its own, suggesting that increased severity of the alcohol dependence among individuals recruited from treatment settings, rather than ethnic differences, may be related to an increased protective association of $ADH1B*2$.

Stratification by ethnicity yielded similar patterns of findings for the association of $ADH1B*2$ with alcohol dependence as was found in the total sample. These analyses included only one Korean sample; thus, only Chinese (n = 9) and Japanese (n = 2) pooled estimates and tests of influence were calculated. Two of the Chinese samples were removed due to empty cells. Chinese pooled ORs were very similar to those found for the total sample, with possession of one and two $ADH1B*2$ alleles reducing the risk for alcohol dependence by approximately one fourth to one sixth (see seventh row of Table 26.5). While following a similar pattern, Japanese pooled ORs were somewhat lower (see eighth row of Table 26.5), with possession of one and two ADH1B*2 alleles reducing the risk for alcohol dependence by approximately one fifth to one tenth. However, the results of the *1/*2 versus *1/*1 analysis had significant influence, indicating that the findings were not robust; this is not surprising given that only two studies were included in this analysis.

There was no evidence of publication bias in any of the models. The 95% CIs of the regressions of z on POR encompassed the origin for each group of studies.

ADH1B–ALDH2*1/*2 Meta-Analyses

Hardy–Weinberg equilibrium was found for all samples except for one case and one control group (see Table 26.4). Disequilibrium was found in the control group of Nakamura et al. (1996), $\chi^2(1, N = 29) = 29.97, p = .022$, and in the case group of Yin and Agarwal (2001), $\chi^2(1, N = 78) = 14.80, p = .001$. Yin and Agarwal aggregated the data from C.-C. Chen et al. (1999),

TABLE 26.4
ADH1B Genotypes of Cases and Controls in
Studies Included in the ADH1B–ALDH2*1/*2 Meta-Analyses

	Participants with ADH1B genotype			Allele frequency	
Study and subsample	*1/*1	*1/*2	*2/*2	*1	*2
W. J. Chen et al. (1996)					
Case	5	1	2	0.69	0.31
Control	0	11	16	0.20	0.80
W. J. Chen et al. (1997)					
Case	0	0	1	0.00	1.00
Control	0	4	4	0.25	0.75
Luczak et al. (2004)					
Chinese American					
Case	0	1	0	0.50	0.50
Control	4	25	51	0.21	0.79
Korean American					
Case	0	4	1	0.40	0.60
Control	7	18	29	0.30	0.70
Nakamura et al. (1996)					
Case	5	1	0	0.92	0.08
Control[a]	0	16	13	0.28	0.72
Tanaka et al. (1996)					
Case	1	2	1	0.50	0.50
Control	2	13	20	0.24	0.76
Yin and Agarwal (2001)					
Case[a]	29	22	27	0.51	0.49
Control	20	106	148	0.27	0.73

Note. Numbers may not match exactly with ALDH2 genotypes due to missing ADH1B genotype data.
[a]Indicates that genotype frequencies significantly differed from Hardy–Weinberg equilibrium ($p < .05$).

Y.-C. Chen et al. (1999), and Thomasson et al. (1991), and both the C.-C. Chen et al. and Thomasson et al. case groups were found to deviate from equilibrium in the *ADH1B–ALDH2*1/*1* meta-analyses. The pooled ORs and 95% CIs for the meta-analyses of *ADH1B* in individuals with *ALDH2*1/*2* are shown in Table 26.5. In the total sample of seven data sets, the pooled OR derived from 105 cases and 521 controls was significant for the *1/*2 versus *1/*1 and *2/*2 versus *1/*1 analyses, but not for the *2/*2 versus *1/*2 analysis. There was also influence in the *1/*2 versus *1/*1 analysis, with the omission of either of two studies resulting in 95% CIs that encompassed 1.0. These studies were the Yin and Agarwal (2001) and W. J. Chen et al. (1996) studies, which accounted for 62% of the cases analyzed in this meta-analysis. The *2/*2 versus *1/*1 pooled ORs was robust, with no indication that the pooled OR was unduly influenced by any single sample. The pattern of pooled ORs was similar to that found in the *ADH1B–ALDH2*1/*1* meta-analyses (see 10th row of Table 26.5). In all samples combined, the pooled OR for the *1/*2 versus *1/*1 analysis was 0.17, 95% CI = 0.04, 0.68, z = 2.50, p = .012, and that for the *2/*2 versus *1/*2 analysis was 0.09, 95% CI = 0.03, 0.32, z = 3.77, p = .000, indicating that, compared with individuals without *ADH1B*2* alleles, individuals who possessed one *ADH1B*2* allele were almost one sixth as likely and individuals who possessed two *ADH1B*2* alleles were approximately one eleventh as likely to be alcohol dependent. The difference between possessing one and two *ADH1B*2* alleles was not significant (OR = 0.72, 95% CI = 0.43, 1.22, z = 1.22, p = .224).

Significant heterogeneity was not observed in any of the analyses, but covariates were still examined to look for potential moderators. As in the *ADH1B–ALDH2*1/*1* meta-analyses, recruitment strategy was a significant covariate in the *1/*2 versus *1/*1 analysis (z = 2.08, p = .038), with recruitment of cases from treatment settings relating to a greater protective effect of *ADH1B*2* from alcohol dependence. There was not sufficient information to test gender or diagnostic criteria as covariates. Mean age of controls, Chinese ethnicity, and Japanese ethnicity were not significant moderators.

When split by ethnicity, patterns of findings similar to those in the total sample were observed in Chinese and Japanese samples. These analyses included just one Korean sample, so only Chinese (n = 4) and Japanese (n = 2) pooled estimates and tests of influence were calculated. The pooled ORs in the Chinese sample were somewhat lower that those in the total sample; the Chinese sample pattern did diverge somewhat from the total sample and Japanese sample patterns in that the pooled ORs did not differ much across the *1/*2 versus *1/*1 and *2/*2 versus *1/*1 analyses (see 11th row of Table 26.5). The pooled ORs in the Japanese samples were lower than those reported for the total sample, but followed a similar pattern (see 12th row of Table 26.5). None of the Japanese ORs were significant, however, likely due to having only two studies in these analyses, and influence was found in the

TABLE 26.5

Odds Ratios (and Confidence Intervals) for Genotype Comparisons

Meta-analysis database ethnicity	Genotype comparison		
	*1/*2:*1/*1	*2/*2:*1/*1	*2/*2:*1/*2
ALDH2			
Total sample (n = 22)	0.22 (0.16, 0.30)[H]	0.12 (0.06, 0.24)[a]	0.49 (0.23, 1.05)[Ib]
Chinese (n = 14)	0.30 (0.24, 0.39)	0.17 (0.07, 0.41)[a]	0.54 (0.20, 1.49)[Ib]
Japanese (n = 4)	0.19 (0.09, 0.42)[H]	0.03 (0.01, 0.11)	0.13 (0.03, 0.57)[I]
Korean (n = 3)	0.13 (0.03, 0.52)[HI]	0.20 (0.03, 1.48)[I]	1.33 (0.27, 6.66)[I]
Covariates	Diagnosis	Recruitment, Japanese	Recruitment, Japanese
ADH1B–ALDH2*1/*1			
Total sample (n = 12)	0.26 (0.16, 0.44)[c]	0.20 (0.10, 0.39)[Hc]	0.81 (0.57, 1.16)[Ic]
Chinese (n = 9)	0.23 (0.15, 0.36)[c]	0.18 (0.09, 0.37)[c]	0.89 (0.58, 1.36)[Ic]
Japanese (n = 2)	0.18 (0.07, 0.52)[I]	0.10 (0.03, 0.27)	0.49 (0.20, 1.21)[I]
Covariates	Gender	Gender, recruitment	Recruitment
ADH1B–ALDH2*1/*2			
Total sample (n = 7)	0.17 (0.04, 0.68)[Id]	0.09 (0.03, 0.32)[d]	0.72 (0.43, 1.22)[Id]
Chinese (n = 4)	0.12 (0.03, 0.48)[Id]	0.12 (0.03, 0.48)[d]	0.88 (0.49, 1.58)[Id]
Japanese (n = 2)	0.07 (0.00, 3.00)[I]	0.03 (0.00, 1.31)[I]	0.39 (0.09, 1.65)[I]
Covariates	Recruitment	—	—

Note. H = heterogeneity; I = influence. Dashes indicate no covariates were significant.
[a]Five studies excluded from analysis. [b]Six studies excluded from analysis. [c]Two samples excluded from analysis. [d]One sample excluded from analysis.

*1/*2 versus *1/*1 analysis for the Chinese samples. In fact, all of the ethnic group analyses in the ADH1B–ALDH2*1/*2 samples should be viewed cautiously due to the low number of studies (n = 2–4).

There was no evidence of publication bias in any of the models. The 95% CIs of the regressions of z on POR encompassed the origin for each group of studies.

DISCUSSION

Magnitude of Effect Sizes

The first aim of this study was to provide estimates of the effect sizes of ALDH2 and ADH1B when controlling for ALDH2 from the body of literature published as of April 2005. The ALDH2 meta-analyses included 15 studies with 1,980 cases and 2,550 controls. The results suggest that possessing one ALDH2*2 allele reduces the risk for alcohol dependence to approximately one fourth and that possessing two ALDH2*2 alleles reduces the risk to approximately one ninth. The difference between possessing one and two ALDH2*2 alleles approached but did not reach statistical significance (p = .066). The lack of significance likely resulted from low power (β = 0.36) because of few individuals (approximately 5%) being ALDH2*2/*2 and only 3 of these individuals being alcohol dependent.

Stratifying individuals into ALDH2*1/*1 and ALDH2*1/*2 groups and then examining ADH1B revealed a protective effect of ADH1B*2 against alcohol dependence above and beyond that of ALDH2*2. The ADH1B–ALDH2*1/*1 meta-analyses included 12 studies with 685 cases and 890 controls. The ADH1B–ALDH2*1/*2 meta-analyses included seven studies with 105 cases and 521 controls. In ALDH2*1/*1 individuals, possession of one ADH1B*2 allele reduced the risk for alcohol dependence to approximately one fourth, and possession of two ADH1B*2 alleles reduced the risk to approximately one fifth. In ALDH2*1/*2 individuals, possession of one ADH1B*2 allele reduced the risk for alcohol dependence to approximately one sixth, and possession of two ADH1B*2 alleles reduced the risk to approximately one eleventh. The difference between the levels of protection of one and two ADH1B*2 alleles, however, was not statistically significant in either the ALDH2*1/*1 (p = .248) or ALDH2*1/*2 (p = .224) analyses. Fewer studies were used in both of the ADH1B analyses because only studies in which ALDH2–ADH1B haplotypes could be determined were included, but there is a high prevalence of the ADH1B*2 allele in Northeast Asians, with about 60% having one and about 30% having two ADH1B*2 alleles. Power was adequate for the ALDH2*1/*1 analyses (β = 0.65), but was low for the ALDH2*1/*2 analyses (β = 0.26). Thus, although the trends were similar across the *ALDH2*1/*1* and *ALDH2*1/*2* analyses and the effect sizes did not differ greatly between the *ADH1B*1/*2* and *ADH1B*2/*2* genotypes, power still remained an issue in these meta-analyses.

The present results for *ADH1B* are consistent with the findings of Whitfield's (2002) meta-analysis of *ADH1B* in some ways, but highlight important influences of methodological issues in determining the effect sizes of these genes. The protective effects of *ADH1B* reported by Whitfield for Han Chinese and Japanese are intermediate to the levels we found for *ADH1B* when stratifying for *ALDH2*. Whitfield reported that Europeans with one *ADH1B*2* allele were about one half as likely to be alcohol dependent as those without an *ADH1B*2* allele, but that Asians were about one fifth as likely to be alcohol dependent. The stronger effect sizes in Asians compared with Whites may be partially accounted for by Asians also possessing *ALDH2*2* alleles. This is supported by Whitfield's (1997) meta-analysis, in which he stratified for *ALDH2* in Asians and found that the effect size of one *ADH1B*2* allele was reduced to one third in *ALDH2*1/*1* individuals and to one fourth in *ALDH2*1/*2* individuals. In the present meta-analyses, the risk for alcohol dependence was also lower for *ADH1B*2* in *ALDH2*1/*2* individuals compared with *ALDH2*1/*1* individuals. The overlap of the CIs indicates that these differences were not significant, but a small interaction effect cannot be ruled out based on the present available data. Examining *ADH1B* in conjunction with *ALDH2* is an important component for the better understanding of genetic influences across ethnic groups.

Genetic Model of Influence

The second aim of this study was to examine models of influence for *ALDH2* and *ADH1B*. The trends of the *ALDH2* data are most supportive of a partial dominant model of the *ALDH2*2* allele, but do not rule out an additive or dominant model. There was a strong protective effect in individuals possessing one *ALDH2*2* allele relative to no *ALDH2*2* alleles and an additional, albeit nonsignificant, increase in protection in individuals possessing a second *ALDH2*2* allele. The increase in protection from fourfold with one *ALDH2*2* allele to ninefold with two *ALDH2*2* alleles suggests a linear trend in protection of *ALDH2*2*, which would be supportive of an additive genetic model of influence. The lack of a significant difference between possessing one and two *ALDH2*2* alleles, but with both having significant protective effects compared with *ALDH2*1/*1*, is more supportive of a dominant model. This lack of significance is likely due to the low power ($\beta = 0.36$) for *ALDH2*2/*2* analyses, and even with the low power, the difference between *ALDH2*2/*2* and *ALDH2*1/*2* protective effects approached significance. A partial dominant model falls between these models, with a difference between the protective effects of each genotype, but without requiring the protection of two *ALDH2*2* alleles to be twice the level of protection of one *ALDH2*2* allele. A partial dominant model is consistent with previous reports of enzyme production levels across the three *ALDH2* genotypes (Wang et al., 1996; Xiao et al., 1995, 1996), but dominant models have also been supported in enzyme analyses (Crabb et al., 1989; Peng et al., 1999; Singh et al., 1989). A partial dominant or additive model is also more consistent with clinical research on *ALDH2*1/*2* and *ALDH2*2/*2* showing heightened response to alcohol (Peng et al., 1999; Wall, Thomasson, Schuckit, & Ehlers, 1992) and lower rates of alcohol consumption (Higuchi et al., 1996; Muramatsu et al., 1995; Sun, Tsuritani, Honda, Ma, & Yamada, 1999; Sun, Tsuritani, & Yamada, 2002; Takeshita & Morimoto, 1999) in *ALDH2*2/*2* compared with *ALDH2*1/*2* individuals. Increased power with additional *ALDH2*2/*2* cases is, however, necessary to draw stronger conclusions.

The most appropriate genetic model of influence for the relationship between *ADH1B* and alcohol dependence appears to be a dominant or partial dominant model. There was a strong protective effect in *ALDH2*1/*1* individuals possessing one *ADH1B*2* allele relative to no *ADH1B*2* alleles and only a slight and nonsignificant increase in protection in *ALDH2*1/*1* individuals possessing a second *ADH1B*2* allele. This slight increase in protection from fourfold with one *ADH1B*2* allele to fivefold with two *ADH1B*2* alleles suggests that a dominant genetic model of influence may be most appropriate for the *ADH1B*2* allele, but because there is still some increase in protection, a partial dominant model might also be appropriate. The pattern of results for *ADH1B* in *ALDH2*1/*2* individuals was similar to that in *ALDH2*1/*1* individuals, with a strong protective effect found for one *ADH1B*2* allele and a nonsignificant increase in protection found for a second *ADH1B*2* allele. Results from clinical studies have been mixed for the effects of one versus two *ADH1B*2* alleles, with some reports suggesting that two *ADH1B*2* alleles may produce greater subjective and objective responses to alcohol (W. J. Chen, Chen, Yu, & Cheng, 1998; Cook et al., 2005), thus supporting a partial dominant model, but other reports finding that both one and two *ADH1B*2* alleles produce similar increases in skin reactions compared with *ADH1B*1/*1* (Takeshita, Yang, & Morimoto, 2001), thus supporting a dominant model.

Taken together, the findings of all three meta-analyses suggest that each gene produces unique protective effects. The protective effect of *ALDH2*2* and *ADH1B*2* in combination was greater than that of either *2 allele alone. One proposed mechanism of influence for both *ALDH2*2* and *ADH1B*2* is that the *2 alleles lead to increased levels of acetaldehyde, which in turn lead to lower rates of alcohol consumption and problems. Quertemont (2004) has further proposed that it is the balance between the unpleasant effects of acetaldehyde in the periphery and the positive effects of acetaldehyde in the brain that lead to the overall reinforcement value of alcohol. *ALDH2*2* and *ADH1B*2* alleles are thought to alter the balance between peripheral and brain acetaldehyde levels, resulting in a greater buildup of acetaldehyde in the periphery before it reaches the brain, thus reducing the overall reinforcing aspects of drinking. Future research should examine the effects of *ALDH2*2* and *ADH1B*2* in combination, as well as their possible interactions, in relation to both acetaldehyde levels and alcohol involvement.

An important caveat to these findings is that the cases and controls in these studies were not matched on drinking history. There is some evidence that *ALDH2*1/*2* individuals develop alcohol dependence at lower levels of alcohol intake compared with *ALDH2*1* homozygotes (Iwahashi, Matsuo, Suwaki, Nakamura, & Ichikawa, 1995) and that their clinical course of alcohol-related life events (e.g., habitual drinking, withdrawal) is delayed between 1 and 5 years (Murayama, Matsushita, Muramatsu, & Higuchi, 1998). Additionally, alcohol metabolism is altered by alcohol consumption, with enzyme induction possible from high rates of drinking as well as from chronic high rates of consumption (Nuutinen, Lindros, Hekali, & Salaspuro, 1985; Nuutinen, Lindros, & Salaspuro, 1983). Moreover, in the presence of alcohol dependence or at lower levels of alcohol intake, Asians with *ALDH2*2* or *ADH1B*2* alleles appear more vulnerable to certain alcohol-related pathologies such as liver disease, pancreatitis, and head and neck cancers, consistent with a role of acetaldehyde in the pathogenesis of organ damage (Day & Bassendine, 1992; Sorrell & Tuma, 1985). Thus, the genetic effects of *ALDH2*2* and *ADH1B*2* on alcohol dependence may change over the course of alcohol use, that is, *ALDH2*2* and *ADH1B*2* may be protective at one stage of alcohol use (e.g., the progression to heavy drinking), but become a risk factor at another stage (e.g., the progression to alcohol-related medical problems). Such effects could alter the relationship between the genetic polymorphisms and alcohol dependence and lead to different conclusions regarding the most appropriate models of protective influence. In this meta-analysis study, such long-term effects of alcohol use on metabolism rates cannot be determined.

These models have implications for how to most appropriately analyze *ALDH2* and *ADH1B* in clinical research. Previous studies have examined *ALDH2* and *ADH1B* genotypes as continuous or ordinal variables, or the genes have been dichotomized by grouping together **1/*2*s and **2/*2*s (e.g., Luczak, Wall, Shea, Byun, & Carr, 2001; Shea, Wall, Carr, & Li, 2001). The *ALDH2* meta-analyses suggest that *ALDH2* can be examined with genotype categorized as an ordinal variable, given the support for a **2* partial dominant model, and possibly as a continuous variable, given the support for an additive model. If genotypes are dichotomized then, based on the finding that *ALDH2*2* may be dominant or partially dominant, there is support for combining *ALDH2*1/*2*s with *ALDH2*2/*2*s, but not *ALDH2*1/*1*s with *ALDH2*1/*2*s. The implications are similar for *ADH1B*, except that the lack of support for an additive model suggests that if the genotype is examined as a three-level variable, it should be ordinal instead of continuous. The prevalence of *ADH1B*1/*1* is low in Asians, but combining *ADH1B*1/*1* with *ADH1B*1/*2* to increase power does not fit with the likely model of influence and could mask differences between the alleles.

Moderators of Effect Sizes

The third aim of this study was to examine potential moderators of the effect sizes, including sample characteristics (e.g., ethnicity, gender, and age of controls) and ascertainment procedures (e.g., diagnostic criteria and recruitment strategy). The meta-analyses demonstrated that several sample characteristics moderated the effect sizes of both genes, including recruitment strategy, Japanese ethnicity, gender, and diagnostic criteria. In Whitfield's (1997) original meta-analysis, he reported that *ADH1B*2* showed greater rates of protection from alcohol dependence in studies of Han Chinese and Japanese than in studies of Korean and non-Han Chinese. In Whitfield's meta-analysis and in the present meta-analyses, however, all of the Han Chinese and Japanese samples were treatment samples, whereas all of the Korean and non-Han Chinese samples were general samples recruited from the community. In the present meta-analyses, we determined that recruiting from treatment settings as well as being Japanese significantly related to a greater protective effect of *ALDH2*2*. Because of the overlap of these two variables, it cannot be determined whether the significance is due to ethnicity, recruitment strategy, or both. In the *ADH1B* meta-analyses, however, recruitment strategy continued to be a significant moderator, whereas Japanese ethnicity was not. It is plausible that recruiting more severe cases from treatment settings leads to greater differences between cases and controls. For example, in the nine studies examining treatment samples reviewed in these meta-analyses, only 1 of 1,327 alcohol-dependent cases (0.1%) was *ALDH2*2/*2* (Y.-C. Chen et al., 1999), but in the five studies using general population samples, 2 of the 535 cases (0.4%) were *ALDH2*2/*2* (Luczak et al., 2004). It is possible that the moderation of recruitment strategy may be masked by its overlap with ethnicity in the published studies.

Gender was also a significant moderator of the association of *ADH1B* with alcohol dependence. Samples with a greater proportion of male cases compared with male controls showed greater protection of *ADH1B*2*. As a whole, men drink greater amounts of alcohol compared with women, regardless of alcohol dependence status (Helzer & Canino, 1992; World Health Organization, 2004). The proposed mechanism for the effect of these genes on alcohol dependence is that possession of variant alleles results in increased levels of acetaldehyde when drinking, so individuals who have *ALDH2*2* or *ADH1B*2* alleles drink less and therefore are less likely to develop alcohol dependence. Thus, if women already drink less than men, the genes may have less of an impact on the development of alcohol dependence for women. Not knowing the distributions of the alleles by gender limited our ability to test for gender differences beyond as a covariate.

Finally, the diagnostic system was a significant moderator in the *ALDH2* meta-analyses. This covariate could not be tested in the *ADH1B* analyses because all studies for which we were able to obtain haplotypes used *DSM–III–R* criteria, with the exception of one sample that used *DSM–III* criteria. It appears that using a more stringent diagnosis of alcohol dependence based on *ICD–10* as opposed to *DSM–III–R* criteria results in greater discrepancies between cases and controls and thus reveals a greater protective effect of *ALDH2*2* with alcohol dependence. Although the diagnostic system could not be tested in the *ADH1B* analyses, linkage analyses of the Collaborative Study on the Genetics of Alcoholism found that regions of chromosome 4 including the ADH gene cluster had different associations with *DSM–IV* and *ICD–10* diagnoses of alcohol dependence (Williams et al., 1999). Thus, it appears that diagnostic systems have different associations with both candidate genes and gene regions.

Study Limitations

There are several limitations to this study. First, the *ALDH2*2/*2* genotype is rare, and the analyses contained only three cases, which resulted in low power to detect significant differences between groups. The difference between *ALDH2*2/*2* and *ALDH2*1/*1* individuals was significant, however, and the difference between *ALDH2*2/*2* and *ALDH2*1/*2* approached significance. Second, 10 of the 22 samples were eliminated from the *ADH1B* analyses because we could not stratify the *ADH1B* data by *ALDH2* genotype. Obtaining haplotypes from additional studies would have increased our power and generalizability. Third, several of the study samples were not in Hardy–Weinberg equilibrium. Disequilibrium in case samples supports evidence that the gene is related to alcohol dependence because the genotype frequencies observed differ from those expected by chance. However, disequilibrium in control samples suggests that the samples are not representative of the expected distribution of the genotypes and thus may distort findings. Of the three control samples that were not in Hardy–Weinberg equilibrium, two samples were small, and the disequilibrium was not highly significant; but in the data of C.-C. Chen et al. (1999) in the *ALDH2* meta-analyses, these differences were notable. Fourth, it is possible that other variables not tested in the present study may moderate the associations of *ADH1B* and *ALDH2* with alcohol dependence. For example, there may be differences in dependence severity required for admission to alcohol treatment across countries or locations that we were unable to detect or test. In addition, the tests of moderation we did conduct were limited by missing information in some of the studies (e.g., age of the control group). Also, in studies in which either cases or controls were of mixed gender but the other was all male, a gender ratio could not be calculated. Finally, as noted by Kidd et al. (2002), *ADH1B* haplotypes have not been fully evaluated, so the protection of these genes could actually be due to a difference in linkage disequilibrium at another site.

Conclusions and Directions for Future Research

Alcohol dependence is a complex disorder with many genetic and environmental factors that contribute to its development. In Asians, both *ALDH2*2* and *ADH1B*2* appear to protect individuals from alcohol dependence in an additive manner. Based on the results of our three meta-analyses, we conclude that a partial dominant, dominant, or additive model would be the most appropriate way to model the influence of *ALDH2* on alcohol dependence and that a dominant or partial dominant model would be the most appropriate way to model the influence of *ADH1B*. This study highlights the importance of methodological issues that need to be taken into consideration when examining the relationships between genes and phenotypes.

Future directions for research should emphasize examination of not just individual genes, but also gene–gene interactions and full haplotypes in relation to phenotypes. Haplotype analyses may help explain discrepancies in biological and clinical research, such as the finding that *ADH1B*2* has a protective effect against alcohol dependence but has not been associated with increased blood acetaldehyde concentrations. It is possible that another gene interacts with or is in linkage disequilibrium with *ADH1B* and that this gene is responsible for changes in acetaldehyde levels or some other alcohol metabolism process that results in protection from alcohol dependence. In a Korean study of 53 cases and 211 controls examining 36 sequence variants and 17 polymorphisms across the *ADH1B* and *ADH1C* gene regions, however, the results suggested that *ADH1B*2* was the locus most strongly associated with alcohol dependence (Choi et al., 2005). More complete haplotype analyses across the entire ADH cluster could reveal additional relationships.

Future research should also include longitudinal studies. Prospective studies will provide the most insight into the causal mechanism by which the *ALDH2* and *ADH1B* genes protect against alcohol dependence. Such studies will also allow for determination of how the effects of these genes may change over the course of lifetime alcohol use.

Finally, continued investigation of gene–environment interactions is needed. Higuchi et al. (1994) first identified a gene–environment interaction for *ALDH2*2*, and Whitfield (2002) was the first to test ethnicity as a moderator of the effects of *ADH1B*2*. The present study extends the examination of potential moderators of these two genes to include sample characteristics and ascertainment procedures of the published research. Obtaining better measures of these moderators, as well as examining other potential moderators, will continue to improve our knowledge of how environmental, genetic, and methodological factors influence our understanding of ALDH2, ADH1B, and other alcohol-related genes.

REFERENCES

American Psychiatric Association. (1980). *Diagnostic and statistical manual of mental disorders* (3rd ed.). Washington, DC: Author.

American Psychiatric Association. (1987). *Diagnostic and statistical manual of mental disorders* (3rd ed., rev.). Washington, DC: Author.

American Psychiatric Association. (1994). *Diagnostic and statistical manual of mental disorders* (4th ed.). Washington, DC: Author.

Assanangkornchai, S., Noi-pha, K., Saunders, J. B., & Ratanachaiyavong, S. (2003). Aldehyde dehydrogenase 2 genotypes, alcohol flushing symptoms and drinking patterns in Thai men. *Psychiatry Research, 118,* 9–17.

Bond, M. H., & Hwang, K.-K. (1986). The social psychology of Chinese people. In M. H. Bond (Ed.), *The psychology of Chinese people* (pp. 213–266). Hong Kong: Oxford University Press.

Brennan, P., Lewis, S., Hashibe, M., Bell, D. A., Boffetta, P., Bouchardy, C., et al. (2004). Pooled analysis of alcohol dehydrogenase genotypes and head and neck cancer: A HuGE review. *American Journal of Epidemiology, 159,* 1–16.

Bucholz, K. K., Helzer, J. E., Shayka, J. J., & Lewis, C. E. (1994). Comparison of alcohol dependence in subjects from clinical, community, and family studies. *Alcoholism: Clinical and Experimental Research, 18,* 1091–1099.

Chen, C.-C., Lu, R.-B., Chen, Y.-C., Wang, M.-F., Chang, Y.-C., Li, T.-K., et al. (1999). Interaction between the functional polymorphisms of the alcohol-metabolism genes in protection against alcoholism. *American Journal of Human Genetics, 65,* 795–807.

Chen, W. J., Chen, C.-C., Yu, J.-M., & Cheng, A. T. A. (1998). Self-reported flushing and genotypes of ALDH2, ADH2, and ADH3 among Taiwanese Han. *Alcoholism: Clinical and Experimental Research, 22,* 1048–1052.

Chen, W. J., Loh, E. W., Hsu, Y.-P. P., Chen, C.-C., Yu, J.-M., & Cheng, A. T. A. (1996). Alcohol-metabolizing genes and alcoholism among Taiwanese Han men: Independent effect of ADH2, ADH3, and ALDH2. *British Journal of Psychiatry, 168,* 762–767.

Chen, W. J., Loh, E. W., Hsu, Y.-P. P., & Cheng, A. T. A. (1997). Alcohol dehydrogenase and aldehyde dehydrogenase and alcoholism among Taiwanese aborigines. *Biological Psychiatry, 41,* 703–709.

Chen, Y.-C., Lu, R.-B., Peng, G.-S., Wang, M.-F., Wang, H.-K., Ko, H.-C., et al. (1999). Alcohol metabolism and cardiovascular response in an alcoholic patient homozygous for the ALDH2*2 variant gene allele. *Alcoholism: Clinical and Experimental Research, 23,* 1853–1860.

Cheng, T. K. (1980). *The world of the Chinese: The struggle for human unity.* Hong Kong: Chinese University Press.

Cho, Y. I., & Faulkner, W. R. (1993). Conceptions of alcoholism among Koreans and Americans. *International Journal of the Addictions, 28,* 681–694.

Choi, I.-G., Son, H.-G., Yang, B.-H., Kim, S. H., Lee, J.-S., Chai, Y.-G., et al. (2005). Scanning of genetics effects of alcohol metabolism gene (ADH1B and ADH1C) polymorphisms on the risk of alcoholism. *Human Mutation, 26,* 224–234.

Cook, T. A. R., Luczak, S. E., Shea, S. H., Ehlers, C. L., Carr, L. G., & Wall, T. L. (2005). Associations of ALDH2 and ADH1B genotypes with response to alcohol in Asian Americans. *Journal of Studies on Alcohol, 66,* 196–204.

Crabb, D. W., Edenberg, H. J., Bosron, W. F., & Li, T.-K. (1989). Genotypes for aldehyde dehydrogenase deficiency and alcohol sensitivity: The inactive ALDH2(2) allele is dominant. *Journal of Clinical Investigations, 83,* 314–316.

Crabb, D. W., Matsumoto, M., Chang, D., & You, M. (2004). Overview of the role of alcohol dehydrogenase and aldehyde dehydrogenase and their variants in the genesis of alcohol-related pathology. *Proceedings of the Nutrition Society, 63,* 49–63.

Day, C. P., & Bassendine, M. F. (1992). Genetic predisposition to alcoholic liver disease. *Gut, 33,* 1444–1447.

DerSimonian, R., & Laird, N. (1986). Meta-analysis in clinical trials. *Controlled Clinical Trials, 7,* 177–188.

Egger, M., Davey Smith, G., Schneider, M., & Minder, C. (1997). Bias in meta-analysis detected by a simple, graphical test. *British Medical Journal, 315,* 629–634.

Enomoto, N., Takase, S., Yasuhara, M., & Takada, A. (1991). Acetaldehyde metabolism in different aldehyde dehydrogenase-2 genotypes. *Alcoholism: Clinical and Experimental Research, 15,* 141–144.

Eriksson, C. J. P. (2001). The role of acetaldehyde in actions of alcohol (Update 2000). *Alcoholism: Clinical and Experimental Research, 25,* 15S–32S.

Ferencz-Biro, K., & Pietruszko, R. (1984). Human aldehyde dehydrogenase catalytic activity in Oriental liver. *Biochemical and Biophysical Research Communications, 118,* 97–102.

Goedde, H. W., Agarwal, D. P., Fritze, G., Meier-Tackmann, D., Singh, S., Beckmann, G., et al. (1992). Distribution of ADH2 and ALDH2 genotypes in different populations. *Human Genetics, 88,* 344–346.

Hasin, D. S., & Grant, B. F. (2004). The co-occurrence of DSM-IV alcohol abuse in DSM-IV dependence: Results of the National Epidemiology Survey on Alcohol and Related Conditions on heterogeneity that differ by population subgroup. *Archives of General Psychiatry, 61,* 891–896.

Helzer, J. E., Burnam, A., & McEvoy, L. T. (1991). Alcohol abuse and dependence. In L. N. Robins & D. Regier (Eds.), *Psychiatric Disorders in America: The Epidemiological Catchment Area Study* (pp. 81–115). New York: Free Press.

Helzer, J. E., & Canino, G. C. (1992). *Alcoholism in North America, Europe, and Asia.* New York: Oxford University Press.

Helzer, J. E., Canino, G. J., Yeh, E.-K., Bland, R. C., Lee, C. K., Hwu, H.-G., et al. (1990). Alcoholism—North America and Asia: A comparison of population surveys with the Diagnostic Interview Schedule. *Archives of General Psychiatry, 47*, 313–319.

Higuchi, S., Matsushita, S., Imazeki, H., Kinoshita, T., Takagi, S., & Kono, H. (1994). Aldehyde dehydrogenase genotypes in Japanese alcoholics. *The Lancet, 343*, 741–742.

Higuchi, S., Matsushita, S., Muramatsu, T., Murayama, M., & Hayashida, M. (1996). Alcohol and aldehyde dehydrogenase genotypes and drinking behavior in Japanese. *Alcoholism: Clinical and Experimental Research, 20*, 493–497.

Higuchi, S., Matsushita, S., Murayama, M., Takagi, S., & Hayashida, M. (1995). Alcohol and aldehyde dehydrogenase polymorphisms and the risk for alcoholism. *American Journal of Psychiatry, 152*, 1219–1221.

Ikawa, M., Impraim, C. C., Wang, G., & Yoshida, A. (1983). Isolation and characterization of aldehyde dehydrogenase isoenzymes from usual and atypical human livers. *Journal of Biological Chemistry, 258*, 6282–6287.

Iwahashi, K., Matsuo, Y., Suwaki, H., Nakamura, K., & Ichikawa, Y. (1995). CYP2E1 and ALDH2 genotypes and alcohol dependence in Japanese. *Alcoholism: Clinical and Experimental Research, 19*, 564–566.

Kidd, K. K., Osier, M. V., Pakstis, A. J., & Kidd, J. R. (2002). Reply to Whitfield. *American Journal of Human Genetics, 71*, 1250–1251.

Lee, H. C., Lee, H.-S., Jung, S.-H., Yi, S. Y., Jung, H. K., Yoon, J.-H., et al. (2001). Association between polymorphisms of ethanol-metabolizing enzymes and susceptibility to alcoholic cirrhosis in Korean male population. *Journal of Korean Medical Science, 16*, 745–750.

Lewis, S. J., & Smith, G. D. (2005). Alcohol, ALDH2, and esophageal cancer: A meta-analysis which illustrates the potentials and limitations of a Mendelian randomization approach. *Cancer Epidemiology, Biomarkers, and Prevention, 14*, 1967–1971.

Li, T.-K. (2000). Pharmacogenetics of responses to alcohol and genes that influence alcohol drinking. *Journal of Studies on Alcohol, 61*, 5–12.

Luczak, S. E., Elvine-Kreis, B., Shea, S. H., Carr, L. G., & Wall, T. L. (2002). Genetic risk for alcoholism relates to level of response to alcohol in Asian men and women. *Journal of Studies on Alcohol, 63*, 74–82.

Luczak, S. E., Wall, T. L., Cook, T. A. R., Shea, S. H., & Carr, L. G. (2004). ALDH2 status and conduct disorder mediate the relationship between ethnicity and alcohol dependence in Chinese-, Korean-, and White-American college students. *Journal of Abnormal Psychology, 113*, 271–278.

Luczak, S. E., Wall, T. L., Shea, S. H., Byun, S. M., & Carr, L. G. (2001). Binge drinking in Chinese, Korean, and White college students: Genetic and ethnic group differences. *Psychology of Addictive Behaviors, 15*, 306–309.

Maezawa, Y., Yamauchi, M., Toda, G., Suzuki, H., & Sakurai, S. (1995). Alcohol-metabolizing enzyme polymorphisms and alcoholism in Japan. *Alcoholism: Clinical and Experimental Research, 19*, 951–954.

Muramatsu, T., Wang, Z.-C., Fang, Y.-R., Hu, K.-B., Hequin, Y., Yamada, K., et al. (1995). Alcohol and aldehyde dehydrogenase genotypes and drinking behavior in Chinese living in Shanghai. *Human Genetics, 96*, 151–154.

Murayama, M., Matsushita, S., Muramatsu, T., & Higuchi, S. (1998). Clinical characteristics and disease course of alcoholics with inactive aldehyde dehydrogenase-2. *Alcoholism: Clinical and Experimental Research, 22*, 524–527.

Nakamura, K., Iwahashi, K., Matsuo, Y., Miyatake, R., Ichikawa, Y., & Suwaki, H. (1996). Characteristics of Japanese alcoholics with the atypical aldehyde dehydrogenase 2*2: A comparison of the genotypes of ALDH2, ADH2, ADH3, and cytochrome P-4502E1 between alcoholics and nonalcoholics. *Alcoholism: Clinical and Experimental Research, 20*, 52–55.

Nuutinen, H., Lindros, K., Hekali, P., & Salaspuro, M. (1985). Elevated blood acetate as indicator of fast ethanol elimination in chronic alcoholics. *Alcohol, 2*, 623–626.

Nuutinen, H., Lindros, K. O., & Salaspuro, M. (1983). Determinants of blood acetaldehyde level during ethanol oxidation in chronic alcoholics. *Alcoholism: Clinical and Experimental Research, 7*, 163–168.

Osier, M., Pakstis, A. J., Kidd, J. R., Lee, J.-F., Yin, S.-J., Ko, H.-C., et al. (1999). Linkage disequilibrium at the ADH2 and ADH3 loci and risk for alcoholism. *American Journal of Human Genetics, 64*, 1147–1157.

Park, J. Y., Danko, G. P., Wong, S. Y. C., Weatherspoon, A. J., & Johnson, R. C. (1998). Religious affiliation, religious involvement, and alcohol use in Korea. *Cultural Diversity and Mental Health, 4*, 291–296.

Park, S. C., Oh, S. I., & Lee, M. S. (1998). Korean status of alcoholics and alcohol-related health problems. *Alcoholism: Clinical and Experimental Research, 22*, 170S–172S.

Peng, G.-S., Wang, M.-F., Chen, C. Y., Luu, S.-Y., Chau, H.-C., Li, T.-K., et al. (1999). Involvement of acetaldehyde for full protection against alcoholism by homozygosity of the variant allele of mitochondrial aldehyde dehydrogenase gene in Asians. *Pharmacogenetics, 9*, 463–476.

Quertemont, E. (2004). Genetic polymorphism in ethanol metabolism: Acetaldehyde contribution to alcohol abuse and alcoholism. *Molecular Psychiatry, 9*, 570–581.

Schuckit, M. A., Anthenelli, R. M., Bucholz, K. K., Hesselbrock, V. M., & Tipp, J. E. (1995). The time course of development of alcohol-related problems in men and women. *Journal of Studies on Alcohol, 56*, 218–225.

Schuckit, M. A., Daeppen, J.-B., Tipp, J. E., Hesselbrock, M., & Bucholz, K. K. (1998). The clinical course of alcohol-related problems in alcohol dependent and nonalcohol dependent drinking men and women. *Journal of Studies on Alcohol, 59*, 581–590.

Schuckit, M. A., Hesselbrock, V., Tipp, J., Anthenelli, R., Bucholz, K. K., & Radziminski, S. (1994). A comparison of *DSM–III–R, DSM–IV* and *ICD–10* substance use disorders diagnoses in 1922 men and women subjects in the COGA study: Collaborative Study on the Genetics of Alcoholism. *Addiction, 89,* 1629–1638.

Shea, S. H., Wall, T. L., Carr, L. G., & Li, T.-K. (2001). ADH2 and alcohol-related phenotypes in Jewish American college students. *Behavior Genetics, 31,* 231–239.

Shen, Y.-C., Fan, J.-H., Edenberg, H. J., Li, T.-K., Cui, Y.-H., Wang, Y.-F., et al. (1997). Polymorphism of ADH and ALDH genes among four ethnic groups in China and effects upon the risk for alcoholism. *Alcoholism: Clinical and Experimental Research, 21,* 1272–1277.

Singh, S., Fritze, G., Fang, B., Harada, S., Paik, Y. K., Eckey, R., et al. (1989). Inheritance of mitochondrial aldehyde dehydrogenase: Genotyping in Chinese, Japanese and South Korean families reveals a dominance of the mutant allele. *Human Genetics, 83,* 118–121.

Sorrell, M. F., & Tuma, D. J. (1985). Hypothesis: Alcoholic liver injury and the covalent binding of acetaldehyde. *Alcoholism: Clinical and Experimental Research, 9,* 306–309.

StataCorp LC. (2005). Stata (Version 8.0) [Computer software]. College Station, TX: Author.

Sun, F., Tsuritani, I., Honda, R., Ma, Z.-M., & Yamada, Y. (1999). Association of genetic polymorphisms of alcohol metabolizing enzymes with excessive alcohol consumption in Japanese men. *Human Genetics, 105,* 295–300.

Sun, F., Tsuritani, I., & Yamada, Y. (2002). Contribution of genetic polymorphisms in ethanol-metabolizing enzymes to problem drinking in middle-aged Japanese men. *Behavior Genetics, 32,* 229–236.

Takeshita, T., & Morimoto, K. (1999). Self-reported alcohol-associated symptoms and drinking behavior in three ALDH2 genotypes among Japanese university students. *Alcoholism: Clinical and Experimental Research, 23,* 1065–1069.

Takeshita, T., Morimoto, K., Mao, X. Q., Hashimoto, T., & Furuyama, J. (1994). Characterization of the three genotypes of low Km aldehyde dehydrogenase in a Japanese population. *Human Genetics, 94,* 217–223.

Takeshita, T., Yang, X., & Morimoto, K. (2001). Association of the ADH2 genotypes with skin responses after ethanol exposure in Japanese male university students. *Alcoholism: Clinical and Experimental Research, 25,* 1264–1269.

Tanaka, F., Shiratori, Y., Yokosuka, O., Imazeki, F., Tsukada, Y., & Omata, M. (1996). High incidence of ADH2*1/ALDH2*1 genes among Japanese dependents and patients with alcoholic liver disease. *Hepatology, 23,* 234–239.

Thomasson, H. R., Crabb, D. W., Edenberg, H. J., Li, T.-K., Hwu, H.-G., Chen, C.-C., et al. (1994). Low frequency of the ADH2*2 allele among Atayal natives of Taiwan with alcohol use disorders. *Alcoholism: Clinical and Experimental Research, 18,* 640–643.

Thomasson, H. R., Edenberg, H. J., Crabb, D. W., Mai, X.-L., Jerome, R. E., Li, T.-K., et al. (1991). Alcohol and aldehyde dehydrogenase genotypes and alcoholism in Chinese men. *American Journal of Human Genetics, 48*, 667–681.

U.S. Department of Health and Human Services. (1998). *Drinking in the United States: Main findings from the 1992 National Longitudinal Alcohol Epidemiological Survey (NLAES)* (DHSS Publication No. 99– 3519). Rockville, MD: Secretary of Health and Human Services.

van den Bree, M. B., Johnson, E. O., Neale, M. C., Svikis, D. S., McGue, M., & Pickens, R. W. (1998). Genetic analysis of diagnostic systems of alcoholism in males. *Biological Psychiatry, 43*, 139–145.

Wall, T. L., Shea, S. H., Luczak, S. E., Cook, T. A. R., & Carr, L. G. (2005). Genetic associations of alcohol dehydrogenase with alcohol use disorders and endophenotypes in White college students. *Journal of Abnormal Psychology, 114*, 456–465.

Wall, T. L., Thomasson, H. R., Schuckit, M. A., & Ehlers, C. L. (1992). Subjective feelings of alcohol intoxication in Asians with genetic variations of ALDH2 alleles. *Alcoholism: Clinical and Experimental Research, 16*, 991–995.

Wang, X., Sheikh, S., Saigal, D., Robinson, L., & Weiner, H. (1996). Heterotetramers of human liver mitochondrial (class 2) aldehyde dehydrogenase expressed in Escherichia coli: A model to study the heterotetramers expected to be found in Oriental people. *Journal of Biological Chemistry, 271*, 31172–31178.

Whitfield, J. B. (1997). Meta-analysis of the effects of alcohol dehydrogenase genotype on alcohol dependence. *Alcohol and Alcoholism, 32*, 613–619.

Whitfield, J. B. (2002). Alcohol dehydrogenase and alcohol dependence: Variation in genotype-associated risk between populations. *American Journal of Human Genetics, 71*, 1247–1250.

Williams, J. T., Begleiter, H., Porjesz, B., Edenberg, H. J., Foroud, T., Reich, T., et al. (1999). Joint multiple linkage analysis of multivariate qualitative and quantitative traits: II. Alcoholism and event-related potentials. *American Journal of Human Genetics, 65*, 1148–1160.

Woolf, B. (1955). On estimating the relation between blood group and disease. *Annals of Eugenics, 19*, 251–253.

World Health Organization. (1993). *International classification of disease and related health problems* (10th ed.). Geneva, Switzerland: Author.

World Health Organization. (2004). *Global status report on alcohol*. Geneva, Switzerland: Department of Mental Health and Substance Abuse. Retrieved March 22, 2005, from http://www.who.int/substance_abuse/ publications/alcohol/en/

Xiao, Q., Weiner, H., & Crabb, D. W. (1996). The mutation in the mitochondrial aldehyde dehydrogenase (ALDH2) gene responsible for alcohol-induced flushing increases turnover of the enzyme tetramers in a dominant fashion. *Journal of Clinical Investigation, 9*, 2027–2032.

Xiao, Q., Weiner, H., Johnston, T., & Crabb, D. W. (1995). The aldehyde dehydrogenase ALDH2*2 allele exhibits dominance over ALDH2*1 in transduced HeLa cells. *Journal of Clinical Investigation, 96*, 2180– 2186.

Yin, S.-J., & Agarwal, D. P. (2001). Functional polymorphism of alcohol and alde-hyde dehydrogenase: Alcohol metabolism, alcoholism, and alcohol-induced organ damage. In P. Agarwal & H. K. Seitz (Eds.), *Alcohol in Health and Disease* (pp. 1–26). New York: Marcel Dekker.

Yu, E. S. H., Liu, W. T., Xia, Z. X., & Zhang, M. (1989). Alcohol use, abuse, and alcoholism among Chinese Americans: A review of the epidemiologic data. In D. Spiegler, D. Tate, S. Aiken, & C. Christian (Eds.), *Alcohol Use Among U.S. Ethnic Minorities* (National Institute of Alcohol Abuse and Alcoholism Research Monograph 18, DHHS Publication No. ADM 89–1435, pp. 329–341). Rockville, MD: National Institute of Alcohol Abuse and Alcoholism.

AUTHOR INDEX

Page numbers in italics refer to listings in the references.

Aasland, O. G., 327, *340*

Abab, T., 607, *614*

Abbott, R. D., 159–161, 163, *182–185,* 261, *283,* 316, *613*

Abeliovich, A., *31*

Abrams, D. B., 38, *50, 53,* 253, 371, 390, *393,* 396, 409, 417, *420, 424–426,* 438, *455, 456,* 461, *462,* 472, 473, *485, 495, 511, 516, 534, 535*

Achenbach, T. M., 60, 61, *82,* 167, *181,* 300n4, 312, *314*

Acierno, R., 635, *652*

Adams, E. K., 479, *485*

Adams, K. M., 345, *362*

Adams, M. E., *495*

Adams, R. A., 497, *513*

Adamse, M., 344, *364*

Addiction Centre Adolescent Research Group, Foothills Medical Centre, 627, *655*

Addis, M. E., 551, *552*

Affleck, G., 412, *427*

Agarwal, D. P., 685, 696, 697, *707, 712*

Ageton, S., 199, *221*

Agrawal, S., 41, *49*

Ahadi, S. A., 287, 290, 300, *318*

Ahern, D. K., 372, *394*

Ahmad, S., *653*

Ahonen, T., 501, *512*

Aiken, L. S., 215, 216, *219,* 271, 275, 282, 292, *314*

Ainette, M. G., 260, *286*

Akaike, H., 74n1, *82,* 97, *111,* 238, 239n, *251*

Albaugh, B., 587, *610*

Albaugh, P., 587, *610*

Albert, P. S., 379, *399*

Aldridge, J., 130, *134*

Alesci, N. L., *494*

Alessi, S. M., 559, *570*

Alkon, A., 289n1, *319*

Allain, A. N., 345, *365*

Allen, B. A., 324, 327, *340*

Allen, D. N., 497, *510*

Allen, J. A., 46, *47*

Allen, J. P., 324, *339,* 406, *424,* 602, *555,* 616, 657, *674*

Allerton, M., *339*

Allison, P. D., 501, *510*

Allison, W. M., 344, *361*

Allsop, S., 407, *419*

Almond, J., *485*

Alpert, A., 301, *316*

Alterman, A. I., 27, *32, 51,* 311n9, *319,* 413, *424, 556,* 559, 569, *570*

Altman, J., 411, *426*

Amado, H., 66, *88*

American Psychiatric Association, 21, *31, 44, 47,* 66, *82,* 93, *111,* 243, *251,* 264, *282,* 346, *361,* 369, *388, 393,* 430, 433, 435, 436, *455, 499, 510,* 518, *533,* 547, *552,* 564, 569, *582,* 610, 663, *674,* 681, 682, *706*

American Psychological Association, 643, 647, 648, *652*

American Psychological Association Division 12 Task Force on Promotion and Dissemination of Psychological Procedures, 623–624, 648, *652*

Amini, F., 628, 635, 637–639, 641, *652*

Ananda, R., 368, *397*

Anda, R. F., 368, 386n8, *393*
Anderson, A. E., 368, *394*
Anderson, H., 516, *534*
Anderson, J. E., *494*
Anderson, K. G., 418, *424*
Anderson, P., 34, *47*
Anderson, S. W., 503, *510*
Andrassy, J., 540, *556*
Andreason, N., 268, *283*
Andreski, P., 368, *393*
Andrews, D. M., 201, *221*
Andrews, D. W., 204, *223*
Andrews, G., 97, *115*
Andrews, J. A., 467, *493*
Andrews, N., 501, *511*
Anglin, D., 539, *554*
Anglin, M. D., 543, 544, 547, *552, 554*
Angold, A., 93, *112*, 582, *612*
Aniskiewicz, R., 194, *196*
Annis, H. M., 42, *47*, 407, *419*, 589, *610*
Anthenelli, R. M., 476, *485*, 682, *709, 710*
Anthony, J. C., 202, *219*, 430, *455*
Applegate, B., *85*
Arana, G., 34, *48*
Arbuckle, J. L., 210, *220*
Armeli, S., 412, *427*
Armenian, H. K., 543, *552*
Armitage, S. G., 348, *361*
Armor, D. J., 543, *552*
Armstrong, S., 411, *422*
Arnett, P. J., 89, *112*
Arnoutovic, A., 368, *394*
Aroian, L. A., 270n4, *285*
Arthur, G. A., 348, *361*
Asarnow, J. R., *182*
Asparouhov, T., 167, *184*
Assaf, A. R., 464, *486*
Assanangkornchai, S., 678, 687, 690, *706*
Athanasou, J. A., 368, *395*
Atkinson, J. H., Jr., 34, *47*
Audrain, J., *491*
Auerbach, A., 42, *51*
Austin, D. F., *252*
Austin, M., 559, *570*
Austin, S. B., 230, 250, *256*
Austin, W. D., 464, *494*

Aveyard, P., 473, *485*
Axelrod, S. R., *87*
Ayers, C. D., 159, *185*
Azjen, I., 595, *612*
Azrin, N. H., 550, *552*, 627, 635, 638, 645, *652*

Babor, R. F., 547, *555*
Babor, T. F., 34, *50, 54*, 66, *87*, 93, *115*, 324, 325, 327, 339, 340, 453, 456
Bachman, J. G., 90, 110, *112, 115*, 118, *133*, 162, 166, *182, 184*, 195, *195*, 200, 201, *223*, 225, 226, 228, 231, 232, 233n4, 248, 249, *251–255*, 296, *316*, 324, *339*, 583, *614*, 620, 657, 661, 674, *675*
Bachmann, M., *486*
Badger, G. J., *50*
Baer, J. S., 38, *51*, 90, *112, 115*, 148, *157*, 254, 325, 328, *339–341*, 387, *393*, 407, 418, *419, 421*, 438, *455*, 600, 603, 606, *610*, *612, 615*
Baggott, M., 118, 130, *132*
Bailey, S. L., 187, *196*
Bailey, W. J., 227, *255, 488*
Baird, S., *363*
Baker, E., 483, *485*
Baker, J. R., 262, *282*
Baker, S., 39, *53*, 499, *512*
Baker, T. B., 370, 371, 388, 390, *393*, 410–412, 414, *419, 423, 425*, 472, 478, *487, 488, 490, 492*, *494, 496*
Balabanis, M. H., *15*, 368, 370, 371, 389, 398, *426*, 496, 532, *534*
Balanda, K., *252*
Baldwin, J. A., 585, *618*
Balfour, D. J. K., 369, *393*
Bandura, A., 160, *181*, 404, 407, *419*, 594, *610*
Bangert-Drowns, R. L., 595, *610*
Baptista, M. A. S., 409, *426*
Barckley, M. F., 467, *493*
Bardone, A. M., 249, *251*
Barendregt, J. J., 479, *485*
Barker, B., 117, *133*

Barlow, D. H., 372, *393*
Barnett, N. P., *487*
Barnhart, R., 430, *456*
Baron, R. M., 270, *282*
Barr, M., 551, *553*
Barrera, M., Jr., 230, *253*, 263, 264, *282*,
    283, 288, 295, *314*, *315*
Barrett, K., *654*
Barrett, M. E., 588, *610*
Barrett, S. P., 117, *133*
Barron, A., 288, *315*
Barrowclough, C., 548, *552*
Barry, K. L., 418, *421*, *554*
Barth, R. P., *619*
Bartholow, B. D., 91, *116*
Barton, S., 413, *419*
Bartosch, W. J., 478, *487*
Basian, E., 324, *341*
Bassendine, M. F., 702, *707*
Bates, C., *486*
Bates, J. E., 287–290, 292, 310, 312,
    315, *318*
Bates, M. E., 226, *251*, 344, 346, 359,
    361, 497, 498, 502, 508, *510*
Bates, S. C., 589, *610*
Battig, K., 370, 371, *396*
Battin-Pearson, S., 161, *183*
Bauer, D. J., 174, *182*, 251, *251*
Bauer, L. O., 109, *112*, 417, *419*
Bauer, R. R., 483, *488*
Bauer, U. E., *485*
Baum, A., 369, *394*
Bauman, K. E., 200, *221*
Baumeister, R. F., 43, *47*, 387, *396*, 411,
    419, 517, 531, 532, *535*
Baxter, L. R., 27, *31*
Bayer, R., 152, *156*
Beals, J., 575, 576, 584, *612*, *614*, *617*
Beamesderfer, A., 349, *361*
Beattie, M. C., 41, *47*, 345, *363*, 412,
    419, 498, *511*
Beauvais, F., 200, 217, *223*, 296, *317*,
    575, 576, 579–589, 591, 592,
    610, *611*, *617*
Bech, K., 264, *282*
Beck, A. T., 349, *361*, 436, 442, 448,
    455, 500, *510*

Beck, J., 129, *132*
Beck, S. J., 372, *393*
Becker, B., 263, 280, 284, 288, *317*
Beckmann, G., *707*
Beede, S., *490*
Begleiter, H., 20, *31*, 95, *112*, *711*
Behm, F. M., 477, *493*
Belcher, M., 495, 531, *536*
Belding, M. A., 559, *570*
Bell, D. A., *706*
Bell, R. M., 160, *183*
Bell-Bolek, C., 587, *620*
Bellido, C., 640, *652*
Bellino, L., 540, *558*
Benally, C. C., 585, *618*
Bencivengo, M., *556*
Benefield, R. G., 41, *51*
Bennett, M. E., 37, *52*, 226, *251*
Bennetto, A., 147, *155*
Benowitz, N. L., 389, *395*, 477, *485*
Benson, D. F., 503, *513*
Bentler, P. M., 34, *53*, 169, *181*, 199,
    223, 262, *285*, 297, 297n3, 313,
    315, *317*, 351, *361*, *363*, 503,
    511, 585, *611*
Benton, A. L., 348, *361*
Benyamina, A., 533, *535*
Bergeisen, L., 584, *611*
Bergeron, J., 539, *552*
Bergman, H., 344, *361*
Bergman, K. S., *31*
Berlin, I., 476, *485*
Bernal, G., 624, 638–640, 643, 646,
    649, 651, *652*
Bernard, B. A., 350, *365*
Bernier, H., *317*
Berns, S. B., 505, *511*
Berridge, K. C., 369, 370, 388, *397*
Berry, C., *491*
Berwick, D. M., 545, *552*
Besalel, V. A., 635, *652*
Bhatta, K., 118, *134*
Bickel, W. K., *50*
Bien, T. H., 40, 41, *47*, *52*, 227, *251*
Biener, L., 461, 462, *485*
Biernacki, P., 538, *552*
Bierut, L. J., 84, *113*

Bigelow, G. E., 370, *394*, 559, 568, 569, *571*

Biglan, A., *221*

Bigler, E. D., 343, 344, 358, *363*

Bihari, B., 95, *112*

Billings, A. G., 34, 36, *47*

Binkoff, J. A., *396*, *424*

Bisighini, R. M., 411, *420*

Bjornson, W., 469, *494*

Blackson, T. C., 300, *315*

Blaine, J., 563n1, *569*, *570*

Blair, J. R., 350, *361*

Blalock, J. A., *420*

Bland, R. C., *708*

Blangero, J., *31*

Blanton, H., 313, *315*

Blaser, B., 551, *553*

Blitz, C., 642, *653*

Block, J. H., 188, *196*, 199, *220*

Blondal, T., 476, *485*

Bloom, B. L., 265, 267, *282*

Bloom, F. E., 91, 109, *115*

Bloom, J., 585, *615*

Blot, W. J., 227, *252*

Blow, F. C., 260, *283*, *286*

Blower, S. M., 145, *155*

Blum, R. W., 575, 584, *611*

Blume, A. W., 603, *610*, *613*, *615*, *616*

Boardman, C. R., *569*

Bobo, J. K., 515, *533*, 600, *611*, *619*

Bock, G. R., 60, *83*

Boerstler, H., *558*

Boffetta, P., *706*

Bohandana, A., 476, *485*

Bohman, M., 23, *31*, 60, 64, *83*

Bohn, M. J., 417, *425*, 530, *534*

Boisvert, J. M., 407, *427*

Boker, S. M., 416, *419*

Boles, S. M., 462, 473, *488*, *491*

Bolger, N., 270, *285*

Bolles, R., 410, *419*

Bonabeau, E., *420*

Bond, G. R., 548, *553*

Bond, M. H., 681, *706*

Bondurant, S., 480, *494*

Bonillo, J., 640, *652*

Bonneux, L., 479, *485*

Bonollo, D. S., *492*

Boomsma, D. I., 109, *116*

Booth, M. W., 543, *552*

BootsMiller, B., *554*

Bor, D. H., *491*

Borden, P., 659, *674*

Borduin, C. M., *653*

Borg, S., 344, *361*

Boroughs, J. M., 41, *47*

Borrelli, B., *491*

Bosron, W. F., 679, *707*

Bott, M., 526, *535*

Botvin, E. M., 483, *485*

Botvin, G. J., 160, *181*, *183*, 219, 220, 483, *485*, *618*

Bouchard, T. J., Jr., *84*

Bouchardy, C., *706*

Boutin, P., *317*

Boutsen, M., 476, *490*

Bovasso, G. B., 543, *552*

Bowers, B. J., 22, *31*

Bowers, C. A., 405, *422*

Bowman, E. D., *491*

Box, G. E. P., *339*

Boyce, W. T., 289n1, *319*

Boyd, C. J., 119, *132*

Boyd, G., *396*

Boyd, J. W., *491*

Boyle, R. G., *494*

Boys, A., *133*

Brady, K., 34, *48*

Braithwaite, J., 144, *155*

Brandon, T. H., 408, *423*

Brave Heart, M. Y., 587, *611*

Brekke, M. J., *490*

Brekke, M. L., *490*

Brenna, D. C., 659, *674*

Brennan, P., 683, 685, *706*

Brent, E. E., 250n12, *255*, 260, *285*

Breslau, N., 121, *132*, 227, *252*, 368, 386n8, *393*, *487*

Brettle, R. P., 40, *48*

Breus, M., 370, *397*

Brewer, R. D., *115*

Brickman, A. L., *655*

Bricolo, R., 130, *134*

Bright, J., *423*

Brill, P., 456, *555*
Brischetto, C. S., 371, *393*
Britt, D. M., 417, *425*
Britton, J., 476, *486*
Brochu, S., 539, *552*
Broderick, J. E., 373, *399, 536*
Brody, C. L., *493*
Brody, G. H., 288, 310, 311, *315, 320*
Brody, J. L., 635, *655*
Broge, M., *492*
Brondino, M. J., 638, *653*
Bronfenbrenner, U., 218, *220*
Bronstone, A., *339*
Brook, D. W., 219, *220*
Brook, J. S., 219, *220*, 660, *674*
Brooks, R. G., 483, *485*
Brooner, R. K., 560, *570*
Brown, B. S., 539, *558*
Brown, C. H., 199, *222, 254*
Brown, J. M., 37, 41, *48, 52*, 324, *339*,
    368, *395*, 411, *419*
Brown, L., 359, *362*, 498, *510*
Brown, R., 545, *558*
Brown, R. A., *420*
Brown, S., *363, 513*
Brown, S. A., 33, 36–39, 43, 45, *48, 53*,
    233, *252*, 408, 412, 418, *419*,
    420, 424
Browne, M. W., 70, *83*, 169, *182*, 351,
    361
Browne, N., 410, *421*
Brownell, K. D., 403, 413, 416, *419, 420*
Browning-Ferrando, M., *55*
Bruce, T. J., 405, *420*
Bruneau, J., 139n1, *155*
Bryant, A. L., *112*, 166, *182*, 249, *252*
Bryk, A. S., 96, *112*, 169, *185*
Buchanan, T., 324, *339*
Bucholz, K. K., 41, *48, 84, 87, 113*,
    116, 244, *254, 284*, 682, 683,
    706, 709, 710
Buckhalt, J. A., 261, 263, 279, 281, *283*
Budney, A. J., *50*, 430, 431, 438, 452,
    453, *455*
Buhringer, G., 418, *420*
Buist, A. S., 469, *494*
Buka, S. L., 657, *675*

Buksten, O. G., 37, *50*
Bulger, D., 473, *485*
Bullock, B. M., 219, *220*
Burch, J. B., 370, 371, *393*
Bureau of Indian Affairs, 577, *611*
Burge, J., 227, *251*
Burgess, E. S., 412, 415, *420*
Burke, E. L., 635, *652*
Burleson, J. A., 627, 641, 642, *653, 654*
Burling, A. S., 515, *533*
Burling, T. A., 407, *420*, 515, *533*
Burnam, A., 541, *557*, 682, *707*
Burns, D. M., 480, *486*
Burns, K. M., 608, *612*
Burns, S., 465, 467, *486*
Burns, T., 109, *115*
Burrows, S., *489*
Burt, S. A., 77, 80, *83*, 96, 111, *112, 116*,
    260, *286*
Burton, S. L., 474, *494*
Buss, A., 290, *315*
Butcher, J. N., 641, 647, 650, *652*
Butler, C. C., 471, *486, 493*
Butters, N., *363, 513*
Butz, M. R., 413n1, *420*
Buyske, S., 227, *256*
Buzzi, R., 370, *396*
Byun, S. M., 702, *708*

Cacciola, J. S., *569*
Cadoret, R. J., 60, *83*, 109, *112*
Caggiula, A. R., 481, *492*
Cahalan, D., 34, *48*
Caldarone, B. J., 477, *493*
Califano, J. A., 89, *113*
Camazine, S., 413n1, *420*
Campbell, D. T., 217, *220*
Campbell, R. T., 226, *252*
Cancilla, A., 324, *340*
Canino, G. C., 681, 703, *708*
Capaldi, D. M., 200, 201, 203, 206, 215,
    220
Caplan, G., 590, *611*
Caporaso, N. E., *491*
Carbonari, J. P., 407, *421*, 435, *456*
Cardon, L. R., 68, *86*
Carey, G., 60, 79, *83, 86*

Carlin, A. S., *362*

Carloni, J. A., *55*

Carlson, C. L., *494*

Carlson, S. R., 61, *84*, 91, 93, *113, 284*

Carlton, R. A., *464, 486*

Carman, J. M., *558*

Carmelli, D., 481, *486, 487*

Carmody, T. P., 371, *393*

Carney, M. A., *412, 427*

Caron, C., *317*

Carpenter, R. A., 595, 596, *611*

Carr, L. G., 678, 679, 681, 702, *707, 708, 710, 711*

Carroll, K., 39, *50, 53, 455,* 499, *511, 512*

Carroll, K. M., 405, 406, 411, *420, 456, 570*

Carter, B., 409, *427*

Carter, B. L., 371, *393,* 409, *420*

Carter-Saltzman, L., 97, *115*

Caruso, J. C., 416, 417, *422, 427*

Caspers, K., *112*

Caspi, A., 59, 63, 64, 79, 83, 85, 96, *112,* 251, *285,* 287, 288, *311n9, 315, 316*

Casswell, S., 118, *134*

Castillo, S., 89, 91, *116*

Castro, F. G., 313, *315*

Castro, R. J., 118, *134*

Castro, S., 34, *48*

Catalano, R. F., 159–161, 163, *182–185,* 200, *222,* 259, 261, *283,* 291, *316,* 406, *422,* 588, *613*

Cattarello, A. M., 187, 194, *195*

Caudill, B. D., 36, *48*

Caulkins, J., 142, *156*

C'de Baca, J., 43, 45, *52*

Center for Substance Abuse Treatment, 639, *653,* 657, 673, *674*

Centers for Disease Control and Prevention, 34, 46, *49,* 460, 461, 467, 483, *486,* 624, 635, 637, *653*

Cestaro, V., *365*

Chai, Y.-G., *707*

Chait, L. D., 371, *393*

Chamberlain, L. L., *413n1, 420*

Chambless, D. L., 550, *552,* 624, 637, 639, 645–647, 650, 651, *653*

Champagne, S. E., 367, *394*

Champion, L., 291, *318*

Chan, D., 42, *47*

Chang, D., 685, *707*

Chang, E., 539, *557*

Chang, G., *31, 38, 54*

Chang, S. Y., 627, *655*

Chang, Y.-C., *706*

Channer, K., *486*

Chaplin, W. F., 311, *315*

Chapman, P. L. H., 41, *49*

Charuvastra, V. C., *396*

Chassin, L., 90, 91, *112, 113,* 160, 180, *182, 184,* 200, 220, 226, *252,* 259–264, 267, 268n2, 268n5, 274, 279, 280, 282–284, 291, 295, *314, 315*

Chassin, L. A., 288, 313, *315*

Chastain, C., *615*

Chau, H.-C., *709*

Chavez, E., 584, *611*

Chen, A., 587, *621*

Chen, C.-C., 677, 678, 685, 687, 689, 690, 694, 696, 701, 704, *706, 710*

Chen, C. Y., *709*

Chen, K., 34, *49,* 210, *222, 225, 252,* 581, *614*

Chen, P., 227, *256*

Chen, W. J., 678, 685, 687, 690, 694, 696, 697, 701, *706*

Chen, Y.-C., 677, 678, 685, 687, 691, 694, 697, 703, *706*

Cheng, A. T. A., 678, 701, *706*

Cheng, K. K., *485*

Cheng, L. S., 481, *487*

Cheng, T. K., 681, *707*

Cherniss, C., 545, *553*

Chesney, M. A., 289n1, *319*

Ch'ien, J. M. N., 38, *56*

Chien, S., 132, *134*

Chilcoat, H. D., 121, *132*

Childress, A. R., 409, *426*

Chin Sue, C., 659, *674*

Chiocchio, F., 539, *552*

Chirinko, R. S., 145, *155*

Cho, Y. I., 681, *707*

Choi, I.-G., 705, *707*

Chou, C., 544, *554*

Chow, T. W., 357, *362*

Christiansen, B. A., 233, *252*, 408, *419*

Christiansen, K., 433, *457*

Christie, R., 152, *155*

Chromy, J., 121, *132*

Chung, N. K., 200, *221*

Chung, T., 410, *420*

Chutuape, M. A., 568, 569

Cicchetti, D. V., 226, *252*, 263, 280, 284, 288, *317*, 331, *339*

Cinciripini, P. M., 415, *420*

Civita, M., 412, *421*

Clapp, J. D., 91, *112*, *114*, 627, 637, 651, *654*

Clare, G., 371, *395*

Clark, G. L., 146, *157*

Clark, L. A., 59, 62–64, 78, *83*, 86, 88, 227, 244, *256*

Clay, D. L., 624, 637, 639, 641, *653*

Clayton, A. C., 464, *494*

Clayton, P. J., 86

Clayton, R. R., 187, 188, 190, 193, 194, *195*, 483, *487*

Cleary, P. D., 369, *395*

Cleary, S. D., 288, 290, 297, 301, 311, 314, *319*, *320*

Cloninger, C. R., 23, *31*, 60, 63, *83*

Coakley, E., 466, *495*

Coatsworth, J. D., *654*

Cockerham, W. C., 583, *611*

Cohen, D., *486*

Cohen, J., 443, *455*, 626, *653*, 664, *674*

Cohen, L. M., 408, 412, *420*

Cohen, P., 660, *674*

Cohen, S. J., 386n8, *393*, 465, 466, *486*, 488, *491*

Coie, J. D., 159, *182*

Colby, S. M., 38, *53*, 253, 418, *424*, 471, *487*, 516, *534–536*, 606, *617*

Colder, C. R., 180, *182*, 226, 230, 234, 238, *252*, 260, *282*

Cole, K. C., 589, 596, *619*

Coleman, H. L. K., *614*

Colletti, G., 368, *397*

Colligan, R. C., *494*

Collins, A. C., 31, 371, 391, *393*

Collins, F. L., 372, *394*

Collins, L. M., 200, *221*

Collins, R. L., 328, *339*, 411, *425*, 517, 535

Colliver, J. D., 582, *620*, 657, *675*

Colon, H. M., 638, *653*

Columbus, M., 46, *47*

Comer, S. D., 430, *455*

COMMIT Research Group, 463, *487*

Committee on Substance Abuse, 430, 455

Compton, W. M., 579, *613*

Conduct Problems Prevention Research Group, 160, *182*

Cone, E. J., *570*

Conger, K. J., 313, *315*

Conger, R. D., 310, *315*

Conn, S. A., *490*

Connell, C. M., 579, *615*

Connor, W., 371, *393*

Connors, G. J., 36, *49*, 407, 408, *421*, *424*, 542, 548, 549, *553*, *555*, *558*

Conrad, K. J., 546, *553*

Convit, A., 344, *361*, 497, *510*

Cook, T. A. R., 678, 679, 701, *707*, *708*, *711*

Cook, T. D., 217, *220*

Cooney, J. L., 516, 530, *533*, *536*

Cooney, N. L., 38, *50*, *53*, 373, *395*, 410, 414, *423*, 438, *455*, *456*, *511*, 516, 517, *533*, *535*, *536*, 547, *555*

Cooper, C. L., 368, *395*

Cooper, M. L., 412, *425*

Cooper, S. M., 620, *675*

Copeland, J., 431, 438, 452, 453, *455*

Coppel, D. B., 328, *340*, 603, *614*

Çorapçioglu, A., 118, *132*

Corbin, W., 404, *422*

Corley, R. P., 61, 88

Cornelisse, P. G. A., *157*

Cornell, G., 584, *611*

Cornish, J. W., 559, *569*

Cornwell, L. W., 270n4, *285*

Corrigan, P. W., 551, *553*

Costa, F. M., 160, *183*, 218, *221*, 245, *253*, 588, *613*
Costa, L., 109, *112*
Costa, P., 270, *283*
Costello, E. J., 93, *112*, 582, *612*
Costello, M., *421*
Cote, R., *317*
Cottler, L. B., 66, *87*, 93, *115*, 500, *512*, 579, *613*
Courage, M. L., 413, *421*
Coutts, A., 546, *554*
Covert, J., 595, *611*
Covey, L. S., 482, *488*
Crabb, D. W., 679, 685, 701, *707*, *710*, *711*
Crabbe, J. C., 22, *31*
Craemer, V. A., 412, *419*
Craske, M. G., 372, *393*
Cremona, A., 34, *47*
Creson, D., 368, *394*
Crits-Christoph, P., 539, 542, *553*
Crockenberg, S., 289, *315*
Croghan, G. A., *490*
Croghan, I. T., *490*, *494*, *534*
Cromwell, J., 478, *487*
Cronkite, R. C., 36, *53*, 538, *556*
Crosby, L., 200, *220*
Croughan, J., 267, *285*
Crowe, R. R., 60, *83*
Crowne, D. P., 660, 661, *674*
Crum, T., *652*
Crusto, C., *184*
Csikszentmihalyi, M., 372, *394*
Cudeck, R., 70, *83*, 169, *182*, 351, *361*
Cui, Y.-H., *710*
Cummings, C., 368, 387, *394*, 412, *421*
Cummings, J. L., 357, *362*
Cummings, K. M., 464, *487*
Cummings, M. E., 260, 261, *283*
Cummins, L. H., 608, *612*, *616*
Cumsille, P., 168, *185*
Cunningham, J. A., 41, *49*, 543, *553*
Curley, R. T., 595, *612*
Curran, G. M., 260, *283*
Curran, P. J., 168, 174, *182*, 251, *251*, 260, *282*, 288, 291, 301, 303, *315*
Currie, S. L., *157*

Curry, S. J., 404, 415, *421*, 478, *487*
Curtin, L., 430, *456*
Cuthbertson, L., *486*
Cutting, J. C., 345, *362*
Cvetkovivh, G. T., *619*

Daeppen, J.-B., 682, *709*
Daisy, F., 602, *612*
Dakof, G. A., 642, *654*
Dalack, G. W., 460, *487*
Dale, L. C., *490*
Dallery, J., 568, *569*
Damasio, A. R., 503, *510*
D'Amico, D., *492*
Daniels, D., 292, *317*
Danko, G. P., 681, *709*
d'Arcy, H., *132*
Darkes, J., 233, *252*
Davenport, A. E., 89, 91, *116*, 325, *341*
Davey Smith, G., 689, *707*
Davidian, M., 417, *421*
Davidson, D., 409, *425*
Davidson, G., *494*
Davidson, W. S., II, *554*
Davies, M., 199, *222*, 288, 297n3, *316*
Davies, P., 260, 261, *283*
Davis, B., 159, *183*, 218, *222*
Davis, C. G., 60, *85*
Davis, C. S., 589, *610*
Davis, E. Z., 344, *362*
Davis, L. J., Jr., *534*
Davis, R. M., 465, *487*
Davis, T., 121, *132*
Dawson, D. A., 28, *31*, 543, *553*
Day, C. P., 702, *707*
Day, L. E., 194, *195*
Day, N. E., 227, *254*
de Almeida, S. P., 118, *133*
Dean, R. S., 357, *363*
DeBakey, S., 34, *55*
DeBaryshe, B. D., 261, *285*, 314, *317*
Debon, M., 390, *395*
DeBruyn, L. M., 587, *611*
DeCato, L. A., *652*
Deffenbacher, J., 584, *611*
de Fiebre, C. M., 370, 371, *393*
DeFries, J. C., 96, *115*

DeGarmo, D. S., 79, 86
Degenhardt, L., 117–119, 130, 131, *133*
de Geus, E. J. C., 109, *116*
De Jong, J. A., 589, *618*
de la Fuente, J. R., 327, *340*
De La Rosa, M. R., 418, *421*
Del Boca, F. K., 233, *252*, 324, *339*, 435, *456*, 501, *512*, 519, *535*
DelBoca, F. K., 547, *555*
De Leon, G., 542, *553*, 659, *674*
DeLucia, C., 260, *282*
Del Vecchio, A. M., 583, *616*
Dembo, R., 659, *674*
DeMers, S. T., 658, *675*
DeMoor, C. A., *496*
Deneubourg, J., *420*
Denny, C., *115*
Dent, C. W., 249, *255*
Department of Health and Human Services, 229, *252*
DePue, J., *488*
DeRoo, L., 438, *455*
Derryberry, D., 287, *318*
DerSimonian, R., 686, *707*
Des Jarlais, D. C., 139, 142, *155*
Désy, M., *155*
Detmer, W. M., 466, *491*
Detwiler, F. R., 368, *394*
DeVries, H., 466, *493*
de Wit, H., 369, *399*
Dey, A. N., *253*, *534*
Deyo, R. A., 585, *613*
Diamond, G. S., *654*
Dias, M. G., 153, *155*
Diaz, T., 483, *485*
Dick, R. W., 584, 586, *612*
Dickson, N., *251*
DiClemente, C. C., 40, 41, *52*, *54*, 324, 328, *340*, 407, 410, *421*, *425*, 466, *491*, *494*, 499, *512*, 601, 605, *618*
Dielman, T. E., 169, *182*
Diener, E., 375, 386, 391, *395*, 522, *534*
DiFranza, J. R., 227, *252*
DiFuria, L., 130, *134*
DiLalla, L. F., 60, *83*
Dillon, P., 117, *134*

DiMarino, M. E., 474, *494*
DiMatteo, M. R., 297, *316*
Dimeff, L. A., 418, *421*, 606, *612*, *615*
Dinges, M. N., 201, 217, *220*
Dinges, N. G., 580, 585, *612*
Dinwiddie, S. H., 84, *87*, *113*
Dishion, T. J., 199–201, 204, 206, 210, 215, 217–219, *220*, *221*, *223*
Disney, E. R., 109, *112*
Doan, B. T., 87
Dobbs, S. D., 387, *394*
Dobkin, P. L., 64, *87*, 412, *421*
Dodge, K. A., *315*, 413, *421*
Dolinsky, Z. S., 34, *54*, *339*
Donaldson, S. I., 312, *315*
Donavan, J. E., 109, *112*
Donnermeyer, J. F., 194, *195*, 587, 588, 594, *617*
Donny, E., 481, *492*
Donohue, B., 624, 628, 635, 638, 645, 652
Donovan, D. M., 50, 43, 49, 348, *365*, 406, 407, 416, 418, *421*, 438, *455*, 497, 503, *510*, *511*, *553*, 620
Donovan, J. E., 218, *221*, 245, *253*
Dorfman, S. F., *488*
Dorpat, N., 594, *612*
Doty, R. M., 152, *157*
Douglas, M., 153, *155*
Dowdall, G. W., 89, 91, *116*
Doyle, A. E., 67, 69, *83*, 84
Drake, E. E., 548, *553*
Dramaix, M., 476, *490*
Draper, R. J., 345, *362*
Drebus, D. W., 417, *425*
Drobes, D. J., 368, *399*, 516, 530, *533*
Drucker, E., 139, *156*
Drummond, D. C., 409, *421*, *424*
Dufour, M. C., 34, *55*
DuHamel, K., 287, *319*
Dukes, R. L., 187, 188, 194, *195*
Duncan, B. L., 541, *554*
Duncan, C., *489*
Duncan, S. C., 168, *182*, 200, *221*, 301, *316*
Duncan, T. E., 168, 169, *182*, *184*, 200, *221*, 301, *316*

Dunn, C., 438, *455*
Dunn, J., *318*
Dunn, M. E., 405, *422*
Dunne, M. P., 87
Duong-Tran, Q., 580, 585, *612*
Durcan, M. J., *489*
Durell, J., *556*
Duryea, E. J., 579, 581, 584, *618*
Dusenbury, L., 483, *485*
Dwyer, J. H., 270, 271n5, 273, *284*, *317*
D'Zurilla, T., 644, *654*

Earls, F., 289, *315*
Eaton, C., *488*
Eaton, W. W., 543, *552*
Eaves, L. J., 64, 85, 88, 97, *114*
Eberman, K. M., *534*
Eckardt, M. J., 344, *362*
Eckert, E. D., *84*
Eckey, R., *710*
Eddy, J. M., 160, *182*, 201, *220*
Edelbrock, C. S., 60, *82*
Edenberg, H. J., *31, 32*, 679, *707, 710, 711*
Edge, K., *426*
Edwards, E. D., 587, 591, 592, *612*
Edwards, G., 41, 49, 387, *394*
Edwards, K., 311n9, *319*
Edwards, M., 472, *496*
Edwards, M. E., 587, 591, 592, *612*
Edwards, R. S., 587, *617*
Edwards, R. W., 576, 605, *611, 612*
Efron, B., 329, *339*
Egert, S., *49*
Egger, M., 689, *707*
Ehlers, C. L., 416, *421*, 701, *707, 711*
Ehrman, R. N., 559, *569*
Eikelboom, R., 369, *399*
Eisen, S. A., 86, 88
Eisenberg, J. M., 478, *487*
Eitle, D., *283*
Ekman, P., 390, *394*
Elash, C. A., 369, 398, *494*
Elder, C., 588, *612*
Elder, G. H., *315*
el Guebaly, N., 411, *422*
Elkins, I. J., 61, 67, *84*, 90, 93, 109, 111, *112, 113, 114*, 116, 260, 286

Ellard, J. H., 324, *340*
Ellickson, P. L., 159, 160, 167, 179, *183*, 226, *255*
Elliott, D., 199, 200, 217, *221*
Elliott, G., *47*
Ellis, D. A., 268, 286, 345, *364*
Ellsworth, P. C., 150, *155*
El-Sheikh, M., 261, 263, 279, 281, *283*
Elvine-Kreis, B., 681, *708*
Emery, G., 500, *510*
Emmons, K. E., 462, *485*
Emmons, K. M., 492, *495*
Emrick, C. D., 543, *553*
Endicott, J., 268, *283*
Eng, T. R., 473, *493*
Engberg, J., *15, 16*, 373, 375, 376, *398*, *426*
Engelbrecktson, K., 344, *361*
Ennett, S. T., 188, 194, *195*, 200, *221*
Ennifar, S., *492*
Enoch, M., 91, *113*
Enomoto, N., 679, *707*
Ensminger, M. E., 199, *222*
Epps, R. P., 466, *491*
Epstein, D. H., 568, *570*
Epstein, E. E., 46, *51*, 548, *555*
Epstein, L. H., 371, 372, 389, 391, *394–397*
Erb, S., 417, *426*
Erickson, D. J., *255*
Erickson, P. G., 151, *155*
Eriksson, C. J. P., 679, *707*
Erkanli, A., 93, *112*, 582, *612*
Errico, A. L., 344, 345, *362*, *364*
Escobedo, L. G., *393*
Estilo, M. J., 146, *157*
Ettner, S. L., 541, *553*
European Monitoring Centre for Drugs and Drug Addiction, *133*
Everingham, S. S., 147, *155*
Eysenck, H. J., 369, *394*

Fabsitz, R., 481, *486*
Fagerström, K. O., 460, 476, *487, 489*, 519, *534*
Faillace, L. A., 36, *49*, 408, *421*
Falissard, B., 533, *535*

Fals-Stewart, W., 344, 347n1, 348, 349, 352, 359, 362, *497, 498, 502, 508, 509, 510*

Fan, J.-H., *710*

Fang, B., *710*

Fang, Y.-R., *709*

Faraone, S. V., 86

Farmer, E. M. Z., 582, *612*

Farmer, M. E., *54, 557*

Farquhar, J. W., 463, *487*

Farringdon, F., 159, 162, *184*

Farrington, D. P., *185*

Faulkner, W. R., 681, *707*

Faust, R., 581, *614*

Fava, J. L., *47, 472, 495*

Federman, B., 539, *556*

Federman, E. B., 582, 599, *612*

Felch, L. J., 560, *571*

Feldman, H. A., 464, *486*

Felix-Ortiz, M., 588, *617*

Feller, D. J., *31*

Fendrich, M., 119, *133*

Feng, Z., *494*

Ferencz,-Biro, K., 679, *707*

Ferguson, F. N., 589, *612*

Ferrence, R., 119, *133*

Fertig, J. B., 324, *339*

Fetrow, B., 204, *221*

Fetrow, R. A., 160, *182*

Feyerabend, C., *495*

Fichtenberg, C. M., 467, *487*

Fidell, L. S., 74n1, *87*

Fiester, S., *490*

Filer, M., 294n2, 311, *320*

Filley, C. M., 348, *363*

Fillmore, K. M., 248, *252*

Fincham, F. D., 262, 279, *283*

Finger, M. S., 62, 69, *85*

Finn, P. R., 109, *114*

Finney, J. W., 36, 38, *49, 53, 538–540, 542, 543, 546–549, 551, 553–558*

Fiore, M. C., 410, 414, *419, 423, 425, 461, 465, 466, 468–473, 477, 478, 481, 482, 487, 488, 490, 494, 496*

Fiorentine, R., 539, *554*

First, M. B., 349, *365, 436, 442, 448, 455, 519, 533*

Fischer, L. A., *398*

Fischman, M. W., 430, *455*

Fishbein, M., 595, *612*

Fisher, C. L. G., *493*

Fisher, K. J., 230, *253*

Fiske, D. W., 217, *221*

Fitzgerald, H. E., 226, 256, 261, 268, *284, 286, 345, 364*

Flammino, F., *425*

Flanagan, E., 261, 263, 279, 281, *283*

Flanders, W. D., 227, *252*

Flay, B. R., 226, *252, 317*

Fleming, C. B., *182*

Fleming, C. M., 577, 589, *612, 617*

Fleming, M. F., 418, *421, 540, 554*

Flewelling, R. L., 188, *195*

Flewelling, R. P., 187, *196*

Flor, D. L., 288, *315*

Flora, D., 259, *282*

Flora, J. A., 464, *487, 488*

Foa, E. B., 405, *422, 547, 554*

Foege, W. H., 34, *51*

Foerg, F. E., *50*

Fogg, C. P., 199, *223*

Foley, D. L., 80, *84*

Follick, M. J., 372, *394*

Foltin, R. W., 430, *455*

Fonte, C., 370, 389, *397*

Foote, F. H., 635, 638, *654, 655*

Forgatch, M. S., 204, *221*

Forman, R. F., 563n1, *569*

Foroud, T., *711*

Forster, J. L., *490*

Fortmann, S. P., 464, *488, 487, 531, 534*

Forza, G., 130, *134*

Foster, R. W., *558*

Foster, S. E., 89, *113*

Foster, W. H., 89, *113*

Fouladi, R. T., *420*

Foulds, J., *489*

Fowler, J. S., *365, 476, 477, 488*

Fox, H. R., 658, *675*

Fox, J. H., 350, *365*

Fox, R., 42, *49*

Foy, B. D., 118, *134*

France, E. K., 467, *488*

Franceschi, D., *488*

Franco, E., *155*
Franco, R. L. H., *489*
Frank, K. A., *554*
Frankforter, T. L., 411, *420*
Franklin, G. M., 348, *363*
Franks, N., *420*
Frecker, R. C., 519, *534*
Freeman, R. C., 638, *653*
Freitas, T. T., 344, 349, *362*
French, D. C., 206, 218, *221*
French, L. A., 575, *612*
French, M. T., *554*
French, S. A., *490*
Frese, F. J., 551, *554*
Freund, G., 344, *362*
Frey, R. M., 548, *556*
Frick, P. J., 85, 281, *286*
Friedman, A. S., 629, 644, 645, *653*
Friedman, L. S., 201, *221*
Friedman, M. J., 547, *554*
Friedman, S. R., 139, 142, *155*
Friesen, W. V., 390, *394*
Frith, C. D., 369, *394*
Fritze, G., *707, 710*
Fromme, K., 328, 340, 404, *422*, 603,
    610, 614
Frone, M. R., 412, *425*
Fryer, G. E., *493*
Fuller, R. K., 38, *49*
Furuyama, J., 681, *710*

Galaif, E. R., 249, *255*
Gamma, A., 118, *133*
Gandour, M. J., 288, *319*
Garcia-Mason, V., 587, *613*
Garmezy, N., 288, *316*
Gauger, K., 311, *315*
Gauvin, T. R., *494*
Gawin, F. H., 344, *364*
Geist, C., 602, *616*
Gelernter, J., 481, *488*
General Accounting Office, 139, *155*
George, T. P., 516, *533*
Gerbert, B., 324, 337, *339*
Gerkovich, M., 526, *535*
Gerrard, M., 310, 313, *315, 316, 320*
Gershuny, B. S., 261, *285*

Gerton, J., 589, *614*
Gfroerer, J., 121, *132*
Giancola, P. R., 290, *316*
Gibbon, M., 349, *365*, 436, *455*, 519, *533*
Gibbons, F. X., 310, 313, *315, 316, 320*
Gieringer, D., 146, *155*
Giffen, C., *492*
Gilbert, D. G., 368, *386n8*, 391, *394*
Gilbert, G. G., 368, *396*
Gilchrist, L. D., *618, 619*
Gill, K., 412, *421*
Gillespie, J., 151, *156*
Gilley, D. W., 350, *365*
Gillin, J. C., *48*
Gillmore, M. R., 406, *422*
Gilpin, E. A., *491*
Giltinan, D. M., 417, *421*
Giovino, G. A., *393*
Gitchell, J., 474, *494*
Gladsjo, J. A., 36, *55*
Glantz, M., 582, *620*
Glantz, M. D., 288, *316*, 657, *675*
Glantz, S. A., 467, 479, 487, *491*
Glanz, K., *494*
Glasgow, R. E., 459, 461, 462, 467, 469,
    473, 478, 488, *491*
Glassman, A. H., 460, 482, *488*
Glassman, B., 473, *490*
Gledhill-Hoyt, J., 461, *495*
Gleghorn, A., 37, *48*
Glenn, S. W., 345, *365*
Glover, E. D., *490*
Glynn, T. J., 466, 483, 488, *491, 492*
Gnys, M., 11, *16*, 369, 398, 411, *422*,
    426, 517, *536*
Goate, A., 31, *32*
Godfrey, A. B., 545, *552*
Godfrey, C., 478, 486, *492*
Godley, M., 550, *552*
Goedde, H. W., 677, 678, 681, *707*
Goehl, L., 35, *51*
Goines, M. A., *615*
Goldberg, B., 469, *494*
Goldberg, J., 86, *88*
Goldberg, S. R., 371, *398, 399*
Goldberger, R., 641, *654*
Goldman, D., 60, 83, 91, *113*

Goldman, M. S., 233, *252*, 408, *419*, 498, *510*

Goldring, E., 500, *512*

Goldsmith, H. H., 60, *84*, 290, *316*

Goldstein, A., 139, *155*

Goldstein, G., 497, *510*

Goldstein, M. G., *420*, *425*, 466, 474, 478, *485*, *488–491*

Golub, A., 581, *613*

Gomez-Dahl, L., *534*

Gonzales, D., *489*

Gonzales, N., 281, 286, 289, *318*

Gonzalez, G., 560, *570*

Goode, J. A., 60, *83*

Goodman, A. C., 41, *49*

Goodman, M. J., 478, *493*

Goodwin, D. W., 60, *84*

Goodwin, F. K., *54*, *557*

Gordon, A., 507n1, *510*

Gordon, J. R., 36, 39, 43, *51*, 368, 371, *394*, *395*, 404, 405, 412, 413, 418, *421*, *424*, 517, *535*, 589, 601, *616*

Gordon, J. S., 467, *493*

Gordon, L. T., 406, *420*

Gorenstein, E. E., 63, *84*

Gorsuch, R. L., 351, *362*, 436, *456*

Gorton, G. E., 507n1, *510*

Gosnell, B., 530, *534*

Gossop, M., 410, 414, *421*

Gotham, H. J., 90, 91, 94, 110, 111, *113–116*, 254, *255*

Gottesman, I. I., 60, *83*, *84*, 290, *316*

Gould, F., *556*

Grabowski, J., 418, *426*

Graham, J. D., *495*

Graham, J. W., 161, 168, *183*, *185*, 200, *221*, 312, *315*, *316*, 416, *419*, *613*

Granic, I., 219, *220*

Grant, B. F., 28, *31*, 93, *113*, 681, *707*

Grant, I., 36, 48, 344, 345, 349, 358, *362*, *363*, 498, *512*

Grant, M., 327, *340*

Green, D., 368, 371, *395*

Green, L., 588, *612*

Green, S. B., 371, *395*, *396*

Green, V. A., 589, *619*

Greenberg, R. S., *252*

Greenfield, S., 407, *421*

Greenley, J. R., 545, *558*

Gregson, R. A. M., 360, *363*

Greig, R., 624, *653*

Grella, C., 544, *554*

Griesler, P., 204, *223*

Griffin, K. W., 160, 161, *181*, *183*

Griffiths, R. R., 370, 371, *393*, *394*

Grissom, G. R., *51*, 456, *511*, *555*

Gritz, E. R., 389, *394*, 465, *486*, *488*

Grob, P. J., 146, *155*

Grobe, J. E., 368, 370, 389, *397*

Grodin, D. M., 345, *362*

Gross, M. M., 387, *394*

Gross, S. R., 117, 119, 131, *133*, 150, *155*

Grossman, D. C., 585, *613*

Grossman, J. L., 530, *534*

Grothaus, L. C., 478, *487*

Grove, W. M., 60, *84*, 195, *195*

Gruenfeld, D. H., 144, *158*

Grunberg, N. E., 369, *394*

Grych, J. H., 262, 279, *283*

Gudmundsson, J., 476, *485*

Guerrera, M. P., 227, *252*

Gulliver, S. B., 38, *53*, 227, *253*, 516, *534*, *536*

Gunzerath, L., 91, *113*

Guo, J., 161, *183*, 261, *283*

Gustafson, D., 473, *493*

Gustafson, G., 476

Gustavsson, G., 476, *485*, *490*

Guthmann, D. R., 659, *674*

Guthrie, S., *49*

Gutierres, S. E., 180, *183*, 591, 592, *613*

Guy, S. M., 199, *223*

Guze, B. H., *31*

Guze, S. B., 60, *84*

Gwaltney, C. J., *15*, 398, 408, 412, *422*, *426*, *494*

Haaga, D. A. F., 389, *396*, 413, *425*

Haas, E., 201, *220*

Haber, J. R., 261, *284*

Haber, R., *284*

Haddock, G., *552*

Hagan, T. A., *556*

Hagekull, B., 290, *316*
Haggerty, K. P., 163, *182, 183*
Haggerty, R. J., 159, *184*
Haidt, J., 153, *155*
Hajek, P., 472, 473, *489, 496, 531, 536*
Hall, J., *653*
Hall, N. G. C., 624, 639, 640, 643, 646,
    647, 651, *653*
Hall, S. M., 412, *422,* 471, 475, 477, *489*
Halstead, W. C., 348, *363*
Hammersley, R., 372, *394*
Hamsher, K., 348, *361*
Han, C., 108, *113*
Handmaker, N. S., *52*
Hando, J., 117, *134*
Haney, M., 430, *455*
Hanger, P., *513*
Hankin, J. R., 41, *49*
Hanrahan, P., 546, *553*
Hansen, W. B., 161, 168, *183, 185,* 187,
    196, 200, *221,* 312, *315, 317*
Hanson, G., 43, *49*
Hanson, T., *570*
Harachi, T. W., 163, *182, 183*
Harada, S., *710*
Harford, T. C., 110, *113*
Harmon, B., 584, *611*
Harper, E. P., 145, *155*
Harris, H., 130, *134*
Harris, J. F., 139, *155*
Harris, J. R., 80, *84*
Harris, L., 584, *611*
Harris, N. A., 530, *536*
Harris, R. A., 22, *31*
Harris, R. J., *52,* 144, *156*
Harrison, A., *394*
Harrison, E. R., 160, *183*
Hart, E. L., *85*
Hartley, M. T., 417, *425*
Hartup, W. W., 217, *222*
Hartwell, T. W., 464, *494*
Hartz, D. T., *489*
Hashibe, M., *706*
Hashimoto, T., 681, *710*
Hasin, D. S., 41, *49,* 681, *707*
Haskell, W. L., *487*
Hasselblad, V., 478, *487*

Hatgis, C., 551, *552*
Hatsukami, D. K., 367, *394*
Haugaard, J. J., 194, *196*
Havassy, B. E., 412, *422*
Hawke, J., 659, *674*
Hawker, A., *49*
Hawkins, C. A., 405, 415, 416, *422*
Hawkins, E. H., 575, 586, 589, 608,
    612, 613, 615, 616
Hawkins, J. D., 159–161, *182–185,* 200,
    222, 259–261, 268n2, 268n5,
    283, 288, 291, 300, *316,* 406,
    422, 585, 588, *613*
Hawkins, R. C., 405, 415, 416, *422, 427*
Hayashida, M., 27, *32,* 677, 681, *708*
Haynes, S. N., 417, *422*
Hays, J. T., 478, *489*
Hays, R. D., 296, *316*
Hayward, P., *423*
Hazel, K., 602, *616*
Healy, D. J., 460, *487*
Heath, A. C., 60, 64, *84, 85, 87,* 91, 97,
    108, *113, 114,* 244, *254, 284,*
    481, *489*
Heather, N., 137, 142, *156,* 407, *422*
Heatherton, T. F., 43, *47,* 411, *419,*
    519, *534*
Heaton, R. K., 344, 348, 358, *363, 364*
Hecht, M. L., 657, *675*
Hedeker, D., 270, *283,* 415, *422,* 491
Hedrick, K. E., 37, *52*
Hegel, M. T., 405, *420*
Heinrichs, S. C., 24, *32*
Heinssen, R. K., 509, *511*
Heishman, S. J., 530, *536*
Hekali, P., 702, *709*
Helzer, J. E., 34, 36, 37, 41, 48, *49, 54,*
    264, 267, *283, 285,* 500, *512,*
    569, 681–683, *703, 706–708*
Hemenway, D., 145, *156*
Hen, R., *31*
Henderson, S., 97, *115*
Henggeler, S. W., 41, *49,* 204, *223,* 626,
    629, 630, 636, 638, 642–645, *653*
Henk, H. J., 530, *534*
Henly, G. A., 658–663, 667, 673,
    674–676

Henningfield, J. E., *253, 369, 399, 465, 494*

Henry, B., 287, 288, *315, 316*

The Henry J. Kaiser Family Foundation, 150, *156*

Hensman, C., *49*

Hequin, Y., *709*

Herjanic, B., 66, 88, 269n3, *283*

Herman, C. P., 369, 371, 387, *394, 395, 404, 406, 425*

Herman, S. E., 548, *554*

Hermann, R. C., 541, *553*

Hermansen, L., 60, *84*

Herrell, J., 433, *457*

Herrera, N., 472, 474, *489*

Hershberger, S., 292, 303, 310, *317*

Hervis, O., 635, 638, *654, 655*

Herz, M. I., 405, *422*

Hesselbrock, M. N., 34, 36, 37, *50*, 498, *511*, 682, *709*

Hesselbrock, V. M., 109, *112*, 339, 682, *709, 710*

Hester, R. K., 38, 39, 43, 46, *50, 52*

Heston, L. L., *84, 86*

Hettema, J. M., 97, *113*

Heurtin-Roberts, S., 575, *615*

Hewitt, J. K., 61, 88, *114*

Heyman, R. E., 261, *283*

Heywood, E., 60, *83*

Hickcox, M., 11, *16*, 398, 411, *426, 517, 536*

Hicks, B. M., 60, *85, 284*

Hieda, Y., *492*

Hietala, R., 501, *512*

Higgins, S. T., 38, *50*, 430, *455, 570*

Higuchi, S., 677, 680, 681, 687, 691, 701, 702, 705, 708, *709*

Hill, D., 497, *510*

Hill, E. M., 260, *283, 286*

Hill, K. G., 160, 161, *183*, 261, *283, 316, 613*

Hill, S. K., 357, *363*

Hill, S. Y., 109, *113*

Hillbom, M., 359, *363*

Himmelstein, D., *491*

Hinde, R. A., 218, *222*

Hinson, R. E., 369, *397*

Hirky, A. E., 295, *320*, 586, *621*

Hirsch, J. A., 227, *256*

Hirsch, L. S., 548, *555*

Hirschi, T., 160, *183*

Hiss, H., 405, *422*

Hitsman, B., 475, *489*

Hitzemann, R., *365*

Hitzman, R., *365*

Hockaday, C., 160, *185*

Hodgins, D. C., 411, *422*

Hoffman, J. M., 270, *284*

Höfler, M., 118, *134*

Hofman, D. A., 145, *157*

Hofmann, M., *339*

Hohmann, A. A., 552, *554*

Holcomb, J., *87*

Holdcraft, L. C., 66, *84*

Holden, G. W., 580, *616*

Holder, H. D., 38, 41, *49, 50*

Holland, D., 605, *618*

Hollis, J. F., 462, *488*

Hollon, S. D., 624, 637, 639, 645, *653*

Holm, L., 359, *363*

Holmes, T., 585, *616*

Holt, C. S., 407, *419*

Homan, S. M., 41, *48*

Honda, R., 701, *710*

Honigmann, I., 589, *613*

Honigmann, J., 589, *613*

Hopkins, R. S., 483, *485*

Hops, H., 159, 169, *183, 184*, 200, 218, *221, 222, 253*

Horn, D., 368, *395*

Horvath, A. T., 35, *50*

House, R. F., *494*

Howard, J., 575, *615*

Howard, M. O., 63, *84*, 579, 586, *613, 620*

Howe, M. L., 413, *421*

Howell, C. T., 61, *82*, 312, *314*

Howell, J. C., 160, *183*, 652

Howie, P., 97, *115*

Hoyt, D. R., 587, *621*

Hromi, A., *427*

Hser, Y., 544, 547, *554*

Hsu, Y.-P. P., 678, *706*

Hu, K.-B., *709*

Hu, L.-T., 351, *363*, 503, *511*
Hu, S., *493*
Hubbell, A., 119, *133*
Hubble, M. A., 541, *554*
Hudson, S., 405, *423*
Hudziak, J. J., 563n1, *569*
Huebert, K. M., 591, 592, *621*
Huebsch, P., 548, *555*
Hufford, M. R., 372, 373, 389, *397–399*,
    416, 417, *421, 422, 427*, 532,
    534, 536
Hughes, A. R., *490*
Hughes, E. F., *558*
Hughes, J. R., 38, *50*, 145, *156*, 430,
    455, 460, 469, 472, 474–477,
    482, 487, 489, 490, 515, *534*
Hughes, S. O., 407, 410, *421*
Huizinga, D., 199, *221*
Hull, J. G., 409, *426*
Humfleet, G. L., *489*
Humphreys, K., 540, 546, 548, 549, 551,
    554, 555
Hunt, W. A., 409, *421, 424*
Hunt-Carter, E. E., *116*
Hur, Y.-M., 66, *84*
Hurley, S. E., 139, 139n1, *156*
Hurt, R. D., 473, 474, 483, 489, *490*,
    515, *534*
Hussong, A. M., 91, *113*, 260, 261, 267,
    279, *282, 284*
Husten, C., 466, *491*
Hutchison, K., 516, *535*
Huygens, I., 41, *49*
Hwang, K.-K., 681, *706*
Hwu, H.-G., *708, 710*
Hymowitz, N., *492*
Hyytia, P., 24, *32*

Iacono, W. G., 59, 61, 63, 65–67, 77,
    78, *83–86*, 90, 91, 93–96, 108,
    109, 111, *112–114, 116*,
    259–261, 263, 284–286
Ialongo, N. S., 160, *184*
Ichikawa, Y., 702, *708, 709*
Idelson, R. K., 466, *495*
Iguchi, M. Y., 559, 560, *570, 571*
Ikard, F. F., 368, 372, 391, *395*

Ikawa, M., 679, *708*
Imazeki, F., *710*
Impraim, C. C., 679, *708*
Inaba, R. K., 36, *48*
Indian Health Service, Office of Public
    Health, Program Statistics Team,
    575, 585, *613*
Ingham, D., *653*
Institute of Medicine, 590, *613*
Institute of Medicine, National Acad-
    emy of Sciences, 35, 38, 40, 44,
    46, *50*
Ippoliti, A., *394*
Irvin, J. E., 405, 406, *422*
Irwin, M. R., *48*, 345, 359, *363, 513*
Isaac, N., 89, *116*, 233, *256*
Israel, A. C., 59, *85*
Istvan, J., 227, *253*, 516, *534*
Iwahashi, K., 702, *708, 709*

Jaccard, J., *114*, 303, 311, *316*
Jack, L. M., 475, *495*
Jackson, D. N., 69, 86, 660, *674*
Jackson, K. M., 91, 111, *114*, 228, 238n7,
    248–250, *253–255*, 657, *675*
Jacob, P., 389, *395*
Jacob, T., 260, 261, *284*
Jacobs, G. A., 436, *456*
Jacobson, K. C., 79, *84*
Jacobson, N. S., 505, *511*, 659, *674*
Jaffe, A. J., *31*, 38, *54*
Jainchill, N., 659, *674*
Janca, A., *569*
Jang, K. L., 64, 69, 81, 82, *84*, 86
Janis, I. L., 41, *50*
Jarvik, M. E., 368, 387, *394–398*
Jarvis, M. J., 486, *495*
Jasinski, D. R., 358, *364*
Jatulis, D. E., 464, *488*
Java, R. I., 357, *364*
Jeddeloh, R. J., 478, *490*
Jeffrey, D. L., 509, *511*
Jeffrey, R. W., 462, *490*
Jelinek, L. C., *253*
Jennison, K. M., 249, *253*
Jensen, A. R., 78, *85*
Jerome, R. E., *711*

Jerrell, J. M., 539, *555*
Jerrom, D. W. A., 344, *361*
Jessor, L., 109, *112*
Jessor, R., 37, *50*, 109, *112*, 160, *183*,
　　199, 217, 218, *221*, *222*, 245,
　　253, 588, *613*
Jessor, S. L., 37, *50*, 199, 217, *222*, *253*
Jo, B., *254*
Joanning, H., 630, 645, *653*
Joe, G. W., 539, *558*
Johnson, B. D., 91, *113*, 581, *613*
Johnson, C. A., *317*
Johnson, E. O., 260, *284*, *711*
Johnson, J. A., 475, *494*
Johnson, J. L., 288, *316*, 585, *618*
Johnson, K. A., 249, *253*, 418, *421*
Johnson, M. B., *114*
Johnson, R. C., 681, *709*
Johnson, R. J., 199, *222*
Johnson, S. B., 576, 609, *615*, *653*
Johnson, T. M., 483, *485*
Johnson, T. P., 119, *133*
Johnson, V., 226, 227, *251*, *256*
Johnston, J. A., *490*
Johnston, J. D., *620*
Johnston, L. D., 90, *112*, *115*, 118, 121,
　　131, *133*, 162, 166, 180, *182*,
　　184, 195, *195*, 200, 201, *223*,
　　225, 226, 228–232, 248, 249,
　　251–255, 296, *316*, 324, *339*,
　　583, *614*, 657, 661, 674, *675*
Johnston, T., 679, *711*
Johnstone, B. M., 187, *195*
Jolley, D. J., 139, 139n1, *156*
Jones, B. L., 230, *253*
Jones, B. T., 404, 408, *422*
Jorenby, D. E., *423*, 476, 488, 490, *494*,
　　496
Jöreskog, K. G., 301, 303, *316*, 351, *363*
Joseph, A. M., 516, *534*
Jouriles, E. N.7, 261, *283*
Judd, C. M., 292, *317*
Judd, L. L., *54*, 344, *362*, *363*, *557*
Julia, H. L., 371, *397*
Juliano, L. M., 408, *423*
Jumper-Thurman, P., 605, *612*
Jung, H. K., *708*

Jung, K., 66, *88*
Jung, S.-H., *708*
Justus, A. N., 109, *114*

Kabela, E., 410, *423*, *456*
Kabene, M., 37, *50*
Kaczynski, N. A., 227, *254*
Kadden, R. M., 38, 39, 40, *50*, *53*, 406,
　　407, 410, *423*, 438, 440, 453, *455*,
　　456, 497, 499, *510*, *511*, 547, *555*
Kagawa-Singer, M., 576, *617*
Kahan, J., 137, 151, *156*
Kahler, C. W., 110, *114*, 420, 548, *556*
Kaiser, P., 289n1, *319*
Kalant, H., 417, *423*
Kaldor, J. M., 139, 139n1, *156*
Kalman, D., 516, *534*
Kaminer, Y., 37, *50*, 627, 631, 641, 642,
　　644, 645, *653*, *654*
Kampman, K. M., 559, *569*, *570*
Kandel, D. B., 34, 49, 199, 200, 202,
　　210, 217, *222*, 224, 225, *252*,
　　288, 297n3, *316*, 581, 585, *614*,
　　660, 675
Kaplan, H. B., 199, *222*
Kaprio, J., 90, *116*
Kardia, S. L. R., 481, *493*
Karkowski, L. M., 80, *85*
Karus, D., 199, *222*
Kassel, J. A., 517, *536*
Kassel, J. D., 11, *16*, 369, 372, 395, 397,
　　398, 409, 411, 412, *422*, *423*, *426*
Katon, W., *423*
Kauffman, S., 413, 415, *423*
Kaufman, N., 219, *221*
Kavanagh, K., 219, *221*
Kazdin, A. E., 194, *195*
Kealey, K. A., 482, *492*
Keane, T. M., 547, *554*
Keeler, G., 93, *112*
Keenan, R. M., *253*
Keener, J. J., 34, *50*
Keiser, T., 348, *364*
Keith, S. J., *54*, *557*
Kelder, S. H., *490*
Kellam, S. G., 160, 167, *184*, *185*, 199,
　　222

Keller, R. T., 493
Kelley, M., 577, 614
Kemnitzer, L. S., 587, 614
Kendall, P. C., 195, 195
Kendler, K. S., 60, 64, 78–80, 84–87,
    97, 108, 113, 114, 490
Kenford, S. L., 412, 423, 475, 481, 490,
    496
Kenny, D. A., 270, 282
Kerr, N., 423
Kessel, K. B., 569
Kessler, D. A., 467, 479, 490
Kessler, R. C., 60, 64, 85, 97, 114, 202,
    219, 269, 284, 430, 455
Keuthen, N., 491
Keyes, S., 199, 220
Keyler, D. E., 492
Khantzian, E. J., 412, 423
Khayrallah, M., 494
Khoo, S. T., 254
Kidd, J. R., 680, 708, 709
Kidd, K. K., 680, 705, 708
Kidorf, M., 560, 566, 570
Kiesler, C. A., 34, 50
Kilbey, M. M., 368, 393
Killen, J. D., 531, 534
Killer, S. H., 155
Kim, J. A., 409, 426
Kim, S. H., 707
King, A. C., 344, 362, 407, 426, 589, 618
King, J., 575, 586, 614
King, K. M., 259, 260, 263, 280, 282, 284
King, S. L., 477, 493
King, S. M., 109, 114
Kinne, S., 494
Kirkcaldy, B. D., 368, 386n8, 395
Kirp, D. L., 139, 152, 156
Kissin, B., 95, 112
Kivlahan, D. R., 63, 84, 90, 112, 328,
    340, 348, 365, 418, 421, 438,
    455, 497, 510, 584, 603, 606,
    610, 612, 614, 615, 619, 620
Klajner, F., 324, 341
Klein, D. J., 159, 183
Klein, W. M., 151, 158
Klesges, R. C., 390, 395
Kline, R. B., 351, 363, 501, 511

Knight, R. G., 497, 500, 511
Knutson, N., 79, 86
Ko, H.-C., 706, 709
Kochanska, G., 312, 317
Kocsis, J. H., 38, 51
Kodya, S., 416, 422
Kogan, E. S., 635, 652
Kok, G. J., 466, 493
Koller, S. H., 153, 155
Kolodner, K., 570
Koob, G. F., 24, 32
Koppenhaver, J. M., 413, 424
Korhonen, H., 493
Kornitzer, M., 476, 490
Koskenvuo, M., 90, 116
Kossak-Fuller, J., 264, 282
Kosten, T. R., 560, 570
Kosterman, R., 160, 183, 184
Kottke, T. E., 465, 466, 486, 490, 534
Kouri, E. M., 430, 456
Kozak, M. J., 405, 422
Kozlowski, L. T., 227, 253, 369, 371,
    387, 395, 519, 534
Krahn, D. D., 530, 531, 534
Krantz, D. L., 545, 553
Kranzler, H. R., 34, 50, 516, 533
Krauter, K. S., 61, 88
Kress, K., 551, 554
Kreuter, M. W., 473, 490
Krisberg, B., 160, 183
Krishnan-Sarin, S., 533, 535
Krueger, R. F., 59–64, 67, 69, 77, 78, 83,
    85, 96, 112, 261, 284
Krull, J. L., 238n7, 254
Ku, L., 341
Kumanyika, S. K., 576, 617
Kumpfer, K. L., 184
Kunitz, S. J., 584, 615
Kunze, M., 487
Kuo, M., 230, 256, 583, 620
Kurtines, W. M., 635, 638, 654, 655
Kushner, H., 37, 51, 456, 511
Kushner, M. G., 51
Kutner, M. H., 235n5, 254

Laaksonen, S., 501, 512
LaBoueff, S., 582, 586, 587, 591, 592, 611

Labouvie, E. W., 324, 327, *341*, 346, *361*, 410, *420*, 498, *510*, 548, *556*, 582, *621*
LaBuda, M. C., 60, 86
Lachance, N., *155*
Ladouceur, R., 407, *427*
Laforge, R. G., 472, *495*
LaFromboise, T. D., 587, 589, 591, 592, 600, 604, 606, *614*
Lahey, B. B., 69, 85
Laird, N., 686, *707*
Lake, J. R., *492*
Lam, D. H., 405, *423*
La Marr, J. C., 607, *614*, *615*
Lamb, A., *55*
Lambert, M. D., *620*
Lamberti, J. S., *422*
Lamoth, E., *155*
Lancashire, R., *485*
Landau, T. C., 602, *614*
Lando, H. A., 464, 473, *490*, *491*, 515, *533*
Landry, M. J., 118, *133*, 539, *552*
Lane, J. D., 371, *395*
Langbehn, D., *112*
Lange, J. E., 91, *114*
Langenbucher, J. W., 265, *285*, 410, *420*
LaPerriere, A., *654*
Lapinski, K. J., *652*
Laplante, B., *317*
Lara, E. A., 474, *494*
Larimer, M. E., 38, *51*, 148, *157*, 328, *340*, 602, *610*, *615*, *616*
Larsen, R. J., 375, 386, 391, *395*, 522, *534*
Larson, R., 372, *394*
Lasater, T. M., 464, *486*
Laser-Wolston, N., 372, *394*
Lasser, K., 460, 482, *491*
Lathrop, M., 204, *221*
Latimer, W. W., 631, 644, 645, *654*, 658, 659, *676*
Latini, D., 515, *533*
Lauerman, R. J., 34, *50*
Launay, J. M., *485*
Lavee, Y., 297, *317*
Lawendowski, L. A., 411, *419*
Lawrence, T., *485*

Laws, D., 405, *423*
Leaver-Dunn, D., 588, *612*
Leccese, M., 657, *675*
Lee, B. L., 389, *395*
Lee, C. K., *708*
Lee, H. C., 230, *256*, 461, *495*, 583, 620, 677, 678, 687, 691, 693, *708*
Lee, H.-S., *708*
Lee, J. E., 230, *256*, 461, *493*, 583, *620*
Lee, J.-F., *709*
Lee, J.-S., *707*
Lee, M. S., 681, *709*
Leed-Kelly, A., 516, *533*
Legrand, L. N., 90, *114*, 263, 281, *284*
Lehman, L. B., 501, *511*
Lehman, W. E., 588, *610*
Lehn, L., 624, *653*
Lei, H., *253*
Leigh, B., 324, *340*
Leigh, G., *253*, 371, *395*
Leischow, S. J., *490*
LeMaster, P. L., 579, 583, 586–588, *615*
Lemery, K. S., 290, *316*
Lennox, K., 348, *364*
Lenton, S., 119, 130, *133*
Leo, G. I., 324, *340*
Leonard, K. E., 110, *114*, 261, *284*
Lepper, M. R., 150, *156*
Leri, F., 417, *423*
Lerman, C., 481, *491*
Lerner, J., 151, *157*
Lerner, R. M., 294, *320*
Lesar, M. D., 543, 548, *558*
Lessov, C. N., *31*
Leventhal, H., 369, *395*
Levine, M. D., *492*, *556*
Levine, S., 466, *495*
Levis, D. J., 368, *397*
Levy, J. E., 584, *615*
Lewin, L. M., 159, *183*, 218, *222*
Lewis, C. E., 169, *185*, 351, 365, 683, *706*
Lewis, M. N., Jr., 357, *363*
Lewis, R. A., 632, 645, *654*
Lewis, S. J., 683, 685, *706*, *708*
Lewis, S. W., *552*
Lewis, Y. P., 638, *653*
Lex, B. W., 576, *617*

Lezak, M. D., *511*

Li, F., 169, *184*, 201, 220, 230, 234, *253, 316*

Li, R., *570*

Li, T.-K., 677, 679, 702, *706–711*

Liang, K., 379, *399*

Licari, P. A., *493*

Lichtenstein, C., 588, *620*

Lichtenstein, E., 201, *221*, 386n8, 387, *393, 403, 407, 419, 459, 461, 462, 467, 469, 473, 478, 490, 491, 493*

Lichtman, K., 483, *494*

Liddle, H. A., 632, 642–645, *654*

Lieb, R., 118, *134*

Liebson, I. A., 370, *394, 559, 571*

Liechti, M. E., 118, *133*

Lightwood, J. M., 479, *491*

Lilienfeld, S. O., 59, *85*

Lilliquist, M. W., 343, 344, 358, *363*

Lim, J., *251*

Lim, K., *364*

Lima, J. C., 479, *491*

Lin, E., *423*

Lin, N., *88*

Lind, J. C., 169, *185*

Lindberg, L. D., *341*

Lindros, K. O., 702, *709*

Lindsay, E. A., *492*

Linnan, L., 462, *485*

Lipscomb, T. R., 36, *48*

Litt, M. D., 373, *395*, 410, 414, 415, *423, 517, 532, 533, 535, 536, 547, 555*

Litten, R. Z., 324, *339, 409, 421, 424*

Little, R. J. A., 97, *114, 168, 184*, 501, *511*

Littleton, J., 417, *423*

Liu, K. S., 15, *398, 422, 426*

Liu, W. T., 682, *712*

Liu, X., 199, *222*

Livesley, W. J., 64, 69, *84, 86*

Lo, Y., 238, *253*

Loberg, T., 344, 356, 358, *363, 364*

Løberg, T., 497, *512*

Locke, B. Z., 39, *53, 54, 557*

Locklear, V. S., *618*

Lockshin, B., *491*

Lockwood, C. M., 270, *284*

Loeber, R., 85, 159, *185*, 199, 200, 217, 218, *221, 222*

Lofaso, D., *493*

Logan, E. A., 43, *51*

Logan, J. A., 488, 585, *614, 660, 675*

Loh, E. W., 678, *706*

Lonczak, H. S., 160, *184*

London, R., 418, *421*

Long, S. W., 115, *228, 254*

Longabaugh, R., 38, 46, 47, 50, 52, 345, *363, 406, 407, 411–413, 419, 423, 425, 427, 498, 507n1, 511, 513, 546, 547, 555, 557, 558*

Longmore, B. E., 497, 500, *511*

Longshore, D., 544, *554*

Lopez, A. D., 483, *491*

Lopez, R. E., 418, *421*

Lord, C. G., 150, *156*

Lorenz, F. O., *315*

Lorvick, J., 146, *157*

Loukas, A., 261, 279, *284*

Lowman, C., 406, 409, *421, 423, 424*

Lu, R.-B., *706*

Luborski, L., 500, *511*

Luborsky, L., 35, 42, *51*, 542, *555*

Luce, D. D., *570*

Lucente, S., 359, *362, 510*

Luchins, D. J., 546, *553*

Lucia, V. C., 121, *132*

Luckie, L. E., *52*

Luczak, S. E., 678, 679, 681, 685, 687, 691, 693, 694, 696, 702, 703, *707, 708, 711*

Ludman, E. J., *423*

Lukas, S. E., 118, *133*

Lukasiewicz, M., 533, *535*

Luker, K., 141, *157*

Lurie, P., 139, 146, *156*

Lushene, R., 436, *456*

Luthar, S. S., 263, 280, *284*, 288, *317*

Luu, S.-Y., *709*

Lydiard, R. B., 34, *48*

Lykken, D. T., 84, *86*

Lyon, R. J., 371, *395*

Lyons, C. A., 595, *611*

Lyons, M. J., 60, 79, 86, 88
Lyyti, H., 501, *512*

Ma, Z.-M., 701, *710*
Maany, I., *569, 570*
Macciocchi, S. N., 360, *363*
MacCoun, R. J., 137–140, 142–144, 146, 150, 151, 153, *156, 157*
MacGregor, R., *488*
MacKinnon, D. P., 270, 271, 273, *284, 286, 317*
MacKinnon, S., *570*
Maddahian, E., 313, *315*
Madden, P. A. F., 84, *87, 113,* 244, *254*
Maes, H. H., 88, 108, *114*
Maezawa, Y., 677, 687, *709*
Magdol, L., *285*
Maggs, J. L., 90, 110, 111, *115,* 162, *184,* 226, 228, 243, *254*
Maglione, M., 547, *554*
Magnan, S., *494*
Magnusson, J., 152, *158*
Maguin, E., *183, 316, 613*
Mahableshwarkar, A., *489*
Mahaddian, E., 262, *285*
Mai, X.-L., *711*
Mail, P. D., 575, 576, 589, 607, 609, *615, 616*
Main, D. S., 466, *491*
Maisto, S. A., 227, *254,* 407, *424*
Majd-Jabbari, M., 227, *255*
Majeskie, M. R., 410, *419*
Malcomb, R., 34, *48*
Malin, D. H., *492*
Malloy, P. F., 345, 359, *363, 365,* 498, 507n1, *511, 513*
Malone, S. M., 90, 91, 93, 94, *113, 114,* 261, *286*
Manderscheid, R. W., 39, *53*
Mankowski, E., 549, *555*
Manley, M. W., 464, 466, *491, 492*
Mann, B. J., *653*
Mann, L., 41, *50*
Mann, S. L., 482, *492*
Manning, A., 345, *362*
Manning, D., 659, *674*
Manning, W., 167, *184*

Manson, S., 585, 589, *615*
Manson, S. M., 575, 579, 584, *612, 614, 615, 617*
Manwell, L. B., 418, *421, 554*
Mao, X. Q., 681, *710*
Marcus, A. C., 467, *488*
Marcus, M. D., *492*
Marek, P. M., 482, *492*
Mariani, J., 294n2, *320*
The Marijuana Treatment Project Research Group, 433, 453, *456, 457*
Markides, K. S., 576, *617*
Markman, H. J., *182*
Marks, J. S., *115*
Marks, M. J., 371, *393*
Marlatt, G. A., 36, 38–41, 43, *49, 51,* 90, *112,* 148, *157,* 328, *339, 340,* 368, 371, *394, 395,* 403–408, 410, 412, 413, 418, *419, 421, 424, 427,* 517, 519, *535,* 589, 600–603, 606, 608, *610, 612, 614–616*
Marlowe, D., 660, 661, *674*
Marsano, L., 501, *511*
Marsden, J., 410, *421*
Marshall, G. D., 515, *533*
Marshall, M. P., 160, *184*
Marshall, W. R., 371, *395, 396*
Martin, B., 560, 566, *570*
Martin, C. S., 227, *254,* 265, *285,* 290, 300, *315, 316,* 409, *426,* 658, *675*
Martin, N. G., 108, *113,* 244, *254,* 481, *489*
Martin, S. E., 575, *615*
Martinet, Y., 476, *485*
Martinson, B. C., 478, *493*
Marx, J., 559, *570*
Mase, T., 533, *535*
Mason, B. J., 38, *51*
Mason, K. M., 465, *494*
Mason, V. G., 589, *616*
Masse, L. C., 64, 86, 287, *317*
Mast, E. E., *393*
Masyn, K., *254*
Matarazzo, J. D., 227, *253,* 371, *393,* 516, *534*
Mathalon, D., *364*

Matsueda, R. L., 160, *184*

Matsumoto, M., 685, *707*

Matsuo, Y., 702, *708, 709*

Matsushita, S., 677, 681, 702, *708, 709*

Matters, M. D., 546, *553*

Matthews, C. G., 358, *363*

Mattia, J. I., 81, 88

Mattson, M. E., 546, *555*

Maughan, B., 290, 291, *318*

Mauldon, J., 141, *157*

Maxwell, P., *490*

Maxwell, W. A., 387, *394*

May, P. A., 582, 583–585, 587, *616*

Mayer, L. S., 160, *184*

Mayhew, K. P., *252*

Maziade, M., 289, *317*

Mazza, J. J., *182*

Mazziotta, J. C., *31*

McAfee, T., 478, *487*

McAuliffe, W. E., 38, *56*

McBride, N., 162, *184*

McCabe, G. P., 331, *340*

McCabe, S. E., *132*

McCaffrey, B., 140, *157*

McCaffrey, D. F., 132, *134*

McCann, M., *425*

McCartan, L., *422*

McCarthy, D. E., 410, 414, *419, 425*

McCarthy, D. M., 408, 418, *420, 424*

McCartney, K., 91, 110, *115*, 291, 292, 311, *318*

McClearn, G. E., 96, *115*

McClelland, G. H., 292, *317*

McClure, J., *496*

McConaughy, S. H., 61, *82*, 312, *314*

McCord, J., 199, *222*

McCormick, D., *491*

McCoy, G., 585, *617*

McCoy, J. F., 371, *396*

McCracken, S. G., 551, *553*

McCrady, B. S., 46, *51*, 226, *251*, 548, *555, 556*

McCrae, R., 270, *283*

McDermut, W., 389, *396*

McDonald, R. V., 409, *426*

McDonough, B. E., 389, *399*

McEvoy, L. T., 199, *223*, 682, *707*

McFall, R. M., 372, *396*

McFarlin, S. K., 349, *362*

McGee, B., *569*

McGee, R. O., 63, 85, 287, *315*

McGinnis, J. M., 34, *51*

McGlinchey, J. B., 505, *511*

McGovern, P. G., *490*

McGrew, J., 200, *220*

McGue, M. K., 59–61, 63, 66, 67, 77, 78, 83–86, 90, 91, 93, 94, 96, 108, 109, 111, *112–116*, 259–261, 263, 279, *284–286, 711*

McGuffin, P., 79, 87, 96, *115*

McGuigan, K. A., 159, *183*

McGuire, W. J., 595, *616*

McHugo, G. J., 548, *553*

McIlvain, H. E., 515, *533*

McKay, J. R., 413, *424, 556, 559, 569*

McKee, S. A., 533, *535*

McKelvey, W. F., *425*

McKennell, A. C., 368, 370, 372, *396*

McKinlay, S. M., 464, *486*

McKnight, P., 603, *610*

McLaughlin, J. K., *252*

McLean, A. R., 145, *155*

McLean, M. G., 600, *610*

McLellan, A. T., 35, 42, 46, *51*, 436, 439, 440, 442, 448, 451, *456*, 500, 501, *511*, 542, 543, 547, 552, *555, 556, 559, 569*

McMahon, J., 408, *422*

McMahon, P. T., 627, *652*

McMahon, R. C., 412, *424*

McMorris, B. J., 587, *621*

McNamara, G., 288, 295, 300, 308n8, 314, *320, 586, 621*

McNeal, R. B., 187, *196*

McNeil, A., *486*

McNeill, A., 468, 478, *492, 493*

McPhee, S. J., *339*, 466, *491, 495*

McPhillips-Tangum, C., 478, *491*

McQuilkin, S. J., *31*

McRee, B., 433, *457*

Meador-Woodruff, J. H., 460, *487*

Meadow, A., *489*

Measham, F., 130, *134*

Mechanic, D., 541, *556*

Meddis, R., 375, 396
Medici Skaggs, N., 200, 221
Meek, D. A., 55
Meeker, W. Q., 270n4, 285
Mehta, P., 252
Meier-Tackmann, D., 707
Mellanby, A. R., 595, 616
Mello, N. K., 370, 396
Melo, J. A., 22, 31
Melton, G. B., 653
Mendell, N. R., 238, 253
Mendelson, J. H., 370, 396
Mendelson, M., 436, 455
Mendoza, D., 260, 286
Mercer-McFadden, C., 548, 553
Meredith, L. S., 541, 557
Merette, C., 317
Mermelstein, R. J., 415, 422, 492
Meshkoff, J. E., 543, 552
Metzger, D. S., 51, 456, 511, 556
Meyer, J. M., 86, 114
Meyer, R. E., 31, 34, 50, 54, 339
Meyers, K., 556
Meyers, R. J., 39, 51, 550, 552
Michel, C., 371, 396
Midanik, L. T., 94, 115
Midford, R., 162, 184
Miles, D. R., 79, 86
Miller, A., 492
Miller, E. T., 323, 337, 340
Miller, I. W., 410, 418, 420
Miller, J. Y., 160, 183, 200, 222, 259, 283, 291, 316, 588, 613
Miller, M., 433, 453, 456, 457
Miller, S. D., 541, 554
Miller, S. M., 151, 157
Miller, W. R., 36–46, 47, 48, 50–54, 411, 419, 424, 438, 456, 499, 501, 512, 519, 535, 541, 542, 548, 549, 553, 556, 558, 595, 601, 602, 611, 616
Milligan, B. C., 585, 613
Mills, S., 473, 485
Minder, C., 689, 707
Mineka, S., 62, 86
Minicuci, N., 130, 134
Mintz, J., 370, 396, 422

Miotto, K., 425
Mitchell, C. M., 576, 579, 581, 584, 585, 615–617
Mitchell, S. L., 389, 397
Mittlemark, M. B., 490
Miyatake, R., 709
Mizes, J. S., 489
Moe, J., 339
Moekens, B., 89, 116
Moffitt, T. E., 59, 63, 64, 79, 83, 85, 96, 112, 188, 196, 251, 285, 287, 288, 291, 311n9, 315–317
Moggi, F., 548, 556
Mohatt, G., 591, 602, 614, 616
Mokdad, A., 115
Molenaar, P. C. M., 109, 116, 413, 417, 427
Molina, B., 288, 315
Molnar, B. E., 325, 341
Molof, M., 180, 183
Moltzen, J. O., 407, 420
Monaco, G. E., 144, 156
Monahan, S. C., 38, 49, 542, 553
Moncher, M. S., 580, 587, 616
Montaner, J. S. G., 157
Montello, D., 200, 220
Montgomery, G. K., 372, 396
Montgomery, R. P. G., 407, 421
Monti, P. M., 38, 50, 53, 253, 371, 396, 405, 409, 415, 418, 424, 426, 438, 455, 456, 487, 511, 516, 535, 536, 606, 617
Montoya, A. G., 118, 133
Montoya, I. D., 563n1, 569, 570
Moolchan, E. T., 530, 536
Moon, D. G., 657, 675
Moore, D. S., 331, 340
Moos, B., 540, 543, 545, 550, 556
Moos, R. H., 34, 36, 47, 53, 410, 420, 424, 543, 546, 538–550, 554–558
Moran, J. R., 585, 589, 591, 597, 599, 604, 606, 616, 617
Mordhorst, M. J., 624, 653
Morgan, S. F., 367, 394
Morgenstern, J., 411, 425, 546, 548, 549, 556, 557
Morimoto, K., 681, 701, 710

Moring, J., *552*
Morland, J., 118, *133*
Morral, A. R., 132, *134, 559, 566, 570*
Morrissey-Kane, E., *184*
Morris-Yates, A., 97, *115*
Morse, E., 370, *393*
Morse, P., 373, *395, 414, 423*
Morse, P. M., 517, *535*
Morse, R. M., *534*
Morton, T. L., 34, *50*
Mosback, C., *493*
Moses, H. D., 226, *256*
Moss, H. B., 290, *316, 319*
Moss, H. M., 290, 300, *315*
Mott, M. A., 36, 37, 48, *53*
Mowbray, C. T., *554*
Moyer, A., 540, 542, 543, *557, 558*
Moyers, T. B., 42, 44, *53*
Mrazek, P. J., 159, *184*
Mudar, P., 110, *114*, 412, *425*
Mudd, S. A., 260, *283, 286*
Mudde, A. N., 466, *493*
Muenz, L., *421*
Mueser, K. T., 548, *553*
Mullen, R., 645, *653*
Muller, E. S., *570*
Mulvaney, F. D., 413, *424*, 559, *569*
Mundt, J. C., 417, *425*
Mundt, M. P., *554*
Munoz, N., 227, *254*
Munoz, R. F., 471, *489*
Munroe, S. M., *424*
Muramatsu, T., 677, 681, 687, 701, 702, *708, 709*
Muraven, M., 387, *396*, 411, *425*, 517, 531, 532, *535*
Murayama, M., 677, 681, 702, *708, 709*
Murphy, K. R., 506, *512*
Murray, C. J. L., 483, *491*
Murray, D. M., 293, *317, 490*
Murrelle, L., *114*
Mustillo, S., 93, *112*
Muthén, B. O., 167, 169, *184*, 228, 230, 234, 238, 248, 251, *254*, 267, *285*, 352, *364*, 501, 503, *512, 513*
Muthén, L. K., 169, *184*, 230, 234, 248, *254*, 267, *285*, 352, *364*, 501, *512*

Myers, H. F., 576, *617*
Myers, M. G., 36–38, 48, *53*, 408, *420*
Myers, M. L., 467, 479, *490*
Myors, B., 506, *512*

Naar, S., 267, *282*
Nabors-Oberg, R. E., *116*
Nadelmann, E., 137, 138, 143, *156, 157*
Naehri, V., 501, *512*
Nagin, D. S., 230, *253, 254*
Nagy, S., 588, *612*
Naimi, T. S., 89, *115*
Najavits, L. M., 42, *53*
Nakamura, K., 677, 687, 694, 696, 702, *708, 709*
Nanda, S., 91, *116*
Nansel, T. R., 585, *618*
Naquin, M. R., 368, 386n8, *396*
Narrow, W. E., 39, *53*
Nathan, P. E., 36, *55*, 63, 82, 86, 550, *557*
Nation, M., 181, *184*
National Institute on Alcohol Abuse and Alcoholism, 34, 40, 46, *53*, 94, 98, *115*
National Institute on Drug Abuse, 46, *53*, 580, *617*, 623, *654*
Neale, M. C., 64, 68, 70, 80, 84–86, 97, *113–115, 711*
Needle, R., 297, *317*
Neinhaus, K., 411, *425*
Nelson, D. B., 516, *534*
Nelson, L. M., 348, *363*
Nelson, M. L., *493*
Nelson, S., 219, *221*, 585, *617*
Neter, J., 235n5, *254*
Newcomb, M., 199, *223*
Newcomb, M. D., 34, *53*, 262, *285*, 297, 313, *315, 317*, 588, *617*
Newman, D. L., 64, *83*, 259, *285*, 311n9, *315*
Newman, J. H., 130, *134*
Newman, J. P., 63, *84*
Nezu, A. M., *425*
Niaura, R. S., 253, 369, 371, *396*, 409, 414, 416, 417, *420, 425, 426*, 475, 478, *485, 488, 489, 491*, *534, 536*

Nich, C., 406, 411, *420, 570*
Nichol, K. L., 516, *534*
Nichols, M., 644, *654*
Nichols, T. R., 160, *183*
Nickless, C. J., *555*
Nides, M. A., *490*
Nienhaus, K., 517, *535*
Nil, R., 370, *396*
Nilsson, F., 476, *485, 489*
Nishiura, E., 41, *49*
Nissinen, A., *493*
Nixon, S. J., 500, *512*
Noel, N. E., *47, 345, 363, 498, 511*
Noi-pha, K., 678, *706*
Norcross, J. C., 41, *54, 541, 550, 557*
Norcross, K., *133*
Norman, G. J., *422*
Novins, D. K., 576, 581, 584, 585, *616, 617*
Novotny, T. E., 461, *488*
Novy, P. L., 430, *455*
Nowinski, J., 39, 40, *53, 499, 512*
Noyes, C., 546, *554*
Nugent, S. M., 516, *534*
Nuutinen, H., 702, *709*

Oberklaid, F., 287, *317*
O'Brien, C. P., 27, *32, 42, 51, 456, 500, 511, 555, 556*
O'Brien, J. L., *558*
O'Brien, R., *552*
Ockene, J. K., 467, 472, *492*
O'Connell, K., 526, *535*
O'Conner, E. J., *558*
O'Connor, P. J., 478, *493*
O'Dell, S., *422*
O'Donnell, R. P., 371, *393*
Oetting, E. R., 200, 201, 217, *220, 223, 296, 317, 576, 582–584, 587, 588, 594, 605, 611, 612, 617*
O'Farrell, T. J., 38, *53, 54, 349, 362*
Offord, D. R., 590, *618*
Offord, K. P., *490, 494, 534*
Ogden, D., *50*
Ogel, K., 118, *132*
O'Gorman, T. W., 60, *83*
Oh, S. I., 681, *709*

O'Hare, P., 137, *156*
Okazaki, S., 658, *675*
Okwumabua, J. O., 579, 581, 584, *618*
Olasfsdottir, I., 476, *485*
O'Leary, K. D., 261, *283*
O'Leary, M. R., 348, *365*
O'Leary, T., 418, *424, 606, 617*
Olivares, R., *485*
Ollendick, T. H., 550, *552*
Olsen, M. K., 167, 180, *185*
O'Malley, P. M., 90, *112, 115, 118, 133, 162, 166, 182, 184, 195, 195, 200, 201, 223, 225, 226, 228, 231, 232, 233n4, 249, 251–255, 296, 316, 324, 339, 583, 614, 620, 657, 661, 674, 675*
O'Malley, S. S., 27, *31, 32, 38, 54, 344, 348, 352, 364, 533, 535*
Omata, M., *710*
Oncken, C. A., 516, *533, 536*
O'Neill, S. E., 94, *115*
O'Nell, T. D., 585, 587, *618*
Orford, J., 43, *49, 54*
Orlandi, M. A., *618*
Orlando, M., 226, *255*
Orleans, C. T., 466, 472, *485, 492*
Orlikov, A., 371, *396*
Osborne, M. L., 469, *494*
Osgood, D. W., 201, *223*
O'Shaughnessy, M. V., *157*
Osier, M. V., 678, 680, *708, 709*
Ossip-Klein, D. J., 473, *491*
Ostafin, B., 516, *535*
Oster, Z., *365*
Osterrieth, P. A., 348, *364*
Ouimette, P. C., 540, 542, 548, *556, 557*
Overall, J., *365*
Owen, E. H., *31*
Oxford English Dictionary Online, 403n1, *425*
Ozechowski, T. J., 642, *654*

Pabiniak, C., 478, *487*
Packer, L., 121, *132*
Padilla, A., 587, *620*
Paik, Y. K., *710*

Pakstis, A. J., 680, *708, 709*
Pakula, A., 324, 337, *340*
Palfai, T. P., 110, *114,* 409, *425,* 516, *535*
Pallonen, U., 483, *494*
Pandina, R. J., 226, 227, *251, 256,* 410,
    420
Panella, D., 204, *223*
Pantilat, S., *339*
Pappas, N., *488*
Paraherakis, A., 412, *421*
Parent, D., 559, *570*
Park, J. Y., 681, *709*
Park, S. C., 681, *709*
Parker, H., 130, *134*
Parker, K., *654*
Parker-Langley, L., 598, *618*
Parkin, A. J., 357, *364*
Parks, G. A., 328, *339*
Paronis, C. A., 369, *395,* 412, *423*
Parra, G. R., 94, *115,* 238n7, *254*
Parrott, A. C., 118, *134,* 370, 386n8, *397*
Parrott, S., 478, *492*
Parsons, O. A., 344, 345, 358, 360, *362,
    364, 365,* 498, *512*
Partidas, A., *489*
Pasveer, K. A., 324, *340*
Patel, U. A., 368, *397*
Paton, A., 34, *47*
Patrick, C. J., 63, 86, 88, *284*
Patrick, D. M., *157*
Patrick, K., 473, *493*
Patten, C. A., *490,* 516, *533*
Patterson, G. R., 79, 86, 201, 203, 206,
    218, 220, *221, 223,* 261, 262,
    279, 285, 314, *317*
Patterson, T. L., 36, *48*
Paty, J., 411, *426,* 474, *494,* 532, *534*
Paty, J. A., 11, *15, 16,* 369, 373–376,
    387–389, 391, *397, 398, 422,
    426,* 474, *494,* 517, *535, 536*
Pavan, D., 324, *341*
Paylor, R., *31*
Payne, T. J., 368, 371, 387, *397*
Pechacek, T., *492*
Pechacek, T. F., *490*
Pedersen, W., 117–119, 131, *134,* 159,
    185

Pedlow, R., 287, 290, *317*
Pedraza, M., 371, *396*
Peele, S., 43, 44, *54*
Peirce, J. M., 561, 566, 567n1, *570*
Peirce, R. S., 412, *425*
Pelham, W. E., 290, *316*
Pelletier, K. R., 462, *492*
Peng, G.-S., 679, 701, 706, *709*
Pentel, P. R., 477, *492*
Pentz, M. A., 312, *317*
Perez-Vidal, A., 635, 638, 654, *655*
Perkins, K. A., 368, 370, 389, *397,* 481,
    482, *492*
Perlick, D., 368, *398*
Peroutka, S. J., 130, *134*
Perrott, M. A., 409, *426*
Perry, C. L., 293, *317*
Perry, M. G., *425*
Perry, R. B., 152, *158*
Perz, W., 16, *398*
Peters, R., *51,* 456, *511*
Peterson, A. V., 482, *492*
Peterson, B. E., 151, 152, *157*
Peterson, L., 261, *285*
Peterson, R., *157*
Peterson, T., 635, *655*
Peto, J., 368, *397*
Petoskey, E. L., 589, 591, 592, *618*
Petry, N. M., 559, 560, 566, 567, *570*
Pettit, G. S., *315,* 413, *421*
Pfefferbaum, A., 343, *364*
Pfeifer, M., *55*
Pfister, H., 118, *134*
Philibert, R., *112*
Phillips, M., 41, *54,* 162, *184*
Phillips, T. J., *31*
Phinney, J. S., 624, *654*
Pianezza, M. L., 481, *492*
Piasecki, T. M., 410, 414, 416, *425,* 472,
    492, 494
Piccinin, A. M., 312, *315*
Picciotto, M. R., 477, *493*
Pickens, R. W., 60, 86, 88, 91, *115,*
    260, *284,* 367, *394, 711*
Pickles, A., 88, 290, 291, *318*
Pickrel, S. G., 638, *653*
Pierce, J. P., 461, *488, 491, 495, 496*

Piercy, F. P., 645, *654*
Pieterse, M. E., 466, *493*
Pietrukowicz, M., *493*
Pietruszko, R., 679, *707*
Pihl, R. O., 64, *87*, 117, *133*
Pilich, A., 501, *511*
Pilkey, D. T., 516, *533, 536*
Pillow, D. R., 288, *315*
Pilskin, J. S., *495*
Pingitore, R., *489*
Pinney, J., 474, *494*
Piper, M. E., 410, *419*
Pirie, P. L., *490*
Pitkanen, T., 287, *317*
Pitts, S. C., 90, *112*, 226, *252*, 260, *282*
Pizacani, B., *493*
Pleck, J. H., *341*
Pledger, M., 118, *134*
Plested, B. A., 605, *612*
Plomin, R., 79, *83*, 96, *112*, 115, 290, 292, 303, 310, *315, 317, 318*
Pociask, K., 22, *31*
Podus, D., 539, *557*
Poe, J., 204, *223*
Polich, J., 91, 109, *115*
Poling, J., 560, *570*
Polinsky, M. L., 547, *554*
Polivy, J., 404, 406, *425*
Pollack, V. E., 91, *115*
Pollock, N. K., 265, *285*
Pomerleau, C. S., 367–369, 387, *397*
Pomerleau, O. F., 367–369, 387, *397*, 481, *493*
Pomrehn, P., *492*
Poon, E., 345, *364*
Pope, H. G., Jr., 430, *456*
Pople, K. S., *653*
Porjesz, B., *31*, 95, *112, 711*
Portnoff, L. A., 344, *364*
Posner, M. J., 287, *318*
Poulos, C. X., 369, *397*
Prange, M., 372, *398*
Prendergast, M. L., 539, 544, *554, 557*
Prescott, C. A., 60, 79, 80, 84–86
Presson, C. C., 200, *220*, 226, *252*
Preston, K. L., 560, 566, 568, *570*
Preston-Martin, S., *252*

Price, B. H., 118, *133*
Price, R., 69, *87*
Prior, M., 287, 289, 300n4, 312, *317, 318*
Pritchard, H. E., 46, *54*
Prochaska, J. O., 41, *54*, 324, 328, *340*, 410, *425*, 472, 473, 475, 477, *485, 495*, 601, 605, *618*
Prochazka, A. V., *493*
Project MATCH Research Group, 26, 27, *31*, 39, 40, *54*, 407, 417, *425*, 499, 501, 508, *512*, 542, *557*
Pronk, N. P., 478, *493*
Prost, J., 90, *112*, 226, *252*
Prue, D. M., 407, *426*, 589, *618*
Pryzbeck, T. R., 34, 36, 37, *49, 54*, 264, *283*
Przybeck, T. R., 199, 202, 218, *223*, 288, *318*, 569
Puech, A. J., *485*
Pulkkinen, L., 199, *223*, 287, *317*
Purcell, T., *492*
Puska, P., 463, 464, 487, *493*

Quertemont, E., 679, 701, *709*
Quigley, L. A., 38, *51*, 148, *157*, 615
Quinn, N., 605, *618*
Quinn, W., 645, *653*
Quinton, D., 290, 291, *318*

Rabois, D., 413, *425*
Radhert, E., 582, *620*
Radin, S., *615*
Radonovich, K. J., 430, *455*
Radziminski, S., *710*
Rae, D. S., 39, 53, 54, *557*
Raftery, A. E., 70, *87*
Rahdert, E., 657, 658, *675*
Rakowski, W., *488*
Ramanaiah, N. V., 368, *394*
Ramirez, A., 559, *570*
Ramsey, E., 261, *285*, 314, *317*
Randall, M., *456, 555*
Ranseen, J. D., 360, *363*
Rapp, S., 407, *426*, 589, *618*
Raskin, G., 261, *285*
Ratanachaiyavong, S., 678, *706*
Ratcliff, K. S., 267, *285*

Raudenbush, S. W., 96, *112*, 169, *174n4*, *185*
Raw, M., 468, 478, *492*, *493*
Rawlings, R. R., 344, *362*
Rawson, R. A., 406, *425*, 559, *570*
Ray, J. W., 390, *395*
Read, J. P., 110, *114*
Reaman, J. A., 591, 597, 599, 604, 606, *617*
Reardon, S. F., 657, *675*
Reavy, R., *114*
Rebok, G. W., 160, *184*
Redmond, C., 160, *185*, 483, *494*
Reed, G. M., 658, *675*
Reed, H. B., 498, *511*
Reed, R., 345, *362*
Rees, J. B., 595, *616*
Regier, D. A., 34, 36, 39, *53*, *54*, 547, *557*
Reiber, C., *425*, 559, *570*
Reich, T., 20, *31*, *32*, *711*
Reich, W., 66, 88, 269n3, *283*
Reid, J. B., 160, *182*, 201, 218, *223*
Reilly, P. M., 407, *420*
Reingold, A. L., 139, 146, *156*
Reitan, R. M., 357, *364*, 500, *512*
Rekart, M. L., *157*
Relapse Research Group, 406, *424*
Remington, P. L., *393*
Renjilian, D. A., *425*
Rennard, S. I., *490*
Rennick, P. M., 348, *362*, *364*
Reppucci, N. D., 194, *196*
Resko, J. A., 260, *286*
Resnick, M. D., 584, *611*
Resnick, M. P., *490*
Reus, V. I., 471, *489*
Reuter, P., 137–140, *142*, *143*, *156*, *157*
Reynaud, M., 533, *535*
Reynolds, N. C., 372, *396*
Reynolds, S., 59, *83*
Rhee, J., 151, *156*
Rhoades, H., 418, *426*
Rhodes, S. S., 358, *364*
Ribisi, K. M., *554*
Rice, C., *555*
Rice, J. P., *32*
Richardson, J. L., 226, *252*

Ridge, B., *315*
Ridgely, M. S., 539, *555*
Ridley, D. L., 369, *393*
Rigdon, E. E., 305n7, *318*
Riggins-Caspers, K., 109, *112*
Rigotti, N. A., 461, 466, *489*, *493*, *495*
Rim, L., 348, *364*
Ringwalt, C. L., 187, 188, *195*, *196*
Ritsher, J., 540, *557*
Ritt, A., 483, *494*
Ritter, J., 259, 262, *282*
Rivara, F. P., 438, *455*
Rivelli, S., 482, *488*
Robbin, A., 577, *618*
Robbins, S. J., 559, *569*
Roberts, L. J., 505, *511*
Roberts, S. B., 64, *87*
Robinette, D., 481, *486*
Robins, L., 500, *512*
Robins, L. M., 66, 69, 87, 93, *115*
Robins, L. N., 36, *54*, 199, 202, 218, *223*, 267, 269, 285, 288, *318*
Robinson, L., 679, *711*
Robinson, T. E., 369, 370, 388, *397*
Robinson, T. N., 473, *493*
Roche, A., *134*
Rock, N., *490*
Rode, S., *31*
Rodgers, W. L., *251*
Rodin, E., 348, *364*
Rodriquez, O., 673, *675*
Roeder, K., 230, *253*
Roessner, J., 545, *552*
Roffman, R. A., 41, *55*, 406, *426*, 430, 431, *455*, *456*
Rogers, C. M., 371, *396*
Rogers, S. M., *341*, 345, *363*, 498, *511*
Rogers, W. H., 541, *557*
Rogosch, F., 263, 283, 295, *314*
Rogosch, F. A., 226, *252*
Rohay, J. M., 474, *494*
Rohde, K., 483, *493*
Rohsenow, D. J., 38, *53*, *253*, 371, *396*, 408, 409, 415, *424*, *426*, 487, 516, *534–536*
Rolando, R., *489*
Rolf, J. E., 585, *618*

Rollnick, S., 41, 42, *52*, 410, 418, *424*, *438*, *456*, 471, *486*, *493*, 601, 602, *616*
Romoli, C., *493*
Roque, C., *365*
Rosales, R., *653*
Rosbrook, B., *491*, *496*
Rose, G., 148, *157*
Rose, J. E., 368, 371, 387, *394–397*, 477, *493*
Rose, R. J., 90, *116*
Rosenbaum, D. P., 187, *196*
Rosenbaum, M., 129, *132*, *364*
Rosenberg, M., 190, *196*
Rosenheck, R. A., 551, *557*
Rosenthal, R. N., 547, *557*
Ross, L., 150, *156*
Rossi, J. S., 472, *495*
Rothbart, M. K., 287–290, 292, 300, 310, *318*
Rothman, K. J., 227, *252*
Rounsaville, B. J., *31*, 34, 36, *54*, *339*, 406, 420, 570, 642, *653*
Rourke, S. B., 344, 356, *364*, 497, 498, *512*
Rowe, W. E., 592, 593, 600, 604, *614*, *618*
Rubin, A., 406, *423*, *427*, 540, *558*
Rubin, B. R., 199, *222*
Rubin, D. B., 97, *114*, 168, *184*, 238, *253*, 501, *511*
Rubonis, A. V., 38, *50*
Rudas, T., 379, 384, *397*
Ruel, E., 226, *252*
Ruggiero, S. D., *55*
Rush, A. J., 500, *510*
Russell, I., *486*
Russell, J. A. 375, 386, 391, *397*, 522, *536*
Russell, M. A. H., 368, 372, *397*, 412, *425*, *495*
Russo, N. F., 591, *613*
Rustine, T., *362*
Rutherford, M. J., *569*
Rutigliano, P., 349, *362*
Rutter, C., *423*
Rutter, M. L., 60, 87, 263, *285*, 288–291, 310, 311, 313, *318*, 588, *618*

Ryan, L., 358, *363*
Ryan, T. M., 543, *552*
Rychtarik, R. G., 40, *52*, 407, *426*, 499, *512*, 589, *618*
Rydell, C. P., 147, *155*
Ryzov, I., 371, *396*

Sabol, S. Z., 481, *493*
Sachs, D. P., *490*
Sadler, G., *496*
Safran, D. G., *495*
Said, S., *485*
Saigal, D., 679, *711*
Saiger, A., 137, *156*
Sakurai, S., 677, *709*
Salasnek, S., 635, *652*
Salaspuro, M., 702, *709*
Salonen, J., *493*
Samuel, S., 507n1, *510*
Sanderson, W. C., *653*
Sandhu, H. K., *112*
Sandler, I. N., 271, *286*
Sandy, J. M., 261, *286*, 287, 290, 311–314, 311n9, *320*
Sankis, L., 59, *88*
Sanson, A., 287, *317*
Santisteban, D. A., 532, 638, 639, 641, 642, 644, 645, *655*, *654*
Sarason, I. G., 482, *492*
Saunders, B., 41, *54*, 407, *419*
Saunders, J. B., 327, *340*, 678, *706*
Sawyer, D. A., 371, *397*
Sayer, A. G., 300, *319*
Sayette, M. A., 389, *397*, 409, *426*, *427*
Scarr, S., 91, 97, 110, *115*, 290–292, 311, *318*
Schachter, S., 368, 387, *398*
Schaefer, J., 540, *556*
Schaeffer, K. W., 344, 345, 359, *364*
Schafer, G. L., *31*
Schafer, J. L., 167, 180, *185*, 359, *362*
Schafer, K., 498, *513*
Schare, M. L., 368, *397*
Scharron-del-Rio, M. R., 624, 638–640, 646, 651, *652*
Schechter, M. T., 139n1, *155*, *157*
Scheier, L. M., 34, 49, 160, *183*

Schelling, T., 138, 143, 146, *156*
Schensky, A. E., *488*
Schifano, F., 130, *134*
Schinke, S. P., 586, 596, 597, 600, 604, *618, 619*
Schmeidler, J., 659, *674*
Schmidt, W. C., 323, *340*
Schmitt, F. A., 360, *363*
Schmitz, J. M., 368, 372, *394, 399,* 418, *426*
Schneider, M., 689, *707*
Schneiger, A., 219, *221*
Schoberberger, J. C., *487*
Schoof, K., *362*
Schottenfeld, R. S., *31,* 38, *54*
Schuckit, M. A., 21, *32,* 34, 36, 37, 40, *47, 48, 54,* 91, *113, 363,* 682, 701, *709–711*
Schulenberg, J. E., 89, 90, 91, 110, 111, *112, 115,* 118, *133,* 162, 166, *182, 184,* 225, 226, 228, 231, 232, 233n4, 243, 249, *251–255, 620, 675*
Schulsinger, F., 60, *84*
Schulteis, G., 24, *32*
Schulz, R., 545, *558*
Schumacker, R. E., 305n7, *318*
Schuster, C. R., *570*
Schwartz, G., 238, 239n1, *255*
Schwartz, J. E., 373, *399,* 517, 526, *535, 536*
Schwartz, J. M., *31*
Schwartz, S. J., *654*
Scott, R., *422*
Scutchfield, F. D., 483, *487*
Seaton, B. E., 497, *510*
Sees, K. L., *489*
Segal, B., 418, *421*
Segal, N., *84*
Segars, L. B., 91, *112*
Segraves, K. A., *489*
Seibring, M., 110, *113*
Seidner, A. L., 515, *533*
Sellers, E. M., 481, *492*
Serdula, M. K., *115*
Severson, H. H., 462, 467, *488, 493*
Seybolt, D., *184*

Seydel, E. R., 466, *493*
Shadel, W. G., 417, *425*
Shaham, Y., 417, *426*
Shanahan, T., 498, *510*
Sharpe, J. P., 368, *394*
Shaw, B. F., 500, *510*
Shayka, J. J., 683, *706*
Shea, S. H., 678, 679, 681, 702, *707, 708, 710, 711*
Shear, M. K., 552, *554*
Shear, P., *364*
Shedler, J., 188, *196*
Sheets, V., 270, *284*
Sheikh, S., 679, *711*
Shelton, K. K., 281, *286*
Shen, Y.-C., 678, 685, 688, *710*
Shendure, J., 22, *31*
Sher, K. H., 37, *54*
Sher, K. J., *51,* 59, 63, 78, 81, 87, 90, 91, 94, 110, *113–116,* 228, 238n7, 244, 250, *253–255,* 260–262, *285,* 294n2, *318*
Sherman, J. E., 370, *393*
Sherman, S. J., 200, *220,* 226, *252*
Shermer, R. L., *425*
Sherratt, E., *485*
Sherwood, H., 411, *426*
Shestowsky, J. S., 117, *133*
Shetty, P., 480, *494*
Shi, J., *535*
Shields, A. L., 416, *422,* 532, *534*
Shields, A. S., 417, *427*
Shiffman, S., 11, *15, 16, 255,* 368–376, 387–391, *394, 397–399,* 408–411, 414, 415, 417, 418, *422, 423, 427,* 465, 470, 471, 474, 475, 480, 490, *494,* 517, 520, 526, 531, 532, *534–536*
Shilling, R. F., *619*
Shillington, A. M., 91, *112,* 627, 636, 637, 651, *654*
Shin, C., 160, *185,* 483, *494*
Shinar, O., 261, *286,* 288, 290, 313, 314, *319, 320*
Shipley, R. H., 464, *494*
Shiratori, Y., *710*
Shoaib, M., 371, *398*

Shoham, V., 653
Shopland, D., 466, 491
Shoptaw, S., 425
Shore, J., 585, 615
Shortell, S. M., 545, 558
Shrout, P. E., 270, 285
Siegel, J. E., 495
Siegel, M., 479, 491
Siegel, S., 36, 54, 55, 369, 397, 409,
    426
Sierra, S., 570
Sigvardsson, S., 23, 31, 60, 64, 83
Silberg, J. L., 88, 114
Silk Walker, P., 579, 584, 613, 619
Silva, M. T. A., 118, 133
Silva, P. A., 59, 63, 64, 83, 85, 251,
    285, 287, 288, 311n9, 315, 316
Silver, L. M., 22, 31
Silverman, K., 560, 566, 568, 569, 570
Silverstein, B., 368, 398
Silverthorn, P., 281, 286
Simcic, F., 560, 570
Simon, G., 423
Simone, S. S., 55
Simonoff, E., 88, 318
Simons, R. L., 315
Simpkins, C. G., 34, 50
Simpson, D. D., 539, 558, 588, 610
Simpson, E. E., 406, 426, 430, 456
Simpson, T. L., 52
Singer, B., 542, 555
Singer, D. E., 466, 495
Singh, S., 679, 701, 707, 710
Singleton, E. G., 409, 427, 530, 536
Sinha, R., 32, 345, 365
Sippel, J. M., 469, 494
Siqueland, L., 539, 542, 553
Sirota, A. D., 536
Sirota, L. A., 493
Sisk, E., 118, 134
Sisson, R. W., 550, 552
Skinner, E. A., 411, 426
Skinner, H. A., 324, 327, 337, 340, 416,
    426
Skitka, L. J., 152, 157
Sklar, S. M., 407, 426
Skog, O. J., 148, 157

Skrondal, A., 117–119, 131, 134, 159, 185
Slade, J., 466, 492
Slesnick, N., 635, 655
Slosson, R. L., 518, 536
Slutske, W. S., 60, 62, 68, 79, 84, 86,
    87, 88, 111, 113, 116, 259, 285
Smith, A., 348, 365, 500, 513
Smith, G. D., 683, 685, 708
Smith, G. E., 313, 315
Smith, G. M., 199, 223
Smith, I., 51, 456, 511
Smith, J., 289, 300n4, 312, 318
Smith, J. E., 38, 39, 51
Smith, J. L., 324, 339
Smith, L. A., 653
Smith, M. A., 324, 340
Smith, R. S., 311n9, 319
Smith, S. S., 423, 472, 488, 490, 494, 496
Smith, T. A., 483, 494
Smith, T. L., 21, 32, 363, 513
Smoking Cessation Clinical Guideline
    Panel and Staff, 520, 536
Sneyd, J., 420
Snyder, F. R., 369, 399
Sobel, M. E., 270n4, 270n5, 285
Sobel, R., 507n1, 510
Sobell, L. C., 41, 45, 49, 55, 324, 340,
    341, 348, 349, 365, 436, 442,
    456, 519, 536, 602, 619, 641,
    654
Sobell, M. B., 41, 45, 49, 55, 324, 340,
    341, 348, 349, 365, 436, 442,
    456, 519, 536, 602, 619, 641,
    654
Sofuoglu, M., 560, 566, 570
Solberg, L. I., 467, 490, 494
Solomon, D. A., 359, 365
Solowij, N., 117, 134
Somervell, P., 589, 617
Son, H.-G., 707
Sonenstein, F. L., 341
Sörbom, D., 301, 303, 316
Sorensen, G., 462, 463, 494
Sorrell, M. F., 702, 710
Sorrentino, R., 118, 133
Soto, J., 155
Sparadeo, F. R., 36, 55

Speckart, G. R., 543, 552
Spellers, R. E., 657, 675
Spencer, V., 55
Spicer, P., 587, 619
Spiegel, D. A., 405, 420
Spielberger, C. D., 436, 442, 456
Spindler, G. D., 587, 619
Spindler, L. S., 587, 619
Spirito, A., 487
Spitzer, R. L., 268, 283, 349, 365, 436,
    455, 519, 533
Spoth, R. L., 160, 185, 483, 494
Spracklen, K., 201, 220
Spracklen, K. M., 200, 201, 220, 221
Spreen, O., 350, 361, 500, 513
Sprenkle, D. H., 645, 654
Spreux-Varoquaux, O., 485
Spring, B., 489, 491
Sprott, J. C., 416, 427
Stacy, A. W., 249, 255, 297, 316
Stafford, R. S., 466, 495
Stallard, A., 407, 422
Stallings, M. C., 61, 88
Stanley, J., 551, 554
Stanley, L. C., 464, 494
Stanton, A. L., 372, 399
Stanton, W. R., 251, 252, 285
Stapelton, J. A., 495
Stapleton, J. M., 344, 362
Stark, M., 493
StataCorp LC, 686, 710
Stata Corporation, 121, 134
Stauffacher, E. A., 554
Stebbins, G. T., 350, 365
Steffens, R. A., 34, 55
Steiger, J. H., 169, 185
Stein, J. A., 187, 188, 195, 199, 223
Steinberg, H. R., 533, 536
Steinberg, K. L., 432, 438, 439, 456
Steiner, L., 551, 553
Steiner, S. S., 418, 427
Steinhauer, S. R., 109, 113
Steinman, K., 226, 254
Steinmetz, J. E., 109, 114
Stephens, R. S., 41, 55, 406, 426, 430,
    431, 435, 436, 438, 440, 442,
    447, 452, 453, 455, 456

Stetner, F., 482, 488
Stetter, M., 585, 617
Stetzer, A., 145, 157
Stevens, L., 358, 364
Stewart, D., 410, 421
Stewart, J., 369, 370, 399, 417, 423, 426
Stewart, M. A., 36, 48, 109, 112
Stice, E., 281, 286, 289, 291, 315, 318
Stinchfield, R. D., 658, 659, 676
Stinson, F. S., 34, 55
Stitzer, M. L., 559, 560, 566, 568, 569–571
Stockwell, T., 38, 55
Stoltenberg, S. F., 260, 268, 283, 286
Stone, A. A., 16, 372, 373, 398, 399,
    408, 417, 427, 517, 536
Stone, S. A., 600, 619
Stoneman, Z., 311, 315
Stoolmiller, M., 220, 291, 318
Stott, N., 471, 486, 493
Stotts, A., 418, 426
Stout, R., 507n1, 513
Stout, R. L., 47, 406, 418, 423, 424,
    427, 435, 456, 540, 558
Stouthamer-Loeber, M., 159, 185
Strada, M. J., 653
Strain, E. C., 559, 571
Strathdee, S. A., 139n1, 157
Stratton, K., 480, 494
Strauss, E., 500, 513
Strecher, V. J., 473, 474, 490, 494
Stretch, V., 496
Strickler, D. P., 387, 394
Stroud, L. R., 369, 395, 412, 423
Strycker, L. A., 301, 316
Stubben, J. D., 587, 621
Sturm, R., 541, 557
Stuss, D. T., 503, 513
Su, S., 297, 317
Substance Abuse and Mental Health
    Services Administration, 118,
    121, 134, 429, 430, 456, 623,
    624, 635–637, 654
Substance Abuse and Mental Health Ser-
    vices Administration, Center for
    Substance Abuse Prevention, Divi-
    sion of Knowledge Development
    and Evaluation, 591, 608, 619

Substance Abuse and Mental Health Services Administration, Office of Applied Studies, 579, 583, 584, 619

Substance Abuse and Mental Health Services Administration Office of Applied Studies, 457

Suchinsky, R., 539, 556

Sue, S., 624, 641, 643, 645–647, 651, 654, 658, 675

Sullivan, E., 364

Sun, F., 701, 710

Sussman, J., 642, 653

Sussman, S., 249, 255, 483, 494

Sutherland, G., 474, 476, 495

Sutker, P. A., 345, 365

Suwaki, H., 702, 708, 709

Suzuki, H., 677, 709

Svikis, D., 563n1, 569

Svikis, D. S., 60, 86, 88, 91, 115, 711

Swaim, R. C., 587, 617

Swan, G. E., 475, 481, 486, 487, 495

Swanner, L. S., 371, 398

Swanson, L., 605, 612

Swearingen, C. E., 540, 543, 557, 558

Swendsen, J. D., 412, 427

Swift, R., 409, 425

Swift, W., 431, 455

Swirsky-Sacchetti, T., 507n1, 510

Sylvain, C., 407, 427

Szapocznik, J., 633, 635, 638, 641–645, 654, 655

Szasz, T. S., 44, 55

Szuba, M. P., 31

Tabachnick, B. G., 74n1, 87

Takada, A., 679, 707

Takagi, S., 677, 708

Takase, S., 679, 707

Takeshita, T., 681, 701, 710

Tanaka, F., 677, 688, 694, 696, 710

Tanaka, J. S., 660, 674

Tanda, G., 371, 399

Tang, H., 541, 553

Tarbox, A. R., 36, 49, 408, 421

Tardif, M., 559, 570

Tarrier, N., 552

Tarter, R. E., 37, 50, 61, 63, 82, 87, 227, 254, 287, 290, 291, 294n2, 300, 311n9, 312, 315, 316, 319

Tate, J. C., 372, 399

Taub, E., 418, 427

Taylor, A., 79, 83, 96, 112

Taylor, B. J., 168, 185

Taylor, C. A., 37, 41, 52

Taylor, C. B., 464, 487, 488

Taylor, G. M., 360, 363

Taylor, J., 61, 63, 84, 86, 93, 113, 261, 279, 286

Taylor, R. C., 530, 536

Taylor, S., 311n9, 320

Taylor-Caldwell, A., 653

Tedford, J., 570

Teichner, G. A., 652

Tein, J., 271, 277, 286

Tejeda, M., 654

Tellegen, A., 64, 67, 87

Tengs, T. O., 478, 495

Tennen, H., 412, 427

Tepavac, L., 596, 619

Terborg, J. R., 462, 488

Tetlock, P. E., 151, 152, 157

Thapar, A., 79, 87

Thayer, J. F., 586, 614

Theraulaz, G., 420

Thijs, J., 476, 490

Thivierge, J., 317

Thomas, F., 645, 653

Thomas, L., 602, 612

Thomas, R. K., 368, 370, 396

Thomasson, H. R., 677, 678, 685, 688, 692–695, 697, 701, 710, 711

Thompson, B., 494

Thompson, G., 55

Thompson, L. L., 348, 363

Thorndike, A. N., 466, 495

Thurman, P. J., 589, 619

Thyer, B. A., 349, 365

Tibshirani, R. J., 329, 339

Tice, D. M., 43, 47, 411, 419

Tiffany, S. T., 368, 370, 371, 387, 390, 393, 399, 409, 420, 427, 531, 536

Timko, C., 543, 547, 548, 554, 558

Tipp, J. E., 682, *709, 710*
Tobler, N. S., 188, *195,* 595, *619*
Toda, G., 677, *709*
Todd, M., 260, *282*
Tomkins, S. S., 368, *399*
Tomlinson, K. L., 418, *424*
Toneatto, R., *365*
Toneatto, T., 41, *49*
Tonegawa, S., *31*
Tong, J. E., 371, *395*
Tonigan, J. S., 40, 41, 46, *47, 51, 52,*
    548, 549, *553, 558*
Tonry, M. H., 152, *157*
Topp, L., 117, 118, 130, 131, *133, 134*
Torabi, M. R., 227, *255*
Toscova, R., 548, *558*
Tracey, D. A., 36, *55*
Treitas, T. T., *362*
Tremblay, R. E., 64, 86, *87,* 287, *317*
Triandis, H. C., 605, *619*
Trim, R., 259, *282*
Trimble, J. E., 575, 580, 587–589, 591,
    610, 614, 616–620
Tripp, J. H., 595, *616*
Troughton, E. P., 60, *83,* 109, *112*
Truax, C. B., 541, *558*
Truax, P., 659, *674*
True, W. R., 63, 86, 88, *284*
Trull, T. J., 59, 78, 81, *87,* 294n2, *318*
Tschann, J. M., 289n1, *319*
Tsuang, M. T., 60, *88*
Tsukada, Y., *710*
Tsuritani, I., 701, *710*
Tucker, J. A., 36, *55,* , 540, *555,* 658,
    675
Tucker, J. S., 159, 169, *183,* 226, 234,
    243, *255*
Tucker, L. R., *185,* 351, *365*
Tuma, D. J., 702, *710*
Tuomilehot, J., *493*
Turbin, M. S., 160, *183,* 588, *613*
Turin, A. C., 371, *397*
Turkheimer, E., 80, *88*
Turner, C. F., 34, *47,* 324, 337, *341,*
    635, *655*
Turner, J. J. D., 118, *134*
Turner, N. E., 407, *426*

Turner, S., 658, *675*
Tyler, J., 588, *620*
Tyndale, R. F., 481, *492*

Uebersax, J. S., 626, *655*
Ullman, J. B., 187, 188, *195*
Umbricht, A., 568, *570*
Umbricht-Schneiter, A., *570*
Ungerleider, S., 180, *183*
United Nations Office for Drug Control
    and Drug Prevention, 118, *134*
Urbanski, L., 591, *613*
U.S. Census Bureau, 577, 599, *620,* 624,
    640, *655*
U.S. Congress, Office of Technology
    Assessment, 35, *55,* 581, 585, *620*
U.S. Department of Commerce, 292,
    319
U.S. Department of Health and Human
    Services, 34, *55,* 90, *116,* 367,
    390, 391, *399,* 461, 482, *495,*
    575, *620,* 623, 624, 635, *655,*
    682, *711*
Useda, J. D., *87*

Vaccaro, D., 287, 288, 295, *319, 320,*
    586, *621*
Vagg, P. R., 436, *456*
Vagge, L., *421*
Vaillant, G. E., 538, *558*
Valle, S. K., 42, *55*
van Baal, G. C. M., 109, *116*
Van Beijsterveldt, C. E. M., 109, *116*
Van De Mass, P. J., 479, *485*
Van Den Bos, J., 160, *183,* 588, *613*
van den Bree, M. B. M., 60, 88, 682,
    711
van den Oord, E. J. C. G., 69, *88*
van der Maas, H., 413, 417, *427*
Vanderryn, J., 160, *183,* 588, *613*
Vanderwagen, W., 585, *617*
Vanderwagen, W. C., 609, *620*
Van Eerdewegh, P., *32*
Van Stelle, K. R., 589, *618*
Van Vunakis, H., *394*
Vanyukov, M. M., 287, 290, *319*
Vartiainin, E., *493*

Vaughan, R. D., *113*
Veiel, H. O. F., 359, *365*
Velarde, J., 587, *617*
Velicer, W., *485*
Velicer, W. F., 461, 472, 473, *495*
Vendetti, J., 433, *457*
Venturelli, P. J., 43, *49*
Vergun, P., 540, *557*
Vernon, P. A., 64, 69, 84, *86*
Verona, E., 63, *88*
Victor, M., 497, *513*
Viegener, B. J., *425*
Vik, P. W., 36, *48*, 412, *419*
Vikander, B., 344, *361*
Viken, R. J., 90, *116*
Vincelette, J., *155*
Vitaro, F., 64, *87*
Voas, R. B., *114*
Voelbel, G. T., 346, *361*, 498, *510*
Vogel-Scibilia, S., 551, *554*
Vogel-Sprott, M., 36, *55*
Volkow, N. D., 343, *365*, 488
Vollenweider, F. X., 118, *133*
Volpicelli, J. R., 27, *32*, 570
von Eye, A., 238n9, *256*, 261, *284*
Von Korff, M., *423*
von Sydow, K., 118, *134*
Voorhees, C. C., *492*
Vuchinich, R. E., 36, *55*

Wachs, T. D., 288, 291, 292, 310, *319*
Wadden, T. A., *420*
Wade, W. A., 551, *552*
Wadsworth, K. N., 90, *115*, 225, 226,
    231, 232, *251*, *255*
Walden, B., 111, *116*, 260, *286*
Walden, K. P., 194, *195*
Waldman, I. D., 59, 68, 85, *88*
Waldron, D. J., 46, *54*
Waldron, H. B., 44, *52*, 623, 634, 635,
    642–645, *655*, 657, *675*
Waldron, M., 80, *88*
Waldstein, S. R., 507n1, *513*
Walitzer, K. S., *255*, 260, *285*, 542, *553*
Walker, D. D., 418, *427*, 584, *619*
Walker, P. S., *620*

Walker, R. D., 63, 84, 348, 365, 515,
    533, 579, 580, 583, 599, *613*, 620
Wall, T. L., 678, 679, 681, 701, 702,
    707, *708*, *710*, *711*
Wallace, J. M., 578–581, *620*, 657, *675*
Wallace, P., 34, *47*
Wallace, R., 480, *494*
Walsh, J. M., 466, *495*
Walters, S. T., 118, *134*
Walton, K. G., 418, *427*
Wan, C. K., 303, 311, *316*
Wandersman, A., *184*
Wang, E., *317*
Wang, G., 343, *365*, 488, 679, *708*
Wang, H.-K., *706*
Wang, M. C., 405, *422*
Wang, M.-F., *706*, *709*
Wang, M. Q., 588, *612*
Wang, X., 679, 701, *711*
Wang, Y.-F., *710*
Wang, Z.-C., *709*
Wangberg, D., 595, *611*
Ward, A. S., 430, *455*
Ward, C. H., 436, *455*
Ward, M. M., 475, *495*
Ward, T. P., 139, 142, *155*, 405, *423*
Warner, K. E., 478, *495*
Warner, L. A., 202, *219*, 430, *455*
Warren, C. A., 389, *399*
Warren, K., 416, *427*
Warsi, G., 273, *284*
Washington State Department of
    Health, 170, *185*
Wasserman, D. A., 412, *422*
Wasserman, W., 235n5, *254*
Waterman, B., *284*
Watkins, E. R., *423*
Watson, D., 59, 62–64, 83, 86, *88*
Watt, N. F., *182*
Watters, J. K., 146, *157*
Weatherspoon, A. J., 681, *709*
Weaver, M. J., *493*
Wechsler, D., 348, *365*
Wechsler, H., 89, 91, 110, *113*, *116*,
    230, 233, 250, *256*, 325, *341*,
    461, 466, *493*, *495*, 583, *620*

Wehner, J. M., *31*
Wei, E., *185*
Weibel-Orlando, J., 587, *620*
Weidenman, M. A., 498, *511*
Weinberg, N. Z., 582, *620*, 657, 658, *675*
Weiner, B., 152, *158*
Weiner, H., 679, *711*
Weingarten, E., 418, *427*
Weinstein, M. C., *495*
Weinstein, N. D., 151, *158*
Weis, J. G., 160, *183*
Weise, K. L., 409, *426*
Weisner, C., 551, *555*
Weiss, R., *421*
Weiss, R. D., 42, *53*
Weissman, K., *487*
Wells, E. A., 406, *422*
Wells, K. B., 541, 551, *557, 558*
Welner, Z., 66, *88*
Wemer, E. E., *319*
Wenger, C. D., *31*
Wenger, J. R., 409, *427*
Werner, E. E., 288, 289, 311, 311n9, 312, *319*
Werthamer-Larsson, L., 167, *185*
Wertz, J. M., 409, *426, 427*
West, J. C., 41, *52*
West, R. J., 468, 472, 474, 478, 489, 492, 493, 495, 531, *536*
West, S. G., *182*, 215, 216, 219, 270, 271, 275, 282, 284, 292, *314*
Westerberg, V. S., 42, 44, *52*
Western Center for the Application of Prevention Technologies, 591, *621*
Westhuis, D., 349, *365*
Westin, A., 476, *485*
Westman, E. C., 477, *493*
Westreich, L., 547, *557*
Wetter, D. W., 420, *423*, 490, *496*
Wetzel, W. W., *569*
Wheeler, L., 167, *185*
Whitaker, D., 406, *426*
Whitbeck, L. B., *315*, 587, *621*
White, H. R., 227, 229n1, 230, *256*, 324, 327, 341, 582, *621*

Whiteman, M., 219, *220*, 660, *674*
Whitfield, C. L., 36, *55*
Whitfield, J. B., 678, 684, 685, 700, 703, 705, *711*
Widaman, K. F., 296, *316*
Widiger, T. A., 59, 62, 63, 87, 88, 227, 244, *256*
Wiebe, J., 591, 592, *621*
Wikler, A., 369, *399*
Wikstroem, P.-O. H., 159, *185*
Wilbourne, P. L., 541, 542, *556*
Wilde, G., 145, 154, *158*
Wilkins, C., 118, *134*
Wilkinson, C., 41, *54*
Wilkinson, D. L., 187, *196*
Willard, A., *427*
Willenbring, M. L., 516, *534*
Willett, J. B., 300, *319*
Willey-Lessne, C., *488*
Williams, E., 328, *340*, 603, 610, *614*
Williams, J., 270, 284, 349, *365*
Williams, J. B. W., 436, *455*, 519, *533*
Williams, J. H., 159, *185*
Williams, J. T., *32*, 682, 704, *711*
Williams, P. T., *487*
Williams, R. J., 627, 642, *655*
Williamson, D. F., *393*
Willoughby, M. T., 174, *182*
Wills, T. A., 260, 261, 286, 287, 288, 290, 294n2, 295, 297, 300, 301, 308n8, 310–314, 311n9, *319*, *320*, 586, *621*
Wilson, G. T., 194, *195*, 390, *393*, 403, *419*
Wilson, J. J., 160, *183*
Wilson, J. K., 201, *223*
Wilson, R. S., 350, *365*
Wilson, V. B., 657, *674*
Windle, M., 199, *224*, 249, *256*, 260, 286, 290, 291, 294, 300, *320*
Winn, D. M., *252*
Winokur, G., 60, *84*
Winter, D. G., 152, *157*
Winters, K. C., 644, 654, 658, 659–663, 667, 673, 674–676

Wirtz, P. W., 435, *456*, 546, 547, *555*,
 558
Wise, R. A., 371, *399*
Wislar, J. S., 119, *133*
Witkiewitz, K., 416–418, *422*, *427*, 517,
 535
Wittchen, H. U., 118, *134*
Wodak, A., 137, *156*
Wolchik, S. A., 271, *286*
Wolf, A., *365*
Wolf, W., 576, *611*
Wolfe, B. L., 46, *54*
Wolfson, D., 357, *364*, 500, *512*
Wolter, T. D., *490*
Wong, C. J., 430, *455*, 568, *570*
Wong, S. Y. C., 681, *709*
Wood, M. D., 37, *51*, 110, *114*
Wood, P. K., 37, *51*, 90, 91, 94, *113*,
 114, 228, 244, 250n12, *253*, *255*,
 260, *285*
Woodcock, R. W., 357, *363*
Woods, S. C., 409, *427*
Woodward, C. E., *114*
Woody, G. E., 35, 42, *51*, 500, *511*,
 556
Woolf, B., 686, *711*
Woolhandler, S., *491*
Wootton, J. M., 281, *286*
World Health Organization, 21, *32*,
 681, 682, 703, *711*
World Health Organization Brief Inter-
 vention Study Group, 40, *55*
Worley, C., 602, *612*
Wothke, W., 305n7, *318*
Wright, D., 194, *196*
Wright, K., *423*
Wugalter, S. E., 200, *221*
Wun, L. M., *491*
Wurschmidt, T. N., 194, *195*
Wyatt, S. W., 483, *487*
Wyer, R. S., 144, *158*
Wysong, E., 194, *196*

Xia, Z. X., 682, *712*
Xiao, Q., 679, 701, *711*
Xiao-Feng, L., 169, 174n4, *185*

Yaeger, A., 261, 286, 287, 290,
 311–314, 311n9, *320*
Yagelka, J., 659, *674*
Yamada, K., *709*
Yamada, Y., 701, *710*
Yamaguchi, K., 199, 202, 210, *222*, *224*,
 581, *614*
Yamauchi, M., 677, *709*
Yang, B.-H., *707*
Yang, C.-C., *254*
Yang, X., 701, *710*
Yardley, J. K., 262, *282*
Yasar, S., 371, *398*
Yasuhara, M., 679, *707*
Yates, W. R., 109, *112*
Yeh, E.-K., *708*
Yi, S. Y., *708*
Yin, S.-J., 685, 696, 697, *709*, *712*
Yoerger, K., 200, 201, *220*, *223*
Yohman, J. R., 345, *364*
Yokosuka, O., *710*
Yoo, S., 160, *185*
Yoon, J.-H., *708*
York, J. L., 227, *256*
Yoshida, A., 679, *708*
You, M., 685, *707*
Young, K., 647, *654*
Young, S. E., 61, 64, 79–82, *88*
Young, T. B., *496*
Young, T. J., 575, *621*
Young, T. L., 479, *485*
Yu, C.-Y., 503, *513*
Yu, E. S. H., 682, *712*
Yu, J.-M., 701, *706*
Yucuis, R., *112*

Zachariou, V., 477, *493*
Zachary, R. A., 499, *513*
Zackon, F., 38, 39, *56*
Zacny, J. P., 227, *256*
Zane, N., 647, *654*
Zanis, D., *456*, *555*
Zaparniuk, J., 311n9, *320*
Zarrett, N. R., 228, *255*
Zeger, S. L., 379, *399*
Zempolich, K. A., 63, *86*

Zhang, M., 682, *712*
Zhang, Q., 85
Zhu, S. H., 473, *496*
Ziedonis, D., *490*
Ziff, D. C., 407, *420*
Zilberg, N. J., 635, *652*
Zimmerman, M., 81, 88
Zitzow, D. A., 585, *621*

Zucker, R. A., 90, *116, 226, 228, 254, 256, 261, 268, 283, 284, 286, 290, 310, 320, 345, 364*
Zuckerman, M., 63, 88
Zweben, A., 40, *52*, 499, *512*
Zwick, W. R., 55, *424*, 540, *558*
Zywiak, W. H., 406, 407, *423, 424*, 540, 547, 550, *558*

SUBJECT INDEX

AA. *See* Alcoholics Anonymous
Absinthe, 154
Abstinence
    from alcohol, 94–95, 105n1
    and craving, 409
    discomfort during, 25
    as goal of treatment, 5
    from marijuana, 447–448
    with methadone maintenance. *See*
        Methadone-maintenance
        abstinence incentives (study)
    moderation vs., 148, 453
    relief of, 24
    from smoking, 376n3, 408
Abstinence violation effect, 404, 405,
    415
Acamprosate, 26, 38
Acculturation level, 649
Acculturation stress, 587
Acetaldehyde, 679, 680, 685, 701–702
Acetylcholine, 476
ACTH (adrenocorticotropin hormone),
    29
Action stage, 601
Active genotype–environment correla-
    tion, 110
Active treatment interventions, 601
Acute detoxification, 34–35
Adaptation, 290
Addiction, as brain disease, 3
Addiction-focused training, 43
Addiction Severity Index (ASI), 436,
    449–451
Additive genetic component (a2), 96
Additive model, of genetic influence,
    15, 679, 686, 700, 701, 705

ADH1B (alcohol dehydrogenase) gene,
    15, 677–682
    and age of onset of alcohol depend-
        ence, 682
    alcohol-dependence risks with, 678
    and ethnicity, 680–681
    and gender, 681–682
    genetic model of influence, 679–680
    potential moderators of effect, 680
    prevalence of, 678
    proposed mechanism of influence,
        679
*ADH1B*1* allele, 678, 680, 685, 694,
    696, 698, 700, 703
*ADH1B*2* allele, 678–682, 684, 685,
    694–703, 705
ADH1B and *ALDH2* genes (study),
    683–706
    coding of sample characteristics,
        685–688
    discussion, 699–706
    inclusion criteria, 684–685
    literature search/gathering data sets,
        684
    method, 684–691
    purpose, 683–684
    results, 689, 692–699
    statistical analyses, 686, 690–691
ADI (Adolescent Diagnostic Inter-
    view), 663
Ad lib smoking, 11, 387, 389, 390
Adolescence/adolescents
    development of alcohol and tobacco
        use during. *See* Developmen-
        tal course of alcohol and
        tobacco use (study)
    drinking during, 28–29

Adolescence/adolescents (*continued*)
 ecstasy use during, 123, 130–131
 family harmony during, 260–261,
  271–274, 278–279
 friendship in. *See* Friendships and
  substance use (study)
 heavy drinking during. *See* Heavy
  drinking during transition to
  young adulthood (study)
 heritability of externalizing factor in
  late, 77–79
 illicit drug use during, 126
 smoking during, 483–484
 substance use in Native Indian/
  Alaska Native. *See* American
  Indian and Alaska Native
  adolescent substance use
Adolescent Assessment and Referral
 Treatment System, 658
Adolescent Diagnostic Interview
 (ADI), 663
Adoption studies, 23, 61–62
Adrenocorticotropin hormone
 (ACTH), 29
ADS. *See* Alcohol Dependence Scale
Adult modeling of substance abuse, 587
Advertising, cigarette, 467
Affect
 and cigarette smoking, 368–370,
  375, 383–388, 391–392
 and relapse prevention, 411–412
Affective disorder, parental, 267, 268n2
African Americans
 AOD use among, 658
 substance use studies of, 636, 638,
  640, 643, 644
Age
 of alcohol-dependence onset, 682
 and drinking behavior, 99–101, 108
 of drinking onset, 28–29, 90, 344
 of initial substance use among American Indians/Alaska Natives,
  585
 of smokers, 460
Aggressiveness, 109, 586
AHCPR. *See* U.S. Agency for Health
 Care Policy and Research

AIDS, 34, 139
AIDS prevention, 150
Alaska Natives. *See* American Indians
 and Alaska Natives
Alcohol
 ecstasy used with, 119, 123, 127,
  128, 130, 131
 gender-related preferences for, 22
 marijuana used with, 126
 reduced sensitivity to effects of, 22
Alcohol, tobacco, and other drug
 (ATOD) use, 592, 593
Alcohol abstention rates, 94–95
Alcohol and drug problems, 33–47. *See
 also* Heavy drinking during transition to young adulthood (study)
 AUDIT/RAPI measures of, 324, 327
 barriers to treatment of, 44
 changing approaches to treatment
  of, 42–45
 comorbidity with, 36–38
 and motivation for change, 40–41
 nature of, 35–36
 prevalence/impact of, 33–35
 psychologist's role in treating, 35–42
 as public health problem, 44
 screening for/assessing, 46
 and smoking comorbidity, 482
 therapist's characteristics, impact of,
  42
 treatment of, 38–40
Alcohol and other drug (AOD) abuse,
 657
Alcohol and tobacco cessation in
 alcohol-dependent smokers
 (study), 515–533
 design/procedure, 519–520
 discussion, 528, 530–533
 EMA protocol, 520–522
 first-cigarette antecedents, 526, 528,
  529
 first-drink antecedents, 526, 527
 measures/instruments, 519
 method, 518–522
 participants, 518–519
 posttreatment abstinence rates,
  522–523

results, 522–529
urge to drink, 523–525
Alcohol craving, 530, 531
Alcohol dehydrogenase gene. *See*
    ADH1B gene
Alcohol dependence, 71, 72
    ADS measure of, 324, 327
    in American Indian/Alaska Native
        adolescents, 586
    in Asians, 677–683
    and childhood conduct disorder,
        60–61
    drug dependence vs., 279–280
    pathway to, 280
    prediction of, 261–262
Alcohol dependence in Asians (study),
    683–706
    coding of sample characteristics,
        685–688
    discussion, 699–706
    inclusion criteria, 684–685
    literature search/gathering data sets,
        684
    method, 684–691
    purpose, 683–684
    results, 689, 692–699
    statistical analyses, 686, 690–691
Alcohol metabolism, 702
Alcohol reinforcement, 24
Alcohol-relevant knockouts, 22
Alcohol research
    future directions for, 28–30
    goals of, 19
    on treatments, 25–27
Alcohol-Specific Role Play Test, 405
Alcohol–tobacco use disorder types, 228
Alcohol use
    adolescent, 28–29
    as adolescent norm, 218
    in American Indian/Alaska Native
        adolescents, 580, 585
    and bicultural competence interven-
        tion, 597
    and cigarette smoking, 13, 370–371,
        383, 389
    controlled drinking of, 148
    DARE effects on, 191, 192

and deviant friendship process,
    201–203
ethnicity studies of, 635, 636
measures of, 93–95
prevalence of problems with, 33–34
in Raising Healthy Children project,
    170–175
self-reported, 208
and smoking relapse, 517
and tobacco use. *See* Developmental
    course of alcohol and tobacco
    use (study)
trajectories of, 238
by underage drinkers, 89
Alcohol use disorders (AUDs), 228
Alcohol Use Disorders Identification
    Test (AUDIT), 324, 327,
    330–332, 334, 335
Alcohol Dependence Scale (ADS),
    324, 327, 330, 332, 334, 335
Alcoholic dementia, 343
Alcoholics Anonymous (AA), 508,
    539, 548–550
Alcoholism
    among American Indians/Alaska
        Natives, 585
    biological/behavioral systems inter-
        action in, 19
    and brain processes, 24–25
    familial. *See* Familial alcoholism
    genetics of, 20–24
    and subjective states, 29
    subtypes of, 90
Alcp1 locus, 22
Alcp2 locus, 22
Aldehyde dehydrogenase gene. *See*
    ALDH2 gene
ALDH2 (aldehyde dehydrogenase) gene,
    15, 23, 677–682. *See also* ADH1B
    and ALDH2 genes (study)
    and age of onset of alcohol depend-
        ence, 682
    alcohol-dependence risks with, 678
    and ethnicity, 680–681
    and gender, 681–682
    genetic model of influence, 679–680
    potential moderators of effect, 680

ALDH2 (aldehyde dehydrogenase)
(*continued*)
prevalence of, 677–678
proposed mechanism of influence, 679
ALDH2*1 allele, 678, 680, 681, 685,
689–694, 696–704
ALDH2*2 allele, 677–686, 689–693,
696–705
American Indian and Alaska Native
adolescent substance use, 578–589
alcohol, 580
consequences/correlates of, 585
cultural factors, 587–588
culture-specific factors, 588–589
environmental influences on,
586–587
gender differences, 583–584
inhalants, 579–580
intrapersonal variables with, 586
marijuana, 581
patterns, 582–583
polysubstance, 581–582
prevalence of, 578
prevention of. *See* Substance-use prevention among American
Indian and Alaska Native youth
protective factors, 588
regional/tribal differences, 584
risk factors of, 586
tobacco, 578–579
universal factors, 588
American Indians and Alaska Natives,
460, 575–578, 584
cultural diversity of, 598–599
demographics of, 576–577
and federal boarding schools, 577
terminology, 577–578
American Psychiatric Association,
468–469
American Psychological Association
(APA), 33
American Stop Smoking Intervention
Trial for Cancer Prevention
(ASSIST), 464
Amnesia, posttraumatic, 345, 349
Amphetamines, 119, 130, 635
Analysis of variance (ANOVA), 96
Animal genetics, 21–22

ANOVA (analysis of variance), 96
Antidepressants, 473, 475, 477
Antisocial behavior
adolescent, 66–67, 71–73
and deviant friendship process, 215
and drug dependence, 262
and parenting, 289
and substance dependence, 59–61
Antisocial personality disorder (ASPD)
and cognitive impairment, 345
and development of alcoholism, 109
and executive ability, 507n1
parental, 267, 268n2
Anxiety and anxiety disorders, 62, 345,
448
AOD abuse assessment instruments
(study), 657–673
data analysis, 663–664
discussion, 671–673
group differences on response distortion, 668, 671
measure, 659–661
method, 659–665
participants, 661–662
procedure, 663
reliability, 664–666
results, 664–671
validity, 665–670
AOD (alcohol and other drug) abuse,
657
APA (American Psychological Association), 33, 45–46, 623–623
Apparently irrelevant decisions, 405
Arizona, 467
Arousal, 369, 383, 384, 528, 531
ASI. *See* Addiction Severity Index
Asian Americans, 639, 643, 644, 658
Asian descent, persons of, 23
Asian Pacific islanders, 460
Asians, alcohol dependence in,
677–683. *See also* Alcohol
dependence in Asians (study)
ASPD. *See* Antisocial personality disorder
Atayal Chinese, 687, 688, 690
ATOD use. *See* Alcohol, tobacco, and
other drug use
Attention-deficit hyperactive disorder,
61, 64

Attitude(s)
    drug-use, 200
    of therapist, 45
AUDIT. *See* Alcohol Use Disorders
    Identification Test
AUDs (alcohol use disorders), 228
Australia, 118, 130, 431
Authoritarianism, 152
Automatic smoking, 370
Aversive smoking procedures, 470
Axis II ASPD module of SCID
    (SCID–II), 349

Bars, smoking in, 382, 390
Beck Depression Inventory (BDI), 349,
    436, 448, 449
Behavioral continuum, 44
Behavioral coping, 410
Behavioral interventions, 40, 470–472
Behavioral reinforcement, 13
Behavioral science, 4
    and alcohol research, 19, 21
    and animal genetics, 21–22
    bio-, 29–30
    in disease etiology, 230
    and environment, 23–24
Behavioral therapies, 38
Behavioral undercontrol, 279–280
Belief formation, 161
Benton Multilingual Aphasia Exam
    (MAE), 348
Bias, 151
Bicultural competence, 589, 596–598,
    606
Bicultural life skills approaches, 603–604
Binge drinking. *See also* Heavy drinking
    during transition to young adult-
        hood (study)
    among American Indians, 583
    among college students, 230
    defined, 121
    with ecstasy, 130
    with marijuana, 127
    measure of, 233
    reducing, 90
    by underage drinkers, 89
Biobehavioral research, 29–30

Biomarker feedback, 471
Biometric modeling, 96–98
Birth defects, 29
Block random assignment by ethnicity,
    647
Bloom's Family Processes Scale, 265,
    267
Boarding schools. *See* Indian boarding
    schools
Bongs, 146–147
Boredom, 587
Brain
    acetaldehyde levels in, 701–702
    addiction as disease of, 3
    alcohol reinforcement in, 24
    cellular adaptation in, 24–25
Brief interventions, 4, 40, 41, 602
Brief strategic family therapy (BSFT),
    644, 645
British Health Education Authority, 468
BSFT. *See* Brief strategic family therapy
Bunun Chinese, 687, 690, 694
Buprenorphrine, 560
Bupropion, 467, 473, 475–478

Cannabis dependence, 430. *See also*
    Marijuana use
Cannabis-dependence treatments
    (study), 429–454
    abstinence/improvement outcomes,
        447–448
    assessment procedures, 436–438
    cannabis use/problems, 443–447
    data analysis, 442
    discussion, 452–454
    follow-up procedures, 441–442
    generalizability of outcomes, 451–452
    method, 432–442
    missing data, effects of, 447
    participants, 432–435
    research design/sites, 435–436
    results, 443–452
    secondary outcomes, 448–451
    therapist training/fidelity of treat-
        ment, 441
    treatment attendance, 443
    treatment interventions, 438–441

Canoe Family, 607
"Canoe Journey," 14, 607–608
Capital punishment, 150
Carbon monoxide (CO), 374, 519
Cardiovascular diseases, 467
CAS. *See* Clinical Anxiety Scale; Commands with auditory sequencing
Case management (CM), 435
Catastrophe model, 416–417
Category Test (CT), 348
Caucasians, 636, 638, 643, 644
CBT. *See* Cognitive–behavioral therapy
CDC. *See* U.S. Centers for Disease Control and Prevention
CDC Behavioral Risk Factor Surveillance System, 460
CDCP, 625
Cellular adaptation, 24–25
Center for Substance Abuse Prevention, 591, 608
Center for Substance Abuse Treatment (CSAT), 625
CFA (confirmatory factor analysis), 351
Chaos theory, 416
Cheng, Andrew T. A., 685
Childhood conduct disorder, 60–61, 64
Childhood learning disorders, 358
Childhood stressors, 249
Children of alcoholics (COAs), 264, 345
Chinese
    *ADH1B*2* allele in, 678
    *ALDH2*2* allele in, 677
    ethnic subgroups of, 685
    gender differences in alcohol dependence in, 681
    study recruitment of, 692, 693
    study sample of, 697–699
Chinese Americans, 687, 691, 694, 696
"Chippers," 226
Christian tradition, 144
Chromosomal "hot spots," 20
Chronic antisocial alcoholism, 90
CIDI. *See* Composite International Diagnostic Interview
Cigarettes, as smoking cues, 371, 389
Cigarette smoking
    and activity, 376–378, 382
    and affect, 368–370, 375, 383–385

by American Indian/Alaska Native adolescents, 586
among American Indian/Alaska Native adolescents, 583, 584
and cigarettes as cues, 371, 383
and coffee, 370–371, 383
DARE effects on, 191, 192
and drinking, 13, 370–371, 383
early, 213
and environmental context, 382
and filters/low-tar tobacco, 145
and food, 383
health risks with, 227
location of, 382
methods for studying antecedents to, 371–373
and peer groups, 200–201
and psychiatric comorbidity, 482
in Raising Healthy Children project, 170–172, 177–178
restrictions on, 380, 381
and setting, 376–378
trajectories of, 226–227, 238
trends in, 229
and urge to smoke, 371, 375, 383, 384
Cigarette smoking antecedents (study), 373–392
    assessments, 375–378
    data reduction/analysis, 376, 379–380
    descriptive statistics, 380, 381
    discussion, 386–392
    environmental contexts, 382
    food/coffee/tea/alcohol consumption, 383
    internal states, 383–385
    lag times between observations/sensitivity testing, 385
    method, 373–380
    participants, 373
    procedure, 373–375
    results, 380–385
    smoking cues, 383
    smoking regulations, 380, 381
Cigars, 229
Classical conditioning, 35

Clinical Anxiety Scale (CAS), 349
Clonidine, 473, 474
CM (case management), 435
CO. *See* Carbon monoxide
COAs. *See* Children of alcoholics
Cocaine Risk Response Test, 411
Cocaine use
    cognitive decrements with, 344
    ecstasy use with, 119, 123, 124, 128,
        129, 131
    ethnicity studies of, 635
    marijuana use with, 126
    and methadone maintenance,
        559–560
    prevalence of, 147
Coffee, 371, 383, 389
COGA. *See* Collaborative Study on the
    Genetics of Alcoholism
Cognitive–behavioral model
    of relapse, 404, 517
    of relapse prevention, 404–405
Cognitive–behavioral mood manage-
    ment, 471
Cognitive–behavioral therapy (CBT), 38
    with alcohol use disorders, 499, 502,
        508, 509
    and ethnicity, 645
    for marijuana-dependent adults,
        430–431, 438–440
    in Project MATCH, 40, 546
    for relapse prevention, 411
Cognitive coping, 410
Cognitive impairments
    risk factors linked to, 344–345
    vulnerability to alcoholism because
        of, 21
Cognitive processes, 28
Cognitive reactions, to stressors, 288–289
Cohort effects, 235–237
Collaborative Study on the Genetics of
    Alcoholism (COGA), 20–21,
    682, 704
Collateral interviews, 437
Collective decision making, 592
College attendance, 111
College of Professional Psychology, 33
College students, as test subjects, 324

Combined therapies, 27
Commands with auditory sequencing
    (CAS), 348
COMMIT. *See* Community Interven-
    tion Trial for Smoking Cessation
Common pathway model, 69, 73–75
Communication, 473
Community awareness, stages of, 605
Community-based care, 39–40
Community-based process, 609
Community collaboration, 600
Community empowerment, 592, 593
Community influence, 586–587
Community Intervention Trial for
    Smoking Cessation (COMMIT),
    463–464
Community involvement, 597, 604–605
Community-level interventions,
    463–465
Community-oriented prevention
    approaches, 591–594
Community readiness model, 605
Community-reinforcement approach, 38
Comorbid conditions, 5
    prevalence of, 34
    psychologist's role with, 35–38
    treating, 547–548
Comorbidity
    developmental, 247–248
    and externalizing disorders, 62
    phenomenon of, 59
    twin studies of, 61
Compensatory behavior, 145
Composite International Diagnostic
    Interview (CIDI), 66, 93
Comprehensive Drinker Profile, 519
Computer-assisted interviews, 121
Computer literacy and access, 337
Computer technology, 4, 473
Conditioning
    and cigarette smoking, 369
    classical, 35
Condom distribution in schools, 141
Conduct disorder
    and alcoholism, 109
    in American Indian/Alaska Native
        adolescents, 586

Conduct disorder (*continued*)
  shared environmental factors con-
    tributing to, 79–80
  and substance dependence, 67, 71,
    72, 76
  and tobacco use, 249
Confidentiality, 293, 338
Confrontational programs, 41, 42, 541
Confucian philosophy, 681
Consciousness, loss of, 345, 349
Consequentialist opposition, to harm
    reduction, 149–150
Constraint, 71, 72, 75
Consumer safety standards, 140, 141
Contemplation stage, 601
Contingency management, 13
Control, need for, 150–151
Controlled drinking programs, 141, 148
Coping families, 411
Coping skills, 35, 410–411
Coping skills training, 606–607
Core values, 597
Cortical shrinkage, 343
Corticotropin releasing factor (CRF), 29
Cotinine, 374
Counter-tobacco advertising, 467
Crack, ecstasy used with, 123, 124, 128,
    130, 131
Craving, 28, 408–409, 530, 531
CRF (corticotropin releasing factor), 29
Criminal behavior, 63
Cross-cultural validation studies, 650
Cross-substance coping response
    hypothesis, 516, 517, 531
Cross-substance cue reactivity model,
    13, 516–517, 530
CSAT (Center for Substance Abuse
    Treatment), 625
CT (Category Test), 348
Cubans, 638
Cue reactivity, 409
Cultural affiliation, 593
Cultural factors
  in American-Indian/Alaska-Native
    adolescent substance use,
    587–589
  in Asian alcohol dependence, 681

Cultural suitability, of instruments,
    641–642

Dangerous drug use, 209, 216, 218–219
DARE. *See* Project Drug Abuse Resis-
    tance Education
DARE America, 194
Data collection methods, 4
Death penalty, 150
Deaths
  among American Indians/Alaska
    Natives, 585
  leading contributors to preventable,
    34
Defensiveness, 661
Delayed emergence effect, 405
Delayed treatment control (DTC), 431
Delinquency, 64, 199, 201, 241–245, 249
Demand reduction strategy, 138
Depression
  and cigarette smoking, 482
  and cognitive impairment, 359
  and neuropsychological impairment,
    345
  and smoking cessation treatment, 475
Depressive episodes, 36
Desipramine, 560
Detoxification, 34–35, 39
Developmental course of alcohol and
    tobacco use (study), 225–251
  alcohol–tobacco comorbidity,
    227–229, 247–248
  analytic procedure, 234
  cohort effects, 235–237
  discussion, 246–251
  extracting trajectories, 238–239
  goal of study, 230–231
  identifying trajectories, 239–240
  measures, 232–234
  method, 231–234
  predicting alcohol–tobacco comor-
    bidity, 248–249
  predicting trajectory group member-
    ship, 240–246
  preliminary analyses, 235
  respondents/procedure, 231–232
  results, 234–246

strengths/limitations of study, 250–251
studying comorbidity, 246–247
third-variable analyses, 229–230
Developmentally limited alcoholism, 90
Developmental theory, 90
Developmental Trends Study, 69
Deviancy training, 201, 202, 206
Deviant friendship process, 201–203,
    206, 207, 213–215
Deviant peer group
  and drinking behavior, 110–111, 260
  substance-using adolescents without, 9
  and temperament, 291, 314
Deviant talk, 204, 205
Diagnosis, 44
Diagnostic and Statistical Manual of Men-
    tal Disorders (DSM), 28
Diagnostic and Statistical Manual of
    Mental Disorders (3rd ed., rev.;
    DSM–III–R), 66, 93, 264, 265, 682
Diagnostic and Statistical Manual of Men-
    tal Disorders (5th ed.; DSM–V),
    62
Diagnostic criteria, 28, 682, 704
Diagnostic Interview for Children and
    Adolescents–Revised (DICA–R),
    66
Diagnostic Interview Schedule (DIS),
    267
Diaries
  electronic. *See* Electronic diaries
  written, 373
DICA–R (Diagnostic Interview for
    Children and Adolescents–
    Revised), 66
Discrimination, perceived, 587–588
DIS (Diagnostic Interview Schedule),
    267
Disease etiology, 230
Disgust, 153
Disinhibition, 67
Disinhibitory personality traits, 63–65,
    81–82
Disulfiram, 26, 38
Diversity, 36–37, 648
Dizygotic (DZ) twins, 96
DNA, 22

Dominant model, of genetic influence,
    15, 679, 680, 686, 700, 701, 705
Dopamine, 3, 476
Dopamine transporter gene polymor-
    phism SLC6A3-9, 481
Dorsolateral prefrontal–subcortical cir-
    cuit, 357
DOT-R (Revised Dimensions of Tem-
    perament Survey), 294
Drinking rates, 328
Drinks consumed, 94, 501
Drug Abuse Warning Network, 118
Drug control strategies, 138–139
Drug dependence
  alcohol dependence vs., 279–280
  gender differences with, 71, 72
  prediction of, 261–262
"Drug naive," 130–131
Drug use history, 661
"Drug use sequence," 131
DSM (*Diagnostic and Statistical Manual*
    of Mental Disorders), 28
DSM–III–R. *See Diagnostic and Statistical*
    Manual of Mental Disorders (3rd
    ed., rev.)
DSM–V (*Diagnostic and Statistical Man-*
    ual of Mental Disorders; 5th ed.),
    62
DTC (delayed treatment control), 431
DZ (dizygotic) twins, 96

Early intervention, 44, 601
Early onset heavy drinking, 90, 98–99
  among American Indians/Alaska
      Natives, 585
  biological influences on, 91
  and heritability of alcoholism, 110
  and P3 amplitude, 106–107, 109
Early substance use
  protective factors against, 160
  risk factors for, 159–160
EAS (Emotionality, Activity, and
    Sociability Inventory), 294
Easy-going temperament, 289
Ecological momentary assessment
    (EMA), 11, 12, 372, 408, 517,
    520–522, 530, 531

Ecstasy (3,4-methylenoioxy-
      methamphetamine; MDMA), 117
Ecstasy use
      age of onset, 119, 127–128
      and binge drinking, 127
      marijuana use vs., 126–127
      with other substances, 119, 123–129
      prevalence of, 7, 118
      and rave movement, 119
      side effects of, 118
      trends in, 121
Ecstasy use (study), 117–132
      demographics of users, 122–123
      discussion, 129–132
      method, 119–120
      results, 122–129
      sample/measures, 119–120
      statistical analysis, 121
EDs. *See* Electronic diaries
Education
      about relapse process, 405
      prevention, 608
Education level
      and alcoholism, 345, 358
      and cigarette smoking, 460
      of parent. *See* Parent education level
EEG (electroencephalographic) activ-
      ity, 95
EFA. *See* Exploratory factor analysis
Effect size (ES), 498
Efficacy trials, 550–551
Electroencephalographic (EEG) activ-
      ity, 95
Electronic diaries (EDs), 11, 12,
      372–374, 517, 532
Electrooculographic (EOG) activity, 95
Elunchun Chinese, 688, 691
EMA. *See* Ecological momentary
      assessment
EM (expectation maximum), 234
Emic approaches, 606
Emotionality, Activity, and Sociability
      Inventory (EAS), 294
Empathy, 42, 541
Empirically supported therapies (ESTs),
      623, 645
Employment, 448, 449, 451
Empowerment, sense of, 337

Enlistment strategies, 650
Environment
      and adolescent heavy drinking, 90–91
      and cigarette smoking, 388–389
      and externalizing factors, 68–69,
            79–81
Environmental approach, 609
Environmental influences
      on adolescent drinking behavior,
            101–105, 109–111
      on alcoholism, 23–24
      on American Indian/Alaska Native
            adolescent substance use,
            586–587
      on smoking behavior, 481
Environment seeking, 91
EOG (electrooculographic) activity, 95
Epigenetic theory, 290, 292
Equal environments assumption, 96–97
ES (effect size), 498
Esophageal cancer, 227
ESTs. *See* Empirically supported therapies
Ethanol, 22, 344
Ethnic differences
      in ecstasy use, 122
      and measurement difficulties, 658
Ethnic dislocation, 587
Ethnic identity, 624
Ethnicity
      and alcohol–tobacco use trajectories,
            241–245, 248
      and Asian alcohol dependence,
            680–681
      and assessment instruments. *See*
            AOD abuse assessment instru-
            ments (study)
      studies incorporating, 14
Ethnicity in adolescent drug abuse treat-
      ment outcomes (study), 623–652
      clinical implications, 648–649
      criteria for study inclusion, 626–627
      demographic characteristics of par-
            ticipants, 637
      discussion, 646–652
      explicit consideration of ethnicity,
            642–646
      future directions, 649–650
      method, 625–633

number of studies, 627, 635
outcome measures, 640–642
reporting of participants' ethnicity, 637–640
research implications, 646–648
results, 627–646
search method, 625
search reliability, 625–626
studies included, 628–634
study inclusion criteria, 625
treatment characteristics, 635–636
Ethnic matching, 643
Etic approaches, 606
Evidence-based guidelines, 468–469, 550–551
Executive functioning, 346, 357, 358, 503, 507–509
Expectancies
and cognitive processes, 28
drug, 35
and motivation for change, 410
and positive reinforcement, 408
Externalizing factor
and disinhibitory personality traits, 63–65, 81–82
distinct syndromes of, 61–63
etiologic basis of, 60–61
heritability in late adolescence, 77–79
hierarchical model, evidence supporting, 79–81
Externalizing factors (study)
correlations, 71–73
data analysis, 68–70
descriptive statistics, 70–71
discussion, 76–82
measures, 66–68
method, 65–70
model fitting, 73–76
participants, 65–66
results, 70–76
Externalizing syndromes
distinct, 61–63
hierarchical model of, 62

Fagerström Test for Nicotine Dependence, 519

Familial alcoholism
and alcohol dependence, 280
and cognitive impairment, 345, 346, 350, 359
and family harmony, 262–263, 280–282
measure of, 501
and substance use disorders in young adults, 260, 275–278
Familial environment, 96
Family-based tobacco intervention, 483
Family conflict, 289n1
Family dynamics, 9–10
Family effects on young adults' substance use disorders (study), 259–282
data analytic strategy, 270–271
differential pathways to substance use disorders, 279–280
discussion, 278–282
familial alcoholism, 260
familial alcoholism–family harmony interaction, 280–282
family harmony during adolescence, 260–261, 271–274, 278–279
measures, 265, 267–270
method, 263–271
participants, 263–264
and personality, 274–275
prediction of substance abuse disorders, 261–262, 275–278
previous studies, 262–263
procedure, 264–265
results, 271–278
selection of subsample, 265, 266
sibling correlations, 271
Family harmony
and familial alcoholism, 262–263, 280–282
and substance use disorders in young adults, 260–261, 271–274, 278–279
Family history density (FHD), 260
Family History–Research Diagnostic Criteria (FH-RDC), 268
Family(-ies)
American Indian/Alaska Native adolescents influenced by, 587

Family(-ies) (*continued*)
    drinking within, 587
    in social development model, 161
    and temperament, 296, 298–300
Family income, 122, 123, 646
Family intervention strategies, 164
Family life events, 295, 310
Family-oriented therapies, 643–644
Family systems therapy, 645
Fast Track project, 160
Fatigue, of self-regulation, 411
Federal boarding schools. *See* Indian
    boarding schools
Federal prison inmates, 8
Feedback, 412
Feedback loops, 414
Fetal alcohol syndrome, 29
Fetus, alcohol effects on, 29
FFT. *See* Functional family therapy
FHD (family history density), 260
FH-RDC (Family History–Research
    Diagnostic Criteria), 268
FIML. *See* Full-information maximum-
    likelihood
First-cigarette predictors, 526, 528, 529.
    See also Cigarette smoking
    antecedents (study)
First-drink predictors, 526, 527
First Nation communities of Canada,
    602
Fluoxetine, 475
Flushing reaction, 23
Foot shock stress, 417
Form 90, 519
"4As" smoking cessation strategy, 466
Frequency, of drunkenness, 94
Friends
    selection of, 200
    substance use by, 295
Friendships and substance use (study),
    199–219
    construct formation, 206–210
    data analytic strategy, 210
    discussion, 217–219
    hypotheses tested in, 202–203
    method, 203–210
    Peer Interaction Task, 204

    procedure, 203–204
    results, 210–217
    sample, 203
    Topic Code, 204–206
    youth interviews, 204
Functional family therapy (FFT), 643, 645

GABA (γ-aminobutyric acid) receptor,
    22
Gamma-glutamine transferase (GGT),
    345, 349, 359
Gateway theory of drug involvement,
    581–582
Gender differences
    with adolescent drinking, 91, 104,
        105, 107–111
    with adolescent drinking behavior,
        99–101
    with alcohol–tobacco use trajectories,
        241–245, 248
    with alcohol use, 170
    in American-Indian/Alaska-Native
        adolescent substance use,
        583–584
    with antisocial behaviors, 67–68,
        71–74
    in Asian alcohol dependence,
        681–682, 703–704
    with cigarette use, 178, 481–482
    with ecstasy use, 122–123
    with family harmony/alcoholism
        effects, 271–273
    in Indian identity, 593
    with marijuana use, 170, 176
    in preference for alcohol, 22
Gene expression, 23–24
Generalized anxiety disorder, 36
General linear model (GLM) analyses,
    442
Genes, 15
Genetic influence
    on adolescent drinking behavior,
        101–105, 108–109
    on Asian alcohol dependence,
        679–680
    models of, 15
    on smoking behavior, 481

Genetic mapping, 24–25
Genetics, of alcoholism, 20–24
    in animals, 21–22
    collaborative study on, 20–21
    and environment, 23–24
GGT. *See* Gamma-glutamine transferase
GLM (general linear model) analyses,
    442
Global issues, 484
Glucose, reduced utilization of, 343
Goals
    guiding clients toward specific, 541
    of treatment, 5
Grandparental alcoholism, 268
Group therapy, 430, 469, 602

Han Chinese, 678, 687, 688, 690, 695,
    700, 703
Haplotype analyses, 705
Hard drugs, ethnicity studies of, 635
Harm reduction, 5, 8, 38, 137–154
    for American-Indian/Alaska-Native
        youth, 602
    consequentialist opposition to,
        149–150
    contagion opposition to, 153
    direct consequences of, 143–144
    drug control vs., 138–139
    effectiveness of macro, 146–147
    and helping drug users, 151–153
    hypotheses for successful, 153–154
    indirect consequences of, 144–145
    micro vs. macro, 142–143
    movement toward, 137
    and predictability/control needs,
        150–151
    public acceptability of, 149–153
    smoking cessation vs., 479–480
    through quantity reduction, 147–149
    U.S. resistance to, 139–140
    in U.S. policy debates, 140–141
    and value trade-offs, 151
Head injuries, 345, 349, 359
Health care costs, 34
Health care provider interventions,
    465–467
Health care work environment, 545
Health problems, 34

Health risks, with cigarette smoking, 227
Healthy People 2010, 90
Heavy drinking
    at age 17, 98–99
    and cognitive impairment, 344
    quantitative measure of, 93–94
    stability/change, 108
Heavy drinking during transition to
        young adulthood (study), 89–111
    age/sex effects, 99–101
    discussion, 108–111
    genetic/environmental influences,
        101–105
    hypotheses about, 92
    later onset, 90–91
    measures, 93–95
    method, 92–99
    modeling P3-amplitude–heavy-
        drinking association, 98–99
    P3 amplitude–heavy drinking associ-
        ation, 106–107
    participants, 92–93
    results, 99–107
    statistical analyses, 96–98
Heavy drugs, 582
HEAVY measure, 94
Heroin
    ecstasy used with, 119, 123, 125,
        126, 128, 131
    marijuana used with, 126
    relapse rates with, 417–418
Hierarchical model, of externalizing dis-
        orders, 62, 63, 76, 79–82
High-risk sexual behaviors, 34
Hispanic Americans
    ecstasy use among, 129
    substance use studies of, 636, 638,
        640–642, 644
HIV exposure, 34, 139
HIV vaccine, 145
Holistic approach to health, 609
Hospitalization, 34, 39
Human Studies Subcommittee of the
        Veterans Affairs, 518
Hunger, 385, 389
Hutchinson Smoking Prevention
        Project, 482–483

ICD–10 (*International Classification of Disease and Related Health Problems—Tenth Edition*), 682

Illicit drug use
    DARE effects on, 191–193
    and disinhibition, 64
    ethnicity studies of, 635
    prevalence of, 34
    reducing riskiness of, 144–145
Illicit drug users, propriety of helping, 151–153
Immigration benefits, 141
Impulsivity, 63, 64, 109, 262
Incentives
    in addiction treatment, 13
    and cigarette smoking, 370
    for methadone maintenance. *See* Methadone-maintenance abstinence incentives (study)
Indian boarding schools
    alcohol use in, 580, 584
    attendance at, 577
    inhalant use in, 579
Indian identity, 589, 593
Indicated prevention programs, 590, 591
Individual counseling, 469
Information dissemination, 608
"Informative" families, 20
Infrequency, 661
Inhalant use
    by American Indian/Alaska Native adolescents, 579–580, 583–584, 586
    ecstasy use with, 123, 128, 131
    marijuana use with, 127
Inhibitory neurotransmitters, 22
Initiating substances, 582
Injection drug use
    and AIDS, 34
    level of substance use as predictor of, 218
    prevalence of, 139
    self-reported, 209–210
Institute of Medicine, 590
Integrated family and CGT, 645
Integrated treatment approach, 5, 39, 548

Intensity, of treatments, 4
Intensive outpatient therapy, 603
Interactive video, 473
Internal consistency, test, 664, 665
International Classification of Disease and Related Health Problems—Tenth Edition (ICD–10), 682
Internet-based assessments
    advantages of, 323–324
    concerns about, 324
    suitability of, 10
Internet-based assessments (study), 323–339
    analytic approach, 329, 331
    assessment format/incentives, 326–327
    discussion, 335–339
    measures, 327–328
    method, 325–328
    participants, 325
    preliminary analyses, 329, 330
    results, 329–335
    subjective convenience/preferences, 335
    test–retest reliability, 331–332
    validity, 333–335
Intrapersonal risk factors, for American-Indian/Alaska-Native adolescent substance use, 586

Japanese culture, 144
Japanese people
    ADH1B*2 allele in, 678
    ADH1B gene in, 700, 703
    ALDH2*2 allele in, 677
    ALDH2 gene in, 680
    study characteristics, 687, 688
    study recruitment of, 692, 693
    study sample of, 697, 698
Journeys of the Circle project, 607, 609

Kauffman, S., 415–416
Knowledge, of substance use disorders, 45–46
Korean Americans, 687, 690, 693, 694, 696
Korean Chinese, 688–690, 693

Koreans
    ADH1B*2 allele in, 678
    alcohol dependence in, 705
    ALDH2*2 allele in, 677
    gender differences in alcohol
        dependence in, 681
    study characteristics, 687
    study recruitment of, 692.693
    study sample of, 698
Korsakoff's syndrome, 343
Kraepelinian approach, 245

Laryngeal cancer, 227
Later onset heavy drinking, 90–91,
    98–99
Learning
    and cigarette smoking, 369
    principles of, 42
Learning disorders, 358
Legalization, of drugs, 138–140, 151
Legislation, smoking, 467
Leisure activities, 382
Life context, 549–550
Life skills, 542, 597, 603–604
Life stress, 586
Lifestyle
    changes in, 29, 39
    and friendship selection, 216–217
Limited strength model, 517, 531
Liver functioning, 349, 645, 702
LSD, ecstasy used with, 119, 123, 125,
    128–131

Macro harm reduction strategy, 138
    effectiveness of, 146–147
    micro vs., 142–143
MAE (Benton Multilingual Aphasia
    Exam), 348
Maintenance stage, 601
Major depression, 64
Major life transitions, 109–110
Mandated treatment, 636
MAO inhibitors, 476–477
Marijuana Problem Scale (MPS), 436
Marijuana-specific relapse prevention,
    406

Marijuana use. *See also* Cannabis
    dependence
    in American Indian/Alaska Native
        adolescents, 581, 584, 585
    and bicultural competence interven-
        tion, 597
    binge drinking with, 127
    with bongs, 146–147
    DARE effects on, 191, 192
    and deviant friendship process,
        201–203, 214–216, 218
    ecstasy use with, 119, 120, 123, 124,
        127, 128, 130, 131
    ethnicity studies of, 635, 636
    legalization of, 151
    motivational therapies with, 41
    with other substances, 126–127
    prevalence of, 429–430
    problems with, 430
    in Raising Healthy Children project,
        170–172, 175–177
    reducing, 12
    self-reported, 208–209
Marijuana withdrawal, 430
Marital conflict, 261
Marital therapy, 38
Marlowe–Crowne Social Desirability
    Scale, 660, 661
"Masked effect," 229, 249
Maternal reports, of child's antisocial
    behavior, 66
MDFT. *See* Multidimensional family
    therapy
MDMA (ecstasy), 117
Mecamylamine, 477
Medical status, 448, 449, 500–501
Memory, 358, 359
Mental health concerns, 35–38
Mental Measurement Yearbook, 658
MET. *See* Motivational enhancement
    therapy
Methadone maintenance, 5, 13, 38
Methadone-maintenance abstinence
    incentives (study), 559–569
    data analysis, 562–563
    discussion, 566–569
    method, 561–563

Methadone-maintenance abstinence
incentives (study) (*continued*)
participants, 561
procedure, 561–562
results, 564–566
Methamphetamines, 636
Mexican Americans, 643
Mexican marijuana crops, 154
Mice, 22
Micro harm reduction strategy, 138,
142–143
MI (motivational interviewing), 471
MI (myocardial infarction), 479
Mindfulness meditation, 418
Minnesota Heart Health study, 464
Minnesota Twin Family Study (MTFS),
64–82, 92–93
correlations, 71–73
data analysis, 68–70
descriptive statistics, 70–71
discussion, 76–82
disinhibitory personality style and
externalizing disorders, 81–82
heritability of externalizing factor in
late adolescence, 77–79
hierarchical model, evidence supporting, 79–81
measures, 66–68
method, 65–70
model fitting, 73–76
participants, 65–66
results, 70–76
Moclobemide, 476
Modeling influences, 35
Mongolian Chinese, 688, 690
Monitoring the Future (MTF) study, 9,
118, 121, 131, 229, 231, 578
Monozygotic (MZ) twins, 96
Mood disorders, 62
Motivation
to change, 40–41, 438–439
to quit smoking, 461
and relapse prevention, 409–410
for smoking, 367
Motivational enhancement therapy
(MET), 40
with alcohol use disorders, 499, 502,
508, 509

for marijuana-dependent adults,
431–432, 438–440
Motivational interviewing (MI), 471
MPQ (Multidimensional Personality
Questionnaire), 67
MPS (Marijuana Problem Scale), 436
MST. *See* Multisystemic therapy
MTFS. *See* Minnesota Twin Family
Study
MTF study. *See* Monitoring the Future
study
Multidimensional family therapy
(MDFT), 643, 645
Multidimensional Personality Question-
naire (MPQ), 67
Multimedia campaigns, 467
Multisystemic therapy (MST), 643, 645
Multi-tribal urban youth, 599
Myocardial infarction (MI), 479
MZ (monozygotic) twins, 96

NAART (North American Adult
Reading Test), 350
Naltrexone, 26, 27, 38
National Cancer Institute (NCI), 464,
469, 484
National Comorbidity Survey, 269
National Drug Abuse Treatment Clini-
cal Trials Network, 561
National Heart, Lung, and Blood Insti-
tute, 469
National Household Survey on Drug
Abuse (NHSDA), 120, 229, 429,
578
National Institute of Mental Health,
636
National Institute on Alcohol Abuse
and Alcoholism (NIAAA),
26–28, 45, 406
National Institute on Drug Abuse
(NIDA), 3, 231, 469, 484, 623,
625, 636, 658
National Institutes of Health, 4
National Longitudinal Alcohol Epi-
demiology Survey, 28
National Survey on Drug Use and
Health, 120

Native Americans
  AOD use among, 658
  substance use studies of, 639, 644
NCI. *See* National Cancer Institute
Neck cancers, 685, 702
Needle exchange programs, 5, 139, 141,
    146, 150
Negative affect, 261, 289
  in American Indian/Alaska Native
      adolescents, 586
  and cigarette smoking, 368, 369,
      383, 384, 386, 391
  and externalizing disorders, 62
  and relapse, 411–412
  and smoking relapse, 517, 531–532
Negative emotionality, 290, 291
Negative life events, 295
Negative reinforcement, 24
NEO Five-Factor Inventory
    (NEO–FFI), 270
Neural systems, 21
Neurological Screening Battery (NSB),
    348
Neuropsychological abilities (study),
    343–361
  analyses, 350–352
  confirmatory factor analysis, 354,
      355
  discussion, 357–361
  exploratory factor analysis, 353–354
  measures, 348
  method, 346–352
  outpatient clinic, 353–354
  participants, 346–347
  previous studies, 345–346
  procedure, 350
  results, 352–357
  risk factors, 348–350, 354–357
  subtest scores, 352
  therapeutic community, 354–356
Neuropsychological abilities with alco-
    hol use disorders (study),
    497–509
  data analysis, 501–502
  executive ability at baseline,
      507–508
  measurement model, 503, 505–506

measures, 499–501
  mediators/executive recovery at
      15 months, 508–509
  method, 499–502
  participants, 499, 500
  procedure, 501
  results/discussion, 502–509
  risk factor correlates of latent abilities,
      506–507
Neuropsychological measurement
    model, 503, 505–506
Neuropsychological subtest scores, 352
Neuropsychological tests, 499, 500, 502
Neuroscience research, 25–26
Neuroticism, 64, 261, 274
Neurotoxicity, 344
Neurotransmitter systems, 25
NHSDA. *See* National Household Sur-
    vey on Drug Abuse
NIAAA. *See* National Institute on
    Alcohol Abuse and Alcoholism
Nicoderm, 520
Nicotine, ecstasy used with, 119
Nicotine craving, 409
Nicotine dependence, 367, 391, 481
Nicotine gum, 473, 474, 532
Nicotine inhaler, 473, 474
Nicotine lozenge, 476
Nicotine nasal spray, 473, 474, 532
Nicotine patch, 38, 473–477, 520
Nicotine replacement therapy (NRT),
    373n2, 465, 467, 473–477, 481
Nicotine vaccine, 477
Nicotine withdrawal, 369, 385, 388
NIDA. *See* National Institute on Drug
    Abuse
Nine-session intervention, 439–440,
    443–453
Nonshared environment (e2), 96,
    110–111
Normative talk, 204, 205
North American Adult Reading Test
    (NAART), 350
Nortriptyline, 475, 477
"Nothing about us without us," 551
Novelty seeking, 61, 63, 64, 81
NPY knockouts, 22

NRT. *See* Nicotine replacement therapy
NSB (Neurological Screening Battery), 348

Obsessive–compulsive disorder, 27
Odds ratio (OR), 377–378
Office of Management and Budget, 577
Offsetting behavior, 145
One-person family therapy (OPFT), 643–645
Operant learning, 35
OPFT. *See* One-person family therapy
Opiate antagonist, 26
Opiates, 559, 562
OR. *See* Odds ratio
Oregon Youth Study (OYS), 203
OTC products. *See* Over-the-counter products
Out-patient treatment, 39–40, 353–354
Over-the-counter (OTC) products, 465, 474
OYS (Oregon Youth Study), 203

Pain killers
    ecstasy used with, 123, 131
    marijuana used with, 127
Pairwise ethnic comparisons, 664
Paiwan Chinese, 687, 690, 694
Pancreatitis, 685, 702
Panic attacks, 36
"Parachute" academic, 600
Parallel treatment, 548
Parent, School and Community Partnership Program, 592–593
Parental alcoholism, 267, 278
Parental discipline, 289, 312
Parental modeling, of tobacco/alcohol use, 291
Parental monitoring, 260
Parental social support, 260
Parental undercontrol, 289
Parent–child conflict, 261, 295, 308–313
Parent–child relationships, 260, 300
Parent education level, 234, 241–245, 248, 303
Parenting
    effective, 281
    and family conflict, 260

Parenting out of wedlock, 200
Parenting practices, 219
Parents
    affective/antisocial personality disorders in, 268n2
    antisocial personality disorder in, 267
    tobacco/alcohol use by, 295, 308–310, 312, 313
Partial dominant model, of genetic influence, 15, 679, 680, 686, 700–701, 705
"Partying," 201, 582
Pattern-centered intervention, 226
Pausing, 205–206
Pawtucket Heart Health Program, 464
PDA (percentage days abstinent), 349
PDD (percentage days drinking), 349
PDDU (percentage days any drug use), 349
PDHD (percentage days heavy drinking), 349
Pearson's reliability coefficients, 331, 332
Peer-clustering theory, 200
Peer-counseling, 595–596
Peer groups
    substance-abusing, 200
    substance use among, 297, 299–300, 302, 303, 308–311, 313–314
Peer influences
    on American Indian/Alaska Native adolescents, 587, 588
    in social development model, 161
Peer Interaction Task (PIT), 204
Peer intervention strategies, 164
Peer-pressure resistance, DARE effects on, 192, 193
Peer rejection, 200
Peer relationships, temperament and, 291–292
PEI. *See* Personal Experience Inventory
Perceived discrimination, 587–588
Percentage days abstinent (PDA), 349
Percentage days any drug use (PDDU), 349
Percentage days drinking (PDD), 349
Percentage days heavy drinking (PDHD), 349

Personal digital assistants, 408
Personal Experience Inventory (PEI),
    14, 658–673
  problem severity part of, 660
  psychosocial risk scales of, 660
  response distortion/drug use history/
    defensiveness items of, 661
Personal feedback report (PFR), 439
Personal Involvement With Chemicals
    scale (PICS), 660
Personality, 262, 270, 274–275, 279
Person-centered interventions, 226
PET (positron emission tomography)
    scans, 27
PFR (personal feedback report), 439
Pharmacotherapies, 3–4, 27, 38
  for alcoholism, 25–26
  relapse prevention with, 418
  for smoking cessation, 467, 473–478
Phasic responses, 414, 415
Physical dependence, on alcohol
  development of, 24–25
  genetic influences on, 22
Physical functioning, 345
Physicians, 465–467
PICS (Personal Involvement With
    Chemicals scale), 660
PIT (Peer Interaction Task), 204
Planfulness, 290
Plasticity, 29
Pleasure centers (in brain), 3
Polysubstance abuse, 41
  in American Indian/Alaska Native
    adolescents, 581–582
  cognitive decrements with, 344,
    358–360
Positive affect
  and cigarette smoking, 368, 370
  and relapse prevention, 411–412
Positive belief formation, 161, 179
Positive emotionality, 290–291, 313
Positive reinforcement, 24, 161, 408
Positive Reinforcement in Drug Educa-
    tion (PRIDE), 594
Positron emission tomography (PET)
    scans, 27
Postprandial cigarette, 389

Posttraumatic amnesia, 345, 349
Poverty, 586
Practicum training, 46
Precocious sexuality, 199, 200
Precontemplation stage, 601
Pregnant smokers, 479, 480
Presence of other smokers, 11
Prevalence reduction strategy, 138, 140
Preventable death, leading contributors
    to, 34
Prevention categories, 590
Prevention education, 608
Prevention–intervention continuum, 601
Prevention programs
  for American Indian/Alaska Native
    youth, 602
  indicated, 590, 591
  primary, 590
  secondary, 590
  selective, 590
  targeted, 590–591, 601–603
  tertiary, 590
  universal, 590, 601, 603–605
Preventive interventions, 161
Preventive measures, 40
PRIDE (Positive Reinforcement in Drug
    Education), 594
Primary prevention programs, 590
Primary socialization theory, 594–595
Principal-components factor analysis,
    666–670, 672
Prison inmates, 8
Problem behaviors, 160
Problem identification and referral,
    608–609
Problem solving, 470, 471
Prohibition of drugs, as source of harm,
    138
Project COMBINE, 27
Project DARE (study), 187–195
  alcohol use, 191, 192
  cigarette use, 191, 192
  efficacy of, 194–195
  illicit drug use, 191–193
  initial DARE intervention, 190
  marijuana use, 191, 192

Project DARE (study) (*continued*)
measures, 189–190
method, 188–190
participants, 188–189
peer-pressure resistance, 192, 193
procedures, 189
results/discussion, 190–195
self-esteem, 192, 193
Project Drug Abuse Resistance Education (DARE), 8, 190
Project MATCH study, 12, 26–27, 40, 417, 498, 500, 542, 547
Proportion of times drunk, 94
Proscription of advertising to minors, 467
Prosocial involvement, 161
Protective factors
in American Indian/Alaska Native adolescent substance use, 588–589
against early substance use, 160
Protestant fundamentalist tradition, 153
Psilocybin, 119
Psychiatric disorders, temperament and, 289
Psychoactive substances, 35
Psychologists
role of, 34–42
training of, 45–46
Psychology of Addictive Behaviors, 4
Psychometric properties, of PEI, 672
Psychopathology
and familial alcoholism, 505
measures of, 500
Psychophysiological assessment, 95
Psychosocial functioning, 448–451
Psychosocial risk scales, 660
Psychotherapy, 411
P3 amplitude, 98–99, 106–107, 109
P3 amplitude reduction (P3-AR), 91
Public health approaches, to smoking cessation, 467–468
Public health problem
alcohol/drug abuse as, 44
cigarette smoking as, 461
ecstasy as, 131
Punitive drug policies, 152

Purdue brief family therapy, 645

QTL mapping and analysis, 22
Quantitative trait locus (QTL), 22
Quantitative traits, 22
Quantity reduction strategy, 138, 147–149
Quit ratio, smoking, 460

Race, 152, 241–245, 248
Raising Healthy Children (RHC) project, 8, 160–181
alcohol use, two-part latent growth model of, 171–175
cigarette use, two-part latent growth model of, 177–178
data analysis, 167–170
discussion, 178–181
intervention/implementation/fidelity/ exposure, 163–165
marijuana use, two-part latent growth model of, 175–177
measures, 166–167
method, 162–170
participants, 162–163
prevalence/frequency of substance use, 170–171
procedure, 165–166
results, 170–178
targeted interventions with, 161
RAPI. *See* Rutgers Alcohol Problem Index
Rats, 22, 24, 417–418
Rave movements, 119
RC (reading comprehension), 348
Readiness to change, 328, 410
Reading comprehension (RC), 348
Recessive model, of genetic influence, 679
Red Cliff Wellness School Curriculum, 592
Reinforcement
alcohol, 24
behavioral, 13
community, 38
positive, 24, 161, 408
and relapse prevention, 408, 410
Reintegrative shaming, 144

Relapse, 11–13
  and affect/alcohol consumption, 517
  among recovering alcoholics, 25
  assessing, 417–418
  cognitive–behavioral model of, 404
  conceptualizing process of, 413–416
  medications for reducing, 38
  psychosocial influences on, 35
  smoking, 368, 388
Relapse prevention (RP), 403–419
  with American Indians/Alaska
      Natives, 601
  for cigarette smoking, 471
  defined, 403
  effectiveness/efficacy of, 405–406
  future research on, 416–417
  interpersonal determinants of, 412
  intrapersonal determinants of,
      407–412
  for marijuana, 406
  previous studies, 403–407
  psychologist's role in, 38
  in 21st century, 418
Relapse Replication and Extension
    Project (RREP), 406–407
Relationships
  and drinking behavior, 109–110
  parent–child, 260, 300
  patterns of social, 290
  peer, 291–292
  and temperament, 297, 299–300
Reliability, test, 331–332, 664–666, 671
Religiosity, 233, 241–245, 248
Religious activities, 588
Research findings, disseminating, 43
Reservation Indians
  alcohol use among, 580, 584
  bicultural competence interventions
      with, 596–605
  bicultural identity of, 589
  and exposure to other cultures, 606
  inhalant use among, 579
  marijuana use among, 581
  unstructured time of, 587
Residential treatment, 39, 603
Resiliency research, 288
Resistance to control, 289

Response distortion, 661, 668, 671, 672
Restaurants, smoking in, 382, 390
Restlessness, 384, 388
Retributive view, 152–153
ReVia 7, 26
Revised Dimensions of Temperament
    Survey (DOT-R), 294
Rey–Osterrieth Complex Figure
    (ROCF), 348
RHC project. See Raising Healthy Chil-
    dren project
Righting reflex, 22
Right Wing Authoritarianism Scale,
    152
Risk compensation, 145
Risk factors
  for American Indian/Alaska Native
      adolescent substance use,
      586–594
  cognitive impairments linked to,
      344–345
  for early substance use, 159–160
  for neuropsychological abilities,
      348–350, 354–357, 506–507
Risk taking, 90
Robert Wood Johnson Foundation, 469,
    484
ROCF (Rey–Osterrieth Complex Figure),
    348
Rogers, Carl, 541
Role playing, 411
RP. See Relapse prevention
RREP. See Relapse Replication and
    Extension Project
Russian Whites, 678
Rutgers Alcohol Problem Index
    (RAPI), 324, 327, 330, 332, 335

SAM. See Substance Abuse Module
SAMHSA. See Substance Abuse and
    Mental Health Services
    Administration
School
  early onset heavy drinking and prob-
      lems in, 585
  in social development model, 161
School-based tobacco prevention, 483

School condom programs, 141

School drop-outs, 584

School–home coordinators (SHCs), 164–165

School intervention strategies, 163–164

SCID. *See* Structured Clinical Interview for *DSM–III–R*

SCID–II (Axis II ASPD module of SCID), 349

SCID-I/P (Structured Clinical Interview for *DSM–IV* Axis I Disorders, Patient Edition), 519

SDM. *See* Social development model

SDMT. *See* Symbol Digit Modalities Test

Seat belts, 145

Seattle Indian Health Board, 607

Seattle Social Development Project (SSDP), 160

Secondary prevention programs, 590

Sedative use
  cognitive decrements with, 344
  ecstasy use with, 123, 131
  marijuana use with, 126

Selective prevention programs, 590

Self-control, 517, 531, 532

Self-efficacy, 404, 407–408, 410, 412, 415, 517

Self-esteem, 42, 192, 193

Self-help groups, 548–549

Self-help materials, 465

Self-medicating, 36

Self-monitoring, 372

Self-organization, 413

Self-reliance, 411

Self-report measures, 294–296, 391

Self-worth, 586

Sensation seeking, 586

Serial treatment, 548

Serotonin 1(knockout, 22

Service episodes, 544

SES. *See* Socioeconomic status

Seventh Generation project, 597

Sexual behaviors
  high-risk, 34
  unsafe, 200

Shared environmental component (c2), 96, 111

SHCs. *See* School–home coordinators

Shipley Institute of Living Scale (SILS), 499

Siblings, 271

Significant other (SO), 439, 440

SILS (Shipley Institute of Living Scale), 499

Single-parent families, 303

"Situational associations" for smoking, 368

Skewness, 178n7, 210

Skills training, 595

"Sleeper effects," 188

Smokeless tobacco, 583, 586, 597

Smokers, presence of other, 11

Smoking. *See* Cigarette smoking; Marijuana use; Tobacco use

"Smoking Cessation Guidelines for Health Professionals" (British Health Education Authority), 468

Smoking cessation treatment(s)
  adoption/implementation of, 479
  in alcohol-dependent smokers. *See* Alcohol and tobacco cessation in alcohol-dependent smokers (study)
  changing trends in, 461–468
  community-level, 463–465
  cost-effectiveness of, 478–479
  evidence-based guidelines for, 468–469
  as global issue, 484
  harm reduction vs., 479–480
  health care provider, 465–467
  and individual differences/special populations, 480–484
  pharmacological, 473–478
  public health related, 467–468
  research issues with behavioral, 470–472
  research issues with pharmacological, 474–478
  stepped-care model of, 472
  structural/psychosocial aspects of, 469–470
  tailored communication in, 473

transdisciplinary focus of, 484
treatment-matching, 472
work-site, 462–463
Smoking cues, 371, 383, 388–389
Smoking restrictions, 379–381, 388, 516
SO. *See* Significant other
Sociability, 294n2
Social bonds, 111
Social desirability, 661
Social development model (SDM),
160–162
Social drinkers, 227
Social environments, 110
Social influence skills, 219
Social influences model, 482–483
Socializing, smoking while, 382
Social learning, 369, 516
Social phobias, 36
Social relationships, patterns of, 290
Social skills training, 38
Social support
and family risk factors, 311
and relapse prevention, 412
for smoking cessation, 470–472
Society for Research on Nicotine and
Tobacco, 484
Socioeconomic status (SES)
of cigarette smokers, 461
of drug users, 152
and ecstasy use, 129–130
Specialist certification, 33, 43
Specialized treatments, 34, 38–39, 46,
540–541
Spectrum disorders, 590
SSDP (Seattle Social Development
Project), 160
SSSE (strategic structural systems
engagement), 644
Stage (gateway) theory of drug involve-
ment, 581–582
Stages of change model, 410, 601–602
STAI. *See* State–Trait Anxiety Inventory
Stake theory, 589
Stanford Five City Project, 464
State–Trait Anxiety Inventory (STAI),
436, 448, 449
Stepped-care model of treatment, 4, 472,
602–603

Stigma, 44
Stimulants
ecstasy used with, 123, 125, 128,
129, 131
marijuana used with, 126–127
Strategic structural systems engagement
(SSSE), 644
Stress
and cigarette smoking, 386n8
and drinking, 29
Stress management, 38
Stressors
childhood, 249
cognitive reactions to, 288–289
Stroke, 479
Structured Clinical Interview for
DSM–III–R (SCID), 349, 436
Structured Clinical Interview for
DSM–IV Axis I Disorders,
Patient Edition (SCID-I/P), 519
Student intervention strategies, 164
Sublingual tablets, 476
Substance Abuse and Mental Health
Services Administration
(SAMHSA), 120, 578, 591, 608,
625
Substance Abuse Module (SAM), 66, 93
Substance experimentation, 61
Substance use
adolescent, 209, 217
adult modeling of, 587
in American Indian/Alaska Native
adolescents. *See* American
Indian and Alaska Native
adolescent substance use
consequences/correlates of, 585
in middle adolescence, 202
patterns of, 582–583
and peer groups. *See* Friendships and
substance use (study)
trends in, 212
Substance use disorders (SUDs)
family effects on young adults'. *See*
Family effects on young adults'
substance use disorders (study)
prevalence of, 34
therapist's knowledge of, 45–46

Substance-use prevention among American Indian and Alaska Native youth, 589–600
for American Indian youth, 591
best practices, 601
bicultural life skills approaches, 603–604
Canoe Journey program, 607–608
community involvement, 604–605
community-oriented approaches, 591–594
concepts of, 590–591
cultural challenge with, 605–607
future steps for, 608–610
for healthier communities, 600–610
individual-oriented approaches, 594–598
limitations of current approaches, 598–600
prevention–intervention continuum approaches, 601–602
stepped-care model, 602–603
SUDs. *See* Substance use disorders
Supply reduction strategy, 138
Symbol Digit Modalities Test (SDMT), 348, 500
Symptom counts, 69, 70–71
Synaptic processing speed, 359

Tactual Performance Test (TPT), 348
Tailored communication, 473
Talking circles, 607
Target Community Partnership Project, 593–594
Targeted prevention programs, 590–591, 601–603
Task attentional orientation, 290–291, 300
Taxes, tobacco, 467
TC. *See* Therapeutic community
TD (tobacco dependence), 228
Teachers, 165, 296
Technological improvements, 144–145, 337
Telephone counseling, 469, 473
Telephone interactive voice recognition, 473

Temperament effects on development of problem behavior (study), 287–314
analyses of moderation effects, 300–303
descriptive statistics, 296–298
difficult-temperament dimensions, multiple-group tests for, 308–310
discussion, 310–314
family/temperament variables, descriptive statistics for, 297, 298
locus/magnitude of moderation effects, 311–313
method, 292–296
multiple-group analysis, 303–305
multiple-group tests for temperament dimensions, 305–310
nature of moderation effects, 313–314
participants, 292–293
previous research, 288–289
procedure, 293–294
protective-temperament dimensions, multiple-group tests for, 305–308
relationships among predictor variables, 297, 299–300
results, 296–310
self-report measures, 294–296
substance use, descriptive statistics for, 296–298
teacher-report measures, 296
theoretical basis, 289–292
Tertiary prevention programs, 590
Thais, 677, 678
Therapeutic alliance, 541
Therapeutic community (TC)
defined, 346
life skills emphasized by, 542
neuropsychological test scores from, 354, 355
risk-factor scores from, 354, 356–357
Therapeutic skills, 42
Therapist
characteristics of effective, 42
ethnicity of, 642–643
Third-party payers, 478
Tiffany's model of urges, 390

Timeline follow-back (TLFB) assessment, 348–349, 374, 436, 519, 641–642
TMT. *See* Trail Making Test
Tobacco
    taxes on, 467
    toxins in, 480
Tobacco dependence (TD), 228
Tobacco-related research, 484
Tobacco settlement, 479
Tobacco use. *See also* Cigarette smoking
    and alcohol use. *See* Developmental course of alcohol and tobacco use (study)
    in American Indian/Alaska Native adolescents, 578–579, 583
    and deviant friendship process, 201, 202, 213
    early, 200
    as leading cause of preventable death, 12
    measure of, 233
    prevalence of, 34
    self-reported, 206, 208
Tolerance mechanism, 22, 24
Tonic processes, 414, 415
TPT (Tactual Performance Test), 348
Trade-offs, value, 151
Traditional treatment methods, 4
Traffic fatalities, 34
Trail Making Test (TMT), 348, 500
Training, 45–46
Tranquilizers, 123, 127, 131
Transdisciplinary Tobacco Use Research Centers (TTURC), 484
Translation, of instruments, 641, 647
Transtheoretical model of change, 41
Treatment careers, 544
Treatment matching, 26–27, 472, 546–547
Treatment setting, 541
Treatment(s) for addictive behaviors, 537–552
    alcoholism, 25–27
    changing approaches to, 42–45
    and cognitive impairment, 360
    common dynamics underlying, 538–539

for comorbid disorders, 547–548
    comparing, 545–546
    contextual perspective on, 538
    duration/continuity of, 539–540
    effective, 38–40
    evidence-based, 550–552
    formal, 542–543
    goals of, 5
    and health care work environment, 545
    intensity of, 4
    life-skills context of, 542, 549–550
    models of, 4, 5
    self-help group, 548–549
    and service episodes/treatment careers, 544
    specialist, 540–541
    therapeutic alliance in, 541
    treatment-matching, 546–547
Tribal differences, 584
Tribal languages, 577
Tri-Ethnic Center for Prevention Research at Colorado State University, 578, 605
TSF. *See* 12-step facilitation
TTURC (Transdisciplinary Tobacco Use Research Centers), 484
Tucker–Lewis fit index (TLI), 169
12-step facilitation (TSF), 40, 499, 502, 508–509, 542, 546, 550
Twin studies, 60–61, 64, 90, 96, 107, 110–111, 481. *See also* Minnesota Twin Family Study
Two-part latent growth model
    of alcohol use, 171–175
    analysis using, 179
    of cigarette use, 177–178
    generally, 167–169
    of marijuana use, 175–177
Two-session MET, 439, 443–453
Type I alcoholism, 23
Type II alcoholism, 23

Unintended harms, 142–143
United States
    age of alcohol-dependence onset in, 682

United States (*continued*)
    antagonism toward drug users in, 152
    ecstasy use in, 118, 131
    resistance to harm reduction, 139–140
    specialized treatments in, 34
    survey of drug use in, 120
Universal factors, in American
    Indian/Alaska Native adolescent
    substance use, 588
Universal prevention programs, 590, 601,
    603–605
University of Rhode Island Change
    Assessment (URICA), 324, 328,
    330, 332, 335
Urban Indians, 594, 599, 607
Urge to drink, 523–525, 528
Urge to smoke, 371, 375–376, 383, 384,
    390, 526, 528
URICA. *See* University of Rhode Island
    Change Assessment
Urinalysis, 437–438, 559–562
U.S. Agency for Health Care Policy and
    Research (AHCPR), 468, 469
U.S. Centers for Disease Control and
    Prevention (CDC), 89–90, 469
U.S. Congress, 140
U.S. Surgeon General, 90, 624
Use reduction paradigm, 138, 140

VA. *See* Veterans Affairs
VA Connecticut Healthcare System, 518
Verbal ability, 346, 357–359
Verbal therapy, 27
Veterans Affairs (VA), 518, 539, 540
Video, interactive, 473
Vigor, 311n9

Violence, adolescent, 201
Vocabulary, 345, 350
Voices of Indian Teens Project, 579
Voucher incentive program, 560

Wall, Tamara L., 685
Warmth, 541
Web-based condition (Web), 325, 326
Web-based psychological assessment
    tools and interventions, 4
Web-based-with interruption condition
    (Web-I), 325–327
Wechsler Memory Scale (WMS), 348
Welfare, 141
WF (written fluency), 348
Whites, ecstasy use among, 129
Withdrawal symptoms, 387–388, 409
WMS (Wechsler Memory Scale), 348
Work environment, health-care, 545
Workplace, smoking in, 382, 389–390
Work-site health promotion interven-
    tions, 462–463
World Health Organization, 484
World Wide Web, 473
Written fluency (WF), 348

Young adults
    family effects on substance use disor-
    ders in. *See* Family effects on
    young adults' substance use
    disorders (study)
    leading contributors to death among,
    34
    smoking rates in, 460–461

Zygosity, 65–66, 95

ABOUT THE EDITORS

G. Alan Marlatt, PhD, is a professor of psychology at the University of Washington and director of the Addictive Behaviors Research Center at that institution. He received his PhD in clinical psychology from Indiana University in 1968. After serving on the faculties of the University of British Columbia (1968–1969) and the University of Wisconsin—Madison (1969–1972), he joined the University of Washington faculty in the fall of 1972. His major focus in both research and clinical work is the field of addictive behaviors. In addition to more than 200 journal articles and book chapters, he has published several books in the addictions field, including *Relapse Prevention*, *Assessment of Addictive Behaviors*, *Harm Reduction*, and *Brief Alcohol Screening and Intervention for College Students (BASICS): A Harm Reduction Approach*. Over the course of the past 30 years, he has received continuous funding for his research from a variety of agencies, including the National Institute on Alcohol Abuse and Alcoholism, the National Institute on Drug Abuse, the Alcoholic Beverage Medical Research Foundation, and the Robert Wood Johnson Foundation. In 1990, Dr. Marlatt was awarded the Jellinek Memorial Award for outstanding contributions to knowledge in the field of alcohol studies, in 2001 he was given the Innovators in Combating Substance Abuse Award by the Robert Wood Johnson Foundation, and in 2004 he received the Distinguished Researcher Award from the Research Society on Alcoholism.

Katie Witkiewitz, PhD, is a research scientist at the Alcohol and Drug Abuse Institute (ADAI), University of Washington, Seattle. She received her PhD from the University of Washington in 2005, where she completed the clinical psychology graduate program and an internship in psychiatry and behavioral sciences. She then took a faculty position in the Department of Psychology at the University of Illinois—Chicago as an assistant professor of psychology until July 2007, when she joined the ADAI staff. Her primary research interests include quantitative methods, latent variable modeling, nonlinear dynamical systems, computer modeling of treatment system case management for chronic alcohol abusers, analysis of clinical treatment outcomes and relapse, mindfulness-based treatments for alcohol and drug abuse, and harm reduction approaches to the treatment of addiction. She was co-editor with G. Alan Marlatt of the book *Therapist's Guide to Evidence-Based Relapse Prevention* and has authored and coauthored articles in *Journal of Abnormal Psychology*, *Clinical Psychology Review*, and *Psychology of Addictive Behaviors*.